Brazil

Regis St. Louis
Gary Chandler, Gregor Clark, Robert Landon,
John Noble, Kevin Raub, Mara Vorhees

Manaus (p641)
Gateway to jungle trips along the mighty Amazon, the once-glorious city has teeming markets and Amazonian culture

Pantanal (p415)
Verdant wonderland with fantastic wildlife viewing coupled with trekking, horseback riding and boat trips

Iguaçu Falls (p326)
More than 250 spectacular waterfalls surrounded by Atlantic rain forest

LEGEND

Freeway
Primary Road
Secondary Road
Tertiary Road

0 ____ 500 km
0 ____ 300 miles

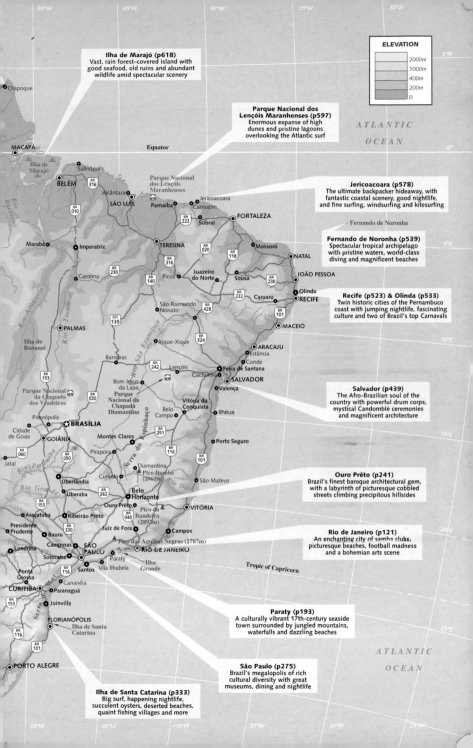

Ilha de Marajó (p618)
Vast, rain forest–covered island with good seafood, old ruins and abundant wildlife amid spectacular scenery

Parque Nacional dos Lençóis Maranhenses (p597)
Enormous expanse of high dunes and pristine lagoons overlooking the Atlantic surf

Jericoacoara (p578)
The ultimate backpacker hideaway, with fantastic coastal scenery, good nightlife, and fine surfing, windsurfing and kitesurfing

Fernando de Noronha (p539)
Spectacular tropical archipelago with pristine waters, world-class diving and magnificent beaches

Recife (p523) & Olinda (p533)
Twin historic cities of the Pernambuco coast with jumping nightlife, fascinating culture and two of Brazil's top Carnavals

Salvador (p439)
The Afro-Brazilian soul of the country with powerful drum corps, mystical Candomblé ceremonies and magnificent architecture

Ouro Prêto (p241)
Brazil's finest baroque architectural gem, with a labyrinth of picturesque cobbled streets climbing precipitous hillsides

Rio de Janeiro (p121)
An enchanting city of samba clubs, picturesque beaches, football madness and a bohemian arts scene

Paraty (p193)
A culturally vibrant 17th-century seaside town surrounded by jungled mountains, waterfalls and dazzling beaches

São Paulo (p275)
Brazil's megalopolis of rich cultural diversity with great museums, dining and nightlife

Ilha de Santa Catarina (p333)
Big surf, happening nightlife, succulent oysters, deserted beaches, quaint fishing villages and more

ELEVATION
2000m
1000m
400m
200m
0

ATLANTIC OCEAN

Equator

Tropic of Capricorn

Ojapoque
MACAPÁ
Ilha de Marajó
Salinópolis
BELÉM
BR 316
Alcântara
SÃO LUÍS
BR 010
Parque Nacional dos Lençóis Maranhenses
Parnaíba
Jericoacoara
Camocim
FORTALEZA
BR 222
Sobral
Fernando de Noronha
Marabá
Imperatriz
TERESINA
BR 020
Mossoró
NATAL
BR 116
BR 230
BR 316
Juazeiro do Norte
Sousa
JOÃO PESSOA
Carolina
BR 140
Picos
BR 232
Caruaru
Olinda
RECIFE
São Raimundo Nonato
BR 428
BR 101
BR 135
MACEIÓ
Xique-Xique
BR 324
Ilha do Bananal
ARACAJU
Estância
Conde
BR 242
Barreiras
Lençóis
Feira de Santana
Cachoeira
SALVADOR
PALMAS
Bom Jesus da Lapa
Parque Nacional da Chapada Diamantina
Valença
BR 020
Parque Nacional da Chapada dos Veadeiros
Belo Campo
Vitória da Conquista
Ilhéus
Pirenópolis
BRASÍLIA
Montes Claros
BR 251
Cidade de Goiás
GOIÂNIA
Pirapora
Porto Seguro
Jataí
BR 060
BR 050
BR 116
BR 101
Curvelo
Diamantina
Pico Itambé (2062m)
São Mateus
Uberlândia
BR 262
Belo Horizonte
Uberaba
Ouro Prêto
Pico da Bandeira (2892m)
VITÓRIA
BR 153
Ribeirão Preto
BR 040
Araçatuba
Juiz de Fora
Campos
Presidente Prudente
BR 330
Pico das Agulhas Negras (2787m)
Bauru
Campinas
SÃO PAULO
Londrina
Sorocaba
Paraty
RIO DE JANEIRO
Ponta Grossa
BR 116
Santos
Vila Ilhabela
Ilha Grande
CURITIBA
Cananéia
Paranaguá
BR 153
Joinville
FLORIANÓPOLIS
Ilha de Santa Catarina
BR 116
BR 101
PORTO ALEGRE

Rio Branco
Rio Araguaia
Rio Tocantins
Rio São Francisco
Rio Paranaíba
Rio Grande
Serra do Espinhaço
Serra do Mar
Rio Doce

50°W 45°W 40°W 35°W 30°W 25°W
5°N 0° 5°S 10°S 15°S 20°S 25°S

On the Road

REGIS ST. LOUIS

If I had to pick just one totem animal for this trip, it would be my four-legged friend, the horse. They seemed to appear in the most unlikely places. After exploring the cobblestone streets of Laranjeiras (p506), I walked up the hillside outside of town and met this handsome fellow.

GARY CHANDLER That's me on a jungle trip in Mamirauá (p659), showing the piranha who's boss. (Bait of choice: beef sirloin.) Our guide said most piranha are harmless, preferring smaller prey. But the red guys are an exception, known to munch on the occasional toe if the river is low and food scarce.

GREGOR CLARK After weeks inland in Minas Gerais, I headed for the beach in Búzios, where it promptly started raining cats and dogs. When the sun finally came out five days later, I celebrated with a stroll to see the fishermen statues along beachfront Orla Bardot (p216). Sunset never felt sweeter!

JOHN NOBLE You could call the Lençóis Maranhenses (p597) a desert if the endless dunes didn't have a freshwater lake in every hollow. It's hot work climbing over them, and this was only the second dune. The best view's from a plane, actually.

KEVIN RAUB I hadn't planned on renting a car in Brasília until a friend said it was obligatory. I conceded. I drove into the city and immediately got confused and lost. I drove straight back to the car rental place but they wouldn't take the car back without charging me full price. So I kept it, learned the city by driving and got this amazing photo of the Congresso (p377) reflecting off its hood!

ROBERT LANDON As an unofficial Carioca (Rio native), I've always felt keenly São Paulo's lack of beachfront. Then I discovered Guarujá (p307), an hour's ride away (when traffic cooperates). Its miles-long beaches are fine, but I felt a particular affection for the 70s-style high-rises that line them – melancholic reminders of the city's heyday.

MARA VORHEES It was my first day 'on the road' and I was still having trouble communicating in Portuguese. But that didn't diminish my awe at the ancient 'stone city' at Vila Velha (p317).

See full author bios page 744

Making friends in
Amazonas (p641)

JOHN BORTHWICK

Nosso Brasil (Our Brazil)

A land of magnificent beaches, vast rain forests and music-fueled cities, Brazil bears an astounding variety of natural and cultural wonders. This is the world's largest country in the tropics, and the only limit to a journey here is your imagination.

Setting the stage are idyllic, palm-covered islands, pristine stretches of coastline fronting emerald seas and jewel-box colonial towns framed against verdant peaks – yet all this is found in just one state. Throughout the other 26 lie dazzling gold-mining towns, futuristic cities of the interior and 18th-century villages whose soul is more African than South American.

Whether or not you come for Carnaval, music is a big part of the Brazilian experience. There are numerous ways to discover the perfect beat, from dancing with Cariocas at Rio's atmospheric samba clubs to following powerful drumbeats through the streets of Salvador. There's dancehall *forró* of the Northeast, twirling *carimbó* of the Amazon, scratch-skilled DJs of São Paulo and an endless variety of regional sounds that extends from the back-country *sertanejo* to reggae-loving Maranhão.

Brazil's rich ecosystems make for some amazing journeys. You can go horseback-riding through the Pantanal in search of monkeys and capybara, or whale-watching off the coast. There are unforgettable river trips along the Amazon, descents into waterfall-cooled canyons, refreshing dips in forest streams and ascents up rocky cliff tops to breathtaking views.

Given the country's many riches, it's no surprise that Brazil has been turning heads for centuries. Among the first to fall under the spell was the Portuguese king himself (Dom João VI), who came, fell in love and just couldn't tear himself away from his adopted homeland – something to keep in mind when booking that return flight.

Cristo Redentor (p150) stands guard over Rio de Janeiro

JOHN MAIER JR

The heavenly blue waters
of Baía dos Porcos (p541),
Fernando de Noronha
PAUL BIGLAND

INTERVIEW 1:
Spectacular Sanctuary

NAME	Fabiana Cava
OCCUPATION	Projects Coordinator, Spinner Dolphin Center, Fernando de Noronha
RESIDENCE	Fernando de Noronha Archipelago
FAVORITE MUSICIAN	Renato Russo of Legião Urbana

Fernando de Noronha (p539) is the best place in the world for observing spinner dolphins – you can see 1000 of them in one day in Baía dos Golfinhos, where they come to rest and reproduce.

'It's vital to involve local communities in conservation'

I study the impact of tourism on the dolphins. Swimming and boating in the bay are no longer allowed, to avoid disturbing them.

I also work on community projects. It's vital to involve local communities in conservation. We give free courses in computing, English, diving instruction and ecotourism. I grew up in southern Brazil but I love the people up here in the Northeast for their open nature and the strong community feeling.

Is Brazil doing enough to protect its environment? No, it's doing about 10% of what it should! Funding is the big problem. Conservation needs indefinite commitments, but whenever the government changes, everything stops and we have to start all over again.

AS RELATED TO JOHN NOBLE

Looking down on Baía dos Golfinhos (Bay of Dolphins; p561)

PAUL BIGLAND

INTERVIEW 2:
Strength Meets Grace

NAME	Jelon Vieira
OCCUPATION	Artistic Director of Dance Brazil and founder of Capoeira Foundation
RESIDENCE	Salvador, Bahia and New York City
FAVORITE PLACE	Salvador da Bahia

'I love being in the Northeast. It's so rich, so full of culture. It feeds me creatively.'

I love being in the Northeast. It's so rich, so full of culture. It feeds me creatively.

I was born in Santo Amaro, where Caetano Veloso, an old friend, is from, but I moved to Salvador when I was 10. That's where I saw capoeira for the first time; I knew right away that's what I wanted to do with my life.

I grew up in a poor neighborhood, where it was easy to take a wrong turn. If it wasn't for capoeira, I would've gotten into a lot of trouble. Capoeira showed me a different world. It brought me tremendous respect for life, and later connected me to so many different people around the world.

My influences were the great *mestres* (masters) of Bahia, though my students are nowadays my biggest source of inspiration. Their excitement keeps me going, reminds me that the self-esteem and positive thinking that my *mestres* inspired in me – I can share this with the next generation.

AS RELATED TO REGIS ST. LOUIS

The streets of Pelourinho, Salvador, come to life with capoeira (p449)

JOHN MAIER JR

INTERVIEW 3:
Life in the Big City

NAME	Alex Cassimiro
OCCUPATION	Fashion designer
RESIDENCE	São Paulo
MUST-SEE	Pinacoteca do Estado (p282)

People come to São Paulo (p275) from all over Brazil, and from every country in the world. The diversity constantly forces you look at things in new ways. For a designer, that's liberating.

'São Paulo is the country's economic capital and pulsing heart'

It's true that people tend to have a 'love-hate' relationship with São Paulo. The social, cultural and economic opportunities are unparalleled. At the same time, traffic, crime and lack of decent public transport or other public investment make life in São Paulo stressful and difficult.

São Paulo is the country's economic capital and pulsing heart. Brazilians who come here and stay for a time never want to leave. After knowing São Paulo, they would only trade it for another of the world's great cities.

Rua 25 de Março is an incredible place to discover new objects, new ideas; as are the markets in Bixiga and Benedito Calixto. But it's impossible to name one place I love best. My relationship with São Paulo is multi-disciplinary.

AS RELATED TO ROBERT LANDON

Overhead the teeming metropolis of São Paulo (p275)

ALFREDO MAIQUEZ

INTERVIEW 4:

Saving the Forest and Its People

NAME	Dercy Teles de Caravalho Cunha
OCCUPATION	President, Union of Rural Workers of Xapuri
RESIDENCE	Seringais Boa Vista
FAVORITE MEMORY OF CHICO MENDES	'How he could talk and relate to anyone.'

'Chico's life and death brought a lot of attention to Xapuri – we need people to see that we are continuing his work, his mission'

Our mission is to improve the lives of rural workers, to be sure they can have the things they see other people have – like TVs, telephones – while still working and living in the forest. Many young people growing up in the forest don't see a future there. But the forest has clean water, clean air; you can grow food or collect it; you have work and security. That's why we're also committed to protecting the environment.

Some unionists are only concerned about people, but to me, allowing the forest to be destroyed only makes our situation more difficult. Chico Mendes understood that: that unionists and environmentalists have a lot in common. And the people responded to his call.

The challenge is to keep up the momentum. Chico's life and death brought a lot of attention to Xapuri – we need people to see that we are continuing his work, his mission.

AS RELATED TO GARY CHANDLER

Home and murder site of Chico Mendes (p689) in Xapuri, Acre

GARY CHANDLER

INTERVIEW 5:
Preserving Gaúcho Traditions

NAME	Luiz Fernando Brilhante
OCCUPATION	Traditional *gaúcho* (cowboy) dancer
RESIDENCE	Porto Alegre
MUST-SEE	Folkloric show at Churrascaria Roda de Carreta (p358)

Dancing is my passion. From the first moment I started to dance, it has been in my blood. In the south, we learn traditional dances as children. Now I have been dancing for 35 years – 15 years at the Churrascaria Roda de Carreta. Of course, the dances we perform here are not truly authentic: they are transformed for the enjoyment of the spectators.

The Centro Traditional Gaúcho preserves many elements of *gaúcho* culture – not just music and dance, but also traditional dress, rodeo competitions and drinking *chimarrão* (p359). Small rodeos are held right in Porto Alegre. Even culinary traditions like *churrascaria* and *caipirinhas* – which are considered typically 'Brazilian' – originated from *gaúcho* culture.

What I love most about Brazil is the diversity of its people and cultures. Every state has a different folkloric tradition. When I attend national dance festivals, I witness the amazing diversity that makes up our country.

AS RELATED TO MARA VORHEES

'When I attend national dance festivals, I witness the amazing diversity that makes up our country'

Modern-day cowboys from Rio Grande do Sul (p353)

JEFFERSON BERNARDES/GETTY IMAGES

INTERVIEW 6:
Astonishing Nature

NAME	Ailton Alves de Lara
OCCUPATION	Tour guide, the Pantanal
RESIDENCE	Cuiabá
FAVORITE MUSICIAN	Tom Jobim

'The most astonishing thing I have ever seen here was an anaconda eating a capybara'

The Pantanal (p415) is a unique and dynamic place that is always changing. If you visit during the dry season and then come back during the wet season, it's almost as if you are going to a different place. You can barely recognize the same trees. For a place of its size, the concentration of animal species one finds here is amazing.

When I'm not guiding, I just observe the birds here and try to catalogue them, record their sounds and match their characteristics to my field guide. For me, the area around Pousada Rio Clarinho is the best for this. It sits on an arm of the Rio Claro and is full of small birds. It's my second home.

The most astonishing thing I have ever seen here was an anaconda eating a capybara. Neither was very big, but the fact that the anaconda's mouth had enlarged 12 times its normal size just to eat the capybara was incredible – how nature adapts and gives the animals the right materials to survive.

AS RELATED TO KEVIN RAUB

Toucans and wildlife aplenty reside in the Pantanal (p415)

JANE SWEENEY

INTERVIEW 7:

Stories in the Stone

NAME	Ángela Leite Xavier
OCCUPATION	Oral historian and storyteller
RESIDENCE	Ouro Prêto
FAVORITE MUSICIAN	Chico Buarque de Holanda

History isn't set in stone; it's always being renewed. I believe that tourists today want something more than what's offered in the usual circuits. There's an official, distant history of monuments and documents told by those who hold power. When I wrote *Treasures, Ghosts and Legends of Ouro Prêto*, I wanted to share the untold oral history of Ouro Prêto's people. It makes history more human and more engaging.

'I believe that tourists today want something more than what's offered in the usual circuits'

The entire hill region around Ouro Prêto (p241) where the highest-carat gold was found, has lots of old mines and remains from the period of discovery, walls from slave times later used to build new houses. And there are many little places – like Lavras Novas (p250) – off the tourist circuit that have beautiful baroque churches, old houses, waterfalls and many stories. Among the famous colonial towns, I also really like Diamantina (p261) for its light, colorful architecture, its pavement of large stones.

AS RELATED TO GREGOR CLARK

Matriz NS da Conceição de Antônio Dias (p244), Ouro Prêto
BRUCE BI

INTERVIEW 8:
Music in the Blood

NAME	Fabio Barreto
OCCUPATION	Samba musician
RESIDENCE	Santa Teresa, Rio de Janeiro
FAVORITE COMPOSERS	Nelson Cavaquinho, Noel Rosa, Wilson Moreira, Paulinho da Viola...

'Samba is philosophy, it's freedom, it's religion. I love samba, but samba doesn't need me, I need it.'

Music was always in my blood. When I was 14, I wanted to play rock'n'roll. I scraped enough money together to take guitar lessons, but at my first lesson, I heard the kid's father playing in the background, some amazing style of music I didn't recognize. Samba. I knew that's what I wanted to play.

I'd go to Bar da Deusa in Santa Teresa, where these old-timers sat around playing samba. 'You, sit there, kid!' they'd bark. I was nervous, but they told me, 'If you don't play, you'll never learn.' That's where I learned to play.

Samba is philosophy, it's freedom, it's religion. I love samba, but samba doesn't need me, I need it. The music scene is tough. I've had steady gigs and hard times. Once, I was on my way to sell my guitar. As I walked past the Lapa arches, a man stopped me and asked if I knew how to play. I played some chords and he offered me a job. He owned a club and his guitarist had just broken his arm. This was a sign. I haven't give up on my music since.

AS RELATED TO REGIS ST. LOUIS

Drum corps – part of Brazil's rich musical heritage
BRUCE BI

Contents

Regional Map Contents

Amazon Region p603

Ceará, Piauí & Maranhão p567

Paraíba & Rio Grande do Norte p548

Pernambuco p522–3

Sergipe & Alagoas p502

Bahia p438

Mato Grosso & Mato Grosso do Sul p407

Brasília pp374–5

Goiás p383

Minas Gerais p234

Espírito Santo p221

São Paulo State p274

Rio de Janeiro State p188

Rio de Janeiro p137

Paraná p313

Santa Catarina p333

Rio Grande do Sul p354

Getting Started

Before you go to Brazil, find out whether you need a visa. Many nationalities require them, including citizens from the US, Canada and Australia. See p711 for more details.

If you're going to Carnaval in Rio, Salvador or Olinda, secure hotel reservations as far in advance as possible. That also holds true for Rio's Reveillon (New Year's Eve; p164). If you're hitting other major festivals (p702), book your room in advance – often easily done over the internet. During the busy summer season (December to March), it's also wise to book ahead.

Brazil is a large country, with vast distances between destinations. If you plan to visit a number of regions, consider purchasing a Brazil Airpass (p720), which allows you between four and nine in-country flights at a set rate. These tickets must be purchased outside the country.

WHEN TO GO

Brazil's high season runs from December to March. This is when the country fills with both foreign visitors and vacationing Brazilian families (school holidays run from mid-December to Carnaval, usually in February). Prices rise during this time and you'll face more crowds, though this is also the most festive time in Brazil. Brazil's low season runs from May to September. With the exception of July, which is also a school-holiday month, this is the cheapest and least-crowded time to visit the country – though it can be utterly vacant in some resort areas and cold in the south.

Depending on where you go, weather may be a significant factor in your travel plans. In Rio, the humidity can be high in summer, with temperatures hovering around 28°C (82°F). Rainfall is another factor, with October to January being the wettest months. In winter Rio temperatures hover around 23°C (73°F), with a mix of both rainy and superb days.

On the northeast coast, from Bahia to Maranhão, temperatures are a bit warmer year-round than in Rio – with days reaching 31°C (88°F) – but due to a wonderful tropical breeze and less humidity, it's rarely stifling. The rainy season runs from about mid-December to July, though even then you'll encounter gorgeous days.

The Amazon region (the north) is one of the world's rainiest places and rainfall occurs most frequently from December to May, making travel exceedingly difficult then. The rest of the year the region still receives plenty of rain, though showers tend to last only an hour or two.

The Pantanal also has rainy and dry seasons, and if you plan to go, do so during the dry season (mid-April to late September). The rest of the year,

See Climate Charts (p698) for more information.

DON'T LEAVE HOME WITHOUT...

- Getting your visa, if you need one (p711).
- Learning a few Portuguese words and phrases (p741).
- Insect repellent containing DEET (p730).
- A yellow fever vaccine (p728), if planning a trip to the Amazon. You may want to take medication against malaria as well (p726).
- A waterproof jacket.
- A Brazil Airpass (p720) if you're planning to cover a lot of ground in a short amount of time.

HOW MUCH?

Admission to samba club in Rio R$15

Two-hour flight from Rio to Salvador (one way) R$220

Double room in a comfy pousada in Arraial d'Ajuda R$120

Eleven-hour bus ride from São Paulo to Florianopolis R$87

Four-day excursion in the Pantanal R$500

For more price information, see the Lonely Planet Index, inside front cover.

the wetlands receive tremendous rainfall, washing out roads and making traveling a nightmare.

The South has the most extreme temperature changes, and during the coldest winter months (June to August), Rio Grande do Sul, Santa Catarina, Paraná and São Paulo have temperatures between 13°C (55.4°F) and 18°C (64.4°F). In some towns, the occasional snowfall is even possible. As elsewhere along the coast, summer is quite hot, and you'll have lots of company on the beach.

COSTS & MONEY

Although still cheaper than North America and parts of Europe, Brazil, with its booming economy and strong real, has become South America's most expensive country.

How much to budget depends on where you stay and how much ground you plan to cover. Some cities, like Rio, have grown particularly pricey in the last few years. Rural and less-visited destinations are often significantly cheaper. Bus travel costs about R$8 (US$4) per hour of distance covered. Flights, which sometimes run fare specials, might not cost much more for long hauls. Decent accommodations and particularly rental cars (which cost about R$100 per day) can quickly eat up a budget.

If you're frugal, you can travel on about R$100 (US$50) a day – paying around R$40 for accommodations, R$30 for food and drink, plus bus travel, admission to sights and the occasional entertainment activity. If

---

TRAVELING RESPONSIBLY

Since our inception in 1973, Lonely Planet has encouraged our readers to tread lightly, travel responsibly and enjoy the serendipitous magic independent travel affords. International travel is growing at a jaw-dropping rate, and we still firmly believe in the benefits it can bring – but, as always, we encourage you to consider the impact your visit will have on both the global environment and the local economies, cultures and ecosystems.

Sustainable travel is fairly easy within Brazil, but with the increasing use of 'eco' splashed about, it can be hard to separate the green from the greedy (see p695 for tips on finding eco-friendly hotels). With a little research – and a healthy sense of adventure – your trip can have a positive impact on both the local economy and the environment.

For more detailed information on the wider environmental issues facing Brazil, and how these are being tackled, see the Environment chapter (p95).

Getting There & Away

Unless you're traveling from a neighboring South American country, it's almost impossible to avoid flying into Brazil. To combat the heavy environmental costs associated with air travel, consider offsetting your carbon emissions (p716). Once in Brazil, flights will prove tempting if you're traveling great distances, but there are other options, including riverboats in the Amazon, buses and even a few rare train lines.

Slow Travel

Slow travel is getting back to basics. Skip the long plane journey in favor of traveling locally, focusing your trip on a region in Brazil, like Bahia or Maranhão. You can always come back and cover another part of the country. And once you get to where you are going, hike, bike and paddle your way to that off-track destination. We're not saying that you should never take busses or planes, far from it. When necessary, take that bus or taxi ride. It directly benefits the Brazilian economy, so you'll know your carbon footprint is going directly toward putting dinner on the plates of locals. You can also take an organized tour (p94) based on sustainable itineraries, or you can volunteer your time (p713).

you just stay in hostels and plan to lie on a beach, eating rice, beans and fish every day, you can probably scrape by on R$70 a day.

If you stay in reasonably comfortable hotels, eat in nicer restaurants, go out most nights and book the occasional flight or guided excursion, you'll probably spend upwards of R$250 a day. Those planning to stay overnight at particularly comfortable guesthouses in resort areas, eat at the best restaurants and not stint on excursions or nightlife can easily spend R$500 a day or more.

Bear in mind that during the December-to-February holiday season, accommodations costs generally increase by around 30%. During Carnaval accommodations prices triple, but a week afterwards, the prices drop to low-season rates. Another thing to remember: resort areas near major cities are often packed on summer weekends. There will be fewer crowds – and sometimes lower prices – if you visit during the week.

Brazil is fair value for solo travelers, as long as you don't mind staying in hostels. Otherwise, a single room generally costs about 75% of the price of a double room.

TRAVEL LITERATURE

A Death in Brazil by Peter Robb is one of the most fascinating travelogues published in recent years (2004). Robb, who spent 20 years in Brazil, explores four centuries of Brazilian history, while detailing his own modern-day travels, creating a compelling portrait of the country.

Accommodations & Food

Your tourist dollar can go a long way to supporting the country if you choose your accommodations carefully. Stay clear of chain hotels and all-inclusive resorts in Brazil's larger cities and beach towns. These chains are often owned by foreign investors who take all profit out of the country. And the battered hotels in town are rarely a good investment – the staff are usually underpaid, the buildings are a health inspector's nightmare and profits are siphoned off to fund less-than-salubrious activities.

You're much better off staying in family-run pousadas (guesthouses). We've made sure to include such recommendations throughout our coverage. By staying in smaller, family-run places, you're guaranteeing that your money will remain in the hands of the local people running the establishment.

In terms of food, Brazil requires some tough choices to be made. Although Brazilian beef is top notch, the explosion of cattle farming continues to fuel the Amazon's destruction, with old-growth forests cleared to make way for pastures. There is a growing number of restaurants serving organic and vegetarian fare, and we've indicated these options where available. Avoid major fast-food chains, as these have played a significant role in fueling the country's deforestation.

Responsible Travel Organizations

Brazil has no certification system to identify the 'green-ness' of accommodations and tour operators. However, various organizations are working to establish sustainable-travel criteria, and the situation may change. Environmentally responsible organizations working in Brazil include the following:

- Rainforest Alliance (www.rainforestalliance.org)

- ResponsibleTravel.com features volunteer opportunities across the country (www.responsible travel.com)

- Rainforest Action Network (www.ran.org)

For a complete list of environmental organizations see p100.

TOP 10

BEST FESTIVALS & EVENTS

Some of Brazil's liveliest festivals are in the Northeast, but no matter where you are, you'll find fantastic, wild and, at times, downright surreal celebrations.

1 Boi-Bumbá (p657), late June, Parintins

2 Bumba Meu Boi (p593), late June to second week of August, São Luís

3 Carnaval, Shrove Tuesday and the days preceding it, February or March, Rio de Janeiro (p114), Salvador (p452) or Olinda (p535)

4 Cavalhadas (p390), 50 days after Easter, Pirenópolis

5 Círio de Nazaré (p610), second Sunday in October, Belém

6 Festa da NS de Boa Morte (p464), mid-August, Cachoeira

7 Reveillon and Festa de Iemanjá (p164), December 31, Rio de Janeiro

8 Folclore Nordestino (p535), late August, Olinda

9 Oktoberfest (p345), mid-October, Blumenau

10 Semana Santa (Holy Week), March or April, Ouro Prêto (p246) or Cidade de Goiás (p387)

BEST ALBUMS

It's no easy task selecting just 10 albums from the scores of Brazil's talented singers and songwriters. Check out some of the great works below, most of which can be found in Brazil.

1 *Africa Brasil*, Jorge Ben

2 *Bossa Negra*, Elza Soares

3 *Elis & Tom*, Elis Reginas and Antonio Carlos Jobim

4 *Feijoada Completa*, Chico Buarque

5 *Gal Costa*, Gal Costa

6 *Getz/Gilberto*, Stan Getz and João Gilberto

7 *Os Afros Sambas*, Baden Powell

8 *Refazenda*, Gilberto Gil

9 *Samba Bossa Nova*, Putumayo compilation

10 *Tropicalia 2*, Caetano Veloso and Gilberto Gil

BEST FILMS & DOCUMENTARIES

A quick and enjoyable way of getting beneath the surface is to explore the films starring Brazil.

1 *Orfeu Negro* (1959)

2 *Pagador de Promessas* (1962)

3 *Bye Bye Brasil* (1980)

4 *Pixote* (1981)

5 *The Mission* (1986)

6 *Central do Brasil* (1998)

7 *Madame Satã* (2002)

8 *Bus 174* (2002)

9 *Cidade de Deus* (2002)

10 *House of Sand* (2006)

Travelers' Tales Brazil, edited by Scott Doggett and Annette Haddad, is a fine anthology of tales of travel and life in Brazil. The excellent 2nd edition (published 2004) includes contributions from writers such as Diane Ackerman, Joe Kane, Petru Popescu and Alma Guillermoprieto.

How to Be a Carioca by Priscilla Ann Goslin is highly recommended for anyone planning to spend time in Rio de Janeiro. Her tongue-in-cheek descriptions of the Carioca (resident of Rio) lifestyle are spot on. Don't miss the hilarious 'essential vocabulary' section for mastering the local lingo.

The Capital of Hope: Brasília and Its People by Alex Shoumatoff is an engaging portrait of Brasília, informed by the author's interviews with government workers and the capital's first settlers.

Peter Fleming's *Brazilian Adventure* is about the young journalist's expedition into Mato Grosso in the 1930s – a wild region then – in search of vanished explorer Colonel Fawcett. What Fleming found is less important than the telling, written with wry humor.

For a fascinating journey from the Andes through Brazilian Amazonia and on to the Atlantic Ocean in the 19th century, read *Exploration of the Valley of the Amazon* by William Lewis Herndon. This recently republished volume is a vivid account of the people and local cultures Herndon encounters, along with observations of the plants, animals and geography of the Brazilian landscape.

After serving as US president, winning the Nobel Peace Prize and surviving an assassin's bullet, Theodore Roosevelt explored parts of Brazil and wrote *Through the Brazilian Wilderness*. It's a great adventure story well worth seeking out.

Although not specifically about Brazil, Redmond O'Hanlon's hilarious *In Trouble Again: A Journey Between the Orinoco and the Amazon* tells of his fretful journey through Latin America.

Also not solely about Brazil is Peter Matthiessen's *The Cloud Forest,* an account of a 30,000km journey across the South American wilderness from the Amazon to Tierra del Fuego. It's well worth a read.

Moritz Thomsen's *The Saddest Pleasure: A Journey on Two Rivers* is an engaging book about the author's experiences in South America, including journeys through Brazil and along the Amazon.

Running the Amazon by Joe Kane is the story of the 10 men and one woman who, in 1986, became the first expedition to cover the entire length of the Rio Amazonas (Amazon River), from the Andes to the Atlantic, on foot and in rafts and kayaks.

INTERNET RESOURCES

Brazilian Embassy in London (www.brazil.org.uk) Excellent country low-down, with links to dozens of local tourism sites in Brazil.

Brazzil (www.brazzil.com) In-depth articles on the country's politics, economy, literature, arts and culture.

Gringoes (www.gringoes.com) Articles written by Anglophones living in Brazil.

Hip Guide to Brazil (www.brazilmax.com) Excellent guide to Brazilian culture and society; good, selective articles and links.

Lanic Brazil (http://lanic.utexas.edu/la/brazil) The University of Texas' excellent collection of Brazil links.

Lonely Planet (www.lonelyplanet.com) Summaries on Brazil travel, the popular Thorn Tree bulletin board, online accommodation booking and links to other web resources.

Terra Brasil (www.terra.com.br/turismo) Portuguese-language travel site with up-to-date information on entertainment, nightlife and dining options in many cities around Brazil.

Itineraries

CLASSIC ROUTES

RIO & THE SOUTHEAST
Three Weeks

Gorgeous beaches, rain forest–covered islands and colonial towns are just some of the things you'll experience on a trip around the Southeast.

Spend a few days discovering **Rio** (p121) and its beaches, restaurants and incredible music scene before heading to **Ilha Grande** (p189), an island blanketed by rain forest and ringed by beaches. Next is **Paraty** (p193), a beautifully preserved colonial town. **Ilhabela** (p305) is another car-free island of beaches, forests and waterfalls. Stop in **São Paulo** (p275) for high culture, including the nation's best museums and restaurants. Then head to exquisite **Ouro Prêto** (p241), **Diamantina** (p261) and **Tiradentes** (p257), some of Brazil's finest colonial gems .

Connect in **Belo Horizonte** (p233) for the picturesque **train ride** (p240) to the coast, or catch a bus to **Parque Nacional de Caparaó** (p270), a hiker's paradise. In **Vitória** (p221), catch a coastal bus south, passing fishing villages and handsome beaches, particularly around **Guarapari** (p226). Further south are equally stunning beaches, from chic **Búzios** (p216), to surf-lovers' **Saquarema** (p212).

On the way back to Rio, detour north to **Petrópolis** (p204), a cool mountain retreat. Great hiking is nearby at the **Parque Nacional da Serra dos Órgãos** (p209). You can also get a taste of Switzerland at **Nova Friburgo** (p210).

This 2300km trip begins and ends in Rio de Janeiro. The circular route passes through picturesque coastal towns, beach-lovers' getaways, surfing spots, idyllic islands, magnificent gold-mining towns and South America's largest metropolis, with opportunities for boat rides and a pretty train journey en route.

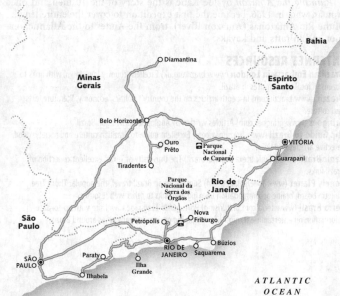

BEST OF BRAZIL

Three Months

On this epic trip you'll experience the rhythm-infused towns of the Northeast, the jungles of the Amazon and the biodiversity of the Pantanal, with beaches, tropical islands and historic towns thrown into the mix.

From **São Paulo** (p275), head east to Rio, stopping at glorious beaches such as **Ubatuba** (p302), **Trindade** (p199) and **Paraty-Mirim** (p200) before reaching **Rio** (p121).

From there head north, visiting the pretty mountain towns of **Ouro Prêto** (p241) and **Diamantina** (p261). The architectural masterpiece that is **Brasília** (p371) is next, and lies near the **Parque Nacional da Chapada dos Veadeiros** (p401), a fantastic wilderness area.

On the way to Bahia, explore the **Parque Nacional da Chapada Diamantina** (p498) before reaching **Salvador** (p439), the country's Afro-Brazilian gem. Further up the coast is **Olinda** (p533), one of Brazil's prettiest towns. From historic **Recife** (p523), fly out to the spectacular archipelago of **Fernando de Noronha** (p539).

Back on the mainland, travel north, stopping in the backpackers' paradise of **Jericoacoara** (p578) en route to the surreal dunes in the **Parque Nacional dos Lençóis Maranhenses** (p597), a stark contrast to the colonial beauty of **São Luís** (p589).

West lies **Belém** (p605), a culturally rich city near the lush island of **Ilha de Marajó** (p618). Catch a boat up the Amazon to **Manaus** (p641), where you can arrange jungle treks.

From Manaus, head south to **Bonito** (p430), and experience the region's waterfalls, crystal-clear rivers, lush forests and subterranean caves. Go south to the awe-inspiring **Iguaçu Falls** (p325), with waterfalls straddling three countries. Before completing the circle, explore the secluded beaches and charming Germanic towns around **Florianópolis** (p334).

This 12,500km (!) trip shows you Brazil's many charms from its nightlife to its wildlife with a survey of pristine islands, storybook towns, steamy jungles and more. To really do the country justice, you'll need six months or a year.

BAHIA & THE NORTHEAST   Six Weeks

Those looking for the soul of Brazil would do well to focus on the Northeast. A confluence of music, history and culture amid spectacular natural scenery makes for an unforgettable journey.

Begin in the pretty towns of **Arraial d'Ajuda** (p486) and **Trancoso** (p487), both blessed with great guesthouses and restaurants, a laid-back nightlife and access to endless walks on the beach. Contine north to **Itacaré** (p475), a lively town with great surf. Then on to **Salvador** (p439), Bahia's most vibrant and colorful city, where drum corps march through the cobblestone streets by day, and nights are devoted to Candomblé, capoeira and dance parties about town.

Detour west to the **Parque Nacional da Chapada Diamantina** (p498) for crisp mountain streams, panoramic views and an endless network of trails. Back on the coast, **Olinda** (p533) is one of Brazil's largest and best-preserved colonial cities and it holds an outstanding Carnaval. From buzzing **Recife** (p523), Olinda's sister city, fly out to **Fernando de Noronha** (p539), an exquisite archipelago of rich marine life and splendid beaches.

Return to the mainland, visit the beautiful and laid-back **Praia da Pipa** (p561), a global village on the coast. The coast from **Natal** (p554) to Fortaleza and Jericoacoara is one of the most spectacular and least developed in Brazil, with scores of spectacular dune-backed beaches ripe for beach-buggy adventures and perfect winds for kitesurfing and windsurfing.

Jericoacoara (p578) itself is a gorgeous beach village with fantastic nightlife. West of there, the **Parque Nacional dos Lençóis Maranhenses** (p597) has one of the most striking landscapes in Brazil, a surreal combination of dunes, lagoons and beaches. The final stop is **São Luís** (p589), a city of colonial beauty that is also Brazil's unquestioned capital of reggae!

> This 4500km trip takes you from gorgeous tropical beaches to culturally rich colonial cities. Porto Seguro, with its many flight connections, is a good gateway. Those with extra time can easily spend three to six months exploring this vibrant region.

ROADS LESS TRAVELED

WATERWAYS OF THE AMAZON   Six Weeks

Few places ignite the imagination like the Amazon. The largest forest on the planet has astounding plant and animal life. Surprising to many visitors, the wetlands also contain historic cities, beautiful river beaches and one of the most important archaeological sites in South America.

Begin in **Belém** (p605), a culturally rich city at the mouth of the great river. From here explore the forest-covered island of **Ilha de Marajó** (p618) or head northeast to **Algodoal** (p616), a rustic fishing hamlet in a splendid setting.

Get a hammock and travel by boat up the Rio Amazonas. Stop in **Monte Alegre** (p627) to see ancient rock paintings, the oldest-known human creations in the Amazon. Upstream is **Santarém** (p621), a pleasant city with many nearby attractions. Across the river, **Alenquer** (p627) is near beautiful, rarely visited countryside. Also reachable is the virgin rain forest of the **Floresta Nacional do Tapajós** (p625) and **Alter do Chão** (p627), a picturesque lagoon with white-sand beaches.

Continue upriver to **Manaus** (p641), Amazonia's largest city and its center for arranging jungle treks or visits to the **Reserva Xixuaú-Xipariná** (p655). You can also travel to **Santa Elena de Uairén** (p671), Venezuela, for treks up **Mt Roraima** (p665). Northwest of Manaus lies the fairly unexplored **Parque Nacional do Jaú** (p656).

You'll see incredible wildlife at the **Mamirauá Reserve** (p659), outside of **Tefé** (p657). From there, continue by river to **Tabatinga** (p660), and into **Leticia** (p662) in Colombia for excursions into the **Parque Nacional Natural Amacayacu** (p664) or for stays at **jungle lodges** (p665) along the Rio Javari.

This 3900km trip begins in Belém, and travels mostly by boat along the world's mightiest river. Several detours include Belém to Ilha de Marajó and Manaus to Santa Elena de Uairén in Venezuela.

SOUTHWARD BOUND   Three Weeks

One of Brazil's most overlooked regions has gorgeous islands and beaches, unexplored national parks and fascinating towns with largely European roots.

Start your journey in **Foz do Iguaçu** (p325) to gaze at some of the most impressive waterfalls on the planet. Take short day trips to Argentina and Paraguay before heading east (by overnight bus or quick flight) to **Curitiba** (p313), a cosmopolitan city with an environmentally responsible design. Next, take the scenic train ride to **Paranaguá** (p319), a sleepy waterfront town that's the jumping-off point to car-free **Ilha do Mel** (p321). The forest-covered island has lovely beaches, low-key guesthouses and is skirted by some pretty trails.

Next head to **Blumenau** (p344) and nearby **Pomerode** (p346), where the Teutonic architecture, blond-haired residents and local brew are more Bavarian than Brazilian. For island beauty, continue on to **Ilha de Santa Catarina** (p333), a forest-covered gem of sand dunes, sparkling beaches, pretty lagoons and sleepy fishing villages.

South of Florianópolis is **Praia do Rosa** (p350), one of Brazil's most glorious beaches – and a great spot for sighting whales off shore. On into Rio Grande do Sul, you'll reach the dramatic canyon and waterfalls of the **Parque Nacional de Aparados da Serra** (p364). Inland, it's worth detouring to the Italian-immigrant town of **Bento Gonçalves** (p359), gateway to the picturesque vineyards of the Serra Gaucho.

Head east to **Santo Ângelo** (p366), which leads on to the Jesuit missions. From there you can visit **São Miguel das Missões** (p366), **São João Batista** (p368) and numerous other holy sites; true grail-seekers can even cross the border into **Paraguay** or **Argentina** (p368).

This 1600km trip begins in Foz do Iguaçu and travels through Brazil's southernmost states. Highlights include forested islands, mountainous national parks, Bavarian-style towns, idyllic beaches and historic missions. At trip's end, go to Porto Alegre for a flight to Rio or São Paulo.

TAILORED TRIPS

WATCHING WILDLIFE   Six Weeks

Brazil contains an astounding variety of fauna and flora with incomparable settings for spying wildlife. Winter (June to September) is probably the best time to go. Despite its urban façade, Rio boasts enticing natural attractions like the **Parque Nacional da Tijuca** (p160) home to coatis, ocelots, three-toed sloths and various species of monkeys. Yet more simians (including howler monkeys) can be spotted on **Ilha Grande** (p189).

Sea turtles are making a comeback in Brazil, and you might see hatchlings in places like **Praia do Forte** (p466) and **Mangue Seco** (p469). Whale-watching is unrivalled in certain parts of Brazil, including the offshore reef of **Parque Nacional Marinho de Abrolhos** (p492) and **Praia do Rosa** (p350), though by far the best place to see aquatic life is **Fernando de Noronha** (p539). **Bonito** (p430), with its crystal-clear rivers, makes for some great snorkeling among river fish, including meter-long catfish. Nearby canyons are home to numerous scarlet macaws.

High on any naturalist's list should be the **Pantanal** (p415), where river otters, caimans, monkeys, jaguars, anacondas and capybara, plus numerous bird species are all part of the mix. The **Amazon** (p601), of course, has many places to see Brazil's wild side, from spotting river dolphins around **Santarém** (p621) to glimpsing toucans outside of **Manaus** (p641).

AROUND BRAZIL IN 80 MEALS   Four Weeks

Brazil has a long history of immigration and cultural diversity across regions. A way of experiencing this is through its cuisine. Food lovers should linger in **São Paulo** (p294) and sample dishes like *camarões à paulista* (marinated shrimp). Although Cariocas didn't invent *feijoada* (bean-and-meat stew), they serve it with finesse, making **Rio** (p169) an essential stop (hint, it's served on Saturdays). *Churrascarias* (barbecued-meat restaurants) are widespread in **Porto Alegre** (p357) and other *gaúcho* cities; it's also the place to try *erva mate*, a tea-like beverage. Other southern delights are the vineyards near **Bento Gonçalves** (p360) and the German restaurants of **Blumenau** (p345). **Minas Gerais** (p104) has its own cuisine, and **Ouro Prêto** (p246) is a good place to try *tutu á mineiro* (mashed black beans and manioc), served with meat dishes. Tasty fish is found in the Central West. Don't miss *dourado*, *pacu* or *pintado* – available in **Bonito** (p433) among other places. The Northeast has many addictive Afro-Brazilian dishes including *moqueca* (spicy fish stew) and *acarajé* (bean-and-shrimp fritters). **Salvador** (p454) is its culinary capital. The Amazon's diversity doesn't end at the waterline. Wonderful dishes like *tacacá* (a spicy soup) and many delicious fish, including *surubim*, *tambaquí*, and the prized *tucunaré*, warrant the trip to **Belém** (p611).

Snapshot

No stranger to the spotlight, Brazil has garnered much attention in the world press in recent years – and for once it's not all bad news. President Lula, re-elected in 2006, continues to bask in the glow of Brazil's huge economic growth along with his administration's effective antipoverty measures – a coupling pleasing to both investors and Lula's labor base.

Back in 2003, economists were calling Brazil the 'next biggest thing' after China and India, with enormous potential for economic growth. Over the next few years, following surprisingly conservative fiscal management, Brazil saw a boom in exports, with Lula taking a US$8 billion deficit to a US$46 billion surplus. The real is among the world's strongest currencies, having surpassed two-to-one parity with the dollar, its highest value since 2001. Following years of stagnation and mounting public debt, Brazil had solid GDP growth, while paying down its debts – it even paid off its debt to the IMF.

Some believe Chinese demand for Brazilian products is fueling the growth, and Brazil and China's strong trade relations have certainly brought benefits. China, however, isn't the only one courting the Latin American giant. Spain, South Korea and Saudi Arabia were all planning new ventures with Brazil. Even the US has thrown a few admiring glances Lula's way. President Bush and Lula met in 2007 to promote international production of ethanol, the plant-based fuel that has helped Brazil transform its economy.

Rising oil prices and a growing acceptance of human-produced climate change has made biofuel an important topic in countries like the US. But in Brazil, ethanol's success is a result of three decades of effort and billions spent on incentives. Brazilian ethanol, made from energy-efficient sugar cane (eight times more efficient than fuel made from US corn), provides 40% of the country's fuel. Brazil is the world's largest exporter of it. Along with expanding oil reserves, it's one of the reasons why Brazil is expected to become energy self-sufficient within the year.

Other good news stems from Lula's progressive social policies. Campaigning years earlier on promises to end hunger in Brazil, Lula delivered the goods with his Bolsa Familia (family grant), a program touted by some (including the World Bank) as a global model for effective social policy. Indeed, it's done much to alleviate the suffering for Brazil's worst off by giving low-income families (those earning less than R$120 a month) a stipend, provided the children stay in school and receive their vaccinations. To date, Bolsa Familia has benefited over 11 million families (44 million people, or 20% of the population). Although it's too early to measure the program's success, a survey of beneficiaries found that more than 80% reported eating better. Critics of the program fear it will leave people addicted to government handouts.

Brazil continues to have notable success at combating AIDS. For over a decade, Brazil has provided free antiretroviral medicine to citizens unable to pay for it, and has become one of the leaders among developing countries in treating its AIDS victims. One of the biggest threats to the program, though, is the rising cost of new drugs (essential for patients resistant to old antiretroviral treatments). In 2007, following a breakdown in negotiations with the large pharmaceutical company Merck, Brazil announced it would bypass Merck's patent and reproduce the drugs inexpensively – a move that even the WTO accepts in the event of national emergencies. It has also had a great deal of success with prevention schemes, educating youth about the dangers of unprotected sex, and distributing free condoms on a massive scale (25 million are distributed nationwide over Carnaval).

FAST FACTS

Population: 190 million

Annual growth: 1.01%

Life expectancy at birth: 68 years (men), 76 years (women)

GDP: R$3.13 trillion

Number of people living below the poverty line: 40 million

Monthly minimum wage: R$380

Infant mortality per 1000 live births: 27 (US: 7)

Unemployment: 10%

Adult literacy: 86%

Number of political candidates charged with fraud: 1535

Despite predictions by the World Bank that more than one million Brazilians would carry HIV by 2000, today the infection rate stands at half that number. Health officials have even developed a working partnership with Brazil's prostitutes, a move that has angered church officials.

Speaking of the church, Brazil received its first visit from Pope Benedict XVI in 2007. He arrived to canonize the first Brazilian-born saint, Antonio de Sant'Anna Galvão, an 18th-century monk credited with some 5000 miracles. Although the numbers of Catholics are declining in Brazil (down from 89% of the population in 1980 to around 73% today), Brazil still has the world's largest Catholic population – and Benedict has clearly made a focal point of Brazil and Latin America (which he described as 'a continent of hope'). Some 1.2 million people gathered outside of São Paulo to hear the pope say Mass. The pope also used his visit to distance himself from the teachings of Liberation Theology, a clerical movement promoting social justice for the poor through activism, which still has many followers in Brazil. Before departing, Benedict denounced the legalization of abortion in Mexico City – a warning to Brazil (which still outlaws abortion) not to follow suit.

As in many places, abortion is a hot topic in Brazil. On the eve of the pope's visit, Lula called abortion a public-health issue that can no longer be ignored. Brazil's newest health minister echoed that statement, calling for wide-ranging debates, and suggested it may be time for a referendum.

On other fronts, grievous social problems still plague Brazil. Crime continues to skyrocket, with the homicide rate doubling in the last two decades. Lula even used the word 'terrorism' to describe one particularly heinous bus attack, perhaps signaling a shift in thinking about the country's relentless urban violence.

Corruption is another never-ending scourge of Brazil, impacting nearly every layer of public life. Lula, who promised a new era of clean government in 2002, has presided over several notorious episodes. The most recent scandal erupted after the arrest of several of Lula's operatives, who were caught with nearly US$800,000 en route to purchase a dossier believed damaging to Alckmin, Lula's presidential rival.

Although some suspected the scandal would cost him the election, ultimately Lula prevailed. Given the progress his administration has made in many fields, it's not difficult to see why. After all, corruption may never disappear from politics. Brazilians only hope the present economic and social gains don't either.

History

Brazil's population, the fifth biggest in the world, reached its lands from Africa, Asia, Europe and other parts of the Americas – diverse origins that have created one of the planet's most racially mixed societies. How they came, intermingled and developed the unique Brazilian identity that charms visitors today is a rough-and-tumble story of courage, greed, endurance and cruelty, eventually yielding a fitful progress towards the democracy the country now enjoys.

BEFORE THE PORTUGUESE

By the time the Portuguese rolled up in AD 1500, what is now Brazil had already been populated for as many as 50,000 years. But unlike the Incas, Brazil's early inhabitants never developed a highly advanced civilization and they left few clues for archaeologists to follow. One of the few certainties is that it wasn't the Portuguese who discovered *terra brasilis*.

It's generally believed that the early inhabitants of the Americas arrived from Siberia in waves between about 60,000 and 8000 BC, crossing land now submerged beneath the Bering Strait, then gradually spreading southward over many millennia. Researchers in the remote Serra da Capivara in the Northeastern state of Piauí (p588) have found evidence of human presence there 50,000 years ago, predating other finds in the Americas by about 30,000 years. The oldest traces of human life in the Amazon region can be seen on a detour from a river trip between Santarém and Belém: a series of rock paintings estimated to be 12,000 years old near Monte Alegre (p627). Other remnants of early civilizations can be found on the Ilha de Marajó (p618 and p628) at the mouth of the Amazon, and at the Gruta da Lapinha (p241) in Minas Gerais.

By the time the Portuguese arrived in AD 1500, there were probably between two and four million people in what's now Brazil, in over 1000 tribes.

CABRAL & CHUMS

The course of Brazilian history was changed forever in 1500, when a fleet of 12 Portuguese ships carrying nearly 1200 men rolled up near what is today Porto Seguro.

The fleet, ostensibly bound for East Africa and Asia to set up trading posts, had headed west after passing the Cape Verde Islands, off the coast of West Africa. Increasingly it is thought that, far from having been simply blown off course, the Portuguese already had reason to suspect there was a large land mass across the southern Atlantic that would make such a giant detour worthwhile. Whatever the motive, on April 22, 1500, Pedro Álvares Cabral and his gang stepped for the first time onto Brazilian soil. Their indigenous reception committee was ready and waiting.

'There were 18 or 20 men,' marveled scribe Pero Vaz de Caminha in a letter back to the Portuguese king. 'They were brown-skinned, all of them naked, without anything at all to cover their private parts. In their hands they carried bows and arrows.'

The festivities didn't last long. Having erected a cross and held Mass in the land they baptized Terra da Vera Cruz (Land of the True Cross), the

The Brazilian NGO Instituto Socioambiental has heaps of fascinating information on the indigenous population, in English and Portuguese, at www.socioambiental .org. Also interesting, and with video clips, is www .survival-international.org.

The first Bishop of Brazil, Bishop Pêro Fernandes Sardinha, was shipwrecked off the coast of Alagoas in 1556, then ceremonially killed and eaten by the local Caeté Indians.

c 50,000 BC	1494
Early Brazilians leave the oldest evidence of human presence in the Americas, in the Serra da Capivara	Treaty of Tordesillas divides the New World between Spain and Portugal

Portuguese took to the waves once again. With lucrative spice, ivory and diamond markets in Asia and Africa to exploit, Portugal had bigger fish to fry elsewhere. It wasn't till 1531 that the first Portuguese settlers arrived in Brazil.

BRAZIL'S INDIANS

For Brazil's Indians, April 22, 1500 marked the first chapter in their gradual extermination. Sixteenth-century European explorers along the Amazon encountered large, widespread populations; some were practising agriculture while others were still nomadic hunter-gatherers. Coastal peoples fell into three main groups: the Guarani (south of São Paulo and in the Paraguai and Paraná basins inland), the Tupi or Tupinambá (along most of the rest of the coast) and the Tapuia (other peoples inhabiting shorter stretches of coast in among the Tupi and Guarani). The Tupi and Guarani had much in common in language and culture. A European adaptation of the Tupi-Guarani language later spread throughout colonial Brazil and is still spoken by some people in Amazonia today.

Over the following centuries a four-front war was waged on the Indian way of life. It was a cultural war, as well as a physical, territorial and biological one. Many *índios* fell victim to the *bandeirantes* – groups of roaming adventurers who spent the 17th and 18th centuries exploring Brazil's interior, pillaging Indian settlements as they went. Those who escaped such a fate were struck down by the illnesses shipped in from Europe, to which they had no natural resistance. Others were worked to death on sugar plantations.

If the *bandeirantes* were responsible for the physical destruction of the Indians, it was the Jesuits who began their cultural destruction, outlawing their traditions and customs and settling them in *aldeias* (missions), though at the same time they did oppose Indian slavery and attempted to protect the Indians from the *bandeirantes*.

By the start of the 21st century Brazil's indigenous population had dwindled to somewhere between 350,000 and 600,000, the majority of them in the relatively isolated Amazonian forests. See the boxed text Brazil's Indians Today (p36) for more on how they are surviving.

For more on Sydney Possuelo and uncontacted tribes, check www .korubo.com and dig out the August 2003 *National Geographic*.

DIVIDING THE LAND

Thirty years after Brazil's 'discovery', Portugal's King João III decided it might actually be worth settling there after all. The first settlement sprang up at São Vicente, when a fleet of five ships carrying some 400 men docked near what is now the port of Santos.

In an attempt to ward off the ambitions of other European countries, the king divided the Brazilian coast into 15 captaincies, each with about 250km of coastline and lands stretching inland to the west. These territories were awarded to *donatários,* minor gentry favored by the king. It was hoped that, through settlement, the long coastline could be secured at minimal cost.

The settlers' lives were made difficult by the climate, hostility from the Indians and competition from the Dutch and French. Four captaincies were never settled and four destroyed by Indians. Only Pernambuco and São Vicente were profitable.

In 1549 the king sent Tomé de Sousa to be the first governor of Brazil, to centralize authority and save the few remaining captaincies. Sousa was

1500	1531
The Portuguese land in Brazil	First Portuguese settlers arrive near what is now the port of Santos

joined by some 1000 settlers; among them Portuguese officials, soldiers, exiled prisoners, New Christians (converted Jews) and the first six Jesuit priests. The city of Salvador was founded as Sousa's base, and remained Brazil's capital until 1763, when Rio de Janeiro took over.

BRAZIL'S INDIANS TODAY

When the Portuguese arrived in 1500, there were, by the most common estimates, between two and four million indigenous people already living in Brazil, in over 1000 different tribes. Five centuries later there are somewhere between 350,000 and 600,000 Indians left, depending whose statistics you look at, in a little over 200 tribes. Slavery, diseases, armed conflict and loss of territory all took a savage toll on Brazil's native peoples, to the point where in the 1980s Indian numbers were under 300,000 and it was feared they might die out completely. Since then there has been a marked recovery in the Indian population, partly thanks to international concern about peoples like the Yanomami, who were threatened with extermination by disease and violence from an influx of gold prospectors into their lands. Government policy has become more benign and huge areas of Brazil are now Terra Indígena (Indigenous Land). Just over 1 million sq km – more than 12% of the whole country – is now either officially registered as Indigenous Land or in process of registration.

Indigenous Lands remain state property, but their Indian inhabitants are granted permanent possession and exclusive use, meaning that this 12% of national territory is reserved for about 0.2% of the national population. Unsurprisingly, there are those who think this is too much and fail to respect Indian rights to these lands. Disputes between Indian groups and loggers, miners, homesteaders, hunters, road builders and reservoir constructors are still common, and sometimes violent. Indian-rights supporters were especially alarmed in 2006 when Mércio Gomes, then president of the government Indian-affairs agency, Fundação Nacional do Índio (Funai), declared that limits ought to be set on the amount of Indigenous Land. This provoked an outspoken attack on Gomes by the legendary Sydney Possuelo, head of Funai's unknown-tribes department. Possuelo, who has spent his life seeking out uncontacted tribes in the depths of the Amazon rain forests in order to protect them from disease, violence and other effects of encroaching settlement, commented that Gomes spoke the language of the Indians' enemies, and was summarily sacked. Gomes himself was replaced by Márcio Meira in 2007.

It's thought there may still be over 50 uncontacted tribes, mostly small groups in the Amazon forests – home to about 60% of Brazil's Indians (and almost all the existing Indigenous Lands).

Most of Brazil's Indians still live traditional lifestyles, hunting (some still with blowpipes and poisoned arrows) and gathering and growing plants for food, medicine and utensils. Their homes are usually of natural materials such as wood or grass. Ritual activity is strong, body- and face-painting is prevalent, and most Indian peoples are skilled in making pottery, basketry, masks, headdresses, musical instruments and other artisanry with their hands. None of those known to the outside world are truly nomadic. Indigenous Lands generally have an exemplary record of environmental conservation because their inhabitants continue to live sustainable lifestyles.

The largest tribes include the Tikuna on the upper Rio Solimões in Amazonia (around 30,000 strong), the Yanomami in the hills straddling the Brazil–Venezuela border (about 12,000 in Brazil), and the Guarani, of whom some 35,000 are scattered around southern Brazil, with further members in Argentina, Paraguay and Bolivia. At the other extreme, several tribes are on the verge of extinction, including the Juma from Amazonia's Purus River, of whom just five members remain – one man, his three daughters and one grand daughter.

Indians in Amazonia have generally had more luck in holding onto their territory and avoiding cultural disintegration. Many Guarani, in the southern parts of Brazil, live on lands too small to support them, and they suffer from a high suicide rate.

1538	1549
The first African slaves arrive in the Northeast	Tomé de Sousa becomes the first governor of Brazil, with his capital at Salvador

SUGAR & SLAVERY

Brazil didn't boast the ivory and spices of Africa and the East Indies, and the only thing that had interested the Portuguese in the early years after they had found it was a rock-hard tree known as *pau brazil* (brazilwood), which yielded a valuable red dye. Merchants began sending a few ships each year to harvest brazilwood and take it back to Europe, and the colony changed its name to Brazil in tribute to the tree. Alas, the most accessible trees were rapidly depleted, and the Indians soon stopped volunteering their labor. But after colonization in 1531, the settlers soon worked out that Brazil was a place where sugarcane grew well. Sugar came to Brazil in 1532 and hasn't left since. It was coveted by a hungry European market, which used it for medicinal purposes, to flavor foods and even in wine.

These days sugar is as popular as ever in Brazil. You can sip it on the beach in the form of a *caldo de cana* (sugarcane juice). You can neck it in one of Brazil's many *pé-sujo* (dirty-foot) bars as a shot of *cachaça* (white spirit made from sugarcane). You can pour copious amounts into your coffee, as do most Brazilians, and you can even run your car on it.

Perhaps envisaging Brazil's sugarcoated future, the colonists turned to this new industry. They lacked just one thing: a work force.

Rio de Janeiro got its name because its Portuguese discoverers arrived in January (Janeiro), 1502, and thought that Guanabara Bay on which it lies was the mouth of a river *(rio)*.

The Slave Trade

Initially the Portuguese seemed to hit it off with Brazil's natives. There was even an exchange of presents between Cabral's men and the Indians on the beach, with a Portuguese sombrero swapped for feather headdresses. Relations cooled when the Portuguese started enslaving their neighbors for work on the sugarcane plantations. Yet, for a variety of reasons the Portuguese felt the Indians didn't make great slaves and turned instead to Africa's already existing slave trade.

African slaves started to pour into Brazil's slave markets from about 1550. They were torn from a variety of tribes in Angola, Mozambique and Guiné, as well as the Sudan and Congo. Whatever their origins and cultures, their destinations were identical: slave markets such as Salvador's Pelourinho (p444) or Belém's Mercado Ver-o-Peso (p608). By the time slavery was abolished in Brazil in 1888, around 3.6 million Africans had been shipped to Brazil – nearly 40% of the total that came to the New World.

Africans were seen as better workers and less susceptible to the European diseases that had proved the undoing of so many Indians. In short, they were a better investment. Yet the Portuguese didn't go out of their way to protect this investment. Slaves were brought to Brazil in subhuman conditions: taken from their families and packed into squalid ships for the month-long journey to Brazil.

Visitors to the beaches of Porto de Galinhas (p537), near Recife, might not pick up on the area's grim past. Even after abolition, slave traders continued to smuggle in slaves often packed into a ship's hull under crates full of *galinhas* (chickens).

Three worthwhile recent 300-page tellings of the whole Brazilian story in English are Joseph Smith's *A History of Brazil* (2002; the most recent), Thomas E Skidmore's *Brazil: Five Centuries of Change* and Boris Fausto's *A Concise History of Brazil* (both 1999).

Masters & Slaves

For those who survived such ordeals, arrival in Brazil meant only continued suffering. A slave's existence was one of brutality and humiliation. Kind masters were the exception, not the rule, and labor on the plantations was

---

1654	1695
Dutch driven out of Recife, ending rival colonial powers' designs on Brazil	Destruction of the Palmares *quilombo* in Brazil's Northeast

relentless. In temperatures that often exceeded 30°C (86°F), slaves were required to work as many as 17 hours each day, before retiring to the squalid *senzala* (slave quarters), and with as many as 200 slaves packed into each dwelling, hygiene was a concept as remote as the distant coasts of Africa. Dysentery, typhus, yellow fever, malaria, tuberculosis and scurvy were rife; malnutrition a fact of life. Syphilis also plagued a slave population sexually exploited by its masters.

A doorstop of a book about the relationship between slaves and masters on Pernambuco's sugar plantations, Gilberto Freyre's *The Masters and the Slaves* (1933) revolutionized Brazilian thinking about the African contribution to Brazilian society.

Sexual relations between masters and slaves were so common that a large mixed-race population soon emerged. Off the plantations there was a shortage of white women, so many poorer white settlers lived with black or Indian women. Brazil was already famous for its sexual permissiveness by the beginning of the 18th century.

Aside from the *senzala*, the other main institution of the sugar plantation was the *casa grande* ('big house') – the luxurious mansion from which the masters would control their slaves.

Resistance & the Quilombos

Resistance to slavery took many forms. Documents of the period refer to the desperation of the slaves who starved themselves to death, killed their babies or fled. Sabotage and theft were frequent, as were work slowdowns, stoppages and revolts.

Other slaves sought solace in African religion and culture. The mix of Catholicism (made compulsory by slave masters) and African traditions spawned a syncretic religion on the sugar plantations, known today as Candomblé. The slaves masked illegal customs with a facade of Catholic saints and rituals. The martial art capoeira (see p449) also grew out of the slave communities.

Quilombo (directed by Cacá Diegues) is an epic history flick in which the vast Palmares *quilombo* – a community of runaway slaves led by the legendary Zumbi – is reconstructed in Rio's Baixada Fluminense. It's blessed with Gilberto Gil's excellent soundtrack.

Many slaves escaped from their masters to form *quilombos,* communities of runaway slaves that quickly spread across the countryside. The most famous, the Republic of Palmares, which survived through much of the 17th century, was home to some 20,000 people. Palmares was a network of *quilombos* covering a broad tract of lush tropical forest straddling the border of Alagoas and Pernambuco states. Under their leaders Ganga Zumba and his son-in-law Zumbi, its citizens became pioneers of guerrilla warfare, repeatedly fending off Portuguese attacks between 1654 and 1695. Eventually Palmares fell to a force of *bandeirantes* from São Paulo.

As abolitionist sentiment grew in the 19th century, many (unsuccessful) slave rebellions were staged, the *quilombos* received more support and ever-greater numbers of slaves fled the plantations. Only abolition itself, in 1888, stopped the growth of *quilombos*. Over 700 villages that started as *quilombos* remain today. Some were so isolated that they remained completely out of contact with white Brazilians until the last couple of decades.

COLONIAL RIVALS

It's hard to picture what Brazil would have been like under French or Dutch rule. Tom Jobim might have composed a track about the *Meisje* from Ipanema; Brazilians might be tucking into frogs' legs and not *feijoada* (bean-and-meat stew) every Sunday. For a time, such outcomes were a distinct possibility.

Technically, the 1494 Treaty of Tordesillas divided the New World between Spain and Portugal. An imaginary line, running north–south from roughly the mouth of the Amazon to what is now Santa Catarina, was drawn on

1710	1727
The Brazilian gold rush begins	The first coffee bean arrives in Brazil

the map. Land to the east became Portuguese territory; land to the west fell under Spanish control.

But the line proved very imaginary indeed. As any traveler brave enough to venture into the further reaches of Mato Grosso will discover, enforcing such a vast border running through thick jungles and swamps was never a particularly viable idea. Brazil's borders remained in flux until as late as 1930.

Over the years, Portugal repeatedly ignored the frontier in an attempt to squeeze more land out of its rivals. France and Holland also had their eyes on Brazil's green and lucrative land.

The French

In 1555 three boatloads of French settlers landed on a small island in Rio's Baía de Guanabara. Obviously liking what they found, the French decided to try to incorporate parts of southern Brazil into their ever-growing empire. Antarctic France would be its name.

Things didn't go to plan – a few years later the *franceses* were expelled by the Portuguese, who landed near Praia Vermelha, at the foot of the Sugarloaf Mountain. It was here that Estácio de Sá founded the city of São Sebastião do Rio de Janeiro on March 1, 1565.

The French made another brief attempt to claw Brazilian soil from the Portuguese, further north, in 1612, when they founded the city of São Luís, which took its name from France's then king, Louis XIII. Three years later, the Portuguese sent the French packing once again.

The Dutch

The challenge from Holland proved harder to shake off. The Dutch West India Company (DWIC), set up in 1621, was much more than a simple trading business. Its business, in fact, was war, and its goal was to take Brazil's Northeast from the Portuguese.

The Dutch bombardment of Salvador began on the morning of May 9, 1624. By the following day, the invading force of 3000 men from 26 ships had captured and ransacked the city. Salvador's return to Portuguese hands was almost as quick; it was just a year before a combined force of 12,000 Spanish and Portuguese troops evicted the Dutch. But five years later the Dutch were back, storming the cities of Olinda and Recife and making Recife the capital of New Holland. In 1637 a Dutch prince, Maurice of Nassau, was brought in to govern the colony. Educated at university back home in, among other things, good manners, Nassau was a definite hit with the locals. His policy of freedom of worship, which left Brazil's Catholics to their own devices despite the Protestant invasion, brought a definite stability to the region.

The Dutch extended their control over much of northeastern Brazil, from the São Francisco river in Bahia to Maranhão. That Brazilians didn't go on to become Dutch speakers is largely down to the exit of Nassau, who returned to Holland in 1644 after a series of disagreements with the boys from the DWIC. New Holland had hardly waved its ruler goodbye when violent uprisings broke out, designed to uproot the Dutch. The following decade saw a series of bloody clashes in the Northeast: two crucial battles, in which the Portuguese came out victorious even though outnumbered, took place in 1648 and 1649. The Dutch were driven back into Recife and eventually surrendered in 1654, drawing a line under Holland's part in Brazilian history.

1763	1807
Rio de Janeiro replaces Salvador as Brazil's capital	The Portuguese royal family escapes from Napoleon to Rio de Janeiro

THE BANDEIRANTES & THE GOLD RUSH

The *bandeirantes,* too, were keen to make inroads into Brazil. These bands of explorers roamed Brazil's interior in search of Indian slaves, mapping out undiscovered territory and bumping off the odd indigenous community along the way.

The *bandeirantes* took their name from the trademark flag-bearer who would front their expeditions. During the 17th and 18th centuries, group after group of *bandeirantes* set out from São Paulo. The majority were bilingual in Portuguese and Tupi-Guarani, born of Portuguese fathers and Indian mothers. They benefited from both Indian survival techniques and European weaponry.

By the mid-17th century they had journeyed as far as the peaks of the Peruvian Andes and the Amazon lowlands. It was the exploits of these discoverers that stretched Brazil's borders to their current extent. In 1750, after four years of negotiations with the Spanish, their conquests were secured. The Treaty of Madrid handed over 6 million sq km to the Portuguese and put Brazil's western borders more or less where they are today.

The *bandeirantes* were known for more than just their colorful flags. Protected from Indian arrows by heavily padded cotton jackets, they waged an all-out war on Brazil's natives, despite the fact that many of them had Indian mothers. Huge numbers of Indians fled inland, searching for shelter in the Jesuit missions. But there were few hiding places – it is thought the *bandeirantes* killed or enslaved well in excess of 500,000 Indians.

Gold

'As yet we have no way of knowing whether there might be gold, or silver or any kind of metal or iron [here],' reported Pero Vaz de Caminha to his king in 1500.

Though it wasn't discovered until nearly two centuries later, there certainly was gold in Brazil. Unsurprisingly, it was the *bandeirantes* who, in between decapitating Indians, discovered it in the Serra do Espinhaço in Minas Gerais.

For part of the 18th century Brazil became the world's greatest gold 'producer', unearthing wealth that helped build many of Minas Gerais' historic cities. The full title of Ouro Prêto (p241), one of the principal beneficiaries of the gold boom, is actually Vila Rica de Ouro Prêto (Rich Town of Black Gold).

Other wild boomtowns such as Sabará (p250), Mariana (p248) and São João del Rei (p253) sprang up in the mountain valleys. Wealthy merchants built opulent mansions and bankrolled stunning baroque churches, many of which remain to this day.

Gold produced a major shift in Brazil's population from the Northeast to the Southeast. When gold was first discovered, there were no white settlers in the territory of Minas Gerais. By 1710 the population had reached 30,000, and by the end of the 18th century it was 500,000. An estimated one-third of the two million slaves brought to Brazil in the 18th century were sent to the goldfields, where their lives were often worse than in the sugar fields.

But the gold boom didn't last. By 1750 the mining regions were in decline and coastal Brazil was returning to center stage. Many of the gold-hunters ended up in Rio de Janeiro, which grew rapidly.

1822	1835
Independence declared from Portugal	Brazil's last big slave revolt, in Bahia, narrowly fails

TIRADENTES

As if the French and Dutch hadn't been enough to deal with, Brazil's Portuguese rulers also faced threats from within. During the 18th century calls for independence grew ever stronger and in 1789 the first organized movement came to life.

In charge was Joaquim José da Silva Xavier – a dentist from Ouro Prêto known as Tiradentes (Tooth Puller). With 11 other conspirators – all outraged by attempts to collect taxes – Tiradentes began talks about how best to uproot the Portuguese.

Though the plotters earned themselves a grand name – the Inconfidência Mineira – their plans were quickly foiled. All 12 were arrested and sentenced to death and, although a royal pardon was eventually issued exiling the rebels to Angola and Mozambique, it came too late for Tiradentes, who was hanged in Rio de Janeiro in 1792. As a warning to other would-be rebels the authorities sliced up his body and displayed the parts across Minas Gerais. His head was put on show in Ouro Prêto, his house destroyed and salt scattered on the ground outside so that nothing would grow there. According to one version of events, soldiers formally recorded the event on a manuscript – using Tiradentes' blood as ink.

Tiradentes became a national martyr – a symbol of resistance – and during the later Vargas era, a museum in his honor was opened in Ouro Prêto's old town hall.

DOM JOÃO VI

Brazil became a temporary sanctuary to the Portuguese royal family in 1807. Running scared from Napoleon, whose army was at that moment advancing on Lisbon, some 15,000 court members fled to Rio de Janeiro, led by the prince regent, Dom João.

Like so many *estrangeiros* (foreigners) arriving in Brazil, the regent fell in love with the place and granted himself the privilege of becoming the country's ruler. He opened Rio's Jardim Botânico (Botanical Gardens; p128) to the public in 1822, and they remain there to this day in the upmarket Jardim Botânico neighborhood.

Even after Napoleon's defeat at Waterloo in 1815, Dom João showed no sign of abandoning Brazil. When his mother, Dona Maria I, died the following year, he became king and declared Rio the capital of the United Kingdom of Portugal and Brazil. Brazil became the only New World colony ever to have a European monarch ruling on its soil.

INDEPENDENCE

Independence eventually came in 1822, 30 years after the Inconfidência Mineira. Legend has it that, on the banks of São Paulo's Ipiranga river, Brazil's then regent, Dom João's son Pedro, pulled out his sword, bellowing, *'Independência ou morte!'* (Independence or death!). With the same breath he declared himself Emperor Dom Pedro I.

The Portuguese quickly gave in to the idea of a Brazilian empire. Without a single shot being fired, Dom Pedro I became the first emperor of an independent Brazil. The *povo brasileiro* (Brazilian people), however, were not as keen on Pedro as he was about their newly born nation. From all accounts he was a blundering incompetent, whose sexual exploits (and resulting string

1888	1889
Princesa Isabel signs the Lei Aurea, officially abolishing slavery	Republic declared

of love children) horrified even the most permissive of Brazilians. After nine years of womanizing he was forced to abdicate, leaving his five-year-old son, Dom Pedro II, to take over.

A period of crisis followed: the heir to the throne was, after all, just a child. Between 1831 and 1840 Brazil was governed by so-called *regências* (regencies), a time of political turmoil and widespread rebellions. The only solution was the return of the monarchy and a law was passed to declare Dom Pedro II an adult, well before his 18th birthday.

The bloodiest and most radical of the 1830s revolts was the Cabanagem War, a popular rebellion in Pará. Rebels held the city of Belém for a year before being evicted and decimated by government troops.

Aged just 15, Dom Pedro II received the title of Emperor and Perpetual Defender of Brazil, precipitating one of the most prosperous spells in the country's history, barring the war with Paraguay in 1865. Invaded by its neighbor, Brazil teamed up with Argentina and Uruguay and thrashed the Paraguayans back across the border.

Paraguay was left crippled – its population slashed to just 200,000, of whom around 180,000 were women. Brazil, too, suffered heavily: around 100,000 men died, many of them slaves sent to war in the place of wealthier Brazilians.

ABOLITION & THE REPUBLIC

Since the 16th century, slavery had formed the backbone of a brutally unequal society in Brazil. 'Every dimension of our social existence is contaminated,' lamented abolitionist Joaquim Nabuco in 1880.

To undo something so deeply ingrained into the Brazilian way of life was never likely to be easy. Brazil prevaricated for nearly 60 years before any sort of resolution was reached. The 19th century was punctuated by a series of halfhearted legislative attempts to lay the slave industry to rest. Repeatedly such laws failed.

Slave trafficking to Brazil was banned in 1850, but continued clandestinely. Another law, in 1885, freed all slaves over the age of 65. The lawmakers had obviously forgotten that the average life expectancy for a slave at this time was 45. Not until May 13, 1888 – 80 years after Britain had freed its slaves – was slavery itself officially banned in Brazil. Unsurprisingly, this didn't make a huge immediate difference to the welfare of the 800,000 freed slaves, who were largely illiterate and unskilled. Thousands were cast onto the streets without any kind of infrastructure to support them. Many died, while others flooded to Brazil's urban centers, adding to the cities' first slums. Still today, blacks overall remain among the poorest and worst-educated groups in the country.

Not far out of the door behind slavery was the Império Brasileiro. In 1889 a military coup, supported by Brazil's wealthy coffee farmers, decapitated the old Brazilian empire and the republic was born. The emperor went into exile, where he died a couple of years later.

A military clique ruled Brazil for the next four years until elections were held, but because of ignorance, corruption, and land and literacy requirements, only about 2% of the adult population voted. Little changed, except that the power of the military and the now-influential coffee growers increased, while it diminished for the sugar barons.

FULL OF BEANS

The first coffee bean found its way into Brazil in the 18th century. The responsible party was, they say, an army officer called Francisco de Mello

1890s	1897
Brazil opens its borders and immigrants come flooding in	First *favela* founded in Rio by soldiers returning from massacring the messianic settlement of Canudos

Palheta, who had journeyed to French Guiana and came back brandishing a handful of coffee beans – a gift from a lover he had left behind. On arrival back in Brazil, the beans were swiftly planted, thus beginning another Brazilian love-hate affair – with *café*.

Whatever the truth, the coffee industry eventually grew into a huge success. By 1889 coffee accounted for two-thirds of Brazil's exports.

Coffee growers filled the gap left in Brazil's export market by the decline of its sugar industry since the 1820s. Unable to compete with the newly mechanized sugar mills in the West Indies, sugar exports plummeted. Coffee, meanwhile, flourished, and coffee plantations soon took up vast tracts of land in São Paulo and Minas Gerais states.

Although coffee was the making of many millionaires in the southern states, it was also the cause of great suffering. The coffee *fazendas* (ranches) in many ways replicated the Northeastern sugar plantations: slaves worked inhuman hours in cramped and fetid conditions. In Rio many such estates have now opened their doors to the public, and provide a chilling insight into Brazilian *escravidão* (slavery). After abolition in 1888, the work force changed, but the conditions did not.

OPEN BORDERS

In the final decade of the 19th century, Brazil opened its borders. Millions of immigrants – from Italy, Japan, Spain, Germany, Portugal and elsewhere – streamed into Brazil to work on the coffee *fazendas,* and to make new lives in the rapidly growing cities, especially Rio and São Paulo, adding further textures to Brazil's ethnic mixture and confirming the shift of Brazil's economic center of gravity from the Northeast to the Southeast. When you tuck into a pizza in São Paulo's Bela Vista district or sample a *pastel chinês* (Chinese pastry) at one of Rio's many street-corner snack bars, it is more than likely to be this generation of border hoppers you have to thank.

Over the next century, immigrants continued to flood into Brazil. The country became a haven for Jews fleeing persecution at the hands of the Nazis, as well as Nazis looking to avoid being put on trial for war crimes. Arabs, universally known as *turcos* by the Brazilians, also joined the influx of newcomers. Many of the traders you'll meet at Rio de Janeiro's Rua Uruguaiana flea market hail from the Middle East.

RUBBER

Toward the end of the 19th century the Amazon region was the scene of another Brazilian economic boom: that of the *Hevea brasiliensis*, the rubber tree.

Demand for rubber rocketed in 1890 with the invention of the pneumatic tire and the start of the automobile industry in the US. The rubber price shot up, bringing huge wealth to the main Amazonian cities of Belém and Manaus. Manaus' spectacular opera house, the Teatro Amazonas (p642), opened in 1896, was one fruit of the rubber boom. Rubber production reached its peak in 1912, when latex exports made up nearly 40% of Brazil's export revenue.

As with all booms, the bust had to come. The British may have given Brazil one of its greatest gifts in football, but they also stole one of Brazil's greatest assets. In 1876 Englishman Henry Wickham had smuggled

Bye-Bye Brasil, directed by Cacá Diegues, is a classic Brazilian film that follows a traveling circus across Brazil's Northeast, charting the profound changes in Brazilian society that characterized the second half of the 20th century.

1937	1938
Fascist Estado Novo (New State) declared by Getúlio Vargas	The last great *cangaçeiro* (bandit of the Northeast), Lampião, is killed by police

The Canudos massacre is the subject of one of the masterpieces of Brazilian literature, *Os Sertões* (Rebellion in the Backlands) by Euclides de Cunha, who witnessed the end of Canudos as a correspondent for a São Paulo newspaper.

70,000 rubber-tree seeds out of Amazonia on a chartered freighter to Kew Gardens in London. Seedlings quickly found their way to the British colonies in Southeast Asia, where large rubber plantations were established. When the plantations started to yield in 1910, the price of latex plummeted on the world market. The Brazilian rubber boom blew out in spectacular fashion.

MILK & COFFEE POLITICS

On November 15, 1894, Prudente de Morais became Brazil's first directly elected civil president. At this time Brazil was dominated by land-owning families from two states: Minas Gerais and São Paulo. These groups controlled national politics, and Brazil's presidents came almost without exception from these states of milk and coffee respectively. Each state was dominated by a series of rural landowners known as *coronéis* (colonels), who controlled the local political, judicial and police systems through friends and family in all the important public posts.

Such political bias was reflected in the electoral system. Ballots were not secret and those who voted against the ruling powers suffered reprisals. Fraud was common: many people would vote more than once and, from time to time, even the dead found the power to vote.

Disillusioned with the dominance of this wealthy few, a new movement among the military, known as *tenentismo*, began to form in opposition to the small oligarchies of Minas and São Paulo.

The world-famous Copacabana beach was the scene of the first rebellion. On July 5, 1922, 18 tenants set out from the fort of Copacabana (p148) and clashed with government troops. Just two of the *tenentes* – Eduardo Gomes and Siqueira Campos – survived, the latter giving his name to the metro station a few blocks from the beach.

For another eight years Brazil's coffee farmers continued to enjoy the status of political untouchables, but the Wall St bust of 1929 changed every-

---

CANUDOS

The 19th century was an era of messianic popular movements among Brazil's poor. Most of these happened in the economically depressed backlands of the Northeast, devastated by the decline of the sugar industry and the terrible droughts in the 1870s and '80s. The most famous was that of Canudos. Its leader, Antônio Conselheiro (Antônio the Counselor), had wandered for years through the backlands preaching and prophesying the appearance of the Antichrist and the end of the world, defending the poor and antagonizing the authorities. He railed against the new republican government and in 1893 eventually settled with his followers at Canudos, in the interior of northern Bahia. Within 1½ years Canudos had grown to a city of 35,000.

The republican government sensed plots in Canudos to return Brazil to the monarchy. Miraculously, the rebels first defeated a force of state police, and then two subsequent attacks by the federal army. Hysterical demonstrations in the cities demanded that the republic be saved from the rebels. A federal force of 8000 well-supplied soldiers eventually took Canudos after vicious, hand-to-hand, house-to-house fighting. The military suffered heavy casualties and was disgraced and the federal government embarrassed, but Canudos was wiped out. The soldiers killed every man, woman and child, and then burned the town to the ground to erase it from the nation's memory. Its site was covered by a reservoir in the 1970s.

1954	1958
President Getúlio Vargas shoots himself through the heart at his Rio palace	Brazil wins its first soccer World Cup, inspired by the young Pelé

thing. The coffee market all but dried up, prices plummeted and many of Brazil's powerful coffee farmers were left ruined. The economic and political upheaval soon translated into revolution.

GETÚLIO VARGAS, POPULIST DICTATOR

The Vargas era began in 1930 when members of the newly formed Liberal Alliance party decided to fight back after the defeat of their candidate, Getúlio Vargas, in the presidential elections. The revolution kicked off on October 3 in Rio Grande do Sul and spread rapidly through other states. Twenty-one days later President Júlio Prestes was deposed and on November 3 Vargas became Brazil's new 'provisional' president.

The formation of the Estado Novo (New State) in November 1937 made Vargas the first Brazilian president to wield absolute power. Inspired by the fascist governments of Salazar in Portugal and Mussolini in Italy, Vargas banned political parties, imprisoned political opponents and censored artists and the press.

Despite this, many liked Vargas. The 'father' of Brazil's workers, he created Brazil's minimum wage in 1938. Each year he introduced new labor laws to coincide with Workers' Day on May 1, to sweeten the teeth of Brazil's factory workers.

Like any fascist worth his salt, Vargas began WWII siding with Hitler's Third Reich. Mysteriously, an offer of US investment to the sum of US$20 million in 1942 led Vargas to switch allegiances. The National War Memorial in Flamengo – a huge concrete monument and museum, which represents a pair of hands begging the skies for peace – today pays testament to the 5000 Brazilians who served in Europe.

Vargas, of course, wasn't exactly practising what he preached. The glaring contradiction of someone fighting for democracy in Europe and maintaining a quasi-fascist state back home soon became impossible. After WWII, the military forced him to step down.

Yet he remained popular and in 1951 was elected president – this time democratically. But Vargas' new administration was plagued by the hallmark of Brazilian politics – corruption. For this, a young journalist called Carlos Lacerda attacked him incessantly. In 1954 Vargas' security chief sent two gunmen to assassinate Lacerda at his home in Copacabana. The troublesome scribe was only slightly wounded but an air force major was killed, precipitating a huge scandal. Amid calls from the military for his resignation, Vargas responded dramatically. He penned a note saying 'I leave this life to enter into history,' and on the following morning, August 24, 1954, fired a single bullet through his own heart.

HEY BIG SPENDER!

Juscelino Kubitschek de Oliveira, whose tongue twister of a name swiftly earned him the *apelido* (nickname) JK, was elected president in 1956. 'Fifty years' progress in five,' had been his election promise. His critics responded with, 'Forty years' inflation in four.' Sadly for JK, the second assessment came closer to the mark, despite an 80% increase in industrial production during his term.

Kubitschek's lasting legacy was Brasília, Brazil's love-it-or-hate-it capital, located slap bang in the center of the country as a symbol of national unity

1960	1962
Brazil's new capital, Brasília, is inaugurated	First public performance of Tom Jobim's much-hummed 'Girl from Ipanema'

and a catalyst for development of the interior. Though the construction of such a city was written into the 1891 constitution, it was Kubitschek who, quite literally, made the idea concrete. The windswept, shadeless streets of Brasília were inaugurated with much fanfare on April 21, 1960.

As if Kubitschek hadn't made enough enemies by taking the honor of capital city from the 'Marvelous City' of Rio de Janeiro, his successor, Jânio Quadros, went one step further. He tried to outlaw bikinis on Brazil's beaches, a serious affront to Brazilian popular culture. Quadros also made the even worse mistake of irritating the military by decorating Che Guevara in a public ceremony in Brasília. This triggered plots among the right-wing military and after seven months in office Quadros resigned, claiming 'occult forces' were at work.

THE GENERALS TAKE OVER

Quadros' vice-president, a leftist by the name of João Goulart, took power. Though Goulart didn't demonstrate an overt aversion to *fio dental* (dental-floss bikinis), the military wasn't keen on him either. In 1964 he was overthrown in a so-called *revolução* (revolution) – really a military coup, believed to have received backing from the US government. President Lyndon Johnson did nothing to dampen such theories when he immediately cabled his warmest wishes to the new Brazilian administration.

> The first *favela* (shantytown) appeared on Rio's landscape in 1897 – but it wasn't until 1994 that the communities (which today number over 600) were included on maps.

Brazil's military regime was not as brutal as those of Chile or Argentina – a reality that led to the somewhat unkind saying, 'Brazil couldn't even organize a dictatorship properly.' Yet for the best part of 20 years, freedom of speech was an unknown concept and political parties were banned. The Lei de Segurança Nacional (National Security Law) of 1967 tightened the noose on political dissidents, who were often tortured, murdered or – perhaps worse – thrown into Brazilian jails.

The dictatorship coincided with one of the most culturally rich periods in Brazilian history, but a generation of composers and academics were exiled for their opposition to the regime – among them sociologist Fernando Henrique Cardoso (who would go on to become president) and musician Gilberto Gil (who decades later would become culture minister in the Lula government).

A draconian censorship law known as the Ato Institutional 5 (AI-5) marked the height of repression in 1968. In response, Brazil's middle-class student movement came to life. In June 1968 the streets of Rio de Janeiro hosted a mass demonstration, known as the Passeata dos cem mil (March of the 100,000), against the dictatorship. Many in the Catholic Church, which had broadly supported the coup, also turned against the government, inspired by Liberation Theology.

Perversely during a time of such repression, the Brazilian economy flourished. Year after year in the late 1960s and early 1970s, the economy grew by over 10%, as Brazil's rulers borrowed heavily from international banks. But in the absence of rural land reform, millions moved to the cities, where *favelas* (slums) filled up the open spaces.

Brazil's obsession with 'mega-projects' was born. Under the quick-spending regime, construction began on numerous colossal (and mostly ill-fated) plans, including the Transamazônica highway, the Rio–Niterói Bridge and the Ilha do Fundão, which was to house Rio's Federal University.

1964	1980
An apparently US-backed coup ushers in two decades of military dictatorship	Brazil's Workers' Party (PT) is founded

THE WORKERS ORGANIZE

By the late 1970s, the economic boom was dying and opposition to the regime began to spread from the educated middle class to the working class. A series of strikes in the São Paulo car industry signaled the intent of the militant new workers' movement. At the helm was Luíz Inácio 'Lula' da Silva, who famously lost one *dedo* (finger) in a factory accident but made up in charisma for what he lacked in the finger department.

The Partido dos Trabalhadores (PT; Workers' Party), Brazil's first-ever mass political party to speak for the poor, grew out of these strikes. Though grass-roots metalworkers formed the PT's base, the party's broad membership extended to some of Brazil's leading left-wing academics, among them literary critic Antonio Candido and historian Sérgio Buarque de Holanda, whose book *Raízes do Brasil* (The Roots of Brazil) remains a defining work in Brazilian scholarship. In January 1980 the PT's first manifesto declared the need to 'build an egalitarian society, where there are neither exploited nor exploiters.'

First came the *abertura* (opening), a slow, cautious return to civilian rule between 1979 and 1985. With popular opposition gathering force, the military announced gradual moves toward a democratic Brazil. Political prisoners and exiles were granted amnesty. Six new political parties – of which the PT was one – emerged. The tail end of this *abertura* was marked by the *direitas já* (elections now) movement, which called for immediate and direct presidential elections.

DEMOCRACY & DEBT

In 1985 a presidential election took place, but the only voters were the members of the national Congress, which caused the PT to boycott such an indirect vote. Unexpectedly, Tancredo Neves, opposing the military candidate, came out on top, and millions of Brazilians took to the streets to celebrate the end of military rule.

Immediately a spanner was thrown in the works: Neves died from heart failure before he could assume the presidency. His vice-presidential candidate, the whiskered José Sarney, took over.

Sarney – who had supported the military until 1984 – held office until 1989, a period in which runaway inflation helped Brazil rack up a gargantuan foreign debt. By 1990 the external debt stood at a crippling US$115 billion. Sarney's stint as president proved a sad rebuttal of his catchphrase, '*tem que dar certo*' (it has to work out). Virtually nothing did – though he can claim to have implemented one crucial law: Brazil's illiterate, previously excluded from the political system, were at last permitted to vote.

In the 1989 direct presidential election, the first ever that could be called democratic, it was a Northeastern political climber by the name of Collor who was victorious, beating Lula, the PT's candidate, by the smallest of margins – and only after the powerful Globo TV network had sabotaged Lula by screening his ex-lover claiming he had tried to force her to have an abortion 16 years before.

The haunting story of a street child turned murderer, Hector Babenco's *Pixote* takes us on a grim trawl through 1980s São Paulo. The leading actor, himself from a poor background, was famously killed by police in 1990.

THE CLIMBER FALLS

Fernando Collor de Mello, former governor of the small state of Alagoas, had a certain superficial charisma and a talent for manipulating TV, and

1985	1985
Tancredo Neves becomes president in the first post-dictatorship election; he dies before taking power	The Movimento Sem Terra (Landless Workers' Movement) is founded

came from a background of established influence – his father was a media boss, his grandfather had been a minister under Getúlio Vargas and his wife hailed from a landowning clan enmeshed in political violence in the Northeastern backlands.

Collor revolutionized consumer laws – when you see a 'best before' date on a tub of Brazilian margarine, it's him you have to thank. 'Sell by' dates, however, couldn't save him from disgrace. An ever-lengthening list of scandals involving Collor and his intimate associate PC Farias – corruption on a vast scale, drug deals, family feuds – led to a congressional inquiry, huge student protests and eventually the president's impeachment.

Though out of office, 'Fernandinho' managed – as is all too often the case with Brazil's white-collar criminals – to wriggle out of a prison sentence, receiving little more than an eight-year ban from politics. Found not guilty of 'passive corruption' by the Supreme Court in 1994, he skedaddled to Miami – and in 2006 re-entered Brazil's Congress as a senator for Alagoas.

TRAVELING HENRIQUE CARDOSO

Following Collor's impeachment, Vice-President Itamar Franco found himself in the hot seat. Despite his reputation as an eccentric, his administration was at least credited with competence and integrity, rare commodities in Brazilian politics.

His greatest achievement was to stabilize Brazil's violently erratic economy, introducing a new currency, the real. The Plano Real produced a brief economic boom in Brazil, during which the real was momentarily pegged to the US dollar. Inflation plummeted from a rate of over 5000% in late 1993 to under 10%.

Lula was an early favorite for the 1994 election (the second in which the ex-shoeshine boy had run), but in the end Fernando Henrique Cardoso, who as Franco's finance minister had devised the Plano Real, rode the real's success to a landslide victory.

Cardoso was a former left-wing sociologist from the University of São Paulo, who had spent time in exile during the military dictatorship. But as president he was far less radical. 'Forget everything I have said and written,' he said on taking power.

Brazil's economy grew steadily during the mid-1990s: the currency remained stable, inflation stayed low, foreign investment hit new heights, and the number of Brazilians without enough income to eat properly fell from 20% to 15%. Cardoso was re-elected in 1998, again defeating Lula. Frequent trips abroad to rub shoulders with the likes of Tony Blair and Bill Clinton earned the president the nickname Viajando (Traveling) Henrique Cardoso.

By the end of his second term (after which he was not allowed to stand again), Cardoso could claim solid progress on several fronts: Brazilians were healthier (infant mortality had fallen from 40 per 1000 to under 30), more of them went to school (up from 87% to 97% of seven- to 14-year-olds), many more of them had houses, and more of those houses had water, drainage and telephones. The government bought tracts of underused land and helped the rural landless set up cooperative farms, settling over 600,000 landless families, three times the total for the previous 30 years.

But with slower economic growth in Cardoso's second term, the official unemployment rate rose from 4% to 8% between 1994 and 2002. Life for the

According to the 1.5-million-member Movimento Sem Terra (MST; Landless Workers' Movement), half the arable land in Brazil is controlled by just 1.6% of landowners.

Brazzil Magazine (www .brazzil.com) focuses a cynical eye on Brazilian history, politics and culture.

Australian Peter Robb weaves the whole of Brazil's history, and most of its literature, into his account of the unbelievable corruption of the Collor de Mello regime, *A Death in Brazil* (2003) – a gripping read.

1988	1994
Amazonia rubber-tappers' leader and environmentalist Chico Mendes is murdered by a local rancher	The Plano Real introduces a new currency, the real, and starts an economic boom

average *favelado* (slum dweller) improved very little. Violent crime, especially in the cities, got worse, and Cardoso could claim little progress against the cancer of corruption.

LULA, THE WORKERS' PRESIDENT

Come the 2002 election, Lula, at the fourth time of asking, toned down his socialist rhetoric, campaigned with the slogan 'Lulinha, Peace and Love,' swapped his jeans for suits, and promised to repay Brazil's international

---

LORDS OF THE JAILS

Brazilians have a happy way of looking on the bright side and making the best of every situation, but like the rest of us, they do worry about some things. Apart from unemployment and the fear of it, Brazilians' biggest concern, according to polls, is violence. The country certainly has an appalling murder rate – around 150 murders a day. Statistics indicate that violent crime is falling in big cities, and indeed none of the country's state capitals is in Brazil's top 10 cities when it comes to murder rates. São Paulo's murder rate halved between 2000 and 2006. This doesn't stop the city's wealthy from building big walls round their houses or sending their kids to school with bodyguards. Tourists too need to exercise special prudence in cities like São Paulo, Rio de Janeiro, Salvador and Recife. But fortunately the worst outbreaks of violent crime are things you're only likely to hear about in the news media, and are mostly to do with the country's infamous prison gangs.

São Paulo lived through a week of horror in 2006 when around 200 people were killed in a series of jail riots, attacks on buses, banks and police stations, and the ensuing police backlash. The protagonists were a jail-based criminal network called the Primeiro Comando da Capital (PCC; First Command of the Capital), who used smuggled mobile phones to direct the violence. The PCC was, in part, protesting against the transfer of 700 of its members to higher-security jails.

The PCC's counterpart in Rio is the Comando Vermelho (CV; Red Command), whose name gives a clue to the way these gangs are organized. The CV was born in 1979 at the now-demolished Cândido Mendes jail on Ilha Grande, Rio de Janeiro state (p189), where left-wing opponents of the military dictatorship rubbed shoulders with common criminals. Regular inmates, influenced by the political prisoners' revolutionary methods, founded the CV to dominate the jail. The organization ended up spreading to other jails, controlling much of Rio's drug trade and taking root in the city's crime-ridden *favelas*.

The origins of the PCC, formed in 1993 by survivors of the Carandiru jail massacre, when 111 prisoners were killed during and after a riot, have certain similarities to those of the CV. Not that these organizations have any political motivation. Their main activities, apart from jail riots and murders, include drug trafficking, kidnappings and robberies. (Which makes the CV's slogan *'Paz, Justiça e Liberdade'* (Peace, Justice and Freedom) – widely seen in Rio – all the sicker.) The gangs enjoy a cult status in the *favelas*, with rappers exalting them at the funk music parties they put on. Much of the slang used in the *favelas* has roots in the prison system too.

Corruption and violence by the police and jail authorities are blamed by some for strengthening the hold of the gangs over the *favelas* and jails. The failure of a 2005 referendum to ban gun sales in Brazil didn't help. But as long as the *favelas* and their poverty and the drug trade remain, there seems little that can be done to diminish the heavily armed gangs' power. They are unlikely to run short of funds: the PCC is thought to have been behind the world's biggest-ever bank robbery in 2005, when thieves tunneled 80m into the vault of a bank in the northwestern city of Fortaleza, drilled through a meter of reinforced concrete and made off with R$164 million (US$80 million) in used banknotes, without setting off a single alarm.

Rio de Janeiro's violent, drug-ridden *favelas* have inspired two of the best recent Brazil-themed films: Fernando Meirelles' *City of God* (2002) and Jeff Zimbalist's *Favela Rising* (2005), which documents the rise of the Afro-reggae musical movement.

InfoBrazil (www.infobrazil .com) features an analysis of Brazilian politics and the economy.

The website of the Brazilian embassy in London (www.brazil.org.uk) has lots of interesting tidbits about Brazil, including a breakdown of its often baffling political system.

debts. This, and the PT's corruption-free reputation, won over enough of the electorate's middle ground – and the media giant Globo – to give Lula a convincing victory over the center-right candidate Jose Serra. For the first time ever, Brazil had a government on the left of the political spectrum and a president who really knew what poverty was like. One of 22 children born to a dirt-poor illiterate farm-worker from Brazil's stricken Northeast, Lula had worked as a shoeshine boy, then a mechanic, then a trade-union leader.

But there were no quick, easy solutions to Brazilian poverty. Forced into alliances with other parties in Congress, Lula's government had to be pragmatic. He managed Brazil's budget prudently enough to repay the country's entire US$15 billion debt to the International Monetary Fund (IMF) ahead of schedule in 2005. Inflation fell, the minimum wage was raised, and – what Lula's first term will probably be most remembered for – the Bolsa Família (Family Fund) program paid up to R$95 (about US$45) a month to 11 million of Brazil's poorest families – about a quarter of the population. Families received these payments in exchange for keeping their kids in school and making sure they received prescribed vaccinations. Half the recipients were in the Northeast.

But the rural landless remained unsatisfied, and land invasions and violent rural conflicts continued. Around 700,000 landless families were settled in four years, but this was chiefly on public land or in existing settlements. The large-scale land expropriations the landless had hoped for did not happen. The 1.5-million-member Movimento Sem Terra (MST; Landless Workers' Movement), which occupies unused land and establishes cooperative farming settlements there, claimed that Lula had failed to live up to his promises.

Nor did Lula's government do much to improve Brazil's low education standards, a big reason why so many of the poor are trapped in poverty. The richest 10% of Brazilians garner nearly half the income in the country, while the poorest 10% get less than 1%.

Meanwhile, big business complained that Brazilian economic growth was being held back by high taxes and the large size of the public sector.

As Lula's first term neared its end, scandals showed that even the PT could not avoid the taint of corruption. A cash-for-votes rumpus in Congress in 2005 was followed in 2006 by the exposure of an attempt by the PT to buy damaging information about the opposition. Lula's re-election hopes were further jeopardized by the continuing drug-gang violence in the main cities (see the boxed text Lords of the Jails, p49).

Nevertheless Lula's popularity and commitment to the poor carried him to a second resounding presidential victory in October 2006, over center-right challenger Geraldo Alckmin. Lula's first significant act after re-election was to raise the minimum wage by 8.5%, well above the rate of inflation. Brazil's poor were a little less desperate than four years previously, but land reform and education now had to join welfare programs as real priorities if the country's first workers' president was to narrow the wealth gap in a lasting way.

2003	2005
Lula launches the Bolsa Família program of cash payments to 11 million of Brazil's poorest families	American missionary nun Dorothy Stang, campaigner for poor Amazonia farmers, is murdered by local rancher

The Culture

THE NATIONAL PSYCHE

Brazilians are known for lively celebrations (Carnaval is but one manifestation), which generally becomes more animated the further north you go. This joie de vivre can be seen in football matches, on the beaches, in the samba clubs and on the streets. The flip side of this trait is *saudade,* that woeful manifestation of homesickness, longing or deep regret, given much play on old bossa nova records.

In a land of profound diversity, the Brazilians themselves exhibit some deep contradictions. A landscape of beaches, mountains and forests that is universally praised receives incredible destruction (the Amazon) – and indifference – from its citizens; Brazilian racial harmony is a widely accepted ideal, yet Blacks are egregiously underrepresented in the government and suffer the lion's share of poverty; Carnaval is a time of wild freedom, while sexual repressiveness lurks the rest of the year.

Perhaps owing to the incredible diversity of the population, it's possible to find Brazilians who profess to be Catholics while also attending a Candomblé ceremony (p57) from time to time, who believe in science and market economies while nurturing beliefs in mystics and fatalism.

Contradictions are most severe in the social-class system, where you can find dirt-poor and filthy-rich living in close proximity, often separated by nothing more than a highway. It's not surprising then that violence is such a prevalent facet of Brazilian society. Nearly every Carioca (Rio resident) and Paulistano (São Paulo city resident) has a horror story of getting mugged. The response is often one of resignation and 'What can be done?'.

Indeed, there is much resignation in the national character. Some suggest this is a holdover from the military dictatorship that ruled people's lives for 20 years (from 1964–84), creating a docile public. But Brazilians have been a nonconfrontational people since the beginning of the Republic. Brazil was the only country in Latin America to gain its independence without spilling a drop of blood, and slavery ended in 1888 (the last in the Americas) without battles or violent showdowns.

In a country noted for its bureaucracy (the legacy of the dictatorship), Brazilians have to put up with serious inefficiencies. This has led to some rather creative solutions to one's problems. There's the official way of doing something, and then there's the *jeitinho,* that characteristically Brazilian way around it. A few friends, and a bit of good humor, can go a long way.

LIFESTYLE

Constructing a portrait of the typical Brazilian is a complicated task, given the wide mix of social, cultural and economic factors in play. One thing that everyone agrees on is the huge chasm separating rich from poor.

The country's middle and upper class live in comfortable apartments or houses, with all the trappings of the first world, including good health care in private clinics, cars, vacation homes and easy access to the latest gadgets and trends. The wealthiest send their children to private schools and abroad to university. Maids are common – even among middle-class Brazilians – and some families have chauffeurs and cooks. Depending on where one lives in the country, crime is likely to be of high concern. Those who can take extra precautions, opting for high-security buildings or even hiring bodyguards.

Blairo Maggi, the governor of Mato Grosso state, is the world's largest individual soybean grower. Greenpeace believes his massive farms have fueled the Amazon's destruction, and in 2006 he received their Golden Chainsaw award.

Meeting Brazilians: one kiss on each cheek for ladies (start at the left – her right); a handshake between gents. The same holds true when bidding goodbye.

THE LOVE MOTEL

Something of a Brazilian institution, the love motel provides a discreet meeting place for a rendezvous. Visited by all rungs of society, love motels are found in every part of the country. Some
are designed with lavish facades – decked out to resemble medieval castles, Roman temples
or ancient pyramids – while others blend more subtly into the landscape. Inside, rooms come
standard with mirror-covered ceilings, heart-shaped beds, rose-tinted lighting, Jacuzzis, televisions
loaded with porn channels, dual-headed showers and a bedside menu of sex toys (and food).
In many countries, love motels scream seediness, but in Brazil, they are viewed as colorful but
perfectly acceptable places. People need a place for their liaisons – they might as well have a
laugh and a bit of fun while they're at it.

Somewhere below the elite are working-class folk struggling to put food
on the table and pay the rent; the children tend to live at home until they
are married. Couples tend to marry younger.

At the bottom of the socioeconomic ladder are *favelados* (slum dwellers),
who are themselves a fairly diverse bunch. According to one survey carried
out in 2005 in Rocinha, Brazil's largest *favela* (slum or shanty town), some
56% of inhabitants use the shopping mall, 23% have a credit card and 93%
have at least one TV – not exactly what you would expect from what is often
referred to as 'South America's largest slum.' *Favelas* are now a feature of
nearly every city in Brazil, with millions of Brazilians living without access
to good schools, adequate health care, roads and other important infrastructure. The *favelas* are often 'governed' by drug lords and their gangs,
who are frequently the communities' only benefactors. They often try to
paint themselves as 'Robin Hood' types, complete with pithy slogans about
peace and justice. Dangers to residents come during gun battles with police
or when rival gangs move in.

In the countryside, conditions for the poor can be even worse. Unequal
land distribution dating back to the colonial era means that thousands of
homeless rural families are left to squat on vacant land or work long hours
as itinerant laborers for low wages.

President Luíz Inácio da Silva, popularly known as Lula, who grew up
among such poverty, has made some improvements in bringing relief to
the neediest. His Bolsa Família (Family Grant) has reached millions of
families, and may very well spell the difference between staying fed and
going hungry.

Domesticas (Maids), the
first film by Fernando
Meirelles (of *City of God*
fame), delves into the
lives of five women who
work as *domesticas*,
creating a compelling and
humanistic portrait of
Brazil's often overlooked
underclass.

ECONOMY

One of the BRIC countries (along with Russia, India and China), Brazil was
noted by economists back in 2003 as a country with enormous economic
potential. Although Brazil's growth hasn't been on par with either that of
China or India, its presence has expanded in world markets, and Brazil is
indisputably Latin America's biggest economy.

Brazil's earnings in exports have boomed since 2003, with its currency
gaining almost 50% against the US dollar since 2004 – spurred by record
gains in the prices of exports. Brazil has also done much to reduce its debt,
cap its inflation (currently 3%), lower its unemployment (9.6%) and grow
its economy.

Despite his left-leaning roots, Lula has run a fiscally conservative administration, focusing on improving the public-debt ratio, and
attracting investment.

The growth has been particularly strong in agribusiness, which generates
10% of Brazil's GDP and employs about 20% of its labor force. Agribusiness

The 1979–83 droughts
in the Northeast were
among the worst the
country has ever experi-
enced, leaving between
250,000 and one million
people dead.

grew almost 100% between 2002 and 2006, leading to record trade surpluses. Today Brazil is the world's biggest exporter of sugar, coffee, orange juice, soy and beef, and a major producer of corn, cotton and other crops. Other important sectors employing Brazil's 96-million-strong work force are mining, manufacturing, and service sectors.

While Brazil has rarely been a source of innovation, it has been putting technology to creative uses in recent years – most notably in its championing of biofuel. During the oil crisis in the 1970s, Brazil transformed its sugarcane into an alternative fuel: ethanol. Today 70% of its cars can run on gasoline, ethanol or some combination of the two, and ethanol provides 40% of the country's fuel. Ethanol exports are on the rise, with plans to export 8 billion liters by 2010 (up from 3 billion liters today).

Economic management has been good, but public debt still remains high, which strains government finances and threatens social security and other important safety nets. This is one of the key issues in Brazil's continued economic health for the future: maintaining sufficient growth to generate employment and reducing government debt. Environmentalists also point out that Brazil's growth in agribusiness has led to the continued destruction of the rain forest. The high prices for soybean products, for instance, has led to huge tracts of forest being chainsawed to make way for fields, a practice with enormously damaging implications for Brazil's environment.

Many uncontacted Indian groups still live in the Amazon. In 2007, 89 Metyktire suddenly emerged in a village in Pará, the first time this particular group (feared dead) had been encountered since 1950.

POPULATION

Brazil is the world's fifth most populous country, but it also has one of the smallest population densities, with 20 people per sq km. Most of Brazil's population lives along the coast, particularly in the South and Southeast, home to 75% of the country's inhabitants. Until the mid-20th century, Brazil was largely a rural country – today, it's more than 70% urban. The population in cities has exploded in the last half-century, though growth is slowing.

The Northeast has the highest concentration of Afro-Brazilians, with Salvador as its cultural capital. In the Amazon live Caboclos (literally 'copper-colored'), the mixed descendents of indigenous peoples and the Portuguese. In the South is the most European of the Brazilian population, descendents of Italian and German immigrants. Overall the population is 54% White, 6% Black, 39% mixed and 1% other (including Japanese, Arabs and indigenous groups).

Greater São Paulo had 2.2 million residents in 1950, compared to 18 million today.

While there is much more mixing between races, Brazil is a long way from being a color-blind society. Afro-Brazilians make up the bulk of low-paid workers, and are far more likely to live in *favelas* than in middle-class neighborhoods. More than 62% of Afro-Brazilians live in poverty. Afro-Brazilians die younger than Whites, earn less and have a greater risk of going to prison. Only 2% of university students are Black – though a new quota system instituted at some universities in 2003 is aiming to create more opportunities for young Afro-Brazilians. A Black political representative or even a high-ranking Black employee is a rarity – clear examples of the lack of opportunities for Blacks in Brazil.

The indigenous population today is around 350,000, comprising 200 tribes – a fraction of the estimated two to six million in Brazil at the time of European arrival. Customs and beliefs vary widely from tribe to tribe – as do the strengths of these traditions in the face of expulsion from traditional lands, declining numbers, missionary activity and other influences. Brazil's largest groups of Indian peoples include the Tikuna on the upper Rio Solimões (numbering 20,000 or more), the Yanomami in northwestern Amazonia (more than 11,000), and the 30,000 or so Guarani in the Central West and South.

Tristes Tropiques, by Claude Lévi-Strauss, is both a well-written travelogue and one of the most important anthropological studies of some of Brazil's indigenous peoples.

After centuries of genocidal attacks, slavery, dispossession and death from imported diseases, Brazil's Indian population is now finally growing again but still faces a host of problems. Most Indians live in the Amazon rain forest, and therefore the threats that the rain forest faces – logging, mining, ranching, farming, roads, settlements, dams, hydroelectric schemes – also threaten the Indians whose way of life depends on it.

MULTICULTURALISM

The Brazilian identity has been shaped not only by the Portuguese, who provided its language and main religion, but also by native Indians, Africans and the many immigrants over the years from Europe, the Middle East and Asia.

Indian culture, though often ignored or denigrated by urban Brazilians, has helped shape modern Brazil and its legends, dance and music. Many indigenous foods and beverages, such as tapioca, manioc (cassava), potatoes, maté and guaraná (a shrub whose berry is a stimulant; also a popular soft drink) have become staples.

The influence of African culture is also evident, especially in the Northeast. The slaves imported by the Portuguese brought with them their religion, music and cuisine, all of which have become a part of Brazilian identity.

Brazil had several waves of voluntary immigration. After the end of slavery in 1888, millions of Europeans were recruited to work in the coffee fields. The largest contingent was from Italy (some one million arrived between 1890 and 1920), but there were also many Portuguese and Spaniards, and smaller groups of Germans and Russians.

Immigration is only part of the picture when considering Brazil's diversity. Brazilians are just as likely to mention regional types, often accompanied by their own colorful stereotypes. Caboclos, who are descendents of the Indians, live along the rivers in the Amazon region and keep alive the traditions and stories of their ancestors. *Gaúchos* populate Rio Grande do Sul, speak a Spanish-inflected Portuguese and can't quite shake the reputation for being rough-edged cowboys. By contrast, Baianos, descendents of the first Africans in Brazil, are stereotyped for being the most extroverted and celebratory of Brazilians. Mineiros (residents of Minas Gerais state) are considered more serious and reserved than Brazil's coastal dwellers, while Sertanejos (residents of the backlands – called *sertão* – of the Northeast) are dubbed tough-skinned individuals with strong folk traditions. Cariocas (residents of Rio city) are superficial beach bums according to Paulistanos (residents of São Paulo city), who are often denigrated as being workaholics with no zeal for life – a rivalry that anyone who's lived in LA or New York can understand.

Today there are dozens of terms to describe Brazilians' various racial compositions, and it is not uncommon for apparently White Brazilians to have a mix of European, African and indigenous ancestors. Yet, despite appearances of integration and racial harmony, underneath is a brutal reality. Although Blacks and mulattoes account for 45% of the population, they are sorely underrepresented in government and business, and often see little hope of rising out of poverty. The indigenous are even more openly discriminated against, continuing a cycle that began with the genocidal policies of the first Europeans.

SPORTS
Soccer

Soccer, or football as it's also called (*futebol* to Brazilians), was introduced in the 1890s when a young student from São Paulo, Charles Miller, returned from studies in England with two footballs and a rule book and began to organize the first league. It quickly became the national passion, and Brazil is the only country to have won five World Cups. The rest of the world

---

Survival International (www.survival-international.org) is a good source of information on Brazilian Indians.

Japanese immigration began in 1908, and today São Paulo has the world's largest Japanese community outside of Japan.

The Ukrainian community in Brazil numbers 550,000, the majority of whom live in the South. Prudentopolis is a city of Orthodox churches and Slavic features, with 75% of the population of Ukrainian descent.

BRAZILIAN FOOTBALL: THE CLUBS

Apart from a couple of short breaks for the Christmas–New Year holiday and Carnaval, professional club competitions go on all year. If you get a chance, don't miss a game in Rio's Maracanã (p156), the world's largest soccer stadium.

Club	Home city	Stadium (capacity)	Jerseys
Bahia	Salvador	Fonte Nova (96,000)	white
Botafogo	Rio de Janeiro	Caio Martins, Niterói (15,000)	black & white stripes
Corinthians	São Paulo	Pacaembu (40,000)	white; black collar
Cruzeiro	Belo Horizonte	Mineirão (90,000)	blue
Flamengo	Rio de Janeiro	Maracanã (100,000)	red; black hoops
Fluminense	Rio de Janeiro	Laranjeiras (10,000)*	red, green & white stripes
Grêmio	Porto Alegre	Olímpico (55,000)	blue, black & white stripes
Internacional	Porto Alegre	Beira-Rio (80,000)	red
Palmeiras	São Paulo	Parque Antarctica (28,000)	green
Santa Cruz	Recife	Arruda (80,000)	white; black & red hoops
Santos	Santos	Vila Belmiro (26,000)	white
São Paulo	São Paulo	Morumbi (65,000)	white; red & black hoops
Sport	Recife	Ilha do Retiro (50,000)	red & black hoops
Vasco da Gama	Rio de Janeiro	São Januário (40,000)	white; black slash

*Fluminense play most of their home games at the Maracanã.

acknowledges that Brazilians are among the best footballers, and Brazilians are, to put it mildly, insane about the sport.

No one goes to work on big international game days, a situation that the government – which is prepared to spend whatever it takes to win a World Cup – laments. When Brazil unexpectedly lost to France in the 1998 World Cup final, millions cried on the streets and depression gripped the country for weeks. Since then some of the shady business that goes on behind the soccer scenes has started to come to light, and parliamentary commissions have investigated corruption in football. The fans may criticize the way football is run, but nothing dims their insane passion for the game itself. Brazil's lackluster 2006 World Cup performance left a few fans calling for investigations once again – with rumors circulating that the Brazilian team must have been bribed by France to lose the match against them (in truth Brazil has never played well in European matches, which some fatuous commentators attributed to some sort of Latin American inferiority complex).

Most of the best players leave Brazil for lucrative contracts with European clubs as was the case with Ronaldinho, FC Barcelona's star forward, who became a Spanish citizen in 2007. And even mid-rank players can earn a decent wage on small European leagues – something impossible to do in Brazil. Yet many gifted kids are waiting to replace the stars. You'll see tiny children playing skilled, rough matches in the streets, on the beaches, in a jungle clearing – just about anywhere.

Volleyball

Volleyball is Brazil's second sport. A natural for the beach, it's also a popular spectator sport on TV. A local variation you'll see on Rio's beaches is *futevôlei* (volleyball played without hands), only for the most talented of players.

Motor Racing

Since the early 1970s Brazilian drivers have won more Formula One world championships than any other nationality. Emerson Fittipaldi was

Brazilian footballers play in some pretty far-flung destinations, including Albania, India, Botswana, Iran, Liechtenstein, Indonesia and even the Faroe Islands.

The site www.ofutebol .com contains articles and video clips of Brazil's great football players, rosters of current and upcoming stars and match results. It's run by Alex Bellos, author of the fascinating *Futebol, the Brazilian Way of Life*.

world champion twice in the 1970s, Nelson Piquet won his third world championship in 1987, and the late, great Ayrton Senna took it out three times. The Brazilian Grand Prix at Interlagos, São Paulo, now takes place in October.

An excellent football website for results, schedules and league tables is http://cbfnews .uol.com.br (in Portuguese, but not hard to decipher).

Tennis

Tennis is increasingly popular, especially in the Southeast and South. Brazil's tennis hero is the highly popular Gustavo 'Guga' Kuerten from Florianópolis. One of the world's great clay-court players, Guga was the French Open champion in 1997, 2000 and 2001.

MEDIA

Until recently, the media and political demagogues worked hand in hand. Shortly after radio arrived in Brazil in the 1930s, President Getúlio Vargas initiated weekday transmissions of the *Voice of Brazil* as a means of distilling government propaganda to the people. The rise of Brazil's great media mogul, Roberto Marinho, was largely assisted by his decision not to criticize the fascistic regimes of the military government from 1964 to 1984. Other newspapers simply foundered if anything remotely critical of the government was published.

Today the empire created by Marinho extends to TV, and Rede Globo is the world's fourth-largest TV network (behind NBC, CBS and ABC). TV is by far the biggest form of media in Brazil, though radio is also popular (with more than 2500 radio stations nationwide). The country publishes 465 daily newspapers and 1600 magazines.

Although there is much more press freedom today than in the days of military dictatorship, Brazil still has some antiquated press laws on the books (for instance 'crimes of opinion', ie published articles that besmirch the names of government officials, are criminal offences). There have been notable advances in an individual's right to freedom of expression. In 2006 President Lula signed the Inter American Press Association's Declaration of Chapultepec on press freedom. He also vetoed a proposed law requiring journalists to have a diploma and belong to a journalism institute (which would have allowed much more governmental control over journalists).

For more information on press freedom in Brazil and other countries around the world, visit www.rsf.org, the website of the international watchdog association, Reporters Without Borders (available in English, Spanish and French).

For its part, the government occasionally puts the heat on journalists. After weekly news magazine *Veja* published a story on unethical maneuvers carried out by Lula's Labor Party (involving a suitcase full of €600,000, and a compromising file up for sale on Geraldo Alckmin, Lula's rival in the 2006 election), police summoned three *Veja* reporters to reveal their sources, while another publication claimed its phones were being tapped by federal police.

In recent years, reporters have been assassinated for speaking out against local authorities (as was the case with the journalist Ajuricaba Monassa, who was beaten to death in 2006 near Rio de Janeiro by a town councillor). Fear of reprisals run large in the Brazilian press world and in 2006 there were 40 cases of threats and physical attacks. The offices of the São Paulo daily *Imprensa Livre* were attacked (and seven staff members assaulted) following the publication of an article about the criminal group First Commando of the City (PCC) inciting riots in the city.

RELIGION

Officially, Brazil is a Catholic country and claims the largest Catholic population of any country in the world. But Brazil is also noted for the diversity and syncretism of its many sects and religions, which offer great flexibility to their followers.

Brazil's principal religious roots have been the animism of the indigenous people, Catholicism, and African cults brought by the Blacks during the period of slavery. The colonists prohibited slaves from practicing their religions, just as they forbade music and dance for fear that they would reinforce the group identity of the captives. Religious persecution led to religious syncretism: to avoid persecution the slaves gave Catholic names and identities to all their African gods. This was generally done by finding the similarities between the Catholic images and the *orixás* (deities) of Candomblé. Thus the slaves worshipped their own deities behind representations of Catholic saints.

In the 19th century Brazil wrote freedom of religion into its constitution, but the African cults continued to suffer persecution for many years. Candomblé was seen by White elites as charlatanism that displayed the ignorance of the poorest classes. But the spectrum of religious life was gradually broadened by the addition of Indian animism to Afro-Catholic syncretism, and by the increasing fascination of Whites with the spiritualism of Kardecism.

Today large numbers of converts are being attracted to Evangelical Christianity, to the Afro-Brazilian cults, and to spiritualist or mystic sects.

Serge Bramly's *Macumba* provides a fascinating portrait of the religion; the highlights are interviews with Maria José, a *mãe de santo* (saint's mother) who explains the philosophy, history and practice of Macumba, and the pantheon of *orixás*.

Christianity

Catholicism retains its status as Brazil's official religion, but is declining in popularity. Many people now merely turn up to church for the basics: baptism, marriage and burial. Evangelical Christianity, however, is booming. All over Brazil, especially in poorer communities where people are most desperate, you will come across simple, recently built churches full of worshipers. Sometimes there will be two or three rival Evangelical churches on the same street, going by names such as the Assembléia de Deus (Assembly of God), Igreja Pentecostal Deus é Amor (God is Love Pentecostal Church) and even the Igreja do Evangelho Quadrangular (Church of the Quadrangular Gospel). In one, worshipers may be moaning and speaking in tongues, in another they'll simply be listening to the stern words of a preacher.

Note: In this book you will find the abbreviation NS used for 'Nossa Senhora' (Our Lady) or 'Nosso Senhor' (Our Lord), for example NS do Pilar.

Afro-Brazilian Cults
CANDOMBLÉ

Candomblé is the most orthodox of the religions brought from Africa by the Nago, Yoruba and Jeje peoples. Candomblé is an African word denoting a dance in honor of the gods, and is a general term for the religion. Afro-Brazilian rituals are directed by a *pai de santo* or *mãe de santo* (literally saint's father or mother – the Candomblé priests) and practiced in a *casa de santo* or *terreiro* (house of worship). This is where the initiation of novices takes place as well as consultations and rituals. The ceremonies are conducted in the Yoruba language.

The religion centers upon the *orixás*. Like the gods in Greek mythology, each *orixá* has a unique personality and history. Although *orixás* are divided into male and female types, there are some that can switch from one sex to the other, such as Logunedé, son of two male gods, Ogun and Oxoss, or Oxumaré, who is male for six months of the year and female for the other six months. (Candomblé, not surprisingly, is much more accepting of homosexuality and bisexuality than other religions.)

Candomblé followers believe that every person has a particular deity watching over them – from birth until death. A person's *orixá* can be identified when a *pai* or *mãe de santo* makes successive throws with a handful of *búzios* (shells), in a divination ritual known as Jogo dos Búzios (Casting of

Sacred Leaves of Candomblé, by Robert Voeks, is a nonacademic work on cultural anthropology and ethnobotany. Voeks explores medicinal plants used in Candomblé and the survival of Afro-Brazilian religion in Brazil.

Shells). The position of the shells is used to interpret one's luck, one's future and one's past relationship with the gods.

To keep themselves strong and healthy, followers of Candomblé give food or other offerings to their respective *orixá*. The offering depends on the *orixá's* particular preferences. For example, to please Iemanjá, the goddess or queen of the sea, one should give perfumes, white and blue flowers, rice and fried fish. Oxalá, the greatest deity, the god and owner of the sun, eats cooked white corn. Oxúm, god of fresh waters and waterfalls, is famous for his vanity. He should be honored with earrings, necklaces, mirrors, perfumes, champagne and honey. Whichever god is receiving the offering, Exú must first be appeased, as he serves as the messenger between the individual and the god. Exú, incidentally, likes *cachaça* (high-proof sugarcane alcohol) and other alcoholic drinks, cigarettes and cigars, strong perfumes and meats.

In Bahia and Rio, followers of Afro-Brazilian cults turn out in huge numbers for the festival held during the night of December 31 and on New Year's Day. Millions of Brazilians go to the beach at this time to pay homage to Iemanjá. Flowers, perfumes, fruits and even jewelry are tossed into the sea to please the mother of the waters, or to gain protection and good luck in the new year.

UMBANDA & QUIMBANDA

Umbanda (white magic) is a mixture of Candomblé and spiritualism with Angolan/Bantu roots. The ceremony, conducted in Portuguese, incorporates figures from all the Brazilian ethnicities: Prêto Velho (the old Black slave), O Caboclo (an Indian – in this context) and other Indian deities, O Guerreiro (the White warrior), and so on. Umbanda is less structured than Candomblé, and rituals vary from region to region. Some sects tend toward practices found in Kardecism (contacting spirits, seances), while others feature more straightforward praying or preaching by the *pai* or *mãe de santo*.

Quimbanda, a form of black magic, is the evil counterpart to Umbanda. Its rituals involve lots of blood, animal sacrifice and nasty deeds, and it's technically illegal.

Kardecism

During the 19th century, Allan Kardec, the French spiritual master, introduced spiritualism to Brazilian Whites in a palatable form.

Kardec's teachings, which incorporated some Eastern religious ideas into a European framework, are now followed by large numbers of Brazilians. Kardecism emphasizes parlor seances, multiple reincarnations and speaking to the dead. Kardec's writings on his teachings include *The Book of Spirits* and *The Book of Mediums*.

Other Cults

A few Indian rites have become popularized among Brazilians without being incorporated into Afro-Brazilian cults. The cults União da Vegetal (in Brasília, São Paulo and the South) and Santo Daime (centered in Acre and Amazonas states) are both based on consumption of the hallucinogenic drink *ayahuasca*, which has been used for centuries by indigenous peoples of South America. *Ayahuasca* aside, these cults are very straight, dictating that moral behavior and dress follow strict codes. The government tolerates the use of *ayahuasca* in these religious ceremonies, and tightly controls its production and supply.

The cult of Santo Daime was founded in 1930 in Rio Branco, Acre, by Raimundo Irineu Serra, a rubber tapper who had been initiated into the use of *ayahuasca* by Indians on the Acre–Peru border. In visions he received instruc-

For more on the relationship between psychoactive plants and mystical experiences, read the excellent work *Cleansing the Doors of Perception*, written by Huston Smith, one of the great scholars on world religions.

tions to set up a base near Rio Branco to spread the doctrine of *ayahuasca*. The name Santo Daime comes from the wording of the cult's prayers, *'Dai-me força, dai-me luz…'* ('Give me strength, give me light…'). Santo Daime and União da Vegetal together have between 10,000 and 20,000 members. Santo Daime's two major communities are Ceú do Mapiá in Amazonas and Colônia Cinco Mil, near Rio Branco.

The Brasília area, believed by some to be especially propitious for supernatural contact, has syncretic cults that can be visited near the city in Vale do Amanhecer (Valley of the Dawn) and Cidade Eclética (Eclectic City) – see the boxed text, p376.

WOMEN IN BRAZIL

Brazil had one of the earliest feminist movements in Latin America, and women were among the first in the region to gain the right to vote, in 1932. Today there is a growing number of feminist NGOs, dedicated to educating women about their legal rights and family planning, while also training police how to handle cases of domestic violence. In Brasília there's even a feminist lobby (Feminist Center for Studies and Advising); they have a Portuguese-language website, www.cfemea.org.br.

In spite of advances, many *machista* (chauvinist) stereotypes persist, and women are still sorely underrepresented in positions of power. Only about 9% of all legislators are women (compared with the 12% to 15% average in the rest of Latin America). Although women represent 44% of the work force, they tend to be concentrated in low-paying jobs. For equal work, a woman earns about 70% of a man's salary.

Instances of domestic abuse are frighteningly common (one report stated that every 15 seconds a woman is beaten in Brazil). In response, the first women's police station opened in 1990 specifically to handle violence against women. Today there are more than 250 women's police stations, largely staffed by female police officers.

The birth rate has declined significantly in recent years (from an average of 4.3 births per woman in 1980 to 2.1 in 2006). Many attribute this to the AIDS epidemic (which is on the rise among women, up 44% between 1995 and 2005) and to sterilization, an option some women opt for as a means of birth control. (The latter is such a large problem that in 1997 the government passed a law allowing sterilization only for women who have had at least two children or are over the age of 25.)

Abortions are still illegal in Brazil (except in cases of rape and maternal health risks), and an estimated one million are performed each year, often with substantial health risks. More than 200,000 women each year are hospitalized from clandestine abortions.

ARTS
Music & Dance

Few countries in the world can compete with Brazil's rich musical heritage. Music here is a deeply ingrained part of life, a form of both celebration and escape, and is heard everywhere. Perhaps because of its African roots, Brazilian music is a collective community act, a *festa* (party), a celebration, and is virtually inseparable from dancing. Genres such as *pagode*, samba, *frevo*, *forró* and lambada all have their corresponding dances.

Shaped by the mixing of varied influences from three continents, Brazilian popular music has always been characterized by great diversity. The *samba canção* (samba song), for example, is a mixture of Spanish bolero with the cadences and rhythms of African music. Bossa nova was influenced by samba and North American music, particularly jazz. *Tropicália* mixed influences

Benedita da Silva: An Afro-Brazilian Woman's Story of Politics and Love are the memoirs of Brazil's first Afro-Brazilian female senator, detailing her rise from the *favelas* to becoming one of the most important political voices in Brazil.

About one in five Brazilian households is headed by a woman.

For a great overview of Brazilian music, from the great funk albums of the '60s to more recent talents, visit www.allbrazilianmusic.com and www.slipcue.com/music/brazil/brazillist.html.

ranging from bossa nova and Italian ballads to blues and North American rock. Brazil is still creating new and original musical forms today.

SAMBA, PAGODE & CHORO

The birth of modern Brazilian music essentially began with the birth of samba, first heard in the early 20th century in a Rio neighborhood near present-day Praça Onze. Here, Bahian immigrants formed a tightly knit community in which traditional African customs thrived – music, dance and the Candomblé religion. Local homes provided the setting for impromptu performances and the exchange of ideas among Rio's first great instrumentalists. Such an atmosphere nurtured the likes of Pixinguinha, one of samba's founding fathers, as well as Donga, one of the composers of 'Pelo Telefone,' the first recorded samba song (in 1917) and an enormous success at the then-fledgling Carnaval.

Samba continued to evolve in the homes and *botequims* (bars with table service) around Rio. The 1930s are known as the golden age of samba. By this point, samba's popularity had spread beyond the working-class neighborhoods of Central Rio, and the music evolved at the same time, into diverse, less-percussive styles of samba. Sophisticated lyricists such as Dorival Caymmi, Ary Barroso and Noel Rosa popularized *samba canção,* melody-driven samba laid over African percussion. Songs in this style featured sentimental lyrics and an emphasis on melody rather than rhythm, foreshadowing the later advent of cool bossa nova. A big radio star of the 1930s was samba singer Carmen Miranda, one of the first ambassadors of Brazilian music.

The 1930s were also the golden age of samba songwriting for Carnaval. *Escolas de samba* (samba schools or clubs), which first emerged in 1928, soon became a vehicle for samba songwriting, and by the 1930s samba and Carnaval would be forever linked. Today's theme songs still borrow from that golden epoch.

Great *sambistas* (samba singers) continued to emerge over the next few decades, although other emerging musical styles diluted their popularity. Artists such as Cartola, Nelson Cavaquinho and Clementina de Jesus made substantial contributions to both samba and styles of music that followed from samba.

Traditional samba went through a rebirth a little over a decade ago with the opening of old-style *gafieiras* (dance halls) in Rio's Lapa district (see the boxed text, p152). Classic *sambistas* such as Alcione and Beth Carvalho still perform, while rising stars Teresa Christina and Grupo Semente continue to provide samba's new sound.

Pagode is a style that branched off from samba and emerged in Rio in the 1970s. This informal, backyard-party samba features the *cavaquinho* (a small four-string guitar, a relative of the ukulele) and a few informal percussion instruments. The style is relaxed, rhythmic and melodic and enjoys widespread popularity. Beth Carvalho (also the queen of *samba canção*), Jorge Aragão and Zeca Pagodinho were pioneer *pagode* singers and are still going very strong.

Choro is a slightly more distant relative of samba. Characterized by its jazzy sound, melodic leaps and sometimes rapid-fire tempo, *choro* is mostly instrumental music and highly improvisational. It's played on the *cavaquinho* or guitar alongside a recorder or flute. The flutist Pixinguinha (1898–1973) is one of the great legends of *choro*, while today's lions include Paulinho da Viola and Paulo Moura, a saxophonist and master of *choro* rhythms.

BOSSA NOVA

In the 1950s came bossa nova (literally, new wave), sparking a new era of Brazilian music. Bossa nova's founders – songwriter and composer Antônio Carlos (Tom) Jobim and guitarist João Gilberto, in association with the lyricist-poet Vinícius de Moraes – slowed down and altered the basic samba rhythm to create a more intimate, harmonic style. This initiated a new style of playing instruments and of singing.

Bossa nova's seductive melodies were very much linked to Rio's Zona Sul, where most bossa musicians lived. Songs such as Jobim's 'Corcovado' and Roberto Meneschal's 'Rio' evoked an almost nostalgic portrait of the city with their quiet lyricism. Bossa nova was also associated with the new class of university-educated Brazilians, and its lyrics reflected the optimistic mood of the middle class in the 1950s.

By the 1960s bossa nova had become a huge international success. The genre's initial development was greatly influenced by American jazz and blues, and over time the bossa nova style came to influence those musical styles in turn. Bossa nova classics were adopted, adapted and recorded by such musical luminaries as Frank Sinatra, Ella Fitzgerald and Stan Getz, among others.

In addition to the founding members, other great Brazilian bossa nova musicians include Marcos Valle, Luiz Bonfá and Baden Powell, whose talented son Marcel Powell carries on the musical tradition. Bands from the 1960s such as Sergio Mendes & Brasil '66 were also quite influenced by bossa nova, as were other artists who fled the repressive military dictatorship to live and play abroad.

Bossa Nova: The Story of the Brazilian Music that Seduced the World, by Ruy Castro, is an excellent book that captures the vibrant music and its urban backdrop of 1950s Rio.

TROPICÁLIA

One of Brazil's unique artistic movements, emerging in the late 1960s, *tropicália* was a direct response to the dictatorship that held power from 1964–84. Leading the movement were Caetano Veloso and Gilberto Gil, making waves with songs of protest against the national regime. (Gil, ironically, is today's much-loved Minister of Culture.) In addition to penning defiant lyrics, *tropicalistas* introduced the public to electric instruments, fragmentary melodies and wildly divergent musical styles. In fact, the *tropicalistas'* hero was poet Oswald de Andrade, whose 1928 *Manifesto Antropofágico* (Cannibalistic Manifesto) supported the idea that anything under the sun could be devoured and recreated in one's music. Hence, the movement fused elements of American rock and roll, blues, jazz and British psychedelic styles into bossa nova and samba rhythms. Important figures linked to *tropicália* include Gal Costa, Jorge Ben Jor, Maria Bethânia, Os Mutantes and Tom Zé. Although *tropicália* wasn't initially embraced by the public, who objected to the electric and rock elements (in fact, Veloso was booed off the stage on several occasions), by the 1970s its radical ideas had been absorbed and accepted, and lyrics of protest were ubiquitous in songwriting of the time.

While 'pure' *tropicália* bands aren't around anymore, the influence can still be heard in the music of groups such as AfroReggae, one of Rio's leading funk bands.

MPB

Música Popular Brasileira (MPB) is a catchphrase to describe all popular Brazilian music after bossa nova. It includes *tropicália, pagode,* and Brazilian pop and rock. All Brazilian music has roots in samba; even in Brazilian rock, heavy metal, disco or pop, the samba sound is often present.

MPB first emerged in the 1970s along with talented musicians such as Edu Lobo, Milton Nascimento, Elis Regina, Djavan and dozens of others, many of whom wrote protest songs not unlike the *tropicalistas*. Chico Buarque is one of the first big names from this epoch, and is one of Brazil's best songwriters. His music career began in 1968 and spanned a time during which many of his songs were banned by the military dictatorship – in fact his music became a symbol of protest during that era.

THE IPOD 20: SOUNDS FROM BRAZIL

One of the world's great music cultures, Brazil has an astounding array of talented musicians, playing in a range of addictive styles. A list of our favorite songs could easily fill this chapter, but we've limited our (highly subjective) pick to 20 songs from 20 different artists.

- 'Aquarela do Brasil' – Ary Barroso
- 'Soy Loco por Ti, America' – Caetano Veloso
- 'Flor de Lis' – Djavan
- 'Alô, Alô Marciano' – Elis Regina
- 'Namorinho de Portão' – Gal Costa
- 'Desafinado' – João Gilberto
- 'A Procura da Batida Perfeita' – Marcelo D2
- 'Recado' – Maria Rita
- 'Panis et Circenses' – Os Mutantes
- 'Velha Infância' – Tribalistas

- 'Samba da Benção' – Bebel Gilberto
- 'Apesar de Você' – Chico Buarque
- 'O Mar' – Dorival Caymmi
- 'ABC da Vida' – Elza Soares
- 'Quilombo, o Eldorado Negro' – Gilberto Gil
- 'Ponta de Lança Africana' – Jorge Ben Jor
- 'Alibi' – Maria Bethânia
- 'Último Desejo' – Noel Rosa
- 'Garota de Ipanema' – Tom Jobim
- 'Felicidade' – Vinícius de Moraes

Jorge Ben Jor is another singer whose career, which began in the 1960s, has survived up to the present day. Highly addictive rhythms are omnipresent in Ben Jor's songs, as he incorporates African beats and elements of funk, samba and blues in his eclectic repertoire. The celebratory album *África Brasil* and his debut album, *Samba Esquema Novo,* are among his best.

More recent MPB stars include Bebel Gilberto, the sweet-voiced daughter of João Gilberto, who blends bossa nova with modern beats. Marisa has also teamed up with Arnaldo Antunes and Carlinhos Brown to create the hit album *Tribalistas* (2003). Other notable singers who hail from a bossa line include Fernanda Porto and Cibelle.

One artist quite active on the scene (in Rio) is Maria Rita, the talented singer and songwriter whose voice is remarkably similar to that of her late mother, Elis Regina – one of Brazil's greatest singers.

Tropical Truth: A Story of Music and Revolution in Brazil, by Caetano Veloso, describes the great artistic experiment of *tropicália* in 1960s Brazil. Although digressive at times, Veloso vividly captures the music, politics and lifestyles of the era.

BRAZILIAN ROCK & RAP

Derived more from English than American rock, this is the least Brazilian of all Brazilian music. Pronounced 'hock', big stars are groups such as Kid Abelha, Legião Urbana (who led a wave of punk-driven bands from Brasília), and the reggae-based Skank and Cidade Negra. The versatile and original Ed Motta, from Rio, injects soul, jazz and traditional Brazilian music into rock. Heavy metal band Sepultura, from Minas Gerais, achieved fame among headbangers worldwide in the 1990s. Other big pop-rock bands include Paralamas do Sucesso and Lula Santos. There's even in-your-face Brazilian punk, with artist Charlie Brown Jr poking fun at different styles of Brazilian music. Today's skater-punk crowd rallies around Raimundos, a witty band that infuses Northeastern rhythms into their rock; and a band that throws nearly everything into the blender – samba, rock, pop and Afro-Brazilian percussion – with surprising success, O Rappa also has fans.

Other talented indie-rock favorites include Los Hermanos, Zeca Baleiro and Monokini Mondo Topless, whose 2004 self-titled album blends pop with electro grooves – think Stereolab in the tropics. More recent successes include the saucy girl-band Cansei de Ser Sexy (Tired of Being Sexy), whose 2006 self-titled album blends '80s new wave and electro-pop and features irreverent lyrics (sung in English) and up-tempo beats.

In the rap world, Racionais MCs, from São Paulo, were among the first big rap artists to emerge, with hard-edged lyrics about life in the *favelas* and jails. Their 1998 album *Sobrevivendo no Inferno* (Surviving in Hell) sold more than a million copies – a record for independent releases in Brazil. Another rap star, Gabriel O Pensador is a White middle-class Carioca who directs a biting wit at…White middle-class Cariocas.

The list of emerging talents gets longer each day, but Brazilian hip-hop is reaching its stride with talented musicians such as Marcelo D2 (formerly of Planet Hemp), who dazzled audiences with big-beat album *À Procura da Batida Perfeita* (Looking for the Perfect Beat). Seu Jorge, who starred in the film *Cidade de Deus* (City of God), has also earned accolades for the release of *Cru* (Raw), an inventive hip-hop album with politically charged beats.

REGIONAL MUSIC

The Northeast has perhaps the most regional musical and dance styles. The most important is *forró*, a lively, syncopated music centered on the accordion and the *zabumba* (an African drum). Although a few artists such as Luiz Gonzaga and Jackson do Pandeiro have achieved national status, *forró* was long dismissed by urbanites as unsophisticated. The film *Eu, Tu, Eles* (Me, You, Them) has brought down-home *forró* back to center stage, aided in part by Gilberto Gil singing the hit *Esperando na Janela*.

Another type of distinctive regional music is the wonderful Bumba Meu Boi festival sound from São Luís, Maranhão (see the boxed text, p593). There is also *frevo*, a frenetic, samba-related, Carnaval-based music specific to Recife and neighboring Olinda.

The *trio elétrico*, also called *frevo baiano*, began more as a result of a change in technology rather than in music. It started as a joke when, during Carnaval in Salvador in the 1950s, a group of musicians spearheaded by innovative musical talents Dodo and Osmar (aka Adolfo Nascimento and Osmar Alvares Macedo) got on top of a truck and played *frevo* with electric guitars. The *trio elétrico* is not necessarily a trio, but it's still the backbone of Salvador's Carnaval, when trucks piled high with speakers – with musicians perched on top – drive through the city surrounded by dancing mobs. It was popularized when Caetano Veloso began writing songs about the *trio elétrico*. Another important element of Carnaval on the streets of Salvador is the *afro bloco* (Afro-Brazilian percussion group). Filhos de Gandhi and Grupo Olodum are the most famous of these – Filhos have deep African roots and are strongly influenced by Candomblé; Olodum invented samba-reggae.

Mangue beat (also known as *mangue bit*), from Recife, combines folkloric and regional styles with international influences as diverse as hip-hop, neo-psychedelic and *tejano* (instrumental folk music with roots in northern Mexico and Southern Texas). The early leaders of the genre were Chico Science and Nação Zumbi – the title of whose 1996 masterpiece, *Afrociber-delia*, kind of summed up what their music was about. Chico Science died in a 1997 car crash, but Nação Zumbi has gone forward without him, and other bands such as Mestre Ambrósio and Mundo Livre S/A continue to carry the *mangue* torch.

Axé is a label for the profuse samba/pop/rock/reggae/funk/Caribbean fusion music that emerged from Salvador in the 1990s. Taking its cue from Salvador's older Carnaval forms, *axé* was popularized by the powerful, flamboyant Daniela Mercury. Other exponents include the groups Ara Ketu and Chiclete com Banana. At its best it's great, superenergetic music – hear Daniela sing 'Toda Menina Baiana' (Every Bahian Girl) – but some bands overcommercialized it at the end of the '90s.

How to Be a Carioca, by Priscilla Ann Goslin, is a humorous portrait of the Rio dweller, with tongue-in-cheek riffs on beach-going, driving, soap operas, football and Carioca slang.

The influence of Brazilian Indian music was absorbed and diluted, as was so much that derived from Brazil's indigenous cultures. The *carimbó* music of the Amazon region (where the majority of Indians live today) is influenced primarily by the Blacks of the coastal zones.

OTHER STYLES

Lambada, a dance style influenced by *carimbó* and by Caribbean rhythms such as rumba, merengue and salsa, became popular in Brazil in the late 1980s and caught on briefly in Europe and the US. The most successful lambada artist was Beto Barbosa with her group Kaoma.

Also hugely popular, *sertanejo* is a kind of Brazilian country and western music that is a favorite with truck drivers and cowboys. It's characterized by soaring harmonies and lyrics about broken hearts, life on the road etc. Exponents like to pair off in duos, such as Milionário e José Rico, Chitãozinho e Xororó, and Leandro e Leonardo.

The Brazilian Sound, by Chris McGowan and Ricardo Pessanha, is a well-illustrated, readable introduction to Brazilian music, with insight into regional styles and musicians (big-name and obscure). Useful discography included.

Literature

The best-selling Brazilian author Paulo Coelho, whose many books have sold more than 80 million copies worldwide, is Latin America's second-most-read novelist (after Gabriel García Márquez). While critics tend to knock his simplistic New Age spiritual fables, books such as *The Alchemist, The Pilgrimage* and, more recently, *The Witch of Portobello* have struck a nerve with his global fan base, bringing him rock-star fame.

A writer of 'actual' rock-star fame is talented singer and songwriter Chico Buarque. The author of two rather mediocre novels, Buarque seemed to jump the fence successfully in his third effort, *Budapest*, an engaging and meditative novel of love and language set in Budapest and Rio.

Brazil's most famous writer is Jorge Amado, who died in August 2001. Born near Ilhéus in 1912, and a longtime resident of Salvador, Amado wrote colorful romances about Bahia's people and places. His early work was strongly influenced by communism. His later books are lighter in subject, but more picturesque and intimate in style. The two most acclaimed are *Gabriela, Clove and Cinnamon*, which is set in Ilhéus, and *Dona Flor and Her Two Husbands*, set in Salvador. *Tent of Miracles* explores race relations in Brazil, and *Pen, Sword and Camisole* laughs its way through the petty worlds of military and academic politics. *The Violent Land* is an early Amado classic.

Joaquim Maria Machado de Assis (1839–1908) is praised as one of Brazil's great writers. The son of a freed slave, Assis worked as a typesetter and journalist in late-19th-century Rio. A tremendous stylist with a great sense of humor and irony, Assis had an understanding of human relations that was subtle and deeply cynical. Look for Gregory Rabassa's good late-1990s translations of *Quincas Borba* and *The Posthumous Memoirs of Bras Cubas*. Machado's other major novel was *Dom Casmurro*.

An Anthology of Twentieth-Century Brazilian Poetry (1972) is a fine introduction to Brazilian poets, famed and obscure. It's edited by American poet Elizabeth Bishop, who planned a short trip to Santos and ended up staying 15 years.

Without a word wasted, Graciliano Ramos (1892–1953) tells of peasant life in the *sertão* in his best book, *Barren Lives*. The stories are powerful portraits. Also read anything you can find by Mário de Andrade (1893–1945), a leader of the country's 1920s artistic renaissance. His comic *Macunaíma*, which pioneered the use of vernacular language in Brazilian literature and was a precursor of magical realism, could only take place in Brazil.

The writings of the existentialist-influenced, Ukrainian-born Clarice Lispector (1925–77) are more subjective, focusing on human isolation, alienation and moral doubt, and conveying a deep understanding of women's feelings. The short-story collections *Family Ties* and *Soulstorm* are among her best works.

Themes of repression and violence gained prominence starting in the late 1960s with the advent of military dictatorship. The bizarre and brutal *Zero*, by Ignácio de Loyola Brandão, was banned by the military government until a national protest lifted the prohibition. *Tower of Glass*, five stories by Ivan Ângelo, is all São Paulo: an absurdist 1970s look at big-city life where nothing that matters, matters. João Ubaldo Ribeiro's *Sergeant Getúlio* is a story of a military man in Brazil's Northeast. No book tells better of the sadism, brutality and patriarchy that run through Brazil's history. Ribeiro's *An Invincible Memory* (which, like *Sergeant Getúlio*, was translated into English by the author himself) is a hugely popular 400-year saga of two Bahian families from opposite ends of the social spectrum.

Márcio Souza is a modern satirist based in Manaus. His biting humor captures the frightening side of the Amazon, and his imaginative parodies of Brazilian history reveal the stupidity of personal and official endeavors to conquer the rain forest. Do your best to obtain *Mad Maria* (a historical novel about the Madeira–Mamoré railway) and *Emperor of the Amazon* if you're going to Amazonia.

Dinah Silveira de Queiroz's *The Women of Brazil* is about a Portuguese girl who goes to 17th-century Brazil to meet her betrothed. Another author of interest is Joyce Cavalcante, who emerged in the 1990s as a writer able to express the experience of women in modern Brazil as well as the enduring social problems of the Northeast. Her *Intimate Enemies* is a tale of corruption, violence and polygamy, told with humor.

Aluísio Azevedo was one of the first in history to bring attention to the harrowing life in Rio's *favelas*. *Slum* brings rich characters and naturalistic scenery to life in this fascinating story from the 1890s, recently republished in the US and Europe.

Inferno, by Patrícia Mello, is a spine-chilling novel about a boy's ascent to the top of Rio's cocaine trade. The author had never set foot in a *favela* before writing it, creating controversy in many quarters.

Cinema & TV

Brazil's film industry has produced a number of major feature films and documentaries. One of the most recent films to achieve worldwide release is Andrucha Waddington's *House of Sand*, a film that follows three generations of women as they struggle on the dramatic but desolate desert landscape in Maranhão. It stars Seu Jorge and Fernanda Montenegro.

Eu, Tu, Eles, Andrucha Waddington's social comedy about a Northeasterner with three husbands, was also well received. It has beautiful cinematography and a score by Gilberto Gil. Waddington is currently at work on a film about singer Maria Bethânia.

Better known for its music than its storyline, the 2005 *Dois Filhos do Francisco* (The Two Sons of Francisco) is a film based on the true lives of two small-town brothers – Zeze and Luciano di Camargo – who became successful country musicians. Caetano Veloso arranged the soundtrack.

Although made by two Americans, *Favela Rising* (2005) has such a powerful message that it deserves mention. This documentary shows a *favela* through the eyes of Anderson Sá, founder of the very talented Grupo Cultural Afro Reggae (Afro-Reggae Group) and symbol of hope for many poor children growing up in the *favela*. In the film, Sá, who turned his life around after involvement in gangs, starts a music school for youths and makes an enormous contribution to a number of lives as the Afro-Reggae movement spreads to other *favelas*.

For a trip back to Rio's Lapa of the 1930s, check out Karim Aïnouz's compelling *Madame Satã* (2002). Rio's gritty red-light district of that time (which hasn't changed much in the last 75 years) is the setting for the true story of Madame Satã (aka João Francisco dos Santos), the troubled but good-hearted *malandro* (con artist), transvestite, singer and capoeira master, who was synonymous with Lapa's midcentury bohemianism.

A more contemporary portrait of Rio's social problems unfolds in José Padilha's harrowing *Bus 174* (2002). This award-winning documentary weaves together the televised footage of a bus hijacking with the story of the hijacker's life, himself a victim of brutality. The work explores Rio's cycle of violence, the social ills leading to crime and the role of the media.

One of Brazil's top directors, Fernando Meirelles earned his credibility with *Cidade de Deus,* the 2002 film based on a true story by Paolo Lins. The film, which showed brutality and hope coexisting in a Rio *favela,* earned four Oscar nominations. More importantly, it brought much attention to the urban poor in Brazil. Following his success with *Cidade de Deus,* Meirelles went Hollywood with *The Constant Gardener* (2004), a conspiracy film shot in Africa.

The highly recommended film *Favela Rising* tells the story of a former drug trafficker who renounces violence and uses music to radically change and inspire his community.

Walter Salles is one of Brazil's best-known directors, whose Oscar award–winning *Central do Brasil* (Central Station; 1998) should be in every serious Brazilianist's film library. The central character is an elderly woman who works in the main train station in Rio writing letters for illiterates with families far away. A chance encounter with a young homeless boy leads her to accompany him into the real, unglamorized Brazil on a search for his father. Salles' more recent film, *Diarios de Motocicleta* (The Motorcycle Diaries; 2004), chronicles the historic journey of Che Guevara and Alberto Granada across South America. As with many filmmakers, some of Salles' best works came much earlier. In fact, his first feature film, *Terra Estrangeiro* (Foreign Land), shot in 1995, holds an important place in the renaissance of Brazilian cinema.

Hector Babenco is another top Brazilian director. *Carandiru* (2003) is an inside look at São Paulo's hellish state penitentiary of the same name. Based on the real-life experiences of a doctor who worked inside the prison, *Carandiru* garnered a number of film-festival awards including the Cannes Palme d'Or. Even more powerful is Babenco's earlier film, *Pixote* (1981), which shows life through the eyes of a homeless child who gets swept from innocent waif to criminal by the currents of the underworld. Babenco went on to direct international Hollywood hits *Kiss of the Spider Woman* (1985), *Ironweed* (1987) and *The Past* (2007), his latest release, which stars Gael García Bernal in a twisted postlove story set in Argentina (where Babenco grew up before becoming a Brazilian naturalized citizen).

Rio de Jano is a colorful portrait of Rio life. It's a documentary about French cartoonist Jean le Guay, aka Jano, who came to Rio and made marvelous work of the Cariocas. Look for the book in Rio's bookstores.

Although it was made by an English director, the film *The Mission* (1986) deserves special mention for its portrait of life in the early colonial days and the brutal relationship between Guarani and the vying world powers of Portugal and Spain. It was shot around Iguaçu Falls and the cinematography is spectacular.

Dealing with Brazil's more recent troubles is Bruno Barreto's *O Que é Isso Companheiro* (released as *Four Days in September* in the US, in 1998). Set during the dictatorship, it was based on the 1969 kidnapping of the US ambassador to Brazil by leftist guerrillas.

Carlos Diegues' *Bye Bye Brasil* (1980) is another important Brazilian film. The first major film produced after the end of the dictatorship, it chronicles the adventures of a theater troupe as they tour the country, witnessing the profound changes in Brazilian society in the second half of the 20th century. Diegues also directed *Orfeu* (1999), a lackluster remake of the Camus classic.

Prior to the dictatorship, which stymied much creative expression in the country, Brazil was in the grip of Cinema Novo. This 1960s movement focused on Brazil's bleak social problems, and was influenced by Italian neorealism. One of the great films made during this epoch was the 1962 *O Pagador de*

Promessas (The Payer of Vows), a poetic story about a man who keeps his promise to carry a cross after the healing of his donkey. It won the Palme d'Or at the Cannes film festival. Another great pioneer of Cinema Novo is the director Glauber Rocha. In *Deus e o Diabo na Terra do Sol* (Black God, White Devil; 1963), Rocha explored the struggle, fanaticism and poverty of Northeastern Brazil. It's one of the great films of the period.

Going back in time, we reach *Orfeu Negro* (Black Orpheus), Marcel Camus' 1959 film, which opened the world's ears to bossa nova by way of the Jobim and Bonfá soundtrack. Music aside, the film did a clever job recasting Ovid's original Orpheus-Eurydice myth in the setting of Rio's Carnaval (a fertile ground for mythmaking).

Neorealism was one of the earliest movements affecting Brazil cinema, and *O Cangaceiro* (The Brigand; 1953) by Lima Barreto was perhaps the first Brazilian film to receive international recognition. The film chronicles the adventures of a roving band of outlaws, and was inspired by the Northeast's most infamous outlaw, Lampião.

The slasher film *Turistas*, about evil Brazilians stealing the organs from well-toned foreign kids, upset many Brazilians, who complained about egregious misrepresentations. Urban violence, Brazil has. Organ harvesters, not the last time we checked.

Painting & Visual Arts

Brazil's best-known contemporary artist outside the country is the photographer Sebastião Salgado. Noted for his masterful use of light, the black-and-white photographer has earned international acclaim for his highly evocative photos of migrant workers and others on the fringes of society. Genesis, his latest project, will take him to the Galapagos Islands, the Himalayas, the Nambian desert, the glaciers of Argentina and other remote regions as he films the peaceful integration of man and nature – a kind of 'planetary anthropology,' as he described it.

Ernesto Neto is another top figure in Brazil's contemporary art scene. His installations – some massive enough to fill an exhibition space – are made of membranelike fabric, sculpted into a wild assortment of shapes, from disturbingly anthropomorphic pieces to subterraneanlike labyrinths, and he often brings the viewer into his work.

One of Neto's inspirations is Hélio Oiticica (1937–80), one of the most significant figures of the avant-garde of the '60s and '70s. He's best known for interactive works, such as his *Cosmococa*, an installation that invited viewers to lie on sand covered with plastic sheeting, while watching a projection in which lines of cocaine were arranged across a photo of Marilyn Monroe.

Although she's sometimes associated with the *tropicália* movement, Lygia Clark (1920–88) had an art career spanning three decades. Her earliest pieces were monochrome constructivist paintings of the 1950s; in the '60s, her work became more conceptual, morphing finally into highly experimental explorations of sensory perception, ultimately entering a kind of psychotherapeutic realm.

Prior to the experimental era of constructivism and the avant-garde, European art was the principal influence on Brazilian artists, and movements such as neoclassicism, romanticism and impressionism were also observed in Brazil. One of the great neo-realists of the 20th century was Cândido Portinari (1903–62). Early in his career he made the decision to paint only Brazil and its people. Strongly influenced by Mexican muralists such as Diego Rivera, he fused indigenous, expressionist influences with a sophisticated, socially conscious style.

The 18th century was the era of Brazilian baroque art. Wealth provided by the gold rush helped talented artists to realize their full potential. The acknowledged genius of this period was the sculptor and architect Antônio Francisco Lisboa (1738–1814), better known as Aleijadinho (see the boxed text, p252, for information on his life and works).

Sebastião Salgado's *Workers* ranks among the great photographic portrait books of our time. In it Salgado shows the toil of laborers in powerful images captured in Spain, France, South Dakota and the gold mines of Brazil.

Brazil's earliest artists were colonial painters in Jesuit and Benedictine missionaries, who brought European sensibility to churches and sacred objects. The 17th-century Dutch invasion in the Northeast brought with it some important Flemish artists, such as Frans Post, who painted the flora and fauna in their tropical surroundings.

One of the most comprehensive surveys of 20th-century Brazilian architecture is *Brazil's Modern Architecture*. It's written by a variety of Brazilian architects and critics, discussing the high-modernism of the mid-20th century plus more recent projects.

Architecture

Salvador, capital of colonial Brazil from 1549 to 1763, has managed to preserve many outstanding Renaissance and baroque buildings. A special feature of its old town, where more than 600 buildings and monuments have been restored since 1992, are the many brightly colored houses, often decorated with high-quality stucco.

Olinda is essentially an 18th-century city. Its architectural wealth and unique atmosphere stem from its 20 baroque churches and many convents, chapels and houses with red-tile roofs. In São Luís the entire street plan of the late-17th-century heart of the city survives, along with many historic buildings, including fine mansions with colorful tiled facades.

The 18th-century mining towns of Minas Gerais also harbor architectural riches from the colonial era. The crown jewel is Ouro Prêto, the focal point of the 18th-century gold rush, which is adorned with the greatest concentration of fine baroque buildings in Brazil, many of them designed or embellished by the genius of Brazilian baroque, Aleijadinho. Lovely Ouro Prêto is joined on the World Heritage List by Diamantina, founded by 18th-century diamond hunters. Other Minas towns, such as Tiradentes and São João del Rei, also have baroque works.

When Brazil Was Modern: A Guide to Architecture: 1928–1960, by Lauro Cavalcanti, is a well-illustrated guide to the 30-odd architects who made important contributions to Brazil's modern landscape.

Brazil's architecture in the 19th and early 20th centuries was much influenced by French styles. Neoclassical tastes yielded grandiose, monumental constructions such as Rio de Janeiro's Museu Nacional de Belas Artes (p154) and Amazonian rubber-boom palaces such as Manaus' Teatro Amazonas (p642) and Belém's Teatro da Paz (p608). Art nouveau style arrived around the turn of the 20th century: an outstanding example in Rio is the interior of the Confeitaria Colombo (p173).

The 1930s was the era of art deco, as exemplified by Rio's central railway station and statue of Cristo Redentor (Christ the Redeemer; p150), the buildings along Belém's Avenida Presidente Vargas and many apartment buildings in Rio de Janeiro. The 1930s also saw the emergence of a new generation of Brazilian architects, led by Oscar Niemeyer and influenced by the modernist ideas of Le Corbusier. Niemeyer was pivotal in breaking away from the neoclassical style and designing without ornamentation, using steel and glass in elemental, aesthetically pleasing shapes. He is considered one of the great pioneers of modernism, and his reach is global. In Rio, Niemeyer's best-known work is his Museu do Arte Contemporânea (p157).

His most outstanding project, however, wasn't a building but an entire city. The nation's new capital, Brasília, was created in the 1950s and '60s from scratch by Niemeyer, urban planner Lúcio Costa and landscape architect Burle Marx. Although Brasília has its critics, it's still considered one of the world's most audacious urban-design projects. Its wild, airplane-shaped street plan has many iconic buildings, including the crown-shaped cathedral, the Santuário Dom Bosco, and dramatic government buildings such as the Palácio do Itamaraty and Palácio da Justiça.

Curves of Time: Oscar Niemeyer Memoirs is recommended for those interested in the art and life of Brazil's great architect (from exile in Paris to romps with Henry Miller).

Many other talented architects emerged in the second half of the 20th century. Lina Bo Bardi (1914–92), born in Rome, immigrated to Brazil following WWII. Highly active in Brazil's intellectual life, her first project was São Paulo's Casa de Vidro (Glass House; 1951), a Zenlike cube atop slender columns that melds into the surrounding landscape. She went on to expand

BRAZIL'S ECOLOGICAL CAPITAL

Although it's not the most exciting destination for visitors, Curitiba (p313) has long garnered praise for being one of the world's best models of urban planning. Over the past four decades, the capital of Paraná has developed an excellent (and much studied) public-transit system, created effective recycling initiatives and transformed urban spaces into parks, all the while promoting environmentally sustainable design long before it was fashionable.

Curitiba would probably resemble any other Brazilian city if it weren't for the bold initiatives of its three-term mayor, Jaime Lerner. Back in the 1960s, urban developers, influenced by Oscar Niemeyer and his followers, were planning to remodel the city around the automobile – tearing down buildings and widening boulevards – just as civil engineers were doing in the US. In Curitiba, a group of young architects and urban planners fought bitterly against the idea, proposing radical zoning and transportation ideas that would save the city from the wrecking ball. Lerner, an architect, who became mayor in 1971, put those ideas into action – and came up with a few brilliant ones of his own.

One of his first daring moves was transforming a six-block length of the downtown into a pedestrian zone. Since local merchants blocked the implementation, Lerner used guerilla tactics. On a Friday evening, under secrecy, he brought in a crew, who laid walkways, installed lights and planters, and completed the task in 72 hours – before anyone could stop the project. With a huge boost in pedestrian traffic, merchants soon asked for an extension of the automobile-free zone. Some drivers, however, were less pleased and when Lerner heard that a group was planning to drive along the road, he was prepared. He gathered several hundred children along the street, where they sat, painting pictures. This cemented the success of the pedestrian district and cast Lerner as a can-do mayor.

Public transit was another big challenge. Since the city couldn't afford to build an underground system, it took the efficiencies of the underground and adapted them to the surface. It created five express-bus avenues, increased frequencies (arriving every 30 seconds at peak time) and built tubular boarding platforms, complete with fare clerks and turnstiles to allow faster boarding and exiting. It also had Volvo make double-accordion, 270-passenger buses. Today, the system transports over two million passengers daily and provides a speedy way around the city.

Lerner spearheaded some highly imaginative methods for dealing with the city's garbage. He encouraged everyone to recycle (22% of garbage is currently separated for recycling) and got poorer citizens in on the city's clean-up act. Since the streets in some *favelas* are too narrow for garbage trucks, people cart out their own trash – 2kg of garbage is given in exchange for 0.5kg of vegetables.

He has also planted trees on an enormous scale (more than one million in the last 30 years) and set aside wetlands and parks (many with lakes to catch run-off in flood-prone areas), even transforming a waste dump into a botanical garden. Despite its explosive population growth, Curitiba increased its green areas from ½ sq meter per person to more than 50 sq meters. The ecology also extends to business, as Curitiba decided in the 1970s to admit only nonpolluting companies to its municipality, which it houses in an industrial district surrounded by large areas of green space.

Despite Curitiba's many successes, the obstacles are growing. The city faces a flood of new, poor immigrants, attracted in part by the city's livability, plus more drivers packing the roads, and declining recycling rates (particularly alarming since the city's only landfill will likely be full by 2009). Perhaps the once visionary city needs a Lerner for the 21st century – although modifying human behavior is likely the only way Curitiba can avoid going the way of other urban behemoths.

on the idea of weight and levity in her design for the Museu de Arte de São Paulo (MASP; p283), a bold design featuring two huge red concrete frames that suspend the interior glass structure above the ground. She remained active in the design world until the 1990s, both as a practitioner and a theorist, collaborating in numerous projects. Her many admirers remark on her 'anthropological architecture,' design based on a respectful attitude toward the user.

One of Brazil's most active contemporary architects is Paulo Mendes da Rocha (b 1929). In 2006, the São Paulo–based architect won the Pritzker prize (the Nobel of the architecture world) for his 'deep understanding of the poetics of human space.' Part of the avant-garde group of 'brutalist' architects in São Paulo, Mendes da Rocha designs with simple materials and forms that could be readily and easily constructed. There's also an ethical dimension to his work that focuses on the harmony between indoor and outdoor space. His work can be seen in São Paulo's Praça do Patriarca, a revitalized public space crowned with a curved steel canopy that appears to float overhead.

Environment

Brazil boasts a truly incredible variety of landscapes and ecosystems with a diversity of flora and fauna unequaled on earth. It's home to the world's largest rain forest, as well as some of the greatest wetlands and most beautiful beaches. The sleek predatory jaguar dwells here, as does the gentle pink river dolphin, and plants range from the mighty mahogany to the delicate orchid.

More known species of plants (over 55,000), freshwater fish (around 3000), amphibians (775) and mammals (522) are found in Brazil than in any other country in the world. Brazil ranks third for the number of birds (nearly 1700) and fifth for reptiles (633). Around 10 to 15 million types of insect fly, hop and wriggle their lives away here too. About a quarter of the mammals in Brazil, more than one-third of the reptiles and over half the amphibians occur nowhere else – and new species are being discovered all the time, including 13 types of monkey since 1990.

Unfortunately, Brazil is also renowned for the destruction of its natural environment. Amazonia, which contains most of Brazil's biological diversity, is in environmental crisis. All of Brazil's other major ecosystems are also threatened. Even as new species are being discovered, others are disappearing. Some 120 Brazilian birds and 70 mammals are threatened with extinction.

But a surge of environmental awareness among Brazilians since the 1990s is finally changing attitudes and practices. Apart from a broader understanding of the irreplaceability of the Amazon rain forest, the value of other Brazilian habitats from scrub to swamps is increasingly appreciated, and high-profile conservation campaigns dedicated to animals, such as sea turtles, dolphins and the golden lion tamarin (a small primate), have caught the attention of millions. Most politicians now at least have to claim that their policies are environmentally sustainable.

Brazil's natural wonders are a huge and growing tourist attraction, and tourism will have a key future influence on Brazil's environment. Along the coasts, while ecologists struggle to protect the shore and waters from damaging development, they can also spread the word through visitors' centers for high-profile projects such as Tamar (dedicated to sea turtles) and Projeto Peixe-Boi (manatees). Hotels and pousadas (guesthouses) built and run on truly ecological principles serve as examples to thousands of visitors. In the inland forests and wetlands, the understanding is growing that nature kept pristine attracts tourists and their money. Travelers can play an important role by giving their custom to businesses with genuinely sustainable practices (see the boxed text Questions to Ask a Local Tour Operator, p96).

This chapter introduces the Brazilian natural environment, including current conservation efforts and the best places to see the country's fascinating wildlife for yourself.

THE LAND

Brazil is the world's fifth-largest country (after Russia, China, Canada and the US). Its 8.5 million sq km occupy almost half of South America and it borders every country in the continent except Chile and Ecuador.

Away from the generally narrow coastal plains, southern, southeastern and northeastern Brazil are composed chiefly of low, hilly country broken by occasional dramatic escarpments, with some mountain ranges, such as the Serra do Espinhaço and Serra do Mar, rarely exceeding 2000m in elevation. Many southern and southeastern rivers flow inland to join the Paraná, the

The international website of WWF, www.panda.org, has a lot of fascinating material on Brazil in English.

Henry Walter Bates' *The Naturalist on the River Amazons* is a classic journal of plant, animal and human life in Amazonia in the 1850s.

The Nature Conservancy website (www.nature .org) includes portraits of Brazil's major ecosystems and information on the country's endangered species.

THE STATES OF BRAZIL

Uruguai or Paraguai, big waterways flowing southward toward the Río de la Plata (River Plate), between Uruguay and Argentina. The Paraguai emerges from the low-lying Pantanal wetlands that straddle Brazil's central west and parts of Bolivia and Paraguay.

The northeastern tip of Brazil is nearer to Africa than it is to far southern or western Brazil.

At the heart of the country spreads a broad, elevated plain, the Planalto Brasileiro, broken by several small mountain ranges but with an average altitude of only about 500m. Apart from the great Rio São Francisco, which empties into the Atlantic north of Salvador, most rivers here flow north to the enormous, low-lying Amazon Basin. There they feed the mighty Amazon, along with hundreds of other tributaries originating in the Andes in Bolivia, Peru, Ecuador and Colombia and in the mountains along the Brazil–Venezuela border and in the Guyana Shield along Brazil's borders with Guyana, Suriname and French Guiana. Pico da Neblina (3014m) on the Venezuelan border is Brazil's highest peak.

Brazil has five principal biomes (major regional plant and animal groupings): Amazonia, Atlantic rain forest, caatinga (semiarid land), cerrado (the central savanna) and the wetlands of the Pantanal.

Amazonia

Blanketing nearly all of northern Brazil plus parts of Mato Grosso and Maranhão states – over 4 million sq km, almost half the country – Brazilian Amazonia incorporates 30% of the world's tropical forest (the planet's most biologically diverse ecosystem). It's home to around 45,000 plant species (some 20% of the world total), 311 mammals (about 10% of the world total), 1000 bird species (15%), 1800 types of butterfly and around 2000 species of fish (in contrast, Europe has about 200). The forest still keeps many of its secrets: to this day, major tributaries of the Amazon River remain unexplored, thousands of species have not yet been classified and it is highly likely that some human communities have still avoided contact with the outside world.

Including a further 2 million sq km in neighboring countries, the entire Amazon Basin holds 20% of the world's fresh water and produces 20% of the world's oxygen. Unfortunately, humanity has been destroying the Brazilian Amazon forests so quickly in recent decades – about 17% of them is already gone – that, before we even start thinking about the consequences for global warming, we must recognize that hundreds of animal and plant species are likely to be extinguished before they're even known to us (see the boxed text, p75, for more on the issue of Amazon deforestation).

Rain forests can occur in areas where more than 2000mm of rain falls annually and where this rainfall is spread over the whole year. In the Amazon, half the rain comes from damp trade winds blowing in from the Atlantic Ocean and the rest results from vapor released by Amazonia's own soil and trees – much of which is recycled rain. Humidity is always greater than 80%, and temperatures range fairly constantly between 22°C (72°F) by night and 31°C (88°F) by day.

FLOODPLAIN & DRY LAND

Seasonal rainfall patterns mean that the water levels of the Amazon River and its tributaries rise and fall at different times of the year. This produces dramatic alterations in the region's geography. Water levels routinely vary by 10m to 15m between low and high marks; during high-water periods, areas totaling at least 150,000 sq km (about the size of England and Wales together) are flooded. The high waters link rivers, creeks and lakes that are otherwise unconnected, providing river travelers with numerous shortcuts. The seasons are not the same everywhere in the Amazon Basin: high water on the Amazon itself and its major northern tributary, the Rio Negro, is in June; while high water on the southern tributaries such as the Madeira, Araguaia and Tocantins occurs in March.

In 2005 the Amazon Basin experienced its worst drought in 50 years, with some lakes and rivers drying up completely. While Greenpeace blamed deforestation, saying that burning of trees had prevented the formation of clouds, Brazilian government meteorologists argued that the drought was due to climate cycles and temperatures in the Atlantic Ocean.

The regularly inundated floodplains of the 'white-water' (actually creamy-brown) rivers flowing down from the Andes are known as *várzea* and sustain forests up to 20m tall. Many of the trees have elevated roots. *Igapó* is the common name for forests flooded by the darker waters of the Rio Negro basin. It's particularly fascinating to boat through a flooded forest because you move along at treetop level and can get closer to the wildlife.

Forests on *terra firme* (higher land, not subject to flooding) typically grow to 30m in height. Here are found the Brazil nut tree and valuable hardwoods such as mahogany, which prefer a drier environment.

The National Geographic documentary *Amazon: Land of the Flooded Forest* (1997) explores this unique region, where water and land life intermingle for six months of the year. The film details the fragile interdependency of the wildlife and its habitat.

The Brazilian research institute Imazon (www .imazon.org.br in Portuguese) reports on various aspects of Amazon ecology.

Jacques Cousteau's two Amazon movies, *Amazon – River of the Future* (1991) and *Amazon – Journey to a Thousand Rivers* (1991), follow the world's greatest oceanographer as he films the intricacies of this unique ecosystem, and makes a persuasive argument for its conservation.

On the waters themselves live aquatic plants, such as the giant *Victoria amazonica* water lily (named after Britain's Queen Victoria and up to 2m in diameter) and even floating islands with amphibious grasses.

The Amazon Basin averages between 130 and 250 rainy days a year, depending on exactly where you are.

FOREST LAYERS

The rain forest is stratified into layers of plant and animal life. Most of the animal activity takes place in the canopy layer, 20m to 30m above ground, where trees compete for sunshine, and butterflies, sloths and the majority of birds and monkeys live. Here hummingbirds hover for pollen, and macaws and parrots seek out nuts and tender shoots. A few tall trees reaching up to 40m, even 50m, poke above the canopy and dominate the forest skyline. These 'emergent trees' are inhabited by birds such as the harpy eagle and toucan and, unlike most other rain forest plants, disperse their seeds by wind.

In *The Last Forest: The Amazon in the Age of Globalization*, authors Mark London and Brian Kelly revisit the great river basin 25 years after writing an earlier book on it, and conclude that all is not yet lost.

The dense foliage of the canopy layer blots out sunlight at lower levels. Below the canopy is the understory. Epiphytes (air plants) hang at midlevels and below them are bushes, saplings and shrubs growing up to 5m in height. Last is a ground cover of ferns, seedlings and herbs – plants adapted to very little light. Down here live ants and termites, the so-called social insects. The *saubas* (leaf-cutter ants) use leaves to build underground nests for raising fungus gardens, while army ants swarm through the jungle in huge masses, eating everything in their path. Insects, fungi and roots fight for access to nutrients, keeping the forest floor quite tidy. At ground level it's cooler than in the canopy, averaging about 28°C (82°F), but humidity is higher, at about 90%.

The forest's soils are typically shallow. Many trees have buttress roots that spread over wide patches of ground to gather more nutrients.

Atlantic Rain Forest

Brazil's 'other' tropical rain forest, the Mata Atlântica (Atlantic rain forest) once extended right along the country's southeast-facing coast, from Rio Grande do Norte to Rio Grande do Sul. It formed a band that gradually widened toward the south, where it reached a width of up to 800km. The Atlantic rain forest covered more than 1 million sq km when the Portuguese arrived.

Today, three-quarters of Brazil's population and all its main industrial cities are located in what used to be the Mata Atlântica, and only 7% of the original forest remains. Brazilwood extraction, sugarcane and coffee cultivation, gold mining, farming, ranching, logging, fires, and acid rain have also taken their toll on the forest.

But if you travel along the coast, you'll still have plenty of opportunities to experience the Mata Atlântica, now split into dozens of separate fragments. The Mata Atlântica is older than the Amazon forest and evolved independently. It's incredibly luxuriant, and some areas boast what may be the highest biodiversity levels on earth. Though the Atlantic rain forest shares many animal and plant families with other Brazilian ecosystems, it also contains many unique species – 21 of its 26 primate types are found only here, as are more than 900 of its 2000-plus kinds of butterflies, and many of its over 600 bird species. Unsurprisingly, many of these species are endangered, including the four types of lion tamarin and the two wooly spider monkeys (the largest primates in the Americas).

With *Broadax and Firebrand: The Destruction of the Brazilian Atlantic Forest*, by Warren Dean, chronicles the history of the other rain forest in Brazil, and serves as a warning for the Amazon and other rain forests.

The Atlantic rain forest's distinctive flora – more than half of its tree species exist nowhere else – includes large trees such as brazilwood, ironwood, Bahian jacaranda and cedar, as well as many rare tree ferns. The 20,000 plant species here, half of them endemic, account for 8% of the world total. Unesco recognized the Mata Atlântica's importance in 1999 when it placed 33 separate areas in Paraná, São Paulo, Espírito Santo and Bahia states, totaling 5820 sq km, on the World Heritage List.

WHY THE RAIN FOREST MATTERS

Measuring greenhouse-gas emissions is an inexact science and no two sets of statistics ever agree, but the general indication is that Brazil is responsible for about 3% of global greenhouse-gas emissions, while China and the US are responsible for around 20% to 25% each, and the European Union (EU) for about 15%. About a quarter of the world's greenhouse-gas emissions come from deforestation, but in Brazil the proportion is more like three-quarters (only Indonesia destroys more forest than Brazil). So halving Brazilian deforestation, such as happened between 2004 and 2006 (see p97), can cut global emissions by between 1% and 2%. In the battle to stem global warming, every bit counts.

The greenhouse theory, in simple terms, is as follows. Much of the sun's heat that reaches the planet is reflected back into space as infrared radiation. Carbon in the atmosphere, however, in the form of carbon dioxide (CO_2) or methane (CH_4), prevents the radiation from leaving and thus traps heat on the planet like a global greenhouse. The more carbon in the atmosphere, the hotter the earth gets.

By day, trees absorb carbon dioxide and release oxygen; by night, they absorb oxygen and release carbon dioxide. In a mature forest, the consumption and release of these two gases is in balance. But growing trees absorb more carbon dioxide than they release, and burning or dead trees release carbon dioxide without absorbing any at all. So when tree-dense areas are burned or otherwise deforested, levels of carbon in the atmosphere increase and, as a result, the earth gets hotter. Burning is a particular problem in the Brazilian Amazon, where ranchers and farmers often use fire to clear land and encourage grass growth. Fires can get out of control and the problem becomes particularly acute when the annual rains do not come as expected after the August-to-September burning season. Preserving rain forests, on the other hand, helps to keep carbon locked away – in the jargon, 'sequestered' – and out of the atmosphere.

Another source of carbon in the atmosphere is the burning of fossil fuels by motor vehicles, electricity plants, industrial processes and so on. In 1997 many of the world's rich countries signed the Kyoto Protocol, under which they must cut their emissions of greenhouse gases by around 5% from 1990 levels by 2012. (Some signatories look set to meet the target, while others such as Canada, Japan and Spain look set to miss it badly. The US in the end did not ratify the agreement at all and remained outside the Kyoto process.)

One important consequence of Kyoto was the first large-scale, carbon-credit trading scheme, initiated in the EU in 2005. Under this program companies in heavily polluting industries were issued with permits to produce set amounts of carbon dioxide, the commonest greenhouse gas. Firms that did not need their full entitlement could sell the 'surplus' to other companies, and companies could also acquire the right to emit more carbon dioxide by paying for carbon-offset schemes, such as planting trees, in the world's poorer countries.

Brazil at first opposed the idea of such payments – national pride resisted the idea of foreigners telling Brazil what to do with its forests, and logging-ranching-agribusiness interests in the country were too strong. But Brazil changed its tune at a UN meeting on climate change in Nairobi in 2006, proposing an international fund to reward Brazil for keeping deforestation below certain agreed levels. The country thus hopes to turn a profit from the service it renders to the rest of the world by simply keeping its forests in existence.

There are plenty of other good reasons for Brazil to protect its rain forests. One is their enormous biodiversity. Tropical forests have a far greater concentration of different plant and animal species than most other ecosystems. For example, of the 250,000 species of higher plants known to science, 45,000 can be found in the Amazon rain forest. This reservoir of genetic diversity is an incredibly vital source of food, medicines and chemicals used worldwide (and of business opportunities for Brazilians). About a quarter of the medicines used in the developed world contain elements extracted from tropical forests. The Amazon rain forest has already given us rubber, manioc (cassava) and cocoa, as well as antimalarial drugs, cancer drugs and hundreds of other medicinal plants. A cure for AIDS, breast cancer or the common cold might be lurking somewhere in forest flora or fauna. The destruction of such a storehouse would be an incalculable loss.

Caatinga

Caatinga is semiarid land, with hardy vegetation composed mainly of cacti and thorny shrubs adapted to a shortage of water and extreme heat – the natural environment of much of the interior of the Northeast region, the *sertão*. Rainfall (300mm to 800mm a year) is irregular, and often torrential when it comes (in the first half of the year). Most rivers rising here are dry for half the year. Despite this, the caatinga harbors surprising biodiversity. When it does rain, the trees break into leaf and the ground turns green. 'Islands' of humidity and fertile soils around the mountain ranges are known as *brejos*. Caatinga is a habitat unique to Brazil, although less than one-tenth of it is in its natural state.

Caatinga wildlife tends to be nocturnal or subterranean, and many species – anteaters and armadillos, for example – have been severely depleted by hunting and habitat destruction. The handsome laughing falcon is a typical sight in caatinga skies, but the last known wild Spix's macaw, a beautiful iridescent-blue bird, disappeared from its haunts near Curaçá, Bahia, in 2000.

Wood and coal from the caatingas are a primary energy source for many of the region's more than 20 million inhabitants, and also fuel hungry brick-works and steel industries. Centuries of cattle ranching, and more recent ill-advised attempts at irrigated, pesticide-aided agriculture, have devastated large areas of caatinga. Some 40,000 sq km of caatinga were desertified in the last 15 years of the 20th century.

Cerrado

Cerrado covers the central high plains of Brazil – 2 million sq km in a rough triangle from southern Minas Gerais to Mato Grosso to southern Maranhão, nearly a quarter of the country in all. Typical cerrado is open savanna grassland dotted with trees, though it can edge into scrub, palm stands or even fairly thick forest. Over 800 bird species are known to live here and plant diversity is great – 10,000 species, of which 45% are found nowhere else in the world. Many plants are used to produce cork, fibers, oils, handicrafts, medicines and food. Medicinal plants native to cerrado include arnica and golden trumpet.

Despite the cerrado's size, it is severely threatened. Only about 20% has intact original vegetation, and with deforestation running at about 30,000 sq km a year, some researchers fear the cerrado will disappear completely by 2030. Less than 1% is under environmental protection. In the past the major problem was mining, which contaminated rivers with mercury and caused erosion and silting of streams. Since the mid-20th century, farming and cattle ranching, with accompanying human settlement, have done even greater damage to the natural balance. Intensive single-crop farming over large areas, especially of soybeans, has depleted soils, and contaminated water and soils with pesticides and fertilizers. The expansion of sugarcane plantations to provide the raw material for ethanol motor fuel (see p99) promises more of the same. From the cerrado, rivers flow north to Amazonia, south to the Pantanal and east to the Atlantic, meaning that the agricultural toxins from here can have a very wide effect. None of this bodes well for such rare and in some cases threatened cerrado inhabitants as the maned wolf, giant anteater, jaguar, cerrado fox, giant and three-banded armadillo, pampas deer, crowned eagle and the largest bird in Brazil, the ground-dwelling rhea.

Pantanal

The Pantanal is a vast swampy wetland in the center of South America, about half the size of France – some 210,000 sq km spread across Brazil, Bolivia and Paraguay. It's the largest inland wetland on earth, and 140,000 sq km of it lies in Brazil, in the states of Mato Grosso and Mato Grosso do Sul.

One hectare (10,000 sq meters) of well-conserved caatinga can be home to 200 different ant species.

The disappearance of the Spix's macaw leaves another caatinga dweller, the Lear's macaw, as the world's rarest macaw, with less than 150 left (near Canudos, Bahia).

The greatest number of different tree species ever found in 1 hectare (10,000 sq meters) was 476, recorded in an area of Atlantic rain forest in the hills of Espírito Santo state. Second prize (454 tree species) goes to another area of Atlantic rain forest in the Ecoparque de Una, Bahia (p480).

During the wet season, from October to March, the waters from the higher surrounding lands run into the Pantanal, inundating as much as two-thirds of it for half the year. The Pantanal, though 2000km upstream from the Atlantic Ocean, is only 100m to 200m above sea level and drains very slowly. Its chief outlet is the Rio Paraguai, which ultimately drains into the Atlantic Ocean via the Rio de la Plata. Waters reach their highest levels, up to 3m above dry-season levels, around March in the northern Pantanal, but not until about June in the south.

This seasonal flooding has made systematic farming impossible, severely limiting human impact on the area, and it creates an enormously rich feeding ground for wildlife. The Pantanal is still one of Brazil's wildest regions. It is the best area to head in all Brazil if you want to see wildlife, boasting greater visible numbers of animals and at least as much variety of creatures as Amazonia, with which it shares many species. The Pantanal supports approximately 650 bird species, 300 fish species, up to 190 mammals and 170 reptile species including iconic creatures like the giant anaconda, the jaguar, the puma, the giant anteater, the hyacinth macaw, the giant otter, and the black howler and brown capuchin monkeys – and somewhere between 10 and 35 million caimans. The most visible mammal is the capybara, the world's largest rodent, which is often seen in family groups or even large herds.

The flood waters replenish the soil's nutrients, the waters teem with fish, and the ponds provide ecological niches for many animals and plants. Birds fly in flocks of thousands, and six different species may nest on a single branch. In the dry season the lagoons and marshes dry out and fresh grasses emerge on the savanna, while hawks and caimans compete for fish in the shrinking ponds.

With cerrado to the east, Amazon rain forest to the north and spots of Atlantic rain forest to the south, Pantanal vegetation – an estimated 3500 plant species – is a mishmash of savanna, forest, meadow and even, on some of the highest points, caatinga.

Despite threats to its ecosystems the Pantanal (see boxed text, p78) is still generally well conserved and the region provides a secure habitat for reduced populations of threatened species such as the hyacinth macaw, giant otter, marsh deer, jaguar and maned wolf.

Other Environmental Zones

The mountainous regions of southern Brazil were once covered by coniferous forests that were dominated by the prehistoric-looking, 30m- to 40m-high *araucária* (Paraná pine) tree. The *araucária* forests have been decimated by timber cutters and now survive only in scattered areas such as the Aparados da Serra national park, generally at altitudes above 500m.

Apart from the cerrado, grasslands occur chiefly in Brazil's far north (northern Roraima) and far south (Rio Grande do Sul). Unlike the cerrado, which has a consistent scattering of medium to tall trees, the Roraima grasslands have only low trees and bushes, while the *campos do sul* (southern fields), on the rolling southern pampas, generally have no trees except where interspersed with patches of woodland.

WILDLIFE

Brazil's teeming flora and fauna make it one of the planet's best destinations for nature lovers. The following brief portraits cover a selection of the most exciting and most often seen species, many of which are widely distributed around the country.

In *Spix's Macaw: The Race to Save the World's Rarest Bird*, Tony Juniper of Friends of the Earth looks beyond his immediate narrative to examine issues of the huge global wildlife trade.

A superb guide for ecotravelers visiting the Pantanal is *Brazil: Amazon and Pantanal* by David L Pearson and Les Beletsky. Although written by a biologist, it's accessible and informative, identifying wildlife, plants, environmental threats and conservation issues.

Rios Vivos (www .riosvivos.org.br) has good information in English and Portuguese on environmental issues in the Pantanal.

Mammals
ANTEATERS, ARMADILLOS & SLOTHS

Zoologists group these animals together in the edentate order. Edentate means 'toothless,' and while that's not strictly true of sloths, these creatures feed chiefly on plants and insects.

The giant anteater can grow well over 2m long. It tears open ant and termite nests with its sharp claws and laps up as many as 35,000 a day with its probing sticky tongue. You're most likely to see the giant anteater in cerrado (savanna) habitat. Its meat is prized in some areas of Brazil, and it's a threatened species. The collared or lesser anteater, up to 1.4m long, is yellow and black, mainly nocturnal and often climbs trees.

Sloths, true to their name, move very slowly. And they're not, by the look of it, too bright. They hang upside down from branches by their strong arms

The giant anteater's Portuguese name, *tamanduá bandeira*, means 'flag anteater' and refers to its long hairy tail, which waves like a flag as the creature forages for ants and termites.

THE PANTANAL STILL UNDER SIEGE

The good news: poaching in the Pantanal has been brought under control after threatening to wipe out several rare and wonderful species in the last decades of the 20th century. Even though commercial wildlife hunting was made illegal in Brazil in 1967, the laws went unenforced for many years. From the late 1970s poachers went on the rampage in the Pantanal, taking as many as a million caiman skins a year to be smuggled out to Bolivia and Paraguay and thence to Europe, North America and the Far East, largely to be made into 'croc-skin' handbags, shoes, belts and other accessories. Poachers also took many thousands of other animals – ocelots, jaguars, giant otters, anacondas, hyacinth macaws, toucans – in some cases alive for the international pet market, in most cases dead for their skins. Further rare animals such as anteaters and marsh deer were hunted for food. The hyacinth macaw and the giant otter were particularly threatened. Some 10,000 beautiful bright-blue hyacinth macaws, each worth thousands of dollars in the US, disappeared in the 1980s, leaving just 3000 in the Pantanal.

In 1988 Brazil strengthened its hunting laws and in 1992 the Convention on International Trade in Endangered Species (cites) banned the export of raw or salted skins, wiping out much of the poachers' market. Though it will never be possible to eliminate poaching in the Pantanal completely, it is now under control, and tougher enforcement of antipoaching laws has seen creatures such as the hyacinth macaw and giant otter making comebacks there. No one is sure which way jaguar numbers are heading. Pantanal ranchers continue, illegally, to kill jaguars that have killed their livestock, at a rate of about 40 a year, because the alternative – government compensation for the livestock – takes too long to arrive. Some ranchers have however signed agreements not to kill these jaguars, in return for more effective compensation from conservation groups.

The bad news: fresh threats to the Pantanal's ecosystems and wildlife are arising all the time, chiefly as a result of the push for economic development. In fact the Pantanal was declared 'Threatened Lake of the Year' by the international foundation Global Nature Fund in 2007.

Arguably the biggest problem is the rapid spread of intensive soy, cotton and sugarcane farming on Brazil's central plains, which are the source of most of the Pantanal's water. The sugarcane is the raw material of ethanol motor fuel, for which Brazil has such high economic hopes. Herbicides, fertilizers and other chemicals from the plantations drizzle their way into Pantanal waters, and forest clearance on the plains leads to erosion and consequent silting of Pantanal rivers.

The growing cities around the Pantanal lack adequate sewage treatment, and further pollution is threatened by plans for industrial development – including a thermal power station, mining operations and chemical and steel plants in Corumbá, and up to 42 new ethanol distilleries in the state of Mato Grosso do Sul by 2010.

And tourism? It could be a blessing or a curse. Despite the Pantanal's international renown as a great place to see wildlife, some 70% of its approximately one million tourists every year go there just to fish, and some fish species are already alarmingly scarce in certain areas. Well-run ecotourism operations have many benefits, but they are small beer beside the bounty that fishing tourism brings in.

and legs, feeding on leaves, sleeping up to 18 hours a day and descending to the ground to excrete just once a week. Surprisingly, they're good swimmers. You have a good chance of seeing some if you get a bit off the beaten track in Amazonia: from a moderate distance they look like clumps of vegetation high in trees. The species you're most likely to see is the brown-throated three-toed sloth.

Brazil's several species of armadillo are mainly nocturnal and rarely seen. Two of them are threatened.

COATIS & RACCOONS

The widespread coati is one of the carnivorous animals that you're most likely to come across – possibly as a pet, for it's easily tamed. It's furry and cute, the size of a small or medium-sized dog, with a long brown-and-yellow-ringed tail, and a long flexible snout that noses around for food on the ground or up in trees. Scientifically the coati is a procyonid – one of the raccoon family. Its distant relative, the crab-eating raccoon, with a ringed tail and black eye mask like the North American raccoon, is found in Amazonia, the Pantanal and in between, always near water, where it seeks out its diet of crabs, fish, mollusks and small amphibians.

DEER, PECCARIES & TAPIRS

These animals are all ungulates (hoofed quadrupeds), though this term is no longer used in formal classification.

In the Pantanal, most people see at least a few deer. The biggest, which is active by day, is the marsh deer, whose antlers can grow to 60cm long. Other species – some found as far north as Amazonia – include the pampas deer, which lives more out in the open than most other deer, and the small (60cm to 70cm long) gray brocket deer and red brocket deer.

Peccaries – looking like small wild boars – are fairly widely distributed in forests. They live in groups, are active by day and feed on fruit, roots, carrion and small animals. The collared peccary, around 1m long and weighing 20kg, is named for the light-colored semicircle below its neck and is found in groups of 10 to 50. The slightly bigger white-lipped peccary travels in groups of 50 or more, chewing and trampling everything in its path.

The Brazilian tapir can be found in most forested parts of the country but is shy and nocturnal. Related to the horse and about the size of a stocky pony (it can weigh 300kg), the tapir has a long snout that helps it forage for leaves, fruit and roots. It rarely strays far from mud, which it uses to keep cool and control parasites.

DOGS, FOXES & WOLVES

The maned wolf inhabits cerrado and the Pantanal. It is russet-colored, fox-faced and long-legged, grows to about 1m long (plus tail) and has a mane of darker hair on the back of the neck. It's commonly hunted and is a threatened species. Other Brazilian members of the dog family include the crab-eating fox and the bush dog, both present in cerrado and the Pantanal. They are pretty rare and in fact you'll be lucky if you see any of these three.

DOLPHINS, MANATEES & WHALES

On many rivers in the Amazon Basin you should catch glimpses of the pink dolphin. One of the world's five freshwater cetaceans, it lives only in the Amazon and Orinoco Rivers and their tributaries – and it really is pink! It's most often seen where tributaries meet larger rivers, and is most active in the early morning and late afternoon. Sightings are tantalizing – and getting good photos virtually impossible – as the dolphin surfaces unpredictably, for just a

The Brazilian version of the yeti or the Loch Ness monster is the Mapinguari, a legendary nocturnal animal of the Amazon jungle that grows to 2m long, is covered in red hair and can rip apart palm trees. Cryptozoologists believe that the legend may be inspired by giant sloths (now extinct).

The giant ground sloth, which grew to the size of an elephant, once inhabited much of Brazil. The slow-moving animal was an easy target for prehistoric hunters and it was presumably hunted to extinction about 10,000 years ago.

A good field guide to the animals of tropical Brazil is *Neotropical Rainforest Mammals* by Louise Emmons.

second or so at a time, to breathe. Often it won't even lift its head above the surface. The pink dolphin has a lumpy forehead, a long beak, no dorsal fin (just a ridge) and tiny eyes – it's almost blind but has a highly evolved sonar system. Adults are 1.8m to 2.5m long, weighing 85kg to 160kg.

Amazonian rivers are also home to the gray dolphin, a bit smaller than the pink and often found together with it. Unlike the pink dolphin, the gray also inhabits the sea, in coastal waters from Florianópolis to Panama. When it surfaces it usually lifts its head and part of its body out of the water.

The Fernando de Noronha archipelago (p539), off Natal in Northeast Brazil, is a good site for observing large groups of the spinner dolphin, a small marine dolphin less than 1.8m long. They gather by the hundreds in the bays at sunrise and playfully swim around the bows of tour boats.

Larger than the dolphins is the Amazon manatee, a slow-moving vegetarian that is illegally hunted for its meat by riverbank dwellers and consequently is in danger of extinction. Prospects are even poorer for the marine West Indian manatee, of which there are just 500 left in coastal waters from the state of Alagoas northward.

Seven whale species occur off Brazil's coasts. The country's first dedicated whale sanctuary, Praia do Rosa (p350), was declared along 130km of the Santa Catarina coast in 2000, to protect the southern right whale, once the abundant raw material of a Brazilian whaling industry but now down to a world population of about 5000. Mothers and calves can be seen from beautiful Praia do Rosa beach between June and October.

Another rare whale, the humpback whale, breeds in the same months in the Parque Nacional Marinho de Abrolhos (p492), off the coast of southern Bahia.

In the captivating *Journey of the Pink Dolphins*, Sy Montgomery recounts some magical experiences with these amazing inhabitants of Amazonian waterways.

Amazonian myth has it that the pink dolphin can turn itself into a handsome man able to seduce young women.

FELINES

Everyone dreams of sighting a wild jaguar, but few have the luck to achieve that dream. This elusive and splendid big cat – the largest American feline – is widely but thinly distributed in Brazil, occurring in Amazonia, the Pantanal, the cerrado and such easterly national parks as Caparaó (p270), Ilha Grande (p189), Monte Pascoal (p490), Chapada Diamantina (p498) and Chapada dos Veadeiros (p401). Yellow with black spots, jaguars can grow to 2.5m long, including tail, and males can weigh 120kg (females weigh up to 90kg). Jaguars hunt at night, covering large distances. They prey on a wide variety of animals, in trees, water and on the ground, including sloths, monkeys, fish, deer, tapirs, capybaras and agoutis – but rarely people. They're generally solitary and, unusually among cats, good swimmers.

The puma, almost as big as the jaguar and similarly elusive, is the same beast as North America's cougar or mountain lion. As well as preying on deer, it sometimes attacks herds of domestic animals such as sheep or goats.

Brazil's four smaller wild cats are also widely but sparsely distributed and rarely seen. Three have markings similar to the jaguar. The largest of the three (up to 1.4m long with tail and weighing 15kg) is the ocelot; next biggest is the margay; and then the oncilla. The jaguarundi is probably more often seen than any other Brazilian feline, because it's active by day. A good swimmer, it's also known as the otter-cat, and is similar in size to the margay, with a uniformly colored coat, which may be black, brown or gray.

The 'black panther' (*onça preta* in Portuguese), found in Amazonia, is just an all-black variety of the jaguar.

MARMOSETS & TAMARINS

Around 20 species of marmoset and tamarin, small – often very small – primates, are found in Brazil. Some are fairly common, but the four species of lion tamarin, inhabitants of the Atlantic rain forests with a resemblance to miniature lions, are all endangered. The golden lion tamarin exists only in the Reserva Biológica Poço das Antas in Rio de Janeiro state (within earshot of interstate Hwy BR-101). A campaign to save this species – a squirrel-sized creature with a brilliant orange-gold color – has, amazingly, brought it back from near-extinction. Its population, down to about 100 in the 1970s, is now above 1000, and the golden lion tamarin has left the critically endangered list. It's a symbol to Brazilians of the whole struggle to save the remaining Atlantic rain forest and indeed of conservation in general.

Photos and concise pen-portraits of Brazilian wildlife are to be found at www.brazilianfauna.com.

MONKEYS

About 80 of the world's approximately 300 primate species (which also include marmosets and tamarins) are found in Brazil, many of them unique to the country. Some monkeys are hunted deep in the forest by settlers and indigenous people for their meat, and others live harmoniously in and around beach towns, much like squirrels in North American city parks. Some species are quite common and on an Amazon jungle trip you're very likely to see groups of monkeys moving through trees.

The most common primate in Amazonia is the little squirrel monkey, with its pale face, dark nose area, big ears and long tail. It moves in small, noisy groups. The black spider monkey, up to 1.5m long with thin, lengthy limbs and a prehensile tail (accounting for 60% of its length), is fairly common in parts of Amazonia where it isn't usually hunted. Southeast Brazil's two species of wooly spider monkey, the southern muriqui and northern muriqui, with their thick brown fur, are the largest primates in the Americas and both are endangered, the northern species critically so and down to a population of under 300.

Howler monkeys are much easier heard than seen: their roar (not really a howl) carries over many kilometers. They're stocky, up to 1.25m long (half tail), and live in groups of up to 20 – usually 10m to 20m high in trees – that are led by a single male. In Amazonia you're most likely to encounter the red howler monkey. Further south, including in the Pantanal, the black howler monkey is the local species. The brown howler monkey inhabits the small remaining areas of the Mata Atlântica. The rumors are true – a howler monkey will try to pelt you with its excrement if it feels threatened, so you may want to listen to its roar from a judicious distance.

The bald uakari's red complexion and lack of head hair have earned it the nickname *macaco-inglês* (English monkey).

The lithe capuchin monkeys are named for the hair atop their heads, which resembles monks' cowls. They're dispersed over almost the whole country – even Rio de Janeiro's Parque Nacional & Floresta da Tijuca (p160) – living in groups of up to 20 led by one male, and active by day in the lower forest stories, so relatively easily seen. The usual species is the brown capuchin monkey, measuring up to 1m (half tail).

The two types of uakari monkey, the black-headed and the bald, inhabit Amazonian flooded forest. The bald uakari has a red or pink bald head and thick, shaggy body fur ranging from chestnut-red to white (giving rise to the popular names red uakari and white uakari). Bald uakaris are threatened, but if you happen to visit the Mamirauá Reserve (Reserva de Desenvolvimento Sustentável Mamirauá; p659) you stand a good chance of seeing the very distinctive white uakari.

OTTERS

The endangered giant otter can measure 2m from nose to tail tip. It inhabits lakes and calm rivers in forests from Amazonia to the Pantanal, usually in family groups of six to eight. The Alta Floresta district (p413) and Reserva Xixuaú-Xipariná (p655) are two areas where visitors regularly see giant otters. The smaller southern river otter is also widely dispersed.

The diet of the giant otter includes fish, snakes, birds and even small caimans.

MAMMAL GLOSSARY

Portuguese names for animals are often the only ones local guides know, and scientific names are the only sure way across language barriers when you're trying to identify a species. Here's a list of Portuguese names for mammals mentioned in this chapter, with scientific names added for individual species.

English	Portuguese	Scientific name
agouti	cutia	
Amazon manatee	peixe-boi amazônico	Trichechus inunguis
armadillo	tatu	
bald uakari	uakari, bicó	Cacajao calvus
black howler monkey	bugio-preto	Alouatta caraya
black spider monkey	macaco prêto, macaco aranha	Ateles paniscus
Brazilian tapir	anta	Tapirus terrestris
brown capuchin monkey	macaco-prego	Cebus apella
brown howler monkey	bugio ruivo	Alouatta fusca
brown-throated three-toed sloth	preguiça de três dedos	Bradypus variegatus
bush dog	cachorro do mato vinagre	Speothos venaticus
capybara	capivara	Hydrochaeris hydrochaeris
coati	quati	Nasua nasua
collared or lesser anteater	tamanduá mirim, tamanduá colete	Tamandua tetradactyla
collared peccary	cateto, caititu	Pecari tajacu
crab-eating raccoon	guaxirim, mão-pelada	Procyon cancrivorus
crab-eating fox	lobinho, cachorro do mato	Cerdocyon thous
giant anteater	tamanduá bandeira	Myrmecophaga tridactyla
giant otter	ariranha	Pteronura brasiliensis
golden lion tamarin	mico-leão-dourado	Leontopithecus rosalia rosalia
gray brocket deer	veado-catingueiro	Mazama gouazoubira
gray dolphin	tucuxi	Sotalia fluviatilis
howler monkey	guariba, bugio, barbado	
humpback whale	baleia jubarte	Megaptera novaeangliae
jaguar	onça pintada	Panthera onca
jaguarundi	gato-mourisco	Felis yaguaroundi
lion tamarin	mico-leão	
maned wolf	lobo guará	Chrysocyon brachyurus
margay	jaguatirica, gato-maracajá, gato-do-mato-grande	Felis wiedii
marmoset	sauim, saguim, sagui, saguinus or soim	
marsh deer	cervo-do-pantanal	Blastocerus dichotomus
northern muriqui	muriqui	Brachyteles hypoxanthus
ocelot	jaguatirica, gato-maracajá	Felis pardalis
oncilla	jaguatirica, gato-do-mato-pequeño	Felis tigrina
paca	paca	Agouti paca
pampas deer	veado-campeiro	Ozotoceros bezoarticus
pink dolphin	boto, boto cor-de-rosa	Inia geoffrensis
porcupine	ouriço, porco-espinho	
puma	suçuarana, onça parda	Felis concolor
red brocket deer	veado-mateiro	Mazama americana
red howler monkey	guariba, bugio	Alouatta seniculus
sloth	preguiça	
southern muriqui	muriqui	Brachyteles arachnoides
southern right whale	baleia franca do sul	Eubalena australis
southern river otter	lontra	Lutra longicaudis
spinner dolphin	golfinho rotador	Stenella longirostris
squirrel monkey	macaco-de-cheiro, mico-de-cheiro	Saimiri sciureus
tamarin	sauim, saguim, sagui, saguinus, soim	
West Indian manatee	peixe-boi-marinho	Trichechus manatus
white-lipped peccary	queixada, porco-do-mato	Tayassu pecari
wooly spider monkey	muriqui, mono-carvoeiro	

RODENTS

The widespread capybara is the world's largest rodent, 1m long and up to 70kg in weight. It has a guinea pig–like face and a bulky hairy body, but no tail. It's vegetarian and at home on land or in water. Herds of up to 40 may be seen in the Pantanal. Smaller rodents – but still up to 60cm or 70cm long – include the paca and various species of agouti. You can distinguish the paca by its rows of white spots. Porcupines are rodents too: Brazil has several tree-dwelling species.

Reptiles
CAIMANS

Brazil has several species of caiman, close relatives of the alligator. They eat fish, amphibians, crustaceans and some birds. In the Pantanal, where caimans survived a devastating bout of poaching for their skins in the 1980s, the most common type is the yacare caiman or Paraguayan caiman. Amazonia has four species. The biggest is the black caiman, which reaches up to 6m long and is still hunted for its skin and meat. The most common Amazonian caiman – the one you may get to handle on nighttime expeditions – is the spectacled caiman, which can grow up to 2.3m long. Caimans lay eggs in nests of leaves and stalks, and these are vulnerable to predators such as coatis and lizards; the hatched young are prey for herons and storks.

Although the caiman is hunted and even farmed for its skin, only a small portion of the skin is actually of any value; the rest is usually discarded.

SNAKES

The infamous anaconda coils around its victims to crush and suffocate them, then eats them whole. On *extremely* rare occasions, an anaconda kills a person. It's not poisonous but can bite viciously. Generally an olive-brown color with black patterning, anacondas grow up to 10m long and can live in water or on land and are considered common in the Pantanal.

Other constrictor snakes – using the same cheerful coil-crush-suffocate technique – include the boa constrictor, which is 3m to 5m long, generally brown patterned and lives off small animals in varied and widespread habitats; and the handsome green-and-white emerald tree boa. A number of other snakes live in trees, but most are harmless.

REPTILE GLOSSARY

English	Portuguese	Scientific name
caiman	*jacaré*	
anaconda	*sucuri*	*Eunectes notaeus* or *Eunectes murinus*
black caiman	*jacaré açu*	*Melanosuchus niger*
boa constrictor	*jibóia*	*Boa constrictor*
Brazilian coral snake	*cobra coral*	*Micrurus frontalis*
coral snake	*cobra coral*	
emerald tree boa	*jibóia-verde*	*Corallus caninus*
false coral snake	*cobra falsa-coral*	
Paraguayan caiman	*jacaré-do-Pantanal*	*Caiman yacare*
rattlesnake	*cascavel*	
river turtle	*quelônio*	
sea turtle	*tartaruga marinha*	
snake	*cobra*	
spectacled caiman	*jacaré tingá*	*Caiman crocodilus*
viper	*vibora, peçonhenta, cobra covinha*	
Wied's lancehead	*jararaca-pintada, boca-de-sapo*	*Bothrops neuwiedi*
Yacare caiman	*jacaré-do-Pantanal*	*Caiman yacare*

ANACONDA LOVE

An anaconda's average life span is around 10 years, but they can live to be well over 30. The male anaconda reaches sexual maturity at 18 months of age or approximately 2m in length. The dominant female does so at three years of age or 3m in length. When they mate, the snakes wind themselves together into a 'breeding ball' that can consist of two to 12 males coiled around a single female. They take their time and can stay like this for two to four weeks. As a sign of endearment, sometimes the postcoital females then cannibalize a couple of males. Experts think that they may eat their breeding partners in order to survive the seven-month fast during pregnancy.

Although it is rare to encounter a venomous snake in the wild, Brazil still has quite a few species of them, including rattlesnakes, vipers and coral snakes. The most dangerous in the Pantanal is Wied's lancehead, a gray, black-and-white patterned viper up to 70cm long that sometimes hides in houses; its bite can be fatal if not treated quickly. Also to be steered clear of is the highly poisonous Brazilian coral snake, with its rings of red, black and white. It lurks under rocks or logs and only bites when it feels threatened. The various false coral snakes are, lucky for them, nearly impossible to distinguish from the real thing.

The official Tamar Project website, www.tamar.com.br, contains plenty of information on Brazilian turtles.

TURTLES

Five of the world's seven species of sea turtle are found along Brazil's coasts and are all under effective official protection, though still endangered or vulnerable. The Tamar Project, founded in 1980, does an impressive job of protecting turtle-nesting beaches from Santa Catarina state to Ceará, and spreading environmental awareness at the same time (see p467 for more on Tamar and sea turtles). Brazil is also home to several species of river turtle, spread throughout the country and mostly not endangered.

Fish

Amazonia is home to at least 2000 freshwater fish species, and the Pantanal to around 300 species.

The pirarucu has gills but they are basically useless. It breathes with lungs instead, and has to surface for air about every 10 minutes, or it will drown. By contrast, it can survive for up to 24 hours out of the water.

The king of Amazonian fish is the beautiful and enormous pirarucu or arapaima, which can grow to 3m long and weigh well over 100kg. Its red and silvery-brown scale patterns are reminiscent of Chinese paintings. The pirarucu is a voracious hunter of other fish, and a rich food source for humans. To try to preserve the shrinking population, catching it is banned if it's less than 1.5m in length or during the October-to-March spawning season. It's a member of the primitive Osteoglossiformes order, characterized by a bony tongue and rear fins that almost join the tail. Unusually, the male protects the young for up to the first six months of their lives. Another Amazonian Osteoglossiform, also with good meat, is the aruanã. Up to 1m long, it can leap 2m into the air to grab fruit or catch insects.

The most important food fish of central Amazonia is the little jaraqui, which swims in shoals of thousands. Another food fish, the tambaqui, is of the same family (Serrasalmidae) as piranhas. The rotund tambaqui can reach 1m in length and weigh up to 25kg. Normally it lives on nuts (which it can crack with its jaws) and seeds, but when the waters recede it can turn carnivorous.

Young aruanãs are nurtured inside the mouths of adult males.

Amazonia harbors at least 100 species of catfish, named for the long bristles that help them search for food on river bottoms. One aggressive catfish, the piraíba, grows up to 3m long and weighs as much as 200kg. It will even attack water birds. The dourado, up to 1m long with pale-gold sides, is common in the Pantanal as well as Amazonia, and is a popular dish in restaurants throughout the country. The piramutaba lays its eggs in the upper Rio Solimões, then descends in big shoals to mature at the mouth of the Amazon. It can grow to more than 1m long and is heavily fished.

You will hear about the infamous candiru in Amazonia. There are many species of these small catfish, most of them pretty obnoxious. The really infamous type is one of the *Vandellia* genus, about 5cm long. This little charmer normally lives inside the gills of other fish to suck their blood, but is attracted to urine and reputedly able to wriggle up humans' urinary tracts, where it lodges itself with sharp spines and can only be removed by surgery. The belief that it can actually swim up a stream of urine to get inside you is almost certainly false, but it's probably not a good idea to urinate in Amazonian waters just the same. Locals wear clothing to exclude the candiru in areas where it's known.

Other best-avoided inhabitants of Brazilian freshwaters include the stingray (*arraia* in Portuguese) and the electric eel (Portuguese: *poraquê*). The stingray lives on river floors and can inflict deep, painful cuts with the barbs in its tail. The electric eel, growing up to 2.75m long, is capable of a 600-volt discharge to stun its prey and could potentially kill a human with a volley of electric pulses.

Much sought after in Amazonia, both for its delicious taste and its famous fighting qualities as a sport fish, is the peacock bass (Portuguese: *tucunaré*). Growing to 50cm or more, it has a peacocklike 'eye' spot on its tail. Also sought – for home aquariums the world over – are the tiny but brightly colored tetra fishes. These come from the murky *igapós* (flooded Amazon forests), where they would doubtless go unseen if more demurely pigmented.

Birds

There are fantastically colorful, plentiful and varied birds in almost every region of Brazil, making the country a major destination for birding trips. The more powerful your binoculars, the better! The biggest Brazilian bird is the flightless rhea (Portuguese: *ema*), found in the cerrado and Pantanal. It grows to 1.4m tall and weighs some 30kg. The smallest are the numerous hyperactive types of hummingbird, found throughout the country.

The website www.jungle photos.com has many images of Amazonian flora and fauna.

BIRDS OF PREY

Much like great cats, birds of prey command respect and are always an object of fascination. Brazil has around 40 species of eagle, hawk, falcon, kite, caracara and kestrel, some quite common, and they're not very easy to tell apart.

The crested caracara is common in many areas – it's 50cm to 60cm long with a 1.2m or 1.3m wingspan. Its broad diet includes fish dying from a lack of oxygen as Pantanal ponds dry up, and animals that have been run over on roads or burnt in forest fires. Also common in Amazonia and the Pantanal are the yellow-headed caracara, about 40cm long, and the black-collared hawk, a reddish-brown fish-catcher, with a white head and chest, that reaches lengths of 45cm. The osprey, or fishing eagle, is bigger (55cm to 60cm; wingspan 1.45m to 1.7m), with a darker brown body.

The stingray will only strike if you step on it. To avoid this, don't raise your feet far off the bottom as you walk in shallow, unclear water.

Brazil's most emblematic bird of prey (and the largest in the Americas) is the ferocious, rare and enormously powerful harpy eagle, weighing up to 10kg, with a wingspan of up to 2.5m, and claws bigger than human hands. It enjoys a diet of monkeys, sloths, armadillos and other large animals, and nests at least 25m above the ground in big jungle trees. Though a few harpies still inhabit Mata Atlântica, the bird is found chiefly in Amazonia. It's not yet endangered but will become so if destruction of its rain-forest habitat continues.

MAN BITES PIRANHA

Why are people scared of piranhas? The fish should be frightened of us, as humans eat piranhas a billion times more often than piranhas eat people. They're reasonably tasty, if a bit small and bony. A standard activity on an Amazon jungle trip is catching your own piranha lunch. You'll be taken by canoe to a promising spot and given a simple fishing rod constructed of cane, line and hook, and small chunks of meat for bait. Put a piece of bait onto the hook, drop it into the water, and – presto – free lunch. For the piranhas, that is, which will nibble the bait right off your hook without getting caught.

Your more-skilled local companions, however, will catch half a dozen of them without even trying – and *these* will be your lunch.

A piranha is not just a piranha, of course. It could be any of about 50 species of the *Serrasalmo* genus. Piranhas are found in the basins of the Amazon, Orinoco, Paraguai and São Francisco Rivers and in the rivers of the Guianas. Some live on seeds and fruits, some on other fish and only a handful of species are potentially a risk to larger creatures. These types are most dangerous when stuck in tributaries, meanders or lakes that get cut off from main rivers in the dry season. When they have eaten all the other fish, the piranhas will attack more or less anything, including wounded mammals entering their waters. The scent of blood or bodily fluids in the water can whip a shoal into a feeding frenzy. Confirmed accounts of human fatalities caused by piranhas are extremely few, but plenty of Amazonian river folk have scars or missing fingers to testify just how sharp and vicious those little triangular teeth can be.

HUMMINGBIRDS

These beautiful little birds, with their dazzling iridescent colors, may be seen all over Brazil, including in cities. They flit rapidly, almost insectlike, from one spot to the next, and can even fly backwards. The lyrical Brazilian name for them is *beija-flor* (flower-kisser). There are many dozens of species (family *Trochilidae*) and they occupy an important role in Brazilian art and folklore, often mentioned in music and poetry. Even one of Rio's best-known samba schools is called Beija-Flor.

Hummingbirds beat their wings up to 80 times a second, allowing them to hover while extracting pollen from flowers – making a light humming noise as they do.

PARROTS

These are the kinds of bird that have come to symbolize tropical rain forests, and people travel from all over the world to see some of Brazil's dozens of species. These charismatic, colorful birds have strong, curved beaks that they use to break open seeds and nuts and they also eat soft clay to temper the acidity of their other foods.

Macaws, the biggest parrots, grab most of the glamor. You can distinguish them by their dead-straight body shape when flying, and straight-as-an-arrow trajectory. They often go about in pairs and make a lot of raucous noise as they travel up to 25km a day foraging for food.

The name scarlet macaw is given to two large, gloriously colored species – *Ara chloroptera*, also called the red-and-green macaw, which grows up to 95cm long, with blue-and-green wings and a red-striped face, and *Ara macao*, which is a bit smaller with blue-and-yellow wings. The latter bird is restricted to Amazonia, but the red-and-green macaw also inhabits the Pantanal, cerrado and even caatinga. The blue-and-yellow macaw, about 85cm long, is also widely distributed. The yellow covers its underside, the blue its upper parts.

Aves Brasileiras by Johan Dalgas Frisch is the classic Brazilian bird-identification guide, with names in Portuguese, Latin, English and Spanish

Unfortunately, macaws' beautiful plumage makes them a major target for poachers. Poaching contributed greatly to the decline of the endangered hyacinth macaw, the world's largest parrot (1m long). This gorgeous bird, deep blue with splashes of yellow, is down to a wild population of about 3000 and conservationists are struggling to bring it back from the brink. Its range extends from Pará state to the Pantanal; the recently established

Parque Nacional das Nascentes do Rio Parnaíba (p588) in Piauí state is a good place to see it.

TOUCANS

Among the best-known and most colorful groups of Latin American birds, toucans have huge rainbow-colored beaks, sometimes as long as

BIRD GLOSSARY

English	Portuguese	Scientific name
anhinga	biguatinga, carará	Anhinga anhinga
bird of prey	gavião	
black-collared hawk	gavião-belo	Busarellus nigricollis
blue-and-yellow macaw	arara-amarela, arara-canindé	Ara ararauna
blue-crowned trogon	surucuá-de-coroa-azul	Trogon curucui
cormorant	biguá	
crested caracara	caracará, carcará	Polyborus plancus
eagle	águia	
egret	garça, garcinha	
falcon	falcão	
harpy eagle	águia real, harpia	Harpia harpyja
heron	garça, socó	
hummingbird	beija-flor	
hyacinth macaw	arara-azul	Anodorhynchus hyacinthinus
ibis	curicaca	
jabiru	tuiuiú, jaburu	Jabiru mycteria
kingfisher	martim-pescador, ariramba	
Lear's macaw	arara-azul-de-lear	Anodorhynchus leari
laughing falcon	acauã	Herpetotheres cachinnans
macaw	arara	
maguari stork	tabuiaiá	Ciconia maguari
osprey	aguia pescadora	Pandion haliaetus
parakeet	periquito	
parrot	papagayo, maracanã	
pavonine quetzal	surucuá açu	Pharomacrus pavoninus
red-and-green macaw	arara vérmela	Ara chloroptera
rhea	ema	Rhea americana
ringed kingfisher	martim-pescador-matraca, martim-pescador-grande, ariramba-grande	Ceryle torquata
roseate spoonbill	colhereiro	Platalea ajaja
scarlet ibis	guará	Eudocimus ruber
scarlet macaw	arara vermelha	Ara chloroptera, Ara macao
snowy egret	garcinha	Egretta thula
southern lapwing	quero-quero	Vanellus chilensis
Spix's macaw	ararinha-azul	Anodorhynchus spix
stork	cegonha	
tiger heron	socó-boi	Tigrisoma lineatum
toucan	tucano, araçari	
toco toucan	tucanuçu, tucano	Ramphastos toco
yellow-ridged toucan	tucano-rouco, tucano pequeno de papo branco	Ramphastos culminatus
trogon	surucuá, saracuã	
white-throated toucan	tucano-assoviador	Ramphastos tucanus
wood stork	cabeça-seca	Mycteria americana
yellow-headed caracara	gavião-pinhé, carrapateiro	Milvago chimachima

their bodies, enabling them to reach berries at the end of branches. But the beak is light and almost hollow, allowing the bird to fly with a surprising agility. Toucans live at forest treetop level and are often best seen from boats.

Brazil's biggest is the toco toucan, whose habitat ranges from Amazonia to the cerrado to the Pantanal. Around 55cm long, including its bright orange beak, the plumage is black except for a white neck area. In Amazonia you may see the white-throated toucan or the yellow-ridged toucan. Both are fairly large birds, with black beaks.

TROGONS

This family of medium-sized, brightly colored, sometimes iridescent birds with long tails includes the celebrated quetzals. You may see them perching and flying at medium heights in tropical forests. Amazonia has at least seven species, including the pavonine quetzal and the blue-crowned trogon. The latter also inhabits the Pantanal.

WATERFOWL

Commoner freshwater fishing birds include types of cormorant and the similar anhinga. You can often see them standing on waterside branches, their wings spread out to dry.

Other highly visible birds in the Pantanal and Amazonia include many of the Ciconiiformes order – herons, egrets, storks, ibises, spoonbills and their relatives. You'll see them flapping inelegantly along waterways or standing motionless ready to jab for fish with their long beaks. The tiger heron, with its brown and black stripes, is particularly distinctive. The sight of hundreds of snowy egrets gathering in a waterside rookery looks like a sudden blooming of white flowers in the treetops.

Of the storks, the tall (1.40m) black-headed and scarlet-necked jabiru has become a symbol of the Pantanal and is also found in Amazonia. In the Pantanal, also look for the similarly sized maguari stork, which is mainly white with a pinkish face, and the smaller wood stork, with its black head and beak with a curved end. The beautiful pink roseate spoonbill is another Pantanal resident. The spectacular scarlet ibis is a deep pink, is 50cm long and is found living in flocks along parts of the Northeast coast and on the Ilha de Marajó (p618), an island located at the mouth of the Amazon River.

Kingfishers fly across or along rivers as boats approach. The biggest species is the 42cm-long ringed kingfisher, which is predominantly bright turquoise with a rust-colored underside.

Endangered Species

From the stealthy jaguar to serene sea turtles, an alarming number of Brazilian animal species are threatened. Government and activist programs attempt to help and protect some of the more charismatic species, including monkeys, whales, turtles, great cats and predatory birds. But numerous lesser-known creatures are disappearing and any species, regardless of how insignificant it may seem, plays an irreplaceable role in the ecosystem. In all, Brazil has 339 threatened wildlife species, according to the 2006 Red List of the International Union for the Conservation of Nature and Natural Resources (IUCN; www .iucnredlist.org). This includes 124 birds, the highest number of any country in the world. Humans may not care about the extinction of the Brazilian spiny rice rat or the bushy-tailed opossum, but if nothing else, they both occupy a spot in the food chain and their disappearance will forever affect the other plants and animals around them.

There are three main reasons for the extinction of Brazilian wildlife. Hunting is responsible for about 25% of extinction. Destruction of habitats accounts for around 36% of the loss. The least known yet most lethal cause of extinction is the introduction of competing species, which is responsible for some 39% of the destruction. Dogs, pigs, rats and lizards (not to mention humans) have wreaked havoc on untold thousands of smaller species.

Even if no one ever hunted a jaguar again it would still be at risk of extinction as it needs a huge amount of territory to hunt and a large gene pool for mating. Its reduced population and habitat may already mean the jaguar is on its way to existing only in zoos.

Sightings of endangered species are much sought by travelers interested in wildlife, but most are difficult if not impossible to spot. Some are found only in small reserves or specific parts of national parks.

Critically endangered mammals are the black-faced lion tamarin, the Brazilian arboreal mouse, the ring-tail monkey, Coimbra's titi monkey, the golden-rumped lion tamarin, the Northern Bahian blond titi monkey and the northern muriqui (northern wooly spider monkey).

Other endangered mammals are the Brazilian spiny rice rat, the buffy-headed marmoset, Cleber's arboreal rice rat, the giant armadillo, the giant otter, the golden-headed lion tamarin, the golden lion tamarin, the maned three-toed sloth, the pygmy short-tailed opossum, the Rio de Janeiro rice rat, the southern muriqui and the white-whiskered spider monkey.

Plants

Brazil's history and future are inextricably tied to its forests and nature. So close is this association that the country even gets its name from the brazilwood *(pau brasil)* tree, which the early Portuguese explorers cut and exported as fast as they could for a valuable red dye found in its core.

The last ice age did not reach Brazil and the rain forests have never suffered long droughts, so the area has had an unusually long period of time to develop plant species that are found nowhere else in the world. Although some of these long-evolved species have been destroyed in the last 30 years through heavy deforestation, there remains an impressive range of flora in Brazil – from over 200 species of delicate orchids and the world's largest variety of palms (390) to 90m-tall hardwood trees.

Though estimates run at around 45,000, it would be impossible to determine an exact number of plant species in the Amazon, let alone in the whole of Brazil, as new plants are being discovered all the time and, unfortunately, others are disappearing with frightening frequency. The great majority of the plants in Brazil's rain forests are trees – estimated at some 70% of the total vegetation. Many rain-forest trees look similar even though they are of different species, but a trained eye can distinguish more than 400 species of tree per hectare (10,000 sq meters) in some areas.

One of the most economically important trees is the rubber tree, which grows in the wild or on sustainable plantations for the large-scale production of latex – yes, condoms too come from the Amazon. Another sustainable forest product is the nut from the Brazil nut tree, a good snack if you are able to get the shell off without having a nervous breakdown. Mahogany trees are the most prized of Brazilian hardwoods and, despite being protected, are still often felled and sold (usually within Brazil).

Many edible fruits also grow in the rain forest, so many in fact that a number of them only have names in Portuguese. Some of the more popular fruits, including *açaí, acerola* and *cupuaçu,* can be found at juice bars throughout the country. Guaraná berries, containing a stimulant similar to caffeine, are also making their way into energy drinks the world over.

Animal Info (www .animalinfo.org) lists Brazil's endangered and vulnerable mammals.

In 1876 English adventurer Henry Wickham smuggled 70,000 rubber seeds from Brazil to London's Kew Gardens, where they were cultivated then transferred to Sri Lanka for planting. The resulting competing rubber crops caused the collapse of the Brazilian rubber industry.

A Brazil nut tree takes 10 years to reach maturity and can produce more than 450kg of nuts per year.

Outside the rain forests the plant life is quite different. In some of the drier parts of the country it may seem that the only plants are palm trees, shrubs or thorny cacti. Let's hope that the rain forests do not soon look the same.

Brazil has 382 threatened plant species, of which 46 are critically endangered.

NATIONAL PARKS & PROTECTED AREAS

Much of Brazil is, officially at least, under environmental protection. Around 1000 areas throughout the country, covering well over 600,000 sq km (approaching one-tenth of the whole country), are protected in a variety of conservation units, ranging from national parks and national forests to extractive reserves and sustainable development reserves. Some of these are run by the federal government, some by state governments and some by private individuals or nongovernmental organizations (NGOs).

The amount of protected territory is growing steadily. At least 20 new national parks have been created since the late 1990s. In 2006 the Amazonian state of Pará announced it was giving protected status to 150,000 sq km of rain forest, much of it virgin forest. A senior researcher from the Brazilian sustainability institute Imazon hailed the move as 'the greatest effort in history toward the creation of protected areas in tropical forests.'

Unfortunately, the degree of protection that Brazil's protected areas actually receive is erratic and in some cases practically nonexistent. The federal government's environmental agency, the Instituto Brasileiro do Meio Ambiente e dos Recursos Naturais Renováveis (IBAMA; Brazilian Institute of the Environment & Renewable Natural Resources), has a small budget and is even unable to protect some of the 62 national parks from illegal logging, ranching, settlement and poaching.

Permits, or at least an official guide, are needed to visit some conservation units legally. Wherever possible, regulations of this type are cited in this book.

Brazil's conservation units fall into two main groups: strictly protected areas (unidades de proteção integral), and sustainable-use areas (unidades de uso sustentável). Strict-protection areas are supposedly under full protection and human habitation is not permitted; people are only allowed in these areas for specific purposes such as scientific research, education and (in some cases) ecological tourism.

Types of strict-protection area are parque nacional (national park); parque estadual (state park); parque natural municipal (municipal nature park); refúgio de vida silvestre (wildlife refuge); monumento natural (natural monument); estacão ecológica (ecological station); and reserva biológica (biological reserve). In the last two categories only scientific and educational activity is permitted.

Sustainable-use areas are intended to combine nature conservation with the sustainable use of natural resources and may contain human populations. The sustainable-use categories are área de proteção ambiental (environmental protection area); área de relevante interesse ecológico (area of ecological interest); floresta nacional (national forest); floresta estadual (state forest); floresta municipal (municipal forest); reserva extrativista (extractive reserve); reserva de desenvolvimento sustentável (sustainable development reserve); reserva de fauna (fauna reserve); and reserva particular do patrimônio natural (private natural heritage reserve). National, state and municipal forests are areas of predominantly native forest, geared to sustainable exploitation and research. Extractive reserves are dedicated to protecting the way of life of human populations dependent on subsistence agriculture and traditional extractive activities – such as rubber tap-

For 15 years Mark Plotkin devotedly tracked down Amazonian witchdoctors to understand some of their encyclopedic knowledge of medicinal plants. His Tales of a Shaman's Apprentice is travelogue and adventure story too.

A Field Guide to Medicinal and Useful Plants of the Upper Amazon by James L Castner, Stephen L Timme and James A Duke combines clear photos, accurate descriptions and interesting information on how Amazonia's huge wealth of medicinal plants is used locally.

Harvard botanist Richard Evans Schultes was an Amazon plant collector and expert in sacred hallucinogens. Wade Davis' The Lost Amazon: The Photographic Journey of Richard Evans Schultes is not only a biography but also reproduces many of Schultes' mid-20th-century black-and-white Amazon photos.

NATURAL BRAZIL

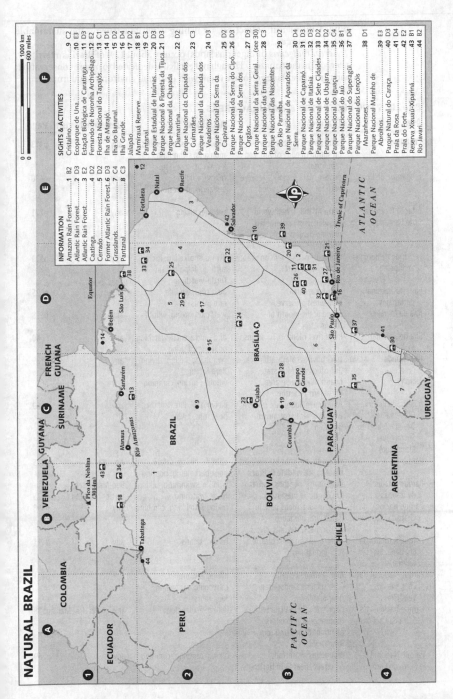

ping, fruit or nut collecting, or fishing – while ensuring the sustainable use of resources.

Terras indígenas (indigenous lands) occupy about 12% of Brazilian territory, nearly all in the Amazon. Though not explicitly dedicated to nature conservation, their inhabitants tend to use them with minimal environmental impact.

BRAZIL'S TOP PROTECTED & NATURAL AREAS

Area	Features	Activities	Best time to visit	Page
Cristalino	state park & private reserve on southern edge of Amazon rain forest	viewing birds, butterflies, monkeys, swimming, kayaking, abseiling	any	p413
Ecoparque de Una	private Mata Atlântica reserve with rare golden-headed lion tamarin	hiking, wildlife, endangered species	any	p480
Estação Biológica de Caratinga	Mata Atlântica, half world population of endangered *muriqui* (largest American primate)	wildlife, hiking	any	p271
Fernando de Noronha archipelago	fabulous marine park on islands 350km from Natal	diving, snorkeling, hiking, surfing, dolphin- and turtle-watching	any	p539
Floresta Nacional do Tapajós	lush Amazonian rain-forest preserve	boat trips, wildlife, rare plants	any	p625
Ilha de Marajó	island in the mouth of the Amazon	wetlands, hiking, wildlife	any	p618
Ilha do Bananal	huge river island in Tocantins	bird- and animal-watching, boat trips, fishing	any	p640
Ilha Grande	tract of virgin Mata Atlântica, just off coast of Rio state	swimming, hiking, diving, flora & fauna	any	p189
Jalapão	beautifully diverse area of eastern Tocantins	wildlife, hiking, camping	any	p639
Mamirauá Reserve (Reserva de Desenvolvimento Sustentável Mamirauá)	Amazonian floodplain reserve with excellent ecotourism program	viewing wildlife & plants, boat trips, hiking	any	p659
Pantanal	vast wetlands that are the best place to see wildlife in Brazil	wildlife, hiking, safaris, horseback riding, boating	Apr-Oct	p415
Parque Estadual de Itaúnas	sand dunes, beaches, Tamar Project turtle preserve	wildlife, swimming, hiking, turtle-watching	Sep-Mar to see turtles hatching	p225
Parque Nacional da Chapada Diamantina	large mountainous park in Bahia with gorgeous landscape, waterfalls, rivers	hiking & trekking, climbing	any	p498
Parque Nacional da Chapada dos Guimarães	waterfalls, canyons, bizarre rock formations	hiking, safaris	any	p411
Parque Nacional da Chapada dos Veadeiros	high-altitude cerrado with sublime landscapes, near Brasília	hiking, swimming, canyoning, rappelling, Jeep tours	Apr-Oct	p401
Parque Nacional da Serra da Capivara	park in southern Piauí with thousands of prehistoric paintings & amazing rock formations	hiking, archaeology	any, cooler Nov-Mar	p588
Parque Nacional da Serra do Cipó	mountains, waterfalls & cerrado, near Belo Horizonte	hiking, camping, climbing	any	p269

Where to Go

Brazil is a huge country and its flora and fauna are scattered across vast regions. Plan ahead to take in areas that meet your interests in nature. The table on opposite lists highlight areas for getting up close with natural Brazil.

Area	Features	Activities	Best time to visit	Page
Parque Nacional da Serra dos Órgãos	mountains & cliffs, 86km from Rio	climbing, hiking	May-Oct for hiking	p209
Parque Nacional da Serra Geral	spectacular canyons, adjoining Aparados da Serra national park	hiking, camping	any	p364
Parque Nacional das Emas	fantastic cerrado preserve with rheas	wildlife, hiking	any	p386
Parque Nacional das Nascentes do Rio Parnaíba	Recently (2002) created park of cerrado savanna and red-rock escarpments	viewing rare wildlife, hyacinth macaws	Apr-Jul	p588
Parque Nacional de Aparados da Serra	stunning canyons, *araucária* forests, in Rio Grande do Sul	hiking	any	p364
Parque Nacional de Caparaó	highest mountains in southern Brazil	hiking, climbing, camping	Feb-Oct	p270
Parque Nacional de Itatiaia	ruggedly beautiful mountainous park, 150km from Rio	hiking, climbing, wildlife	any	p203
Parque Nacional de Sete Cidades	unique rock formations in Piauí	hiking, cycling, swimming, archaeology	any	p587
Parque Nacional de Ubajara	small Ceará park with large caves, lush vegetation, dramatic escarpments	hiking	any	p582
Parque Nacional do Iguaçu	Brazilian side of the international waterfalls park	wildlife	any	p326
Parque Nacional do Jaú	one of the world's largest tracts of protected tropical rain forest; no infrastructure	rare flora & fauna, boat trips	any	p656
Parque Nacional do Superagüi	large area of coastal Mata Atlântica	abundant wildlife, rare flora, hiking, beaches	any	p324
Parque Nacional dos Lençóis Maranhenses	enormous expanse of sand dunes & clear rain pools, near coast	hiking, swimming, wildlife	any	p597
Parque Nacional & Floresta da Tijuca	Mata Atlântica & mountains right in Rio	hiking, great views	any	p160
Parque Nacional Marinho de Abrolhos	marine park 80km off the Bahia coast, coral reefs	whale-watching, marine & bird life	any	p492
Parque Natural do Caraça	variety of terrain, from Mata Atlântica to wild mountain vegetation	hiking, swimming	any	p268
Praia do Rosa	beach town in Santa Catarina, whale sanctuary	whale-watching, surfing	Jun-Oct	p350
Praia do Forte	ecological beach resort, headquarters of Tamar Project	hiking, cycling, turtle-viewing	any	p466
Reserva Xixuaú-Xipariná	remote ecotourism project, 1½-day boat trip from Manaus	rare flora & fauna, boat trips	any	p655
Rio Javari	area near Peruvian border with some pristine rain forest	wildlife, jungle, boat trips, hiking	any	p665

SOUTHEAST

Many national parks in this region cover mountainous terrain, with some of Brazil's highest peaks, and make for spectacular hiking and climbing. Vegetation ranges from lush Mata Atlântica (Atlantic rain forest) to *araucária* forest and cerrado.

Itatiaia is Brazil's oldest national park, declared in 1937.

SOUTH

Abundant wildlife is a big attraction of the Superagüi and Iguaçu national parks – and also of the Argentine Parque Nacional del Iguazú on the other side of the Iguaçu Falls. The Aparados da Serra and Serra Geral national parks contain stunning canyons and rock formations.

CENTRAL WEST

If you're keen to see animals in the wild, don't miss the Pantanal, which has the greatest concentration of fauna in the New World – visible to the most casual observer in the Pantanal's open spaces. The Chapada dos Veadeiros and Chapada dos Guimarães national parks have gorgeous scenery with spectacular waterfalls, canyons and deep valleys. Parque Nacional das Emas is Brazil's best-preserved tract of cerrado, with abundant visible wildlife, including the *emas* (rheas) for which it's named.

The Iguaçu Falls, along with other scenic Brazilian locations, featured in both the James Bond movie *Moonraker* (1979) and the Oscar-winning *The Mission* with Robert de Niro and Jeremy Irons (1986).

NORTHEAST

The Northeast's natural highlights range from the escarpments, peaks, waterfalls and rivers of the Parque Nacional da Chapada Diamantina (a great hiking area) to the vast dune fields of the Parque Nacional dos Lençóis Maranhenses. Marine attractions rank high here too, with two national marine parks, Fernando de Noronha and Abrolhos. The Fernando de Noronha archipelago, 350km out into the Atlantic, abounds in dolphins, sea turtles and bird life and has some of the world's best diving, snorkeling and beaches.

The government-backed Tamar Project (p467), protecting Brazil's five sea-turtle species, has 21 stations along Brazil's coasts, mainly in the Northeast. The headquarters, which you can visit, is at Praia do Forte, Bahia.

NORTH

The Amazon region, with its dense jungles and countless rivers, is easily Brazil's richest for wildlife and plant diversity, but getting to see the best of it is a challenge. The further you get from sprawling, urban Manaus, the more wildlife you're likely to see. On a trip of less than five days from Manaus you will probably see pink and gray river dolphins, caimans, piranhas, a fair variety of birds and a few monkeys, but it won't be the teeming jungles you might have imagined. Further afield – and harder to reach and more expensive to visit – the Mamirauá Reserve, Parque Nacional do Jaú, Reserva Xixuaú-Xipariná, Ilha do Bananal, the Rio Javari and the Cristalino area offer much greater variety and abundance of visible wildlife.

Brazilian director Andrucha Waddington's *Casa de Areia* (The House of Sand; 2005) is set entirely amid the desertlike dunescapes of the Lençóis Maranhenses.

ORGANIZED TOURS

Operators specific to single localities are covered in the regional chapters in this book. The following are some of the companies offering a wider range of trips.

Brazil Ecojourneys (☎ 0xx48-3232 9270; www.brazilecojourneys.com; Servidão Ilha Paraíso 132, Campeche, Santa Catarina) Recommended southern Brazil specialist with whale-watching, off-the-beaten-track hiking expeditions in the Serra Geral and Mata Atlântica.

Brazil Ecotravel (☎ 0xx21-2512 8882; www.brazil-ecotravel.com; 2nd fl, Rua Visconde de Pirajá 572, Ipanema, Rio de Janeiro) A professional firm offering tailor-made trips to a complete range of Brazil's best natural destinations, emphasizing environmentally responsible travel. Visits to emblematic conservation projects such as the Tamar Project in Bahia and the Reserva Biológica Poço das Antas in Rio de Janeiro state, home of the golden lion tamarin, are high on its menu.

Ecotour Expeditions (☎ 401-423-3377; www.naturetours.com; PO Box 128, Jamestown, RI 02835, USA) US-based provider of 'thoughtful nature trips' – boat based in Amazonia, lodge based in the Pantanal.

Field Guides (☎ 800 728 4953; www.fieldguides.com; Suite 150, Bldg 1, 9433 Bee Cave Rd, Austin, TX 78733, USA) Well-established US-based birding-tour operator. It runs eight specialized bird-watching tours in Brazil with expert guides.

Focus Tours (☎ 505-989-7193; www.focustours.com; PO Box 22276, Santa Fe, NM 87502, USA) Highly rated birding and nature-tour firm using English-speaking naturalist guides. It uses tape recorders to record and play back calls, encouraging wildlife to come into view. It's active in conservation too. Destinations include the Pantanal, Chapada dos Guimarães, Cristalino, the Emas and Itatiaia national parks, and the Parque Natural do Caraça. Focus' founder and president, Doug Trent, has been running ecological tours to Brazil since before the word 'ecotourism' was coined, and what he doesn't know about birds isn't worth knowing.

Tropical Nature Travel (☎ 877-888-1770; www.tropicalnaturetravel.com; PO Box 5276, Gainesville, FL 32627-5276, USA) Part of a nonprofit organization promoting conservation through ecotourism. It offers Amazonia, Pantanal and cerrado trips using some of Brazil's best ecolodges.

Victor Emanuel Nature Tours (VENT; ☎ 800 328 8368; www.ventbird.com; Suite 1003, 2525 Wallingwood Dr, Austin, TX 78764, USA) Another highly professional US-based birding-tour company, with a number of experienced guides.

ENVIRONMENTAL ISSUES

In the year from August 2005 to July 2006, 13,100 sq km of the Brazilian Amazon forest disappeared, adding to a total deforested area of some 700,000 sq km – about 17% of the whole Brazilian part of the forest. Apart from its effects on the global climate – see the boxed text, p75, for more on the global aspects of Amazon deforestation – such destruction has devastating results on wildlife, leading to extinction of species and loss of valuable biodiversity. It can also devastate the lives of the forests' traditional human inhabitants.

There are no simple solutions to these problems. Some 20 million Brazilians are trying to eke out an existence among the Amazon forests and any answers to Amazonia's problems have to address the needs of these people, who are mostly poor and in desperate need of better education, medical care and sanitation, as well as jobs. Illegal logging is one of Amazonia's biggest problems, but the logging industry is the third-largest employer in the region (after agriculture and fishing).

Deforestation in Brazil was accelerated rapidly by the military government in the 1970s as it attempted to tame Amazonia with the ambitious Plano de Integração Nacional. Long roads, such as the 2500km of the Transamazônica highway from Aguiarnópolis (Tocantins state) to Labrea (Amazonas), were constructed through the jungle. Thousands left Brazil's drought-stricken Northeast to build homesteads in the newly cleared forest. But the lushness of the Amazon is deceptive. The jungle ecosystem recycles most organic matter before it can even be absorbed into the soil. Only about 17% of Amazonia is suitable for sustained agriculture. Most of the hopeful settlers failed to establish a foothold and abandoned the land for the *favelas* (shantytowns) of Amazonia's growing cities. Cattle ranchers took over cheap lands abandoned by settlers, but eventually they too faced the same problems and had to move on to new tracts of cleared forest as the land became depleted.

Loggers also moved into the jungles and during the 1980s Brazil treated the forests as assets that could be used to pay back the international debt incurred during the 20 years of military dictatorship. Encouraged by the International Monetary Fund and the World Bank, the government provided

John Kricher's *A Neotropical Companion*, while not specific to Brazil, is a good introductory text for neotropical ecology and explains many of the forest's intricacies in straightforward terms.

The International Ecotourism Society (www .ecotourism.org) is a great source of ideas, news, facts and recommendations on sustainable travel the world over, Brazil included.

One River: Explorations and Discoveries in the Amazon Rain Forest by Wade Davis reflects on the importance of the Amazon and its contents to the planet as a whole.

large incentives to coax multinational timber and mining firms to exploit the Amazon.

A turning point, of sorts, was the 1988 assassination of Chico Mendes, a leader among the rubber tappers and a prominent opponent of rain-forest destruction (see p689). The incident focused international attention on the plight of the Brazilian rain forest and its poorer inhabitants.

QUESTIONS TO ASK A LOCAL TOUR OPERATOR

Half the tourism businesses anywhere in Brazil promoting natural attractions seem to have those three letters 'eco' in their names. And the rest have them in their propaganda. Especially in Manaus and the Pantanal, hosts of rival 'eco' operators are eager to snap you up for 'ecotours' of the jungles, rivers, lakes or wetlands. Some of these are reputable and dependable, some are just out for a quick buck, and a few will scam you. As you attempt to pick one, weighing up costs, quality, reliability, comfort and all the other factors, it's worth remembering the definition of ecotourism as provided by the International Ecotourism Society: 'Responsible travel to natural areas that conserves the environment and improves the well-being of local people.' A guiding principle of genuine ecotourism is that it benefits resident human communities too and thus encourages them to look after the local environment.

Throughout this book you'll find recommendations for local tour operators. Here are some pointers, applicable anywhere, to finding outfits who will give value for money and tread lightly in the environments they take you to. First, identifying and dealing with a likely operator:

Don't be hurried into a decision – reputable operators know you need time to consider the options.

- Use an agency or guide with appropriate accreditation, such as that provided by Amazonastur in Manaus. Local tourism offices can often tell you about registration and certification schemes and provide lists of accredited operators.

- Go to the operator's office rather than just dealing with a representative at an airport, bus station or hotel.

- Try to meet the guide in person before you commit to a trip, to assess their knowledge, training, experience, language skills and capabilities.

- Ask for an itinerary or trip plan in writing, with details about meals, accommodations, activities, transport, group size and exactly what's included in your price.

- Find out what equipment the company provides to help you observe fauna and flora, such as binoculars and reference materials.

- Pay your money to the person in charge, not a go-between. Many reputable operators will not expect full payment beforehand.

As well as being satisfied that you'll get value for money, you can inquire about the impact of your trip:

- Ask what is done with waste generated on the trip.

- Ask about policy on handling or disturbing wildlife and observing rules of parks and reserves. Operators who interfere with natural behavior are likely to alter that behavior for the future. Genuine operators can rarely *promise* sightings of wild animals.

- Your lodgings: do they use energy-saving techniques and manage waste properly; were they built with sustainable materials (not too much concrete or excavation or endangered hardwoods)?

- What benefit will your visit bring to local communities? Will you be using local guides or staying in accommodations owned or run by local people; will locally made crafts be available to buy? Best of all, if possible, give your business to an ecotourism venture run by the community itself.

In general, you will get what you pay for. Cheaper operators are more likely to cut corners not only on your lodgings, meals and transport but also in the way they treat the environment. That said, there are responsible and reputable operators at all price levels. You don't have to stay in the latest state-of-the-art, upmarket ecolodge to enjoy a satisfying, and sustainable, trip.

But economics brought another twist to the rain-forest story in 1999 when the Brazilian government stepped up financial support for exporters of primary products in order to increase the country's foreign-currency reserves. This encouraged a major spurt in deforestation to clear land for cattle ranching and soybean cultivation.

Forward again to 2005–06. The deforestation rate was now equivalent to five soccer fields per minute, but the Brazilian government was pleased with it – and so, up to a point, were many environmentalists, for the figure was a lot lower than a couple of years earlier. From 2001 to 2004 Amazon deforestation had run at an average of 25,000 sq km a year (10 soccer fields a minute).

Environmentalists had held high hopes for the leftist Luíz Inácio 'Lula' da Silva when he was elected president in 2002. Many had hoped that the new, more humanistic administration and its green environment minister Marina Silva would be able to make a real difference to Brazil's environmental record. The burning question as the pair entered their second term of office in 2007: was the Lula government really making a difference on the environment, and if so, would it be able to sustain it?

The Burning Season: The Chico Mendes Story (1994) stars Raul Julia as Mendes and is a quick way to get an overview of this man's important life and legacy.

Enforcement

The government attributed the drop in deforestation between 2004 and 2006 to more effective control and to a greater emphasis on sustainable-development projects. During Lula's first four-year term of office (2002–06) enforcement of environmental laws was significantly stepped up, spurred in part by the international outcry at the 2005 murder of American missionary Dorothy Stang at Anapu, 700km southwest of the Amazonian city of Belém. Stang had been a high-profile campaigner for sustainable development and against illegal logging (see the Chico Mendes boxed text, p689). Between 2003 and 2006 a series of large coordinated operations between the police and IBAMA, the national environmental agency, resulted in the breakup of several large gangs illegally removing and selling Amazonian timber, with 380 people jailed and 814,000 cu meters of wood seized.

For the Chico Mendes story in words, read *The World is Burning* by Alex Shoumatoff.

Protected Areas

Between 2002 and 2006 the Lula government created 195,000 sq km of new federal environmentally protected areas – an increase of 57% on the previous total. Despite difficulties in supervising these huge areas on limited budgets and with a history of corruption within IBAMA, deforestation inside protected areas still runs at only one-seventh of the rate outside protected areas. Protected status usually decreases the value of land, making it less attractive to illegal land-grabbers and speculators. The government's target is 500,000 sq km of federally protected land in Amazonia by 2012. In addition to federal parks and reserves, large Amazonian areas are under state-level protection, including the 150,000 sq km of virgin rain forest with enormous biodiversity that was given protection by Pará state in 2006. Altogether, nearly 20% of Brazilian Amazonia is now covered by parks and reserves, and a further 25% is indigenous territory, which tends to be at least equally well conserved.

Illegal Logging (www .illegal-logging.info) is good for news and background on logging issues.

Infrastructure

The government also demonstrated some recognition that large economic-development projects in sensitive areas such as Amazonia needed to incorporate environmental safeguards. When it was announced in 2003 that the 1765km Hwy BR-163 – from Cuiabá in Mato Grosso state to Santarém on the Amazon River – was to be fully paved, making access to a huge swath of southern Amazonia a whole lot easier, speculators indulged in a frenzied grab for land near the highway. Roads are the number-one trigger of deforestation in Amazonia, bringing in settlers, loggers, ranchers and mining prospectors, and by some estimates as much as 80% of Amazon deforestation has occurred within 50km of roads. The government postponed paving the BR-163 pending assessment of its environmental effects and placed a temporary stop on forest clearance on 82,000 sq km of land near the road. When the project was finally given the go-ahead in 2006, it included the declaration of seven new protected areas and a 160,000 sq km 'sustainable forest district' on lands near the road, of which only 50,000 sq km would be available for forestry conforming to strict environmental rules. Even so, environmentalists still fear the fully paved BR-163 will significantly increase forest destruction.

Environmentalists are also worried by the government's Growth Acceleration Plan, announced in 2007. A number of controversial Amazonian dam projects are envisaged and the plan gives high priority to three big hydroelectric installations – Belo Monte on the Rio Xingu in Pará, and Santo Antônio and Jirau on the Madeira River in Rondônia. Belo Monte is slated to flood more than 240 sq km of one of the most biologically diverse parts of Amazonia, while it's argued that the Madeira projects, set to increase Brazil's electricity-generating capacity by 8%, would displace 850 people, block the flow of nutrients to the Amazon floodplains, and inundate important wildlife habitats.

Beans, Beef & Mato Grosso
A large part of the fall in deforestation figures was attributable to a circumstance for which the Lula government could take no credit. This was the slump in profitability of Brazilian soybean and beef exports as Brazil's currency, the real, strengthened after 2003.

Cattle ranching and agriculture are to blame for at least as much Amazon deforestation as logging. Brazil is the world's biggest soy and beef exporter, and the state of Mato Grosso is Brazil's largest grain and beef producer. Northern Mato Grosso is an 'agricultural frontier' where farmers and ranchers are advancing into the southern Amazon region and clearing forests as they go. Mato Grosso has been responsible for some 40% of Amazon deforestation in recent years.

Between 1998 and 2004 the area of Mato Grosso under soybean cultivation doubled from 26,000 sq km to 52,000 sq km, while the number of cattle in Amazonia (a large proportion of which are in Mato Grosso) jumped from 38 million to 66 million. This period coincided with a dramatic rise in Amazon deforestation figures, from 18,000 sq km in the year 1999–2000 to 27,000 sq km in 2003–04. When export prices fell due to the strengthening currency, ranchers and soy growers lost the incentive to spend money on clearing more forest to expand their production. Should market conditions again become more favorable for them, deforestation rates could start climbing again.

Land Grab
A major hurdle to bringing deforestation under control is the chaotic state of Brazil's property laws. At the very least 1 million sq km of Brazil's 8.5 million sq km of land has been illegally appropriated. The reasons for this go way back in history but include laws that enabled people to claim title to previously unoccupied public land if they could demonstrate that they were occupying it – for which clearing the forest was often taken as sufficient evidence. Since the 1970s large tracts of Amazonia have been illegally commandeered by loggers and ranchers with the collusion of corrupt officials. In many cases small-scale settlers have been forced off their land, and hundreds have been murdered for resisting this. The state of Pará, where only one-third of land is officially registered, is particularly notorious. According to the Brazilian Catholic Church more than 500 people

Brazil's beef exports have quintupled since 1998 and the country overtook Australia as the world's largest beef exporter in 2004. One-third of the exports go to the EU, but more than three-quarters of the 9 million tonnes of production is eaten at home. About 80% of new pasture land is in the Amazon region.

Europe (49%) and China (20%) are the biggest export markets for Brazilian soy (used chiefly for cattle feed).

Mato Grosso state's governor Blairo Maggi, the largest soybean grower in the world, was awarded Greenpeace's 'Golden Chainsaw' award in 2005.

SUGAR POWER, SWEET OR SOUR?

At least one pump at almost every Brazilian gasoline station bears the name of a fuel as yet uncommon elsewhere in the world. Beside the pumps for various grades of gasoline and diesel, there are pumps labeled Álcool Comum, and they're usually among the busiest on the forecourt. This fuel alcohol, known in English as ethanol, is widely considered Brazil's big lucky break in the field of energy. Since 2003, when new 'flex-fuel' cars – able to run on any combination of gasoline and ethanol – were developed in Brazil, they have sold like hot cakes. By 2007 three million had been bought and ethanol accounted for 45% of transport fuel.

Álcool, made from sugarcane, gives fewer kilometers per liter than gasoline but is cheaper, so overall it works out more economical for drivers. It's also considered better for the environment. It still yields carbon dioxide emissions like gasoline – but a comparable amount of carbon dioxide is absorbed from the atmosphere by the growth of the plants from which the fuel is processed, greatly reducing the fuel's contribution to greenhouse gases.

Brazil was producing some 18 billion liters of ethanol a year by 2007 and planned to raise this to 26 billion liters by 2010, and to keep on raising it thereafter. It has suddenly found itself the world leader in a commodity that looks set to boom worldwide. As countries across the world attempt to reduce their dependence on expensive, polluting fossil fuels, biofuels (made from living organisms or their waste) such as ethanol look like being a big part of the future. This was made more than clear in 2007 when US president George W Bush visited Brazil and signed an agreement with President 'Lula' da Silva to pool their countries' experience and technology in developing biofuels for an international market.

The US is already a bigger ethanol producer than Brazil (the two countries account for 70% of world production), but Brazil is the biggest exporter. Brazil aims to lift its ethanol exports from 3 billion liters in 2006 to 8 billion liters in 2010, at the same time rapidly expanding the area of sugarcane plantations (currently around 60,000 sq km) and building scores of new distilleries to turn the cane into motor fuel.

Unfortunately, ethanol is not the win-win solution to the world's fuel needs that its fans claim. The carbon absorbed by the growing plant may cancel the carbon emitted by the fuel, but the fuel's production also consumes large amounts of fossil fuel through fertilizer and fungicide use, the distillation process, and transport. On this score, Brazil has a big advantage over the US, where ethanol is made chiefly from corn (maize) and burns up about seven times as much fossil fuel in its production than Brazilian sugarcane ethanol. By some estimates US-produced corn ethanol may not even reduce overall carbon dioxide emissions at all.

Even Fidel Castro waded into the debate after the Bush–Lula accord, commenting that using grains to produce vehicle fuel instead of food could push up the price of staple foods on which the world's poor depend. Castro drew attention, too, to the slavery-based history of sugarcane in Brazil and the generally low wages paid for the hard labor of cutting it.

Environmentalists also fear that Brazilian rain forest will be felled to make way for sugar plantations, and that chemical runoffs from the plantations – chiefly in Brazil's central highlands – will damage the Pantanal and Amazon ecosystems. Responding to this concern, President Lula proposed in 2007 that new plantations be located only on already degraded land without native vegetation. Meanwhile Brazilian scientists are working to develop methods of converting the whole cane plant – instead of the current one-third – into ethanol. Using the whole plant would require a lot less land to produce the fuel.

have been killed in such land disputes in Pará since 1986 – among them, in 2005, American missionary Dorothy Stang, who campaigned against exactly this kind of illegal land grabbing.

One reason the Lula government has created so many new protected areas is to combat this kind of land theft, making it more difficult for the grabbers to obtain land titles. But the measure needs to be combined with effective surveillance if it is to have genuine effect.

The government is now issuing *protocolos* – official recognition of land claims – in the form of bar codes rather than documents that can be sold or used as collateral, short-circuiting the illegal trade in land titles.

Sustainability Initiatives

The environmental initiatives that seemingly offer the best prospects of success are those that make conservation act in the interests of the local populace – such as extractive reserves and sustainable-development reserves (see p90 for an elaboration of these terms), fish-farming, and community ecotourism projects. Unfortunately, most of these are alarmingly small-scale compared with the size of the Amazonian population.

Hopes for more rational logging practices have been raised by international certification schemes, such as the one operated by the Forest Stewardship Council. Such schemes seek to certify timber that has been produced by sustainable methods, something that is increasingly demanded by domestic and international consumers of Brazilian timber. This type of consumer demand encourages reduced-impact logging, whereby forestry areas are divided into blocks to be exploited on a rotating basis and given time to regenerate. At the same time, the largest specimens of valuable tree species are left standing in order to reseed the block, and care is taken to minimize damage to trees that are not being felled. Some major Brazilian home-supply stores and a number of international stores carry certified lumber. However, it's also true that most illegal timber from the Amazon stays in Brazil, a large proportion of it being used in the construction industry in the south of the country.

Other Issues

Amazon deforestation grabs all the headlines and is undoubtedly the number-one environmental issue for Brazil, but what's often forgotten, especially by those outside the country, is that all Brazil's other main ecosystems are also under severe pressure. The Atlantic rain forest, older than the Amazon forest and once a quarter of its size, is now down to just 7% of its original area. The Pantanal wetlands are subjected to a variety of serious threats, including the side effects of intensive soybean and sugarcane cultivation on Brazil's central plains. See the Land section in this chapter (p71) and the boxed text The Pantanal Still Under Siege (p78) for more on some of these challenges.

On Brazil's coasts, growth of cities and burgeoning tourism developments threaten many delicate coastal marine ecosystems despite the creation of protected areas on extensive tracts of land and sea.

Environmental Organizations

The Brazilian conservation movement and the level of environmental awareness in the country have progressed and matured fast over the last few years. While more and more Brazilians know that the environment matters – they're as scared about global warming as anyone – environmental activists have at the same time understood that conservation won't succeed unless it also protects people's economic needs. Increasingly, conservation programs include social components, both to spread their message and to provide sustainable employment for local populations in affected areas.

As ever, the biggest single battle is to persuade politicians, at all levels, to give the environment priority alongside economic development. The 'megaproject' mentality, which looks to large-scale human interference in nature – building long-distance roads through rain forest, flooding large

For sustainable forestry and sustainable tourism initiatives in Brazil, check the Rainforest Alliance (http://rainforest-alliance.org).

www.sustainabletourismbrazil.org explains Brazil's sustainable-tourism certification system.

Amazonia Program (www.amazonia.org.br) is a superb resource for Amazonia news and other information in English and Portuguese.

areas for hydroelectricity, planting vast areas of bush with chemically fertilized soybeans – remains a temptation to any politician looking for ways to employ desperate people and pump money into the economy.

The following organizations are among those working actively to protect Brazil's environment. Strategies range from campaigns to save a single animal species to lobbying in Brasília and pressuring institutions to stop financing destructive projects. A few groups concentrate primarily on research and some do hands-on activist work – a number of them can arrange volunteer work for those interested. Many of their websites are in English as well as Portuguese.

AUSTRALIA
Greenpeace (☎ 02-9261 4666; www.greenpeace.org.au; Level 4, 35-39 Liverpool St, Sydney, NSW 2000)

BRAZIL
Amazonia Program (☎ 0xx11-3887 9369; www.amazonia.org.br; Rua Bento de Andrade 85, São Paulo) Amazonia is an Amazon monitoring and information program run by Amigos de Terra (Friends of the Earth). The website is a terrific resource.

Conselheiro Brasileiro de Manejo Florestal (☎ 0xx61-3248 7274; www.fsc.org.br in Portuguese; Room 228-B, Block F, Centro Comercial Gilberto Salomao, SHIS QI 05, Brasília) Brazilian representative of the Forest Stewardship Council, working for sustainable forestry via a certification scheme.

Conservation International (☎ 0xx31-3261 3889; www.conservation.org.br in Portuguese; 7th fl, Av Getúlio Vargas 1300, Belo Horizonte) This is the Brazilian branch of a large international field-based organization working for biodiversity and sustainable development. In Brazil it's involved in grassroots conservation projects, ecotourism and national policy initiatives.

Ecológica (☎ 0xx63-3215 1279; www.ecologica.org.br; Lote 28, Rua SO 11, Conjunto 03, ACSO (103 Sul), Palmas, Tocantins) This one's a dynamic institute involved in carbon-sequestration research, climate-change consultancy, environmental education and ecotourism.

Greenpeace (☎ 0xx11-3035 1155; www.greenpeace.org.br in Portuguese; Rua Alvarenga 2331, Butantã, São Paulo) Campaigns actively and publicly for renewable energy, and against illegal logging and whaling.

Instituto de Pesquisa Ambiental da Amazônia (IPAM; ☎ 0xx91-3283 4343; www.ipam .org.br in Portuguese; Av Nazaré 669, Belém, Pará) An environmental research institute and pressure group, IPAM is dedicated to sustainable development in Amazonia and organizes environmental education and training around Brazil. It's partnered by the Woods Hole Research Center of Massachusetts, a US ecological research institute.

Instituto do Homem e Meio Ambiente da Amazônia (Imazon; ☎ 0xx91-3182 4000; www.imazon.org.br; Rua Domingos Marreiros 2020, Bairro Fátima, Belém, Pará) This research organization promotes sustainable development with an eye on both social and environmental concerns in the Amazon.

Instituto Socioambiental (ISA; ☎ 0xx11-3515 8900; www.socioambiental.org; Av Higienópolis 901, São Paulo) ISA campaigns and lobbies for Brazil's indigenous peoples and environment. It publishes books, maps and other interesting information, and has several offices around Brazil.

Nature Conservancy (☎ 0xx61-3421 9100; www.nature.org; Office 246, Centro Empresarial Brasília Design Center, Block A, Conjunto D, Block 701, SRTVS, Brasília, Distrito Federal) This is the Brazil office of a US-based organization geared to protecting fragile ecosystems, endangered species and biodiversity; in Brazil it works with local communities and partner organizations to preserve ecosystems and promote sustainable economic development.

SOS Mata Atlântica (☎ 0xx11-3055 7888; www.sosmatatlantica.org.br in Portuguese; Rua Manoel da Nóbrega 456, Paraíso, São Paulo) SOS carries out political pressure work and environmental education, chiefly in defense of the Atlantic rain forest.

Tamar Project (Projeto Tamar; ☎ 0xx71-3676 1020; www.tamar.com.br; PO Box 2219, 40223-970 Rio Vermelho, Salvador, Bahia) Tamar is the official Brazilian government project to protect

Bad news for all those who quit eating meat because cattle ranching was killing the rain forest: soybean farming is now one of the biggest causes of deforestation in Brazil.

Breakfast of Biodiversity: The Truth about Rainforest Destruction, by John Vandermeer and Ivette Perfecto, is an insightful look at tropical deforestation and the many social and political reasons that lead to this complex and unfortunate situation.

Conservation International's website, www .conservation.org, covers various aspects of ecotourism and the global conservation movement, including CI's extensive work in Brazil.

sea turtles. Cooperating strongly with local communities, it has 21 stations and six visitors' centers along the coasts. National coordination is done from the Rio Vermelho branch, at Praia do Forte, 50km north of Salvador.

WWF Brasil (☎ 0xx61-3364 7400; www.wwf.org.br in Portuguese; Conjunto E, QL 6/8, SHIS EQ, Brasília, Distrito Federal) Part of the largest nature-protection network in the world, WWF Brazil has a very wide range of programs around the country working to balance human activity with biodiversity and sustainable use of resources.

CANADA
Greenpeace (☎ 416-597 8408; www.greenpeacecanada.org; Suite 605, 250 Dundas St W, Toronto, Ontario M5T 2Z5)

UK
Friends of the Earth (☎ 020-7490 1555; www.foe.co.uk; 26-28 Underwood St, London N1 7JQ)
Greenpeace (☎ 020-7865 8100; www.greenpeace.org.uk; Canonbury Villas, London N1 2PN)
Survival (☎ 020-7687 8700; www.survival-international.org; 6 Charterhouse Bldgs, London EC1M 7ET) Helps tribal peoples protect their lands.

US
Conservation International (☎ 800-429-5660; www.conservation.org; Suite 500, 2011 Crystal Dr, Arlington, VA 22202)
Environmental Defense (☎ 212-505-2100; www.environmentaldefense.org; 257 Park Ave S, New York, NY 10010) Environmental Defense organizes a number of environmental and human campaigns.
Greenpeace (☎ 202-462-1177; www.greenpeace.org/usa; 702 H St NW, Washington DC 20001)
Nature Conservancy (☎ 703-841-5300; www.nature.org; Suite 100, 4245 N Fairfax Dr, Arlington, VA)
Rainforest Action Network (RAN; ☎ 415-398-4404; www.ran.org; 221 Pine St, 5th fl, San Francisco, CA 94104) RAN works to protect rain forests and support inhabitants' rights through education, grassroots organizing and nonviolent direct action.
Rainforest Alliance (☎ 212-677-1900; http://rainforest-alliance.org; Suite 500, 665 Broadway, New York, NY 10012) Works on sustainable forestry, sustainable tourism and sustainable agriculture. Has a forestry certification program in Brazil and is involved in developing a sustainable-tourism certification scheme there.
Rainforest Foundation US (☎ 212-431-9098; www.rainforestfoundation.org; Suite 1614, 32 Broadway, New York, NY 10004) Supports local people living in protected areas in Amazonia.

Ron Mader's brilliant www.planeta.com has many ecotourism resources on Brazil and elsewhere, from photos and practical information to more theoretical online symposiums.

The illicit wildlife trade is a global industry worth more than US$12 billion a year, exceeded only by drugs and arms as a source of criminal earnings, according to the Convention on International Trade in Endangered Species of Wild Flora and Fauna (CITES).

The Smithsonian Atlas of the Amazon is a gorgeous treat for anyone who falls under the spell of Amazonia – 150 maps, 300 photos and lots of fascinating information.

Food & Drink

In Brazil, eating is, like so many other things, another pretext for pleasure-taking. There is no such thing as Brazilian haute cuisine per se, but the food tastes damned good just about anywhere you go. Even more remarkable is the cultural know-how about what, where, when and how to eat.

This *arte de comer bem* (art of eating well) has nothing to do with either fussiness, *á francesa,* or pseudoscientific taboos, *á americana.* Brazilians simply understand that the body feels better when it's kept hydrated with fruit and water while at the beach, or that a fattening little snack and a few sips of strong, hot coffee or ice-cold beer make the ride home from work infinitely more pleasant.

The food is as syncretic as the country itself. The most basic 'Brazilian' meal can include Portuguese olive oil, native manioc, Japanese sushi, African okra, Italian pasta, German sausage and Lebanese tabbouleh. Still, the cuisine can be reduced to three delightful principles: generosity, freshness and simplicity.

First, you should plan for some of the largest portions on the planet – a single main course can leave two people stuffed. It's hard to go hungry here, even on a modest budget. As for freshness, the fertile soil and luxuriant climate ensure that a stunning variety of produce is available at all times. Many of the local fruit and vegetable names have no translation simply because they exist nowhere else. Packaged foods are generally frowned upon, and farm animals are rarely pumped full of hormones, if only because of the prohibitive cost.

Given the richness and variety of fresh ingredients, Brazilians generally eat their food neat. They feel no need for fancy sauces or rarefied cooking processes. Meat is coated in salt and set on the grill, while veggies are steamed and served straight up. Simply add a drizzle of olive oil and a bit of salt to taste. That said, there are complex regional dishes that are well worth their careful preparation.

Travelers are often surprised to learn that Brazilians tend to eschew spicy food. In fact, restaurants rarely include pepper shakers as part of the normal table service, though it's generally available upon request, as is hot sauce. There are exceptions, of course, especially in the Northeast, where the burn of *malagueta* pepper laces many dishes.

One thing, though, you can be sure of – in Brazil, you're going to eat exceedingly well.

Maria-Brazil.org (www.maria-brazil.org/brazilian_recipes.htm) has a very good section on Brazilian food, including easy-to-follow recipes and a guide to shopping in the country's supermarkets and street fairs.

STAPLES & SPECIALTIES

Just as there's no 'typical' Brazilian face, there's no single Brazilian cuisine. Foodies prefer to say it's a conglomeration of regional cuisines, each itself a hybrid of ethnic cuisines adapted to local conditions. That said, here follows a description of a typical Brazilian meal – available just about anywhere you go.

BRAZIL'S TOP FIVE

- **Olympe** (p172) Rio de Janeiro
- **ZUU a.Z.d.Z** (p380) Brasília
- **Fasano** (p296) São Paulo
- **Restaurante Carcará** (p580) Jericoacoara
- **Cafeteria do Largo** (p648) Manaus

Certainly, the meal will include *arroz e feijão* (rice and beans), the principle staples of the Brazilian diet. Each is cooked with garlic and onions. To the rice add tomatoes, and to the beans add bay leaves and perhaps some bacon. On top of the beans, sprinkle *farofa* – manioc flour sautéed in butter, perhaps with bits of egg or bacon.

Grilled meats, known as *churrasco* or *grelhadas,* are the meal's crowning glory: chicken, beef or pork is dredged in salt and grilled over an open fire. A green salad or sautéed or steamed vegetables (beets, carrots, green beans, broccoli or kale) round out the main course. French fries, usually served in great quantities, are also hugely popular, though you might go even more local and ask for fried manioc – a crunchy delight.

A digestive pause is followed by *sobremesa* (dessert), which could include either fresh or preserved fruit, a pudding enlivened with coconut or passion fruit, deliciously creamy cakes, caramel (aka *doce de leite*) in several forms, or the flanlike *quindim*. The meal only comes to a conclusion with the consumption of a strong, sweet shot of coffee – Brazilian, of course.

Note that, except in higher-end restaurants, food is generally served family-style – that is, with generous helpings on communal plates. Also, all the dishes (except dessert) are served at once – there are no formal courses.

Churrasco (barbecued meat) is so important to Brazilians that a built-in barbecue grill is a key selling point for real-estate agents, whether they're offering a vacation villa or a family home.

Bahia & the Northeast

Brazilian restaurants outside of Brazil tend to serve, more specifically, Bahian cuisine, perhaps because it's the most obviously exotic. It developed in the kitchens of the region's slave-based sugar plantations, and its African origins reveal themselves in the three main ingredients: coconut milk; the spicy *malagueta* pepper; and *dendê* oil, a reddish-orange extraction of west African palm, which is deliciously distinctive though it can also be very hard to digest for those who are unused to it. The delicious stew known as *moqueca* includes all three, plus meat or seafood, and is a classic Bahian specialty. On the streets of Bahia you can't escape the smell of *acarajé* – fritters made with brown beans and shrimp fried in *dendê* oil.

By contrast, the much drier inland areas of the Northeast known as the Sertão produce a very different cuisine. Perhaps the most famous ingredient is *carne seca* or *carne de sol,* both of which consist of beef that has been salted and dried to preserve it against the region's punishing heat. Squash, which manages to survive in difficult growing conditions, is also very popular.

Looking to reproduce Brazilian dishes you've tried on your travels? Check out *The Art of Brazilian Cookery* by Dolores Botafogo. It's the classic text on Brazilian cuisine, with recipes adapted for North American and European cooks.

The Amazon

Amazonian cuisine is strongly influenced by the region's native Tupi people, who live largely on manioc, freshwater fish, yams and beans, and exotic fruit. *Caldeirada* is a popular fish stew not unlike bouillabaisse, and *pato no tucupi* is a regional favorite made with duck, garlic, *jambú* herb and the juice of both lemons and manioc roots. *Jacaré* (caiman meat) is another delicacy.

The Central West

Occupying the prairie-like cerrado, the Central West is dominated by sprawling *fazendas* (ranches) that produce pork and beef, as well as staples such as corn, rice, kale and manioc. The region's rivers offer up the meaty *dourado* fish, the *pintado* (a type of catfish), and, of course, the infamous piranha. Recipes tend to be simple but delicious, relying on the freshness of local ingredients.

In his fourth book, *Açúcar* (an antique spelling of *Açúcar* or 'sugar'), legendary anthropologist Gilberto Freyre brilliantly unravels the relationship of sugar, slavery and the 'sweetness' of Brazilian culture.

Rio, São Paulo & the Southeast

The mountainous state of Minas Gerais offers the most distinctive regional cuisine of the Southeast. Pork is particularly popular, as is the kalelike *couve*, which is sautéed in oil with garlic and onions. *Frango ao molho pardo* (chicken stewed in its own blood with vegetables) sounds gruesome but tastes delicious. *Queijo minas* is a soft, vaguely sweet white cheese that, when served with *goiabada* (guava paste), makes a refreshing dessert.

São Paulo is the gastronomic capital of Brazil, thanks to high levels of disposable wealth and a large Italian community that places a high social value on refined eating. Here you'll find temples of fine dining as well as humble ethnic restaurants that reflect the city's dazzling number of immigrant communities, among whom the Japanese deserve special mention. Forming the largest colony outside of Japan, they have made sushi popular throughout Brazil. Note that pizza baked in a wood-burning oven is a Sunday-night tradition.

Rio doesn't have its own cuisine per se, but as the adopted home of Brazilians of all stripes, it offers excellent food from every region. As the former colonial capital, the Portuguese influence is less adulterated here than elsewhere, evidenced by the popularity of *bacalhau* (codfish). *Feijoada*, a bean-and-meat stew served with rice, *farofa*, kale and sliced orange, is the city's contribution to the national cuisine. Because it takes a few hours to cook as well as digest, it is traditionally served on Saturday. Food in Rio tends be lighter than elsewhere, at least in the upscale places in the Zona Sul neighborhoods such as Ipanema, where the body beautiful is held in higher esteem than gastronomic delight. Expect lots of delicious (and often quite creative) salads and sandwiches.

The recipes may be hard to follow, but who cares? Christopher Idone's *Brazil: A Cook's Tour* provides a terrific photographic tour of Brazil and its varied cuisine.

The South

Italian and German food rules the day in the South. The country's love affair with pasta and beer began here – both have become Brazilian staples. Expect to see lots of sausage and sauerkraut in the German enclaves of Joinville and Blumenau. Brazilian wine, whose quality improves year by year, comes from grapes lovingly imported from Italy and planted in the accommodating soil of Rio Grande do Sul.

As in Argentina, the pampas (grassy plains) of the far south were long dominated by *gaúchos* – Brazilian cowboys who taught the region to love beef above all other meats. *Churrasco* is better here than anywhere else in the country. In fact, throughout Brazil it is considered a mark of a good grill restaurant that its meat carvers are *gaúchos* (which also used to describe natives of Rio Grande do Sul). The region preserves another cowboy tradition – *erva maté* tea (see the boxed text on p359).

Experts trace Brazil's present-day love of very sweet desserts to Moorish origins, via the Arab occupation of Portugal.

TRAVEL YOUR TASTEBUDS

Acarajé Eat these Bahian fritters, made of brown beans and dried shrimp, as soon as they've been fished from a spattering pot of *dendê* (palm) oil.

Açaí This addictive, deep-purple, vitamin-rich berry from the Amazon is a staple of both Tupi Indians and Rio bodybuilders.

Caipirinha The divine national cocktail is made from limes, sugar, ice and *cachaça* (a high-proof sugarcane alcohol).

Cafezinho A small shot of Brazilian coffee that should be strong as the devil, hot as hell and sweet as love.

Feijoada completa Plan for a long, digestive nap after indulging in this stew of black beans and well-larded meat and sausage.

Jambú This Amazonian herb makes the tongue tingle, then go slightly numb.

Picanha Not to be confused with piranha, Brazil's favorite cut of beef comes from the cow's rump; it's eaten pinkish, salty and fresh from the grill.

Piranha Take a bite out of this flesh-eater; the meat is delicious, but beware of sharp bones.

Pan-Brazilian Fusion

Like much of the world, Brazil has undergone a kind of culinary renaissance in the last decade. One result has been a new, high-end, pan-Brazilian fusion cuisine. It begins with a renewed excitement about native ingredients, from the Amazonian fruits of the north to the grass-fed beef of the south. Up-and-coming chefs fuse these with cordon bleu and other classic European cooking methods to create novel, often exquisite, combinations. Asian and Arab influences are also evident, especially in São Paulo, home to the largest Japanese and Lebanese communities outside their respective countries. Indeed, São Paulo is in many ways the capital of this new Brazilian-fusion cuisine, though it is quickly spreading to the more prosperous enclaves around the country.

FEIJOADA *Regis St. Louis*

Brazil's national dish, *feijoada* is a delicious stew of black beans slowly cooked with a great variety of meat, including dried tongue and pork offcuts, seasoned with salt, garlic, onion and oil. The stew is accompanied by white rice and finely shredded kale, fried *farofa* (manioc flour) and pieces of orange.

The popular myth is that *feijoada* originated in the kitchens of African slaves, who had to make the most of otherwise unsavory cuts of pork and beef. Others argue that the recipe is essentially a Portuguese invention adapted to Brazilian climes. Kale, a typical accompaniment, is certainly a Portuguese favorite. Fried *farofa*, on the other hand, was inherited from Brazil's indigenous peoples. Certainly it began life as a humble dish, though it has long been adopted by the middle and upper classes as 'classically' Brazilian.

Ingredients

6 cups dried black beans
1/4 kg smoked ham hocks
1/4 kg Brazilian *lingüiça* (Brazilian sausage; substitute chorizo or sweet sausage)
1/4 kg Brazilian *carne seca* or lean Canadian (loin-cut) bacon
1kg smoked pork ribs
(the intrepid can add one each of a pork ear, foot, tail and tongue)
2 bay leaves
3 garlic cloves, minced
1 large onion, chopped
3 tablespoons olive oil
4 strips smoked bacon
salt and black pepper
orange slices to garnish
rice, *farofa*, kale or collard greens to serve
hot sauce (optional) to serve

Preparation

After soaking beans overnight, bring them to the boil in 3L of water and then keep them on low to medium heat for several hours, stirring occasionally. Meanwhile, cut up the ham hocks, *lingüiça* and *carne seca* into 3cm or 4cm chunks, separate the pork ribs by twos and place them all in a separate pan full of water and bring to the boil. After the first boil, empty out the water and add the mixture, along with the bay leaves and salt and pepper, to the beans. As the pot simmers, in a separate pan sauté the garlic and onion in olive oil, adding in the smoked bacon. Take two ladles of beans from the pot, mash them and add to the frying pan. Stir around, cook for a few more minutes, then add frying-pan contents to the pot; this will thicken the mixture. Simmer for another two to three hours, until the beans are tender and the stock has a creamy consistency. Remove bay leaves and serve over rice with *farofa* and kale or collard greens. Garnish with fresh orange slices. Add hot sauce as desired.

DRINKS
Nonalcoholic Drinks

JUICES

Brazilian *sucos* (juices) are divine. Staples include known qu3antities such as orange, lime, papaya, banana, passionfruit, carrot, beet, pineapple, melon, watermelon and avocado. Then there are the Amazonian fruits that hardly exist outside Brazil. The berrylike *açaí* is prized for its nutritional value and addictive taste, while guaraná (a type of berry) is loaded with caffeinelike stimulants. They defy translation, as do *graviola, cupuaçu* and *fruta do conde.*

Caldo de cana is extracted directly from lengths of sugarcane, usually with a machine that's a hand-cranked, multicogged affair. *Agua de côco* (coconut juice) is available anywhere that it's hot and where there are people. With a few strokes of a butcher's knife, vendors open a hole large enough for a straw. It sounds touristy but it's not – the juice is high in electrolytes, and Brazilians value its hydrating properties.

In Rio, where juice is a way of life, corner bars can offer 30 or 40 different varieties, made from fresh fruit and vegetables or from pulp. Request them *sem açúcar e gelo* or *natural,* if you don't want sugar and ice. Juices often have water mixed in; this is almost certain to be purified but if you're worried about it, ask for juices mixed with *suco de laranja* (orange juice) instead of water, or for a *vitamina* (juice with milk). Orange juice is rarely adulterated.

CAFFEINE

Brazilians like their coffee as strong as the devil, as hot as hell and as sweet as love. In the morning they take it with milk *(café com leite)*. For the rest of the day, it's *cafezinhos,* regular coffee served either in a drinking glass or an espresso-sized coffee cup and often presweetened. It is sold in stand-up bars, and dispensed free in large thermoses in restaurants, at hotel reception desks and in offices to keep the general population perky the whole day through. Espresso is increasingly available in more upscale establishments, and just about everywhere in São Paulo, which boasts a highly evolved coffee culture.

A good cup of tea is harder to come by, but *erva maté* (called simply *maté*) is a potential alternative. It's available throughout the country and is usually served cold and cloyingly sweet. Only in the state of Rio Grande do Sul is it drunk hot (see the boxed text on p359).

Made from an Amazonian berry, guaraná 'champagne' rivals Coca Cola as Brazil's favorite soft drink. It's served cold, carbonated and sweet, and it's reputed to have all sorts of health-giving properties.

Alcoholic Drinks

BEER

Brazilians enjoy their beer served *bem gelada* (icy cold). In general, a *cerveja* refers to a 600ml bottled beer, a 'longneck' is a 300ml bottle, and a *cervejinha* is a 300ml can. Antárctica (ant-*okt*-chee-kah) and Brahma are the best national brands. Keep your eyes peeled for regional brands, including Bohemia from Petrópolis, Cerpa from Pará, Cerma from Maranhão and the tasty Serramalte from Rio Grande do Sul. For thicker palates, try the stoutlike Caracu or Xingu, sweet black beers from Santa Catarina.

Chope (*shop*-ee) is a pale blond pilsner draft that's lighter and generally superior to canned or bottled beer. Antárctica and Brahma produce the two most widespread versions. In big cities you may even find *chope escuro,* a kind of light stout. Key phrase: *Moço, mais um chope, por favor!* (Waiter, another draft, please!). Many a Brazilian evening is whiled away in plastic chairs at plastic tables set up pell-mell on sidewalks and terraces, the empty bottles and glasses left to pile up as a sort of badge of honor.

Foodies who read Portuguese should keep their eye out for *Gula*, Brazil's leading gourmet magazine. You can also read many articles online at www.gula.com.br.

Even Oprah considers *açaí*, a delicious Amazonian berry, a 'superfood' for its remarkable nutritional attributes, including high levels of fiber, omega-6 acids, potassium, vitamins C and E, and antioxidant anthocyanins.

Capital amassed by São Paulo's coffee barons, plus the creation of infrastructure (including trains and port facilities) for the exporting of coffee, fueled the city's startlingly rapid industrialization, beginning in the 1880s.

CACHAÇA

Also called *pinga* or *aguardente, cachaça* is a high-proof sugarcane alcohol produced and drunk throughout the country. It can be cheaper than water (literally) or as dear as whiskey, and yes, price definitely signals a difference in taste and effect (and aftereffect!). Velho Barreiro, Ypioca, Pitú, Carangueijo, and São Francisco are some of the better labels.

The *caipirinha* is the unofficial Brazilian national drink. Ingredients are simple – *cachaça* with crushed lime, sugar and ice – but the results are sublime when sipped in the cool of an evening. You can replace the *cachaça* with vodka (to make a *caipirosca*) and the lime with a variety of fruit, including strawberries, kiwi, the cherrylike *pitanga* and the bracingly tart *limao da Pérsia* (a light-yellow lime).

> The Maué Indians so revere guaraná – an Amazonian fruit whose caffeine-packed seed resembles the human eye – that its plant is said to have given birth to the tribe's founder.

CELEBRATIONS

Brazilians love to eat (then again, who doesn't?), and holidays and celebrations are another excuse for the hearty consumption of both food and alcohol. Any day off from work is an occasion for *churrasco*. Many of the gastronomic traditions are borrowed wholesale from European and American culture: turkey at Christmas, chocolate at Easter, champagne at the New Year, iced cakes for birthdays and weddings. In addition, pork and lentils augur good luck at the New Year, and during the winter feast days known as Juninas (June saints' days), *cachaça* is spiced with cinnamon, cloves and ginger and served warm. Despite the cultural importance of Carnaval, there is not a specific cuisine – alcohol trumps food.

WHERE TO EAT & DRINK

Eating out in Brazil can mean fried treats at the corner *lanchonete* (snack bar or greasy spoon); a lunchtime *prato feito* (ready-to-eat hot meal including rice, beans, a meat dish and salad) at a *bar* (pub) or *botequim* (working man's restaurant); a gorge session at a sit-down *rodízio* (all-you-can-eat) restaurant; or à la carte dining on white linen.

> Unable to grow grapes, Italian immigrants to Espírito Santo made wine out of *jabuticaba*, a purplish-black grapelike fruit native to the Atlantic rain forest. The fruit grows out of a tree's trunk rather than on a vine.

To eat quickly, cheaply and well, head to a *por-kilo* restaurant, which, as the name suggests, serves food by weight, and costs from R$15 to R$30 per kilogram. Offerings generally include fresh veggies, rice, beans, grilled meat and fish, plus regional specialties. It's a great option for travelers, as you don't have to decipher a menu. Try to get there early (noon for lunch or 7pm or 8pm for dinner), when offerings are freshest and available in abundance.

Churrascarias are generally *rodízio*-style and include a salad bar, plus, at higher-end places, meat that's brought to your table fresh from the grill and carved for you. *Rodízio* restaurants serving pizza and *massa* (pasta) are also popular and cost between R$10 and R$25.

Lone travelers will be made to feel at home wherever they go. If you want to strike up a conversation, head to the closest corner bar or food stand, where bonhomie is almost certain to abound.

> *Delightful Brazilian Cooking,* by Eng Tie Ang and Martine Fabrizio, has a range of Brazilian recipes that tend to be healthy as well as straightforward to execute.

Tipping is not necessary – your bill will include a 10% service charge. In restaurants frequented by tourists, count your change and make sure your check is itemized: *Pode discriminar?* (Can you itemize?). There is no pressure to turn a table – you can linger as long as you like just about anywhere you go.

Quick Eats

In Brazil, you're never far from a *lanchonete,* where you can get *salgadinhos* (savory snacks, usually fried) – also known as *tira-gostos* and *petiscos* – for around R$1. Try *quibe,* which is cracked wheat stuffed with spiced meat then deep fried – it's both delectable and rib-sticking. *Pasteis* (dough filled with meat, cheese or seafood then deep fried) are unbeatable when eaten piping hot. *Pão de queijo* (a concoction of cheese and tapioca dough) is also deliciously ubiquitous.

For a few more centavos, you can get a *sanduiche*, a term that covers a multitude of hot sins from the *X-tudo* (cheeseburger with everything) to the dependable *misto quente* (toasted ham-and-cheese sandwich). Cold sandwiches, usually on crustless white bread, are called *sanduiche natural*.

VEGETARIANS & VEGANS

Vegetarianism is very much a minority activity in Brazil. Many Brazilian waiters consider *sem carne* (without meat) to include such 'vegetable' groups as chicken, pork and animal fats, so be very clear when ordering in restaurants. Beware especially the typical black-bean dishes, which are often flavored with meat.

Most cities offer a few all-vegetarian options, but where this is neither convenient nor possible, head to a *por-kilo* restaurant – they usually offer at least half a dozen different salad, vegetable and bean dishes.

EATING WITH KIDS

Brazilians love children, and except at the finest establishments yours will be welcome wherever you go, as long as they're reasonably behaved. Note that bratty behavior is little tolerated by Brazilian parents, who consider a quick swat far more constructive than a mere 'time-out.'

Familiar food is available for unadventurous palates just about anywhere you go, from burgers and pizza to grilled-cheese sandwiches. Prepackaged baby food is generally available from supermarkets, though not from corner stores.

HABITS & CUSTOMS

Brazilians tend to have a small *café da manha* (breakfast; often shortened to *café*) of coffee with milk and a sweet or savory baked good; a big *almoço* (lunch) any time from noon to 3pm; a hearty *lanche* (late-afternoon snack) of a *salgadinho* with juice, coffee or beer; and a light *jantar* (dinner) of soup and/or sandwiches or a smaller recapitulation of lunch, usually sometime around 9pm or even later. Extended families religiously gather for Sunday lunch, the most important meal of the week. It can last until 5pm or later and may seamlessly blend into *lanche* and *jantar*. Snacking is perfectly acceptable at any time of the day or night, as is a quick shot of ultrasweet coffee.

COOKING COURSES

Based in the colonial town of Paraty, the **Academy of Cooking & Other Pleasures** (chefbrazil.com) offers five-day courses with respected chef and educator Yara Robert and includes cooking classes as well as *cachaça* tasting, visits to local farms and more.

Philadelphia-based **Amerispan Study Abroad** (☎ 215-751-1100; www.amerispan.com) offers very reasonably priced Bahian cooking classes, including home stay, from about US$400 per week in Salvador da Bahia.

EAT YOUR WORDS

Use the following guide to help you order correctly and better understand – and enjoy – the dishes once they arrive. For pronunciation guidelines see the Language chapter, p732.

Cookbrazil.com (www .cookbrazil.com) offers a range of classic Brazilian recipes, from appetizers through desserts. There are also commentaries by readers who have actually made the recipes and offer their own tips.

You'll find a nice summary of Brazilian cuisine, plus easy-to-follow recipes for select classic dishes, at www.sallys -place.com/food/ethnic _cusine/brazil.htm.

In Brazil, Saint John the Baptist (São João) is considered a protector of the corn crop, and his saint's day on June 24 is often celebrated with a profusion of corn dishes.

DOS & DON'TS

Brazilians are casual about many things. Table manners are not one of them. Where possible, avoid eating with your hands – middle-class Brazilians often eat sandwiches with a knife and fork. Eat finger food with a napkin. If you dine in someone's home, bring a small gift such as wine or flowers – or win permanent friends with a liter of duty-free whiskey.

Smoking is generally acceptable, sometimes even in designated nonsmoking areas. It's considered polite, however, to ask fellow diners if it's OK to light up, especially in private homes. Brazilians love their cell phones – you can make or receive a quick call on any occasion except the most formal.

Brazilians consider avocado a fruit rather than a vegetable (which it technically is), and it is most commonly consumed as a juice that includes a healthy dose of sugar. Avocado served with salt is generally considered distasteful.

For a deeper understanding of Brazilian table manners as well as other matters of custom and etiquette, check out *Brazil – Culture Smart!* by Sandra Branco.

Joaquim Machado de Assis, Brazil's greatest 19th-century writer, was also a famous gourmand. Cooking and eating are essential ingredients of his eerily postmodern novels.

Useful Phrases

The menu (in English), please.	O cardapio (em inglês), por favor.	o kar-*da*-pyo eng eeng-*gles* porr fa-*vorr*
What would you recommend?	O que você recomenda?	o ke vo-*se* he-ko-*meng*-da
I'm a vegetarian.	Eu sou vegetariano/a. (m/f)	e-oo so ve-zhe-ta-ree-*a*-no/a
I'd like...	Queria...	ke-ree-a...
I'm full/I've eaten well.	Estou satisfeito/a. (m/f)	es-to sa-tees-*fay*-to/a
Do you have...?	Tem...	teng...
The check, please.	A conta, por favor.	a *kong*-ta porr fa-*vorr*

Menu Decoder

MENU BASICS

almoço	ow-*mo*-so	lunch
arroz	a-*hoz*	rice
aves	*a*-ves	poultry
azeite	a-*zay*-te	olive oil
bebida	be-*bee*-da	drink
café da manha	ka-*fe* da ma-*nyang*	breakfast
carne	*kar*-ne	meat (usually beef)
churrasco	shoo-*has*-ko	barbecue
comida caseira	ko-*mee*-da ka-*zay*-ra	home-style cooking
comida por kilo	ko-*mee*-da porr *kee*-lo	pay-by-weight buffet
dendê	deng-*de*	reddish palm oil
entrada	eng-*tra*-da	first course, appetizer
farinha de mandioca	fa-*ree*-nya de mang-*dee*-o-ka	manioc flour; the staple food of Brazil's Indians before colonization and the staple for many Brazilians today, especially in the Northeast and Amazon
farofa	fa-*ro*-fa	garnish of manioc flour sautéed with butter
feijão	fay-*zowng*	bean
frutos do mar	*froo*-tos do marr	seafood
grelhadas	gre-*lya*-das	grilled meat or fish
lanche	*lang*-she	hearty, late-afternoon snack
lanchonete	lang-sho-*ne*-te	snack bar
molho	*mo*-lyo	sauce
peixe	*pay*-she	fish
por-kilo	porr-*kee*-lo	per kilogram; used for self-serve restaurants
prato	*pra*-to	main course

prato feito	*pra*·to *fay*·to	literally 'made plate'; plate of the day; typically, an enormous and cheap meal
pratos típicos	*pra*·tos *tee*·pee·kos	local dishes
refeição	he·fay·*sowng*	meal
refeição comercial	he·fay·*sowng* ko·merr·*syow*	meal/serving of various dishes (normally comes with enough food for two to share)
rodízio	ho·*dee*·zyo	smorgasbord, usually with lots of meat
sobremesa	so·bre·*me*·za	dessert

MAIN DISHES

barreado	ba·rre·*a*·do	a mixture of meats and spices cooked in a sealed clay pot for 24 hours and served with banana and *farofa;* the state dish of Paraná
bobó de camarão	bo·*bo* de ka·ma·*rowng*	manioc paste flavored with dried shrimp, coconut milk and cashew nuts
canja	*kang*·zha	soup made with rice and chicken broth
carne de sol	*kar*·ne de sol	tasty, salted meat, grilled and served with beans, rice and vegetables
casquinha de siri	kas·*kee*·nya de *see*·ree	stuffed crab
cozido	ko·*zee*·do	a meat stew heavy on vegetables
feijoada	fay·zho·*a*·da	bean-and-meat stew served with rice and orange slices, traditionally eaten for Saturday lunch
frango ao molho pardo	*frang*·go ow *mo*·lyo *par*·do	chicken pieces stewed with vegetables and the blood of the bird
moqueca	mo·*ke*·ka	Bahian fish stew cooked in a clay pot with *dendê* oil, coconut milk and spicy peppers
pato no tucupí	*pa*·to no too·koo·*pee*	roast duck flavored with garlic, juice of the manioc plant and jambú; a favorite in Pará
pirarucu ao forno	pee·ra·hoo·*koo* ow *forr*·no	a preparation of Brazil's most famous fish from the rivers of Amazonia, in which the fish is oven-cooked with lemon and other seasonings
tutu á mineira	too·*too* a mee·*nay*·ra	savory black-bean mash typical of Minas Gerais
vatapá	va·ta·*pa*	a seafood dish of African origins with a thick sauce of manioc paste, coconut and *dendê* oil
xinxim de galinha	sheeng·*sheeng* de ga·*lee*·nya	pieces of chicken flavored with garlic, salt and lemon

Food Glossary

FRUIT & VEGETABLES

abacate	a·ba·*ka*·te	avocado
abacaxí	a·ba·ka·*shee*	pineapple
açaí	a·sa·*ee*	gritty, deep-purple forest berry
acerola	a·se·*ro*·la	acidic, cherry-flavored fruit; a megasource of vitamin C
alface	ow·*fa*·se	lettuce
alho	*a*·lyo	garlic

Brazil is one of the world's largest food exporters, and number one in sugar, coffee, beef and orange juice.

The Brazil Nut Effect – the tendency of the larger Brazil nut to rise to the top when a bowl of mixed nuts is shaken – is actually a serious point of scientific inquiry into separation of granular mixtures by size and density.

GlobalGourmet.com (www.globalgourmet .com/destinations/brazil/) provides a good introduction to the history and culture of Brazilian cuisine, with pages highlighting two much-loved staples – guaraná and manioc.

batata	ba·*ta*·ta	potato
beterraba	be·te·*ha*·ba	beetroot
caju	ka·*zhoo*	fruit of the cashew plant
carambola	ka·rang·*bo*·la	starfruit
cenoura	se·*no*·ra	carrot
cupuaçu	koo·poo·*a*·soo	acidic, slightly pearlike fruit
fruta do conde	*froo*·ta do *kong*·de	sugar-apple fruit
goiaba	go·*ya*·ba	guava
graviola	gra·vee·*o*·la	custard apple
jaca	*zha*·ka	jackfruit
laranja	la·*rang*·zha	orange
limão	lee·*mowng*	lime or lemon
maçã	ma·*sang*	apple
mamão	ma·*mowng*	papaya
mandioca	mang·dee·*o*·ka	manioc, cassava (also known as *aipim*)
manga	*mang*·ga	mango
maracujá	ma·ra·koo·*zha*	passion fruit
melancia	me·lang·*see*·a	watermelon
melão	me·*lowng*	honeydew melon
morango	mo·*rang*·go	strawberry
pupunha	poo·*poo*·nya	a fatty, vitamin-rich Amazonian fruit taken with coffee
uva	*oo*·va	grape

SNACKS

acarajé	a·ka·ra·*zhe*	Bahian fritters made of brown beans and dried shrimp fried in *dendê* oil
empadão	eng·pa·*downg*	a tasty pie, typical of Goiás, made from meat, vegetables, olives and eggs
quibe	*kee*·be	cracked wheat stuffed with spiced meat then deep fried
pão de queijo	powng de *kay*·zho	balls of cheese-stuffed tapioca bread
pastel	pas·*tel*	thin square of dough stuffed with meat, cheese or fish, then fried
salgadinhos	sow·ga·*dee*·nyos	savory snacks; also *salgados*
salgados	sow·*ga*·dos	savory snacks; also *salgadinhos*

MEAT, FISH & DAIRY

camarão	ka·ma·*rowng*	shrimp
carne	*kar*·ne	meat in general, also beef; also known as *bife* and *carne de vaca*
carneiro	karr·*nay*·ro	lamb
dourado	do·*ra*·do	meaty freshwater fish
frango	*frang*·go	chicken
leite	*lay*·te	milk
ovos	*o*·vos	eggs
porco	*porr*·ko	pork
queijo	*kay*·zho	cheese
requeijão	he·kay·*zhowng*	cream cheese
siri	*see*·ree	crab
tainha	*tai*·nya	a meaty but tender local fish

DESSERT

arroz doce	a·*hoz* do·se	rice pudding
bolo	*bo*·lo	cake

Rock-hard, often bitter, and sometimes poisonous, manioc root – once properly processed – forms the basis for everything from cakes and bread to stews and the ubiquitous *farofa* (manioc flour sautéed with butter).

Descendants of Swiss immigrants around the town of Novo Friburgo, who first arrived in 1818, still produce goat's cheese in what they call 'cremeries' (pronounced kre-me-*hees*).

brigadeiro	bree·ga·*day*·ro	*doce de leite* covered with chocolate
cocada	ko·*ka*·da	baked coconut treat
doce de leite	*do*·se de *lay*·te	creamy milk-and-sugar concoction
goiabada	go·ya·*ba*·da	sweet guava paste
pavé	pa·*ve*	creamy cake
quindim	*keen*·deem	egg-based sweet
sorvete	sorr·*ve*·te	ice cream

DRINKS

agua	*a*·gwa	water
aguardente	a·gwarr·*deng*·te	firewater, rotgut; any strong drink, but usually *cachaça*
batida	ba·*tee*·da	blended drink
cachaça	ka·*sha*·sa	sugarcane spirit
café	ka·*fe*	coffee
caipirinha	kai·pee·*ree*·nya	drink made from *cachaça* and crushed citrus fruit, such as lemon, orange or *maracujá*
cerveja	serr·*ve*·zha	beer
chope	*sho*·pe	draft beer
erva maté	err·va *ma*·te	popular tea of southern Brazil
guaraná	gwa·ra·*na*	soft drink made from Amazonian berry
pinga	*peen*·ga	another name for *cachaça*
refrigerante	he·free·zhe·*rang*·te	soft drink
suco	*soo*·ko	juice
vitamina	vee·ta·*mee*·na	juice with milk

Eat Smart in Brazil, by Joan and David Peterson, provides an excellent introduction to Brazil's culinary history, some classic recipes, and an extensive and very useful glossary.

Carnaval in Rio

One of the world's largest parties, Carnaval – in all its colorful, hedonistic bacchanalia – is virtually synonymous with Rio. Although Carnaval is ostensibly just five days of revelry, from the Friday to the Tuesday preceding Ash Wednesday, Cariocas (residents of Rio) begin the partying months in advance. The parade through the Sambódromo, featuring elaborate floats flanked by thousands of pounding drummers and twirling dancers, is the culmination of the festivities – though the real action, Cariocas profess, is at the wild parties about town.

Adding to the welcome mayhem are visitors, who can join Cariocas in the revelry, heading to nightclubs and bars that throw special costumed events. There are free live concerts happening all over the city (like those in Largo do Machado, Arcos da Lapa and Praça General Osório), while those seeking a bit of decadence can head to the various balls about town. Whatever you do, prepare yourself for sleepless nights, an ample dose of *caipirinhas* (the unofficial Brazilian national drink: *cachaça* with crushed lime, sugar and ice) and samba, and mingling with the joyful crowds spilling out of the city.

Joining the *bandas* (street parties, also called *blocos*) is one of the best ways to celebrate à la Carioca. These consist of a procession of drummers and vocalists followed by anyone who wants to dance through the streets of Rio. Some *bandas* require costumes (drag, Amazonian attire etc), while others simply expect people to show up and add to the good cheer.

Although the city is blazing with energy during Carnaval, don't expect the party to come to you. See opposite to get some ideas on how to celebrate the return of King Momo, the lord of the Carnaval. For those unacquainted with Momo, he's the modern embodiment of Momos, the Greek god of trickery, and when the chosen Momo is announced, Cariocas expect a portly, jolly ruler who can dance a mean samba. The revelry officially begins when the mayor hands King Momo the keys to the city on the Friday before Carnaval.

More information on events during Carnaval is in *Veja* magazine's Veja Rio insert (sold on Sunday at newsstands) or visit Riotur (p126), Rio's tourism and Carnaval authority.

For a complete rundown on the latest Carnaval info, including street parties, samba schools and balls, visit the excellent website www.rio-carnival.net.

King Momo is slimming down these days. Following the heart attack of several of the city's portliest Momos (weighing in at over 200kg), the city seems to be losing its taste for obese Carnaval kings.

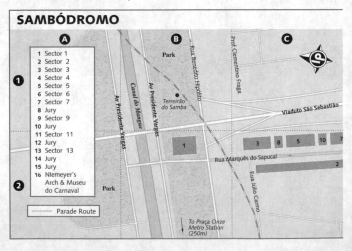

SAMBÓDROMO

1 Sector 1
2 Sector 2
3 Sector 3
4 Sector 4
5 Sector 5
6 Sector 6
7 Sector 7
8 Jury
9 Sector 9
10 Jury
11 Sector 11
12 Jury
13 Sector 13
14 Jury
15 Jury
16 Nlemeyer's Arch & Museu do Carnaval

Parade Route

Park

Rua Benedito Hipólito

Prof. Clementino Fraga

Canal do Mangue

Av Presidente Vargas

Av Presidente Vargas

Terreirão do Samba

Viaduto São Sebastião

Rua Marquês do Sapucaí

Rua Júlio Carmo

Park

To Praça Onze Metro Station (250m)

HISTORY

Carnaval, like Mardi Gras, originated from various pagan spring festivals. During the Middle Ages, these tended to be wild parties until tamed, in Europe, by both the Reformation and the Counter-Reformation. But not even the heavy hand of the Inquisition could squelch Carnaval in the Portuguese colony, where it came to acquire Indian costumes and African rhythms.

Some speculate that the word *carnaval* derives from the Latin *carne vale*, meaning 'goodbye meat,' owing to the 40 days of abstinence (from meat and other worldly pleasures) that Lent entails. To compensate for the deprivation ahead, they rack up sins in advance with wild parties in honor of King Momo, the king of Carnaval.

SIGHTS & ACTIVITIES

Bandas: Carnaval on the Streets

Attending a *banda* is one of the best ways to celebrate Carnaval. *Bandas*, also called *blocos*, consist of a procession of drummers and singing, followed by anyone who wants to dance through the streets. To join in, all you have to do is show up. Note that some *bandas* ask you to march in one of their colors. Many sell shirts on the spot (R$20) or you can just show up in the right colors. Some *bandas* are featured below; for complete listings, check with Riotur (p126) or visit the website **Samba & Choro** (www.samba-choro .com.br/carnaval in Portuguese).

Banda de Ipanema (Map pp138-9; Praça General Osório, Ipanema; ⏰ 4pm 2nd Sat before Carnaval & Carnaval Sat) This longstanding *banda* starts from Ipanema. It's a wild crowd, complete with drag queens and others in costume. Don't miss it.

Barbas (Map pp142-3; cnr Rua Assis Bueno & Rua Arnaldo Quintela, Botafogo; ⏰ 2pm Carnaval Sat) One of the oldest *bandas* of the Zona Sul parades through the streets with a 60-piece percussion band. A water truck follows along to spray the crowd of some 2500. Colors: red and white.

Bloco de Bip Bip (Map pp140-1; Rua Almirante Gonçalves 50, Copacabana; ⏰ midnight Carnaval Fri, 7pm Mon) Has perhaps the best music of any *banda*, owing to the professional musicians who drop in from time to time. Leaves from the old samba haunt, Bip Bip (p179).

Bloco de Carioca da Gema (Map pp144-5; Rua do Lavradio, Lapa; ⏰ 4pm Carnaval Sat) One of best new *blocos* in town, this one meets near the classic samba club Carioca da Gema (p179).

Bloco de Segunda (Map pp142-3; Cobal Humaitá, Rua Voluntários de Pátria 446, Botafogo; ⏰ 5pm Carnaval Mon) An excellent percussion band joins 2000 or so revelers.

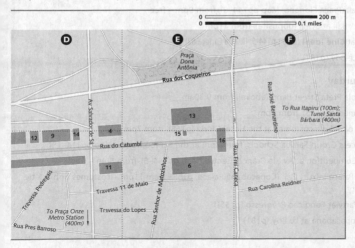

Some *blocos* are rather colorfully named – like *Suvaco de Cristo* (armpit of Christ), which parades in Jardim Botânico, below the savior's outstretched arms.

Carmelitas (Map pp144–5; cnr Rua Dias de Barros & Ladeira de Santa Teresa, Santa Teresa; ☺ 5pm Carnaval Fri, 6pm Carnaval Tue) An excellent and popular *bloco* through Bohemian Santa Teresa. Some *bloco* devotees dress up as Carmelite nuns.

Cordão do Bola Preta (Map pp144–5; Praça Mauá, Centro; ☺ 5pm Carnaval Sat) The oldest *banda* in activity, features lots of men dressed as women (who are often straight) and a chaotic march that leads the group to stop at bars along the way. Costumes always welcome – especially those with black and white spots.

Dois Pra Lá, Dois Pra Cá (Map pp142–3; Carlinho de Jesus Dance School, Rua da Passagem 145, Botafogo; ☺ 2pm Carnaval Sat) This fairly long parade travels from the dance school to the Copacabana Palace hotel. *Banda* T-shirts are obligatory.

Monobloco (Map pp138–9; western end of Leblon Beach, marching to *posto* 10, Ipanema; ☺ 5pm Sun 5 days after Shrove Tuesday) This post-Carnaval *bloco* is a fun option if you arrived in the city after the big event. There's a huge percussion band with thousands of young partiers in attendance. Monobloco is sometimes held on Copacabana Beach; verify the locale before heading out.

Simpatia É Quase Amor (Map pp138–9; Praça General Osório, Ipanema; ☺ 3pm 2nd Sat before Carnaval & Carnaval Sun) A big *bloco*, with 10,000 participants and a 50-piece percussion band.

CARNAVAL PARTY PLANNER *Marcos Silviano do Prado*

Saturday Two Weeks Before Carnaval

■ Banda de Ipanema (p115)

■ Rehearsals at samba schools

Weekend Before Carnaval

■ Saturday – Banda Simpatia é Quase Amor (above)

■ Sunday – Monobloco (above)

■ Rehearsals at samba schools

Carnaval Friday

■ Carnaval King Momo is crowned by mayor at 1pm on Av Rio Branco, Centro

■ Shows start at Terreirão do Samba (Map pp114–15) and Rio Folia (Map pp144–5), near the Arcos do Lapa, next to the Catedral Metropolitana, from 8pm

■ Cinelândia Ball (Praça Floriano; Map pp144–5), from 9pm – free

■ Red and Black Ball at Scala (opposite), from 11pm

■ Dance Party at **Cine Ideal** (Map pp144–5; Rua da Carioca 62)

■ Gay Balls at Le Boy (p181)

Carnaval Saturday

■ Cordão do Bola Preta Street Band (above), from 9:30am

■ Banda de Ipanema (p115), from 4pm

■ Competition of deluxe costumes at the Hotel Glória (p168), from 7pm

■ Parade of Access Group Samba Schools, from 7pm at the Sambódromo (Map pp114–15)

■ Street Band Competition at Av Rio Branco, Centro (Map pp144–5), from 8pm – free

■ Copacabana Palace Luxury Ball (Copacabana Palace; p168), from 11pm – costumes or black tie are mandatory

■ X-Demente Party at Fundição Progresso (p155)

■ Gay Ball in Copacabana at Le Boy (p181)

Carnaval Balls

Carnaval balls are surreal and erotic events. The most famous one is held at the Copacabana Palace (p168). It's a formal affair, so you'll need a tux or a ball gown. You'll have the opportunity to celebrate with Rio's glitterati as well as the occasional pop star who turns up. Tickets cost a whopping R$800 to R$1800.

Other balls that are decidedly less upper-class are held at **Scala** (Map pp138-9; Av Afrânio de Melo Franco, Leblon); **Canecão** (Av Venceslau Brás 215, Botafogo); and **Help** (Map pp140-1; Av Atlântica 3432, Copacabana). The most extravagant gay balls are found at Le Boy (p181) in Copacabana. The most popular ball is held in Centro at Praça Floriano (p154), which attracts around 60,000 revelers. Every night of Carnaval weekend (from 9pm onward, Friday to Tuesday), bands take the stage in front of the Câmara Municipal, in the northwest corner of the plaza. This ball is free.

Rio's excellent insider website www.ipanema .com has loads of up-to-date info on Carnaval events about town.

Tickets go on sale roughly two weeks beforehand, and the balls are held nightly for the week preceding and all through Carnaval.

- Shows at Terreirão do Samba (Map pp114–15) and Rio Folia (Map pp144–5), near the Arcos do Lapa, next to the Catedral Metropolitana

Carnaval Sunday

- Samba Parade at the Sambódromo (Map pp114–15), from 9pm to 6am
- Carnaval Balls at Scala (above) and Help (above), from 11pm
- Gay Balls at Le Boy (p181) and **Elite** (Map pp146-7; Rua Frei Caneca, Centro)
- Parties at 00 (p180) and other dance clubs
- Shows at Terreirão do Samba (Map pp114–15) and Rio Folia (Map pp144–5), near the Arcos do Lapa, next to the Catedral Metropolitana, from 8pm

Carnaval Monday

- Samba Parade at the Sambódromo (Map pp114–15), from 9pm to 6am
- Carnaval Balls at Scala (above), Help (above) and other venues, from 11pm
- Gay Balls at Le Boy (p181) and Elite (Map pp146–7)
- Parties at 00 (p180) and other dance clubs
- Shows start at Terreirão do Samba (Map pp114–15) and Rio Folia (Map pp144–5), near the Arcos do Lapa, next to the Catedral Metropolitana, from 8pm

Carnaval Tuesday

- Banda de Ipanema (p115), from 4pm
- Parade of Group B Samba Schools at Sambódromo (Map pp114–15), from 9pm
- Scala Gay Costume Ball in Leblon (Map pp138–9), from 11pm
- Carnaval Balls at Help (above) and other venues, from 11pm
- Gay balls at Le Boy (p181) and other venues.
- X-Demente Party at Marina da Glória (Map pp142–3)
- Parties at 00 (p180) and other dance clubs
- Shows at Terreirão do Samba (Map pp114–15) and Rio Folia (Map pp144–5), near the Arcos do Lapa, next to the Catedral Metropolitana, from 8pm

Samba-School Parades

The main parade takes place in the **Sambódromo** (Map pp114-15; Rua Marques do Sapuçai), near Praça Onze metro station, and it's nothing short of spectacular. Before an exuberant crowd of some 30,000, each of 14 samba schools has their hour and 20 minutes to dazzle the audience.

The parades begin in moderate mayhem and work themselves up to a higher plane of frenzy. The announcers introduce the school, the group's theme colors and the number of wings. Far away the lone voice of the *puxador* (the interpreter of the theme song) starts the samba. Thousands more voices join him, and then the drummers kick in, approximately 200 to 400 per school. The pounding drums drive the parade. Sambas, including the themes for each group, flood the airwaves for weeks before the beginning of Carnaval.

Next come the main wings of the school, the big allegorical floats, the children's wing, the drummers, the celebrities and the bell-shaped *baianas* (women dressed as Bahian 'aunts') twirling in elegant hoopskirts. The *baianas* honor the history of the parade itself, which was brought to Rio from Salvador da Bahia in 1877.

The *mestre-sala* (dance master) and *porta-bandeira* (flag bearer) waltz and whirl. Celebrities, dancers and tambourine players strut their stuff. The costumes are fabulously lavish, complete with 1.5m feathered headdresses, long, flowing capes that sparkle with sequins, and rhinestone-studded G-strings.

More than an hour after the parade begins, the school makes it past the arch and the judges' stand. The whole procession is also an elaborate competition. A hand-picked set of judges chooses the best school on the basis of many components, including percussion, the *samba do enredo* (theme song), harmony between percussion, song and dance, choreography, costumes, story line, floats and decorations. The championship is hotly contested, with the winner becoming the pride of Rio and all of Brazil.

> Those seeking an insider's perspective on what it's like to join a samba school should read Alma Guillermoprieto's excellent book *Samba*.

CARNAVAL BEYOND RIO

Around Carnaval, if you bump into any Salvadorenhos (inhabitants of Salvador) en route to Rio, they'll be quick to tell you that the world's best Carnaval happens not in Rio, but in Bahia. Brazil has plenty of other cities that throw a wild party:

- Carnaval in Salvador (p452) happens on the streets, where music and spontaneity rule and *trios elétricos* (electrically amplified bands playing atop speaker-laden trucks) work thousands of revelers into a frenzy.

- Everyone dons a costume for the 11 days and nights of Olinda's Carnaval (p535). Balls, nights of samba and *afoxé* (the music of Bahia, which has strong African rhythms and close ties to Candomblé), and plenty of street-style merriment characterize the *festas*.

- Recife (p527) starts its Carnaval weeks in advance, with *bailes* (dances) in the clubs and *blocos* (drumming and dancing processions) on the streets. The pounding rhythms of *maracatu* (slow, heavy Afro-Brazilian drumbeats) aren't for wallflowers.

- Porto Seguro (p482) throws an impressive and hedonistic bash, complete with plenty of dancing in the streets, round-the-clock music jams and no-holds-barred partying.

- In Rio state, Paraty (p196) has its own odd version of the party, more akin to Woodstock than Carnaval, as hundreds of young revelers cover themselves in mud and dance through the cobblestone streets.

- Carnatal is Natal's (p558) out-of-season Carnaval, held the first week of December. The same festive atmosphere and rhythm-charged music prevails.

SAMBÓDROMO GLOSSARY

alas – literally, the 'wings.' These are groups of samba-school members responsible for a specific part of the central theme *(samba do enredo)*. Special *alas* include the *baianas*, women dressed as Bahian 'aunts' in full skirts and turbans. The *abre ala* of each school is the opening wing or float.

bateria – the drum section. This is the driving beat behind the school's samba and the 'soul' of the school.

carnavalescos – the artistic directors of each school, who are responsible for the overall layout and design of the school's theme.

carros alegóricos – the dazzling floats, usually decorated with near-naked women. The floats are pushed along by the school's maintenance crew.

desfile – the procession. The most important samba schools *desfilar* (parade) on the Sunday and Monday night of Carnaval. Each school's *desfile* is judged on its samba, drum section, master of ceremonies and flag bearer, floats, leading commission, costumes, dance coordination, and harmony.

destaques – the richest and most elaborate costumes. The heaviest ones usually get a spot on one of the floats.

diretores de harmonia – the school organizers, who usually wear white or the school colors; they run around yelling and 'pumping up' the wings and making sure there aren't any gaps in the parade.

enredo – the central theme of each school. The *samba do enredo* is the samba that goes with it. Themes vary tremendously.

passistas – a school's best samba dancers. They roam the parade in groups or alone, stopping to show their fancy footwork along the way. The women are usually scantily dressed and the men usually hold tambourines.

puxador – the interpreter of the theme song. He (they're invariably male) works as a guiding voice leading the school's singers at rehearsals and in the parade.

The Sambódromo parades start on Friday night with the *mirins* (young samba-school members) and continue on through Saturday night when the Group A samba schools strut their stuff. Sunday and Monday are the big nights, when the Grupo Especial – the best 14 samba schools in Rio – parade: seven of them on Sunday night and into the morning, and seven more on Monday night. The following Saturday, the eight top schools perform once more in the Parade of Champions. Each event starts at 9pm and runs until 6am.

TICKETS

Getting tickets at legitimate prices can be tough. Tickets go on sale in September. **Riotur** (Map pp144-5; www.rio.rj.gov.br/riotur; 9th fl, Rua Assembléia 10) can advise on where to get them, as the official outlet can vary from year to year. People line up for hours, and travel agents and scalpers snap up the best seats. Riotur reserves seats in private boxes for tourists for around R$400, but you should be able to pick up regular tickets from a travel agent for around R$150. Try to get seats in the center, as this is the liveliest section – and the best views are from here.

By Carnaval weekend, most tickets will have sold out, but there are lots of scalpers. If you buy a ticket from a scalper (no need to worry about looking for them – they'll certainly find you!), make sure you get both the plastic ticket with the magnetic strip and the ticket showing the seat number. The tickets for different days are color-coded, so be sure to double-check the date as well.

If you haven't purchased a ticket but still want to go, you can show up at the Sambódromo at around midnight, three or four hours into the show. This is when you can get grandstand tickets for about R$40 from scalpers outside the gate. Make sure you check your sector. Most ticket sellers will try to pawn off their worst seats.

And if you can't make it during Carnaval proper, there's always the cheaper (but less exciting) Parade of Champions the following Saturday.

Imperatriz holds the most Carnaval victories among Rio's samba schools, with six titles – three taken in successive years (1999, 2000 and 2001).

Though not traditionally a Carnaval destination, São Paulo has its own elaborate parades held in a sambadrome modeled on Rio's Sambódromo. The main parades are held Friday and Saturday night (Rio's begins Sunday night).

JOINING A SAMBA SCHOOL

There's nothing to stop you from taking part in a Carnaval parade. Most samba schools are happy to have foreigners join one of the wings. To get the ball rolling, you'll need to contact your chosen school far in advance; they'll tell you the rehearsal times and when you need to be in the city (usually one or two weeks before Carnaval). You'll also need to memorize their theme song, make it to the rehearsals and master that winning smile. For a list of samba schools and contact information see p180. The biggest investment, aside from making it to Rio, is buying a *fantasia* (costume), which will cost between US$300 and US$500. You can order costumes through agencies like **Rio Carnaval** (www.rio-carnival.net).

GETTING TO THE SAMBÓDROMO

Don't take a bus to or from the Sambódromo. It's much safer to take a taxi or the metro, which runs round the clock during Carnaval until 11pm Tuesday. It's also a great opportunity to check out the paraders commuting in costume.

The old classic film *Orfeu Negro* cleverly sets the Orpheus myth in the setting of a Rio *favela* (shanty town) during Carnaval. The bossa nova soundtrack is excellent.

Make sure you indicate to your taxi driver which side of the stadium you're on. If you decide to take the metro, remember the stop you get off at depends on where your seats are. For sectors 2, 4 and 6, exit at Praça Onze. Once outside the station, turn to the right, take another right and then walk straight ahead (on Rua Júlio Carmo) to sector 2. For sectors 4 and 6, turn on Rua Carmo Neto and proceed to Av Salvador de Sá. You'll soon see the Sambódromo and hear the roar of the crowd. Look for signs showing the entrance to the sectors. If going to sectors on the other side (1, 3, 5, 7, 9, 11 and 13), exit at Central station. You'll then have to walk about 700m along Av Presidente Vargas until you see the Sambódromo.

Samba City, Samba Land

One of the biggest new developments in Rio is **Cidade do Samba** (Samba City; Map pp146-7; ☎ 2213 2503; Rua Rivadávia Correa 60, Gamboa; admission R$20; 🕑 noon-6pm), which opened in 2006. Near the port, the 70,000-sq-meter 'city' is actually made up of 14 large buildings, where competing schools build their Carnaval floats. Visitors can wander the grounds and perhaps see a show (R$80; currently held at 7pm on Thursday). These are rather touristy affairs, but if you're not around during Carnaval, they'll give you a small taste of what the event is like.

The **Terreirão do Samba** (Samba Land; Map pp114-15; Praça Onze, Av Presidente Vargas), is an open-air courtyard next to sector 1. Performances are presented the weekend before Carnaval, then continue from the following Friday all the way through to Tuesday. Samba Land also hosts a party the Saturday after Carnaval, which is the Parade of Champions.

Samba-School Rehearsals

Around August or September, rehearsals start at the *escolas de samba* (samba 'schools' or clubs). Rehearsals usually take place in the *favelas* and are open to visitors. They're fun to watch, but go with a Carioca for safety. Mangueira and Salgueiro are among the easiest to get to, and their rehearsals are popular with a mix of Cariocas and tourists. See p180 for a complete listing of samba schools.

DATES

The following are Carnaval dates (Friday to Tuesday):

2008 February 1 to 5
2009 February 20 to 24
2010 February 12 to 16
2011 March 4 to 8

Rio de Janeiro City

Be warned: Rio's powers of seduction can leave you with a bad case of *saudade* (indescribable longing) when you leave. Planted between lush, forest-covered mountains and breathtaking beaches, the Cidade Maravilhosa (Marvelous City) has many charms at her disposal.

Although joie de vivre is a French invention (as is the bikini), it's the Cariocas (Rio dwellers) who've made it their own. How else to explain the life-lusting zeal with which the city's inhabitants celebrate their days? While large-scale festivities like Carnaval make Rio famous, there are countless occasions for revelry – Saturday at Ipanema Beach, a *festa* (party) in Lapa, soccer at Maracanã, or an impromptu *roda de samba* (samba circle) on the sidewalks of Leblon, Copacabana or any other corner of the city.

Music is the meeting ground for some of Brazil's most creative artists and nets an audience as diverse as the city. This is another of Rio's disarming traits: its rich melting pot of cultures. Cariocas they may call themselves, but the city's enticing variety of cuisines speaks volumes about its history of immigration.

The spectacular landscape is another of Rio's shameless virtues. Verdant mountains and white-sand beaches fronting deep blue sea offer a range of adventure: surfing great breaks off Prainha, hiking through Tijuca's rain forests, sailing across the Baía de Guanabara (Guanabara Bay) or rock climbing up the face of Pão de Açúcar (Sugarloaf Mountain).

As with any city in the tropics, there is always a downside, and Rio is no exception with its high crime rates and alarming social inequalities. Yet despite her many problems, Rio rarely fails to seduce, and most visitors arrive home already daydreaming of their return.

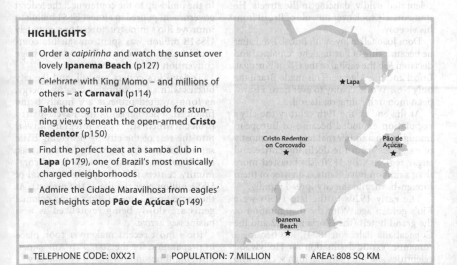

HIGHLIGHTS

- Order a *caipirinha* and watch the sunset over lovely **Ipanema Beach** (p127)
- Celebrate with King Momo – and millions of others – at **Carnaval** (p114)
- Take the cog train up Corcovado for stunning views beneath the open-armed **Cristo Redentor** (p150)
- Find the perfect beat at a samba club in **Lapa** (p179), one of Brazil's most musically charged neighborhoods
- Admire the Cidade Maravilhosa from eagles' nest heights atop **Pão de Açúcar** (p149)

★ Lapa

Cristo Redentor on Corcovado ★

Pão de Açúcar ★

Ipanema Beach ★

■ TELEPHONE CODE: 0XX21   ■ POPULATION: 7 MILLION   ■ AREA: 808 SQ KM

RIO DE JANEIRO CITY

HISTORY

The Tamoio people were living on the land surrounding the Baía de Guanabara when Gaspar de Lemos sailed from Portugal for Brazil in May 1501 and entered the huge bay in January 1502. Mistaking the bay for a river, Lemos named it Rio de Janeiro. The French, however, were the first Europeans to settle along the great bay in 1555. After a brief alliance with the Tamoio – who hated the Portuguese for their cruelty – the French were expelled in 1567. The Portuguese victors then drove the Tamoio from the region in another series of bloody battles.

By the 17th century, the Tamoio had been wiped out. Those who weren't taken into slavery died from disease. Other Indians were 'pacified' and taken to live in settlements organized by the Jesuits. The Portuguese had set up a fortified town on the Morro Castelo in 1567 and, by the 17th century, Rio became Brazil's third-most important settlement (after Salvador da Bahia and Recife-Olinda). African slaves streamed in and the sugar plantations thrived. Even more slaves arrived to work in the gold mines of Minas Gerais during the 18th century.

In 1807 Napoleon's army marched on Lisbon. Two days before the invasion, 40 ships carrying the Portuguese prince regent (later known as Dom João VI) and his entire court of 15,000 set sail for Brazil. When the prince regent arrived in Rio, his Brazilian subjects celebrated wildly, dancing in the streets. He immediately took over the rule of Brazil from his viceroy.

Dom João fell in love with Brazil. Even after he became king of Portugal, he remained and declared Rio the capital of the UK of Portugal, Brazil and the Algarve. This made Brazil the only New World colony to ever have a European monarch ruling on its soil.

At the end of the 19th century the city's population exploded because of European immigration and internal migration (mostly of ex-slaves from the declining coffee and sugar regions). By 1890 Rio boasted more than a million inhabitants, a quarter of them foreign-born, and the city spread rapidly.

The early 1920s to the late 1950s were Rio's golden age. With the inauguration of the grand hotels (the Glória in 1922 and the Copacabana Palace in 1924), Rio became a romantic, exotic destination for Hollywood celebrities and international high society who came to play and gamble at the casinos and dance or perform in the nightclubs.

Rio continued to change. Three large landfill projects were undertaken to ease the strain on a city restricted by its beautiful surroundings. The first was to become Aeroporto Santos Dumont, near Centro. The second resulted in Flamengo Park, and the third expanded the strand at Copacabana.

Rio remained the political capital of Brazil until 1960, when the government moved to Brasília. During the 1960s, modern skyscrapers rose in the city, and some of Rio's most beautiful buildings were lost. During the same period, the *favelas* (shantytowns) of Rio grew to critical mass with immigrants from poverty-stricken areas of the Northeast and interior, swelling the number of Rio's urban poor. The Cidade Maravilhosa began to lose its gloss as crime and violence increased.

The final decade of the military dictatorship that ruled Brazil from 1964 to 1985 was not kind to Rio. There were numerous protests during that period (notably in 1968 when some 100,000 marched upon the Palácio Tiradentes). Even Rio's politicians opposed the military regime, which responded by withholding vital federal funding. The administration was forced to tighten its belt, and infrastructure deteriorated as the city's coffers dried up.

A turning point for Rio came when it was chosen as host city for Eco 92, the UN Conference on Environment and Development. In the build-up to the conference, the federal government poured in almost US$1 billion to improve Rio's infrastructure. Approximately US$18 million was spent on satellite communications alone, and Riocentro, a huge convention center, was built.

Today Rio's coffers are full, and the city buzzes with an unstoppable creative energy, as long-awaited projects are finally being financed. The biggest is the Favela-Bairro project, which strives to integrate *favelas* into the rest of the city by providing basic sanitation and by planning leisure areas, health clinics, schools, preschools and community centers (Rio has pledged a total of US$1 billion over the life of the project). At the same time, some of Rio's aging colonial gems are slowly being revitalized as new businesses arrive.

Rio's most recent makeover took place in preparation for the 2007 Pan Am games, bringing thousands of visitors to the city.

Ongoing efforts of the Favela-Bairro project continue to be a major focus of development. This project, begun in 1994, has brought infrastructure and city services to numerous *favelas*.

ORIENTATION

Rio is a city of unusual urban diversity, with beaches, mountains, skyscrapers and the omnipresent *favelas* all woven into the fabric of the landscape. The city itself can be divided into two zones: the Zona Norte (North Zone), which consists of industrial, working-class neighborhoods, and the Zona Sul (South Zone), full of middle- and upper-class neighborhoods and Rio's well-known beaches. Centro, Rio's business district and the site of its first settlement, marks the boundary between the two, and a number of the important museums and colonial buildings are there.

The parts of Rio you are most likely to explore stretch along the shore of the Baía de Guanabara and the Atlantic Ocean. South from Centro are the neighborhoods of Lapa, Glória, Catete, Flamengo, Botafogo and Urca – where the striking peak of Pão de Açúcar dominates the landscape. Further south lie the neighborhoods of Copacabana, Ipanema and Leblon, the only stops for many travelers to the city.

Other areas of interest include the quaint, colonial neighborhood of Santa Teresa, on a hill overlooking Centro, and the looming statue of Cristo Redentor, atop Corcovado in Cosme Velho, from where there are fabulous views of both zones of the city.

Aside from the bus station, Maracanã Football Stadium and the international airport, most travelers have few reasons to visit the Zona Norte.

Rio de Janeiro's international airport, Aeroporto Galeão (GIG; also called Aeroporto Tom Jobim), is 15km north of the city center. Santos Dumont airport, used by a few domestic flights, is by the bayside in the city center, 1km east of Cinelândia metro station. Rio's central bus station, Rodoviária Novo Rio, lies several kilometers northwest of Centro. For information on getting into town from the bus station or from the airports, see p185.

Maps

Guia Quatro Rodas publishes an excellent city map of Rio de Janeiro (R$16), available at most newsstands. Lonely Planet also produces a good city map. Riotur, the city's tourist information center, provides free street maps at its offices. For physical and topographical maps, head to **Editora Geográfica J Paulini** (Map pp144-5; ☎ 2220 0181; Shop K, Rua Senador Dantas 75, Centro).

RIO IN...

Two Days

Start your day off with a refreshing glass of *açaí* (nutritious berry-like fruit) at a neighborhood juice bar and head to lovely **Ipanema Beach** (p127). For lunch, stroll up the sands to **Leblon** (p126) and grab a bite on restaurant-packed **Rua Días Ferreira**, followed by window-shopping on the streets of Leblon and Ipanema. End the saunter at Praia do Arpoador, one of Rio's best places to watch the sunset. After a powernap (or a *cafezinho* – strong, espresso-sized coffee), have dinner at a **lakeside kiosk** in Lagoa (p128). On day two, take the cable car to **Pão de Açúcar** (p149), followed by a stroll around **Urca** (p149). Around lunchtime, ride the *bonde* (tram) to **Santa Teresa** and dine at **Espírito Santa** (p176) or another well-placed Santa spot. In the evening, go to a samba club in **Lapa** (p179) for Rio's best music scene.

Five Days

On your third day, do something active – hire a bike for a ride along the beachfront or go hiking in **Parque Nacional da Tijuca** (see the boxed text on p160). In the evening, dine in one of Ipanema's great restaurants. On day four, explore the old streets of **Centro** (p152), stopping in some of its excellent museums, cultural centers and churches. In between sightseeing, have lunch at **Brasserie Rosário** (p175) or one of the outdoor cafés nearby. In the evening, catch a football match at **Maracanã** (p156). On your last day, rise early for a stroll along Copacabana beach, stopping for coffee at the idyllic **Confeitaria Colombo** (p173). Afterwards, take the cog train up Corcovado to **Cristo Redentor** (p150), for outstanding views. Have dinner that night in **Yorubá** (p174).

INFORMATION

Bookstores

Argumento (Map pp138-9; ☎ 2239 5294; Rua Días Ferreira 417, Leblon) Small but decent selection of foreign-language books and magazines. Café in back.

Bar das Artes (Map pp144-5; ☎ 2215 5795; Praça XV de Novembro 48, Centro) Combination bistro/bookstore/music shop, inside the Paço Imperial.

Letras e Expressões Ipanema (Map pp138-9; ☎ 2521 6110; Rua Visconde de Pirajá 276, Ipanema; ⊙ 8am-midnight); Leblon (Map pp138-9; ☎ 2511 5085; Av Ataulfo de Paiva 1292, Leblon; ⊙ 24hr) Foreign-language books and magazines, plus an internet café at each branch.

Livraria da Travessa Av Rio Branco (Map pp144-5; Av Rio Branco 44, Centro); Rua Visconde de Pirajá (Map pp138-9; ☎ 2249 4977; Rua Visconde de Pirajá 572, Ipanema); Travessa do Ouvidor (Map pp144-5; Travessa do Ouvidor 17, Centro; ⊙ 9am-8pm Mon-Fri, 10am-1pm Sat) Books and periodicals, CDs and an excellent café at the Ipanema branch.

Livraria Prefácio (Map pp142-3; ☎ 2527 5699; Rua Voluntários da Pátria 39, Botafogo) Occasionally hosts readings in its back café.

Nova Livraria Leonardo da Vinci (Map pp144-5; ☎ 2533 2237; Av Rio Branco 185, Centro) One of Rio's best collections of foreign-language books.

Cultural Centers

Casa de Cultura Laura Alvim (Map pp138-9; ☎ 2267 1647; Av Vieira Souto 176, Ipanema) Ipanema's beachside cultural center has a cinema, gallery space, and an enticing café.

Casa França-Brasil (Map pp144-5; ☎ 2253 5366; www.casafrancabrasil.rj.gov.br; Rua Visconde de Itaboraí 78, Centro; admission free; ⊙ noon-8pm Tue-Sun) Opened in 1990, this cultural center hosts Franco-Brazilian exhibitions. A lovely bistro is hidden out the back.

Centro Cultural Banco do Brasil (Map pp144-5; ☎ 3808 2020; www.cultura-e.com.br; Rua Primeiro de Março 66, Centro; ⊙ noon-8pm Tue-Sun) One of Rio's best cultural centers, with excellent exhibitions, a film series and lunchtime and evening concerts.

Centro Cultural Carioca (Map pp144-5; ☎ 2242 9642; www.centroculturalcarioca.com.br; Rua do Teatro 37, Centro; ⊙ noon-8pm Mon-Sat) On Praça Tiradentes, this cultural center hosts musical groups along with dance recitals and ongoing exhibitions.

Centro Cultural Laurinda Santos Lobo (Map pp144-5; ☎ 2224 3331; Rua Monte Alegre 306, Santa Teresa; ⊙ 8am-5pm) The large mansion built in 1907 occasionally hosts exhibitions and open-air concerts.

Fundição Progresso (Map pp144-5; ☎ 2220 5070; Rua dos Arcos 24, Cinelândia; admission free; ⊙ 9am-6pm Mon-Fri) This former foundry stages avant-garde exhibitions and performances.

Instituto Moreira Salles (Map p137; ☎ 3284 7400; www.ims.com.br; Rua Marquês de Sao Vicente 476, Gávea; admission free; ⊙ 1-8pm Tue-Sun) A beautiful cultural center that hosts impressive exhibitions. Leafy gardens and a café lie next door.

Emergency

Report robberies to the **tourist police** (Map pp138-9; ☎ 3399 7170; Rua Afrânio de Melo Franco 159, Leblon; ⊙ 24hr).

Other useful numbers:

Ambulance (☎ 192)

Fire department (☎ 193)

Police (☎ 190)

Internet Access

Internet cafés charge R$4 to R$8 per hour.

Central Fone (Map pp138-9; Rua Teixeira de Melo 47, Ipanema; ⊙ 9:30am-9:30pm)

iCafé (Map pp138-9; Rua Prudente de Morais 167B, Ipanema; per hr R$10; ⊙ 10am-10pm) For Mac lovers.

Letras & Expressões Ipanema (Map pp138-9; Rua Visconde de Pirajá 276; ⊙ 8am-midnight); Leblon (Map pp138-9; Av Ataulfo de Paiva 1292; ⊙ 24hr)

Fone Rio (Map pp140-1; Rua Constante Ramos 22, Copacabana; ⊙ 9am-midnight)

Locutório (Map pp140-1; Av NS de Copacabana 1171, Copacabana; ⊙ 8am-2am)

Tele Rede (Map pp140-1; Av NS de Copacabana 209A, Copacabana; ⊙ 8am-2am)

Eurogames (Map pp142-3; Rua Corrêa Dutra 39B, Catete; ⊙ 10am-10pm)

Central Fone (Map pp144-5; basement level, Av Rio Branco 156, Centro; ⊙ 9am-9pm Mon-Fri, 10am-4pm Sat)

Cyber Café Fundição Progresso (Map pp144-5; Rua dos Arcos 24, Lapa)

Internet Resources

www.ipanema.com Dubbed 'the insider's guide to Rio,' this website has excellent up-to-date city info.

www.riodejaneiro-turismo.com.br Riotur's comprehensive website, in Portuguese and English.

Laundry

A drop-off, wash-and-fold service costs around R$15 per load.

Laundromat (Map pp140-1; Rua Barata Ribeiro 181B, Copacabana) Across from the metro station.

Laundromat (Map pp140-1; Av NS de Copacabana 1226, Copacabana)

Media

Rio's main daily papers are *Jornal do Brasil* (www.jbonline.com.br) and *O Globo* (www.globo.com.br). Both have entertainment and event listings, particularly strong on Thursday and Sunday. The national publication *Veja* has a *Veja Rio* insert, which details weekly entertainment options (it comes out on Sunday).

Medical Services

There are scores of pharmacies in town, a number of which stay open 24 hours, including two branches of **Drogaria Pacheco** Av NS de Copacabana 115 (Map pp140-1; Av NS de Copacabana 115, Copacabana; ✸ 24hr); Av NS de Copacabana 534 (Map pp140-1; Av NS de Copacabana 534, Copacabana; ✸ 24hr); Rua Visconde de Pirajá (Map pp138-9; Rua Visconde de Pirajá, Ipanema) and **Farmácia do Leme** (Map pp140-1; Av Prado Júnior 231, Copacabana; ✸ 24hr). Meanwhile, in Leblon, **Farmácia Piauí** (Map pp138-9; ☎ 2274 8448; Av Ataulfo de Paiva 1283, Leblon; ✸ 24hr) also stays open 24 hours.

For medical emergencies visit one of the following:

Hospital Ipanema (Map pp138-9; ☎ 3111 2300; Rua Antônio Parreiras 67, Ipanema)

Miguel Couto Hospital (Map pp138-9; ☎ 2274 2121; Av Bartolomeu Mitre 1108, Gávea)

Money

ATMs can be found throughout the city. Banco do Brasil, Bradesco, Citibank and HSBC are the best banks to try when using a debit or credit card. Even though many ATMs advertise 24-hour service, these '24 hours' usually fall between 6am and 10pm. On Sundays and holidays, ATM access ends at 3pm. Money changing is speedier at *casas de câmbio* (exchange offices) than at banks. At the **airport**, international ATMs and money exchange are located on the 3rd floor of arrivals.

CENTRO

A number of exchange offices can be found on either side of Av Rio Branco, several blocks north of Av Presidente Vargas. Other options include the following, located on Map pp144-5:

Banco 24 Horas (near Ave Rio Branco) ATM outside Carioca metro stop.

Banco do Brasil (Rua Senador Dantas 105) ATM on 1st floor, money exchange on 2nd fl.

Casa Aliança (☎ 2224 4617; Rua Miguel Couto 35C) ✸ 9am-5:30pm) A recommended *câmbio*.

Citibank (Rua da Assembléia 100) Has ATM and money exchange.

HSBC (Praça Floriano 23) ATM.

COPACABANA

Câmbios can be found on Av NS de Copacabana, right near the Copacabana Palace hotel. The following places are also on the main streets of Copacabana; see Map pp140-1.

American Express (Av Atlântica 1702, Copacabana) The usual Amex services.

Banco do Brasil (Av NS de Copacabana 1292) ATM.

Banco do Brasil (Av NS de Copacabana 594) Money exchange.

Casa Universal (Av NS de Copacabana 371) A recommended *câmbio*.

Citibank (Av NS de Copacabana 828) ATM.

HSBC (Av Princesa Isabel 186) ATM.

IPANEMA

Find other *câmbios* scattered along Rua Visconde de Pirajá, west of Praça NS de Paz.

Citibank (Map pp138-9; Rua Visconde de Pirajá 459A, Ipanema) ATM and money exchange.

Post

Most *correios* (post offices) open from 8am to 6pm Monday to Friday, and on Saturday until noon. Any mail addressed to Posta Restante, Rio de Janeiro, Brazil, ends up at the **main post office** (Map pp144-5; Rua Primeiro de Março 64, Centro).

Other branches include the following:

Botafogo post office (Map pp142-3; Praia de Botafogo 324, Botafogo)

Copacabana post office (Map pp140-1; Av NS de Copacabana 540, Copacabana)

Ipanema post office (Map pp138-9; Rua Prudente de Morais 147, Ipanema)

Telephone

For local telephone calls – and other calls within Brazil – you will need to buy a *cartão telefônico* (phone card; R$5 to R$20). These cards are available from newsstands and street vendors. See p707 for more info. Many internet cafés offer an international calling service, and Skype is also widely available.

Central Fone (Map pp138-9; Rua Teixeira de Melo 47, Ipanema; ✸ 9:30am-9:30pm)

Fone Rio (Map pp140-1; Rua Constante Ramos 22, Copacabana; ✸ 9am-midnight)

Locutório (Map pp140-1; Av NS de Copacabana 1171, Copacabana; ✸ 8-2am)

Tele Rede (Map pp140-1; Av NS de Copacabana 209A, Copacabana; ✸ 8-2am)

Central Fone (Map pp144-5; basement level, Av Rio Branco 156, Centro; ✸ 9am-9pm Mon-Fri, 10am-4pm Sat)

Tourist Information

Riotur is Rio's tourism agency. It has a tourist information hot line called **Alô Rio** (☎ toll-free in Brazil 0800-285 0555, 2542 8080; ⏲ 9am-6pm). The helpful receptionists speak English. Riotur's useful multilingual website, www.riodejaneiro-turismo.com.br, is also a good source of information.

All of the Riotur offices distribute maps and the excellent (and updated) quarterly *Rio Guide*, listing the major events of the season. The **Riotur Centro** (Map pp144-5; ☎ 2588 9134; 9th fl, Rua Assembléia 10, Centro; ⏲ 9am-6pm Mon-Fri) is the best office for obtaining information. English-speaking staff are always on hand, and they'll call around for you to find a hotel if you show up without a reservation. There is a second branch in **Copacabana** (Map pp140-1; ☎ 2541 7522; Av Princesa Isabel 183, Copacabana; ⏲ 9am-6pm Mon-Fri). At the tourist offices, you can also pick up a **Riopass** (www.riopass.com), a free discount card launched in 2007 that gives 5% to 15% off certain shops and restaurants.

Riotur also has the following information booths:

Aeroporto Galeão (Map p137; Arrival Terminals 1 & 2; ⏲ 6am-midnight;)

Rodoviária Novo Rio (Map pp146-7; Av Francisco Bicalho, São Cristóvão; ⏲ 8am-8pm)

Travel Agencies

American Express (Map pp140-1; ☎ 2548 2148; Av Atlântica 1702, Copacabana CEP 20040; ⏲ 9am-5:30pm Mon-Fri)

Andes Sol (Map pp140-1; ☎ 2275 4370; Av NS de Copacabana 209, Copacabana) A good multilingual agency.

Casa Aliança (Map pp144-5; ☎ 2224 4617; casaalianca@casaalianca.com.br; Rua Miguel Couto 35C, Centro; ⏲ 9am-5:30pm)

G Brazil (Map pp138-9; ☎ 2247 4431; www.gbrazil.com; Suite 303, Rua Farme de Amoedo 76, Ipanema) Rio's gay specialist.

Le Bon Voyage (Map pp144-5; ☎ 2287 4403; lebonvoyage@hotmail.com; Rua Visconde de Pirajá 82, Ipanema)

DANGERS & ANNOYANCES

Rio is indeed a crime-ridden city. But if you travel sensibly when visiting, you will likely suffer nothing worse than a few bad hangovers. All the same, theft is not uncommon, and you should do what you can to minimize the risks of getting robbed.

Buses are well-known targets for thieves. Avoid taking them after dark, and keep an eye out while you're on them. Take taxis at night to avoid walking along empty streets, and never walk on the beach at night. Centro, which is deserted in the evening and on weekends, should only be explored during weekdays.

Purse- and bag-snatching is extremely common on the beaches of Copacabana and Ipanema, where thieves work with lightning speed. Always keep an eye on your stuff and don't take anything of value to the beach. Unfortunately, armed robberies are on the rise and have occurred on the streets of Lapa, Santa Teresa and Copacabana (where 40% of the city's tourist robberies occur).

Maracanã Football Stadium is worth a visit, but take only spending money for the day and avoid the crowded sections. Don't wander into the *favelas* unless you're with a guide who really knows the area.

If you have the misfortune of being robbed, slowly hand over the goods. Thieves in the city are only too willing to use their weapons.

Scams

A common beach scam is for one thief to approach you from one side and ask you for a light or the time. While you're distracted, the thief's partner grabs your gear from the other side.

SIGHTS

The once mighty 'capital of the Brazilian empire' (as one Portuguese king called it), Rio has much more than just pretty beaches. From the bohemian lanes of old Santa Teresa to the village-like charm of Urca, Rio's colonial streets, magnificent churches and leafy plazas provide urban wanderers with days of exploration. Its lake (Lagoa Rodrigo de Freitas), the lush Jardim Botânico (Botanical Gardens) and the Atlantic rain forest still trimming many parts of the city make for idyllic retreats after discovering its historic center. There are also the fantastic overlooks from Pão de Açúcar (Sugarloaf) and Cristo Redentor (Christ the Redeemer), tranquil islands in the bay, wildly beautiful beaches to the west, and vibrant markets, with vendors peddling everything from vintage bossa records to tangy *jabuticaba* (a native fruit).

Ipanema & Leblon

Truly among the world's most enchanting addresses, Ipanema and Leblon are blessed with a magnificent beach and open-air cafés,

A VISIONARY PLAN FOR A TROUBLED STATE

In Brazil, where it's business-as-usual in many public offices, Sérgio Cabral, the 44-year-old newly elected governor of Rio brings a bold new vision to the state.

One of Cabral's role models is former New York City mayor Rudolph Giuliani, whose 'zero tolerance' crime policies are often credited with cleaning up the city. Cabral has promised to root out corruption in the police force and bring reform to a justice system of short sentences, rampant inefficiencies and often bribed officials. He plans to build more prisons to alleviate the overcrowding that stigmatizes the Brazilian penal system.

Cabral seems determined. He has already moved some of the most dangerous criminals from local prisons to a new facility in another state, where their influence and means of communicating with gang leaders will be compromised. In his first four months in office, he fired more than 100 police officers and has said that perhaps as many as 10,000 of Rio's military police are corrupt.

Cabral plans to bring new roads and city services into *favelas*, hoping to break the stranglehold gangs have on communities there. He has jumpstarted a family-planning program in poor neighborhoods, making condoms and the pill more widely available.

Critics of Cabral's 'tough-on-crime' approach say it's the same message that's been tried and has failed in the past. Whether Cabral brings meaningful change to Rio will undoubtedly play out on city streets in the coming years.

bars and restaurants scattered along tree-lined streets. This is Rio's premier zip code and favored stomping ground for wealthy Cariocas, young and old, gay and straight.

Ipanema acquired international fame in the early '60s as the home of the bossa nova character 'The Girl from Ipanema.' It became the hangout of artists, intellectuals and wealthy liberals, who frequented the sidewalk cafés and bars. After the 1964 military coup and the resulting crackdown on liberals, many of these bohemians were forced into exile. During the '70s, Leblon became the nightlife center of Rio. The restaurants and bars of Baixo (Lower) Leblon, on Av Ataulfo de Paiva, between Ruas Aristídes Espínola and General Artigas, were the meeting points for a new generation of artists and musicians. Evenings continue to be very animated here today, even though the heart of Rio's nightlife has moved to Lapa.

IPANEMA & LEBLON BEACHES

Although the beaches of Ipanema and Leblon (Map pp138–9) are really one long beach, the *postos* (posts) along them subdivide the beach into areas as diverse as the city itself. **Posto 9**, right off Rua Vinícius de Moraes, is **Garota de Ipanema**, which is where Rio's most lithe and tanned bodies tend to migrate. The area is also known as the **Cemetério dos Elefantes** because of the old leftists, hippies and artists who hang out there. The beach in front of Rua Farme de Amoedo, also called **Bolsa de Valores** and **Crystal Palace**, is the gay section, while **Posto 8**

is mostly the domain of *favela* kids. **Arpoador**, between Ipanema and Copacabana, is Rio's most popular surf spot, while Leblon attracts a broad mix of Cariocas.

Whatever spot you choose, you'll enjoy cleaner sands and sea than those found in neighboring Copacabana. Keep in mind that if you go on Saturday or Sunday, it gets very crowded. Incidentally, the word *ipanema* is Indian for 'bad, dangerous waters' – an apt description given the strong undertow and often oversized waves crashing on the shore. Be careful, and swim only where the locals do.

A few fishermen, casting out to sea, mingle with couples admiring the view from the lookout known as **Mirante do Leblon**, at the west end of Leblon Beach, stretching down Leblon and Ipanema Beaches.

MUSEU H STERN

The headquarters of H Stern, the famous jeweler, contains the **Museu H Stern** (Map pp138–9; ☎ 2274 3447; www.hstern.com.br in Portuguese; Rua Garcia D'Ávila 113; admission free; ⏰ 8:30am-6pm Mon-Fri, to noon Sat), an interesting fine-jewelry museum.

If you're in the market for it, the adjoining store has an array of finely crafted jewelry, watches and other accessories for sale.

MUSEU AMSTERDAM SAUER

Next door to Museu H Stern, the **Museu Amsterdam Sauer** (Map pp138–9; ☎ 2512 1132; www .amsterdamsauer.com; Rua Garcia D'Ávila 105; admission free; ⏰ 9:30am-2:30pm Mon-Fri, 10am-2pm Sat) also houses an impressive collection of precious stones – over 3000 items in all. It also has two life-size replicas of mines.

Like H Stern, the Amsterdam Sauer store is the place to lay down some serious cash if you're looking for precious gems or well-made accessories.

Gávea, Jardim Botânico & Lagoa

Beginning just north of Ipanema and Leblon, these well-heeled neighborhoods front the Lagoa Rodrigo de Freitas, a picturesque saltwater lagoon ringed with a walking/biking trail and dotted with lakeside kiosks serving cuisine alfresco and live music on warm nights. The other big draw here is the royal garden (Jardim Botânico) that gave the neighborhood its name. Here you'll find stately palms, rare orchids and colorful flowering plants. Aside from its natural attractions, these neighborhoods have some excellent restaurants, trendy bars, a planetarium and the city's horseracing track.

JARDIM BOTÂNICO

The exotic **Jardim Botânico** (Map pp138-9; ☎ 3874 1808; www.jbrj.gov.br; Rua Jardim Botânico 920, Jardim Botânico; admission R$4; ☻ 8am-5pm), housing over 5000 varieties of plant, was designed by order of the Prince Regent Dom João in 1808. It's quiet and serene on weekdays and blossoms with families and music on weekends. A pleasant outdoor café overlooks the gardens.

LAGOA RODRIGO DE FREITAS

One of the city's most picturesque spots, **Lagoa Rodrigo de Freitas** (Map pp138-9) is encircled by a 7.2km cycling/walking path. Bikes are available for hire (R$16 per hour) near **Parque Brigadeiro Faria Lima**, as are paddle boats (R$25 per half hour). For those who prefer *caipirinhas* (drinks made from sugarcane spirit, crushed lime, sugar and ice) to plastic swan boats, the kiosks on either side of the lake offer food and drinks, often accompanied by live music.

PARQUE DA CATACUMBA

Brazil's first outdoor sculptural garden, **Parque da Catacumba** (Map pp138-9; Av Epitácio Pessoa, Lagoa; ☻ 8am-7pm) sits atop the Morro dos Cabritos, which rises from the Lagoa Rodrigo de Freitas. During the summer, Catacumba often hosts free Sunday-afternoon concerts in its outdoor amphitheater.

SUNDAY SUNNY SUNDAY

Many museums in Rio are free on Sunday, making it a good day to pack in your sightseeing. If the weather is simply too lovely for staying indoors, head to the shore. Sunday is also the day when the beachfront road running from Leblon to Leme closes to traffic. Cyclists, joggers and skaters fill the seaside lanes; further north, the road through Parque do Flamengo also closes to traffic.

PARQUE LAGE

Beautiful **Parque Lage** (Map pp138-9; ☎ 2527 2397; www.eavparquelage.org.br; Rua Jardim Botânico 414, Jardim Botânico; ☻ 8am-5pm) has English-style gardens, little lakes and the **Escola de Artes Visuais** (School of Visual Arts), which often hosts art exhibitions and an occasional performance. A lovely café lies on the grounds.

PARQUE DA CIDADE & MUSEU HISTÓRICO DA CIDADE

The 19th-century mansion on the lovely grounds of the **Parque da Cidade** (Map pp138-9; admission free; ☻ 7am-6pm) now houses the **Museu Histórico da Cidade** (City History Museum; ☎ 2512 2353; Estrada de Santa Marinha 505, Gávea; admission R$6; ☻ 11am-5pm Tue-Sun), which portrays Rio from its founding in 1565 to the mid-20th century. The museum also has exhibitions of furniture, porcelain, photographs and paintings by well-known artists.

INSTITUTO MOREIRA SALLES

The beautiful **Instituto Moreira Salles** (Map p137; ☎ 3284 7400; www.ims.com.br in Portuguese; Rua Marquês de Sao Vicente 476, Gávea; admission free; ☻ 1-8pm Tue-Sun), next to the Parque da Cidade, contains an archive of more than 80,000 photographs, many portraying old streets of Rio. The gardens, complete with artificial lake and flowing river, were designed by Brazilian landscape architect Burle Marx. There's also a craft shop and a café serving lunch and afternoon tea.

PLANETÁRIO

Gávea's stellar attraction, the **Planetário** (Planetarium; Map pp138-9; ☎ 3523 4040; www.rio.rj.gov.br/planetario in Portuguese; Av Padre Leonel Franca 240, Gávea; admission R$6; ☻ 10am-6pm Tue-Sun, 3-7pm

(Continued on page 148)

JUDY BELLAH

On the descent from Cristo Redentor
(p150), high on Corcovado mountain

Cariocas unwind on Ipanema Beach (p127)

JOHN MAIER JR

Serene views of Pão de Açúcar (p149) and Baía de Guanabara (p156)

JOHN PENNOCK

JOHN MAIER JR

All ages welcome at the Carnaval parades, Sambódromo (p118), Rio de Janeiro

JOHN MAIER JR

The *bonde* (p154) rattling over the Arcos do Lapa

Opposite:
A riot of color at Carnaval, Rio de Janeiro (p114)
JOHN MAIER JR

Cruising past *posto* 9, Ipanema (p127)

JOHN MAIER JR

Heading out from Búzios' beaches (p217)

KATHLEEN MUNNELLY

TOM COCKREM

Colonial relic turned craft shop, Paraty (p193), Rio de Janeiro state

Dawn breaks over Capela de NS das Dores (p194) and Matriz NS dos Remédios (p194), Paraty, Rio state

JOHN PEN

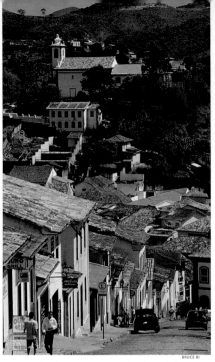

Stepping back in time, Ouro Prêto (p241), Minas Gerais

All aboard the 'Smoking Mary' (p257) steam train, Tiradentes railway station

JOHN PENNOCK

The heart of Ouro Prêto: Praça Tiradentes (p242) and the Museum da Inconfidência (p244)

BRUCE BI

KATHLEEN MUN...

São Paulo's Theatro Municipal (p281) in all its splendor

Architectural genius reflected at the Memorial da América Latina (p286), São Paulo

ALFREDO MAIQUEZ

GUY MO...

Potatoes and everything else under the sun – for sale at São Paulo's street markets (p300)

KATHLEEN MUNNELLY

Lagoa da Conceição (p340) and surrounds on the Ilha de Santa Catarina, Santa Catarina

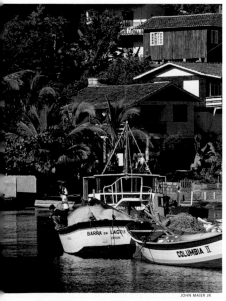

JOHN MAIER JR

Colorful fishing boats anchor down in Florianópolis (p334), Santa Catarina

The Iguaçu River puts on a dramatic show at Garganta do Diablo (p326), Iguaçu Falls

JOHN PENNOCK

136

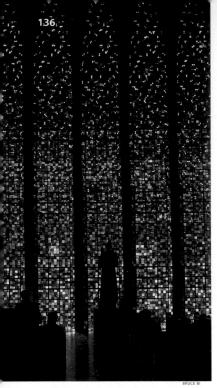

The celestial inner sanctum of the Santuário Dom Bosco (p377), Brasília

Catedral Metropolitana (p376) in Brasília – the futuristic capital of Brazil

Congresso Nacional (p377) lit up at night, Brasília

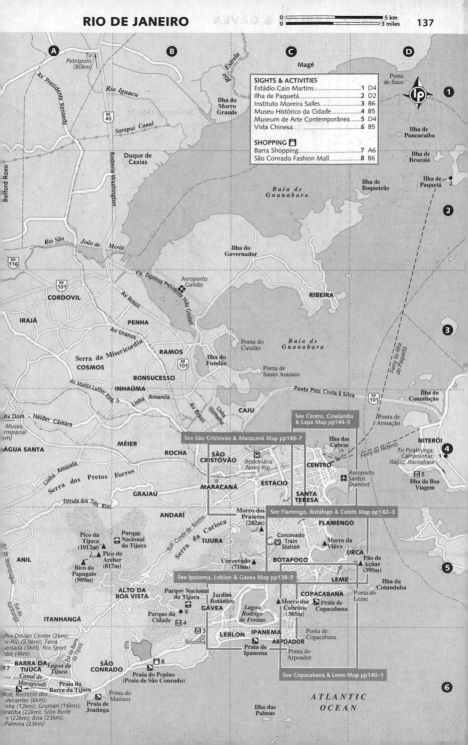

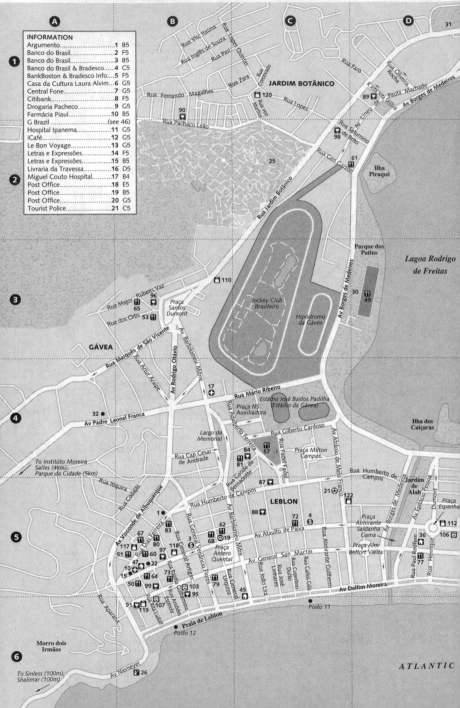

Rua Visc Itaúna
Rua Inglês de Souza
Rua Lopes Quintas
Rua Peri
Rua Corcovado
Rua Faro
Rua Oliveira Rocha
31
Rua Zara
JARDIM BOTÂNICO
Rua Paula Machado
Av Borges de Medeiros
Rua Fernando Magalhães
120
Rua vPr Martins
Rua Lopes
89
R João de Barro
L'neu de
Rua Saturnina
90
98
de Brito
Rua Pacheco Leão
61
Rua Gen Garzon
25
Ilha Piraquê
Rua Jardim Botânico
110
Parque dos Patins
Lagoa Rodrigo de Freitas
Jockey Club Brasileiro
30
49
Rua Major Rubens Vaz
96
Praça Santos Dumont
65
Rua dos Oitis
53
GÁVEA
Hipódromo da Gávea
Av Borges de Medeiros
Rua Marquês de São Vicente
Rua Artur Araripe
Av Rodrigo Otávio
Av Bartolomeu Mitre
17
Rua Mário Ribeiro
Estádio José Bastos Padilha (Estádio da Gávea)
Praça NS Auxiliadora
32
Av Padre Leonel Franca
Rua Adalberto Ferreira
Rua Gilberto Cardoso
Ilha dos Caiçaras
Largo da Memória
84
81
57
Praça Milton Campos
Av Alfaia de Melo Franco
Rua Cap Cesar de Andrade
To Institúto Moreira Salles (4km); Parque da Cidade (5km)
Rua Conde de Bernadotte
87
Rua Humberto de Campos
Rua Itiquira
Rua Codajá
21
122
Jardim de Alah
Rua Humberto de Campos
LEBLON
Praça Espanha
Av Visconde de Albuquerque
1
Rua General Venâncio Flores
88
72
4
112
67
83
62
3
68
Av Ataulfo de Paiva
Praça Almirante Saldanha Gama
36
106
117
80
97
Praça Antero Quental
Av Borges de Medeiros
Rua Paul Redfern
77
51
60
118
Av Epitácio Pessoa
Rua General Artigas
Rua Bartolomeu Mitre
47
22
Av General San Martín
Praça Alm Belfort Vieira
Rua Henrique
10
73
64
Rua João Lira
Rua José Linhares
Rua Cupertino Durão
Rua Carlos Góis
50
99
79
Rua General Urquiza
45
Av Delfim Moreira
91
103
119
107
95
Posto 11
Rua Aperana
Rua Lúdio
Praia de Leblon
Posto 12
Morro dois Irmãos
ATLANTIC
To Sinless (100m); Shalimar (100m)
Av Niemeyer
26

0 ___ 500 m
0 ___ 0.3 miles

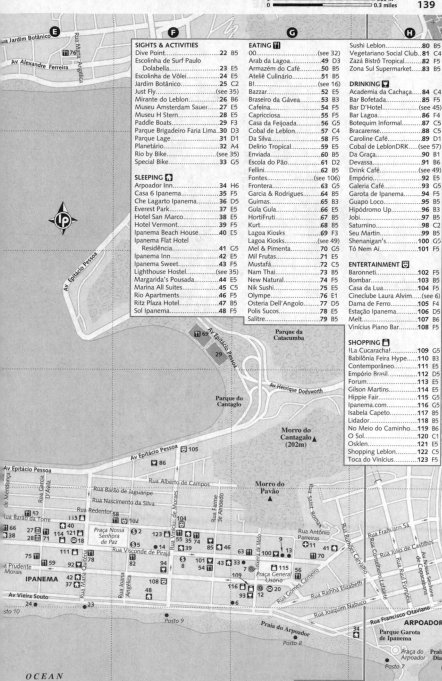

SIGHTS & ACTIVITIES
Dive Point.................................22 B5
Escolinha de Surf Paulo
　Dolabella.............................23 E5
Escolinha de Vôlei...................24 E5
Jardim Botânico........................25 C2
Just Fly...............................(see 35)
Mirante do Leblon.....................26 B6
Museu Amsterdam Sauer....27 E5
Museu H Stern...........................28 E5
Paddle Boats............................29 F3
Parque Brigadeiro Faria Lima...30 D3
Parque Lage..............................31 D1
Planetário................................32 A4
Rio by Bike..........................(see 35)
Special Bike............................33 G5

SLEEPING
Arpoador Inn...........................34 H6
Casa 6 Ipanema........................35 F5
Che Lagarto Ipanema.............36 D5
Everest Park...............................37 F5
Hotel San Marco.......................38 E5
Hotel Vermont..........................39 F5
Ipanema Beach House.............40 E5
Ipanema Flat Hotel
　Residência.............................41 G5
Ipanema Inn.............................42 E5
Ipanema Sweet..........................43 E5
Lighthouse Hostel.................(see 35)
Margarida's Pousada...............44 E5
Marina All Suites.......................45 C5
Rio Apartments........................46 F5
Ritz Plaza Hotel........................47 B5
Sol Ipanema.............................48 F5

EATING
OO............................(see 32)
Arab da Lagoa.........................49 D3
Armazém do Café....................50 B5
Ateliê Culinário........................51 B5
B!...(see 16)
Bazzar......................................52 E5
Braseiro da Gávea...................53 B3
Cafeína.....................................54 F5
Capricciosa...............................55 F5
Casa da Feijoada......................56 E5
Cobal de Leblon........................57 C4
Da Silva....................................58 F5
Delírio Tropical.........................59 E5
Enviada.....................................60 B5
Escola do Pão..........................61 D2
Fellini.......................................62 B5
Fontes...................................(see 106)
Frontera...................................63 G5
Garcia & Rodrigues.................64 B5
Guimas.....................................65 B3
Gula Gula................................66 E5
HortiFruti..................................67 B5
Kurt..68 B5
Lagoa Kiosks.............................69 F3
Lagoa Kiosks.........................(see 49)
Mel & Pimenta.........................70 G5
Mil Frutas.................................71 E5
Mustafá....................................72 C5
Nam Thai..................................73 B5
New Natural.............................74 E5
Nik Sushi..................................75 B5
Olympe.....................................76 E1
Osteria Dell'Angolo..................77 D5
Polis Sucos...............................78 E5
Salitre......................................79 B5

Sushi Leblon............................80 B5
Vegetariano Social Club.........81 C4
Zazá Bistrô Tropical................82 F5
Zona Sul Supermarket............83 B5

DRINKING
Academia da Cachaça.............84 C4
Bar Bofetada............................85 F5
Bar D'Hotel...........................(see 45)
Bar Lagoa.................................86 F4
Botequim Informal..................87 C5
Bracarense...............................88 C5
Caroline Café...........................89 D1
Cobal de LeblonDRK............(see 57)
Da Graça..................................90 B1
Devassa....................................91 B6
Drink Café.............................(see 49)
Empório....................................92 E5
Galeria Café.............................93 G5
Garota de Ipanema..................94 F5
Guapo Loco.............................95 F5
Hipódromo Up.........................96 B3
Jobi...97 B5
Saturnino.................................98 C2
Seu Martin...............................99 B5
Shenanigan's.........................100 G5
Tó Nem Aí..............................101 F5

ENTERTAINMENT
Baronneti................................102 F5
Bombar....................................103 B5
Casa da Lua............................104 E5
Cineclube Laura Alvim........(see 6)
Dama de Ferro........................105 F4
Estação Ipanema....................106 D5
Melt...107 B6
Vinícius Piano Bar..................108 F5

SHOPPING
¡La Cucaracha!.......................109 G5
Babilônia Feira Hype..............110 B3
Contemporâneo.......................111 E5
Empório Brasil........................112 D5
Forum......................................113 E5
Gilson Martins........................114 E5
Hippie Fair..............................115 G5
Ipanema.com..........................116 E5
Isabela Capeto.......................117 B5
Lidador....................................118 E5
No Meio do Caminho..............119 B6
O Sol.......................................120 C1
Osklen.....................................121 E5
Shopping Leblon....................122 C5
Toca do Vinícius.....................123 F5

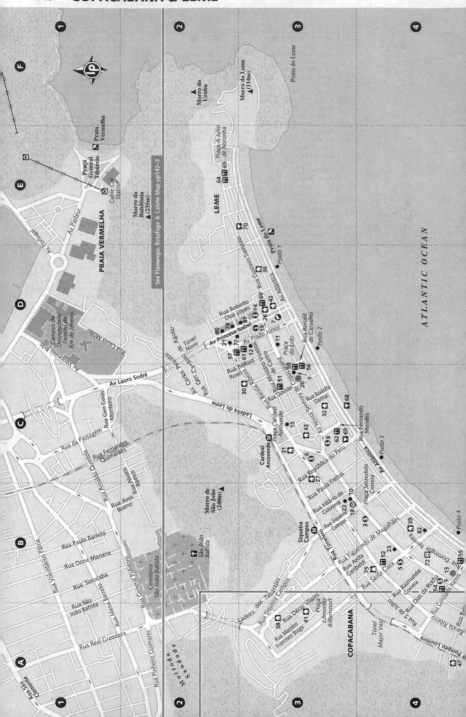

0 — 500 m
0 — 0.3 miles

INFORMATION

American Express	(see 32)
Andes Sol	1 C3
Banco do Brasil	2 A5
Banco do Brasil	3 B4
Bradesco ATM	4 A5
Bradesco ATM	5 B4
Bradesco ATM	6 C3
Canadian Consulate	7 D3
Casa Universal	8 C3
Citibank	9 B4
Drogaria Pacheco	10 B3
Drogaria Pacheco	11 D3
Farmácia do Leme	12 D3
Fone Rio	13 B4
HSBC	14 D3
Laundromat	15 C3
Laundromat	16 A6
Locutório	17 A5
Post Office	18 B3
Riotur	19 D3
Tele Rede	20 C3

SIGHTS & ACTIVITIES

Ciclovia	21 D2
Clube Excursionista Carioca	22 B3
Instituto Brasil-Estados Unidos	23 B4
Museu Histórico do Exército e Forte de Copacabana	24 B6
Zaga Bike	25 A5

SLEEPING

Acapulco	26 D3
Apa Hotel	27 C3
Atlantis Copacabana	28 A6
Blame It On Rio 4 Travel	29 B5
Copacabana Holiday	30 C3
Copacabana Hotel Residência	31 C3
Copacabana Palace	32 C3
Copacabana Praia Hotel	33 A6
Design Hotel Portinari	34 A6
Ducasse Rio Hotel	35 A5
Fantastic Rio	36 D3
Hotel Debret	37 A5
Hotel Santa Clara	38 A3
Hotel Toledo	39 B4
Hotel Vilamar	40 A5
Jucati	41 A3
Le Meridien	42 D3
Mellow Yellow Hostel	43 C3
Orla Copacabana	44 B6
Parthenon Arpoador	45 B6
Residencial Apart	46 A6
Rio Backpackers	47 A4
Rio Guesthouse	48 A6
Yvonne Reimann	49 B6

EATING

Amir	50 C3
Azumi	51 C3
Bakers	52 B4
Botequim Informal	53 B5
Caféina	54 B4
Capricciosa	55 B4
Carretão	56 C3
Cervantes	57 D2
Confeitaria Colombo	58 B6
Copa Café	59 B5
Galeria 1618	60 D3
HortiFruti	61 D3
La Trattoria	62 C3
Le Blé Noir	63 A5
Marius	64 E2
Marius Crustáceos	65 E2
Siri Mole	66 A6
Yonza	67 A5

DRINKING

Allegro Bistrô Musical	(see 75)
Bar Luiz	68 C3
Copacabana Palace Poolside Bar	(see 32)
Manoel & Juaquim	69 C3
Sindicato do Chopp	70 E3

ENTERTAINMENT

Bip Bip	71 A5
Espaço Sesc	72 B4
La Girl	(see 73)
Le Boy	73 A6

SHOPPING

Galeria River	74 A6
Modern Sound	75 B4
Top Sound	76 A5

TRANSPORT

Actual	77 D2
American Airlines	(see 32)
Avis	78 D2
Ciclovia	79 B6
Hertz	80 D2
Localiza	81 D3
United Airlines Office	82 B4

See Ipanema, Leblon & Gávea Map pp138-9

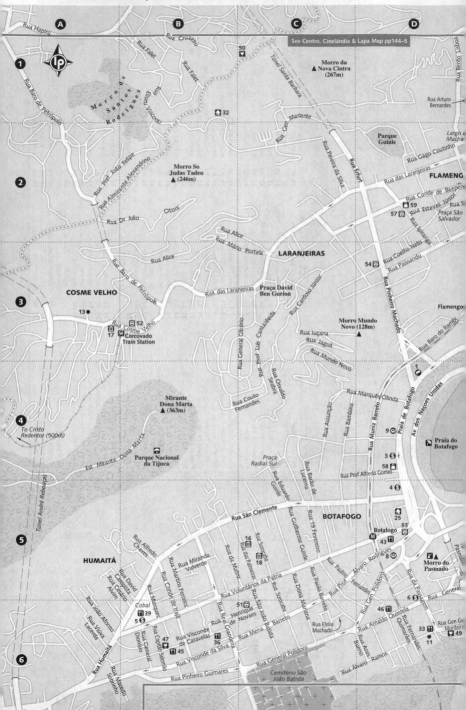

See Centro, Cinelândia & Lapa Map pp144–5

Rua Hapiru

Rua Cruzeiro

Rua Falet

Rua Falet

Morro de
Santos
Rodriguez

Morro da
Nova Cintra
(267m)

Rua Arturo
Bernardes

Largo
Macha

Rua Baro de Petrópolis

Rua Prof. João Felipe

Rua Almirante Alexandrino

Elisa Visconti

Rua Cier Mariante

Rua Pereira da Silva

Rua Erfurt

Parque
Guine

Rua Gago Coutinho

Rua das Laranjeiras

FLAMENG

Morro So
Judas Tadeu
(246m)

Otoni

Rua Dr. Julio

Rua Alice

Rua Mário Portela

Rua Conde de Baepen

Rua Esteves Júnior

Rua S

Praça São
Salvador

LARANJEIRAS

Rua Alice

Rua Baro de Petrópolis

Rua das Laranjeiras

Praça David
Ben Gurion

Rua Cardoso Júnior

Rua Coelho Neto

Rua Paissandu

COSME VELHO

Rua General Glicério

Rua Prof. Luis Cantanheda

Morro Mundo
Novo (128m)

Flamengo

Rua Cosme Velho

Corcovado
Train Station

Rua Juçana

Rua Jaguá

Rua Mundo Novo

Rua Baro do Itambi

Rua Osvaldo
Seihra

Rua Pinheiro Machado

Mirante
Dona Marta
(363m)

Rua Couto
Fernandes

Rua Marquês Olinda

To Cristo
Redentor (500m)

Est. Mirante Dona Marta

Parque Nacional
da Tijuca

Rua Assunção

Rua Bambina

Praia de Botafogo

Av. dos Nações Unidas

Praia do
Botafogo

Praça
Radial Sul

Rua Muniz Barreto

Rua Prof. Alfredo Gomes

Túnel André Rebouças

Rua São Clemente

Rua Barão de
Lucerna

BOTAFOGO

Botafogo

Rua Alfredo
Chaves

Rua Guilherme Guinle

Rua 19 Fevereiro

Morro do
Pasmado

HUMAITÁ

Rua Miranda
Valverde

Rua da Matriz

Rua das Palmeiras

Rua David
Campista

Rua Osório
Alvim

Rua Martins Ferreira

Rua Conde de Irajá

Rua Sorocaba

Rua Voluntários da Pátria

Rua Paulino

Rua Paulo Barreto

Rua Prof. Fernandes

Rua Álvaro Rodrigues

Rua Gen. Polidoro

Rua General

Rua Humaitá

Rua João Afonso

Rua Viúva
Lacerda

Cobal

Rua General
Dionisio

Rua Capitão Salomão

Rua Visconde
de Caravelas

Rua Henrique
de Novaes

Rua Visconde da Silva

Rua João Batista

Rua Mena Barreto

Rua Elvira
Machado

Rua Arnaldo Quintela

Rua Fernandes
Guimarães

Rua Gen G
Monteiro

Rua Nascido
Sobrinho

Rua Pinheiro Guimarães

Rua General Polidoro

Rua Álvaro Ramos

Rua Assis

Rua Bueno

Cemitério São
João Batista

Rua Dona Mariana

50

32

59

57

54

13

52

17

9

3

4

1

25

53

58

43

8

16

18

51

39

5

47

45

36

46

33

11

49

6

INFORMATION

Argentinian Embassy	**1** D4
Banco do Brasil	**2** E1
Banco do Brasil	**3** D4
Bradesco ATM	**4** D5
Bradesco ATM	**5** B6
Bradesco ATM	**6** D5
Eurogames	**7** E1
Livraria PrefácioINF	(see 43)
Post Office	**8** D5
Post Office	**9** D4
UK Embassy	**10** E2

SIGHTS & ACTIVITIES

Casa de Dança Carlinhos de Jesus	**11** D6
Centro Cultural Telemar	**12** E2
Largo do Boticário	**13** A3
Museu Carmen Miranda	**14** E4
Museu da República	(see 19)
Museu de Folclórico Edson Carneiro	**15** E1
Museu do Índio	**16** C5
Museu Internacional de Arte Naïf do Brasil	**17** A3
Museu Villa-Lobos	**18** C5
Palácio do Catete	**19** E1
Pão de Açúcar	**20** H5
Parque do Catete	**21** E1
Parque do Flamengo	**22** D2
Pista Cláudio Coutinho	**23** G5
Trilharte Ecoturismo	**24** E2

SLEEPING

El Misti Hostel	**25** D5
Hotel Caxambu	**26** E1
Hotel Ferreira Viana	**27** E1
Hotel Monterrey	**28** D1
Hotel Riazor	**29** E1
Imperial Hotel	**30** E1
Mengo Palace Hotel	**31** E1
Pousada Favelinha	**32** B1

EATING

Adega do Valentim	**33** D6
Armazem do Chopp	**34** E3
Belmonte	**35** E2
Botequim Informal	(see 58)
Carême	**36** B6
Catete Grill	**37** E1
Churrascaria Majórica	**38** E2
Cobal de Humaitá	**39** B6
Estação República	**40** E1
Garota da Urca	**41** G4
Lamas	**42** E2
Livraria Prefácio	**43** D5
Porção Rio's	**44** F3
Stravaganze	**45** B6
Yorubá	**46** D6

DRINKING

Aurora	**47** B6
Bar Urca	**48** G4
Miam Miam	**49** D6
Mike's Haus	**50** C1

ENTERTAINMENT

Casa da Matriz	**51** C6
Clan Café	**52** B3
Espaço Unibanco de Cinema	**53** D5
Fluminense Football Stadium	**54** D3
Praia Vermelha	**55** F6
São Luiz	**56** E2
Severyna	**57** D2

SHOPPING

Botafogo Praia Shopping	**58** D4
Pé de Boi	**59** D2
Rio Sul	**60** E6

TRANSPORT

Buses to Centro or Zona Sul	**61** F5

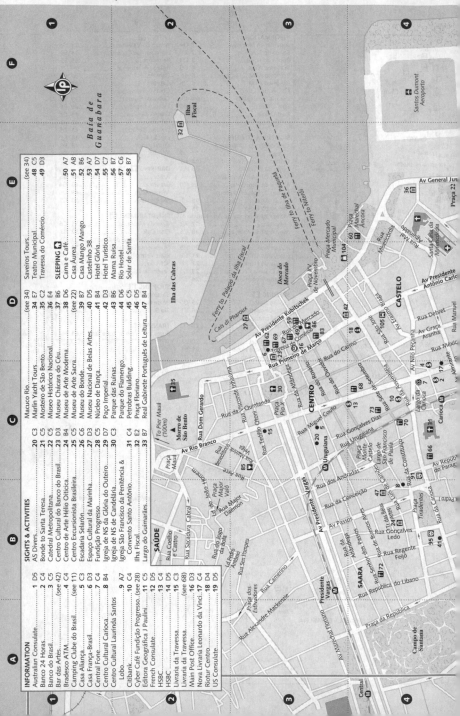

Baía de Guanabara

0 500 m
0 0.3 miles

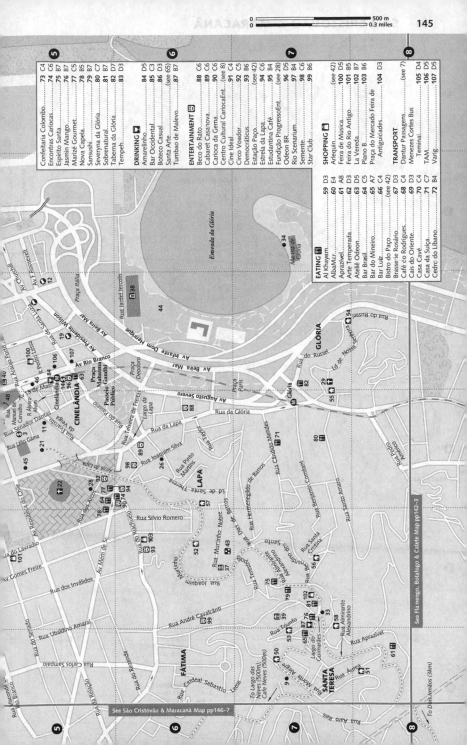

Confeitaria Colombo	73 C4
Encontras Cariocas	74 C6
Espírito Santa	75 B7
Jasmin Mango	76 C5
Marizé Gourmet	77 C5
Nova Capela	78 B5
Sansushi	79 B7
Severyna da Glória	80 C7
Sobrenatural	81 B7
Taberna da Glória	82 D7
Tempeh	83 D3

DRINKING

Amarelinho	84 D5
Bar Occidental	85 C3
Boteco Casual	86 D3
Santa Arte	(see 65)
Tumbao de Malevo	87 B7

ENTERTAINMENT

Beco do Rato	88 C6
Cabaret Casanova	89 C6
Carioca da Gema	90 C6
Centro Cultural CariocaEnt	(see 8)
Cine Ideal	91 C5
Circo Voador	92 C5
Democráticus	93 B6
Estação Paço	(see 42)
Estrela da Lapa	94 C6
Estudantina Café	95 B4
Fundição ProgressoEnt	(see 28)
Odeon BR	96 D5
Rio Scenarium	97 B4
Semente	98 C6
Star Club	99 B6

SHOPPING

Arlequim	(see 42)
Feira de Música	100 D5
Feira do Rio Antigo	101 A8
La Vereda	102 B7
Plano B	103 B6
Praça do Mercado Feira de Antiguicades	104 D3

TRANSPORT

Dantur Passagens	(see 7)
Menezes Cortes Bus Terminal	105 D4
TAM	106 D5
Varig	107 D5

EATING

Al Khayam	59 D3
AlbaMar	60 E4
Aprazível	61 A8
Arte Temperada	62 D3
Ateliê Odeon	63 D5
Bar Brasil	64 C5
Bar do Mineiro	65 A7
Bar Luiz	66 C4
Bistro do Paço	(see 42)
Brasse'e Rosário	67 D3
Café co Rodrigues	68 C4
Cais do Oriente	69 D3
Casa Cavé	70 C7
Casa da Suíça	71 C7
Cedrc do Líbano	72 B4

See São Cristóvão & Maracanã Map pp146–7

See Flamengo, Botafogo & Calete Map pp142–3

To Larga das
Neves (500m);
Café Neves (500m)

To Dhikramos (3km)

INFORMATION

Riotur	(see 3)
Riotur	(see 10)

SIGHTS & ACTIVITIES

Fiera Nordestina	1 C1
Jardim Zoológico	2 A3
Maracanã Football Stadium	3 A4
Museu da Fauna	(see 5)
Museu do Carnaval	4 G4
Museu Nacional	5 B3
Quinta da Boa Vista	6 B3
Sambódromo	7 F3
Sports Museum	(see 3)
Universidade da Pesca	8 D6

DRINKING 🍸

Café Neves	9 G5

TRANSPORT

Rodoviária Novo Rio	10 D1

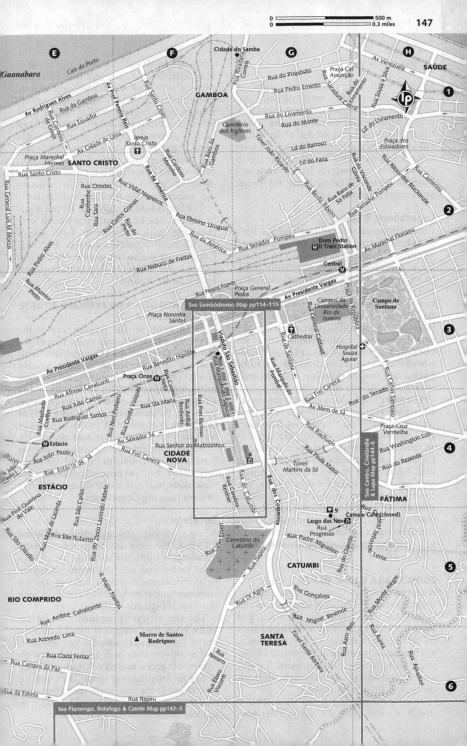

0   500 m
0   0.3 miles

Guanabara

Cais do Porto

Cidade do Samba

GAMBOA

SAÚDE

Av Venezuela

Rua do Propósito

Praça Cel
Assunção

Rua Pedro Ernesto

Av Rodrigues Alves

Rua da Gamboa

Rua Equador

Rua Cordeiro
de Graça

Av Prof Pereira Reis

Rua Santo Cristo

Av Cidade de Lima

Igreja
Santo Cristo

Praça Marechal
Hermes

SANTO CRISTO

Rua do Livamento

Rua do Monte

Cemitério
dos Ingleses

Rua Bão de
So Félix

Túnel João Ricardo

Ld do Barroso

Ld do Faria

Praça dos
Estivadores

Ld do Livramento

Rua Souza e Silva

Rua Camerino

Rua Alexandre Mackenzie

Rua Barão de
Gamboa

Rua Gardoso
Marinho

Rua Santo Cristo

Rua General Luís M Morais

Rua Orestes

Rua Vidal Negreiros

Rua
Capiberibe

Rua Sara

Rua Carlos Gomes

Rua do
Pinto

Rua Ebroíno Uruguai

Rua da América

Rua da América

Rua Senador Pompeu

Rua Senador Pompeu

Rua Bento Ribeiro

Rua Barão de
So Félix

Rua da
Gamboa

Rua Nabuco de Freitas

**Dom Pedro
II Train Station**

Av Marechal Floriano

Rua Pedro Alves

Rua Moreira
Pinto

Rua Pereira Franco

Praça General
Pedra

Av Presidente Vargas

Central

Campus da
Universidade
Rio de
Janeiro

Campo de
Santana

Praça Noronha
Santos

See Sambódromo Map pp114–115

Praça da República

Rua de Santana

Cathedral

Rua Central Caldwell

**Hospital
Souza
Aguiar**

Av Presidente Vargas

Rua Benedito Hipólito

Viaduto São Sebastião

Rua Marquês do Sapucaí

Rua de Santana

Rua Marquês de
Pombal

Rua Frei Caneca

Praça Onze

Rua Neuro

Rua Carmo

Av Mem de Sá

Rua do Senado

Rua Carlos Sampaio

Rua Afonso Cavalcanti

Rua Aníbal
Benévolo

Rua Riachuelo

Praça Cruz
Vermelha

Rua Julio Carmo

Rua Corrêa Vasques

Rua Prés Barroso

Rua Paula Matos

Rua Washington Luís

Rua Machado
Coelho

Rua Sta Maria

Rua Rodrigues Santos

Rua Neri Pinheiro

Av Salvador Sá

Rua do Rezende

Estácio

Rua Senhor do Matozinhos

**CIDADE
NOVA**

Túnel
Martins da Sá

FÁTIMA

Rua João Paulo I

Rua Estácio de Sá

Rua Frei Caneca

Rua Carolina
Reidner

Rua do Catumbi

Rua dos Coqueiros

ESTÁCIO

Rua Prof Quintino
do Vale

Rua São Carlos

Rua Maia de Lacerda

Camã e Café (closed)

Rua
Progresso

Largo das Neves

Rua Maria
José

Rua São Claudio

Rua São Roberto

Rua do Zuco Laurindo Rabelo

Cemitério do
Catumbi

Rua Padre Miguelino

Rua do Oriente

Rua do Leme

Rua Ven Enverri

CATUMBI

Rua Monte Alegre

RIO COMPRIDO

Rua Ambiré Calvalcante

Rua Dr Agra

Rua Gonçalves

Rua Aurea

Rua Azevedo Lima

Morro de Santos
Rodrigues

Rua Miguel Resende

Rua Azro

Rua Costa Ferraz

Rua Navarra

**SANTA
TERESA**

Túnel Santa Bárbara

Rua Campos da Paz

Rua Elibeu
Visconti

Rua Alpeável

Rua da Estrela

Rua Itapiru

Rua Itapiru

See Flamengo, Botafogo & Catete Map pp142–3

See Centro, Cinelândia & Lapa Map pp144–5

(Continued from page 128)

Sat & Sun) features a museum, a *praça dos telescópios* (plaza of telescopes) and two state-of-the-art operating domes, each capable of projecting over 6000 stars on its walls. Several times a week, there are guided observations (R$6 extra), several through the far-reaching telescopes. Periodically, the Planetário plays host to live concerts. Its hypermodern **Museu do Universo** (Universe Museum) houses permanent exhibitions.

Copacabana & Leme

Framed by mountains and deep blue sea, Rio's most beautiful beach curves 4.5km from end to end. No longer a symbol of Rio's glam, Copacabana is a fascinating but chaotic place, its art-deco buildings, aging beachfront hotels and tree-lined sidestreets form the backdrop to a wildly democratic mix of tourists, elderly middle-class Cariocas, and *favela* dwellers (who live in the hillsides surrounding the neighborhood). Despite its faults (crime for one), the neighborhood has its charms – old-school *botecos* (small, open-air bars), eclectic restaurants, vibrant street life, and the handsome beach still entrance some visitors.

The name Copacabana comes from a small Bolivian village on Lake Titicaca. Historians believe a statue of the Virgin Mary (Our Lady of Copacabana) was brought to Rio and consecrated inside a small chapel near Arpoador. Copacabana remained a small fishing village until Túnel Velho opened in 1891, connecting Copacabana with the rest of the city. The construction of the neoclassical Copacabana Palace hotel in 1923 heralded Copacabana's golden era as a tropical getaway for the rich and fabulous. Copacabana remained Rio's gem until the 1970s, when the area began to fall into decline.

COPACABANA & LEME BEACH

A magnificent confluence of land and sea, the long, scalloped beach of Copacabana and Leme (Map pp140–1) always has a flurry of activity stretching its length: overamped footballers singing their team's anthem, Cariocas and tourists lining up for *caipirinhas* at kiosks, *favela* kids showing off their football skills, and beach vendors picking their way through the mass of bronzed bodies.

As in Ipanema, each group stakes out its stretch of sand. Leme is a mix of older residents and *favela* kids, while the area between the Copacabana Palace and Rua Fernando Mendes is the gay and transvestite section, known as the Stock or Stock Market – easily recognized by the rainbow flag. Young football and *futevôlei* (volleyball played without hands) players hold court near Rua Santa Clara. Posts 5 and 6 are a mix of *favela* kids and Carioca retirees, while the beach next to the Forte de Copacabana is the unofficial *posto de pescadores* (fishermen's post). In the morning, you can buy the fresh catch of the day.

The beach is lit at night and there are police in the area, but it's still not wise to walk there after dark – stay on the hotel side of Av Atlântica if you take a stroll. Av NS de Copacabana is also dangerous – watch out on weekends, when the shops are closed and few locals are around.

MUSEU HISTÓRICO DO EXÉRCITO E FORTE DE COPACABANA

Built in 1914, on the promontory of the former Our Lady of Copacabana chapel, the Forte de Copacabana (Copacabana Fort) was one of Rio's premier defenses against attack. You can still see its original features, including walls up to 12m thick, defended by Krupp cannons. The several floors of exhibits in the **Museu Histórico do Exército e Forte de Copacabana** (Map pp140-1; ☎ 2521 1032; cnr Av Atlântica & Rua Francisco Otaviano, Copacabana; admission R$4; ⏱ 10am-4pm Tue-Sun), tracing the early days of the Portuguese colony to the mid-19th century, aren't the most tastefully done, but the view alone warrants a visit. There's a lovely café overlooking Copacabana.

Botafogo

A largely middle-class residential area, Botafogo lacks the sensuality of Ipanema and the decadence of Copacabana, but it's one of Rio's most traditional neighborhoods. It boasts small museums, excellent theaters, quaint bookstores, neighborhood bars and a welcome shortage of high-rise buildings.

The area attained prominence in the late 1800s when the Portuguese court arrived in Brazil. Dom João VI's wife, Carlota Joaquina, had a country villa built in Botafogo with convenient access to Baía de Guanabara, one of her favorite bathing spots. With royalty established in the area, many mansions were constructed, some of which still stand – as schools, theaters and cultural centers.

MUSEU DO ÍNDIO

Featuring multimedia exhibitions on Brazil's northern tribes, the small **Museu do Índio** (Map pp142-3; ☎ 2286 8899; www.museudoindio.org.br; Rua das Palmeiras 55, Botafogo; admission R$3, free Sun; 9:30am-5:30pm Tue-Fri, 1-5pm Sat & Sun) provides an excellent introduction to the economic, religious and social life of Brazil's indigenous people.

MUSEU VILLA-LOBOS

Housed in a century-old building, the modest **Museu Villa-Lobos** (☎ 2266 3845; Rua Sorocaba 200, Botafogo; admission free; 10am-5:30pm Mon-Fri) is dedicated to the memory of Brazil's greatest classical composer, Heitor Villa-Lobos. Here you'll find personal items, scores and musical instruments, including the piano on which Villa-Lobos composed. The gardens were designed by landscape architect Burle Marx.

Urca

The tranquil, shady streets of Urca offer a pleasant escape from the urban bustle of other parts of the city. An eclectic mix of building styles and manicured gardens lines its streets, with local residents strolling among them. Along the sea wall, which forms the northwestern perimeter of Pão de Açúcar, fishermen cast for dinner as couples lounge beneath palm trees, taking in views of Baía de Guanabara and Cristo Redentor off in the distance. Tiny Praia Vermelha, in the south, has one of Rio's finest beach views. A lovely walking trail begins from here.

Although it was the site of one of the first Portuguese garrisons in the region, almost 300 years elapsed before Urca developed into a residential neighborhood. Today it holds the distinction of being one of the safest and – in spite of Pão de Açúcar being in its midst – least discovered by foreign visitors.

PÃO DE AÇÚCAR

Seen from the peak of **Pão de Açúcar** (Sugarloaf Mountain; Map pp142-3; ☎ 2546 8400; Praça General Tibúrcio, Urca; adult/child R$35/17.50; 8am-10pm), Rio is undoubtedly the most beautiful city in the world. There are many good times to make the ascent, but sunset on a clear day is the most rewarding.

A visit to Pão de Açúcar is a must, but if you can, avoid it from about 10am to 11am and 2pm to 3pm, which is when most tourist buses arrive. Avoid cloudy days as well. Two cable cars connect to the summit, 396m above Rio.

The first ascends 220m to **Morro da Urca**. From here, you can see Baía de Guanabara and the winding coastline. On the ocean side of the mountain is Praia Vermelha, in a small, calm bay. Morro da Urca has its own restaurant, souvenir shops, a playground, an outdoor theater and a helipad (for helicopter tours, see p164). Beneath the shadow of Morro da Urca, the narrow **Praia Vermelha** has superb views of the rocky coastline from the shore. Its coarse sand, unlike that of any other beach in Rio, gives the beach the name *vermelha* (red).

The second cable car goes up to Pão de Açúcar. At the top, the city unfolds beneath you, with Corcovado mountain and Cristo Redentor off to the west, and Copacabana Beach to the south. If the breathtaking heights unsteady you, a drink stand serves *caipirinhas* or *cerveja* (beer). The two-stage cable cars depart every 30 minutes.

Those who'd rather take the long way to the summit should sign up with one of the granite-hugging climbing tours offered by various outfits in Rio (see p159).

PISTA CLÁUDIO COUTINHO

A paved 2km path, **Pista Cláudio Coutinho** (Map pp142-3; 6am-sunset) winds along the southern contour of Morro da Urca. It's a lush area, shaded by trees, with the waves crashing on the rocks below. Keep an eye out for families of small *micos* – capuchin monkeys with ringed tails. About 300m along the path, there's a small unmarked trail that leads up to Morro da Urca. Pão de Açúcar can also be climbed – but it's not recommended without climbing gear.

Flamengo

Flamengo was once Rio's finest residential district, but lost its glitter after the tunnel to Copacabana opened in 1904. Today, Flamengo maintains its largely residential roots. Along tree-shaded sidewalks, old-school restaurants and historic bars lie beside fragrant juice bars and Música Popular Brasileira–playing internet cafés. Flamengo also boasts the Parque do Flamengo, which fronts a scenic beach (too polluted for swimming).

PARQUE DO FLAMENGO

The result of a landfill project that leveled the São Antônio hill in 1965, **Parque do Flamengo** (Map pp142–3 and Map pp144–5) now spreads all the way from downtown Rio through Glória, Catete and Flamengo, and on around to Botafogo. Cyclists and rollerbladers glide along the paths winding through the park, while the many football fields and sports courts are framed against the sea. On Sunday and holidays, the avenues through the park are closed (from 7am to 6pm), bringing a welcome calm to the verdant park.

Designed by famous Brazilian landscaper Burle Marx (who also landscaped Brasília), the park features some 170,000 trees of 300 different species. In addition there are several museums in the park, including the Museu de Arte Moderna and the Museu Carmen Miranda.

MUSEU DE ARTE MODERNA
At the north end of Parque do Flamengo, the **Museu de Arte Moderna** (MAM; Map pp144-5; ☎ 2240 4944; www.mamrio.org.br in Portuguese; Av Infante Dom Henrique 85, Flamengo; adult/child R$5/2; ☺ noon-6pm Tue-Fri, to 7pm Sat & Sun) is immediately recognizable by the striking postmodern edifice designed by Alfonso Eduardo Reidy. The landscaping of Burle Marx is no less impressive. After a devastating fire in 1978 that consumed 90% of its collection, the museum is finally back on its feet and now houses 11,000 permanent works, including pieces by Brazilian artists Bruno Giorgi, Emiliano Di Cavalcanti and Maria Martins. You'll find excellent photography and design exhibits, and the cinema hosts regular film festivals throughout the year.

MUSEU CARMEN MIRANDA
Although Carmen Miranda is largely forgotten in Hollywood, the once-great Brazilian singer still has her fans, and has become a cult icon among Rio's gay community. In addition to photographs and music of her era, the tiny **Museu Carmen Miranda** (Map pp142-3; ☎ 2551 2597; facing Av Rui Barbosa 560, Flamengo; adult/child R$3/1; ☺ 11am-5pm Tue-Fri, 2-5pm Sat & Sun) showcases the starlet's iconographic costumes and jewelry.

Cosme Velho
Cosme Velho lies west of Laranjeiras and is one of the city's most visited neighborhoods – if only for the statue of Christ the Redeemer soaring above its streets.

CRISTO REDENTOR
Atop Corcovado (which means 'hunchback'), **Cristo Redentor** (Christ the Redeemer; Map pp142-3; ☎ 2558 1329; Cog station: Rua Cosme Velho 513, Cosme Velho; adult/child R$35/17.50; ☺ 8:30am-6:30pm)

gazes out over Rio, a placid expression on his well-crafted face. The mountain rises straight up from the city to 710m, and at night, the brightly lit, 38m-high statue is visible from nearly every part of the city – all 1145 tons of the open-armed redeemer.

The view from the top of Corcovado provides a spectacular panorama of Rio and its surroundings. Corcovado lies within the Parque Nacional da Tijuca. You can get there by car or taxi (taxi drivers typically charge around R$60 for return trips with waiting time), but the best way is to go up in the cog train (departures every 30 minutes). For the best view, sit on the right-hand side going up. Be sure to choose a clear day to go up.

LARGO DO BOTICÁRIO
The brightly painted houses on the picturesque square of **Largo do Boticário** (Map pp142-3; Rua Cosme Velho 822) date from the early 19th century. Largo do Boticário was named in honor of the Portuguese gentleman – Joaquim Luiz da Silva Souto – who once ran a *boticário* (apothecary) utilized by the royal family.

MUSEU INTERNACIONAL DE ARTE NAÏF DO BRASIL
The collection of arte naïf (primitivist) paintings in the **Museu Internacional de Arte Naïf do Brasil** (Map pp142-3; ☎ 2205 8612; www.museunaif.com .br; Rua Cosme Velho 561, Cosme Velho; adult/child R$8/4; ☺ 10am-6pm Tue-Fri, noon-6pm Sat & Sun) is extensive: over 8000 pieces, executed by artists from 130 countries, dating from the 15th century to the present. Visitors receive a 50% discount by showing a ticket stub from the Corcovado cog train, which is a block away.

Catete & Glória
Like Flamengo, these twin districts flourished in the mid-19th century, when their location at the outskirts of the city made them desirable places to live. The area's star attraction is the Palácio do Catete, the republic's seat of power before the capital was transferred to Brasília.

IGREJA DE NS DA GLÓRIA DO OUTEIRO
The tiny **Igreja de NS da Glória do Outeiro** (Map pp144-5; ☎ 2225 2869; www.outeirodagloria.org.br in Portuguese; Praça de NS da Glória 135; ☺ 8am-5pm Mon-Fri, 8am-noon Sat & Sun) commands lovely views over Parque do Flamengo and the bay. Considered one of the finest examples of religious colonial architecture in Brazil, the church dates from

RIO'S FAVELAS: BEYOND THE BANG BANG

Residents of Rio de Janeiro's *favelas* (shantytowns) face enormous obstacles. Many families live in communities lacking basic essentials (sewers, medical clinics, roads). Children attend some of the city's worst schools (many indeed drop out). The long bus commute to work can often take hours on traffic-snarled roads for a salary that may not even meet living expenses. There's also the social stigma of living in the slums, some of which are run by local drug lords.

Yet it isn't all gloom for Rio's estimated one million *favela* residents. In the last two decades, locally managed organizations have begun appearing in *favelas* across the city. While small in scale, these non-profit organizations offer residents the chance to learn new skills, gain a sense of pride, and give something often in short supply: hope.

For many poor *favela* children, the Grupo Cultural Afro Reggae (GCAR) is a lifeline. In 1997, in the Vigário Geral *favela*, GCAR opened a cultural centre offering workshops in music, theater, dance, hip-hop and capoeira. The center provides kids with a chance to get off the street, tap into their Afro-Brazilian heritage and gain self-esteem in setting and fulfilling goals. Owing to the center's wide popularity, the ideas have spread. GCAR and its *favela* affiliates now offer more than 60 different programs for poor residents around Rio.

Rocinha, Brazil's largest *favela*, creates similar opportunities for local residents at its Casa da Cultura. Founded in 2003 by Gilberto Gil, Minister of Culture, singer and neighbor, the center draws on the *favela's* rich artistic tradition, and offers classes in music, theater and painting. The *favela* next door, Vidigal, perched on a hillside overlooking Ipanema Beach, is the base of the group 'Nos do Morro' (We of the Favela). This theater group won fame after some of its young actors appeared in the award-winning film *Cidade de Deus (City of God)*. Ten of its members performed in *Two Gentlemen of Verona* for the Royal Shakespeare Company in August 2006.

As many have discovered, the *favela* has a deep well of talent, but few opportunities. Opportunity is exactly what sociologist Maria Teresa Leal had in mind when she founded a sewing collective in Rocinha in the 1980s. The idea began during Leal's repeat trips to the *favela* when she encountered many talented seamstresses who had no chance to earn money for their skills. So began **Coopa Roca** (www.coopa-roca.org.br), a small group of women, each working from home to produce quilts, pillows and craft items made of recycled fabrics and other materials. Today the co-op employs some 150 women, and has even caught the eye of the fashion world, with commissions from Brazilian designers Osklen and Carlos Miele, as well as British designer Paul Smith.

For their part, *favelas* have made numerous contributions to the city. Rio's biggest party, Carnaval, was born in the *favelas*, and they continue to be pivotal to the fest. That *favelas* throw the best parties has long been known to many Cariocas. Today, Baile Funks are the biggest party craze to lure both rich and poor to the gritty neighborhoods on the hillsides. There, DJs spin a blend of Rio's bass-heavy funk music to packed dance floors.

Travellers interested in seeing beneath the stereotypes can visit a *favela* on a tour (p163), volunteer (p713) or even overnight in a *favela* (Pousada Favelinha, p169).

1739 and became the favorite of the royal family upon their arrival in 1808. Attached to the church is a small religious art **museum** (R$1; ۞ 9am-5pm Tue-Fri, 9am-noon Sat & Sun).

MUSEU DA REPÚBLICA

Located in the Palácio do Catete, the **Museu da República** (Map pp142-3; ☎ 3235 2650; www.museu darepublica.org.br in Portuguese; Rua do Catete 153, Catete; admission R$6, free on Wed & Sun; ۞ noon-5pm Tue, Thu & Fri, 2-5pm Wed, 2-6pm Sat & Sun) has a good collection of art and artifacts from the Republican period, and also houses an outdoor café, cinema and bookstore. Built between 1858 and

1866 and easily distinguished by the bronze condors on the eaves, the palace was home to the president of Brazil from 1896 until 1954, when President Getúlio Vargas killed himself. The bedroom in which the suicide occurred is eerily preserved on the 3rd floor.

Behind the Palácio lies the **Parque do Catete**, a small, nicely landscaped park complete with a pond and the occasional swan.

MUSEU DE FOLCLÓRICO EDSON CARNEIRO

Next door to the Palácio do Catete, the **Museu de Folclórico Edson Carneiro** (Map pp142-3; ☎ 2205 0090; Rua do Catete 181, Catete; free admission; ۞ 11am-6pm

Tue-Fri, 3-6pm Sat & Sun) provides an excellent introduction to Brazilian folk art. Its collection includes Candomblé costumes, ceramic figurines and religious costumes used in festivals, though our favorite exhibits are the delightful, mechanized scenes (the circus, bull riding, samba show, rubber tree workers).

CENTRO CULTURAL TELEMAR

One of Rio's intriguing new additions, **Centro Cultural Telemar** (Map pp142-3; ☎ 3131 6060; www.centroculturaltelemar.com.br in Portuguese; Rua 2 de Dezembro 63; admission free; ⏰ 11am-8pm Tue-Sun) is a six-story ultra-modern exhibition space featuring multimedia installations focusing on architecture, urban design and video art. The top-floor auditorium of this cultural center has a regular line-up of film screenings and concerts. While the first floor functions as a library where visitors can peruse art books and design mags; a listening station features eclectic music.

Centro

Rio's bustling commercial district, Centro is a blend of high-rise office buildings with remnants of its grand past still present in looming baroque churches, wide plazas and cobblestone streets.

Many pedestrian-only areas crisscross Centro. The most famous of these is known as **Saara**, a giant street bazaar crammed with discount stores. In the last century, Saara attracted an influx of immigrants from the Middle East, and still has a few authentic Lebanese restaurants.

BOHEMIAN RIO

The Zona Sul may have lovely beaches, but the city's soul has long since migrated inland. Today, the neighborhood of Lapa and its hilltop sister Santa Teresa form the backdrop to an explosive renaissance.

On weekend nights, Av Mem de Sá is a jumble of dance halls and restaurants, with samba and *chorinho* (an informal, instrumental music genre) seeming to spill from every doorway. Meanwhile in Santa Teresa, old haunts like **Bar do Mineiro** (p176) continue to be the meeting ground for a new wave of artists and intellectuals as the old tram rattles through the streets.

The area is known for its colorful characters, although the latest crop of eccentrics is hardly the first. Lapa's grand days of bohemia came in the 1920s and '30s, when a jumble of artists, writers and intellectuals mingled among the rough underworld of dance halls, cabarets and brothels. It was the era of colorful *malandros* (con artists) and samba, which was the music of the city. Films like *Madam Satã*, in which Lapa plays a starring role, recall the era of intrigue on the streets, with hush men and corrupt cops, villains and prostitutes wandering dark street corners as samba ballads spilled out of dimly lit clubs.

Yet the place lost its soul in the 1940s, when then president Getúlio Vargas shuttered the cabarets and dance halls and the energy moved elsewhere. Hard times ensued, and escalated as Rio lost its federal prominence (and much cash) to Brasília in the 1960s. Lapa soon became a no-go area of crime and decay, and samba went underground. Although *sambistas* never forget about Lapa, the city forgot about samba – and the appetite for the old-fashioned sound waned as youth flocked to the new bossa nova bars in the beachside neighborhoods of Ipanema and Leblon. Later, rock and disco replaced bossa.

Then in the last decade, Lapa has emerged, phoenix-like, from the ashes. Its rebirth has much to do with samba's renewed popularity. The area's first samba club, **Carioca da Gema** (p179), opened in 2000, and Cariocas slowly started coming into the neighborhood – although they were wary of returning at first. Today there are dozens of music venues in Lapa, and the city seems to have an insatiable appetite for samba.

On a Thursday night, the democratic mix in the neighborhood is startling: white-clad sambistas slinging *cavaquinhos* (small, four-string guitars), alongside young Zona Sul couples and tourists from across the globe, watched over by a new wave of *malandros* (picaresque con artists) and oldtimers, who've seen it all even though they haven't left the neighborhood. Cariocas once again gather in old-fashioned clubs with grand staircases and soaring ceilings – making the glass and vinyl bars of the Zona Sul seem downright soulless. As one *sambista* recently said, 'Lapa is eternal. It's like a phoenix. It decays, dies, then rises again.'

CENTRO CULTURAL DO BANCO DO BRASIL

Housed in a beautifully restored building dating from 1906, the **Centro Cultural do Banco do Brasil** (CCBB; Map pp144-5; ☎ 3808 2020; www.cultura-e.com.br in Portuguese; Rua Primeiro de Março 66; admission free; ❤ noon-8pm Tue-Sun) is now one of Brazil's best cultural centers, with a cinema, two theaters and some of the city's best (and free) exhibitions. There's always something going on at CCBB – visit its website for listings.

CENTRO DE ARTE HÉLIO OITICICA

This avant-garde **museum** (Map pp144-5; ☎ 2242 1012; Rua Luis de Camões 68; admission free; ❤ 11am-7pm Tue-Fri, 11am-5pm Sat & Sun) is set in a 19th-century neoclassical building that originally housed the Conservatory of Music and Dramatic Arts. Today, the center displays permanent works by the artist, theoretician and poet Hélio Oiticica, as well as bold contemporary art exhibitions, well-tuned to Oiticica's progressive aesthetics.

ESPAÇO CULTURAL DA MARINHA

On the waterfront, the **Espaço Cultural da Marinha** (Map pp144-5; ☎ 2104 6992; Av Alfred Agache s/n; admission free; ❤ noon-5pm Tue-Sun) is a sailor's delight. Moored along the dock are the *Riachuelo* submarine and the *Bauru* (a small WWII destroyer), which have been turned into floating museums. You'll also find a 19th-century vessel used by Dom João VI, countless ship models, and maps and navigational instruments charting the history of imperial and Brazilian navigation. The boat tour to Ilha Fiscal (p156) leaves from here.

IGREJA SÃO FRANCISCO DA PENITÊNCIA & CONVENTO SANTO ANTÔNIO

Overlooking the Largo da Carioca is the baroque **Igreja São Francisco da Penitência & Convento Santo Antônio** (Map pp144-5; ☎ 2262 0197; Largo da Carioca 5, Centro; ❤ 9am-noon & 1-4pm Tue-Fri), dating from 1726. Recently restored to its former glory, the church's sacristy has blue Portuguese tiles and an elaborately carved altar made out of jacaranda wood. It also has a roof panel by José Oliveira Rosa depicting St Francis receiving the stigmata. The church's statue of Santo Antônio is an object of great devotion to many Cariocas in search of a husband or wife.

IGREJA DE NS DE CANDELÁRIA

The construction of the original church to NS de Candelária (dating from the late 16th century), on the present site, was credited to a ship's captain who had almost been shipwrecked at sea. Upon his safe return he vowed to build a church to her. A later design led to its present-day grandeur, which rated **Igreja de NS de Candelária** (Map pp144-5; ☎ 2233 2324; Praça Pio X, Centro; ❤ 8am-4pm Mon-Fri, 9am-1pm Sat & Sun) among the largest and wealthiest churches of imperial Brazil. The interior is a spectacular combination of baroque and Renaissance styles. The ceiling above the nave features six large panels that depict the romanticized version of the sea captain's journey and the subsequent origin of the church. The cupola, fabricated entirely from limestone shipped from Lisbon, is one of its most striking features.

MOSTEIRO DE SÃO BENTO

Another fine colonial gem, the **Mosteiro de São Bento** (Map pp144-5; ☎ 2291 7122; Rua Dom Gerardo 68, Centro; ❤ 8-11am & 2:30-6pm) was built between 1617 and 1641 on Morro de São Bento, one of the four hills that once marked colonial Rio. The simple facade hides a baroque interior richly decorated in gold. Among its historic treasures are wood carvings designed by Frei Domingos da Conceição and paintings by José Oliveira Rosa. On Sunday, the High Mass at 10am includes a choir of Benedictine monks singing Gregorian chants. To reach the monastery from Rua Dom Gerardo, go to number 40 and take the elevator to the 5th floor.

MUSEU HISTÓRICO NACIONAL

Housed in the colonial arsenal, which dates from 1764, the impressive **Museu Histórico Nacional** (Map pp144-5; ☎ 2550 9224; www.museuhistoriconacional.com.br; off Av General Justo; adult/child R$6/3, free Sun; ❤ 10am-5:30pm Tue-Fri, 2-6pm Sat & Sun) contains over 250,000 historic relics relating to the history of Brazil from its founding to its early days as a republic. The museum is located near Praça Marechal Âncora and features many well-designed displays, from gilded imperial coaches and the throne of Dom Pedro II to massive oil paintings depicting the horrific combat in the war with Paraguay. There's some attention paid to Brazil's indigenous population and to curious relics like the writing quill that Princess Isabel used to sign the document abolishing slavery in Brazil and a full-sized model of a colonial pharmacy.

MUSEU NACIONAL DE BELAS ARTES

Rio's **Museu Nacional de Belas Artes** (Map pp144-5; Av Rio Branco 199, Centro; admission US$1.50; ☺ 10am-6pm Tue-Fri, 2-6pm Sat & Sun) houses more than 800 original paintings and sculptures ranging from the 17th to the 20th centuries. One of its most important galleries is the Galeria de Arte Brasileira, with 20th-century classics such as Cândido Portinari's *Café*. Other galleries display Brazilian folk art, African art and furniture, as well as contemporary exhibits. Guided tours are available in English (call ahead).

PAÇO IMPERIAL

Built in 1743, the **Paço Imperial** (Imperial Palace; Map pp144-5; ☎ 2533 4407; cnr Praça XV de Novembro & Rua Primeiro de Março, Centro; free admission; ☺ noon-6:30pm Tue-Sun) today hosts an excellent range of changing exhibitions (recent shows included the mobiles of Alexander Calder and a history of Brazilian music, complete with dozens of listening stations). Originally built as a governor's residence, it later served as the home to Dom João and his family when the Portuguese royals fled Napoleon and transferred the throne to the colony. In 1888 Princesa Isabel proclaimed the Freedom from Slavery Act from the palace's steps. In addition to exhibitions, there are restaurants, a music store and a cinema on the 1st floor.

Adjoining the Paço is the **Praça XV de Novembro**, the broad plaza where Brazil's two emperors (Pedro I and Pedro II) were crowned. It was later the site of the deposition of Emperor Pedro II in 1889.

PRAÇA FLORIANO

The heart of modern Rio, **Praça Floriano** (Map pp144-5; Av Rio Branco, Centro) comes to life at lunchtime and after work when the outdoor cafés are filled with beer drinkers, samba musicians and political debate. The square is also Rio's political marketplace. There's daily speechmaking, literature sales and street theater. Most city marches and rallies culminate here on the steps of the old Câmara Municipal (Town Hall), in the northwest corner of the plaza.

REAL GABINETE PORTUGUÊS DE LEITURA

Built in the Manuelin Portuguese style in 1837, the gorgeous **Real Gabinete Português de Leitura** (Portuguese Reading Room; Map pp144-5; ☎ 2221 3138; Rua Luís de Camões 30; admission free; ☺ 9am-6pm Mon-Fri) houses over 350,000 works, many dating from the 16th, 17th and 18th centuries. It also has a small collection of paintings, sculptures and ancient coins.

TEATRO MUNICIPAL

Built in 1905 in the style of the Paris Opera, the magnificent **Teatro Municipal** (Municipal Theater; Map pp144-5; ☎ 2299 1711; Rua Manuel de Carvalho; guided tour R$6; ☺ 1-4pm Mon-Fri) is the home of Rio's opera, orchestra and ballet. It's well worth booking a tour (call ☎ 2299 1667), if you don't attend a performance there.

TRAVESSA DO COMÉRCIO

Beautiful two-story colonial townhouses line the narrow cobblestone street of **Travessa do Comércio** (Map pp144-5; Near Praça XV de Novembro), leading off of Praça XV de Novembro. The archway known as Arco de Teles leading into the area was once a part of an old viaduct running between two buildings. Today, the street contains half a dozen restaurants and drinking spots that open onto the streets. It's a favorite spot for Cariocas after work.

Santa Teresa

Set on a hill overlooking the city, the cobbled streets and aging mansions of Santa Teresa are a vision of days long past. Named after the Carmelite convent founded here in 1750, Santa Teresa was the uppermost residential neighborhood in the 19th century, when Rio's upper class lived here and rode the *bonde* (tram) to work in Centro. During the 1960s and 1970s many artists and bohemians moved into Santa Teresa's mansions, initiating a revitalization process that still continues. Throughout the year, impromptu festivals and street parties fill the air, making it one of Rio's most exciting neighborhoods.

Although there is a police presence in the area, the *favelas* down the hillsides still make this a high-crime area. Don't take any valuables when walking around; it's best to stick close to Largo do Guimarães and the *bonde* line.

BONDE

The **bonde** (Map pp144-5; ☎ 2240 5709; station at Rua Lélio Gama 65, Centro; ticket R$0.60; ☺ departures every 30min, 7am-10pm) that travels up to Santa Teresa from Centro is the last of the historic streetcars that once crisscrossed the city. Its clatter through the cobbled streets has made it the icon for bohemian Santa Teresa. The tram travels over the Arcos do Lapa and up Rua Joaquim Murtinho before reaching Largo do Guimarães. From there, one line (Paula Matos) takes a northwestern route, terminating at Largo das Neves. Unfortunately, security is an issue, and travelers have been mugged walking to and from this plaza. The safest time to go is on a weekend night, when the Largo is at its liveliest – but take a taxi or a tram; don't walk. The longer route (Dois Irmãos) continues from Largo do Guimarães uphill and southward before terminating near the water reservoir at Dois Irmãos.

Tram tours depart every Saturday highlighting historic points in the neighborhood (see p164 for details).

MUSEU CHÁCARA DO CÉU
The former mansion of art patron and industrialist Raymundo Ottoni de Castro Maya is now the **Museu Chácara do Céu** (Map pp144-5; ☎ 2507 1932; Rua Murtinho Nobre 93, Santa Teresa; admission R$6; ☼ noon-5pm Wed-Mon), with a small collection of modern art. In addition to works by Portinari, Di Cavalcanti, and a good assortment of European and Asian works, the museum displays furniture and Brazilian maps dating from the 17th and 18th centuries. Beautiful gardens surround the museum, with fine views of Centro and Baía de Guanabara. Sadly, four of the museum's most valuable paintings were stolen during an armed robbery in 2006.

PARQUE DAS RUINAS
Connected to the Chácara do Céu by a walkway, the **Parque das Ruinas** (Map pp144-5; ☎ 2252 1039; Rua Murtinho Nobre 169, Santa Teresa; admission free; ☼ 10am-8pm Tue-Sun) contains the ruins of the mansion that belong to Brazilian heiress Laurinda Santos Lobo. Her house was a meeting point for Rio's artists and intellectuals for many years until her death in 1946. Today the park often stages open-air concerts and performances. Don't miss the view from the top floor.

Lapa
Formerly a residential neighborhood of the wealthy, Lapa had its best days before the 20th century, and its mansions are now sadly neglected. Today Lapa recalls decades of dereliction in the minds of some Cariocas, while others cite the cultural renaissance happening here. Undoubtedly, Lapa is the center of a vibrant bohemian scene in Rio, with dozens

of music clubs, bars and old-fashioned restaurants scattered along its avenues.

On weekend nights, revelers pack the neighborhood's samba clubs, its streets and the wide plaza in front of the Arcos do Lapa, the neighborhood's prominent landmark. Narrow tracks course over the 64m-high structure, carrying the famous *bonde* to and from Santa Teresa.

CATEDRAL METROPOLITANA
The enormous cone-shaped **Catedral Metropolitana** (Map pp144-5; ☎ 2240 2669; Av República do Chile 245, Lapa; admission free; ☼ 7am-5:30pm) was inaugurated in 1976 after 12 years of construction. Among its sculptures, murals and other works of art are four breathtaking stained-glass windows, which stretch 60m to the ceiling.

The small **Museu de Arte Sacra** (Museum of Sacred Art; admission R$2) is in the basement. It contains historical items such as the throne of Dom Pedro II, the baptismal basins used at the christenings of royal princes and the golden roses Princess Isabel received from Pope Leo XIII after signing the law abolishing slavery in Brazil.

ESCADARIA SELARÓN
An ever-expanding installation, the **Escadaria Selarón** (Selarón Staircase; Map pp144-5; btwn Rua Joaquim Silva, Lapa & Rua Pinto Martins, Santa Teresa), leading up from Rua Joaquim Silva, became a work of art when Chilean-born artist Jorge Selarón decided to cover the steps with colorful mosaics. A dedication to the Brazilian people, the 215 steps are a vivid riot of color.

FUNDIÇÃO PROGRESSO
Once a foundry for safes and ovens, the **Fundição Progresso** (☎ 2220 5070; Rua dos Arcos 24, Lapa; admission free; concerts R$10-50; ☼ 9am-6pm Mon-Fri) today hosts avant-garde exhibitions, performances and popular samba parties during the summer.

Greater Rio
To the west of Centro lie some of Rio's big-name attractions, including the Sambódromo, the Maracanã Football Stadium and the Feira Nordestina, one of Brazil's wildest markets. You'll also find the Quinta da Boa Vista, a large park containing the Museu Nacional and the Jardim Zoológico (zoo). These latter

sites lie in São Cristóvão, which in the 19th century was home to the nobility, including the monarchs themselves. It has since become one of the most populous suburbs in Rio.

To the east of Centro lies Rio's scenic bay. Unfortunately, it's too polluted for swimming, but it makes a fine setting for sailing out to Ilha de Paquetá or Niterói. For cruises on the bay, see p163.

CIDADE NOVA
Sambódromo

The epicenter of Rio's Carnaval, the **Sambódromo** (Map pp146-7; Rua do Catumbi) was designed by Oscar Niemeyer and completed in 1984. The small **Museu do Carnaval** (Map pp146-7; free admission; 11am-5pm Tue-Sun) has information on the history of Rio's samba schools, and you can try on costumes, but aside from that, there isn't much to see when the parades aren't happening.

SÃO CRISTÓVÃO
Feira Nordestina

The enormous **Feira Nordestina** (Map pp146-7; 3860 9976; www.feiradesaocristovao.com.br in Portuguese; Campo de São Cristóvão, São Cristóvão; 10am-4pm Tue-Thu & 10am Fri-10pm Sun) is not to be missed. The fair (32,000 sq meters with 658 stalls) showcases the culture from the Northeast, with *barracas* (stalls) selling Bahian dishes as well as beer and *cachaça* (sugarcane spirit), which flows in great abundance. Bands perform *forró* (popular music of the Northeast), samba and Música Popular Brasileira (MPB). On Friday, the fair turns into a huge party which runs nonstop until Sunday.

Maracanã Football Stadium

Brazil's temple of soccer, **Maracanã Football Stadium** (Map pp146-7; 2299 2941; Rua Professor Eurico Rabelo, São Cristóvão; admission R$12-30) easily accommodates more than 100,000 people. On certain occasions, such as the World Cup match of 1950 or Pelé's last game, it has squeezed in close to 200,000 crazed fans – although it's now been modified to hold fewer.

For a quasi-psychedelic experience, go to a *futebol* (football) match – preferably a championship game or one between local rivals Flamengo, Vasco da Gama, Fluminense or Botafogo. See p182 for details.

A **sports museum** (admission R$14; 9am-5pm daily except game days) inside the stadium displays photographs, posters, and the uniforms of Brazilian sporting greats, including Pelé's famous number 10 shirt. There's a recording of cheering fans overhead, giving you an idea of the energy that runs through this place. There's also a store that sells football shirts. Enter through gate number 16 on Rua Professor Eurico Rabelo.

Quinta da Boa Vista

The residence of the imperial family until the Republic was proclaimed, today **Quinta da Boa Vista** (Map pp146-7; 2234 1609; Rua Paula e Silva, São Cristóvão; 7am-6pm) is a large and busy park with gardens and lakes. On weekends it's crowded with soccer games and families from the Zona Norte. The former imperial mansion houses the **Museu Nacional** (Map pp146-7; 2568 8262; admission R$3; 10am-4pm Tue-Sun) and **Museu da Fauna**. In addition to Etruscan ceramics, Egyptian mummies and stuffed prehistoric animals, the Museu Nacional contains a small Brazilian section with relics from the country's early indigenous people. For a chance to see a wide assortment of plants and flowers – both native and imported species – visit the Museu da Fauna.

The **Jardim Zoológico** (Map pp146-7; 2569 2024; admission R$5; 9am-4:30pm Tue-Sun), Rio's zoo, is 200m away from Boa Vista. It boasts a medium-sized collection of Brazilian mammals and endangered species. Highlights include the tropical-bird aviary (the gardens are a good place for birdwatchers) and the Nocturnal House, offering visitors a close-up view of sloths, bats and other creatures of the night.

BAÍA DE GUANABARA
Ilha Fiscal

The lime-green, neo-Gothic palace of **Ilha Fiscal** (Map pp144-5; 2233 9165; admission R$8; 1pm, 2:30pm & 4pm Thu-Sun except on the 2nd weekend of each month), sitting in the Baía de Guanabara, looks like something out of a fairy tale. It was designed by engineer Adolfo del Vecchio and was the location of the last Imperial Ball on November 9, 1889. Today it's open for guided tours, which leave from the Espaço Cultural da Marinha (p153), north of Praça XV de Novembro.

Ilha de Paquetá

The **Ilha de Paquetá** (Map p137), in the Baía de Guanabara, was once a popular tourist spot and remains a pleasant escape from the city's bustle. There are no cars on the island. Transport is by foot, bicycle (with hundreds for rent) or horsedrawn carts. There's a certain decadent charm to the colonial buildings, unassuming beaches and businesses catering to local tourism. The place gets crowded on weekends.

Go to Paquetá for the boat ride, the pretty scenery across the bay and to see Cariocas at play – especially during the Festa de São Roque, which is celebrated over five days in August.

Boats leave from near the Praça XV de Novembro in Centro. The regular **ferry** (☎ 4004 3113; weekday/weekend return R$7.20/12) takes 70 minutes and offers seven to nine trips daily from 7.10am to 11pm. At the time of research, the **hydrofoil** (☎ 2533 4343; return R$16) took 30 minutes and was operating infrequently.

NITERÓI
The city of Niterói's principal attraction is the famous Museu do Arte Contemporânea. The cruise across the bay, however, is perhaps just as valid a reason for leaving Rio. The ferry costs about R$4.60 return and leaves from Praça XV de Novembro in Centro; it's usually full of commuters. The faster and more comfortable alternative is the jumbo catamaran, which runs every 15 minutes from 7am to 4pm and costs R$11 return. Once you reach the dock, there isn't much to see in the immediate area. It's a busy commercial area, full of pedestrians and crisscrossing intersections. From here catch a bus to the MAC or to one of the beaches.

Museu do Arte Contemporânea
Designed by Brazil's most famous architect, Oscar Niemeyer, the **Museu do Arte Contemporânea** (MAC; Map p137; ☎ 2620 2400; www .macniteroi.com.br in Portuguese; Mirante da Boa Viagem s/n, Niterói; admission R$5; ⏲ 11am 6pm Tue-Sun) is a curvilinear building with breathtaking views, but the expositions inside aren't always very notable. To get here from the Niterói ferry terminal, turn right as you leave and walk about 50m across to the bus stop in the middle of the road; a 47B minibus will drop you at the museum door.

BEACHES EAST OF NITERÓI
A number of beaches lie just east of Niterói. The ones closest to town are too polluted for swimming, but as you continue out, you'll reach some pristine beaches – Piratininga, Camboinhas, Itaipu and finally Itacoatiara, the most fabulous of the bunch. Framed by two looming hills on either side and backed by vegetation, the white sands of Itacoatiara seem a world removed from the urban beaches of Rio. *Barracas* sell scrumptious plates of fish, and there are also food stands overlooking the beach (try Sanduiches Onda for a *natural* – a sandwich of tuna, chicken or cottage cheese, with additional ingredients such as carrots, raisins or olives). The surf is strong here – as evidenced by the abundance of surfers – so swim with caution. To get here, you can take bus 38 from the ferry terminal (R$4, 50 minutes) or any bus labeled 'Itacoatiara.' If you're traveling in a group you can negotiate a return fare with a taxi driver.

BARRA DA TIJUCA & WEST OF RIO
Ten kilometers west of Leblon, Barra da Tijuca (Barra) is the Miami of Rio, with malls and shopping centers set against the tropical landscape. At 12km long, the lovely beach here is the city's longest. Beyond this, the region gets less and less urban. Some of Rio's most beautiful beaches lie out this way (see the boxed text on p158 for details). Further west begins Brazil's gorgeous coastal road that travels through the region known as the Costa Verde.

Praia da Barra da Tijuca
The best thing about Barra is the beach, **Praia da Barra da Tijuca** (Map p137). It's a long, scenic spot with blue sea lapping at the shore; the first few kilometers are filled with bars and seafood restaurants.

The young and beautiful hang out in front of *barraca* number 1 – also known as the Barraca do Pepê, after the famous Carioca hang gliding champion who died during a competition in Japan in 1991.

The further out you go the more deserted it gets, and the stalls turn into trailers. It's calm on weekdays and crazy on hot summer weekends.

Sitio Burle Marx
The enormous 350,000-sq-meter estate, **Sitio Burle Marx** (Map p137; ☎ 2410 1412; burlemarx@alternex .com.br; Estrada da Barra de Guaratiba 2019, Guaratiba; admission R$5; ⏲ 7am-4pm, by advance appointment only) was once the magnificent home of Brazil's most famous landscape architect, Roberto Burle Marx. The beautifully lush gardens of the estate, 22km west of the city, easily warrant a visit. Strolling the verdantly landscaped area allows visitors the chance to see and smell

BEACHES WEST OF RIO

Although Copacabana and Ipanema are Rio's most famous stretches of sand, there are many stunning beaches in the area, some in spectacular natural settings.

Pepino/São Conrado

The first major beach you'll reach heading west of Leblon is **Praia do Pepino** (Map p137) in São Conrado. Pepino is a beautiful beach, and is less crowded than Ipanema. It's also where hang gliders like to lounge when they're not soaring overhead.

Recreio dos Bandeirantes

Although it gets crowded on weekends, **Recreio dos Bandeirantes** is almost deserted during the week. The large rock acts as a natural breakwater, creating a calm bay. The 2km-long stretch of sand is popular with families.

Prainha

The secluded 700m-long **Prainha** lies just 6km past Recreio. It's one of the best surfing beaches in Rio, so it's always full of surfers. Waves come highly recommended here.

Grumari

The most isolated and unspoiled beach close to the city, **Grumari** is quiet during the week and packed on weekends with Cariocas looking to get away from city beaches. It is a gorgeous setting, surrounded by mountains and lush vegetation.

Guaratiba

From Grumari, a narrow road climbs over a jungle-covered hillside toward **Guaratiba**. West of here is a good view of the **Restinga de Marambaia** (the vegetation-rich strip between the beach and the mainland), closed off to the public by a naval base. Cariocas enjoy eating lunch at several of the seafood restaurants in the area.

---

thousands of exotic plant species from both Brazil and abroad. A lovely 17th-century Benedictine chapel, along with Burle Marx's original farmhouse and studio, completes the idyllic setting.

ACTIVITIES

Given the mountains, beaches and forests in their backyard, it's not surprising that Cariocas are an active bunch. The coastline brings an array of options: jogging, hiking, walking, cycling, and surfing. The mountains offer their own allure: you can hang glide off them or rock climb up them. Great hiking trails through Atlantic rain forest lie just outside the city.

Cycling

There are over 74km of bike paths around Rio, including those around Lagoa Rodrigo de Freitas, along Barra da Tijuca and the oceanfront from Leblon to Leme. This last path also connects to Praia de Botafogo and Parque do Flamengo, running all the way to Centro. In the Tijuca forest, a 6km bikeway runs from a waterfall (Cascatinha) to a mu-

seum (Açude). On Sundays the beach road from Leblon to Leme closes to traffic, as does the road through Parque do Flamengo. Bilingual bike tours are available through **Rio by Bike** (Map pp138-9; ☎ 2247 7269; Hostel Ipanema, House 14, Rua Barão da Torre 175, Ipanema).

You can rent bikes from a stand along the west side of Lagoa Rodrigo de Freitas for R$10 per hour. A few other places to rent bikes:

Ciclovia (Map pp140-1; ☎ 2275 5299; Av Prado Junior 330 & Rua Francisco Otaviano 55, Copacabana; per hr/day R$8/50; ☒ 9am-7pm Mon-Fri, 9am-4pm Sat) Rents bikes from posto 6 on Sundays (from 9am to 2pm).

Special Bike (Map pp138-9; ☎ 2521 2686; Rua Visconde de Pirajá 135B, Ipanema; per hr/day R$15/45; ☒ 9am-7pm Mon-Fri, to 3pm Sat)

Zaga Bike (Map pp140-1; ☎ 2287 7616; Rua Miguel Lemos 51F, Copacabana; per hr/day R$10/50; ☒ 9am-6pm Mon-Fri, to 2pm Sat) Good mountain bikes.

Diving

Dive Point (Map pp138-9; ☎ 2239 5105; www.divepoint .com.br in Portuguese; Shop 5, Av Ataulfo de Paiva 1174, Leblon) offers diving courses and tours around Rio's main beaches and Cagarras Island (in front of Ipanema), as well as trips to Angra dos Reis and Búzios.

Calypso (☎ 9939 5997, 8144 6574; www.calypsobrasil .com.br in Portuguese) provides diving courses (up to Dive Master) in waters near Rio. You can pick up information about courses at the dive shop **AS Divers** (Map pp144-5; ☎ 2252 8852; mezzanine, Rua da Alfândega 97, Centro).

Fishing

Universidade da Pesca (Map pp146-7; ☎ 3971 7211; www.upesca.com.br in Portuguese; Rua do Bispo 94/1207, Rio Comprido) features a wide range of fishing tours – from day trips in Baía de Guanabara and Cagarras Island to weeklong adventures in the Amazon.

Hang gliding

If you weigh less than 100kg (about 220lb) and can spare R$250, you can do the fantastic hang glide off 510m-high Pedra Bonita – one of the giant granite slabs that tower above Rio – onto Praia do Pepino in São Conrado. No experience is necessary; tandem riders are secured in a kind of pouch attached to the kite.

Flights typically last from 15 to 25 minutes and naturally depend on weather and wind conditions. You can usually fly on all but three to four days per month, and conditions during winter are even better. If you fly early in the day, you have more flexibility to accommodate weather delays. Prices include pick-up and drop-off from your hotel. Travel agents also book tandem flights, but tack on their own fee. To cut out the middlemen, call direct.

Just Fly (☎ 2268 0565; www.justfly.com.br; Hostel Ipanema, House 14, Rua Barão da Torre 175, Ipanema) Paulo Celani is a highly experienced tandem flyer with over 6000 flights to his credit.

SuperFly (☎ 3322 2286; www.riosuperfly.com.br in Portuguese; House 2, Estrada das Canoas 1476; São Conrado) Ruy Marra, founder of SuperFly, has more than 25 years of experience flying and is an excellent tandem glider pilot.

Tandem Fly (☎ 2422 6371, 3322 5817, 2493 4324; www.riotandemfly.com.br) Three experienced pilots run this tandem flight outfit. They also give lessons for those wanting to fly solo.

Hiking & Climbing

Aside from access to nearby national parks like Parque Nacional da Serra dos Órgãos (p209) and Parque Nacional de Itatiaia (p203),

Rio has many trails through the rain forest of Floresta da Tijuca. Visitors can also take part in hikes around Corcovado, Morro da Urca, Parque Lage and other areas. It's advisable to go with a guide for a number of reasons – to avoid getting lost and robbed are top of the list. Group outings can also be a good way to meet Cariocas.

Rio is also the center of rock climbing in Brazil, with around 350 documented climbs within an hour's drive. Rio has several well-organized climbing clubs, which have regular weekly meetings to discuss upcoming outings.

Centro Excursionista Brasileira (CEB; Map pp144-5; ☎ 2252 9844; www.ceb.org.br in Portuguese; 8th fl, Av Almirante Barroso 2, Centro; ⊙ meeting 7pm Thu, office 2-6pm Mon-Fri) CEB sponsors day hikes and weekend treks (with camping).

Clube Excursionista Carioca (Map pp140-1; ☎ 2255 1348; www.carioca.org.br in Portuguese; Rua Hilário de Gouveia 206/71, Copacabana; ⊙ meeting 8:30pm Thu) typically arranges hikes and technical climbs, as well as rappelling and rafting trips.

Rio Hiking (☎ 2552 9204, 9721 0594; www.riohiking .com.br) Founded by a mother-and-son team of outdoor enthusiasts, Rio Hiking offers a wide variety of hikes. Popular treks go up Pico da Tijuca (the highest point in the national park), Pedra da Gávea (eight hours, R$142.50), Pão de Açúcar (five hours, R$114) and Corcovado. Cycling, rafting, kayaking and rappelling trips can also be arranged.

Tangara Ecological Hikes (☎ 2252 8202, 9656 1460; www.tangarapasseios.com.br) Tangara arranges day hikes and outings on weekends on Tijuca trails, up Corcovado and Pedra Bonita, and to other nearby sites. Hikes are affordable (around R$20 to R$25 per person), although you'll have to arrange your own transport to the sites.

Trilharte Ecoturismo (Map pp142-3; ☎ 2225 2426; www.trilharte.com.br in Portuguese; Suite 1, Rua Almirante Tamandaré 77, Flamengo) This organization offers hiking trips that attract those with a passion for nature photography; hikes cost around R$35 (hike up Morro de Urca) and are held on Saturdays.

Surfing

When the surf is good, it gets crowded. Praia do Arpoador, between Copacabana and Ipanema, draws large flocks of surfers, though there are much better breaks further out in Barra, Grumari, Joá and Prainha – by far the

PARQUE NACIONAL DA TIJUCA

The Floresta da Tijuca (another name for Parque Nacional da Tijuca) is all that's left of the Atlantic rain forest that once surrounded Rio de Janeiro. In just 15 minutes you can go from the concrete jungle of Copacabana to the 120-sq-km tropical jungle of the **Parque Nacional da Tijuca** (Map p137). A more rapid and dramatic contrast is hard to imagine. The forest is an exuberant green, with beautiful trees, creeks and waterfalls, mountainous terrain and high peaks. It has an excellent, well-marked trail system. Candomblistas (devotees of the Candomblé religion) leave offerings by the roadside, families have picnics and serious hikers climb the 1012m to the summit of **Pico da Tijuca**.

The heart of the forest is the Alto da Boa Vista area, which has many lovely natural and artificial features. Among the highlights of this beautiful park are several waterfalls (**Cascatinha Taunay**, **Cascata Gabriela** and **Cascata Diamantina**), a 19th-century chapel (**Capela Mayrink**) and numerous caves (**Gruta Luís Fernandes**, **Gruta Belmiro** and **Gruta Paulo e Virgínia**). Also in the park is a pleasant picnic spot (**Bom Retiro**) and several restaurants (Restaurante Os Equilos and Restaurante a Floresta, which is near the **Ruínas do Archer**, the ruins of Major Archer's house). A recommended culinary experience is the open-air brunch at the **Museu do Açude** (☎ 2492 2119; Estrada do Açude 764, Floresta da Tijuca), held on the last Sunday of the month.

The park is home to many different bird and animal species, including iguanas and monkeys, which you might encounter on one of the excellent day hikes you can make here. Maps can be obtained at the small artisan **shop** (☺ 7am-9pm), just inside the park entrance.

The entire park closes at sunset. It's best to go by car, but if you can't, catch a number 221, 233 or 234 bus. Alternatively, take the metro to Saens Peña then catch a bus going to Barra da Tijuca and get off at Alto da Boa Vista. The best route by car is to take Rua Jardim Botânico two blocks past the Jardim Botânico (heading east from Gávea). Turn left on Rua Lopes Quintas and then follow the Tijuca or Corcovado signs for two quick left turns until you reach the back of the Jardim Botânico, where you turn right. Then follow the signs for a quick ascent into the forest and past the **Vista Chinesa** (get out for a good view) and the **Mesa do Imperador**, both of which offer some fantastic views of Rio's mountainous seascape. As soon as you seem to come out of the forest, turn right onto the main road and you'll see the stone columns at the entrance of Alto da Boa Vista on your left after a couple of kilometers. You can also drive up to Alto da Boa Vista by heading out to São Conrado and turning right up the hill at the Parque Nacional da Tijuca signs.

Warning: There have been occasional reports of armed robberies within the park. Most Cariocas recommend going on weekends when there are more people around.

---

best surf spot in Rio. Across the bay, Itacoatiara also has good breaks. For transportation to the beaches, grab your board and hop on the **Surf Bus** (☎ office 2539 7555, bus 8702 2837; www.surfbus .com.br in Portuguese; 1-way R$3), a bright yellow-orange bus that makes four return trips daily (beginning at 7am) from Largo do Machado (near Flamengo) to Prainha, with stops at beaches along the way.

If you don't have a board, you can hire or buy one in Arpoador at **Galeria River** (Map pp140-1; Rua Francisco Otaviano 67, Arpoador; per day R$30), a commercial center full of surf shops and boutiques.

You'll find informal surf schools scattered along the beaches of Ipanema, Leblon and Barra da Tijuca. Most charge around R$20 per hour.

Escolinha de Surf Paulo Dolabella (Map pp138-9; ☎ 2259 2320; in front of Rua Maria Quitéria, Ipanema Beach) Although you'll have to ask around to find him, Paulo gives private lessons.

Escolinha de Surf Barra da Tijuca (☎ 3209 0302; 1st kiosk after Post 5, Av Sernambetiba, Praia da Barra da Tijuca) This surfing school is run by a Brazilian ex-champion and former professional surfer.

Volleyball & Other Beach Sports

Volleyball is Brazil's second most popular sport (after football) and a natural activity for the beach. A local variation of the sport, seen on Rio's beaches, is *futevôlei*. It's a cross between volleyball and football – but no hands allowed.

Usually played on the firm sand at the shoreline, *frescobol* involves two players, each with a wooden racquet, hitting a small rubber ball back and forth as hard as possible.

Those interested in improving their volleyball game – or just meeting some Cariocas – should pay a visit to Pelé at **Escolinha de Vôlei** (Map pp138-9; ☎ 9702 5794; www.voleinapraia.com.br in Portuguese; near Rua Garcia D'Ávila, on Ipanema Beach). Pelé, who speaks English, has been giving one-hour volleyball lessons for over 10 years. Lessons are in the morning (from about 8am to 11am) and in the afternoon (5pm to 7pm). He charges around R$50 for the month and you can come as often as you like. Look for his large Brazilian flag on the beach.

Walking & Jogging
Good walking and jogging paths in the Zona Sul include Parque do Flamengo (Map pp144-5), which also has workout stations. Around Lagoa Rodrigo de Freitas (Map pp138-9), a 7.5km track provides a path for cyclists and joggers. Along the seaside, from Leme to Barra da Tijuca, there's a bike path and footpath. On Sunday, the road is closed to traffic from 7am to 6pm. The road skirting through Parque do Flamengo is also closed on Sundays.

Located between the mountains and the sea at Praia Vermelha in Urca is the Pista Cláudio Coutinho (Map pp142-3). It's closed to bicycles but open to walkers and joggers from 7am until 6pm daily, and is very secure because of the army post nearby.

WALKING TOUR
A blend of historic buildings and young skyscrapers, the center of Rio makes an excellent place to discover the city's charm away from its beaches and mountains. Among the hustle and bustle, you'll find museums, charming bars, theaters and open-air bazaars. This tour is best done during the week, when Centro is at its most vibrant (and safest).

Start at **Praça Floriano (1**; p154), which is the heart of modern Rio. Praça Floriano comes to life at lunchtime and after work when the outdoor cafés fill with Cariocas. The neoclassical **Teatro Municipal (2**; p154) overlooking the plaza is one of Rio's finest buildings.

On the east side of Av Rio Branco, facing Praça Floriano, is an open-air music market, **Rua Pedro Lessa (3**), where you can browse the

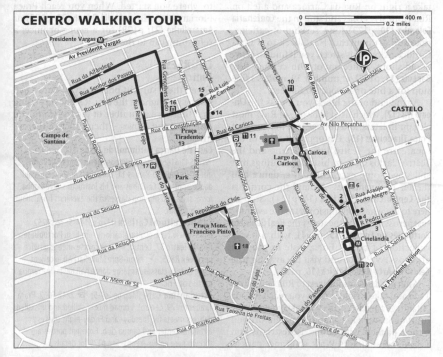

CENTRO WALKING TOUR

record and CD stalls. Next to it is the **Centro Cultural Justiça Federal** (4; ☎ 2510 8846; Av Rio Branco 241; admission free; ☽ noon-7pm Tue-Sun), which hosts changing contemporary exhibitions. The solid **Biblioteca Nacional** (5; ☎ 2262 8255; Av Rio Branco 219; admission free; ☽ noon-8pm Mon-Fri) is next door, while north on Av Rio Branco is another historic building, today hosting the **Museu Nacional de Belas Artes** (6; p154). Take a peek inside to see some of Rio's best-known 19th-century painters.

Now cross Av Rio Branco and walk in front of the Teatro Municipal, then take a left down Av 13 de Maio. Cross Av Almirante Barrosoa and you're in the **Largo da Carioca** (7), a pedestrian area that gets packed with vendors during the week. Up on the hill is the recently restored **Convento Santo Antônio** (8; p153). The original church here was started in 1608, making it one of Rio's oldest.

Gazing south from the convent, you'll notice the **Petrobras building** (9), whose boxlike metal chassis seems to cast an ominous shadow over the area. Behind it is the ultramodern Catedral Metropolitana.

Come back down from the church and take a right on Rua da Carioca and a left on Rua Gonçalves Dias and stop in the **Confeitaria Colombo** (10; p173) for a serving of caffeine, cake and art nouveau. Head back to Rua da Carioca. Along this street, you'll find an array of old shops, a slice out of 19th-century Rio. **Bar Luiz** (11; p175), at number 39, makes a fine stop for a bite or a *chope* (draft beer).

At the end of the block you'll pass the **Cinema Iris (12)**, which used to be one of Rio's most elegant theaters, and emerge into the hustle of **Praça Tiradentes (13)**. On opposite sides of the square are the Teatro João Caetano and the Teatro Carlos Gomez, historic buildings that still stage some excellent music, dance and theater performances. Around the corner is the **Centro Cultural Carioca** (14; p124). Stop in here to see what's on musically for the evening. Just across from the theater is the **Real Gabinete Português de Leitura** (15; p154), with a lovely collection of books. For a taste of modern art, cross Av Passos and visit the avant-garde **Centro de Arte Hélio Oiticica** (16; p153).

Afterwards, continue west to Rua Gonçalves Ledo and take a right. When you reach Rua da Alfândega turn left. This will take you into the heart of Saara, a longstanding neighborhood bazaar packed with shops, pedestrians and Lebanese restaurants. Walk, shop and snack as far as Campo de Santana. Make a U-turn there and proceed back along Rua Senhor dos Passos. Take a right on Rua Regente Feijó. When this street ends take a short left and then a right and head down Rua do Lavradio. This street is famous for its antique shops set in colorful 19th-century buildings. A number of great nightspots, such as **Rio Scenarium** (17; p180), feature excellent samba bands playing in restored colonial buildings.

When you reach Av República do Chile take a left and stop in the **Catedral Metropolitana** (18; p155) for a glimpse of the church's marvelous stained-glass windows. When you leave, head back to Rua do Lavradio for more window shopping. When you reach Av Mem de Sá, take a left and follow the road around the curve as you pass beneath the **Arcos do Lapa (19)**. This is Rio's big samba center at night, with clubs and old-school bars scattered all over the neighborhood. When you reach the Largo da Lapa, a small plaza along which a restaurant and a few samba clubs are scattered, take a left and walk along Rua do Passeio. You'll have great views of the arches from here. In two more blocks you'll be back to where you started. When you reach Praça Floriano, stop in at **Ateliê Odeon** (20; p175) or **Amarelinho** (21; p178) for a *chope* or juice, a refreshing cap to the walk.

COURSES
Dance
Given the resurgent popularity of dance hall samba throughout the city, it's not surprising that there are a number of places where you can learn the moves – then practice them – in Lapa.

Casa de Dança Carlinhos de Jesus (Map pp142-3; ☎ 2541 6186; www.carlinhosdejesus.com.br in Portuguese; Rua Álvaro Ramos 11, Botafogo) At this respected dance academy, Carlinhos and his instructors give samba, *forró*, salsa and hip-hop classes in the evenings from about 7pm to 10pm.

Centro Cultural Carioca (Map pp144-5; ☎ 2252 6468; www.centroculturalcarioca.com.br in Portuguese; Rua do Teatro 37, Centro; 4-week course, meeting twice per week R$65; ☽ noon-8pm Mon-Sat) An excellent place to take classes. Its large dance hall hosts live samba parties on Friday.

Estudantina Café (Map pp144-5; ☎ 2242 5062; Praça Tiradentes 79, Centro) A broad mix of skilled and unskilled dancers meets for Tuesday- and Friday-night classes at a cultural center and samba club. Excellent parties are thrown here on weekends. See p179 for details.

Núcleo de Dança (Map pp144-5; ☎ 2221 1011; 2nd fl, Rua da Carioca 14, Centro) On the northern edge of Lapa; offers classes on *forró*, tango, salsa and samba. Instructor Marcia Pinheiro is flexible – you can usually drop in and join a class. Most are held during the day – around noon – so stop in to see what's on.

Language

Many hostels advertise freelance language teachers who offer private and small-group lessons, which are often more economical than studying through a school.

Instituto Brasil-Estados Unidos (IBEU; Map pp140-1; ☎ 2548 8430; www.ibeu.org.br in Portuguese; 5th fl, Av NS de Copacabana 690, Copacabana; 4-week course, meeting 3 times per week R$1000) One of the most respected language institutions in the city, IBEU has four levels of classes (beginner to advanced). Classes typically meet for two hours a day, Monday through Thursday for four weeks.

RIO FOR CHILDREN

Brazilians are very family-oriented. Many hotels let children stay free, although the age limit varies. Babysitters are readily available and most restaurants have high chairs.

Lonely Planet's *Travel with Children*, by Cathy Lanigan, gives a lot of good tips and advice on traveling with kids in the tropics.

There's plenty of good spade and sand-bucket fun to be had on Rio's beaches, particularly Leblon's *posto* 12, known as Baixo Bébe for its mini-playground and all the moms and tots around. Other amusement for kids includes the shows and exhibits at the **Planetário** (p128), the animals of **Jardim Zoológico** at **Quinta da Boa Vista** (p156), the impressive ships at **Espaço Cultural da Marinha** (p153), and the mechanized displays at the **Museu de Folclórico Edson Carnerio** (p151). You can also hire bikes (including big, shaded four-seaters) and visit the playground near the bike stand at **Lagoa Rodrigo de Freitas** (p128).

In addition, children may also enjoy the following sights:

Mini-Rio (Map p137; 1st fl, Barra Shopping, Av das Américas, Barra da Tijuca; ☽ 10am-10pm) Small amusement area with bumper cars, boat and plane rides for little ones.

Museu Aerospacial (Map p137; ☎ 2108 8954; www.musal.aer.mil.br in Portuguese; Av Marechal Fontenele 2000, Campo dos Afonsos; admission free; ☽ 9am-3pm Tue-Fri, 9:30am-4pm Sat & Sun) Expositions on Santos Dumont (the Brazilian father of aviation) and the role of Brazil's air force in WWII. Lots of old planes, including replicas of Santos Dumont's planes: the *14 Bis* and the *Demoiselle*.

Terra Encantada (Map p137; ☎ 2421 9444; www.terra-encantada.com.br in Portuguese; Av Ayrton Senna 2800, Barra da Tijuca; adult/child R$36/18; ☽ 2-9pm Fri-Sun) The Enchanted Land includes Cabhum, a 64m, 100km/h free fall, and Ressaca, a toboggan ride that goes over a waterfall, among many other rides.

TOURS
Favela Tours

Marcelo Armstrong (☎ 3322 2727; www.favelatour.com.br; per person R$60) The pioneer of *favela* tourism, Marcelo takes small groups to visit the *favelas* of Rocinha and Vila Canoas near São Conrado, where he does an excellent job explaining the social and political context of the *favela* in relation to greater Rio de Janeiro. Marcelo's outfit donates a portion of its profits to *favela* social projects.

Paulo Amendoim (☎ 3322 8498, 9747 6860; paulo amendoim@hotmail.com; 2-3hr tour per person R$60) Former president of Rocinha's resident association, Paulo leads tours through Rio's biggest *favela* and offers visitors the chance to see beneath the stereotypes that characterize *favela* life.

Walking Tours

Cultural Rio (☎ 3322 4872, 9911 3829; www.culturalrio.com.br; 4hr tour per person from R$100) Run by the loquacious and erudite Carlos Roquette, this tour offers visitors an in-depth look at social and historical aspects of Rio de Janeiro. Itineraries include a night at the Teatro Municipal, colonial Rio, baroque Rio, imperial Rio and a walking tour of Centro. Professor Roquette has been in business for over 20 years.

Fabio Sombra (☎ 2275 8605; www.fasombra.cjb.net; tour for 4 people R$200) A multilingual artist still active as an arte naïf painter, Fabio leads tours around Centro and Santa Teresa. His most popular tour covers the ruins of the old port and historical sites around Praça XV de Novembro, the Mosteiro de São Bento and the Catedral Metropolitana, passing through Lapa and ending in Santa Teresa.

Luiz Amaral Tours (☎ 2259 5532; www.travelrio.com; tour per person around R$100) A friendly, well-traveled Carioca with a good command of English, Luiz offers small-group tours around Rio, including visits to Santa Teresa, an exploration of beaches south of Barra and nightlife tours in Rio.

Private Tours (☎ 2232 9710; www.privatetours.com.br) Pedro Novak has been leading excursions around the city and further afield since 1992. He also offers jeep tours to Tijuca and Praia de Grumari as well as trips to Paraty, Parque Nacional de Itatiaia and beyond. He speaks English, French, Spanish, Italian and Portuguese.

Bay Tours

Macuco Rio (Map pp144-5; ☎ 9200 3569; www.macuco rio.com.br; Marina de Glória, Glória; cruise R$50-100) Macuco's high-velocity 28-seat speedboat offers a more exhilarating bay tour. Trips circle around the bay or head to Cagarras Archipelago, for bird- and possibly dolphin-spotting.

Marlin Yacht Tours (Map pp144-5; ☎ 2225 7434; www.marlinyacht.com.br; Marina da Glória, Glória; cruise R$40-70) Marlin offers several tours aboard their large 30-person schooners to Cagarras Island, stopping for a beach swim along the way. They also offer a sunset cruise and sailing and diving trips.

Saveiros Tours (Map pp144-5; ☎ 2225 6064; www .saveiros.com.br; Marina de Glória, Glória; cruise R$40-70) These bay tours involve two-hour cruises out over Baía de Guanabara in large schooners.

Other Tours

Bonde Histórico (☎ 2215 8581; per person R$12; ☽ depart 10am & 2pm Sat) Three-hour tram tours run by the Museu do Bonde (Tram Museum). Guided tours of the Santa Teresa neighborhood illuminate historic points along the journey from downtown to the neighborhood of Silvestre and back, with a stop at the Museu do Bonde. Trams depart from the *bonde* station (Map pp144–5) on Rua Lélio Gama in Centro.

Be a Local (☎ 9643 0366; www.bealocal.com; per person R$30-60) Popular with backpackers, Be a Local offers group tours with a younger, edgier flavor. They offer *favela* tours (where you'll ride to the top of the *favela* by mototaxi), outings to football matches at Maracanã and trips to evening *favela* parties. Tours include pickup from your hostel/hotel.

Helisight (☎ 2511 2141, 2542 7895; www.helisight.com .br; per person 6min/30min R$150/520) Offering helicopter tours since 1991, Helisight has eight different itineraries, all giving a close-up view of Cristo Redentor and gorgeous views over the city. Price includes pick-up and drop-off from hotel. There is a three-person minimum.

Jeep Tour (☎ 2589 0883; www.jeeptour.com.br; 4hr-tour incl hotel pick-up & drop-off per person around R$150) Jeep Tour offers travel to the Parque Nacional da Tijuca atop a large, convertible jeep. The tour includes a stop at the Vista Chinesa, then on to the forest for an easy hike and a stop for a swim beneath a waterfall, before making the return journey.

FESTIVALS & EVENTS

Aside from Carnaval, there are many other exciting events happening throughout the year.

Dia de São Sebastião January 20 – The patron saint of the city is commemorated with a procession that carries his image from the Igreja de São Sebastião dos Capuchinos in Tijuca (Rua Haddock Lobo 266) to the Catedral Metropolitana, where it's blessed in a Mass celebrated by the archbishop of Rio de Janeiro.

Dia da Fundação da Cidade March 1 – The founding of the city by Estácio de Sá in 1565 is commemorated with a Mass in the church of its patron saint, São Sebastião.

Sexta-Feira da Paixão March or April – Good Friday is celebrated throughout the city. The most important ceremony is a reenactment of the Stations of the Cross under the Arcos do Lapa, carried out by more than a hundred actors.

Portas Abertas One weekend in May and in November – Santa Teresa's artists open their studios and the neighborhood becomes a living installation in this twice-yearly event. Dates change so stop by at Cama e Café (p169) or Parque das Ruinas (p155) for more information.

Festas Juninas June – The June Festival is one of the most important folkloric festivals in Brazil. In Rio, it's celebrated in various public squares throughout the month, primarily on June 13 (Dia de Santo Antônio), June 24 (Dia de São João) and June 29 (Dia de São Pedro).

Festa da São Pedro do Mar July 13 – The fishing community pays homage to its patron saint in a maritime procession. Decorated boats leave from the fishing district of Caju and sail to the statue of São Pedro in Urca.

Festa de NS da Glória do Outeiro August 15 – A solemn Mass is held in the Igreja de NS da Glória do Outeiro, which is ablaze with decorated lights, with a procession into the streets of Glória to mark the Feast of the Assumption. This festival includes music and colorful stalls set up in the Praça NS da Glória. Festivities start at 8am and continue all day.

Dia de Independência do Brasil September 7 – Independence Day is celebrated with a big military parade down Av Presidente Vargas. It starts at 8am at Candelária and goes just past Praça Onze, north of the Sambódromo.

Rio International Film Festival September and October – The festival is one of the biggest in Latin America. Over 200 films from all over the world are shown at some 35 theaters. The festival usually runs for 15 days from the last week of September through to the first week of October. Check the website (www.festivaldorio.com.br in Portuguese) for details.

Rio Jazz Festival October – Features three nights of great music. National and international acts present a wide variety of music – not just jazz. Dates vary from year to year.

Festa da Penha October and November – This is one of the largest religious and popular festivals in the city. It takes place every Sunday in October and the first Sunday in November, at Igreja NS da Penha de França, Largo da Penha 19 in Penha. It's very lively.

Reveillon & Festa de Iemanjá December 31 – New Year's Eve (Reveillon) in Rio is celebrated by millions of people. Tons of fireworks explode in the sky over Copacabana. New Year's Eve coincides with the festival of Iemanjá, the sea goddess. Wearing white, the faithful carry a statue of Iemanjá to the beach and launch flowers and other offerings into the sea.

SLEEPING

Reservations are a good idea in Rio, and you can often save by booking ahead. Hotel rates rise during the summer months

LONG-TERM RENTALS

If you're planning to stay in Rio for longer than a few nights, you may consider renting an apartment, which is often much better value than staying in a hotel. The following agencies are adept at accommodating foreign visitors and can often arrange airport transportation, cell phone hire and provide other services. Apartments start at R$120 per night.

Blame it on Rio 4 Travel (Map pp140-1; ☎ 3813 5510; www.blameitonrio4travel.com; Rua Xavier da Silveira 15B, Copacabana) This popular agency rents many types of apartments; it also rents cell phones and provides many other services.

Copacabana Holiday (Map pp140-1; ☎ 2542 1525; www.copacabanaholiday.com.br; Rua Barata Ribeiro 90A, Copacabana) Specializing in Copacabana, this agency rents apartments for a minimum of three days.

Fantastic Rio (Map pp140-1; ☎ 2543 2667; Apt 501, Av Atlântica 974, Leme) Multilingual Peter Corr of Fantastic Rio rents everything from modest one-bedrooms to spacious four-bedrooms with beach views.

Rio Apartments (Map pp138-9; ☎ 2235 7180; www.rioapartments.com; Suite 301, Rua Farme de Amoedo 76, Ipanema) This highly professional outfit offers a wide selection of apartments in the Zona Sul, and can arrange cell phone rental, airport transport and more.

Vanna Rocha (☎ 2548 5030; www.vannarioflats.com.br) Vanna maintains a website of competitively priced apartment listings for Leblon, Ipanema and Copacabana. English spoken.

Yvonne Reimann (Map pp140-1; ☎ 2227 0281; Apt 605, Av Atlântica 4066, Copacabana) Yvonne rents a range of apartments in the area. She speaks French, German and English.

(December through February), and triple during New Year's Eve and Carnaval. Most hotels will only book in four-day blocks around these holidays.

Keep in mind that some hotels add in a combined 15% service and tax charge, though cheaper places don't generally bother with this.

Ipanema & Leblon

Ocean views with access to Rio's loveliest beaches, restaurants and bars make Ipanema and Leblon a magnet among travelers. Not surprisingly, prices here are higher than elsewhere.

BUDGET

Casa 6 Ipanema (☎ 2247 1384; www.casa6ipanema.com; House 14, Rua Barão da Torre 175, Ipanema; dm/d with fan R$40/120) On Ipanema's hostel row, this place has clean, basic, and extremely small rooms (with triple bunk beds), but staff is friendly and helpful and it's in a great location.

Lighthouse Hostel (☎ 2522 1353; www.thelighthouse.com.br; House 20, Rua Barão da Torre 175, Ipanema; dm/d R$45/120; 🔀 🖳) Along with a handful of other budget spots on this quiet lane, the Lighthouse has an easygoing vibe and clean, simple rooms that attract a good mix of backpackers. Accommodations consist of eight-bed dorm rooms and one private double.

Che Lagarto Ipanema (Map pp138-9; ☎ 2512 8076; www.chelagarto.com; Rua Paul Redfern 48, Ipanema; dm/d R$45/130) Part of a small empire of hostels in the Zona Sul, Che Lagarto's Ipanema branch is a five-story hostel, with tiny, basic rooms and not much common space – aside from the pricey bar on the 1st floor.

Ipanema Beach House (Map pp138-9; ☎ 3202 2693; www.ipanemahouse.com; Rua Barão da Torre 485, Ipanema; dm/d R$45/140; 🖳 🏊) One of Rio's loveliest hostels, the Ipanema Beach House is a converted two-story house with six- and nine-bed dorms (with three-tiered bunk beds). There are also several private rooms, spacious indoor and outdoor lounge spaces, a small bar and a pool.

MIDRANGE & TOP END

Margarida's Pousada (Map pp138-9; ☎ 2239 1840; margaridacaneiro@hotmail.com; Rua Barão da Torre 600, Ipanema; s/d/apt from R$75/120/140; 🔀) This excellently located Ipanema guesthouse has pleasant, simply furnished rooms popular with young (French) travelers. There's also a bigger private apartment available for rent in a building nearby.

Hotel San Marco (Map pp138-9; ☎ 2540 5032; www.sanmarcohotel.net; Rua Visconde de Pirajá 524, Ipanema; s/d from R$150/160; 🔀 🏊) It's all about location if you stay at the San Marco. Rooms are clean but cramped, and the green bedspreads aren't winning any style awards.

Hotel Vermont (Map pp138-9; ☎ 2522 0057, fax 2267 7046; Rua Visconde de Pirajá 254, Ipanema; s/d R$150/185; 🔀 🏊) The Hotel Vermont offers no-frills accommodations in a high-rise a few blocks from the beach. Hotel Vermont's small rooms are in need of renovation. Still, the location can't be beat.

Ipanema Flat Hotel Residência (Map pp138-9; ☎ 2523 1292; ipanemaflat_ipanema@yahoo.com.br; Rua Gomes Carneiro 137, Ipanema; s/d R$170/190) The place is suffering from a bad case of style envy: cheaply furnished rooms are seriously short on it and just aching to get some. The simple apartments have kitchens, balconies (no view) and bland but clean bedrooms at prices hard to find elsewhere in this neighborhood.

Ipanema Sweet (Map pp138-9; ☎ 2551 0488; Rua Visconde de Pirajá 161, Ipanema; s/d apt from R$200; 🔊) The modern, furnished apartments at this amiable spot each have a kitchen, lounge and balcony (no view), and are good value. A mix of Brazilians and international visitors consistently rate the place well.

Arpoador Inn (Map pp138-9; ☎ 2523 0060; www .riodejaneiroguide.com/hotel/arpoador_inn.htm; Rua Francisco Otaviano 177, Ipanema; d with/without ocean view R$390/205; 🏊) This six-story is the only hotel in town that doesn't have a busy street between it and the beach. That said, Arpoador Inn is disappointing, with worn carpets and small rooms, and it's not worth staying if you don't pay for an ocean view.

Ipanema Inn (Map pp138-9; ☎ 2523 6092; www .riodejaneiroguide.com/hotel/ipanema_inn.htm; Rua Maria Quitéria 27, Ipanema; s/d from R$240/270; 🏊) Simple but attractive, Ipanema Inn's rooms are pleasant with nice touches including woodblock prints on the walls and modern bathrooms with full tubs. Friendly, multilingual staff.

Everest Park (Map pp138-9; ☎ 2525 2200; www .everest.com.br; Rua Maria Quitéria 19, Ipanema; d from US$140) Just a block from the beach in a fantastic neighborhood, Everest Park is a fine hotel. The multilingual staff is very approachable, and the rooms are comfortable and nicely maintained. A woodsy smell in the corridors brings a scent of the country to the place.

Ritz Plaza Hotel (Map pp138-9; ☎ 2540 4940; www .ritzhotel.com.br; Av Ataulfo de Paiva 1280, Leblon; d R$310-345, apt R$450; 🏊) This elegant all-suites hotel is in a sublime part of Leblon. Rooms are nicely furnished with artwork on the walls, good lighting and spotless bedrooms, and all have balconies – some with partial ocean views. The one-bedroom apartments have small kitchens and a separate lounge/dining area.

Sol Ipanema (Map pp138-9; ☎ 2525 8484; www .solipanema.com.br; Av Vieira Souto 320, Ipanema; s/d from R$322/360; 🔊) The 15-story Sol Ipanema has an enviable position overlooking the beach. The well-decorated rooms feature dark-wood furnishings and good lighting. Oceanfront rooms cost about 20% more and are a worthy splurge if you can swing it.

Marina All Suites (Map pp138-9; ☎ 2540 5212; www .marinaallsuites.com.br; Av Delfim Moreira 696, Leblon; ste from R$695) Marina All Suites offers style and comfort with wonderful ocean views. Elegantly furnished suites have decent sound systems and space enough for you to host your own small parties. The rooftop pool, lounge space and small movie theater are nice touches. Bar D'Hotel (p177), on the 2nd floor, attracts the beauty crowd.

Copacabana & Leme

Copacabana, particularly Av Atlântica, is packed with hotels. Quality and price varies considerably, and many places are in dire need of a makeover.

BUDGET

Rio Backpackers (Map pp140-1; ☎ 2236 3803; www .riobackpackers.com.br; Travessa Santa Leocádia 38, Copacabana; dm/d from R$30/90; 🔊 💻) Young backpackers flock to this popular three-story hostel. The rooms are small and basic, and there are choice spots to chill out. Staff has all the lowdown on the city's nightlife.

Mellow Yellow Hostel (Map pp140-1; ☎ 2547 1993; www.mellowyellow.com.br; Rua General Barbosa Lima 51, Copacabana; dm/d from R$30/100; 🔊 💻) Copacabana's biggest hostel, Mellow Yellow attracts young travelers, who are willing to endure rustic accommodations in exchange for party atmosphere – complete with a bar, ample lounge space, a patio with spa and barbecue nights. Dorm rooms have anywhere from four to 24 beds; the cheapest lack air-conditioning.

Jucati (Map pp140-1; ☎ 2547 5422; www.edificiojucati .com.br; Rua Tenente Marones de Gusmão 85, Copacabana; dm R$30, apt s/d/tr/q R$100/120/140/160; 🔊 💻) Overlooking a leafy park, this unsigned building hides one of Copacabana's best deals. In addition to dorms, there are simple apartments with small kitchens and room enough to sleep up to six.

MIDRANGE & TOP END

Residencial Apartt (Map pp140-1; ☎ 2522 1722; www .apartt.com.br; Rua Francisco Otaviano 42, Arpoador; s/d R$116/182) Located in Arpoador between Copacabana and Ipanema, this hotel has 25 one-bedroom suites, each with a small kitchen, a lounge room (with cable TV) and a bedroom. Furnishings here are dated – floral patterns, dingy yellows and greens dominate – but for the price it's a good deal.

Hotel Santa Clara (Map pp140-1; ☎ 2256 2650; www .hotelsantaclara.com.br; Rua Décio Vilares 316, Copacabana; s/d from R$140/153) Up the street from a neighborhood park lies the Hotel Santa Clara, with its whitewashed exterior and blue shutters. The upstairs rooms are best, complete with wood floors, a writing desk and a refreshing balcony.

Ducasse Rio Hotel (Map pp140-1; ☎ 2522 1191; www .hotelducasse.com.br in Portuguese; Rua Sá Ferreira 76, Copacabana; s/d R$160/170; ☒) At this price bracket, the Ducasse is ahead of the rest. The medium-sized rooms are simply furnished but bright and cozy. All rooms ending in 1, 2, 3 and 4 have balconies, which are just large enough to step out onto and take a breath of ocean air.

Hotel Vilamar (Map pp140-1; ☎ 3461 5601; www .hotelvilamarcopacabana.com.br; Rua Bolívar 75, Copacabana; s/d from R$160/180; ☒ ☒) Fairly new on the block, the 15-story Vilamar is on a quiet street and has pleasant clean-swept rooms with cheery bedspreads and big windows.

Apa Hotel (Map pp140-1; ☎ 2548 8112; www.apahotel .com.br; Rua República do Peru 305, Copacabana; s/d R$165/180) The Apa is dated but has helpful staff and clean rooms. Some rooms have balconies.

Hotel Toledo (Map pp140-1; ☎ 2257 1995; www .hoteltoledo.com.br; Rua Domingos Ferreira 71, Copacabana; s/d R$165/195; ☒) A block from the beach, the Toledo has aging, simply furnished rooms with either carpet or tile floors. Some have ocean views.

Atlantis Copacabana (Map pp140-1; ☎ 2521 1142; www.atlantishotel.com.br; Rua Bulhões de Carvalho 61, Copacabana; s/d R$180/200; ☒) Between Copacabana and Ipanema, Atlantis is in a good location for exploring either neighborhood. The rooms here are short on elegance and inexpensively furnished, but rooms above the 9th floor have views.

Acapulco (Map pp140-1; ☎ 2275 0022; www.acapulco hotel.com.br; Rua Gustavo Sampaio 854, Leme; d from R$190; ☒) After a much-needed renovation in 2005, Acapulco offers modern, streamlined rooms on a quiet street one block from the beach. It has a handful of suites for those seeking a bit more room.

Copacabana Praia Hotel (Map pp140-1; ☎ 2522 5646; www.copacabanapraiahotel.com.br; Rua Francisco Otaviano 30, Copacabana; d R$200; ☒ ☒) All rooms in the 11-story hotel have balconies and top-floor digs

have partial sea views. Rooms are comfortable but compact.

Copacabana Hotel Residência (Map pp140-1; ☎ 2548 7212; www.copahotelresid.com.br; Rua Barata Ribeiro 222, Copacabana; d R$220; ☒ ☒) A few blocks from the beach, the Copacabana Hotel Residência has 70 spacious suites with small kitchen units, living rooms and clean, well-maintained quarters, though it's very cheaply furnished.

Hotel Debret (Map pp140-1; ☎ 2522 0132; www .debret.com; Av Atlântica 3564, Copacabana; d from R$230) The Hotel Debret is a traditional hotel in a converted apartment building. It has simple colonial-style furnishings and great views from the top-floor restaurant. The ocean-fronting rooms (luxos; luxury rooms) are recommended.

Orla Copacabana (Map pp140-1; ☎ 2525 2425; www .orlahotel.com.br; Av Atlântica 4122, Copacabana; d from R$275; ☒ ☒) The entrance to the Orla Copacabana is past sleek lounge chairs, artfully lit flower arrangements and giant canvases along the wall. Upstairs, the design falters a bit but still presents modern furnishings, marble-fixtured bathrooms and decent views. There's a rooftop pool and patio.

our pick Rio Guesthouse (Map pp140-1; ☎ 2521 8568; www.rioguesthouse.com; Rua Francisco Sá 5, Copacabana; d R$280-450; ☒) On the top floor of a high-rise overlooking Copacabana Beach, this small guesthouse offers handsomely decorated rooms in a welcoming setting. There's also a sunny patio overlooking Copacabana Beach.

Design Hotel Portinari (Map pp140-1; ☎ 3222 8800; www.hotelportinari.com.br; Rua Francisco Sá 17, Copacabana; d from R$290; ☒) This stylish 13-story hotel has artfully lit rooms with comfortable beds, big windows and tile floors. The top-floor restaurant is set with tropical plants and boasts fine views through the floor-to-ceiling windows.

Parthenon Arpoador (Map pp140-1; ☎ 3222 9600; www.mercure.com.br in Portuguese; Rua Francisco Otaviano 61, Copacabana; ste from R$340; ☒ ☒) The all-suites Parthenon Arpoador has rooms with sleek white leather sofas that open into beds, modern kitchenettes, TVs with stereo and DVD player, ambient lighting and comfortable bedrooms. All have verandas – though there's no view. In addition to a long, narrow swimming pool, there's also a sauna and workout room.

Le Meridien (Map pp140-1; ☎ 3873 8888; mail@ lemeridien-riodejaneiro.com; Av Atlântica 1020, Leme; d from R$380) A decadent affair, Le Meridien has all the trappings of luxury: crisply dressed staff, elegant lobby, excellent French restaurant on the 37th floor. The rooms are comfortable and spacious but hardly inspiring. The view, however, is, so be sure to book the *luxo*.

Copacabana Palace (Map pp140-1; ☎ 2548 7070; www.copacabanapalace.com.br; Av Atlântica 1702, Copacabana; d from R$880) The city's most famous hotel, the Palace has hosted heads of state and rock stars (including the Rolling Stones in 2005). The dazzling white facade dates from the 1920s, when the hotel became a symbol of the city. Inside you'll find a range of rooms, a wonderful pool and excellent restaurants.

Botafogo

Although there aren't many accommodations in the area, this is where you'll find an authentic slice of Rio – its tree-lined streets, old-school *botecos* and non-touristy restaurants.

El Misti Hostel (Map pp142-3; ☎ 2226 0991; www.elmistihostel.com; Praia do Botafogo 462, House 9, Botafogo; dm/s/d R$25/100/140, s/d without bathroom R$80/120; ▣) Located along Botafogo's hostel row, El Misti is a popular budget spot among Brazilian and foreign travelers for its cheap dorm rooms (with triple bunk beds) and lively atmosphere. It's a short walk to the Botafogo metro station.

O Veleiro (☎ 2554 8980; s/d from US$62/69; ▣ ▣) O Veleiro is a B&B surrounded by remnants of Atlantic rain forest, offering attractive rooms in a friendly, welcoming setting. There's a pool, backyard and splendid garden views over the hillside. It's a 20-minute walk up from Botafogo beach. The owners only give out the address to those confirming reservations. For more information, call the telephone number provided.

Flamengo, Catete & Glória

These middle-class neighborhoods have affordable options if you don't mind being far from the beach.

BUDGET

Hotel Monterrey (Map pp142-3; ☎ 2265 9899; Rua Arturo Bernardes 39, Catete; s without bathroom R$30, s/d with fan R$50/70) It's a bit of a dump, but if you're short on cash, and have sworn off hostels, Monterrey might be for you. Rooms are small and basic and some lack windows.

Hotel Riazor (Map pp142-3; ☎ 2225 0121; hotel riazor1@hotmail.com; Rua do Catete 160, Catete; s/d R$50/75; ▣) The pretty colonial facade of the Riazor hides basic quarters, which are not bad for the price. Sparkling wall paint and round

beds are features in some. Others are simple, straightforward affairs.

Hotel Ferreira Viana (Map pp142-3; ☎ 2205 7396; Rua Ferreira Viana 58, Catete; s/d R$55/75; ▣) The best rooms here have good light, bright tiled floors, modern furnishings and plenty of space. Not all the rooms are decent, however, so see a few before committing.

Hotel Turístico (Map pp144-5; ☎ 2557 7698; fax 2558 9388; Ladeira da Glória 30, Glória; s/d R$60/80; ▣) On a quiet street near the Igreja de NS da Glória do Outeiro, the Turístico is a friendly spot with clean, well-maintained rooms – some with balconies.

Hotel Caxambu (Map pp142-3; ☎ 2265 9496; Rua Corrêa Dutra 22, Catete; s/d R$65/75; ▣) This nicely renovated place maintains a higher standard than other budget options. Rooms are clean, though some lack natural light.

MIDRANGE & TOP END

Imperial Hotel (Map pp142-3; ☎ 2556 5212; www.imperialhotel.com.br; Rua do Catete 186, Catete; d from R$120; ▣ ▣) A fair choice for Catete, this hotel is set in a lovely white three-story building. The rooms here are clean and modern, and *luxos* have whirlpool tubs.

Mengo Palace Hotel (Map pp142-3; ☎ 2556 5343; mengohotel@infolink.com.br; Rua Corrêa Dutra 31, Flamengo; s/d ste from R$150/180; ▣) Mengo Palace is a clean, modern all-suites hotel with a forlorn air about it. The rooms are small with pressed wood floors, carpeting on the walls and whirlpool bathtubs big enough for two. The beds are a little stiff.

Hotel Glória (Map pp144-5; ☎ 2555 7373; www.hotelgloriario.com.br; Rua do Russel 632, Glória; d from R$165; ▣ ▣) Once a grand 1920s beachfront hotel, Glória still retains the aura of its past splendor, when it overlooked prime beachfront. Red carpets and old paintings line the hallways, along with antique fixtures and liberal use of brass. Glória lost its glory when the tunnel to Copacabana was constructed. If you stay here, book your room in the old part of the hotel, with its antique-filled rooms, fine verandas and sitting rooms.

Santa Teresa

A growing number of hotels have opened in Santa Teresa in recent years, drawing travelers to this intriguing, arts-loving neighborhood. Do take care when walking around, day or night, as muggings are not uncommon.

BUDGET & MIDRANGE

Pousada Favelinha (Map pp142-3; www.favelinha.com; Rua Antonio Joaquim 13, Morro do Pereirão da Silva; dm/d R$35/75) This clean, attractive guesthouse is one of the only guesthouses of its kind in Brazil. Located in the Favela Pereirão da Silva, Favelinha has four double rooms and a 5-bed dorm room, all with balconies that have stunning views over the city to Pão de Açúcar. There's also a terrace, a lounge for guests, and lots of insider info from the welcoming Brazilian-German owners. While the Pereirão da Silva is one of Rio's more peaceful *favelas*, this place isn't for everyone – some love it; some don't. To get there, take the *bonde* to Colegio Asunção (Rua Almirante Alexandrino 2024) and enter the favela through the school grounds.

Rio Hostel (Map pp144-5; ☎ 3852 0827; www.rio hostel.com; Rua Joaquim Murtinho 361, Santa Teresa; dm/ d/chalet R$37/100/120; ☒ ☒) A favorite among travelers, Rio Hostel provides a home away from home, with handsomely designed rooms, a cozy lounge and a backyard patio. The spirit of bonhomie prevails with barbecues and occasional jam sessions by guests and local musicians.

Cama e Café (Map pp144-5; ☎ 2224 5689; www .camaecafe.com.br; Rua Pascoal Carlos Magno 5; d from R$90) Cama e Café is a B&B network that links travelers with local residents, making it a brilliant way to get an insider take on the neighborhood. There's a pool of some 50 houses to choose from, and guests can select their accommodations by location and comfort level. Accommodations range from modest to lavish, with a decent breakfast and sizable rooms with private bathrooms common to all. Check the website for listings.

Casa Áurea (Map pp144-5; ☎ 2242 5830; www .casaaurea.com.br; Rua Áurea 80; d R$90-140) Set on a quiet street, this handsome two-story house has been converted into a simple guesthouse with pleasant, airy rooms and a small garden with hammocks out back.

Casa Mango Mango (Map pp144-5; ☎ 2508 6440; www.casamangomango.com; Rua Joaquim Murtinho 587; dm R$35, d without/with bathroom R$120/168; ☐ ☒) In an atmospheric Victorian mansion, this friendly guesthouse has comfortable, spacious rooms and a lush garden and patio. Excellent breakfasts.

Castelinho 38 (Map pp144-5; ☎ 2252 2549; www .castelinho38.com; Rua Triunfo 38; s/d from R$120/150; ☒) Opened as a guesthouse in 2006, Castelinho

offers a range of spacious rooms with high ceilings, wood floors and a light, airy design. It's set in a mid-19th-century mansion and has an outdoor terrace with a garden and lounge space.

our pick Solar de Santa (Map pp144-5; ☎ 2221 2117; www.solardesanta.com; Ladeira do Meireles 32; d R$385-565; ☒ ☒) Set in a converted colonial villa, this marvelous boutique hotel has beautifully designed rooms with wood floors and colorful details. Rooms open onto a veranda with splendid views through the lush foliage out front to downtown. Overlooking the lush grounds is a patio, ideal for an afternoon drink.

Mama Ruisa (Map pp144-5; ☎ 2242 1281; www .mamaruisa.com; Rua Santa Cristina 132; d from €220; ☒ ☒) Another of Santa Teresa's new boutique hotels, Mama Ruisa aims for bohemian chic in its seven spacious, uniquely designed guestrooms. Every whim is catered for in this lovely converted colonial mansion, and guests can opt for massages, private tours or just enjoy the spectacular view over the bay from the swimming pool.

EATING

Rio has an impressive array of restaurants, serving Brazilian regional cuisine along with international and fusion fare. In general, Ipanema and Leblon boast Rio's best dining scene, though every neighborhood has its gems.

You can eat on the cheap (try per-kilo places and juice bars), but it's worth splashing out for a meal once and a while (dinner for two averaging R$80 to R$120) to enjoy fantastic cuisine in some beautiful settings. Among Rio's quintessential dining experiences: feasting at a *churrascaria* (all-you-can-eat barbecued meat restaurant), dining alfresco beside the lake in Lagoa, joining the fashion parade at a sidewalk café in Ipanema, chowing on local favorites at a neighborhood *boteco* and lingering over the sweeping views from a restaurant patio in high-up Santa Teresa.

Ipanema & Leblon

By day, Ipanema's busy cafés and juice bars fill with bronze bodies heading to and from the beach, while at night its tree-lined streets make a picturesque setting for open-air dining. Leblon's Rua Días Ferreira and Ipanema's Rua Garcia D'Ávila are packed with dining options.

For fresh tropical fruits, visit the *feiras* (produce markets), which are on Monday on Rua Henrique Dumont (Ipanema), Tuesday on Praça General Osório (Ipanema), Thursday on Rua General Urquiza (Leblon) and Friday on Praça NS de Paz (Ipanema). On Sunday, the Hippie Fair, in Praça General Osório (Ipanema), has a stall in the southeast corner of the plaza where you can buy tasty Northeastern cuisine. Don't miss it.

BUDGET

Polis Sucos (Map pp138-9; ☎ 2247 2518; Rua Maria Quitéria 70, Ipanema; juices R$3-4; ☾ 7am-midnight) Serving 40 or so juices, Polis Sucos is a great place to get your vitamins, and you can pair those tangy beverages with sandwiches (vegetarian, chicken, filet mignon).

Fontes (Map pp138-9; ☎ 2512 5900; Rua Visconde de Pirajá 605D, Ipanema; mains R$7-10; ☾ 11am-10pm Mon-Sat, noon-8pm Sun) Hidden in a nondescript shopping plaza, this tiny, low-key restaurant serves decent vegetarian meals. The menu changes daily but features shiitake-filled manioc pastries, green salads, roasted eggplant and the like. On Saturday, the rich, smoked-tofu *feijoada* draws a crowd.

Mel & Pimenta (Map pp138-9; ☎ 2227 1477; Rua Visconde de Pirajá 44B, Ipanema; mains R$7-15; ☾ 9am-6pm) This attractive, airy bistro serves fresh salads, quiches, sandwiches, crepes and other light fare.

Delírio Tropical (Map pp138-9; ☎ 3201 2977; Rua Garcia D'Ávila 48, Ipanema; salads R$8-12; ☾ 9am-9pm) Delírio Tropical serves 16 different varieties of salad along with soups and hot dishes (veggie burgers, grilled salmon). The open layout has a pleasant, casual vibe, with big windows overlooking the street. Breakfast also served.

New Natural (Map pp138-9; ☎ 2287 0301; Rua Barão da Torre 167, Ipanema; lunch specials R$12; ☾ 11am-6pm Tue-Sun) Featuring an excellent lunch buffet with many vegetarian options, New Natural has fresh pots of soup, rice, veggies and beans for rock-bottom prices.

MIDRANGE & TOP END

Vegetariano Social Club (Map pp138-9; ☎ 2540 6499; Rua Conde de Bernadotte 26L, Leblon; mains R$14-24; ☾ noon-5:30pm) On Saturday vegetarians can sample Brazil's signature dish at this zenlike spot when tofu *feijoada* is served. Other offerings include salads, soups, *sucos* (juices) and organic wine.

Gula Gula (Map pp138-9; ☎ 2259 3084; Rua Aníbal de Mendonça 132, Ipanema; mains R$20-30; ☾ noon-midnight) Gula Gula is a popular, low-key spot serving quiches and salads, as well as grilled meats and other Brazilian dishes. For dessert, try the rich chocolate mousse (order it *quente*, hot).

Nam Thai (Map pp138-9; ☎ 2259 2962; Rua Rainha Guilhermina 95B, Leblon; mains R$28-40; ☾ lunch Tue-Sun, dinner nightly) The charming, colonial Nam Thai features Thai and fusion dishes, such as spicy shrimp curry with pineapple and squid salad. Don't miss the *caipivodca de lychee* (litchi vodka *caipirinha*).

Capricciosa (Map pp138-9; ☎ 2494 2212; Rua Vinícius de Moraes 134, Ipanema; mains R$29-41; ☾ dinner) This trendy spot serves a huge variety of handsomely prepared, thin-crust pizzas.

Nik Sushi (Map pp138-9; ☎ 2512 6446; Rua Garcia D'Ávila 83, Ipanema; all-you-can-eat lunch/dinner R$29/41; ☾ lunch & dinner) Nik Sushi is an attractively set Japanese restaurant that's much liked among neighborhood regulars for its all-you-can-eat sushi specials.

Bazzar (Map pp138-9; ☎ 3202 2884; Rua Barão da Torre 538, Ipanema; mains R$30-45; ☾ lunch & dinner) On a quiet, tree-lined street, Bazzar is a handsomely designed contemporary restaurant, serving unique dishes like grilled *namorada* (a type of perch) with whole grain rice, citrus and pesto, and lamb with polenta and mushrooms. Outdoor seating in front.

Osteria Dell'Angolo (Map pp138-9; ☎ 2259 3148; Rua Paul Redfern 40, Ipanema; mains R$32-50; ☾ noon-4pm & 6pm until last customer Mon-Fri, 6pm until last customer Sat & Sun) Northern Italian cuisine is served here with consummate skill, and the *risotto nero di sepia* (squid risotto in ink sauce) is one of the best dishes on the menu. President Lula, among other notable visitors, has dined here.

Salitre (Map pp138-9; ☎ 3205 6977; Av General San Martín 857, Leblon; mains R$34-52; ☾ breakfast, lunch & dinner Tue-Sun) Above a wine store and gourmet delicatessen, Salitre serves unique international fare like sweet potato gnocchi with salmon as well as grilled dishes, and luscious desserts (just visit the counter on the first floor). Breakfast features homemade breads (a rarity in these parts).

our pick Zazá Bistrô Tropical (Map pp138-9; ☎ 2247 9101; Rua Joana Angélica 40, Ipanema; mains R$35; ☾ 7:30pm-midnight) French-colonial decor and delicately spiced cuisine await those venturing inside this charming converted house in Ipanema. Inventive combinations, blending

East and West, match the seductive mood inside. Upstairs, diners lounge on throw pillows, with candles glowing along the walls. Those who prefer fresh air can dine on the porch out front.

Casa da Feijoada (Map pp138-9; ☎ 2247 2776; Rua Prudente de Morais 10B, Ipanema; feijoada R$37; ☺ noon-11:30pm) At this longstanding institution, any day is fine to sample the rich, black bean and salted pork dish. The *feijoada* is served with the requisite orange slices, *farofa* (manioc flour sautéed with butter) and grated kale, all of which pair nicely with a *caipirinha*.

Fellini (Map pp138-9; ☎ 2511 3600; Rua General Urquiza 104, Leblon; per kg R$44; ☺ lunch & dinner) Fellini's high-quality buffet has something for everyone: salads, pastas, grilled fish and shrimp, sushi and roast meats.

Sushi Leblon (Map pp138-9; ☎ 2512 7830; Rua Días Ferreira 256, Leblon; dinner for 2 R$75-150; ☺ lunch & dinner) Leblon's premier sushi destination, Sushi Leblon boasts creative additions to its award-winning sashimi. The usual stylish crowd gathers here – and the wait can be exhausting – so steel yourself with a few rounds of sake.

CAFÉS & DESSERT SHOPS

Kurt (Map pp138-9; ☎ 2294 0599; Rua General Urquiza 117B, Leblon; desserts R$3-6; ☺ 8am-5pm Mon-Fri) At Kurt, flaky strudels and palm-sized tortes with strawberries and kiwifruit pair nicely with cappuccinos.

Armazém do Café (Map pp138-9; ☎ 2259 0170; Rua Rita Ludolf 87B, Leblon; cappuccino R$4; ☺ 9am-midnight) Dark wood furnishings and the scent of freshly ground coffee lend an authenticity to this Leblon coffeehouse. Armazém also serves snacks and desserts.

Cafeína (Map pp138-9; ☎ 2521 2194; Rua Farme de Amoedo 43, Ipanema; desserts R$6-8; ☺ 9am-8pm Sun & Mon, 8am-11:30pm Tue-Sat) The popular café, in the heart of Ipanema, has outdoor tables for enjoying the waffles, desserts, coffees and espressos.

Ateliê Culinário (Map pp138-9; ☎ 2239 2825; Rua Días Ferreira 45, Leblon; desserts R$6-10; ☺ 6pm-1am Mon-Fri, 1pm-1am Sat & Sun) Offering a tempting assortment of desserts, this small outdoor café is a good place to linger over dense cheesecake with guava sauce and/or moist chocolate cake.

Enviada (Map pp138-9; ☎ 2512 1313; Rua Días Ferreira 45, Leblon; desserts R$6-10; ☺ noon-6pm) An elegant café with heavenly chocolates, ice cream, cakes, teas and coffees.

B! (Map pp138-9; ☎ 2249 4977; Rua Visconde de Pirajá 572, Ipanema; salads R$12-16; ☺ 9am-midnight Mon-Sat, 1pm-midnight Sun) On the 2nd floor of the bookstore Livraria da Travessa, this stylish café makes a cozy setting for a coffee, desserts or a light meal.

QUICK EATS & TAKE-OUT

Cobal de Leblon (Map pp138-9; ☎ 2239 1549; Rua Gilberto Cardoso, Leblon; ☺ closed Sun) This charming market has lots of fruit and veggies for sale. You can also grab a bite at one of the many restaurants and cafés here.

HortiFruti (Map pp138-9; ☎ 2512 6820; Rua Días Ferreira 57, Leblon; ☺ 8am-8pm Mon-Sat, to 2pm Sun) Leblon's popular indoor fruit and vegetable market.

Zona Sul Supermarket (Map pp138-9; ☎ 2259 4699; Rua Días Ferreira 290, Leblon; ☺ 24hr, closed midnight Sun to 7am Mon) The best branch of Rio's supermarket chain stocks plenty of freshly baked breads, imported cheeses, wine, prosciutto and thousands of other products.

Mustafá (Map pp138-9; ☎ 2540 7299; Av Ataulfo de Paiva 1174, Leblon; snacks R$2-8; ☺ noon-7pm) This small take-out counter in Leblon serves fresh pita bread, tabbouleh, hummus and *quibe* (cracked wheat stuffed with spiced meat, then deep-fried).

Mil Frutas (Map pp138-9; ☎ 2521 1384; Rua Garcia D'Ávila 134A, Ipanema; ice cream R$6-10; ☺ 10:30am-1am Mon-Fri, 9:30am-1am Sat & Sun) Mil Frutas serves sandwich wraps, as well as tasty ice cream that showcases fruits from the Amazon and abroad. Try the *jaca* (jackfruit), litchi or *açaí* (berrylike fruit). There's a small patio in front.

Frontera (Map pp138-9; ☎ 3289 2350; Rua Visconde de Pirajá 128, Ipanema; per kg R$35-38; ☺ 11am-11pm) Run by a Dutch chef, Frontera offers more than 60 plates at its delectable lunch buffet, featuring a medley of French, Thai, Italian, Indian and other world flavors. It has cozier atmosphere than most per-kilo places.

Da Silva (Map pp138-9; ☎ 2521 1289; Rua Barão da Torre 340, Ipanema; per kg R$36; ☺ 11:30-2am) Da Silva spreads a fine buffet of excellent Portuguese cuisine, including lamb stew, pork tenderloin and delicate desserts.

Garcia & Rodrigues (Map pp138-9; ☎ 3206 4100; Av Ataulfo de Paiva 1251, Leblon; per kg R$40; ☺ 8am-midnight Mon-Thu & Sun, to 1am Fri & Sat) This French restaurant has a lovely deli where you'll find fresh bakery items, imported cheeses, salads, wines and desserts.

Gávea, Jardim Botânico & Lagoa

During the summer, live music fills the air as diners eat, drink and stroll along the lake. Rua Jota Jota Seabra is Jardim Botânico's most happening eating and drinking spot.

Braseiro da Gávea (Map pp138-9; ☎ 2239 7494; Praça Santos Dumont 116, Gávea; mains R$16-24; ☺ 11am-midnight Mon-Sat) Extremely popular with the weekend crowd, this breezy bistro serves large portions of its popular steak, pot roast and fried chicken.

Arab da Lagoa (Map pp138-9; ☎ 2540 0747; Parque dos Patins, Av Borges de Medeiros, Lagoa; platter for 2 R$46; ☺ 10am-1am) One of numerous outdoor restaurants on the lake, this popular spot serves traditional Middle Eastern specialties like hummus, baba ghanoush, tabbouleh, *quibe* and tasty thin-crust pizzas. The large platters for two or more are a good option for sharing. During the day, it's a peaceful refuge from the city, while at night you can hear live samba, *choro* (romantic, intimate samba) or jazz from 9pm (music charge R$6).

Guimas (Map pp138-9; ☎ 2259 7996; Rua José Roberto Macedo Soares 5, Gávea; mains R$24-36; ☺ noon-1am) A classic open-air *boteco* with creative flair, Guimas has been going strong for over 20 years. Trout with leeks and roast duck go well with superfine *caipivodcas* (vodka *caipirinhas*).

00 (Zero Zero; Map pp138-9; ☎ 2540 8041; Planetário, Av Padre Leonel Franca 240, Gávea; mains R$30-45; ☺ 8pm-late) Inside Gávea's planetarium, 00 is a sleek restaurant-lounge that serves Brazilian cuisine with Asian and Mediterranean accents. After dinner, have a few cocktails and stick around: some of Rio's best DJs spin at parties here.

Escola do Pão (Map pp138-9; ☎ 2294 0027; Rua General Garzon 10, Lagoa; brunch R$40; ☺ 5pm-midnight Tue-Sat, 9am-1pm Sat & Sun) In a converted colonial mansion, this beautifully decorated restaurant serves delightful French fare by night, but their decadent weekend brunch is famed.

Olympe (Map pp138-9; ☎ 2539 4542; Rua Custódio Serrão 62, Lagoa; mains around R$78; ☺ dinner Mon-Sat, lunch Fri) One of Rio's best chefs, Claude Troisgros continues to dazzle guests with unforgettable meals at his award-winning restaurant. Originally from France, Troisgros mixes old-world with new in ever inventive combinations. The setting is in a lovely house on a tree-lined street.

Copacabana & Leme

Copacabana has everything from five-star dining rooms atop beach-fronting hotels to charming old-fashioned bistros. Although the open-air restaurants along Av Atlântica have a nice view, the food isn't so hot, and things get a little seedy at night.

For fresh fruits, visit Copacabana *feiras*, which happen on Wednesday on Rua Domingos Ferreira, Thursday on Rua Belford Roxo and Rua Ronald de Carvalho, and Sunday on Rua Décio Vilares. Supermarkets include **Pão de Açúcar** (Av NS de Copacabana 497; ☺ 24hr) and the fruit-filled **HortiFruti** (Map pp140-1; Av Prado Junior 277; ☺ 8am-8pm Mon-Sat, 8am-2pm Sun).

BUDGET

Yonza (Map pp140-1; ☎ 2521 4248; Rua Miguel Lemos 21B, Copacabana; crepes R$10-16; ☺ 1pm-midnight lunch Tue-Fri, 6pm-midnight Sat & Sun) A young crowd flocks to this colorful creperie at night to fill up on hearty, inexpensive plates. Among the favorites: *picanha com gorgonzola* (steak with gorgonzola).

Cervantes (Map pp140-1; ☎ 2275 6147; Av Prado Júnior 335B, Copacabana; sandwiches R$12-18; ☺ noon-late Tue-Sun) This Copacabana institution gathers a mixed crowd who feast on trademark meat-and-pineapple sandwiches. Fussy waiters are quick to the tap when your *chope* runneth dry. Around the corner, at Rua Barato Ribeiro 7, is Cervantes' stand-up *boteco*, good for a meal in a hurry.

MIDRANGE & TOP END

Galeria 1618 (Map pp140-1; ☎ 2295 1618; Rua Gustavo Sampaio 840, Leme; mains R$15-26; ☺ 9am-11pm) Equal parts bookstore, art gallery and bistro, Galeria 1618 serves tasty quiches, coffee, juices and desserts to an attractive middle-class crowd. It also serves an excellent daily special – risotto with shrimp and the like.

Botequim Informal (Map pp140-1; ☎ 2255 4746; Rua Domingos Ferreira 215, Copacabana; mains R$17-23; ☺ lunch & dinner) One of the neighborhood's popular meeting points, this airy bar and restaurant serves Brazilian standards and cold beer on a quiet tree-lined street.

La Trattoria (Map pp140-1; ☎ 2255 3319; Rua Fernando Mendes 7A, Copacabana; mains R$18-32; ☺ 11am-1am) This casual but festive Italian trattoria has been a neighborhood favorite for over 25 years. Seafood pasta dishes are particularly recommended.

Azumi (Map pp140-1; ☎ 2541 4294; Rua Ministro Viveiros de Castro 127, Copacabana; plates R$20-40; ☺ dinner Tue-Sat) This low-key sushi bar is a favorite among the *nisei* (second-generation Japanese born in Brazil) community. Azumi's *sushiman* (sushi chef) masterfully prepares delectable sushi and sashimi. Tempuras and soups are also excellent.

Copa Café (Map pp140-1; ☎ 2235 2947; Av Atlântica 3056, Copacabana; mains R$20-44; ⏰ 7pm-2am Tue-Sun) Facing the beach, this sleek, loungelike place has black wood floors, white bar stools, an open layout and electronic music. The menu features high-end bistro fare: fresh fish, steak and gourmet burgers.

Carretão (Map pp140-1; ☎ 2542 2148; Rua Ronald de Carvalho 55, Copacabana; all-you-can-eat R$28; ⏰ 11:30am-midnight) It's all about the meat at this inexpensive *churrascaria*. There is another branch in Ipanema, at Rua Visconde de Pirajá 112.

Amir (Map pp140-1; ☎ 2275 5596; Rua Ronald de Carvalho 55C, Copacabana; mains R$28-35, all-you-can-eat R$35; ⏰ lunch & dinner) Serving some of Rio's best Middle Eastern dishes, this enticing two-story restaurant near the beach offers consistently good plates of hummus, *kaftas* (savory meatballs), falafel and salads. The truly ravenous can opt for the *rodízio* (all-you-can-eat smorgasbord), brought to your table.

Capricciosa (Map pp140-1; ☎ 2255 2598; Rua Domingos Ferreira 187, Copacabana; mains R$29-41; ⏰ dinner) This stylish spot serves excellent thin-crust pizzas.

Le Blé Noir (Map pp140-1; ☎ 2287 1272; Rua Xavier da Silveira 15A, Copacabana; mains R$30-45; ⏰ dinner) Flickering candles, subdued conversation and tasty crepes make this popular restaurant a real date-pleaser.

Siri Mole (Map pp140-1; ☎ 2267 0894; Rua Francisco Otaviano 50, Copacabana; mains for two R$80; ⏰ dinner daily, lunch Tue-Sun) Understated elegance is the key to Siri Mole's long-standing success – both in ambience and in the perfectly prepared seafood. Among the favorites at this award-winning restaurant: *moqueca de siri mole* (spicy, soft-shell crab stew) and *acarajé* (spicy, shrimp-filled croquettes).

Marius Crustáceos (Map pp140-1; ☎ 2104 9002; Av Atlântica 290A, Leme; per person R$130; ⏰ lunch & dinner) Although the price is sky-high here, this all-you-can-eat seafood restaurant has many fans. The waiters file through the dining room bearing delectable fruits of the sea – lobster, mussels, oysters, tuna, salmon, scallops and more. Next door is **Marius Carnes** (☎ 2104 9102; Av Atlântica 290B, Leme; per person R$85; ⏰ lunch and dinner), serving delicious cuts of steak.

CAFÉS & DESSERT SHOPS

Cafeína (Map pp140-1; ☎ 2547 8651; Rua Constante Ramos 44, Copacabana; pastries R$2-4; ⏰ 8:30am-11:30pm Tue-Sat, 9am-8:30pm Sun & Mon) A few blocks from the beach, Cafeína is a pleasant indoor and outdoor spot that serves good coffee and a variety of baked goods.

Bakers (Map pp140-1; ☎ 2256 7000; Rua Santa Clara 86B, Copacabana; Danishes R$4; ⏰ 9am-8pm Mon-Fri, to 6:30pm Sat, 9am-5pm Sun) Behind shiny countertops are tasty banana Danishes, apple strudels and flaky croissants.

Confeitaria Colombo (Map pp140-1; ☎ 3201 4049; Forte de Copacabana, Praça Coronel Eugênio Franco, Copacabana; snacks R$4-10; ⏰ 10am-8pm Tue-Sun) Located inside the Forte de Copacabana (admission R$2), this café has shady outdoor tables with magnificent views of Copacabana Beach.

Botafogo & Urca

Cobal de Humaitá (Map pp142-3; Rua Voluntários da Pátria 446, Botafogo; ⏰ closed Sun) This place is a fruit and flower market by day, with lively cafés and restaurants that open at night.

Livraria Prefácio (Map pp142-3; ☎ 2527 5699; Rua Voluntários da Pátria 39, Botafogo; mains R$14-24; ⏰ 2-10pm) In the back of a small bookshop, this café is a charming spot for a light meal or a drink.

Garota da Urca (Map pp142-3; ☎ 2541 8585; Av João Luís Alves 56, Urca; mains for two R$30-50; ⏰ noon-2am) Overlooking the small Praia da Urca, this neighborhood restaurant serves standard Brazilian fare, but the stunning views from the open-air veranda are the real draw.

Botequim Informal (Map pp142-3; ☎ 3171 6442; Praia de Botafogo 400, Botafogo; mains R$18-30; ⏰ noon-8:30pm) Located on the 7th floor of the Botafogo Praia Shopping, Botequim Informal has a fairly standard menu, but boasts spectacular views of the bay and Pão de Açúcar. It's one of many eateries in the mall.

Stravaganze (Map pp142-3; ☎ 2535 0591; Rua Visconde de Caravelas 121, Botafogo; pizzas R$25-35; ⏰ 6pm-midnight Mon-Sat) This small, elegant restaurant serves piping-hot pizzas cooked in a wood-burning oven. Fresh ingredients and excellent variety, along with attentive service, make this one of Rio's top pizza picks.

Adega do Valentim (Map pp142-3; ☎ 2541 1166; Rua da Passagem 178, Botafogo; mains R$26-42; ⏰ noon-1am) *Bacalhau* (cod) is the specialty at this old-fashioned Portuguese restaurant, which offers over a dozen different ways of preparation. Jocular waiters serve up plenty of other favorites.

Carême (Map pp142-3; ☎ 2537 2274; Rua Visconde de Caravelas 113, Botafogo; mains R$30-50; ☯ 8pm-midnight Tue-Sat) This French bistro serves excellent plates of marinated snapper, braised rabbit, and apple-and-nut risotto (among other vegetarian offerings). The desserts at Carême are legendary.

Yorubá (Map pp142-3; ☎ 2541 9387; Rua Arnaldo Quintela 94, Botafogo; mains for two R$70-90; ☯ 7-11pm Wed-Fri, 2-11pm Sat, noon-6pm Sun) Candlelit Yorubá looks as if it's always ready for the arrival of an *orixá* (deity of Candomblé). And if the goddess Iemanjá were to pay a surprise visit, she'd find heavenly plump shrimp and rich coconut milk blended to perfection in *babão de camarão*, and outstanding *moqueca* (Bahian fish stew).

Flamengo, Catete & Glória

On weekend nights, the restaurants and bars lining Rua Marquês de Abrantes crowd with neighborhood diners. In Catete, the streets near Largo do Machado have a few popular outdoor restaurants.

BUDGET

Estação República (Map pp142-3; ☎ 2225 2650; Rua do Catete 104, Catete; per kg R$19; ☯ 11am-11pm) Estação's buffet table is a neighborhood institution. Featuring an extensive selection of salads, meats, pastas and vegetables, it's easy to indulge without breaking the bank.

Catete Grill (Map pp142-3; ☎ 2285 3442; Rua do Catete 239, Catete; per kg R$21; ☯ 11am-11pm) This modern per-kilo restaurant is a good inexpensive lunch or dinner choice when exploring the neighborhood. Good variety of salads, pastas, seafood and grilled meats.

MIDRANGE & TOP END

Severyna da Glória (Map pp144-5; ☎ 2224 6604; Rua Santo Amaro 38, Glória; mains R$12-16; ☯ 11am-11pm) One of the rare gems of the neighborhood, Severyna is a cozy restaurant with rustic décor and satisfying plates of *carne seca* (dried meat with spices), *moqueca* and other classic Northeastern fare. There's live music Thursday to Sunday nights at 8pm (R$6).

Armazem do Chopp (Map pp142-3; ☎ 2557 4052; Rua Marquês de Abrantes 66, Flamengo; mains R$14-20; ☯ noon-midnight) In a barnlike structure above the street, Armazem do Chopp is a neighborhood favorite for its tasty grilled dishes and traditional inexpensive Brazilian fare (with

lunch specials). At night, its open-air front deck is a lively place for ice-cold drafts.

Taberna da Glória (Map pp144-5; ☎ 2265 7835; Rua do Russel 32A, Glória; mains R$17-25; ☯ noon-1am) On a small plaza in the heart of Glória, this large outdoor eatery serves filling Brazilian grilled meats and fish, and its *feijoada* on Saturday still draws crowds.

Belmonte (Map pp142-3; ☎ 2552 3349; Praia do Flamengo 300, Flamengo; mains R$18-36; ☯ 7am-late) One of the city's classic *botecos* (and now a popular chain), Belmonte is a vision of 1950s Rio. Beneath globe lights, a few patrons steel their nerves with *cachaça* as unhurried waiters make their way across the tile floors, carrying plates of trout or steak sandwiches.

Churrascaria Majórica (Map pp142-3; ☎ 2285 6789; Rua Senador Vergueiro 11, Flamengo; mains for two R$50; ☯ noon-midnight Tue-Sat) Meat is very serious business at Majórica, and if you're looking for an authentic *churrascaria* experience, look no further.

Lamas (Map pp142-3; ☎ 2556 0799; Rua Marquês de Abrantes 18A, Flamengo; mains R$25-45; ☯ dinner) This classic restaurant opened in 1874, and in spite of the mileage, dishes here hold up well. You can't go wrong with grilled *linguiça* (garlicky pork sausage) or filet mignon.

Casa da Suíça (Map pp142-3; ☎ 2552 5182; Rua Cândido Mendes 157, Glória; fondues R$42; ☯ lunch Sun-Fri, dinner daily) Tucked away on a quiet street in Glória lies a slice of Switzerland in the tropics. Featuring flambés, fondues and an ever-changing menu, Casa da Suíça has a strong culinary reputation.

Porcão Rio's (Map pp142-3; ☎ 2554 8535; Av Infante Dom Henrique, Flamengo; all-you-can-eat R$60; ☯ 11:30am-midnight) Set in the Parque do Flamengo with a stunning view of Pão de Açúcar, this is an excellent *churrascaria*.

Centro

It's worth lunching in Centro, where you can rub elbows with Rio's workaday crowds and take advantage of weekday specials, offered at even the toniest restaurants. An area worth exploring is Travessa do Comércio, just after work when the restaurants and cafés fill with chatter. The cafés and restaurants around Praça Floriano are also popular gathering/quaffing spots.

BUDGET & MIDRANGE

Confeitaria Colombo (Map pp144-5; ☎ 2232 2300; Rua Gonçalves Dias 34, Centro; desserts R$4-8; ☯ 8am-8pm

Mon-Fri, 10am-5pm Sat) Stained-glass windows, brocaded mirrors and marble countertops create one of the most lavish settings for coffee or a meal.

Bistro do Paço (Map pp144-5; ☎ 2262 3613; Praça XV de Novembro 48; mains R$10-17; ⓨ lunch Mon-Sat) Inside the Paço Imperial, this airy lunchtime spot serves fresh salads, tasty sandwiches and piping hot quiches, with decent vegetarian options. A more formal restaurant lies inside the same building.

Casa Cavé (Map pp144-5; ☎ 2222 2358; Rua Sete de Setembro 137; mains R$10-20; ⓨ 9am-7pm Mon-Fri, to 1pm Sat) This simple but historic coffeehouse has a few stand-up tables and a long counter full of tasty desserts.

Café do Rodrigues (Map pp144-5; ☎ 3231 8015; Travessa do Ouvidor 17, Centro; mains R$12-20; ⓨ 9am-8pm Mon-Fri) Inside the quaint bookstore Livraria da Travessa, Café do Rodrigues serves lighter fare such as *torta do palmito* (heart of palm quiche), soups and flavorful salads.

Cedro do Líbano (Map pp144-5; ☎ 2224 0163; Rua Senhor dos Passos 231; mains R$14-22; ⓨ 11am-5pm) Along a bustling pedestrian strip, this 70-year-old institution serves traditional Lebanese cooking: *quibes*, *kaftas*, lamb – tender portions of perfection.

Al Khayam (Map pp144-5; ☎ 2252 6261; www .alkhayam.com.br; Rua do Ouvidor 16; mains R$16-24; ⓨ lunch & dinner Mon-Fri) Al Khayam has modern decor and serves up excellent Middle Eastern cuisine. Hookahs and fortnightly belly dance shows add spice to the ample menu.

Ateliê Odeon (Map pp144-5; ☎ 2240 0746; Praça Floriano, Cinelândia; mains R$16-26; ⓨ noon-10pm Mon-Fri) Next to the cinema of the same name, the new Ateliê Odeon serves up decent Brazilian fare to a festive crowd on its open-air terrace. On weekends, Ateliê opens around film screenings next door.

Bar Luiz (Map pp144-5; ☎ 2262 6900; Rua da Carioca 39, Centro; mains R$18-30; ⓨ 11am-11:30pm Mon-Sat) A festive air fills this old saloon (opened in 1887), where you can get your fill of traditional German cooking – potato salad and smoked meats – along with ice-cold drafts.

Tempeh (Map pp144-5; ☎ 2232 8007; 2nd fl, Rua Primeiro de Março 24; per kg R$22; ⓨ lunch Mon-Sat) One of Centro's best vegetarian restaurants, Tempeh has a wide assortment of nicely prepared dishes, including soups, pastas, veggie burgers, vegan sushi and desserts. The old colonial walls add to the charm.

Brasserie Rosário (Map pp144-5; ☎ 2518 3033; Rua do Rosário 34, Centro; lunch specials R$23; ⓨ 8am-8pm Mon-Fri, 10am-5pm Sat) Set in a handsomely restored 1860s building, this atmospheric bistro has a hint of Paris. Croissants, *pain au chocolat* (chocolate croissant) and other bakery items fill the front counters, while the restaurant menu features roast meats and fish, soups, baguette sandwiches and the like.

Arte Temperada (Map pp144-5; ☎ 2253 2589; Rua Visconde de Itaboraí 78, Centro; mains R$24-36; ⓨ lunch Mon-Fri) Hidden in a tiny alley behind the Casa França-Brasil, this charming restaurant serves delicious Franco-Brazilian cuisine. Top choices are crepes, bouillabaisse, and the chicken breast served with passion-fruit sauce and polenta.

TOP END

Cais do Oriente (Map pp144-5; ☎ 2203 0178; Rua Visconde de Itaboraí 8, Centro; mains R$33-46; ⓨ lunch daily, dinner Tue-Sat) Brick walls lined with tapestries stretch high to the ceiling in this almost cinematic 1870s mansion. Set on a brick-lined street hidden from the masses, Cais do Centro blends West with East in dishes such as filet steak and sesame tuna.

AlbaMar (Map pp144-5; ☎ 2240 8378; Praça Marechal Âncora 186; mains for two R$50-120; ⓨ lunch & dinner) Perched over the water, this old favorite offers excellent views of the Baía de Guanabara and Niterói and serves up tasty seafood dishes. Favorites include shrimp curry.

Santa Teresa & Lapa

Santa Teresa has superb views, while Lapa has an unrivaled music scene, and both are excellent places to discover a mix of new and old-fashioned eating and drinking haunts.

BUDGET

Marizé Gourmet (Map pp144-5; ☎ 2221 0919; Av Mem de Sá 82, Lapa; sandwiches R$5-12; ☎ 8am-5pm Mon, to 11pm Tue & Wed, to 3am Thu & Fri, 8pm-3am Sat) This airy two-story restaurant is ideally suited to samba-club-goers in the area. It has big windows from which to watch the street action, and tasty salads, sandwiches and bar snacks. There's live music Thursday to Saturday (R$10 admission).

Jasmin Mango (Map pp144-5; ☎ 2242 2605; Largo do Guimarães 143, Santa Teresa; mains R$10-21; ⓨ 10am-11pm) Well-placed beside the *bonde* stop, Jasmin Mango is a charming spot to linger over sandwiches, quiches, pastas, pizzas and desserts. There's an airy patio in back.

MIDRANGE & TOP END

Encontras Cariocas (Map pp144-5; ☎ 2221 0028; Av Mem de Sá 77, Lapa; pizzas R$14-35; ☎ 6pm-5am Wed-Sun) This late-night pizza parlor is a good place to stop in while exploring Lapa's music scene. You'll find 24 pizza varieties amid old-fashioned charm – high wooden ceilings, brick walls and warm lighting.

Sobrenatural (Map pp144-5; ☎ 2224 1003; Rua Almirante Alexandrino 432, Santa Teresa; mains R$16-36; ☎ noon-midnight Mon-Sat) The exposed brick and old hardwood ceiling set the stage for feasting on the *frutos do mar* (seafood). Lines gather on weekends for grilled fish and *moqueca*. During the week, stop by for lunchtime specials.

Bar do Mineiro (Map pp144-5; ☎ 2221 9227; Rua Paschoal Carlos Magno 99, Santa Teresa; mains R$18-30; ☎ 11am-2am Tue-Thu, to 4am Fri & Sat, to 8pm Sun) Photographs of old Rio cover the walls of this old-school *boteco* in the heart of Santa Teresa. The *feijoada* is tops on Saturday. Good anytime dishes include *carne seca* and *linguiça* (garlicky pork sausages) along with strong *caipirinhas*.

Bar Brasil (Map pp144-5; ☎ 2509 5943; Av Mem de Sá 90, Lapa; mains R$18-40; ☎ 11:30am-11pm Mon-Fri, to 4pm Sat) This restaurant serves traditional German cuisine: sauerkraut, wursts, lentils, and an ever-flowing tap quench the appetites of the sometimes-rowdy Lapa crowd.

Nova Capela (Map pp144-5; ☎ 2252 6228; Av Mem de Sá 96, Lapa; mains R$18-40; ☎ 11am-late) Like Bar Brasil next door, Nova Capela stays open late into the night, and fills with a garrulous mix of neighborhood regulars, party kids and assorted characters who stumble in off the street. Legendarily bad-tempered waiters (no surprise given what they have to work with) serve up big plates of traditional Portuguese cuisine. *Cabrito* (goat) is very popular.

Espírito Santa (Map pp144-5; ☎ 2508 7095; Rua Almirante Alexandrino 264, Santa Teresa; mains R$20-36; ☎ noon-6pm Tue-Wed, to midnight Thu-Sat, to 7pm Sun) Espírito Santa is set in a beautifully restored mansion in Santa Teresa, with sweeping views from its back patio. The cuisine is no less amazing: The chef expertly prepares rich meat and seafood dishes from the Amazon.

Sansushi (Map pp144-5; ☎ 2224 4658; Rua Almirante Alexandrino 382, Santa Teresa; sushi platter R$46; ☎ 7pm-midnight Tue-Fri, 1pm-midnight Sat, to 8pm Sun) This tiny sushi spot on Santa Teresa's main strip attracts a loyal local following with its delectable sushi and sashimi (36 different varieties) as well as teriyaki and other hot dishes.

our pick **Aprazível** (Map pp144-5; ☎ 3852 4935; Rua Aprazível 62, Santa Teresa; mains R$53; ☎ noon-1am Thu-Sat, 1-7:30pm Sun) Hidden on a windy road high up in Santa Teresa, Aprazível has beautiful views and a lush garden setting. The menu features gourmet Brazilian fare: grilled fish with orange chutney and coconut rice, mixed mushroom lasagne and roast beef with onion torte. Thursday night is dedicated to live *chorinho* (R$15 cover). Reservations are recommended.

Barra & Greater Rio

Outside the city limits one can find fresh seafood in open-air spots overlooking the coast.

Bira (Map p137; ☎ 2410 8304; Estrada da Vendinha 68A, Barra de Guaratiba; mains for two R$80-125; ☎ noon-6pm Thu & Fri, noon-8pm Sat & Sun) Splendid views of Restinga de Marambaia await diners who make the trek to Bira, about 45 minutes outside of the city. On a breezy, wooden deck, you can feast on *moquecas*, sea bass, shrimp and crabmeat pastries.

Tia Palmira (Map p137; ☎ 2410 8169; Caminho do Souza 18, Barra de Guaratiba; set lunch R$60; ☎ 11:30am-5pm Tue-Sun) A venerable destination for 40 years, Tia Palmira wins fans with its seafood *rodízio*. Plate after plate of *vatapá* (a seafood dish with a thick sauce of manioc paste, coconut and *dendê* or palm oil), crabmeat, grilled fish, shrimp pastries and other fruits of the sea come to your table until you can eat no more.

DRINKING

Leblon and Ipanema offer flashy nightspots, as well as old-school watering holes. A youthful bar scene draws revelers to Gávea, while a more sedate crowd enjoys Lagoa's scenic spots. Centro's narrow pedestrian streets attract drinkers during weekday cocktail hours, while a mix of old and new clutters the streets of Lapa and Santa Teresa.

Ipanema & Leblon

Academia da Cachaça (Map pp138-9; ☎ 2239 1542; Rua Conde de Bernadotte 26G, Leblon; ☎ noon-2am Mon-Sat, to 1am Sun) Although *cachaça* has a bad reputation in some parts, here the fiery liquor is given the respect it nearly deserves. This pleasant spot serves over 500 varieties.

Botequim Informal (Map pp138-9; ☎ 2259 6967; Rua Humberto de Campos 646, Leblon; ☎ noon-1am Tue-Sun) This charming neighborhood bar with outdoor seating is hidden away on a quiet, tree-lined street and makes a fine place to start the evening.

TICKET MATTERS

When entering some bars (and self-serve restaurants) you might be handed a ticket, which is used to track your consumption throughout the evening. When you're ready to move on, you'll pay a cashier for the goods (and possibly an admission fee). The cashier will then give you another ticket to pass onto the door attendant as you exit. It's all wonderfully Brezhnevian – but saves you the trouble of having to cough up every time you order a cocktail. Don't lose that ticket, as you may be charged R$100 or more. You'll see this system in many areas of Brazil.

Bar D'Hotel (Map pp138-9; ☎ 2540 4990; 2nd fl, Marina All Suites, Av Delfim Moreira 696, Leblon; ⏰ 7pm-1am Sun-Thu, to 2am Fri & Sat) The waves crashing on the shore are part of the ambience at this bar overlooking Ipanema Beach. The intimate space is a magnet for the style set.

Bracarense (Map pp138-9; ☎ 2294 3549; Rua José Linhares 85B, Leblon; ⏰ 7am-midnight Mon-Sat & 9am-9pm Sun) Cariocas consider Bracarense one of Rio's classic *botecos*, for its unpretentious atmosphere, garrulous mixed crowd, ice-cold *chope* and heavenly *salgados* (snacks). It gets packed on weekends.

Cobal de Leblon (Map pp138-9; Rua Gilberto Cardoso, Leblon; ⏰ closed Mon) Leblon's popular market features a number of open-air bars and restaurants, and it's a major see-and-be-seen destination in the summer.

Devassa (Map pp138-9; ☎ 2540 6087; Av General San Martín 1241, Leblon; ⏰ 5pm-late Mon-Fri, noon-late Sat & Sun) Serving Rio's best beer, Devassa makes its own creamy brews (in Vargem Grande), before offering them up to thirsty, festive crowds at the two-story *chopperia* (beer hall). Weekend bands playing upstairs add to the din.

Empório (Map pp138-9; ☎ 2267 7992; Rua Maria Quitéria 37, Ipanema; ⏰ noon-2am) A young mix of Cariocas and gringos stirs things up over cheap cocktails and blaring music at this battered Ipanema favorite.

Garota de Ipanema (Map pp138-9; ☎ 2523 3787; Rua Vinícius de Moraes 49, Ipanema; ⏰ 10:30-2:30am) The famed spot where Tom Jobim and Vinícius de Moraes wrote 'A Garota de Ipanema' (The Girl from Ipanema) is now pretty touristy, but the beer is ice-cold and the crowd is lively.

Guapo Loco (Map pp138-9; ☎ 2294 2915; Rua Rainha Guilhermina 48, Leblon; cover R$10-40, mains R$15-30; ⏰ 7pm-midnight Mon, to 4am Tue-Fri, noon-4am Sat, to midnight Sun) This colorful Mexican restaurant and bar is one of Leblon's livelier spots for the under-30 crowd. It offers a variety of tequilas to keep things rowdy. Filling quesadillas, tacos and fajitas are also available if hunger strikes after working the dance floor.

Jobi (Map pp138-9; ☎ 2274 0547; Av Ataulfo de Paiva 1166, Leblon; ⏰ 9am-4am) A favorite since 1956, Jobi is one of Leblon's most traditional drinking spots. Grab a seat by the sidewalk, order a cold beverage and watch the night unfold.

Seu Martin (Map pp138-9; ☎ 2274 0800; Av General San Martín 1196, Leblon; ⏰ noon-1am Tue-Sat, noon-11pm Sun) This small, inviting bar in Leblon is an intimate setting for a drink. Jazz plays overhead as young friends and couples work their way through cocktails and conversation. Seu Martin also serves tasty appetizers and sandwiches.

Shenanigan's (Map pp138-9; ☎ 2267 5860; Rua Visconde de Pirajá 112A, Ipanema; ⏰ 6pm-3am Mon-Fri, 2pm-3am Sat, to 2am Sun) Overlooking the Praça General Osório, Shenanigan's is one of many Irish pubs in town that continues to draw a young mix of locals and pale out-of-towners over games of pool. Dark, festive and pubby ambience.

Tô Nem Aí (Map pp138-9; ☎ 2247 8403; Rua Farme de Amoedo 57, Ipanema; ⏰ noon-3am) A popular new watering hole that attracts a fun, very mixed crowd to its indoor and outdoor tables. Excellent appetizers and light fare.

Gávea, Jardim Botânico & Lagoa

Bar Lagoa (Map pp138-9; ☎ 2523 1135; Av Epitácio Pessoa 1674, Lagoa; ⏰ 6pm-2am Mon, noon-2am Tue-Sun) Overlooking the lake, Bar Lagoa is one of the neighborhood's classic haunts. A youthful air pervades the ever-crowded tables.

Caroline Café (Map pp138-9; ☎ 2540 0705; Rua JJ Seabra 10, Jardim Botânico; ⏰ 6pm-3am Sun-Thu, to 4am Fri, 7pm-4am Sat) The usual sexy, young crowd fills the tables at this sceney indoor-outdoor spot.

Da Graça (Map pp138-9; ☎ 2249 5484; Rua Pacheco Leão 780, Jardim Botânico; ⏰ 6pm-1:30am Tue-Thu, noon-1:30am Fri & Sat) Colorful Da Graça is one of Jardim Botânico's liveliest bars, with a festive and colorfully kitsch decor and sidewalk tables packed on weekends.

Drink Café (Map pp138-9; ☎ 2239 4136; Parque dos Patins, Av Borges de Medeiros, Lagoa; live-music charge R$5; ☼ 5pm-2am Mon, 9am-2am Tue-Sun) One of several, open-air restaurants along the lake, the Drink Café hosts live jazz and bossa nova most nights.

Hipódromo Up (Map pp138-9; ☎ 2274 9720; Praça Santos Dumont 108, Gávea; ☼ 8pm-3am) Hipódromo Up is one of several bars in the area responsible for the local residents' chronic lack of sleep. A young college-age crowd celebrates here most nights.

Saturnino (Map pp138-9; ☎ 3874 0064; Rua Saturnino de Brito 50, Jardim Botânico; ☼ 6pm-2am Sun-Wed, to 3am Thu-Sat) Saturnino has high ceilings and touches of tropical decor, with a 20-something crowd mingling over fruity cocktails (that could use a touch more alcohol).

Copacabana & Leme

Bar Luiz (Map pp140-1; Kiosk 10, Av Atlântica, Copacabana; ☼ 8am-midnight) One of many shiny, new kiosks on Copacabana's sands, serving up cold beer and tasty bites (the kitchen is concealed underground).

Copacabana Palace Poolside Bar (Map pp140-1; ☎ 2548 7070; Copacabana Palace hotel, Av Atlântica 1702, Copacabana; ☼ noon-11pm) Even if you can't swing the pricey rooms, you can still soak up some decadence at the Palace's lovely outdoor terrace bar. For something less open, head inside to the elegant piano bar (4pm to midnight).

Manoel & Juaquim (Map pp140-1; ☎ 2523 1128; Av Atlântica 3806, Copacabana; ☼ noon-2am) Facing the beach, this outdoor spot is a longstanding favorite, attracting a garrulous mix of locals and tourists.

Sindicato do Chopp (Map pp140-1; ☎ 2541 3133; Av Atlântica 514, Leme; ☼ 11am-3am) With a peaceful beachfront location, this casual bar is a relaxing and largely local spot to enjoy a draft or a filling meal.

Botafogo & Urca

Aurora (Map pp142-3; ☎ 2539 4756; Rua Capitão Salomão 43, Botafogo; ☼ 11am-midnight Mon-Thu, to 2am Fri & Sat, to 9pm Sun) This classic *boteco* is 100% Carioca. A comfortable, roomy bar with a lively, talkative crowd spilling onto the sidewalk tables.

Bar Urca (Map pp142-3; ☎ 2295 8744; Rua Cândido Gaffré 205, Urca; ☼ 6am-10pm Tue-Sat, to 7pm Sun) This simple neighborhood bar and restaurant is in a marvelous setting near the waterfront. At night patrons take a seat along the seaside wall as waiters bring cold drinks and appetizers.

Miam Miam (Map pp142-3; ☎ 2244 0125; Rua General Góes Monteiro 34, Botafogo; ☼ noon-3pm Tue-Fri, 8pm-1am Tue-Sat) A cozy new edition to Botafogo's drinking scene, this bar and bistro has a nicely lit lounge with exposed brick walls and modish furniture and a Brazilian electronic soundtrack. Cocktails and Italian fare (bruschetta, pastas, panini) fill the menu.

Centro

Amarelinho (Map pp144-5; ☎ 2240 8434; Praça Floriano 55, Cinelândia; ☼ 11am until last customer) Facing Praça Floriano, Amerilinho packs its outdoor tables during that oh-so-refreshing after-work drink.

Bar Occidental (Map pp144-5; Rua Miguel Couto 124, Centro; ☼ 5-10pm Mon-Fri) One of several sidewalk bars in the area, Bar Occidental is the place to go for icy *chope* and fried sardines.

Boteco Casual (Map pp144-5; ☎ 2232 0250; Rua do Ouvidor; ☼ 11am-midnight Mon-Fri; 11am-6pm Sat) Boteco Casual serves ice-cold beer and filling plates to its sidewalk tables; it gets packed after work, particularly as the weekend nears. Numerous other open-air spots lie nearby.

Santa Teresa & Lapa

Café Neves (Map pp144-5; ☎ 2221 4863; Largo das Neves 11, Santa Teresa; ☼ 6pm-late Tue-Sat) Small but charming, Café Neves faces peaceful Largo das Neves, with the occasional tram rattling by. The open-sided bar draws a vibrant mix on weekends, and there's often live music somewhere on hand. Several other bars lie around the square.

Tumbao de Malevo (Map pp144-5; Rua Paschoal Carlos Magno 121, Santa Teresa; ☼ 4-10pm Thu-Sun) High up above the street, this casual, open-air café attracts an eclectic neighborhood crowd. In addition to beer and cocktails, Tumbao serves sandwiches and other light bites. Live music some nights.

Santa Arte (Map pp144-5; ☎ 2242 9366; Rua Paschoal Carlos Magno 103B, Santa Teresa; ☼ 7pm-midnight) A casual, dimly lit spot to hear live music nightly among neighborhood regulars. Santa Arte is at its liveliest on weekends.

Mike's Haus (Map pp142-3; ☎ 2509 5248; Rua Almirante Alexandrino 1458A, Santa Teresa; ☼ noon-midnight Tue-Sun) This German-style pub attracts a mix of expats and Cariocas on weekend nights and serves frothy German beers and filling pub grub. It's a bit off the beaten path, so plan on sticking around before moving on.

ENTERTAINMENT
Music & Dancing

Rio's music scene features some incredibly talented performers playing in atmospheric settings to a truly democratic crowd. Lapa is the heart of samba, and its old clubs are a must-see for visitors. The widest assortment of music venues is along Av Mem de Sá. In the summer, the city hosts its Noites Cariocas, big parties atop Pão de Açúcar that feature the likes of Caetano Veloso, Jorge Ben Jor and other big names.

LIVE MUSIC

Allegro Bistrô Musical (Map pp140-1; ☎ 2548 5005; www.modernsound.com.br; Modern Sound, Rua Barata Ribeiro 502, Copacabana; admission free; ☼ 9am-9pm Mon-Fri, to 8pm Sat) The small café in Copacabana's excellent music store, Modern Sound, features live music most nights of the week, typically from 5pm to 9pm.

Beco do Rato (Map pp144-5; ☎ 2221 8062; Rua Morais e Vale 5, Lapa; admission free; ☼ 7pm-2am Tue-Sun) One of Lapa's classic samba spots, this small outdoor bar has excellent live groups playing to a laid-back crowd. Friday nights are particularly recommended.

Bip Bip (Map pp140-1; ☎ 2267 9696; Rua Almirante Gonçalves 50, Copacabana; ☼ 8pm-midnight) A neighborhood institution, Bip Bip has been hosting samba jams for more than 15 years. The ambience is simple: just a breadbox-sized storefront with tables spilling onto the sidewalk, great music and a diverse crowd of music lovers. Sunday is the current fave.

Circo Voador (Map pp144-5; ☎ 2533 5873; www.circovoador.com.br in Portuguese; Rua dos Arcos, Lapa; admission R$20-40) In a curvilinear building behind the Arcos do Lapa, this concert space hosts big names like Chico Buarque and Jorge Ben Jor as well as up-and-coming bands playing rock, ska, funk and samba.

Clan Café (Map pp142-3; ☎ 2558 2322; Rua Cosme Velho 564, Cosme Velho; admission R$10-15; ☼ 6pm-2am Tue-Sat) Set against the hillside of Corcovado, Clan Café has a large open-air patio that makes a great spot for live jazz, bossa nova and Música Popular Brasileira. Bands play around 9pm.

Estrela da Lapa (Map pp144-5; ☎ 2507 6686; Av Mem de Sá 69, Lapa; admission R$10-20; ☼ 7pm-1am Mon, 9pm-2am Tue-Sun) Inside a restored 19th-century mansion, Estrela da Lapa has an eclectic music scene and hosts samba bands playing *choro*, blues and hip-hop. On weekends, shows are

followed by a DJ who keeps the dance floor going until late.

Estudantina Café (Map pp144-5; ☎ 2232 1149; Praça Tiradentes 79, Centro; admission R$12-20; ☼ 10pm-3:30am Wed-Sat) Overlooking the Praça Tiradentes, the old dance hall packs in crowds who come for a line-up of samba, rock, soul and *forró* (popular Northeastern music). The open-air veranda provides a nice spot to cool off.

Fundição Progresso (Map pp144-5; ☎ 2220 5070; www.fundicao.org in Portuguese; Rua dos Arcos 24, Lapa; admission R$20-35) Inside this enormous old factory are several stages that host some of the best concerts and arts events in Lapa. Check the website for the latest line-up.

Praia Vermelha (Map pp142-3; ☎ 2275 7292; Praça General Tibúrcio, Urca; admission R$6-10; ☼ noon-midnight) Perched over the beach of the same name, Praia Vermelha has gorgeous views of Pão de Açúcar looming overhead. By night, jazzy MPB bands play from 6pm onward, making for an enviable open-air setting. The food, unfortunately, is less spectacular.

Semente (Map pp144-5; ☎ 9781 2451; Rua Joaquim Silva 138, Lapa; admission R$10; ☼ 8pm-1am Sun-Thu) This tiny bar hosts up-and-coming samba and *choro* groups and is a more authentic space to find samba's soul. Sunday and Monday nights are current picks.

Severyna (Map pp142-3; ☎ 2556 1296; Rua Ipiranga 54, Laranjeiras; admission R$5-10; ☼ 11:30am-2am) At night this barnlike dining hall hosts live bands playing *forró* and other music from Northeastern Brazil. Shows begin at 8:30pm.

Vinícius Piano Bar (Map pp138-9; ☎ 2523 4757; Rua Prudente de Morais 34, Ipanema; admission R$10-30) Billing itself as the 'temple of bossa nova,' Vinícius Piano Bar has been an icon in the neighborhood since the late '80s. The small, intimate upstairs music space hosts a fine assortment of jazz and bossa nova groups.

SAMBA CLUBS

Gafieiras (dance halls) are a big attraction in Lapa. Here you'll find restored colonial buildings hiding dance floors and large samba bands – along with their many admirers.

Carioca da Gema (Map pp144-5; ☎ 2221 0043; Av Mem de Sá 79, Lapa; admission R$10-20; ☼ closed Sun & Mon) One of the first to bring samba back to Lapa, this small, colorful club hosts an excellent line-up of bands and a good mixed crowd that packs the dance floor most nights.

Centro Cultural Carioca (Map pp144-5; ☎ 2242 9642; www.centroculturalcarioca.com.br; Rua do Teatro 37, Centro; admission R$16; ❂ 7pm-1am Mon-Thu 8:30pm-2am Fri & Sat) This restored theater, on Praça Tiradentes, books top samba groups throughout the year, and it's a historic setting in which to hear – and dance to – live music.

Democráticos (Map pp144-5; ☎ 2252 4611; Rua do Riachuelo 91, Lapa; admission R$12-24; ❂ 10pm-4am Wed, 11pm-4am Thu-Sat, 8pm-midnight Sun) This spacious, 19th-century dance hall has an enormous dance floor and a long stage, covered with musicians. For an authentic slice of Rio's old-fashioned love of samba, Democráticus is hard to beat.

Rio Scenarium (Map pp144-5; ☎ 3147 9005; Rua do Lavradio 20, Lapa; admission R$15-25; ☎ 7pm-2:30am Tue-Sat) Perhaps Rio's most beautiful nightspot, Rio Scenarium has three antique-filled floors with balconies overlooking the stage on the 1st floor. Talented samba bands play to a dance-happy crowd, about half of whom are tourists.

SAMBA SCHOOLS

Starting in September, in preparation for Carnaval, most big samba schools open their rehearsals to the public. These are large dance parties, and provide a good chance to mingle with Cariocas. Schools typically charge R$5 to R$15 at the door. Many samba schools are in the *favelas*, so use common sense when going.

You can visit the samba schools on a tour or you can go by yourself: you can catch a taxi there, and there are always cabs outside the schools waiting to take people home. It's a good idea to confirm that the rehearsals are on before heading out. Following is a list of some of the more popular samba schools, rehearsal days and contact information. The most popular schools for tourists are Mangueira and Salgueiro.

Beija-Flor (☎ 2791 2866; www.beija-flor.com.br in Portuguese; Pracinha Wallace Paes Leme 1025, Nilópolis; ❂ 8pm Thu)

Caprichosos de Pilares (☎ 2592 5620; www .caprichosos.com.br; Rua Faleiros 1, Pilares; ❂ 10pm Sat)

Grande Rio (☎ 2775 8422; www.granderio.org.br in Portuguese; Rua Almirante Barroso 5-6, Duque de Caixas; ❂ 11pm Fri)

Imperatriz Leopoldinense (☎ 2560 8037; www .imperatrizleopoldinense.com.br in Portuguese; Rua Professor Lacê 235, Ramos; ❂ 7pm Sun)

Mangueira (☎ 2567 4637; www.mangueira.com.br in Portuguese; Rua Visconde de Niterói 1072, Mangueira; ❂ 10pm Sat)

Mocidade Independente de Padre Miguel (☎ 3332 5823; Rua Coronel Tamarindo 38, Padre Miguel; ❂ 10pm Sat)

Porto da Pedra (☎ 3707 1518; www.gresuportoda pedra.com.br in Portuguese; Av Lúcio Tomé Feteiro 290, São Gonçalo; ❂ 10pm Fri)

Portela (☎ 2489 6440; www.gresportela.com.br in Portuguese; Rua Clara Nunes 81, Madureira; ❂ 10pm Fri)

Rocinha (☎ 3205 3303; www.academicosdarocinha .com.br in Portuguese; Rua Bertha Lutz 80, São Conrado; ❂ 10pm Sat)

Salgueiro (☎ 2238 5564; www.salgueiro.com.br in Portuguese; Rua Silva Teles 104, Andaraí; ❂ 10pm Sat)

Tradição (☎ 3350 5668; Estrada Intendente Magalhães 160, Campinho; ❂ 10pm Fri)

Unidos da Tijuca (☎ 2516 4053; www.unidosdatijuca .com.br in Portuguese; Clube dos Portuários, Rua Francisco Bicalho 47, Cidade Nova; ❂ 11pm Sat)

Viradouro (☎ 2628 7840; Av do Contorno 16, Barreto, Niterói; ❂ 10pm Sat)

NIGHTCLUBS

Flyers advertising dance parties and raves (pronounced '*hah*-vees') can be found in record stores and clothing shops in Ipanema and Leblon, and in the surf shops in Galeria River shopping center, near Praia de Arpoador. Some clubs give a discount if you've got a flyer.

Melt (Map pp138-9; ☎ 2249 9309; Rua Rita Ludolf 47A, Leblon; admission R$10-30; ❂ 10pm-3am) The sinewy Melt club is one of those places that couldn't possibly be anywhere but Leblon. Models and their admirers lie draped around the candlelit lounge, while wait staff glide between the tables delivering colorful cocktails. Upstairs, DJs break beats over the dance floor, occasionally accompanied by a few percussionists.

00 (Zero Zero; Map pp138-9; ☎ 2540 8041; Planetário, Av Padre Leonel Franca 240, Gávea; admission R$20-30; ❂ 10pm-4am Thu-Sun) Housed in Gávea's planetarium, 00 (Zero Zero) is a restaurant by day, sleek lounge by night. With an outdoor patio and some of Rio's best DJs, 00 has a solid reputation in the fashion-literate party crowd.

Baronneti (Map pp138-9; ☎ 2522 1460; Rua Barão da Torre 354, Ipanema; admission R$5-15; ❂ 11pm-5am Tue-Sun) One of Ipanema's only nightclubs, Baronneti has a sleek and trim interior with two dance floors. Given its prime Zona Sul location, you'll find a young, well-heeled crowd here. Eclectic DJs and fruity cocktails keep the fans returning.

Bombar (Map pp138-9; ☎ 2249 2161; Av General San Martín 1011, Leblon; admission R$10-30; ☯ 10pm-4am Mon-Sat) This popular Leblon nightclub attracts a festive, neighborhood crowd to fill the upstairs dance floor. Downstairs is a bar, for mingling among a mostly Zona Sul crowd.

Casa da Matriz (Map pp142-3; ☎ 2266 1014; www .casadamatriz.com.br in Portuguese; Rua Henrique de Novaes 107, Botafogo; admission R$10-25; ☯ 11pm-4am Mon-Sat, 8pm-2am Sun) Artwork decorates the walls of this avant-garde space in Botafogo. With numerous little rooms to explore – lounge, screening room, dance floors – this old two-story mansion embodies the most creative side of the Carioca spirit. Check the website for party listings.

Classical Music, Theater & Dance

The city's most lavish setting for a performance is the beaux-arts **Theatro Municipal** (Map pp144-5; ☎ 2299 1711; www.theatromunicipal.rj.gov.br in Portuguese; Rua Manuel de Carvalho, Centro). You'll find a more exciting repertoire of modern dance, theater and performance art at the excellent **Espaço Sesc** (Map pp140-1; ☎ 2547 0156; Rua Domingos Ferreira, Copacabana).

Cinemas

One of Latin America's film centers, Rio remains remarkably open to foreign and independent films, documentaries and avant-garde cinema. For listings and show times pick up *O Globo*, *Jornal do Brasil* newspapers or *Veja Rio* magazine.

Casa França-Brasil (Map pp144-5; ☎ 2253 5366; www .casafrancabrasil.rj.gov.br; Rua Visconde de Itaboraí, Centro)

GAY & LESBIAN RIO Dan Littauer

Rio has been a major destination for gays since the beginning of the 20th century. Gay balls date as far back as the 1930s, and Carnaval celebrations have long given gays a chance to dress up, dance and mingle. Nowadays the GLBT (gay, lesbian, bisexual, transgender) scene, especially for visitors, is in Ipanema, with Rua Farme de Amoedo, and the beachfront intersecting it, at center stage. Keep in mind that the Carioca definition and idea of a 'gay friendly' area is very different from, say, the Castro or the Marais, where there are clearly demarcated areas for GLBT businesses. Rainbow flags are still a rarity in Rio, and people prefer mixing to exclusivity.

Bar Bofetada (Map pp138-9; ☎ 2227 1675; Rua Farme de Amoedo 87A, Ipanema; ☯ 8am-2am) Frequented by gay guys enjoying a beer after the beach, Bofetada is a good place to watch the boys catwalking up and down Rua Farme de Amoedo.

Cabaret Casanova (Map pp144-5; ☎ 2221 6555; Av Mem de Sá 25, Lapa; ☯ 11pm-4am Fri & Sat) One of Rio's oldest clubs, Casanova features a good mixed crowd, drag queens and slightly trashy music.

Casa da Lua (Map pp138-9; ☎ 2247 4652; Rua Barão da Torre 240A, Ipanema; ☯ 5pm-2am Tue-Sun) One of Rio's only lesbian hangouts, Casa da Lua is in a leafy part of Ipanema and serves great drinks.

Cine Ideal (Map pp144-5; ☎ 2252 3460; www.cineideal.com.br in Portuguese; Rua da Carioca 62, Centro; ☯ Fri & Sat) An old movie theater, and now an electronic music club, Ideal has an outdoor terrace with views of old Rio.

Dama de Ferro (Map pp138-9; ☎ 2247 2330; Rua Vinícius de Moraes 288, Ipanema; admission R$12-25; ☯ 11pm-8am Thu-Sat) Dama de Ferro has one of the best dance floors in town. A fun, mixed crowd packs this place in the late hours (around 4am) on weekend nights.

Galeria Café (Map pp138-9; ☎ 2523 8250; www.galeriacafe.com.br; Rua Teixeira de Melo 31, Ipanema; ☯ Thu-Sat) This bar has lovely decor and a very mixed crowd.

Le Boy (Map pp140-1; ☎ 2513 4993; Rua Raul Pompéia 102, Copacabana; admission R$12-25; ☯ 11pm-4am Tue-Sun) Trannies and pretty boys gather at this festive Copacabana dance club for dancing, drinking and perhaps debauchery. Super popular, Le Boy shouldn't be missed.

La Girl (Map pp140-1; ☎ 2247 8342; Rua Raul Pompéia 102, Copacabana; admission R$12-25; ☯ 11pm-2am Tue-Sun) Rio's best-known girl bar, La Girl is a great party scene for lesbians. It's run by the owner of Le Boy.

Buraco da Lacraia (Map pp144-5; ☎ 2242 0446; Rua André Cavalcante 58, Lapa; ☯ Thu-Sat) This wicked place has entertained for over 12 years. You'll find glamorous and trashy visitors, bizarre drag shows, karaoke, a dark room and other attractions.

Cineclube Laura Alvim (Map pp138-9; ☎ 2267 1647; Av Vieira Souto 176, Ipanema) Set in the charming Laura Alvim cultural center.

Espaço Unibanco de Cinema (Map pp142-3; ☎ 3221 9221; Rua Voluntários da Pátria 35, Botafogo) A café and used bookshop are also inside.

Estação Ipanema (Map pp138-9; ☎ 2540 6445; Rua Visconde de Pirajá 605, Ipanema)

Estação Paço (Map pp144-5; ☎ 2529 4829; Paço Imperial, Centro) Set in the historic Paço Imperial.

Odeon BR (Map pp144-5; ☎ 2262 5089; Praça Mahatma Gandhi 5, Cinelândia) Rio's landmark cinema is a beautiful old theater.

São Luiz (Map pp142-3; ☎ 3221 9292; Rua do Catete 307, Catete)

Spectator Sports

FOOTBALL

Maracanã Football Stadium (Map pp146-7; ☎ 2568 9962; Rua Professor Eurico Rabelo, São Cristóvão; admission R$12-30) Nearly every child in Brazil dreams of playing in Maracanã, Rio's enormous shrine to football. Matches here rate among the most exciting in the world, and the behavior of the fans is no less colorful. The devoted pound huge samba drums as their team takes the field, and if things are going badly – or even very well – fans are sometimes driven to sheer madness. Some detonate smoke bombs in team colors, while others launch beer bottles, or cups full of urine or dead chickens into the seats below. As well, enormous flags are spread across large sections of the stadium's bleachers, while people dance in the aisles (this has been known to inspire a goal or two).

Games take place year round and can happen any day of the week. Rio's big four clubs are Flamengo, Fluminense, Vasco da Gama and Botafogo. Although many buses run to the stadium, the metro is safer and less crowded on game days. Keep in mind that the safest seats are on the lower level *cadeiras* (chairs), where the overhead covering protects you from descending objects. After the game, avoid the crowded buses, and go instead by metro or taxi.

To see some of Rio's favorite teams in action, go to their home stadiums:

Botafogo (☎ 2611 2656; Estádio Caio Martins, Rua Presidente Backer, Niterói)

Flamengo (Map pp138-9; ☎ 2529 0100; Estádio José Bastos Padilha, Av Borges de Medeiros 997, Lagoa) This stadium is also known as Estádio da Gávea. Most of Flamengo's home games are, however, played at Maracanã.

Fluminense (Map pp142-3; ☎ 2553 7240; Estádio Laranjeiras, Rua Álvaro Chaves, Laranjeiras)

Vasco da Gama (☎ 2580 7373; Estádio de São Januário, Rua General Almério de Moura 131, São Cristóvão)

HORSE RACING

Jockey Club Brasileiro (Map pp138-9; ☎ 2512 9988; www.jcb.com.br in Portuguese; Jardim Botânico 1003, Gávea) The Jockey Club seats 35,000 and lies on the Gávea side of the Lagoa Rodrigo de Freitas opposite Praça Santos Dumont. It's a beautiful track, with a great view of the mountains and Corcovado, and a nice bar and restaurant overlooking the track. Races are held on Saturday and Sunday afternoons and Monday and Friday nights. The big event of the year is the Brazilian Grand Prix, which falls on the first Sunday in August.

SHOPPING

Rio has much in the way of shopping, from colorful markets to eye-catching Zona Sul boutiques. Some of the major strips in the city for window shopping include the following:

Av Ataulfo de Paiva, Leblon (Map pp138-9) Boutiques selling haute couture sprinkled among cafés, bookshops and restaurants.

Rua Visconde de Pirajá, Ipanema (Map pp138-9) Ipanema's vibrant shopping strip.

Rua do Lavradio, Lapa (Map pp144-5) Rows of antique stores.

Clothing & Spirits

Contemporâneo (Map pp138-9; ☎ 2287 6204; Rua Visconde de Pirajá 437, Ipanema; ☙ 9am-8pm Mon-Sat) A stylish boutique selling unique pieces, Contemporâneo is a good place to see Brazil's best designers. Café attached.

Forum (Map pp138-9; ☎ 2521 7415; www.forum.com .br; Rua Barão da Torre 422, Ipanema; ☙ 10am-6pm Mon-Fri, 10am-2pm Sat) Much vaunted Brazilian designer Tufi Duek has set up his flagship store on a peaceful, tree-lined street. You'll find elegant, beautifully made pieces from his men's and women's collections.

Gilson Martins (Map pp138-9; ☎ 2227 6178; Rua Visconde de Pirajá 462, Ipanema; ☙ 10am-8pm Mon-Fri, 10am-4pm Sat) Designer Gilson Martins turns the Brazilian flag into a fashion statement in this colorful store. Glossy handbags, wallets and other accessories sport the green and yellow.

Ipanema.com (Map pp138-9; ☎ 2227 1288; Rua Prudente de Morais 237C, Ipanema; ☙ 10am-7pm Mon-Fri, 10am-4pm Sat) Ipanema.com carries colorful men's T-shirts, sneakers, and denim: A good spot if you need a new look in a hurry.

Isabela Capeto (Map pp138-9; ☎ 2540 5232; Rua Días Ferreira 45B, Leblon; ☼ 10am-8pm Mon-Fri, 10am-3pm Sat) Brazilian designer Isabela Capeto sells her beautifully handmade pieces for women from this cheerful Leblon boutique.

!La Cucaracha! (Map pp138-9; ☎ 2522 0103; Rua Teixeira de Melo 31H, Ipanema) This small, curious Ipanema store sells T-shirts, zines, comics, some CDs and various tchotchkes.

Osklen (Map pp138-9; ☎ 2227 2911; Rua Maria Quitéria 85, Ipanema; ☼ 10am-7pm Mon-Fri, 10am-2pm Sat) One of Brazil's hottest labels, Osklen has an excellent selection of men's and women's beachwear, outerwear, shirts, skirts and shoes.

Handicrafts & Artwork

In addition to shops listed below, good places to browse include the handicrafts shop at the Museu do Índio (p149; featuring works made by indigenous artists) and the colorful contemporary design store at the Museu de Arte Moderna (p150).

La Vereda (Map pp144-5; ☎ 2222 1848; Rua Almirante Alexandrino 428, Santa Teresa) Brazilian handicrafts as well as work from local artists and artisans are featured here. Several other handicraft shops are nearby.

Empório Brasil (Map pp138-9; ☎ 2512 3365; Store 108, Rua Visconde de Pirajá 595, Ipanema; ☼ 10am-6pm Mon-Fri, 10am-4pm Sat) Hidden in the back of a small shopping center, Empório Brasil sells jewelry, vases, instruments, baskets and other unique handicrafts.

No Meio do Caminho (Map pp138-9; ☎ 2294 1330; Av General San Martín 1247, Leblon; ☼ 10am-7pm Mon-Fri, 10am-2pm Sat) Showcasing the work of Brazilian artisans, No Meio do Caminho has two floors full of pottery, vases, ceramics and woodwork. Pieces here are more akin to artwork and priced accordingly. Located in Leblon, No Meio do Caminho will ship anywhere.

O Sol (Map pp138-9; ☎ 2294 5099; Rua Corcovado 213, Jardim Botânico; ☼ closed Sun) Run by a nonprofit organization, this delightful store displays the works of regional artists and sells baskets, woven rugs and Brazilian folk art in clay, wood and porcelain.

Pé de Boi (Map pp142-3; ☎ 2285 4395; Rua Ipiranga 55, Laranjeiras; ☼ 9am-7pm Mon-Fri, 9am-1pm Sat) One of Rio's best handicrafts stores, Pé de Boi sells works in wood and ceramic as well as tapes-tries, sculptures and weavings that showcase the talent of artists from Amazonia, Minas Gerais and further afield.

Liquors

Lidador (Map pp138-9; ☎ 2512 1788; Av Ataulfo de Paiva 1079, Leblon; ☼ 10am-8pm Mon-Fri, 10am-5pm Sat) One of Leblon's best wine shops, Lidador stocks Chilean, Argentinean and even Brazilian wines as well as *cachaça* and other spirits.

Markets

Rio's biggest market is found at the Feira Nordestina (p156) in São Cristóvão.

Babilônia Feira Hype (Map pp138-9; www.babilonia hype.com.br; Jockey Club Brasileiro, Rua Jardim Botânico 971, Jardim Botânico; admission R$6; ☼ 2-10pm Sat & Sun) A huge fair of clothing, sunglasses and jewelry stalls, with live bands and food stalls. You can also get your fortune read by *místicos* (fortune tellers) or receive a henna tattoo.

Hippie Fair (Feira de Arte de Ipanema; Map pp138-9; Praça General Osório, Ipanema; ☼ 9am-5pm Sun) The Zona Sul's big market, the Hippie Fair has lots of artwork, jewelry, handicrafts and clothing. A stall in the southeast corner of the plaza sells tasty plates of *acarajé*.

Praça do Mercado Feira de Antiguidades (Map pp144-5; Praça Mercado Municipal, Centro; ☼ 9am-5pm Sat) This antique market, next to the Niterói ferry terminal, is a browser's paradise with a vast array of antiques – silverware, carpets, pocket watches, jewelry, typewriters, records, art-deco and art-nouveau items.

Feira do Rio Antigo (Rio Antiques Fair; Map pp144-5; Rua do Lavradio, Centro; ☼ 10am-6pm 1st Sat of month) Although the Rio Antiques Fair happens just once a month, don't miss it if you're in town. The colonial buildings become a living installation as the whole street fills with antiques and music.

Music

Most places will let you listen to CDs before you buy.

Modern Sound (Map pp140-1; ☎ 2548 5005; www .modernsound.com.br; Rua Barata Ribeiro 502, Copacabana) One of Brazil's largest music stores stocks an impressive selection, including staff recommendations, top Rio artists and imports. Live music shows are staged here most days, at Allegro Bistrô Musical (p179).

Plano B (Map pp144-5; ☎ 2507 9860; Rua Francisco Muratori 2A, Lapa) An underground favorite among local DJs, Plano B has new and used records and CDs, as well as a tattoo parlor in the back.

Arlequin (Map pp144-5; ☎ 2220 8471; Av Primeiro de Março, Centro) Set inside the Paço Imperial, Arlequin is a pleasant place to browse for CDs, records and used books (in Portuguese) while exploring the area.

Feira de Música (Map pp144-5; Rua Pedro Lessa, Centro; ☺ 9am-5pm Mon-Fri) During the week browse through bins of records and CDs at this open-air market in Centro.

Toca do Vinícius (Map pp138-9; ☎ 2247 5227; www .tocadovinicius.com.br; Rua Vinícius de Moraes 129, Ipanema) Bossa nova's smooth sound lives on in this shop dedicated to old and new artists of the genre. Upstairs, Vinícius de Moraes fans can get a glimpse of his life's work in the small museum dedicated to him.

Top Sound (Map pp140-1; ☎ 2267 9607; Av NS de Copacabana 1103C, Copacabana) A small store with a decent selection of new and used CDs.

Shopping Malls

Rio has many large *shoppings* (malls), particularly in Barra. Most keep hours from 10am to 10pm Monday through Saturday. Some open on Sunday as well (3pm to 10pm, typically).

Barra Shopping (Map p137; Av das Américas 4666, Barra da Tijuca) Enormous! It has 500 stores, 42 restaurants and five movie screens.

Botafogo Praia Shopping (Map pp142-3; Praia de Botafogo 400, Botafogo) Great views from top-floor restaurants.

Rio Design Center (Map p137; Av das Américas 7770, Barra da Tijuca) Art galleries and high-end shops selling home furnishings and decorative pieces.

Rio Sul (Map pp142-3; Rua Lauro Müller 116, Botafogo)

São Conrado Fashion Mall (Map p137; Estrada da Gávea 899, São Conrado) The city's most upscale boutiques and pretty cafés, too.

Shopping Leblon (Map pp138-9; Av Afrânio de Melo Franco 290, Leblon) Rio's newest, with glitzy shops and enticing eateries.

GETTING THERE & AWAY
Air

Most flights depart from Aeroporto Galeão (Map p137; also called Aeroporto António Carlos Jobim), 15km north of the center. Some flights to/from São Paulo and other nearby cities use Aeroporto Santos Dumont (Map pp144–5), in the city center. Many international airlines have offices on or near Av Rio Branco, Centro.

Gol (☎ 0800 701 2131; www.voegol.com.br; Aeroporto Galeão, Aeroporto Santos Dumont) All travel agents sell Gol tickets.

TAM (☎ 3212 9300; www.tam.com.br; Av Rio Branco 245, Centro)

Varig (Map pp144-5; ☎ 2510 6650; www.varig.com.br; Av Rio Branco 277, Centro)

The following lists sample prices on Gol and TAM, Brazil's major carriers. Prices quoted are one-way and leave from Aeroporto Galeão. Given frequent specials and volatile prices, this information is subject to change.

Destination	Airline	Cost	Frequency
Belém	Gol	R$369-625	3-4 daily
	TAM	R$420-650	7-10 daily
Fortaleza	Gol	R$379-520	12-20 daily
	TAM	R$369-550	12-20 daily
Foz do Iguaçu	Gol	R$180-565	4-6 daily
	TAM	R$220-370	5-7 daily
Manaus	Gol	R$349-805	5-9 daily
	TAM	R$500-620	3-4 daily
Recife	Gol	R$209-349	5-7 daily
	TAM	R$289-489	12-20 daily
Salvador	Gol	R$129-289	5-7 daily
	TAM	R$259-320	12-20 daily
São Paulo	Gol	R$89-209	4-7 daily
	TAM	R$189	3-5 daily

Bus

Buses leave from the **Rodoviária Novo Rio** (Novo Rio Bus Station; Map pp146-7; ☎ 3213 1800; www.novorio .com.br; Av Francisco Bicalho, São Cristóvão), about 2km northwest of Centro. Several buses depart daily to most major destinations, but it's best to buy tickets in advance. Some travel agencies in the city sell bus tickets. If you're in Centro, try **Dantur Passagens** (Map pp144-5; ☎ 2262 3424; downstairs, Store 134, Av Rio Branco 156, Centro; ☺ 10am-5pm Mon-Fri).

If you arrive in Rio by bus, it's a good idea to take a taxi to your hotel, as the bus station is in a seedy area. To arrange a cab, go to the small booth near the Riotur desk, on the 1st floor of the bus station. Average fares are R$35 to the international airport and R$30 to Copacabana or Ipanema.

In addition to destinations below, buses leave Novo Rio every 30 minutes or so for São Paulo (R$57 to R$74, six hours) operated by **Viação 1001** (☎ 4004 5001) and **Itapemirim** (☎ 0800 723 2121).

Destination	Duration	Cost	Frequency	Company
International				
Buenos Aires, Argentina	46hr	R$310	daily	Pluma (☎ 2233 0336)
Santiago, Chile	72hr	R$362	daily	Pluma (☎ 2233 0336)
National				
Angra dos Reis	3hr	R$31	2 daily	Costa Verde (☎ 2233 3809)
Belém	52hr	R$290	daily	Transbrasiliana (☎ 2516 8284)
Belo Horizonte	7hr	US$57-95	8 daily	Viação Cometa (☎ 4004 9600)
Brasília	17hr	R$142-162	2 daily	Util (☎ 2518 1133)
Cabo Frio	3½hr	R$18-20	20 daily	Viação 1001 (☎ 4004 5001)
Curitiba	13hr	R$108-140	5 daily	Penha (☎ 0800 723 2122)
Florianópolis	18hr	R$179	daily	Itapemirim (☎ 0800 723 2121)
Foz do Iguaçu	23hr	R$184	2 daily	Pluma (☎ 2233 0336)
Ouro Prêto	7hr	R$60-90	2 daily	Util (☎ 2518 1133)
Paraty	4hr	R$39	7 daily	Costa Verde (☎ 2233 3809)
Petrópolis	1½hr	R$12	10 daily	Facil/Unica (☎ 2263 8792)
Porto Alegre	26hr	R$200	daily	Itapemirim (☎ 0800 723 2121)
Recife	38hr	R$235	daily	São Geraldo (☎ 2263 9008)
Salvador	26hr	R$176	daily	Aguia Branca (☎ 4004 1010)
Vitória	8hr	R$55-69	4 daily	Itapemirim (☎ 0800 723 2121)

GETTING AROUND
To/From the Airports

Rio's international airport, Aeroporto Galeão (GIG) is 15km north of the city center, on Ilha do Governador. Aeroporto Santos Dumont, used by some domestic flights, is by the bayside in the city center, 1km east of Cinelândia metro station.

Real Auto Bus (☎ 0800 240 850) operates buses with air-con from the international airport (outside the arrivals floor of Terminal 1 or the ground floor of Terminal 2) to Rodoviária Novo Rio, Av Rio Branco (Centro), Aeroporto Santos Dumont, southward through Glória, Flamengo and Botafogo and along the beaches of Copacabana, Ipanema and Leblon to Barra da Tijuca (and vice versa). The buses run every 30 minutes, from 5:20am to 12:10am, and will stop wherever you ask. Fares are around R$6, and it takes anywhere from one to two hours to reach the Zona Sul from the airport depending on traffic. You can also transfer to the metro at Carioca metro station.

Heading to the airports, you can catch the Real Auto bus in front of the major hotels, along the main beaches, but you have to look alive and flag them down.

Taxis from the international airport may try to rip you off. The safest course, a radio taxi for which you pay a set fare at the airport, is also the most expensive (R$72/86 to Copacabana/Ipanema). A yellow-and-blue *comúm*

(common) taxi should cost around R$60 to Ipanema if the meter is working.

Boat

Rio has several islands in the bay that you can visit by ferry, though you can also get fine views on the commuter ferry to Niterói. See p156 for more information.

Ilha de Paquetá (Map p137 ; ☎ ferries 4004 3113, hydrofoils 2533 4343) The regular ferry (weekday/weekend return R$7.20/12, 70 minutes, seven to nine daily) runs from 7:10am to 11pm. The hydrofoil (return R$16, 30 minutes, two to four daily) often cancels service for no apparent reason.

Niterói (Map p137) The ferry (return R$4.60, 20 minutes) leaves every 20 minutes from Praça XV de Novembro in Centro (Map pp144-5). Faster and more comfortable catamarans (return R$11, 10 minutes) run every 15 minutes from 7am to 4pm.

Car

Driving can be frustrating even if you know your way around. If you do drive in Rio, it's good to know a couple of things: The first is that Cariocas don't always stop at red lights at night, because of the small risk of robberies at deserted intersections. Instead they slow at red lights and proceed if no one is around. Another thing to know is that if you park your car on the street, it's common to pay the *flanelinha* (parking attendant) R$2 for looking after it. Some of them work for the city; others are 'freelance,' but regardless, it's a common practice throughout Brazil.

HIRE

Car-hire agencies can be found at either airport or scattered along Av Princesa Isabel in Copacabana. At the international airport, **Hertz** (☎ 3398 4377), **Localiza** (☎ 3398 5445) and **Unidas** (☎ 3398 3452) provide hire cars. In Copacabana the following are worth a try: **Avis** (Map pp140-1; ☎ 2543 8481; Av Princesa Isabel 350, Copacabana), **Localiza** (Map pp140-1; ☎ 2275 3340; Av Princesa Isabel 150, Copacabana), **Actual** (Map pp140-1; ☎ 2541 3444; Av Princesa Isabel 181, Copacabana) and **Hertz** (Map pp140-1; ☎ 2275 7440; Av Princesa Isabel 500, Copacabana).

For more information on renting a car, see p721.

Public Transportation

METRO

Rio's subway system is an excellent, speedy way to get around. It's open from 5am to midnight Monday through Saturday and 7am to 11pm on Sunday and holidays. During Carnaval the metro operates nonstop from Friday morning until Tuesday at midnight.

Both air-conditioned lines are clean, fast and safe. The main line goes from Cantagalo (which opened in 2007) in Copacabana to Saens Peña, connecting with the secondary line at Estácio (which provides service to São Cristóvão, Maracanã and northern suburbs). More stations are planned in the coming years, and eventually Ipanema (Praça General Osório) will be linked to the system. You can buy one-way, round-trip or 10-ride tickets. A basic single costs R$2.30, and there's no discount for round-trip or multiple-ride tickets – although you can connect to an Integração bus for free. Just be sure to request a *bilhete integração* (integrated ticket) at the ticket booth. Free subway maps are available at most ticket booths.

BUS & VAN

Rio buses (R$1.90 to R$2.30) are fast and frequent, and because Rio is long and narrow it's easy to get the right bus and usually no big deal if you're on the wrong one. Most buses going south from the center will go to Copacabana, and vice versa. The buses are, however, often crowded, stuck in traffic, and driven by raving maniacs. They're also the sites of many of the city's robberies, and it's not wise to ride late at night. On most buses you now board at the front, and pay the fare to the money collector. To avoid pickpockets and muggers, try to sit near the front of the bus. Avoid packed buses.

Minibuses (Cariocas call them vans) provide a faster alternative between Av Rio Branco in Centro and the Zona Sul as far as Barra da Tijuca. The destination is written in the front window. The flat fare costs around R$4.

Taxi

Rio's taxis are quite handy for zipping around town. Metered taxis charge around R$4.30 flat rate, plus around R$3 per km – slightly more at night and on Sunday. Radio taxis are 30% more expensive, but safer.

A selection of radio taxis includes **Centraltáxi** (☎ 2593 2598), **Coopatáxi** (☎ 3899 4343), **JB** (☎ 2501 3026) and **Transcoopass** (☎ 2560 4888).

Rio de Janeiro State

Say the name Rio de Janeiro and people automatically think of the city. But there's another Rio out there, the stunningly beautiful state of Rio de Janeiro, home to some of Brazil's most alluring destinations, all within a three-hour drive of the Cidade Maravilhosa (Marvelous City).

To the southeast, the Costa do Sol is a land of dunes and lagoons, blinding white sands and limpid waters ranging from deep blue to jade green. Saquarema delights surfers with some of Brazil's best breakers. Arraial do Cabo has paradisiacal beaches and picturesque harbors tucked between steep promontories. And Búzios, chic but casual, sparkles day and night, with 330 days of annual sunshine and countless nightspots buzzing till dawn.

Just north of Rio, a jagged mountain wall forms the backdrop for the imperial city of Petrópolis and the climbers' paradise of Parque Nacional da Serra dos Órgãos. Nearby Teresópolis and Nova Friburgo straddle an equally picturesque landscape dotted with dairies, Swiss chalets and peaks whose names hint at their fantastic shapes: Friar's Wart, Finger of God, Woman of Stone.

West along the Costa Verde lies one of Brazil's true gems, the colonial town of Paraty, whose geographic backdrop of green forest, waterfalls and flowering trees is as dazzling as the town's colorful 18th-century architecture. Offshore, the vast traffic-free island of Ilha Grande offers over 100km of hiking trails leading to over 100 of Brazil's most secluded beaches.

To the northwest is Brazil's oldest national park, Parque Nacional de Itatiaia, where stark high country plateaus and rocky spires intermingle with lush, low country jungle. Bordering the park, the towns of Visconde de Mauá and Penedo welcome visitors with rustic cabins, rushing streams and fresh-grilled trout.

HIGHLIGHTS

- On **Ilha Grande** (p190), surf the south shore's wild waves, or chill at the floating bar on a tranquil cove nearby
- Snorkel, swim and slide down waterfalls all day, then spend the evening learning to cook gourmet Brazilian food in picturesque, colonial **Paraty** (p193)
- Rappel up the rocky face of 2787m Pico das Agulhas Negras in **Parque Nacional de Itatiaia** (p203)
- Stroll at sunset, or party all night on breezy beachfront Orla Bardot in **Búzios** (p216)
- Sample local honey *cachaça* (high-proof sugarcane alcohol) and Alpine-style goat cheese while enjoying spectacular mountain scenery along the **Teresópolis-Friburgo Scenic Circuit** (p210)

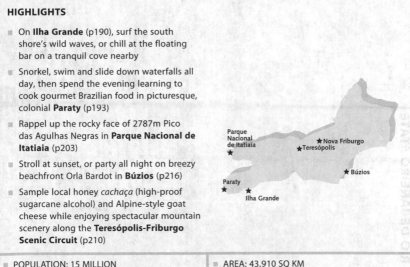

- POPULATION: 15 MILLION
- AREA: 43,910 SQ KM

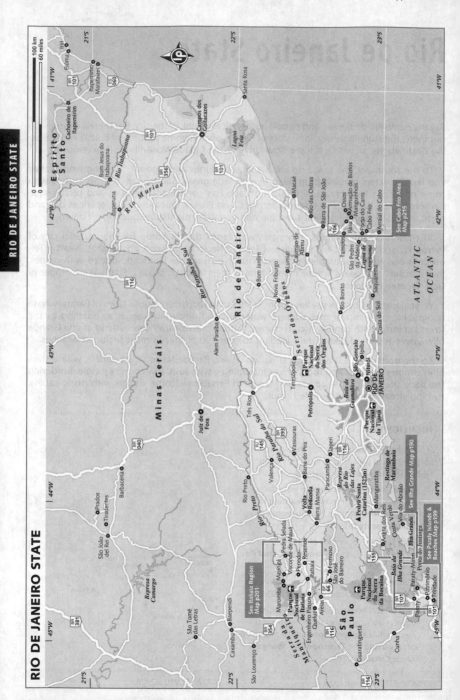

RIO DE JANEIRO STATE

History
The first European visitors to Brazil arrived by ship on January 1, 1502. For a short while it appeared that the newcomers were going to cohabit peacefully with the indigenous people, but once colonizing started in earnest in the early 16th century, everything changed. Great effort was put into enslaving indigenous people to work plantations and converting them to Christianity.

The state's development moved inland with the construction of Brazil's first major overland thoroughfare, linking coastal Paraty with the valley of the Rio Paraíba and continuing into Minas Gerais. Another important chapter in Rio's development was the establishment of coffee plantations here in the early 19th century. The crop was taken by mule train to new ports along the coast, and these roads were the main means of communication until the coming of the railways after 1855.

Modern Rio de Janeiro state is one of Brazil's economic powerhouses, where spurting oil and sun-baked tourists compete with traditional industries like steel and shipbuilding to see which can generate the most income.

Climate
The best time to visit the coastal areas of Rio state is between May and August, when balmy trade winds cool the region and the average temperature hovers around the mid-80°F mark (around 30°C). But beware – during the same period it can get downright cold (single digits centigrade) in the mountains of Petrópolis and Itatiaia. Between December and March, the rainy season, the entire state is hotter and wetter.

National Parks
For such a small state, Rio de Janeiro has an impressive array of national parks, including two of Brazil's oldest. Parque Nacional de Itatiaia, established in 1937, preserves large sections of lowland Mata Atlântica (Atlantic rain forest), plus significant high-altitude habitats. Parque Nacional da Serra dos Órgãos, established just north of Rio in 1939, gets its name from the remarkable organ-pipe shapes of its sheer rock walls. And little-visited Parque Nacional Serra da Bocaina encompasses a gorgeous swath of steep coastal jungle where the intrepid hiker can discover idyllic waterfalls and a section of the 17th-century gold route leading inland from Paraty.

Getting There & Around
International and domestic flights fly into Rio de Janeiro's Galeão and Santos Dumont airports, linking Rio state to cities throughout Brazil and the world. Rio's local bus station is a hub for virtually every bus line in the country, with fast, frequent service to nearby towns via well-maintained modern highways.

COSTA VERDE

West of Rio city is a captivating stretch of coastline where jungled hillsides dotted with flowering trees dive precipitously into a blue-green sea. The sinuous shoreline here is perfect for meandering, taking time to appreciate the ever-changing panorama of bays, islands, peaks and waterfalls.

ILHA GRANDE & VILA DO ABRAÃO
☎ 0xx24 / pop 3500
The fabulous island retreat of Ilha Grande owes its pristine condition to its unusual history. First it was a pirates' lair, then a leper colony and, finally, a prison for some of Brazil's most violent and deranged criminals. All that remains of those days are some half-buried stone foundations, but the island's unsavory reputation kept developers at bay for a long time. Consequently, beautiful tropical beaches and virgin Atlantic rain forest (now protected by the federal government) abound on Ihla Grande, and there are still only a few settlements on the island.

Vila do Abraão, the only town of any size on Ilha Grande, was itself a sleepy fishing village until 30 years ago. Recently, there's been a steady stream of new pousadas and bars popping up, but this palm-studded beachfront town with its tidy white church is still incredibly picturesque, and remains small by mainland Brazil standards. Except for Abraão's lone garbage truck, fire engine and police vehicle, cars are not allowed in town, so the only transport here is by foot or boat. The village comprises a few dirt roads, and everybody congregates down near the dock and beach at night. On weekends and during high season it can get a bit claustrophobic in Vila do Abraão, but you can easily escape the crowds by hiking a few steps out of town in any direction.

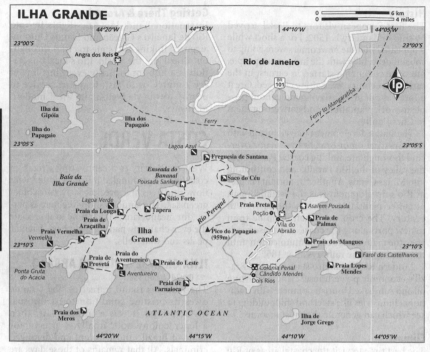

ILHA GRANDE

RIO DE JANEIRO STATE

Orientation & Information

Ferries from the mainland (Angra dos Reis and Mangaratiba) dock on the far west of Abraão's beach. As you disembark, look for the **Centro de Informações Turísticas e Hospedagem** (☎ 3361-5508; www.ilhagrande.com.br; ☺ 9am-noon & 3-6pm) kiosk on the right side at the end of the dock. Meme speaks English and can suggest lodging options, make reservations, hook you up with local guides and get you on boats going to the other side of the island. The ferry ticket office is also on the dock, directly adjacent to the tourist office.

West of the dock is the road to Praia Preta and the ruined Lazareto prison. East lies the heart of Abraão village, with its main street, the cobbled Rua da Igreja, curving to become Rua Getúlio Vargas. At the far eastern end of the beach, Ilha Grande's most popular hiking trail leads to Praia de Palmas, Praia dos Mangues and Praia Lopes Mendes.

Note that there are no ATMs on the island, although credit cards are accepted at many places and it's possible to change cash in a pinch.

Internet Station (Rua Getúlio Vargas; per hr R$12; ☺ 9am-3pm & 5-11pm) has several computers, plus facilities for Skype.

Sights & Activities

Outdoor adventure options on Ilha Grande just don't quit. The tourist office gives out a free map showing 16 different signposted trails leading through the lush forest to several of the island's 102 beaches. When visiting some beaches, it's possible to hike one way and take a boat the other. The most popular hike is the three-hour, 6.1km (each way) trek from Abraão to **Praia Lopes Mendes**. This seemingly endless beach with good surfing waves (shortboard/longboard rental onsite R$25/40 per day) is considered by some the most beautiful in Brazil. **Praia de Parnaioca** also ranks up there, accessible via an 8km (each way) trail that passes through **Dois Rios**, a picturesque beach where two separate rivers flow into the open Atlantic. Dois Rios served as the site of the **Colônia Penal Cândido Mendes**, Ilha Grande's last functioning prison, used to hold political prisoners during the military regime that took power in 1964, and finally destroyed (literally blown up!) by order of the state government in 1994.

A much shorter jaunt is the Circuito do Abraão, a 1.7km return hike that leads past two small beaches to the claustrophobic moss-covered stone ruins of Ilha Grande's other former prison, **Lazareto**, shut down in 1954. This easy hike affords some pretty views of Pico do Papagaio and takes you past an old aqueduct adjoined by a large swimming hole called **Poção**, perfect for a picnic and a dip. Along the way you can hear all sorts of birds and jungle creatures, and you may run into local kids jumping into the water on their way home from school.

Before hitting the trail, let people at your pousada know where you're going and when you'll be back, stock up on water and bug repellent and bring a flashlight, as darkness comes swiftly under the jungle canopy. Guides are advisable for exploring beyond the most heavily traveled routes – poorly marked trails and poisonous snakes can make things challenging.

The **Associação de Barqueiros** (☎ 3361 5920; Rua da Praia s/n) has an information booth near the dock. This outfit organizes day cruises to northern beaches such as Saco do Céu (from R$25 per person) and from December to March offers a circumnavigation tour of the island for R$100, weather permitting.

Numerous other tour operators have sprung up recently and in low season rates are very reasonable. **Sudoeste SW Turismo** (☎ 3361 5516; www.sudoestesw.com.br; Rua da Praia 647)

and **Phoenix Turismo** (☎ 3361 5822; www.phoenix turismo.com.br; Rua da Praia 703) both have excellent bilingual guides available for treks around the island. Both also offer private boat tours, kayak rentals and daily schooner excursions to prime snorkeling spots such as Lagoa Azul and Lagoa Verde (from R$30).

Elite Dive Center (☎ 3361 5501; Travessa Buganville 1-2A) offers courses and two-tank dives with English-speaking guides in some fantastic spots. Ask about diving around the sunken helicopter – quite a sight!

Sleeping

Note that prices quoted here are for high season (December to February). Prices drop by as much as 50% between March and November.

BUDGET

The cheapest option is the slew of camping areas set back from the beach near Rua Getúlio Vargas. Some locals also rent out rooms, especially in high season.

Santana's Camping (☎ 3361 5287; www.ilhagrande .com; Rua Santana; per person R$15) This conveniently located camping ground has hot showers, big shade trees and a kitchen and barbecue area for guests' use. They rent out tents for R$10 extra per night.

Holandês Hostel (Ilha Grande Hostel) (☎ 3361 5034; www.holandeshostel.com.br; Rua da Assembleia s/n; dm/s/d/tr R$25/45/65/90) Uphill and inland from the center of town, this shady, peaceful retreat has banana trees, chirping parrots

VILA DO ABRAÃO

0 ———————— 200 m
0 ———————— 0.1 miles

To Praia Preta (1km);
Lazareto (1km);
Aqueduct (1km)

Ferry To
Angra dos Reis

Ferry To
Mangaratiba

Baía de
Ilha Grande

Praia do
Canto

To Restaurante Lua e
Mar (50m); Aquário (400m);
Asalem (1.5km); Praia de Palmas
(3km); Praia dos Mangues (4km);
Praia Lopes Mendes (6km)

Rua da Praia

Igreja de
São Sebastião

Buganville

Rua Getúlio Vargas

Rua da Assembleia

Assembléia
de Deus

Rua do
Bicão

Rua do
Cemeterio

To Holandês
Hostel (100m)

INFORMATION		
Centro de Informaçoes Turística e Hospedagem	1	B1
Health Center	2	C2
Internet Station	3	C2
Phoenix Turismo	4	C1
Post Office	5	B1
Telephone Office	6	B1

SIGHTS & ACTIVITIES		
Associação de Barqueiros	7	B1
Elite Dive Center	8	C1
Sudoeste SW Turismo	9	C1

SLEEPING		
Beto's Pousada	10	C1
Pousada Beira Mar	11	C1
Pousada Casablanca	12	C1
Pousada d'Pillel	13	C2
Pousada Mare et Claude	14	D1
Pousada Portal das Borbas	15	C1
Santana's Camping	16	C1

EATING		
Hamelote	17	C2
O Pescador	18	C1
Pizza na Praça	19	B1
Queijos e Tal	20	B2
Sorveteria Boca Gelata	21	B1

TRANSPORT		
Ferry Dock	22	B1
Ferry Ticket Office	23	B1

and a terrace full of hammocks. Rooms are somewhat musty but affordable. HI members save R$5 per person off rates quoted above.

Aquário (☎ 3361 5405; www.aquariohostel.com; dm/d R$35/90; 🖭) The spacious sundeck overlooking the ocean, natural swimming pool and lively evening barbecues have earned this beachfront hostel/pousada a loyal following among backpackers. To get there, head 1km east along the beach from the ferry dock.

Pousada Beira Mar (☎ 3361 5051; beiramar 2000@uol .com.br; Rua da Praia; s/d from R$80) This good beachfront choice is just 300m from the dock. Lutz, a German who has made Abraão his home, enjoys meeting fellow travelers and speaks many languages. The lovely front rooms, featuring terraces with hammocks and ocean views, cost R$60 extra.

MIDRANGE & TOP END

Beto's Pousada (☎ 3361 5312; www.ilhagrande.com.br; Travessa Buganville 63; s/d/tr/q R$70/90/117/144) You'll find spotless rooms at Beto's, including some with multiple bunks for friends or family members traveling together. Air-conditioning is available at R$20 extra per night. There's a helpful staff and a nice breakfast.

Pousada d'Pillel (☎ 3361 5075; www.ilhagrandedpillel .com.br; Rua do Bicão; s/d from R$95) This friendly, family-run pousada, a few blocks from the beach, has a cool, shady garden with comfortable seating under a thatched roof out back.

Pousada Mara et Claude (☎ 3361 5922; www .ilhagrande.org; Rua da Praia 333; s/d from R$90/130) This extremely attractive French-run pousada, with stone walls and blue French doors, is set in a pretty garden just off the beach. Front rooms with ocean views are worth the R$50 extra.

Pousada Portal das Borbas (☎ 3361 5085; www .portaldasborbas.ilhagrande.org; Rua das Flores 4; s/d/tr/q R$150/160/204/245) A few blocks back from the beach, just off Rua Getúlio Vargas, this pousada has rooms with verandas facing a nice garden courtyard and some with views to the hill and forest.

Pousada Casablanca (☎ 3361 5040; www.casablanca pousada.com.br; Travessa Buganville; s/d R$190/210) On the picturesque shopping alley called Buganville, Casablanca features some upstairs rooms with small balconies overlooking the mountains.

Asalem (☎ 3361 5602; www.asalem.com.br; Praia da Crena s/n; s/d/tr R$215/260/305) Despite its remote, immersed-in-nature atmosphere, Asalem is only five minutes from Abraão by boat, or a 25 minute walk via a scenic beachfront trail.

Owned by an internationally acclaimed photographer, it commands gorgeous views of the forest and adjoining bay from its hillside location. Pickup and dropoff at Abraão dock, plus kayak rental, are included in the price.

Pousada Sankay (☎ 3365 1090; www.pousadasankay .com.br; s/d with meals R$160/290) If you really, really want to get away from it all, this is the remotest place you can go and still have protection from the mosquitoes. It's on Enseada do Bananal, on the northwestern side of the island. Breakfast, dinner and boat transfer from Angra dos Reis are included in the rate.

Eating

Restaurants abound along Rua da Praia, Rua da Igreja, Rua Getúlio Vargas and the small pedestrian street Travessa Buganville. During busy periods you'll see sweets carts being pushed about, as well as entrepreneurial islanders selling grilled seafood and *caipirinhas* (the national cocktail made from limes, sugar, ice and high-proof sugarcane alcohol).

Queijos e Tal (Rua Dona Romana 55; 🖭 8am-noon & 4-9pm Mon-Sat) Hikers can stock up here on cheese, salami and other sandwich fixings before hitting the trail.

Sorveteria Boca Gelata (Abraão pier; R$3 per 100g; 🖭 9am-midnight) With three dozen flavors of self-serve ice cream, this is a great place to ward off the midday heat or enjoy a late night dessert. Be bold and try some of the less conventional offerings – fig with cognac and walnuts is surprisingly tasty, as are corn and plum flavors.

Hamelote (Rua Getúlio Vargas 161; snacks from R$4; 🖭 7am-midnight) Hamelote caters to the breakfast needs of nearby campers, but also serves an affordable and varied menu – soups, salads, sandwiches, seafood and vegetarian offerings – late into the evening.

Pizza na Praça (Praça São Sebastião; pizzas from R$14; 🖭 11am-late Fri-Sun, from 3pm Mon-Thu) Always bustling, this simple eatery with outdoor seating on the main church square serves pizza and pasta into the wee hours.

Lua e Mar (Praia do Canto; meals per person from R$30; 🖭 6:30pm-late) Candlelit tables on the sand make a tranquil place to watch the crashing waves and scurrying crabs while you enjoy tasty seafood dishes for two.

O Pescador (☎ 3361 5114; Rua da Praia; meals per person from R$30; 🖭 6:30pm-late) The cozily furnished, romantically lit Pescador is one of the island's best choices for a fancy beachfront dinner.

They make a mean *caipirinha*, plus delicious appetizers – try the *casquinha de siri* (stuffed crab) – and decadent combos such as *mare e monti* (filet mignon and shrimp). The friendly owners speak English.

Getting There & Away

Barcas SA (www.barcas-sa.com.br) runs daily ferries between Ilha Grande and the mainland ports of Angra dos Reis and Mangaratiba. Ferries are sometimes added during high season and the schedule can fluctuate, so it's wise to confirm locally before departure. The ferry between Angra dos Reis and Abraão (R$6 Monday to Friday, R$15 Saturday to Sunday, 80 minutes) leaves Angra at 3:30pm Monday to Friday and 1:30pm Saturday to Sunday, returning from Abraão at 10am daily. From Mangaratiba, east of Angra along the coast, the ferry (R$5.90 Monday to Friday, R$15 Saturday to Sunday, 80 minutes) leaves for Abraão at 8am daily and 10pm Friday, returning to Mangaratiba at 5:30pm daily. The Barcas ferry also offers nice opportunities to observe fishermen at the docks unloading fish and locals returning from Angra with boxes of supplies.

The regular Barcas SA ferry service is supplemented by smaller tourist boats operated by the Associação de Barqueiros (see p191) and **Ilha Grande Turismo** (IGT; ☎ 3365 6426; igt@ilhagrandeturismo.com.br). Depending on demand, each company schedules multiple daily departures between Angra dos Reis and Abraão, ranging in price from R$15 to R$20. Check schedules with IGT at their desk inside Angra's bus station or with the Associação de Barqueiros at their office in Abraão.

ANGRA DOS REIS

☎ 0xx24 / pop 97,000

The savage beauty of Angra dos Reis's tropical, fjordlike coastline has been badly blemished by industrialization. Supertankers dock in Angra's port, a railway heads inland to the steel town of Volta Redonda, and the nearby Petrobras oil refinery and nuclear power plant stick out like sore thumbs. If you've got your own wheels, there are plenty of gorgeous beaches to explore east and west of town, but for those traveling by bus, the main reason to pass through Angra is to catch the ferry for Ilha Grande.

Angra's helpful **Centro de Informações Turísticas** (☎ 3367 7826; cit@angra.rj.gov.br; Av Ayrton Senna 580; ⏰ 8am-7pm Mon-Fri & 9am-4pm Sat & Sun) between

---

INDIAN NAMES
Many place names in Rio state have their origins in Indian words, including the following: **Geribá** – a kind of coconut palm **Guanabara** – arm of the sea **Ipanema** – place that gives bad luck or place of dangerous sea **Itatiaia** – many-pointed rock **Mangaratiba** – banana orchard **Paraty** – a kind of fish **Saquarema** – lagoon without shells **Tijuca** – putrid-smelling swamp

the bus station and the ferry docks provides local hotel referrals and information on Ilha Grande. Along Av Julio Maria near the docks, you can stock up on cash at Bradesco or HSBC ATMs before heading out to Ilha Grande. There's also a post office at Praça Lopes Trovão.

A great lunch option only steps from the ferry is **Fogão de Minas** (Rua Júlio Maria 398; per kg R$15.95) serving delicious and inexpensive self-serve *mineiro* food.

Getting There & Around

Angra's **bus station** (☎ 3365 1280; Largo da Lapa) is northeast of the center. Costa Verde buses leave for Rio (R$31, 2½ hours) every hour from 4am to 10:45pm daily, while Colitur buses run to Paraty (R$7, two hours) at least hourly from 6am to 11pm daily.

During high season and on weekends the Costa Verde bus line that runs between Angra and Rio will have a bus idling at the Angra docks to greet ferries returning from Ilha Grande, reservations not needed. If that bus fills up (very likely) before you can get in line, walk out to the main road from the dock and turn right, heading up the road until you see a plaza. Costa Verde buses to Rio stop here, as do local buses to Paraty. You don't have to double back to the bus station itself.

PARATY

☎ 0xx24 / pop 31,000

Set amid jutting peninsulas and secluded beaches, with a backdrop of steep, jungled mountains plunging into an island-studded bay, Paraty is one of Brazil's most appealing and exquisitely preserved historical gems.

Paraty's colonial center is remarkable not only for its centuries-old architecture, but also for its lack of automobile traffic. The irregular cobblestone streets are closed to motor vehicles, making it a delightful place to stroll about. Elegant white buildings adorned with fanciful multi-hued borders and latticed windows blend harmoniously with the natural beauty that envelops the town.

Dozens of pristine beaches are within a couple of hours of Paraty by boat or bus, while inland, the Parque Nacional da Serra da Bocaina provides protection for a lush remnant of Mata Atlântica.

The Brazilian government has recognized Paraty as a National Historic Site since 1966, and the town is currently petitioning Unesco for World Heritage status.

Paraty is crowded and lively throughout the summer holidays, brimming with Brazilian and European vacationers and good music. The town's cosmopolitan flavor is further enhanced by the large number of artists, writers and chefs, both Brazilian and foreign, who have settled here and opened shops, galleries and restaurants in recent years.

History

Paraty was inhabited by the Guianas Indians when Portuguese settlers first arrived here in the 16th century. With the discovery of gold in Minas Gerais at the end of the 17th century, Paraty became an obligatory stopover between Rio de Janeiro and the mines, as it was the only point where the escarpment of the Serra do Mar could be scaled.

As gold poured from the interior, Paraty became a busy, important port, and the wealthy built churches and fine houses. Paraty's glory days didn't last long. After the 1720s, a new road from Rio via the Serra dos Órgãos cut 15 days off the journey to Minas Gerais, and Paraty started to decline. In the 19th century, the local economy revived with the coffee boom, but until the mid-20th century the sea remained the only viable commercial route to Paraty. In 1954 a modern road was built through the steep Serra do Mar, passing the town of Cunha, 47km inland. Then in 1960 the coastal road from Rio, 253km away, was extended to Paraty and 330km beyond to São Paulo, ushering in a new era of tourism-based prosperity.

Orientation

Paraty is small and easy to navigate, although street names and addresses can get confusing. Some streets have more than one name, and house numbers don't always follow a predictable pattern.

Information

Banco do Brasil (Av Roberto Silveira) ATM.
Bradesco (Av Roberto Silveira) ATM.
Centro de Informações Turísticas (☎ 3371 1897/6553; www.paraty.com.br; Av Roberto Silveira; ☼ 9am-9pm) Staffed by friendly locals, including some English speakers.
Internet access (Av Roberto Silveira) Internet, including Skype, is available at several places along Av Roberto Silveira just outside the historic center.
Nova Paraty Livraria e Café (☎ 3371 6042; Rua da Praia 159) Sells books in Portuguese and English, newspapers, magazines, maps, postcards and stamps. The attached café serves coffee, juice and snacks.
Paraty Wash (☎ 3371 3027; Shopping Martins, Loja 15; per good-sized basket R$15) Just across from the bus station, Paraty Wash will wash and dry clothes in an hour.
Post office (cnr Rua Marechal Deodoro da Fonseca & Rua Domingo Gonçalves de Abreu)

Sights & Activities

CHURCHES

The **Igreja NS do Rosário e São Benedito dos Homens Pretos** (Largo do Rosario; admission R$2; ☼ 9am-noon & 1:30-5pm Tue-Sat) was built in 1725 by and for slaves. Renovated in 1857, the church has gilded wooden altars dedicated to Our Lady of the Rosary, St Benedict and St John. The pineapple-like chandelier base in the roof is a symbol of prosperity.

The **Igreja Santa Rita dos Pardos Libertos** (Rua Santa Rita) was the church for freed mulattos (persons of mixed black and European parentage). Built in 1722, it houses a tiny **museum of sacred art** (admission R$2; ☼ 9am-noon & 2-5pm Wed-Sun) and has some fine woodwork on the doorways and altars.

Capela de NS das Dores (Rua Fresca), the church of the colonial white elite, was built in 1800 and renovated in 1901. Open only sporadically, it hides a fascinating cemetery in the inner courtyard.

Matriz NS dos Remédios (Praça Monsenhor Hélio Pires) was built in 1787 on the site of two 17th-century churches. Inside, there is art from past and contemporary local artists. According to legend, the construction of the church was financed by pirate treasure found hidden on Praia da Trindade. At the time of writing, Matriz NS dos Remédios was closed for renovation.

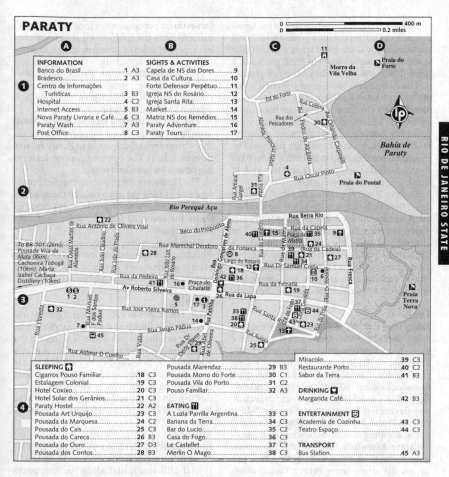

PARATY

0 _____ 400 m
0 _____ 0.2 miles

INFORMATION		SIGHTS & ACTIVITIES	
Banco do Brasil...................1	A3	Capela de NS das Dores..........9	
Bradesco...............................2	A3	Casa da Cultura...................10	
Centro de Informações		Forte Defensor Perpétuo......11	
Turísticas...........................3	B3	Igreja NS do Rosário............12	
Hospital...............................4	C2	Igreja Santa Rita.................13	
Internet Access.....................5	B3	Market................................14	
Nova Paraty Livraria e Café...6	C3	Matriz NS dos Remédios.......15	
Paraty Wash.........................7	A3	Paraty Adventure................16	
Post Office............................8	C3	Paraty Tours........................17	

RIO DE JANEIRO STATE

Bahía de Paraty

SLEEPING			Pousada Marendaz...................29	B3	Miracolo.............................39	C3
Cigarros Pouso Familiar...........18	C3		Pousada Morro do Forte.............30	C1	Restaurante Porto..............40	C2
Estalagem Colonial.................19	C3		Pousada Vila do Porto..............31	C2	Sabor da Terra....................41	B3
Hotel Coixxo..........................20	C3		Pouso Familiar.......................32	A3		
Hotel Solar dos Gerânios.........21	C3				DRINKING	
Paraty Hostel.........................22	A2		EATING		Margarida Café...................42	B3
Pousada Art Urquijo................23	C3		A Luzia Parrilla Argentina.........33	C3		
Pousada da Marquesa.............24	C2		Banana da Terra......................34	C3	ENTERTAINMENT	
Pousada do Cais.....................25	C3		Bar do Lucio...........................35	C3	Academia de Cozinha..........43	C3
Pousada do Careca.................26	B3		Casa do Fogo..........................36	C3	Teatro Espaço.....................44	C3
Pousada do Ouro....................27	D3		Le Castellet............................37	C3		
Pousada dos Contos................28	B3		Merlin O Mago........................38	C3	TRANSPORT	
					Bus Station.........................45	A3

CASA DA CULTURA

Opened in 2004 in a beautiful colonial mansion, Paraty's **Casa da Cultura** (☎ 3371 2325; www .casadaculturaparaty.org.br; Rua Dona Geralda 177; admission R$5; ☽ 10am-6:30pm Wed-Mon) has a fascinating permanent exhibition documenting local culture through photos and videotaped interviews with residents. The museum also displays relics from Paraty's past, with signs in English and Portuguese. There are fabulous views of town from the main gallery upstairs.

FORTE DEFENSOR PERPÉTUO

Forte Defensor Perpétuo (admission R$2; ☽ 9am-noon & 2-5pm Wed-Sun) was built in 1703 to defend against pirate raids on the gold passing through Paraty's port, then rebuilt in 1822

upon Brazil's independence from Portugal. It's a 20-minute walk north of town. To get there, cross the bridge over the Rio Perequê Açu, then climb the Morro da Vila Velha, the hill past Praia do Pontal. The fort commands sweeping views over the bay and houses the **Casa de Artista e Centro de Artes e Tradições Populares de Paraty** (admission R$2; ☽ 10am-5pm Tue-Sun), a museum and gallery that displays fishing implements and baskets, and sells local handicrafts.

ISLANDS & BEACHES

Paraty has some 65 islands and 300 beaches in its vicinity. To visit the less accessible beaches, take an organized schooner tour; tickets average about R$25 per person (see Tours on p196).

Alternatively, you can hire one of the small motorboats at the port for a private tour. Local captains know some great spots and will take you out for roughly R$45 to R$50 per hour, a good deal if you have a large enough group.

The closest fine beaches on the coast – **Vermelha** and **Lulas** (northeast of Paraty) and **Saco da Velha** (to the east) – are an hour away by boat. The best island beaches nearby are probably **Araújo** and **Sapeca**; many other islands have rocky shores and are private. The mainland beaches tend to be better; most have *barracas* (stalls) serving beer and fish and, at most, a handful of beachgoers.

Back in Paraty, walking north across the river, the first beach you'll reach is **Praia do Pontal**. A handful of open-air restaurants lines its shore, but the water can get a bit murky. The cleaner and relatively secluded **Praia do Forte** lies a quick walk north from there. Another 2km further north is **Praia do Jabaquara**, a spacious beach with great views, shallow waters and a small restaurant overlooking the sand.

Tours

Paraty Tours (☎ 3371 1327; www.paratytours.com.br; Av Roberto Silveira 11; ☯ 8am-9pm), located next door to the tourist information office, Paraty Tours offers hiking (R$35 to R$45, six hours), biking (self-guided, R$6 per hour or R$30 per day), horseback riding (R$90, three hours) and diving (R$165 to R$180) adventures. Especially popular are five-hour schooner cruises, which cost R$25 and depart daily at 10am, 11am and noon, stopping at various beaches en route.

    Paraty Adventure (☎ 3371 6135; www.paraty adventure.com; Av Roberto Silveira 40; ☯ 8am-10pm), just across the street from Paraty Tours, offers similar itineraries and prices.

Festivals & Events

Carnaval here is a big street party – check out the Saturday procession of the Bloco da Lama, in which young people come in droves to cover themselves in mud and dance through the streets.

    Holy Week celebrations include the beautiful **Procissão do Fogaréu**, a torchlit procession through the historic center starting just past midnight on the Thursday before Easter. The **Festa do Divino Espírito Santo** begins with colorful street decorations and processions nine days before Pentecostal Sunday (the seventh Sunday after Easter), and ends with a huge community lunch prepared by local women.

Corpus Christi processions in June are also magnificent, with the cobblestone streets covered in carpets of colored sawdust, leaves, flowers, coffee grounds and chalk.

The **Festas Juninas**, throughout June, showcase local dances, music and street theater, culminating in late June with a maritime procession to Ilha do Araújo.

The **Festival Literária Internacional de Parati** (www.flip.org.br), launched in 2003, brings authors from around the world to Paraty for five days each July. The opening concert features big names in Brazilian music.

The Paraty region produces excellent *cachaça*, and in 1984 the town council inaugurated the annual **Festival da Pinga**. The pinga (another name for *cachaça*) party lasts for four days each August.

New festivals keep springing up each year. Recent additions include festivals of photography, gastronomy and seafood. See www.paraty.com.br/eventos.asp for a full list.

Sleeping

From December to February, and during festivals, hotels fill up and room prices double, so reservations are advisable. The rest of the year, finding accommodations is relatively easy and inexpensive. Prices quoted here are high-season rates; you can bargain for better deals during the off-season. Paraty is a favorite destination for gay and lesbian crowds and all locations should be considered gay-friendly.

BUDGET

Paraty Hostel (☎ 3371 2223; www.paratyhostel.com; Rua Antônio de Oliveira Vidal 120; dm/d R$30/60; ☐ ☒) Paraty's HI-affiliated hostel, along the river north of the bus station, has dorms plus a couple of private rooms. A riverside deck and swimming pool, hammocks, a shady sitting area, laundry facilities and free internet give it a homey feel. The hostel also organizes excursions to local beaches.

    Pousada do Careca (☎ 3371 1291; Praça do Chafariz s/n; s/d R$30/60) This affordable pousada features bright, no-frills rooms just inside the historic center.

    Pouso Familiar (☎ 3371 1475; Rua José Vieira Ramos 262; s/d R$40/50) A friendly place close to the bus station, run by Joseph and Lúcia, a Belgian/Brazilian couple. The pousada has clean rooms around a central courtyard, with clothes-washing facilities. Joseph speaks English, German, French, Spanish and Dutch.

Hotel Solar dos Gerânios (☎ 3371 1550; www.paraty .com.br/geranio; Praça da Matriz; s/d R$60/80; 🖳) Run by the same family for decades, this rustic hotel on lively Praça da Matriz is the best budget choice in Paraty's colonial center. Wood and ceramic sculptures, stone walls and floors, columns and beamed ceilings, and a courtyard full of plants, cats and (occasionally) monkeys all add character. Some rooms have balconies overlooking the square.

There are a few camping grounds on the north edge of town, just over the bridge.

MIDRANGE

Pousada Marendaz (☎ 3371 1369; www.paraty.com .br/marendaz in Portuguese; Rua Dr Derly Ellena 9; s/d/tr R$50/90/120) Run by three sisters, this welcoming pousada is more of a family home than a hotel; attractions include a big Jacuzzi tub in the courtyard.

Pousada Vila do Porto (☎ 3371 8600; www.eco -paraty.com/camping/en.htm; Rua do Pontal 60; s/d R$80/ 130; 🞎) Vila do Porto is the most accessible of several places directly across the bridge from colonial Paraty, towards the fort and city beaches. Rooms are laid out along an ersatz colonial street.

Pousada dos Contos (☎ 3371 7505; www.pousadados contos.com.br; Rua Marechal Deodoro 1; s/d R$105/125; 🞎) Just west of the historic center, this popular place has stylish modern rooms with king-sized beds. English and German spoken.

Cigarros Pouso Familiar (☎ 3371 1497; www.paraty .com.br/cigarras; Largo do Rosario 7; r from R$120/150) Decorated with colorful lamps and run by a retired professor, this elegant colonial building retains the feel of a family home. Each room is unique, and two have kitchenettes. The upstairs TV room is charming, as is the veranda with views of the adjoining square.

Pousada Vila da Mata (☎ 3371 7948; www.pousada viladamata.com.br in Portuguese; Estrada Paraty/Cunha, 6.5km; d/q R$130/260) Several kilometers uphill from town, right next to a waterfall along the Penha bus route, Vila da Mata features attractive, creatively designed rooms sleeping up to four, with decks facing the jungle and the sound of rushing water in the background.

Pousada Morro do Forte (☎ 3371 1211; www .pousadamorrodoforte.com.br; Rua Orlando Carpinelli 21; s/d R$150; 🞎 🞎) This pousada's incomparable vistas of the town and bay are well worth the uphill climb. Perched on the Morro do Forte, it has comfortable rooms with small balconies. Owners speak English and German.

Estalagem Colonial (☎ 3371 1626; www.paraty .com.br/estalagemcolonial; Rua da Matriz 9; s/d R$100/160) This historic mansion in the heart of colonial Paraty features a cheerful downstairs common area filled with natural light, plus fantastic views from the upstairs corner rooms.

Hotel le Gite d'Indaiatiba (☎ 3371 7174; www .legitedindaiatiba.com.br; Rodovia Rio-Santos, 562km; d/tr R$150/200, bungalow d/tr/q R$200/250/300; 🞎) Next to a waterfall in a gorgeous jungle setting 16km north of Paraty, this French-owned hotel is a spectacular getaway. Its two *apartamentos* (room with a bath) and three bungalows all come equipped with fireplace and verandas offering breathtaking views. Daytime activities include horseback riding, jungle treks and visits to local fruit plantations or the beach below.

TOP END

There are several splendid colonial pousadas in Paraty.

Pousada do Cais (☎ 3371 1200; www.pousadadocais .com.br; Travessa Santa Rita 20; s/d/tr R$130/200/240, ste tr/q R$260/320; 🞎). This waterfront pousada is modern but built in colonial style. Despite its luxurious feel, rooms are relatively affordable because it lacks the pool and large garden typical of Paraty's pricier hotels. Book ahead for the front rooms with gorgeous French doors overlooking the harbor.

Pousada da Marquesa (☎ 3371 2163; www.pousada damarquesa.com.br; Rua Dona Geralda 69; r from R$190; 🞎) This pousada's charming historical atmosphere begins in the lobby, with its stone pillars and high beamed ceilings. Bedrooms, some on two levels, are attractive, and the interior poolside garden is among the nicest in Paraty.

Pousada do Ouro (☎ 3371 2045; www.pousadaouro .com.br; Rua da Praia 145; s/d from R$145/190, ste R$225/ 300; 🖳 🞎) It's easy to imagine bumping into Mick Jagger, Sonia Braga or Tom Cruise here, especially when you enter the lobby and see photos of them posing in front of the pousada. The hotel has everything – bar, pool, sauna and a gorgeous garden.

Hotel Coxixo (☎ 3371 1460; www.hotelcoxixo.com.br; Rua do Comércio 362; r from R$190; 🞎) Centrally located, this top-end hotel has cozy colonial decor, medieval-looking stone walls, a beautiful courtyard with pool and bar and artistic nighttime lighting.

Pousada Art Urquijo (☎ 3371 1362; www.urquijo .com.br; Rua Dona Geralda 79; r from R$270; 🞎) This wonderfully inviting pousada is obviously a labor of love for artist-owner Luz Urquijo. The downstairs sitting area features plush cushions, a stylish bar and a bubbling pool. Especially nice rooms are Sofia, with its deck, flowering tree and ocean view, and Xul, with its futon and floor-level window imparting a Japanese feel.

Eating

Paraty has many pretty restaurants, but once your feet touch the cobblestones in the picturesque historic center, prices rise.

BUDGET

Sabor da Terra (☎ 3371 2384; Av Roberto Silveira 180; per kg R$19.90; ☼ 11am-10pm) An affordable self-serve restaurant just outside the historic center, Sabor da Terra's tasty offerings include shrimp and fish.

Bar do Lucio (☎ 3371 8261; Praça da Matriz 3; sandwiches R$7, meals from R$17; ☼ 6pm-1am) On the quieter side of the same square, this newly opened local hangout has its own art gallery and is a great spot for a simple meal, with live music nightly.

Le Castellet (☎ 3371 7461; Rua Dona Geralda 44; crepes R$8-14; ☼ 5-11pm) The French-Brazilian couple who run this small eatery have created a vibrant, colorful ambience, serving up French favorites such as *salade niçoise*, *croque monsieur* and sweet and savory crepes.

Miracolo (☎ 3371 1045; Praça da Matriz 8; pizzas R$10; ☼ 10am-midnight) Buzzing with activity day and night, this popular snack spot features outdoor seating on the cobblestones of Paraty's biggest square. Run by an Italian expat, it's a relaxing place to watch the world go by while sipping a beer.

MIDRANGE

A Luzia Parrilla Argentina (☎ 3371 9647; Rua do Comércio 58; meals $21; ☼ 3pm-midnight) Specializing in grilled meats, Argentine-style, Luzia offers atmospheric candlelit seating on the cobblestones, plus a good wine list.

Casa do Fogo (☎ 3371 6359; Rua da Ferraria 38; meals R$25; ☼ 5pm-midnight) The name says it all here – everything's on fire! The menu focuses on seafood set ablaze with the local *cachaça*, and desserts don't escape a fiery death either.

TOP END

Restaurante Porto (☎ 3371 1058; Rua do Comércio 15; meals $35; ☼ 2pm-midnight) The delicious

European-influenced Brazilian cuisine at Porto recently earned it a spot on the Condé Nast list of the world's 100 best restaurants.

Merlin O Mago (☎ 3371 2157; Rua do Comércio 376; meals R$40; ☼ dinner) At this candlelit restaurant with only eight tables, the globetrotting German chef and his Japanese wife have created a delightful fusion of Brazilian, Asian and European flavors.

Kontiki (☎ 3371 1666; Ilha Duas Irmãs; meals R$48; ☼ noon-5:30pm Thu-Tue) For a unique dining experience, check out this island restaurant in the middle of the bay. Kontiki specializes in seafood paella, and will pick you up at the Paraty pier for the 10-minute crossing.

Banana da Terra (☎ 3371 1725; Rua Dr Samuel Costa 198; meals R$50; ☼ 6pm-midnight Mon, Wed & Thu, noon-4pm & 7pm-midnight Fri, Sat & Sun, closed Tue) One of the classiest restaurants in Paraty, Banana da Terra's trademark is creative taste combinations and artistic presentation. Try the fish, shrimp, mussels, vegetables and banana with wine and saffron, wrapped in banana leaves.

Drinking

Margarida Café (☎ 3371 2441; Praça do Chafariz; pizzas R$16, meals R$30; ☼ noon-late) At the edge of the old town, this cozy, intimate café has great drinks and live music nightly, plus wood-fired pizzas and inventive fish and pasta dishes.

Entertainment

Academia de Cozinha (☎ 3371 6468; www.chefbrazil.com; Rua Dona Geralda 288; all-included dinner R$170) Mixing theater with haute cuisine, the Academy of Cooking and Other Pleasures stages cooking classes – in Portuguese, English, French and Spanish. Guests learn about Brazilian regional cuisines, see chef Yara Castro Roberts in action, assist with the cooking (optional), then sit down to a leisurely dinner and an evening of lively conversation. Groups are often international – residents of over 60 countries have participated to date. The price includes cocktails, wine, desserts and recipes.

Teatro Espaço (☎ 3371 1575; www.ecparaty.org .br; Rua Dona Geralda 327; admission R$20) This small playhouse presents puppetry, music and dance performances by the internationally acclaimed resident theater company, Contatores de Estórias.

Getting There & Away

The **bus station** (Rua Jango Pádua) is 500m west of the old town. The Costa Verde bus line has frequent buses to Rio de Janeiro (R$40, four hours, every one to three hours from 6am to 9pm). Colitur has buses to Angra dos Reis (R$7, two hours, at least hourly from 4:40am to 10:30pm) and Reunidas buses head to São Paulo (R$36, six hours, three to four daily).

AROUND PARATY
Cachoeira Tobogã
In the hills 10km inland, this natural water slide is a blast! Take a local Colitur bus to Penha (R$2.60, 30 minutes), and get off at the white church. Follow signs 100m downhill to an idyllic pool surrounded by jungle, with a slick rock face that makes a perfect natural slide (once featured in the movie *The Emerald Forest*). Tourists who value their skulls should heed the

posted warnings against surfing (ie standing instead of sitting), although local teenagers have mastered the technique and it's exciting (if terrifying!) to watch. Afterwards, don't miss the great *caipirinhas* at Bar do Tarzan, across the swinging bridge above the falls.

Praia da Trindade
About 25km south of Paraty, Trindade occupies a long sweep of stunningly beautiful coastline. Here you can lounge or hike along four of Brazil's most dazzling beaches (Cepilho, Ranchos, Meio, and Cachadaço), with surging breakers, enormous boulders, vast expanses of mountain-fringed white sand, steep trails threading through the dense jungle, and a calm-watered natural swimming

RIO DE JANEIRO STATE

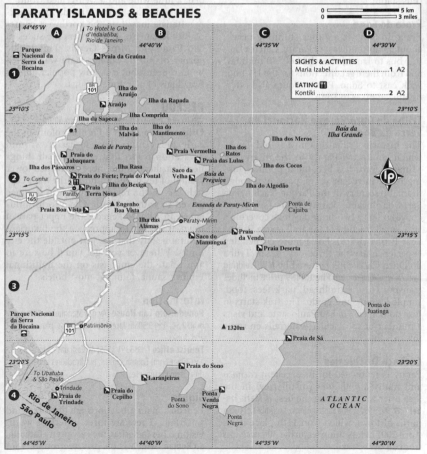

PARATY ISLANDS & BEACHES

SIGHTS & ACTIVITIES
Maria Izabel......................1 A2

EATING
Kontiki...............................2 A2

pool opposite the furthest beach, Cachadaço. The town itself has the somewhat scraggly quality of a frontier outpost that's grown up too fast (indeed, 15 years ago, there was only a small fishing village here), but the sizeable cluster of pousadas, camping grounds and restaurants permits an overnight stay. Hourly Colitur buses (R$2.60, 40 minutes) serve Trindade from Paraty's bus station.

Praia de Paraty-Mirim

For accessibility, cost and beauty, this tranquil beach is hard to beat. Paraty-Mirim is a small town 17km southeast of Paraty, with *barracas* serving simple meals and an 18th-century church. Colitur runs buses here (R$2.60, 40 minutes) from Paraty's *rodoviária* (bus station).

Praia do Sono

Praia do Sono is another stunning beach, about 35km southeast of Paraty. Catch a Colitur bus to Laranjeiras (R$2.60, 40 minutes) and from there get directions for the 1½-hour walk east to Sono. Paraty Tours also offers organized hikes to Sono.

Trilha do Ouro/Parque Nacional da Serra da Bocaina

The historic Trilha de Ouro (Gold Trail), which connected Paraty to the interior of Minas Gerais, has become a popular hiking route in recent years, passing through dramatic scenery in the Parque Nacional da Serra da Bocaina. Paraty Tours (see Tours above) offers a two-hour day hike covering a very small fraction of the trail above Paraty, near Penha (R$15). For a more challenging experience, try the three-day, 42km Trilha do Ouro Classic hike offered by **MW Trekking** (www.mwtrekking.com.br). The R$489 price includes transport to the trailhead, park fees, food, simple lodging and guide. The trek starts in José do Barreiro in São Paulo state and visits a number of spectacular waterfalls en route towards the coast.

Cachaça Distilleries

Paraty is renowned for its excellent *cachaça* and many *alambiques* (distilleries) in the area offer tours. Among the best is **Maria Izabel** (☎ 9999 9908; Sítio Santo Antônio, Corumbê), 10km north of town, which won 11th place in an April 2007 competition featuring 300 *cachaças* from all over Brazil.

ITATIAIA REGION

The Itatiaia region is a curious mix of Old World charm and New World jungle. The climate is Alpine temperate and the chalets are Swiss, but the vegetation is tropical and the warm smiles are pure Brazilian. There are neatly tended little farms with horses and goats, and small homes with clipped lawns and flower boxes side by side with large tracts of dense forest untouched by the machete. This is a wonderful place to tramp around green hills, ride ponies up purple mountains, splash in waterfalls and hike trails without straying too far from the comforts of civilization: a fireplace, a soft bed, a little wine and a well-grilled trout!

The region lies in the Serra da Mantiqueira's Itatiaia massif, in the northwest corner of Rio de Janeiro, and borders the states of São Paulo and Minas Gerais. This idyllic corner of Rio de Janeiro state was settled by Europeans, but it is now popular among Brazilians of all ethnic groups.

PENEDO

☎ 0xx24 / pop 40,000 / elevation 600m

Originally started as a Finnish colony in the early 20th century, Penedo has grown into a vacation resort that embraces all things non-Brazilian. In the more developed lower section of town, you'll find tourist traps capitalizing on the region's European heritage mixed in with authentic Old World influences. In Alto do Penedo, the upper part of town, it's easier to appreciate the luxuriant natural beauty that lies just outside the city limits. Wherever you go, you'll be sure to appreciate the emphasis on the traditional Finnish sauna, found at most hotels.

Information

Penedo.com Lan House (Av das Mangueiras 800; per hr R$2.50; ☟ 9:30am-late) Internet access, plus snacks and drinks.

Tourist office (☎ 3351 3535; Av Casa das Pedras 766; ☟ 10am-6pm) English spoken, but brochures and information are in Portuguese.

Sights

Penedo's main attractions are the forest and waterfalls. There are three waterfalls worth visiting: **Três Cachoeiras**, the very pretty **Cachoeira do Roman**, which is on private grounds (but

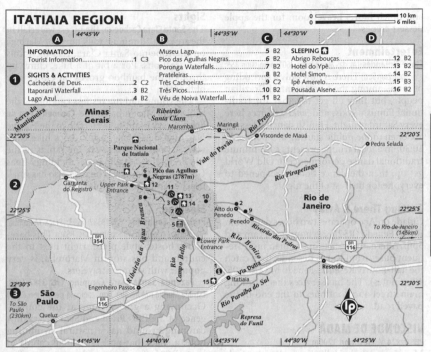

ITATIAIA REGION

INFORMATION			
Tourist Information	1 C3	Museu Lago	5 B2
		Pico das Agulhas Negras	6 B2
SIGHTS & ACTIVITIES		Poronga Waterfalls	7 B2
Cachoeira de Deus	2 C2	Prateleiras	8 B2
Itaporani Waterfall	3 B2	Três Cachoeiras	9 C2
Lago Azul	4 B2	Três Picos	10 B2
		Véu de Noiva Waterfall	11 B2

SLEEPING		
Abrigo Rebouças	12 B2
Hotel do Ypê	13 B2
Hotel Simon	14 B2
Ipê Amerelo	15 B3
Pousada Alsene	16 B2

RIO DE JANEIRO STATE

accessible to the public), 10 minutes' walk uphill from the Pousada Challenge, and **Cachoeira de Deus**, which is right near the Pousada Challenge. About one hour of uphill **hiking** from the end of the asphalt takes you into very dense forest with trails and opportunities to observe wildlife, including monkeys.

In town, you can hire horses at **From Penedo** (☎ 3351 1380; www.penedo.com/frompenedo; Rua das Palmeiras; 90-min ride with guide R$35).

Sleeping & Eating

Penedo is expensive, due to the large number of weekend tourists who come up from Rio, but the accommodations and food are above average.

Pousada Trilha (☎ 3351 1349; www.hospede-se.com in Portuguese; s/d from R$79; 🖳)) Just downhill from Três Cachoeiras, this simple pousada resembles a log cabin. Rooms are small but comfy.

Pousada Challenge (☎ 3351 1389; www.encante-se.com/challenge in Portuguese; Alameda Áustria 43; d R$100; 🖳) Tucked into a hilly suburb of Alto do Penedo, this pousada has clean prefabricated chalets with fireplaces, plus a pool and sauna.

Pequena Índia (☎ 3351 1702; www.pequenaindia .com.br in Portuguese; Rua Romeo de Vasconcelos 25; s/d with half board from R$150) Like so many places in Penedo, Pequena Índia strives to create a non-Brazilian atmosphere. The spa-like hotel way uphill in Alto do Penedo offers yoga classes, daily hikes, massage, and vegetarian breakfast and lunch.

Casa do Chocolate (☎ 3351 1127; Av Casa das Pedras 10; sandwiches R$6) Besides the delicious chocolate cake and hot chocolate you'd expect, Casa do Chocolate serves up big sandwiches, apple strudel, as well as 50 different ice-cream flavors.

Com Agua na Boca (☎ 3351 1077; Av das Mangueiras 1775; per kg R$24; ⏰ 11:30am-11pm) The self-service buffet features fresh trout, and you can people-watch from the outdoor patio along Penedo's main street.

Koskenkorva (☎ 3351 2532; Estrada Três Cachoeiras 3955; dinner from R$20; ⏰ noon-11:30pm Mon-Sat, to 6pm Sun) With a lovely outdoor seating area by a creek, Koskenkorva specializes in Finnish and German food. For a splurge, try Voileipäpöyta, a smorgasbord-like platter featuring smoked trout, marinated salmon, herring, trout pâté and much more. Leave room for the apple dessert crepes.

Entertainment

Clube Finlandês (Av das Mangueiras 2601; admission R$5; 🕙 9pm-2am Sat;) There is now only a sprinkling of Finns among the assortment of Brazilian people, but they all get together for traditional Finnish *letkiss* and *jenkiss* dances here every Saturday night. Finnish dancing lessons are open to the public starting at 9:00pm. At 10:30pm a local troupe presents a 40-minute traditional dance performance in Old World get up, then the dance floor is reopened to everyone for the rest of the night.

Getting There & Away

Cidade do Aço operates two buses daily from Rio to Penedo (R$25, 2½ hours) at 11am and 5pm. Alternatively, take one of their more frequent buses from Rio to Resende, then catch the half-hourly Resende-Penedo bus (R$2.05, 45 minutes). The bus services the 3km-long main street and continues to the end of the paved road.

VISCONDE DE MAUÁ

☎ 0xx24 / elevation 1200m

Mauá is an utterly idyllic river valley that feels like a world unto itself. Prettier and more tranquil than Penedo, it has rushing streams, tinkling goat bells, cozy chalets and country lanes graced with wildflowers. Its isolation is largely thanks to the town's limited access routes, all via rutted dirt roads over precipitous mountaintops – however you get here, be ready for a bumpy ride!

Information

Visconde de Mauá consists of three small villages a few kilometers apart along the Rio Preto. The bus stops first at Mauá, the largest village, and then heads uphill to Maringá, 6km to the west (one side is actually in Minas Gerais). Maromba is further upstream at the end of the bus route and about 2km west of Maringá. Most travelers stay in Maromba or Maringá. Maromba has the feel of a hippie hangout, while Maringá attracts a slightly more upscale crowd.

At the entrance to the village of Mauá, the **tourist information hut** (🕙 10am-1pm & 2-6pm, closed Thu morning, Sun afternoon & all day Wed) has helpful photos of area accommodations and can call ahead to reserve.

Sights

The **Santa Clara Cachoeira**, the nicest waterfall in the area, is a 40-minute walk north of Maringá on the Ribeirão Santa Clara. Ask the locals for directions. For a bit of a hike, climb up through the bamboo groves on either side of the falls.

The young and the restless can follow the trail from Maromba to the **Cachoeira Veu de Noiva**, a very beautiful waterfall, in the Parque Nacional de Itatiaia, a full day's hike each way. It's possible to kayak the rapids of the Rio Preto, the cascading river dividing Minas Gerais from Rio state. The river also has small beaches and natural pools.

Sleeping

Pousada Sonhador (☎ 3387 1533; Praça Maromba, Maromba; per person without breakfast R$10) This barebones hostel-style place, right next to the church and bus stop in Maromba, is very popular with younger travelers.

Fazenda Santa Clara Camping (☎ 3387 1508; Estrada Maringá/Moromba 1km; camping per person R$10) Occupying a grassy slope at the convergence of the Rios Preto and Santa Clara, this camping ground has a natural swimming hole, a snack bar and *very* small cabins to rent (R$35) for those without a tent. The bus stop across the river is accessible via a pedestrian bridge.

Pousada na Colina (☎ 3387 1392; colina.web.terra .com.br; Vale do Pavão; s/d R$85; 🏊) This is the highest place you can stay in the Vale do Pavão, a lovely side valley between Mauá and Maringá. Cute cabins in well-tended grounds overlook the forest. The homey comforts include porches with hammocks, fireplaces artfully pre-loaded with wood and pine needles, a sauna and a pool.

Olho d'Agua (☎ 3387 1386; www.olhodaguamaua .com.br in Portuguese; Maringá; d from R$130) If you prefer a less isolated setting, try Olho d'Agua, in the heart of Maringá's shopping district. The onsite restaurant is excellent too.

Pousada Moriá (☎ 3387 1505; www.pousadamoria .com.br in Portuguese; Estrada da Maromba s/n; d R$130, with whirlpool tub R$220) This idyllic hideaway is opposite the Cachoeira do Escorrega, a natural water slide above Maromba. Chalets all have electric blankets and fireplaces, there's a DVD library and the onsite restaurant serves trout and fondue. Breakfast is served in a glass-walled cabin or out on the deck overlooking the waterfall.

Eating

Agua Viva (☎ 3387 1594; Estrada Maringá/Moromba 7km; meals from R$11; ⏰ 11am-10pm Fri-Wed) Trout and *mineiro* (Minas Gerais cuisine) food is served in this delightful riverside location. Outdoor seating and hammocks allow you to relax to the sound of rushing water during and after the meal. The owner speaks some English.

Zorba Budda (☎ 3387 1170; Alto Maringá; pizza from R$15; ⏰ 7pm-1am Fri-Sun) This sweet little pumpkin-colored restaurant serves excellent pizza and is packed on weekend nights.

Filho da Truta (☎ 3387 1527; Vale do Pavão; meals from R$20; ⏰ 11am-11pm) Run by an enterprising couple of Lebanese-French descent, this cozy restaurant has won national acclaim for its 37 different trout recipes. The brand-new attached pousada is a great deal at R$98 per couple, including all meals.

Rosmarinus Officinalis (☎ 3387 1550; Estrada Maringá 4km; meals R$30; ⏰ 7-10pm Fri-Wed) Beautifully set amid gardens, with smoke pouring out its chimney in chilly weather, this restaurant looks like a fairy-tale house, but the food is strictly gourmet. The glass-walled eating area is especially cozy when lit with reflected candlelight at night.

Getting There & Around

Visconde de Mauá has no bus station. The two main bus stops are at the shops in Maringá and up at the Praça da Maromba in Maromba.

Four buses from Monday to Saturday and three on Sunday travel between Visconde de Mauá and Resende, just east of Itatiaia, (R$4.65, two hours). Transfer in Resende for buses to/from Rio. Cidade de Aço also runs one direct bus daily between Rio and Mauá (R$28, 4½hrs)

PARQUE NACIONAL DE ITATIAIA

☎ 0xx24

Parque Nacional de Itatiaia is Brazil's oldest national park, and one of its most ruggedly beautiful. Its lush, dark foliage contains more than 400 species of native birds and is also home to monkeys and sloths. Divided into upper and lower sections, the park features lakes, rivers, waterfalls, alpine meadows and primary and secondary Atlantic rain forests. Don't let the tropical plants fool you; temperatures drop below freezing in June and, occasionally, the park even has a few snowy days! Bring warm clothes, even in summer.

There is a 24-hour tourist information booth in the town of Itatiaia, 1km north of the Via Dutra, the main east–west superhighway between Rio and São Paulo. The lower park entrance is 5.5km north of town.

Sights & Activities

Each section of the park (upper and lower) has its own entrance station (admission R$3 low country, R$12 high country, plus R$5 per vehicle). Park headquarters and the adjacent museum (admission free; ⏰ 8am-5pm Tue-Sun) are 9km north of Itatiaia town, in the park's lower, tamer section. From headquarters, a simple 400m walk takes you to **Lago Azul** (Blue Lake). A few kilometers up the road, short trails lead to the **Poranga, Véu de Noiva and Itaporani waterfalls**. For a longer hike in the low country, try the five-hour, 15km return trip to **Três Picos** (1600m).

Climbing and trekking enthusiasts will want to pit themselves against the high country's more challenging peaks, cliffs and trails. The park's diminutive upper entrance station – almost two hours from Itatiaia town – is reached via an extremely rugged unpaved 15km road from a junction called Garganta do Registro, on the border between Rio state and Minas Gerais. Prominently visible as you enter the park are the dramatic pointy profile of the **Agulhas Negras** (at 2787m, the highest peak in the area) and, a bit further on, the boulders of the **Prateleiras**. A guide is required for climbs to these peaks. One highly recommended guide is the park ranger **Levy** (☎ 8812 0006; levyecologico@bol .com.br), who charges R$40 to R$100, depending on the itinerary. You can also contact the **Grupo Excursionista de Agulhas Negras** (☎ 3352 1734), which organizes climbs every other week, or ask local pousadas to help you find a guide.

At the time of writing, the brand new **Travessia Rui Braga** trail, starting at the foot of Prateleiras, was scheduled to open in late 2007, linking the upper and lower parts of the park and allowing visitors to experience Itatiaia's alpine and Atlantic rain forest ecosystems in a single long day hike (nine hours one way, descending).

Sleeping & Eating

The fancier hotels inside the national park offer full board as noted in individual reviews. However, you'll want to bring your own food if staying in one of the area's simpler accommodations (first three listings below).

RIO DE JANEIRO STATE

Abrigo Rebouças (☎ 3352 1461; bunk per person R$10) This hikers' shelter in the high country, with a gas stove and electricity, provides basic accommodations for up to 20 people but no food or other supplies. Advance reservations are required, as the place can fill up fast.

Pousada Alsene (☎ 0xx35-3363 1773; www.alsene .com.br in Portuguese; campsite/room per person R$15/85) If the shelter inside the park is full, high country visitors can try this pousada/camping ground at 2400m, just below the park's upper entrance station. The hotel has a bar and limited food, but it's highly advisable to bring extra supplies (especially chocolate, snacks and warm clothes). Alsene is colder and bleaker than your average Brazilian pousada and it's a long, bumpy drive out. Book in advance and let them know if you need a ride in (for a fee).

Ipê Amarelo (☎ 3352 1232; www.pousadaypeamarelo .com.br in Portuguese; Rua João Mauricio de Macedo Costa 352; campsite/room per person R$18/35; 🐾) This combination hostel/campground just north of the Via Dutra has a pool, a sauna and bicycles for rent. It's a 15-minute walk west of the bus station (R$5 by taxi). They'll organize day trips to Itatiaia's high country (R$80 to R$100 per person, including meals and transportation).

Hotel do Ypê (☎ 3352 1453; www.hoteldoype.com.br; s/d with meals from R$180/252; 🖵 🐾) About 8.5km north of the lower park entrance, this wonderful place at the end of the road is close to several hiking trails, with adorable chalets for rent. Toucans and hummingbirds feed in abundance outside the breakfast room window, and at lunchtime there's a great outdoor barbecue served around the pool.

Hotel Simon (☎ 3352 1230; www.hotelsimon.com .br; s/d with meals from R$198/259) About 7km north of the lower park entrance is the spiffy Hotel Simon (officially renamed the Itatiaia Park Hotel, but still known by its old name, including on road signs and the hotel's own website). It has gorgeous rustic furnishings and its own orchid garden.

Getting There & Around

The village of Itatiaia is most easily reached from the nearby city of Resende (the hub for buses to/from Rio). Service between Itatiaia and Resende runs every 20 minutes on weekdays, every 40 minutes on weekends. There are a few daily buses from Itatiaia village into the park (leaving the bus station at 7am, noon and 4pm, and returning from the park at 8am, 1pm, and 4:45pm; R$2 one-way). A

taxi ride from Itatiaia town to the places to stay within the main section of the park costs R$20 to R$25.

NORTH OF RIO DE JANEIRO

The mountains north of Rio rise up with shapes so improbable and dramatic, they catch your attention even from a great distance. Landing at Galeão international airport or surveying the northern skyline from the top of Rio's Pão de Açúcar (Sugarloaf Mountain), your eye is automatically drawn to the intriguing sawtooth ridge on the horizon. In the 19th century, the allure of these mountains led Brazil's imperial family to set up a summer residence in Petrópolis, and inspired the country's first Swiss immigrants to choose Nova Friburgo as their New World home. More recently, climbers from all over the world have become enamored of the vertiginous rocky faces of the Serra dos Órgãos (Organ Pipe Range). To this day, the cooler climate and recreational opportunities, along with the region's imperial and immigrant legacy, continue to attract visitors from Rio and beyond.

PETRÓPOLIS

☎ 0xx24 / pop 279,000 / elevation 809m

A lovely mountain retreat with a decidedly European flavor, Petrópolis is a favorite weekend getaway for Cariocas (residents of Rio city). This is where the imperial court spent the summer when Rio got too muggy, and it's still the home of the heir to the throne, Dom Pedro II's great-great-grandson Dom Luiz Gastão de Orleans e Bragança. Wander around or ride by horse and carriage through the squares and parks, past bridges, canals and old-fashioned street lamps.

Information

Bradesco (Rua do Imperador 268) One of many banks with ATMs along the town's main street.

Job Net (☎ 2231 7331; Rua 16 de Março 80; per hr R$3; ☯ 9am-9pm Mon-Sat) Internet and Skype access.

Laundromat (☎ 2242 8145; Rua 16 de Março 334; per machine R$8; ☯ 8am-8pm Mon-Sat)

Post office (Rua do Imperador 350)

Tourist information booth (☎ 2246 9377; www.petro polis.rj.gov.br/fctp; Praça Expedicionários; ☯ 9am-6pm)

PETRÓPOLIS

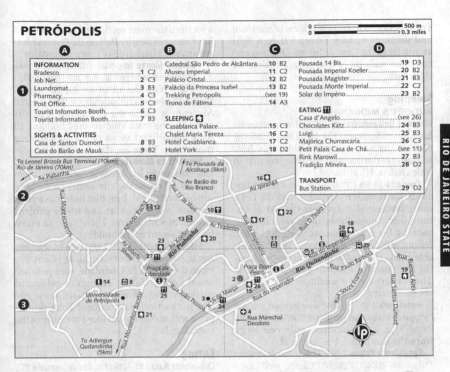

INFORMATION		
Bradesco	1	C2
Job Net	2	C3
Laundromat	3	B3
Pharmacy	4	C3
Post Office	5	C3
Tourist Infomation Booth	6	C3
Tourist Information Booth	7	B3
SIGHTS & ACTIVITIES		
Casa de Santos Dumont	8	A3
Casa do Barão de Mauá	9	B2
Catedral São Pedro de Alcântara	10	B2
Museu Imperial	11	C2
Palácio Cristal	12	B2
Palácio da Princesa Isabel	13	B2
Trekking Petrópolis	(see 19)	
Trono de Fátima	14	A3
SLEEPING		
Casablanca Palace	15	C3
Chalet Maria Tereza	16	C2
Hotel Casablanca	17	C2
Hotel York	18	D2
Pousada 14 Bis	19	D3
Pousada Imperial Koeller	20	B2
Pousada Magister	21	B3
Pousada Monte Imperial	22	C2
Solar do Império	23	B2
EATING		
Casa d'Angelo	(see 26)	
Chocolates Katz	24	B3
Luigi	25	B3
Majórica Churrascaria	26	C3
Petit Palais Casa de Chá	(see 11)	
Rink Marowil	27	B3
Tradição Mineira	28	D2
TRANSPORT		
Bus Station	29	D2

Tourist information booth (☎ 2246 9377; www.petro polis.rj.gov.br/fctp; Praça da Liberdade; ☺ 9am-6pm)

Trekking Petrópolis (☎ 2235 7607; www.rioserra.com .br/trekking) Organizes hikes, mountain-biking, rafting and bird-watching trips through nearby Mata Atlântica rain forest. You can also book through Pousada 14 Bis (p206).

Sights & Activities

Most of the museums and other attractions are closed on Monday.

A fun way to get oriented is by taking a **horse and carriage ride**. Nineteenth-century *vitórias*, carriages of British design, make fixed-price circuits of the downtown area lasting twenty minutes (R$20) to one hour (R$50).

Petrópolis' main draw is the **Museu Imperial** (☎ 2237 8000; Rua da Imperatriz 220; admission R$8; ☺ 11am-5:30pm Tue-Sun), housed in the impeccably preserved and appointed palace of Dom Pedro II. You're given felt slippers at the entrance so you won't scuff the fine wood floors – great fun to slide around in! On display is the 1.7kg imperial crown, with its 639 diamonds and 77 pearls, as well as the ruby-encrusted, feather-shaped gold pen used to sign the *Lei Aurea*, freeing Brazil's remaining slaves in 1888.

The **Catedral São Pedro de Alcântara** (☎ 2242 4300; Rua Sao Pedro de Alcantara 60; ☺ 8am-noon & 2-4pm Wed-Mon) houses the tombs of Brazil's last emperor, Dom Pedro II, his wife Dona Teresa and their daughter, Princesa Isabel. Its steeple is lit up with beautiful bluish-purple lights at night.

Downtown has fine mansions that can be viewed from the outside only, including the **Palácio da Princesa Isabel** (Av Koeller) and the **Casa do Barão de Maua** (Praca da Confluencia), across Rio Piabanha.

The **Palácio Cristal** (Alfredo Pachá) is an iron and glass structure built in France and imported in 1879 to serve as a hothouse in which to grow orchids. It now serves as a venue for evening cultural events.

West of Praça da Liberdade, the **Casa de Santos Dumont** (admission R$5; ☺ 9am-5pm Tue-Sun) was the summer home of Brazil's diminutive father of aviation and inventor of the wristwatch. The house itself is charming and there are interesting photos of Dumont's many inventions.

The **Trono de Fátima** is a 3.5m sculpture of NS de Fátima Madonna, imported from Italy.

RIO DE JANEIRO STATE

From here you have a great view of the town and surrounding hills. To reach it, turn right as you leave the Casa de Santos Dumont and continue walking uphill, always taking the right fork.

Sleeping

BUDGET & MIDRANGE

Albergue Quitandinha (☎ 2291 4483; www.quitandinha hostel.com.br; Rua Uruguai 570; dm/s/d from R$33/50/75) Out of the way but affordable, this hostel offers dorms and private rooms in little chalets. HI-affiliated.

Pousada 14 Bis (☎ 2231 0946; www.pousada14bis .com.br; Rua Buenos Aires 192; s/d from R$80/130) On a quiet residential street near the old downtown bus station, the restored colonial Pousada 14 Bis has handsome, well-appointed rooms with lovely wood floors and comfortable beds. The best have balconies overlooking the peaceful street or garden out back. The owners have a wealth of information about the city.

Hotel York (☎ 2243 2662; www.hotelyork.com.br in Portuguese; Rua do Imperador 78; s/d R$90/130) The big draw here is the location, only one block from the downtown bus terminal.

Casablanca Palace (☎ 2242 0162; Rua 16 de Março 123; s/d/tr/q R$110/130/200/245) Clean, well cared for and close to the main shopping district.

TOP END

Pousada Magister (☎ 2242 1054; www.pousadamagister .com.br; Rua Monsenhor Bacelar 71; r from R$165) This century-old mansion near the Casa de Santos Dumont blends old-world elegance with modern amenities.

Hotel Casablanca (☎ 2242 6662; www.casablanca hotel.com.br; Rua da Imperatriz 286; s/d/tr/q from R$145/180/ 245/300; 🅟) Almost next door to the Museu Imperial, the Casablanca has a range of rooms – the best feature high ceilings, old shutters, long bathrooms with tubs and antique furnishings.

Chalet Maria Tereza (☎ 2242 7107; www.chaletmaria tereza.com.br; Av Ipiranga 405A; r R$180) Reached via a long trellised garden archway, the friendly, homelike Maria Tereza doesn't advertise itself prominently but is full of understated historic charm.

Pousada Imperial Koeller (☎ 2243 4330; www.pousada monteimperial.com.br; Av Koeller 99; r R$195; 🅟) One of the newest pousadas in town, the Imperial Koeller is right in the heart of things, along architecturally stunning Av Koeller. It's set back a bit from the main road, but front rooms still have views of nearby Palácio da Princesa Isabel against a backdrop of green mountains.

Pousada Monte Imperial (☎ 2237 1664; www .pousadamonteimperial.com.br; Rua José Alencar 27; r R$215; 🖳) With the air of an Alpine retreat, this pousada on a hillside above the Imperial Museum is worth the stiff climb. Upstairs rooms in the main vine-covered building all have magnificent views of the surrounding mountains. There are also three chalets.

Pousada da Alcobaça (☎ 2221 1240; www.pousada daalcobaca.com.br; Rua Agostinho Goulão 298; d from R$300; 🅟) Outside the city center in the suburb of Corrêas, this beautiful hotel has a pool, a sauna, a tennis court and lovely gardens crossed by a small river. There's also an excellent restaurant in the building.

Solar do Império (☎ 2103 3000; www.solardoimperio .com.br; Av Koeller 376; r from R$431; 🖳 🅟) Centrally located on Praça da Liberdade, with polished wood floors, 15-foot ceilings, a columned entryway, grand fireplaces, a pool, sauna and spa, the meticulously restored Solar do Império will make you feel like a member of the royal family.

Eating

Chocolates Katz (☎ 2245 1818; Rua do Imperador 912; coffee R$2.40, apple strudel R$4) This German-style coffee shop and patisserie makes excellent cappuccinos, hot cocoa and chocolate torte.

Tradição Mineira (☎ 2242 5592; Rua do Imperador 148; per kg R$16.90; ⏰ 11am-4pm) One of downtown's most popular self-serve lunch spots.

Luigi (☎ 2246 0279; Praça da Liberdade 185; lunch $9; ⏰ 11am-midnight) A charming Italian restaurant set in an old house with tall ceilings and creaky floors. The regular menu is supplemented by daily lunch specials for under R$10 and an evening *rodízio de pizza* (all-you-can-eat pizza), where countless varieties are offered for R$14.

Casa d'Angelo (☎ 2242 0888; Rua do Imperador 700; mains from R$12; ⏰ 8am-1am) Opposite the obelisk at the corner of Ruas Imperador and Imperatriz, Casa d'Angelo has long been a Petrópolis institution. Always popular for beers and reasonably priced meals, Angelo is especially worth visiting on Saturday when they serve *feijoada* (the Brazilian national dish, a bean-and-meat stew) for only R$13.90.

Rink Marowil (☎ 2243 0743; Praça da Liberdade 27; meals from R$13; ⏰ 8am-2am) This long glass-walled building in the center of Praça da Liberdade affords lovely views of trees, mansions and the canal running nearby. The menu features pasta, risotto, meat and fish.

Petit Palais Casa de Chá (☎ 2237 8000; Av Imperatriz 220; afternoon tea R$20; ☷ noon-7pm Tue-Sun) On the Museu Imperial grounds, this charming bistro and teahouse serves soups, sandwiches and full meals. Its crowning glory is the *chá imperial* – a lavish afternoon tea featuring cakes, croissants, pâté and a full range of hot beverages.

Majórica Churrascaria (☎ 2242 2498; Rua do Imperador 754; mains R$20; ☷ 11:45am-10pm Sun-Thu, to 11pm Fri & Sat) A traditional favorite, with white tablecloths, wood paneling and dignified waiters, Majórica serves excellent cuts of meat à la carte.

Getting There & Around
Única and Fácil buses from Rio (R$13, 1½ hours, half-hourly from 5:30am to midnight) drop you at Leonel Brizola bus terminal in Bingen, 10km outside downtown Petrópolis. To reach the old downtown bus station (Terminal de Integração), transfer to a local Esperança bus, number 100 or 10, (R$1.90, 30 minutes).

VASSOURAS
☎ 0xx24 / pop 29,000 / elevation 434m
Vassouras, a quiet resort 118km north of Rio, was the most important city in the Paraíba valley in the first half of the 19th century. Local coffee barons, with titles of nobility granted by the Portuguese crown, built huge *fazendas* (farms) in the surrounding hills. With the abolition of slavery in 1888 and the resulting decline in coffee production, the importance of Vassouras diminished, but several historic buildings from the boom days still survive in the pleasant town center.

The area's biggest attractions are the coffee *fazendas* several kilometers outside of town, some of them on the scale of French châteaux and with gardens to match. To visit these, you really need your own vehicle – without it, you'll run up some hefty cab fares or calf muscles!

For two weeks in late July, Vassouras is buzzing with more than just coffee during the annual **Festival Vale do Café**. Daily concerts are scheduled, and some *fazendas* host dinners featuring period food and dress.

Information
Casa de Cultura (☎ 2471 2765; Praça Barão do Campo Belo; ☷ 9am-5pm Mon-Fri, to 4pm Sat, to 2pm Sun)

Displays photos and distributes informational brochures (in Portuguese) about nearby coffee *fazendas*.

Sights
The town's large central square, known as the **Campo Belo**, is a picturesque grassy slope dotted with palm trees and a fountain. Twin roosters crown the spires of the **Matriz NS de Conceição** church at the top of the hill.

Museu Casa da Hera (Rua Dr Fernandes Jr 160; admission free; ☷ 11am-5pm Wed-Sun), former home of the aristocratic heiress Eufrásia Teixeira Leite, displays antique handcarved furniture and other colonial relics.

The countryside around Vassouras is teeming with old coffee *fazendas* protected by historical preservation institutes. Most are still privately owned, so prior permission is required before touring them. The most popular are the imposing **Fazenda do Secretário** (☎ 2488 0150), **Mulungú Vermelho** (☎ 9828 2825), **Santa Eufrásia** (☎ 2471 1065), **Cachoeira do Mato Dentro** (☎ 8114 9655) and **Cachoeira Grande** (☎ 2471 1264; www.fazendacachoeiragrande.com.br in Portuguese). The Casa de Cultura has detailed information and can help arrange visits.

Sleeping & Eating
Hotel Jardim Imperial (☎ 2471 1877; Rua Barão de Vassouras 82; s/d R$60/90) Clean modern rooms complement the convenient location one block from the main square.

Mara Palace (☎ 2471 1993; www.marapalace.com.br; Rua Chanceler Dr Raul Fernandes 121; s/d from R$85/99, with meals R$173/216; ☷ ☷) A centrally located three-star with attractive rooms, pools and a sauna, the Mara is one of the best options in town.

Restaurante Salão Brasil (☎ 2471 8901; Rua Barão de Capivari 60; per kg R$12.90; ☷ 11am-3pm) Right on the main square, this place is popular with students and old folks alike. Delicious home cooking, tasty desserts and the kind of high-quality *cafezinho* you'd expect in Vassouras.

For fine dining and a good wine list, try **Hipólito** (☎ 2471 2805; Rua Anna Jesuina 47; meals from R$20; ☷ 7pm-late Mon-Fri, from noon Sat & Sun), down a side street off the main square.

Getting There & Around
There are six daily buses to Rio (R$22, 2½ hours) from the **bus station** (☎ 2471 1055; Praça Juiz Machado Jr).

To get to the *fazendas*, you'll need your own wheels or a taxi.

TERESÓPOLIS

☎ 0xx21 / pop 128,000 / elevation 871m

Do as Empress Maria Tereza used to do and escape from the steamy summer heat of Rio to the cool mountain retreat of Teresópolis, the highest city in the state, nestled in the strange, organ-pipe rock formations of the Serra dos Órgãos. The gorgeous winding road from Rio to Teresópolis climbs steeply through a padded green jungle, with bald peaks towering dramatically overhead the entire way.

The Quebra Frascos, the royal family of the Second Empire, once resided here. Today the city's principal attraction is the surrounding landscape and its natural treasures. Teresópolis is not merely for alpinists: it's a center for sports lovers of all varieties. There are facilities for volleyball, motocross and equestrian activities – many of Brazil's finest thoroughbreds are raised here – not to mention soccer (see right).

Information

HSBC (Av Delfim Moreira 746) One of several banks with ATMs along this street.

Post office (Av Lúcio Meira)

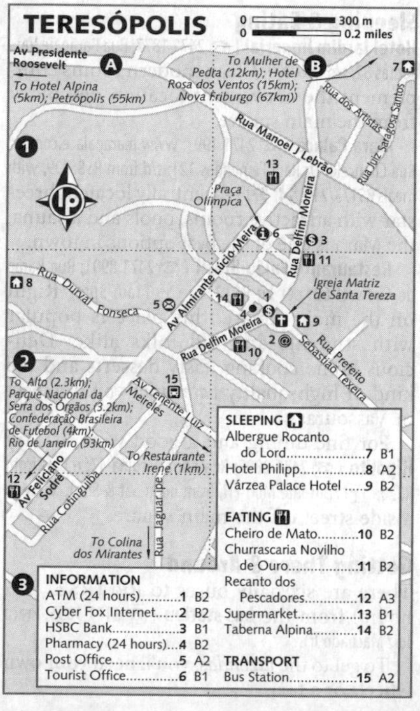
TERESÓPOLIS
0 300 m
0 0.2 miles
Av Presidente Roosevelt
To Hotel Alpina (5km); Petrópolis (55km)
To Mulher de Pedra (12km); Hotel Rosa dos Ventos (15km); Nova Friburgo (67km))
Rua dos Artistas
Rua Juiz Saragosa Santos
Rua Manoel J Lebrão
Praça Olímpica
Rua Delfim Moreira
Av Almirante Lúcio Meira
Rua Durval Fonseca
Igreja Matriz de Santa Tereza
Rua Delfim Moreira
Rua Prefeito Sebastião Texeira
To Alto (2.3km); Parque Nacional da Serra dos Órgãos (3.2km); Confederação Brasileira de Futebol (4km); Rio de Janeiro (93km)
Av Tenente Luiz Meireles
To Restaurante Irene (1km)
Av Feliciano Sodré
Rua Cotinguiba
Rua Jaguar Ipe
To Colina dos Mirantes
SLEEPING
Albergue Recanto do Lord 7 B1
Hotel Philipp 8 A2
Várzea Palace Hotel 9 B2
EATING
Cheiro de Mato 10 B2
Churrascaria Novilho de Ouro 11 B2
Recanto dos Pescadores 12 A3
Supermarket 13 B1
Taberna Alpina 14 B2
INFORMATION
ATM (24 hours) 1 B2
Cyber Fox Internet 2 B2
HSBC Bank 3 B1
Pharmacy (24 hours) 4 B2
Post Office 5 A2
Tourist Office 6 B1
TRANSPORT
Bus Station 15 A2

Tourist office (☎ 2742 5561; turismotere@ig.com.br; Praça Olímpica; 9am-6pm Mon-Fri, to 5pm Sat, to 1pm Sun) In the town center. There's another location in the hills above town, along the road from Rio.

Cyber Fox Internet (☎ 2742 5240; Praça Santa Tereza; per hr R$2.50; 9:30am-11pm) In the shopping center on the main square.

Sights & Activities

The area's main attraction is the Parque Nacional da Serra dos Órgãos. The **Dedo de Deus** (God's Finger) is the town symbol, a dramatic rock spire visible from all over town. **Colina dos Mirantes**, in the southern suburb of Fazendinha, is an especially good place to view the city and its mountain backdrop. On clear days you can see as far as Rio's Pão de Açúcar and the Baía de Guanabara.

Many more attractions lie outside town along the road to Nova Friburgo (see the boxed text, p210).

Teresópolis bears the distinction of being the training base of Brazil's World Cup squad. Check with the tourist office to see if the Brazilian national team is in town during your visit. If so, you can watch players training at the **Confederação Brasileira de Futebol (CBF)** in the Comary neighborhood south of town.

Sleeping

BUDGET & MIDRANGE

Albergue Recanto do Lord (☎ 2742 5586; www.teresopolishostel.com.br, www.recantodo lord.com.br; Rua Luiza Pereira Soares 109; dm/s/d R$25/40/65;) This highly recommended hostel, designed to look like an orange castle, commands amazing views of the Dedo de Deus and other nearby peaks from its hillside perch north of downtown. The friendly owner offers transfers to/from the bus station (R$5) and the national park (R$10) and can provide a wealth of information about the surrounding area.

Várzea Palace Hotel (☎ 2742 0878; www.varzea.palace.nafoto.net (photos only); Rua Prefeito Sebastião Teixeira 41/55; ste R$55-90) This grand old white building with red trim, right off the main square, has been a Teresópolis institution since 1916. Its historic grandeur has faded with time, but there are still plenty of atmospheric touches, including ornamental tiles, parquet wood floors, spacious rooms and high ceilings. The nicer suites have terraces.

Hotel Philipp (☎ 2742 2970; www.hotelphilipp.com.br; Rua Durval Fonseca 1333; s/d/tr/q R$75/95/135/175;) Straight uphill and west of the bus station, the

Philipp feels a bit like a German mountain lodge, with a fireplace, pool and nice views of the surrounding mountains.

TOP END

The more expensive hotels are out of town.

Hotel Alpina (☎ 2741 4999; www.hotelalpina.com.br; Rua Cândido Portinari 837; s/d from R$220/250) The enormous Swiss-style Hotel Alpina, across the street from a swanky golf course, has spacious *apartamentos* and offers full board for a small surcharge. It's 4km out of town, towards Petrópolis.

Hotel Rosa dos Ventos (☎ 2644 9900; www.hotelrosadosventos.com.br; Estrada Tere-Fri 22.6km; d from R$298; master ste R$600) This luxurious Alpine-style resort belongs to the international Relais & Châteaux chain. Way up in the mountains, it has its own lake and network of hiking trails. Magnificent views abound from the many terraces and onsite restaurants. It's 22km out of town along the road to Nova Friburgo.

Eating

For self-caterers, there's a supermarket on Av Almirante Lúcio Meira.

Taberna Alpina (☎ 2742 0123; Rua Duque de Caxias 131; sandwiches from R$3; ☉ noon-10pm Tue-Sun) The Taberna's cozy interior room, sporting wooden benches with heart-shaped cutouts, is reminiscent of the Alps. So is the menu, featuring German mustard, brown bread, goulash, and smoked pork with sauerkraut.

Cheiro de Mato (☎ 2742 1899; Av Delfim Moreira 140; per kg R$18.90; ☉ 11am-3:30pm) A good place for self-serve health food, including brown rice, a large salad buffet and other vegetarian options.

Churrascaria Novilho de Ouro (☎ 2641 6384; Av Delfim Moreira 720, per kg from R$18.90; ☉ 11am-midnight Tue-Sun, to 4pm Mon) Delicious grilled meats are the specialty here, but sushi and other Japanese delights are also available.

Recanto dos Pescadores (☎ 2742 9988; Av Feliciano Sodré 221; meals from R$25; ☉ 11am-11pm Sun-Thu, to 2am Fri & Sat) Excellent service and variety make this one of Teresópolis' most appealing restaurants. Amazingly good seafood is brought up from the coast daily. Try the shrimp in cognac and cream sauce.

Restaurante Irene (☎ 2742 2901; Rua Tenente Luís Meirelles 1800; dinner R$70) In the suburb of Bom Retiro, Irene's is considered the best haute cuisine in Teresópolis. Reservations are required.

Getting There & Around

The **bus station** (Rua Primeiro de Maio) is south of the main square. Buses head to Rio (R$18, 1½ hours, half-hourly from 5am to 10pm), Petrópolis (R$11, 1½ hours, several between 6am and 7pm) and Novo Friburgo (R$8, two hours, five daily).

PARQUE NACIONAL DA SERRA DOS ÓRGÃOS

Created in 1939, this national park covers 118 sq km of mountainous terrain between Teresópolis and Petrópolis. A distinctive feature of the park is the strangely shaped peaks of the **Pedra do Sino** (2263m), **Pedra do Açu** (2230m), **Agulha do Diabo** (2020m), **Nariz do Frade** (1919m), **Dedo de Deus** (1651m), **Pedra da Ermitage** (1485m) and **Dedo de Nossa Senhora** (1320m). With so many peaks, it's no wonder that this is the mountain-climbing, rock climbing and trekking center of Brazil. The region has extensive trails, the most famous of which is the 42km, three-day traverse over the mountains from Teresópolis to Petrópolis. Unfortunately, most of the trails are unmarked and off the available maps. Hiring a guide, however, is easy and inexpensive. Inquire at the **national park entrance** (☎ 2642 1070; admission R$3; ☉ 8am-5pm) or go with a group organized by one of the hiking and mountaineering clubs in Rio. The best time for walks is from May to October (the drier months).

The main entrance to the national park is at the southern edge of the township of Teresópolis, off Hwy BR-116 from Rio, about 4km from the center. Walking trails, waterfalls, natural swimming pools and tended lawns and gardens make this a very pretty place for a picnic.

From the main entrance, the road extends into the park as far as Barragem Beija Flor. There are several good walks from near here. The highlight is the **Trilha Pedra do Sino** – a round-trip of about eight hours from the end of the park road (R$9 trail fee). The trail passes Cachoeira Veu da Noiva, the vegetation changes from rain forest to grassland, and the reward is a panoramic view stretching all the way to Rio de Janeiro and the Baía de Guanabara. For a shorter walk, head up to the **Mirante Alexandre Oliveira** (1100m), from where there is a good view of Teresópolis – it's about a one-hour round-trip from the park road.

THE TERESÓPOLIS-FRIBURGO SCENIC CIRCUIT

Where can you find an Alpine goat cheese dairy, a wacked-out sculpture garden, a beekeeper who makes his own honey *cachaça*, beautiful peaks and waterfalls, and some of Brazil's spiffiest hotels? They're all on the **Circuito Turístico Tere-Fri** (www.terefri.com.br), a 68km highway connecting the towns of Teresópolis and Nova Friburgo. Points of interest are indicated on a handy map available throughout the region. Starting from Teresópolis, highlights include the **Mulher de Pedra** (Woman of Stone) viewpoint at 12km, where a distant mountain really does look like a reclining woman; the **Cremerie Geneve** at 16km, where you can pet baby goats, buy local cheese, stroll the gardens or indulge in a fine French meal; the **Cachoeira dos Frades** turnoff at 21.5km, where an unpaved side road leads through an idyllic valley to a waterfall with a swimming hole; **Hotel Rosa dos Ventos** (see p209) at 22.6km, one of many opulent hotels along the route; the **Queijaria Suíça** at 49km, where a Swiss cheese factory sits adjacent to an excellent museum tracing two centuries of Swiss culture in the Friburgo area; the **Apiário Amigos da Terra** at 51km, where you can learn about bees in the bee museum and drink local honey *cachaça* while the kids play in a honeycomb-shaped play structure; and **Jardim do Nêgo** at 55km, where a local sculptor has created a bizarre landscape of moss-covered human and animal forms. It's easiest to drive the route in your own car, although local buses travel through here and will let you off wherever you like.

There is another, secondary entrance down in the southeast corner of the national park, off the road from Rio. It also has an information center, walking trails and waterfalls.

Tours are also available from Petrópolis (see p205).

Getting There & Around

To get to the park's main entrance from the city center of Teresópolis, take the hourly 'Soberbo' bus (R$1.80). Alternatively, take the more frequent 'Alto' bus and get off at the Pracinha do Alto, from which it's a short walk south to the park's main entrance. A taxi ride from town to the park entrance costs about R$20.

NOVA FRIBURGO

☎ 0xx22 / pop 171,000 / elevation 846m

In 1818, newly crowned Portuguese King Dom João VI started recruiting immigrants from Switzerland and Germany to help settle his vast Brazilian territory. The first 30 families to arrive, from the Swiss canton of Friburg, immediately set out to create a perfect little village reminiscent of their home country in the mountains north of Rio. Traces of Swiss and German heritage remain in modern Friburgo, in the local architecture, the town's passion for floral decoration and the fair-haired, blue-eyed features of some residents. There are also plenty of resplendent natural attractions: waterfalls, woods, trails, sunny mountain mornings and cool evenings.

Information

746 Cyber Café (☎ 2523 8000; Praça Getúlio Vargas; ☽ 10am-late) Internet access, plus coffee and hard liquor to keep you fully wired.

Banco do Brasil (Praça Dermeval B Moreira 10)

Post office Opposite Praça Getúlio Vargas.

Tourist office (☎ 2543 6307; www.friweb.com.br/ turismo; Praça Dermeval B Moreira 10; ☽ 8am-8pm, to 6pm Sun) Has maps and a complete list of hotels, including the cheapest, with updated prices.

Sights & Activities

Most of the sights are a few kilometers out of town. Survey the surrounding area from **Morro da Cruz** (1800m). The chairlift to Morro da Cruz runs on weekends and holidays from 9am to 6pm. Its station is in the center of town at Praça Teleférico. **Pico da Caledônia** (2310m) offers fantastic views and launching sites for hang gliders. It's a 6km uphill hike, but the view is worth it.

North of town, you can hike to **Pedra do Cão Sentado**, a rock formation resembling a sitting dog that serves as Friburgo's town symbol, or visit the mountain town of **Bom Jardim** (23km northeast on Hwy RJ-116). To the southeast, **Lumiar** (34km from Nova Friburgo) is a popular destination for Brazilian ecotourists, with cheap pensions, waterfalls, walking trails, a brand new Alê Friburgo hostel (see opposite) and white-water adventures centered around the Encontro dos Rios, the tumultuous confluence of three local rivers. Guided adventure tours of the area are available through the Alê

Friburgo hostel or **Lumiar Aventura** (☎ 2523 6506; www.lumiaraventura.com in Portuguese).

Sleeping

Alê Friburgo Hostel (☎ 2522 0540; www.friburgohostel .com; Rua Ernesto Bizzotto Filho 2; dm/s/d R$23/40/60; 🖳 🖳) This hostel, 2km straight uphill from Friburgo's town square, compensates for its remote location with friendly staff and great amenities including a pool, sauna and shuttle service from downtown. The owners have recently opened a sister hostel in the pretty forested valley of Lumiar, less than an hour away, where they offer bike rentals and excursions to nearby waterfalls.

Hotel Maringá (☎ 2522 2309; Rua Monsenhor Miranda 110; s/d/tr/q R$50/85/105/125) There are sim-ple *quartos* (room with shared bathroom) and more expensive *apartamentos*, but both choices are clean and nicely decorated. The popular restaurant downstairs features all-you-can-eat home cooking for R$20 at lunchtime.

Primus (☎ 2523 2898; www.hotelprimus.com.br; Rua Adolfo Lautz 128; s/d/tr/q R$60/90/120/150; 🖳) This is up on a very steep hill, but the breakfast alone is worth the hike. There's a pool, pet peacocks and great views.

Hotel São Paulo (☎ 2522 9135; www.hotelsaopaulo .com.br; Rua Monsenhor Miranda 41; s/d/tr/q R$65/90/115/ 140; 🖳) Some rooms are in the more modern part of the building but the real winners at Hotel São Paulo are the high-ceilinged rooms located in the old section.

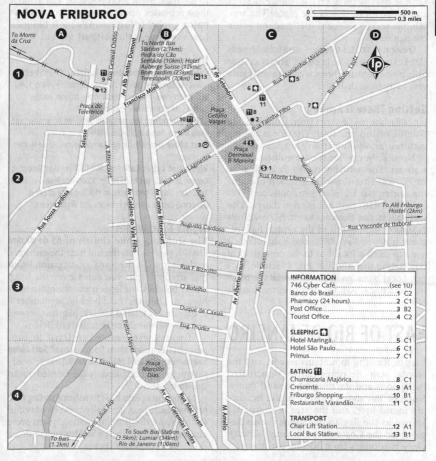

NOVA FRIBURGO

Hotel Auberge Suisse (☎ 2541 1270; www.auberge suisse.com.br; Rua 10 de Outubro, Amparo; chalets from R$200; ☒) The luxury chalets here, in the Amparo district, 12km north of Nova Friburgo, all have fireplaces and pretty landscaped grounds. There are indoor and outdoor pools, and the restaurant serves traditional Swiss cuisine: raclettes, fondues and trout.

Eating

Friburgo Shopping (Praça Getúlio Vargas) Has a variety of bars and cafés.

Restaurante Varandão (2522 5021; Rua Monsenhor Miranda 46; per kg from R$14.90; ☒ 11am-11pm, to 4pm Sunday) This very popular self-serve restaurant features *bacalhau* (codfish) on Sundays.

Churrascaría Majórica (☎ 2523 1510; Praça Getúlio Vargas 74; meals from R$15; ☒ 11am-10pm) For meat and more meat, this is the place. The restaurant serves a decent filet mignon – it's enough for two.

Crescente (☎ 2523 4616; Rua General Osório 21; meals R$30; 11:30am-11pm Thu-Tue, to 5pm Sun) This is a classy little place featuring French cuisine and some very tasty trout dishes.

Getting There & Around

Nova Friburgo is a short jaunt from Rio, via Niterói, on bus line 1001. The ride is along a picturesque, winding, misty jungle road.

Novo Friburgo has two long-distance bus stations. The **north bus station** (Rodoviária Norte; ☎ 2522 6095; Praça Feliciano Costa), 2.5km north of the center, has buses to Petrópolis and Teresópolis (R$8, two hours, five daily). The **south bus station** (Rodoviária Sul; ☎ 2522 0400; Ponte da Saudade), 4km south of the center, has frequent buses to Rio (R$22, two hours). You'll need to catch a local bus to the central, local bus station just north of Praça Getúlio Vargas. Local buses go to just about all the tourist attractions. Ask for details at the tourist office.

EAST OF RIO DE JANEIRO

East of Rio, the mountains recede, and the coastal strip becomes flatter, punctuated by lagoons and dazzling white sand dunes. Some of Rio state's most beautiful beaches are found here, and the area is alternately known as the Região dos Lagos (Lakes Region) or the Costa do Sol (Sunny Coast). Only two hours from Rio by car, the area has rapidly grown into a weekend playground for Cariocas, with plenty of opportunities for nightlife and outdoor recreation.

SAQUAREMA
☎ 0xx22 / pop 49,000

Straddling a spit of sand between a gorgeous lagoon and the open Atlantic, Saquarema is a laid-back little town 100km east of Rio. Polluting industries are forbidden in the municipality; the waters are clean and fish and shrimp are abundant. Touted as the surfing capital of Brazil, its unmarred shoreline also attracts sportfishing enthusiasts and sun worshipers. The surrounding area is a horse-breeding and fruit-growing center; you can visit the orchards and pick fruit, or rent horses or a jeep and take to the hills. Most local pousadas can arrange these activities. About 3km east of town is **Praia Itaúna**, probably Saquarema's most beautiful beach and one of the best surf spots in Brazil.

Information

Centro de Atendimento ao Turista (☎ 2651 2254; www.saquarema.rj.gov.br; Av Saquarema; ☒ 9am-5pm) In a brand-new office overlooking the lagoon, on the Itaúna side of the downtown bridge.

Lakes Shopping This tiny mall, between downtown and Praia Itaúna, has a multi-bank ATM.

Post office (Praça Oscar de Macedo Soares) Close to the bus stop.

World Net Cyber Café (☎ 9974 1207; Lakes Shopping Center, Shop 65; per hr R$2; ☒ 10am-late Mon-Sat, from 1pm Sun) One of two places on the 2nd floor of Lakes Shopping Center offering internet and Skype access.

Sights & Activities

The stunning white church of **NS de Nazaré** (1837), perched on the hill near the entrance to the lagoon, is the town's focal point. From this strategic spot you can survey the long, empty beaches, the lagoon and the mountains beyond. The mass held here on September 7 and 8 attracts around 150,000 pilgrims, second only to the Nazaré celebrations of Belém.

If you've ever wanted to learn to surf, what better place then Saquarema? **Surf Camp Saquarema** (☎ 2651 8651; Praia da Vila) has friendly instructors, all certified by the Confederação Brasileira de Surfe.

Saquarema plays host to **national surfing competitions** each year, generally between May and October. At the time of writing, plans were also underway to open a **Surf Museum** at Praça do Casarão on Praia Itaúna.

Sleeping

Prices quoted here are for high season. Discounts of up to 30% apply in low season. Some of the nicer places are out at Praia Itaúna, R$6 by taxi from the city center.

BUDGET

Sobre O Mar Hostel (☎ 2651 4762; Av Salgado Filho 2412; www.saquaremahostel.com.br; dm/d per person R$26/36; 🖳 🖢) With ocean views, a pool and internet access, this hostel on Boqueirão beach, 2km west of downtown, is a great deal.

Garota da Itaúna (☎ 2651 2156; Av Oceânica 165; s/d R$50/80) A perfectly adequate option near Itaúna beach just behind the restaurant of the same name. With a little effort, you can see the ocean from the upstairs balcony, and you can be dipping your toes in the waves in just two minutes.

MIDRANGE & TOP END

Maasai Hotel Beach & Resort (☎ 2651 1092; www .maasai.com.br; Travessa Itaúna 17; s/d/tr R$80/120/150, s/d/tr ste R$180/250/310; 🖳) An appealing fullsize resort right on the beach, the Maasai has a restaurant, sauna, swimming pool (complete with waterfall!) and a pretty bar facing the water.

Pousada Canto da Vila (☎ 2651 1563; www.pousada cantodavila.com.br; Av Salgado Filho 52; d/tr/q from R$90/130/182) This friendly beachfront place, just downhill from Saquarema's historic church, features happy, airy rooms, many with great views of surfers riding the waves.

Pousada do Suíço (☎ 2651 7842; Rua das Pitangas 580; rooms without/with air-con R$90/130; 🖳) The former Swiss owner has passed on, but the pleasant palm-filled courtyard and location a couple blocks from Itaúna beach continue to draw visitors from around the world.

Eating

Marisco Restaurante (☎ 2651 1884; Praça Oscar de Macedo Soares 35; per kg from R$15.90; 🖢 9am-late) Marisco is always packed, thanks to its reasonably priced per kilo seafood and its pleasant setting on Saquarema's main square.

Forno à Lenha (☎ 2651 7847; Rua dos Mariscos 511; pizza from R$10; 🖢 noon-midnight) A few blocks back from Itaúna beach, this place has a cozy back room with a wood-burning oven, plus a front patio area where you can enjoy their pizza and grilled meats.

Churrascaria Picanha do Gugu (☎ 2651 1165; Av Saquarema 567; meals R$15; 🖢 noon-10pm) One of several dining options in Lakes Shopping Center between downtown and Itaúna beach, Gugu's is a meat-lover's paradise.

Garota da Itaúna (☎ 2651 2156; Av Oceânica 165; meals from R$15; 🖢 8am-late) The Garota's many attractions include a fabulous beachfront terrace and a wide variety of seafood specials. Enjoy the views but hang on to your beers – the wind can be vicious.

Getting There & Around

The 1001 bus company buses leave Rio for Saquarema every other hour between 6:15am and 8:40pm (R$15, two hours).

To get to Cabo Frio, take a local Salineira bus to Bacaxá. From there, buses depart for Cabo Frio every half-hour. The bus stop in Saquarema is across from the bridge, one block from the main square in the town center.

ARRAIAL DO CABO

☎ 0xx22 / pop 23,000

Arraial do Cabo, 45km east of Saquarema, is surrounded by gleaming white sand dunes and offers all the beauty of Búzios with half the fuss. The sign at the town entrance proclaims that this is 'where the sun spends the winter,' and indeed, it's easy to feel that this little town at the end of the peninsula is a charmed world unto itself. Arraial is home to a working fishing port, Porto do Forno, which lends it a welcoming working-class demeanor. Funny little lighthouse statues at intersections around town also add a touch of charm. Some of the best beaches – pristine swaths of gorgeous sand and bright-green waters – are within an easy 15-minute stroll of the downtown bus station, while others are just a short boat ride away.

Arraial is a good place to observe humpback whales (*Megaptera novaeangliae*) and several other marine mammal species. Since 1999, scientists at the Projeto Baleias e Golfinhos de Arraial (Arraial Whale and Dolphin Project) have been studying the local whales and their migration routes, which pass directly offshore.

Information

The **tourist office** (☎ 2622 1949; www.arraial.rj.gov .br/turismo; 🖢 9am-5pm) at the town's formal entry portico 3km from the center has English- and Spanish-speaking staff, and provides a helpful map.

Av Getúlio Vargas is home to the **post office** (Av Getúlio Vargas 19) and several internet places, including **Arraial Online Cyber Cafe** (☎ 2622 7198; Av Getúlio Vargas 16)

Sights & Activities

Arraial's prime attractions lie along the shoreline. **Praia dos Anjos** has beautiful turquoise water but a little too much boat traffic for comfortable swimming. Just above the beach, look for the plaque commemorating Amerigo Vespucci's landing here in 1503. Vespucci left 24 men behind to start a settlement, making Arraial one of the first European toeholds in the Americas.

Favorite beaches within short walking distance of town are **Prainha** to the north of town; **Praia do Forno** (accessed by a 1km walking trail from Praia dos Anjos) to the northeast; and the vast **Praia Grande** to the west, where wilder surf races in off the open Atlantic.

Ilha de Cabo Frio is accessed by boat from Praia dos Anjos. **Praia do Farol** on the protected side of the island is a gorgeous beach with fine white sand. From here there is a 2½-hour walk to the lighthouse. The **Gruta Azul** (Blue Cavern), on the southwestern side of the island, is another beautiful spot. Be alert, though: the entrance to the underwater cavern is submerged at high tide.

Tour operators who organize dives in these waters abound – the tourist office keeps a complete list. One good company is **Sandmar** (☎ /fax 2622 5703; www.sandmar.com.br in Portuguese; Rua Epitácio Pessoa 21).

Sleeping

Prices quoted here are for the high season. Discounts of up to 40% are common in low season.

Marina dos Anjos Hostel (☎ /fax 2622 4060; www.marinadosanjos.com.br; Rua Bernardo Lens 145; dm/d R$35/98) Located one block back from Praia dos Anjos, this youth hostel is a wonderful base from which to explore the area. The helpful staff rents bicycles, canoes, snorkels, surfboards and diving equipment. Marina dos Anjos Hostel's central courtyard, with hammocks and pillows for lounging, is the venue for spontaneous evening barbecues and jam sessions. See if you can find the two unusual Buddhas before they find you.

Praia dos Anjos (☎ 2622 1378; Av Roberto Silveira 10; s/d R$79/115) Only 50m from Praia dos Anjos,

this is one of the least expensive places so close to the beach.

Capitão n'Areia Pousada (☎ 2622 2720; www.capitao pousada.com.br in Portuguese; Rua Santa Cruz 7; s/d from R$100/130; 🖳) A fancier option in the same neighborhood. Rooms here are elegant and big, just like the pool.

Hotel Pousada Caminho do Sol (☎ 2622 2029; www.caminhodosol.com.br; Rua do Sol 50; rooms from R$135; 🖳) Right on Praia Grande, this pretty resort hotel with a pool and beautiful views is a big hit with visiting Brazilians looking for a romantic weekend.

Estalagem do Porto (☎ 2622 2892; www.estalagem doporto.com.br in Portuguese; Rua Santa Cruz 12; s/d/tr/q R$130/160/208/256) Also near the beach, in the most charming section of town, Estalagem is highly recommended for its comfortable rooms, delicious breakfast and rooftop terrace with beautiful panoramas of the harbor below.

Eating

Agua na Boca (☎ 2622 1106; Praça da Bandeira 1; per kg R$27; ⏱ 11:30am-5pm) A stone's throw from the bus station, the highly recommended self-serve includes plenty of seafood in its daily offerings.

Forno á Lenha (☎ 2622 5333; Rua Roberto Silveira 19; pizzas from R$18; ⏱ 6pm-midnight Tue-Sun) The wood-fired pizzas are delicious here and the atmosphere is cheerful, with floral tablecloths, a lion fountain and a giant Brazilian flag.

Saint Tropez (☎ 2622 1222; Praça Daniel Barreto 2; meals from R$20 ⏱ 6pm-midnight Mon-Tue, noon-midnight Wed-Sun) Just a block up from Praia dos Anjos, Saint Tropez is one of the best spots in town for fresh fish.

Viagem dos Sabores (☎ 2622 2892; Rua Santa Cruz 12; meals R$25; ⏱ 2-10:30pm) Inside the pousada Estalagem do Porto, this well-run restaurant serves up delectable dishes with all sorts of eclectic influences. Bahian flavors, Italian and French are prominent.

Getting There & Away

The Arraial do Cabo **bus station** (☎ 2622 1488; Praça da Bandeira) is situated in the town center. Direct buses run by the 1001 bus company leave for Rio every two hours between 6:40am and 6:40pm (R$19, three hours).

An alternative is to catch a municipal bus to Cabo Frio (R$2.70), then transfer to one of the half-hourly Rio-bound buses leaving from the Cabo Frio bus station.

CABO FRIO

☎ 0xx22 / pop 120,000

Built up around sand dunes and beaches, with plenty of fresh breezes, Cabo Frio's naturally gorgeous settings have been stunted by the salt and tourism industries that dominate in the area. If you are able to overlook the encroaching overdevelopment, Cabo Frio remains a relaxed little beach town, ready to greet newcomers with a smile. Every weekend, and throughout the summer holidays, it attracts scores of visitors – the bars are invariably filled with happy-go-lucky Brazilians whooping it up, and the merrymaking spirit is clearly Cabo Frio's strongest attraction.

Orientation

The town of Cabo Frio is at the end of the long sweeping beach that extends northward from Arraial do Cabo. Cabo Frio lies to the west of the Canal do Itajuru, which links the Lagoa de Araruama to the Atlantic Ocean. Near the bridge is the town's focal point – a hill with a small white chapel. The town center is east of here, and the bus station is to the west (about 2km from the center) near the end of Av Júlia Kubitschek. This road runs almost parallel to the Praia do Forte, named after the fort at its eastern end.

Information

Bradesco (Av Assunção 904) Bank and ATM.

HSBC (Av Assunção 793) Bank and ATM.

Lan House Shotzone (☎ 2645 6878; Av Nilo Peçanha 415; per hr R$3; ☺ 9-1am) Internet access into the wee hours.

Post office (Largo de Santo Antônio 55)

Tourist office (☎ 2647 1689; www.cabofrio.rj.gov.br in Portuguese; Av do Contorno 200; ☺ 8am-7pm) Near the end of Av João Pessoa near Praia do Forte. It has hotel information and maps; English and some Spanish spoken.

Forte São Mateus

This **stone fortress** (admission free; ☺ 10am-4pm Tue-Sun), a stronghold against pirates, was built between 1616 and 1620 to protect the lucrative brazilwood trade. You will find the fort at the eastern end of Praia do Forte.

Dunes

There are three sand-dune spots in and about Cabo Frio. The dunes of **Praia do Peró**, a super beach for surfing and surf casting, are 6km north in the direction of Búzios, near Ogivas and after Praia Brava and Praia das Conchas. The **Dama Branca** (White Lady) sand dunes are

on the road to Arraial do Cabo. The **Pontal** dunes of Praia do Forte town beach stretch from the fort to Miranda hill. Robberies can pose a danger at the dunes, so get advice from locals before heading out.

Sleeping

BUDGET

Camping Club do Brasil (☎ 2644 1226; Estrada dos Passageiros 700; per person R$16) A favorite camping site for youngsters, you get to choose: sling a hammock between scrubby pines or pitch a tent.

Peró Hostel (☎ /fax 2644 3123; Rua Coutrin 13; www .perohostel.com.br; dm/d per person R$26/30; ☒) Northeast of town, just a few blocks off Peró beach, this HI-affiliated hostel offers chalets, dorms and kitchenettes. They give tours of the region by boat and in their antique 1958 jeep.

Atlantico (☎ /fax 2643 0996; www.hotelatlantico.tur .br in Portuguese; Rua Jose Bonifacio 302; s/d R$60/80) One of the most popular budget hotels in town, Atlantico has large rooms at bargain prices.

MIDRANGE & TOP END

Porto Peró (☎ 2644 5568; www.portopero.com.br; Av dos Pescadores 2002; s/d/tr/q R$90/100/130/160; ☒)

This pousada is near a very pretty stretch of beach. It has clean, airy rooms and a lovely pool area.

Malibu Palace Hotel (☎ 2647 8000; www.malibu palace.com.br; Av do Contorno 900; s/d R$275) For views and location, it's hard to beat this central place overlooking the dazzling blue and white landscape of Cabo Frio's main beachfront.

Eating

Restaurante Gosto Bom (☎ 2643 4417; Travessa Nações Unidas 29; all-you-can-eat R$8.99; ☼ 11:45am-4:30pm) A good place to fill up on self-serve fare in the heart of town.

Restaurante do Zé (☎ 2643 4277; Blvd Canal 100; meals from R$16; ☼ 11am-midnight) The sidewalk tables at this animated eatery overlook the canal, one of the most picturesque spots in town.

Tia Maluca (☎ 2647 4158; Blvd Canal 109; meals from R$20; ☼ 11am-midnight) Just across the street from Restaurant do Zé, Tia Maluca has the same pretty views, plus good prices for their delicious seafood and *picanha* (rump steak).

Getting There & Away

The **bus station** (☎ 2643 2291; Av Júlia Kubitschek) is 2km west of the center. Buses to and from Rio, run by the 1001 bus company, leave every half hour between 5am and midnight (R$20, 2½ hours).

To Arraial do Cabo, catch Salineira bus 402 from the bus stop just to the left as you leave the bus station (R$2.70, 30 minutes). To get to Búzios, catch a bus from the stop across the road (R$2.70, one hour).

BÚZIOS

☎ 0xx22 / pop 17,000

Beautiful Búzios sits on a jutting peninsula scalloped by 17 beaches. A simple fishing village until the early '60s, when it was 'discovered' by Brigitte Bardot and her Brazilian boyfriend, Búzios is now one of Brazil's most animated seaside resorts, littered with boutiques, fine restaurants, villas, bars and posh pousadas. The Mediterranean touch introduced by the Portuguese has not been lost – indeed, the narrow cobblestone streets and picturesque waterfront add to Búzios' appeal, and contribute to its image as Brazil's St Tropez.

Orientation

Búzios is not a single town but rather three settlements on the peninsula – Ossos, Man-guinhos and Armação de Búzios – and one on the mainland called Rasa. Ossos (Bones), at the northern tip of the peninsula, is the oldest and most attractive. It has a pretty harbor and yacht club, plus a few hotels and bars. Manguinhos, on the isthmus, is the most commercial. Armação, in between, has the most tourist amenities; it's here that you'll find Rua das Pedras, the hub of the Búzios' nightlife. Northwest along the coast is Rasa, where Brazil's rich and powerful relax.

Information

Banco do Brasil (Rua Manoel de Carvalho 70) In Armação.
Bradesco (Av José Bento Ribeiro Dantas 254)
Centro Médico Búzios (☎ 2623 2919, after hr 9972 9749; Rua César Augusto São Luiz 100; ☼ 8am-10pm) A private clinic in downtown Armação.
ClickNet (☎ 2623 7395, Trav Germiniano José Luiz 194; per hr R$2; ☼ 10-1am) One of the best internet cafés in downtown Armação, with excellent prices and hours, plus Skype service.
Internet cafés Can be found in the blocks surrounding Rua Manoel Turibio de Farias.
Itaú (Av José Bento Ribeiro Dantas 223) ATM.
Lave Já (Travessa Oscar Lopez Campos 63; per basket full service/self-service R$28/R$22; ☼ 10am-7pm Mon-Sat). Wash your own laundry or let them do it for R$6 extra.
Multi-bank ATM (Praça Santos Dumont) Convenient but charges a R$6 service fee.
Secretaria de Turismo (☎ 2633 6200, 0800-249 999; www.buziosturismo.com); town entrance portal (Av José Bento Ribeiro Dantas; ☼ 24hr); Armação (Praça Santos Dumont; ☼ 10am-10pm) City maps and hotel information are available in these offices.

Sights & Activities

The biggest draws in Búzios are the natural setting plus the intoxicating mixture of opportunities for relaxation, nightlife, shopping and ocean sports.

Cobblestoned **Rua das Pedras** is Búzios' main venue for shopping, dining and evening entertainment, overflowing with revelers on weekend nights. Its eastward continuation, **Orla Bardot**, is a delightful winding oceanfront promenade linking the two oldest and most picturesque sections of town (Armação and Ossos). As you walk along the beachfront, you'll notice several wonderful statues by sculptor Christina Motta, including representations of Brigitte Bardot and former Brazilian president Juscelino Kubitschek, plus some remarkably realistic-looking fishermen hauling in their nets.

There are some fine **swimming, diving and snorkeling** sites near Búzios. See below for more details.

BEACHES

In general, the southern beaches are trickier to get to, but they're prettier and have better surf. The northern beaches are more sheltered and closer to the towns.

Going counterclockwise from south of Manguinhos, the first beaches are **Geribá** and **Ferradurinha** (Little Horseshoe). These are beautiful beaches with good surf, but the Búzios Beach Club has built condos here. Next on the coast is **Ferradura**, which is large enough for windsurfing and **Lagoinha**, a rocky beach with rough water. **Praia da Foca** and **Praia do Forno** have colder water than the other beaches. **Praia Olho de Boi** (Bull's Eye) is the area's only nude beach. It's reached by a little trail from the long, clean beach of **Praia Brava**.

Both **João Fernandinho** and **João Fernandes** are good for snorkeling, as are **Azedinha** and **Azeda**, reached by a short trail from Ossos. **Praia dos Ossos**, **Praia da Armação**, **Praia do Caboclo** and **Praia dos Amores** are pretty to look at, but a bit public and not so nice for lounging around on. **Praia da Tartaruga** is quiet and pretty. **Praia do Gaucho** and **Manguinhos** are town beaches further along.

Offshore, the islands of **Âncora**, **Gravatás**, **Filhote** and **Feia** are especially good diving destinations.

Tours

Several local operators offer tours to local beaches and islands.

Tour Shop Búzios (☎ 2623 2763; www.tourshop.com .br; Orla Bardot 550; tours from R$30) This outfit runs the Búzios Trolley, an open-sided bus that visits 12 of the peninsula's beaches daily. They also operate rafting tours and trips by glass-bottomed catamaran.

Queen Lory (☎ 2623 1179; www.queenlorytours.com .br; Rua João Fernandes 89; tours from R$40) Daily 2½- and five-hour schooner tours to Ilha Feia, Tartaruga and João Fernandinho beaches offer opportunities for swimming and snorkeling.

Buziosnauta (☎ 2623 9005; www.buziosnauta.com.br; Orla Bardot 712; tours from R$40) Boat tours to beaches and islands on both the north and south sides of the peninsula, as well as night tours and trips to Arraial do Cabo and Cabo Frio.

Casamar (☎ 2623 2441; www.casamar.com.br; Rua das Pedras 242; 2-tank dives from R$110) Offers day and night excursions for experienced divers, plus a full range of courses.

Sleeping

Búzios caters to couples, so things can get pricey for solo travelers. In general, rooms to rent are cheaper than pousadas. Rates quoted here are for the high season: December through March, plus July.

BUDGET

Hostel Ville Blanche (☎ 2623 2892; villeblanche buzios@hotmail.com; Rua Manoel Turibio de Farias 222; dm/d/ tr/q R$30/100/130/160) One block from the nightlife of Rua das Pedras, Ville Blanche is primarily a pousada but also offers limited dorm space. The private rooms can be a good deal for three or four people traveling together.

Alegravila (☎ 2623 2329; www.alegravila.com.br; Av José Bento Ribeiro Dantas 1475; dm/d with HI membership R$33/100, dm/d without HI membership R$43/120; 🖳 🖳) The HI-affiliated Alegravila has attractive, clean rooms centered on a garden with a small pool, plus a guest kitchen. It's 600m from the Armação waterfront, along the main road from Rio, 300m west of the bus station.

Pousada Portal das Palmeiras (☎ 2623 2677; Rua César Augusto São Luiz 11; s/d without breakfast R$70) If you're willing to do without breakfast, this is one of the most affordable centrally located places in Búzios. The rooms are as basic as the price implies.

MIDRANGE

Brigitta's Guest House (☎ 2623 2940; www.brigittas .com.br; Rua das Pedras 131; s/d from R$80/100) Brigitta's privileged location between Rua das Pedras and the Armação waterfront is just one of many reasons to stay here. There are only four rooms, two with doors opening directly onto the beach. The staff speaks nine languages, and the excellent restaurant downstairs serves an award-winning mix of international food. Street noise is the only downside.

Pousadinha em Búzios (☎ 2623 1448; annabina@ hotmail.com; Rua Turíbio de Farias 202D; s/d R$100/120, with air-con R$150; 🔀) Right in the town center, Pousadinha has attractive rooms set around a little courtyard.

Pousada Amendoeira (☎ 2623 2613; www .amendoeira.net; Rua João Fernandes 1449, Ossos; s/d R$100/120) The rooms at this simple pousada are decorated in various cheerful shades of blue, and the affable owner adds to the generally bright atmosphere.

Pousada Moana (☎ 2623 1355; www.buziosexplorer .com.br/pousadamoana; Praça Eugenio Honold 173, Ossos; s/d R$112/140) Cozily situated on a square one block from the Ossos waterfront, Moana's four upstairs rooms are the nicest, with spacious floor plans and ocean views.

Zen-do Suites (☎ 2623 1542; Rua João Fernandes 60; s/d from R$140) This sweet little guesthouse only has three rooms. The upstairs unit is especially bright and cheery, with a balcony overlooking the spacious backyard. The friendly staff speaks multiple languages.

TOP END

Solar do Peixe Vivo (☎ 2623 1850; www.solardopeixevivo .com.br; Orla Bardot 994; s/d R$180) Directly across from the fishermen statues along Búzios's premier waterfront promenade, this lovely historical house is a real treat. President Juscelino Kubitschek stayed here during his summer visits to Búzios, hence the statue of him sitting across the street.

Pousada Hibiscus Beach (☎ 2623 6221; www.hibiscus beach.com.br; House 22, Block C, Rua 1, João Fernandes; r R$275; 🏊) The comfortable private chalets here cascade down the grassy hillside to a pleasant outdoor swimming pool. It's also just a short walk from beautiful João Fernandes beach.

Chez Pitú (☎ 2623 6460; www.chezpitu.com.br in Portuguese; Aldeia de Geribá 10; d from R$300; 🏊) Right on the beach in Geribá, this place has an artsy feel, decorated with sculptures, mosaic designs and brightly painted French doors. There are two pools (one with a small bar), and lounge chairs on a wooden deck with tantalizing views of the ocean a few feet away. The nicest rooms are upstairs, with small verandas where you can watch the best sunset in Búzios.

Glenzhaus Lodge (☎ 2623 2823; www.glenzhaus.com .br; Rua dos Coqueiros 28; s/d from R$480; 🏊 🖥 🏊) New on the scene, the Argentine-owned Glenzhaus is already winning accolades from elite international travel magazines (second best hotel in all of South America, per Condé Nast), as well as from clients in the guestbook who rave about the relaxing vibe and the attentive service. The grounds include a massage hut and a pool surrounded by beautifully landscaped greenery that feels a world apart from downtown Búzios.

Pérola Búzios (☎ 2620 8507; www.perolabuzios.com; Rua Av José Bento Ribeiro Dantas 222; s/d from R$485/570; 🏊 🖥 🏊) This is the most central of Búzios'

trendy new luxury hotels, only two blocks from Rua das Pedras, but far enough removed to guarantee you a good night's sleep. The electric blue pool, seductively surrounded by curtained lounging beds, is fun and inviting day or night. The whole place is artistically decorated, although for the price, it's disappointing that none of the rooms have ocean views.

Casas Brancas (☎ 2623 1458; www.casasbrancas.com .br; Rua Alto do Humaitá 10; r from R$564; 🏊 🖥 🏊) If you just won the lottery or are here for your honeymoon, head straight for Casas Brancas, the best of several top-end places on Alto do Humaitá hill in Armação. The ocean views from the upstairs terrace are stupendous, and the world-class spa, swimming pool and restaurant are nice enough to keep you here all day. Despite the exclusive price tag, Casas Brancas has a rather low-key, friendly attitude.

Eating

For good, cheap food, eat grilled fish at the little thatched-roof places on Brava, Ferradura and João Fernandes beaches. Most of the better restaurants are in or near Armação.

QUICK EATS

Sorvetes Mil Frutas (☎ 2623 6436; Orla Bardot 362) Offers dozens of ice cream flavors right on the waterfront.

BUDGET

Botequim do Baiano (☎ 9214 0317; Rua Luis Joaquim Pereira 265; meals R$10; ⏰ 10am-11pm) You'll understand why locals love this place once you've eaten one of Botequim's homemade *pratos feitos* (fish or meat with rice, beans and salad). Prices are geared for residents rather than tourists.

Chez Michou Crêperie (☎ 2623 2169; Rua das Pedras 90; crepes from R$10; ⏰ 5:30pm-late Mon-Wed, noon-late Thu-Sun) A popular hangout thanks to the incredible sweet and savory crepes. Of course, the outdoor bar serving delicious *pinha coladas* (piña coladas) might also be bringing in the crowds.

Restaurante da Carla (☎ 2623 0302; Rua Turíbio de Farias 152; per kg R$24.90; ⏰ noon-midnight) Not as chichi as Búzios's other per kilo places, Carla's focuses on traditional specialties at a reasonable price. Freshly grilled fish is available for the asking at the back counter, for the same per kilo price.

MIDRANGE

Bananaland (☎ 2623 2666; Rua Turíbio de Farias 50; per kg R$36.50; ☯ 11:30am-late) Touted as the largest self-serve around, this place will have something for everyone. The range of choices is simply astounding.

Boom (☎ 2623 6254; Rua Turíbio de Farias 110; per kg R$39.90; ☯ noon-10pm, to midnight in summer) Another excellent and varied buffet.

Botequim da Corrente (Praça dos Ossos; meals from R$14; ☯ 11am-6pm, to midnight in summer) Opposite the main square of Ossos, this friendly corner place with outdoor seating under the delicate shade of a *framboia* tree serves extremely tasty fish, rice, beans and juices.

Bistrô da Baiana (☎ 2623 7480; Rua Manoel de Carvalho 11; meals R$15; ☯ 1:30pm-late Thu-Tue) With delicious Bahian fish specialties served at small tables on the cobblestones, this place is great for a low-key dinner, or a beer and a snack (try the wonderfully fresh *acarajé* – Bahian style fitters).

TOP END

Cigalon (☎ 2623 1249; Rua das Pedras 199; meals R$30; ☯ 7pm-midnight) This fabulous French restaurant is right on the waterfront along Rua das Pedras. Candlelight dancing off the water and crisp white tablecloths prepare you for the elegance of the food to come.

Sushi Jardin (☎ 2623 6898; Praça dos Ossos 135S; mains from R$35; ☯ 6pm-midnight Tue-Sun) Set in a cozy candlelit sculpture garden, this new addition to the Búzios dining scene has tempting seafood concoctions such as *sequencia de camarões* (series of different shrimp dishes) to go along with the more traditional Japanese fare.

Restaurante David (☎ 2623 2981; Rua Turíbio de Farias 260; meals R$40; ☯ noon-11:30pm) Still going strong after 35 years, David's serves high quality seafood at little wooden tables with checkered tablecloths. You can even choose your own lobster from the tank.

Sawasdee (☎ 2623 4644; Orla Bardot 422; mains from R$40; ☯ 6pm-2am Thu-Tue) Expensive but excellent, Sawasdee specializes in Thai cuisine showcasing the area's fresh seafood. The *kaipilychia* (litchi *caipirinhas*) are quite tasty.

Entertainment

Action on the Rua das Pedras really gets going after midnight.

Patio Havana (☎ 2623 2169; Rua das Pedras 101; ☯ 6pm-late Wed-Sun) is worth checking out if you're a fan of jazz, samba or bossa nova. Fabulous musicians from all over Brazil (and the world) regularly pop in here.

Privilège (☎ 2623 0150; Orla Bardot 510; ☯ 11pm-late Thu-Sat) For house music among the A-list crowd, head to this sleek nightclub with two dance floors and four bars.

Devassa (☎ 2623 2169; Orla Bardot 550; ☯ 5pm-late Wed-Sat) A new *cervejaria* (brewery) right along the waterfront, Devassa dares you to enjoy its beer to the fullest, with all-you-can-drink Thursdays (R$29 men, R$24 women) and two-for-the-price-of-one deals daily till 8pm. Live music on weekends.

Gran Cine Bardot (☎ 2623 1466; Travessa dos Pescadores 88; R$16) Shows movies on weekend nights, including some in English with Portuguese subtitles.

Getting There & Around

Viação 1001 runs buses between Rio and Búzios seven times daily (R$22.90, three hours), eastbound from 6:30am to 7:30pm, westbound from 7am to 7pm. The Búzios **bus station** (☎ 2623 2050; Estrada da Usina Velha 444) is a simple bus stop with no building attached, five blocks south of the Armação waterfront and easily reachable on foot.

Municipal buses between Búzios and Cabo Frio (R$2.70, one hour, 20km) make regular stops along Avenida Ribeiro Dantas and Estrada da Usina, including one directly opposite the Rio-bound bus stop.

Espírito Santo

One of the best reasons to come to Espírito Santo is that so few other tourists will be joining you. Often completely ignored by foreigners due to its lack of high-profile attractions, the state nonetheless has several hidden treasures. It's an enjoyable place to mingle with Brazilians without the hype and higher prices of neighboring Rio and Bahia states.

In the north of the state is the idyllic little hideaway of Itaúnas, a tiny beach town literally buried in the sand dunes. Its attractions include the tranquil beauty of its natural setting and the frenzied nightlife that unfolds every summer when it converts itself overnight into the *forró* capital of Brazil.

South along the coast, the beaches are more developed for family-style tourism, making them very popular with visitors from the neighboring state of Minas Gerais. Here you'll find low-key beach resorts interspersed with fishing villages, plenty of good restaurants and the happy summertime buzz of Brazilian social life.

Inland, Espírito Santo's mountains form an exquisite patchwork of jungled greenery and domed rocky outcroppings, the most dramatic of which is Pedra Azul, a bare mountain crag preserved in a state park less than 100km west of Vitória.

Even without all these scenic attractions, it would be worth visiting Espírito Santo just to eat. Seafood here is fresh and abundant, and local specialties such as *moqueca* and *torta capixaba* are famous throughout Brazil.

HIGHLIGHTS

- See the sun rise over the dunes after dancing all night to *forró* (popular music of the Northeast) in **Itaúnas** (p226)
- Enjoy **moqueca capixaba** (p228), Espírito Santo's tantalizingly tasty seafood stew, up and down the coast from Vitória to Ubu
- Hold on to that rope as you scale the steep granite face of **Pedra Azul** (p230)
- Watch a baby turtle make its way to the sea in **Parque Estadual de Itaúnas** (p225).
- Eat strudel and sip hot chocolate by the fire in the German-style mountain town of **Domingos Martins** (p230)

Parque Estadual de Itaúnas

Itaúnas ★

Domingos Martins ★

★ Vitória

Pedra Azul ★

Ubu ★

- POPULATION: 3.1 MILLION
- AREA: 46,184 SQ KM

History

Colonized in the 16th century, Espírito Santo became an armed region to prevent gold from being smuggled out of Minas Gerais state. Coffee plantations, the prime source of income up until the 1960s, have since been superseded by mining and shipping. The capital city, Vitória, serves as headquarters to Garoto, Brazil's famous (and delicious) chocolate, as well as several chemical and agribusiness concerns.

Climate

Not quite as searingly hot as equatorial Bahia, Espírito Santo can nonetheless get quite uncomfortable in the summer months, especially along the damp, low-lying seaboard. In the mountainous interior, daytime temperatures are pleasantly warm year-round, but can drop surprisingly close to 0°C (32°F) on winter nights. Rains are common, especially in the north, but rarely last long.

State Parks

Espírito Santo has several lovely state parks. Up near the border with Bahia, the vast dune- and lagoonscape of Parque Estadual de Itaúnas includes many kilometers of undeveloped beaches where sea turtles come ashore to lay their eggs. In the western mountains near Minas Gerais, the dramatic soaring granite outcrop of Pedra Azul forms the centerpiece of Parque Estadual da Pedra Azul. South of Vitória, the coastal lagoons and *restinga* (zone of low trees and shrubs that thrive in sandy, nutrient-poor soil) of Parque Estadual Paulo César Vinha demonstrate the potential for habitat preservation even at the edge of a major urban area.

Getting There & Around

Vitória is the biggest city in Espírito Santo and as such boasts a domestic and international airport. Air service is offered to all major cities throughout Brazil and the rest of South America. A well-run bus service connects Vitória to Rio, São Paulo and other neighboring cities throughout Minas Gerais, as well as Bahia to the north. Regular buses also run up and down Espírito Santo's coastline.

VITÓRIA

☎ 0xx27 / pop 271,000

Vitória doesn't have much to show from its colonial past and is often dismissed as being

aesthetically unappealing (despite having a lush backdrop of mountains rushing down to meet sandy beaches that's vaguely reminiscent of Rio). Export coffee and timber pass through Vitória's harbor, and the port at nearby Tubarão is the outlet for millions of tons of iron ore. But that doesn't mean Vitória is devoid of all charm. Local residents, known as Capixabas, are warm and friendly, and the city has a flourishing economy, which translates into many bars, universities, nightclubs, restaurants and hotels.

Orientation

The remnants of old Vitória, built on an island just off the coast, are connected to the mainland via a series of bridges. The city's best beaches are Canto and Camburí to the north, and the renowned Praia da Costa to the south in Vila Velha. The teeming, modern **bus station** (☎ 3222 3366; Ilha do Principe) is located in the center of the old town (don't let the name fool you – it's not a separate island). Trains coming from Belo Horizonte (see p240) arrive at **Estação**

Ferroviária Pedro Nolasco (☎ 3226 4169), 1km west of the bus station in the mainland district of Cariacaca.

Information

ATMs for several banks are clustered together inside the bus station.

Bradesco (Av Jerônimo Monteiro 400) In the city center.

Main post office (Av Jerônimo Monteiro 310)

Net.Point Lan House (☎ 3222 2933; Av República; per hr R$2.50; ◷ 9am-9pm) Offers internet and Skype access directly across from Parque Moscoso.

Tourist booths bus station (◷ 8am-8pm Mon-Sat); airport (☎ 3327 2031; ◷ 6am-midnight daily) There's a branch located opposite track 10 at the bus station and one in the airport arrivals area.

Sights

CITY CENTER

The yellow **Anchieta Palace** (Praça João Climaco) is a 16th-century former Jesuit college and church. It's now the seat of state government, and the only part you can enter is the **tomb of Padre José de Anchieta** (admission free), 1534–97, the cofounder of São Paulo and an early missionary who was hailed as the 'Apostle of Brazil.'

Close by is the **Catedral Metropolitana**, with its neo-Gothic exterior and interesting stained-glass windows.

Teatro Carlos Gomes (Praça Costa Pereira) is a replica of La Scala in Milan. It stages national-caliber theatre and dance productions at very reasonable prices. Check with the tourist office to see what's currently playing.

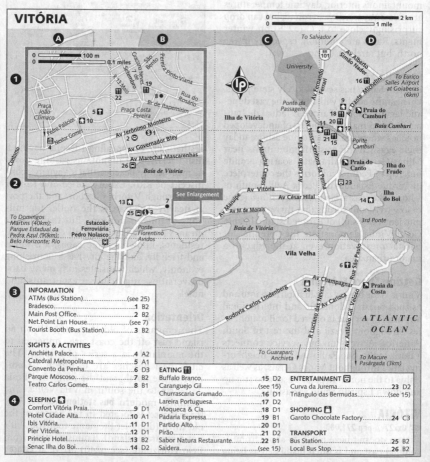

VITÓRIA

Capixabas like to walk and relax in the leafy **Parque Moscoso** (Av Cleto Nunes), just west of the city center.

VILA VELHA

Across the river and south of Vitória sits Vila Velha, the first place in Espírito Santo to be colonized. Don't miss seeing the **Convento da Penha**, atop the densely forested 154m Morro da Penha. The panoramic city views are magnificent and the chapel (founded in 1558) isn't too bad either. It's a major pilgrimage destination – around Easter expect massive crowds all paying homage to NS da Penha, some climbing the hill on their knees.

BEACHES

Praia do Camburí, a 5km stretch of beach, is punctuated by kiosks, restaurants, nightspots and midrange hotels. Don't swim near the bridge – it's polluted there.

Praia da Costa in Vila Velha is the city's nicest beach. It has fewer hotels and restaurants than Camburí, but you can swim and bodysurf. Keep a close eye on the horizon – huge supertankers often pop up with surprising speed!

Sleeping

BUDGET

Hotel Cidade Alta (☎ 3223 0653; Rua Dionizio Rosendo 213; s/d/tr R$20/30/40) A decent hotel with affordable beds, the Cidade Alta is directly across from the cathedral in the so-called 'historic district.'

Principe Hotel (☎ 3322 2799; hotelp@terra.com.br; Av Dario L Souza 120; s/d/tr/q R$36/56/84/105) Ugly as sin but extremely convenient, the Principe is a clean, well-run budget hotel just steps from the bus station.

MIDRANGE & TOP END

our pick **Ibis Vitória** (☎ 2104 4850; www.accorhotels .com.br; Rua João da Cruz 385, Praia do Canto; s/d R$99/119) One of the best values in town, this chain hotel sits right at the edge of the Triângulo das Bermudas, Vitória's nightlife hub, and is only a few blocks from Praia do Canto.

Pier Vitória (☎ 3434 0000; www.piervitoriahotel .com.br; Av Dante Michelini 321; s/d R$179/199) Geared toward business travelers, the Pier Vitória is conveniently located on Camburí beach, only 10 minutes from the airport.

Mercure Pasárgada (☎ 3399 6500; www.accorhotels .com.br; Av Antônio Gil Veloso 1856; s/d R$190/218) Right on the Praia da Costa waterfront in Vila Velha, this hotel feels like a splurge despite

its moderate price tag. It's got spacious, airy rooms and is supremely comfortable.

Comfort Vitória Praia (☎ 3041 9500; www.atlantica hotels.com.br; Av Dante Michelini 1057; s/d R$210/230) Also on Camburí beach, this place is as comfortable as the name implies, despite its bland exterior.

Senac Ilha do Boi (☎ 3345 0111; www.hotelilhadoboi .com.br; Rua Braúlio Macedo 417; s/d standard R$265/300, luxury R$290/330; ❄ 🖳 🖨) For a real night of luxury, this is an excellent choice. It's located on top of a hill with fabulous views of the surrounding bay. The service is impeccable and the amenities delightful, especially the saunas.

Eating

Make sure you try the regional specialty known as *moqueca capixaba*, a savory mixture of local seafood stewed in an earthenware casserole dish.

BUDGET & MIDRANGE

Sabor Natura Restaurante (Rua 13 de Maio 85; per kg R$12.90; ⏰ 11am-3pm Mon-Thu, to 2:30pm Fri) A veggiefriendly self-serve place downtown that's very popular with students.

Padaria Expressa (☎ 3223 1091; Rua Graciano Neves 22; per kg R$12.95; ⏰ 11am-7pm) Just off Praça Costa Pereira, this is an excellent place to stock up on bread, cheese and snacks.

Saidera (☎ 3235 2687; Rua João da Cruz 241, Praia do Canto; drinks & snacks from R$13; ⏰ 6pm-midnight Mon-Tue, 6pm-2am Wed-Fri, noon-2am Sat & Sun) The outdoor terrace here is packed every night with revelers enjoying the cornucopia of drinks and snacks.

Caranguejo Gil (Rua João da Cruz 80; meals R$20; ⏰ 11-1am) As the name implies, you'll find plenty of *caranguejo* (crab) along with other local seafood at this restaurant opposite Buffalo Branco in the festive Triângulo area.

Partido Alto (☎ 3227 4086; Av Dante Michelini 797, Praia do Camburí; meals from R$20; ⏰ 11am-midnight) Another highly recommended seafood place on Camburí beach.

Churrascaria Gramado (☎ 3225 1311; Av Rosendo Serapião Souza 43; meals from R$22; ⏰ 11am-3pm & 6:30-10:30pm Mon-Sat, 11am-4pm Sun) Meat lovers with big appetites will love this place, the best *churrascaria* (restaurant featuring barbecued meat) in the city.

Moqueca & Cia (☎ 3227 6899; Av Dante Michelini 977, Praia do Camburí; meals R$24; ⏰ noon-midnight) Another great place for traditional *capixaba* seafood dishes.

Buffalo Branco (☎ 3227 2933; Rua Joaquim Lírio 723; meals from R$25; ☺ 5pm-midnight Sun-Tue, to 1am Wed-Thu, to 3am Fri & Sat) This is one of the hottest eateries in town. It serves varied meat and seafood dishes, including the house special, Espeto Buffalo Branco (1kg of tri-tip beef with rice, beans, fried potatoes and garlic bread).

TOP END

Lareira Portuguesa (☎ 3345 0331; Av Saturnino de Brito 260, Praia do Canto; mains from R$25; ☺ 11:30am-3pm & 6:30-11pm Mon-Sat, 11:30am-4pm Sun) A gorgeous garden and beautiful Portuguese tiles make this a very sexy and sophisticated location. Delicious fish dishes form the backbone of the menu, but there are also risottos and inventive desserts. A particular standout main is the *bacalhau à lareira* (cod deep fried with a crushed-almond coating).

our pick **Pirão** (☎ 3227 1165; Rua Joaquim Lírio 753, Praia do Canto; meals from R$30; ☺ 11am-3pm & 6:30-11pm Tue-Fri, 11am-5pm Sat-Mon) With award-winning *moquecas* and *tortas capixabas*, Pirão has earned a reputation as one of the city's best restaurants over the past 25 years. On Friday it serves a delicious regional specialty – grouper prepared with *banana da terra* (plantain).

Entertainment

Capixabas like the nightlife – check out the Triângulo das Bermudas, a neighborhood packed with bars, eateries and nightclubs centered on the intersection of Ruas Joaquim Lírio and João da Cruz. Hip crowds also gather at Curva da Jurema, populated by shacks that serve snacks and food into the wee hours.

Shopping

Garoto chocolate factory store (☎ 3320 1522; Praça Meyerfreund 1) Visit the factory store, where the best chocolate in Brazil is really fresh. It's off Rodovia Carlos Lindenberg in Vila Velha – take bus 500 from the city center.

Getting There & Away

Buses leave Vitória for Belo Horizonte (R$60, eight hours, seven daily), Ouro Prêto (R$51, eight hours, direct bus at 9pm), Porto Seguro (R$65, 10, twice daily at 2pm and 9pm) and Rio (R$56, eight hours, seven daily from 10am to 10:50pm).

There's also one daily train from Vitória to Belo Horizonte (see p240) in Minas Gerais state.

Flights leave regularly for Belém, Belo Horizonte, Brasília, Porto Alegre, Recife, Rio, Salvador and São Paulo.

Getting Around

Eurico Salles airport (☎ 3235 6300) is 10km northeast of the city center, in Goiabeiras. Take local bus 212 marked 'aeroporto/rodoviária' to and from the center (R$1.70). Taxis from the airport into town cost about R$20.

Local buses (R$1.70) run from the various stops outside the bus station; the route is written on the side of each bus. For the center, catch any bus that goes along Av Vitória and get off after you pass the yellow Anchieta Palace on your left. For Praia do Camburí, catch any bus that goes along Av Dante Michelini. For Praia do Canto and Triângulo das Bermudas, take any bus that goes along Av Saturnino de Brito. To Vila Velha and Praia da Costa catch the all-yellow Transcol bus 500 or any bus marked Praia da Costa.

THE COAST

ITAÚNAS

☎ 0xx27 / pop 2500

Surrounded by a majestic state reserve and encroaching sand dunes, Itaúnas masquerades as a sleepy fishing village eight months a year. However, from early December through early March, and again in July, it's a party-mad town filled with young students who come for the lively *forró* dance parties as much as for the beautiful surroundings.

Itaúnas is one of those rare places that manages to retain a delightful 'end of the road' feel despite the intermittent barrage of tourists. In recent years, the number of pousadas (guesthouses) has increased from just a handful to well over 50, yet locals and outsiders still seem to mix with ease. Many visitors fall under the town's easygoing spell and end up staying longer than they expected.

Sand dunes once engulfed the original village of Itaúnas, which was set about 1km closer to the ocean than it is now – nowadays the old church tower is buried in sand, indicated only by a small sign. From atop the dunes you have a great view of the Atlantic Ocean and the neighboring Parque Estadual de Itaúnas, with its gorgeous mangrove forest and wetlands.

Orientation & Information

Things are made somewhat confusing by the lack of posted street names in Itaúnas, but a pair of handy maps, on the main square and near the bridge to the dunes, can help you get oriented. Basically, it's a four-road town. Buses stop just a few yards from the village square, and most stores, restaurants and pousadas are concentrated nearby. The main road leading into town loops around the square and back out again. The other roads feed off the main square but don't go far. The beach is 1km from town, across the bridge over the Rio Itaúnas.

There are no banks in Itaúnas.

Positivo.com (☎ 3762 5036; Rua Maria Ortiz Barcelos; per hr R$3; ☷ 11am-midnight) provides internet access, but beware – the game-playing teenage boys can get pretty rowdy.

Sights & Activities

The 3674-hectare **Parque Estadual de Itaúnas** extends for 25km along the coast and has impressive 20m- to 30m-high sand dunes. The wilderness here is home to monkeys, sloths and *jaguatiricas* (wildcats). The park is also a base for the Tamar Project (see the boxed text, p467). From September to March you can accompany local biologists to the beach to observe sea turtles. November and December are the best months to see the females coming onshore to lay eggs, while January and February mark the peak of the hatching season.

The Itaúnas **park office** (☎ 3762 5196; pei@iema .es.gov.br) is in the village next to the bridge over the Rio Itaúnas. It has a souvenir shop, as well as informative displays about the local flora, fauna and culture. There's a trail map posted on the wall, but at the time of writing no such map was available for public distribution.

By far the most popular hike is the 1km **dunes trail** to the nearby beach. From town, simply cross the bridge over the Rio Itaúnas and follow the dirt road until the dunes slope down to meet it, then start climbing. At the crest of the first dune, you'll already have a panoramic view of the ocean, with several beachside *barracas* (stalls) visible straight ahead, and a sign indicating the ruins of the old *igreja* (church) off to the right.

More ambitious hikers can follow the beach 8km north to **Riacho Doce**, a small river that forms the border between Espírito Santo and Bahia. You'll know you've arrived when you see the handpainted sign on the other side '*Sorria – voce está na Bahia!*' (Smile, you're in

Bahia!) Riacho Doce has a restaurant serving simple but tasty meals. For the return trip, retrace your steps down the beach (best done at low tide), or hitch a ride in the back of one of the pickup trucks that occasionally drive the 16km road back to town. If school's in session, you can also try hopping one of the three daily school buses back to Itaúnas.

The **Casinha de Aventuras** (☎ 3762 5081; www .casinhadeaventuras.com.br; Rua Paulino Guanandy 13; ☷ 9am-noon year-round, plus 1:30-6:30pm high season), near the bus stop in the center of town, arranges kayaking trips along the Rio Itaúnas, horseback and dune-buggy excursions, bike rentals, and more.

Festivals & Events

In the second half of July, Itaúnas hosts two week-long *forró* festivals, the **Festival de Forró** and **Circuito Nacional de Forró**. Both events draw big-name performers from all over Brazil, and there's music and dancing all day and night.

Sleeping

Camping da Vila (☎ 3964 2462; Rua Honório Pinheiro da Silva s/n; camp site per person R$10) This place has dozens of grassy, shaded sites.

Pousada Vila Sossego (☎ 3762 5193; itaunasvila sossego@ig.com.br; Rua Paulino Souza Leite Guanandy; s/d R$30/60) In a breezy location on a side street, Vila Sossego has a couple of rooms (numbers 7 and 10) with great views of dunes and the river.

Pousada Ponta de Areia (☎ 3762 1644; Rua Manoel Joaquim Junior; s/d R$35/70) A delightfully simple and welcoming pousada, run by the gracious and well-traveled Bixão.

Pousada do Celsão (☎ 9951 9834; Riacho Doce; r from R$60) In the little settlement of Riacho Doce on the Bahian border, this is a simple place to get away from it all. Tucked between horse pastures and the beach, it also has an on-site restaurant. Just watch out for the intrepid pet parrot – he'll try to climb in the hammock with you!

Pousada das Araras (☎ 3762 5273; www.pousada dasararas.tur.br; Rua Manoel Joaquim Junior; s/d from R$60/80, with air-con R$100/120; ☒ ☖) This place straddles both sides of the street next door to Ponta de Areia. It's got a fabulous swimming pool, and a nice courtyard garden.

Pousada Zimbaue (☎ 3762 5023; www.guiaitaunas .com.br/zimbaue.htm; Rua Teófilo Cabral da Silva 6; s/d from R$70/90, with air-con R$90/120; ☒) This cheerful pousada just off the main square has clean white sheets and a kitchen for guests' use.

ESPÍRITO SANTO

Pousada A Nave (☎ 3762 5102; www.anave.tur.br; Rua Ítalo Vasconcelos; s/d/tr R$70/100/130) Rustic rooms with carved wooden doors abound at this attractive pousada, which is a labor of love for its sculptor/owner, Júlio. The round, open-sided thatched bar is a great place for a few late-night drinks. The attached camping ground, overlooking a mangrove forest and sand dunes, is also attractive.

Casa da Praia (☎ 3762 5028; www.casadapraia itaunas.com.br; Rua Prof Deolinda Lage; s/d R$80/120) This is one of Itaúnas' loveliest pousadas, on a back street with a deck overlooking the river. The likeable manager, Lico, takes pride in keeping the grounds and rooms spotless.

Pousada dos Corais (☎ 3762 5200; www.pousadados corais.com.br; Rua Maria Ortiz Barcelos 154; s/d/tr R$80/120/140; ⊠ ⚊) If you're suffering from the heat, try this friendly pousada with its air-con rooms, comfortable sitting areas and pool.

Eating
There are plenty of inexpensive eateries around Itaúnas. Especially appealing are the half dozen *barracas* out at the beach, serving seafood and beer with ocean views. Note that hours are seasonal and prone to change.

McDunas (☎ 3762 5248; Av Bento Daher; snacks from R$3; ⊗ 11am-midnight) Until the corporate lawyers from McDonald's come knocking, McDunas will continue to display its subtle modification of the golden arches logo. A good place for a snack, serving tasty burgers, juices and other fast food in the heart of town.

Dona Tereza (☎ 3762 5031; Rua Demerval Leite da Silva; meals from R$9; ⊗ 11am-midnight, to 8pm low season) A highly recommended family-run restaurant with pretty etched wooden menus and a breezy outdoor patio. You can eat extremely well here for very little money. From the central square, go one block towards the river.

Dona Pedrolina (☎ 3762 5296; Rua Linoria Lisboa Vasconcelos; meals from R$9; ⊗ 11:30am-late, to 8pm low season) Another excellent family-run place just around the corner from Dona Tereza's. Simple meals of fish, rice and beans are very affordable.

Pizzaria Oasis (☎ 3762 5111; Rua José Basilio dos Santos; meals from R$9; ⊗ 6pm-late daily high season, Sat only low season) A friendly place just across from the main square, with wood-fired pizza, lasagne, and other Italian specialties.

Barraca do Coco (☎ 3762 50424; Praia de Itaúnas; meals from R$15; ⊗ noon-late) Out at the beach, Coco's got seafood, beer and *forró* music from 2pm onwards during the busy season.

Entertainment
During high season the pounding beats of *forró* and *axé* (an Afro-Brazilian pop style incorporating samba, rock, soul and other influences) spill from every open window and doorway in Itaúnas. Things don't really start swinging till after midnight, and the party lasts till dawn. Ask locals to point you toward Buraco do Tatu, Bar Forró and Forró do Coco, festive little shacks that get packed full of dancers. Casa da Praia (see left) also opens up its whole veranda for dancing and gives strong encouragement to beginners.

Getting There & Away
Itaúnas is not exactly a major transport hub. The closest place you can make connections for long-distance buses is in Conceição da Barra, 23km south. From Itaúnas a local bus goes to Conceição (R$4.70, 40 minutes) at 8am, 1:30pm and 4:30pm daily, returning to Itaúnas at 7am, 12:30pm and 3:30pm. There are extra buses in summer, and on Monday and Friday throughout the year.

From Conceição da Barra to Vitória (R$34, five hours), Aguia Branca runs buses at 6:20am, 2pm and 6pm, returning from Vitória to Conceição at 6:40am, 11:40am and 4pm.

GUARAPARI
☎ 0xx27 / pop 80,000
There are some lovely beaches just waiting to be enjoyed about an hour south of Vitória. This stretch of coast is usually passed over by foreigners, but Guarapari is a favored resort destination for Brazilians and as such retains a relaxed, fun and family-friendly atmosphere. There are 23 beaches in the municipality, each with a lovely mountain backdrop.

Orientation & Information
The center is 500m south of the bus station, across the bridge; the beach is 200m further on. The **tourist office** (☎ 3262 8759; Rua Paulo Soares de Aguiar) has maps and information in Portuguese. There are several banks with ATMs along Rua Joaquim da Silva Lima in the center. Internet places are clustered in the center and along Praia do Morro.

Sights
The best beach is **Praia do Morro**, north of the city (be aware that its so-called 'healing' black monazitic sand is, in fact, said to be radioactive!). Also consider **Praia dos Namo-**

rados (small but surrounded by rocks creating beautiful pools), **Praias Castanheiras** and **Areia Preta** (more radioactive sand but crystal-clear waters), **Praia do Meio**, aka Siribeira (great rock pools with gorgeous snorkeling), **Praia Enseada Azul** (a long stretch with lots of natural beauty) and **Praia dos Padres** (accessible only by trail from Enseada Azul with stunning green waters). At the far southern end of town is **Meaípe**, another good place to spend the night.

Sleeping

Camping Club do Brasil (☎ 3262 1325; Praia de Setiba; per person/tent R$22/5) This camping spot a few kilometers north of town is just a stone's throw from lovely Setiba beach.

Hotel Guara Pousada (☎ 3262 5210; guarapousada@ guaratur.com.br; Av Antonio Guimarães, Quadra 40; s/d R$28/56) This former hostel has basic rooms, with bathrooms, on large, walled grounds not far from the bus station and the beach. This area is known as Muquiçaba (Mosquito Nest), so bring repellent!

Pousada Enseada Verde (☎ 3272 1376; www.enseada verde.com.br; Rua Duarte Mattos 27; s/d R$90/100) A great option down the coast in Meaípe, Pousada Enseada Verde has vibrantly colored rooms not far from the beach.

Hotel Coronado (☎ 3361 0144; www.hotelcoronado .com.br; Av Desembargador Lourival de Almeida 312; s/d from R$100/120, ocean view r R$165; 🅇 🅡) Directly opposite the point where Praias Castanheiras and Areia Preta meet, this centrally located older hotel has sweeping views of both beaches and the city.

Porto do Sol Guarapari (☎ 3361 1100; www.hotelporto dosol.com.br; Av Beira Mar 1; s/d from R$195/240; 🅇 🅠 🅡) Porto do Sol, surrounded by water on three sides, has an unbeatable location between downtown and Praia do Morro. All rooms have panoramic ocean views, with wifi, DVD and whirlpool tubs in the deluxe suites. Sea turtles sometimes come up onto the rocks directly below the rooms.

Eating

Up and down all the beaches, but particularly on Praia do Morro, you'll find dozens of *barracas* selling inexpensive fresh seafood and regional dishes.

Delícia Mineira (☎ 3361 0506; Rua Joaquim da Silva Lima 393; per kg R$14.90; 🕙 11am-2:30pm) This downtown self-serve is heavy on the *comida mineira* (the cuisine of Minas Gerais).

Pilão (☎ 3361 6035; Av Maria de Lourdes C Dantas 141; per kg R$15.90; 🕙 11am-late) Two blocks back from Praia do Morro, this self-serve has excellent food at bargain prices. Wood-fired *mineiro* dishes share the menu with seafood specialties such as *moqueca* and codfish lasagne.

Peixada do Irmão (☎ 3261 0636; Rua Jacinto de Almeida 72; meals R$15; 🕙 11:30am-midnight) Near the tourist office, this restaurant has a bilingual menu and an excellent reputation for seafood dishes.

our pick **Cantinho do Curuca** (☎ 3272 1262; Av Santana 96; meals from R$19; 🕙 11am-10pm) Few restaurants can boast such a perfect combination of setting, quality and price. The *moqueca* at this beachfront eatery in Meaípe has been voted the best in Brazil multiple times. Grab a table facing the water and enjoy.

Getting There & Away

Buses run between Vitória and Guarapari's **bus station** (☎ 3261 1308; Rua Araxa 50) hourly from 6am to 9pm (R$7, 1¼ hours). Half-hourly buses also make the 28km trip to Anchieta (R$4, 40 minutes).

AROUND GUARAPARI
Parque Estadual Paulo César Vinha

Ten kilometers north of Guarapari lies this **state park** (☎ 3242 3665; Hwy ES-060, km37.5; 🕙 8am-5pm Tue-Sun), part of Brazil's Atlantic Rain Forest Biosphere Reserve. The park's 1500 hectares shelter a variety of habitats, including dunes, lagoons and coastal *restinga*. The park's lone trail leads 2.5km from park headquarters to **Lagoa de Caraís**, a tranquil lagoon teeming with bird life just inland from the beach. Alvorada buses run frequently from Guarapari to the park (R$1.60, 20 minutes).

ANCHIETA
☎ 0xx28 / pop 19,000

About an hour south of Vitória, Anchieta is one of the oldest settlements in Espírito Santo and, as the name would suggest, contains many relics dedicated to the work of famed 16th-century Jesuit priest José de Anchieta. The beaches aren't as attractive as those leading up to Guarapari (20km to the north) or to neighboring Iriri and Ubu (to the south and north respectively), but this small port town does have its own relaxed appeal – the quiet, rhythmic life of a fishing village is still very much apparent, especially at Praia dos Castelhanos just north of town.

ESPÍRITO SANTO

BRAZIL'S BEST MOQUECA

The state of Espírito Santo is renowned throughout Brazil for the quality of its seafood. Topping the list of local culinary specialties is *moqueca capixaba*, a savory stew made from fish, shellfish, tomatoes, peppers and cilantro cooked in a *panela de barro* (earthenware casserole dish). Espírito Santo's *moqueca capixaba* is similar to the *moqueca baiana* so popular in neighboring Bahia, except that it's made without coconut milk.

Wherever you travel in the state, you'll see signs advertising *a melhor moqueca do Brasil* (Brazil's best *moqueca*). But who really makes the best *moqueca*? Visitors to the Vitória region have a golden opportunity to taste-test for themselves. Several award-winning restaurants can be found in a relatively small geographic area here. Three leading contenders are Pirão (p224) in Vitória, which won *Veja* magazine's 2007 'Best Moqueca in Espírito Santo' prize; Cantinho do Curuca (p227) in Meaipe, which has taken four Rodas' 'Best Moqueca in Brazil' honors four years in a row; and Moqueca do Garcia (opposite) in Ubu, which hasn't won any awards lately, but whose 40 years in business and constant lunchtime crowds speak for themselves.

Sights

You'll have no problem locating the **Santuário Nacional Padre Anchieta** (☺ 9am-noon & 2-5pm Mon-Fri, 9am-5pm Sat & Sun), which dominates the town from its impressive hillside location. A 250-year-old chestnut tree spreads gracefully in front of this striking white church with its bold blue shutters and doors. The complex includes the **Museu Padre Anchieta** (admission R$1), highlighting the evangelical work of the Jesuit priest José de Anchieta among indigenous peoples. The church walls, built by local Indians and Padre Anchieta, are original. The museum contains relics uncovered during restoration. If you'd rather get your history at the seashore, then stroll to the end of Anchieta beach. Just before the road goes over a small, white, wooden bridge you'll find a gold-colored **statue** of José de Anchieta giving blessings to a Goitacá warrior (see opposite).

Festivals & Events

Devoted followers of Padre Anchieta participate in an annual pilgrimage commemorating his missionary work along the Espírito Santo coast. The popular 100km **Steps of Anchieta** walk along the beach from Vitória to Anchieta takes place in June (exact dates vary each year) and lasts four days. Contact the state tourism office in Vitória for specifics.

Sleeping & Eating

Anchieta doesn't provide many tourist services and several downtown hotels have closed in recent years, so you're better off staying in nearby Iriri or Ubu, or on the coast just north of town.

Pousada Beira Mar (☎ 3536 1256; Rua Marechal Deodoro da Fonseca 86; s/d R$30/60) If you decide to spend the night in Anchieta, this is your best bet, 100m north of the bus stop. Very basic but reasonable rooms.

Pousada do Sol (☎ 3536 1643; www.pousadadosol .com; Av Beira Mar, Guanabara; s/d R$60/100; ☒) A much more inviting choice 4km north of Anchieta, this pousada sits a few steps from Guanabara Beach, directly across from the Tamar Project turtle research station (below). Bright artsy rooms, some with terraces overlooking the sea, surround a central pool.

Anchieta has several *lanchonetes* (snack bars) near the bus stop.

Getting There & Away

Buses (R$4, 40 minutes) to Guarapari run every half-hour or so between 5:15am and 9:30pm. To Vitória (R$10) they run 12 times daily (every one to two hours between 6am and 8:40pm). The **bus station** (☎ 3536 1150; Av Carlos Lindenberg 183) is opposite the waterfront on the main road through town.

AROUND ANCHIETA
Praia da Guanabara Turtle Research Station

Four kilometers north of Anchieta, the Tamar Project (see The Sea Turtles of Tamar boxed text on p467) operates the **Praia da Guanabara Turtle Research Station** (☎ 3536 3547; ☺ 10am-7pm daily Dec-Feb, 9am-noon & 1-6pm Mon-Fri Mar-Nov). At the station site, there is a 2km stretch of protected beach where turtles come onshore to lay their eggs every summer, plus an interesting museum of marine turtle exhibits. Between December and

February, you can arrange to accompany researchers on their regular excursions to observe turtles on the beach. To get here, take any northbound Planeta or Sudeste bus from Anchieta. Ask to be let off at Praia da Guanabara and follow the signs 300m downhill to the beach.

Iriri
☎ 0xx28

This delightful coastal getaway is one of Brazil's best-kept secrets. The town's pretty beach is tucked into a sheltered cove flanked by rocky ledges on either side. Iriri is very popular with Mineiros, who come in droves during the summer months and turn the tiny town into an upbeat, family-focused resort.

SLEEPING & EATING
Hotel Maringá (☎ 3534 1252; www.hotelmaringairiri .com; Av Dom Helvecio 665; s/d R$50/90; 🏊) Bland but friendly, the centrally located Maringá, one block back from the beach, is one of Iriri's more affordable choices. There's a self-serve restaurant attached.

Recanto da Pedra (☎ 3534 1599; www.recantodapedra .com.br; Av Beira Mar s/n; s/d R$85/110) Hands down the best value in town, Recanto da Pedra is picturesquely sited on rocks at the northern end of Iriri beach. Many rooms have terraces with bird's-eye views of the gracefully curving shoreline. The attached restaurant serves excellent food – it's fun to lounge here and watch swimmers popping up out of the water for a quick drink at the bar.

Hotel Pontal das Rochas (☎ 3534 1369; www .pontaldasrochas.com.br; Av Beira Mar s/n; r from R$211; 🏊 🖥 🍴) On the same point as Recanto da

Pedra, this first-rate hotel offers fabulous amenities, including a panoramic restaurant, and a sauna and pool built into the rocks overlooking the water.

Restaurante do Português (☎ 3534 1222; Av Dom Helvecio 558; meals from R$11; 🕑 lunch & dinner) Generous portions of tasty local seafood are served at this unpretentious eatery decorated with pretty blue-and-white tiles half a block from the beach.

Ubu
☎ 0xx28

A sleepy little seaside town 9km north of Anchieta, Ubu has a picturesque waterfront with a cliff at one end and a pretty mermaid statue marking the beach's midpoint. The usual Brazilian hospitality is muted somewhat here by the locals' desire to keep their low-key haven from being overrun by developers (something that can happen all too quickly in Brazil), but as long as you don't talk about buying up huge tracts of land and building superhotels, you will eventually be embraced with customary warmth.

SLEEPING & EATING
Pousada de Ubu (☎ 3536 5112; Praia de Ubu; r from R$80) This simple pousada is conveniently located just above the mermaid statue in the heart of town.

Pousada Aba Ubu (☎ 3536 5067; www.abaubu.com .br; Rua Manoel Miranda Garcia; d/tr R$110/130; 🏊 🍴) Just uphill from the beach, the Swiss-run Aba Ubu has a pool, a sauna, a tennis court and nice rooms around a garden.

Moqueca do Garcia (☎ 3536 5050; Av Magno Ribeiro Muqui 17; meals from R$30) Down by the waterfront,

ESPÍRITO SANTO

THE GOITACÁ WARRIORS

Early European explorers reported encounters with the fearsome, long-haired, tall, robust and formidable Goitacá warriors, coastal dwellers of the Rio state–Espírito Santo border region. The tribe had long resisted invasions by rival Tupi nations and, despite the technological advantage of guns, the Europeans found the Goitacá almost impossible to capture. The Goitacá were excellent runners and swimmers, and seemed by all reports to be equally at home on land and in the water. When chased, they were so fast through the waters and jungle that nobody could catch them on foot, on horseback or by boat.

According to legend, a Goitacá could run after a wild deer and capture it with his arms, and could catch a shark using only a piece of wood. (This was accomplished by forcing a stick inside the shark's mouth to stop the jaws from closing, and pulling its guts out by hand until it died.) The Goitacá nation (around 12,000 people), never defeated in battle, was exterminated at the end of the 18th century by an epidemic of smallpox – a disease deliberately introduced by the Portuguese for that very purpose.

the 40-year-old Moqueca do Garcia lives up to its proud reputation as Ubu's best place for top-notch Capixaba cuisine. Don't miss it!

INLAND

DOMINGOS MARTINS

☎ 0xx27 / pop 26,000 / elevation 620m

Tucked into the highlands of the Serra Capixaba, this pretty little German-style town has bracingly cold nights and gorgeous panoramic views of surrounding forests. Also referred to as Campinho by locals, it makes a good base for exploring the nearby streams and mountains.

Sights

Tourist information is available at **Casa da Cultura** (☎ 3268 2550; Av Presidente Vargas 531; admission free; ☯ 9am-noon & 1-5pm Tue-Sun), opposite the first bus stop in town. The museum upstairs features photos, documents and household objects dating from 1847, when Pomeranians first settled this colony. Check out the old pink gramophone.

Further along the same road you'll find the town's main square, a pretty gathering spot with benches, trees and an old Lutheran church. Flora lovers should definitely head out to the **Reserva Kautsky** (☎ 3268 2300; ☯ by arrangement), run by dedicated botanist Roberto Kautsky, who has cultivated more than 100 species of orchid at his home at the southern end of town (ask anyone) and on his mountainside reserve. He'll drive you, free for the asking, to the reserve in his ancient Jeep and talk your ear off in German, 'bad English' or Portuguese – people come from miles around and it's a great experience.

In the second half of July, the **Festival Internacional de Inverno** is an annual gathering of Brazilian and international musicians who offer daily classes and nightly concerts on Domingos Martins' main square.

Sleeping & Eating

Hotel e Restaurante Imperador (☎ 3268 1115; www .hotelimperador.tur.br; Av Senador Jefferson de Aguiar 275; r with breakfast R$68, s/d with breakfast & lunch R$98/118; ☒) Directly opposite the Lutheran church on the main square, the Imperador is an older hotel with traditional German architecture, a pool and sauna, and plenty of quirky charm.

Pousada Germânia (☎ 3268 1131; lvc_30@hotmail .com; Rua de Lazer 204; r from R$70) This sweet little private home looks like it was lifted straight out of the Alps. You'll find it tucked just off the main pedestrian thoroughfare.

Café Expresso Koehler (☎ 3268 3263; Rua de Lazer 54; coffee & strudel R$6; ☯ 11am-10pm) Homemade strudel, cake, and hot chocolate with whipped cream are the specialties at this lively sidewalk café in the heart of the pedestrian zone.

Restaurante Caminho do Imigrante (Rua de Lazer 155; per kg R$15.90 ☯ 10:30am-4pm & 6pm-late Sat & Sun, 10:30am-2:30pm Mon-Fri) For a delicious and inexpensive per-kilo buffet, try this place a little further down the pedestrian mall.

Choperia Fritz Frida (☎ 3268 1808; Av Presidente Vargas; mains from R$15; ☯ 5-10pm) Very popular at dinnertime, this cute half-timbered building on the main square serves pizza, beer and old German favorites.

Getting There & Away

Ten buses daily Monday to Saturday and nine on Sunday make the 42km trip (R$7, one hour) from Vitória to Domingos Martins' **bus station** (☎ 3268 1243; Rua Bernardino Monteiro). Upon request, any bus between Vitória and Belo Horizonte will stop on the main highway just outside the town entrance gate.

AROUND DOMINGOS MARTINS
Parque Estadual da Pedra Azul

Vitória–Belo Horizonte buses also stop at the best reason to come inland: the 500m Pedra Azul, 50km west of Domingos Martins down Hwy BR-262. The dramatic rock, tinted by a bluish moss, forms the centerpiece of **the state park** (☎ 3248 1156; admission R$10; ☯ 8am-5:30pm). Rangers escort hikers to the rock's nine **natural pools**, a moderately difficult hike affording magnificent views of Pedra Azul and the surrounding forest and farmland. Bring a swimsuit and sturdy shoes – there's a short section where ropes are used to scale a steep rock face. The round trip takes 2½ hours and must be booked in advance; departures are scheduled at 9am and 1:30pm on weekends, or by arrangement during the week. Note that independent climbing and camping are no longer permitted in the park.

Cavalgada Ecológica Pedra Azul (☎ 3248 0054; trail rides from R$30) leads horseback excursions around the foot of Pedra Azul, on beautiful Fjorde horses from Norway.

SLEEPING & EATING

The area is dotted with fancier resort hotels, many offering full board.

Pousada Peterle (☎ 3248 1243; www.pousadapeterle .com.br; Hwy BR-262, km88; s/d with meals R$130/170) Two kilometers below the park entrance and opposite a bus stop, Pousada Peterle has attractive log cabins with fireplaces and balconies. The affordably priced snack bar and restaurant below are open to the public.

Pousada Pedra Azul (☎ 3334 2420; www.pousada pedraazul.com.br; Rota do Lagarto, km1.5; r with meals R$375; 🏊) Set in lovely gardens only 500m from park headquarters, this high-end pousada is one of the region's oldest. The main brick-and-wood building with Alpine-style balconies and pagoda-like roofs was designed by Brazilian architect Zanine. Amenities include a pool, sauna, tennis courts, lake and waterfall.

Guest rooms are spacious, with high ceilings, big tubs and armchairs.

Valsugana (☎ 3248 1126; off Hwy BR-262 at km89.5; mains R$20; 🕑 11:30am-3:30pm Sat & Sun, 7pm-late Fri & Sat) Hearty Italian fare and spectacular views of Pedra Azul make this one of the area's nicest restaurants. The inventive recipes feature fresh local produce, and the wine list is excellent.

GETTING THERE & AWAY

Aguia Branca buses pass within 2km of the park entrance. In Vitória, buy a ticket for Fazenda do Estado (R$14, two hours, eleven daily 5:10am to 6:30pm) and ask to be let off at km88. The km88 bus stop is directly opposite Peterle's pousada and restaurant. From here, it's a 2km uphill walk to the park entrance along a lovely winding cobblestone road, Rota do Lagarto.

ESPÍRITO SANTO

Minas Gerais

Geographically close to Rio and São Paulo, but with a culture entirely its own, Minas Gerais is easy to reach and hard to leave behind. The people are among Brazil's friendliest, the food is great, the natural setting is spectacular and there's more beautiful historical architecture per square kilometer than any other place in Brazil.

In the early 18th century, colonial towns like Ouro Prêto, Mariana and Diamantina sprang up along the gold road linking Minas to the coast. Built on Minas's mineral wealth, they soon developed a cultural and architectural wealth all their own. Minas was the birthplace of Tiradentes, leader of Brazil's first great independence movement, and Aleijadinho, the country's finest baroque artist.

Although Minas's natural wonders get less press than the Amazon or the Pantanal, the state is home to some magnificent scenery and wildlife. In 2005 the Serra do Espinhaço, a rocky spine running the length of the state, was recognized for its remarkable biodiversity as Brazil's newest Unesco Biosphere Reserve. Parks throughout Minas provide critical habitat for endangered species such as the northern muriqui.

Lacking beaches, Mineiros (residents of Minas) compensate with fabulous food and drink. Minas cheese and *cachaça* (a high-proof sugarcane alcohol) are considered the best in Brazil. Meals are often cooked on the *fogão à lenha* – a traditional wood-burning stove – and local hospitality is as abundant as the food.

Rich as it is in history, Minas is also a forward-looking state, as epitomized in its capital, Belo Horizonte. Built in the 1890s as Brazil's first planned city, Belo's ongoing openness to innovation is evidenced by Oscar Niemeyer's audacious 1940s building designs and today's burgeoning arts scene.

HIGHLIGHTS

- Wander the picturesque cobblestone streets and marvel at the baroque architectural wonders of **Ouro Prêto** (p242)
- Cruise from one colonial town to the next on Minas's historic **Maria-Fumaça** (p257) steam trains
- Climb Brazil's third-tallest mountain, 2892m Pico da Bandeira in **Parque Nacional de Caparaó** (p270)
- Wait by starlight for the maned wolves to appear at the old monastery at **Parque Natural do Caraça** (p269)
- Check out the nine galleries of contemporary international art and the fabulous gardens at **Centro de Arte Contemporânea Inhotim** (p240), near Brumadinho

Parque Natural do Caraça

Ouro Prêto ★
Brumadinho ★

Parque Nacional de Caparaó

★ São João del Rei

- POPULATION: 18 MILLION
- AREA: 588,384 SQ KM

History
In the late 1600s gold was discovered in Minas. It didn't take long for the word to get out, and Brazilians flocked to Minas, while Portuguese flocked to Brazil. Slaves were brought from Bahia's sugar fields and the savannas of Angola, as few Whites did their own mining. Until the last quarter of the 18th century, the slaves of Minas Gerais were digging up half the world's gold.

Minas set the gold-rush standard – crazy, wild and violent – more than 100 years before the Californian and Australian gold rushes. Disease and famine were rampant, and the mine towns were known for their licentiousness. Minas's gold was siphoned off to Portugal; among the few lasting benefits to Brazil was the creation of the beautiful, church-clad mining cities that dot the hills of Minas Gerais.

As Minas enters the 21st century, the old Estrada Real (Royal Rd) connecting the colonial mining towns has become one of Brazil's prime tourist draws. The government has invested heavily in promoting the route, inviting visitors to rediscover the country's past through a modern lens.

National Parks
Parque Nacional Serra do Cipó – forming the heart of Unesco's brand-new Serra do Espinhaço Biosphere Reserve – is Belo Horizonte's backyard wilderness area. Its vast mountain and river landscapes lie just 100km from the city center. Parque Nacional Caparaó, on Minas's eastern border with Espírito Santo, is home to waterfalls, spectacular vistas and Brazil's third-highest peak. Both parks offer excellent hiking opportunities.

Climate
Minas is a moody place. Drab fogs drift in and out amid almost daily showers (of short duration) from October through February. It's warm, so you only really need an umbrella for protection from the wet. From July to September, the dry season, things can get frostier and a light jacket is sometimes called for, particularly at night.

Getting There & Around
Capital city Belo Horizonte is the arrival point for most travelers. Pampulha and Tancredo Neves/Confins airports handle domestic and international flights, while the large downtown bus station serves as a hub for ground transport (see p240). Direct buses from Rio and São Paulo also serve some of the historic towns.

BELO HORIZONTE
☎ 0xx31 / pop 2.5 million / elevation 858m
Known to locals as Bay-Agah (that's Portuguese for BH), Belo Horizonte was named for its beautiful view of nearby mountains. If you climb into the hills south of town at sunset and survey the vast checkerboard of streets below, the city can still be strikingly beautiful. Still, many people give Belo a miss altogether, based on reports that it's smoggy and overdeveloped. There's some truth there, but the city has considerable other charms.

The longer you stay in Belo, the more it grows on you. Walk down the buzzing cosmopolitan streets of the Savassi neighborhood on a Saturday evening, eat at one of the fine restaurants in Lourdes, stroll through the densely packed market stalls at the Mercado Central, attend a concert at the Palácio das Artes, or visit the brand-new Inhotim art museum west of the city, and you'll see that Belo has countless dimensions. Add to all this the friendly, welcoming nature of Belo's people and you've got a winning combination. Stick around a few days – you might grow fond of the place.

History
In the late 19th century, as the Brazilian Republic was coming into its own, Mineiros began planning a new capital to replace hard-to-reach Ouro Prêto, which had fallen out of favor as a symbol of colonialism. Belo Horizonte sprang up as an art-nouveau city, influenced by the spirit of Ordem e Progresso (Order and Progress), the new slogan on the Brazilian flag.

In the 1940s, Belo expanded northward. Then-mayor Juscelino Kubitschek commissioned young architectural-school graduate Oscar Niemeyer to design the brand-new Pampulha district. These two men are largely responsible for the wide avenues, large lakes, parks and jutting skylines that characterize the city today.

More than 100 years after its founding, Belo still has the young, contagious energy of a community reinventing itself. Plans are currently underway to move a complex of government ministries north of the center, onto the road to Confins airport, liberating

MINAS GERAIS

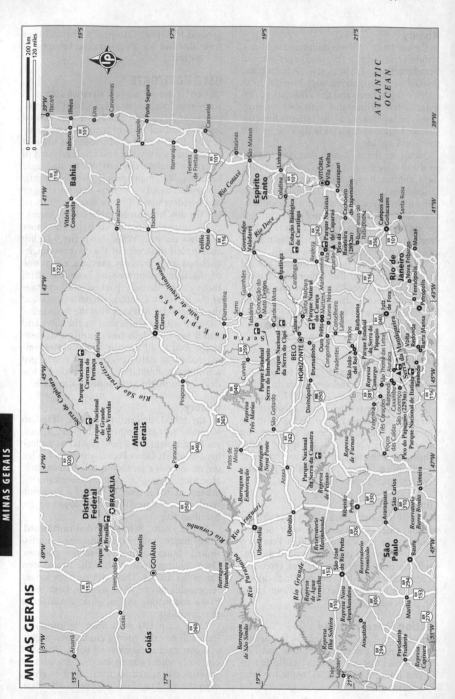

space around beautiful palm-fringed Praça da Liberdade to house the city's symphony orchestra and other arts organizations.

Orientation

Central Belo has a grid of large *avenidas* (avenues) and another smaller grid superimposed at a 45-degree angle. The boundaries of the original planned city are defined by the ring road called Av do Contorno. It's a hilly town, so trips are sometimes less straightforward than they appear on the map. The main drag is Av Afonso Pena, which runs diagonally from northwest to southeast, starting at the bus station at the northern end of downtown and running past leafy green Parque Municipal. From northwest to southeast, there are three pivotal *praças* (squares): bustling Praça Sete, just southeast of the bus station; serene Praça da Liberdade, heart of the government district called Funcionarios; and trendy Praça da Savassi, the center of Belo nightlife and café society.

Outside of downtown, Pampulha is the section of town with most tourist amenities.

Information

BOOKSTORES

Livraria da Travessa (Rua dos Guajajaras 416; 🕑 8am-9:30pm, closed Sun) and **Café com Letras** (☎ 3225 9973; Rua Antônio de Albuquerque 781; 🕑 noon-midnight Mon-Thu, to 1am Fri & Sat, 5-11pm Sun) are two wonderful bookstore-cafés that double as eateries and cultural centers.

EMERGENCY

Ambulance (☎ 192)
Fire department (☎ 193)
Police (☎ 190) For nonurgent matters, call ☎ 3330 5200.

INTERNET ACCESS

Internet places abound throughout the city. One especially good deal:
Pró Terra (☎ 3226 7610; Av Augusto de Lima 134, Loja 11-13; per hr R$1.50 or less; 🕑 8am-10pm) Skype access, photo transfer, and fast connections.

INTERNET RESOURCES

www.descubraminas.com.br Everything you ever wanted to know about Minas, in one easy site (English, Spanish, Portuguese).

LAUNDRY

Laundromat (☎ 3224 5383; Rua dos Timbiras 1264; 🕑 8am-7pm Mon-Fri, to 2pm Sat) Wash your own clothes

(R$7.50 per machine), or let them do it (R$21.50 a basket). Quick service, plus ironing for a small surcharge.

MEDICAL SERVICES

For any nonurgent health matters call ☎ 3222 3322.

MONEY

There are numerous downtown banks with ATMs between Praça Sete and Parque Municipal.
Banco do Brasil (Rua Rio de Janeiro 750)
Bradesco (Rua da Bahia 951)
HSBC (Rua da Bahia 932)

POST

Main post office (Av Afonso Pena 1270) There's another post office at the bus station.

TOURIST INFORMATION

If you read a little Portuguese, check out the weekly listings in the Espetáculo section of the Estado de Minas newspaper. Another great source of local information is the Roteiro Cultural supplement of the Pampulha paper, published every Saturday.
Alo Turismo (☎ 3220 1310; 🕑 8am-10pm) Belotur's tourist-inquiry hotline.
Belotur (☎ 3277 9777; www.belohorizonte.mg.gov .br) Belo's municipal tourist bureau is among the best in Brazil. Its several offices distribute an exceptionally helpful trilingual guide (English, Spanish, Portuguese) cataloguing the city's restaurants, museums, cultural events and other tourist attractions, with instructions on how to get there using local buses. The Guia Turístico also includes a city map, airline and bus company information, and everything else you wanted to know about Belo but didn't know how to ask. Locations around the city include:
Belotur Confins airport (☎ 3689 2557; 🕑 8am-9:30pm) At the main airport exit, outside baggage claim.
Belotur Mercado Central (☎ 3277 4691; 🕑 8am-6pm Mon-Sat, to 1pm Sun) On the ground floor of Belo's famous indoor market.
Belotur Mercado das Flores (☎ 3277 7666; Av Afonso Pena 1055; 🕑 8am-7pm Mon-Fri, to 3pm Sat & Sun) At the flower market on the edge of Parque Municipal.
Belotur Rodoviaria (☎ 3277 6907; 🕑 8am-10pm) Inside the bus station, right near the main exit.

Dangers & Annoyances

There are more dangerous places in the world than Belo Horizonte, but you should remain alert for petty theft, as in any big city, especially near the bus station.

Sights

One of Belo's most appealing spots is **Parque Municipal**, an enormous sea of tropical greenery with artificial lakes and winding pathways, just 10 minutes southeast of the bus station along Av Afonso Pena. It's especially fun on Sunday, when everyone's out strolling and socializing.

The free **Museu Histórico Abílio Barreto** (☎ 3277 8861; Av Prudente de Morais 202, Cidade Jardim; 10am-5pm Tue-Wed & Fri-Sun, to 9pm Thu), just south of Savassi, features a renovated colonial farmhouse, the solitary remnant of Curral del Rey, the rural village destroyed in the 1890s to make room for Belo. There are some fascinating historical photos and other bric-a-brac.

The brand-new **Museu de Artes e Ofícios** (☎ 3248 8600; www.mao.com.br; Praça Rui Barbosa; admission R$4, students/over 60 R$2, free Sat; noon-7pm Tue-Fri, 11am-5pm Sat & Sun), in Belo's historic train station, houses a wide-ranging collection of objects used in the daily lives of Mineiros past and present. There are interpretive cards in English adjacent to each exhibit.

The **Museu Giramundo** (☎ 3446 0686; www.giramundo.org; Rua Varginha 235, Floresta; admission R$5, under 12/over 60/student R$2.50; 9:30am-5pm Tue-Sat) has a fanciful display of 400 marionettes, from performances by the internationally acclaimed, Belo-based Teatro Giramundo.

Fans of modernist architect Oscar Niemeyer won't want to miss his creations dotted around a huge artificial lake in the Pampulha district, north of downtown. The **Igreja de São Francisco de Assis** (☎ 3427 1644; Av Otacílio Negrão de Lima s/n; 9am-5pm Mon-Sat, to 1pm Sun) is an architectural delight and the paintings by Portinari are beautiful.

The **Museu de Arte de Pampulha** (☎ 3277 7946; Av Otacílio Negrão de Lima 16585; 9am-7pm Tue-Sun), with its cute garden designed by landscape architect Roberto Burle Marx, is also worth a look. It was designed as a casino and shows the obvious modernist influence of Le Corbusier. The **Casa do Baile** (☎ 3277 7443; Av Otacílio Negrão de Lima 751; 9am-7pm Tue-Sun), a former dance hall, now holds all types of temporary art exhibits. Its lovely onsite café is a great place to take a break.

Sleeping

BUDGET

Madrid (☎ /fax 3201 1088/6330; Rua dos Guaranis 12; s/d/tr/q with bathroom R$28/45/65/80, without bathroom R$40/55/75/90) Noisy, but convenient for an over-

night between buses, the Madrid is directly across from the *rodoviária*. Ask for a room away from the street bustle.

Albergue de Juventude Chalé Mineiro (☎ 3467 1576; www.chalemineirohostel.com.br; Rua Santa Luzia 288; dm with/without HI membership R$16/21, s/d without breakfast from R$27/50;) The dorm rooms at this hostel 2km east of downtown are decent, despite the grumpy staff. Take bus 9801 from near the bus station. The central pool is a nice touch in an otherwise no-frills experience.

Hotel São Bento (☎ 3271 3399; www.hotelsaobento.com.br; Rua Guarani 438; s/d/tr R$48/52/63, s/d/tr with air-con R$69/76/84) The pleasant, comfortable rooms at this hotel a few blocks south of the bus station are one of downtown's best values.

Pousada Sossego da Pampulha (☎ 3491 8020; www.sossegodapampulha.com.br; Av Cel José Dias Bicalho 1258, Pampulha; dm/s/d with HI membership R$34/82/100, without membership R$41/89/110;) This new HI-affiliated hostel is friendly, clean, well-run and convenient for people arriving by plane. Amenities include a small pool, shared kitchen and rooftop terrace with views of Belo Horizonte and the mountains. From the Pampulha airport, a taxi costs R$7, or take bus 5401 (R$2).

MIDRANGE

Hotel Metrópole (☎ 3273 1544; www.hotelmetropolebh.com.br; Rua da Bahia 1023; s/d/tr R$64/88/120) It's hard to beat the Metrópole for price, location and service. A quick walk from the Parque Central, this faded Art Deco building has comfortable rooms and a friendly staff. To avoid the street noise out front, request a room with a veranda facing quieter Rua Goiás.

BH Palace (☎ 3330 6500; www.hotelbhpalace.com.br; Av Augusto de Lima 1147; s/d R$65/80;) Very near the Mercado Central, but a bit out of the way for the rest of Belo's attractions, this place straddles the line between budget and midrange. Very basic but pretty and clean rooms and all the amenities of a larger hotel at much lower rates.

Evora Palace (☎ 3227 6220; www.orgbristol.com.br; Rua Sergipe 1415; s/d R$105/115, ste R$200;) In the heart of Savassi, the dining and drinking center of Belo's nightlife, Evora stands out as a great midpriced choice. Rooms are large and comfortable.

Hotel Wimbledon (☎ 3222 6160; www.wimbledon.com.br; Av Afonso Pena 772; s/d R$90/105, ste R$128/154;) A delightful place, with warm, welcoming rooms, hardwood floors, Mineiro art, modern bathrooms and a rooftop pool.

CENTRAL BELO HORIZONTE

0 _____ 400 m
0 _____ 0.2 miles

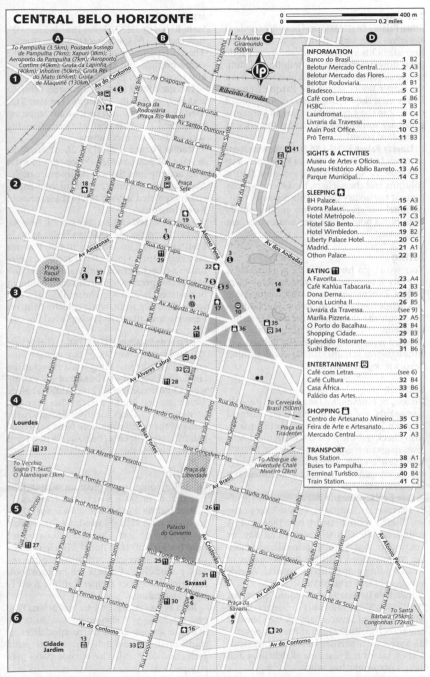

INFORMATION
Banco do Brasil.............................1 B2
Belotur Mercado Central..............2 A3
Belotur Mercado das Flores.........3 C3
Belotur Rodoviária........................4 B1
Bradesco.......................................5 C3
Café com Letras............................6 B6
HSBC..7 B3
Laundromat...................................8 C4
Livraria da Travessa......................9 C6
Main Post Office.........................10 C3
Pró Terra.....................................11 B3

SIGHTS & ACTIVITIES
Museu de Artes e Ofícios...........12 C2
Museu Histórico Abílio Barreto...13 A6
Parque Municipal........................14 C3

SLEEPING
BH Palace....................................15 A3
Evora Palace................................16 B6
Hotel Metrópole.........................17 C3
Hotel São Bento.........................18 A2
Hotel Wimbledon.......................19 B2
Liberty Palace Hotel...................20 C6
Madrid...21 A1
Othon Palace..............................22 B3

EATING
A Favorita....................................23 A4
Café Kahlúa Tabacaria.................24 B3
Dona Derna.................................25 B5
Dona Lucinha II...........................26 B5
Livraria da Travessa...............(see 9)
Marília Pizzeria............................27 A5
O Porto do Bacalhau...................28 B4
Shopping Cidade.........................29 B3
Splendido Ristorante...................30 B6
Sushi Beer....................................31 B6

ENTERTAINMENT
Café com Letras.....................(see 6)
Café Cultura................................32 B4
Casa África..................................33 B6
Palácio das Artes........................34 C3

SHOPPING
Centro de Artesanato Mineiro....35 C3
Feira de Arte e Artesanato.........36 C3
Mercado Central.........................37 A3

TRANSPORT
Bus Station..................................38 A1
Buses to Pampulha......................39 B2
Terminal Turístico.......................40 B4
Train Station...............................41 C2

MINAS GERAIS

TOP END

Othon Palace (☎ 3273 3844; www.hoteis-othon.com.br; Av Afonso Pena 1050; s/d/tr R$145/170/220; ✿ ☐ ☒) The four-star Othon's many advantages include great downtown location, multilingual staff, spacious rooms and spectacular views from the upper floors across the Parque Central. Don't miss the rooftop bar and pool, one of the best in the city, and feel free to bargain – suites are sometimes offered for the price of a standard room!

Liberty Palace Hotel (☎ 2121 0900; www.liberty palace.com.br; Rua Paraíba 1465; s/d R$209/230, s/d ste R$462/508; ✿ ☐ ☒) With its marble floors, columns and chandeliers, the Liberty's lobby hints at the luxury that awaits. Savassi's toniest hotel has spacious rooms and big comfy beds, plus a pool, sauna, gym and an excellent restaurant.

Eating

You won't go hungry in Belo Horizonte! The city is teeming with good food for every budget. Downtown is the best place for cheap eats, while further south, Savassi and Lourdes constitute the epicenter of the city's fine dining scene. The lion's share of the city's non-Mineiro restaurants specialize in Italian food, although you can also find a world of other flavors if you look around.

BUDGET

Dozens of *lanchonetes* (snack bars), per-kilo restaurants, and fast-food places are clustered between Praça Sete and Praça da Liberdade. Also check out the food courts in the downtown malls such as **Shopping Cidade** (☎ 3271 3707; Rua Rio de Janeiro 910), where fast-food offerings mingle congenially with per-kilo buffets and full-service restaurants.

Café Kahlúa Tabacaria (Rua dos Guajajaras 416; coffee with roll or sandwich R$4-10; ✹ 8am-9:30pm, closed Sun) There's more brewing here than java. A young, artistic clientele pops in all day for sandwiches, and the fully enclosed back smoking room is filled with the bright chatter of locals trading quips with the owners. A wide selection of teas is also available.

Livraria da Travessa (Rua dos Guajajaras 416; light meals R$10; ✹ 8am-9:30pm, closed Sun) For budget dining with a touch of Savassi flair, try the sidewalk café at this bookstore just off Praça da Savassi. It's a great place to enjoy local street life. Sandwiches, salads and pasta are all delicious, and there's occasional live music.

MIDRANGE

Sushi Beer (☎ 3282 7755; Rua Tomé de Souza 1121; meals from R$16; ✹ 6pm-midnight Mon-Sat, to 11pm Sun) There's Japanese food and beer here, as the name implies, but the wide-ranging menu also incorporates pizza and steak.

Cervejaria Brasil (☎ 3287 3299; Rua dos Aimorés 90; lunch R$17; ✹ 11am-late Tue-Sun, from 6pm Mon) This hard-core *churrascaria* (restaurant featuring barbecued meat) is absolutely overflowing with options for meat lovers.

Marília Pizzeria (☎ 3275 2027; ☎ Rua Marília de Dirceu 189; pizza from R$20; ✹ 6pm-late) Electric with activity into the wee hours every night, Marilia's has a trendy, youthful vibe and is routinely voted among the best pizzerias in Belo Horizonte.

Xapuri (☎ 3496 6198; Rua Mandacaru 260, Pampulha; meals R$21 per person; ✹ 11am-11pm Tue-Thu, to 2am Fri & Sat, to 6pm Sun) This local institution features fabulous Mineiro food served at picnic tables under a thatched roof, with hammocks close at hand for premeal children's entertainment or postmeal relaxation. The traditional wood stove blazes up front, while colorful Mineiro desserts are attractively displayed in two long cases.

O Porto do Bacalhau (☎ 3222 7300; Rua Espírito Santo 1507; fish dinner for 2 from R$49; ✹ 11am-midnight) Fine seafood isn't the first thing you'd expect in the landlocked capital of Minas, but it's exactly what O Porto delivers. This traditional place with a covered outdoor terrace has been delighting local palates for three decades, with some of the best *bolinhas de bacalhau* (codfish fritters), *moqueca* (Bahian fish stew) and grilled fish this side of the Atlantic.

TOP END

Belo Horizonte has a plethora of standout restaurants, many in Savassi and Lourdes.

Dona Lucinha II (☎ 3261 5930; Rua Sergipe 811; all-you-can-eat buffet R$28; ✹ noon-3pm & 7pm-midnight Mon-Sat, noon-5pm Sun) The sumptuous buffet here features 50 traditional Mineiro dishes daily. Prices have climbed thanks to the recent publication of a best-selling cookbook featuring Lucinha's recipes, but the food is still outstanding.

Dona Derna (☎ 3223 6954; Rua Tomé de Souza 1331; meals from R$35; ✹ 11:30am-midnight Mon-Thu, to 1am Fri & Sat, to 6pm Sun) Dona Derna specializes in traditional Tuscan delights, replete with garlic and olive oil. The outside patio gets jam-packed.

A Favorita (☎ 3275 2352; Rua Santa Catarina 1235; meals from R$37; ⊗ noon–1am Mon-Thu, to 2am Fri & Sat, to midnight Sun) This combination bar, restaurant and bakery, with display shelves full of delicious homemade bread, exudes a relaxed yet classy charm. Specialties include ceviche, carpaccio, oysters, salads and risottos.

Splendido Ristorante (☎ 3227 6446; Rua Levindo Lopes 251; meals from R$40; ⊗ noon–3pm & 7pm-late Mon-Fri, dinner only Sat, lunch only Sun) Visiting dignitaries and celebrities often stop by this Savassi eatery, mingling with the local beautiful people. The French- and Italian-influenced meat dishes go well with imported wines, and local vegetables are used to surprising effect as fillers for pasta entrees.

Vecchio Sogno (☎ 3292 5251; Rua Martim de Carvalho 75; meals from R$42; ⊗ noon-midnight Mon-Thu, noon-2am Fri, 6pm-2am Sat, noon-6pm Sun) Repeatedly voted Belo's best restaurant (not just its best Italian one), Vecchio's is worth the splurge. Entrees range from lamb and saffron risotto to delicate grilled fish. Reserve ahead.

Entertainment

Belo is a cosmopolitan town with a vibrant arts scene and plenty of nightlife.

The **Palácio das Artes** (☎ 3237 7234; www.palacio dasartes.com.br; Av Afonso Pena 1537), an art gallery and performing arts center near the southern end of Parque Municipal, is the hub of Belo's theater, dance, and music concert scene. Current shows are listed in the Art and Culture section of Belotur's free guide.

The city's world-class dance and theater companies, **Grupo Corpo** (www.grupocorpo.com.br) and **Grupo Galpão** (www.grupogalpao.com.br) are often on tour but sometimes perform at home. Their websites show current tour details. Also inquire at any Belotur office.

If you can, catch a performance by Grupo Uakti, a fascinating local music group that invents its own unconventional instruments and creates some truly remarkable sounds.

If you're visiting mid-April to mid-May, check out the **Comida di Buteco festival** (www .comidadibuteco.com.br), in which dozens of neighborhood bars compete to see who makes the best bar food.

Late-night club- and pub-based nightlife gravitates towards Savassi. **Café com Letras** (☎ 3225 9973; Rua Antônio de Albuquerque 781; ⊗ noon-midnight Mon-Thu, to 1am Fri & Sat, 5-11pm Sun) has wonderful live music on weekends, DJs spinning tunes on weeknights, and an intoxicating

bohemian buzz between sets. It's a fun place to kick back, have a drink, browse the shelves or check email using one of the free internet computers in back. Also in Savassi is **Casa África** (☎ 3344 1803; Rua Leopoldinha 48), which has a rotating menu of live entertainment from all over Africa, and a dedicated local following.

Other interesting options include **Café Cultura** (☎ 3222 1347; Rua da Bahia 1416), which is packed on weekends, when the bar features live music, and **O Alambique** (☎ 3296 7188; Av Raja Gabaglia 3200, Estoril), where the décor, the music, the drinks and the food all conspire to make this one of Belo's most entertaining nightspots. There's an old water wheel, tables made from barrels with stone tops, 70 different *cachaça*-based drinks, and *forró* (popular music of the Northeast)and *sertanejo* music to keep things lively all night long.

Shopping

The most vibrant shopping streets are clustered around Praça Savassi. Locals also favor the many highrise shopping centers downtown and the wonderful street markets.

Feira de Arte e Artesanato (Av Afonso Pena, btwn Rua da Bahia & Rua das Guajajaras; ⊗ 6am-noon, but often still going at 3pm) One of Belo's major community events, this enormous Sunday street fair attracts massive crowds searching for clothing, jewelry, street food and lots more. Bordered by the soothing greenery of the Parque Municipal, it's a fun place to wander and enjoy a slice of city life, even if you're not in a shopping mood.

Centro de Artesanato Mineiro (☎ 3272 8572; Av Afonso Pena 1537; ⊗ 9am-6pm Mon-Fri, to 1pm Sat, 10am-2pm Sun) Inside the Palácio das Artes at the edge of Parque Municipal, this government store specializes in Mineiro crafts. The selection is good, although prices are not as cheap as in the colonial towns.

Mercado Central (cnr Rua Curitiba & Rua dos Goitacazes; ⊗ 8am-6pm Mon-Sat, to 1pm Sun) You'll find everything from parrots to perfume at this indoor market, a true Belo Horizonte institution. Sample the delicious local produce, socialize with locals at one of the bars or just roam the aisles aimlessly.

Getting There & Around
AIR

Belo Horizonte has two airports. Most planes use the international **Aeroporto Confins** (CNF; 40km north). The **Aeroporto da Pampulha** (PLU; 7km north) is much more convenient but only has domestic flights.

Flights from the two airports serve most locations in Brazil. The most frequent destinations are Rio, Brasília, Vitória and São Paulo. A full list of airline offices, with phone numbers, appears in the back of the free Belotur guide.

BUS

Belo's **bus station** (☎ 3271 3000) is near the northern end of downtown on Praça da Rodoviária. The free Belotur guide lists bus company phone numbers in the back pages.

Destinations include Brasília (Penha and Itapemirim bus lines, R$80, 11 to 12 hours, three daily); Caxambú (Gardénia, R$54, six hours, two daily at 7:30am and 11pm); Congonhas (Sandra, R$16, two hours, two daily at 7am and 10:15am); Diamantina (Pássaro Verde, R$53, five hours, six daily from 5:30am to midnight); Mariana (Pássaro Verde, R$21, two hours, eight daily from 6am to 11pm); Ouro Prêto (Pássaro Verde, R$19, two hours, nine daily from 7am to 8:15pm); Rio de Janeiro (Cometa and Útil, R$56, 6½ hours, 12 daily from 8am to 12:30am); Salvador (Gontijo and São Geraldo, R$161, 22 hours, two daily at 6pm and 7pm); São João del Rei (Sandra, R$33, 3½ hours, five daily from 8:30am to 7pm); São Paulo (Cometa, R$72, 8½ hours, 12 daily from 7:45am to midnight); Serro (R$56, five to six hours, four daily); Vitória (São Geraldo and Itapemirim, R$75, eight to 12 hours, 10 daily from 8:15am to 11:45pm).

LOCAL BUSES

Belo Horizonte's local buses are color-coded. Blue buses go up and down main avenues in the city center, white express buses only stop at select points, red buses connect outlying suburbs to downtown, and yellow buses have circular routes through the city.

AIRPORT BUSES

Expresso Unir (☎ 3224 1002; www.expressounir.com.br) runs frequent, comfortable Conexão Aeroporto buses between downtown and Belo's two airports (Pampulha and Confins). The conventional bus (R$6.45 to either airport) leaves Belo's bus station every 30 minutes on weekdays, hourly on weekends. First/last departures from the bus station are 4:45am/10:45pm, from Confins 6:15am/1am. An *executivo* (express) bus (R$14.75 to Confins,

R$7 to Pampulha) leaves from the **Terminal Turístico** (Av Alvares Cabral 387), just southwest of Parque Municipal, every 45 minutes to one hour. First/last departures from downtown are 4:30am/10:10pm, from Confins 6:00am/1:30am Mon-Sat, 6:00am/midnight Sunday. Travel time is approximately 30 minutes to Pampulha airport, one hour to Confins.

TRAIN

Companhia Vale do Rio Doce (☎ 3273 5976; www.cvrd .com.br/cvrd/media/horarios.xls) operates a daily train to Vitória in Espírito Santo state (regular/*executivo* class R$39/60, 13 hours), departing at 7:30am from the train station at Praça da Estação, just north of Parque Municipal.

AROUND BELO HORIZONTE
Centro de Arte Contemporânea Inhotim

Greater Belo's newest tourist attraction is the sprawling **Centro de Arte Contemporânea Inhotim** (☎ 3227 0001; www.inhotim.org.br; adults R$10, students/ over 60 R$5; ⊙ 9:30am-4:30pm Thu-Sun), an impressive complex of gardens dotted with nine modern-art galleries, 50km west of the city near the town of Brumadinho. Much of the international artwork is monumental in size. The gardens, which were opened to the public in October 2006 and are expanding constantly, boast 1600 different species of plants (including 200 types of palm alone), peacocks and lakes with swans. You can wander at will, or attend daily scheduled programs led by guides trained in visual arts and natural science. The onsite restaurant and café are both excellent. Saritur runs buses (R$11.40, 80 minutes, 7am, 11am and 3pm) from Belo Horizonte to Brumadinho, where you can catch a taxi to the museum (R$10).

Caves

Three fascinating caves are within two hours of downtown Belo and make great day jaunts.

Gruta Rei do Mato (☎ 3773 0888; adult/child R$8/4; ⊙ 8am-5pm) is the most interesting of the three caves. Near Sete Lagoas, north of Belo, it has prehistoric paintings and petroglyphs. Setelagoano buses (R$12.80, 80 minutes) leave hourly from Belo between 7am and 11pm.

Gruta de Maquiné (☎ 3715 1078; adult/child R$12/6; ⊙ 8am-5pm) is the most famous and crowded of the caves. Maquiné's seven huge chambers are well lit for guided tours. Setelagoano runs daily buses there (R$23.90, 2¼ hours, leaving at 8am, returning at 4pm) from the Belo Horizonte bus station.

The highlight at **Gruta da Lapinha** (☎ 3689 8422; adult/child R$10/5; ⏰ 8:30am-4:30pm) is the Véu da Noiva, a crystal formation in the shape of a bride's veil. Saritur runs five buses daily to Lagoa Santa (R$7.25, one hour, 6:30am to 4:15am); from there, Atual bus 306 goes to the cave (R$2, 35 minutes, every 40 minutes from 7am).

COLONIAL TOWNS

The *cidades históricas* (colonial towns) are Minas' standout attraction. Collectively, they constitute one of Brazil's most alluring and accessible tourist circuits. All the towns covered here bear marks of their common Portuguese ancestry – cobblestone streets, baroque belltowers, winding alleys decked in flowers – but each has unique charms. The colonial remnants of Congonhas and Sabará have been almost entirely eclipsed by modern development, yet each still contains artistic masterpieces that warrant a day trip. Mariana's colonial center has fared better, preserved as perfectly as a pearl inside the surrounding 21st-century oyster. São João del Rei is a unique hybrid, peppered with enough 18th-century churches and bridges to hold their own and provide an interesting contrast to the encroaching highrises and urban bustle. Tiradentes, Serro and Diamantina – thanks to their relative isolation, gorgeous settings and unadulterated architectural integrity – are perfect places to experience rural Minas' 'lost in time' quality. Ouro Prêto stands alone as the largest and best-preserved colonial center in Minas, having benefited from over 70 years of conservation efforts, dating back to 1933, when the Brazilian government declared it a national monument.

OURO PRÊTO

☎ 0xx31 / pop 61,000 / elevation 1179m

Of all the exquisite colonial towns scattered around Minas Gerais, Ouro Prêto is the jewel in the crown. Significant historically as a center of gold mining and government, and as the stage for Brazil's first independence movement, the city remains vital in modern times as a center for education and the arts, and as one of Brazil's three most visited tourist destinations.

Built at the feet of the Serra do Espinhaço range, Ouro Prêto's colonial center is larger, and has steeper topography, than any other historical town in Minas. The narrow, crooked streets of the upper and lower towns tangle together and in places are too rough and precipitous for vehicles. Navigating the vertiginous cobblestoned slopes on foot can be exhausting, but the views of 23 churches spread out across the hilly panorama are spectacular. The city is a showcase of outstanding Mineiro art and architecture, including some of Aleijadinho's finest works (see p252 for more information on Aleijadinho).

History

Legend has it that a mulatto servant in an early *bandeirante* (a group of roaming adventurers who spent the 17th and 18th centuries exploring Brazil's interior, searching for gold and Indians to enslave) expedition pocketed a few grains of an odd black metal he found while drinking from a small river near the current site of Ouro Prêto (Portuguese for 'black gold'). It turned out to be gold, and within a few years, the local deposits were discovered to be the largest in the New World.

Gold fever spread fast. In 1711, Vila Rica de Ouro Prêto, the predecessor of the present town, was founded, and in 1721 it became the capital of Minas Gerais. The finest goods from India and England were made available to the simple mining town. The gold bought the services of baroque artisans, who turned the city into an architectural gem. At the height of the gold boom in the mid-18th century, there were 110,000 people (mainly slaves) in Ouro Prêto, as contrasted to 50,000 in New York and about 20,000 in Rio de Janeiro.

In theory, all gold was brought to *casas de intendéncias* (weighing stations) to be turned into bars, and a *quinto do ouro* (royal fifth) was set aside for the Portuguese crown. Tax shirkers were cast into dungeons or exiled to Africa.

The greed of the Portuguese led to sedition by the inhabitants of Vila Rica. As the boom tapered off, the miners found it increasingly difficult to pay ever-larger gold taxes. In 1789, poets Claudio da Costa, Tomás Antônio Gonzaga, Joaquim José da Silva Xavier (nicknamed Tiradentes, meaning 'Tooth Puller', for his dentistry skills) and others, full of French-Revolutionary philosophies, hatched an uprising against Portuguese colonization known as the Inconfidência Mineira.

The rebellion was crushed in its early stages by agents of the crown. Gonzaga was exiled to Mozambique and Costa did time in prison. Tiradentes, the only man not to deny his role in the conspiracy, was abandoned by his friends, jailed for three years without defense, then drawn and quartered in Rio de Janeiro. His head was paraded around Ouro Prêto, his house demolished and its grounds salted to ensure that nothing would grow there.

In 1897 the state capital was shifted from Ouro Prêto to Belo Horizonte. This was the decisive move that preserved the city's colonial flavor. The ensuing century has seen a steady increase in appreciation for Ouro Prêto's unique cultural legacy, notably marked by Unesco's 1980 decision to enshrine it as Brazil's first World Heritage site.

Climate

Ouro Prêto is 1km above sea level, and temperatures vary from 2°C to 28°C (36°F to 82°F). Winters are pretty cold. It can be rainy and foggy all year round, with showers most frequent in December and January.

Orientation

Ouro Prêto is divided into parishes, each with its own Matriz (mother church). If you stand in Praça Tiradentes facing the Museu da Inconfidência, the parish of Pilar is to the right (west), the parishes of Antônio Dias and Santa Efigênia to the left (east).

Most streets in town have two names: the official one and another used by locals because the official one is too long. For example, Rua Conde de Bobadela, the major thoroughfare descending from Praça Tiradentes, is known as Rua Direita, and Rua Conselheiro Quintiliano, the road to Mariana, is also Rua das Lajes. Adding to the confusion, street names are rarely posted.

The hillside just below the bus station can feel a bit seedy at night, despite the presence of two police stations in the area. As in any city, remain alert when walking around after dark.

Information

INTERNET ACCESS

Internet and Skype access are available at **Lan House Internet** (Rua São José 119A; per hr R$3; ☺ 8:30am-10pm) and **Rai Tai** (☎ 3551 5151; Rua Paraná 100; per hr R$4; ☺ 9am-10pm), both just two blocks from Praça Tiradentes.

LAUNDRY

Down near the train station, **Nascente Lavanderia** (☎ 3551 5070; Rua dos Inconfidêntes 5; ☺ 8am-5pm Mon-Fri, to noon Sat) washes and dries clothes for R$3 per kilo and irons them for an extra R$1 per kilo. They'll pick up and deliver upon request.

MONEY

There's a Bradesco ATM on the northwest corner of Praça Tiradentes. Several other cash machines can be found along Rua São José, including **Banco do Brasil** (Rua São José 189), **Itaú** (Rua São José 105) and **HSBC** (Rua São José 201).

POST

Main post office (cnr Rua Direita & Rua Coronel Alves)

TOURIST INFORMATION

The **Centro Cultural e Turístico** (☎ 3559 3269; Praça Tiradentes 4; ☺ 8:15am-6:15pm), in the heart of town on the eastern side of Praça Tiradentes, offers information in English, Spanish and French. They distribute a free leaflet listing museum and church hours, plus a rough map of the town.

The Livraria Cultural downstairs sells books about Ouro Prêto in various languages. If you read Portuguese, check out the fascinating *Tesouros, Fantasmas e Lendas de Ouro Prêto* (Treasures, Ghosts and Legends of Ouro Prêto), published in 2007 and filled with local lore about the town.

Sights

There are virtually no 20th-century buildings to defile this stunning colonial town. For a panoramic view of the churches and rooftops, head northeast out of Praça Tiradentes and walk five minutes along Rua Conselheiro Quintiliano towards Mariana.

Except where otherwise noted, local attractions charge admission of between R$2 and R$6.

PRAÇA TIRADENTES & AROUND

Praça Tiradentes is the heart of town, surrounded by some of Ouro Prêto's finest museums and churches.

If you only visit one church in Ouro Prêto, make sure it's **Igreja de São Francisco de Assis** (☺ 8:30-11:50am & 1:30-5pm Tue-Sun), one block downhill from Praça Tiradentes. After *The Prophets* in Congonhas (see p251), Aleijadinho's masterpiece, this is the most important

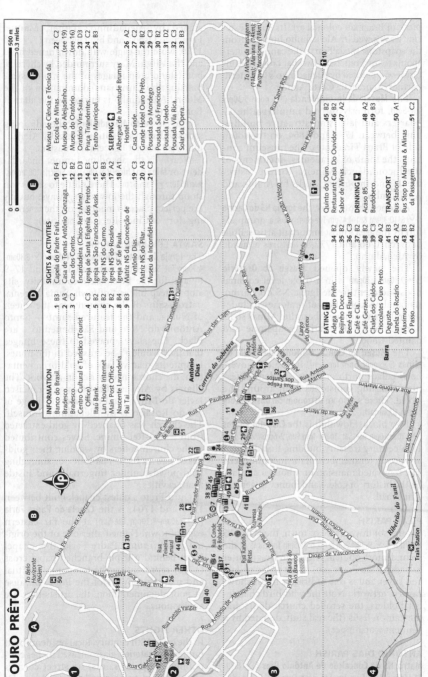

OURO PRÊTO

To Belo
Horizonte
(964m)

To Minas da Passagem
(11km); Mariana (14km);
Parque Itacolomy (18km)

Antônio Dias

Barra

Córrego do Sobreira

Train Station

Ribeirão do Funil

MINAS GERAIS

0   500 m
0   0.3 miles

piece of Brazilian colonial art. Its entire exterior was carved by Aleijadinho himself, from the soapstone medallion to the cannon waterspouts to the Franciscan two-bar cross. The interior was painted by Aleijadinho's long-term partner, Manuel da Costa Ataíde.

The **Museu da Inconfidência** (noon-5:30pm Tue-Sun), formerly the old municipal headquarters and jail, is an attractive building built between 1784 and 1854, on the south side of Praça Tiradentes. The museum contains the tomb of Tiradentes, documents of the Inconfidência Mineira, torture instruments and important works by Ataíde and Aleijadinho.

A stone's throw away, the **Igreja NS do Carmo** (8-10:30am & 1-4:45pm Tue-Sun) was a group effort by the area's most important artists. Built between 1766 and 1772, it features a facade by Aleijadinho.

The newly opened **Museu do Oratório** (9:30am-5:30pm) is in a triple-level colonial house adjacent to the Igreja NS do Carmo. Its fabulous collection of oratories includes several in the uniquely beautiful Minas style, harmoniously integrating soapstone and painted wood.

The **Museu de Ciência e Técnica da Escola de Minas** (noon-5pm Tue-Sun), in the old governor's palace north of Praça Tiradentes, features dazzling gemstones from around the world. There's also an **astronomical observatory** (8-10pm Sat).

Two blocks downhill is the **Casa dos Contos** (10am-6pm Tue-Sat, 10am-4pm Sun, 2-6pm Mon), the 18th-century treasury building that doubled as a prison for members of the Inconfidência. The renovated mansion now houses displays on the history of gold – and money in general – in Brazil.

PILAR PARISH

On the southwest side of town, the **Matriz NS do Pilar** (9-10:45am & noon-4:45pm Tue-Sun) is the second-most-opulent church in Brazil (after Salvador's São Francisco). It has 434kg of gold and silver and is one of Brazil's finest showcases of artwork. Note the wild-bird chandelier holders, the scrolled church doors and the hair on Jesus (the real stuff, donated by a penitent worshipper).

ANTÔNIO DIAS PARISH

Matriz NS da Conceição de Antônio Dias (8:30-11:45am & 1:30-5pm Tue-Sat, noon-5pm Sun) was de-

signed by Aleijadinho's father, Manuel Francisco Lisboa, and built between 1727 and 1770. Note the eagle with downturned head and the Virgin Mary surrounded by cherubs: both stand atop images of the moon, symbolizing the Christians' domination of the Moors. Aleijadinho is buried by the altar of Boa Morte.

The **Museu do Aleijadinho** in the adjoining sacristy displays beautiful works by Aleijadinho and other 18th-century masters.

Nearby is the abandoned mine, Encardadeira or **Mina do Chico-Rei** (Rua Dom Silvério 108; admission R$10; 8am-5pm). There's little to see as you stoop through the low passageways, but it's the perfect place to meditate on the fascinating story of Chico-Rei (see opposite).

SANTA EFIGÊNIA PARISH

The **Igreja de Santa Efigênia dos Pretos** (8:30am-4:30pm Tue-Sun), built between 1742 and 1749 by and for the Black slave community, sits atop a steep hill east of town. Santa Efigênia, patron saint of the church, was the queen of Nubia, and the featured saints – Santo Antônio do Nolo and São Benedito – are Black. The slaves prayed to these images that they wouldn't be crushed in the mines. Despite its relative lack of gold ornamentation, the church is very rich in artwork. The altar is by Aleijadinho's master, Francisco Javier do Briton, and the exterior image of NS do Rosário is by Aleijadinho himself. The church was financed by gold extracted from Chico-Rei's mine. Slaves contributed to the church coffers by washing their gold-flaked hair in baptismal fonts, or smuggling gold powder under fingernails and inside tooth cavities

Ouro Prêto's oldest chapel, built between 1701 and 1704, is the **Capela do Padre Faria** (8:30am-4:30pm Tue-Sun) at the far eastern edge of town. Named after one of the original *bandeirantes*, Padre Faria, this chapel is set behind a triple-branched papal cross (1756) representing the temporal, spiritual and material powers of the Pope. Because of poor documentation, the artists here are anonymous.

OTHER SIGHTS

In the early 18th century, local residents built numerous **oratories** (glass-encased niches containing images of saints) on street corners around town, to keep evil spirits at bay. Of

CHICO-REI

Brazil's first abolitionist was Chico-Rei, an African tribal king. In the early 1700s, amid the frenzy of the gold rush, an entire tribe, king and all, was captured in Africa, sent to Brazil and sold to a mine owner in Ouro Prêto.

The king, Chico-Rei, worked as the foreman of the slave miners. Working Sundays and holidays, he finally bought his freedom from the slave master, then freed his son Osmar. Together, father and son liberated the entire tribe.

This collective then bought the fabulously wealthy Encardadeira gold mine, and Chico-Rei assumed his royal functions once again, holding court in Vila Rica and celebrating African holidays in traditional costume. News of this reached the Portuguese king, who immediately prohibited slaves from purchasing their freedom. Chico-Rei is now a folk hero among Brazilian Blacks.

the few that remain, there's one on Rua dos Paulistas, another on Rua Antônio Dias, and the most famous of all, the **Oratório Vira-Saia**, at the corner of Ladeira de Santa Efigênia and Rua Barão do Ouro Branco.

Launched in 2005, Ouro Prêto's *Museu Aberto/Cidade Viva* program invites you to keep your eyes open at every turn, treating the entire city as an open-air museum. Informative **historical plaques** have been placed on 150 houses around town to heighten visitors' curiosity and expand their knowledge of the city's treasures.

Now the seat of the municipal government, **Tomás Antônio Gonzaga's house** (Rua do Ouvidor 9) is where Gonzaga and the other Inconfidêntes conspired to put an end to Portuguese rule in Brazil.

Built in 1769, the **Teatro Municipal** (Rua Brigadeiro Musqueira; concerts US$2-15; ✆ noon-6pm) is the oldest theater in Minas Gerais. Under renovation at the time of writing, it's expected to reopen in 2008.

Tours

Official city guides (R$60 for four-hour tours, R$120 for eight hours for up to 10 people) are available at the tourist office (see p242). The office also organizes treks and horseback rides into the surrounding hills. Beware of unofficial guides, as there are some nasty characters hanging around.

Festivals & Events

Semana Santa (Holy Week) processions in Ouro Prêto are quite a spectacle (see p246).

The Congado is to Minas what Candomblé is to Bahia and Macumba is to Rio: the local expression of Afro-Christian syncretism. The major **Congado celebrations** are for NS do Rosário (October 23 to 25, at the Capela do Padre Faria), for the New Year and for May 13 (the anniversary of abolition).

You'd also be wise to reserve accommodations in July, when a month-long annual **winter festival** is held.

Ouro Prêto reclaims the symbolic role of state capital once a year, on **Tiradentes Day**, April 21.

Sleeping
BUDGET
Pousada São Francisco (✆ 3551 3456; www.pousadasao franciscodepaula.com.br; Rua Padre José Marcos Penna 202; dm/s/d/tr R$25/40/60/90; 🖳) Set in a 50,000-sq-m garden full of chirping birds, this hostel-like pousada has great views, a friendly multilingual staff and a guest kitchen. The two private upstairs rooms (R$20 to R$30 extra) are nicest. From the bus station, walk five minutes downhill toward Igreja São Francisco de Paula and follow the signs. If you pass the church you've missed the turn. Late-night arrivals should phone from the bus station for an escort – it's close, but impossible to see in the pitch dark.

Albergue de Juventude Brumas Hostel (✆ 3551 2944; www.brumashostel.com.br; Ladeira São Francisco de Paula 68; dm/d HI members R$25/60, nonmembers R$30/70; 🖳) Just a few meters downhill from Pousada São Francisco, this HI-affiliated hostel also has clean rooms, great views and a friendly, multilingual staff. Amenities include a guest kitchen and TV room with fireplace.

Pousada Vila Rica (✆ 3551 4729; pousada@antiga .com.br; Rua Felipe dos Santos 165; s/d/tr R$40/70/90) The beds are a bit tatty, and it's a trek uphill to the center of town, but the 250-year-old Villa Rica still retains some historical charm, with high ceilings, pretty wood floors and a façade covered in blue and white *azulejos* (Portuguese tiles).

MINAS GERAIS

MIDRANGE

Pouso do Chico Rei (☎ 3551 1274; www.pousodochico rei.com.br; Rua Brigadeiro Musqueira 90; s/d/tr/q from R$55/ 88/143/176; 🖵) The best midrange pousada in Ouro Preto, Chico Rei occupies a beautifully preserved 18th-century mansion in the heart of town and has a long tradition of receiving famous guests (see the photos in the lobby). Each room is unique, and most have antique furniture and fabulous views. The two least expensive rooms share a bath. Owners speak French and some English.

Pousada Nello Nuno (☎ 3551 3375; www.pousada nellonuno.com; Rua Camilo de Brito 59; s/d/tr R$70/98/129) In a quiet location just northeast of Praça Tiradentes, this family-run pousada is highly recommended. It has clean and airy *apartamentos* with lots of artwork around a cute courtyard. French and English spoken.

Pousada Toledo (☎ 3551 3366; toledo@ouropreto .com.br; Rua Conselheiro Quintiliano 395; s/d/tr/q R$119/ 132/165/180) Rooms at this pousada are furnished with antiques and beautiful hand-sewn quilts. Ask for a room in the back to avoid the street noise.

Casa Grande (☎ 3551 4314; www.hotelpousadacasa grande.com.br; Rua Conselheiro Quintiliano 96; s/d R$120/135, ste d/tr R$175/220; 🖵) Casa Grande's rooms are spacious, and the pricier suites have balconies with great views of town.

TOP END

Grande Hotel Ouro Prêto (☎ 3551 1488; www.hotelouro preto.com.br; Rua Senador Rocha Lagoa 164; s/d R$145/178, with views R$211/253; 🕿) Oscar Niemeyer's Grande Hotel is not as nice to look *at* as it is to look *from*. Very central, with a pool and bar area overlooking the town, it's the only modernist structure for miles and something of an eyesore.

Pousada do Mondego (☎ 3551 2040; www.mondego .com.br; Largo de Coimbra 38; s/d from R$202/252, deluxe ste R$506; 🖵) This classy inn with close-up views of Igreja de São Francisco de Assis belongs to the exclusive international network Hotels de Charme. The 18th-century colonial mansion features period furnishings, fine artwork and outstanding service.

Solar da Opera (☎ 3551 6844; Rua Direita 75; www .hotelsolardaopera.com.br; s/d from R$232/261, ste R$350; 🕵 🖵) A few steps down from Praça Tiradentes, this is a historic building replete with modern amenities, including broadband internet in every room, hydromassage tubs in the pricier suites and sound-reducing double windows in the rooms facing busy Rua Direita.

Eating
QUICK EATS

Ouro Prêto's endless labyrinth of hills, cobblestone streets, museums and churches can

---

SEMANA SANTA IN OURO PRÊTO

Semana Santa (Holy Week) is celebrated all over Brazil, but Ouro Prêto's festivities are especially dazzling. For four days, the town becomes a giant stage, starting with Thursday night's ceremonial washing of feet and the deposition of Christ from a giant cross in front of Igreja de São Francisco on Good Friday.

The most wonderful event is saved for the wee hours preceding Easter Sunday. Around midnight Saturday, locals begin opening bags of colored sawdust on street corners all over town, unleashing an all-night public art project in which 3km of Ouro Prêto's cobblestoned streets are covered with fanciful designs, a giant carpet marking the route for the following morning's Easter processions. Until the early 1960s, Ouro Prêto observed the old Portuguese tradition of decorating Easter parade routes with flowers and leaves. More recently, colored scraps of leather, sand, coffee grounds, and sawdust have become the media of choice for these *tapetes coloridos* (colored carpets).

Tourists are welcome to participate in laying out the designs, but be prepared for a late night. Things really don't get going until well after midnight. Music and general merrymaking erupt unpredictably all night long, and a few stragglers stick around till dawn to put finishing touches on Praça Tiradentes, the last spot cleared of vehicle traffic. If you prefer your beauty rest, go to bed early Saturday evening, then wake up at 5am Sunday to see the magic that's unfolded while you slept. It's like awakening to a technicolor snowfall!

The designs – some religious, some profane – change every year and only last a few short hours. Within moments of the procession's passing, the public-works crew is out in force with brooms and shovels to clean the streets, until next year.

MINAS GERAIS

wear you out in a hurry. Recharging your batteries is easy, thanks to the city's many snack spots.

Chocolates Ouro Preto (☎ 3551 7330; Rua Getúlio Vargas 66; snacks from R$4; ☼ 9am-7pm Mon-Tue, to 10pm Wed-Sun) A popular spot for hot chocolate and other sinful indulgences, between Rua São José and the Igreja do Rosário.

Café e Livraria Cultural (☎ 3551 3239; Rua Cláudio Manuel 15; snacks from R$4; ☼ 9am-7pm) Tucked away just below the tourist office, this little café with exposed stone walls has simple food, fancy coffee drinks and a clean, relaxed feel. A good place to pore over the map and get your bearings.

Beijinho Doce (☎ 3551 2774; Rua Direita 134; cakes from R$5; ☼ 11:30am-10pm) A half block downhill from Praça Tiradentes, this coffee shop and bakery is perfect for a sweet or savory snack between museums.

BUDGET
Many of Ouro Prêto's eateries are clustered along lively Rua Direita and Rua São José.

Sabor de Minas (☎ 3551 7455; Rua São José 214; per kg R$12.90, pizza from R$10; ☼ 11:30am-3pm & 4:30pm-midnight) Sabor Minas has a varied menu and some of the best prices in town; meals are from R$17. Its *picanha na pedra* (tri-tip steak grilled on a stone) is especially recommended; plates are large enough to share.

Café e Cia (☎ 3551 1901; Rua São José 187; per kg R$14.99; ☼ noon-4pm & 6-11pm) An old favorite with an airy back seating area overlooking the creek. The self-service lunch focuses on Mineiro fare, while dinner (from R$12) includes Italian food and grilled meats.

Maximus (☎ 9914 1209; Rua Direita 151; per kg R$19.90; ☼ 11:30am-5pm Sun-Thu, to 11:30pm Fri & Sat) One of the best per-kilo places, with an upstairs dining area; very popular with locals.

Adega Ouro Prêto (☎ 3551 4171; Rua Teixeira Amaral 24; all-you-can-eat lunch R$10; ☼ 11:30am-4pm daily, plus 6pm-midnight Wed-Sat) The cozy, cavelike Adega is a great deal at lunchtime and also serves reasonable pizza four nights a week.

Quinto do Ouro (☎ 3552 2633; Rua Direita 76; per kg R$23.90; ☼ 11am-3pm Tue-Sun) Prices are higher than at other per kilo restaurants, but the quality and variety of the Mineiro food, including meat grilled to order, is superb.

MIDRANGE
Janela do Rosário (☎ 3551 3132; Rua Gabriel Santos 16; soups, salads & sandwiches R$10-15; ☼ 5-11pm) This sweet little restaurant with candlelit tables on the cobblestones overlooking Igreja do Rosário serves salads, sandwiches and some creative vegetarian and fish offerings. Dinner is R$25. There's live music on weekends.

Chalet dos Caldos (☎ 3551 3992; Rua Carlos Tomaz 33; mains R$14-25; ☼ 7pm-late Tue-Sun) This rustic spot with beautiful stone walls serves delicious soup and local dishes large enough to share.

O Passo (☎ 3552 5089; Rua São José 56; dinner R$22; ☼ noon-late) In a lovely historical building, this restaurant has intimate candlelit rooms with marbled walls; outside, the relaxed terrace overlooking the Casa de Contos is ideal for an after-dinner drink. Everything's superb – pizza, pasta, salads and the wine list!

Deguste (☎ 3551 6363; Rua Coronel Alves 15; all-you-can-eat lunch R$21; ☼ noon-11:30pm) Deguste has a 26-item lunchtime buffet; the á la carte evening menu focuses on fish and meat entrées, accompanied by live music on weekends. Dinner costs from R$24.

TOP END
Café Geraes (☎ 3551 5097; Rua Direita 122; meals from R$25; ☼ 11am-late) Well-heeled students and artists favor this trendy spot to sip wine, talk shop and linger over creative offerings such as *salada mineira* (greens with Minas cheese and basil ice cream) or salmon with crunchy cinnamon crust.

Bené da Flauta (☎ 3551 1036; Rua São Francisco de Assis 32; meals from R$28; ☼ noon-midnight Tue-Sat, to 5pm Sun) Directly below Igreja de São Francisco, this place occupies two levels of a gorgeous colonial *sobrado* (mansion). The open, airy atmosphere, the views and the wine list nicely complement the trout, salmon and Mineiro specialties.

Restaurant Casa Do Ouvidor (☎ 3551 2141; Rua Direita 42; dinner with drinks R$40; ☼ 11am-3pm & 7-10pm) Just downhill from Praça Tiradentes, Ouvidor has garnered numerous awards for its *comida mineira* (typical cuisine of Minas Gerais) entrees. Be prepared for a crowded room, and definitely come with an empty stomach – portions are immense.

Drinking
Students assemble in Praça Tiradentes at night and on weekends. Follow them – or your own ears – to the spontaneous music pouring from bars and buskers along nearby Rua Direita.

MINAS GERAIS

Bardobeco (☎ 3551 1429; Travessa do Arieira 15; ⏰ 6pm-late) This spirited bar has more than 40 brands of *cachaça* – beware! You can ask for *meia doses* (half shots served at half price) if you want to retain some semblance of sobriety while you sample. There are also creative *caipirinhas* (the unofficial national cocktail made from limes, sugar, ice and high-proof sugarcane alcohol; try the *tangerina do beco*), tasty snacks and live music.

Acaso 85 (☎ 3551 2397; Largo do Rosário 85; ⏰ 6:30pm-late Tue-Sun) This bar, with live music and a large selection of whiskey and other drinks, attracts a late-night crowd. The stone walls and high ceilings impart a medieval feeling to the split-level building.

Getting There & Away
BUS
Long-distance buses leave from Ouro Prêto's main **bus station** (☎ 3559 3225; Rua Padre Rolim 661) at the northwest end of town. During peak periods, buy your tickets a day in advance. Destinations include Belo Horizonte (Pássaro Verde, R$17, two hours, 10 daily from 6am to 8pm); Rio de Janeiro (Útil, R$57, 6½ hours, daily at 10pm); São Paulo (Vale do Ouro, R$88, 10 hours, 7:30am daily, plus night bus with varying schedule); São João del Rei (Vale do Ouro, R$40, 3½ hours, daily at 7:30am); Santa Bárbara (Pássaro Verde, R$18, three hours, 7:25am and 1:45pm daily); Brasilia (Pássaro Verde, R$100, 11 hours, 7:30pm daily).

To get to Mariana or Minas de Passagem, catch a local Transcotta bus (R$2.20, at least twice hourly) from the local bus stop just northeast of Praça Tiradentes.

TRAIN
A newly-renovated historic tourist train runs on weekends between Ouro Prêto and Mariana (one hour, R$18/30 one-way/round trip), leaving Ouro Prêto's **train station** (☎ 3551 7705; Praça Cesário Alvim 102) at 11am and 4pm Friday to Sunday, returning at 9am and 2pm from Mariana. The 18km journey is pretty but slow, snaking along a river gorge the whole way.

Getting Around
The town is hilly, but you can go everywhere on foot. A small bus (R$1) circulates between the bus station and Capela do Padre Faria on the eastern side of town, making various stops along the way.

AROUND OURO PRÊTO
Minas de Passagem
This old **gold mine** (☎ 3557 5000; minadapassagem @bol.com.br; admission R$17; ⏰ 9am-5pm Mon-Tue, to 5:30 Wed-Sun) is a kick, starting with the descent underground in a rickety antique cable-car.

The mandatory guided tour, in English or French upon request, covers the mine's history and local gold-extraction methods. Opened in 1719, the mine was worked by Black slaves, many of whom died dynamiting into the rock. There's a shrine to dead miners at the bottom, plus a shallow, crystal-clear 2km-wide subterranean lake, where you can swim if you can handle the 16°C to 18°C (61°F to 65°F) water temperature.

The mine is between Ouro Prêto and Mariana. Take any local bus running between the two (R$2.20 from Ouro Prêto, R$1.40 from Mariana) and ask the driver to let you off at Minas de Passagem.

MARIANA
☎ 0xx31 / pop 42,000 / elevation 712m
Lovely Mariana, founded in 1711, is graced with fine colonial architecture and two of Minas' prettiest squares. Since it's only 14km from Ouro Prêto, Mariana can be used as a base to explore both cities. Its compact historical center is easier to navigate than Ouro Prêto's, not only because of its smaller size, but also because the hills are less steep. The ground floors of many historic mansions have been transformed into stores, boutiques and artists' workshops where you're invited to wander at will.

Information
INTERNET ACCESS
Mundo Virtual Lan House (☎ 3557 3307; Praça da Sé 52; per hr R$2.50; ⏰ 9am-9pm) has relatively fast connections and Skype service.

MONEY
Banco do Brasil and Itaú both have ATMs on the downhill side of Praça da Sé.

POST
The post office is on Rua Padre Gonçalves Lopes, just below Praça da Sé.

TOURIST INFORMATION
Mariana's **tourist information office** (☎ 3557 9044; Praça Tancredo Neves; ⏰ 9am-5pm) is in the Terminal

Turistico building just outside the historic center, near the river where the bus from Ouro Prêto stops.

Sights

All the sights are close together. Two blocks uphill from the tourist information office and the Ouro Prêto bus stop, Praça Minas Gerais boasts one of the state's nicest arrangements of public buildings on a single square. **Igreja São Francisco de Assis** (☺ 9am-5pm) is the final resting place of the painter Ataíde – Aleijadinho's partner – and 94 other lucky souls. **Igreja NS do Carmo** (☺ 9am-4pm) was severely damaged by fire in 1999 but has now been reopened.

One block downhill from Praça Minas Gerais, leafy **Praça Gomes Freire** is a gorgeous place to sit and watch the world go by, with a pond, a gazebo and park benches shaded by grand old trees.

Doubling back downhill, the **Museu Arquidiocesano de Arte Sacra** (☎ 3557 2516; Rua Frei Durão 49; ☺ 9am-noon & 1:30-5pm Tue-Sun) has sculptures by Aleijadinho, paintings by Ataíde, and other religious objects. **Catedral Basílica da Sé** (Praça Cláudio Manuel; ☺ 8am-6pm Tue-Sun), with its fantastic German organ dating from 1701, holds **organ concerts** (admission R$12; ☺ 11am Fri, 12:15pm Sun).

At the top of town is the **Basílica de São Pedro dos Clérigos** (Rua Dom Silvério; ☺ 9am-4pm), which was never completed. There's a great view from the elevated site.

While walking through the old part of town, you'll come across artists at work in their studios. Especially interesting are the **Ateliê do Oratório** (☎ 9916 1558; Praça Gomes Freire 48), tucked into a grassy courtyard down an inviting side alley off Praça Gomes Freire, where beautiful oratories and other antique-inspired religious art are created; and the **Catin Nardi Puppet Theater** (☎ 3557 3927; Rua Do Seminário 290; ☺ 10am-8pm), where you can see new puppets under construction, plus old ones that have appeared on Brazilian national TV miniseries.

To witness some modern-day **gold mining**, head for the *garimpo* (mining camp), just across Mariana's last bridge at Carmo Creek, a short walk from town. Look upstream and you'll see people digging and panning.

Sleeping

Hotel Central (☎ 3557 1630; Rua Frei Durão 8; s/d/tr/q R$28/50/69/88) The drab Hotel Central's only selling point is the low price for its attractive location.

Hotel Providência (☎ 3557 1444; www.hotelprovidencia.com.br; Rua Dom Silveiro 233; s/d/tr/q R$55/99/140/170; ⌨ ☒) This welcoming hotel is colonial Mariana's best value. Guest rooms in the 1849 building are airy and inviting, with clean white sheets, lovely high ceilings and internet connections. It shares a swimming pool with the Catholic school next door.

Pousada Gamarano (☎ 3557 1835; www.pousadagamarano.com.br; Rua Raimundo Gamarano 1; s/d R$50/100) If you don't mind a long uphill trek, this place rewards you with outstanding views and beautiful furniture designed by the owner.

Pouso da Typographia (☎ 3557 1577; Praça Gomes Freire 220; s/d R$75/130) It's worth staying here just to see the antique printing presses in the foyer. The wonderful central location on Mariana's prettiest square can't be beat, although front rooms get noisy on the weekends.

Pousada Solar dos Correa (☎ 3557 2080; www.pousadasolardoscorrea.com.br; Rua Direita 124; s/d R$70/120) Close to the Ouro Prêto train and bus stops, Pousada Solar features nice airy apartments in an 18th-century colonial mansion.

Eating

Vagão Bonomi (Estaçao Ferroviária; sandwiches R$9; ☺ 9am-5pm) A fun place for a snack, housed in a train car at Mariana's railway station.

Gaveteiros (☎ 3557 2273; Praça da Sé 26; per kg R$13.90; ☺ 10:30am-9pm) Centrally located Gaveteiros offers self-serve till 3pm, then pizza, pasta and Mineiro food into the evening. Dinner costs from R$11.

Lua Cheia (☎ 3557 3232; Rua Dom Viçoso 23; per kg R$14.80; ☺ 11am-3pm daily & 6-8pm Tue-Fri & Sun) Mariana's best per-kilo place, just a few steps from lovely Praça Gomes Freire.

O Rancho (☎ 3558 1060; Praça Gomes Freire 108; meals from R$12; ☺ 11am-3pm & 6:30pm-midnight) Cozy and welcoming, O Rancho has earned a loyal following among locals and visitors alike for its hearty Mineiro fare. There are always several pots of delicious soup bubbling on the wood-fired stove, plus pizzas for those needing a break from rice and beans.

Dom Silvério (☎ 3557 2475; Praça Gomes Freire 242; pizza from R$12; ☺ 6.30pm-midnight) has been serving up tasty pizza in the historic center for almost two decades.

Drinking

Deservedly popular for its wide selection of drinks and homemade snacks, **Bar Scotch & Art** (Praça Minas Gerais 57; snacks from R$5; ☺ 6:30pm-2am

MINAS GERAIS

Tue-Sun), a new addition to Mariana's late-night scene, is a wonderful place to while away the evening, with cozy indoor seating plus a slate terrace overlooking lovely Praça Minas Gerais.

Getting There & Away

There are regular Transcotta buses between Ouro Prêto and Mariana (R$2.20, 35 minutes, twice hourly from 6.30am to 11pm). In Mariana, the bus stop is across from the tourist information office on Praça Tancredo Neves.

Mariana's long-distance bus station, Rodovia dos Inconfidêntes, is located at km72, on the edge of town. Destinations served include Belo Horizonte, Rio de Janeiro and São Paulo. The Transcotta bus from Ouro Prêto also stops here en route to downtown Mariana.

Mariana's picturesque peach-and-white-colored train station is just two blocks away from the local bus stop for buses to Ouro Prêto. Trains leave Mariana for Ouro Prêto at 9am and 2pm Friday to Sunday and holidays. There's a restaurant and museum to keep you happy while you wait.

LAVRAS NOVAS

☎ 0xx31 / pop 1000 / elevation 1400m

Lavras Novas, named for the new gold strikes discovered here in 1704, sits on a high plateau 17km from Ouro Prêto. Surrounded by wide-open mountain scenery, its cobblestone main street runs between colorful single-storey houses to the town's focal point, the **Igreja NS dos Prazeres**. Lavras has seen a rapid influx of tourism over the past decade, and on busy weekends it sometimes feels like outsiders outnumber the locals. For a better understanding of the town's history and a taste of its traditional off-the-beaten-path tranquility, it pays to visit Lavras Novas midweek and stay a while.

Activities

You can ride or trek to several nearby waterfalls: **Três Pingos** and **Namorados** are the most popular. For horseback tours or riding lessons, contact Júlio Montresor at **Tropa da Taberna** (☎ 3554 2040; galocamp@terra.com.br; R$40 to R$100, depending on itinerary). Several tour companies around town offer guided hikes, but prices can be steep. An alternative resource for independent hikers is the free trail-map distributed at Pousada Palavras Novas.

Sleeping & Eating

Pousadas are generally empty during the week, but reservations are advisable on weekends and holidays.

Serra do Luar (☎ 3554 2021; www.lavrasnovas.com.br/serradoluar; Rua NS dos Prazeres 119; s/d R$40/60) Run by locals, this is one of the oldest establishments in town. Serra do Luar offers simple *apartamentos* in rustic cabins, and the onsite restaurant serves very inexpensive Mineiro food.

Palavras Novas (☎ 3554 2025; www.pousadapalavrasnovas.com.br; Rua NS dos Prazeres 1110; s/d from R$125; 🖳) With a heated pool and nice mountain views, Palavras Novas caters to a more luxury-minded crowd. The pousada leads group hikes every weekend.

Taberna Casa Antiga e Chalés Galo do Campo (☎ 3554 2040; www.tabernacasaantiga.kit.net; Rua Alto do Campo 213; full board s/d R$120, r with fireplace from R$150-170; 🕙 10am-midnight) At the edge of town, this cozy bar and restaurant (meals from R$20) has a fireplace, live music and a varied menu. Nestled among trees next door are several cute chalets with views of horse pastures and mountains. Chalet rates include breakfast and lunch at the Taberna.

Getting There & Away

Local buses to Lavras Novas (R$5, one hour) leave from in front of the Ouro Prêto train station (not the bus station) daily at 6:40am, 2pm and 5pm, returning daily at 5:45am, 10am and 3pm. Of the 17km to Lavras Novas, 9km is unpaved; it's scenic, despite the bumps!

SABARÁ

☎ 0xx31 / pop 108,000 / elevation 723m

Sabará, 25km southeast of Belo, is filled with houses, mansions, churches, statues, fountains and sacred art, all dating from the town's 18th-century glory days when it was Minas' first major gold-mining center and one of the world's wealthiest cities. In the boom years, when the Rio das Velhas was 15 times wider, boats would sail all the way up the Rio São Francisco from Bahia. Sabará produced more gold in one week than the rest of Brazil produced in a year.

Nowadays Sabará is a poor town dominated by a Belgian metalworks. Since it's only 30 minutes by bus from Belo, it makes an easy and interesting day trip. Don't bother visiting on a Monday – all sites are closed.

There's an information booth at the entrance to town, but major attractions are easy to find, since there are signposts at Praça Santa Rita telling where everything is.

Sights

Most of the churches, museums and other colonial attractions charge admission fees of R$1 or R$2.

A testament to the wealth of bygone days, Sabará's elegant opera house, **O Teatro Imperial** (Rua Dom Pedro II; 8am-noon & 1-5pm Tue-Sun), was built in 1770. It has crystal lamps and three tiers of carved bamboo seats.

Housed in an old gold foundry (1730), the **Museu do Ouro** (Rua da Intendência; admission US$1.50; noon-5:00pm Tue-Sun) houses art and artifacts of Sabará's glory years.

The triple-naved **Matriz de NS de Conceição** (Praça Getúlio Vargas; 9am-noon & 2-5pm, closed Mon), finished in 1720, is a fascinating blend of Asian arts and Portuguese baroque, with gold leaf, red Chinese scrolls and pagodas on the sanctuary door panels.

A riot of gold, red and blue, the diminutive **Igreja de NS do Ó** (Largo NS do Ó; 9am-noon & 2-5pm Tue-Sun) is one of Minas's little gems. Dedicated to the Virgin Mary in her role as protector of pregnant women and those praying for fertility, it also features many Oriental details.

The half-built **Igreja de NS do Rosário dos Pretos** (Praça Melo Viana; 8-11am & 1-5pm) – started and financed by slaves but never finished – now stands as a memorial to the abolition of slavery in 1888.

Aleijadinho was instrumental in the decoration of the **Igreja NS do Carmo** (Rua de Carmo; 9-11:30am, closed Mon). His touch is everywhere, especially in the faces of São Simão and São João da Cruz.

Getting There & Away

The Cisne company runs buses to Sabará (R$2.35, 30 minutes, every 15 minutes from 5am to 11pm) from the local section behind Belo's main bus station. Return buses leave the bus stop on Av Victor Fantini in Sabará; you can also catch one on the road out of town.

CONGONHAS

☎ 0xx31 / pop 42,000 / elevation 871m

This small industrial town has been saved from complete obscurity by the beautiful, brooding presence of Aleijadinho's extraordinary *Prophets* at the Basílica do Bom Jesus de Matosinhos. The dramatic statues almost seem to be performing a balletic dance and it's a wondrous experience to be able to walk freely among them. They are Aleijadinho's masterpiece and Brazil's most famed work of art. It's worth taking the trouble to get to Congonhas just to see them.

Congonhas is 72km south of Belo Horizonte, 3km off Hwy BR-040. The city grew up with the search for gold in the nearby Rio Maranhão, and the economy today is dominated by iron mining in the surrounding countryside.

Sights

Already an old man, sick and crippled, Aleijadinho sculpted *The Prophets* between 1800 and 1805. Symmetrically placed in front of the **Basílica do Bom Jesus de Matosinhos**, each of the 12 Old Testament figures was carved from one or two blocks of soapstone. Each carries a Latin message: some are hopeful prophecies, others warn of the end of the world.

Much has been written about these sculptures – their dynamic quality, the sense of movement (much like a Hindu dance or a ballet), how they complement each other and how their arrangement prevents them from being seen in isolation. The poet Carlos Drummond de Andrade wrote that the dramatic faces and gestures are 'magnificent, terrible, grave and tender' and commented on 'the way the statues, of human size, appear to be larger than life as they look down upon the viewer with the sky behind them.'

Before working on *The Prophets*, Aleijadinho carved (or supervised his assistants in carving) the wooden statues that were placed in the six little **chapels** below. The chapels themselves – also of Aleijadinho's design – and their placement on the sloping site are superb. The way the light falls on the pale sculpted domes against the dark mountain backdrop is truly beautiful.

Each chapel depicts a scene from Christ's Passion, and several portray Jesus with a red mark on his neck. While little is known of Aleijadinho's politics, some local historians interpret this to mean that Aleijadinho intended to draw parallels between the martyred Christ and slain independence fighter Tiradentes. Aleijadinho's sculptures of Roman soldiers lend support to this theory – they all have two left feet and sport ankle boots, a shoe style favored by the colonizing Portuguese.

Festivals & Events

Held September 7 to 14, the **Jubileu do Senhor Bom Jesus do Matosinhos** is one of Minas' great religious festivals. Every year approximately 600,000 pilgrims arrive at the church to make promises, do penance, receive blessings, and give and receive alms. **Holy Week** processions in Congonhas are also famous, especially the dramatizations on Good Friday.

Sleeping & Eating

It's possible to catch an early bus into Congonhas and another one out that same afternoon. Since there's little to see beyond Aleijadinho's artwork, most people don't spend the night. One pleasure of staying over is the opportunity to see the statues in the early-morning light, when they're especially beautiful.

Colonial Hotel (☎ 3731 1834; Praça da Basílica 76; s/d R$50/85) Conveniently situated right across the street from Aleijadinho's masterpieces, the Colonial still wears faded remnants of its former glory in the huge hallways and immensely high ceilings. Most rooms are spacious and the bathrooms surprisingly modern.

Max Mazza (☎ 3731 1970; www.hotelmaxmazza .br; Av Júlia Kubitschek 410; s/d R$42/87) A 15-minute walk from the *Prophets* (all uphill), Max Mazza is a basic but appealing option.

Mineiro food reigns supreme in Congonhas; there's not too much variety in the town's restaurants. The most convenient option for day trippers is **Cova do Daniel** (☎ 3731 1834; Praça da Basílica 76; meals R$15; ❍ 11am-8pm Sun-Thu, to 10pm Fri & Sat) in the basement of the Colonial Hotel. Other eateries are clustered in the industrial center near Av Júlia Kubitschek.

Getting There & Away

Congonhas is on the direct bus route between Belo Horizonte and São João del Rei, so these two towns make the best starting points for a day trip. Viacão Sandra serves this route several times daily (R$16, 90 minutes from Belo Horizonte; R$19, two hours from São João).

Ouro Prêto and Congonhas are very close to each other as the crow flies, but unfortunately there's no direct bus. The best transfer point is Ouro Branco, which is midway between the two towns, but unpredictable connections can lead to some long and frustrating delays. From Ouro Prêto to Ouro Branco, Vale do Ouro buses leave at 7:30am, noon and 6pm, returning at 9:30am, 11am and 4:25pm (R$8, one hour). Onward buses between Ouro Branco and Congonhas leave every two hours or so.

ALEIJADINHO

Antônio Francisco Lisboa (1738–1814), known worldwide today as Aleijadinho (Little Cripple), was the son of a Portuguese architect and a Black slave. His nickname was given to him sometime in the 1770s, when the artist began to suffer from a terrible, debilitating disease. It might have been syphilis or possibly leprosy – either way, he lost his fingers and toes and the use of his lower legs.

Undaunted, Aleijadinho strapped hammers and chisels to his arms and continued working, advancing the art in his country from the excesses of the baroque to a finer, more graceful form known as Barroco Mineiro.

Mineiros have reason to be proud of Aleijadinho – he is a figure of international prominence in the history of art. He studied European baroque and rococo traditions through pictures, but went on to develop his own unique style, using only native materials like soapstone and wood. Aleijadinho's angels have his stylistic signature: wavy hair, wide-open eyes and big, round cheeks.

For many years Manuel da Costa Ataíde, from nearby Mariana, successfully collaborated with Aleijadinho on many churches. Aleijadinho would sculpt the exterior and a few interior pieces, and Ataíde would paint the interior panels. With his secretly concocted vegetable dyes, Ataíde fleshed out many of Aleijadinho's creations

Aleijadinho was buried in the Matriz NS da Conceição, within 50 paces of his birth site. He was named patron of Brazilian arts by federal decree in 1973. *The Prophets* in Congonhas, the Igreja de São Francisco de Assis and the facade of the Igreja de NS do Carmo, both in Ouro Prêto, were all carved by Aleijadinho, as were innumerable relics in Mariana, Sabará, Tiradentes and São João del Rei. The best places to see Aleijadinho's work are Congonhas, Ouro Prêto, Sabará and São João del Rei.

Getting Around

The bus station is on Av Júlia Kubitschek, across town from the sites of interest. From here the Basílica buses leave every half-hour to 40 minutes and cost R$1. It's a 15-minute ride up the hill to the basilica and *The Prophets*. For the best approach and first view of the statues, get off just after the bus passes the church (as it heads downhill). The same bus returns you to the bus station, or you can have the Colonial Hotel staff call you a taxi (R$10).

SÃO JOÃO DEL REI

☎ 0xx32 / pop 78,000 / elevation 910m

São João del Rei affords a unique look at a *cidade historica* that didn't suffer a great decline when the gold boom ended in the 1800s. Modern São João has the unselfconscious urban vitality of a modern city, which can come as a welcome contrast to the preserved-in-amber quality of neighboring Tiradentes or some of the other more studiously conserved historical towns. Downtown there are plenty of high-rises and other trappings of 21st-century Brazil, yet around every corner lurk unexpected colonial surprises. The historic city center, which is protected by Brazil's Landmarks Commission, features two good museums, several of the country's finest churches and some gorgeous old mansions – one of which belonged to the late and still-popular never-quite-president Tancredo Neves. Floodlights illuminate the churches every night, adding to the city's aesthetic appeal.

Orientation

São João sits between mountain ridges, near the southern end of the Serra do Espinhaço. The city is bisected by the Rio Lenheiro – really just a glorified creek in a concrete channel. Two lovely 18th-century stone bridges serve as convenient landmarks in the colonial center. The railway station is just east of downtown, while the bus station is an additional 15-minute walk to the northeast.

Information

INTERNET ACCESS

City 10 (Av Andrade Reis 120; ⊙ 8am-10:30pm; per hr R$3) A tight squeeze and only has a few computers, but also close to the old city center.

World Games Lan House (Rua Ministro Gabriel Passos 281; ⊙ 9am-midnight; per hr R$2.50) Just south of Av Tiradentes, next door to Café del Rei.

MONEY

Several ATMs are available in the historic center. Bradesco and Banco do Brasil are at Av Hermilio Alves 200 and 234; Caixa and Itau are directly across the river at Av Presidente Tancredo Neves 169 and 201.

POST

Post office (Av Tiradentes 500)

TOURIST OFFICES

The **main tourist office** (☎ 3379 2952; Av Hermilio Alves 366B; ⊙ 8am-6pm) is in the train station building, one door down from the Maria Fumaça ticket window. At the time of writing, plans were underway to move the office across the river to the park with bandstand on Av Tancredo Neves, but no certain date was established. There's also tourist information at the bus station.

Sights

Opening times vary widely, as noted below. Monday is not a good day to visit, since most attractions are closed.

IGREJA DE SÃO FRANCISCO DE ASSIS

This 1774 baroque **church** (Rua Padre José Maria Xavier; admission R$2; ⊙ 8am-5:30pm Mon-Sat, 7am-4pm Sun) is exquisite. It's on the south side of the river and faces an elegant lyre-shaped plaza filled with towering palms. Inside the church are two **Aleijadinho sculptures**: the figures of São João Evangelista and São Gonçalo do Amarante in the second altar to the left. The façade, with sculptures of the Immaculate Virgin and angels executed by Francisco Vieira Servas based on Aleijadinho's design, is one of the finest in Minas.

Politician Tancredo Neves is buried in the church graveyard. He was the first elected president after the 1960s-to-'80s period of military dictatorship in Brazil, though he died before he could take office. His grave is something of a pilgrimage site for Brazilians. Follow the arrows painted on the pavement behind the church.

During the 9:15am Mass on Sunday, the local Ribeiro Bastos women's orchestra and choir perform sacred baroque music.

IGREJA DE NS DO ROSÁRIO

This simple **church** (⊙ 8-11am Tue-Sun) was built in 1719 to honor the patron saint who was protector of the slaves.

MINAS GERAIS

SÃO JOÃO DEL REI

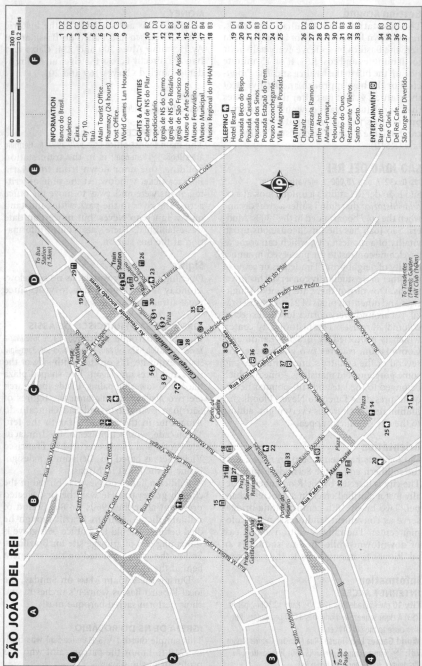

0 — 300 m
0 — 0.2 miles

INFORMATION
Banco do Brasil..................1 D2
Bradesco.........................2 D2
Caixa............................3 C2
City 10..........................4 D2
Itaú.............................5 C1
Main Tourist Office..............6 D1
Pharmacy (24 hours)..............7 C3
Post Office......................8 C3
World Games Lan House............9 C3

SIGHTS & ACTIVITIES
Catedral de NS do Pilar.........10 B2
Expedicionário..................11 D3
Igreja de NS do Carmo...........12 C1
Igreja de NS do Rosário.........13 B3
Igreja de São Francisco de Assis..14 C4
Museu de Arte Sacra.............15 B2
Museu Ferroviário...............16 D2
Museu Municipal.................17 B4
Museu Regional do IPHAN.........18 B3

SLEEPING
Hotel Brasil....................19 D1
Pousada Beco do Bispo...........20 B4
Pousada Casarão.................21 C4
Pousada dos Sinos...............22 B3
Pousada Estação do Trem.........23 D2
Pouso Aconchegante..............24 C1
Villa Magnolia Pousada..........25 C4

EATING
Chafariz........................26 D2
Churrascaria Ramon..............27 B3
Entre Atos......................28 C2
Maria-Fumaça....................29 D1
Pelourinho......................30 D2
Quinto do Ouro..................31 B3
Restaurante Villeiros...........32 B4
Santo Gosto.....................33 B3

ENTERTAINMENT
Bar do Zotti....................34 B3
Cine Glória.....................35 D2
Del Rei Cafe....................36 C3
São Jorge Bar Divertido.........37 C3

MUSEU REGIONAL DO IPHAN

This **museum** (☎ 3371 7663; Rua Marechal Deodoro 12; admission R$1; ☼ 12-5:30pm Tue-Fri, 8am-1pm Sat & Sun) is one of the best in Minas Gerais. It is full of antique furniture and sacred art, and is housed in a colonial mansion that was built around 1859.

MUSEU DE ARTE SACRA

This building served as the public jail between 1737 and 1850. The **museum** (Praça Embaixador Gastão da Cunha 8) – closed indefinitely for renovation at the time of writing – has a small but impressive collection of art from the city's churches.

CATEDRAL DE NS DO PILAR

Begun in 1721, this **church** (☼ 6-10:30am & 1-8pm Tue-Sun) has exuberant gold altars and fine Portuguese tiles. On Wednesday, Thursday and Friday the Lira Sanjoanense, or Coalhada (all-White) orchestra and choir accompany the 7pm Mass.

IGREJA DE NS DO CARMO

This 18th-century **church** (Rua Getúlio Vargas; ☼ 8-noon & 3-7pm), dominating a lovely triangular *praça*, was designed by Aleijadinho, who also did the frontispiece and the sculpture around the door. In the second sacristy is a famous unfinished sculpture of Christ.

Festivals & Events

Someone's always celebrating something in São João. There are literally dozens of festivals, both religious and secular – stop by the tourist office for a full calendar.

Locals boast, credibly, that their **Carnaval** is the best in Minas Gerais, and **Semana Santa** is also quite colorful. The **Semana da Inconfidência**, from April 15 to 21, celebrates Brazil's first independence movement, culminating in a horseback procession between São João and Tiradentes.

Sleeping

Be sure to book ahead in December, when the town is filled with students sitting for exams, and during holidays such as Carnaval and Easter.

BUDGET

Several former budget hotels in the historic center have closed recently, but there are still a couple of good lower-priced options.

Pouso Aconchegante (☎ 3371 2637; Rua Marechal Bittencourt 61; s/d R$15/30) This place offers 10 very simple rooms, all with shared bath, in a family home full of colorful kitsch near the Carmo church.

Hotel Brasil (☎ 3371 2804; Av Presidente Tancredo Neves 395; s/d without breakfast R$20/40) A funky, rambling 19th-century relic with high-ceilinged but slightly shabby rooms, some facing the river; it's a convenient walk from the train station.

MIDRANGE

Pousada Estacão do Trem (☎ 3372 1985; www .pousadaestacaodotrem.com.br; Praça Estação 45; s/d R$50/100) This pousada, right next to the train station, has lovely arched windows and a beautifully decorated lobby. The rooms are a bit small, but the breakfast is abundant.

Pousada dos Sinos (☎ 3371 3867; www.saojoao delreisite.com.br; Av Eduardo Magalhães 106; s/d R$72/100; ☐) This centrally located pousada sits halfway between the two old stone bridges on the south side of the river. The nicest room is No 5, whose veranda overlooks the river and church towers. Interior rooms can be a bit claustrophobic.

Pousada Casarão (☎ 3371 7447; www.pousada casarao.com; Rua Ribeiro Bastos 94; s/d R$70/120; ☒ ☒) In an elegant old mansion behind the Igreja de São Francisco, the Pousada Casarão tastefully blends old with new; many rooms are decorated with antiques, yet all have modern marble-floored bathrooms. The French doors in the breakfast room overlook the pool.

TOP END

Villa Magnolia Pousada (☎ 3373 5065; www.pousada villamagnolia.com.br; Rua Ribeiro Bastos 2; s/d/tr R$105/125/158; deluxe ste R$200; ☒ ☐ ☒) A delightful refuge just across from Igreja de São Francisco, this stylishly renovated 19th-century mansion features pure cotton bedding, oversized towels, spacious rooms, a large pool, shade trees and elegant common areas filled with art books.

Pousada Beco do Bispo (☎ 3371 8844; www.becodo bispo.com.br; Beco do Bispo 93; s/d/tr R$100/150/200; ☒ ☒) Tucked down a peaceful dead-end street a block from Igreja de São Francisco, this pousada has cheerful, cozy rooms and a pool with palm trees.

Eating

BUDGET

Entre Atos (Av Hermilio Alves 146; lunch from R$6.50; ☼ 11am-3pm Tue-Sun, 6pm-late Tue-Sat) Directly adjacent to the Municipal Theater, Entre Atos has a breezy upstairs terrace with wonderful views of the city. Its lunchtime *prato feito* (plate of the day) is a bargain at R$8.50, or R$6.50 for the vegetarian version.

Restaurante Villeiros (Rua Padre José Maria Xavier 132; per kg R$17.90; 🕙 11am-5pm) A fabulous self-serve with great variety near the Igreja de São Francisco, Villeiros is very popular with locals and has a cheerful patio out back.

Chafariz (Rua Quintino Bocáiuva 100; per kg R$17.90, meat only per kg R$30; 🕙 11am-3pm) Chafariz, just behind the train station, is also very popular – it seems half the town is in there for lunch on any given day.

Pelourinho (Rua Hermilio Alves 276; per kg from R$19.90; 🕙 11am-3pm daily, 6-12pm Wed-Sat) Chef Tadeu brings a creative twist to the self-serve concept. On weekends and holidays, he supplements his everyday offerings with gourmet local specialties and adjusts the per-kilo price accordingly.

MIDRANGE & TOP END

Churrascaria Ramon (Praça Severiano Resende 52; meals for 2 R$25-38; 🕙 10am-10pm) Ramon prides itself on perfectly cooked meats and all the traditional Mineiro favorites.

Quinto do Ouro (☎ 3371 7577; Praça Severiano de Resende 4; meals for 2 R$34-47; 🕙 11am-10pm) Regional dishes are served with a lot of attention and flair at Quinto. Many say this is the best Mineiro food in town.

Santo Gosto (☎ 3371 8124; Rua Aureliano Mourão 15; meals from R$30; 🕙 7:30pm-midnight Tue-Sun) This fabulous little place with only four tables is a labor of love for its owner, who specializes in artisanal pastas, risottos and exquisite desserts.

Entertainment

Most of the city's nightlife is on the south side along Av Tiradentes.

Bar do Zotti (Av Tiradentes 805; 🕙 6pm-late) A cozy little place resembling a rustic cabin transplanted into the big city. Lots of people pack in here every night for delicious nibbles, drinks and dancing.

Del Rei Cafe (Av Tiradentes 553; 🕙 5pm-late) This busy corner bar, with numerous sidewalk tables, is great for people-watching. Locals congregate here daily for early evening beers and late-night snacks.

São Jorge Bar Divertido (☎ 3371 2582; Av Balbino da Cunha 18; www.saojorgebardivertido.com.br; 🕙 11pm-5am) Very popular with the 20- to 30-year-old

crowd, who come to dance and flirt the night away to live music.

Cine Gloria (Av Tiradentes 390) This old theater screens multiple films nightly, including many in English with Portuguese subtitles.

Getting There & Away

AIR

In early 2007, **Total Airlines** (☎ 0300 789 6464; www.total.com.br) launched air service from São João del Rei to Rio (R$119) and Belo Horizonte (R$95). The airport is just north of downtown São João.

BUS

The **São João bus station** (☎ 3371 5617; Rua Cristóvão Colombo) is about 1.5km northeast of town.

Direct buses go to Rio, via Petrópolis (Paraibuna bus company, R$51, 5½ hours, 8am and 2pm Monday to Friday, with extra buses on weekends); Belo Horizonte, via Congonhas (Sandra, R$32, 3½ hours, seven daily from 6am to 7pm, with extra buses on Sunday); São Paulo (Gardénia and Vale do Ouro, R$59, 7½ hours, seven daily from 9:20am to 11:20pm); Caxambu (Sandra, R$32, 3½ hours, one daily at 3pm), Ouro Prêto and Mariana (Vale do Ouro, R$40, 3½ to four hours, two daily at 5:30pm and 3:30am – for the early morning bus, buy tickets the day before).

For buses between São João and Tiradentes, see Getting There & Away under Tiradentes (p260).

TRAIN

The wonderful Maria-Fumaça tourist train runs on weekends between São João del Rei and Tiradentes (see opposite).

Getting Around

Local Presidente buses (gray with red letters) run between the bus station (R$1.40, 10 minutes) and the center. The local bus stop in the center is in front of the train station.

The local bus stop is to your left and across the street as you walk out of the bus station, (in front of the Drogaria Americana).

From the main bus station, you have two taxi options – traditional taxis (R$10) or the cool and totally cheap **motorbike taxi** (☎ 3371 6389; R$2.50). Look for the orange Cooperativo Moto Taxi sign to your left as you exit the station. Drivers carry a helmet for the passenger. Use it!

MINAS GERAIS

SMOKING MARY

Sure, there are buses that will get you back and forth between São João del Rei and Tiradentes, but how can they compare to a trip on a 19th-century steam train in pristine condition? Jump aboard as this little engine hisses and belches its way through the winding valley of the Serra de São José, which gradually gets rockier and bleaker as you approach Tiradentes. The trail goes through one of the oldest areas of gold mining in Minas and you'll see the remnants of 18th-century mine workings all around. Keep a sharp eye out for modern *garimpeiros* (gold panners) still hoping to strike it rich.

Built in the 1880s as the textile industry began to take hold in São João, the *Maria-Fumaça* (Smoking Mary) to locals) was one of the first rail lines in Brazil. More history is available at the **Estação Ferroviária** (☎ 3371 8485; Av Hermílio Alves; museum admission R$1; ⏰ 9–11am & 1-5pm Tue-Sun). The trains run out of the same location on Friday, Saturday, Sunday and holidays, leaving São João at 10am and 3pm, returning from Tiradentes at 1pm and 5pm (R$15/25 one-way/round-trip). When leaving São João the best views are on the left side. If you need more time in Tiradentes than the train schedule allows, you can always bus back (there are regular connections between the two cities).

A similar historic train just resumed service between Mariana and Ouro Prêto, with imaginative museums and train-car restaurants greeting visitors at either end of the line. See details in the Getting There & Away section for Ouro Prêto (p248).

TIRADENTES

☎ 0xx32 / pop 6000 / elevation 927m

Perhaps nowhere else in Minas do colonial charm and picturesque natural setting blend so perfectly as in Tiradentes. Quaint historic houses, fringed by exuberant wildflowers, stand out against a backdrop of pretty blue mountains with wonderful hiking trails. If you can, visit midweek, when the town's abundant attractions are most easily appreciated. On weekends, the swarms of visitors who come to gawk at Tiradentes' antique stores and boutiques can make the place feel a bit like a theme park, and the sudden increase in horse-drawn carriages creates some strong aromas!

History

Originally called Arraial da Ponta do Morro (Hamlet on a Hilltop), Tiradentes was renamed to honor the martyred hero of the Inconfidência (see p241), who was born at a nearby farm. In recent years, the town, which sits at the center of a triangle formed by Brazil's three largest cities, has become a magnet for artists and other urban escapees. Today the historic center is home to only a couple dozen original Tiradentes families, intermingled with new arrivals from around the world.

Information & Orientation

Tiradentes' center is a compact and picturesque cluster of cobbled streets and flowery gardens. The town's colonial buildings run up a hillside from the main square, **Largo das Forras**, culminating in the beautiful **Igreja Matriz de Santo Antônio**. From the terrace in front of the church there's a stunning view of the terracotta-tiled colonial houses, the green valley and the towering wall of stone formed by the Serra de São José. For another picture postcard view of town, climb the hill just above the bus station to the grassy square in front of **Igreja de São Francisco de Paula**.

The **Secretária Municipal de Turismo** (☎ 3355 1212; www.tiradentes.mg.gov.br; Rua Resende Costa 71; ⏰ 9am-5:45pm), in the three-story building on the main square, provides maps, plus information on hotels and guided tours.

Broadband internet access, including Skype, is available at **Game Mania Lan House** (☎ 3355 2002; Rua dos Inconfidentes 340A; per hr R$2.50; ⏰ 9am-10:30pm Sun-Fri, 8:30pm Sat).

Sights

IGREJA MATRIZ DE SANTO ANTÔNIO

Named for the town's patron saint, this **church** (admission R$2; ⏰ 9am-5pm) is one of Brazil's most beautiful, and among the last designed by Aleijadinho. Leandro Gonçalves Chaves made the famous sundial out front in 1785.

The all-gold interior is rich in Old Testament symbolism. The polychrome organ was built in Portugal and brought to Tiradentes by donkey in 1798. Also striking are the seven golden phoenixes (symbols of Christ's resurrection), suspending candleholders from long braided chains.

IGREJA NS ROSÁRIO DOS PRETOS

This beautiful stone **church** (Praça Padre Lourival, Rua Direita; admission R$1; ☺ 10am-5pm Tue-Sun), with its many images of Black saints, was built in 1708, by and for slaves. Since they had no free time during daylight hours, construction took place at night – note the nocturnal symbolism in the ceiling paintings of an eight-pointed black star and a half-moon.

MUSEU DO PADRE TOLEDO

This **museum** (Rua Padre Toledo 190; admission R$3; ☺ 9am-5pm Tue-Sun) is dedicated to another

hero of the Inconfidência, Padre Toledo, who lived in this 18-room house where the Inconfidêntes first met. It features regional antiques and documents from the 18th century.

CHAFARIZ DE SÃO JOSÉ

Constructed in 1749 by the town council, this beautiful **fountain** (Rua do Chafariz, north of Córrego Santo Antônio) has three sections: one for drinking, one for washing clothes and one for watering horses. The water comes from a nearby spring, Mãe d'Agua, via an old stone pipeline.

SERRA DE SÃO JOSÉ

At the foot of these mountains there's a 1km-wide stretch of protected Atlantic rain forest, with several nice **hiking trails**.

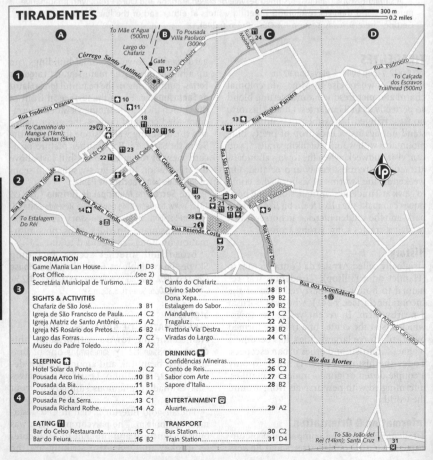

TIRADENTES

MINAS GERAIS

The most popular and simple leads to **Mãe d'Agua**, the spring that feeds the Chafariz de São José fountain. From the fountain square, cross through a gate (open from 9am to 4pm) and follow the trail north for 15 minutes along the stone viaduct into the jungle. It's a magical spot, with sun-dappled glens and monkeys cavorting in the tall trees.

A Calçada dos Escravos is a three-hour round trip that climbs through open fields to a windswept saddle with gorgeous views of the *serra* (mountain range). Also known as Calçada do Carteiro, it includes a section of the old stone-paved road built by slaves between Ouro Prêto and Rio de Janeiro. Finding the trailhead can be tricky: head northeast on Rua Nicolau Panzera past Igreja de São Francisco de Paula, then join Rua Padroeiro Santo Antônio; after you pass house No 878 (left side), cross through a gate and look for a signpost indicating the Calçada dos Escravos. Fork left on the rickety bridge over the stream, then start climbing towards the saddle.

Caminho do Mangue is a walk that heads up the *serra* from the west side of town to Aguas Santas and takes about two hours. There you'll find a mineral-water swimming pool and a very good Portuguese-owned *churrascaria*.

You can link the latter two trails by continuing along the ridgeline, a six-hour loop. Trails are not clearly marked, and locals advise against carrying valuables or trekking alone on the Caminho do Mangue. For up-to-date English-language information on trail safety, independent hiking opportunities and local guides, try Bia at Pousada da Bia or John Parsons at the Hotel Solar da Ponte.

Festivals & Events

Tiradentes is increasingly popular as a center for national events. Two of the biggest and longest established are the **Mostra de Cinema** (second half of January) and the **Festival Internacional de Cultura e Gastronomia** (second half of August), respectively bringing international films and world-class chefs to Tiradentes.

Sleeping

BUDGET

Tiradentes caters to a well-heeled crowd and couples looking for romance. Budget-minded and/or solo travelers can save money by renting rooms in private homes or visiting midweek, when pousadas grant discounts of 10% to 30%.

Pousada da Bia (☎ 3355 1173; www.pousadadabia .com.br; Rua Frederico Ozanan 330; s/d R$50/70; 🖳) An absolute gem! Simple but delightfully friendly, thanks to the efforts of the English-speaking owner, this pousada will make your stay extra pleasant. The sunny breakfast house and fragrant herb garden are especially nice. Milk for coffee is kept warm on the wood stove.

Pousada Arco Iris (☎ 3355 1167; Rua Frederico Ozanan 340; s/d/tr R$45/85/110; 🖳) If Pousada da Bia is full, this place next door has similar prices and amenities. Rooms out back are brighter and more spacious than those in the main house.

MIDRANGE

Pousada do Ó (☎ 3355 1699; www.pousadadoo.com.br; Rua do Chafariz 25; s/d R$80/110) On a lovely plaza and boasting a fabulous garden, this pousada has seven rooms, most of them overlooking the street. Book ahead for No 7, which is set apart from the rest and has a garden view.

Pousada Pe da Serra (☎ 3355 1107; www.pedaserra .com.br; Rua Nicolau Panzera 51; d from $80/100; 🖳 🖳) This family-run, friendly little place sits on a ridge just above the bus station. The nine small but spotless rooms have panoramic views – the location makes up for the otherwise simple décor. Guests have free rein in the garden and sitting rooms.

Estalagem do Rei (☎ 3355 2654; www.estalagem dorei.com.br; Rua Santíssima Trindade 420; s/d R$90/150) This pousada is a short distance out of town but it's worth the trip. The rooms surround a vast garden, and most are palatial, with 3.5m-ceilings, large windows and gorgeous mountain views. One suite features a fireplace.

TOP END

Pousada Richard Rothe (☎ 3355 1333; www .pousadarichardrothe.com.br; Rua Padre Toledo 124; s/d from R$230; 🖳) On a picturesque street in the historic center, this stylish pousada has spacious suites, an elegant reading room with fireplace, and a small protected forest out back where monkeys come to play at dawn.

Pousada Villa Paolucci (☎ 3355 1350; www.villa paolucci.cjb.net; Rua do Chafariz; d from R$328; 🖳 🖳) This stunning mid-18th-century *fazenda* (ranch) just outside town has a palm-lined drive, a pond, tennis courts and outdoor pavilions. Rooms are immense, with fireplaces, solar hot water and antique furniture. The chef here is renowned for his *leitão à pururuca* (roast suckling pig), which he shows off at Tiradentes' summer culinary festival.

Hotel Solar da Ponte (☎ 3355 1255; www.solar daponte.com.br; Praça das Mercês; s/d from R$348; 🞐 🖭) This magnificent re-creation of a colonial mansion is one of Brazil's finest hotels, with first-rate food and service across the board. The rooms have fresh flowers, beautiful antiques, and comfortable chairs and beds. There's a reading room, complete with fireplace, and complimentary afternoon tea is served in the garden.

Eating

BUDGET

Bar do Feiura (☎ 8854 3674; Rua da Cadeia 262; snacks from R$5; ⏲ 7-11:30pm Mon-Thu, 12:30pm-late Fri & Sat, & noon-7pm Sun) This charming spot for a snack or a simple meal is especially fun on chilly nights when the wood stove is blazing and conversation and drinks are flowing freely. For a good story, ask Geraldo to tell you how the bar got its name.

Mandalum (☎ 3355 2176; Largo das Forras 88; sandwiches & omelettes R$8; ⏲ noon-late Wed-Mon) The high-quality fast food at Mandalum includes everything from Lebanese sandwiches to banana splits, and from milkshakes to *caipirinhas*.

Divino Sabor (☎ 3355 1633; Rua Ministro Gabriel Passos 300; per kg R$20.90; ⏲ 11:30am-3:30pm) Very popular with locals for its self-serve offerings, including grilled meats and the normal range of Mineiro specialties.

MIDRANGE

Dona Xepa (☎ 3355 1767; Rua Ministro Gabriel Passos 26A; meals from R$12; ⏲ 11am-6pm Mon, Wed & Thu, to 10pm Fri-Sun) With a *cachaça* menu twice as long as in most places, locally run Dona Xepa's is lots of fun.

Estalagem do Sabor (☎ 3355 1144; Rua Ministro Gabriel Passos 280; meals for 2 R$35; ⏲ 11am-4pm & 7-10pm Mon-Fri, 11am-10pm Sat, 11am-4pm Sun) One of Tiradentes' finest restaurants, Estalagem specializes in meat and *comida mineira*, supplemented by a good wine list.

Bar do Celso Restaurante (☎ 3355 1193; Largo das Forras 80A; meals R$19; ⏲ 11:45am-9pm Wed-Mon) On the main square, this is another locally run Mineiro restaurant with reasonable prices.

TOP END

Viradas do Largo (☎ 3355 1111; Rua do Moinho 11; meals from R$29; ⏲ 1-10pm Wed-Mon) This place is among Tiradentes' best restaurants for traditional Mineiro cuisine. Crowds pack into it on weekends, spilling over into the pleasant outdoor patio and garden area.

Trattoria Via Destra (☎ 3355 1906; Rua Direita 45; meals from R$30; ⏲ noon-5pm Fri-Sun & 7pm-late Wed-Sun) A romantic little Italian restaurant whose chef-owner migrated from Italy to Tiradentes in 2001.

Tragaluz (☎ 3355 1424; Rua Direita 52; meals from R$40; ⏲ 7-10:30pm Sun-Mon & Wed-Thu, to 12:30am Fri & Sat) This restaurant prides itself on innovative home cooking served with artistic flair. Desserts here are especially divine; try the *goaiabada frita Tragaluz*, guava paste mixed with cashews, fried and served on a bed of *catupiry* cheese with guava ice cream.

Drinking & Entertainment

Confidências Mineiras (☎ 3355 2770; Rua Ministro Gabriel Passos 26; ⏲ 6pm-late Wed-Thu, noon-late Fri & Sat, noon-8pm Sun) Cozy and candlelit, this is one of Tiradentes' newest nocturnal draws. Where else can you compare notes on over 500 brands of artesanal *cachaça*, most of them locally brewed in Minas Gerais?

Aluarte (☎ 3355 1608; Largo do Ó 1; meals from R$30; ⏲ 8:30pm-late Thu-Sun) Featuring live music every weekend, this alluring and romantic cavelike nightspot is whimsically lit with perforated metal lamps decked with colored streamers. Lounge on the cushions with your paramour while eating fondue, or duck out back to the herbal hot tub under the trees (by reservation only, R$110 per couple for 1½ hours, including tea, fruit, water and candles). On quiet nights, Pedro may invite you into the kitchen to chat while he cooks you pizza on top of the wood stove.

Three popular bars, Conto de Reis, Sabor com Arte and Sapore d'Italia – all with outdoor seating and live music – vie nightly for visitors' attention on Largo das Forras.

Getting There & Away

Tiradentes is 30 minutes by bus from São João del Rei. Two companies, Presidente (R$2.25) and Vale do Ouro (R$2.10) run regular buses between the two cities. Thanks to this friendly rivalry, you'll never wait longer than 45 minutes for a bus during daylight hours. After 7pm, only Vale do Ouro operates, and departures are less frequent – 7:15pm, 8:45pm and 10:25pm from São João; 7:20pm, 8:20pm, 9:20pm and 11pm from Tiradentes.

It's possible to catch a bus directly from Tiradentes to Rio if you plan ahead. The morning

Pariabuna bus originating in São João del Rei (8am Monday to Friday, 6am Saturday) will pick passengers up in front of the Tiradentes train station (not the bus station), but you must buy your ticket in São João and indicate that you're boarding in Tiradentes. Coming from Rio, you can do the same thing in reverse – take Paraibuna's 7am bus Monday through Friday and let the driver know you want to disembark in Tiradentes.

Tiradentes' bus station is just north of the main square, across the stream. The train station is about 700m southeast of the main square.

DIAMANTINA
☎ 0xx38 / pop 43,000 / elevation 1113m

Isolated but fabulous, Diamantina is one of Brazil's prettiest and least-visited colonial towns. Surrounded by desolate mountains, it was the remotest mining town in Minas and the starting point for the **Caminho dos Escravos**, the old road to the coast built with the sweat, blood and tears of thousands of African slaves. Diamantina's fine mansions and winding streets haven't changed much in the last 200 years. Designated a Unesco World Heritage site in 1999, this *cidade histórica* is also the birthplace of Juscelino Kubitschek, former Brazilian president and founder of Brasília.

Orientation & Information
As with most Mineiro cities, Diamantina is built on precipitous slopes. The bus station sits high on a bluff, so the 500m descent into town can be tough on the knees, and the return climb is a true workout. There are occasional city buses along this route, but taxis (R$5) are the easiest option. The central square is Praça Conselheiro Mota, dominated by **Santo Antônio** cathedral – both colloquially known as Sé.

Two conveniently located ATMs are at **Banco do Brasil** (Praça da Sé), behind the cathedral, and **Bradesco** (Praça Barão do Guaicuí), just below the Mercado Municipal.

Internet and Skype services are available downtown at **JK Net** (☎ 3531 7772; Rua Direita 140; per hr R$4; ☼ 8am-6pm Mon-Fri, to noon Sat).

The bookstore-café **Livraria Café Espaço** (☎ 3531 6005; Beco da Tecla 31; meals from R$15; ☼ 9am-midnight Mon-Thu, to 2am Fri & Sat, to 2pm Sun) is a relaxing spot to mingle with Diamantina's bohemian set. You can browse books, linger over wine and fondue (snacks from R$5), lis-

ten to live music nightly or surf the net using its lone computer.

Staff at the **municipal tourist office** (☎ 3531 8060; catdiamantinaturismo@yahoo.com.br; Praça JK; ☼ 9am-6pm Mon-Sat, to 2pm Sun) will give you a guide in Portuguese that includes a map.

The post office is on Rua do Bonfim.

Sights
Casa de Juscelino Kubitschek (admission R$1; Rua São Francisco 241; ☼ 9am-5pm Tue-Sat, to 2pm Sun), childhood home of the former president, reflects his simple upbringing as the grandson of poor Czech immigrants. Kubitschek himself believed that his early life in Diamantina influenced him greatly. There are some good photos of JK along the staircase in the Hotel Tijuco (see p263).

Between Praça JK and the cathedral is the house of Padre Rolim, one of the Inconfidêntes. It's now the **Museu do Diamante** (admission R$1; ☼ noon-5.30pm Tue-Sat, 9am-noon Sun), exhibiting furniture, coins, instruments of torture and other relics of the diamond days.

The fine colonial mansion known as **Casa da Chica da Silva** (Praça Lobo de Mesquita 266; admission R$2; ☼ noon-5:30pm Tue-Sat, 9am-noon Sun) was the home of diamond contractor João Fernandes de Oliveira and his longtime partner, the former slave Chica da Silva. Here it's possible to get a feeling for the lifestyle of the extravagant mulata.

Consisting of two houses on opposite sides of the street connected by an enclosed, vivid-blue 2nd-storey passageway, **Casa da Glória** (Rua da Glória 298; admission R$2; ☼ 8am-noon & 2-6pm Tue-Sat, 9am-noon Sun) was originally the residence of the diamond supervisors and the palace of Diamantina's first bishop. Today, appropriately, the building houses the Institute of Geology, together with a fine collection of old maps.

Diamantina's **churches** (admission R$2; ☼ 8am-noon & 2-6pm Tue-Sat, 8am-noon Sun, closed Mon) all maintain identical hours and entrance fees.

Igreja de NS do Carmo – adorned with rich, golden carvings, and with a gilded organ made in Diamantina – is the town's most opulent church. Constructed between 1760 and 1765, its tower was built at the rear – lest the bells awaken Chica da Silva.

The oldest church in town is the **Igreja de NS do Rosário dos Pretos**, dating from 1731. It's downhill on Largo do Rosário.

MINAS GERAIS

The **Mercado Municipal** (Municipal Market), built by the army in 1835, is in Praça Barão Guaicuí. The building's wooden arches inspired Niemeyer's design for the presidential palace in Brasília. On Saturday it has a food and craft market and live music. People from the Vale de Jequitinhonha still arrive on horseback with their wares. A small museum here, the Centro Cultural David Ribeiro, has some fascinating old photos.

A couple of kilometers outside of town, there's a short reconstructed section of the **Caminho dos Escravos** – the stone-paved road, built by slaves, that linked Diamantina with Paraty and Rio de Janeiro. From Praça JK, take Rua Macau do Meio and Rua Arraial dos Forros north, then follow the signs. There are numerous other interesting excursions near Diamantina, including the **waterfalls** at Toca, 5km south, and the picturesque historical town of **Biribiri**, 14km north.

Festivals & Events

Diamantina has recently revived an old tradition of evening serenades known as the **Vesperata**. These evening concerts are only scheduled on a few Saturdays throughout the year, so you need to plan ahead. At 8pm on Vesperata night, dozens of local musicians parade into the small triangular *praça* at the north end of Rua da Quitanda, disappear into various doorways, then re-emerge on the illuminated balconies of the surrounding mansions. A conductor standing in midsquare

DIAMANTINA

0   300 m
0   0.2 mile

INFORMATION
Banco do Brasil	1 C3
Bradesco	2 C2
JK Net	3 C3
Livraria Café Espaço	4 C3
Municipal Tourist Office	5 C3
Post Office	6 D3

SIGHTS & ACTIVITIES
Casa da Chica da Silva	7 C4
Casa de Juscelino Kubitschek	8 B3
Igreja de NS do Carmo	9 D3
Igreja de NS do Rosário dos Pretos	10 D4
Igreja de São Francisco de Assis	11 C2
Mercado Municipal	12 D2
Museu do Diamante	13 C3

SLEEPING
Hotel JK	14 B4
Hotel Tijuco	15 B2
Pousada Ariana	16 C3
Pousada Dos Cristais	17 C4
Pousada Gameleira	18 D3
Pouso de Chica	19 B2
Relíquias do Tempo	20 C2

EATING
Apocalipse Point Bar	21 C3
Apocalipse Restaurante	22 C3
Café à Baiuca	23 C3
Cantinha do Marinho	24 C3
Pizza Chic	25 C3
Recanto do Antônio	26 C3

TRANSPORT
Bus Station	27 B4

To Caminho dos Escravos (2km); Biribiri (14km)

Rua Arraial Forros

Rua Nacoes Unidas

To Casa da Glória (150m)

Rua do Ouro

Rua Sofrer R. Couto

Rua Acaiaca

Beco da Paciência

Rua do Burgalhau

Rua Espírito Santo

Santo

Beco das Gaivotas

Rua Rio Grande

Rua da Candade

Rua Álvaro Matta

Rua Macau de Baixo

Rua do Tijuco

Rua Macau de Cima

Rua Macau do Meio

Beco dos Bereiros

Rua São Francisco

Rua Joaquim Felício

Praça JK

Praça Correa Rabelo

Praça Barão Guaicuí

Rua do Amparo

Rua da Quitanda

Rua Campos Carvano

Beco da Tecla

Beco da Peña

Beco Erezuel

Rua do Rosário

Av Francisco de Sá

Rua Augusto Nelson Lessa

Rua Zé de Lota

Rua Direita

Rua Traviessa do Carmo

Rua Viera Couto

Beco Monteiro

Beco do Mota

Rua Monsenhor Neves

Rua do Carmo

Rua do Contrato

Largo do Rosário

Rua Silvério Lessa

Rua das Merces

Praça Conselheiro Mota

Praça Lobo de Mesquita

Rua dos Coqueiros

Rua Samambaia de Cima

Rua Vicente do Figueiredo

Rua Jogo de Bola

Rua Adélio Barreto

To O Garimpo (1km); Serro(87km)

To Toca (5km)

leads the performance. For the best seats in the house, pay for a table in front of Apocalipse Bar or Café Baiuca. Alternatively, watch for free from anywhere on the surrounding sidewalks. For a full list of this year's dates, contact the Diamantina tourist office.

Sleeping
BUDGET

Hotel JK (☎ 3531 8715; Largo Dom João 135; s/d R$25/40; 🖵) This bare-bones hotel is directly across from the bus station, saving you a long uphill trek when you leave town. Internet access is available in the lobby, and rooms are clean, if a bit noisy.

Pousada Gameleira (☎ 3531 1900; Rua do Rosário 209; s/d R$40/80) A family-run place in a historical home, with a cheerful courtyard full of plants. All rooms have high ceilings, and the two front ones face the Igreja de NS do Rosário.

Pousada Dos Cristais (☎ 3531 2897; www.diamantinanet.com.br/pousadadoscristais; Rua Jogo do Bola 53; s/d/tr R$50/80/115; 🖭) In a lovely 18th-century mansion with stunning views of the surrounding countryside, this is Diamantina's most appealing budget option. The adjacent modern wing offers rooms with hammocks and private verandas, in a garden setting, for only R$10 more.

MIDRANGE & TOP END

Pousada Ariana (☎ 3531 3624; www.pousadaariana.com.br; Praça JK 27; s/d R$80/100) Just downhill from the Museu do Diamante, and close to the atmospheric local bustle of Praça JK, the Ariana is unexceptional, but cheaper than other places in the heart of historic Diamantina.

Relíquias do Tempo (☎ 3531 1627; www.pousadareliquiasdotempo.com.br; Rua Macau de Baixo 104; s/d R$96/128, with view R$121/143) Take a trip back in time at this gorgeous historical house with fantastic views, antique furniture and local artwork. Afternoon tea in the rustic dining room is a real treat. Ask to see the chapel in the back.

Hotel Tijuco (☎ 3531 1022; www.hoteltijuco.com.br; Rua Macau do Meio 211; s/d standard R$110/132, deluxe R$121/143) The modernist Tijuco is a Niemeyer creation with spacious, airy rooms. It's worth paying extra for a veranda with panoramic views.

Pouso da Chica (☎ 3531 6190; www.pousodachica.com.br; Rua Macau de Cima 115; s/d R$85/170; 🖵) This attractive new pousada features a main colonial building supplemented by individual chalets out back. Each room features unique amenities, such as a small private patio, disabled access or a sauna. All are wired for the internet.

Eating
BUDGET

Café à Baiuca (Rua da Quitanda 13; snacks from R$4; 🕑 8am-late Mon-Sat) A great place to watch the world go by over a morning cup of coffee or a late-night snack.

Apocalipse Point Bar (Rua da Quitanda s/n; snacks from R$4, meals from R$12; 🕑 8am-late Mon-Sat) Apocalipse is usually packed with people enjoying a beer and a bite on the cobblestones. During the weekend Vesperata it's the perfect place to listen to music pouring from the surrounding windows. Full meals are served, plus affordable omelets and sandwiches.

Apocalipse Restaurante (Praça Barão do Guaicuí 78; per kg R$20.95; 🕑 11am-3pm) Apocalipse's sister restaurant serves an excellent per-kilo lunch in an upstairs room affording great views of the municipal market.

Pizza Chic (☎ 3531 3838; Rua Direita 44; pizza from R$12; 🕑 noon-11:30pm) A popular pizzeria on the cathedral square.

MIDRANGE & TOP END

Recanto do Antônio (☎ 3531 1147; Beco da Tecla 39; dinner R$15; 🕑 6pm-midnight Tue-Thu, to 2am Fri & Sat, 11am-3pm & 6-11pm Sun) With stone walls and wood beams, this cozy and convivial nightspot features live music on weekends (R$3 extra), and its *sanduiche de filé* (R$6) is one of the tastiest bar snacks anywhere in Minas.

Cantinha do Marinho (☎ 3531 1686; Rua Direita 113; meals from R$18; 🕑 10:30am-3pm daily, 6-10:30pm Mon-Sat) The lunchtime *especial do dia* is unbeatable at R$8.50 for a full Mineiro meal (ask and they'll produce the menu from under the counter). But the real specialties here are *bacalhau* (imported codfish – check out the Norwegian box proudly posted on the wall) and *doce de limão*, a sweet lemony dessert made from an old family recipe.

O Garimpo (☎ 3531 1044; Av da Saudade 265; mains from R$25; 🕑 6-10pm Mon-Fri, noon-10pm Sat & Sun) For fine dining, there's no better place than this restaurant just south of town, famous for its regional dishes.

Getting There & Away

Pássaro Verde runs six daily buses from Diamantina to Belo Horizonte (R$53, five hours,

MINAS GERAIS

from 1am to 6pm). To the neighboring historical town of Serro, there are two buses daily (R$16, 2½ hours); schedules vary, but there's always one morning and one afternoon bus.

SERRO

☎ 0xx38 / pop 21,000 / elevation 781m

Founded in 1714, the charming colonial town of Serro snakes down a hillside in beautiful rural country south of Diamantina. While quite popular with Brazilians, this region remains little visited by foreigners and therefore retains a tranquil and traditional Mineiro air. Its cheese is considered the best in Minas.

Heading north from Serro towards Diamantina, the tranquil high-altitude hamlets of Milho Verde and São Gonçalo (less than 35km away but two hours by bus along a steep, rutted dirt road) also make lovely stopovers. The entire region offers fabulous hiking opportunities.

Information

The **Centro de Informações Turísticas** (☎ 3541 2754; www.serro.tur.br; Praça João Pinheiro 154; ⊙ 8am-6pm Mon-Fri, 9am-5pm Sat & Sun) hands out a useful map of Serro's old mansions and churches and also provides information about São Gonçalo and Milho Verde.

Internet and Skype access are available at **Nova Infor Lan House** (☎ 3541 2737; Praça João Pinheiro 186; per hr R$4; ⊙ 8am-noon & 1-10:30pm).

Festivals & Events

In early July, Serro hosts one of Minas' oldest festivals, the **Festa de NS do Rosário**, dating back to 1728. Townspeople representing Brazil's three traditional social groups parade through the streets in colorful attire: *caboclos* (literally 'copper-colored'; the mixed descendents of indigenous peoples and Portuguese) beat out rhythms on bows and arrows, holding mock confrontations with sword- and guitar-wielding *marujos* (Europeans), while *catopês* (Africans) speak an ancient dialect and beat on instruments symbolizing empty plates.

Sights

The most striking building in town is the graceful, single-steepled **Capela de Santa Rita** (⊙ 9am-1pm Mon-Sat), straight uphill from the main square via a steep series of steps. Three other 18th-century churches keep regular hours and are worth a visit: the **Igreja de NS do Carmo** (⊙ 9am-5pm), the **Igreja do Bom Jesus do Matozinhos** (⊙ 1-5pm Mon-Sat) and the **Capela de NS do Rosario** (⊙ 1-5pm Mon-Sat). Admission to each costs R$2.

Just downhill from town, the **Chácara do Barão do Serro** (⊙ 1-5pm Mon-Fri) is a lovely old mansion affording a glimpse of 19th-century baronial life in Serro.

Sleeping & Eating

Pousada Riques Matriz (☎ 3541 1770; Rua Alferes Luiz Pinto 82; s/d R$15/40) Rooms in this historic house near the Praça Matriz are quite basic. Singles all share a bathroom, hence the rock-bottom price.

Pousada Vila do Príncipe (☎ 3541 1485; Rua Antônio Honório Pires 38; s/d without bathroom R$25/50, with bathroom R$35/70) Housed in a 19th-century mansion, this centrally located pousada features gleaming broad-board floors and antique furniture. Rooms above the main street have little balconies with great views

Restaurante Itacolomi (☎ 3541 1227; Praça João Pinheiro 20; per kg lunch R$13.90, pizza from R$12; ⊙ 10:30am-3pm & 4-10pm) The best of the many *por-kilo* restaurants in town, with an airy upstairs dining room overlooking the main square.

Getting There & Away

The bus station is one block downhill from the historical center. Destinations include Belo Horizonte (R$56, five hours, four daily), Conceição do Mato Dentro (R$13, two hours, four daily) and Diamantina (R$16, 2½ hours, two daily).

SOUTHERN MINAS

Such unexpected surprises lurk in this corner of Brazil! Tucked away in the green hills near Minas' southern border with Rio and São Paulo states, you'll find spa towns whose curative waters have been garnering international acclaim since the 19th century, peaceful little valleys just beginning to draw the attention of Brazilian and international ecotourists, and even a hilltop village allegedly favored by extraterrestrials. For anyone who has overdosed on baroque architecture or burned themselves to a crisp at the beach, this quiet corner of Minas is the perfect remedy.

CAXAMBU

☎ 0xx35 / pop 23,000 / elevation 895m

Caxambu is a tranquil resort for the middle class and the elderly, who come here to escape the heat of Rio and the madness of Carnaval. Some couples have been coming here every summer for 30 years or more.

History

Long before Perrier hit Manhattan singles bars, Caxambu water was being celebrated on the international water circuit. Springs were first tapped here in 1870 and medical practitioners were quick to realize the waters' curative properties. Caxambu water took the gold medal in the 1903 Victor Emmanuel III Exposition in Rome, and again in the St Louis International Fair of 1904. It was also awarded the Diploma of Honor in the University of Brussels Exposition of 1910.

Caxambu's turn-of-the-century glory is still reflected in its old hotels, and the famous waters continue to be sold throughout Brazil, by the private firms Supergasbras and Superagua, who took over the government concession in 1981.

Information

Banco do Brasil (Rua Oliveira Mafra)

Post office (Av Camilo Soares) Just east of Parque das Aguas.

Tourist office (☎ 3341 9055; axambu@netzoom.psi.br; Praça Cônego José de Castilho Moreira; ⊗ 1-6pm Mon-Fri) Obtain maps and other information from this helpful office next to the bus station.

Sights

The **Parque das Aguas** (admission US$3, separate fees for attractions inside R$3-10; ⊗ 7am-6pm) is a rheumatic's Disneyland; people come to take the waters, smell the sulfur, compare liver spots, watch the geyser spout, rest in the shade by the canal and walk in the lovely gardens. There's a spring-fed outdoor **swimming pool** where you can do laps, plus the ornate **Balneário Hidroterápico**, dating from 1912, where you can soak in a hot bath, take a shower or relax in a sauna.

The park has 12 founts, each housed in its own architectural folly, and each with different properties. Liver problems? Drink from the Dona Leopoldina **magnesium fountain**. Skin disorders? Take the **sulfur baths** of Tereza Cristina. VD? The **Duque de Saxe fountain**

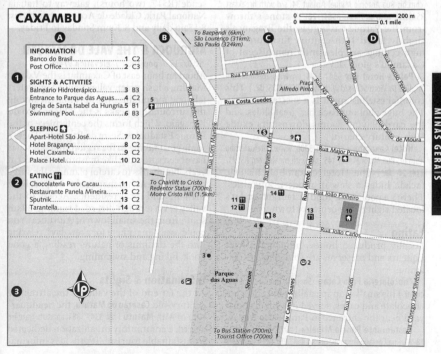

CAXAMBU		0 — 200 m
		0 — 0.1 mile

INFORMATION
Banco do Brasil.................................1 C2
Post Office.......................................2 C3

SIGHTS & ACTIVITIES
Balneário Hidroterápico................3 B3
Entrance to Parque das Aguas.....4 C2
Igreja de Santa Isabel da Hungria.5 B1
Swimming Pool..............................6 B3

SLEEPING
Apart-Hotel São José.....................7 D2
Hotel Bragança..............................8 C2
Hotel Caxambu..............................9 C2
Palace Hotel.................................10 D2

EATING
Chocolateria Puro Cacau............11 C2
Restaurante Panela Mineira.......12 C2
Sputnik...13 C2
Tarantella.....................................14 C2

To Baependi (6km);
São Lourenço (31km);
São Paulo (324km)

Rua Dr Mário Milward
Praça Alfredo Pinto
Rua Costa Guedes
Rua Manoel João
Rua Afonso Pena
Rua NS dos Remédios
Rua Américo Mazzaro
Rua Cons Mavrink
Rua Oliveira Mafra
Rua Pinto de Moura
Rua Major Penha
Rua Alfredo Pinto
Rua João Pinheiro
Rua João Carlos

To Chairlift to Cristo Redentor Statue (700m); Morro Cristo Hill (1.5km)

Parque das Aguas
Stream
Av Camilo Soares
Rua Dr Viotti
Rua Cônego José Silvério

To Bus Station (700m); Tourist Office (700m)

MINAS GERAIS

helps calm the bacteria that cause syphilis. Itchy trigger finger? Hit the **rifle range**. And there's much more, from kidney-stone cures to stomach-ailment alleviators to the chairlift climbing 800m to the image of Jesus atop the **Morro Cristo** hill.

Caxambu gained notoriety when Princesa Isabel (daughter of Brazil's last emperor, Dom Pedro II) visited in 1868. Having tried various treatments for infertility, she finally managed to conceive after taking the miraculous waters of Caxambu. In thanks she built the **Igreja de Santa Isabel da Hungria** on Rua Princesa Isabela.

Sleeping

If you're in Caxambu outside peak holiday times you can get some good deals. The fancier hotels include meals, and many have spas and offer massages.

Apart-Hotel São José (☎ 3341 3133; www.aptsaojose .hpgvip.ig.com.br; Rua Major Penha 264; s/d R$40/80; 🏊) Quite a lot of amenities are offered at this budget location – including a pool and a gorgeous sauna.

Hotel Bragança (☎ 3341 3366; www.hotelbraganca .com.br; Rua Antônio Miguel Arnaut 34; s/d with breakfast R$43/84, with all meals R$84/126) A stone's throw from the Parque das Aguas, the Bragança's slightly faded 19th-century furniture and high ceilings are pleasantly reminiscent of Caxambu's glory days.

Palace Hotel (☎ 3341 3341; www.palacehotel .br; Rua Dr Viotti 567; s/d with meals R$90/125; 🏊) This colonial establishment is a spectacular deal. The huge pool out back has great slides, and the card-playing rooms downstairs exude 19th-century charm.

Hotel Caxambu (☎ 3341 3300; www.hotelcaxambu .com.br; Rua Major Penha 145; s/d with meals from R$171/214; 🖳 🏊) The Hotel Caxambu's historic facade hides a slew of modern amenities. There's a pool and a good restaurant, and it's located right in the center of town.

Eating

Locally produced honey, homemade fruit liqueurs and preserves are sold all over Caxambu.

Chocolateria Puro Cacau (Shop 20, Rua Caetano Furquim) This small shop specializes in coffee, hot chocolate and cakes, served in a small courtyard near the entrance to Parque das Aguas.

Restaurante Panela Mineira (☎ 3341 2511; Shop 18-19, Rua Caetano Furquim; per kg R$13.90; 🕙 11am-2pm & 6pm-midnight) Next door to the *chocolateria*, Panela Mineira serves a good *prato feito* for R$9, as well as Mineiro food by the kilo.

Sputnik (☎ 3341 2511; Av Camilo Soares 648; per kg R$15.90; 🕙 11am-3:30pm) It's tempting to overdose on Sputnik's 18 self-serve hot dishes, but save some room for dessert. Its ice cream is good too!

Tarantella (☎ 3341 2161; Rua João Pinheiro 326; meals from R$17; 🕙 6pm-late) In addition to its classic Italian fare, this cozy restaurant with red-checked tablecloths also specializes in smoked trout.

Getting There & Away

The **bus station** (☎ 3341 9048) is about 1km south of the center on Praça Cônego José de Castilho Moreira. A horse and buggy into town costs about R$10.

Destinations include Belo Horizonte (Gardénia, R$54, six hours, 8:10am daily and 10:40pm Sunday to Friday), São Thomé das Letras (Coutinho, R$13, 2½ hours, 2:15pm, in good weather only) and São Paulo (Cometa, R$39, six hours, four daily from 8am to midnight). For Rio de Janeiro (R$36, five hours) and Resende (R$17, two hours), gateway to Itatiaia National Park, Cidade de Aço runs two buses: 8:15am daily and 8:30pm Sunday to Friday.

AIURUOCA & THE VALE DO MATUTU

☎ 0xx35 / pop 7000 / elevation 974m

About an hour east of Caxambu is the Vale do Matutu, a lush green valley flanked by waterfalls and mountains. Most prominent among the surrounding peaks is the 2293m Pico do Papagaio, which forms the centerpiece of the Parque Estadual da Serra do Papagaio. There's some great hiking in the region, and pousadas have been sprouting like mushrooms in recent years, but thanks to careful planning the surge of development has managed to respect both the land and local residents. Access to the valley is via a rough dirt road running 20km south from the small town of Aiuruoca. You could easily linger here for a few days, relaxing into the rhythms of nature, reading a good book, hiking and swimming.

Information & Sights

At the far end of the valley is the attractive century-old **Casarão do Matutu**, the headquarters of **AMA-Matutu** (☎ 3344 1881; amatutu@atuarq .com.br), a community organization dedicated to sustainable tourism. It provides information about the valley and can arrange for local guides. Recommended destinations are **Cachoeira do Fundo**, a nearby waterfall (R$8 to R$10 per person) or the valley's standout attraction, **Pico do Papagaio** (R$20 to R$30 per person).

MMA Ecoturismo (☎ 3344 1601; www.ajuru.com .br/mmaecoturismo.com.br; Rua Antônio Gonçalves 149, Aiuruoca) also guides trips throughout the Aiuruoca region. Prices are R$10 per person if you meet guides at the trailhead, higher if the outfit provides transportation.

Sleeping & Eating
There are hotels throughout the valley, most of which serve meals. Closer to Aiuruoca, you'll also find a couple of very nice restaurants and some basic accommodations.

Pousada Dois Irmãos (☎ 3344 1373; Rua Coronel Oswaldo 204; s/d R$30/60) This simple hotel is the best option if you arrive in Aiuruoca at night and don't want to miss the scenery further down the valley. Meals are available at the attached restaurant.

Pousada Pé da Mata (☎ 3344 1421; www.pousada pedamata.com.br; Estrada Aiuruoca/Matutu, km12; s/d R$65/130, chalet with full board R$80/160) Near a waterfall at the foot of Pico do Papagaio, this lovely pousada has sweeping views over the valley. Meals are cooked on a traditional *fogão à lenha* (wood stove).

Mandala das Águas (☎ 3344 1725; www.mandala dasaguas.com; Vale do Matutu, km15; s/d with full board R$70/80) Near the valley's far end, delightfully tranquil Mandala features spacious rooms, verandas with hammocks, panoramic views of Pico do Papagaio and a raging river below. The American-Brazilian owners use produce from their garden in the hearty homemade meals.

Restaurante Mirante das Corredeiras (☎ 3344 1403; Estrada Aiuruoca/Alagoa, km4; per kg R$19.90; 🕑 noon-3pm Tue-Fri, to 4:30pm Sat & Sun) The self-serve Mineiro food here is especially enjoyable thanks to the scenic deck overlooking the rapids of the Aiuruoca River.

Getting There & Away
Aiuruoca's **bus stop** (☎ 3341 3839) is on the central Praça Côn José Castilho. Viação Sandra operates three daily buses (R$10, one hour) from Caxambu to Aiuruoca, at 10am, 3:30pm and 6:20pm. Three morning buses return to Caxambu, at 5:20am, 9:15am and 11:15am.

To reach the more remote pousadas in the Vale do Matutu, you'll need your own car (beware the rough road) or a taxi (R$40 to R$60). Once settled in the valley, walking is the most pleasant way to get around.

SÃO THOMÉ DAS LETRAS
☎ 0xx35 / pop 6000 / elevation 1291m
If you're into mysticism or superstition, or just looking for a cheap, fun and idyllic place to relax, consider a detour to the quaint village of São Thomé das Letras, north of Caxambu and southwest of São João del Rei. High on a plateau, with a bird's-eye view of the surrounding farmland, São Thomé feels like a world apart. Perhaps this accounts for its reputation among Brazilian mystics as one of the seven sacred cities of the world. The town's name refers to the puzzling inscriptions on some of the many caverns in the region, and stories of flying saucers and visiting extraterrestrials abound. More down-to-earth attractions include the nearby mountains, caves and waterfalls, as well as the town's buildings, made from beautiful slabs of quartzite.

Information
São Thomé's **tourist information office** (☎ 3237 1461; www.saothome.mg.gov.br; Rua José Cristiano Alves 4; 🕑 9am-noon & 2-5pm) is just off the main square, Praça da Matriz. It provides a brochure in Portuguese with a rudimentary map of town and can point you to surrounding natural attractions.

Sights & Festivals
There are two nice churches in town: **Igreja Matriz de São Thomé** (1785), on beautiful, leafy Praça da Matriz, and the raw-stone **Igreja de Pedra**, downhill towards the bus station.

Next to the Matriz church is the **Gruta de São Thomé**, a small cave containing a shrine to São Thomé, as well as some strange inscriptions. Other nearby caves with inscriptions include **Carimbado** (3km) and **Chico Taquara** (3.5km).

There's a **lookout** 500m uphill from town, with great views at sunset or sunrise.

The popular waterfalls for excursions are **Euboise** (3km), **Prefeitura** (7km) and **Véu de Noiva** (12km).

In August the **Festas de Agosto** attract lots of pilgrims. The **Mystic Festival**, from late December to early January, attracts students and teachers of mysticism – it's a scene.

Sleeping & Eating
Pousada Serra Branca (☎ 3237 1362; www.catalogode hoteis.com.br; Rua Capitão João de Deus 7; R$25/45; 🖳) One block uphill from the Gruta de São

MINAS GERAIS

Thomé, this pousada offers bargain-priced *apartamentos* plus a sauna and a pool.

Pousada Arco Iris (☎ 3237 1212; www.pousarcoiris .com.br; Rua João Batista Neves 19; s/d R$35/70; ⊠) Very centrally located, in a old stone building, Pousada Arco Iris is the prettiest of São Thomé's budget pousadas. It also has a pool and sauna.

Pousada Reino dos Magos (☎ 3237 1300; www .reinodosmagos.com.br; Rua Gabriel Luiz Alvarez 47; s/d/tr/q R$38/55/80/105) Despite an unpromising exterior, the friendly Pousada Reino provides clean, fan-cooled rooms, including some triples and quads.

Restaurante da Sinhá (☎ 3237 1348; Rua Capitão Pedro José Martins 31; per kg R$15.90; ⏰ 11am-4pm Sun-Fri, to 10pm Sat) This family-run self-service place cooks delicious Mineiro food over the wood fire. There's pleasant outdoor seating in the courtyard of their old stone house.

Pizzaria Ser Creativo (☎ 3237 1266; Praça Getúlio Vargas 18; pizzas from R$12; ⏰ 6am-late), near the top of town, wins rave reviews for its pizza.

Restaurante das Magas (☎ 3237 1326; Rua Camilo Rios 2; meals from R$24; ⏰ 11:30am-5pm & 7-11pm Thu-Tue) A friendly spot for a sit-down meal, in a 180-year-old stone house. It specializes in Mineiro food, but also serves pizza.

Getting There & Away

São Thomé's bus station is at Praça Barão de Alfenas, 1km from the center.

Coutinho runs one direct bus between Caxambu and São Thomé along a rugged but scenic dirt road, in good weather only (R$13, 2½ hours, leaving Caxambu at 2:15pm, returning from São Thomé at 9am). Alternatively, Trectur buses (R$8, one hour, five daily) connect São Thomé and the nearby town of Três Corações, where you can make onward connections to Caxambu (1½ hours further) or São João del Rei (2¼ hours).

PARKS

PARQUE NATURAL DO CARAÇA

☎ 0xx31 / elevation 1297m

Near the town of Santa Bárbara, 105km east of Belo Horizonte, the Parque Natural do Caraça is a blissful spot. Isolated from the rest of the world by a mountain ridge, the park encompasses 110 sq km of transition zone between the Mata Atlântica (Atlantic rain forest) and cerrado (savanna) ecosystems. The

park's centerpiece, nestled in a bowl-shaped valley, is a former monastery and boarding school attended by several Brazilian presidents. Now converted to a pousada, it's still owned and run by the Catholic congregation who use the neo-Gothic church for services. The surrounding countryside includes several mountains – including **Pico do Sol** (at 2070m, the highest point in the Serra do Espinhaço) – as well as creeks forming waterfalls and natural swimming pools. The hillsides are lined with easily accessible hiking trails, all marked on a useful map provided at the park entrance. Some of the more treacherous trails (indicated in red) require you to hike with a local guide (R$40 to R$60), but most, including the four-hour round trip to the gorgeous **Cascatona waterfall**, can be undertaken solo.

Sleeping & Eating

Rooms at the **Pousada Santuário do Caraça** (☎ 3837 2698; s/d with meals without bathroom R$50/80, with bathroom R$90/130) range from simple *quartos* off the garden courtyard to swank private doubles with bathroom. Rates include three meals, and advance reservations are required. The kitchen (open 8am to 6pm daily) serves awesome Mineiro cuisine featuring local produce. In the mornings you can fry your own eggs on the wood-fired stove. The big highlight of staying here is the nightly feeding of the wolves (see opposite). Visit midweek if you can, as it's easier to see the wolves and appreciate Caraça's isolation and tranquility without the crowds of weekend escapees from Belo. During less crowded periods meals are served in the more intimate downstairs dining room, which leads to some wonderful spontaneous conversations.

Getting There & Away

Pássaro Verde operates nine buses daily between Belo Horizonte and Santa Bárbara, the town nearest the park (R$21, 2½ hours, from 6am to 9pm). The once daily Belo–Vitória train (see p240) also makes a stop near the park, in Dois Irmãos (regular/*executivo* R$8/15, leaving Belo Horizonte at 7:30am and arriving at Dois Irmãos at 9:05am).

From Santa Bárbara or Dois Irmãos, the 30-minute taxi ride to Caraça will cost R$40 to R$50. Note that the park gate is only open from 7am to 5pm (or to 9pm for pousada guests).

PARQUE NACIONAL DA SERRA DO CIPÓ

☎ 0xx31

Parque Nacional da Serra do Cipó, 100km northeast of Belo Horizonte, is one of the most beautiful parks in Minas. Most of the park's vegetation is cerrado and grassy highlands, straddling the Serra do Espinhaço that divides the water basins of the São Francisco and Doce rivers. At lower elevations there are waterfalls and lush, ferny river valleys containing a number of unique orchids. Fauna here includes maned wolves, tamarin monkeys, banded anteaters, jaguars, bats and the small, brightly colored *sapo de pijama* (pyjama frog).

The park is vast, and the most popular trails involve multiday traverses of the *serra*. Information and trail maps are available at **park headquarters** (☎ 3718 7237; parnacipo@ligbr.com.br; admission R$3), a few kilometers southeast of the town of Cardeal Mota. The most accessible day hike is the 16km round-trip from headquarters to a 70m waterfall called **Cachoeira da Farofa**.

Three excellent local tour operators offering hiking, rafting, horseback and mountainbike excursions to the park are **Cipó Aventuras** (☎ 9605 5413; www.cipoaventuras.com.br), **Cipoeiro Expediciones** (☎ 9611 8878; www.cipoeiro.com.br) and **Tropa Serrana** (☎ 3344 8986; tropaserrana.zip.net). Check their websites for enticing photos. Prices for day trips start at R$50.

Sleeping & Eating

Hotel Cipó Veraneio (☎ 3718 7000; www.cipoveraneiohotel.com.br; Rodovia MG 10, km95; s/d with meals R$267; ❌ ❑) The most convenient place to stay if you're arriving by bus and want easy access to park headquarters, Cipó Veraneio is right on the road but has great facilities, including a pool.

Camping in the park is not permitted, but there are two campsites near the Veu de Noiva waterfall, 4km north of the turnoff for park headquarters. **Grande Pedreira** (☎ 3291 0734; per site R$15) and **Veu da Noiva** (☎ 3799 1177; per site R$15) are both at km99 along the main road. Buses will drop you there upon request.

Getting There & Away

Serro and Saritur run buses to the park from Belo Horizonte (R$17, three hours, several daily from 6am to 4:45pm). For park headquarters, get off at the Hotel Cipó Veraneio, then walk or hitch 4km east down the signposted dirt road on your right, just past the hotel but before the Rio Cipó bridge.

For camping, continue 4km further north through the town of Cardeal Mota.

AROUND SERRA DO CIPÓ
Cachoeira Tabuleiro

North of Serra do Cipó National Park, but still within Unesco's Serra do Espinhaço Biosphere Reserve, is one of Minas' most spectacular natural treasures, the 273m Tabuleiro waterfall. It's the third-highest waterfall in Brazil and can most easily be reached from the small town of Tabuleiro, approximately 180km north of Belo Horizonte.

Five kilometers east of the falls, the brandnew **Tabuleiro Eco Hostel** (☎ 96389641; www.tabuleiroecohostel.com.br; Rua Joaquim Costinha 1B, Vila do Tabuleiro; camp sites/dm/r per person R$15/20/35) offers grassy terraces

---

THE MANED WOLVES OF CARAÇA

The maned wolf – *lobo guará* in Portuguese – is South America's largest wild canine, living happily in the protected cerrado environment of the Parque Natural do Caraça. A few years back, one of Caraça's priests had the idea of befriending the wolves, St Francis style. After two years of patient work gradually tempting them towards the church with offerings of food, he gained the wolves' trust. Nowadays the feeding has become a nightly spectacle, open to the public.

There's no guarantee that you'll see the wolves, but the ritual itself is pure magic. After dinner in the monastery's old stone refectory, people drift out to the patio. The ceremonial plate of scraps for the wolves is placed on the flagstones just past sunset, while popcorn, herb tea, and *cachaça* (a high-proof sugarcane alcohol) are provided for the humans. Then the waiting begins. Whether or not the wolves come hardly matters: the pleasure of so many people sitting in one place, trading conversation or looking at the stars, is meaningful in itself.

And then… the patter of feet, a sudden hush rippling through the assembled crowd, the scamper up the steps, the wild eyes of this beautiful creature come to steal a quick meal and then vanish again into the night.

If you see it, it will stick with you for life. If not, you'll find yourself scheming a way to return.

MINAS GERAIS

for camping, plus dorms and private rooms in a series of colorful buildings running down the hillside. Breakfast is included (other meals are available for R$7 per person when there's enough demand). There are also some simple restaurants in town. The hostel owners organize trips to nearby cliff paintings, waterfalls, canyons and swimming holes.

To get from the hostel to the falls, proceed west through downtown Tabuleiro approximately 3km to **Parque Estadual Serra do Intendente** (admission R$5). From the entrance station, a well-marked 2km-long trail descends steeply to the river, then peters out, requiring you to boulder-hop the rest of the way upstream. The views of the waterfall are spectacular the whole way. During the dry season you can swim in the natural pool at the foot of the falls.

Getting There & Away

Take a Viação Serro bus from Belo Horizonte to Conceição do Mato Dentro (R$31, four hours, several daily). The trick is getting from Conceição to Tabuleiro; local buses only leave at 3pm on Monday, Wednesday and Friday, and at 2pm on Saturday, returning from Tabuleiro at 8am the same days (R$2, one hour). When the bus isn't running, a taxi from Conceição to Tabuleiro will cost about R$40. Buses from Conceição back to Belo Horizonte run six times daily between 7am and 6:15pm (4:30pm on Sunday).

PARQUE NACIONAL DE CAPARAÓ

☎ 0xx32

This 250-sq-km national park contains southern Brazil's highest mountains, including **Cristal** (2798m), **Calçado** (2766m) and the third-highest peak in the country, **Pico da Bandeira** (2892m). Popular with climbers and hikers from all over Brazil, it affords panoramic views of the Caparaó Valley that divides Minas Gerais and Espírito Santo. The wide-open, rocky highlands that predominate here are complemented by a few lush remnants of Mata Atlântica at lower elevations.

Park headquarters (admission R$3; ⏱ 7am-10pm) is 2km straight uphill from the nearest town, Alto do Caparaó. Between November and January there's lots of rain. The best time for clear weather is between June and August – although these are the coldest months. Bring warm clothes!

The classic hike to the summit of Pico da Bandeira can be made without climbing gear

or a guide, as the trail is gradual and well-marked. It costs about R$40 for a taxi from town to the trailhead at Tronqueira camp-site, 8km up a steep dirt road from the park entrance. Cars are prohibited beyond Tronqueira. From here, a gradual 9km climb leads to the summit. Most people go straight up and back to Alto Caparaó the same day, but with your own tent, you can cross over to the Espírito Santo side of the park, camp overnight, and retrace your steps the following day. The dropoff from Pico da Bandeira on the Espírito Santo side is steeper than on the Minas side, making for some very dramatic views, and there are three waterfalls with idyllic swimming holes – **Farofa**, **Aurélio** and **Sete Pilões** – near the last campground, Macieira.

Sleeping & Eating

There are two official campsites on the Minas Gerais side of the park: Tronqueira (above) and Terreirão, 4.5km beyond, which marks the halfway point of the 9km hiking trail from Tronqueira to the summit. On the Espírito Santo side of the park there are two additional campsites: at Casa Queimada, 4.5km down from the summit by trail; and Macieira, 4.5km further by dirt road. Bring all food and supplies with you, and reserve sites in advance by calling **IBAMA** (☎ 3747 2555; per site R$6). All sites have flush toilets and showers.

Pousada Querência (☎ 3747 2566; www.picodaban deiratur.hpg.com.br; Av Pico da Bandeira 1061; with/without HI membership per person R$30/35) Despite its inconvenient location at the bottom of town, this HI-affiliated hostel has good facilities, including a guest kitchen. It organizes rafting trips and predawn excursions to see sunrise atop Pico da Bandeira. Querência's owners can also drive you to the smaller Rio Claro Hostel, in an ecological reserve 14km away, with hydro power supplied by a waterfall, and lodging for up to 12 people (R$120 per night regardless of group size).

Pousada Vale Verde (☎ 3747 2529; Praça da Matriz; s/d R$30/60) This place offers simple rooms, right near the bus stop on the main square. Meals are available at the restaurant next door.

Pousada do Bezerra (☎ 3747 2538; www.pousada dobezerra.com.br; Av Pico da Bandeira; s/d/tr/q with breakfast R$65/115/165/214, with all meals R$90/162/223/284; 🖳 🖻) The lodging option closest to the park entrance, Bezerra serves delicious trout at its attached restaurant. Full or half pension is available, and there's a sauna.

AN ENDANGERED PRIMATE'S LAST STAND

The muriqui, largest primate of the New World, is a stunning creature. Adult males stand roughly 1.5m tall, and their movements and physical presence can be startlingly humanlike. The muriqui's photogenic qualities have made it a poster child for wildlife preservation in Brazil, but actually seeing one in the wild can be challenging. At the time of writing, there were only about 2500 animals left in the world – including only 500 of the rarer northern muriqui – down from an estimated 400,000 at the time of Portuguese colonization.

Three factors explain the muriquis' drastic drop in numbers: destruction of their native Mata Atlântica habitat, their docile nature (their Tupi Indian name means 'easygoing folks') and the slow pace of their reproductive cycle. Female muriquis generally give birth to a single baby after a gestation period of eight months, and newborns stay with their mothers for up to three years, during which time no new mating occurs. Muriquis are slow-moving and less combative than most other primates – indeed, they spend most of their time eating, playing and hugging each other! – so they've historically been easy targets for hunters.

Brazil still has a couple of preserved patches of Mata Atlântica where muriquis thrive: the Estação Biológica de Caratinga in Minas Gerais, and the Parque Estadual Carlos Botelho in São Paulo state. The former is the easiest place to spot them. Whether or not you visit the preserve, you can donate money to muriqui preservation efforts through **Preserve Muriqui** (www.preserve muriqui.org.br/ing/abraco.htm) or **Conservation International** (www.conservation.org).

Getting There & Away

Caparaó is accessible from Belo Horizonte or Vitória (Espírito Santo), connecting at Manhumirim. Pássaro Verde operates buses from Belo to Manhumirim (R$65, six hours, twice daily at 7am, and 7:30 or 10pm). From Vitória, take Aguia Branca's daily 6:30pm bus direct to Manhumirim (R$27, 4½ hours), or its 6:30am bus from Vitória to Manhuaçu (4½ hours), where a Rio Doce bus connects to Manhumirim (R$3.60, 45 minutes).

Rio Doce runs seven daily buses from Manhumirim to Alto Caparaó (R$3.45, 80 minutes, from 6:30am to 8pm, returning 6:25am to 9:10pm). Alternatively, it's a half-hour taxi ride (R$30). Manhumirim's **Palace Hotel** (☎ 33 3341 2255; Av Lauro Silva 656; s/d R$35/55), diagonally across from the bus station, is perfectly adequate if you're stuck here overnight.

ESTAÇÃO BIOLÓGICA DE CARATINGA
☎ 0xx33

This remote and little-visited nature preserve has played a critical role in rescuing the northern muriqui (see the boxed text above) from extinction. In 1944 there were only eight muriquis on record here, when local coffee farmer Feliciano Abdalla committed himself to preserving a large chunk of the native Atlantic rain forest on his property. Forty years later, the protected status of these lands became official with the establishment of the Estação Biológica de Caratinga, and in the

quarter-century since, research and preservation efforts have led to greater understanding of the muriqui and an impressive resurgence of its numbers. Today there are approximately 270 northern muriquis living within the Estação Biológica, representing more than half the world's population. Seeing the primates in their natural habitat is an amazing experience, and visitors have a better-than-average chance of a sighting, thanks to the expert skills of local guides.

Sleeping & Eating

Simple bunks are available at park headquarters, and you can share meals with the researchers, but advance planning is essential. To arrange a visit, write or call the **park office** (☎ 3322 2540; reservemuriqui@hotmail.com) in Caratinga.

Getting There & Away

Pássaro Verde and Presidente buses run from BH to Ipanema (R$70, nine hours, two daily) and Caratinga (R$54, six hours, four daily), the towns nearest the park. From either, take a Rio Doce bus (R$11, two hours from Caratinga; R$5, one hour from Ipanema) and ask to be let off at the Estação Biológica. From the bus stop, it's a 2km walk up a dirt road to park headquarters. With prior notice, **Antônio Bragança** (☎ 9962 5434; antonio_braganca@hotmail .com), the research station's field director, can sometimes provide a ride from Ipanema to the park.

MINAS GERAIS

São Paulo State

It is hard to speak of São Paulo state without using superlatives. The region is home to Brazil's largest industrial output, its largest (and most ethnically diverse) population, the richest of its rich, its biggest stock exchange, its busiest port, its finest museums, its worst traffic and its vastest slums. Paulistas, as residents of São Paulo state are known, take pride in their ascendancy, sometimes irking residents of other states in the process, particularly their tetchy neighbors in Rio. But that, to a good Paulista, only proves the point. Everyone's just envious, you see.

With Rio's economic star in eclipse and Brasília limited to governmental functions, the sprawling city of São Paulo in many ways serves as the country's de facto capital – commercially, financially, industrially and culturally. If you're doing business in Brazil, this is where you're likely to end up, and there has been an explosion of interest among sophisticated travelers who are catching wind of the city's extraordinary restaurants, art scene and nightlife.

Still, there are good reasons to escape the capital's clutches. Just beyond the jungle-draped coastal mountains lie some of southern Brazil's finest beaches. The mountainous stretch of coast around Ubatuba is particularly winning. Inland, the area around Campos do Jordão delivers the stunning vistas – and chilly air – of the Serra da Mantiqueira, whose green peaks reach more than 2500m. Further afield, Iporanga sits amid one of the least disturbed areas of Brazilian Atlantic Forest, while the nearby state park boasts hundreds of cataloged caves, making it Brazil's Capital das Grutas (Cave Capital).

HIGHLIGHTS

- Gape at the sheer size of São Paulo from the art-deco heights of the **Banespa building** (p281)
- Stalk the rich at their preferred watering holes in São Paulo's leafy **Jardins district** (p283)
- Determine which of **São Paulo's legendary nightclubs** (p297) best cater to your unique nightlife needs
- Seek out wild, deserted beaches where mountains meet sea just north of **Ubatuba** (p302)
- Hike amid the green peaks of the **Serra da Mantiqueira** (p310), known as 'Brazil's Switzerland'

Serra da Mantiqueira ★
São Paulo ★
Ubatuba ★

| ■ TELEPHONE CODE: 11 | ■ POPULATION: 40.4 MILLION | ■ AREA: 248,800 SQ KM |

SÃO PAULO STATE

History

Like the rest of Brazil, São Paulo began its life essentially as a series of coastal sugar plantations. However, unlike northeast Brazil, mountains limited growing areas and, while it seems hard to believe now, the region remained a colonial backwater well into the 18th century.

Two groups dominated early Paulista life: Jesuits, who crossed the coastal range to found the future city of São Paulo in 1554, and the *bandeirantes* who followed them – groups of pioneers who conducted raids into the interior, enslaving indigenous peoples to work the coastal plantations. The interior was so remote that even people of European descent spoke not Portuguese but a simplified form of the indigenous Tupi-Guarani language.

When Africans began to replace indigenous peoples on the slave plantations in the late 17th century, the *bandeirantes* tried their fortune hunting for gold, eventually discovering rich veins in neighboring Minas Gerais. The town of São Paulo profited as an important market for *bandeirantes* to stock up on supplies for their expeditions. The land around it also proved relatively good for growing sugar cane.

By the early 19th century, however, sugar growers discovered that their soil was ideal for an even more profitable crop: coffee. By the 1850s vast stretches of the state were given over to coffee plantations. A rail connection over the coastal range began carrying hugely profitable quantities of the bean to the port at Santos, and then on to world markets. When slavery was abolished in 1888, growers encouraged mass immigration of Europeans, particularly Italians, to work the plantations. The next great wave of immigrants came from Japan, starting around 1910 and peaking in the 1930s.

Crashing coffee prices in the early 20th century convinced investors that they needed to spread their bets, and by the 1950s São Paulo had transformed itself into the industrial engine that drove the national economy. Cars had replaced coffee as São Paulo's new cash crop. At the same time, the vast automotive plants that sprung up in São Bernardo do Campo, south of São Paulo city, became a hotbed of leftist union activity and proving grounds for future president Luíz Inácio Lula da Silva.

In fact, the trade unionists were part of a long tradition of liberalism and dissent in the state, from the independence and abolition movements of the 19th century through to opposition to the military junta that, with support from the US, ruled the country from the 1960s to the 1980s.

While immigration slowed dramatically by the 1980s, millions of Brazilians continued to stream into São Paulo, particularly from the Northeast. As the capital failed to cope with its growth, and crime and congestion spiraled out of control, many entrepreneurs began to migrate to the more stable cities of the interior. Today, Campinas and Riberão Preto, once small towns, sit amid one of the richest regions in Latin America.

While the state's dominance remains unchallenged within Brazil, the mega-growth of China and India has raised alarm bells among Brazilian industrialists. At the same time, the maturing economy is more stable and diversified than it has ever been, even if São Paulo, like the rest of the Brazil, must still address the gaping divide between haves and have-nots.

Climate

São Paulo's coastline is skirted by the Sierra do Mar, below which is a narrow coastal zone broken by lagoons, tidal channels and mountain spurs. In the mountains the state has a mild, temperate climate that can be very bracing – jackets are needed in winter. In the coastal zone the temperatures are moderate in winter and very hot and humid in summer with frequent tropical downpours. The city of São Paulo has somewhat more moderate temperatures in summer and cool but not cold winters.

Getting There & Around

The state's capital, São Paulo city, is Brazil's principal hub for international travel. Dozens of airlines have direct international services to São Paulo's Guarulhos airport, and there are also direct bus services from neighboring countries. The city is also a major center for domestic air travel, with affordable airfares available to cities around Brazil. The state's highway system is among the best in South America, making driving a good option, though São Paulo city itself can be maddening because of poor signage and horrendous traffic. Alternatively, there are also frequent and good long-distance bus services, within the state and to other parts of Brazil.

SÃO PAULO STATE

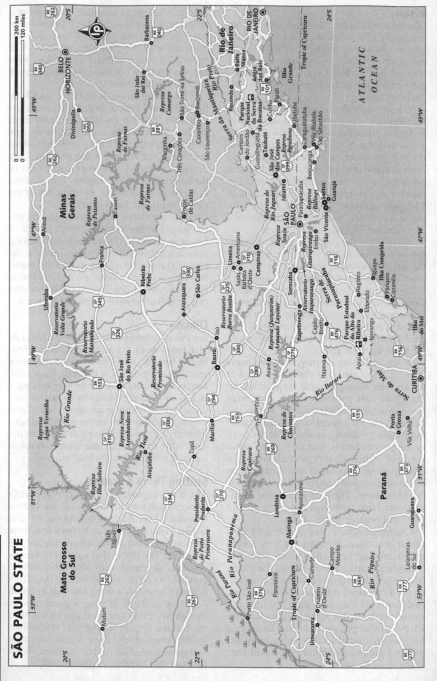

SÃO PAULO CITY

☎ 0xx11 / pop 12.6 million / elevation 760m

São Paulo is enormous, intimidating and, at first glance at least, no great beauty – a difficult city for the traveler to master and one that, initially, may not seem worth the sweat. Even the most partisan Paulistana – resident of São Paulo city – will rail about the smog, the traffic, the crumbling sidewalks and the gaping divide between poor and rich. But in the same breath, they'll tell you they'd never live anywhere else.

Let them guide you to their favorite haunts, and the reason for this will begin to unfold. Maybe they will introduce you to the city's innumerable art-house cinemas and experimental theatres. If they're gourmands, you'll focus on the smart bistros and jewels of ethnic cuisine. If they're partiers, double up on espresso before embarking on a tour of raucous underground bars and the 24/7 clubbing scene. Whatever manmade pleasure you might covet, Sampa – as the city is known – probably has it in spades.

This fertile cultural life is supported by Brazil's biggest and best-educated middle class and further enriched by literally hundreds of distinct ethnic groups – including the largest community of people of Japanese descent outside Japan. It also has the largest openly gay community in Latin America. Sheer numbers helps too. An estimated 20 million people live in greater São Paulo, making it the third-largest metropolis on earth. Its relentless, round-the-clock pulse – a close cousin of London's or New York's – can prove taxing. Then again, it may just deliver the charge you need to discover one of the world's great cities.

Sampa has always been much more interested in making its fortune than preserving its past, and public spaces are largely neglected in favor of private oases. Beyond a handful of good museums and an increasingly well-preserved historic centre, there are relatively few sights per se. By way of compensation, higher-end restaurateurs, shop owners and impresarios tend to turn their establishments into delightful little worlds unto themselves that are, for better or worse, sealed off to the city's nuisances.

The city occupies a high plateau, making it chilly in the Brazilian winter and very warm, but rarely stifling hot, in summer. Unfortunately, São Paulo's millions of cars and its position in a flat basin ringed by mountains, can make smog a serious problem, especially on dry, sunny days. Frequent gray, drizzly weather can be oppressive at times but does keep temperatures moderate and the air relatively clean.

HISTORY

Founded by Jesuit brothers Manoel da Nóbrega and José de Anchieta in 1554, São Paulo remained a tiny provincial backwater for almost three centuries. However, it did serve as a base for groups of slave-trading pioneers, known as *bandeirantes*, who helped establish Portuguese control of Brazil's interior, including incursions into Spanish territory.

By the 18th century the *bandeirantes* had turned their attention to mineral exploration, discovering gold mines in Minas Gerais, Goiás and Mato Grosso. São Paulo began to grow as a posting station for an increasing number of fortune hunters heading for the interior, and for traders who gathered sugar from nearby plantations for shipment to the port at Santos.

Upon Brazil's independence in 1822, São Paulo was declared a state capital, a decision that in turn led to the founding of the Law Faculty – arguably Brazil's first public institution of higher learning. An increasingly important political and intellectual center, the city was soon leading the fight both to end slavery and to found the republic.

Meanwhile, the city's economic fortunes were on the rise as planters realized they could make themselves rich by replacing sugar with the world's new, favorite cash crop: coffee. Some of the mansions the successful planters built still line Av Paulista today. To get the beans to international markets, railroads were built to Santos and other Brazilian cities. When slavery was abolished in 1888, the first great wave of immigrants arrived to work the plantations, first from Italy and Spain, and then Japan.

Coffee prices plummeted at the beginning of the 20th century, but there was plenty of capital left from the boom days to fund the city's transformation into an industrial powerhouse; the coffee-built railroad was improved and soon used to ship manufactured goods. Factory jobs attracted a new wave of immigrants from around the world. At the same time, the union movement grew in the shadow of the industrialists and bankers.

By the 1980s the city was by some accounts the fastest-growing in the world as laborers from drought-stricken northeast Brazil streamed in, many of whom found work building the city's new skyscrapers.

In recent years, São Paulo's explosive growth has slowed, though it is now firmly established as Brazil's banking, industrial and cultural capital. As São Paulo matures, it's making strides toward modernizing its infrastructure, including significant expansions of its metro system. At the same time, it's rediscovering its heritage, and has finally begun to protect its historic center as well as to improve the condition of its public spaces.

ORIENTATION

Because it grew at dizzying speeds and without a master plan, São Paulo has no single grid of streets but rather a hodgepodge of grids in more or less concentric circles from the historic center. This, together with a dearth of easily identifiable landmarks, means it's easy to get hopelessly lost.

There is some good news. First, most places of interest are clustered between the historic center and Av Paulista, an area that can easily be navigated by foot – if you have a good map. Second, a safe, efficient metro also connects most central sites as well as a number of further-flung neighborhoods.

Sitting atop a low ridge and lined with skyscrapers, Av Paulista is the city's main drag, dividing its largely working-class Centro from tonier neighborhoods to the south. At its western end, Av Paulista is crossed by the corridor made up of Av Rebouças and Rua da Consolação, which roughly divides the city's eastern and western halves.

To the north of Av Paulista lies what is generally called the Centro, including Praça da República and around; the traditionally Italian Bela Vista area (also known as Bixiga); Luz, a newly refurbished cultural hub; the traditionally Japanese Liberdade; and the old commercial and historic core around Praça da Sé and its cathedral, including Triângulo and Anhangabaú.

Extending for about 10 blocks south of Paulista is the leafy neighborhood known as Jardins (the neighborhood's official name is Jardim Paulista), which has a lion's share of the city's tony restaurants and boutiques. Further south is the leafy, low-rise and exclusively residential area known as Jardins Europa and also the slightly less exclusive Jardim America. East of Jardins Europa is sprawling Parque do Ibirapuera, while to the west lie the upscale neighborhoods of Pinheiros and Vila Madalena. South of Jardim Europa lie the upmarket bastions of Vila Olímpia and Itaím Bibi, both of which are increasingly important business centers.

The city's international airport is located 30km east of the city center and has good connections by airport bus as well as taxi. The city's domestic airport is about 8km south of the city center and easily reached by taxi or city bus. Four intercity bus stations are spread around the city, though all are at or very near a stop of the city's excellent metro. For more information on getting around the city, see p301.

Maps

The *Guia São Paulo* by Quatro Rodas is probably the best guide for navigating the city, with street maps, hotel and restaurant listings and bus lines. It has the clearest presentation of any street directory. Pick one up at any kiosk around town for about R$28.

Tourist offices also offer a free, decent map of the city's central neighborhoods, as well as very helpful walking maps of individual neighborhoods.

INFORMATION
Bookstores

Livraria Cultura (Map pp292-3; ☎ 3170 4033; Av Paulista 2073) Spread out over three stores on the ground floor of the Conjunto Nacional building, this store is a big favorite with students and intellectuals, and has a large collection of both English-language books and travel guides.

Emergency

Deatur Tourist Police (Map ppp280-1; ☎ 3214 0209 or 5090 9032; Av São Luís 95; ⏰ 8am-8pm Mon-Fri, 1-6pm Sat-Sun) A special police force just for tourists with English-speaking officers.

Internet Access

Blenz Café (Map pp292-3; Rua Augusta 1526; per hr R$8; ⏰ Mon-Fri 7:30am-8pm, Sat 11am-6pm) Comfortable, secure underground café with free wi-fi access if you have your own device. The coffee is excellent.

Cyber (Map pp292-3; Rua Augusta 2346, Jardins; per hr R$8; ⏰ 24hr) Comfortable, air-conditioned and conveniently located, with fast connections. Also has phone cabins (R$1/minute to US, R$1.20/minute to Europe).

SÃO PAULO STATE

SÃO PAULO

INFORMATION
Federal Police........................1 B1
Tourist Information Booth......(see 30)
Tourist Information Booth......(see 32)
US Consulate...........................2 C4

SIGHTS & ACTIVITIES
Auditório Ibirapuera..................3 D3
Bosque da Leitura.....................4 D3
Centro Brasileiro de Estudos Latino
 Americano (CBEAL)................5 C1
Fundação Maria Luísa e Oscar
 Americano..............................6 B3
Instituto Butantan.....................7 B2
Instituto Tomie Ohtake..............8 C2
Jardim Botânico.......................(see 9)
Jardim Zoológico.......................9 E4
Memorial da América Latina......10 C1
Memorial do Imigrante..............11 E2
Monumento Bandeiras...............12 D3
Museu Afro-Brasil....................13 C3
Museu da Casa Brasileira..........14 C3
Museu de Arte Contemporânea...15 D3
Museu de Arte Moderna............16 D3
Museu de Arte Sacra.................17 D1

SLEEPING
Albergue da Juventude
 Praça da Árvore......................18 D4
Hotel Unique...........................19 C3

EATING
Green......................................20 D3

DRINKING
Bar do Unique........................(see 19)

ENTERTAINMENT
Bourbon Street Music Club.......21 C4
Canto da Ema.......................(see 8)
Disco......................................22 C3
D-Edge...................................23 C4
Lotus......................................24 C4
Love Club & Lounge................25 C3
Tom Brazil..............................26 B4
Week.....................................27 C1

SHOPPING
Daslu.....................................28 C3
Feira Bendito Calixto...............29 C2
Shopping Iguatemi..................30 C2

TRANSPORT
Terminal Intermunicipal do
 Jabaquara.............................31 D4
Terminal Tietê.........................32 D1

To Aeroporto São
José dos Campos
(75km); Mojí das
Cruzes (28km)

To Rio de
Janeiro
(429km)

To Belo
Horizonte
(586km)

To Paranapiacaba
(32km)

To Embu
(16km)

0   2 miles
0   4 km

Medical Services

Einstein Hospital (☎ 3747 1233; Av Albert Einstein 627, Morumbi) Located on a southwestern corner of the city in Morumbi, Einstein is one of the best in Latin America. To get there, catch bus 7241 to Jardim Colombo from Av Paulista.

Sírio-Libânes Hospital (Map pp292-3; ☎ 3155 0200; Rua Dona Adma Jafet 91) Another recommended hospital in Bela Vista, near Av Paulista.

Money

Except on weekends, changing money at banks and exchange offices is easy. ATMs are widely available throughout the city, with many clustered on Av Paulista, which is home to a range of banks from around the world. Many travel agencies and exchange offices around the city offer good rates, but avoid the smaller ones downtown – some are illegal and may rip you off.

Action Cambio (Map pp280-1; Shopping Light, Rua Xavier de Toledo; ☿ 10am-7pm Mon-Fri, to 4pm Sat) Changes money.

American Express Aeroporto São Paulo/Guarulhos (☎ 4004 7797; ☿ 7am-10:30pm); Central branch (Map pp292-3; ☎ 4004 7797; Av Paulista 2300, enter at Rua Haddock Lobo 400; ☿ 9am-3pm Mon-Fri).

Post

Post Office Shopping Light (Map pp280-1; Rua Xavier de Toledo; ☿ 10am-6pm); Av Paulista (Map pp292-3; Av Santos 2224; ☿ 9am-5pm Mon-Fri)

Telephone

Baratofone (Map pp280-1; Rua Quitanda 144, Centro; ☿ 8am-6:45pm Mon-Fri, 10am-3pm Sat) R$0.80/minute to US, R$1.50 to Europe.

Lig Center (Map pp280-1; Rua 7 de Abril 253; ☿ 8am-7:30pm Mon-Fri, 10am-5pm Sat) International calls from R$1/minute. Situated 200m from Praça da República.

Tourist Information

Designed for both travelers and Anglophone expats, www.gringoes.com has lots of information covering restaurants to nightclubs, plus a free weekly newsletter about goings-on about town. Pick up a *Guia da Folha* at any newsstand for reviews of the city's dining, entertainment and nightlife options (also available at www1.folha.uol.com.br/guia in Portuguese). The weekly magazine *Veja São Paulo* also has listings.

City tourist information booths (☎ 6224 0400; www.cidadedesaopaulo.com in Portuguese, English & Spanish; ☿ 9am-6pm) all have good city and state maps, as well as helpful walking maps for individual neighborhoods. They are also good for bus and metro information. English is spoken. Locations include the following:

Aeroporto São Paulo/Guarulhos (☿ 6am-10pm) Kiosks in Terminals 1 & 2 at the international airport.

Avenida Paulista (Map pp292-3; ☿ 9am-6pm) Just across from Museu de Arte de São Paulo (MASP).

Avenida São João (Map pp280-1; Av São João 473; ☿ 9am-6pm)

Iguatemi (Map p277; Av Brigadeiro Faria Lima 2232; ☿ 9am-6pm Mon-Fri, noon-6pm Sat & Sun) In front of Shopping Iguatemi.

Parque da Luz (Map pp280-1; Parque da Luz; ☿ 10am-4pm) Kiosk in the park just outside the Pinacoteca do Estado.

Terminal Tietê bus station (Map p277; ☿ 6am-10pm Mon-Fri, 8am-8pm Sat & Sun) In the city's main intercity bus station.

Visas

Polícia Federal (Map p277; ☎ 3616 5166, 3616 5177; Rua Hugo Dantola 95, Lapa; ☿ 8am-5pm Mon-Fri) For visa extensions, head to this office about 4km west of the Barra Funda metro.

DANGERS & ANNOYANCES

While crime levels remain high in São Paulo, the worst is largely limited to the city's periphery. During the day, you can walk most places in central São Paulo, though always exercise normal precautions. After dark, you can still walk around Av Paulista, Jardins and Rua Augusta as well as the chicer neighborhoods of the Zona Sul (Vila Madalena, Pinheiros, and Vila Olímpia), but avoid empty side streets and carry as few valuables as possible. Centro and Praça da República require more vigilance, and walking should be avoided after dark where possible – grab a taxi instead.

If you're driving, be aware that carjackings and red-light robberies can occur anywhere in the city. São Paulo recently changed a traffic law – it's now legal (and recommended) to just slow down at red lights at night. If there's no traffic, continue without stopping. The subway is generally safe, although you should keep your eyes open; on buses, look out for pickpockets, and at night consider taxis over public transportation.

SIGHTS

Praça da Sé & Around

The old heart of the city, **Praça da Sé** (literally, 'Cathedral Square') has seen better days but still draws animated crowds, from street hawkers and nose-down business types to – unfortunately – more than its fair share of pickpockets. Crowning the square is the domed **Catedral da Sé** (Map pp280-1; ☾ 8am-5pm Mon-Sat, 8am-1pm & 3-6pm Sun), a huge neo-Byzantine concoction that, for better or worse, replaced the original 18th-century structure in the 1920s. Still, its lush interior is worth a gander. On the other side of Praça da Sé stands the more modest but also more authentic **Igreja do Carmo** (Map pp280-1), which dates to the 1630s and still preserves its original high altar. At writing it was closed for major restoration.

North of the cathedral, **Rua 25 de Março** is the traditional preserve of the city's Lebanese merchants and remains a lively, crowded wholesale shopping district where you can find remarkable deals on a variety of goods, from clothing to electronics. A little further on, the recently refurbished **Mercado Muncipal** (Map pp280-1; Rua Cantareira 306; ☾ 6am-6pm Mon-Sat, 6-4pm Sun, closed last Sun of month) is a Belle Epoque confection of stained glass and a series of vast domes. Inside is a humble but delightful market specializing in fresh produce and dried goods. It's also a great place to sample a classic Sampa delight: *pasteis*, pockets of dough stuffed with meat, cheese or fish and then fried.

IGREJA DE SÃO FRANCISCO DE ASSIS

This **church** (Map pp280-1; Largo de São Francisco) just west of the cathedral is one the best-preserved colonial structures in the city. Built in the 17th and 18th centuries, it is a classic example of Portuguese baroque. At the time of writing the church was closed for a major restoration. Next to it is the prestigious **College of Law** (Map pp280-1). Founded in 1827 it is Brazil's oldest institution of higher learning, though the current building dates to the early 20th century.

SOLAR DA MARQUESA

Down a narrow side street near the cathedral stands the city's last surviving 18th-century residence, **Solar da Marquesa** (Map pp280-1; ☎ 3241 4238; Rua Roberto Simonsen 136; admission free; ☾ 9am-5pm Tue-Sun). It is a simple but delightful villa that was once home to a lover of Emperor Dom Pedro I and which now houses a modest museum devoted to the history of the city.

PÁTEO DO COLÉGIO

Just up the street from Solar da Marquesa lies the **missionary** (Map pp280-1; ☎ 3105 6898; www .pateodocolegio.com.br in Portuguese; Praça Páteo do Colégio; admission R$5; ☾ 9am-5pm) that occupies the exact spot where São Paulo was founded in 1554 by Jesuit brothers José de Anchieta and Manoel da Nóbregra. The current structure is actually a 1950s replica of the monastery that once stood here, although inside it does possess a nice little collection of original relics from the city's first days. The museum's café also makes for a tranquil pit stop.

Triângulo & Anhangabaú

Just north of Praça da Sé lies the Triângulo, a triangle bounded roughly by Praça da Sé, Mosteiro São Bento and the Prefeitura (city hall). It has narrow, pedestrian-only streets and towering office buildings that in the late 19th and early 20th centuries served as the city's commercial heart. Even if Av Paulista and Vila Olímpia now attract the big money, the Triângulo still does a brisk trade, thanks largely to presence of **BOVESPA** (Map pp280-1; ☎ 3233 2000; www.bovespa.com.br in English & Portuguese; Rua XV de Novembro 275), Latin America's largest stock exchange.

Just west of BOVESPA rises the 35-story **Edifício Martinelli** (Map pp280-1; Rua São Bento 405). São Paulo's first skyscraper, the soaring 1929 Beaux Arts structure seems to have been imported wholesale from turn-of-the-century Manhattan. The building doesn't accept visitors.

At the northern edge of the Triângulo, you'll find the austere but impressive **Mosteiro São Bento** (Map pp280-1; ☎ 3328 8799; admission free; ☾ 6am-6pm Mon-Fri, 6am-noon & 4-6pm Sat & Sun), which is among the city's oldest and most important churches, though its neo-Gothic façade dates only to the early 20th century. Step inside the church to witness its impressive stained glass.

On the small Praça do Patriarca at the southwestern entrance to Triângulo, the more modest, better-preserved **Igreja de Santo Antônio** (Map pp280-1; admission free; ☾ 6am-6pm Mon-Fri, 6am-noon & 4-6pm Sat & Sun) retains many of its original 18th-century contours.

Heading west from Praça do Patriarca, you'll cross the 1892 **Viaduto de Chá**, which crosses the Vale do Anhangabaú, along with the **Viaduto Santa Efigénia** a little to the north and dating from the same era. Both of these elaborate cast-iron bridges were long synonymous with São Paulo's cultural and economic ascendancy. In the Tupi-Guarani language, Anhangabaú means Demon's Valley, and indigenous peoples believed evil spirits dwelled there. The area

CENTRAL SÃO PAULO

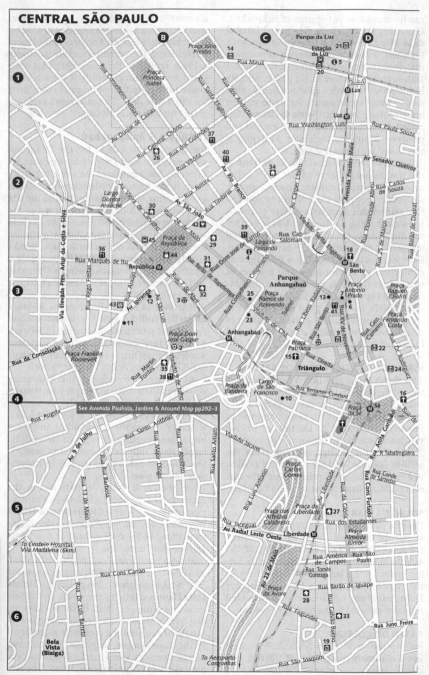

can still be dicey after dark. Across Viaduto de Chá bridge lies **Shopping Light** (Map pp280-1; ☎ 3154 2299; Viaduto do Chá; ⏱ 9am-9pm Mon-Fri, 10am-7pm Sat), a modern, midrange mall that occupies a rather grand building once belonging to the Light English Company. There's a good food court on the 5th floor.

CENTRO CULTURAL BANCO DO BRASIL
Housed in an extraordinarily and lovingly restored Beaux Arts building, this **cultural center** (Map pp280-1; ☎ 3113 3651; www.cultura-e.com. br in Portuguese; Rua Álvares Penteado 112; admission free; ⏱ noon-6:30pm Tue-Sun) holds innovative exhibitions of contemporary art as well as excellent film series and theater performances.

BANESPA
For one of Sampa's best panoramas, head to the top of this **skyscraper** (Map pp280-1; Rua João Brícola 24; ⏱ 10am-5pm Mon-Fri), Brazil's version of the Empire State Building, completed in 1939. Ride free to the observation deck on the top floor for views of the city. Note, you will need some form of ID to sign in.

THEATRO MUNICIPAL
São Paulo's most splendid construction, this **theater** (Map pp280-1; ☎ 3223 3022; www.prefeitura .sp.gov.br/theatromunicipal; Praça Ramos de Azevedo) was begun in 1903 in the style of Paris' Palais Garnier. Its heavily ornamented façade seems to combine every architectural style imaginable, from baroque to Art Nouveau, and its interior is clad in gold and marble. The theater hosts the city's top classical music and opera performances. There are guided visits at 1pm Tuesdays and Thursdays; reservations are required at least one day in advance.

Praça da República & Around
Just a few blocks northwest of Anhangabaú lies Praça da República, an always-lively square that turns into an open-air market on Sundays, specializing in crafts, paintings, coins and gemstones. The area north of the square has become a center popular with the gay community (p298), while to the south lies a dense nest of business hotels, huge office buildings and, especially along **Avenida São Luís**, what were once some of the city's most prestigious apartment buildings.

For Caetano Veloso fans, a visit to the corner of **Avenida Ipiranga** and **Avenida São João**, which features in his beloved song 'Sampa,' is mandatory. There are no sights to speak of, but the bustling intersection does do a good job of summing up the city.

EDIFÍCIO ITÁLIA
With 46 stories, this **skyscraper** (Map pp280-1; Av Ipiranga) just south of the Praça da República, and near Av São Luís, is the tallest in the city center. Its top-floor restaurant offers some of the best views of São Paulo, though meal prices are high and the food only passable. Strictly speaking, you're supposed to be a customer to go there; if you're not, act like one.

EDIFÍCIO COPAN
Shorter but architecturally more remarkable, the nearby **Edifício Copan** (Map pp280-1; Av Ipiranga 200) was designed by modernist master Oscar Niemeyer. The building's serpentine façade and narrow brises-soleil have become a symbol of the city. You can visit its snaking, sloping ground-floor shopping arcade, but the upper floors are made up of private apartments and thus off-limits. Note that the leftist architect designed the building to bring together all classes by including sprawling apartments for the rich as well as tiny studios for the working poor – a real rarity in class-conscious São Paulo.

Luz
Located in a tough area just north of the city center, the Luz neighborhood has become an unlikely cultural hub thanks to major restoration of a series of grand turn-of-the-century buildings around the **Parque da Luz**. The park has also undergone a careful restoration, with spreading, tropical trees, discreetly placed modern sculpture and a generous police presence.

Across the street from the park sits **Estação da Luz** (Map pp280-1; Praça da Luz), a classic late-Victorian train station constructed with materials entirely shipped in from Britain and completed in 1901. It too has been returned to its original splendor. It services São Paulo's extensive suburban lines, with a long tunnel linking it to the Luz metro station.

PINACOTECA DO ESTADO
This elegant neoclassical **museum** (Map pp280-1; State Art Museum; ☎ 3229 9844; Parque da Luz; adult/student R$4/2 incl admission to Estação Pinacoteca; ☼ 10am-6pm Tue-Sun) houses an excellent collection of Brazilian – and especially Paulista – art from the 19th century to present, including works by big names such as Portinari and Di Cavalcanti. Extensive renovations have made it a pleasant place to while away a rainy afternoon, and there is an attractive café that spills out into the adjacent Parque da Luz.

MUSEU DA LÍNGUA PORTUGUESA
Half of Estação da Luz has been given over to this recently inaugurated **museum** (Map pp280-1; ☎ 3326 0775; www.estacaodaluz.com.br; Praça da Luz; adult/student R$4/2; ☼ 10am-6pm, last admission 5pm), with fascinating permanent exhibits documenting the rise of the Brazilian language as distinct from European Portuguese, as well as creative temporary installations celebrating Brazilian literature. Note, though, that all accompanying signs are in Portuguese only.

ESTAÇÃO JÚLIO PRESTES
A short walk west of Estação da Luz is this far larger and grander **train station** (Map pp280-1; Praça Júlio Prestes) in turn-of-the-century Beaux Arts style, though only completed in the 1930s. One wing houses the **Estação Pinacoteca** (adult/student R$4/2 incl admission to Pinacoteca do Estado; ☼ 10am-6pm Tue-Sun), an annex of the Pinacoteca do Estado, which hosts large and often very good temporary exhibitions, mostly of Brazilian art. The ground floor houses the **Memorial da Liberdade** (admission free;

LITERATURE TO GO
Need a copy of Marx's *Das Kapital* to brighten up your commute? How about a Portuguese version of *Chicken Soup for the Soul*? Select Sampa metro stations are now fitted out with vending machines that dispense not chips and soda but low-cost paperbacks, both literary and popular. It sounds more like Paris than São Paulo, but in fact Sampa has cultivated a reverence for learning at least since the founding of Brazil's first higher education institution here in 1827. Besides its vending machines, São Paulo's literary ways are evidenced in fine bookstores such as Livraria Cultura (p276), its highly respected newspaper the *Folha de São Paulo*, its Bosque da Leitura (open-air library; p284) and its 50-plus theaters, many of which are devoted to experimental works.

(🕒 10am-6pm Tue-Sun), a simple but powerful exhibit occupying cells used to imprison and torture political dissidents during Brazil's military dictatorship of the 1960s and '70s. Also in the Estação Júlio Prestes complex is the world-renowned **Sala São Paulo** (🕾 3292 4875; www.salasaopaulo.art.br in Portuguese), a classical music venue that cleverly occupies the station's principle waiting room. Part of the station is still a stop on the suburban train system.

Liberdade

São Paulo is home to the largest population of Japanese descendants outside Japan, and the Liberdade neighborhood – a short walk south of Praça da Sé – has long been the traditional center of this community. Though most new Asian immigrants these days come from China and Korea, the gritty neighborhood is lined with traditional Japanese shops and eateries.

Praça da Liberdade is the neighborhood's main square and also the location of its metro stop. It hosts an open-air market on Sundays. A short walk south on Rua Galvão Bueno takes you past many Asian shops and restaurants as well as some rather neglected Japanese-style gardens.

MUSEU DA IMIGRAÇÃO JAPONESA

This modest but fascinating **museum** (Museum of Japanese Immigration; Map pp280-1; 🕾 3209 5465; Rua São Joaquim 381; adult/child R$5/1; 🕒 1:30-5:30pm Tue-Sun), on the 7th floor of a Liberdade office building, documents the arrival and integration of the Japanese community. Photos, period objects and a full-scale reconstruction of a typical immigrant's farm lodging tell a poignant story, from the arrival in Santos of the first 781 settlers aboard the *Kasato-Maru* in 1908 through to today. Signage is in Japanese and Portuguese only.

Avenida Paulista, Jardins & Around

Once the domain of coffee barons and their sprawling manses, Av Paulista (often known simply as 'Paulista') began to go 'Manhattan' in the 1950s and today is lined with towering modernist office buildings. Though few of these buildings have much architectural merit, the sum of the parts is impressive. It's also a lively area both day and night, packed with restaurants, shops, theaters and cafés. Just off Paulista across from Museu de Arte de São Paulo (MASP; see below) lies **Parque Siqueira Campos**, a beautifully designed and maintained park that recreates the Atlantic rain forest that was leveled to build São Paulo. It's a remarkably tranquil refuge just off the city's busiest street.

North of Paulista, **Rua Augusta** is São Paulo's traditional red-light district, and at night the traffic slows to a crawl as johns troll the sidewalks from their cars. The area is slowly being taken over by the city's alternative crowd, however, and its simple bars and restaurants are packed after 10pm with the young, high-minded and multiply pierced.

On the southern slope of Paulista lies Jardins, the city's leafiest and chicest central neighborhood. This is where you will find some of the city's most over-the-top shopping, especially along Alameda Lorena and, above all, **Rua Oscar Freire**, with its show-stopping series of boutiques and super-refined eateries. A recent face-lift has Oscar Freire looking better than ever (and the same can be said for many of its most avid shoppers).

MUSEU DE ARTE DE SÃO PAULO (MASP)

Sampa's pride, this **museum** (Map pp292-3; 🕾 3251 5644; masp.uol.com.br; Av Paulista 1578; adult/student R$15/7; 🕒 11am-6pm Tue-Sun, to 8pm Thu) possesses Latin America's most comprehensive collection of Western art. Hovering above a concrete plaza that turns into an antiques fair on Sundays (p300), the museum, designed by architect Lina Bo Bardi and completed in 1968, is considered a classic of modernism by many and an abomination by a vocal few. The collection, though, is unimpeachable, and ranges from Goya to El Greco to Manet. The impressionist collection is particularly impressive. There are also a few great Brazilian paintings, including three fine works by Cândido Portinari. The museum hosts temporary exhibits, and there is a bright, pleasant cafeteria on the lower level, though the food is only OK.

Parque do Ibirapuera

The biggest green space in central São Paulo, **Parque do Ibirapuera** makes a fine escape from the city's seemingly infinite stretches of concrete. In addition, the leafy 2-sq-km park serves as a thriving center of the city's cultural life, with a series of museums, performance spaces and the grounds for São Paulo's renowned **Bienal** (see p299).

Inaugurated in 1954 to commemorate the city's 400th anniversary, the park was designed by renowned landscape architect Roberto Burle Marx. A series of landmark buildings in the park are the work of modernist master Oscar Niemeyer; most of them are linked by a long and distinctively serpentine covered walkway. At the north entrance stands Victor Brecheret's huge **Monumento Bandeiras** (Map p277), erected in 1953 in memory of the city's early pioneers. A meandering duck pond takes up much of the western half of the park, and around it are arranged a series of shaded walks, including the **Bosque da Leitura**(Map p277) – a woodsy section that on Sundays turns into an open-air library where you can check out books for the afternoon.

To get the park, take the metro to Vila Mariana station and then bus 775-A 'Jardim Aldagiza.' There are lots of snack stands in the park, or you can get a full meal at the **Green** (Map p277; R$25/kilo; ❤ lunch daily), between the Museu de Arte Moderna and the Museu Afro-Brasil, which serves a hearty per-kilo buffet.

MUSEU DE ARTE CONTEMPORÂNEA

A small branch of the University of São Paulo's **contemporary art museum** (Map p277; ☎ 3091 3039; adult/student R$2; ❤ 10am-7pm Mon-Fri, to 4pm Sat) displays a rotating collection of mostly local, contemporary artists in the same Niemeyer building that houses most of the Bienal's exhibits. If the current show is not to your liking, concentrate on the building's huge spaces and Niemeyer's distinctly curving ramps.

MUSEU DE ARTE MODERNA

Brazil's oldest **modern art museum** (Map p277; ☎ 5085 1300; www.mam.org.br; admission adult/student R$5.50/2.75, free Sun; ❤ 10am-6pm Tue-Sun) possesses a fine collection of Brazilian modernists such as Anita Malfatti and Di Cavalcanti as well as works by Miró, Chagall, Picasso and Dufy. However, the public spaces are devoted exclusively to temporary exhibits. Check the museum's website for current offerings.

MUSEU AFRO-BRASIL

With a permanent collection of some 5000 objects ranging from paintings to religious objects to historical documents, this remarkable **museum** (Map p277; ☎ 5579 8542; www.museu afrobrasil.prodam.sp.gov.br; admission adult/student R$5/2.50; ❤ 10am-5.30pm Tue-Sun), is another winningly open and bright Niemeyer pavilion. Opened

in 2004, it sheds light on the lives of Brazil's African diaspora, from slave times through to the present.

AUDITÓRIO IBIRAPUERA

The park's most recent addition, the **Auditório Ibirapuera** (Map p277; www.auditorioibirapuera.com.br) is another Niemeyer design that dates to the park's founding, though it was only completed five decades later, in 2005. Nicknamed 'a língua' ('the tongue') for the bright-red metal awning that sticks out rather lewdly from an otherwise bunkerlike concrete trapezoid, the hall hosts a wide variety of musical styles, from classical to experimental. Concert bookings can be made through Ticketmaster Brasil (☎ 6846 6000).

Pinheiros, Vila Madalena & Butantã

West of Jardins lies Pinheiros, a sprawling, mostly residential neighborhood of identikit high-rise apartments. One exception is the **Instituto Tomie Ohtake** (Map p277; ☎ 2245 1900; www.institutotomieohtake.org.br; Av Brigadeiro Faria Lima 201; admission free; ❤ 11am-8pm Tue-Sun), a cultural institute founded by Ruy Ohtake, São Paulo's most prominent contemporary architect. The building itself is a curving, colorful affair, perhaps not to all tastes but certainly striking. Inside, an attractive gallery space features changing exhibits of prominent, mostly local artists.

At the heart of the larger Pinheiros neighborhood is the distinctly low-rise and pedestrian-friendly Vila Madalena. Something of a Bohemian enclave, it has in recent years become a popular alternative to the high-end, attitude-heavy clubs and restaurants of nearby Vila Olímpia. The epicenter of the bar and restaurant scene is the corner of Rua Mourato Coelho and Rua Aspicuelta, which grow crowded at happy hour and, on weekends, stay that way until the wee hours. Rua Fidalga has a number of woodcraft and furnishing shops. It's about a 10-minute walk from the Vila Madalena station to the center of the action.

West of Pinheiros across the Rio Pinheiros lies the Cidade Universitária, home of the prestigious University of São Paulo. The quiet, tree-lined streets play home to the school's faculty and staff and make for pleasant strolling.

INSTITUTO BUTANTAN

One of the city's most popular attractions – at least among non-ophidophobes – this **institute**

(Map p277; ☎ 3726 7222; Av Vital Brazil 1500, Cidade Universitária; admission adult/student R$5/2; ☼ 9am-4:30pm Tue-Sun) is highly respected for its ground-breaking biomedical research. The biggest draw, however, is its venom farm. Researchers milk a total of 54,000 snakes of their poison, which is used to make antidotes to snake and spider bites, as well as in research for other medicines. You can see the snakes in their cages, which attempt to recreate their native habitat – apparently happy snakes produce more poison.

South of Jardins

Extra-wide **Avenida Brigadeiro Faria Lima** (called just 'Faria Lima') marks the southwestern edge of the Jardins neighborhoods. Faria Lima is also the main corridor connecting Pinheiros with the ritzy, though mostly un-inviting, neighborhoods of Morumbi, Vila Olímpia, Itaim Bibi and Moema. All of these areas are composed largely of congested streets, forbidding luxury high-rises and glittering complexes that house the majority of the city's most-profitable businesses, from banking to technology. Unfortunately, poor public transport makes a taxi or your own vehicle a necessity. That said, there are plenty of fine restaurants, nightclubs and shopping opportunities that die-hards may want to seek out.

Occupying an extravagant Palladian-style villa built by a local tycoon and his wife in the 1940s, the small but charming **Museu da Casa Brasileira** (Map p277; ☎ 3032 2499; www .mcb.sp.gov.br; Av Brigadeiro Faria Lima 2705; adult/student R$4/2; ☼ 10am-6pm Tue-Sun) has a hodgepodge collection of Brazilian and European furnishings from the 17th to 20th centuries. The muse-um's café-restaurant is its best feature, with good food and lovely outdoor seating.

Home of the couple who developed the leafy, upscale suburb of Morumbi, **Fundação Maria Luisa e Oscar Americano** (Map p277; ☎ 3742 0077; www.fundacaooscaramericano.org.br; Av Morumbi 4077, Morumbi; adult/student R$8/4; ☼ 11am-5pm Tue-Fri, 10am-5pm Sat-Sun) makes a fine retreat as much for its gardens as for its collection of painting, sculpture and objets d'art from the 18th to 20th centuries. The 1950s house turned museum is a small masterpiece of Brazilian modernism, and there's also a lovely **café** (☼ 11:30am-5:45pm Tue-Sun) that serves traditional high tea for R$40.

PARQUE DO ESTADO

In the southern suburb of Cursino, **Parque do Estado** is far from the action but worth seeking out if you find yourself craving greenery in cement-heavy Sampa. Its northern tip is given over to the **Jardim Botánico** (Map p277; ☎ 5073 6300; adult/student R$3/1; ☼ 9am-5pm Wed-Sun), a well-tended botanical garden that includes a promenade of imperial palms, an orchid farm, picturesque ponds, a stand of brazilwood trees and a herb garden where you are encouraged to smell the aromatic flowers and leaves.

Nearby in the park is the **Jardim Zoológico** (Map p277; ☎ 5073 0811; www.zoologico.sp.gov.br; adult/children under 13 R$12/3; ☼ 9am-5pm Tue-Sun), Brazil's largest zoo. It's home to some 3000 animal species and is spread out over some 900 hectares, much of which is old-growth Mata Atlântica (Atlantic rain forest).

The best way to get to the park is by metro to the São Judas station, where you can catch bus 4742 'Jardim Climax.'

CLASS AIRFARE

Why has a helicopter been swaddled in cashmere and hung in the main hall of Daslu (p300), São Paulo's most exclusive shopping emporium? The answer is simple: a private chopper is the ultimate Paulistano status symbol. The city's elite took to the skies in a big way during the 1990s, rebelling against congested roads and kidnappers targeting wealthy residents. Today São Paulo is said to have more helicopter traffic than any other city, with some 300 heliports versus a mere 60 in New York City.

The problem, however, is that only the super-rich can afford their own bird. What are the merely 'very rich' to do? In a fit of class solidarity, they have founded helicopter 'collectives,' enabling members to share the cost of purchase and maintenance of the choppers, and also pilot hire. After an initial outlay of about US$50,000, members need only pony up as little as US$40,000 a year – a bargain when you consider it's a mere 10 times the typical annual salary of a domestic servant.

North of Centro

The neighborhoods north of Centro don't invite lingering, as they're mostly unsafe, bleak-looking or both. However, there are a few sights worth seeking out.

MUSEU DE ARTE SACRA

The best of its kind in Brazil, the **museu de Arte Sacra** (Museum of Sacred Art; Map p277; ☎ 3326 1373; http://artesacra.sarasa.com.br in Portuguese; Av Tiradentes 676, adult/student R$4/2; ⏰ 11am-6pm Tue-Fri, 10am-7pm Sat & Sun) includes works by renowned 18th-century sculptor Antônio Aleijadinho, along with some 2000 other ecclesiastical works from the 17th to 20th centuries. The museum is housed in the 18th-century Luz monastery, which is one of São Paulo's best-preserved buildings of the period and also a fine example of Portuguese colonial architecture.

MEMORIAL DA AMÉRICA LATINA

Another Niemeyer creation, the **Memorial da América Latina** (Map p277) is easily identifiable by the 7m-high cement hand slashed with red just outside its main building. The complex is home to the **Centro Brasileiro de Estudos Latino Americano** (CBEAL; Map p277; ☎ 3823 4600; www.memorial.sp.gov.br in Portuguese; Av Auro Soares de Moura Andrade 664; ⏰ 9am-6pm Tue-Sun), a cultural and research foundation, and includes an auditorium that stages free concerts, and various interesting handicraft exhibits from regional Brazil and other Latin American countries. Cândido Portinari's painting *Tiradentes* hangs in the Salão de Atos, and

---

BRAZIL'S MELTING POT

Brazil's unparalleled racial and ethnic diversity means there is no such thing as a typical Brazilian face. That's why Brazilian passports are highly sought after on the black market. Many faces could pass for being Brazilian.

It is especially hard to say someone is a typical Paulistano. The city has been multiracial from its foundation in the 16th century, bringing together Portuguese, African and indigenous peoples. Since then, wave after wave of immigration has given the city a truly global face. Italian and Spanish immigrants poured into the country to pick coffee after Brazil emancipated slaves in 1888, and today their descendants number about five and three million respectively. These were followed by Japanese immigrants, and today São Paulo has more Japanese descendants (about 1.5 million) than anywhere else outside of Japan. Likewise, São Paulo has more Lebanese descendants (850,000) than anywhere outside Lebanon. Sampa is also home to Brazil's largest Jewish community, with some 130,000 members. There are one million people of German stock and, as well, sizable Chinese, Armenian, Lithuanian, Greek, Syrian, Korean, Polish and Hungarian communities.

For a deeper understanding of the history of immigration to São Paulo, head to the **Memorial do Imigrante** (Map p277; ☎ 6693 0917; www.memorialdoimigrante.sp.gov.br in Portuguese; Rua Visconde de Paraíba 1316; admission adult/student R$4/2; ⏰ 10am-5pm Tue-Sun) in the eastern suburb of Moóca. The museum has a permanent collection of period furnishings, some old documents and photographs, and often hosts visiting exhibitions that explore the nature of emigration and national identity.

The biggest attraction, however, is the memorial structure itself. Built in 1887, it was called the **Hospedaria dos Imigrantes**, and it functioned as a holding place for immigrant labor. The dorm rooms are immense, and one can still see the huge sliding rails that were used to bring in truckloads of people and luggage, fresh from the dock. To the millions of immigrants who came to São Paulo hoping for a better life, it must have seemed more of a prison than a hostel. Designed to hold up to 4000 people, records show that as many as 10,000 individuals were housed there at one time. Translators had to be brought in to help recent arrivals understand the work contracts they were signing – many of which proved punishingly unfair. There were guards and wardens to make sure people didn't slip away in the middle of the night – not everyone who got off the boat wanted to break their back picking coffee. Of course, a guarantee of work was the only way out of the hospedaria.

To get to the memorial take the metro to Bresser. It's a five-minute walk from there, or on weekends you can take the little tram that shuttles visitors back and forth.

huge panels by Carybé and Poty Lazzarotto represent the people of South America.

WALKING TOUR

If you really want a feel for the historic parts of São Paulo, follow this meandering three-hour stroll that brings you past all the best-known landmarks and sights of Sampa.

The start is at **Praça da República (1)**, near the metro stop with the same name. Look for the big yellow edifice known as the **Caetano de Campos building (2)** – it used to be a high school but is now the headquarters for the State Department of Education. On Sunday this plaza is the venue for the Feira da República (see p300), which has a huge variety of crafts, paintings, coins and stones.

Head down Av Ipiranga and then turn onto Av São Luís to get a look at what's still one of the tallest buildings in town – the 46-story **Edifício Itália (3**; p282).

Continuing down Av São Luís (there are lots of travel agencies and money exchange bureaus on this street), check out the rather squat, grey building at the end of the small park on the left. It looks like a prison, but it's

the **Mario de Andrade Municipal Library (4)**, housing the largest book collection in the city.

Turning left onto Rua Xavier de Toledo, keeping the library on your left, follow the road downhill toward the Anhangabaú metro station a few blocks away. Keep a sharp lookout – it's easy to miss in the hustle and bustle. To the right of the station and down a few steps into a park is **Ladeira da Memória** (Memory Hill; **5**), where the Chafariz dos Piques fountain used to supply the city and cattle dealers with water. Now it's the site of the Piramide dos Piques, an obelisk-like structure pointing at the sky.

Continue down Rua Xavier de Toledo until the **Theatro Municipal (6**; p281) appears – this baroque building, with its art nouveau features, is the pride of the city. Across the street from the Teatro is **Shopping Light (7**; p281) Opposite

---

WALK FACTS

Start/Finish Praça da República
Distance 3.5km
Duration 2-3 hours

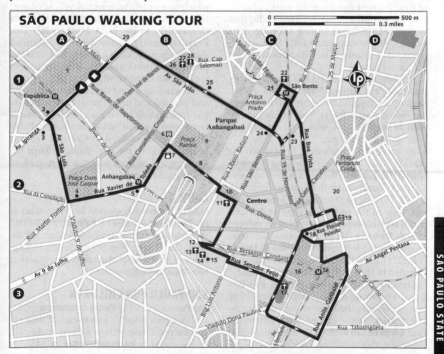

SÃO PAULO WALKING TOUR

SÃO PAULO STATE

the Teatro, on the right, is the **Viaduto do Chá (8)**, a metal bridge built in 1892 and named after an old tea plantation that used to be in the area. Pedestrian traffic became too heavy for the old bridge and a new one was inaugurated in 1938.

Crossing the bridge, look out over the **Parque Anhangabaú (9)** on the left. In the Tupi-Guarani language, Anhangabaú means Demon's Valley, because indigenous peoples believed bad spirits once dwelled there. At the other side of the bridge, enter **Praça do Patriarca (10)** straight ahead. Here you'll find the **Igreja de Santo Antônio (11**; p279), the central church of the settlement of São Paulo at the start of the 17th century.

Some 20 paces beyond that is Rua São Bento, a pedestrian street loaded with shops. Turn right onto Rua São Bento and eventually you'll step into the **Largo de São Francisco (12)**, a little plaza triangulated by the **Igreja de São Francisco de Assis (13**; p279), the **Igreja do Carmo (14**; p279) and the city's well-respected **College of Law (15**; p279). The churches contain a vast number of 18th-century paintings and are well worth a look. In front of the law school is one of Brazil's most controversial works of art – a statue by Swiss artist William Zadig that depicts a Frenchman kissing an indigenous woman. If you can read a little Portuguese, the statue's history is well documented by a plaque on its base.

Just beyond the statue is Rua Senador Feijó, leading to the famous **Praça da Sé (16**; p278). Soak up the joyous atmosphere in the square, but watch your pockets. Step inside the **Catedral da Sé (17**; p279), which reportedly can hold up to 8000 people.

As you exit the cathedral, head down the plaza and continue toward the **Caixa Economica Federal (18)**, home to the city's coffers and also a great cultural center that features Brazilian artists. Turning right onto Rua Floriano Peixoto, walk to the end (it's a dead-end street) and feast your eyes upon the pinkish colored **Solar da Marquesa (19**; p279). Follow the street around to the left and **Praça Páteo do Colégio (20**; p279), the actual site where São Paulo was founded in 1554, will appear on your right.

Directly in front of this plaza is Rua Boa Vista. Following it away from Praça da Sé brings you into the heart of the city's financial district. At the end of Boa Vista, you'll find **Largo de São Bento (21)**, the square that launched thousands of *bandeirante* expe-

ditions. Now it is home to the **Mosteiro São Bento (22**; p279), a monastery and basilica built in an eclectic style and still putting on Gregorian-chant concerts.

Leaving the square, walk up Rua São Bento, a pedestrian street, until reaching Av São João. Turn left at Av São João and another quick left at the next street, where on the right stands the art-deco **BANESPA building (23**; p281). Head to the top floor for a sweeping view of São Paulo. Back track to Rua São Bento and then keep heading straight down Av São João. On the left just past São Bento stands **Edifício Martinelli (24**; p279). You are now crossing the Vale do Anhangabaú that you saw earlier from the Viaduto do Chá. Ahead is the **Prédio dos Correios (25)**, the largest post office in the country. It's currently being restored and will soon be a cultural center and postal museum.

To finish this tour, go up Av São João as far as **Largo de Paiçandú (26)**, where you'll find **NS do Rosário dos Homens Pretos (27)**, a church that was built in 1906 by Black Brazilians on a site where sacred African religious rites were formerly performed. Behind this pretty church, which is painted an unusual yellow/orange tone, is the magnificent **Monumento á Mãe Preta** (Monument to the Black Mother; **28**). This heart-wrenching statue depicts an African slave woman suckling a white child, and the poem underneath gives voice to her lament for her own children who must go hungry.

To wrap up a long day, continue forward and you will end up at the intersection of Av São João and Av Ipiranga, a **corner (29)** that is considered the most famous in all of São Paulo and was immortalized in Caetano Veloso's beautiful ode to the city, 'Sampa.' Turn left and you will be back where it all started, in the Praça da República.

COURSES

One of the most respected language schools for Portuguese courses is **Polyglot** (☎ 3744 4397; www.polyglot.com.br; Rua Hastimphilo de Moura 179, Morumbi). **CEL-LEP** (www.cellep.com) specializes in English and Spanish but also offers Portuguese at locations throughout the city.

SÃO PAULO FOR CHILDREN

São Paulo's sprawling **Parque do Ibirapuera** (p283) makes a great place for kids to run off their excess energy. Those without a fear of snakes will be fascinated by **Instituto Butantan** (p284).

The large and very good zoo, **Jardim Zoológico** (p285), is a definite kid-pleaser. If you have a car, don't miss the **Zôo Safari** (R$8 per person), which is a kind of drive-through petting zoo in which animals, from llamas to monkeys, come right up to your vehicle.

TOURS

For higher-end day tours of the city (from R$135 per person) or nearby destinations such as Campos do Jordão (p310) or Guarujá (p307) from R$200, consider **Easygoing Brazil** (☎ 3801 9540; www.easygoing.com.br). A less-expensive option is one of the Sunday tours organized by the city tourist office (p278), usually lasting a half day and costing about R$20 – though English-speaking guides are not guaranteed. You can also ask your hotel to arrange a city tour with a trusted operator. Expect to pay around R$50, including one meal.

FESTIVALS & EVENTS

The city's two biggest events are the **Bienal de São Paulo** (p299) and the **Gay Pride events** (below).

Also worth a mention:

Carnaval (February and/or March) Celebrations don't approach those of Rio, but there are parties throughout the city.

Virada Cultural (One Saturday in late April or early May) A nonstop, 24-hour party of cultural, especially musical, events around the city.

Festa de Nossa Senhora Achiropita (every weekend in August) A series of street fairs in Bixiga celebrating the city's Italian heritage.

SLEEPING

Ironically, travelers will find that the biggest discounts are given in São Paulo during the vacation months of December, January and February when prices elsewhere in Brazil sky-rocket. Weekend discounts of up to 50% are common at large business hotels.

Praça da República & Around
BUDGET

Hotel Rivoli (Map pp280-1; ☎ 3231 5633; www.hotel rivoli.com.br in Portuguese; Rua Dom José de Barros 28; s/d R$36/47) Once the top choice of backpackers, the Rivoli's tiny rooms and thin mattresses have seen better days. Still, it has some of the cheapest private rooms in the city and is near Praça da República and adjacent metro.

Hotel Joamar (Map pp280-1; ☎ 3221 3611; www .hoteljoamar.com.br; Rua Dom José de Barros 187; s/d R$42/56) A frilly, canary-yellow, turn-of-the-century façade hides basic but well-kept, recently remodeled rooms with fans. It's located on a pedestrian street that is perfectly safe during the day but requires vigilance after dark.

Gavea Palace Hotel (Map pp280-1; ☎ 3331 7921; Rua Conselheiro Nébias 445; s/d without breakfast R$50/60) Situated on a block full of motorbike shops, this no-frills place northeast of Praça da República gets its fair share of biker types. Basic rooms are well kept and better than the bleak façade suggests.

Hotel Itamarati (Map pp280-1; ☎ 3222 4133; fax 3222 1878; Av Doutor Vieira de Carvalho 150; s/d R$70/88; 🐾) Friendly but threadbare, this budget option occupies a fine, old building just a short walk from Praça da República. Rooms at the front are brighter but noisier. Some have fans only.

MIDRANGE & TOP END

Normandie Design Hotel (Map pp280-1; ☎ 3311 9855; www.normandiedesign.com.br; Av Ipiranga 1187; s/d R$100/121) Inspired by the work of Philippe Starck, this hotel manages to be at once fashion-forward and reasonably priced. The stark and striking lobby raises expectations that

---

PRIDE, SAMPA-STYLE

In 1997, São Paulo's first Gay Pride parade drew a meager 3000 people. In less than a decade, it has grown into the world's largest Pride event, attracting nearly three million. That growth is a testament to the profound change in cultural attitudes toward homosexuality in Brazil, but also Sampa's long tradition of tolerance. Indeed, most of the crowd are *simpatizantes* – gay-friendly straights. Rio is often touted as Brazil's gay mecca, yet you almost never see overt displays of affection in the streets. In São Paulo, PDA (public display of affection) is becoming commonplace, at least in certain neighborhoods (p298).

During Pride week, the city's gay and lesbian venues are packed to the gills in the lead-up to the big parade, which traditionally takes place on a Sunday, usually in mid-June. There are also political meetings, street fairs, concerts and other special events.

SÃO PAULO STATE

the rooms can't quite deliver. Still, they're perfectly adequate for the price – and rigorously black-and-white.

Hotel Excelsior (Map pp280-1; ☎ 3331 0377; www .hotelexcelsiorsp.com.br; Av Ipiranga 770; s/d R$162/204; Ⓟ ⊠ ⬜) While ready for a face-lift, this classic business hotel just off Praça da República offers respectable rooms that are good value if you take advantage of their frequent promotional prices.

Novotel Jaraguá São Paulo (Map pp280-1; ☎ 6802 7000; www.accorhotels.com.br; Rua Martins Fontes 71; s/d R$250/300) The Accor chain has refurbished the old Hotel Jaraguá, which had long been central São Paulo's chicest hotel. Digs are large, plush and cheerfully done up in saturated hues. Rooms above the 20th floor have breathtaking city views.

Liberdade

Akasaka (Map pp280-1; ☎ 3207 1500; www.akasaka hotel.com.br; Praça da Liberdade 149; s/d R$69/79) Conveniently located across from the metro, this recently opened budget option offers good value with simple, no-frills but impeccable rooms. Breakfast is available for R$9.

Hotel Barão Lu (Map pp280-1; ☎ 2142 0950; www .hotelbaraolu.com.br; Rua Barão de Iguape 80; s/d R$150/210; ⊠ ⬜) The rooms at this business hotel are starting to look a little dated and tatty but offer comfort, and still deliver good value if you can get the regularly offered 40% discount. Opt for the usual buffet breakfast or an Asian version with rice, soybean soup and grilled fish.

Nikkey Palace Hotel (Map pp280-1; ☎ 3207 8511; www.nikkeyhotel.com.br; Rua Galvão Bueno 425; s/d R$205/260; Ⓟ ⊠ ⬜) Geared to Asian business travelers, the Nikkey hides its charming quirks behind a forbidding, 1960s-style concrete façade. Rooms have a distinctly Asian flair. There is a good spa (a 45-minute shiatsu massage plus sauna costs R$85), and service is courteous and attentive. Japanese and English are spoken.

Around Avenida Paulista

BUDGET

Pousada dos Franceses (Map pp292-3; ☎ 3262 4026; www.pousadadosfranceses.com.br; Rua dos Franceses 100; dm R$30, s/d from R$45/65; ⬜) On a quiet, almost suburban street, yet just a short walk from Av Paulista, this newly renovated hostel offers decent communal digs, bright and pleasant common areas, and private rooms of varying sizes and comfort levels. From the Brigadeiro

metro station, walk northwest along Av Paulista (toward MASP for one block) and turn right down Rua Joaquin Eugênio de Lima. The third street on your left is Rua dos Franceses.

Hospedaria Mantovani (Map pp292-3; ☎ 3889 8623; www.residenzamantovani.com.br; Rua Eliseu Guilherme 269; s/d R$64/84) In what looks like an Italian farmhouse on steroids, this neatly kept inn offers rooms of various sizes and shapes, all spotless and attractive, if simple.

Formule 1 Paulista (Map pp292-3; ☎ 3123 7755; www. accorhotels.com.br; Rua da Consolação 2303; r from R$80; ⊠ ⬜) Large and rather soulless but with a great location and price, this chain hotel is worth considering. Rooms are spartan and rather dormitory-like but perfectly adequate.

Paulista Garden Hotel (Map pp292-3; ☎ 3885 1362; www.paulistagardenhotel.com.br; Alameda Lorena 21; r from R$80; ⊠ ⬜) It may be on a busy intersection, but this friendly place is popular with foreign travelers for its largish and good-value, if uninspiring, rooms.

MIDRANGE

Augusta Park Hotel (Map pp292-3; ☎ 3124 4400; www.augustapark.com.br; Rua Augusta 922; s/d R$100/125; Ⓟ ⊠ ⬜ ⬜) Set amid the action of Rua Augusta, the Augusta Park offers respectable if slightly dated rooms and convenient location. Rooms aren't luxurious but perfectly comfortable, all with separate sitting room and small kitchen. Rooms on higher floors have winning views; rooms at the back of the hotel are quieter.

Paulista Center Hotel (Map pp292-3; ☎ 3062 0733; www.paulistacenterhotel.com.br; Rua da Consolação 2567; s/d without air-con R$100/155, with air-con R$110/170; ⊠ ⬜) Good value considering its location close to Paulista and the action in Jardins, this standby offers smallish rooms without air-con and much larger rooms with air-con for just a few reais more.

Massis Five Stars (Map pp292-3; ☎ 3141 4400; www .massisfivestars.com.br; Rua Luís Coelho; s/d from R$120/140; Ⓟ ⊠ ⬜ ⬜) Near both work and play, this rather imposing high-rise remains a fairly well-kept secret. While rooms aren't likely to dazzle (the name definitely overpromises), all include a small kitchen and balcony and make for a good price-to-value ratio. Rooms on higher floors have fine views.

TOP END

Quality Hotel (Map pp292-3; ☎ 2182 0400; www.atlantica hotels.com.br; Alameda Campinas 540; s/d from R$175/200;

(P) (X) (□) (Q)) While it may be a cookie-cutter affair, this business hotel has two things in its favor: reasonable prices and a fine location. Rooms are small but comfortable and have a dollop of character with touches such as Japanese-print duvets.

Transamerica Flat International Plaza (Map pp292-3; ☎ 3146 5966; www.transamericaflats.com.br; Alameda Santos 981; d from R$220; (P) (X) (□) (Q)) Set in a narrow, ochre-colored high-rise with white trim, the attractive Transamerica Plaza has bright, cleverly designed rooms that are good for the price, plus a small but inviting rooftop pool.

Crowne Plaza Hotel (Map pp292-3; ☎ 4501 8000; www.saobr.com.br; Rua Frei Caneca 1360; s/d R$220/250; (P) (X) (□) (Q)) Located a few steps from Av Paulista, the Crowne Plaza is a favorite with business travelers. This large hotel may not be cozy but it does have large, comfortable rooms specially designed for a good night's sleep, including relaxing music, soft lighting and lavender spray.

Gran Meliá Mofarrej (Map pp292-3; ☎ 3146 5900; www.granmeliamofarrej.solmelia.com; Alameda Santos 1437; s/d from R$575/650; (P) (X) (□) (Q)) Hidden behind a concrete-skyscraper façade, one of São Paulo's top business hotels indulges tropical themes, from its artwork to luxuriant greenery in the lobby and pool room. Rooms are plush, though not overflowing with character.

L'Hotel (Map pp292-3; ☎ 2183 0500; www.lhotel.com.br; Alameda Campinas 266; d from R$800; (P) (X) (□) (Q)) Possibly São Paulo's coziest high-end hotel and certainly among its poshest, this boutique sleep just off Paulista offers deluxe digs, impeccable service and rather traditional continental decor.

Jardins
MIDRANGE

ourpick Pousada Dona Ziláh (Map pp292-3; ☎ 3062 1444; www.zilah.com; Alameda Franca 1621; s/d R$112/136) A rare find, this lovely, briskly run pousada (guesthouse) occupies a Spanish-style villa in the heart of Jardins. Rooms, arranged around a pretty courtyard, are very simple but also well maintained. Attractive common areas promote sociability among a largely international clientele.

Blair House (Map pp292-3; ☎ 3083 5988; Alameda Franca 1645; www.blairhouse.com.br; s/d from R$115/135) The little studio apartments here are rather basic but comfortable – and very well situated near the action in Jardins. Angle for the brighter corner (odd-numbered) rooms.

TOP END

Transamerica Flat 21st Century (Map pp292-3; ☎ 3886 8400; www.transamericaflats.com.br; Alameda Lorena 473; d from R$180) For your own one- or two-bedroom apartment in Jardins, and at a reasonable price, this simple place is well worth considering. Rooms are Ikea-inspired but attractive enough. Some rooms on high floors have good views.

Regent Park Suite Hotel (Map pp292-3; ☎ 3065 5555; www.regent.com.br; Rua Oscar Freire 533; s/d R$245/265) A tony location plus fully equipped, one-bedroom apartments that are both plush and mutedly stylish. Ask for a room on a high floor for views over the Jardins district.

Hotel Emiliano (Map pp292-3; ☎ 3068 4399; www.emiliano.com.br; Rua Oscar Freire 384; d from R$870; (P) (X) (□) (Q)) Sleek, bright and minimalist, Emiliano is more brash than Fasano (see below) but every bit as luxurious, with high-thread-count sheets, impeccable service and a sun-drenched rooftop pool.

Hotel Fasano (Map pp292-3; ☎ 3896 4000; www.fasano.com.br; Rua Vittorio Fasano 88; d from R$950; (P) (X) (□) (Q)) This small but ultrarefined hotel seems to have been plucked straight from Milan, with muted gray marble set off with exquisite 1930s-era antiques in rooms and common areas, and a reserve and formality rare in Brazil. The Zen-like rooftop pool area alone is worth the price of admission. Many rooms have fine views.

South of Jardins

Albergue da Juventude Praça da Árvore (Map p277; ☎ 5071 5148; www.spalbergue.com.br; Rua Pageú 266; dm/d R$33/82; (□)) Set amid semiurban sprawl east of Parque do Ibirapuera, this hostel is worth considering despite its rather inconvenient location about a kilometer from the nearest metro station. Inside the modern house, there are decent dorm rooms, several basic doubles, a pleasant-enough common area and a good communal kitchen. To get there take the north–south (Tucuruvi–Jabaquara) metro line and get off at the Praça da Árvore station. Walk north for a block and turn right at Rua Orissanga and left at Rua Caramurú. Continue north until you get to No 260 and turn onto Rua Pageú.

Hotel Unique (Map p277; ☎ 3055 4710; www.hotelunique.com.br; Av Brigadeiro Luis Antônio 4700; d from R$875; (P) (X) (□) (Q)) Designed by Ruy Ohtake, the shiplike Unique is certainly the city's most architecturally ambitious hotel as well as one of

AVENIDA PAULISTA, JARDINS & AROUND

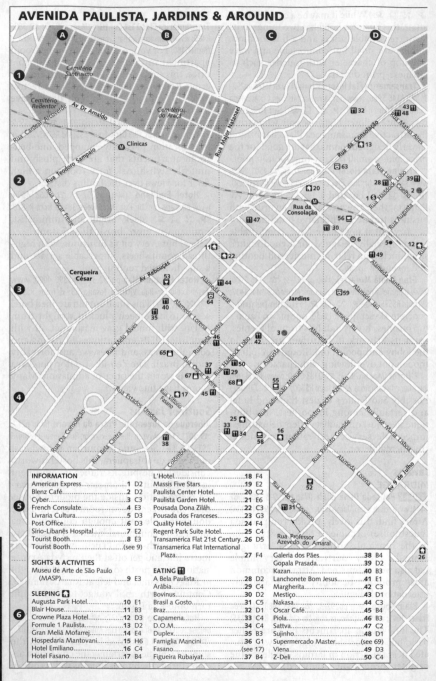

INFORMATION
American Express.....................1 D2
Blenz Café..............................2 D2
Cyber....................................3 C3
French Consulate.....................4 E3
Livraria Cultura.......................5 D3
Post Office..............................6 D3
Sírio-Libanês Hospital...............7 E2
Tourist Booth..........................8 E2
Tourist Booth.....................(see 9)

SIGHTS & ACTIVITIES
Museu de Arte de São Paulo
 (MASP)................................9 E3

SLEEPING
Augusta Park Hotel................10 E1
Blair House...........................11 B3
Crowne Plaza Hotel...............12 D3
Formule 1 Paulista.................13 D2
Gran Meliá Mofarrej..............14 E4
Hospedaria Mantovani...........15 H6
Hotel Emiliano......................16 C4
Hotel Fasano.........................17 B4

L'Hotel.................................18 F4
Massis Five Stars....................19 E2
Paulista Center Hotel.............20 C2
Paulista Garden Hotel............21 E6
Pousada Dona Ziláh...............22 C3
Pousada dos Franceses..........23 G3
Quality Hotel........................24 F4
Regent Park Suite Hotel..........25 C4
Transamerica Flat 21st Century..26 D5
Transamerica Flat International
 Plaza.................................27 F4

EATING
A Bela Paulista......................28 D2
Arábia..................................29 C4
Bovinus................................30 D2
Brasil a Gosto........................31 C5
Braz.....................................32 D1
Capamena.............................33 C4
D.O.M..................................34 C4
Duplex..................................35 B3
Famiglia Mancini...................36 G1
Fasano............................(see 17)
Figueira Rubaiyat..................37 B4

Galeria dos Pães....................38 B4
Gopala Prasada......................39 D2
Kazan...................................40 B3
Lanchonete Bom Jesus............41 E1
Margherita............................42 C3
Mestiço.................................43 D1
Nakasa..................................44 C3
Oscar Café............................45 B4
Piola....................................46 B3
Sattva..................................47 C2
Sujinho.................................48 D1
Supermercado Master........(see 69)
Viena...................................49 D3
Z-Deli...................................50 C4

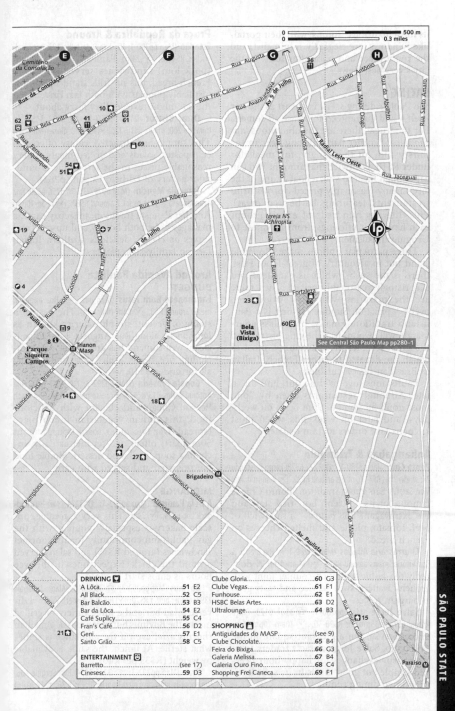

SÃO PAULO STATE

its most luxurious. Rooms, with their portal-like windows, are elegantly minimalist, and the rooftop bar and pool offer some of the city's very best views.

EATING

São Paulo's dining scene is as vast as the city itself – and guaranteed to please all comers. For the frugal, there are the ubiquitous *lanchonetes* – corner bars offering beer to the thirsty, and, for the hungry, full meals for under R$10. For twice that amount you can eat enough meat to sink a boat at one of the city's many reasonably priced *churrascarias* (restaurants featuring barbecued meat). Plus, literally hundreds of ethnic groups each have their offerings, from Lebanese to Uruguayan cuisine.

Three particular options make São Paulo stand out in a country of great food. First, there is the sushi, which is excellent and surprisingly reasonably priced. Then there are the pizzerias with their wood-fired ovens – pizza on Sunday evening is a Paulistano tradition. Finally, high-class gourmands will swoon over the chic bistros and the great temples of gastronomy, most of which are devoted to either French, Italian or Brazilian-fusion cuisines.

Paulistanos love to dine out, and do so late. Although restaurants open by 7pm, most don't fill up until 9pm or so on weekdays, and later on weekends when most kitchens take orders to 1am or later.

Anhangabaú & Triângulo

Ponto Chic (Map pp280-1; ☎ 3222 6528; Largo Paissandu 27; sandwiches R$7-10, mains around R$20; ☻ 7am-midnight Mon-Sat) A São Paulo tradition, Ponto Chic is famous for its efficient, bow-tied staff and the extravagant R$8 *bauru* – a sandwich of beef, tomato, pickle and melted cheeses on French bread.

Churrascaria Aliados (Map pp280-1; Av Rio Branco & Rua Vitória; mains around R$10; ☻ 11am-4am) A doggedly old-fashioned lunch-counter joint with grouchy waiters, swift service and tasty grub at bargain prices.

Salve Jorge (Map pp280-1; ☎ 3107 0123; Praça António Prado 33; mains R$20-30; ☻ 10am-10pm Mon-Fri, noon-6pm Sat) On a pleasant square in the Triângulo, Salve Jorge attracts traders from the nearby exchanges for happy hour beers and simple but good meals in its split-level, wine-lined dining room.

Praça da República & Around

Estadão (Map pp280-1; Viaduto 9 de Julho 193; hot sandwiches R$4-10; ☻ 24hr) Famous for its *pernil* (pork loin) sandwiches served on crusty French bread, this no-frills stand-up joint is justifiably popular with both taxi drivers and the late-night revelers they ferry about.

Oscar Bistrot (Map pp280-1; ☎ 3237 3458; Av Ipiranga 200; mains R$10-12; ☻ lunch & dinner Mon-Sat) This simple but attractive eatery offers decent pastas, salads and grilled meats at very reasonable prices in the serpentine ground-floor gallery of Edifício Copan (p282).

Famiglia Mancini (Map pp292-3; ☎ 3256 4320; Rua Avanhandava 81; mains for 2 around R$60; ☻ noon-10pm) Another Paulista tradition, this cozy cantina manages to be both homey and upscale, and serves up classic, delicious northern Italian fare on family-style platters.

Around Avenida Paulista
BUDGET

Lanchonete Bom Jesus (Map pp292-3; Rua Augusta; meals around R$8; ☻ 8am-midnight) The best of a string of decent, simple eateries known as *lanchonetes* along Rua Augusta, Bom Jesus is clean, well run and has great-value meals including rice, beans, grilled meat and a drink, all for under R$10.

Gopala Prasada (Map pp292-3; ☎ 3289 1911; Rua Antônio Carlos 413 & 429; 3-course meals R$14; ☻ lunch Mon-Sat) Cheap and elegant with delicious food, this Indian vegetarian lunch place (spread over two older town houses about 50m apart) offers two set menus daily, including soup, main and dessert. Simple food but prepared and served with care.

MIDRANGE

A Bela Paulista (Map pp292-3; ☎ 3214 3347; Rua Haddock Lobo 354; ☻ 24hr) This very agreeable, upscale bakery is especially popular with the gay Paulistano community for its gourmet sandwiches (around R$15) and salads served around the clock. Expect lines in the wee hours as clubs start to close.

Bovinus (Map pp292-3; ☎ 3088 6103; Alameda Santos 2393; dinner buffet R$20; ☻ lunch & dinner) With a diverse salad bar and a huge variety of grilled meats, the Bovinus buffet is a classic Brazilian *churrascaria*, even if the ambiance is somewhat sterile. At lunch, the same is available by weight (R$33 per kilo).

Braz (Map pp292-3; ☎ 3231 1554; Rua Sergipe 406, Higienópolis; individual pizza from R$20; ☻ 6:30pm-12:30am)

Cooking up what many consider Sampa's best pizza in wood ovens, this rather upscale but always animated spot is worth the 10 to 15 minute walk from Av Paulista.

Viena (Map pp292-3; ☎ 3283 4130; cnr Rua Augusta & Alameda Santos; buffet R$27; ◷ 11am-10:30pm) In the bright, ground-floor of the enormous Conjunto Nacional building, this winningly straightforward café offers a fine lunchtime buffet with the freshest ingredients, plus an evening all-you-can-eat pizza special with excellent salad bar.

TOP END

Sujinho (Map pp292-3; ☎ 3256 8026; Rua da Consolação 2078; mains around R$25; ◷ 11:30am-3am Sun-Thu, 11:30am-5am Fri-Sat) This no-nonsense steak house is a local favorite for its combination of fine, reasonably priced grilled meats, old-fashioned service and late hours. They have another dining room just across the street on Rua Consolação.

Mestiço (Map pp292-3; ☎ 3256 3165; Rua Fernando de Albuquerque 277; mains R$30-40; ◷ lunch & dinner) Both the creative menu and the colorful-yet-chic design are a delightful combination of Brazilian and Asian influences, from Bahian fritters to Thai curries. Mestiço attracts an upscale, artsy crowd.

Jardins

Jardins is your place to splurge; it offers an incredibly dense collection of Brazil's most-illustrious restaurants, plus some surprisingly reasonable choices to boot.

BUDGET & MIDRANGE

Galeria dos Pães (Map pp292-3; ☎ 3064 5900; Rua Estados Unidos 1645; sandwiches R$8-15; ◷ 24hr) This gourmet grocery store also has a great deli where the beautiful people of Jardins come to hash out their social lives over an excellent selection of gourmet sandwiches and fresh juices. There's also a buffet breakfast during the week (R$14), brunch at weekends (R$18) and a daily buffet of soups and baked goods (R$20; 6pm to 5am).

Sattva (Map pp292-3; ☎ 3083 6237; Alameda Itu 1564; mains around R$10-15; ◷ noon-10pm) Claiming to be Brazil's first veggie restaurant, Sattva still serves up decent meat-free fare, plus live music most Sundays, in a ramshackle but pleasant series of rooms. Try the two-course weekday lunch with drink for R$10.

Z-Deli (Map pp292-3; ☎ 3088 5644; Alameda Lorena 1689; mains R$10-20; ◷ 11am-6:30pm Mon-Fri, to 4:30pm

Sat) A Sampa classic, this upscale, invitingly bright Jewish deli specializes in Eastern European comfort food such as gefilte fish and potato dumplings.

Piola (Map pp292-3; ☎ 3064 6570; Alameda Lorena 1765; 2-person pizzas R$25-40; ◷ 6pm-1am) Serving fine, thin-crust wood-oven pizza in a colorful, relaxed, chic dining room, Piola attracts a youngish and hip crowd. Expect a line Sunday evenings.

Margherita (Map pp292-3; ☎ 6014 3000; Alameda Tietê 255; 2-person pizzas R$25-40; ◷ 6:30pm-1am) Classic thin-crust Italian pizza is cooked up in wood ovens and served in an attractive dining room that draws the young, and young-looking, of Jardins neighborhood. Expect a line on weekends, especially Sundays.

Kazan (Map pp292-3; ☎ 3068 9665; Rua Doutor Melo Alves 343; sushi buffet R$28; ◷ lunch & dinner Mon-Sat) A bright, pleasant Japanese restaurant in the heart of Jardins, Kazan offers good sushi at great prices. The buffet includes soup, tempura, teriyaki and dessert, as well as all the sushi you can eat.

TOP END

Duplex (Map pp292-3; ☎ 3085 8853; Rua Melo Alves 445; mains R$25-35; ◷ lunch & dinner Tue-Sat, lunch Sun-Mon) This chic-yet-cozy bistro serves creative salads, pastas, risottos, and delicious mains that mix Italian, French and Asian methods and ingredients.

Arábia (Map pp292-3; ☎ 3061 2203; Rua Haddock Lobo 1397; mains R$25-35; ◷ lunch & dinner) Widely considered São Paulo's best Middle Eastern restaurant, Arábia sticks closely to classic recipes but stands out for their careful preparation and, above all, the excellence and freshness of the ingredients.

Nakasa (Map pp292-3; ☎ 3064 0970; Rua da Consolação 3147; all-you-can-eat sushi lunch/dinner R$25/55; ◷ lunch & dinner) The decor – a stylish take on rustic Japanese architecture – is alluring, and so is the excellent sushi at this rather romantic Jardins option.

Oscar Café (Map pp292-3; ☎ 3063 5209; Rua Oscar Freire 727; mains around R$30; ◷ 9:30am-10pm Mon-Sat, 9:30am-8pm Sun) New but already a Jardins classic, this restaurant-café is a world unto itself, with natural-wood decor, a pretty waterfall, excellent coffee and baked goods, and creative Brazilian-fusion mains.

ourpick Brasil a Gosto (Map pp292-3; ☎ 3086 3565; Rua Professor Azevedo do Amaral 70; mains from R$35; ◷ lunch & dinner Tue-Sat, lunch Sun) At once cozy and modern, this remarkable new Jardins institution has won kudos for its innovative takes on classic Brazilian dishes and ingredients, from *carne do sol* (tasty, salted meat, grilled and served with beans, rice and vegetables) to Amazonian fruits such as the berry-like *açaí*.

Figueira Rubaiyat (Map pp292-3; ☎ 3063 3888; Rua Haddock Lobo 1738; mains R$50-75; ☻ lunch & dinner) Sprawling and luxurious like the ancient fig that graces its outdoor terrace, this top-of-the-line grill-restaurant serves up perhaps Sampa's best meat, plus other delicacies from fresh oysters to foie gras with figs.

D.O.M. (Map pp292-3; ☎ 3088 0761; Rua Barão de Copamena 549; mains R$50-75; ☻ lunch & dinner Mon-Fri, dinner Sat) Foie gras with a crust of wild rice? Gnocchi with oxtail sauce? Duck breast with banana? This small and deceptively casual Italo-French restaurant serves up some of the finest food in Sampa, which is saying a lot.

Fasano (Map pp292-3; ☎ 3896 4077; Rua Vittorio Fasano; mains from R$75; ☻ dinner Mon-Sat) São Paulo's most feted restaurant sits splendidly on the ground floor of the hotel of the same name, its decor a remarkable combination of opulence and restraint. Its menu features dishes from around Italy, with tasting menus (around R$250) focused on a single region. Need to close a billion-dollar deal? This is your place.

Vila Madalena
MIDRANGE & TOP END
L'Aperô (Map p296; ☎ 3814 2445; Rua Mourato Coelho 1343; mains R$18-24; ☻ dinner Tue-Fri, lunch & dinner Sat & Sun) The French-born owner has created a relaxed, Sampa-style bistro that serves up big portions of classic French dishes with Brazilian inflections, plus creative and delicious salads.

Martín Fierro (Map p296; ☎ 3814 6747; Rua Aspicuelta 683; mains for 2 R$70; ☻ noon-10:30pm Mon-Fri, noon-5:30pm Sat & Sun) Even Brazilians admit that Argentines are the masters of barbecue, and this humble-looking but convivial spot proves their point. The grilled beef is outstanding, while the grilled veggies and empanadas make first-rate accompaniments.

Santa Gula (Map p296; ☎ 3812 7815; Rua Fridalga 340; mains R$25-50; ☻ dinner Mon, lunch & dinner Tue-Sat, lunch Sun) This remarkable restaurant at the end of a leafy court serves up creative Brazilian-fusion dishes such as shrimp with apricots and cashew-encrusted salmon. It doubles as a showcase of Brazilian crafts, so you can literally take home the table you ate on.

Groceries
Self-caterers can stock up at **Supermercado Master** (Map pp292-3; Rua Frei Caneca 569; ☻ 10am-10pm Mon-Sat, 2-8pm Sun), on the ground floor of the Shopping Frei Caneca mall, or at **Pão de Açúcar** (Map pp280-1; Av Rio Branco).

For good quality deli items, baked goods and gourmet groceries 24 hours a day, head to Galeria dos Pães (p295) in Jardins or the smaller A Bela Paulista (p294) just off Av Paulista.

DRINKING
Sampa's raucous and varied nightlife is an easy rival of that in London and New York. Whether you prefer chirpy cafés or after-hour raves, live metal or flow-in electronica, the city of São Paulo is your place. For complete, up-to-the-minute listings, check out the city agenda at www.erikapalomino.com.br (in Portuguese). For more general information in English, head to www.gringoes.com. You can also check out the *Guia da Folha*, the cultural supplement in the Friday edition of *Folha de São Paulo* newspaper for entertainment options.

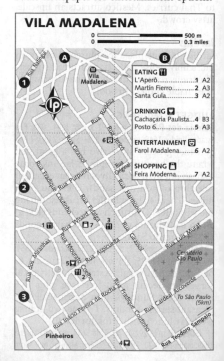

VILA MADALENA

0 _____ 500 m
0 _____ 0.3 miles

EATING 🍴	
L'Aperô.....................1	A2
Martín Fierro............2	A3
Santa Gula................3	A2

DRINKING 🍷	
Cachaçaria Paulista...4	B3
Posto 6......................5	A2

| ENTERTAINMENT 🎭 | |
| Farol Madalena.........6 | A2 |

| SHOPPING 🛍 | |
| Feira Moderna..........7 | A2 |

Cafés

Brazil grows a lot of coffee, but in general doesn't know how to brew it very well – plus the best beans end up in foreign markets. São Paulo is the exception, thanks largely to its Italian heritage. Virtually all the cafés listed below serve Brazil's best beans – mountain-grown arabicas, mostly from Minas Gerais.

Café Floresta (Map pp280-1; Av Ipiranga 200; 7am-midnight, from 8am Sun) With its antique murals, excellent brew and location on the ground floor of Niemeyer's Edifício Copan building near Praça da República, this stand-up-only café is a favorite of traditionalists.

Santo Grão (Map pp292-3; 3082 9969; Rua Oscar Freire 413; 9am-midnight Tue-Sun, noon-midnight Mon) Connoisseurs say Santo Grão (Sacred Bean) offers the city's best coffee. Join the crowd at this Jardins institution and judge for yourself.

Café Suplicy (Map pp292-3; 3061 0195; Alameda Lorena 1430; 8am-midnight Mon-Fri, 9am-midnight Sat & Sun) Santo Grão's rival is smaller, with a refined industrial-chic feel and also outrageously good coffee and pastries.

Bars

In São Paulo you are never more than a few yards from a lively drinking establishment. The young and alternative need just wander up and down Rua Augusta north of Av Paulista and choose from a dozen or so dead-simple places that, after 9pm, grow highly animated. Vila Madalena is the new hot spot for more mainstream types, with dozens of bars, most with outdoor terraces and often with live music, clustered around the intersection of Rua Mourato Coelho and Rua Aspicuelta. For more button-down fun, try the hotel bars at high-flying hotels such as Fasano and Emiliano (p291) in Jardins.

Bar Brahma (Map pp280-1; 3333 0855; Av São João 677; 11am-midnight) A Sampa classic near Praça da República with a well-preserved wood-panelled interior, Brahma remains a popular after-work hangout for professionals, and offers up live music (sometimes with cover) most nights after 9pm.

Bar da Lôca (Map pp292-3; cnr Rua Frei Caneca & Rua Peixoto Gomide; 8am-4am) Presided over by Saddam, beloved for his kind attention as well as his myriad gold chains, this simple place attracts a mixed gay-alternative-punk crowd until very late. Located just off the Rua Augusta corridor.

Geni (Map pp292-3; 3129 9638; Rua Bela Cintra 539; 6pm-2am Mon-Sat) Geni serves up live music, private upstairs rooms, stylish but low-key decor, freshly prepared snacks and an attractive younger crowd – all in a handsome old mansion.

Bar Balcão (Map pp292-3; 3063 6091; Rua Dr Melo Alves 150; 6pm-2am) With good wine, excellent light meals and a simple but elegant design built around a cleverly serpentine bar, this Jardins delight is especially popular with well-heeled designers and artists.

All Black (Map pp292-3; 3088 7990; Rua Oscar Freire 163, Jardins; 6pm-2am Mon-Thu, to 4am Sat & Sun) For your dose of Guinness, fish, chips and Irish good cheer check out Sampa's best approximation of a Dublin pub, with live music most nights (cover R$10 to R$20).

Cachaçaria Paulista (Map p296; 3815 4756; Rua Mourato Coelho 593, Vila Madalena; 6pm-1am Thu, 9pm-1am Fri & Sat) Serving more than 300 kinds of *cachaça* (high-proof sugarcane alcohol), Brazil's national drink, plus live Brazilian music on weekend nights, this Vila Madalena institution is remarkably relaxed and convivial.

Posto 6 (Map p296; 3812 7831; Rua Aspicuelta, Vila Madalena; 5pm-1am Mon-Fri, 2pm-3am Sat, noon-midnight Sun) At Vila Madalena's ground zero, this popular happy hour spot has old-fashioned, wood-paneled rooms that open up onto the street.

Bar do Unique (Map p277; 3055 4710; Av Brigadeiro Luis Antônio 4700; noon-2am) Dress up at least a little for the rooftop bar on the top floor of the Hotel Unique, whose sleek design and unparalleled views make it the perfect place for a sundown cocktail.

ENTERTAINMENT
Nightclubs

Discos don't open until midnight, don't really get going until after 1am, and keep pumping until 5am or later. Then there are the after-hours places... Partying isn't always cheap: covers can range from R$10 to R$50 or more for the high-end places (this often includes a free drink or two). Keep the card they give you on the way in – bartenders record your drinks on it, then you pay on the way out.

Clube Gloria (Map pp292-3; 3287 3700; www .clubegloria.com.br; Rua 13 de Maio 830, Bela Vista (Bixiga); 11:30pm-late Fri & Sat) A church remade into a temple to house and electro music, Glória is inspired by '80s-style European discos and attracts an upscale-alternative crowd.

GAY & LESBIAN SÃO PAULO

Latin America's largest and most visible gay community supports a dizzying array of options, day and night. There are not only gay bars and discos but also restaurants, cafés, even a gay shopping center – **Shopping Frei Caneca** (Map pp292-3; Rua Frei Caneca 569; ☺ 10am-10pm Mon-Sat, 2-8pm Sun), also known as 'Shopping Gay Caneca,' with a shamelessly cruisey food court. And **São Paulo Pride** (p289), usually celebrated in mid-June, is by most estimates the largest gay gathering in the world. São Paulo is also the only city in Brazil where same-sex public displays of affection are a fairly common sight, at least in certain 'safe' neighborhoods. These include the area just north of Praça da República that tends to be more working class; Av Paulista just north of Av Paulista, which attracts an alternative crowd; and Rua da Consolaçao in Jardins, largely the domain of Sampa's upscale gay guys and gals.

In addition to the places listed below, don't miss **A Bela Paulista** (p294), the 24-hour restaurant where everyone ends up after the clubs close; **Bar da Lôca** (p297), where alternative types go when they can't afford entrance at the nearby A Lôca nightclub; the largely gay **D-Edge** (below) and **Lov.e Club & Lounge** (below) nightclubs.

Fran's Café (Map pp292-3; ☎ Rua Haddock Lobo 586, Jardins; ☺ 10am-midnight) Fight the local boys for an outdoor table at this cozy and very gay branch of a classic Sampa café.

ABC Bailão (Map pp280-1; ☎ 3333 3537; Rua Marquês de Itu 182; ☺ 11pm-late Thu-Sat) The Bailão is definitely *'brega'* ('tacky'), but that's the point. Basically just one big dance floor, it features everything from Whitney Huston to *forró* – the music of the Northeast, where many of the patrons were born. Crowd is refreshingly multiracial and multigenerational.

Week (Map p277; ☎ 3872 9966; www.theweek.com.br; Rua Guaicurus 324, Lapa) Both luxurious and cavernous, this club is the place to go if you like sweaty, shirtless, gym-hardened bodies. With two dance floors, three lounges, six bars, state-of-the-art light and sound, and an outdoor pool, it is like a big gay world unto itself.

A Lôca (Map pp292-3; ☎ 3159 8889; www.aloca.com.br; Rua Frei Caneca 916; ☺ midnight-late Wed-Sun) Still the reigning queen of trash chic, this sprawling club is the point of reference for Sampa's *alternativos* – gay, straight, male, female and various combinations thereof. Music varies from punk to electronica to classic disco.

Ultralounge (Map pp292-3; ☎ 3062 0385; www.ultralounge.com.br; Rua da Consolação 3031, Jardins; ☺ midnight-late Wed-Sun) In the heart of Jardins, this smallish disco lays the attitude on thick, but by way of compensation the clientele – and especially the staff – tend to be easy on the eyes. Decor is distinctly Asian-inspired; there is a pleasant lounge area, and the music ranges from classic dance music to electronica.

Farol Madalena (Map p296; ☎ 3032 6470; www.farolmadalena.com.br; Rua Jericó 179, Vila Madalena; ☺ 7pm-2am Tue-Sat, 4pm-midnight Sun) One of the city's top lesbian clubs, this smallish place packs in the young ladies for dinner (mains R$20 to R$30) as well as both live music and DJs as the evening progresses.

Love Story (Map pp280-1; ☎ 3231 3101; Rua Araújo 232; ☺ 1am-late Mon-Sat) Sampa's classic after-hours nightclub, Love Story attracts a rare combination of bourgeois kids, bohemians, celebrities and off-duty sex workers to its huge dance floor. Prices can be steep.

Clube Vegas (Map pp292-3; ☎ 3231 3705; Rua Augusta 765; ☺ midnight-late Tue-Sun) Hidden in a basement in a seedy area just north of Av Paulista, neon-lit Vegas delivers a varied program, with music styles spanning jazz to rock to electronica, and attracting an eclectic, mixed crowd of die-hard night owls, both gay and straight.

Funhouse (Map pp292-3; ☎ 3259 3793; Rua Bela Cintra 567; ☺ 11pm-late Wed-Sat, 8am-late Sun) With its good sound system, though diminutive dance floor, this little club regularly attracts indie British and American bands.

D-Edge (Map p277; ☎ 3667 8334; Alameda Olga 170, Barra Funda) With one of the city's most remarkable sound systems and a roster of world-famous DJs, this mixed gay-straight club is a 'don't miss' for fans of electronica.

Lov.e Club & Lounge (Map p277; ☎ 3044 1613; Rua Pequetita 189, Vila Olímpia; ☺ midnight-6am Tue-Fri, midnight-8:30am Sat) Yet another temple to electronic music, with a superb sound system,

SÃO PAULO STATE

a mixed gay-straight clientele, and a varied line-up, including drum-and-bass and Rio-style funk

Canto da Ema (Map p277; ☎ 3813 4708; Av Brigadeiro Faria Lima 364, Pinheiros; ⏰ 10:30pm-4:30am Tue-Sat, 7pm-midnight Sun) For a break from São Paulo's upmarket danceterias, this relaxed, intimate club specializes in *forró universitário*, a more approachable version of the high-octane dance music from Brazil's Northeast.

Disco (Map p277; ☎ 3813 4708; www.clubdisco.com.br; Rua Professor Atílio Innocente 160, Vila Olímpia; ⏰ 11pm-late Thu-Sat) So fancy it doesn't need a proper a name, Disco is fitted out with glittering, futuristic decor by the same firm that designed Hotel Fasano. Music is more electronica than disco. Dress up and bring plenty of money – drinks are expensive, as is the cover.

Lotus (Map p277; ☎ 3043 7130; www.lotussp.com.br; Av das Nações Unidos 12551, Brooklin; ⏰ 11pm-late Wed-Sat) Complete with its own heliport, Lotus is the place where wealth and beauty meet amid glossy, sleek decor. Music varies from electronica to bossa nova. Very expensive.

Live Music

Bourbon Street Music Club (Map p277; ☎ 5095 6100; Rua dos Chanés 127; cover R$25-35; ⏰ 9pm-2am Tue-Sun) The top spot for live jazz and blues in Sampa, Bourbon Street has hosted the likes of BB King and Ray Charles.

Tom Brazil (Map p277; ☎ 2163 2100; www.tombr.com.br; Rua Bragança Paulista 1281) This medium-sized hall attracts big-name Brazilian and international acts with its state-of-the-art sound system.

Barretto (Map pp292-3; ☎ 3896 4000; Rua Vittorio Fasano 88) Hands down one of the best places to see live music in the world, this bar inside the Hotel Fasano (p291) recalls prewar Milan and attracts top jazz and popular Brazilian musicians who normally only play large venues.

Keep in mind that entrance fees match the glamor levels.

Cinema

Virtually every big shopping center has a multiplex, mostly offering standard Hollywood fare. For high art, check out the film series at the **Centro Cultural Banco do Brasil** (p281). Most films, especially higher quality films, are subtitled rather than dubbed.

Also worthwhile:

HSBC Belas Artes (Map pp292-3; ☎ 3258 4092; Rua da Consolação 2423) Six screens showing new, high-quality foreign and domestic films.

Cinesesc (Map pp292-3; ☎ 3082 0213; Rua Augusta 2075) Features excellent retrospectives.

Classical, Ballet & Opera

Theatro Municipal (Map pp280-1; ☎ 3223 3022; Praça Ramos de Azevedo) Operas, classical ballets and symphonic music in São Paulo's most ornate theater (p281).

Sala São Paulo (Map pp280-1; ☎ 3292-4875; www.salasaopaulo.art.br in Portuguese; Praça Júlio Prestes) Excellent classical music venue, renowned for its fine acoustics, in refurbished train station, Estação Júlio Prestes.

SHOPPING

For remarkable bargains head to Rua 25 de Março, just north of the historic center, where wholesalers sell a dizzying variety of deeply discounted goods from around the world. For high fashion and high-end home furnishings, wander Rua Oscar Freire and surrounding streets in the Jardins district. Not fancy enough for you? There is always **Daslu** (see the boxed text, p300).

Clothing & Shoes

Clube Chocolate (Map pp292-3; Rua Oscar Freire 913, Jardins; ⏰ 10am-8pm Mon-Sat, to 6pm Sun) Set around a

---

THE SÃO PAULO BIENAL

Modeled on the Venice Biennale, the **Bienal de São Paulo** (bienalsaopaulo.globo.com; Parque do Ibirapuera), founded in 1951, has grown into one of the world's most important arts events. Many of the participants are working artists who have been nominated by their home country. In addition, a guest curator chooses a theme and invites his or her own favorites. At its best, the Bienal offers the world a chance to view mind-bending contemporary art. Certainly it cannot fail to be impressive for its sheer size and diversity.

The event is held during even-numbered years, generally from October to December, in a sprawling pavilion designed by modernist master Oscar Niemeyer in the leafy Parque do Ibirapuera (p283). In recent years, admission has been free, though this is subject to funding.

DASLU WILL DAZZLE YOU

Don't plan on walking to **Daslu** (Map p277; ☎ 3841 4000; Av Chedid Jafet 131, Vila Olímpia; ☷ 10am-8pm Mon- Sat, to 10pm Tue). It's against the rules to arrive on foot at São Paulo's most over-the-top shopping emporium. A taxi is one option, though a much chicer option is to arrive by chopper at the rooftop heliport (p285). The store itself looks like an all-white Roman villa on steroids, and over its three floors you can find every top designer, from Gucci to Tumi. Servants in black-and-white uniforms dole out free espresso, biscotti and sparkling water at bars spread throughout the store. Still hungry? There's a tearoom, a sushi bar and a more formal dining room. Daslu even has its own harem – a sprawling series of lounges and changing rooms where mirrors are ubiquitous and men are forbidden to set foot.

Despite the glittering façade, Daslu has known its share of shame. Just after the store opened in its current location in 2005, the owner Eliana Tranchesi was arrested for flagrant and massive tax fraud. She never had to serve a prison sentence, but the store did end up paying a fine of more than US$100 million.

---

winning courtyard complete with its own artificial beach, this super-refined store is Daslu's closest rival for high-end fashions for men and women. Your source for US$500 jeans.

Galeria Melissa (Map pp292-3; Rua Oscar Freire 827, Jardins; ☷ 10am-8pm Mon-Fri, 10am-6pm Sat) This temple to high-end footwear is worth checking out for its bold design – but don't expect bargains.

Galeria Ouro Fino (Map pp292-3; Rua Augusta 2690; ☷ 11am-8pm Mon-Sat) From hip-high boots to camouflage club gear, this old-fashioned, three-story mall has been turned into ground zero for *alternativo* shoppers.

Markets

There are several markets worth checking out.

Feira do Bixiga (Map pp292-3; Praça Dom Orione 1246, Bixiga/Bela Vista; ☷ 9am-5pm Sun) Flea market featuring crafts, antiques, clothing and live music.

Feira da República (Map pp280-1; Praça da República; ☷ 9am-5pm Sun) Open-air market specializing in handicrafts and painting.

Antiguidades do MASP (Map pp292-3; Av Paulista 1578; ☷ 9am-7pm Sun) Antiques fair that's good for browsing, but bargains are limited.

Feira Benedito Calixto (Map p277; Praça Benedito Calixto, Pinheiros; ☷ 9am-7pm Sat) Open-air market for handicrafts and antiques, plus food stalls and live music.

Malls

Sampa's favorite high-end hulk of a mall, **Shopping Iguatemi** (Map p277; Av Brigadeiro Faria Lima 2232; ☷ 10am-10pm) has all the top Brazilian brands, from Osklen to Ellus.

Relatively modest in size, **Shopping Frei Caneca** (Map pp292-3; Rua Frei Caneca 569; ☷ 10am-10pm Mon-Sat, 2-8pm Sun) is nevertheless fully equipped with food court, cinema and good midrange shops.

Souvenirs

Feira Moderna (Map p296; Rua Fradique Coutinho 1246, Vila Madalena; ☷ 10am-10pm Mon-Sat, noon-7pm Sun) is a high-end, high-quality shop featuring Brazilian handicrafts displayed amid a tranquil, flower-filled courtyard. It also has a delightful café.

GETTING THERE & AWAY

Air

From São Paulo's airports there are flights to just about every airport in Brazil and to many of the world's major cities. São Paulo is also the Brazilian hub for most international airlines, and thus the first stop for many travelers. The international airport is **Aeroporto São Paulo/Guarulhos** (☎ 6445 2945; airport code GRU), which is 30km east of the center. Most domestic flights leave from **Aeroporto de Congonhas** (Map p277; ☎ 5090 9000; airport code CGH), 14km south of the center, though as traffic grows, more domestic flights are also leaving from Guarulhos.

A tragic accident at Congonhas in July 2007 is likely to result in a long-term reduction in traffic. In the meantime there has been talk of opening of a third passenger airport in the city, although this may take years.

Most of the major airlines have offices on Av São Luís, near the Praça da República, or along Av Paulista.

Bus

São Paulo has four different bus stations, all accessible by metro. If you need to check which terminal services your destination, consult www.socicam.com.br (in Portuguese) or, in São Paulo, call ☎ 3235 0322.

The main bus station, **Terminal Tietê** (Map p277; ☎ 3235 0322; Tietê metro station), located north of the historic center, is really easy to reach thanks to a metro stop inside the station itself. It is an enormous building but it's generally safe and well-organized. Buses leave for destinations throughout Brazil and also for international destinations. Bus tickets are sold on the upper floor of the station. The hard part can be finding which bus company is headed in your direction. If you can't find a company serving your destination, ask at the information desk in the middle of the main concourse.

Prices listed are for buses with air-con. Expect to pay about 20% to 30% less to travel without air-con, and about 50% to 80% more for a *leitos* (sleeper bus).

International destinations include Asunción in Paraguay (R$120, 20 hours), Buenos Aires in Argentina (from R$200, 34 hours), Montevideo in Uruguay (R$150, 30 hours) and Santiago in Chile (R$330, 54 hours).

Domestic buses leave from Terminal Tietê for Belém (R$325, 48 hours), Belo Horizonte (R$67, eight hours), Brasília (R$120, 14 hours), Cuiabá (R$100, 13 hours), Curitiba (R$70, six hours), Florianópolis (R$110, 12 hours), Foz do Iguaçu (R$125, 15 hours), Rio (R$80, six hours), Salvador (R$240, 32 hours) and Ubatuba (R$37, four hours).

Buses to Santos, Guarujá and São Vicente leave about every half hour from a separate bus station – the Terminal Intermunicipal do Jabaquara (Map p277), which is at the end of the southern metro line (metro Jabaquara). There is also Terminal Bresser, near the Memorial do Imigrante (Map p277) in the east zone district of Brás, with services to the south of Minas Gerais state, and Terminal Barra Funda in the west zone, near the Memorial da América Latina (Map p277), for destinations in São Paulo state and Paraná.

GETTING AROUND
To/From the Airport
A taxi between Aeroporto de Congonhas and the city center costs R$30 to R$40 and takes around 30 to 45 minutes, depending on traffic. For buses to the center, walk out of the terminal and then to your right,

where you'll see a busy street with a pedestrian overpass. Head to the overpass but don't cross; you should see a crowd of people waiting for the buses along the street. Local buses 875A and 875M run all the way to Av Paulista. Alternatively, you can take a taxi to the São Judas metro stop (R$10 to R$15) and take the metro from there to the center.

Aeroporto São Paulo/Guarulhos, São Paulo's international airport, is 30km northeast of the city center. There are 'Airport Service' buses (☎ 6221 0244) to Praça da República, Terminal Tietê bus station, Congonhas airport and high-end hotels in Jardins and the city center. Buses leave approximately every half hour from 6am to 11pm, with less frequent service from 11pm to 6am. All trips cost R$27 and leave from the stop just in front of the arrivals terminal. Taxis from the international airport charge a set fee depending on your destination. Fares to the city center cost around R$75.

Bus
City buses, which are run by the city agency **EMTU** (☎ 0800 724 0555; www.emtu.sp.gov.br in Portuguese), cost R$2.30, and most lines run from around 6am to 1pm. They can be slow going, crowded and prone to pickpockets. Fortunately, there is now a series of *corredores* – special, bus-only lanes that help speed up travel times. The city tourist information booths are excellent sources of information about buses (see p278).

Public Transportation
A combination of metro and walking is the easiest way to see the city. São Paulo's efficient **metro** (www.metro.sp.gov.br/ingles/index.asp; 1-way ticket R$2.40; ☽ 5am-midnight) is one of the best in the world, with clean, modern stations – many of which are decorated with huge murals by local artists.

Taxi
Taxis are plentiful and relatively reasonably priced in São Paulo. For example, a ride from Jardins to the historic center should cost between R$15 to R$20. All taxis should be metered – if your driver doesn't turn the meter on, be sure to mention it. If the driver still doesn't, ask to be let out. If you need to call a taxi, try **Ligue Táxi** (☎ 2101 3030) or **Coopertax** (☎ 6195 6000).

SÃO PAULO STATE

AROUND SÃO PAULO

PARANAPIACABA

☎ 0xx11 / pop 4000

Founded by the British-owned São Paulo Railway Company, the town of Paranapiacaba may sit amid the Atlantic rain forest of the Serra do Mar 40km southeast of São Paulo, but it still retains distinctly English traits, right down to a rough replica of Big Ben. The Brits made the town their headquarters as they laid the tracks that by 1867 would carry São Paulo's coffee to the port at Santos – a remarkable feat given the sheer mountainsides and rapid elevation drops. The British retained control of the railway until 1947.

Because of its remoteness, the town has been remarkably well preserved, with a neat grid of streets populated by English-style buildings of wood and brick. The home of the railway's chief engineer, a classically Victorian wood construction known as 'Castelinho,' has been converted into the **Museu do Castelo** (Rua Caminho do Mendes; admission free; ⊙ 9am-4pm Tue-Sun), a small museum with period furnishings and fine views.

Paranapiacaba also makes a good base for day hikes into the **Parque Estadual Serra do Mar**, with its dense forest that harbors a remarkable profusion of bromeliads and orchids. Trails are not marked, however, so it's best to seek out a licensed guide at the **Associação dos Monitores** (☎ 4439 0155), located near the old train station.

The best way to arrive in Paranapiacaba is by train. Take the Linha D train from São Paulo's Estação Luz to the Rio Grande da Serra station (R$4.50, one hour). From here, there is an hourly bus ($2.20, 15 minutes) to nearby Paranapiacaba.

EMBU

☎ 0xx11 / pop 245,000

Founded in 1554, Embu spent most of its life as a quiet colonial village until, in the 20th century, it was swallowed up by São Paulo, whose center sits about 30km to the west. Yet Embu has managed to retain much of its colonial core, thanks largely to the hippies, artists and intellectuals who made the town their refuge from São Paulo's concrete jungle, starting in the 1970s. Today the town makes a popular Sunday retreat for Paulistanos, when local artisans offer their wares at the **feira** (outdoor market; Largo dos Jesuitas; ⊙ 9am-6pm Sun). The area around the *feira* is full of antique and craft shops that make good browsing on other days of the week.

There is a **tourist office** (☎ 4704 6565; Largo 21 de Abril; ⊙ 9am-6pm), just off the main square. **O Garimpo** (☎ 4704 6344; Rua da Matriz 136; mains from R$25; ⊙ 11:30am-10pm) is a pleasant spot for the peckish, with a veranda, colonial dining room, and a huge menu ranging from *ceviche* (raw fish marinated in lime juice) to suckling pig.

From just outside São Paulo's Tietê bus station, catch the 'Embu das Artes' bus (R$4.50, one hour, about every 30 minutes).

PAULISTA COAST

São Paulo's coast, known in Portuguese as the Litoral Paulista, is most spectacular in its northern reaches, especially around Ubatuba, thanks to jungle-covered peaks of the Serra do Mar that reach all the way down to the Atlantic. Closer to the capital, the scenery is tamer but the beaches remain good, even in overbuilt Guarujá. Inviting strands stretch south all the way to the border with Paraná, including the largely undeveloped Ilha Comprida, an island that shelters the colonial towns of Iguape and Cananéia.

Note that prices along the coast tend to be quite high by Brazilian standards, especially from December to March.

UBATUBA

☎ 0xx12 / pop 76,000

Draped with the rich flora of the Mata Atlântica (Atlantic rain forest), the peaks of Serra do Mar provide a dramatic, emerald green backdrop to the winding Ubatuba coastline. This region has become a preeminent resort for well-heeled Paulistanos, with its elegant beach homes and a number of stylish hotels and pousadas, especially south of the town. Heading north toward neighboring Paraty in the state of Rio de Janeiro, beaches tend to be harder to reach but also wilder and more pristine.

Orientation & Information

The town is a relatively compact grid of streets centered on Praça 13 de Maio, which is just north of Rua Professor Thomaz Galhardo – the main road into town. A number of restaurants and inns are located about 1km south of the center along beachfront Rua Guarani.

Banco 24 Horas (Av Iperoig) ATM located just next to the tourist office.

Post office (Rua Ernesto de Oliveira; ☯ 9am-4pm Mon-Fri, 9am-noon Sat)

Tourist office (☎ 3833 7300; ☯ 8am-6pm) Situated where Rua Professor Thomaz Galhardo hits the bay; it has useful maps of surrounding beaches.

Sights & Activities

The town itself is uninspiring except for its handsome waterfront promenade. The real trick is to get to the remote beaches and picturesque islands outside the city.

BEACHES

Within the district of Ubatuba, there are some 74 beaches and 15 islands. Regular buses run along the coastal road. Some of the best beaches south of Ubatuba include **Praia Vermelha** (3km), **Enseada** (8km), **Flamengo** (12km, on the Ponta do Flamengo), **do Lázaro** (16km) and **Domingos Dias** (18km). The big, loud party scene is 6km south of Ubatuba at **Praia Grande**.

North of town, the beaches are hidden away down steep hillsides. They're harder to find, but good for boogie boarding and surfing and well worth the effort. Among the best are **Vermelha do Norte** (9km), **Itamambuca** (15km), **Promirim** (23km) and **Ubatumirim** (33km).

BOAT TRIPS

Boat trips leave from the port at Praia de Saco da Ribeira, 12km south of Ubatuba. You can book cruises (R$22, four hours, departing around 11am Thursday to Tuesday) into the Baía da Enseada and out to the Ilha Anchieta. Ilha Anchieta is a lovely island, now protected by the national government. The island offers rare glimpses of beautiful fish and birds undisturbed in their natural habitats. You can also see the local Tamar Project, which protects native turtles and their eggs. These minicruises offer enviable views of the coast and its beautiful, deep-green waters.

You can make reservations at the tourist office or many hotels and guesthouses. However, you might get a better deal by heading to the port – it won't be hard to find people who are willing to set you up for a run around the nearby islands.

Sleeping

If you're without a car, the town center is the most convenient place to stay. From here you can catch local buses to the beaches.

BUDGET & MIDRANGE

Camping Itamambuca (☎ 3834 3000; www.itamam buca.com.br; Praia Itamambuca; per person low/high season R$34/60) This eco-resort about 15km north of town offers excellent facilities near one of the region's most beautiful beaches. Rustic chalets are also available (for two people low/high season R$85/130).

Hotel Xareu (☎ 3832 1525; www.hotelxareubatuba .com.br; Rua Jordão Homem da Costa 413; s/d R$65/90; ☒) Located near the bus station, the Xareu may look like an unpromising motel but does offer simple but comfortable, well-maintained rooms, some of which have a certain colonial charm.

Pousada Jofisa (☎ 3832 4515; www.jofisa.com.br; Praia Perequê-Açu; s/d R$100/150) This decent midrange option sits just across the street from the lovely Perequê-Açu beach, about 2km north of the town center. Rooms are uninspiring but clean and have overhead fans.

A Pousadinha (☎ 3832 2136; www.ubatuba.com .br/pousadinha; Rua Guarani; d from $130; ☒) This former boarding house has been totally refurbished and now offers small and simple but airily stylish rooms around a narrow, lemon-yellow courtyard, making for very good value on this expensive stretch of coast.

TOP END

Hotel Parque Atlântico (☎ 3832 1336; www.hotel parqueatlantico.com.br; Rua Conceição 185; d from R$220; ☒) A fine, moderately priced option in the town center, this impeccably kept hotel offers simple but comfortable digs and attractive common areas, all with polished tiled floors.

A Casa do Sol e da Lua (☎ 3848 9412; www.acasa dosoledalua.com.br; Rua do Refúgio do Cosário 580, Praia da Fortaleza; s/d R$180/240) This cozy, welcoming, family-run place sits right on a great stretch of beach about 10km south of town. Meals are served around a communal table, and rooms are casually but tastefully decorated.

Hotel Recanto das Toninhas (☎ 3842 1410; www .toninhas.com.br; Praia das Toninhas; d from R$500; ☒ ☐ ☒) This sprawling, all-inclusive resort, on a privileged stretch of Toninhas beach, offers a pool, tennis courts, sauna and gym. Built largely of local straw, wood and thatch, it manages to be charming despite its size.

Eating

Don't miss *azul-marinho,* a delicious local stew of fish, rice and green bananas. There are a number of cheap eateries in the town center where you can get a simple meal of fish, rice and beans for around R$10 to R$15.

Bucaneiros (Rua Conçeição 61; pizza about R$10; 🕑 lunch & dinner) The good-value and tasty wood-oven pizza at this simple joint is popular with tourists and locals alike.

Spaghetto (☎ 3833 3377; Rua Guarani 686; mains for 2 R$45-60; 🕑 noon-midnight Tue-Fri, to midnight Sat & Sun) This bright, cheerful Italian eatery brings São Paulo's Italian culinary tradition to the beach, with pasta, fish and meat dishes that are simple but made with fine ingredients and prepared and served with care.

O Rei do Peixe (☎ 3832 3272; Rua Guarani 480; mains for 2 R$50-60; 🕑 noon-10pm Tue-Sun) This large, rustic open-air place feels touristy – and it is. But it also serves up first-rate seafood, including an excellent version of *azul-marinho.*

Refúgio da Louca (Rua Guarani 737; buffet meal R$26; 🕑 noon-10:30pm Dec-Feb, lunch Thu-Tue Mar-Nov) This relaxed, airy and attractive spot offers up a health-conscious buffet including grilled fish and savory salads, as well as versions of the classic Brazilian meat-rice-and-bean meal.

Getting There & Around

Ubatuba has two intercity bus stations. For São Paulo (R$37, four hours, eight daily), São Sebastião (R$5, 70 minutes, hourly; change in Caraguátatuba) and other destinations within the state, head to **Litorânea bus station** (☎ 3832 3622; Rua Maria Victória Jean 381), located two kilometers from the town center. A taxi to the center from the bus station costs around R$10.

For buses to Paraty and Rio de Janeiro, head to the **São Jose bus station** (☎ 3432 6912; Rua Professor Thomaz Galhardo 513).

Local buses (R$2.20, hourly from 7am to 8pm) head up and down the coastal highway and come at least within hiking distance of most beaches. The main stop in the center is at Rua Hans Staden 488.

SÃO SEBASTIÃO

☎ 0xx12 / pop 65,000

One of the only towns on the Paulista coast that has preserved a portion of its colonial charms, São Sebastião sits on a dramatic channel dividing the mainland from Ilha de São Sebastião (popularly known as 'Ilhabela'; see p305), a 15-minute ferry trip away. Prices are

moderate by local standards, but for good reason. There are no beaches at hand, and the town is also a major oil depot, with huge tankers somewhat diminishing the natural beauty. Still, it makes a fine stopover if you're traveling to Ilhabela or along the coast. And the windy channel is ideal for windsurfing. For information, check out the **tourist office** (☎ 3892 2620, ext 4; Av Doutor Altino Arantes 174; 🕑 10am-7pm Mon-Fri, 10am-8pm Sat & Sun) on the waterfront in the small colonial center of town.

Sleeping

Hotel Roma (☎ 3892 1016; www.hotelroma.tur.br; Praça Major João Fernandes 174; s/d R$60/80; 🐱) In the heart of the colonial quarter, Hotel Roma has newer, no-frills rooms with air-con ranged around a plain courtyard, plus a few rooms without bathroom and with fan only (single/double $R25/35) in the main colonial-style building.

Pousada da Ana Doce (☎ 3892 1615; www.pousada anadoce.com.br; Rua Expedicionários Brasileiros 196; s/d R$100/120) With neat, cheerful little rooms arranged around a charming, plant-filled courtyard in the colonial center, this inn is the most charming in the region, especially at such reasonable rates. Book ahead.

Pousada da Sesmaria (☎ 3892 2347; Rua São Gonçalo 190; s/d from R$100/150) The most upscale central option, the Sesmaria offers attractive, recently remodeled, if slightly impersonal, modern rooms, plus a good buffet breakfast that includes homemade jams and jellies.

Eating

Tip Top (☎ 3892 2685; Av Doutor Altino Arantes; mains around R$10) Just down the street from A Canoa is this no-nonsense eatery that serves simple meals of grilled meat, beans, rice and salad.

A Canoa (☎ 3892 1772; Av Doutor Altino Arantes 134; mains R$15-25; 🕑 lunch & dinner) This simple waterfront joint serves simple but good seafood, including the regional specialty, *azul-marinho.*

Atobá (☎ 3892 1487; Praça Major João Fernandes 218; mains R$15-25; 🕑 lunch & dinner) A rather stylish eatery on the town's main square, Atobá offers a high-quality lunch buffet (R$22 per kilo) as well as an à la carte menu of pizzas and pasta at dinner.

Getting There & Away

The **bus station** (Praça da Amizade 10), located just off the main coastal highway and a short walk from the colonial center, has service to São

Paulo (R$37, four hours, 12 daily) and Boiçucanga (R$10, one hour, six daily). The quickest route by car to São Paulo (200km) is to head north from Caraguátatuba on Hwy SP-099.

ILHABELA

☎ 0xx12 / pop 23,000 (winter), 120,000 (summer)

Rising steeply from the narrow strait that divides it from the continent, the 350-sq-km Ilhabela (Beautiful Island) earns its name from its volcanic peaks, beautiful beaches, dense tropical jungle and some 360 waterfalls. Almost 85% of the island has been turned into a park and Unesco-protected biosphere, which shelters a remarkable profusion of plant and animal life, including toucans and capuchin monkeys. A haunt of pirates in the 16th and 17th centuries, its waters are scattered with shipwrecks, many of which make for excellent diving. The island also proffers jungle hiking, windsurfing and beach-lazing.

Be aware that in the height of summer the bugs are murder, especially the little bloodsuckers known as *borrachudos*. Use plenty of insect repellent at all times. Summer is also when the island is packed with vacationing Paulistas.

Information & Orientation

The ferry arrives from the mainland in Perequê. About 4km north along the straight lies the historic town of Vila Ilhabela. Good roads run along the western coast of the island; however, the south and east coasts are reachable only by boat or foot except for a rough road accessible by 4WD that reaches Praia dos Castelhanos on the west coast.

The **tourist office** (☎ 3896 1091; Av Almirante Tamandaré 651, Itaquanduba; ☒ 9am-6pm Mon-Fri, 10am-4pm Sat, 10am-2pm Sun), about 2km north of the ferry stop on the road to Vila Ilhabela, provides an excellent map of the island. You can also preview your visit at www.ilhabela.org, which includes history, hiking itineraries, listings for diving and other adventure activities, and more – in English. For those bringing a car to the island, avoid huge lines at the **ferry** (☎ 0800-55 5510) by booking in advance.

Sights

Vila Ilhabela, on the northwestern part of the island, has quite a few well-preserved colonial buildings, including the slave-built **Igreja NS da Ajuda** (founded 1532); the **Fazenda Engenho d'Agua** in Itaquanduba (founded 1582); and

Fazenda Santa Carmen at Feiticeira beach. Two kilometers inland from Perequê beach (near the ferry terminal), **Cachoeira das Tocas** has various small waterfalls with accompanying deep pools and water slides.

BEACHES

Of the sheltered beaches on the north side of the island, **Praia Jabaquara** is recommended; it's accessed by a 5km-long walking trail. On the east side, where the surf is stronger, try beautiful **Praia dos Castelhanos** (good for camping and surfing), which is backed by the steeply rising jungle. From the town of Borrifos you can take a four-hour walk to **Praia Bonete**, a windy surf beach lying on the southern side of the island that you will share with a local community of fishermen.

Activities

Maremar Turismo (☎ 3896 1418; www.maremar.tur .br; Rua Antonio Lisboa Alves 728; d R$200) in Perequê near the ferry organizes all kinds of outdoor activities, including schooner trips around the island (from R$35 per person), diving to offshore wrecks (full day including equipment from R$200), and horseback riding (two hours from R$50).

Sleeping

Reservations are a good idea on weekends – mandatory on summer weekends. Prices are high, so some travelers choose to stay in São Sebastião where rates are more reasonable.

Camping Canto Grande (☎ 3894 1506; www.canto grande.com.br in Portuguese; Av Riachuelo 5638, Praia Grande; per person R$30) This beachside camping ground about 6km south of the ferry landing offers hot-water showers, a simple restaurant, wi-fi and has beach chairs and umbrellas for hire.

Pousada Caravela (☎ 3892 8295; www.caravelaresi dence.com.br in Portuguese; Rua Carlos Rizzini 70; ste R$140; ☒) This place offers good value, with simple but attractive little suites with kitchen and balconies arranged around a grassy courtyard with pool. Located about 500m from the ferry

Pousada dos Hibiscos (☎ 3896 1375; www.pousada doshibiscos.com.br; Av Pedro de Paula Moraes 714; s/d from R$150/180) On the beach and a short walk from the ferry, this place offers decent value, with simple but trim rooms around a flower-filled courtyard, just 800m from the ferry landing.

SÃO PAULO STATE

Refúgio das Pedras (☎ 3894 1756; www.refugiodas pedras.com.br in Portuguese; Av Governador Mário Covas 11495, Ponta da Sela; d R$400) Located near the southern end of the strait facing the mainland, this quirky-but-chic guesthouse takes its name from the natural rocks that have been incorporated in both the landscaping and the rooms. Amenities include a small fitness center and Jacuzzi bath.

Maison Joly (☎ 3896 1201; www.maisonjoly.com.br; Rua Antônio Lisboa Alves 278; d from R$550; ⊠ ⊑ ⧆) With privileged ocean views, festive yet sophisticated decor, 'Zen' lounge for yoga and massage, and a long list of luxury amenities, this inn is a favorite romantic getaway. Children under 12 not allowed.

Eating

In Vila Ilhabela there are a few good, cheap *lanchonetes:* two in the pedestrian mall, and a couple on Rua da Padroeira.

Cheiro Verde (Rua da Padroeira 109; meals from R$12) The best place in Vila Ilhabela for a generous *prato feito* (plate of the day) with rice, beans, salad and grilled meat or fish.

A Redonda (Av Riachuelo 6852; Curral; pizza for 2 from R$20) This simple spot near Praia Curral, about 7km south of the ferry, attracts summer crowds with its good pizza.

Deck (☎ 3896 1489; Av Almirante Tamandaré 805, Itaguassu; mains from R$25; ⧆ noon-10pm Tue-Sun) About 1km north of the ferry lies this popular seafood restaurant that also makes good pizzas. It sometimes closes at 9pm in the low season.

Troia (☎ 3894 2121; Av José Pacheco do Nascimento 7668, Curral; mains around R$30; ⧆ noon-midnight) A seafacing terrace, a misting system that keeps diners cool even on hot days and creative takes on Mediterranean cuisine (shrimp with sauce of orange and vanilla beans) make this the island's top-rated restaurant.

For self-catering, hit the **Ilha da Princesa supermarket** (Av Princesa Isabel 2467), located in Barra Velha.

Getting There & Around

The 15-minute ferry trip between São Sebastião and Ilhabela runs every half hour from 6am to midnight (often until much later in summer). Cars cost R$11 weekdays and R$16 on weekends, motorcycles cost R$5 weekdays and R$8 on weekends, and it's free for pedestrians. A local bus (R$2) links the ferry with the nearby town of Vila Ilhabela.

A decent road runs the length of the western coast. Another unsealed road (22km) crosses the island. To get to the other side of the island requires either a 4WD, a boat or a good strong pair of hiking legs.

BOIÇUCANGA & AROUND

☎ 0xx12 / pop 5800

The laid-back surfer town of Boiçucanga makes a good base to explore the stretch of coast that runs almost due west from São Sebastião. The variety of beaches, many backed by the steeply rising Serra do Mar, is remarkable, and there's good surf at nearby Camburi and Maresias, which have also developed into major party towns.

Information

Boiçucanga has a **tourist office** (☎ 3865 4335; ⧆ 8am-6pm Mon-Fri) right off the main highway about 200m west of the town center. You can also get information from José Mauro, who runs a tourist information service called **Amart** (☎ 3465 1453, 9144 4434; Av Walkir Vergani 319) and speaks English, Spanish and Italian.

Sights & Activities

Some great beaches are strung along this stretch of coastline, all accessible by bus. Both **Maresias** (9km east of Boiçucanga), and **Camburi** (3km west) are great surf beaches. A creek and a small island divide Camburi – the western end is bigger, rougher and good for surfing, and the eastern end is calmer and good for swimming. **Juqueí** (15km west) offers calm waters, making it popular with families. There are a series of deserted islands nearby. Ask at the tourist office to organize passage. Expect to pay around R$20 to R$30 per person.

Sleeping

BUDGET & MIDRANGE

Camping Porongaba (☎ 3865 1384; www.porongaba .com.br; Travessa dos Periquitos 99, Boiçucanga; per person R$20) This camping ground has a pool, snack bar and pleasant grounds. From the bus station in Boiçucanga, head up Estrada do Cascalho about 2km and cross a wooden bridge. The camping ground is 50m on the left.

Hostel Camburi (☎ 3865 1561; Rua Tijucas 2300, Camburi; www.ajcamburi.com.br; dm from R$25, r from R$75; ⊑ ⧆) Though a bit pricey, this hostel is the best budget option in Camburi; it has clean, basic rooms with fans, and a swimming pool amid green grounds. It's about 2.5km from

Camburi Sertão bus stop, from where you can call to be picked up.

Pousada Boiçucanga (☎ 3865 2668; pousada boicucanga@yahoo.com.br; Av Walkir Vergani 522, Boiçucanga; r R$100) The cheapest place in town offers clean, basic rooms that feature tile floors, well-used furnishings and ceiling fans, set around a potentially noisy courtyard.

Dani Hotel (☎ 3865 1299; www.danihotel.com .br; Av Walkir Vergani 455, Boiçucanga; d R$120; P 🔁) Clean, fairly basic rooms set around an attractive-enough courtyard.

TOP END

Pousada das Praias (☎ 3865 1474; www.pousada daspraias.com.br; Rua Piau 70, Camburi; d R$180) Handsomely rustic apartments, most of which are built with local wood, make this higher-end option worth seeking out. Located just off the main road near the eastern end of the beach.

Pousada Portal do Cacau (☎ 3865 1611; www.portal docacau.com.br; Rua Tijucas 895, Camburi; s/d R$220; 🔁) You get good value at this rather plush miniresort, which has a sauna, tennis courts, a pool and massage studio. Rooms at this pousada are comfortable, if undistinguished, and there are walks from here to several nearby waterfalls.

Pousada DiMari (☎ 3865 4711; www.dimari.com.br; Av Walkir Vergani 833, Boiçucanga; d R$440; 🔁) Tranquil, airy rooms with sea views, colorful high-end decor and a lovely beachfront garden with pool. DiMari is the classiest choice in the town of Boiçucanga.

Eating

There are some bargain restaurants (meals from R$10) in Boiçucanga's new American-style mall in the center of town. Restaurants also line the beachfront in Maresias.

Big Pão (🕑 6am-midnight) This old-fashioned bakery café, located at the bend in the highway in the center of Boiçucanga, serves sandwiches and grill food (mains around R$5).

Restaurante Caravela (☎ 3865 1541; Rua Itabira 21, Boiçucanga; mains for 2-3 around R$70; 🕑 noon-10pm Wed-Mon) Head here for delicious *caldeiradas* and *moquecas* (both a kind of fish stew) served on an attractive outdoor terrace.

Getting There & Around

The intercity bus station in Boiçucanga has services to São Paulo (R$30, four hours, eight daily), Guarujá (R$19, two hours, six daily) and São Sebastião (R$10, one hour, six

daily). Intercity buses usually stop at smaller towns such as Camburi and Maresias. There is also a local bus service (R$2.50) connecting Boiçucanga with Maresias, Camburi and other nearby coastal towns.

GUARUJÁ

☎ 0xx13 / pop 285,000

With its fine beaches along the stretch of coast closest to São Paulo, once-glamorous Guarujá has suffered from overdevelopment. Still, if you can't get further afield, it makes a good getaway from the 'other' big city – even if concrete towers line the beaches, which get packed with weekend day-trippers. A recent cleanup of waters and sands has renewed interest in a town that was the extreme of chic back in the '70s. Surfers should note that there are good waves along **Praia do Tombo**.

Information

The helpful **tourist information office** (☎ 3344 4600; Rua Marechal Deodoro da Fonesca 723; 🕑 10am-6pm) sits on the beach at the end of the main road into town.

Sleeping & Eating

Restaurants and bars and accommodations line the waterfront area.

Hotel Rio (☎ 3355 9281; www.hotelrio.com.br; Rua Rio de Janeiro 131; s/d R$90/125) The old-fashioned, whitewashed Hotel Rio is more charming outside than in, but its clean, basic rooms are good value and are situated less than 100m from the beach.

Pousada Canto do Forte (☎ 3354 2860; www .cantodoforte.com.br; Rua Horácio Guedes Barreiro 133; s/d R$100/150; 🔁 🖥 🔁) Simple, clean rooms with fridge and tiled floors are a good deal at this well-run option at the end of Praia do Tombo. Reservations are recommended in summer and at weekends.

Nutris (Av Leomil 538; meals R$10; 🕑 11am-3pm) A good self-service eatery with a decent assortment of vegetarian dishes, Nutris also serves a few chicken and fish dishes.

Combinati (☎ 3386 9005; Rua Mário Ribeira 600; mains from R$20; 🕑 lunch & dinner Wed-Mon) Good, midrange Italian food a short walk from the tourist office.

Getting There & Around

Guarujá is on a large island separated from the mainland by the Canal de Bertioga. The **bus station** (☎ 3386 2325) is at the edge of town

SÃO PAULO STATE

on Via Santos Dumont. From there, cross the street and catch local bus 1, 15 or 41 (R$2.10) to the beach. Buses leave every half hour for São Paulo, cost R$16, and take between 75 minutes and two hours, depending on traffic.

IGUAPE & AROUND

☎ 0xx13 / pop 28,400

Founded by the Portuguese in 1538 to defend Brazil from the Spanish, Iguape is one of the oldest towns in Brazil and one of the few along São Paulo's coast to retain its colonial contours. While beaches are a bit of a hoof, the town makes a tranquil base from which to explore the region.

Information

There is a **tourist information booth** (☎ 3841 3358; Largo da Basílica; ☺ 8am-5:30pm) on the town's main square.

Sights

The town's colonial charms are clustered around the whitewashed main plaza, **Largo da Basílica**, and the 18th-century **basilica**. About 1.5km on the road to Barra do Ribeira is a turnoff to the **Mirante do Morro do Espia**, a lookout with a good view of the port and region.

Barra do Ribeira, the closest beach on the mainland that is good for swimming, is popular with surfers. To get there, grab a boat from Iguape (20 minutes, R$10 return).

Iguape looks across a narrow strait to **Ilha Comprida**, a long, skinny island (86km by 3km) that shelters Iguape from the open ocean. The island is covered with gorgeous forest and has an uninterrupted beach that stretches the entire Atlantic-facing length of the island. A toll bridge now connects Iguape with the island. To go even further off the beaten track, head for the beautiful 15km-long **Praia da Juréia**, 40km northeast of Iguape.

Sleeping & Eating

Silvi Hotel (☎ 3841 1421; www.silvihotel.com.br; Rua Ana Cândida Sandoval Trigo 515; s/d without air-con R$30/45, with air-con R$45/70; ☒) A humble but decent yellow-and-green, motel-style sleep, with clean and largish, if plain, rooms.

Pousada Casa Grande (☎ 3841 1920; Rua Major Rebello 768; s/d R$45/70) Rooms in this colonial one-story structure are definitely small and simple, but open onto a pleasant, shared veranda. Rooms have fans only.

Pousada Solar Colonial (☎ 3841 1591; www.guiadei guape.com.br/solarcolonialpousada; Praça da Basílica 30; s/d R$50/70) This lemon-yellow colonial building right on Largo da Basílica offers old-fashioned but clean, well-maintained digs at good value.

Panela Velha (☎ 3841 1869; Rua 15 de Novembro 190; mains from R$15; ☺ lunch & dinner) This no-nonsense place serves up some of the best, freshest seafood in town at remarkable prices.

Itacurumins (Rua Porto do Rosário 2; mains R$15-25; ☺ lunch & dinner Mon & Wed-Sat, lunch Sun, lunch & dinner Dec-Feb) Another simple, good seafood joint for the local catch of the day.

Getting There & Around

There is a direct bus service from Iguape to São Paulo (R$35, four hours, about four daily) and Cananéia (R$18, two hours, about two daily). Local buses cross the bridge to Ilha Comprida. If you have a 4WD, it is possible to drive along the long, flat beach on Ilha Comprida and take the ferry across to Cananéia (R$7 per vehicle, passengers free), though you must time your trip for low tide.

CANANÉIA

☎ 0xx13 / pop 13,600

Smaller and prettier than neighboring Iguape, Cananéia has an even longer lineage. Founded in 1531, it's considered one of the oldest European settlements in Brazil, and while the bulk of the old town was built in the 19th century, there are a few buildings that date to the 16th century, such as the **Igreja São Batista** (Praça Martim Afonso de Souza; ☺ 9am-noon, 2-6pm Wed-Sun). Unfortunately, many buildings in the town are in varying states of disrepair.

Beaches

The beaches of **Ilha Comprida** are only a 10-minute ferry ride (R$7 per vehicle, every 30 minutes from 6am to midnight). Passengers on foot ride free.

The highlight of the region is **Ilha do Cardoso**, an ecological reserve of gorgeous natural pools, waterfalls and untouched beaches, which has only 400 residents and no cars. There are daily boats (R$45 return, three hours) from the port in Cananéia.

Sleeping & Eating

Hotels are often booked up during peak holiday season (January and February) and on weekends all summer long.

Golfinho Plaza Hotel (☎ 3851 1655; www.golfinho plazahotel.com.br; Av Independencia 885; s/d R$55/65) Located on the main road leading to town from the highway, this hotel offers simple but clean, well-equipped rooms at a good price.

Costa Azul Club (☎ 3851 8288; www.hotelcostazul .com.br; Estrada da Ponte, Km 06; d without/with air-con R$90/120; ✖ ✖) This well-maintained resort hotel on the highway leading into Cananéia has pretty grounds and good-value rooms. Tours and boat rides are available from the hotel's marina.

Hotel Marazul (☎ 3851 1407; www.hotelmarazul .com.br; Av Luís Wilson Barbosa 408; s/d R$100/140; ✖ ✖) With a seaside pool and terrace as well as rather simple but colorful guestrooms, this brick pousada is as upscale as Cananéia gets.

Restaurante Tia Inês (Rua João Carlos Muller 264; mains R$15-25; ✖ lunch & dinner) For an inexpensive meal of rice, beans, salad and grilled meat or fish, head to this simple eatery in the center of town.

Kurt Kaffe (☎ 3851 1262; Av Beira Mar 71; mains R$15-25; ✖ 4-8pm Mon-Thu, to 2am Fri-Sun) A café, restaurant and antique store, this charming waterfront place attracts travelers and local Bohemians alike with its live music, fresh oysters (for which Cananéia is renowned) and, of course, booze.

Getting There & Around

A direct bus leaves Cananéia for São Paulo twice daily (R$42, five hours). There are also two daily buses to Iguape (R$18, two hours).

The ferry terminal to Ilha Comprida is down from the main plaza. The 10-minute ride ferry is free for foot passengers (vehicles cost R$7), with boats leaving every half hour from 6am to midnight.

INLAND

IPORANGA

☎ 0xx15 / pop 4500

Nestled in the Vale do Ribeira in the hills near the São Paulo–Paraná border, Iporanga was founded in 1576 after gold was discovered here. Today, the surrounding region remains one of the least-disturbed stretches of the Brazilian Atlantic Forest and is of international importance for its biodiversity. It also makes a good base for visiting the

Parque Estadual do Alto do Ribeira (Petar). This 360-sq-km state park, with its 280 cataloged caves, is known as Brazil's Capital das Grutas (Cave Capital).

Information

Iporanga has no tourist information office. For information as well as camping and caving reservations, call **Petar** (☎ 3552 1528; www .geocities.com/yosemite/trails/7630), the state park administration in Iporanga. **Ecocave** (☎ 3556 1574; www.ecocave.com.br) organizes expeditions to the caves, as well as kayaking, biking, horseback riding and more.

Caves

The **Núcleos de Visitação** (☎ 3552 1875) are well-set-up visitors centers with information on cave trips, guides (all in Portuguese) and camping grounds.

There are four Núcleos: Núcleo Santana (17km northwest of town) has good facilities for visitors and campers, four caves and a 3.5km-long trek to a beautiful waterfall; Núcleo Ouro Grosso (16km northwest of town) has basic accommodations for groups and offers cooking facilities, two caves and a walking trail; Núcleo Casa de Pedra (9km by road plus 3km by walking trail, northwest from town) is the base for visiting the cave Casa de Pedra, famous for its 215m-high entrance and pristine Atlantic forest; and Núcleo Caboclos (centrally located in the park, 86km by road from town) has good camping facilities, basic visitors' lodgings and several caves.

Sleeping & Eating

Accommodations are mostly clustered in the Bairro da Serra, near the entrance to the park about 13km from the town center. Most places offer full board options.

Pousada Casa de Pedra (☎ 3556 1157; www.pousada casadepedra.com.br; Rua Rio Ribeira de Iguape 517; dm/s/d R$25/30/60) Near the river just west of town, this pousada has rustic dormitory accommodations. The restaurant has tasty homemade meals (R$10), but you need to place your order for food a day in advance.

Pousada das Cavernas (☎ 38149153; www.pousadadas cavernas.com.br in Portuguese; d without/with air-con incl breakfast & dinner R$92/138; ✖) One of the most attractive options around, this inn in the Bairro da Serra area offers wide verandas, colonial-style construction and simple but well-kept rooms, some with views over a pretty

TUDO BEM, Y'ALL?

When the South lost the American Civil War in 1865, Brazil's emperor Dom Pedro II saw dollar signs. Offering cheap land to planters in exchange for the state-of-the-art techniques for growing cotton that they would bring with them, he lured as many as 10,000 southerners to his country.

Most of the new immigrants settled in central São Paulo state, where they found growing conditions remarkably similar to those of the southern US. They planted pecans, peaches, corn and cotton just as they had in their native soil. They also made a concerted effort to stay aloof from Brazilian culture, venerating the Confederate flag and preserving their language and many of their customs. However, they did have to forgo one luxury: slavery, the institution they had fought so hard to defend. Recent research indicates only a few former Confederates actually owned slaves in Brazil.

In the neighboring towns of Americana and Santa Bárbara d'Oeste, both about 100km northwest of São Paulo, you can still hear descendants of the *confederados* speaking English with a distinctly Southern lilt. And every year, the Fraternity of American Descendants – the community's main social institution – holds a picnic, complete with fried chicken, biscuits and peach pie.

The Cemitério do Campo, located in a sea of sugarcane fields about 12km from Santa Bárbara d'Oeste, is the *confederado*'s spiritual epicenter. Founded in the 1870s when Catholic authorities refused burial to the Protestant immigrants, its gravestones are inscribed with names such as Braxton and Bloxom, Sharpley and Shippey, Meriwether and Maxwell.

To explore São Paulo's Confederate heritage, head to Santa Bárbara d'Oeste's **Museu da Imigração** (☎ 0xx19-3455 5082; Praça 9 de Julho; free admission; ✆ 8-11:30am, 1-5pm Tue-Fri, 8-11:30am, 1-2:30pm Sat), whose collections include photographs, letters and household objects. The city has direct services to and from São Paulo's Tietê bus station (R$20, two hours). Ask at the museum about arranging transportation to the Cemitério do Campo, which can be difficult to find, even for local drivers.

valley. Pousada das Cavernas also has a great restaurant/lounge area.

Churrascaria do Abel (Rua Barão de Jundiaí 88; mains from R$15) Grilled meats as well as local home cooking are available at what is generally considered the best place in town.

Getting There & Away

There is generally one early-morning bus daily from São Paulo's Barra Funda bus station to Eldorado (R$30, five hours). From Eldorado you can get the bus to Iporanga.

CAMPOS DO JORDÃO

☎ 0xx12 / pop 47,000 / elevation 1628m

Nestled in the green peaks of Serra da Mantiqueira, 180km northeast of São Paulo, Campos do Jordão is at once a kitsch and rather plain confection. Still, it makes a comfortable base from which to explore the nearby peaks, which are home to some of the last remaining virgin *araucária* (Paraná pine) forests and proffer spectacular views of the Paraíba valley. There is also a renowned winter classical-music festival in July.

Be aware that the town is a hugely popular winter weekend getaway for Paulistas

who enjoy the novelty of wearing woolens. Traffic and prices spike accordingly.

Orientation & Information

Campos is made up of three main districts: Abernéssia (the oldest), Jaguaribe (where the bus station is located) and Capivari, the center. The three districts are connected by a tram (R$2).

The **tourist office** (☎ 3664 3525; ✆ 8am-8pm) is at the gateway to the valley, on the main road into town about 2km before Abernéssia, and offers a helpful map.

Sights

The **Horto Florestal state park** (admission R$4 per vehicle; ✆ 8am-5pm), 14km east from Capivari, is home to the largest *araucária* reserve in the state and offers fine walks of varying levels of difficulty. The **reception desk** (☎ 3663 3762), near the trout farm, can supply you with maps.

Close to Capivari is a *teleférico* (chairlift; R$5; ✆ 1-5pm Fri, 9am-5:30pm Sat & Sun) that takes you to the top of the **Morro do Elefante**, which has a good view of the town.

The **Palácio Boa Vista** (☎ 3662 1122; Av Dr Ademar de Barros 3001; admission R$5; ✆ 10am-noon & 2-5pm Wed-

Sun), 3.5km north of Abernéssia, is the state governor's sprawling, English-style, antiques-filled summer residence.

The 19km **electric train ride** (☎ 3663 1531; 2½hr round-trip R$30) from Campos do Jordão to Santo Antônio do Pinhal is one of Brazil's best. There are five trains daily on weekends, but only two daily on weekdays. The train leaves from Campos (from the Capivari terminal at the end of Av Emílio Ribas). For the best views, sit on the right-hand side when leaving Campos.

Sleeping

July is peak tourist period in Campos, when the town receives up to a million tourists. Many places require a minimum one-week stay at this time. You can expect steep discounts weekdays and outside winter months.

Camping Clube do Brasil (☎ 3663 0425; www .campingclube.com.br; members/nonmembers R$11/33) This decent facility offers hot water and is located about 10km east of Capivari on the road to Horto Florestal.

Campos do Jordão Hostel (☎ 3662 2341; www .camposdojordaohostel.com.br; Rua Pereira Barreto 22; d R$90) Friendly staff and reasonable prices (by local standards) make up for the slightly tattered rooms and thin mattresses at the town's closest approximation to a youth hostel.

Duas Quedas Park Hotel (☎ 3662 2492; http://duas quedas.vilabol.uol.com.br; Rua Leonor Przirembel 255; chalets for up to 4 people R$180) With rustic but comfortable, well-kept (though slightly musty) chalets arranged around a pretty garden complete with waterfall, this is one of the town's most-charming options.

Grande Hotel Campos do Jordão (☎ 3260 6000; www .sp.senac.br/hoteis; Av Frei Orestes Girardi; d incl full board R$800; ✗ ❑ ☑) Set in its own private forest, this sumptuous, European-style resort is run by a prestigious hotel school. It has lovely grounds, pool and tennis courts, plus views from many rooms of the surrounding countryside.

Eating & Drinking

Bia Kaffe (☎ 3663 1507; Rua Isola Orsi 33; mains from R$20; ✇ noon-midnight Fri & Sat, to 8:30pm Sun) This cozy haunt in Capivari serves quality coffee, cakes and other sweets, as well as grilled sausage, goulash and trout. Recommended.

Baden-Baden (☎ 3663 3659; Rua Djalma Forjaz 93; mains around R$30; ✇ 11am-midnight) Located on one of Capivari's kitschier corners, this German-style place draws the crowds with its good sausages, excellent home-brewed beer, attractive outdoor seating and lots of pretty, preening Paulistas.

Harry Pisek (☎ 3663 4030; Av Pedro Paulo 857; mains from R$30; ✇ 10am-5pm Sun-Fri, 10am-11pm Sat) Chef Pisek studied the art of sausage-making in Germany and is celebrated for his homemade production, which he serves up in his cozy restaurant, complete with Teutonic decor on the road to Horto Florestal.

Getting There & Away

The new **bus station** (☎ 3262 1996; Av Dr Januário Miraglia) is near Supermercado Roma, between Jaguaribe and Capivari. Buses travel to São Paulo (R$22, 2½ hours, about six daily) and to Rio de Janeiro (R$42, five hours, two daily).

AROUND CAMPOS DO JORDÃO

The **Gruta dos Crioulos** (Creoles' Cave) was used as a hideout by slaves escaping from the surrounding farms. It's 7km from Jaguaribe on the road to Pedra do Baú, a 1950m-high mountain peak that consists of a huge, rectangular granite block. To get to the top of Pedra do Baú you have to walk 2km north and climb 600 steps carved into the rock. It's about 25km from Campos do Jordão.

For a day trip up **Pedra do Baú**, mountain-bike tours or guided hikes to waterfalls around Pedra do Baú, check out the ecofriendly **Altus Turismo Ecologico** (☎ 3663 4122; www.altus.tur.br; Av Brasil 108). German and English are spoken.

Paraná

Since seceding from São Paolo state in 1853, Paraná has been endlessly compared to its larger neighbor to the north. Indeed, Paraná shares with São Paolo a slew of superlatives, rating among Brazil's highest standards of living, most productive economies and best educated populations.

Paraná's enviable position near the top of these lists is due to many factors. But one is undoubtedly its ancestry, which is mostly German, Italian, Polish and Ukrainian. These hardworking European immigrants established an economy based on small family farms, as opposed to plantations, resulting in a relatively equitable, democratic social order. Add to that a thoughtful approach to economic development and a progressive stance on social issues, and you have the pleasant, prosperous place to live that Paraná is today.

The capital, Curitiba, exemplifies the state's successes. Travelers can take advantage of efficient public transportation as they admire the city's innovative architecture and outstanding urban parks.

Outside of Curitiba, the state of Paraná boasts geological and ecological wonders that will delight any heart. Ilha do Mel and Parque Nacional Superagüi include large swathes of unspoiled rain forest and pristine coastline. Sunbathers and surfers sigh for these beaches, which are the least developed and most idyllic in all of southern Brazil. From the coast, the stunning Serra do Mar stretches up to the Planalto, the high plain that is further inland.

And all the way across the state, straddling Brazil's border with Argentina, is perhaps Paraná's most amazing asset. The power and the splendor of Iguaçu Falls has always earned the awe and admiration of travelers, from indigenous tribes to Jesuit missionaries to modern-day tourists.

HIGHLIGHTS

- Hear the roar and feel the spray from the **Garganta do Diablo** (p326), the mother of all waterfalls at Iguaçu Falls

- Dance the *fandango* (folk dance) in the remote village of **Barra do Superagüi** (p324), in the Parque Nacional do Superagüi

- Watch the sunset from **Farol das Conchas** (p321), the lighthouse on Ilha do Mel

- Marvel at the ancient 'stone city' of **Vila Velha** (p317)

- Attend a concert at Curitiba's unusual **Opera de Arame** (p317), constructed completely of steel tubes and glass

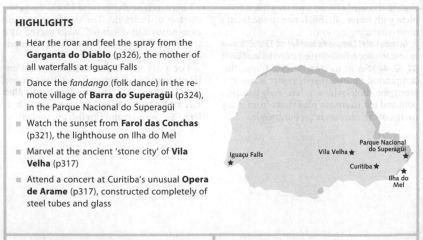

Iguaçu Falls ★   Vila Velha ★   Parque Nacional do Superagüi ★

Curitiba ★

Ilha do Mel ★

- POPULATION: 10.4 MILLION
- AREA: 199,544 SQ KM

History

Like the rest of southern Brazil, Paraná was neglected by the Portuguese colonists; even a brief gold rush in the 17th century withered when bigger finds were discovered in Minas Gerais. When the state seceded from São Paulo in 1853, the economy was based on cattle and *erva maté* tea. The government encouraged immigration from Italy to develop the economy. Italians were followed by waves of Germans, Ukrainians and Poles.

Curitiba had been little more than a stage stop in the cattle trade. But with immigration and railroad construction, the city grew at a remarkable rate, developing into one of the country's richest cities.

Climate

Both the coast and the area around Iguaçu Falls are semitropical regions dominated by the Mata Atlântica (Atlantic rain forest). Summers are hot and humid; winters are mild. Curitiba, which lies on an upland plain, is significantly cooler than the coast.

National Parks

Parque Nacional do Superagüi (p324) is part of a huge, 4700-sq-km reserve of the Mata Atlântica, including a few largely uninhabited islands and miles of mangrove swamps. The famous falls are surrounded by the 1550-sq-km Parque Nacional do Iguaçu (p327), which also protects the ecosystem of the Mata Atlântica.

Getting There & Around

Curitiba is the state's transportation hub, with bus and air services to every major city in Brazil. A passenger train links Curitiba with the coastal town of Paranaguá. Foz do Iguaçu also has a small international airport, as well as direct bus service to São Paulo, Rio de Janeiro and every big city in the South.

CURITIBA

☎ 0xx41 / pop 1.76 million

Curitiba is not particularly sophisticated nor sexy, but its residents enjoy a quality life unparalleled in other parts of the country. With the help of a vibrant local economy,

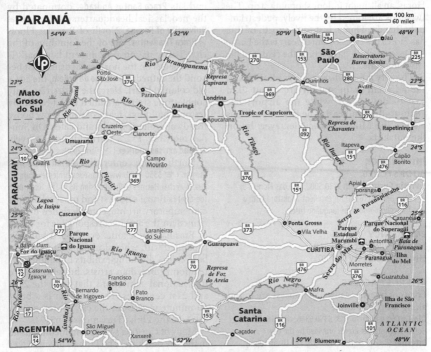

PARANÁ

the modern city has managed to preserve historic buildings and green space.

In the 1970s and 1980s, the city launched progressive incentives to get people out of their cars, lowering bus prices and improving service. The strategy worked: today it's easier to get around Curitiba than any other large city in Brazil. The city has also taken innovative approaches to urban ills such as homelessness, pollution and poverty. To help bridge the technological divide, free internet access is provided at locations around the city.

It is not a beautiful city. However, it is pleasant to promenade along the pedestrian streets or circle the city on the Linha Turisma. The Museu Oscar Niemeyer is fascinating for anyone interested in contemporary art and architecture. The large university population injects a youthful energy and a vibrant music scene, which is on display after dark.

Orientation

Curitiba's historic center is bounded in the east by Praça Santos Andrade and the nearby Passeio Público, a pleasant city park, and in the west by Praça General Osório and Rua 24 Horas, an all-night indoor shopping strip. The two ends are joined by the lively, pedestrian-only Rua das Flores. Just to the north of Rua das Flores the city's colonial heart is the Largo da Ordem, which has become the center of the city's nightlife.

The city's long-distance bus station and the adjacent train station are about 2km east of downtown, while the airport lies 18km to the southeast. The largest parks, as well as the Museu Oscar Niemeyer, lie on the outskirts.

Information

BOOKSTORES
Livraria Curitiba (☎ 3330 5002; Rua das Flores 78; ☩ 8am-6pm Mon-Sat) An excellent bookstore with a small selection of foreign-language titles.

EMERGENCY
Federal Police (☎ 3360 7674)
Medical Emergency (☎ 192)

INTERNET ACCESS
Loads of internet cafes (lan houses) are found along Rua das Flores.
Digitando o Futuro (☎ 3350 6366; shop 16, Rua 24 Horas) Free internet access provided by the city.
Internet (Rua 15 de Novembro 18; ☩ 10am-10pm)

MONEY
Banco do Brasil (Praça Tiradentes 410)
HSBC (cnr Rua 15 de Novembro & Av Marechal Floriano Peixoto)

TOURIST INFORMATION
Both tourist information offices (www.viaje .curitiba.pr.gov.br) are well stocked with glossy brochures and well staffed with willing employees, who may speak a little English.
Bus station information office (☎ 3352 8000; ☩ 7am-midnight Mon-Sat, 7am-7pm Sun)
Rua 24 Horas information office (☎ 3324 7036; Shop 18; ☩ 8am-midnight)

Sights

For an overview of Curitiba, head to the 109m-high **Torre Panorâmica** (☎ 3339 7613; Rua Prof Lycio Grein de Castro Vellozo 191; adult/child R$3/1.50; ☩ 9am-7pm Tue-Sun), which offers 360-degree views from its observation deck. Walk about 2km west from the Largo da Ordem, or take the Linha Turismo (p317).

The focal point of Curitiba's downtown is **Rua das Flores**, a 500m pedestrian mall ideal for shopping and strolling. At its eastern end sits **Praça Santos Andrade**, dominated by the neoclassical headquarters of the **Federal University of Paraná**. North of Rua das Flores is **Praça Tiradentes**, site of the founding of the city. Today its most prominent landmark is the **cathedral** on the northeast corner. Just beyond the cathedral is **Largo da Ordem**, the city's old colonial heart. Here, the pedestrian-only cobblestone streets are lined with beautifully restored buildings, many of which now house trendy art galleries, pubs and cafés. On Sunday morning, Praça Garibaldi hosts a lively **art and artisan market** (☩ 9am-2pm).

North of the center, the **Museu Oscar Niemeyer** (☎ 3350 4400; www.museuoscarniemeyer.org.br; Rua Marechal Hermes 999; admission R$3; ☩ 10am-6pm Tue-Sun) is Brazil's newest and most celebrated contemporary art museum, designed by and named for the architect responsible for much of Brasília. The exotic, eye-shaped building is painted with whimsical dancing figures in bold colors. Rotating exhibits highlight contemporary Brazilian artists, but also feature international exhibitions that span the 20th and 21st centuries. The museum is a brisk 30-minute walk from the city center, or you can take the Linha Turismo (see p317).

Many of Curitiba's parks and memorials lie in the city outskirts. The Linha Turismo takes

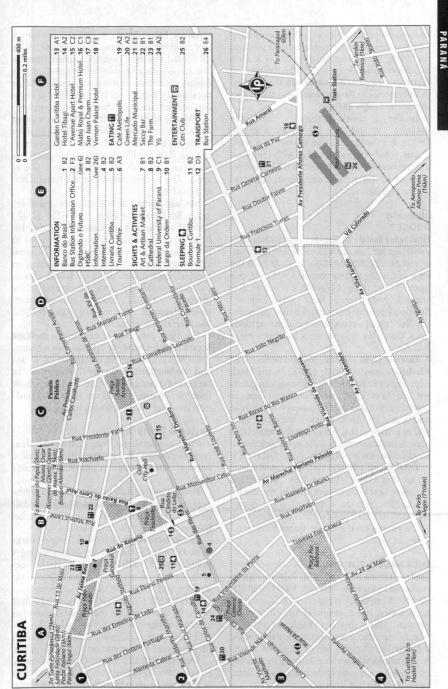

CURITIBA

0 — 400 m
0 — 0.2 miles

INFORMATION	
Banco do Brasil..............................	1 B2
Bus Station Information Office.......	2 F3
Digitando o Futuro.........................	(see 6)
HSBC..	3 B2
Information....................................	4 B2
Internet..	(see 26)
Livraria Curitiba............................	5 B2
Tourist Office...............................	6 A3

SIGHTS & ACTIVITIES	
Art & Artisan Market.....................	7 B1
Cathedral......................................	8 C2
Federal University of Paraná..........	9 C1
Largo da Ordem............................	10 B1

SLEEPING 🅰	
Bourbon Curitiba...........................	11 B2
Formule 1......................................	12 D3

Garden Curitiba Hotel....................	13 A1
Hotel Tibagi..................................	14 A2
L'Avenue Apart Hotel....................	15 C2
Mabú Royal & Premium Hotel........	16 C1
San Juan Charm............................	17 C3
Vernon Palace Hotel......................	18 F3

EATING 🅰	
Café Metrópolis.............................	19 A2
Green Life.....................................	20 A2
Mercado Municipal........................	21 E3
Saccy Bar.....................................	22 B1
The Farm......................................	23 B1
Yo..	24 A2

ENTERTAINMENT 🅰	
Cats Club......................................	25 B2

TRANSPORT	
Bus Station...................................	26 E4

passengers past a series of monuments honoring the region's immigrant communities, including the Italian neighborhood known as Santa Felicidade with its **Portal Italiano**; the German memorial **Bosque Alemão**; the Ukrainian memorial in **Parque Tingui**; and the Polish memorial **Bosque do Papa**.

In the far south of the city, the **Jardim Botânico** (☎ 3264 1800; Rua Eng Ostoja Roguski; ☽ 6am-9pm Dec-Mar, 6am-8pm Apr-Nov) is a vast, flower-filled expanse, studded with sculpture and crisscrossed by cobblestone. The centerpiece glass and metallic greenhouse displays native vegetation.

Sleeping

BUDGET

Curitiba Eco Hostel (☎ 3029 1693; www.curitibaecohostel .com.br; Rua Luiz Tramontin 1693; HI-member/student/non-member dm R$20/23/26, d R$45/50/55; 🖳 🖳) On the edge of the city and surrounded by forest, this hostel is the budget traveler's best bet. For starters, your friendly host speaks English! Spacious rooms have bright-orange walls, tile floors and access to a fabulous outdoor deck. Catch the 'Tramontina' bus from Praça Rui Barbosa.

Formule 1 (☎ 3218 3838; www.accorhotels.com.br; Rua Mariano Torres 927; r R$55; 🔀 🖳) In the stark white lobby at Formule 1, staff check in guests with all the efficiency and charm of a race-car crew. Every one of the 263 rooms is brightly lit and spotlessly clean. You know exactly what you're getting at this Accor hotel: comfortable accommodation at an unbeatable price, two blocks from the bus station. Breakfast is R$5.

Hotel Tibagi (☎ 3223 3141; www.hoteltibagi.com .br; Rua Cândido Lopes 318; r from R$69; 🔀 🖳) This business hotel is a decent deal in the center of Curitiba. Service is efficient, if not overly friendly. Rooms are adequate, if not elegant. Some rooms on the upper floors have great views of the city.

MIDRANGE & TOP END

Garden Curitiba Hotel (☎ 3222 2524; www.garden curitiba.com.br; Rua Ebana Pereira 405; s/d/tr R$69/87/105; 🖳) Nothing fancy happens at this cozy little hostelry, but it is one of the city's more pleasant places to stay. Thanks to its small size, homey decor and welcoming reception, the Garden Curitiba offers an air of small-town intimacy otherwise lacking in this big city. Rooms are simply decorated with floral curtains and plaid linens.

Vernon Palace Hotel (☎ 3362 1222; www.vernon hotel.com.br; Av Presidente Afonso Camargo 455; s/d R$83/105; 🔀 🖳 🖳) The most luxurious option near the bus station, this marble-heavy hotel attracts a business crowd. It wins no extra points for personality, but it does offer the level of comfort and service of an international hotel.

L'Avenue Apart Hotel (☎ 3222 5525; www.lavenue aparthotel.com.br; Rua XV de Novembro 526, Rua das Flores; s/d R$110/130; 🔀 🖳) One of the few places to stay on Rua das Flores, this stylish hotel has 63 suites, all with kitchenettes and sitting areas. The accommodations are tasteful but not too trendy.

San Juan Charm (☎ 3219 9900; www.sanjuanhoteis .com.br; Rua Barao do Rio Branco 354; r R$120; 🔀 🖳) Behind a beautiful neoclassical façade, this hospice is charming indeed. Renovated in 2002, the hotel retains much of its original architectural detail, but does not skimp on modern amenities. Stained wood floors, painted moldings and black-and-white photos give the 24 rooms an aura of understated elegance. Also on site is an excellent Mediterranean restaurant.

Curitiba's swankiest hotels include the **Mabú Royal & Premium Hotel** (☎ 3219 6000; www.hoteismabu .com.br; Praça Santos Andrade 830; s/d R$158/170; 🔀 🖳 🖳) and the **Bourbon Curitiba** (☎ 3221 4600; www.bour bon.com.br; Rua Cândido Lopes 102; s/d; 🔀 🖳 🖳), both four-star chains, decked out to cater to business travelers and discerning tourists.

Eating & Drinking

There is a collection of cheap fast-food restaurants with sidewalk seating on Rua das Flores, between Rua Westfalen and Rua Alameda Dr Murici.

Mercado Municipal (cnr Rua General Carneiro & Av Presidente Afonso Camargo; ☽ 8am-6pm Mon-Sat) Just across from the bus station, the municipal market has food stalls on the lower level.

Café Metrópolis (☎ 3233 6034; Rua Carlos de Carvalho 15; snacks R$4-10; ☽ 8am-10pm Mon-Fri, 8am-9pm Sat) A popular spot for a drink or a light snack. Sidewalk seating means this is a good place to sip a coffee and watch the city come alive.

Saccy Bar (☎ 3222 9922; Rua de São Francisco 350; meals R$8-12; ☽ 10am-1am) This red colonial house has a crowded bar downstairs and a loftlike second floor, both ideal to drink beer and munch on pub grub. Live music on weekend nights.

Green Life (☎ 3223 8490; Rua Carlos de Carvalho 271; per kg R$10 Mon-Fri, R$12 Sat & Sun; ☽ 11am-3pm) Most of the ingredients at this all-organic vegetarian restaurant come from the owners' farm. The menu changes daily according to what's fresh and what's in season.

Yü (☎ 3232 3500; Praça General Osório 485; per kg R$12; ☺ 11:30am-3pm Mon-Sat) In a stylish brick and glass building, the big buffet features Asian fare, including sushi and sashimi, salads and plenty of hot Chinese and Japanese main dishes.

The Farm (☎ 3019 9376; Av Jaime Reis 40; meals R$12-15) This rustic place features large portions of Brazilian fare and a variety of pizzas. The food is tasty, but the real draw is the deck overlooking Praça Garibaldi. Another bonus: live music Tuesday to Sunday from 6pm.

Casa dos Arcos (☎ 3372 2323; Av Manoel Ribas 5999; meals R$15-20) A landmark in the Italian neighborhood of Santa Felicidade. True to its name, this popular restaurant is housed in a 19th-century arcaded edifice. Inside, the decor evokes the Tuscan countryside; and so does the menu. The house special is filet mignon with risotto.

Entertainment

Curitiba has an active live-music and club scene. On warm nights, revelers spill out of pubs and cafés onto the streets around Largo da Ordem.

Cats Club (☎ 3224 5912; Rua Dr Muricy 949; cover R$15-30; ☺ 11:30pm-5am Fri-Sun) It's a lovely pink colonial mansion with a smoky, underground club inside. DJs spin house music and the dance floor fills up with the young and the restless.

Opera de Arame (☎ 3355-6071; Rua João Gava; ☺ 8am-10pm Tue-Sun) Constructed from wire with a transparent roof, this theater is among Curitiba's most unusual and enigmatic landmarks. It is surrounded by the stone quarry park, which contains an outdoor stage. These venues host musical events, from José Carreras to Tom Jobim.

Getting There & Away
AIR

From Curitiba's **Alfonso Pena Airport** (☎ 3381 1153) there are direct flights to São Paulo (45 minutes), Rio de Janeiro (one hour), Foz do Iguaçu (40 minutes), Florianópolis (40 minutes), Porto Alegre (one hour) and Brasília (two hours).

BUS & TRAIN

The long-distance **bus and train stations** (☎ 3320 3121) form a single complex called the *rodof-*

erroviária, which is about 2km from downtown. Within Paraná, Viação Graciosa goes to Paranaguá (R$16, 1½ hours, hourly), while Sulamericana goes overnight to Foz do Iguaçu (R$80 to R$100, 10 hours). Catarinense runs hourly buses to Joinville (R$17, two hours) and Florianópolis (R$37 to R$65, four hours). Longer-distance buses include São Paulo (R$49 to R$66, six hours, 15 daily); Porto Alegre (R$79 to R$85, 11 hours, three daily); and Rio (R$99 to R$159, 13 hours, five daily).

The train between Curitiba and Paranaguá via the Serra do Mar (see p318) is one of the marvels of travel in Brazil.

Getting Around
TO/FROM THE AIRPORT

Alfonso Pena Airport is 18km from the city. The **Aeroporto Executivo** (☎ 3283 4321; www .aeroportoexecutivo.com.br; R$6) runs every half-hour between the train station and the airport, looping around the city center along the way. The bus will stop in front of your hotel if it is on the route. The total trip takes about 50 minutes.

BUS

The **Linha Turismo** (R$15; ☺ 9am-5:30pm Tue-Sun) is a tourist bus that loops around the city, stopping at all the major tourist attractions as well as the parks and monuments on the outskirts of the city. It starts from Praça Tiradentes every half-hour, but you can also pick it up at the bus station or at any other stop. You can get on and off up to four times. A timetable is posted at each stop.

Around Curitiba
VILA VELHA

Located in Campos Gerais, 93km west of Curitiba, Vila Velha is known as the 'stone city.' The park's centerpiece is the 23 *aretinhas* (sandstone pillars), created over millions of years. The mysterious red earth rock formations – some taking recognizable shapes like boots and bottles – create striking silhouettes against the blue sky and green foliage. A bus drops you near the formations, where you can choose to follow a 40-minute walking trail or a 90-minute walking trail around the stone structures.

Within the boundaries of the same park, visitors can witness another geological marvel: a series of *furnas* (craters) that are the result of underground erosion. A 90-minute bus tour stops first at the Lagoa Dourada, a lovely lagoon that attracts ample birdlife. The next stop features two yawning craters that reach depths of 54m. In theory, an elevator descends to water level in one, but it has not functioned in several years.

From Curitiba, catch a Princesa dos Campos bus to Ponta Grossa and ask to get out at the Vila Velha park entrance (R$14, 1½ hours, hourly). Stop first at the **park center** (☎ 0xx42-3228 1138; rock formations R$7, craters R$5; ⏰ 8:30am-5:30pm Wed-Mon), where you can watch an introductory video and buy tickets for the various tours. There's also a snack bar.

MORRETES
☎ 0xx41 / pop 15,300

Founded in 1721 on the banks of the Rio Nhundiaquara, this tranquil colonial town rests on an emerald-green plain at the foot of the Serra do Mar. The loveliest colonial buildings are clustered around Praça Lamenha Lins and along Rua das Flores,

the cobblestone walkway that runs along the river. The **tourist office** (☎ 3462 1024; Largo Dr Jose Pereira 43) occupies a white colonial house along this stretch, and the grand Igreja Matriz anchors one end.

The region's culinary gift to the world is *barreado*, a rib-sticking meat stew that cooks in a clay pot. Originally, it served to keep revelers nourished over the course of several days of Carnaval, but you can test its sustaining qualities any time of year.

Sights & Activities

Besides the quaint colonial center, the biggest attraction in Morretes is the **Parque Estadual Marumbi** (☎ 3462 1155), a paradise for rock climbers and nature lovers. It contains a network of old pioneer trails that were the only connections between the coast and the highland in the 17th and 18th centuries. The **Graciosa Foot Trail** passes close to the Estrada da Graciosa, while the **Itupava Colonial Trail** is a four-hour excursion that ends in the

---

SERRA VERDE EXPRESS

In Curitiba, with hardly a ripple on the horizon, it's hard to believe that a few dozen kilometers to the west lie sharp, jungle-covered peaks with sweeping views down to the Baía de Paranaguá and the ocean beyond. That's because Curitiba sits above the mountains on the Planalto (high plains). As the plains break apart and give way to the sea, they form the stunning Serra do Mar.

Although beautiful to behold, the landscape was a drag on the city's economy. It took two days to transport products from Curitiba to the port of Antonina, only 75km east. Finally, a railway was inaugurated in 1885, connecting Curitiba to the sea. Engineers managed to build 67 bridges and viaducts, dig 13 tunnels through granite mountainsides, and lay track along dizzyingly steep heights.

Today, the train is known as the **Serra Verde Express** (☎ 3323 4007; www.serraverdeexpress.com .br; Esação Ferroviária), and its primary purpose is to awe tourists as they head down the perilous path from Curitiba to the coast. Between Curitiba and Morretes, the view is sublime. Depending on conditions, it encompasses threatening mountain canyons, tropical green lowlands and the vast, blue Atlantic. As you descend, watch as the climate and environment change – the weather becoming hotter and muggier, the vegetation lusher and greener. The segment between Morretes and Paranaguá is less scenic and the train inches along at an excruciating pace.

The *litorina* (tourist train) departs from Curitiba at 9:15am on Sunday only, and goes only as far as Morretes (adult/child R$112/53, three hours). The *litorina* offers passengers panoramic windows, air-conditioning, snack service and a 10-minute stop for the stunning views at Santuário do Cadeado.

The less-luxurious *trem* (regular train) leaves daily at 8:15am, stopping in Marumbi (two hours) and Morretes (three hours), and returning to Curitiba in the afternoon. It goes all the way to Paranaguá only on Sundays. Three classes are available: *executiva* (adult/child R$75/40), *turística* (adult/child R$49/35) and *econômica* (R$25). The return ticket i s about 25% less.

Views are most spectacular from the left side of the train (right side on the return trip) but the tickets are sold in order, so there is no way to guarantee where you will sit. In any case, reservations are highly recommended during summer. Prices and times change frequently, so be sure to stop by the train station or check the website in advance.

village of Porto de Cima, about 5km from Morretes. Views from both are stunning.

The trails are well signposted from the train station and within the park, so a guide isn't necessary. Take the Serra Verde Express from Curitiba (see opposite) to Marumbi station.

The Rio Nhundiaquara is navigable by inner tube, which you can rent at the **Pousada Itupava** (☎ 3462 1925; www.itupava.com.br; per day R$8), in the village of Porto de Cima.

Sleeping & Eating

Hotel Nhundiaquara (☎ 3462 1228; www.nundiaquara .com.br; Rua General Carreiro 13; per person with/without bathroom R$40/20) This old-fashioned place on the riverfront offers plain, wood-paneled rooms with high ceilings but minute bathrooms. The on-site restaurant is famous for its *barreado* (R$15), served on the breezy colonial-style terrace overlooking a lovely bend in the Rio Nhundiaquara.

Pousada Cidreira (☎ 3462 1604; Rua Rômulo Pereira 61; s/d R$50/90) Upstairs from the post office, this lovely little pousada overlooks the rooftops of the Rua das Flores. Twelve rooms are simply decorated with tile floors and heavy wood furniture. Potted plants and original artwork add a touch of home.

Estação Graciosa (☎ 3462 2009; Rua Cons Sinimbú 271; meals R$15) Opposite the train station, Estação Graciosa occupies a blue clapboard house, decorated with folk art and mismatched furniture. A spacious porch overlooks the garden, where lemon trees bloom and a small stream gurgles. It's an ideal setting to indulge in the local specialty *barreado*.

Most of the restaurants are along Largo Dr José Pereira on the riverfront. Here you will find **Restaurante Casarão** (☎ 3462 1314; Largo Dr José Pereira 25; meals R$15-25), an upmarket place with a balcony on the river.

Getting There & Away

The Morretes train station is on a pretty square in the center of town. Trains to Curitiba depart daily at 3pm (see opposite).

The bus station is about 1km from the center of town. A local bus runs from Antonina (R$3, 30 minutes) to Paranaguá (R$3, one hour) via Morretes every hour. There are also regular buses to Curitiba (R$10, one hour, four daily).

ANTONINA

☎ 0xx41 / pop 20,000

Once an important colonial port, Antonina has slipped into charming irrelevance. Fortunately, its economic decline has preserved its colonial center, which fronts the beautiful Baía de Paranaguá. The pace is languid – except during Carnaval, which is one of the region's best. Walk along the tree-lined waterfront, then head uphill toward Praça Coronel Macedo, a pretty square lined with stately homes built with shipping fortunes.

Local buses link Antonina to Morretes and Paranaguá every hour, while a direct bus goes to Curitiba (R$15, two hours, four daily). Trains no longer stop here.

Sleeping & Eating

Hotel Monte Castelo (☎ 3432 1163; Praça Coronel Macedo 46; dm US$7, per person with/without bathroom R$30/20) A friendly budget option on the main square. An inviting entry leads to clean rooms with wood floors and sea green walls.

Atlante Pousada (☎ 3432 1256; www.atlante.com .br; Praça Coronel Macedo 266; s/d R$70/100; 🍴 🛒) Antonina's top-end option is this restored 19th-century mansion. A fresh peach-colored paint job and breezy balconies bedeck the outside. The rooms do not quite live up to the lavish exterior, but they are comfortable and fully equipped.

Restaurante Le Bistrô (☎ 3432 3393; Travessa 7 de Setembro 01; meals R$12-20; 🕑 11:30am-3pm Wed-Mon & 6:30-11:30pm Wed-Sun) Just below the church, this popular restaurant offers bay views and a seafaring theme in its glass-enclosed dining room. As the decor implies, seafood is on the menu. Save room for the specialty dessert, banana flambé.

Restaurante Buganvil (☎ 3432 1434; Praça Coronel Macedo 10; meals R$20; 🕑 11:30am-10pm Tue-Sun) You can't miss this pretty pink colonial building, serving European cuisine. Bold colors and whimsical light fixtures add a modern touch, and the namesake bougainvillea is not lacking.

PARANAGUÁ

☎ 0xx41 / pop 144,800

This colorful old port, sitting serenely on the banks of the Rio Itiberê, has an appealing atmosphere of tropical decadence. Commercially important since the late 18th century, the city has some impressive churches and other public buildings, many of which are

PARANÁ

being carefully restored. Paranaguá remains an important port for corn, soy, cotton and vegetable oils; but for travelers, it serves primarily as a point of departure to Ilha do Mel.

Information

MONEY

Banco do Brasil (Largo Conselheiro Alcindino 103) ATMs.

TOURIST INFORMATION

Tourist Office Waterfront (☎ 3425 4542; Rua General Carneiro 258; 🕓 8am-6pm); Train station (🕓 noon-4pm)

Sights

Housed in an 18th-century Jesuit college, the **Museu de Arqueologia e Etnologia** (Archeology & Ethnology Museum; ☎ 3422 8844; www.proec.ufpr.br; Rua XV de Novembro 575; admission R$3; 🕓 9:30am-noon & 1-6pm Tue-Sat, noon-6pm Sun) displays indigenous artifacts, primitive and folk art, and old tools and machines. Closed at the time of research, it is expected to reopen in early 2008.

The city's colonial churches are simple but striking. The oldest is **Igreja de NS do Rosário** (Rua Marechal Deodoro), parts of which date to 1578. Several churches were constructed during the 18th century, including **Igreja São Francisco das Chagas** (Rua XV de Novembro) and **Igreja de São Benedito** (Rua Conselheiro Sinimbu), built specifically for the town's slaves.

Sleeping

Hostel Continente (☎ 3423 3224; www.hostelcontinente .com.br; Rua General Carneiro 300; dm HI-member/nonmember R$17/22, r per person R$28/35, d R$45/55; 🖵) This HI hostel is across from the tourist port, so you can enjoy your breakfast while watching the boats come in. Rooms are well-lit and colorfully decorated. Facilities include laundry and communal kitchen.

Hotel Ponderosa (☎ 3423 2464; Rua Prescilinio Corrêa 68; s/d R$35/45, d with view R$55; 🛏) Occupying a restored colonial building on a prominent corner, the Hotel Ponderosa evokes a grand past, with its high ceilings and wide plank wood floors. The rooms facing the port are particularly pleasing, with lots of light and lovely views of the waterfront.

San Rafael Hotel (☎ 3432 2123; wwwsanrafaelhotel .com.br; Rua Júlia da Costa 185; s/d/tr from R$150/188/210; 🛏 🖵) The sleek modern façade and tinted glass doors front a contemporary tile lobby, appropriately chilled. The rooms are slightly less sophisticated, but no less cush.

Eating & Drinking

Mercado Municipal do Café (cnr Rua General Carneiro & Rua 29 de Julho) The lively courtyard of this old public market is a good spot for a cheap coffee, beer, seafood snacks or freshly fried pastry.

Gruta da Garoupa (☎ 3423 3896; Rua XV de Novembro 120; per kg R$10) This popular 'fast grill' has something for everyone, with a daily-changing buffet of seafood, grilled meats, pasta and sushi.

Deck 110 (☎ 3425 2927; Rua General Carneiro 110; meals R$20-25; 🕓 11:30am-midnight Tue-Sun) Sip champagne or munch on a savory appetizer under the umbrellas on the classy outdoor deck; or slip into the swanky interior for a

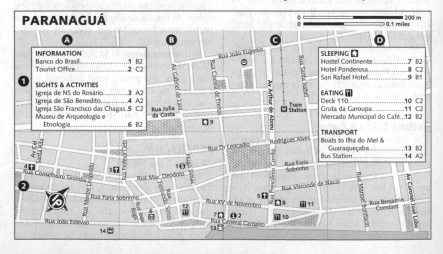

PARANAGUÁ

0 ——— 200 m
0 ——— 0.1 miles

INFORMATION	
Banco do Brasil.................1 B2	
Tourist Office...................2 C2	

SIGHTS & ACTIVITIES	
Igreja de NS do Rosário.........3 A2	
Igreja de São Benedito...........4 A2	
Igreja São Francisco das Chagas..5 C2	
Museu de Arqueologia e	
Etnologia.....................6 B2	

SLEEPING 🏨	
Hostel Continente...............7 B2	
Hotel Ponderosa................8 C2	
San Rafael Hotel................9 B1	

EATING 🍴	
Deck 110......................10 C2	
Gruta da Garoupa...............11 C2	
Mercado Municipal do Café....12 B2	

TRANSPORT	
Boats to Ilha do Mel &	
Guaraqueçaba...............13 B2	
Bus Station...................14 A2	

cocktail from the dark wood bar. The menu features an impressive wine list and lots of fresh seafood.

Getting There & Away

Six or seven boats to Ilha do Mel leave throughout the day (one-way/roundtrip R$12/20), with stops at both Nova Brasília (one hour) and Encantadas (1½ hours). Boats also go to Guaraqueçaba (R$20, three hours, two daily), an access point for Parque Nacional do Superagüi.

From the **bus station** (☎ 3420 2925) on the waterfront, destinations include Curitiba (R$16, 1½ hours, hourly), Antonina (R$3, 1½ hours, hourly) and Morretes (R$3, one hour, hourly). The Serra Verde Express goes all the way to Paranaguá only on Sunday. See p318 for details).

ILHA DO MEL

☎ 0xx41 / pop 1200

This oddly shaped island at the mouth of the Baía de Paranaguá is the most pristine and picturesque beach resort in all of southern Brazil. The island's sense of tranquility and lack of development are thanks in part to its isolation. Accessible only by boat, the Ilha do Mel is traversed by sandy paths; it lacks even a single car. The fatter, northern half of the island is an ecological preserve, closed to any inland exploration. The hillier southern portion is the locale of three small villages: Nova Brasília and Praia do Farol near the isthmus; and Encantadas at the far southern tip. They can be rowdy during the summer holidays, when young crowds descend on the island. But for the most part, Ilha do Mel, or 'honey island,' is the territory of surfers, campers, birders and other escapists in search of simplicity and serenity.

Orientation

Most of the hotels are clustered in the village of Nova Brasília, which occupies the isthmus that links the island, and Praia do Farol, the beach that stretches east from here. The landmark lighthouse sits atop a *morro* (hill) on its easternmost point. Another, smaller settlement, Encantadas, sits at the southern end of the island, the closest point to the mainland. A 6km trail on the east coast links the two towns, traversing a series of undeveloped beaches, including Praia da Fora, Praia do Miguel and Praia Grande.

Information

INTERNET ACCESS

Ilha do Mel Online (☎ 3426 8065; www.ilhadomel online.com; per hr R$9; ☺ 9am-9pm) This charming blue house is on the path between Nova Brasília and Farol das Conchas. Offers internet access, as well as rooms for rent and loads of information about the island.

MONEY

There is no reliable place on the island to get cash, so plan ahead.

TOURIST INFORMATION

There are tourist information offices at the docks in both Brasilia and Encantadas:
Encantadas tourist information office (☎ 3426 9091; ☺ 8am-7pm)
Nova Brasília tourist information office (☎ 3426 8005; ☺ 8am-7pm)

Sights

The picturesque **Fortaleza de NS dos Prazeres** (Fort of Our Lady of the Pleasures), which dates to the 1760s, is a 40-minute hike from Nova Brasília via Praia da Fortaleza. Inspect the deserted fortress before climbing up to the lookout for an incredible vista of the bay.

The **Farol das Conchas** (Conchas Lighthouse), built in 1872 on orders from Dom Pedro II, stands picturesquely atop a hill at the island's most easterly point. From here you have panoramic views of the island, the bay, and the Serra do Mar. It's a popular spot to watch the sun drop below the horizon.

Legend has it that the small caves at the island's southern tip, known as the **Grutas das Encantadas**, are inhabited by beautiful mermaids who enchant all who come near. Signs clearly mark the way to the caves from Encantadas and from Praia da Fora beach.

Activities

SURFING & SWIMMING

There is no shortage of beaches on Ilha do Mel. Those facing the bay enjoy warm waters gently lapping at the white sand, while those facing the ocean boast the big surf. But almost all of them are unspoiled, marked only be windswept dunes, forested hills and rocky outposts. **Praia de Fora** and **Praia Grande** are a 20-minute walk (2km) from Nova Brasília and a 40-minute walk (4km) from Encantadas. According to local surfers, in winter, these beaches have the best waves in Paraná.

The **Praia do Farol** is the long stretch of sand between the Brasília dock and the Farol das Conchas. It is backed by the swampy, grassy protected area of the *retinga,* which also preserves the natural beauty of the beach. Surfers congregate at the base of the hill and ride the legendary **Ondas das Paralelas**.

Stop in at the Grajagan Surf Resort (opposite) on Praia Grande to inquire about renting a surfboard or taking a lesson.

If you didn't bring your surfboard, you might prefer the calmer, warmer waters of the beaches that face the shallow bay. In the north, **Praia da Fortaleza**, often nearly deserted, allows you to bathe in the shadow of the 18th-century Portuguese fort. The

best beach near the settlement of Encantadas is **Praia da Fora**, which has big waves and a few stalls selling *cervejas* (beers) and *sucos* (juice).

BOATING

In the harbors of Nova Brasília and Encantadas, you can hire a boat to explore the nearby islands, including Ilha do Superagüi, Ilha das Palmas and Ilha das Peças.

Pousada das Meninas (☎ 3426 8023; Praia da Farol) The owners of this pousada (see opposite) can organize day trips to any of the islands.

Sea Calm Passeios & Pescaria (☎ 3426 9073; seacalm@bol.com.br; ☉ 10am) This five-hour excursion departs from Encantadas and makes a complete tour around Ilha do Mel.

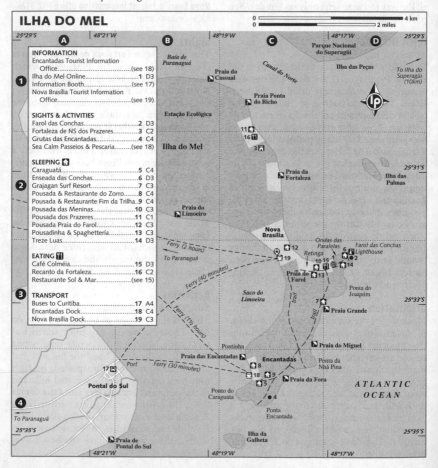

ILHA DO MEL

0 ___ 4 km
0 ___ 2 miles

INFORMATION
Encantadas Tourist Information
   Office.............................(see 18)
Ilha do Mel Online.........................1 D3
Information Booth...................(see 17)
Nova Brasília Tourist Information
   Office.............................(see 19)

SIGHTS & ACTIVITIES
Farol das Conchas........................2 D3
Fortaleza de NS dos Prazeres........3 C2
Grutas das Encantadas..................4 C4
Sea Calm Passeios & Pescaria......(see 18)

SLEEPING
Caraguatá.....................................5 C4
Enseada das Conchas....................6 D3
Grajagan Surf Resort.....................7 C3
Pousada & Restaurante do Zorro......8 C4
Pousada & Restaurante Fim da Trilha..9 C4
Pousada das Meninas....................10 C3
Pousada dos Prazeres...................11 C1
Pousada Praia do Farol.................12 C3
Pousadinha & Spaghettería............13 D3
Treze Luas..................................14 D3

EATING
Café Colméia..............................15 D3
Recanto da Fortaleza...................16 C2
Restaurante Sol & Mar.................(see 15)

TRANSPORT
Buses to Curitiba........................17 A4
Encantadas Dock........................18 C4
Nova Brasília Dock......................19 C3

Sleeping & Eating

Book ahead for holidays and any summer weekend. Prices listed are for high season. Expect discounts of 20% to 40% between April and November. See www.pousadailhadomel .com.br for more options.

NOVA BRASÍLIA & PRAIA DO FAROL

Pousadinha & Spaghettería (☎ 3426 8026; www .pousadinha.com.br; d with/without bathroom R$90/60) It's hard to say what is the bigger draw: the simple, affordable rooms 200m from the boat landing; or the menu of irresistible homemade pastas and South American wines. Rooms are tiny, but the newer *apartamentos* – built out of cultivated hardwood – are quite stylish. Two larger rooms sleep up to six people.

Pousada Praia do Farol (☎ 3426 8014; www.praia dofarol.com.br; d/tr/q with bathroom R$90/120/140, d/tr/q without bathroom R$65/83/90; 😮) Set on the isthmus, this hotel boasts access to both Praia de Brasilia and Praia do Farol. Rooms are small and dark, but there are plenty of comfy common areas, including a beachside deck that is well hung with hammocks.

Pousada das Meninas (☎ 3426 8023; www.pousada dasmeninas.com.br; d with bathroom R$150-200, without R$100-120) Built from driftwood and recycled material, this pousada offers the charm of a guesthouse and the friendliness of family. Hung with hammocks and decorated with nature's bounty, the simple but tasteful rooms are set around a cozy garden.

Treze Luas (☎ 3426 8067; www.pousadatrezeluas.com .br; d Mon-Thu R$100-130, d Fri-Sun R$120-160, q R$160; 😮) This place is surprisingly slick for Ilha do Mel. Brightened by whimsical artwork and bold-colored linens, all the rooms have shiny stained wood walls and cool tile floors. The common area is decked out with modern furniture and a flat screen TV, while a porch overlooks the palm-fringed garden.

Enseada das Conchas (☎ 3426 8040; www.pousada enseada.com.br; s/d/tr/q 110/153/180/210) This lovely pousada is as 'upscale' as this island goes. Four spacious guest rooms are painted in striking colors and decorated according to themes, such as 'Sunlight' and 'Sea Blue.' A wide deck is shaded by a thatch roof and scattered with lounge chairs. It is steps from the lighthouse and the island's best surf beach.

Restaurante Mar & Sol (☎ 3426 8021; meals R$15-20) Serves simple but tasty seafood dishes, including a tasty crab *moqueca* (Bahian stew). Wash it down with an ice cold *cerveja*. For something lighter, go next door to **Café Colméia** (☎ 3426 8029; snacks US$1-3). Follow the path to Farol das Conchas.

PRAIA GRANDE & PRAIA DE FORA

Grajagan Surf Resort (☎ 3426 8043; www.grajagan .com.br; s without bath R$50, d with bath R$170-290; 😮) This pousada caters to surfers who like their creature comforts, including a huge breakfast buffet and a lively beach bar. The rooms with ocean views (R$250 to R$290) are arguably the best on the island: each has a private veranda and hammock facing the sea. Ask the owner Rogério about renting boards or taking lessons.

ENCANTADAS

Restaurants and cafés line the beach at Praia das Encantadas. Head north from the pier.

Pousada & Restaurante do Zorro (☎ 3426 9052; www.hostelzorro.com.br; HI members dm/d/tr R$20/60/80, nonmembers dm/d/tr R$25/80/100; 🖥 🍴) This friendly HI hostel has a great vibe, thanks to its beachfront location, helpful English-speaking staff and happy guests lounging out front. Look for a fun rec room, communal kitchen, and comfy clean rooms, fully equipped with fridges and TVs.

Caraguatá (☎ 3426 9097; www.caraguata-ilhadomel .com.br; d with/without bathroom R$140/110; 😮) Just a few steps from the pier, Caraguatá's pretty chalets are adorned with flowerboxes and greenery. Rooms vary in size but they all have stained wood ceilings, whitewashed walls and crisp linens.

Pousada & Restaurante Fim da Trilha (☎ 3426 9017; www.fimdatrilha.com.br; d R$150; 😮) Off the trail to the Grutas, an enticing winding path leads to this tropical paradise. The spacious terrace is overflowing with blooming foliage and gurgling fountains. Here, you'll find one of the island's best restaurants, specializing in spicy paella. In the back, the six spacious and modern guestrooms are fully equipped and tastefully decorated.

FORTALEZA

Fewer and further between, accommodations around Fortaleza are effective for escaping the summer crowds. However, it's a good 40-minute hike (3km) from the Nova Brasília pier. Otherwise, catch a boat across the isthmus for about R$20.

Pousada dos Prazeres (☎ 3243 9649; www.pousada dosprazeres.com.br; per person R$40) This friendly place has bright yellow cabins with basic rooms and swinging hammocks, catering to guests in search of peace and quiet and not much more. The beachside café will sate your appetite with big plates of fresh seafood. Walk 200m past the fort.

Recanto da Fortaleza (☎ 3275 4455; www.pousada recantodafortaleza.com.br; meals R$10-12) This breezy deck is an ideal place to indulge in a seafood feast or quench your thirst with a cold one after a day on the beach. Out back are a few rooms for rent.

Getting Around

The ferries that run to/from Paranaguá stop in both Nova Brasília and Encantadas, so you can get a lift from one village to the other (R$5, 20 minutes, six daily).

Getting There & Away

TO/FROM PARANAGUÁ

See p321 for information on boats to the island.

TO/FROM PONTAL DO SUL

Viação Graciosa runs buses from Curitiba (R$21, two hours, 10 daily) that bypass Paranaguá and head straight to the pier in Pontal do Sul, which is closer to the island and offers more frequent service. Boats depart to both Nova Brasília and Encantadas every half-hour from 8am to 8pm (one-way/round-trip R$12/20). Schedules vary, so check at the **information booth** (☎ 3455 1144) at the port in Pontal do Sul.

PARQUE NACIONAL DO SUPERAGÜI

☎ 0xx41

Composed of the Superagüi and Peças islands, this national park in the Baía de Paranaguá is covered by mangroves and salt marshes, which support an amazing variety of bird and plant life. The national park is part of the 4700 sq km of Atlantic forest reserves in Paraná and São Paulo states that were given Unesco World Heritage status in 1999.

The park is famous for its array of orchids. Hummingbirds, kingbirds and toucans live here, not to mention the roseate spoonbill and the stunning Brazilian tanager. Every evening at sunset, hundreds – sometimes thousands – of red-tailed parrots return to roost in the canopy on **Papagaio Island**. Dolphins are often sighted in the waters between Ilha do Superagüi and Ilha do Mel. Other mammals

are more elusive, but include agoutis, pacas, deer, howler monkeys and pumas. The park is also home to the endangered black-faced lion tamarind, though he is rarely sighted.

The national park is not open to visitors, although boats are allowed to motor around the islands. Boat trips depart from Ilha do Mel, as well as the tiny fishing village of **Barra do Superagüi**, one of the few settlements within the confines of the protected area. It's worth spending a day in the village to get a taste of life in a place still relatively untouched by tourism. If you're lucky, you might catch a *fandango*, a local folk music and dance tradition that is dying out in other places, but thriving here.

From Barra do Superagüi, one trail leads through the *mata* (rain forest) and across the island. An hour's walk brings you to **Praia Deserta**, a 38km strip of sand and sea with no development and no people.

Sleeping & Eating

Pousada Superaguí (☎ 3482 7149; www.pousada superagui.com.br; Superagüi; per person R$30) In this sweet blue clapboard cottage with yellow trim, rooms are simple and bathrooms are shared, but the place is lovingly decorated with local artwork. Owners Dalton and Olga eagerly share their encyclopedic knowledge of the area; they also provide transportation and offer boat tours of the islands.

Pousada Costa Azul (☎ 3482 7136; www.pousada costazul.com.br; per person R$25) Another option with similar facilities but less charm. The on-site restaurant faces the sea.

The best restaurants in town both overlook the bay, serving fresh seafood and cold beer: **Restaurante Golfinos** (☎ 9959 8852; ⏱ 11am-11pm) and **Restaurante Crepúsculo** (☎ 9959 6709; ⏱ noon-2pm & 6-8pm). It's best to order your lunch in advance.

Getting There & Away

There is no regular transportation to Ilha do Superagüi. On weekends and holidays, boats run from Paranaguá and Guaraqueçaba, but the schedule is erratic. You may have to negotiate a ride with the fishermen at the docks. Expect to pay about R$20 on a boat that is already making the journey. Otherwise, you will likely pay upwards of R$100 to hire a boat for up to five people. To make transportation arrangements in advance, contact:

Claudinei Juruna (☎ 3424 0780; Paranaguá) Offers fishing trips and transport on his boat Anjo Elchadag.
Dalton (☎ 3482 7149; Superagüi) Proprietor of Pousada Superaguí (opposite).

FOZ DO IGUAÇU & AROUND
☎ 0xx45 / pop 309,000

Rising in the coastal mountains of Paraná and Santa Catarina, the Rio Iguaçu snakes west for 600km, picking up a few dozen tributaries along the way. It widens majestically and sweeps around a magnificent forest stage, before plunging and crashing in the tiered falls known as Iguaçu Falls. A total of 275 individual falls occupy an area more than 3km wide and 80m high, which makes them wider than Victoria, higher than Niagara and more beautiful than either.

Thousands of years before they were 'discovered' by Europeans, the falls were a holy burial place for the Tupi-Guarani and Paraguas tribes. Spaniard Don Alvar Nuñes happened upon the falls in 1541, dubbing them 'Saltos de Santa María'. But this name didn't stick and the Tupi-Guarani name, Iguaçu (Great Waters), did. In 1986 Unesco declared the region a World Heritage site.

The falls are unequally shared between Brazil and Argentina, with Argentina claiming the majority. On either side, a national park surrounds the waterfalls and offers extra opportunities for adventure. It's impossible to say which side of the border is the more rewarding: the Parque Nacional do Iguaçu in Brazil offers a more panoramic view of the totality of the 275 falls, while the Parque Nacional Iguazú in Argentina provides an up-close and personal experience. Both are absolutely thrilling.

That said, it's not possible to do justice to both sides of the falls in a single day – plan to spend a full day in either park.

The Brazilian city of Foz do Iguaçu went through a period of frenzied growth during the 18 years that Itaipu Dam was under construction, when the population increased by more than five times. It was an edgy place then, but it has since settled down. That said, muggings have been reported along the riverfront, on the bridge from Ciudad del Este (Paraguay) and on the road from the youth hostels near the airport. So take precautions and watch your back.

Orientation
Av Brasil is the town's main street, running north to south. The long-distance bus station is located 4.5km to the northeast, but the local bus station – just north of Av República Argentina – serves the airport (15km southeast) and Parque Nacional do Iguaçu (17km southeast).

Just south of town, the junction of the Paraná and Iguaçu rivers forms the tripartite Paraguayan, Brazilian and Argentine border (marked by obelisks). The Ponte Presidente Tancredo Neves crosses the Rio Iguaçu about 6km from the center of town, connecting Brazil with the Argentine town of Puerto Iguazú. Just north of the center, the Ponte da Amizade spans the Rio Paraná, crossing to the shabby Paraguayan town of Ciudad del Este.

Information
EMERGENCY
Bombeiros (☎ 193) Handles fires as well as medical emergencies.
Federal Police (Map p326; ☎ 3523 1828; Av Jorge Schimmelpfeng)

INTERNET ACCESS
Most hotels and hostels offer internet access on site.
US Net (Map p326; ☎ 3523 2289; Av Brasil 549; per hr R$3; ◷ 9am-10pm, closed 1-6pm Sun) Internet access and international phone calls.

MEDICAL SERVICES
Hospital Internacional (Map p326; ☎ 523 1404; Av Brasil 1637)

MONEY
Dozens of money-exchange houses are all over town.
Banco do Brasil (Map p326; Av Brasil) AIMs and money exchange.
Caribe Turismo (☎ 3529 7173) Located in the airport, this travel agency exchanges Visa and American Express traveler's checks. It's the only place in town open on Sunday.

TOURIST INFORMATION
The region's **tourist board** (☎ 0800-451 516; www .iguassu.tur.br; ◷ 7am-11pm) maintains an excellent website and a toll-free English-speaking information line, as well as three information booths:
Airport tourist office (◷ noon-1am)
Long-distance bus station tourist office (Map p326; ◷ 6:30am-6:30pm)

PARANÁ

Praça Getúlio Vargas tourist office (Map p326; Praça Getúlio Vargas; ☼ 7am-11pm)

Sights & Activities

PARQUE NACIONAL DO IGUAÇU (BRAZIL)

You can't miss the shiny new entrance to the **Parque Nacional do Iguaçu** (Map p329; ☎ 3521 4400; www.cataratasdoiguacu.com.br; adult/child R$20/5; ☼ 9am-6pm Oct-Mar, 9am-5pm Apr-Sep), which houses bathrooms, ATMs, lockers, souvenir shops and vast parking facilities. Once you buy your ticket, you will be directed to board a free double-decker bus.

To visit the falls, take the bus to the third stop, site of the Hotel Tropical das Cataratas (see p330). Here, you can pick up the **Trilha das Cataratas**, or 'Waterfall Trail.' This 1200m

trail follows the shore of the Iguaçu River, providing innumerable photo ops along the way. It terminates at the **Garganta do Diablo**, the most spectacular part of the falls. A manmade walkway allows you to go out to the middle of the river so you are seemingly surrounded by the force of rushing water. Expect to be dazzled – and doused.

From here, take the panoramic elevator to get a view of the falls from above. At the top, a short walk along the road leads to **Porto Canoas** station, where you will find a nice restaurant with an excellent lunch buffet (R$20), as well as a food court with less expensive options. Both have seating on a pleasant outdoor terrace overlooking the flats of the river.

FOZ DO IGUAÇU

INFORMATION	
Argentine Consulate	1 B4
Banco do Brasil	2 C4
Federal Police	3 C4
Hospital Internacional	4 C4
Paraguayan Consulate	5 C3
Tourist Office	6 B4
US Net	7 C2

SLEEPING	
Albergue Paudimar Falls	8 C4
Bambú Hostel	9 D3
Dany Hotel	10 C2
Hotel Bavieria	11 C4
Hotel del Rey	12 B2
Hotel Rafain Centro	13 C4
Hotel Tarobá Express	14 B1
Pousada El Shaddai	15 B2
Pousada Sonho Meu	16 B1

EATING	
Armazém	17 C3
Búfalo Branco	18 B2
Famiglia Maran	19 C2
Sabor Brazil	20 C2
Tempero da Bahía	21 C3

DRINKING	
Bars & Nightclubs	22 C4
Biergarten	23 C4

TRANSPORT	
Buses to Argentina	24 B1
Buses to Itaipu	25 B1
Local Bus Terminal (Buses to Iguaçu Falls, Argentina, Paraguay)	26 B1

Remember, it's always wet at the falls, and water attracts sunlight. Pack raingear *and* sun block. Also note that lighting for photography is best in the morning on the Brazilian side.

Boating

While admiring the falls from above, you will surely spot fearless adventurers experiencing the falls from below. Such boating excursions are offered on both sides of the falls, but the Brazilian version is more elaborate (and more expensive). Get off the double-decker bus at the second stop for **Macuco Safari de Barco** (☎ 3574 4244; www.macucosafari.com.br; per person R$150; ☼ 8am-5pm).

The excursion starts with a 3km ride through the jungle, with an English-speaking guide pointing out the park's flora and fauna. The second phase is a short hike (600m) to a small waterfall called Salto de Macuco, where you can take a dip. Finally, climb aboard a Zodiac for a 4km journey over flat water and rapids, and under the falls known as the Three Musketeers. You *will* get soaked. The boat ride is 30 minutes, but the whole excursion takes about two hours.

Macuco Safari also offers a more sedate, 3½-hour boat trip on the flats above the falls.

Hiking

Parque Nacional do Iguaçu covers 550 sq km of rain forest, most of which is inaccessible to anybody but the wildlife. You can explore a few hiking trails in the company of a guide provided by the park. (English-speaking guides are available.) The **Trilha Poço Preto** (per person R$135) is a 9km trail that starts near the entrance (get off the bus at the first stop), and leads to the Lagoa do Poço Preto, a small lagoon that attracts birdlife. A quick boat ride and an optional paddle in a kayak complete the well-choreographed outing. The return trip is via the **Trilha das Bananeiras**, but you can get a lift.

Hiking is more rewarding in the morning, when weather is cooler and birds and animals are more active. Look for butterflies, parrots, parakeets, woodpeckers, hummingbirds, toucans, lizards and spiders. Other more elusive creatures include monkeys (especially mono caí), deer, sloths, anteaters, raccoons, jaguars, tapirs, caimans, armadillos and of course coatis. Countless varieties of orchids, lianas and vines are on display. Mosquitoes are plentiful – don't forget your insect repellent.

Challenge Range

For more excitement, stop off at the **Campos de Deafios** (☎ 3529 6040; www.campodedesafios.com.br) for rock-climbing, rappelling and whitewater rafting. The entrance is at the third bus stop, opposite the Hotel Tropical das Cataratas.

PARQUE NACIONAL IGUAZÚ (ARGENTINA)

The **Parque Nacional Iguazú** (Map p329; ☎ 0xx54-3757 420 722; www.iguazuargentina.com; admission A$30; ☼ 8am-6:30pm, to 5:30pm Sep-Mar) is 18km from Puerto Iguazú, the town on the Argentine side of the border.

From the entrance, follow the **Sendero Verde**, a short trail through the jungle that offers a chance to spot butterflies, birds and coatis. You can also opt to ride the free Tren Ecológico de la Selva (Green Train of the Jungle, every 30 minutes). In any case, your first destination is Estación Cataratas. Two walking trails depart from this point, offering incredibly varied perspectives of the waterfalls.

Start with the short **Circuito Superior**, or Upper Circuit, which is the least spectacular, but builds anticipation. The **Circuito Inferior**, or Lower Circuit, is a 1.5km loop offering views of the falls from below. From here you can take a free boat (every 15 minutes) to **Isla San Martín**, which has trails and more close-up views.

Saving the best for last, **Garganta do Diablo** will be your final destination. Take the train to Estación Garganta del Diablo. Here, the catwalk begins at a quiet point upstream from the falls, passing a number of tranquil islands. At the Garganta, the serene river suddenly turns violent, as 13,000 cu meters of water per second plunge 90m in 14 falls around a horseshoe-shaped canyon. It's a hypnotizing, multisensory experience – hearing the falls roaring in your ears, feeling the mist on your face and seeing huge rainbow arcs stretching across the rush. Watch for the swifts, which drop like rocks into the misty abyss, catch insects in mid-air, shoot back up and dart to perch on the cliffs behind the falls.

For lunch, you will find snack bars at Dos Hermanas (at the Circuito Inferior). Near the entrance is a more upscale restaurant, La Selva, with a buffet serving typical Argentine food.

On the Argentine side of the falls, the light is best for photographs in the late afternoon. If you get your ticket stamped when you exit the park, you can return the following day for half-price.

Boating

Many claim that the way to truly experience the falls is to feel their wrath raining down on you. Boats from both sides of the border take adventurous passengers under the falls, but it is significantly less expensive on the Argentinean side.

Iguazu Jungle Explorer (☎ 0xx54-3757 421 696; www.iguazujunglexplorer.com) offers two versions of this adventure. The **Gran Aventura** (A$90) is a one-hour excursion that includes an 8km ride through the jungle on the back of a jeep and a 6km ride down the Iguazú river. The trip culminates in an up-close-and-personal tour of Salto San Martin and Garganta del Diablo. This excursion departs hourly from the visitors center near the entrance.

If your primary interest is the so-called 'waterfall baptism,' you can opt for the abbreviated **Aventura Nautica** (A$45). The 12-minute trip departs from the dock opposite Isla San Martín (every 20 minutes), giving passengers a quick tour of the canyon and a sousing shower. Protective bags are provided for cameras and other gear; anything not contained therein – including you – will get wet.

Buy tickets at the park entrance or at the Iguazu Jungle Explorer office near Estación Cataratas.

Hiking

To explore the rain forest in the national park, stop at the **Interpretation Center** (☎ 0xx54-3757 491 469) near the entrance and inquire about the **Sendero Macuco**. This 7km trail is a rare opportunity to explore the park independently. Six interpretive stations explain the flora, including bamboo, palmitos and pioneer plants. The white-bearded manakin and toco toucan live in these parts, as does a troupe of brown capuchin monkeys. The trail's end point is the **Arrechea Waterfall**, a 20m cascade that has gouged out a lovely natural pool below.

Early morning is best for hiking. Departure before 4pm (3pm in winter) is required.

ITAIPU DAM

On the Paraná river 14km north of town, the **Itaipu Dam** (☎ 3520 6999; www.itaipu.gov.br) is the largest hydroelectric power plant *on the planet*.

The numbers are impressive. The dam is 8km long and 65 stories high. The plant provides 22% of the electric energy consumed in Brazil, and more than 90% of the energy consumed in Paraguay. Even more extraordinary is the massive size of the construction that spans the river, the palpable power of the water rushing out of the spillway, and

---

A DAM SHAME?

For some, it's a wonder of the modern world. For others, it's a man-made disaster. But there's no doubt that Itaipu Dam has permanently changed the face of southern Brazil.

First, the startling statistics. The dam's structures stretch for almost 9km and reach a height of more than 200m. The concrete used in its construction would be sufficient to build a two-lane highway from Moscow to Lisbon. At the height of construction, crews worked at a blinding pace, equivalent to building a 20-storey office-building every hour. No wonder it cost US$18 billion.

So was it worth it? The answer is not easy. Its generating capacity is 12,600 megawatts of clean energy – enough to supply 22% of Brazil's electricity needs and 90% of Paraguay's. To produce an equivalent amount in oil-burning thermoelectric plants, you'd need 434,000 barrels of oil per day. That's a lot of carbon dioxide emissions.

At the same time, critics of the dam estimate that 700 sq km of forest has been lost or compromised. Several species of plant life have been driven into extinction. Many native Guarani and Tupi settlements were destroyed, as was the impressive Sete Quedas waterfalls. Some speculate that the huge new body of water will bring about unforeseen changes in the climate.

For its part, the Itaipu Binacional – a joint Brazilian–Paraguayan agency that administers the dam – has been sensitive to such criticisms. Innovative programs have relocated animals displaced by flooding, reforested the land along the reservoir's banks and compensated communities affected by the construction.

It's tough to come up with a final tally of costs and benefits – especially as you are being dazzled by vivid colors illuminating the dam's concrete face.

the endless array of power lines emanating from the plant.

Construction of the dam was controversial (see opposite), and Itaipu's public relations team is eager to publicize its immensity and accomplishments, if not its downsides. So, expect a barrage of propaganda when you take the **free tour** (8am, 9am, 10am, 2pm, 3pm & 3:30pm Mon-Sat). A short film is followed by a visit to the central observation deck, providing a panoramic view of the complex. All information is in Portuguese and English. For a more technical tour, inquire about the **special circuit** (☎ 3520 6667; adult/senior R$30/16; 8am, 8:30am, 9:30am, 10am, 2pm, 2:30pm, 3:30pm, 4pm). This in-depth, two-hour tour is fascinating for anyone with engineering tendencies.

The last option to visit the dam is the hokey **sound-and-light show** (R$5; 8:30pm Fri & Sat Mar-Nov, 9:30pm Fri & Sat Dec-Feb).

If you are wondering how construction of the dam affected the area's flora and fauna, check out the **Ecomuseu** (admission free; 8:30-11:30am & 2-5:30pm Tue-Sat, 2-5:30pm Sun).

To get to Itaipu Dam, catch a Conjunto C bus from any stop along Av Juscelino Kubitschek (R$2, 30 minutes, every 20 minutes).

PARQUE DAS AVES
This five-hectare **bird park** (Map p329; ☎ 3529 8282; www.parquedasaves.com.br; admission R$23; 8:30am-5:30pm), located 300m from the entrance to Parque Nacional do Iguaçu, is home to 800-plus species of birds. They live in 8m-high aviaries that are constructed right in the forest. Other exhibits are devoted to snakes, butterflies and other species.

CIUDAD DEL ESTE (PARAGUAY)
Across the Ponte da Amizade lies this Paraguayan city – dynamic but dingy, animated but impoverished. Here, you can play baccarat at the casinos or shop for duty-free imported goods: you might find some good deals but imitations are ubiquitous. Walking over the bridge is not safe, so catch a bus from the local bus terminal in Foz (R$3, every 10 minutes) from 6am to 7:30pm.

Tours
If you want to see both sides of the falls in a single day, an organized tour is the only way to make it happen. Almost all hotels in Foz

do Iguaçu offer tours to Argentina for about R$50. One recommended guide is **Diogo Marcel** (Digo71@hotmail.com), based at the **Bambu Hostel** (☎ 3523 3646; Rua Edmundo de Barros 621).

Both parks have some organized adventures, including rafting, rappelling, kayaking, biking and guided nature walks:

Macuco Ecoaventura (☎ 3529 9626; www.macuco ecoaventura.com.br; Brazil) For rafting, rappelling and other activities.

Iguazu Jungle Explorer (☎ 0xx54-3757 421 600; www.iguazujunglexplorer.com; Argentina) Offices are in the Sheraton Hotel inside the park.

Sleeping
Don't be shy about trying to negotiate a lower price if the hotel is not full.

BUDGET
Albergue Paudimar Falls (Map p329; ☎ 3028 5503; www.paudimarfalls.com.br; Rua Antônio Raposo 820; dm HI-member/nonmember $20/26;) Everything an HI hostel should be: a great place to meet up with other travelers, with on-site recreation options, helpful staff and good facilities. The original branch of this hostel – Paudimar Campestre – is a bigger, resortlike place near the airport. Spacious and green, it has excellent facilities and space to pitch a tent; unfortunately, readers have reported muggings on the road from the highway to the hostel, so take precautions.

Hostel Natura (Map p329; ☎ 9116 0979; www.hostel natura.com; Alameda Buri 333; dm/camping R$35/20;) This new hostel is set on a gorgeous piece of land, amid two small lakes and lush scenery. The rooms themselves are pleasant and tidy, and there's ample outdoor lounge space and a fun bar. Service is top-notch, including transportation, dinner and other perks. It's 13km from town on the way to the falls (same turnoff as Paudimar).

MIDRANGE

Pousada El Shaddai (Map p326; ☎ 3025 4493; www .pousadaelshaddai.com.br; s without bathroom R$25, s/d with bathroom R$70/80; ☐ 🗷) On a quiet residential street, this pousada occupies a rambling old house – a rare case of architectural preservation in a town of high-rise hotels. Budget rooms are very plain and rather cramped. But pricier rooms are delightful, with hardwood floors, shuttered windows and glue-chip glass. Common areas include a clean kitchen and a sweet terrace.

Pousada Sonho Meu (Map p326 ☎ 3573 5764; www .sonhomeufoz.com.br; Rua Men de Sa 267; r per person R$40; 🗷 🗷) Sonho Meu – or 'My Dream' – feels like home away from home. Rooms are simple and sweet, with pastel-colored walls, bamboo furniture and ceiling fans. Stands out for its small size and family-friendly atmosphere.

Dany Hotel (Map p326; ☎ 3523 1530; www.danyhotel .com.br; Av Brasil 509; s/d/tr/q R$80/120/150/180; 🗷) The lobby of this little hotel has a homey atmosphere, with worn furniture and interesting artwork. The rooms are more institutional – and very dark.

Hotel Baviera (Map p326; ☎ 3523 5995; www.hotel bavieraiguassu.com.br; Av Jorge Schimmelpfeng 697; s/d/t/q R$81/106/140/180; 🗷) The faux-German façade may be kitschy, but at least this place has a bit of style. The German theme extends to the interior, which is clean, orderly and efficiently run. Appropriately, it's across the street from the popular Biergarten (see opposite).

Hotel del Rey (Map p326; ☎ 3523 2027; www.hoteldel reyfoz.com.br; Rua Tarobá 1020; s/d/tr/q R$94/119/145/172; 🗷 ☐ 🗷) The Hotel del Rey has refurbished its rooms and raised its prices, making this place a solid midrange choice. The rooms are rather utilitarian – think 'white' as a decorating theme – but they are spacious, clean and comfortable.

Hotel Tarobá Express (Map p326; ☎ 2102 7700; www.hoteltaroba.com.br; s/d/tr/q R$100/150/170/200; 🗷 ☐ 🗷) This certified three-star hotel is bustling. Between the travel agency, gift shop and restaurant (dinner R$10), and guests frequenting the busy reception, the atmosphere is

energetic and enthusiastic. Rooms are simple, but absolutely spotless, and fully equipped.

TOP END

Hotel Rafain Centro (Map p326; ☎ 3521 3500; www .rafaincentro.com.br; Rua Marechal Deodoro 984; s/d/tr R$180/220/275; 🗷 ☐ 🗷) This straightforward hotel does not quite justify its four-star rating. But the semi-swanky place offers affordable prices for a high level of comfort and service – especially during slow periods, when prices are negotiable.

Hotel Tropical das Cataratas (Map p329; ☎ 2102 7000; www.tropicalhotel.com.br; d R$280-350; 🗷 ☐ 🗷) Nowhere on either side of the falls is as delightful, delicious and de-luxe as the Tropical das Cataratas. The grand pink colonial edifice is located within the confines of Nacional Parque do Iguaçu, not far from the falls. So yes, you might enjoy a million-dollar view from your window.

Eating

Sabor Brasil (Map p326; ☎ 3028 7778; Av Brasil 638; meals R$8-10; 🕙 11am-10pm Mon-Sat, 3-10pm Sun) Sandwiches and ice cream are the specialties at this tiny café. Baguettes stuffed with meats and cheeses make for a hearty lunch – perfect for a picnic.

Famiglia Maran (Map p326; ☎ 3027 1212; Rua Almirante Barroso 1968; meals R$10-15; 🕙 24hrs) There is something for everyone at this bakery and cafeteria. Sandwiches, pastas and filling hot dishes will sate your hunger, as will the irresistible soup buffet (R$7, 🕙 6pm-5:30am). Enjoy sidewalk seating in pleasant weather.

Búfalo Branco (Map p326; ☎ 3523 9744; Rua Rebouças 530; buffet R$25) The best *churrascaria* (restaurant serving grilled meat) in town is known for its succulent meat and fine service. Arrive hungry to take full advantage of the endless *rodízio* (smorgasbord) of grilled beef and pork.

Tempero da Bahía (Map p326; ☎ 3025 1144; Rua Marechal Deodoro da Fonseca 1228; meals R$25-30; 🕙 6pm-1am) You are nowhere near the northeast, but you wouldn't know it when you taste the spicy *moquecas* (Bahian fish stews cooked in a clay pot with *dendê* oil, coconut milk and spicy peppers) served up at this Bahian café. Live music nightly from 8pm.

Armazém (Map p326; ☎ 3572 7422; Rua Edmundo de Barros 446; mains US$10; 🕙 6pm-2am) Seat yourself on the shady terrace at this attractive, colonial-style house – a lovely setting to enjoy gourmet Brazilian food and a nice selection of wines.

Drinking & Entertainment

Nightlife is hopping along Av Jorge Schimmelpfeng, where you will find breezy beer gardens for early evening and hot-to-trot nightclubs that stay open late. A good place to start is **Biergarten** (Map p326; cnr Af Jorge Schimmelpfeng & Rua Marechal Deodoro da Fonseca; ☑ 11am-4am).

Getting There & Away

AIR

Daily flights go from the **international airport** (☎ 3523 4244) to Asunción (one hour), Buenos Aires (two hours), Rio (two hours), São Paulo (one hour) and Curitiba (40 minutes).

BUS

The **long-distance bus station** (☎ 3522 3336) is 4.5km from the center of town. Destinations include Curitiba (R$80, *leito* – overnight sleeper – R$105, 10 hours), Florianopolis (R$108, *leito* R$226, 14 hours), São Paulo (R$123, *leito* R$190, 16 hours) and Rio de Janeiro (R$185, *leito* US$82, 22 hours). For service to Buenos Aires (20 hours), head to Puerto Iguazú; for Asunción (five hours), head to Ciudad del Este.

Getting to Argentina & Paraguay

To enter Paraguay, Americans and other nationalities need a visa. Most nationalities can enter Argentina without a visa, but always confirm before crossing the border. Obtaining a visa takes about 24 hours.

Argentine consulate (Map p326; ☎ 3574 2969; 26 Travessa Eduardo Ramón Bianchi; ☑ 10am-2pm Mon-Fri)

Paraguayan consulate (Map p326; ☎ 3523 2898; Rua Marechal Deodoro da Fonseca 901; ☑ 8:30am-4:30pm Mon-Fri)

To enter Ciudad del Este, Paraguay, walking across the bridge is inadvisable because of robberies, so take a bus or taxi. At the immigration posts, be sure to request your exit and entry stamps, as it may not happen automatically. From the border post, catch the next bus to Ciudad del Este (buses don't wait for travelers to complete their proceedings) or grab a taxi.

To enter Puerto Iguazú, Argentina, again, you'll have to request your exit and entry stamps if you are staying for longer than a day. Local bus drivers won't stop at the Brazilian border unless you ask, and they probably won't wait around while you finish formalities. Both borders are open 24 hours, but bus service ends around 7pm.

Getting Around

TO/FROM THE AIRPORT

To reach the airport, 15km southeast of the center, catch a bus marked 'Aeroporto/P Nacional' (R$3, 40 minutes) from any stop along Av Juscelino Kubitschek. Buses run every 22 minutes, and every hour after 7pm. A taxi from the center costs around R$30.

TO/FROM THE BUS STATION

From outside the bus station, catch any Centro bus to town (R$2). A taxi costs around R$10

TO/FROM THE FALLS

For the Brazilian side of the falls, catch the 'Aeroporto/P Nacional' bus (R$3, 50 minutes) to the park entrance. You can catch it in the local bus terminal, or at stops along Av Juscelino Kubitschek and Av Jorge Schimmelpfeng.

To get to the Argentine side, catch a Puerto Iguazú bus (R$5, every 20 minutes) from the bus stop behind the local bus station or from any stop along Av Juscelino Kubitschek. In Puerto Iguazú, transfer to a 'Cataratas' bus to the falls (A$8 or R$6, hourly).

Santa Catarina

Life's a beach. Certainly that's true in sunny Santa Catarina, which boasts 560km of spectacular coastline.

If you like your beach deserted, there is a spot of sand for you in the south of Ilha de Santa Catarina. If you prefer a party scene, head further north on that same island. Crave the life aquatic? You'll find excellent snorkeling and diving at Praia Bombinhas. If you're all about big surf, take your pick from any number of beaches south of Florianópolis.

While beaches might be the main draw, there is more to this southern state than sun and sand. Running parallel to the coast, the Serra Geral offers cool temperatures and stunning mountain scenery, promising rewarding hiking and horseback riding.

The inland regions are also where Santa Catarina exhibits the profound influence of its German ancestry. It is most evident during Oktoberfest, Blumenau's huge festival for folk dancing, accordion playing and beer drinking. But the Alpine architecture and fresh-brewed beer are here to enjoy year-round.

Like the other southern states, Santa Catarina enjoys some of Brazil's highest standards of living. The state's prosperity means that its infrastructure is sound and the people are welcoming.

Keep in mind that, on the coast, crowds and prices go up with the temperature. Visit outside of January and February to avoid the craziness and costliness of summer in Santa Catarina.

HIGHLIGHTS

- Watch the sun drop behind the mountains while slurping oysters in **Ribeirão da Ilha** (p341)

- Snorkel in the crystalline waters off **Ilha do Campeche** (p341)

- Sample brews straight from the barrel at the **Eisenbahn Cervejaria & Fábrica** (p346) in Blumenau

- Swim and snorkel from the docks of the floating restaurants in **Caixa d'Aço** (p348) near Porto Belo

- Catch a wave at **Praia da Joaquina** (p340) and you're sittin' on top of the world

Blumenau ★
Porto Belo ★
Praia da Joaquina ★
Ilha do Campeche ★
Ribeirão da Ilha ★

- POPULATION: 5.8 MILLION
- AREA: 95,433 SQ KM

History

In the 1820s, a newly independent Brazil realized the strategic importance of this region on the frontier between the Spanish and Portuguese Americas. The emperor invited German-speaking immigrants to develop the land and serve as a buffer against Spanish insurgency. The German immigrants – and Italians who followed – never adopted the plantation culture of the Northeast. Instead, the economy was based on small, family-owned farms, a legacy that lives on in the region's egalitarian politics and equitable distribution of income.

Climate

The coastal lowlands of Santa Catarina enjoy a semitropical climate, with hot, humid summers and mild winters. The central highlands are drier in summer and colder in winter. At the highest elevations of the Serra Geral, snow is surprisingly common.

Getting There & Around

Florianópolis is the state's transportation hub, with direct bus and air services to every major city in Brazil. Joinville also has direct air services to São Paulo, with connections to other major cities. Most destinations within Santa Catarina are accessible from Florianópolis by bus service, which is extensive and dependable.

ILHA DE SANTA CATARINA

Ilha de Santa Catarina has a vibrant and varied coastline, from the calm, crowded bays of the north, to the wild, cliff-hugging beaches of the south. But it's not just the beaches that make this island so enchanting. A forest of protected pines protect the east coast, while the dunes near Praia da Joaquina create a lunar landscape. The spine of mountains, luxuriant with the Mata Atlântica (Atlantic rain forest), drops precipitously down to the lovely Lagoa da Conceição. The gateway to the island is Florianópolis, political capital of Santa Catarina and cultural capital of southern Brazil.

The north of the island borders on being overdeveloped, and the shores of Lagoa da

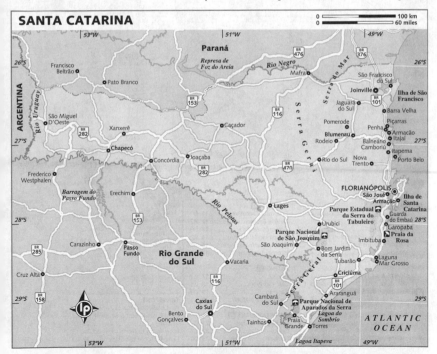

SANTA CATARINA

Conceição are crowded with restaurants, hotels and pubs. The best beaches lie along the east coast, especially for surfers. In general, further south means less developed.

Plan on big crowds and high prices (listed here) between Christmas and early March. Prices can fall 20% to 40% outside peak times.

FLORIANÓPOLIS

☎ 0xx48 / pop 406,600

There are two sides to Florianópolis. On the mainland, the industrial zone occupies the districts of Estreito and Coqueiros. Across the bay, the island holds the historic center and the chic district of Beira-Mar Norte. Two picturesque bridges link these halves. The old suspension bridge, the Ponte Hercílio Luz, is no longer open to traffic, but it still lights the night sky, acting as the defining feature of Floripa's spectacular skyline.

Florianópolis is a convenient transportation hub, with all of the island's 42 beaches within an hour's drive. While in the center, travelers can explore the colonial, cobblestone streets that fan out from the recently renovated Praça XV de Novembro, or take a sunset stroll along the embankment in Beira-Mar Norte.

Orientation

The city's major sights – as well as a range of hotels and restaurants – are just east of the long-distance and local bus stations. The upscale Beira-Mar Norte neighborhood sits on the bay 2km north of the center.

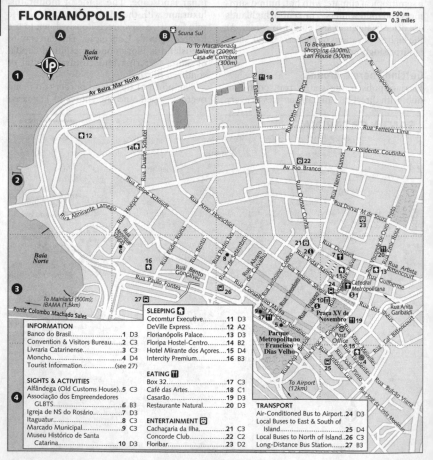

FLORIANÓPOLIS

INFORMATION		EATING 🍴	
Banco do Brasil.........................1 D3		Box 32......................................17 C3	
Convention & Visitors Bureau...2 C3		Café das Artes..........................18 C1	
Livraria Catarinense.................3 C3		Casarão....................................19 D3	
Moncho....................................4 D4		Restaurante Natural..................20 D3	
Tourist Information................(see 27)			
		ENTERTAINMENT 🎭	
SIGHTS & ACTIVITIES		Cachaçaria da Ilha...................21 C3	
Alfândega (Old Customs House)..5 C3		Concorde Club..........................22 C2	
Associação dos Empreendedores		Floribar....................................23 D2	
GLBTS..................................6 B3			
Igreja de NS do Rosário............7 D3		SLEEPING 🛏	
Itaguatur.................................8 C3		Cecomtur Executive................11 D3	
Marcado Municipal...................9 C3		DeVille Express.......................12 A2	
Museu Histórico de Santa		Florianópolis Palace................13 D3	
Catarina..............................10 D3		Floripa Hostel-Centro..............14 B2	
		Hotel Mirante dos Açores....15 D4	
		Intercity Premium....................16 B3	

TRANSPORT	
Air-Conditioned Bus to Airport..24 D3	
Local Buses to East & South of	
Island....................................25 D4	
Local Buses to North of Island..26 C3	
Long-Distance Bus Station.......27 B3	

GAY FLOR-EE

Floripa is becoming Brazil's second gay capital. Its Pride celebration, **Parada da Diversidade** (www .diversidadefloripa.com.br), has grown into one of Brazil's biggest, attracting 30,000 people in 2006. The city also hosts GLBT-centered 'Gay Pop' events during Carnaval. Gay and lesbian travelers from around the world descend on Florianópolis, which is safer and more affordable than Rio.

One agency that caters primarily to gay and lesbian clients is **Outing Turismo** (☎ 8419 7184; www.outingturismo.com.br). Popular hangouts include Floribar (p336), Concorde Club (p336) and Praia Mole (p339).

For more information, including the useful *Guia GLBTS*, visit the **Associação dos Empreend-edores GLBTS** (☎ 4009 2595; www.diversidadefloripa.com.br; Rua Henrique Valgas 112).

Information

BOOKSTORES
Livraria Catarinense (Rua Felipe Schmidt 60; ✆ 10am-8pm Mon-Sat) Small selection of foreign-language titles.

EMERGENCY
Bombeiros (☎ 193) Fire and medical emergencies.
Federal Police (☎ 3281 6500)

INTERNET ACCESS
Lan House (☎ 3028 0477; Beiramar Shopping; per hr R$3; ✆ 10am-10pm Mon-Sat, 2-8pm Sun)
Moncho (☎ 2106 2775; Rua Tiradentes 181; per hr R$4; ✆ 9am-10pm Mon-Fri, to 8pm Sat)

MONEY
Change your cash at one of the money-exchange houses on Rua Felipe Schmidt.
Banco do Brasil (Praça 15 de Novembro 20) For traveler's checks and ATMs.

TOURIST INFORMATION
The city suffers from a shortage of maps, but otherwise the information offices are helpful.
Convention & Visitors Bureau (☎ 3222 4904; www .florianopolisscvp.com.br; Rua Jerônimo Coelho 393)
Tourist information (☎ 3248 0002; long-distance bus station; ✆ 8am-10pm)

Sights
The center of town is the inviting **Praça XV de Novembro**, with its shady walks and 100-year-old fig tree. On one side sits the **Museu Histórico de Santa Catarina** (☎ 3221 3504; Praça 15 de Novembro 227; admission R$3; ✆ 10am-6pm Tue-Fri, 10am-4pm Sat-Sun), formerly the colonial governor's palace. Its collection of indigenous and colonial artifacts is perhaps less interesting than the building itself, which boasts ornate parquetry floors and outrageous 19th-century ceilings.

Catedral Metropolitana sits grandly at the high end of the square, covered by scaffolding at the time of research. The best-preserved colonial church, **Igreja de NS do Rosário**, sits picturesquely atop the steps at Rua Trajano.

At the other end of the square, the busy promenade **Rua Felipe Schmidt** is fine for people-watching and window-shopping. Or continue down to the waterfront to the well-preserved **Alfândega** (Customs House) and **Mercado Municipal** (Municipal Market).

North of the center, **Av Beira Mar Norte** runs along the coast of the Baía Norte. The waterfront promenade attracts runners, bikers and walkers, enjoying the breeze off the bay and a sweeping view across to the mainland.

Tours
Itaguatur (☎ 3225 3939; www.itaguatur.com.br; Suite 208, Rua Felipe Schmidt 515; adult/child R$45/22.50) Day tours visit destinations around the island.
Scuna Sul (☎ 3225 1806; www.scunasul.com.br; tours R$28-35) Boat tours of the bay stop at some pretty 18th-century Portuguese forts.

Sleeping
Florianópolis suffers from a lack of budget sleeping options, although prices drop dramatically outside the high season, making many midrange places more affordable.

BUDGET & MIDRANGE
Floripa Hostel – Centro (☎ 3225 3781; www.floripa hostel.com.br; Rua Duarte Schutel 227; dm HI-member/ student/regular R$22/28/30, d R$50/59/65; 🖳) On a residential street, halfway between the city center and Beira-Mar Norte, this orderly HI hostel is an easy walk from either. Kitchen and shared bathroom facilities are spotless. Sturdy wooden bunk beds are lined up in the dorms, which are segregated by gender.

SANTA CATARINA

Hotel Mirante dos Açores (☎ 3224 6998; www.hotel mirantedosacores.com.br; Rua Tiradentes 167; s/d R$75/88; ✹ ▣ ▤) Located on a quiet cobblestone street, a blue-arched entry leads into a lobby streaming with sunlight and painted in vibrant colors. Murals adorn the guest rooms, which have wood furniture and institutional carpeting.

Cecomtur Executive (☎ 2107 8800; www.cecomtur hotel.com.br; Rua Arcipreste Paiva 107; s/d from R$80/100; ✹ ▣ ▤) There's nothing super fancy about this efficient business hotel. But it's got everything you need: modern, spotless, spacious rooms; congenial, English-speaking service and a few perks besides.

Centro Sul Hotel (☎ 3222 9110; www.centrosulhotel .com.br; Av Hercílio Luz 652; s/d R$86/116; ✹ ▣) CSH – as it is called – is a comfortable, kitschy midrange option. Free wireless access is a bonus; although if you are traveling *sem computador* (without a computer) you will be relegated to the local internet cafe.

Florianópolis Palace (☎ 2106 9633; ww.floph.com .br; Rua Artista Bittencourt 14; r R$130; ✹) The fanciest hotel in the historic center receives mixed reviews for its service and style. But perks like free parking and the sprawling breakfast buffet are enticing. Rooms on the upper floors offer panoramic views of the city.

ourpick DeVille Express (☎ 3225 6002; www.deville .com.br; Rua Felipe Schmidt 1320; s/d R$137/154; ✹ ▣) This all-suite hotel offers the trappings of luxury at midrange prices – great value. Higher-priced rooms have balconies, from which to enjoy some of Floripa's loveliest views.

TOP END

Intercity Premium (☎ 3027 2200; www.intercityhoteis .com.br; Av Paolo Fontes 1210; s/d R$168/184; ✹ ▣ ▤) This classy, accommodating high-rise hotel is convenient to the bus station. The lobby sparkles with white marble, while plush couches are scattered with pillows. Guest rooms are fully equipped and tastefully decorated, and some enjoy impressive views of the bay and mainland.

Eating & Drinking

For a cluster of cheap eats, head to the food court in **Beiramar Shopping** (cnr Rua Bocaiúva & Av Beira Mar Norte; ✹ 10am-10pm Mon-Sat, 11am-10pm Sun), 2km north of the center.

Restaurante Natural (☎ 3223 4507; Rua Visconde de Ouro Preto 298; meals R$10-12; ✹ 11am-3:30 Mon-Fri) This all-vegetarian joint offers an appetizing buffet in a handsome, colonial-style home.

ourpick Café das Artes (☎ 3322 0690; Rua Esteves Júnior 734; sandwiches R$5-10; ✹ 11:30am-11pm Mon-Sat, 4-11pm Sun) An artsy, upscale café in Beira-Mar Norte, this cozy option offers good coffee and baked goods as well as salads and sandwiches.

Casarão (☎ 3222 9092; Praça 15 de Novembro 320; meals R$10-12; ✹ 11am-11pm Mon-Sat) Housed in an old colonial building, this breezy place has a huge per-kilo lunch buffet and an á la carte menu in the evenings. Live music nightly.

Casa de Coimbra (☎ 3222 9017; Av Beira Mar Norte 2568; meals R$10-15; ✹ 11:30am-midnight Tue-Sat) Heavy wood doors open up to a cool, country casa, right in the heart of the city. The rustic interior, filled with folk art, is a perfect atmosphere to enjoy hearty, home-cooked Brazilian fare.

Macarronada Italiana (☎ 3223 2666; Av Beira Mar Norte; meals R$20-30; ✹ 11am-1am) The vast dining room and terrace are often crowded with families, feasting on pasta, pizza, seafood and grilled meats. The Italian fare is delicious, and wine flows freely.

Box 32 (☎ 3224 5588; Mercado Municipal; meals R$25-30; ✹ 10am-10pm Mon-Sat, to 5pm Sun) This historic bar and restaurant in the Mercado Muncipal claims to be 'the most democratic box in Brazil.' Maybe that's what attracts the city's local celebrities, who come during happy hour for frothy beer and fresh seafood.

Entertainment

While many people flock to Lagoa for its nightlife, Floripa center has a few hot spots too.

Cachaçaria da Ilha (☎ 3224 0551; Av Osmar Cunha 164; ✹ 5pm-2:30am Mon-Fri, 8pm-4am Sat) This sophisticated bar is famous for its *cachaça*, but also has a fine selection of draft beers. Live music makes it a popular spot for happy hour.

Floribar (☎ 3322 2550; Rua Dorval Melchíades de Souza 638; ✹ 6pm-2am Thu-Sun) A cool bi-level lounge, where Floripa's most beautiful people sip fancy cocktails and groove to house music.

Concorde Club (☎ 3222 1981; Av Rio Branco 729; cover R$15-25) Two dance floors pulse to the beat of a heavy bass, while swirling bodies are lost in the movement of flashing lights. Three bars ensure that dancers do not get dehydrated.

Getting There & Away

AIR

Direct flights go to São Paulo (one hour), Porto Alegre (one hour), Rio de Janeiro (1½ hours) and Curitiba (40 minutes), with connections to most other cities.

The **airport** (☎ 3226 0229) is 12km south of the city (R$20 by taxi). Red local buses marked Correador Sudoeste run to the airport (R$2, 45 minutes) every 15 minutes from the local bus terminal on Rua Antônio Luz.

BUS

From the long-distance **bus station** (☎ 3212 3100), buses link Florianópolis with every major city in southern Brazil. Destinations include Blumenau (R$26, three hours, hourly); Joinville (R$33, 2½ hours, hourly); Porto Alegre (US$14, 6½ hours); Curitiba (R$37 to R$65, four hours, hourly); São Paulo (US$28, 12 hours); Rio de Janeiro (US$42, 18 hours); Foz do Iguaçu ($108, *leito* – overnight sleeper – R$226, 14 hours). International destinations include Buenos Aires (24 hours) and Montevideo (20 hours).

Getting Around

The city is the transportation hub for the rest of the island, all within a one-hour drive.

BUS

The island of Santa Catarina has a remarkably efficient bus service (R$2). Buses for the east coast and south island (including Lagoa and Joaquina) depart from the local bus terminal on Rua Antônio Luz. Buses for the north depart from the local bus terminal on Rua Francisco Tolentino. Additional yellow microbuses (R$4) follow the same routes: their advantages include air-conditioning, fewer stops, direct routes to the beaches and room for surfboards.

CAR

Consider renting a car for easier exploration of the island's beaches. Beware that prices are generally high (per day without/with air-con R$85/110) and traffic can be deadly on weekends.

Latina Rent a Car (☎ 9945 6652; latinarc@terra.com.br) Includes pick-up and drop-off at the airport, bus station or hotel.

Yes Rent a Car (☎ 3236 0229; Rua Deputado Diomício Freitas 3241) Offices at the airport, in central Floripa and in Canasvieiras; also offers car delivery.

NORTH ISLAND

From Praia de Jurerê to Praia dos Ingleses, the north of the island is designed for mass tourism: calm, family-friendly waters; newly widened roads that provide easy access to the

international airport; and lots of anonymous hotels and restaurants.

Santo Antônio de Lisboa

On the west coast, Santo Antônio de Lisboa is among the oldest communities on the island. This picturesque place retains an old-fashioned fishing-village atmosphere in its cobblestone streets and Azorean architecture. The most prominent edifice is the **Igreja da Nossa Senhora da Necessidade**, dating from 1750. Many other 18th-century colonial buildings now house restaurants and art galleries. Stop by the delightful **Casa Açoriana** (☎ 3235 1262; Rua Cônego Serpa 30) to peruse the collection of island arts and enjoy some sweets in the courtyard café.

Santo Antônio's seaside setting and fishing heritage guarantee that you can enjoy delicious seafood. Try **Bar & Restaurante Açores** (☎ 3235 1377; Rua Cônego Serpa 20; meals R$15-30) or **Sobrado** (☎ 3334 2403; Rua XV de Novembro 123; meals R$10-20), both in historic houses.

Canasvieiras

Canasvieiras is not the most atmospheric place on the island, but it has easy access to **Praia de Jurerê** and **Praia de Canasvieiras**. Both beaches offer options for windsurfing, jet-skiing and fishing. Nightlife in town is hopping, as crowds of young people flock to local bars and clubs. Outside the season, however, this town is pretty sleepy, and many hotels are closed altogether.

Open only in summer, **Floripa Hostel – Canasvieiras** (☎ 3266 2036; Rua Dr João de Oliveira 517; dm HI-member/student/regular R$20/24/26, d R$46/55/56; 🖳) subscribes to all the hostel norms: friendly, English-speaking reception; bunk beds and lockers; shared bathrooms, common kitchen and TV room. The location two blocks from the town beach is hard to beat.

The 'apart-hotel' **Lacabana** (☎ 3266 0400; www .lacabana.com.br; Av das Nações 525; d/q R$80/120; 🖭) is no beauty, but it is practical, offering comfortable but small rooms with kitchenettes. About 150m from the beach, it's a decent option for families who require the convenience of Canasvieiras.

Praia da Lagoinha & Praia Brava

The northeastern tip of the island is a slender peninsula, accessed by slow-moving roads that wind around the hills to the beach. These towns are ritzier than their neighbors,

SANTA CATARINA

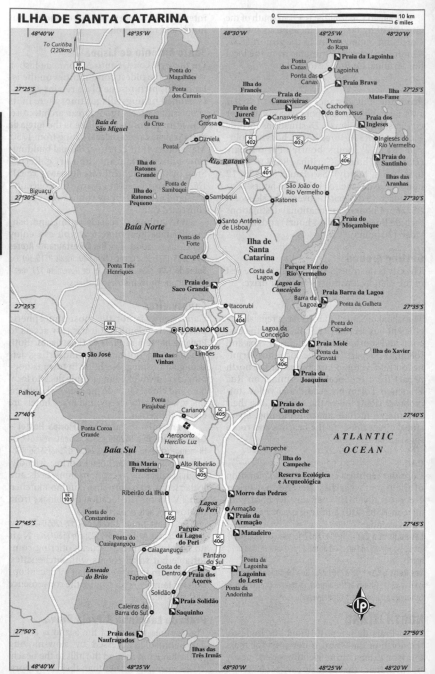

ILHA DE SANTA CATARINA

SANTA CATARINA

though the beaches are still overbuilt. **Praia da Lagoinha** is a crescent-shaped patch of sand, surrounded on three sides by rocky cliffs that keep the water calm. Further south, **Praia Brava** has wilder waves that attract a steady stream of surfers. Adventure-seekers can try **paragliding** (OVNI Parapente; ☎ 9985 8393; www.ovniparapente.com; per person R$120) for an unusual and exhilarating perspective on the peninsula.

Santa Catarina's Italian heritage is lovingly showcased in the design and decor at the luxurious **Villabella Villaggio** (☎ 3284 2017; www.villabella villaggio.com.br; Av Epitácio Bittencourt 470, Praia Brava; d R$150-220, chalets R$250; ✖ ⛻ ⛹). Every guest room has an expansive view toward either Praia da Lagoinha or Praia Brava. You'll want to catch your rays or waves at the latter, which is about 300m away.

Perched high atop a hillside, the picturesque, pink **Pousada da Vigia** (☎ 3284 1789; www .pousadadavigia.com.br; Rua Côn Walmor Castro 291, Lagoinha; d with garden/ocean view R$250/290; ✖ ⛻ ⛹) overlooks Praia da Lagoinha. Ten guest rooms, scattered around lovely gardens, all exude upper-class style. The long arm of attentive service reaches the beach, which is accessible by a 200m footpath.

Praia dos Ingleses & Praia do Santinho

Once among the island's finest beaches, **Praia dos Ingleses** has suffered from its popularity. It's now crowded with high-rise hotels and overpriced restaurants.

Further south, **Praia do Santinho** is quieter, thanks to the protected area of dunes behind it. Santinho is the north island's best surfing beach, acclaimed for its consistent waves and uncrowded conditions. Check out **Floripa Surf Camp** (☎ 9615 6282; www.floripasurfcamp.com; Av Madre Maria Vilac esq Com Vidal Ramos 100; rental/classes per day R$25/75) for equipment rental, classes and multiday camps.

You are guaranteed a warm welcome at the friendly, family-run **Pousada do Santinho** (☎ 3269 2836; www.pousadasantinho.com.br; Rodovia Vereador Onildo Lemos 1259, Praia do Santinho; d R$120-140; ✖ ⛹). The rooms are plain but clean; just as the grounds are barren but perfectly pleasant, with the beautiful beach just across the dunes.

EAST COAST

Facing the open ocean, the east coast boasts the island's cleanest waters, longest beaches and most challenging surf.

Barra da Lagoa & Around

In the north, **Praia do Moçambique** merges with **Praia Barra da Lagoa** to form a stunning, 14km strand. The beach is hidden from the road by pine forest, which thrives in the sandy soil. Surfing is sweet all along here: Praia Barra da Lagoa has gentle swells and shallow waters that are good for beginners, while the long stretch of Moçambique has more challenging peaks.

Praia do Moçambique is protected, so the only construction is around the town of Barra da Lagoa. This town borders on shabby, despite the canal that atmospherically winds its way through the center. Restaurants, bars and pousadas are plentiful.

At **Pousada 32** (☎ 3232 4232; www.pousada32.com .br; Rua Angelina Joaquin dos Santos 300; s/d/q with kitchen R$60/90/120), colorful rooms have ceiling fans and balconies, making this a decent option if you must stay in town. The '32' refers to the number of meters to the beach.

The congenial owner of **Pousada Rio Vermelho** (☎ 296 1337; www.riovermelhopousada.com.br; São João de Rio Vermelho; d R$110-120; ⛻ ⛹), Carlota, claims that her pousada (guesthouse) is the oldest on the island, dating back some 25 years, but its age does not show. The spacious grounds and chic chalets are clean and contemporary. The grounds cover almost 0.5 sq km, extending from the road to Praia do Moçambique.

Praia Mole

Praia Mole is famous for its world-class waves and happening social scene, especially among the gay and lesbian community. The beach is absolutely beautiful, as are most of the bodies sunning and surfing. It does get crowded, but that's part of the appeal of this hot spot.

To take full advantage of the surf, sign up with **Nexus Surf Experience** (www.nexussurf.com; Rodovia Jornalista Manoel de Menezes 2031/29). Otherwise, you can partake of paragliding, kitesurfing or beach volleyball. But the most competitive sport on Praia Mole is cruising; so don your teeniest bikini and your darkest sunglasses and check it out.

SLEEPING

Bangalôs da Mole (☎ 3232 0723; www.bangalosdamole .com.br; Rodovia Jornalista Manoel de Menezes 1007; d R$100-160; ✖) Directly across from the beach, this place has spacious suites and bi-level bungalows, all with cool tile floors and high ceilings. Higher-priced units have kitchens and sea views.

Parque Flor Essência (☎ 3232 3903; www.parqu essencia.com.br; Rodovia Jornalista Manoel de Menezes 631; d R$120-200; 🍽 🕹) Nestled into the side of a hill, 10 charming cottages each offer a fabulous panorama of the lagoon and the mountains beyond. If you can pull yourself away, you are 150m from the waves of Praia Mole.

Praia da Joaquina

About 3km south of Praia Mole, the huge white dunes of 'Joaca' are visible for miles. These massive sandy mounds have inspired a new sport: sand surfing. Rent a sand board and haul it up to the top of the dune, from where it is a fast, dirty ride down.

Good old-fashioned surfing is still the number one activity at Praia da Joaquina, which boasts long, fast, powerful waves that are up to 3m high. Stop in at the surf shop **Swell** (☎ 3232 0366; Estrada Geral da Joaquina 834; 🕑 9am-9pm) for more information and lots of gear.

A handful of places to stay are along the road to Joaquina, including the simple **Pousada Aloha** (☎ 3232 5862; Estrada Geral da Joaquina 834; per person R$20-30) above the surf shop. Alternatively, **Cris Hotel** (☎ 3232 5104; www.crishotel.com; Estrada Geral da Joaquina 1; s/d/tr/q R$99/119/150/180; 🍽) wins points for its prime location on the beach.

Lagoa da Conceição

For spectacular scenery, exhilarating water sports or all-night parties, Lagoa da Conceição is a popular alternative to the beaches. Forested hills form a fabulous backdrop for the pretty lagoon.

The town of Lagoa sits on a sandbar that divides the two halves of the lagoon; it is often packed with tourists. Driving through town can take hours on a summer weekend, so seek an alternative route if you are actually trying to get somewhere.

Get off the beaten track by hiking along the lagoon's undeveloped west coast. From the center of town, it is 6km to the tiny village of **Costa da Lagoa**, which is otherwise accessible only by boat (see Activities, below).

INFORMATION

For more information, see www.lagoavirtual .com. The aptly named **Internet** (☎ 3232 1882) is at the turnoff to Praia da Joaquina.

ACTIVITIES

The lagoon is ideal for windsurfing, kayaking and boating:

Passeio de Escuna (☎ 3232 5083; per person R$4) Boats depart from the dock at the north end of Rua das Rendeiras.

Toscani Náutica (☎ 9912 8392; per hr R$5) One of many places along the southern shore to rent kayaks.

Water taxis (per person R$3) Get a lift from the dock in the center of town (under the bridge) to Costa da Lagoa and other destinations around the lake.

SLEEPING

Loads of pousadas are along the southern shore of the lake. Drive over the bridge and continue east on Rua das Rendeiras.

Vento Forte (☎ 3232 5263; www.pousadaventoforte .com.br; Servidão Evaristo Manoel Pedro 122; d from R$80; 🖥) This hot-pink triple-decker features hammock-strung balconies, fully equipped kitchens, bold colors and avant-garde art. Follow signs from the road to Praia da Joaquina.

Pousada Ilha da Magia (☎ 3232 5038; www.pousada ilhadamagia.com.br; Av Santiago 23; s/d R$95/122) Right across from the lagoon, these cute, colorful cottages come in a variety of styles, from Alpine to A-frame.

EATING & DRINKING

Lagoa is the center for nightlife on the island.

Barracuda (☎ 3232 5301; Rua das Rendeiras; meals R$30-40) This place has a huge, airy dining room, often packed with patrons feasting on fresh seafood. It's known for its *bacalhau* (salted cod), served any way you like it.

John Bull Pub (☎ 3232 8535; Rua das Rendeiras 1046; meals R$20; 🕑 9am-4am Tue-Sun Dec-Mar, Thu-Sun Apr-Nov) Live music and lovely views over the lagoon make this English pub a popular spot for a drink.

SOUTH ISLAND

With white-sand beaches and mountains that drop into the sea, the South is the most pristine and picturesque part of the island. But south-island residents are engaged in the inevitable struggle between developers and preservers: the former see the potential for more tourists and big bucks; the latter fear that their piece of paradise will soon resemble the North. The balance is delicate and ever shifting.

For now, these towns retain their idyllic appeal. The beaches are less crowded (the hottest surf spots excepted), and the atmosphere is more laid-back, than other island destinations.

At the southern tip, **Praia dos Naufragados** is accessible only by hiking 4km on a flat, shady trail from the village of Caieiras da Barra do Sul. Your reward is a picturesque lighthouse and a fantastic vista of the islands in the vicinity.

Ribeirão da Ilha

More than any other town, the tiny village of Ribeirão da Ilha has preserved its Azorean heritage, evident in its cobblestone streets and colorful tile-roof houses. The main square centers on the lovely **Igreja Nossa Senhora da Lapa do Riberão**, which dates to 1806. Locals gather in the waterside park to play chess and watch the sun set behind the mainland mountain range.

Given its location overlooking the tidal flats, it is no surprise that the local specialty is oysters – as plump, juicy and fresh as you'll find anywhere. Sit on the dock at **Ostradamus** (☎ 3337 5711; Rod Baldicero Filomeno 7640; meals R$20-30) and slurp a dozen or two.

Campeche

Campeche is an alternative outpost, home to artists, massage therapists and other bohemian types, seeking to escape the crowds of the city and the tourist hot spots.

The 5km **Praia do Campeche** is protected, so there is no development on the beach. Desolate dunes and pounding surf – stretching for miles in either direction – guarantee solitude for swimmers and sunbathers. At the southern end of the beach, catch a boat (R$15 round-trip) to **Ilha do Campeche**, an ecological reserve with opportunities for hiking and snorkeling.

The grand neoclassical façade of **Pau de Canela Pousada** (☎ 3338 3584; www.pousadapaude canela.com.br; Rua Pau de Canela 606, Rio Tavares; d without/ with air-con R$120/150; 🖳 🖳) looks out of place on this rundown, residential road, 1km from the beach. The eight guest rooms are simple but luxurious, fitted with box-spring beds and Jacuzzi tubs, and decorated with shiny wooden floors and sophisticated artwork.

The owner of **Pousada Natur Campeche** (☎ 3237 4011; www.naturcampeche.com.br; Servidão Familia Nunes 59; s/d R$160/240, ste R$270-370; 🖳 🖳) has traveled the world, bringing back treasures to decorate this pousada. The exotic rooms are arranged around a green garden, just 100m from Praia de Campeche.

The friendly pousada **Vila Tamarindo** (☎ 3237 3464; www.tamarindo.com.br; Av Campeche 1836; d R$200-260, ste R$260-380; 🖳) has generous gardens,

airy rooms and views across the dunes to the open ocean.

Armação

This little town dates to the 18th century, when it served as a whaling center. The impressive **Igreja Santa Anna** still stands from these days. While whaling is no longer practiced, the fishing industry still thrives here.

Armação provides access to three beaches, all excellent surfing spots. North of town, **Morro das Pedras** is popular for its consistent right, but you'll probably have to fight for a chance to ride it. Further south, **Praia da Armação** is a surfer's delight, especially at the north end of the beach. For a little adventure, follow a winding trail inland the rocky coastline to the gorgeous **Matadeiro**, a near-deserted beach surrounded by lush greenery.

Inland from Armação, the **Lagoa do Peri** is a pretty lake surrounded by parkland. Lesser known and less visited than Conceição, it offers wonderful opportunities for swimming, hiking and otherwise escaping the summer crowds.

Follow the rough dirt road 300m from the beach, through the iron gate, and enter **Pousada Alemdomar** (☎ 3237 5600; www.alemdomar .com.br; Rua Lagoa do Peri 403; d R$180), a little plot of New Age paradise. Six simple guest rooms evoke tranquility and harmony with nature. Behind the main house, guests can follow a woodsy trail all the way to Lagoa do Peri.

'An overdose of health' is how **Nutri Lanches** (☎ 3237 5182; meals R$8-12) lauds its all-organic sandwiches, salads and pastries. The lunchtime buffet is an incredible array of healthy, homemade goodness.

Pântano do Sul

Fishermen of Azorean descent still inhabit the village of Pântano do Sul, so its beach is dotted with fishing boats and seafood shacks. Ringed by mountains, the protected cove contains calm, cool waters that are ideal for sunning and swimming.

From here, you can catch a lift from a local fisherman or hike about 1½ hours to the deserted beach of **Lagoinha de Leste**. The hike is hot, so leave early and bring plenty of water. Lagoinha do Leste offers some of the island's most consistent and powerful waves, so don't be surprised when surfers run past you on the trail.

Set 30m from the beach and surrounded by forest, **Pousada do Pescador** (☎ 3237 7122; www.pousadadopescador.com.br; Rua Manoel Vidal 257; s/d/tr R$80/100/120; ⊠) has simple, sweet one- and two-room chalets. The rustic seafood shack **Arante** (☎ 3237 7022; meals R$15-20) has become an island institution, its walls covered with handwritten messages, poetry and artwork, which patrons have contributed over the years.

Costa de Dentro & Around

This is the end of the road, and it feels like it. These tiny towns are home to a handful of places to stay and eat, but they are left largely to their fishing and farming residents. Costa de Dentro has access to the lovely, calm waters of the **Praia dos Açores**; or continue all the way to **Praia Solidão** or **Saquinho**.

Just before the paved road turns into a packed dirt path, 500m from the beach, you'll find **Albergue do Pirata** (☎ 3389 2727; www .alberguedopirata.com.br Ra Rosália Ferreira 4973, Costa de Dentro; dm/d per person R$28/35; ⊠), an 'international hostel.' Perks include English-speaking owners, free internet access and a lively outdoor restaurant and bar.

Vila dos Escargôs (☎ 3389 2301; www.viladosescargos .com.br; Rua Maurício Rosar 10, Praia dos Açores; s/d/tr R$150/170/190; ⊠ ⊠ ⊠), a stucco hotel, is far enough from the beach so as not to impede the natural landscape of the dunes, but close enough to allow ocean views from its upper floors. Spacious, comfortable rooms are all adorned with tile mosaics depicting the creatures of the sea.

About 1.5km past Costa de Dentro, **Pousada Sítio dos Tucanos** (☎ 3237 5084; www.pousada sitiodostucanos.com; s/d R$140/175; ⊠) sits in the midst of jungly wilderness on the southern edge of the Parque da Lagoa do Peri. Rustic rooms have balconies overlooking a gurgling mountain stream. Creative, delicious dinners (R$15) are also available with advance notice.

THE MAINLAND

Santa Catarina is famed for its beaches, and rightly so. But it is not only the Ilha de Santa Catarina that has such a marvelous coastline. Both north and south of Florianópolis, fine sand and big surf attract beachcombers, sunbathers and surfers. Inland, the Serra Geral runs parallel to the coast, protecting some of southern Brazil's most remote destinations. This is where Santa Catarina's German and Italian heritage endures most tenaciously.

JOINVILLE

☎ 0xx47 / pop 478,000

While Joinville does not have the historic center (or the beer festival) of Blumenau, it does have decidedly German roots. They are evident in the city's nouveau-Alpine architecture and in the well-manicured lawns and litter-free parks around town. The economy thrives on metallurgy, plastics and information technology, but this industrial activity is tucked neatly away from the eyes of visitors. The result is a big city with the good manners of a small town. Joinville's citizens are proud of their prosperous, orderly home, and they welcome visitors with warm hospitality and a surplus of helpful information.

Information

Banco do Brasil (cnr Rua Luiz Neimeyer & Rua do Principe) Money exchange and Visa ATMs.

Information posts Long-distance bus station (☟ 8am-noon & 2-6pm) Shopping Mueller (cnr Rua Pedro Lobo & Rua Senador Felipe Schmidt; ☟ 10am-6pm Mon-Fri, 8am-noon & 2-6pm Sat & Sun)

Sights

In an elegant palace dating from 1870, the **Museu Nacional da Imigração e Colonização** (National Museum of Immigration & Colonization; ☎ 3433 3736; www .museunacional.com.br; Rua Rio Branco 229; admission R$5; ☟ 9am-5pm Tue-Fri, 11am-5pm Sat & Sun) documents the history of immigration to Santa Catarina. The impressive stand of palms along **Alameda das Palmeiras** will lead you there.

Art lovers might prefer the **Museu de Arte de Joinville** (☎ 3433 4677; Rua 15 de Novembro 1400; admission free; ☟ 9am-5pm Wed-Fri, 11am-5pm Sat & Sun), with rotating exhibits by local and national artists.

For a vista of Joinville and Baía da Babitonga, head to the Morro do Boa Vista, about 10km east of the center. The 250m-high **Mirante** (Rua Saguaçu) is a tall tower with a circular staircase and a 360-degree panorama.

Tours

Cruise ship **Barco Príncipe III** (☎ 3455 4444; adult/ child R$70/35; ☟ 10am; ⊠) offers tours around the Baía da Babitonga, ending at São Francisco do Sul (see p347). Departs from the Espinheiros neighborhood, 10km from the center.

Sleeping

Hotel Trocadero (☎ 3422 1469; Rua Visconde de Taunay 185; s/d R$45/60, with air-con R$50/70) Angels herald your arrival in this bright, baroque hotel. The pewlike furniture in the lobby and crucifixes on the wall evoke an air of devotion. Rooms are less than divine, but cleanliness is next to godliness, and they have that going for them.

Hotel Germânia (☎ 3433 9886; www.hotelgermania .com.br; Rua Ministro Calógeras 612; s/d R$78/90; 🍴 🖳 🔊) It looks like a chain hotel from the outside, but inside it's spotlessly clean, tastefully appointed and attentively run.

our pick Anthurium Parque Hotel (☎ 3433 6299; www.anthurium.com.br; Rua São José 226; s/d/tr R$80/105/130; 🍴 🖳 🔊) This former residence of the Bishop

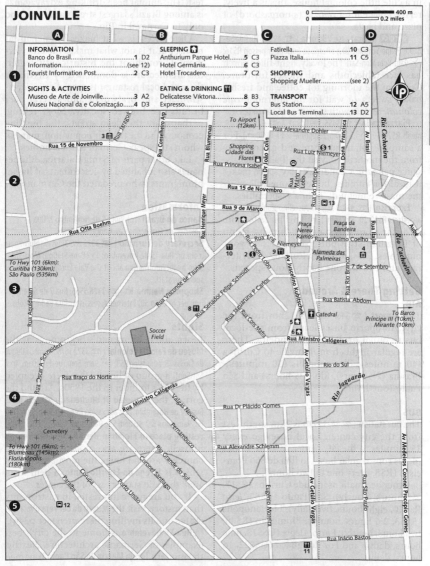

JOINVILLE

SANTA CATARINA

0 — 400 m
0 — 0.2 miles

of the Joinville diocese is appropriately located opposite the city's avant-garde cathedral. Set back from the road, the fine colonial building is surrounded by lush, blooming gardens.

Eating & Drinking

Fatirella (☎ 3433 8136; Rua Visconde de Taunay 299; all-you-can-eat pizza R$12; ☯ lunch daily, dinner Mon-Sat) Set in a cute little colonial house, this is a lively, relaxed place for a *rodízio* (smorgasbord) of pizza and pasta.

our pick **Delicatesse Viktoria** (☎ 422 0570; Rua Senador Felipe Schmidt 400; afternoon buffet per person R$16; ☯ 9am-8pm Mon-Sat) The lovely, light-filled porch has lace tablecloths and wicker furniture. Come in the morning for coffee and freshly baked sweets, or wait for the afternoon *café colonial*, replete with sweets and savories.

Piazza Italia (☎ 3455 3991; Rua Anita Garibaldi 79; meals R$20-30; ☯ 11:30am-2:30pm & 6:30-11:30pm) For a sampling of architecture and gastronomy from the motherland, visit this Italian Renaissance palazzo. A children's play space makes it ideal for families, but everyone will enjoy the massive menu of 'nonna's' specialties.

Expresso (☎ 433 9451; Av Juscelino Kubitschek 536; appetizers R$10-20; ☯ 5pm-1am) This place is more of a bar than a restaurant, but its menu of Brazilian-style pub grub will sate your munchies. Plus, it has a pleasant, shady terrace and two-for-one happy-hour specials.

Getting There & Around

AIR

The **airport** (☎ 3467 1000) is 12km from the city; Aeroporto buses leave from the local bus terminal on Praça da Bandeira. There are regular flights from Joinville to Curitiba (40 minutes), Florianópolis (30 minutes), Brasília (2½ hours), Rio (1½ hours) and São Paulo (one hour).

BUS

The **bus station** (☎ 3433 2991) is 2km southwest from the city center. Local buses go every 15 minutes to the city center. Viação Verdes Mares runs regular buses to Ilha de São Francisco (R$8, every one to two hours).

Other destinations include Curitiba (R$17, 2½ hours, hourly); São Paulo (R$62, *leito* R$110, eight hours, five daily); Florianópolis (R$33, 2½ hours, hourly); Blumenau (R$20, two hours, hourly); Porto Alegre (US$18, nine hours, daily); and Foz do Iguaçu (US$22, 16 hours, daily).

BLUMENAU

☎ 0xx47 / pop 288,600

Blumenau is not the only city in Santa Catarina that was founded by German settlers who transplanted their beer-brewing expertise and their taste for Alpine architecture to South America. But it is the best known, thanks in part to its uninhibited, over-the-top Oktoberfest. The annual beer-drinking extravaganza is among Brazil's largest street parties, second only to Carnaval in Rio.

Oktoberfest is what makes Blumenau famous, but it is not what makes the city German. Throughout the historic city center, the architecture is dominated by Germanic themes. Local restaurants specialize in *jägerschnitzel* and bratwurst, and several beer brands are brewed locally. Most telling, perhaps, are the clean streets, the bustling economy and the tall, fair population, many of whom still speak German in their homes.

Like other parts of Santa Catarina, Blumenau is also inhabited by descendents of Italian immigrants (who predated the Germans).

Information

Banco do Brasil (cnr Rua 15 de Novembro & Rua Amadeu da Luz) Money exchange and ATMs.

Secretary de Turismo (☎ 3322 6933; www.blumenau.com.br; Rua 15 de Novembro; ☯ 8am-5:30pm Mon-Fri) Stop by for information about the Vale Europeu. German-speaking staff.

Shopping Neumarkt (☎ 3326 5566; Rua 7 de Setembro; per hr US$4.50) Internet access, near Rua Padre Jacobs.

Sights

Learn about Blumenau's beginnings at the **Museu de Família Colonial** (☎ 3322 1676; Alameda Duque de Caxias 78; admission R$3; ☯ 9am-5pm Tue-Fri, 10am-4pm Sat-Sun), a group of houses that were occupied by the city's founder in the 1850s. Around the corner, the **Mausoléu Dr Blumenau** (☎ 3226 6990; Rua XV de Novembro 161; admission free; ☯ 9am-5pm Tue-Fri, 9am-noon & 2-4:30pm Sat, 9am-noon Sun) is the final resting place of Herman Bruno Otto Blumenau himself. There are also models of Lutheran churches around town, the most beautiful of which is **Igrega do Espírito Santo**, a gem from 1858 that still stands east of the center.

If you are more interested in gastronomy than history, visit the **Museu da Cerveja** (Praça Hercilio Luz) and its inviting Biergarten (see p346).

Rua XV Novembro is home to the city's best examples of Germanic architecture. Nearby, the modern **Igreja Matriz do São Paolo** is named for the only Brazilian saint, who incidentally was born in Italy.

Festivals & Events

All of the city's major festivals and events are held at Vila Germânica, a huge convention hall modeled after an Alpine villa.

Oktoberfest (☎ 3326 6901; www.oktoberfestblumenau .com.br; admission R$5-10 per day) A festive parade kicks off two weeks of folk music, dancing and beer drinking. Free admission for anyone in traditional German dress.

Fest Itália (☎ 3323 4043; www.festitalia.com.br) Celebrates the city's Italian heritage, with a week of pasta, wine and music in mid-July.

Sleeping

Book accommodations well in advance if you plan to be in Blumenau during Oktoberfest.

Pousada Grün Garten (☎ 3339 6529; www.grun garten.com.br; Rua São Paulo 2457; dm R$30, s/d without bath R$35/70, d/tw/tr with bath R$85/95/106) This clean, attractive HI hostel is 6km from the center in the suburb of Itoupava Seca. Laundry facilities and a restaurant are on site. Take bus 10 toward Fonte Aterro/Via Rua São Paulo. Discounted rates for HI members.

our pick **Hotel Glória** (☎ 3326 1988; www.hotelgloria .com.br; Rua 7 de Setembro 954; s/d/tr standard R$70/100/130, superior R$90/120/150; 🅿 🖳) With its wood-paneled entrance and a traditional German *kaffeehaus* (coffeehouse) attached, this hotel offers comfortable rooms and an old-world flair. Perks at Hotel Glória include free parking and free internet access.

Hotel Garden Terrace (☎ 3326 3544; Rua Padre Jacobs 45; s/d R$90/120/150; 🅿 🖳) The hotel does not exactly earn the four stars it claims, but it does boast a prime location just across from the city's modern cathedral. Higher floors have lovely views of Blumenau and the surrounding valley.

Himmelblau Palace Hotel (☎ 3036 5800; www .himmelblau.com.br; Rua 7 de Setembro 1415; s/d R$130/150; 🅿 🖳 🖭) This attractive brick façade fronts the city's main drag. Rooms are brightened by light yellow walls, fresh white moldings and simple, modern furniture.

Eating

Cafehaus Glória (☎ 3322 6944; Rua 7 de Setembro 954; buffet R$8-16) This old-world coffeehouse is famous for its *café colonial*, an afternoon

SANTA CATARINA

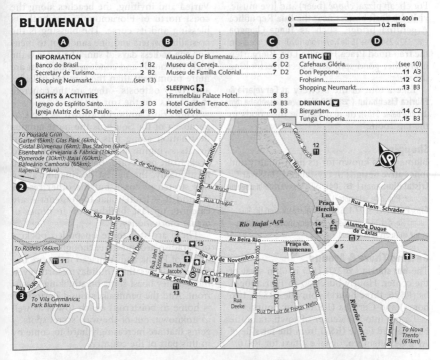

BLUMENAU

| 0   400 m |
| 0   0.2 miles |

INFORMATION
Banco do Brasil.................................1 B2
Secretary de Turismo.......................2 B2
Shopping Neumarkt.....................(see 13)

SIGHTS & ACTIVITIES
Igrego do Espírito Santo..................3 D3
Igreja Matriz de São Paulo...............4 B3

Mausoléu Dr Blumenau....................5 D3
Museu da Cerveja.............................6 D2
Museu de Família Colonial................7 D2

SLEEPING 🛏
Himmelblau Palace Hotel.................8 B3
Hotel Garden Terrace.......................9 B3
Hotel Glória....................................10 B3

EATING 🍴
Cafehaus Glória..........................(see 10)
Don Peppone..................................11 A3
Frohsinn..12 C2
Shopping Neumarkt........................13 B3

DRINKING 🍷
Biergarten......................................14 C2
Tunga Choperia..............................15 B3

To Pousada Grün Garten (5km); Glas Park (6km); Cristal Blumenau (6km); Bus Station (6km); Eisenbahn Cervejaria & Fábrica (10km); Pomerode (30km); Itajaí (60km); Balneário Camboriú (65km); Itapema (75km)

To Rodeio (46km)

To Vila Germânica; Park Blumenau

Rua Cidnal Sieich

Rua Itajaí

Rua República Argentina

2 de Setembro

Av Brasil

Rua Utugaí

Praça Hercílio Luz

Rua Alwin Schrader

Alameda Duque de Caxias

Rua São Paulo

Rua Amadeu da Luz

Rua N Deeke

Rua John Kennedy

Rua Padre Jacobs

Rua Dr Curt Hering

Rua XV de Novembro

Rio Itajaí-Açú

Av Beira Rio

Praça de Blumenau

Rua Floriano Peixoto

Rua Ângelo Dias

Rua Nereu Ramos

Av Rio Branco

Rua 7 de Setembro

Rua Deeke

Rua Dr Luiz de Freitas Melro

Riberião Garcia

Rua João Pessoa

Rua Amazonas

To Nova Trento (61km)

buffet (3pm to 8pm) that features cakes, pastries, pies and sandwiches. Lunchtime (11am to 2pm Monday to Saturday) means a more traditional Brazilian buffet, while evening brings out the soup buffet (6pm to 10pm Monday to Friday).

Don Peppone (☎ 3322 8682; Rua 7 de Septembro 2013; meals R$12-20) When you tire of sausages and sauerkraut, stop by this pizzeria to sample Blumenau's 'other' ethnic cuisine.

our pick **Park Blumenau** (☎ 3326 5000; Rua Alberto Stein 215; meals R$20) This typical biergarten is one of many on the fringes of Vila Germânica. Even if you are not here for Oktoberfest, it's worth visiting this Disneylike complex to celebrate your German heritage, or at least your love of German beer. *Ein Prosit!*

Frohsinn (☎ 3326 6050; Rua Gertrud Sierich; meals R$20-30) Perched atop Morro do Aipim, this fancy restaurant offers lovely views of Blumenau. Excellent selection of European fare.

For good variety and cheap prices, head to the food court at **Shopping Neumarkt** (☎ 3326 5566; Rua 7 de Setembro).

Drinking

For cheap pizza, *chope* (beer) and live music, visit the draft houses near the Rua República Argentina bridge, such as **Tunga Choperia** (☎ 3322 2549; Rua 15 de Novembro 1020). Located on the tree-lined Praça Hercílio Luz, Biergarten is another good spot for a beer overlooking the river.

Take a tour of the brewery at **Cervejaria & Fábrica Eisenbahn** (☎ 3330 7371; www.eisenbahn.com.br; Rua Bahia 5181), or just sample the goods in the tap room.

Shopping

Blumenau is known for its high-quality and innovative designs in crystal and glassware.

Cristal Blumenau (☎ 3041 5525; www.cristalblumenau.com.br; Rua 2 de Setembro 1330)

Glas Park (☎ 3327 1261; www.glaspark.com.br; Rua Rudolf Roedel 147) An onsite museum shows the history of the industry and the art.

Getting There & Around

The **bus station** (☎ 3323 2155) is 6km west of the center. Hourly buses go to Florianópolis (R$26, three hours), Joinville (R$20, two hours) and Curitiba (R$26, four hours).

To get into the center of town, take the bus marked Fonte (R$2) from the far side of Av 2 de Setembro, or take a taxi for R$10.

Around Blumenau

The collection of towns and villages around Blumenau that were settled by Italian and German immigrants is sometimes called **Vale Europeu**, as they still preserve their European culture today. During the 17 days of Oktoberfest, many of these villages host their own unique ethnic festivals.

For a profound insight into the region's Germanic roots, head 30km north of Blumenau to **Pomerode** (www.pomerode.com.br), where an estimated 80% of the population still speaks German (see the boxed text, opposite). Pomerode is home to the region's most renowned German restaurant, **Wunderwald** (☎ 3395 1700; Rua Ricardo Bahr 200), set in a 19th-century country house. Local buses go from Blumenau to Pomerode throughout the day.

The region's Italian heritage is alive and well in small towns like **Nova Trento** (61km south of Blumenau) and **Rodeio** (46km west). For more information, pick up the comprehensive booklet *Vale Europeu* from the tourist office in Blumenau.

NORTH OF FLORIANÓPOLIS

Varied and inviting, the beaches along the coast north of Florianópolis are both its blessing and its curse. The blessing is the crystalline waters and fine sand, not to mention the endless days of sun. The curse is the high-rise hotels and condominiums that are more prominent than the forested hillsides and rocky outposts – they are the concrete that blocks out the sun and sky.

Balneário Camboriú, known as the Copacabana of the South, is the most famous destination along this stretch, renowned for its swinging nightclubs and crowded oceanfront boulevard. Balneário Camboriú is, arguably, the ugliest destination along this stretch of coast, but the other resorts around it – from Itajaí to Itapema – are catching up fast, building up in hopes of luring more money.

There are still some unspoiled pockets of paradise around here, though. The twin towns of Penha and Armação feel more like fishing villages than holiday resorts, even though they boast some breathtaking beachfront. And the peninsula around Porto Belo is home to boisterous beach towns as well as unknown, out-of-the-way 'secret spots' – gems that are increasingly hard to come by in this part of the country.

SPRECHEN SIE DEUTSCH?

The first German immigrants arrived in the 1820s at the behest of Dom Pedro I. The southern part of the newly independent Brazil was still disputed by Argentina and Uruguay, and the emperor wanted to populate the region with loyal followers. Successive waves of immigrants arrived in the 1850s and the 1890s, then again around the two world wars. Contrary to popular imagination, most Germans who arrived in the 1940s were political and economic refugees, rather than Nazi leaders on the run.

For a century, German was the dominant language in many parts of southern Brazil. German speakers came from different regions of Germany and spoke different dialects, so they faced their own linguistic Babel. They often resorted to a kind of Creole, which incorporated Portuguese and local Indian languages. Italians facing a similar problem relied on 'Taliã,' an amalgamation of dialects based mainly on those of the Veneto region.

The 20th century took a toll on the German language in Brazil. The world wars led to the suppression of German in public institutions like schools and government. Industrialization and increasing economic integration brought the region into closer contact with Portuguese speakers. Finally, the arrival of radio and television, dominated by national networks, reinforced the use of Portuguese, especially among the young.

In the town of Pomerode, a confluence of forces has ensured the preservation of German language. Only in the last generation have decent roads linked Pomerode to Blumenau, so the town remained physically isolated from its neighbors. In addition, nearly all of its original settlers spoke the same dialect (Pomeranian), so there was no need to resort to Portuguese as a lingua franca. And the settlers were Lutheran, so German remained their language of worship. These days, there is a growing movement to preserve Brazil's bilingual communities.

Ilha do São Francisco

☎ 0xx47 / pop 37,700

The lovely city of São Francisco do Sul, 45km east of Joinville, is Brazil's third-oldest, founded in 1504 by the French explorer Binot Paulmier de Gonneville (only Bahía and São Vicente are older). A century later, the Portuguese arrived, in hopes of exploiting the city's strategic position at the mouth of Baía da Babitonga.

These days, the historical center is on the Patrimônio Histórico (National Heritage list), for its decadent, colonial feel. The bus from Joinville lets you off about 2km from the historic center, which lies on the island's west coast. Walk down Rua Fernandes Dias to the waterfront **Rua Babitonga**, which is lined with colonial houses, seafood restaurants and the beautifully restored **Mercado Público**.

BEACHES

The city acts as a gateway to the rest of the Ilha do São Francisco, a popular destination for sun-worshippers and surfers. The closest beaches are 12km to 15km from São Francisco do Sul, but they are all served by local bus.

At the southern end of the island, both **Prainha** and **Praia Grande** are ocean beaches exposed to a lot of swell. Closer to the city, **Praia da Ubatuba** and **Praia de Enseada** are safe for swimming, but they're developed and get very crowded on weekends. Some of the more secluded beaches are **Praia Itaguaçu** and **Praia do Forte** on the island's northern tip.

TOURS

Boats run by **Marujo Amigo** (☎ 3449 0875; www.maru joamigo.com.br; ☼ 10am-3pm) leave from Praia de Enseada for island tours. Fishing trips as well.

SLEEPING & EATING

In the city center, the sweetest spots overlook Baia Babitonga, including the lovely colonial **Kontiki Hotel** (☎ 3444 2232; www.hotelkontiki.com.br; Rua Babitonga 211; s/d R$50/90; ❄ ☐), and the larger and more luxurious **Zibamba Hotel** (☎ 3444 2020; Rua Ferndes Dias 27; s/d R$120/166, s/d/tr with sea view R$153/208/258; ❄ ☒).

Portela (☎ 3444 1579; Rua Babitonga 84; meals R$15-20) is a bustling seafood restaurant situated on a pier that juts out into the bay.

There are several hotels along Praia de Enseada (served by direct bus from Joinville). A more out-of-the-way option is **Hotel Porto de Paz** (☎ 3442 5706; Rua Roma 555, Praia de Itaguaçu; ❄ ☒), a charming colonial building on the island's most remote beach.

Penha & Armação

☎ 0xx47 / pop 16,600

These two villages are side by side along the north shore of a peninsula that juts out into the ocean, 110km north of Florianópolis. The crescent-shaped beach wraps around a bay dotted with colorful fishing boats. This beach – called **Praia do Quilombo**, **Praia da Armação** or **Praia da Fortaleza**, depending exactly where you are standing – is calm, clean and quiet. The idyllic village atmosphere changes slightly on summer weekends, however, when the main beachfront turns into one big *festa* (party).

To escape the crowds, head to **Praia Grande** (5km) at the peninsula's eastern tip, or **Praia Vermelha** (9km), south of Armação village. The latter requires a taxing drive over a rocky, red-earth *morro* (hill), which gives way to fine pink sand and iridescent blue waters.

For better or for worse, the landscape of this peninsula is changing rapidly, especially with the endless expansion of **Beto Carrero World** (☎ 3261 2354; www.betocarrero.com.br; Rua Inácio Francisco de Souza 1597; child/adult/senior R$65/78/39; ☺ 10am-6pm daily Nov-Feb & Jul, Thu-Sun Mar-Jun & Aug-Oct), a massive theme park.

The **tourist information office** (☎ 3345 3428; www.penha.sc.gov.br), located at the turnoff from Hwy SC-414, has information about local hotels and restaurants.

TOURS

Escuna Vónica (☎ 9981 2709; tickets R$15; ☺ 9am, 11am, 3pm & 5pm) takes a tour of the bay, departing from the village of Sul Piçarras.

SLEEPING & EATING

A few hotels and restaurants are clustered around the town center on the beach. Two options are **Hotel Itapocoroí** (☎ 3345 5015; www.hotelitapocoroi.com.br; Rua Maria da Costa 62; d without/with sea view R$70/90; ☒) and **Costamar Hotel** (☎ 3345 6861; www.costamarhotel.com; Av Elizabeth Kondor Reis 556; d R$70), both well located near the dock.

Sample the local cuisine, influenced by the flavors of the Azores, at the excellent **Peixe na Telha** (☎ 3398 0079; Rua Maria Emíila da Costa 92; meals R$30), which enjoys lovely waterside seating.

GETTING THERE & AWAY

Three buses a day come to Penha from Blumenau (three hours) and one from Joinville (four hours). Otherwise, there is a bus terminal at Piçarras (6km north), where you can take a local Circular or Navagantes bus to Penha and Armação.

Porto Belo & Around

☎ 0xx47

A small peninsula fans out from Porto Belo about 60km north of Florianópolis. Here, clear, emerald-green waters offer some of the best diving in southern Brazil.

Porto Belo is a fishing village, so the town beach is dominated by a big dock and boats moored in the bay. The principle swimming beaches are **Praia Bombinhas** (9km from Porto Belo) and the adjacent **Praia Bombas** (3km). These sandy stretches also offer accommodations – indeed they are lined with small-scale hotels and seafood restaurants. The crowd includes bikini-clad bathers and sand-covered kids – all lounging under colorful umbrellas and cooling off amidst the welcoming waves.

Experienced surfers should check out **Praia do Mariscal**, which faces the open sea; while beach bums in search of seclusion should head to **Praia Canto Grande**. The sparkling blue waters of **Caixa d'Aço** are protected by the rocky outpost that makes a tail off the tip of the peninsula. There is no beach, but you can hire a boat taxi to go to the **floating restaurants**, which invite swimming, snorkeling and sunbathing off their docks.

At the western end of Porto Belo, the **tourist office** (☎ 3369 5638; www.portobelo.com.br) has information about the whole peninsula.

SIGHTS

Located 900m off the coast, **Ilha de Porto Belo** (☎ 3369 4146; www.ilhadeportobelo.com.br; child/student/adult R$2/2/4; ☺ 9am-5:30pm daily Dec-Feb, Sat & Sun only Mar & Sep-Nov) is a nature reserve and *ecomuseu*. A well-marked hiking trail leads to scenic overlooks, ancient petroglyphs and a sandy beach. There are also a few decent snorkeling spots. Get a lift from a boat taxi (R$7) at Praça dos Pescadores in Porto Belo or at Bombinhas pier.

Back on the mainland, another educational opportunity is at the **Instituto Kat Schürmann** (☎ 3369 3690; www.schurmann.com.br; Av Vereador Manoel José dos Santos 220, Bombinhas; admission R$8; ☺ 2-8pm daily Dec-Feb, Sat only Mar-Nov). The Schürmann family are local celebrities, known for their worldwide travels and their research on marine biology. The visitor center in Bombinhas

has a 400m ecological trail, as well as exhibits and films about the family's expeditions.

DIVING

The **Reserva Biológica do Avoredo** consists of three islands surrounded by coral reefs that are home to fish, dolphins, stingrays and turtles. Day-long diving and snorkeling tours leave from the Bombinhas pier (baptism/discovery/certification/open-water R$150/170/500/700; 9am to 4pm). All three schools can arrange English-speaking instructors:

HyBrasil Mergulho (☎ 3369 2545; www.hybrazil.com .br; Av Vereador Manoel José dos Santos 205)

Patadacobra Adventures (☎ 3369 2119; www.patada cobra.com.br)

Submarine (☎ 3369 2473; www.submarinescuba.com.br; Rua Ver Manoel José dos Santos 1353)

SLEEPING & EATING

Both Porto Belo and Bombinhas are packed with places to stay. Expect discounts of up to 50% if you arrive outside of the busy summer months.

Pousada Sonho Meu (☎ 3369 4624; www.pousada sonhomeu.com; Rua São Luiz 500, Porto Belo; 🅿 🖨) Chalets are surrounded by greenery, with trails for those who wish to explore. The wide veranda offers views of the ocean in the distance.

Villa Oceânica (☎ 3393 6985; www.villaoceanica.com .br; Rua Cascudo; r R$150; 🅿 🖨) At the near end of Praia Bombinhas, this sweet retreat offers stylish guest rooms with cool white-tile floors and comfy king-size beds.

Pousada Vila do Farol (☎ 3393 9000; www.viladofarol .com.br; Av Vereador Manoel José dos Santos 800, Bombinhas; d R$590; 🅿 🖨 🖨) One of the biggest places in Bombinhas, this cluster of colorful, colonial-style buildings is right on the beach. Indeed, while sunning your bum, chairs, umbrellas and fruity cocktails are at your disposal, thanks to attentive beach service.

GETTING THERE & AWAY

You probably have to connect in Balneário Camboriú, from where 12 buses a day travel to Bombinhas, stopping in Porto Belo on the way. Hourly buses go to Balneário Cambroriú from Florianópolis, Joinville and Blumenau.

SOUTH OF FLORIANÓPOLIS

The waves have put this stretch of coastline on the map. Long gone are the quiet fishing villages and near-deserted beaches that once dotted the coast south of Florianópolis. While the local population is still largely descended from Azorean fishermen, you'll be hard pressed to find them amidst the suntanned surfers and bikini-clad beauties. The beaches that don't have big surf – and there are a few – are given over to fun-seeking families who show up every summer for their fix of sun and sand.

The coast south of Florianópolis is not as built up as that north of the city: your sun will not be blocked by the overgrowth of a concrete jungle. But most of the beaches are littered with smaller-scale hotels, campgrounds, beach bars, seafood shacks and all the business that caters to holidaymakers – during summer months you are unlikely to find a secluded spot. But that, again, may be part of the fun.

Guarda do Embaú

☎ 0xx48

Famous for its excellent left that breaks at the mouth of the river, Guarda do Embaú often makes the list of Brazil's best surfing beaches. But this spot 44km south of Florianópolis is virtually unknown outside the surf community. The place has a laid-back, hippy vibe – an excellent destination for wave riders, backpackers and other bohemian types.

For information on Guarda, see www.guarda doembau.com. Otherwise, check out **Sun Hostel da Guarda** (☎ 3283 2316; fernando@garopaba .com.br; Estrada Geral 713; d/tr/q R$45/70/80, chalets d/tr/q R$80/90/100; 🅿) or **Pura Vida Pousada** (☎ 3283 2252; puravidapousada@yahoo.com.br; d/tr/q R$150/200/240; 🅿).

Three daily Paulotur buses stop in Guarda en route to/from Pinheira and Garopaba. Some buses between Florianopolis and Garopaba also stop in Guarda.

Garopaba

☎ 0xx48 / pop 13,164

Garopaba – 95km south of Florianópolis – could well be the future of Guarda. Once a quiet Azorean fishing village, it was discovered by surfers, and then by the rest of the world. Now the quaint cobblestone village and the 18th-century architecture are nearly lost amidst the sprawl of souvenir shops. The long, smooth stretch of beach is beautiful – crowned at either end with tree-covered *morros* – but in summer it is inevitably packed.

Sunbathers and sand castle builders spread their beach towels out along the town beach, where waters are calm and cool. Surfers head 5km north to **Praia da Ferrugem** (www .praiadaferrugem.com.br) or 2km south to **Praia do**

SANTA CATARINA

Silveira, both of which have a few options for accommodations. For information on local surf schools, head to **Mormaii Surf Shop & Café** (☎ 3254 3733; www.mmsurfboards.com.br; Rua João Orestes do Araújo 1143; 🕙 10am-10pm), which doubles as a cool café and the flagship store for Brazil's most chic surf gear.

There are a bunch of internet cafés, as well as a Banco do Brasil, on Rua Pref João Orestes de Araujo, the main drag that leads to the beach.

SLEEPING & EATING

For a cheap sleep, there are a number of camp-grounds along the town beach.

Lobo Hotel (☎ 3254 3745; www.lobohotel.com.br; Rua Marques Guimarães 81; s/d R$30/40) This affordable hotel – one block from the beach – is excellent value. Basic rooms are spacious and airy; service is laid-back and friendly.

Pousada da Praia (☎ 3254 3334; www.pousadada praiagaropaba.com.br; Av dos Pescadores 121; s/d R$77/77, with ocean view R$98/110; 😭) This beachfront, family-run pousada is not particularly original, but its brick walls and white linens do lend an element of rustic sophistication. Rooms with sea views boast spacious balconies.

Pousada Barramares (☎ 3254 341; www.garopaba surf.com.br/barramares; Rua Maria Antônia dos Santos 489; s/d R$55/75; 😭) An affordable, comfortable option near the bus station.

Sandwich shops and pizza places line the Rua Pref João Orestes de Arajuo. One of the region's finer dining options is **Bistro do Cais** (☎ 3254 3325; Praça 21 de Abril 2; meals R$30-40; 🕙 6pm-midnight), a delightful seafood restaurant in a charming old Azorean-style house on the town's old main square.

GETTING THERE & AROUND

The **bus station** (☎ 3355 0090) is 1km north of the center. Regular buses connect Garopaba with Florianópolis (R$14, two hours), while there are local buses to Guarda do Embaú (R$8), Praia do Rosa (R$2) and other local beaches.

Praia do Rosa

☎ 0xx48 / pop 900

Santa Catarina's swankiest seaside town, Praia do Rosa, is about 15km south of Garopaba. Rosa has two things going for it: a set of stunning, nearly pristine beaches and a sophisticated, eco-aware population. Not to mention the many opportunities for surfing.

In winter, the bay becomes a breeding ground for southern right whales, and mothers and calves can be seen from the beach. Instituto Baleia Franca, a conservation group created to protect and study these unique mammals, is based here (see the boxed text on opposite).

Rosa has no tourist office but there is plenty of information on the website of the **Pousadas da Praia do Rosa Associadas** (PROA; www.praiadorosa -brasil.com.br).

SLEEPING & EATING

The highest road in town, Caminho do Rei, is home to accommodations options with sweeping views.

Albergue do Rosa (☎ 3355 6614; www.gsurf.com .br/dindarosa; r per person US$25; 🖳) Head here for cheap digs in the middle of town. Rooms are tiny and bathrooms are shared. Bonus: onsite internet access and 24-hour snack bar.

La Roca (☎ 3355 6471 www.laroca.com.br; Caminho do Rei; d R$100) Built into rocky hillside, this Bed-rock-style place has cool stone walls and shiny wood floors that evoke an eco-stylish atmosphere. The shared balcony offers ocean views from the upper floors, while the lower floors are engulfed in greenery.

Pousada Caminho do Rei (☎ 3355 6062; www.caminho dorei.com.br; Caminho do Rei d R$220-320, plus R$40 per person; 😭 🖳) Each of the eight units in this complex boasts a jaw-dropping, gorgeous view of the beach below and the sea beyond. Perks include private verandas, king-size beds and bathtubs with a view.

Fazenda Verde do Rosa (☎ 3355 7272; www.fazenda verdedorosa.com.br; chalets R$300-500; 😭 🖳 😭) Spread across a stunning bluff above the beach, this place has colorful chalets that sleep four to six people, all with kitchen facilities and private terraces. Facilities include guided hikes, surf lessons and horseback riding (open to the public). The hotel also has three excellent restaurants – French, seafood and pizza – all with breezy decks and fabulous ocean views.

GETTING THERE & AWAY

Local buses run to Garopaba (R$2, every two hours), from you where you can continue on to Florianópolis; or to Imbituba (R$2, five daily), for Porto Alegre.

Laguna

☎ 0xx48 / pop 47,600

About 110km south of Florianópolis, Laguna has a quaint colonial center. Over the

---

THE WHALES ARE ALL RIGHT

Every winter, between June and October, hundreds of southern right whales return to the Santa Catarina coast. These massive mammals can be 18m long and can weigh more than 60 tons. They come north from the frigid waters of Antarctica, in search of a warmer, calmer place to spawn. When the calves are born, they are usually 3m or 4m long, already weighing as much as five tons.

The right whales were on the brink of extinction in the 1970s. Their huge size and slow speeds made them prime targets for commercial fishermen. The primary goal of the **Instituto Baleia Franca** (IBF; ☎ 3355 6111; www.baleiafranca.org.br) is to monitor and protect these amazing creatures. The organization contributed to the creation of the Right Whale Environmental Protection Area off the Santa Catarina coast in 2001; now the population is estimated at 7000 and growing rapidly.

The whales and their calves frolic in the waters very close to shore, and are often visible from the beach. Take your binoculars and go to high ground and you may spot their mammoth forms breaching or batting their fins. For a closer encounter, take a whale-watching tour with **Turismo Vida Sol e Mar** (☎ 3355 6111; www.vidasolemar.com.br; per person R$90 Mon-Fri, R$140 Sat & Sun; ☑ 8am & 11am). The tours last for 90 minutes or more, depending on the location of the whales. Each boat has an IBF scientist on board, but whale sightings are not guaranteed. It's best to allow a couple of days for this outing, as it also depends on weather conditions.

---

hill, the beach at **Mar Grosso** is less enticing. For more elbow room, head to the terrific beaches around **Farol da Santa Marta**, 18km south of town.

The old town dates to 1676. While wandering its cobblestone streets and squares, peek in the **Museu Anita Garibaldi** (Praça Anita Garibaldi; admission US$1; ☑ 8am-6pm), which honors the Brazilian wife of the Italian leader. Nearby, the **Casa de Anita Garibaldi** (Praça Vidal Ramos; admission US$1; ☑ 8am-6pm) is where she grew up.

The main drag in Mar Grosso is Avenida Senador Gallotti, which runs parallel to the beach. Here you'll find the **tourist office** (☎ 3646 0533; www.laguna.sc.gov.br) as well as a slew of hotels and restaurants.

TOURS
Associação de Guias (☎ 9977 6352) Leads tours to the Farol Santa Marta and to some archaeological sites in the area.
Scuna Garibaldi (☎ 9129 8761; per person R$15; ☑ 10am, 3pm & 6pm) This two-hour boat ride departs from the historic center.

SLEEPING & EATING
Many hotels in Mar Grosso are only open on weekends from March to November.
Hotel Recanto (☎ 3644 0902; Rua Engenho Colombo Salles 108; r per person R$25) No-frills rooms near the bus station.
Atlântico Sul Hotel (☎ 3647 1166; www.atlanticosul laguna.com.br; Av Senador Gallotti 360; s/d/tr from

R$70/98/120; ☒ ☒) This block along the main drag in Mar Grosso is no beauty, but it does offer good value.

In Mar Grosso, there are several old-style seafood restaurants, including **Arrastão** (☎ 3647 0418; Av Senador Galotti 629; meals R$20-25). In the old town, the per-kilo **Restaurante Praç de Anita** (Praça República Juliana; per kg R$10; ☑ 11am-3pm Mon-Sat) serves excellent, Azorean-influenced food in an airy colonial house.

GETTING THERE & AROUND
The long-distance **bus station** (☎ 3646 0119) is on the edge of the old town. From here you can catch a local bus to Mar Grosso or to the Farol da Santa Marta. Long-distance destinations include Porto Alegre (R$25, six hours) and Torres (R$20, four hours, two daily) in Rio Grande do Sul; and Florianópolis (R$15, two hours, five daily) and Imbituba (R$5, one hour, eight daily) in Santa Catarina.

SERRA GERAL
Santa Catarina is better known for its beaches than its mountains, but this gorgeous mountain range – located about 250km west of Florianópolis – should not be overlooked. With peaks up to 1800m, this is the coolest part of Brazil, often accumulating snow during the winter months. The mountains and canyons offer opportunities for hiking, horseback riding and otherwise getting off the beaten track.

SANTA CATARINA

São Joaquim

☎ 0xx49 / pop 19,000

High in the mountains of the Serra do Rio do Rastro (an offshoot of the Serra Geral), São Joaquim is about 290km southwest of Florianópolis. This little town in the Rio Canoas valley is famous for its apple orchards, many of which were planted by the local Japanese population. São Joaquim's other claim to fame is its snowfall: come in early July for the annual **Festival de Inverno**.

About 45km from here, via a hair-raising but spectacular winding road, the **Parque Nacional de São Joaquim** boasts a breathtaking landscape of grassy highlands and thick *araucária*

forests. Here, you'll find Santa Catarina's highest peak, the **Morro da Igreja** (1822m). The park does not have much infrastructure, but there are hiking trails leading to panoramic lookouts and freefalling waterfalls. Inquire for more information at the **tourist information center** (☎ 3278 4245) in Urubici.

The most affordable sleeping option is **Nevada Hotel** (☎ 3233 0259; Rua Manoel Joaquim Pinto 190; r R$80). For a bit of rustic luxury, try the **Villa da Montanha** (☎ 3278 4132; www.villadamontanha.com; d R$180), 10km from the center, with hiking trails and horseback riding.

There are daily buses to and from Florianópolis (R$22, 5½ hours).

Rio Grande do Sul

Brazil's southernmost state is covered largely by pampas, the grassy plains that supported centuries of cattle-herding. Much of this land is now actually used to cultivate soybean crops; but the cowboy culture endures.

So it is that residents of Rio Grande do Sul call themselves *gaúchos,* after the independent-minded ranchers and cattle herders that settled the state. In the countryside, it is not unusual to see old-timers sporting wide-brimmed hats and other traditional dress. Grilled meat, or *churrasco,* is still the state's favorite food, and everywhere, everywhere, locals suck down *chimarrão,* the distinctive tea made from the maté plant. Such traditions remain, even in the cosmopolitan capital of Porto Alegre.

The unique *gaúcho* culture is not the only thing that lures visitors to Rio Grande do Sul. In the state's northeastern corner, the earth opens up in an amazing geological display, giving way to the spectacular Serra Gaúcha. These mountains offer unlimited opportunities for hiking and other adventures, from the forest-covered canyons of the national parks near Cambará do Sul to the cascaded river valleys around Canela.

In the Vale dos Vinhedos, Italian-descended vintners are producing wines that rival the best vintages from Chile and Argentina. Inspired by the mountain scenery and influenced by their German and Italian heritage, towns like Gramado cast themselves as Brazilian alpine villages, selling fancy chocolates and publicizing their annual snowfall. In so many ways, Rio Grande do Sul defies notions of typical Brazil, which only makes this southern state more alluring.

RIO GRANDE DO SUL

HIGHLIGHTS

- Bargain for trash and treasures at the Sunday morning flea market at **Parque Farroupilha** (p357) in Porto Alegre

- Sample the crisp whites and earthy reds from the **Vale dos Vinhedos** (p360)

- Admire the views from the *teleférico* (chairlift) In **Parque Floresta Encantada** (p362) in Canela

- Hike the **Trilha do Mirante** and peer over the edge of the **Cânion da Fortaleza** (p364) in the Parque Nacional da Serra Geral

- Uncover the mystery of the Jesuit mission at **São Miguel das Missões** (p366)

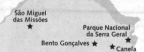

São Miguel das Missões ★
Parque Nacional da Serra Geral ★
Bento Gonçalves ★   ★ Canela
Porto Alegre ★

- POPULATION: 10.8 MILLION | - AREA: 282,062 SQ KM

History

Living on land long disputed by the Spanish and Portuguese, the people of Rio Grande do Sul used the conflict to create an identity distinct from the rest of Brazil. The region even declared its independence during the ill-fated Guerra dos Farrapos, a decade-long civil war ending in 1845. A wave of immigrants, mostly German, Italian and Swiss, began arriving in the late-19th century, reinforcing the region's cultural differences.

Climate

The Brazilian state sitting furthest from the equator, Rio Grande do Sul has the most temperate climate in Brazil, with hot summers and cool winters. The mountains of the Serra Gaúcha north of Porto Alegre even see occasional snow. That said, the climate is subtropical in the coastal lowlands, with hot, humid summers.

National Parks

Parque Nacional Aparados da Serra occupies 10,250 hectares on the border between Rio Grande do Sul and Santa Catarina. North and south of Aparados da Serra, the parkland was extended in 1992 with the creation of the Parque Nacional da Serra Geral. These parks preserve some of the country's last araucaria forests, as well as a series of stunning canyons that offer opportunities for hiking, horseback riding and rock climbing.

RIO GRANDE DO SUL

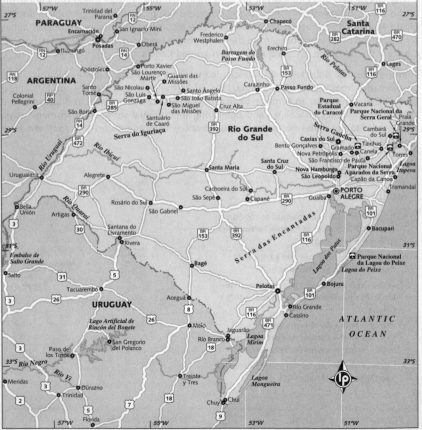

Getting There & Around

Porto Alegre is the state's transportation hub, with air and bus services to every major city in Brazil. Excellent roads and the efficient regional bus service makes traveling within the state relatively easy, with most long-distance routes originating in Porto Alegre.

PORTO ALEGRE

☎ 0xx51 / pop 1.44 million

On the banks of the huge freshwater Lagoa dos Patos, Porto Alegre is southern Brazil's most important port city and a key player in Mercosul (South American free-trade agreement). It is also, thanks to its well-educated and forward-thinking population, one of the most sophisticated cities in Brazil.

The downtown area has benefited from a thoughtful approach to development, including the creation of transportation hubs and the preservation of much of the grand, neoclassical architecture. A long tradition of progressive politics has helped nurture vibrant arts and alternative music scenes, and the well-organized gay and lesbian community recently won the right to register domestic partnerships.

Unfortunately, crime levels in the city have risen in recent years and the downtown area can be dangerous after dark.

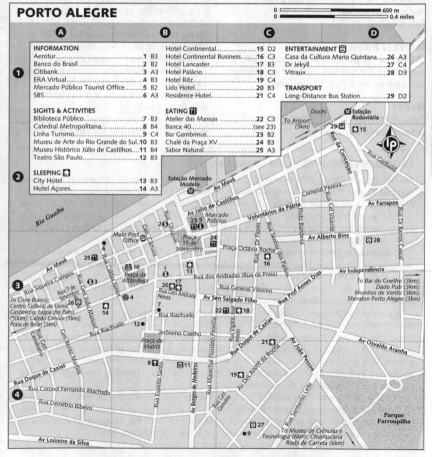

PORTO ALEGRE

0 ————— 600 m
0 ————— 0.4 miles

INFORMATION
Aerotur...1 B3
Banco do Brasil..............................2 B2
Citibank...3 A3
ERA Virtual....................................4 B3
Mercado Público Tourist Office.........5 B2
SBS..6 A3

SIGHTS & ACTIVITIES
Biblioteca Público..........................7 B3
Catedral Metropolitana...................8 B4
Linha Turismo.................................9 C4
Museu de Arte do Rio Grande do Sul..10 B3
Museu Histórico Júlio de Castilhos...11 B4
Teatro São Paulo............................12 B3

SLEEPING
City Hotel.......................................13 B3
Hotel Açores..................................14 A3

Hotel Continental...........................15 D2
Hotel Continental Business.............16 C3
Hotel Lancaster..............................17 B3
Hotel Palácio..................................18 C3
Hotel Ritz.......................................19 C4
Lido Hotel......................................20 B3
Residence Hotel.............................21 C4

EATING
Atelier das Massas.........................22 C3
Banca 40.................................(see 23)
Bar Gambrinus...............................23 B2
Chalé da Praça XV..........................24 B3
Sabor Natural.................................25 A3

ENTERTAINMENT
Casa da Cultura Mario Quintana......26 A3
Dr Jekyll..27 C4
Vitraux..28 D3

TRANSPORT
Long-Distance Bus Station.............29 D2

RIO GRANDE DO SUL

ORIENTATION

The Mercado Público (Public Market) is the focal point of the city center and the transportation hub, with a metro station and a local bus terminal. The vibrant shopping and nightlife district, Moinhos de Vento, is about 3km east of the center. Praia de Belas is a long city park that runs along the lakeshore south of the center.

INFORMATION

Bookstores

SBS (☎ 3228 1260; Rua Caldas Júnior; ◷ 9am-6pm Mon-Fri, 9am-1pm Sat) Small selection of English-language classics.

Emergency

Bombeiros (☎ 193) Handles fire emergencies.
Medical emergencies (☎ 192)
Polícia Federal (☎ 194)

Internet Access

ERA Virtual (☎ 3061 7333; Rua dos Andradas 1001; per hr R$4.20; ◷ 9am-9pm Mon-Sat) One of several internet cafés inside the Rua da Praia Shopping Center.

Money

Aerotur (☎ 3228 8144; Rua dos Andradas 1137) Exchanges traveler's checks and cash.

Banco do Brasil (Av Uruguai 185) Offers cash exchange and ATMs.
Citibank (Rua 7 de Setembro 722)

Tourist Information

Airport tourist office (☎ 3358 2000; www.portoalegre.rs.gov.br; ◷ 7:30am-midnight)
Mercado Público Tourist Office (◷ 9am-8pm Mon-Sat) Inside the main entrance of the Mercado Público.

SIGHTS

Praça 15 de Novembro, site of the 1869 **Mercado Público** (www.mercadopublico.com.br), is the centerpiece of the city. The old building bustles during daytime hours, when vendors sell fresh produce, meats and seafood, as well as the all-important *erva maté* for *chimarrão* (see the boxed text on p359).

A pedestrian promenade runs into Praça Alfândega, the leafy square that is home to the **Museu de Arte do Rio Grande do Sul** (MARGS; ☎ 3227 2311; www.margs.org.br; Praça Alfândega; admission free; ◷ 10am-7pm Tue-Sun). The neoclassical building is an impressive venue for regional artists. On the ground floor, the inviting Bistrot de MARGS takes advantage of the leafy setting, which is a lovely spot for lunch.

Three blocks south, the picturesque Praça da Matriz is dominated by the early-20th-century,

---

PROGRESSIVE POLITICS IN RIO GRANDE DO SUL

Rio Grande do Sul has a long history of contrariness. The state's *farroupilhas* (political extremists) revolted against the Brazilian emperor in the 1830s and 1840s, declaring a short-lived republic. In the late 1970s, strikes by *gaúcho* (cowboy) trade unions helped weaken the military junta ruling the country. In 2001, the city hosted the first World Social Forum (like a World Economic Forum for lefties). And in March 2004, in a country that is overwhelmingly Catholic, the state's high court declared same-sex unions a civil right.

In progressive political circles, Porto Alegre is best known for its innovative approach to local politics called Orcamento Participativo, or participatory budgeting. In the late 1980s, the Workers' Party instituted this radical reform in attempt to improve democratic institutions and to create citizen ownership. It is a complex system that gives residents a direct role in setting priorities and creating the municipal budget.

In principle, participatory budgeting creates opportunities for the impoverished, the uneducated and the otherwise disenfranchised to get involved in the decision making process. In practice, the trend seems to be increased spending in lower-income neighborhoods. More generally, studies suggest that it results in greater government transparency and increased levels of public participation. Now throughout Brazil, hundreds of municipalities are experimenting with participatory budgeting, as they see the results achieved in Porto Alegre. This system has also been replicated in other cities throughout Latin America.

In 2004, the Workers' Party suffered a surprising defeat in local elections. Despite the changing of the guard, however, participatory budgeting continues (at least in principle). How this plays out in practice remains to be seen. But it will be difficult to deter the thousands of citizens who have become educated about local issues and are active in community groups.

neoclassical **Catedral Metropolitana**. On the northern side, you'll find the elegant mid-19th-century edifice of the **Teatro São Pedro** and the sculpted façade of the **Biblioteca Público**. Nearby is the **Museu Histórico Júlo de Castilos** (☎ 3221 3959; Rua Duque de Caxias 1231; admission free; ☽ 10am-7pm Tue-Fri, 1:30-5pm Sat & Sun), displaying *gaúcho* artifacts in a typical 19th-century home.

About 2km southeast of the cathedral lies **Parque Farroupilha**, the city's largest park and home to a sprawling flea market on Sunday morning.

Also southeast of the center, the **Museu de Ciências e Tecnologia** (MCT; ☎ 3320 3597; www.mct .pucrs.br; Av Ipiranga 6681; adult/student/child R$10/7/7, planetarium R$2; ☽ 9am-5pm Tue-Sun) is the huge impressive science museum of the Pontifícia Universidade Católica. Exhibits cover everything from astronomy to physics to biology, with plenty of opportunities for hands-on experimentation. Take bus 343 or 353 from the Mercado Público.

TOURS
Cisne Branco (☎ 3224 5222; www.barcocisnebranco.com .br; Av Presidente João Goulart 551) River trips include one-hour cruises down the river (R$15; ☽ 10:30am, 3pm & 4:30pm), two-hour happy hour cruises and all-day cruises. They depart from the Centro Cultural do Usino Gasômetro.
Linha Turismo (☎ 3212 3464; Travessa do Carmo 84; R$3.50; ☽ 10:30am, 1:30pm, 3pm & 4:30pm Tue-Sun) Offers 90-minute rides on a double-decker bus. Some tour guides speak English.

SLEEPING
Budget
our pick **Hotel Ritz** (☎ 3225 0693; hotelritz_ptoalegre @hotmail.com; Av Des André da Rocha 225; s/d without bathroom R$28/42, s/d with bathroom R$35/55) Tiny, clean rooms surround a sweet courtyard that is filled with blooming trees – a fantastic place to meet other travelers. Breakfast not included.

Hotel Palácio (☎ 3225 3467; Rua Vigário José Inácio 644; s/d without bathroom R$33/52, s/d with bathroom R$45/70) The spacious rooms in institutional green feel like dorms. Fortunately the rooms are clean and well lit, making this a decent budget choice.

Hotel Lancaster (☎ 3224 4737; www.hotel-lancaster -poa.com.br; Travessa Eng Acelino de Carvalho 67; s/d/tr R$60/90/130; ⊠) Yellow shutters adorn this art-deco facade, which you enter from the pedestrian passageway. Inside, the quarters are cozy, clean and cramped.

Hotel Açores (☎ 3321 7588; www.acoreshotel.com .br; Rua dos Andradas 85; s/d/tr R$78/92/102; ⊠ ☐) The main advantage is its excellent location – central yet tranquil. Rooms are looking a little worse for wear, but they are spacious and comfortable.

Midrange
Lido Hotel (☎ 3228 9111; www.lidohotel.com.br; Rua General Andrade Neves 150; s/d R$82/106; ⊠ ☐) The lobby at the Lido is refreshingly crisp and uncluttered, though the staff takes itself too seriously. Simple, sparkling rooms are invariably fresh – a welcome retreat from the nonstop bustle outside.

Hotel Continental Business (☎ 3027 1600; www .hotelcontinentalbusiness.com.br; Praça Otávio Rocha 49; r weekend/weekday R$90/120; ⊠ ☐) Short on charm but long on comfort, this towering hotel offers reasonable rooms and professional service. As per the name, it caters mainly to business travelers. Its sister property near the bus station has slightly higher rates.

Residence Hotel (☎ 3225 8644; www.residence hotel.com.br; Av Des André da Rocha 131; s/d R$110/138, ste s/d R$129/158; ⊠ ☐) Long-term guests are attracted to in-room kitchenettes and reduced rates for extended stays. Even if you are only in town for a few days, you will appreciate the fresh simple style at this new hotel, not to mention the attractive location near Parque Farroupilha.

City Hotel (☎ 3212 5488; www.cityhotel.com.br; Rua Dr José Montaury 20; s/d/tr R$140/160/190; ⊠ ☐) In the heart of downtown, this Beaux Arts classic maintains a sense of grandeur. The lobby is small but swanky in an old-fashioned way, while guestrooms are modern.

Top End
Sheraton Porto Alegre (☎ 2121 6000; www.sheraton -poa.com.br; Rua Olavo Barreto Viana 18; r from R$300; ⊠ ☐ ☒) The fanciest digs in town are 3km east of the center, in the upscale neighborhood of Moinhos de Vento. Streets lined with quaint cafés and chic boutiques and the popular Parque Moinhos make this a prime locale for splurge seekers.

EATING
Many of the entertainment venues along Rua Fernando Gomes (see Entertainment, p358) are also excellent eating options.
Banca 40 (☎ 3226 3533; Mercado Público; ice cream R$3-6; ☽ 9am-7pm) This family-owned bakery

and creamery serves up distinctive ice cream made from 50-year-old recipes. Try a scoop (R$2.30) of an exotic flavor like *coco* (coconut) or *milho* (corn).

Sabor Natural (☎ 3028 0539; Rua Siqueira Campos 890; buffet R$10; ☒ lunch Mon-Fri) Vegetarians will delight at this all-organic, meat-free all-you-can-eat buffet that caters to the downtown lunch crowd. Enjoy limitless soups, salads and other animal-friendly fare.

Bar Gambrinus (☎ 3226 6914; Mercado Público; meals R$25-30; ☒ lunch daily, dinner Mon-Fri) This Portuguese restaurant in the Mercado Público is popular for its old-world aura and extremely fresh seafood.

Churrascaria Roda de Carreta (☎ 3336 0817; Av Ipiranga 5300; buffet R$30; ☒ lunch & dinner) This *churrascaria* was founded by the local Center of Gaúcho Tradition (CTG) to celebrate *gaúcho* customs, from food and drink to song and dance. The huge buffet features 17 kinds of grilled meats and countless other hot and cold dishes. The highlight is the rousing cabaret (see the Local Voices chapter, p13). Churrascaria Roda de Carreta is located near the Shopping Bourbon Ipiranga.

Galpão Crioulo (☎ 3226 8194; Parque Maurício Sirotsky Sobrinho; buffet R$30; ☒ lunch & dinner) Considered one of the city's best *churrascaria* for its extensive all-you-can-eat buffet and well-stocked wine cellar. The designated Mestre do Chimarrão (Chimarrão Master) means that this is an excellent place to sample that local specialty (see opposite).

our pick **Atelier das Massas** (☎ 3225 8888; Rua Riachuelo 1482; meals R$30-40; ☒ 11am-11pm Mon-Sat) An artistic flair shines bright at this downtown joint, where the walls are crammed with original artwork and funky photographs. The menu is no less creative, with an irresistible antipasti buffet and delectable homemade pastas.

Chale da Praça XV (☎ 3225 2667; Praça 15 de Novembro; meals R$30-40; ☒ noon-midnight) Housed in a pleasant, Victorian-style garden house and surrounded by a sprawling terrace, this Porto Alegre institution buzzes with activity starting at happy hour, around 6pm.

ENTERTAINMENT

Pick up a copy of *Jornal do Nuances* for nightlife listings.

Casa da Cultura Mario Quintana (☎ 3221 7147; www.ccmq.rs.gov.br; Rua dos Andradas 736) The cultural center in this pink baroque building has a cinema and two busy cafés. The 7th-floor Café

Concerto Majestic is a lovely place to listen to live music and watch the sunset over Lagoa dos Patos.

Centro Cultural do Usino Gasômetro (☎ 3212 5979; Av Presidente João Goulart 551; admission free) On the banks of the Lagoa dos Patos, this former factory now houses art cinemas, temporary art exhibitions and a pleasant café.

Dr Jekyll (☎ 3226 9404; Travessa do Carmo 76) This underground club hosts alternative rock bands and their raucous fans.

Other bars and clubs are concentrated around Av Goethe and Rua Fernando Gomes (known as 'The Walk of Fame') in Moinhos de Vento. A couple of favorites:

Dado Pub (☎ 3395 1468; Rua Fernando Gomes 80)

Bar do Goethe (☎ 3222 2043; Rua 24 de Outubro 112)

Porto Alegre has an active gay and lesbian social scene, with hotspots such as the dance club **Vitraux** (☎ 3221 7799; Rua Conceição 492; ☒ 11pm Fri & Sat & 10pm Sun).

GETTING THERE & AWAY
Air

Porto Alegre's modern **Aeroporto Internacional Salgado Filho** (☎ 3358 2000) is located 6km from downtown. Take a taxi (R$25, 15 minutes) or ride the metro (R$2, 30 minutes).

Direct flights go to São Paulo (one hour), Rio de Janeiro (1½ hours), Florianópolis (40 minutes), Curitiba (one hour) and Brasília (2½ hours), as well as Montevideo and Buenos Aires.

Bus

The busy **long-distance bus station** (☎ 3210 0101; www.rodoviaria-poa.com.br), on Largo Vespiano Júlio Veppo, is accessible by metro; Alternatively, a taxi costs R$8.

Destinations within Rio Grande do Sul include Torres (R$30 to R$38, three hours, six daily), Gramado (R$22, two hours, seven daily), Canela (R$24, 2½ hours, seven daily), Pelotas (R$38, three hours, eight daily), Cambará do Sul (R$23, six hours, one daily) via São Francisco de Paula, and Santo Ângelo (R$68, *leito* R$108, seven hours, eight daily). One overnight *semidireto* (semidirect) bus goes to Chuí on the Uruguayan border (R$77, seven hours); otherwise you can connect in Pelotas.

Buses travel interstate to Foz do Iguaçu (US$28, 14 hours), Florianópolis (R$32, seven hours), Curitiba (R$79 to R$85, 11 hours, three daily) and Rio de Janeiro city (R$208, 25 hours, twice daily). International

RIO GRANDE DO SUL

destinations include Montevideo (12 hours), Buenos Aires (18 hours), and Santiago (36 hours).

GETTING AROUND

Porto Alegre has a clean and efficient one-line metro that connects downtown with both the long-distance bus station and the airport. Once you are downtown, virtually all the city's main attractions are within a 15-minute walk of the metro's final stop, just behind the Mercado Público.

SERRA GAÚCHA

North of Porto Alegre, the flat coastal land disappears, as the roads climb into the mountains of the Serra Gaúcha. This scenic stretch – particularly beautiful between Nova Petrópolis and Gramado – is characterized by forested hillsides and unexpected rocky cliffs, often sparkling with waterfalls.

The region was first settled by Germans (beginning in 1824) and later by Italians (starting in the 1870s), and this heritage is still a source of pride and fascination. Although the mountains don't reach much more than 1000m, Gramado and Canela resemble Swiss villages in their architecture and atmosphere. In Bento Gonçalves and the nearby Vale dos Vinhedos, fountains flow with *vino*, as descendants of Italian immigrants foster a burgeoning wine industry.

Many visitors come to the Serra Gaúcha in winter (June to August) in hopes of catching sight of snow; higher altitudes get a couple of inches a year. In spring the hills are blanketed with wildflowers, while thousands of hydrangeas bloom well into summer. Hiking is excellent year-round, particularly in the Parque Nacional Aparados da Serra.

BENTO GONÇALVES

☎ 0xx54 / pop 103,000

Considering the region's Italian heritage and its dry, mountainous landscape, it makes sense that Rio Grande do Sul would be a center for wine production. Since the 1970s, Brazilian vineyards have been implementing higher quality standards and upgrading production techniques, turning out tempting cabernets and chardonnays. The region's sparkling wines have received particularly high marks, so don't bypass the bubbly.

The center for this burgeoning wine industry is Bento Gonçalves, 124km north of Porto Alegre. It is a large, loud city that does not offer much besides convenient access to the region's vineyards. West of here, however, in the Vale dos Vinhedos, rows of grapevines blanket the hills; stone farmhouses and steepled churches dot the landscape. This is the idyllic setting for more than two dozen wineries, ranging from small family-run enterprises to larger, more industrial operations.

Every year in January and February, the city hosts **Fenavinho** (www.fenavinhobrasil.com.br) to celebrate and promote the wine industry.

CHEERS TO CHIMARRÃO

Rio Grande do Sul is among Brazil's most modern and most sophisticated states. Yet even the most *moderno gaúcho* (modern cowboy) reaches for a gourd when he needs a lift.

It was the Guarani Indians who taught Spanish settlers the pleasures of *chimarrão* (tea from the maté plant) and how to sip it not from a cup but through a *bomba* (straw) stuck into a hollowed-out *cuia* (gourd). Also known as *erva maté*, this tea-like beverage is made from the leaves of the maté tree, which is native to the pampas (grassy plains) that extend from Argentina and Uruguay through southern Brazil.

The original *gaúchos*, the men who tended the region's vast cattle herds, quickly became addicted to maté's pleasurable effects, which are at once energizing and calming. They even grew to love its bittersweet taste, perhaps because it reflected the lives they led on the empty plains. Even the act of sucking at the straw seems to satisfy an ancient yearning. *Chimarrão* is an acquired taste and a serious addiction.

These days, this ancient tradition is getting a boost from scientists and pseudoscientists alike, who make claims about maté's health benefits, from lower blood pressure to increased intelligence. Hard results are yet to come. However, you might make your own study by sampling *chimarrão* at Galpão Crioulo (opposite).

Orientation & Information

The main drag in Bento is Rua Marechal Deodoro, where you will find a few hotels and the **tourist information office** (☎ 3453 6699; www.bentogoncalves.rs.gov.br; Rua Marechal Deodoro 70; ☷ 9am-6pm Mon-Sat).

Sights & Activities

The entrance to Bento Gonçalves is marked by the **Pórtico da Pipa**, a gigantic wine barrel that straddles the street. This is also the gateway to the **Vale dos Vinhedos** (☎ 3451 9601; www.valedosvinhedos.com.br), the wine region that stretches 5km to the west along the Estrada do Vinho and Via Trento. Most of the wineries in the Vale dos Vinhedos are open for tours and tastings. Pick up a map and directory from the tourist office in Bento.

The only winery in the city center is the **Vinícola Aurora** (☎ 3455 2000; www.vinicolaaurora.com .br; Rua Olavo Bilac 500; tours & tastings free; ☷ 8:15am-5:15pm Mon-Sat, 8:30-11:30am Sun), located one block north of the train station. From the Aurora vineyards on the outskirts of town, the grape juice flows to this production facility via an underground pipe network.

Twice a week, the steam engine **Maria Fumaça** (☎ 3455 2788; www.mfumaca.com.br; adult/child R$40/free; ☷ 9am & 2pm Thu & Sat Feb-Jun & Aug-Nov, daily in Dec, Jan & Jul) chugs along the track between Bento Gonçalves and the small towns of Garibaldi and Carlos Barbosa. At each stop, passengers are herded onto the platforms to partake of cheap wine. Riding the old steam engine has a certain appeal, but the trip is otherwise overrated.

Tours

Caminhos de Pedra (☎ 3454 5702; www.caminhosde pedra.org.br; per person R$30) Visits architectural relics from the 19th century.

Vale das Vinhas (☎ 3451 4216; www.valedasvinhastur .com.br; Rua Barão do Rio Branco 245; per person R$30) This three-hour tour visits four facilities in the Vale dos Vinhedos. You may pay extra for tastings, although this amount is deductible from any purchases you make. Located in the lobby of the Hotel Vinocap (see right).

Sleeping & Eating

The most appealing option is to stay at one of the rural hotels in the Vale dos Vinhedos. If you are dependent on public transportation, however, it is more convenient to stay in Bento.

Pousada da Pipa (☎ 3453 3157; mapellis@terra.com .br; Travessa Silva Paes 415; s/d R$30/50; ☐) This sweet yellow house is near the Pórtico da Pipa. Simple, sunlit rooms with wood floors and ruffled linens offer excellent value, although the location is inconvenient for those relying on public transport.

Hotel Vinocap (☎ 3455 7100; www.vinocap.com.br; Rua Barão do Rio Branco 245; s/d R$60/80; ☒ ☐) It's not the most beautiful building in Bento, but it might be the most central. The 126 rooms are pretty plain but perfectly comfortable, and you can upgrade to a newly renovated 'luxury' room (singles/doubles R$120/150) if you desire.

Villa dei Fiori (☎ 3453 7866; www.villadeifiori.com.br; Rua Herdiros Refatti 185; r R$129-179) You might not expect to discover an Italian villa so close to the bus station, but here it is. The old stone structure and the lovely garden setting make this the most charming place to stay in the city proper.

Pousada Borghetto Sant'Anna (☎ 3453 2355; www.borghettosantanna.com.br; Linha Leopoldina 868; s/d R$180/200, cottages s/d R$225/250; ☒ ☐) About 4km from Bento, perched above the Vale dos Vinhedos, this cluster of romantic stone houses gives a fantastic view of the valley below. Reminiscent of Tuscany, the lodgings mix rustic charm with sumptuous comfort.

Canta Maria (☎ 3453 1099; ☷ lunch daily, dinner Mon-Sat) The city's most celebrated restaurant is located near the Pórtico da Pipa. A buffet of soups, salads and pastas is accompanied by a *rodízio* (smorgasbord) of grilled meats, fish and lamb. If you're in need of transportation, call the restaurant and they'll pick you up from anywhere in town or the vicinity.

There is a decent food court in the Shopping Bento Gonçalves, on Rua Marechal Deodoro.

Getting There & Around

The **long-distance bus station** (☎ 3452 1311) is about 1km north of the center, at the corner of Rua Osvaldo Aranha and Rua Gen Gomes Carneiro. Buses travel hourly to Porto Alegre (R$17, 2½ hours) and Caxias do Sul (R$7, one hour), where you can connect to Canela, Gramado or Cambará do Sul. One daily bus goes to Santo Ângelo (R$58, seven hours).

There is no public transportation to the Vale dos Vinhedos. If you don't have your own vehicle, sign on for one of the reasonably priced tours (see left).

GRAMADO

☎ 0xx54 / pop 26,200

This tony mountain resort bills itself as 'naturally European,' and it does indeed feel like a Swiss mountain village. Boutiques sell avant-garde glassworks and gourmet chocolate, while local restaurants specialize in fondue. Hotels are decked out like Swiss chalets. At times the insistence on Alpine themes crosses over into kitsch, but the overall affect is pleasant.

In August, Gramado hosts **Festival de Gramado** (www.festivaldegramado.com.br), Brazil's most prestigious film festival.

Information

Banco do Brasil (cnr Rua Garibaldi & Rua Augusto Zatti) Has ATM and money exchange.

Posto Telefônico (☎ 3286 0864; Av Borges de Medeiros 2889; Internet access per hr R$5; ☷ 9am-9pm Mon-Sat, noon-6pm Sun) Internet access and booths for international phone calls.

Tourist information office (☎ 3286 1475; www.portalgramado.com.br; Praça Major Nicoletti; ☷ 9am-7pm)

Sights

About 1.5km southeast of the center, **Lago Negro** is an attractive, man-made lake surrounded by hydrangeas and crowded with swan boats. Closer to the center, **Parque Knorr** offers inspiring views of the Vale do Quilombo, a beautiful valley that stretches along the road between Gramado and Canela.

Tours

Black Bear Adventur (☎ 9939 7191; www.blackbearadventure.com.br; Rua Bruno Ernest Riegel 713) Organizes white-water rafting, rappelling down waterfalls and hiking in the Cânion do Itaimbezinho (p364) and Cânion da Fortaleza (p364). The office is near Lago Negro.

Passeio Panorâmico Gramado (☎ 3286 9324; www.jardineiradashortensias.com.br; Av das Hortênsias 1710; per person R$10; ☷ 10am, noon, 2pm & 4pm) This 90-minute bus tour gives an overview of the town's history, architecture and nature highlights.

Sleeping

Prices listed are for weekends in summer (December to February). Rates rise significantly over Christmas and during the film festival.

Pousada Metodista (☎ 3286 2299; www.gramadosite.com.br/pousadametodista; Av Borges de Medeiros 2889; s/d R$50/80; ☒) Sleep in the hallowed halls behind the Methodist church. Six small rooms have private bathrooms, plain walls and linoleum floors; larger dormitories usually cater to church groups, go figure.

Hotel Vovó Carolina (☎ 3286 2433; www.vovocarolina.com.br; Av Borges de Medeiros 3129; s/d from R$104/127) This cheery hotel has recently been revamped, receiving a fresh coat of paint and new carpeting. Don't confuse it with the Pousada Vovó Carolina, which is a much larger place 5km south of the center.

Pousada Bernadete (☎ 3286 1569; www.pousadabernadete.com.br; Rua Augusto Zitti 200; s/d R$120/210; ⌨) This homey, hospitable B&B is located dead center. Décor is simple but sophisticated.

Pousada da Colina (☎ 3286 7355; www.pousadadacolina.com.br; Rua Arthur Zwetsch 111; d from R$150) The delight is in the details, like beds adorned with patchwork quilts and throw pillows, walls hung with quirky, colorful art, and cozy common areas.

Bella Terra Pousada (☎ 3286 3333; www.pousadabellaterra.com.br; Av Borges de Medeiros 2870; s/d/ste R$150/165/250; ⌨) This building sits back from the road, which means it does not suffer from street noise. Indeed, the place is a

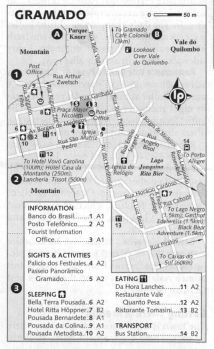

GRAMADO   0 ⸺ 50 m

INFORMATION	
Banco do Brasil........1	A1
Posto Telefônico........2	A2
Tourist Information Office........3	A1

SIGHTS & ACTIVITIES	
Palicio dos Festivales........4	A2
Passeio Panorâmico Gramado........5	A2

SLEEPING	
Bella Terra Pousada........6	A2
Hotel Ritta Höppner........7	B2
Pousada Bernadete........8	A2
Pousada da Colina........9	A1
Pousada Metodista........10	A2

EATING	
Da Hora Lanches........11	A2
Restaurante Vale Quanto Pesa........12	A2
Ristorante Tomasini........13	B2

TRANSPORT	
Bus Station........14	B2

RIO GRANDE DO SUL

center of peace and tranquility; large, light-filled rooms have big box-spring beds and marble bathrooms.

Hotel Casa da Montanha (☎ 3286 2544; www
.hotelcasadamontanha.com.br; Av Borges de Medeiros 3166;
r weekday/weekend from R$165/254; 🕸 🖳 🔊) Re-sembling a rustic chalet on the outside, this hotel is sumptuous and luxurious on the in-side. Guestrooms have fancy, old-fashioned flair. Other onsite amenities include a rich, dark-wood library, a slick spa and a gour-met restaurant specializing in fresh trout and wild game.

Hotel Ritta Höppner (☎ 3286 1334; www.ritta
hoppner.com.br; Rua Pedro Candiago 305; r/ste R$180/230;
🖳 🔊) Situated in a lovely residential dis-trict, this plush inn takes kitsch seriously. The breakfast room is a lace-filled affair, and the garden is replete with gnomes and elves.

Eating

Gramado has no shortage of Italian, German and Swiss cuisine, reflecting the ethnic makeup of the region's original settlers. Fresh-water trout is a local specialty.

Da Hora Lanches (☎ 3286 5256; Av Borges de Medeiros;
meals R$10-12; 🕙 11am-7pm) Floating flowers and fishbowls serve as centerpieces at this cool lit-tle café. The daily changing lunchtime buffet is excellent, while simple sandwiches and fresh juices are available throughout the day. Enjoy sidewalk seating in a shady alleyway.

Restaurante Vale Quanto Pesa (☎ 3286 3457; Rua
São Pedro 401; meals R$12-15; 🕙 lunch & dinner Tue-Sun) A massive buffet at midday and a pizza *rodízio* by night guarantee to sate your appetite. The buffet features over 50 dishes, and the *rodízio* offers almost as many types of pizza pie.

Ristorante Tomasini (☎ 3286 4311; Av das Hortênsias
1189; meals R$30-40; 🕙 lunch & dinner) In a warm, fire-lit dining room, Tomasini serves up tasty pasta dishes, grilled meats and seafood from its á la carte menu. Or try the excellent *seqüência de fondues*, which includes meat cooked on a hot rock, as well as cheese and chocolate fondue.

Gasthof Edelweiss (☎ 3286 1861; Rua da Carriérie
1119; meals R$30-40; 🕙 lunch & dinner) Situated pic-turesquely just across from Lago Negro, this homey restaurant serves up the town's best German cuisine.

Getting There & Around

The town is small enough to get everywhere by foot. There are frequent buses to Porto Alegre (R$22, two hours, seven daily). Buses for Canela leave the main bus station every 10 to 20 minutes (R$1.50, 20 minutes).

CANELA

☎ 0xx54 / pop 33,600

While lacking Gramado's sophistication, Canela has a small town charm of its own. Centered around a leafy green square, the village center is anchored at one end by an impressive Gothic Catedral de Pedra (stone cathedral). The streets are lined with shops and cafés. And though they are not as chic as those in Gramado, Canela offers a wider range of budget accommodations and more convenient access to the state parks, which are popular hiking spots.

Information

Banco do Brasil (Praça João Corrêa) Money exchange and Visa ATMs.
Posto Telefônico (☎ 3303 1107; per hr R$3.50; Av Julio de Castilhos 319) Internet access and call center.
Tourist information (☎ 3282 2200; www.canela
turismo.com.br; Praça João Corrêa)
War Zone Lan House (Av Oaldo Aranha 333; per hr R$3;
🕙 10am-10:30pm) Internet access and computer games.

Sights & Activities

The major attraction of **Parque Estadual do Cara-col** (☎ 3278 3035; admission R$8; 🕙 8:30am-5:30pm), 9km from Canela, is the spectacular Cascata do Caracol, a 130m free-falling waterfall. It's particularly attractive in the morning sun, when the water sparkles as it cascades over the granite lip. If you're feeling fit, you can walk to the base of the waterfall down (and back up) the 900-plus steps.

About 3km from Caracol, the **Parque Floresta Encantada de Canela** (☎ 3504 1405; www
.canelateleferico.com.br; adult/child R$4/free; 🕙 9am-5pm) offers another perspective from across the canyon. A *teleférico* (chairlift) travels 830m up and down the mountainside, providing 20 minutes' worth of fabulous views – of the canyon, the waterfall and Gramado in the distance. You can get off at either end and hike back to the entrance.

A 6km hike from Caracol brings you to **Parque da Ferradura** (☎ 9969 6785; admission R$8;
🕙 9am-5:30pm), named for the 420m horseshoe-shaped canyon formed by the Rio Santa Cruz. There are three lookouts that you can hike to along well-marked trails. Also along the road to the park you'll come across **Castelinho**, the

oldest house in the area. This pioneer German home was built without the luxury of metal nails.

Tours

The following companies offer tours of adventure activities such as trekking, rappelling, rafting and cycling.

At!tude Ecologia & Tourismo (☎ 3282 6305; www .atitude.tru.br; Shop 16, Av Osvaldo Aranha 391; per person R$80; ⏱ 8:30am-noon & 2-5:30pm) Twice daily trips visit Caracol, Ferradura and Castelinho, as well as Lago Negro in Gramado.

Vida Livre (☎ 3286 7326; www.vidalivreturismo.com.br; Room 302, Rua Madre Verônica 30; per person R$50; ⏱ 8:30am & 2pm) The standard four-hour trip visits all the local parks.

Sleeping

Prices listed here are for the high summer season (Dececember to March).

Pousada do Viajante (☎ 3282 2017; www.pousadado viajante.com.br; Rua Ernesto Urban 1; r HI members/nonmembers R$23/30) 'Sleep good and cheap.' So promises this HI-affiliated hostel. And it lives up to its motto, with clean, quiet, single and double rooms, all with shared facilities.

Vila Vecchia (☎ 3282 4220; Rua Melvin Jones 137; s/d R$60/90) This sweet Swiss-style chalet is trimmed with flower boxes and shutters. Inside, the rooms are simple and cheap. A wood-burning stove warms the common area.

Alpes Verdes Parque Hotel (☎ 3282 1162; www .alpesverdes.com.br; Rua Gilda T Bolognese 1001; s/d/tr R$100/130/150; 🖳 🖳) In a lovely green setting 2km from town, this hotel features private chalets with excellent views of the Vale do Quilombo. Hospitable hosts are happy to ferry you back and forth to town.

Laje de Pedra (☎ 3278 9000; www.lajedepedra.com .br; Rua dos Flores 222; s/d from R$230/255; 🖳 🖳 🖳) Perched at the edge of the Vale do Quilombo, this sumptuous resort offers spectacular views and wonderful walking trails, as well as five-star comforts and service. Tennis courts, game room and spa guarantee a good time for the whole family.

Pousada Cravo & Canela (☎ 3282 1120; www .pousadacravoeconela.com.br; Rua Tenente Manoel Correa 144; d R$295-395; 🖳 🖳 🖳) Once the home of the German governor of the region, this plush pousada (guesthouse) retains a sense of history. Many architectural details have been preserved, including the tile fireplace in the dining room and the original owner's collection of cuckoo clocks.

Eating

Olimpia Restaurante (☎ 3282 3888; Av Osvaldo Aranha 456; buffet R$10; ⏱ lunch & dinner) This per-kilo restaurant is packed by noon, and for good reason. The well-stocked buffet is fresh and filling, and includes grilled meats as well as fresh vegetables and salads.

Coelho Cantina e Galeteria (☎ 3282 4224; Av Osvaldo Aranha 287; buffet R$15; ⏱ lunch & dinner) The noon-time meal at Coelho is like a buffet, but they bring it to you. Save room for dessert, as you have your choice of 15 options!

RIO GRANDE DO SUL

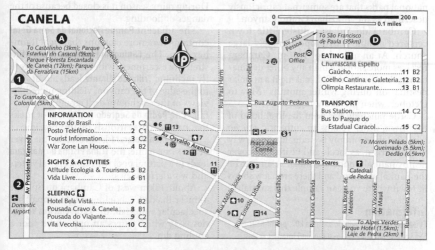

CANELA

| 0 | 200 m |
| 0 | 0.1 miles |

To Castelinho (3km); Parque Estadual do Caracol (9km); Parque Floresta Encantada de Canela (12km); Parque da Ferradura (15km)

To Gramado Café Colonial (5km)

Rua Teixeira Manoel Correa

Rua Paul Harris

Rua Ernesto Dornelles

Rua Augusto Pestana

Av João Pessoa

Post Office

To São Francisco de Paula (35km)

INFORMATION
Banco do Brasil..................1 C2
Posto Telefônico................2 C1
Tourist Information...........3 C2
War Zone Lan House........4 B2

SIGHTS & ACTIVITIES
At!tude Ecologia & Tourismo.5 B2
Vida Livre..........................6 B1

SLEEPING 🏠
Hotel Bela Vistá................7 B2
Pousada Cravo & Canela...8 B1
Pousada do Viajante.........9 C2
Vila Vecchia.....................10 C2

EATING 🍴
Churrascana Espelho Gaúcho..................11 B2
Coelho Cantina e Galeteria.12 B2
Olimpia Restaurante.........13 B1

TRANSPORT
Bus Station......................14 C2
Bus to Parque do Estadual Caracol....15 C2

Av Osvaldo Aranha

Praça João Correa

Rua Felisberto Soares

Av Presidente Kennedy

To Morros Pelado (5km); Queimado (5.5km); Dedão (6.5km)

Catedral de Pedra

Rua Melvin Jones

Rua Ernesto Urbani

Av Júlio de Castilhos

Rua Dona Carlinda

Rua Borges de Medeiros

Av Visconde de Mauá

Rua Teixeira Soares

Domestic Airport

To Alpes Verdes Parque Hotel (1.5km); Laje de Pedra (2km)

Churrascaria Espelho Gaúcho (☎ 3282 4348; just off Av Osvaldo Aranha; meals R$15-20 ☺ lunch & dinner) A decent *churrascaria* with an all-the-meat-you-can-eat option.

Gramado Café Colonial (☎ 3282 2317; Estrada Canela-Gramado; per person R$25 ☺ lunch & dinner) This amazing *café colonial* features more than 80 dishes, ranging from fresh salads and cold cuts to freshly baked bread to tasty *salgados* (snacks) – fried polenta being a specialty – to sweet pastries and desserts. Pay one price and you can sample them all. Midway between Canela and Gramado.

Getting There & Around

Buses for Gramado leave the main bus station every 10 to 20 minutes (R$1.50, 20 minutes). There are also buses to São Francisco de Paula (R$5, one hour), where you can connect to Cambará do Sul (R$10, two hours); and to Caxias do Sul (R$10, seven daily), where you can connect to Bento Gonçalves (R$5, hourly). Buses go frequently to Porto Alegre (R$24, 2½ hours, seven daily).

Two buses a day go to Parque do Caracol (R$1.50, 20 minutes), departing from Praça João Corrêa at 8:15am and noon and returning at 12:30pm and 6pm.

CAMBARÁ DO SUL

☎ 0xx54 / pop 7000

Located 186km northeast of Porto Alegre, this town serves as a base for both Parque Nacional de Aparados da Serra (18km) and Parque Nacional da Serra Geral (23km), the national parks that are somewhat capriciously described as the 'Brazilian Grand Canyon.'

Cambará do Sul is a dusty little town centered around a disproportionately large church. At an altitude of 1000m, Cambará receives more snowfall than any other destination in Rio Grande do Sul, making it a popular destination during winter months (May to October; when prices are higher).

Cattle ranching has been the livelihood of this town, which retains an authentic *gaúcho* aura. But the economy is gradually giving way to ecotourism, as locals and visitors discover nearby natural wonders. Cambará claims to be the 'capital of honey,' and there are a few shops in town where you can sample this specialty.

Information

Cyber Serra (Rua Padre João Pazza 802; per hr R$2; ☺ 9am-11pm Mon-Sat, 6-10pm Sun) Internet access.

Tourist information office (☎ 3251 1320; www.cambaraonline.com.br; Rua 15 de Março, Cambará do Sul) Across from the town's main church.

Sights & Activities

The magnificent **Parque Nacional de Aparados da Serra** (☎ 3251 1262; admission R$3; ☺ 9am-4pm Wed-Sun) stretches across the state line into Santa Catarina. Here, the vast, uninspired pasturelands give way to a series of stunning canyons, where the earth opens up and drops to depths of 720m.

The park is 18km from the town of Cambará do Sul, which serves as the base for visitors. It preserves one of the country's last araucaria forests, which has earned it its protected status. But the main attraction is the **Cânion do Itaimbezinho**, a narrow, 5800m-long canyon with sheer parallel escarpments, ranging from 600m to 720m. Two waterfalls drop into this incision in the earth, which was formed by the Rio Perdiz's rush to the sea.

Three trails wind through the park. **Trilha do Vértice** runs for 2km to an observation point for the canyon and the Cascata do Andorinhas. **Trilha Cotovelo** is a 3km trail (2½ hours round-trip) passing by the Véu de Noiva waterfall, with wonderful vistas of the canyon.

For a completely different perspective, **Trilha do Rio do Boi** follows the base of the canyon for 7km, from the Posto Rio do Boi entrance. This last route is most easily accessed from the town of Praia Grande in Santa Catarina. A professional guide (see opposite) is recommended for the challenging, loose, rocky trail. During rainy season it is closed because of the danger of flooding.

The adjacent **Parque Nacional da Serra Geral** contains two more canyons that rival Itaimbezinho. The **Cânion da Fortaleza** is an 8km stretch of escarpment with 900m drops. A gently inclining **Trilha do Mirante** leads about 7km to the edge of the canyon, yielding incredible views of the Cachoeira do Tigre Preto waterfall. The **Pedra do Segredo** is a tower of rocks that balances precariously on this precipice.

The **Cânion Malacara** is formed by the river of the same name; the **Trilha Piscina do Malacara** leads to a natural pool with cool, crystal waters and wonderful views.

About 18km west of Cambará do Sul, the 4km Trilha da Cachoeira leads to a small but spectacular waterfall, the **Cachoeira dos Venâncios** (R$3), which offers an opportunity for a cooling dip.

Tours

Local companies provide transportation and guides for the canyons (at a cost of R$35 per person for Itaimbezinho or Fortaleza). Meanwhile, a guided trek on the Trilha do Rio do Boi is about R$90. Horseback-riding and mountain-climbing expeditions are also available.

Canyon Turismo (☎ 3251 1027; www.canyonturismo .com.br; Av Getúlio Vargas 1098)

Nativa Ecoturismo (☎ 3251 1013; www.nativaeco turismo.com.br; Av Getúlio Vargas 1282)

Sleeping

Cambará has many economical, family-run pousadas, while higher-end options are outside of town. Unfortunately there is no camping in the parks.

Prices quoted here are for the high season (May to October). In other seasons, expect a discount of 25% or more.

Pousada Itaimbeleza (☎ 3251 1367; www.itaim bezinho.tur.br; Rua Dona Úrsula 648; s/d without bathroom R$30/60, d with bathroom R$65-80) Cute, comfy chalets are clustered around a garden bursting with birds and flowers. The accommodating owner, Loreni, is ever willing to assist with arrangements for trips to the canyons.

Pousada Paraíso (☎ 3251 1352; www.paraiso pousada.com.br; Rua Antonio Raupp 678; r per person R$40) Set on the edge of the village, this two-story home can house 40 guests in its fresh, simple rooms.

Pousada Corucacas (☎ 3251 1123; www.corucacas .com; per person r R$80) About 1km from town on the road to Ouro Verde, this working farm has rustic rooms and a big-sky setting. On the grounds, guests can go horseback riding and fishing. Price includes both breakfast and dinner.

Estalagem da Colina (☎ 3251 1746; www.estalagem dacolina.com.br; Av Getúlio Vargas 80; d R$167-187, q R$275; 🖳) On the edge of Cambará, this place boasts 10 stylish wooden chalets built from recycled materials. In the main lodge, guests can congregate around the fire or enjoy an excellent dinner.

Refúgio Ecológico Pedra Afiada (☎ 0xx48-3532 1059; www.pedraafiada.com.br; s/d/tr R$210/270/360) Splendidly located within the Canión Malacara, this isolated inn boasts a gorgeous stone fireplace for chilly nights and a fabulous rooftop deck for clear days. Hiking, horseback riding, rafting and rappelling are all at your doorstep.

Parador Casa da Montanha (☎ 3286 2544; www .paradorcasadamontanha.com.br; s/d R$295/350) Midway between Cambará and Itaimbezinho, the parador is the poshest place in the region. Surrounded by pine forests and waterfalls, lodging is in heated, elevated tents that somehow combine luxury and rusticity. Prices include half-pension and local tours.

Eating

Dining options in Cambará are limited.

Cafe Expresso Mata Bicho (☎ 3251 1203; Rua 20 de Septembro 90; meals R$9-10; ☽ lunch & dinner) Heading out on the trail? Stop by Cafe Expresso Mata Bicho for a sandwich, a piece of fruit, a granola bar and a juice – packed to go.

Restaurante Bom Paladar (☎ 3251 1280; Rua João Francisco Ritter 842; meals R$10-20; ☽ lunch & dinner) Has a homey wood interior and offers filling food.

O Casarão (☎ 3251 1711; Rua João Francisco Ritter 969; meals R$15-20; ☽ Tue-Sun) This is a slightly upscale option with organic produce, homemade pastas and local wines.

Galpão Costaneira (☎ 3251 1005; Rua Dona Úrsula 1069; meals R$20-30; ☽ lunch & dinner) If the *gaúcho* atmosphere has got you in the mood for *churrascaria*, try this option with live music on weekends.

Getting There & Around

Two daily buses go to São Francisco de Paula (R$10, two hours), with connections to Porto Alegre or Canela and Gramado. One daily bus goes to Caxias do Sul, where you can connect to Bento Gonçalves.

If you are coming from the north, a direct bus runs to Torres three times a week. Otherwise, you can connect in Tainhas. Alternatively, taxis can make the run between Cambará and Praia Grande for about R$93.

The parks are not serviced by public buses. You can take a taxi from Cambará to the parks (R$60 to R$70, one way). Local tour companies (see left) are a reasonable alternative, especially if they can hook you up with a small group.

ROTA MISSÕES

Soon after the discovery of the New World, the Portuguese and Spanish kings authorized Catholic orders to create missions to convert the natives. The Jesuits were the most successful order, establishing a series of missions across Paraguay, Brazil and Argentina. At its height in the 1720s, this prosperous 'nation' claimed 30 mission villages inhabited by more than 150,000 Guarani Indians (see Paradise Lost, opposite).

Today, all 30 missions are in ruins. Together, they form the Rota Missões, or 'Missions Route,' a network of pilgrimage sites for the faithful and the curious. Seven are in Brazil (in the northwestern part of Rio Grande do Sul), eight are in southern Paraguay and 15 are in northeastern Argentina. For an excellent overview of the Brazilian missions see the website of the **Rota Missões** (www.rotamissoes.com.br in Portuguese).

SANTO ÂNGELO

☎ 0xx55 / pop 80,100

This small, pleasant city is the regional transportation hub and jumping-off point for exploring the Brazilian missions. The impressive cathedral, on **Praça da Catedral**, is a contemporary replica of the church at São Miguel das Missões (right). A few blocks north, the **Monumento ao Índio** remembers Sepé Tiaraju, the leader of the indigenous resistance during the Guarani War.

Orientation

Av Brasil is the main commercial street that runs east–west through the center of town. The Praça da Catedral is four blocks south along Rua Marquêes do Herval.

Information

Maps of the city are available at the hotels listed under Sleeping & Eating (right).

Banco do Brasil (cnr Av Brasil & Rua Marques do Herval) Money exchange and ATMs.

Suprema Internet (☎ 3313 2016; R Marques do Herval 1448; per hr R$3; ☺ 10am-10pm)

Tours

Without your own vehicle, it is difficult to visit all of the missions independently. An organized tour offers a reasonable alternative.

Caminho das Missões (☎ 3312 9632; www.caminho dasmissoes.com.br) Leads walking and biking tours of the missions, ranging from three to 14 days.

Golden Travel (☎ 3314 2773; www.goldentravel .br; Rua Marques do Herval 1446) The traditional three-day circuit (R$266) includes São João Batista (p368), São Miguel das Missões (right) and the Caaró Sanctuary (p368). Also offers a four-day international circuit (R$868).

Sleeping & Eating

Turis Hotel Santo Ângelo (☎ 3313 5255; www.santo angeloturishotel.com.br; Rua Antônio Manoel 726; s/d R$30/47, s/d with air-con R$65/85; ☒) Rooms vary widely, but none of them are going to win any design awards. Nonetheless, it's a decent budget option, just one block west of the Praça da Catedral.

Hotel Maerkli (☎ 3313 2127; Av Brasil 1000; s/d R$107/156; ☒) A more upscale option, this hotel caters to business travelers and tourist groups, who appreciate the attentive service and well-appointed rooms. It's on the main drag, one block west of Praça Leônidas Ribas.

Quick (☎ 3313 4488; cnr Av Brasil & Rua Marques do Herval; meals R$10-20; ☺ lunch & dinner) Featuring a hearty lunchtime buffet and an extensive late-night menu, this is the best of several options located along this stretch between Av Brasil and the main square.

Getting There & Around

The **bus station** (☎ 3313 2618) is 1km west of the center. One daily bus goes to Bento Gonçalves (R$58, seven hours) and one overnight bus goes to Foz do Iguaçu (12 hours) in Paraná. Buses run frequently between Santo Ângelo and Porto Alegre (R$68, *leito* R$108, seven hours, eight daily).

Four times a day, buses go to São Miguel das Missões (R$7, one hour). Renting a car from **Sulmive** (☎ 3312 1000; Rua Marechal Floriano 747) is a good option for visiting the Brazilian missions, but it is difficult to take a rental car over the border to visit international missions.

SÃO MIGUEL DAS MISSÕES

☎ 0xx55 / pop 7700

The best preserved and most moving of the Brazilian missions is **São Miguel Arcanjo** (adult/student R$5/2.50; ☺ 9am-noon & 2-6pm), located in the village of São Miguel das Missões, 53km southwest of Santo Ângelo. The elegant church, designed by an Italian architect who was also a Jesuit friar, earned Unesco World Heritage status in 1984. It is surrounded by mystical ruins of the Jesuit settlement, which evokes 'paradise lost' (see opposite).

The archaeological site also includes an excellent little **Museu das Missões**. Designed by Lúcio Costa of Brasília fame, the museum contains an impressive collection of religious artifacts that were rescued from the ruins. A few Guarani families hang around selling handicrafts. A spectacular, if campy, **sound-**

RIO GRANDE DO SUL

PARADISE LOST

In 1608, the governor of the Spanish province of Paraguay ordered the local Jesuit leader, Fray Diego de Torres, to convert the local Tupi and Guarani people. The Jesuits established missions across a vast region that encompassed much of southern Brazil, as well as portions of southern Paraguay and northern Argentina.

Unlike their brethren elsewhere in the New World, the Jesuits made a concerted effort to convert the indigenous people without destroying their culture or language. The missions became centers of culture and intellect, as well as religion. The arts flourished, combining elements of European and Guarani music and painting. Scholars created a written form of the Tupi-Guarani language and, beginning in 1704, published several works, using one of South America's earliest printing presses. The missions produced sophisticated sculpture, metallurgy, ceramics and musical instruments. In an age of monarchies and institutionalized slavery, the missions were an island of idealism, where wealth was divided equitably; and religion, intellect and arts were cultivated in tandem.

From the beginning, the missions faced threats from the outside world. In the 1620s, they were harassed by Portuguese *bandeirantes*, bands of Paulistas who raided the interior in search of gold and Indians to enslave. Thousands of Indians were captured, and the 13 missions of Guayra (present-day Paraná) were eventually abandoned. Beginning in the 1630s, the Jesuits consolidated their position in 30 sites across the northwest corner of present-day Rio Grande do Sul, as well as in Argentina and Paraguay. These sites, now in ruins, constitute the contemporary Rota Missões, or Missions Route.

In large part, it was the success of the missions that brought about their downfall. The independent-minded Jesuits became an embarrassment to Rome, and to the Spanish and Portuguese kings. In 1750 the Treaty of Madrid dictated that the sites be handed over to Portuguese rule, which would not protect the Indians from enslavement. The Guarani were commanded to evacuate in 1754, but they refused to abandon their settlements and thus incited the Guarani War. In 1756, a combined Spanish-Portuguese army attacked the missions, killing more than 1500 Indians and selling many more into slavery, thus decimating the Guarani population. It was a tragic, bloody end to a great social experiment.

The missions were lauded by great thinkers from Voltaire to Montesquieu as a real incarnation of Christian utopia and destroyed by the very forces that created it. Robert De Niro and Jeremy Irons relive this story in the 1986 film, *The Mission,* a moving, fictional account of these events (see also p66).

RIO GRANDE DO SUL

and-light show (R$5; 8:30pm Dec-Feb, 8pm Mar-Nov) illustrates the history of the missions.

Orientation & Information

The mission is about 500m west of the bus station, and the small commercial center lies in between. The **tourist office** (3381 1294) is near the entrance of the mission.

Sleeping & Eating

The last bus to Santo Ângelo leaves before the sound-and-light show, so it's worth spending the night. There are a couple of casual restaurants clustered around the bus station, and a snack bar opposite the entrance to the mission.

Pousada das Missões (3381 1202; www.pousada tematica.com.br; Rua São Nicalau 601; r per person R$32;) Student groups utilize the dorm-style accommodation at this HI hostel, but more discerning travelers will be comfortable in the private rooms, each labeled with a Guarani name and accompanying explanation. It is located just behind the archaeological site; follow signs from the entrance.

Wilson Park Hotel (3381 2000; www.wilson parkhotel.com.br; Rua São Miguel 664; s/d/tr R$91/130/170;) Boasting mission-style architecture, stylish rooms and an international restaurant, this fancy resort is not exactly catering to pilgrims. Excellent facilities include tennis courts, a football field and a fancy swimming pool.

Getting There & Around

From the **bus station** (3381 1226) in Missões, four daily buses go to Santo Ângelo (US$4, one hour).

OTHER BRAZILIAN SITES

São João Batista

Midway between Santo Ângelo and São Miguel, little remains from the mission at **São João Batista** (☎ 3329 1170; admission free; ☒ 9am-5pm). With a little imagination, it is possible to make out the structures of the church, the cemetery and the school.

Caaró

About 20km west of São Miguel, the **Caaró Sanctuary** (☎ 3505 7427; ☒ 8:30-11:30am & 1:30-6pm Mon-Fri) is the place where the region's spiritual history is most alive. A modest monument honors three priests who were killed by *bandeirantes* in 1626. One of the victims, Roque González, has been canonized. This site attracts a stream of pilgrims, especially in November, around the anniversary of St Roque's martyrdom.

Saõ Lourenço Mártir

In 1690, a group from the Argentine reduction of Santa Maria founded **São Lourenço Mártir** (☎ 3352 2699; admission free; ☒ 8am-noon & 1:30-6pm). It is located about 18km west of the turn-off to São Miguel, 9km north off the road to São Luiz Gonzaga (BR-285). The church, cemetery and school are still discernable and there is a small exhibit of findings from excavations. The most impressive find – the grand image of São Lourenço that once graced the church – is now held at the Museu das Missões (p366) in São Miguel.

São Nicolau

About 120km west of Santo Ângelo, this mission was an artistic center, producing painting, ceramics and wood sculpture. Today, all that remains at the **archaeological site** (☎ 3363 1441; ☒ 8am-noon & 2-6pm Mon-Fri, 2-6pm Sat & Sun) is the Jesuits' stone cellar. The **Museu Municipal** (☎ 3356 1247; Rua João Fagundes 131; admission free; ☒ 9-11:30am & 1:30-4:45pm Mon-Fri) contains an interesting exhibit on Jesuit-Guarani culture.

If you make it this far, you can spend the night at the **Pousada dos Jesuítas** (☎ 3363 1101; pousada_dos_jesuitas@yahoo.com.br; Cel Mamed de Souza 1046), 50m from the archaeological site.

ARGENTINE & PARAGUAYAN MISSIONS

Posadas is the best base for exploring the Argentine missions, the highlight of which is San Ignacio Miní (60km northeast), not to be confused with San Ignacio Guazú, which is in Paraguay. Use either Encarnación or Posadas (just across the border) as a base for visiting the missions of Paraguay, where the most important site is the red stone ruins of Trinidad de Parana, 25km northeast of Encarnación.

The most direct route to the Argentine and Paraguayan missions is via the border town of Porto Xavier, 145km northwest of Santo Ângelo. From here it's possible to cross the Rio Uruguai by barge to the Argentine town of São Tomé, where there are buses to Posadas and Encarnación.

LITORAL GAÚCHO

On paper, it sounds amazing: a 500km strip of Brazilian coastline that forms one seemingly endless beach, stretching from Torres on the Santa Catarina border, all the way to Chuí at the Uruguayan border. Unfortunately, the reality is less enticing. The water tends to be murky and the beaches are undistinguished, with little geographical variation.

TORRES

☎ 0xx51 / pop 40,000

On the border with Santa Catarina, Torres is the exception to the state's uninviting coastline. The town, 205km north of Porto Alegre, has attractive (if crowded) beaches punctuated by basalt rock formations. In winter, Antarctic currents bring cold, hard winds to the coast; the crowds disappear, and most hotels shut down from May to November.

Every year in April, Torres hosts a **hot-air balloon festival** (www.festivaldebalonismo.com.br), a spectacular sight.

Orientation

Av Barão do Rio Branco runs west from the beach at Prainha. Praia Grande stretches north from here, while Praia da Cal is to the south. The bus station is on the west side of the violin-shaped Lagoa do Violoão on Av José Bonifácio.

Information

Banco do Brasil (Av Barão do Rio Branco 236) For money exchange or ATMs.

Loja de Conveniência (Av Barão do Rio Branco 217; per hr R$3) One of many internet cafés along the main streets.

RIO GRANDE DO SUL

Tourist information office (☎ 3626 1937; www.torres
.tur.br; cnr Avs Barão do Rio Branco & Silva Jardim) Publishes
a useful city map.

Sights & Activities

Praia Grande, the town's main beach, is quite
calm, but surfers can head 2km south to **Praia
da Cal** for decent waves. Nearby, an 18m-high
lighthouse sits atop the **Morro do Farol**, an excellent vantage point to view the city.

Further south, the gardens of **Parque Guar-
ita** provide a gorgeous natural setting for
cultural events and other recreation. The
nearby beach of the same name is considered the most beautiful in Torres.

Tours

Passeios Náuticos (☎ 3626 2933; per person R$10) of-
fers boat trips to Ilha dos Lobos, an ecological reserve that is home to a colony of sea
lions between March and November. From
the end of Av Silva Jardim, walk along the
Rio Mampituba to Ponte Pênsil.

Sleeping

Prices listed are for summer season (December to February) – expect discounts of 20%
to 40% between March and November.

Hotel Costa Azul (☎ 3664 3291; Av José Bonifácio 382;
s/d R$30/60; ﹡) This small, friendly place is an
excellent option near the bus station. Rooms
are slightly cramped, but they are clean, car-
peted and fresh-smelling.

Pousada da Prainha (☎ 3626 2454; www.pousada
daprainha.com.br; Rua Alferes Feirreira Porto 138; s/d R$65/80;
﹡) This attractive, colonial-style hotel is just
one block from the quiet beach at Prainha.

Pousada La Barca (☎ 3664 2925; www.pousadala
barca.com.br; Av Beira Mar 1020; s/d R$100/180, s/d with
sea views R$120/200; ﹡ ▯ ▣) Sleek and so-
phisticated, this contemporary pousada is
an upscale option on the beach. Rooms are
equipped with ceiling fans and big balconies
for maximum sea-breeze action.

Solar Inn (☎ 3626 3731; Av Beira Mar 1713; r R$160-
230; ﹡ ▣) For its excellent beachfront location and welcoming small size (18 rooms),
you can't beat this new inn on Prainha
beach. Less luxurious – but more convivial –
than the hulking Dunas Hotel next door.

Eating

Doce Art (☎ 3664 5591; Av Silva Jardim 295; meals R$10-
20; ﹡ breakfast & lunch) Come here for hot coffee,
fresh juice and tasty pastries in the morning,

or sandwiches and pastas at lunchtime. Outdoor seating overlooks Praça XV.

Nápole Roda Pizza (☎ 3664 2657; Av Benjamin Constant 163; meals R$10-20; ﹡ dinner) With 40 types
of pizza, you're bound to find something
you like. It's one block south of Av Barão
do Rio Branco.

Restaurante A Prainha (☎ 3626 4566; Rua Joaquim
Porto 151; meals R$15-25; ﹡ lunch & dinner) Two
blocks from the beach of the same name,
this casual restaurant serves seafood. and
typical Brazilian platters on its pleasant,
shady porch.

Getting There & Away

The town is small and all conveniences are
accessible by foot, including the **bus station**
(☎ 3664 1787). Destinations include Porto Alegre (R$30 to R$38, three hours, six daily)
and Florianópolis (US$12, five hours, five
daily). A direct bus goes to Cambará do Sul
three times a week; otherwise, you can connect in Tainhas.

RIO GRANDE

☎ 0xx53 / pop 183,400

Located at the mouth of Lagoa dos Patos,
Rio Grande was founded in 1737 to guard
the disputed southern border of the Portuguese empire. The region's oldest city, it
blossomed during the 19th century, when its
port became a vital link in the profitable beef
trade. Rio Grande has a charming historic
center that is home to some interesting colonial and neoclassical buildings. The excellent
Museu Oceanográfico (☎ 3232 9107; Rua Capitão Heitor
Perdigão 10; admission free; ﹡ 9-11:30am & 2-5:30pm Tue-
Sun) is one of the best in Latin America.

Sleeping & Eating

Paris Hotel (☎ 3231 3866; www.hotelvillamoura.com.br; R
Marechal Floriano 112; s/d R$60/80) This historic hotel
dates to 1826, exhibiting its bygone grandeur
in its high ceilings, antique furnishings and
leafy courtyard.

Atlântico Rio Grande (☎ 3231 3833; www.hoteis
atlantico.com.br; Rua Duque de Caxias 53; s/d R$74/84, s/d
with views R$98/109; ﹡ ▯) It may not be beauti-
ful, but it has lovely views of the waterfront
and adjacent park.

Getting There & Away

From the **bus station** (☎ 3232 8444), buses connect
Rio Grande with all major cities in southern
Brazil, as well as Chuí (R$26, 3½ hours, two

daily) on the Uruguayan border. However, Pelotas (R$10, one hour, every 30 minutes) is the major transportation hub.

CHUÍ

☎ 0xx53 / pop 5700

Located 245km south of Rio Grande, this border town is both Brazilian and Uruguayan (Chuí and Chuy, respectively). The main drag acts as the border: on the northern (Brazilian) side it is Av Uruguaí, while on the southern (Uruguayan) side it is Av Brasil. Tourists can wander freely on both sides of the town; Portuguese and Spanish are spoken interchangeably.

The Uruguayan side is home to many duty-free shops and casinos, so Chuy attracts its fair share of smugglers and gamblers. Unless these are your games, you may not wish to stick around longer than necessary.

Information

CONSULATES

Both Brazil and Uruguay maintain consulates here. It takes about 24 hours to get a visa for either country, so plan accordingly.

Brazilian consulate (☎ 3265 1011; Rua Tito Fernandez 147)

Uruguayan consulate (☎ 3265 1151; Rua Venezuala 311)

MONEY

Most establishments accept Brazilian and Uruguayan currency as well as US dollars. There is a **Banco do Brasil** (cnr Rua Venezuela & Rua Chile) two blocks from the Brazilian bus station. There are also money-exchange offices near the corner of Avs General Artigas and Brasil.

Sleeping & Eating

If you're stuck in Chuí, you can stay at the **Rivero Hotel** (☎ 3265 1271; Calle Colombia 163; s/d R$10/20) on the Brazilian side or **Nuevo Hotel Plaza** (☎ 598-474 2309; www.hotelplaza.chuynet.com; Plaça de Chuy; s/d R$20/40; 🐱) in Uruguay. A semi-upscale option is **Bertelli Chuí Hotel** (☎ 3265 1266; www.bertellichuihotel.com.br; r R$100; 🐱 🏊), about 2km north of town on BR-471. There are some good *churrascarias* on the Uruguayan side of Av Brasil.

Getting There & Away

BORDER CROSSINGS

The Brazilian border post is on Av Argentina, several kilometers north of town. You do not need a visa or entry or exit stamp to visit the town; however, if you are continuing into Uruguay, you will need to tell the driver to stop at the border post for an exit stamp.

In Uruguay, the border post is 2.5km south of town. The bus will stop again for the Uruguayan officials to check your Brazilian exit stamp and Uruguayan visa (if you need one). Stop here for an exit stamp if you are entering Brazil.

BUS

The Brazilian bus station is located on Rua Venezuela about three blocks from Av Brasil. There are buses to Pelotas (R$20, four hours, six daily) and Rio Grande (R$26, four hours, two daily), as well as one overnight bus to Porto Alegre (R$77, seven hours). You can buy tickets to Montevideo (five hours) and other Uruguayan destinations from the bus agencies along Calle Leonardo Oliveira on the Uruguayan side.

RIO GRANDE DO SUL

Brasília

Brazil's futuristic capital is the closest attempt on earth to a create a modern utopia. It's the result of a long-harnessed Brazilian dream of an inland capital, carved out of nowhere in the 1950s in a spectacular feat of urban planning, architectural design and political prophecy.

The purpose-built city and its surrounding area, known as the Distrito Federal (DF), occupies part of the Brazilian central plateau – the Planalto – totaling 5802 sq km, with rolling hills and a large artificial lake, Paranoá. Wide-open, spectacular cerulean skies characterize the whole area, a picturesque backdrop to Brasília's clean-lined design and marvelous architecture.

For a nation often tapped as the country of the future, Brasília is its revolutionary testament to that end, a living museum lauded the world over for everything from its avant-garde grid of perfectly planned streets to its über-organized residential apartment and commercial blocks. As Brazil's seat of government, it's a city of bureaucrats and government workers, all of whom relish the national capital as a '60s version of a third-millennium city. It remains the only city in the world constructed in the 20th century to achieve World Cultural Heritage designation by Unesco.

Nearly 50 years after its inauguration, Brasília is affluent, well-manicured and lively. If you're interested in modern architecture, you'll easily spend a few days visiting the city's impressive buildings and monuments, each day fueled by some of Brazil's top restaurants and vibrant *vida nocturna*. Otherwise, come here as a stopover en route to the Pantanal (p415), Chapada dos Veadeiros in Goiás (p401) or Ilha do Bananal in Tocantins (p640).

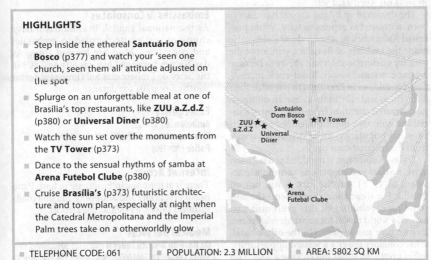

HIGHLIGHTS

- Step inside the ethereal **Santuário Dom Bosco** (p377) and watch your 'seen one church, seen them all' attitude adjusted on the spot

- Splurge on an unforgettable meal at one of Brasília's top restaurants, like **ZUU a.Z.d.Z** (p380) or **Universal Diner** (p380)

- Watch the sun set over the monuments from the **TV Tower** (p373)

- Dance to the sensual rhythms of samba at **Arena Futebol Clube** (p380)

- Cruise **Brasília's** (p373) futuristic architecture and town plan, especially at night when the Catedral Metropolitana and the Imperial Palm trees take on a otherworldly glow

Santuário Dom Bosco ★
ZUU a.Z.d.Z ★
Universal Diner ★
★ TV Tower
★ Arena Futebal Clube

- TELEPHONE CODE: 061   - POPULATION: 2.3 MILLION   - AREA: 5802 SQ KM

BRASÍLIA

HISTORY

Brasília and DF are the result of an ambitious urban project, which was set in motion by heroic President Juscelino Kubitschek, and orchestrated by architect Oscar Niemeyer, urban planner Lúcio Costa and landscape architect Burle Marx. The whole thing was built in just 41 months, though it was a long time coming.

The concept of an inland capital was first conceived in 1823 by Brazilian statesman José Bonifácio, who believed moving the capital from Rio de Janeiro was central to capitalizing on the country's vast inland resources and would bring an economic shock to the interior. His idea was shrugged off until years later, when Dom Bosco, a Salesian priest living in Turin, Italy, prophesied a new civilization would emerge in Brazil, somewhere between the 15th and 20th parallels. That caught Brazil's attention and land was allocated in the 1891 Constitution for a new capital.

Still, it wasn't until 1955 that Brasília started to become a reality. After almost 150 years of debate, President Kubitschek ordered the DF be carved out of the state of Goiás to house the new capital, Brasília. With millions of poor peasants from the Northeast working around the clock, Brasília was built, incredibly, in just three years (Niemeyer later admitted that it was all done too quickly) – it wasn't exactly finished, but it was ready to be the capital. The capital was officially moved from Rio to Brasília on April 21, 1960.

The dream of an inland capital had always been dismissed as expensive folly. What possessed Kubitschek to actually do it? Politics. He made the building of Brasília a symbol of the country's determination and ability to become a great economic power. Kubitschek successfully appealed to all Brazilians to put aside their differences and rally to the cause. In doing so, he distracted attention from the country's social and economic problems, gained enormous personal popularity, and borrowed heavily from the international banks.

Today, Kubitschek is heralded as a national hero (he died in a suspicious automobile accident in 1976) and the jury is still out on Brasília. For some, the city represents the outstanding capabilities of this great and vast nation, a world model for urban development, architecture and society. On the other hand, some consider the city a wasted opportunity, full of pretty buildings but lacking a soul. You can judge for yourself. Meanwhile, Niemeyer's original plans for the city continue to this day, with the opening most recently of the National Museum.

ORIENTATION

From the air, Brasília's millennial design evokes the image of an airplane, with each of its architectural marvels strategically laid out along the Eixo Monumental (which forms the fuselage); and its residential and commercial blocks along its outspread wings, known as *asas*.

The *plano piloto* (pilot plan) specified that the city would face the giant artificial Lago do Paranoá. In the fuselage are all the government buildings and monuments. The plaza of three powers – with the Palácio do Planalto, the Palácio do Congresso and the Palácio da Justiça – is in the cockpit. Out on the *asas* are block after numbered block of apartment buildings (known as *superquadras* or *quadras*) but little else.

To get the full effect, you must take a tour of the city by air, bus or foot. See p377 for details.

INFORMATION

Bookstores

Siciliano has branches on the 2nd floor of the Conjunto Nacional and Pátio Brasil, and the 1st floor of the Shopping Brasília malls. All locations have a good selection of English books and magazines.

Embassies & Consulates

As the national capital, Brasília has a large chunk of real estate devoted to embassies and consulates. Most are located along Av das Nações between Quadras 801 and 809 in the Setor de Embaixadas Sul (Embassy Sector South). See p701 for details.

Emergency

Ambulance (☎ 192)
Fire department (☎ 193)
Police (☎ 190)

Internet Access

There is at least one internet café in both Pátio Brasil (1st floor) and Shopping Brasília malls (ground floor), as well as the airport.

Medical Services

Da Base do Distrito Federal (☎ 3325 5050; SMHS 101)
Santa Lúcia (☎ 3445 0000; SHLS, Quadra 716, Conjuncto C)

ADDRESSES FOR THE LOGICAL MIND

Brasília's addresses are as futuristic as its architecture – a series of numbers and letters that look baffling at first but are easy to decipher once you know what all the acronyms mean.

For example, the address to Pensão da Zenilda is SQS 704, Bloco Q, Casa 29. That means it's in Super Quadra South 704, *bloco* (building) Q, *casa* (house) 29. The first digit in the address (7) shows the position east or west of the Eixo Rodoviário (the main north–south arterial road) – odd numbers to the west and even to the east, increasing as they move away from the center. The last two digits (04) show the distance north or south of the Eixo Monumental. So Pensão da Zenilda is four blocks to the south of the Eixo Monumental and four blocks east of the Eixo Rodoviário (1, 3, 5, 7). The higher the number of the Super Quadra, the further it is from the center.

Get to know these acronyms:

Asa Norte/Asa Sul The two 'wings' of the city, connected by main roads, *eixo rodoviários*. The N (Norte) or S (Sul) after an acronym indicates on which side of the Eixo Monumental it's located.

SBN/SBS (Setor Bancário Norte/Sul) The banking areas either side of the Eixo Monumental.

SCLN/SCLS (Setor Comércio Local Norte/Sul) The main shopping blocks between the *superquadras*.

SCN/SCS (Setor Comercial Norte/Sul) The commercial office block areas next to the main shopping centers.

SDN/SDS (Setor de Diversões Norte/Sul) The main *conjuntos* (shopping centers) either side of the Eixo Monumental.

SEN/SES (Setor de Embaixadas Norte/Sul) The embassy sectors.

SHIN/SHIS (Setor de Habitações Individuaís Norte/Sul) The residential areas around the lake. SHIN is reached on the Eixo Norte. SHIS is accessed via the bridges off Av das Nações.

SHN/SHS (Setor Hoteleiro Norte/Sul) The hotel sectors each side of the Eixo Monumental.

SMHN/SMHS (Setor Médico Hospitalar Norte/Sul) The hospital sectors each side of the Eixo Monumental, next to the SCN and SCS respectively.

SQN/SQS (Super Quadras Norte/Sul) The individual *superquadras* in the main residential wings of the *plano piloto*.

If all of this seems too logical, make sure you write down the address, as all these *superquadras* start to look the same after a very short while.

Money

There are banks with money-changing facilities in the Setor Bancário Sul (SBS; Banking Sector South) and Setor Bancário Norte (SBN; Banking Sector North). Both sectors are close to the city bus station. The airport also has a variety of ATMs, most with Cirrus/MasterCard/Visa networking. Travel agencies will change cash dollars and often give better rates.

Banco do Brasil (SCS Quadra 5, Bloco B, loja 158; ☽ 11am-4pm Mon-Fri) Has a Visa/MasterCard ATM. Its handy branch at the airport changes money, has a Visa/MasterCard ATM and is open on Saturday.

Post

Main post office (SHS Quadra 2, Bloco B; ☽ 9am-5pm Mon-Fri) There is also a branch conveniently located in the arrivals hall of the airport.

Tourist Information

If all you need is a map or a list of attractions, simply pick up a brochure from the front desk of any large hotel or travel agency.

C.A.T. tourist office (airport; ☽ 8am-10pm) Don't leave the airport without stopping here. Most of the staff speak English and they offer a wealth of information. You will not receive nearly the same level of service at the TV Tower location.

Travel Agencies

CTR Turismo (☎ 3323 1713; Hotel Nacional, SHS Quadra 1; ☽ 8:30am-7pm Mon-Sat) Useful for booking flights, renting cars, and organizing city tours and the like around the city.

SIGHTS
Memorial JK

The tomb of JK (President Juscelino Kubitschek) lies underneath eerily beautiful stained-glass by French artist Marianne Peretti inside the **Memorial JK** (☎ 3226 7868; Praça do Cruzeiro; admission R$4; ☽ 9am-6pm Tue-Sun). The museum houses JK's 3000-book strong personal library as well as a pictorial history of Brasília. Don't miss JK's 1973 Ford Galaxie just outside the back door.

TV Tower

The 75m-high **observation deck** (☎ 3325 5735; Eixo Monumental; admission free; ☽ 8am-8pm) of the TV

BRASÍLIA

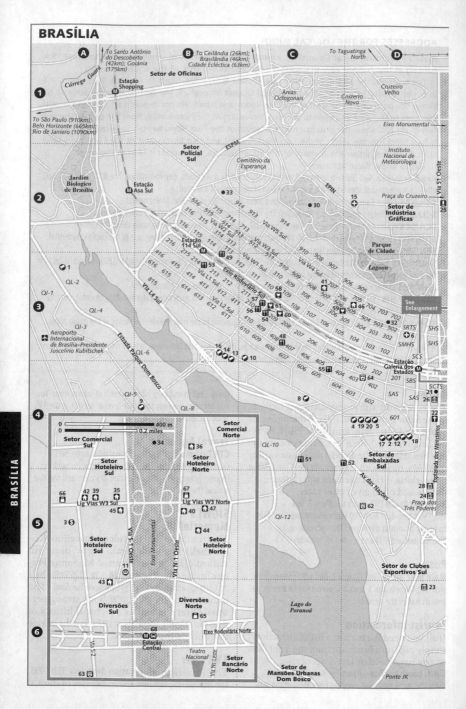

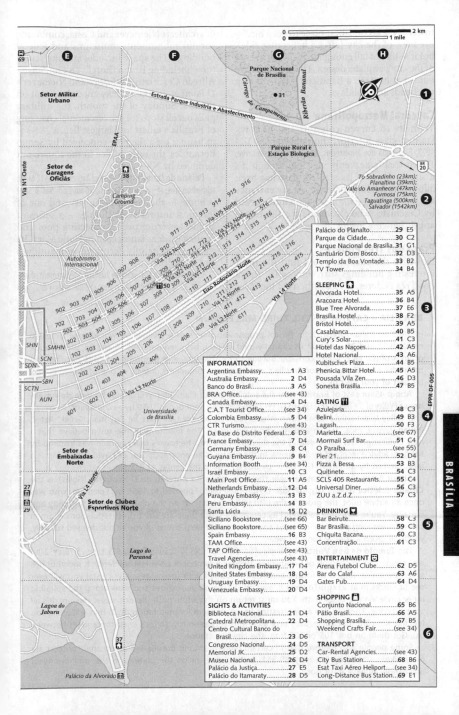

tower is the second-best place to get a bird's-eye view of the city (after a helicopter ride), but it's still not tall enough to really get a sense of the city's airplane design. That's not a *favela* (slum) at its base; a handicrafts fair runs on weekends and holidays.

Catedral Metropolitana

With its 16 curved columns and its wavy stained-glass interior, the **cathedral** (☎ 3224 4073; Esplanada dos Ministérios, Asa Sul; admission free; ☼ 8am-6pm) is heavenly viewing, though it's a shame some of its stained glass has been allowed to fall into disrepair. At the entrance are the haunting *Four Disciples* statues carved by Ceschiatti, who also made the aluminum angels hanging inside.

Praça dos Trés Poderes

Down in the cockpit, you'll find the most interesting buildings surrounding the Praça dos Trés Poderes. It's a synthesis of the ideas of architects Niemeyer and Costa, combining various monuments, museums and federal buildings. The space includes striking sculptures, including Bruno Giorgi's *Os Candangos*, Alfredo Ceschiatti's *A Justiça* and Niemeyer's *O Pombal*. If you're lucky enough to visit on the first Sunday of the month, the military pulls out all stops for the ceremonial changing of Brasília's tallest and largest flag, a 286-sq-m banner on a flagpole conceived by Sergio Bernardes, the only edifice in the square not designed by Niemeyer.

Palácio do Itamaraty (Palace of Arches; ☎ 3411 6640; admission free; ☼ 3-5pm Mon-Fri, 10am-2pm Sat & Sun) is home to the Foreign Ministry and one of the most impressive buildings – a series of arches towering over a reflecting pool and floating gardens landscaped by Burle Marx. Its rooms are tastefully decorated with antiques and art objects.

Outside the **Palácio da Justiça** (Department of Justice; ☎ 3218 3223; admission free; ☼ 8am-noon & 2-6pm

---

BRASÍLIA – CAPITAL OF THE THIRD MILLENNIUM

In 1883 an Italian priest, John Bosco, prophesied that a new civilization would arise between parallels 15 and 20, and that its capital would be built between parallels 15 and 16, on the edge of an artificial lake. Many consider Brasília to be that city, and a number of cults have sprung up in the area. If you tire of Brasília's architectural monuments, a visit to one of the cults may be part of your destiny.

About 45km east of Brasília, near the satellite city of Planaltina, you'll find the **Vale do Amanhecer** (Valley of the Dawn; ☎ 3388 0537; ☼ 10pm-midnight), founded in 1959 by a clairvoyant, Tia Neiva. The valley is actually a small town where you can see (or take part in) Egyptian, Greek, Aztec, Indian, Gypsy, Inca, Trojan and Afro-Brazilian rituals. The mediums in the town believe that a new civilization will come during the third millennium. The town's main temple was inspired by spiritual advice received by Tia Neiva. In the center is an enormous Star of David, which forms a lake, pierced by an arrow. Get there by bus 617 from the center of Brasília.

About 63km west of Brasília, near the town of Santo Antônio do Descoberto (Goiás), is the **Cidade Eclética** (Eclectic City; ☎ 3626 1391; ☼ 8am-6pm). Founded in 1956 by Yokanam, who was once an airline pilot, the group's aim is to unify all religions on the planet through fraternity and equality. You're welcome to attend its ceremonies, but there are strict dress regulations. Women cannot wear long pants (skirts only) and men cannot wear shorts. If you're not dressed suitably, you'll be given a special tunic to wear.

The **Templo da Boa Vontade** (Temple of Goodwill; ☎ 3245 1070; SGAS, Quadra 915, Lotes 75/76; ☼ 24hr) was created by the Legion of Goodwill in 1989 as a symbol of universal solidarity. It incorporates seven pyramids, joined to form a cone that is topped with the biggest raw crystal you will ever see (it clocks in at 21kg). To view it, you must take off your shoes and walk along the spiraling inner circle via the black path. You must return on the white path (do not screw this up). It's all a bit dizzying. There is also an interesting Egyptian room for meditation (R$2) that will make you feel like King Tut (of course, they take all of this very seriously, so let's keep these jokes between us). Get there on bus 105 or 107 from the city bus station.

Some people also believe that in certain regions around Brasília extraterrestrial contacts are more likely – at km69 on Hwy BR-351, for instance, or on the plateau in the smaller city of Brasilândia. Believe it, or not!

Mon-Fri), water cascades between its arches into a koi fish pond; inside is a lovely internal garden. Don't show up in shorts or Havaianas.

Featuring the photogenic 'dishes' and twin towers, the congress building, **Congresso Nacional** (Parliament; admission free; ⏰ 9:30am-4:30pm Mon-Fri, 9am-1:30pm Sat & Sun), is one of the more interesting buildings on the inside as well. In addition to the color-coded chambers of the Senate (blue) and House of Representatives (green) – *so* '60s gauche – there is an architecturally interesting 'Tunnel of Time' and an exhibit of antique Senate benches and microphones from 1867. English tours are available by appointment. Same dress code as Palácio da Justiça.

The president's office, the **Palácio do Planalto** (Presidential Palace; ☎ 3411 2317; admission free; ⏰ 9:30am-2:30pm Sun), is another Niemeyer design that's worth seeing, both inside and out. From the curved lines of the exterior to the lustrous columns and sweeping curved ramp inside, it's one of the best examples of architectural modernism in the world. On the tour, which is only available on Sunday, you can even peek into the President's office. There is a ceremonial changing of the guard outside the gates every hour on weekends and every two hours during the week.

Complexo Cultural da República

As Niemeyer's original plans for Brasília continue to come to fruition, new attractions are popping up just east of Catedral Metropolitana. The first to open, inaugurated in late 2006 with a tribute to Niemeyer, is the **Museu Nacional** (admission free; ⏰ 9am-5pm Tue-Sun). Another spherical half dome by the architect, the inside features a discreet mezzanine mostly held up by columns suspended from the roof. A signature curved ramp juts out from its base and runs around the outside like a ring of Saturn. The massive exterior of the new working national library, the **Biblioteca Nacional** (⏰ 9am-5pm Tue-Sun), is finished, though city planners were rushing to fill its walls with the promised 60 years of books during our visit.

Santuário Dom Bosco

Even more impressive than the cathedral, **Dom Bosco's Shrine** (☎ 3223 6542; Via W3 Sul; admission free; ⏰ 7am-7pm) is made of concrete columns that support 7400 pieces of illuminated Murano glass symbolizing a starry sky. It casts an otherworldly blue and purple glow over the

whole interior. It's near the budget hotels at Quadra 702.

Centro Cultural Banco do Brasil

Brasília's most important **contemporary museum** (☎ 3310 7087; admission to expositions free; SCES, Trecho 2, Conjunto 22; ⏰ 10am-9pm Tue-Sun) is in a giant building in the South Sports Club Sector. It houses fascinating exhibitions in two galleries, an indie cinema, a café and a bookstore. There is a free bus every hour from Hotel Nacional (look for the white and yellow bus that says CCBB).

Parks

In the northern reaches of the city limits, the 30,000-hectare **Parque Nacional de Brasília** (☎ 3465 2013; admission R$3; ⏰ 8am-4pm) is a good place to relax. It has natural swimming pools and is home to a number of endangered animals, including deer, banded anteaters, giant armadillos and maned wolves. Bus 128.1 from the city bus station goes past the front gate. The park is very popular on weekends. There's a visitors' center where you can get information about the park and walking trails.

A good park not far from the city center is the **Parque da Cidade** (Eixo Monumental, Asa Sul; admission free; ⏰ 5am-midnight), where you'll find a swimming pool with artificial waves and kiosks where you can grab a snack.

TOURS

If you want to save your feet, half-day guided tours of the city start at around R$75. Hotel Nacional houses several travel agencies offering sightseeing tours. You can also book bus tours through the tourist office at the airport. For fluent English tours, **Billy Deeter** (☎ 8112 3434; billyvango@yahoo.com), an American who has lived in Brasília since he was a child, organizes group and/or private customized tours that include some off-the-beaten-track points of interest starting at R$100.

Apart from relocating, there are only two ways to make quick sense of Brasília's über-sensible layout. The quickest and most exhilarating is a breathtaking 10-minute helicopter flight with **Esat Aerotaxi** (☎ 3323 8777). Departures are from the heliport near the back of the base of the TV Tower, and trips cost R$120 per person with a four-person minimum.

Otherwise, although renting a car is trial by fire, the city is a driving dreamland whose big picture becomes all the more clearer with wheels, and driving here is incalculably safer and more comfortable than in other cities in Brazil. Its (☎ 3223-0161; www.itsrentacar.com.br; ⏰ 8am-8pm Mon-Fri) rents cars from the Hotel Nacional complex for as little as R$20 per day with a kilometer cap.

If that sounds too hairy, you can do a bus tour or combine a ride on local buses from the city bus station (104 or 108 are the best) with some long walks to see the bulk of Brasília's attractions. Some buildings are closed on weekends and at night, so double check before setting out.

SLEEPING
Budget
Good budget accommodations are hard to come by. If you plan to stay over a weekend, a lot of midrange and high-end hotels often slash prices by almost half, and everyone offers significant discounts from the posted rates if you ask. The most inexpensive places to stay are on or near Via W3 Sul, 1km or 2km southwest of the Eixo Monumental, but hygiene is not a top priority in many, and your safety (and that of your belongings) is far from guaranteed. They cater mostly to long-term-stay Brazilians and aren't exactly traveler friendly.

Pousada Villa Zen (☎ 3443 2548; www.pousadavillazen .com.br in Portuguese; SQS Quadra 705, Bloco G, Casa 51; s/d R$30/60; 🖳) You'll have to check your English at the door, but this 21-room pousada is clean and has a pleasant lobby with free internet, as well as a big kitchen and laundry facilities.

Cury's Solar (☎ 3244 1899; SQS Quadra 707, Bloco I, Casa 15; s/d R$35/70; 🖳) The 19 rooms here are practically on top of each other, and some guests complain that's it's too hot, but if you don't mind those mild inconveniences, it's clean, family-run, and very safe. Add R$7 for breakfast, though guests are welcome to use the kitchen and laundry facilities. Get off at the stop between Quadras 707 and 708, walk up through the park and turn right at the third row of houses.

Brasília Hostel (☎ 3343 0531; SRPN Quadra 2, Lote 2; s/d R$37/71; 🖳) This 20-room hostel has big, open breezeways, spanking-clean rooms and individual lockers in dorms of six beds each (there are a few doubles as well). It's located just west of Asa Norte in Brasília's designated camping sector.

Midrange & Top End
Most hotels offer substantial discounts on weekends throughout the year (prices plummet 30% on average), making some of the top-end hotels very affordable, as well as discounts when reserved ahead. Hotels within the *plano piloto* are in either the SHN (Setor Hoteleiro Norte) or the SHS (Setor Hoteleiro Sul). Those in the SHN are more conveniently located to shopping centers, but those in the SHS are better value. The tourist office at the airport can help organize discounts at these hotels.

Bristol Hotel (☎ 3962 6162; www.bristolhotel.com.br in Portuguese; SHS Quadra 4, Bloco F; s/d R$110/140; 🖂 🖳 📧) A pleasant lobby and spacious rooms with marble floors and a small desk make this hotel good value. The rooms were touched up in 2005, so they don't feel quite as outdated as others in this category.

Casablanca (☎ 3328 8586; www.casablancabrasilia .com.br; SHN Quadra 3, Bloco A; s/d R$115/144; 🖂 🖳) Worn carpets and photographs of vaguely Bavarian landscapes are signatures at this simple yet friendly hotel near the TV Tower. All rooms have a double and single bed. If you get one near the lobby, you can pick up the free wi-fi.

Hotel das Naçoes (☎ 3322 8050; www.hoteldas nacoes.com.br in Portuguese; SHS Quadra 4, Bloco I; s/d R$120/160; 🖂 🖳) Clean and comfortable rooms with hardwood floors and a giant minibar make this a good option for stocking up on food. The location across the street from Patío Brasil shopping center is ideal.

Alvorada Hotel (☎ 2195 1122; www.alvoradahotel .com.br in Portuguese; SHS Quadra 4, Bloco A; s/d R$134/ 174; 🖂) Alvorada is good value, with clean and compact standard rooms. Breakfast is great and there are fine views from the restaurant. Ask for a room facing away from W3 to lessen the traffic noise.

Phenicia Bittar Hotel (☎ 3218 5858, 0800-707 5858; www.hoteisbittar.com.br; SHS Quadra 5, Bloco J; s/d R$S135/165; 🖂 🖳) Third-floor nonsmoking rooms with ceramic floors are the nicest and brightest in this large hotel.

Aracoara Hotel (☎ 3424 9222, 0800-614 881; www .aracoara.com.br in Portuguese; SHN Quadra 5, Bloco C; s/d R$188/229; 🖂 🖳) It's sporadically decorated in funky 1970s decor, which is exactly its charm. Rooms made over in 2006 are spacious and comfortable.

Blue Tree Alvorada (☎ 3424 7080; www.bluetree .com.br; SHTN Trecho 1, Conjunto 1B, Bloco C; s/d R$303/

351; ⬡ ▢ ⬢) The capital's most stylish hotel is a horseshoe-shaped complex overlooking Lago do Paranoá, right next door to the President's residence. Famed architect Ruy Ohtake designed a futuristic, open lobby with wavy hallways that climb up towards a wiry, Zeppelinesque ceiling. It's a haven for celebs, models and, of course, architects.

Sonesta Brasília (☎ 3424 2500; www.sonesta.com /brasília; SHN Quadra 5, Bloco B; s/d R$305/345; ⬡ ▢ ⬢) Inaugurated in late 2006, this is Brasília's newest hotel, so naturally it's in better shape than the majority. Rooms decked out in warm colors like olive green and tangerine are a soothing change of pace from the ivory-toned dominance of Brasília's cityscape.

our pick Kubitschek Plaza (☎ 3329 9649; www .kubitschek.com.br; SHN Quadra 2, Bloco E; s/d R$370/390; ⬡ ▢ ⬢) The halls and lobby of this classic choice feature wonderful art by local artists and famous photographs of Juscelino Kubitschek's administration. Rooms on the 12th, 14th and 15th floors got a modern makeover in 2006, including gorgeous hardwood floors and earth-toned pinstriped headboards.

EATING

Brazilians may say that Brasília is boring, but foodies flock here with abandon – the capital has one of the highest concentrations of starred restaurants in the country and eating here is definitely a highlight. The best selections are centered around SCLS 209/210, 409/410 and 411/412, which forms a sort of 'gourmand triangle' (it is also home to the city's most lively nightlife, packed from Thursday to Sunday).

Another good selection of restaurants is clustered in SCLS 405. Here you'll find Tex-Mex, Portuguese, German, Thai, Japanese, Chinese and vegetarian eateries. It's packed on weekends.

Elsewhere, Brazilians in need of sustenance head to Brasília's shopping malls. With buildings so spread out and few street stalls, finding somewhere to eat out of the heat during the day can drive one to drink, except it's hard to find that as well. Not surprisingly, three centrally located oases – Shopping Brasília, Pátio Brasil and Conjunto Nacional – all have small cafés and food courts with enough variety to cater to most tastes and cranked-up air-conditioning.

There are also many excellent restaurants and bars scattered around the city. In the fol-lowing addresses, SCL means Setor Comércio Local, which is the space provided in the *quadras* for shops, restaurants etc. The letter N or S immediately after SCL means *norte* (north) or *sul* (south), and is followed by the *quadra* number, the block number and the *loja* (shop) number.

Budget

Belini (☎ 3345 0777; SCL Quadra 113, Bloco D, Loja 35; sandwiches R$5-11; ⏱ 7am-11:30pm) Though housed inside a very expensive-looking Italian mansion, this high-end food emporium/restaurant offers reasonably priced sandwiches at the counter of its small coffee shop (anything on ciabatta should sort you out).

Marietta (☎ 3327 3892; Shopping Brasília, Praça de Alimentação; sandwiches R$6.50-7.30) This sandwich shop turns out the capital's best: a triangular triple-decker of arugula, buffalo mozzarella and sun-dried tomatoes. It has killer juices as well.

O Paraíba (☎ 3244 2221; SCL Quadra 405, Bloco B, Loja 6; dishes R$6.50-15.50; ⏱ noon-3pm & 4-11pm Mon-Thu, 11am-3pm & 4pm-midnight Fri-Sun) Indigenous art lines the walls at this upscale *tapiocaria* where quesadilla-like dishes are made from tapioca, a specialty of the Northeast. Try the signature dish, *queijo coalho* and *carne de sol* served with homemade butter from the countryside.

Midrange

Azulejaria (☎ 3443 0698; SCL Quadra 408, Bloco D, Loja 1; meals R$10-18; ⏱ noon-3pm & 6pm-late Mon-Fri, 12:30-3:30pm & 6pm-late Sat) This trendy spot dotted with painted tiles from local artists offers excellent fresh oysters and champagne on Thursday, but its filet-mignon sandwich for R$9.80 is one of the best deals in town.

Mormaii Surf Bar (☎ 3248 1265; SHIS, Quadra do Lago 10, Bloco E, Lote 8; sandwiches R$12-20; ⏱ 10am-2am) Locals park themselves on the outdoor lakeside patio every afternoon for tasty sandwiches and the house specialty, *açaí na tigela*, a refreshing sorbet-like meal of blended palmberries, guaraná syrup, bananas and honey. On weekends, the waterfront location (located in the Pontão) attracts a roaring nightlife crowd as well.

Pizza à Bessa (☎ 3345 5252; SCL Quadra 214, Bloco C, Loja 14; pizza rodízio R$16.90; ⏱ 6pm-midnight) The all-you-can eat option here is implausibly cheap and the best way to try some inventive ingredients like pureed pumpkin, broccoli, and an outrageous dessert pizza with a huge

BRASÍLIA

scoop of ice cream. The *queijo coalho* (cured white cheese) and *rapadura* (dried sugarcane juice) pizza is a masterpiece. It's packed with a fun and rambunctious crowd.

Quitinete (☎ 3242 0506; SCLS Quadra 209, Bloco B, Loja 22; desserts R$3-5, sandwiches R$17; ◷ 7am-2am) This chic emporium/restaurant/bakery serves exquisite desserts (try the *tartellete de limão*) and the best coffee in the city (roasted in-house).

Top End

Lagash (☎ 3273 0098; SCLN Quadra 308, Bloco B, Loja 11/17; dishes R$25-45; ◷ noon-4pm & 7pm-midnight Mon-Sat, noon-6pm Sun) A mix of Moroccan, Lebanese and Syrian cuisine earns this sparsely decorated restaurant top Middle Eastern food in town year after year. Anything with lamb is delightful.

ZUU a.Z.d.Z (☎ 3244 1039; SCLS Quadra 210, Bloco A, Loja 38; dishes R$42-69; ◷ noon-3pm & 8pm-midnight Mon-Fri, 8pm-midnight Sat) The city's hottest contemporary table honors the slow food tradition in an exotic atmosphere that highlights fresh produce from Amazonas and Pará. Chef Mara Alcamim, who trained in New York and Italy, is Brasília's *chef du moment*. Her grilled shrimp in apricot chutney served alongside Brie risotto is cause for genuflecting.

ourpick **Universal Diner** (☎ 3442 2089; SQS Quadra 210, Bloco B, Loja 30; dishes R$47-64; ◷ noon-3pm & 7pm-midnight Mon-Thu, noon-3pm & 7pm-1:30am Fri, noon-4pm & 7pm-1:30am Sat, noon-4pm Sun) A junkyard-chic aesthetic greets patrons at this eclectic eatery (it's overflowing with funky bric-a-brac and antique knickknacks), another of the city's Brazilicious culinary gems. Mouth-watering tenderloin *au poivre* is the way to go, served up on vinyl LP placemats.

DRINKING

Bar Brasília (☎ 3443 4323; SCLS Quadra 506, Bloco A, Loja 15A; dishes R$16-25; ◷ 5pm-2am Mon-Thu, 11:30am-2am Fri & Sat, 11:30am-midnight Sun) A Brasília institution in the same vein as the classic bars from Rio and São Paulo, complete with a hardwood bar relocated from a pharmacy in 1928, and antique tiled floors. It's great for draft beer, and the Friday to Saturday *feijoada* (bean-and-meat stew served with rice, R$25.50) is highly recommended as well.

Bar Beirute (☎ 3244 1717; SCLS Quadra 109, Bloco A, Lojas 2/4; 2-person dishes R$35; ◷ 11am-2am) This Brasília institution has a massive outdoor patio packed with an edgier crowd than most spots. It's a GLS point – the clever Brazilian acronym for gays, lesbians and sympathetics –

but it's really a free-for-all. There's no better spot for a cold Bohemia; the Middle Eastern cuisine is an afterthought.

Concentração (☎ 3242 3426; SCLS Quadra 209, Bloco C, Loja 03/05; ◷ 11am-late) Another reliable option on the same street as Chiquita Bacana, featuring a lively bar that is home to a cavalcade of tragically hip with projection screens and a nightly DJ.

ENTERTAINMENT

If you're after live music, check the listings in the 'Caderno C' section of the daily *Correio Brasiliense* newspaper or the bi-monthly minimag, *Tablado*.

ourpick **Arena Futebol Clube** (☎ 3224 9401; SCES, Trecho 3, Lote 1; cover R$10-15; ◷ 10pm-late Thu-Sat, 7pm-midnight Sun) It's well worth the taxi fare to the Setor de Clubes Esportivos Sul, southwest of Praça dos Trés Poderes, for this live-music mecca that takes over the soccer club on weekends. Daughters of ministers and politicos sweat out to hip-shaking *forró* (popular Northeastern music), samba and samba-funk. The best we've seen outside Rio.

Bar do Calaf (☎ 3325 7408; SBS Quadra 2, Bloco S, Loja 51/57; cover R$10-15; ◷ 10pm-late) Though technically a Spanish restaurant, the food is an afterthought to the wildly mixed crowd, all of whom rate the excellent live samba, *pagode* (popular samba) and *choro* (improvised samba) over the paella. Monday is the biggest draw for samba-funk. Located in the Ed Empire Center office complex.

Gate's Pub (☎ 3225 4576; SCLS Quadra 403, Bloco B, Loja 34; cover R$15-20; ◷ 9pm-3am Tue-Sun) Gate's claims to be the longest-established bar in the city. Most nights there's live music with a rock, reggae and funk flavor, then dance music until closing.

Chiquita Bacana (☎ 3242 1212; SCLS Quadra 209, Bloco A, Loja 37; ◷ 5:30pm-2am Mon, noon-2am Tue-Sun) The *patricinhas* and *mauricinhos* – as Brazil's beautiful people have been affectionately coined – spill out onto Bloco 210 at this trendy open-air *chopperia* (beer hall). A daily happy hour from 5pm to 8pm nets an excellent *chope* for R$2.20.

SHOPPING

The weekend crafts fair at the base of the TV Tower is a good place to pick up leather goods, ceramics and art objects.

You should be able to satisfy your other shopping needs in one of Brasília's shopping malls:

BRASÍLIA OR BUST?

As Brasília approaches its 50th anniversary in 2010, the question remains: does it work? Well, it depends on who you ask. Brasília tends to be very polemic. Brasiliense, as locals are referred to, regard the capital as a well-organized Brazilian utopia: roads are well maintained, grass is green, vehicles actually stop for pedestrians in crosswalks (a miracle in Brazil) and there are no *favelas* in the city. Large trucks are forbidden from entering the city limits, keeping pollution in check, and there is a height limit to signs and billboards, ensuring the city's big, open skies remain unobstructed (see the oddly short golden arches at McDonald's – you can nearly reach up and touch it). For Brazil, it's an impressive standard of living. On the other hand, most folks in the rest of the country see the city as a soulless bore, a sterile metropolis full of bureaucratic nonsense. Dig a little deeper and you'll find holes in the city's perfect plan, mostly concerning traffic. If a bus breaks down or there's an accident, it can be snarled for hours. With very few exit points on the city's roadways, a missed turn can be disastrous. At the end of the day, Brasília is a lot like Los Angeles – residents love it while everyone else loves to hate it.

Conjunto Nacional (Asa Norte SCN) Brasília's first mall, right across from the bus station. Contains a post office, pharmacies, restaurants and a supermarket.

Pátio Brasil (Asa Sul, W3 SCS) The nicest of the capital's centrally located malls. More modern than the Conjunto Nacional, with a better restaurant selection.

Pier 21 (Setor de Clubes Esportivos Sul) Has the largest concentration of restaurants, bars and nightclubs but very few actual stores. Very popular with the young and well-off.

Shopping Brasília (Asa Norte SCN Quadra 5) All amenities, including cinemas and restaurants.

GETTING THERE & AWAY

As the capital, Brasília has a large daily influx of sightseers and lobbyists. The international airport connects with all major Brazilian cities. Most visitors fly in, but those who choose to go overland will cover some long distances.

Air

Many domestic flights make stopovers in Brasília, so it's easy to catch a plane to almost anywhere in Brazil. Flights to Rio are 1½ hours; to São Paulo, one hour 20 minutes.

The easiest way to book a flight is through the travel agencies in the Hotel Nacional complex. Nearly all the domestic and international airline offices here have been consolidated into travel agencies. Exceptions:

BRA (☎ 2105 0909; www.voebra.com.br)
TAM (☎ 4002 5700; www.tam.com.br)
TAP (☎ 3223 7138; www.flytap.com)

That said, to book *most* domestic and international airlines, see the following agencies at Nacional, respectively:

Air Brazil Viagens (☎ 3322 8822)
Ventur Viagens (☎ 3223 5002)

Bus

From the **train and long-distance bus station** (rodoferroviária; ☎ 3363 4045), due west of the city center, there are buses to places you've never heard of, but no trains. Prices noted here are for *executivo* services. Bus destinations include Goiânia (R$34, three hours), Rio (R$179, 17 hours), São Paulo (R$186, 14 hours) and Salvador (R$170, 22 hours). There are also buses to Cuiabá (R$171, 20 hours) and Porto Velho (R$239, 42 hours). Buses run north along Hwy BR-153 to Belém (R$243, 35 hours, three daily), but the road around the Tocantins border can be impassable during the rainy season.

Buses go to Pirenópolis (R$17, three hours, seven daily) and Alto Paraíso (R$27, 3½ hours, two daily) for access to the Parque Nacional da Chapada dos Veadeiros.

Getting Around

President Juscelino Kubitschek international airport (☎ 3364 9000) is 12km south of the center. To get to the airport from the city, take a 102 or 102.1 bus (R$2, 40 minutes) from the city bus station. Conversely, catch either bus at the bus stop to your right as you exit the airport arrivals hall. A taxi to/from the airport from the center costs R$30 to R$35.

To get from the city bus station to the long-distance bus and train station, take local bus 131 (R$2).

There are car-rental agencies at Brasília's airport and the Hotel Nacional.

Inaugurated in 2001, **Metro DF** (one-way ticket R$3; ☯ 6am-8pm Mon-Fri) is pretty much useless for travelers. It runs from the city bus station to the outer suburbs of Taguatinga and Samambaia.

Goiás

Goiás is Brazil's road less traveled, though not for good reason: fiery red sunsets over never-ending skies and lush, rolling hills set the stage for this sparsely populated state's unparalleled postcard-perfect views. While oftentimes almost criminally overlooked by tourists, Goiás is home to one of the country's most important and beautiful landscapes, the savannalike cerrado, which is the backdrop to the unspoiled splendor of the state's flawlessly preserved national parks and sleepy colonial towns.

Sweeping across Brazil's central high plains, the endangered cerrado, characterized by dense forests and gentle, sloping plateaus, is a worldwide biodiversity hot spot. In recent years, Goiás became the center of a campaign aimed to protect this important biome, all too much of which was plowed under at a rapid rate over the years to make way for immense soy plantations. Agriculture is big business here (Goiás once boasted more millionaires per capita than any other state), but soy has lost steam in recent years after too many eager beavers jumped on the bandwagon. Eventually, the banks pulled the plug on easy loans. These days, the biodiesel and ethanol industries are paying the bills.

Goiás is most often traversed by intrepid travelers looking to break their journey between the futuristic metropolis of Brasília and the Pantanal, the world's largest wetlands. Major attractions include the picturesque colonial villages of Cidade de Goiás and Pirenópolis, the therapeutic hot springs at Caldas Novas, and the rivers, waterfalls and forest trails of the Parque Nacional da Chapada dos Veadeiros.

With its vast distances and excellent regional food, it's easy to get lost in Goiás for a few weeks. It's not as hectic as Rio or the Northeast, the people and towns are more prosperous, and the raw beauty of the South American savanna is spectacular.

HIGHLIGHTS

- Soak up the alternative atmosphere in colonially cool **Pirenópolis** (p388)
- Wander lazily the cobblestone streets of **Cidade de Goiás** (p386) in a sugar-induced coma
- Trek through the unique high-cerrado flora in **Parque Nacional da Chapada dos Veadeiros** (p401)
- Rock-hop the naturally formed lunarscape at **Vale da Lua** (p402), near Chapada dos Veadeiros
- Mingle with emas (the biggest birds in Brazil) and anteaters in **Parque Nacional das Emas** (p386)

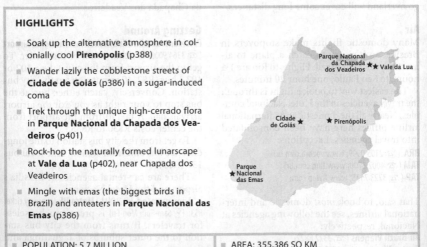

- POPULATION: 5.7 MILLION
- AREA: 355,386 SQ KM

History

On the heels of the gold discoveries in Minas Gerais, *bandeirantes* (groups of roaming adventurers who explored the interior) pushed further inland in search of more precious metals and, as always, Indian slaves. In 1682 a *bandeira,* headed by the old Paulista Bartolomeu Bueno da Silva, visited the region. The Goyaz Indians gave him the nickname *anhanguera* (old devil) when, after burning some *cachaça* (sugarcane rum) – which the Indians believed to be water – on a plate, he threatened to set fire to all the rivers if they didn't show him where their gold mines were. Three years later, having been given up for dead, the old devil returned to São Paulo with a few survivors, and with gold and Indian slaves from Goiás.

In 1722, da Silva's son, who had been on the first trip, organized another *bandeira.* The gold rush was on. It followed a pattern similar to that in Minas Gerais: first came the Paulistas, then the Portuguese Emboadas (immigrants who had arrived for the earlier gold rush in Minas Gerais) and soon the Black slaves. With everything imported from so far away, prices in Goiás were high. Many suffered and died, particularly the slaves. The gold rush ended quickly.

Goiás achieved official statehood in 1889. Things were relatively quiet until the mid-1950s, when the Brazilian dream of an inland capital was realized and a portion of Goiás was carved out to build Brasília. Shortly thereafter, Goiás thrived. Under the wing of a colossal

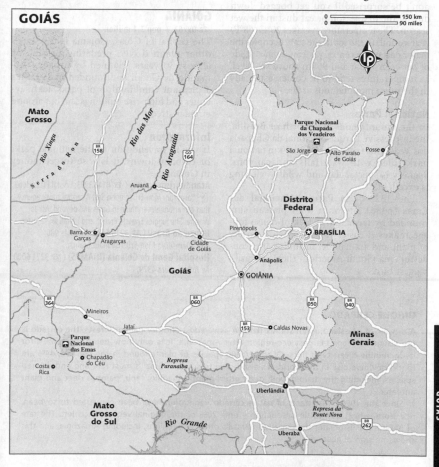

agriculture boom (sugarcane and soy paid the bills), the state flourished, and many farmers were made into millionaires nearly overnight. That has settled some in recent years, although the state remains an agricultural hotbed.

In 1989, due to the vastness of its borders, Goiás once again forfeited some of its land, when the northern half of the state split off to become the separate state of Tocantins. Today, Goiás remains one of Brazil's most prosperous and livable states.

Climate
Most of Goiás lies within the Brazilian highlands, which have a tropical climate. Between October and March it's hot and humid. April to September it's hot and dusty. That said, don't be surprised if you get bogged down during the dry season or eat dust in the wet season. The temperature averages 20°C (68°F) year-round. In the south the state occupies the major part of the central plateau, at an altitude of between 750m and 900m above sea level, so temperatures tend to be cooler, especially in the more mountainous areas.

National Parks
In the mountainous area north of Brasília, the impressive Parque Nacional da Chapada dos Veadeiros (p401) is a 650-sq-km national park filled with waterfalls and canyons. Scenery is spectacular and wildlife viewing is excellent.

The 132-sq-km Parque Nacional das Emas (p386) sits on a high plateau surrounded by farmland. A lack of dense foliage makes it easier to spot a wide variety of plant and animal life, including the wonderful ema (South American rhea) – Brazil's biggest bird.

Getting There & Away
The gateway to Goiás is Brasília, with daily flights to all major Brazilian cities. It's also possible to travel overland via some long bus rides. The majority of travelers coming from the coast first pass through Minas Gerais, or from the north through São Paulo. Minas is the more scenic and interesting route.

Getting Around
Goiás offers many attractions and is a popular stopover for travelers wanting to break their journey between the coast and the Pantanal wetland to the west. Regular bus services connect all the major towns and cities. Road conditions are generally good and renting a car is a viable option.

GOIÂNIA
☎ 0xx62 / pop 1.1 million
The capital of Goiás, Goiânia is the state's other planned city, predating Brasília by almost 30 years. Planned by urbanist Armando de Godói and founded in 1933, it's a pleasant combination of parks, leafy avenues and high-rise buildings laid out around circular streets.

Information
If you're traveling on to the national parks or colonial towns, it is wise to get money in Goiânia.

Atan tourism agency (☎ 8146 3993; Crystal Plaza Hotel; ☽ 8am-7pm Mon-Fri, to noon Sat) A central travel agency that can arrange everything in Goiás and beyond. Ask for Wanira. She juggles English, French and Italian like a jester.

Banco do Brasil (☎ 3216 5500; Av Goiás 980; ☽ 10am-4pm Mon-Fri) The main branch.

Hospital Geral de Goiânia (INAMPS) (☎ 3221 6000; Av Anhanguera 4379)

UNIQUE CERRADO

A mosaic of grassland, palm stands (known as *veredas*) and dry gallery forests, the cerrado is the country's second-largest eco-region after Amazonia. It is only now being recognized for its incredible diversity of flora. Of the 10,000 species of plants found in the cerrado, 44% are found nowhere else in the world. It's also home to some of Brazil's most rare and endangered species, including the maned wolf, giant otter, giant armadillo, tapir, pampas deer and giant anteater.

Since the 1970s, vast tracts of native cerrado vegetation have been converted to soybean, rice, corn, wheat and cattle production – only 20% of the original vegetation is left. The rate of habitat loss is greater than in any of Brazil's other eco-regions, including Amazonia, and this shows no sign of abating.

GOIÂNIA

INFORMATION
Atan Travel Agency...........(see 6)
Banco do Brasil.................**1** C1
HSBC............................**2** B2
Post Office......................**3** B3
Yes Internet Café................**4** B2

SIGHTS & ACTIVITIES
Museu de Arte de Goiânia....**5** A3

SLEEPING
Crystal Plaza Hotel.............**6** B3
Goiânia Palace.................**7** B2
Hotel Serras de Goyaz.........**8** A1

HSBC (Av Anhanguera 5271; ✆ 9am-5pm Mon-Fri) Visa/MasterCard ATM.

Post office (☎ 3226 2110; Praça Cívica 11; ✆ 9am-5pm Mon-Fri)

Yes Internet Café (Av Tocantins 488, Setor Central; per hr R$2; ✆ 8am-10pm Mon-Fri, 8am-9pm Sat) Internet access.

Sights & Activities

Goiânia isn't exactly a tourist mecca, but it's not a bad place to break your onwards travel to Parque Nacional da Chapada dos Veadeiros or other attractions in the state. It's clean, relatively safe and efficiently organized. There is some great regional food to try as well as some thriving nightlife.

Smack downtown near the Praça Cívica, the lush **Bosque dos Buritis** makes a nice spot to relax for a bit; it's home to fountains and lakes overflowing with bird life. The **Museu de Arte de Goiânia** (☎ 3254 1189; admission free; ✆ 9am-9pm Tue-Fri) is in the western part of the park and worth a quick look. It hosts about 30 exhibits a year specializing in modern art and sculptures.

The weekend markets – **Feira da Lua** (Praça Tamandaré), a few blocks west of the Praça Cívica on Saturday afternoon, and **Feira do Sol** (Praça do Sol), 7km from downtown on Sunday afternoon – are both a great way to spend a weekend afternoon.

Sleeping

Ask for discounts at all city hotels on weekends. The midrange and top-end hotels in particular drop as much as 50% off their prices on weekends.

Goiânia Palace (☎ 3224 4874; Av Anhanguera 5195, Setor Central; s/d R$41/62, apt R$72/102; ✖) French owner Jean Luc finished off a six-year renovation in late 2006, including spiffying up his brick-and-wood *apartamentos* with new wardrobes and full-length mirrors. English is spoken.

Hotel Serras de Goyaz (☎ 3224 2310; www.hotel serrasdegoyaz.com.br in Portuguese; Av Paranaíba 1445, Setor Central; s/d R$85/120; ✖ 🖵) This tastefully decorated hotel is close to the convention center. It's full of regional local art, and the exposed brick gives it more character than other hotels in town.

Crystal Plaza Hotel (☎ 3267 4500; www.crystalplaza hotel.com.br in Portuguese; Av 85 30, Setor Sul; s/d R$100/110; ✖ 🖵) Standard rooms at this centrally located

GOIÁS

hotel just off Praça Cívica are double the size of those elsewhere. There is a handy tourist agency on the premises.

Eating & Drinking

Chão Nativo I (☎ 3233 5396; Av República do Líbano 1809, Setor Oeste; fixed price R$21.90; ⏰ 11:30am-3:30pm Mon-Fri, 11am-4pm Sat & Sun) An all-you-can-eat staple for authentic Goiânian dishes. West of Praça Cívica.

Piquiras (☎ 3223 8168; Rua 146 464, Setor Marista; dishes R$26-58; ⏰ 5pm-late Mon-Fri, 11:30am-late Sat & Sun) A Goiânia institution serving great examples of local fare. South of downtown, the expansive outside deck is packed with the city's young and fun on weekends.

Celson & Cia (☎ 3215 3043; Rua 15 539, Setor Oeste; ⏰ 4pm-3am Mon-Fri, 11-3am Sat, 11am-5pm Sun) Goianienses of all ilks drink in droves here, filling the 65 outdoor tables under illuminated almond trees day and night.

Getting There & Around

Aeroporto de Goiânia (☎ 3265 1500) is 6km northeast of the city center (R$18 by taxi). You can fly to Rio (R$439), São Paulo (R$379) and other major Brazilian cities.

From the huge bus station/shopping mall, hourly buses leave for Brasília (R$36.15, three hours, hourly), Cuiabá (R$112.75, 16 hours, six daily), Caldas Novas (R$23, 2½ hours, three daily), Pirenópolis (R$30, 2½ hours, one daily), Alto Paraíso (R$53.50, six hours, one daily) and Cidade de Goiás (R$20, three hours, hourly). Two of the buses to Goiás Velho continue on to Aruanã (R$34, six hours), for access to the Rio Araguaia.

From outside the bus station, take a Rodoviária–Centro bus to town, or grab a taxi (R$12).

CIDADE DE GOIÁS

☎ 0xx62 / pop 27,000

Straddling the Rio Vermelho and surrounded by the rugged Serra Dourada, Cidade de Goiás is a sleepy town of lamplit cobblestone streets and whitewashed colonial homes. The former state capital, once known as Vila Boa (and briefly later on as Goiás Velho), was awarded Unesco World Heritage status in 2002. Its gorgeous baroque churches shine and the town's population swells during Semana Santa (Holy Week). Every July 25, the anniversary of the town's foundation in 1727, the state governor visits Cidade de Goiás, which becomes the state capital for three days.

Information

Banco do Brasil (Av Sebastião Fleury Curado; ⏰ 11am-4pm Mon-Fri) Visa/MasterCard ATM.

Bradesco (Praça do Coreto; ⏰ 11am-4pm Mon-Fri) Visa/MasterCard ATM.

Extreme Net (Praça do Coreto 33; per hr R$1.50; ⏰ 8am-midnight Mon-Sun) Internet access.

Ouro Tur (☎ 3371 3346; Praça do Coreto) Helpful agency that can arrange tours and ecotourism adventures.

Sights & Activities

Strolling through town, you quickly notice the magnificent 18th-century colonial architecture, much of which is home to narrow streets and low houses hawking the region's famous *frutas cristalizados*, sugar-coated fruit concoctions that come in a plethora of flavors. Fuel up and make your way around the town's seven churches. The most impressive is the oldest, **Igreja de Paula** (Praça Zaqueu Alves de Castro), built in 1761.

The fascinating **Museu das Bandeiras** (Praça Brasil Caiado; admission R$2; ⏰ 8am-5pm Tue-Sat, to 3pm Sun) is an old jail (1766) and also a former town hall that's full of interesting antiques

---

DETOUR: PARQUE NACIONAL DAS EMAS

Parque Nacional das Emas is a relatively small (132-sq-km) park in the remote southwest corner of Goiás, where it meets the states of Mato Grosso and Mato Grosso do Sul. Situated on a high plateau surrounded by farmland, this park is considered the best-preserved cerrado in the country. There's not much foliage to obstruct the sighting of wildlife, including tapirs, anteaters, deer, capybaras, foxes, peccaries, armadillos, blue and yellow macaws, and the emas that give the park its name. The flightless ema is Brazil's biggest bird, growing to a height of 1.4m and weighing around 30kg. The park is also the exclusive sanctuary of the jacamari (a species of wolf) and other endangered wolves. Another interesting spectacle is the 2m-high termite mounds that 'glow' in the dark (most often at the start of the rainy season in October) – the result of bioluminescence produced by the termite larvae.

and original furniture (the 1.5m-thick cells made of *aroeira* (pepper-tree) wood are a museum in themselves). Outside in the square, the **Chafariz de Cauda fountain** (1778) is perfectly preserved, save the water. Other interesting museums are the **Museu de Arte Sacra** (admission R$2; ☺ 8am-5pm Tue-Fri, 9am-5pm Sat, 9am-3pm Sun) in the old **Igreja da Boa Morte** (Praça Castelo Branco), with a good selection of 19th-century works by renowned Goiânian sculptor Viega Vale; the **Casa de Cora Carolina** (Rua Dom Cândido Penso 20; admission R$3; ☺ 9am-5pm Tue-Sat, to 4pm Sun), birthplace and home of the area's renowned poet; and the **Palácio Conde dos Arcos** (Praça Castelo Branco; admission R$2; ☺ 9am-5pm Tue-Sat, to 3pm Sun), the restored colonial governor's residence.

The **Espaço Cultural de Goiandeira do Courto** (☎ 3371 1303; Rua Joaquim Bonifácio 19; admission R$2; ☺ 9am-noon & 1-4pm Tue-Sat, 9am-1pm Sun) is well worth a visit. This amazing artist in her 90s 'paints' using 551 varieties of sparkling colored sands found in the Serra Dourada, predating pixilation by decades (and by hand, it should be noted). She maintains an exposition in her studio and will talk your ear off, reciting the list of countries that house her work quicker than the alphabet.

Festivals & Events

Semana Santa Cidade de Goiás' big occasion takes place the week before Easter. The week's highlight is the Wednesday-night procession re-enacting the arrest of Christ. The streetlights are turned off and thousands of

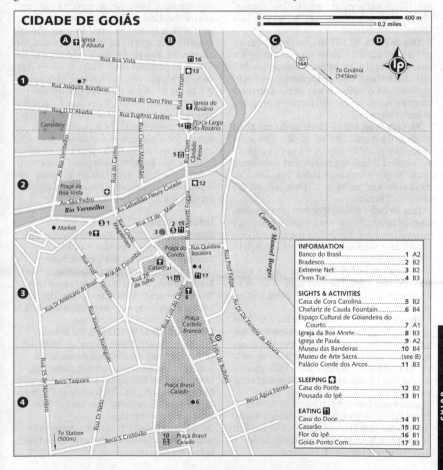

CIDADE DE GOIÁS

0 ————— 400 m
0 ————— 0.2 miles

To Goiânia (141km)

GOIÁS

people march through the streets carrying torches, led by 40 eerie, pointy-hooded figures – the *farricocos* – whose colorful dress harks back to the days of the Inquisition.

Festival International de Cinema Ambiental (International Environmental Film Festival) Over five days in early June, the festival includes film and video screenings, workshops, live shows, lectures and exhibitions – all environmentally themed. It was started in 1999 in an attempt to draw worldwide attention to the town.

Sleeping & Eating

Cidade de Goiás is a popular getaway from Goiânia, so it's a good idea to book ahead if you're arriving on a weekend. The town is packed during Semana Santa and for the International Environmental Film Festival. The *empadão* reigns here – the tasty savory pie filled with meat, vegetables, cheese, olives and sometimes egg is served just about everywhere.

Casa do Ponte (☎ 3371 4467; Rua Moretti Foggia s/n; s/d R$80/100; ☒ ☐) There's no accounting for taste with regards to the floral bedspreads, but this kitschy hotel is on a nice corner overlooking the Rio Vermelho. It was spruced up most recently, so the rooms and common areas are more modern.

Pousada do Ipê (☎ 3371 2065; Rua do Forum 22; s/d apt R$120/129, chalets R$147/165; ☒ ☒) The most charming place to stay. A tranquil property set around a lush courtyard and swimming pool. Enjoy the sugar-laden breakfast of local jams and jellies in a room just off the old-style kitchen.

Casa do Doce (☎ 3371 1824; Praça Largo do Rosário; sweets per kg R$20; ☺ 8am-noon & 1-5pm) If you don't mind a few bees, you'll find the colorful display of 28 crystallized fruits here too much to walk away from.

Casarão (☎ 9917 8913; Rua Moretti Foggia 8; dishes R$3-6; ☺ 10am-11pm) The best spot in town to try piping-hot *empadão*, served in traditional ceramic crockery.

Flor do Ipê (☎ 3372 1133; Rua da Boa Vista; dishes for 2 R$16-36; ☺ noon-3pm & 6pm-midnight Tue-Sat, noon-3pm Sun) For lunch, there's a wealth of regional choices laid out in fiery hot clay pots for R$16. In the evenings, the shady garden setting fills up quickly for excellent à la carte local dishes.

Goiás Ponto Com (☎ 3371 1691; Praça do Coreto 19; dishes R$32-41; ☺ 11am-4pm & 6:30-midnight Thu-Sat, 11am-4pm Sun-Wed) Does excellent *dourado* fish in the town's most stylish setting, inside a colonial home lined with modern art.

Getting There & Away

The bus station is 500m south of Praça Brasil Caiado. There are frequent buses running between Cidade de Goiás and Goiânia (R$19.15, three hours). There are also buses to Aruanã (R$25, three hours) for access to the Rio Araguaia, and a few to Barra do Garças (R$33, four hours), where there are regular connections to Cuiabá (Mato Grosso).

PIRENÓPOLIS

☎ 0xx62 / pop 21,000

A curious mix of Art Deco and Portuguese colonial architecture first strikes visitors to Pirenópolis, but that's far from the only thing slightly odd about this quirky town, on the Patrimonio Nacional (National Heritage) register since 1989. Set on striking red earth astride the Rio das Almas, it's another colonial gem with a history steeped in gold, though quite it's different from others in the state. An alternative movement took hold here in the '70s and remains today. There is a New Age, vaguely hippie vibe to this laid-back spot – it's home to more Volkswagen Beetles per capita than any other city in Brazil – and it is committed to a major grassroots sustainable - tourism movement. It's a popular weekend retreat for Goianienses and Brasiliense, who come to town for its wide range of ecotourism options and budding slow food movement. You'll be sick of waterfalls by the time you leave, but it's an excellent base from which to explore the 73 around the area.

Information

Banco do Brasil (☎ 3331 1183; Rua Sizenando Jayme; ☺ 11am-4pm Mon-Fri) Visa/MasterCard ATM.

Bradesco (☎ 3331 1141; Rua Sizenando Jayme; ☺ 11am-4pm Mon-Fri) Visa/MasterCard ATM.

Brasil Central (☎ 3331-3677; www.brcentral.tur.br; Rua dos Pireneus 67; ☺ 9am-noon & 2-6pm Mon-Sat) A fantastic agency run by a cute young couple specializing in sustainable ecotourism and cultural tours.

CAT tourist office (☎ 3331 2633; Rua do Bonfim; ☺ 8am-5pm Sun-Fri, 8:30am-6:30pm Sat) Provides info on accommodations and activities in the area as well as transportation and guides. Accredited guides charge between R$50 and R$60 per day, excluding transportation.

Center Vídeo (☎ 3331 3724; Rua do Bonfim 15; per hr R$3; ☺ 9am-11pm Mon-Sat, 10am-5pm Sun) Video-rental spot with internet access.

Delegacía de Polícia (☎ 3331 1813; Rua do Fuzil 6)

Hospital Nossa Senhora do Rosário (☎ 3331 1592; Av Neco Mendonça 38)

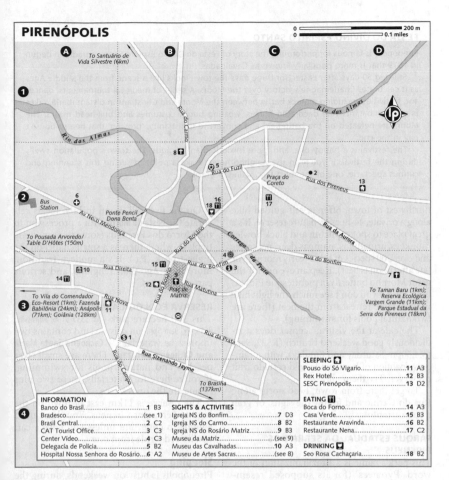

PIRENÓPOLIS

0 — 200 m
0 — 0.1 miles

To Santuário de Vida Silvestre (6km)

Rio das Almas

Rua do Carmo

Rua do Fuzil

Praça do Coreto

Rua dos Pireneus

Rio das Almas

Ponte Pencil Dona Benta

Av Neco Mendonça

Bus Station

To Pousada Arvoredo/ Table D'Hôtes (150m)

Rua do Rosário

Córrego da Prata

Rua da Aurora

Rua Direita

Rua do Bonfim

Rua do Bonfim

Rua Nova

Praç de Matriz

Rua Matutina

To Vila do Comendador Eco-Resort (1km); Fazenda Babilônia (24km); Anápolis (71km); Goiânia (128km)

To Taman Baru (1km); Reserva Ecológica Vargem Grande (11km); Parque Estadual da Serra dos Pireneus (18km)

Rua da Prata

Rua Sizenando Jayme

Rua do Campo

To Brasília (137km)

SLEEPING
Pouso do Só Vigario.................11 A3
Rex Hotel................................12 B3
SESC Pirenópolis.....................13 D2

EATING
Boca do Forno.........................14 A3
Casa Verde..............................15 B3
Restaurante Aravinda..............16 B2
Restaurante Nena....................17 C2

DRINKING
Seo Rosa Cachaçaria...............18 B2

INFORMATION
Banco do Brasil...............................1 B3
Bradesco.................................(see 1)
Brasil Central.................................2 C2
CAT Tourist Office..........................3 C3
Center Vídeo...................................4 C3
Delegacía de Polícia.......................5 B2
Hospital Nossa Senhora do Rosário...6 A2

SIGHTS & ACTIVITIES
Igreja NS do Bonfim.......................7 D3
Igreja NS do Carmo........................8 B2
Igreja NS do Rosário Matriz............9 B3
Museu da Matriz........................(see 9)
Museu das Cavalhadas..................10 A3
Museu de Artes Sacras................(see 8)

Sights & Activities

CHURCHES & MUSEUMS

Unfortunately, three of the town's main sights, the **Igreja NS do Carmo** (1750), the **Museu de Arte Sacra** inside it, and the Portuguese-built **Igreja NS do Bonfim** (1750), have been closed for several years. They are all caught up in money scrabbles and church bureaucracy (imagine that). Depending on whom you talk to, it's either due to a crabby owner who doesn't want to mess with tourism, or because church leaders in nearby Anápolis are short on funds. Regardless, they may or may not be open when you visit.

The town's oldest church, the 1732 **Igreja NS do Rosário Matriz** (Praça de Matriz; admission R$1; 7-11am & 1-5pm Wed-Sun, 7-11am Mon) is open again

after being tragically gutted by fire in 2002 (arson is suspected). Inside, the **Museu da Matriz** explains the history and ongoing renovation. The new altar was ironically restored and brought in from the former slave church (a necessary house of worship since slaves were banned from this one). Another interesting spot is the **Museu das Cavalhadas** (☎ 3331-1166; Rua Direita 39; admission R$2; 10am-5pm), with its bright and colorful artifacts from the annual Festo do Divino Espírito Santo (p390). The sign says to knock if the museum appears closed.

SANTUÁRIO DE VIDA SILVESTRE – FAZENDA VAGAFOGO

The **Vagafogo Farm Wildlife Sanctuary** (☎ 3335 8515; adult/child R$10/5; 8:30am-5pm Mon-Sun), 6km

GOIÁS

FESTA DO DIVINO ESPÍRITO SANTO

Pirenópolis is famous for performing the story of Festa do Divino Espírito Santo, a tradition begun in 1819 that is more popularly known as Cavalhadas.

Starting 50 days after Easter, for three days the town looks like a scene from the Middle Ages as it celebrates Charlemagne's victory over the Moors. A series of medieval tournaments, dances and festivities, including a mock battle between the Moors and Christians in distant Iberia, takes place. Combatants ride decorated horses, wearing bright costumes and bull-head masks. The Moors are defeated on the battlefield and convert to Christianity, 'proving' that heresy doesn't pay in the end.

The festival is a happy one, and more folkloric than religious. The town's population swells during the festival. If you're in the neighborhood, make a point of seeing this stunning and curious spectacle, one of the most fascinating in Brazil.

---

northwest of town, offers a self-guided hike along a private, 44-hectare nature reserve. It's a great place to spot capuchin and black howler monkeys, armadillos, pampas deer, peccaries and over 200 species of birds (early morning or late afternoon is best). Keep an eye out for the giant Morpho butterfly, a picturesque Picasso blue. Even if you don't see much, the light hike is a welcome retreat from the heat (there are two natural pools for swimming).

The café at the visitors' center does a ridiculously good weekend brunch (R$22; 9am to 4:30pm Saturday and Sunday), with a rainbow coalition of homemade wild cerrado fruit preserves. Try them all.

To get there from town, head north along Rua do Carmo and follow the signs, or grab a cab or mototaxi.

PARQUE ESTADUAL DA SERRA DOS PIRENEUS

This park's name is a Brazilianization of the word 'Pyrenees' (for its supposed resemblance). It contains three peaks, Pai (the tallest at 1385m), Filho and Espírito Santo, all of which can be climbed. It's also the top spot in the state for bouldering (rock climbing without a rope). It's 18km northeast of town, and there are waterfalls and interesting rock formations to see along the way, some dating back to Gondwanaland.

You'll need an accredited guide to enter (admission R$3), who can be hired for a combo day trip with Viagem Grande for around R$130 including transport but not entrance fees. A local agency or the tourist information office can facilitate this. **Cachoeira do Abade** (admission R$10) is worth checking out en route as you can actually swim under the falls.

On the first full moon in July, locals celebrate the **Festa do Morro** with a procession to the Morro dos Pireneus (some to pray, some to play), where there is a small chapel on the highest peak (Pai). It's a modern tradition, more New Age than religious, and serious partying ensues.

RESERVA ECOLÓGICA VARGEM GRANDE

This 360-hectare **park** (☎ 3331 3166; admission R$15; ✆ 9am-5pm) on private land contains two impressive waterfalls – **Cachoeira Santa Maria** and **Cachoeira do Lázaro**. There are small river beaches and natural pools for swimming. If you're here for waterfalls, these two plus Abade are the ones to see.

The reserve is 11km east of town on the road to Serra dos Pireneus. You don't need a guide to enter, but unless you have a car, you'll need a ride from one.

Sleeping

Pirenópolis is busy on weekends, during the Cavalhadas festival and for Carnaval, when prices can double those quoted.

Rex Hotel (☎ 3331 1121; Praça de Matriz 15 37; s/d R$25/50) A dirt-cheap option in a house originally built for slaves. It's a bit of a shambles, but it'll do if you've busted your budget.

Pousada Arvoredo (☎ 9617 2659; Av Abercio 15; www .arvoredo.tur.br; s/d R$60/80; ❄ ⚍) This excellent-value pousada is steeped in sustainable tourism (all the bricks were recycled from old homes in Goiânia) and features lovely verandahs and large rooms full of natural handicrafts. There is an interesting French-leaning Slow Food restaurant as well. Highly recommended.

SESC Pirenópolis (☎ 3331 1383; www.sescgo.com.br in Portuguese; Rua dos Pireneus 45; with/without air-con s R$51/42, d R$80/65; ⚍) If you can manage to book rooms 1 to 3, you've scored the best deal in town: well-appointed suites with a separate living room, very nice stone bathroom, and vaulted ceilings for the same price as a double.

Pouso do Só Vigario (☎ 3331 1206; www.pousada spirenopolis.com.br; Rua Nova 25; s/d R$87/100; 🅿 🖵) It's showing its age and there is some questionable use of Rembrandt, but otherwise this pousada in a converted colonial house is nicely located and decently priced.

Taman Baru (☎ 3331 3880; www.tamanbaru.com.br; Estrada dos Pireneus km2; s/d apt R$140/160, bungalows R$240; 🅿 🖵 🖵) A romantic retreat with the occasional Balinese touch set inside a forest, located just east of town. The colorful bungalows and gorgeous new infinity pool both offer outstanding views across the cerrado (it looks a bit like Africa).

Villa do Comendador Eco-Resort (☎ 3331 1162; GO 431 km1; www.villadocomendador.com.br; s & d R$180; 🅿 🖵 🖵) Opened in 2007 1km outside town, this is the first pousada in Pirenópolis to be sanctioned by national environmental watch groups as truly eco. It offers pools, playgrounds, horseback riding, volleyball and outstanding cerrado views. A haven for kids!

Eating & Drinking

Most restaurants close on Monday, and some only open on weekends. Rua do Rosário,

aka Rua do Lazer, is the main restaurant-café strip and turns into a pedestrianized free-for-all of outdoor tables and lively Goianienses on the weekends.

Pireneus Café (☎ 3331 3042; Rua dos Pireneus 41; sandwiches R$4-9; 🕒 10am-midnight Thu-Sat, to 10pm Sun) A sophisticated spot overlooking Praça do Coreto for life-changing grilled focaccia sandwiches and first-rate coffee.

Casa Verde (☎ 3331 2537; Rua do Rosário 5; dishes R$12-24; 🕒 noon-9pm Mon-Thu, to midnight Fri & Sat, to 6pm Sun) An excellent cheapie, with great risotto, salads and filets. One of Monday's few options.

Restaurante Nena (☎ 3331 1470; Rua da Aurora 4; buffet R$14; 🕒 noon-4pm Fri-Sun) One of the nicer buffets you'll come across, with great regional food and a varied selection of salads. Get in early before the offerings are picked thin.

Boca do Forno (☎ 3331 1790; Travessa Santa Cruz s/n; pizza R$18-29; 🕒 6pm-midnight) The owner of this cozy pizzeria is from Brazil's pizza capital, São Paulo. If that means nothing to you, it will once you try the pizza.

Table D'Hôtes (☎ 3331 3479; Salão de Pousada Arvoredo; meals R$10-52; 🕒 noon-2pm Mon-Fri, 8pm-midnight Thu-Sat) There's no menu at this upscale organic French restaurant inside Pousada Arvoredo – you get what Slow Food chef Murielle Dargaud wants to make that evening. Vegetarian lunches are one course

---

CAFÉ COLONIAL: THE FOOD OF THE TROPEIROS

After the *bandeirantes* swept Goiás clean of its gold, the *tropeiros* (the famed muleteers of Brazil) followed in their path, conquering the region and bringing slaves from Brazil's coast. It was these entrepreneurial cowboys who commercialized an impressive chunk of Brazil stretching south from Minas Gerais, expanding borders and connecting routes of commerce along the way. The journey took months and Pirenópolis sat right on the crossroads between the only two highways in Goiás, one to São Paulo and the other to Bahia. The journey was deadly hot (40% of the slaves died en route) and food was obviously scarce. As a result, the *tropeiros* adapted various foods from Afro-Brazilian, Portuguese and Indian cultures to allow for the lengthy journey without refrigeration. This long-lost subculture of Brazilian cuisine has been resurrected at **Fazenda Babilônia** (☎ 3331 1226; GO 431A, km24; 🕒 8:30am-4:30pm Sat & Sun), a sugar plantation and farm (1800) on the Patrimonial Nacional (National Heritage) register since 1965. Every weekend, this restored *fazenda* (farm), 24km southwest of Pirenópolis, breaks out the historical gastronomy for a fascinating breakfast called Café Colonial. Hearty meats, cheeses and pastries highlight the near-endless options. *Carne de porco* (a succulent pork dish stored in its own fat for conservation), *mané pelado* (a sweet cake of grated manioc, eggs, cheese and coconut milk) and *matula galinha* (chicken with saffron, eggs, aromatic peppers and toasted corn wrapped in a corn husk) highlight an absolutely thrilling meal that includes some 28 dishes that you're likely to have never seen before. The whole thing costs R$25 and includes a tour of the *fazenda* itself, a fascinating glimpse into life in this part of Brazil in the 18th century. Get there via taxi (R$50 round-trip) or local agencies can arrange a tour.

for R$10; dinner is five courses for R$52 and features a wonderful cheese course from an artisanal farmstead nearby.

Seo Rosa Cachaçaria (☎ 3331 2046; Rua do Rosário 17; ⏰ from 5pm Sun-Thu, from 10am Fri & Sat; cachaça R$3-5) More than 150 different *cachaças* to choose from. Go off menu and ask for Gabriela.

Getting There & Away

The tiny bus station is 500m west of Igreja Matriz. There are buses to Brasília (R$16, three hours, 165km, seven daily), one to Goiânia (R$12, three hours, 128km, 6am), and Anápolis (R$7, 1½ hours, five daily), where you can also catch a connection to Goiânia. Getting around town is easily done on foot or by mototaxi.

CALDAS NOVAS

☎ 0xx64 / pop 63,000

Suffering from high blood pressure after your visit to Brasília? Poor digestion after your visit to a truck-stop café in Minas? Exhausted after your extended Carnaval in Salvador? If your answer is yes to any of these questions, then Caldas Novas, with more than 30 curative hot springs, may be just the place for you. Now an upmarket resort, the town's population swells to around 200,000 during holidays.

Information

Banco do Brasil (Rua Capitan João Crisostomo 325) Visa/MasterCard ATM.

CAT tourist office (☎ 3454 3564; Praça Mestre Orlando; ⏰ 8am-6pm) Located on the main square and can help with accommodations and hot-springs info.

Hospital Aparecida (☎ 3453 1290; Rua Eça de Queiroz 13)

Las Vegas LAN House (Praça Mestre Orlando 436; per hr R$3; ⏰ 8am-11pm) Internet access.

Police station (☎ 3453 4011; cnr Alameda do Contono & Rua Crisostómo)

Post office (Rua Crisostómo 361)

Hot Springs

Nearly everyone in Caldas Novas has a thermal pool to cure what ails ya, but not all of them are open to the public. Besides the hotels and pousadas, there are a few good options in and around the city for day use only. Working your way from the city center out, **SESC Caldas Novas** (☎ 3455 9400; Av Ministro Elias Bufáiçal 600; admission R$11; ⏰ 8am-10pm) is the most conveniently located and favorably priced. The 11 thermal pools in the SESC complex are well-maintained and within walking distance of Praça Matriz. There is also a good pousada here. A little further out is **di Roma Acqua Park** (☎ 3453 1868; Rua São Cristovão 805; admission R$20; ⏰ 8am-8pm, closed Mon & Thu), an all-out aquatic extravaganza featuring the world's first thermal wave pool, water slides, lazy river, restaurants and numerous therapeutic waters.

Sleeping & Eating

During holidays and long weekends the town is packed, so reservations are advisable. Rooms in all categories tend to be nearly identical – pick based on hot-springs action.

SESC Caldas Novas (☎ 3455 9400; www.sescgo.com .br in Portuguese; Av Ministro Elias Bufáiçal 600; s with/without air-con R$71/35, d R$91/119; 🖳 🖳) A large recreation area with 11 thermal pools. One of the best deals in town.

Hotel Roma (☎ 3453 1335; www.hotelroma.com.br in Portuguese; Praça Mestre Orlando 368; s/d R$136; ✖ 🖳) The six thermal pools, whirlpool and massive sauna skew a bit toward *On Golden Pond*, but the location on the main square is hard to beat. The bedside condoms next to the New Testament are an interesting dilemma.

di Roma Thermas Hotel (☎ 3453 9393; www .diroma.com.br in Portuguese; Av Santo Amaro 1800; r R$235; ✖ 🖳 🖳) A recently renovated megaresort a few kilometers out of town, di Roma has nine thermal pools and lots of action for kids (a zip line!). In January and July there's a three-day minimum stay.

Hotel Parque das Primaveras (☎ 3453 1268; www .hpprimaveras.com.br; Rua do Balneário 1; s/d R$240/270; ✖ 🖳 🖳) Feisty macaws roam the jungly grounds at this lush pousada, the top digs in town. The four thermal pools feel more private than others.

Picanha Na Brasa (☎ 3453 8023; Rua José Luiz Pereira & Pedro Branco de Souza 241; rodízio R$13.90; ⏰ 11am-midnight) This popular rodízio-style *churrascaria* (all-you-can-eat barbecue restaurant) is one of the cheapest and tastiest you'll find.

Paneteria Famigli Amoroso (☎ 3453 6623; cnr Rua do Turismo & Rua da Madalena; pizzas R$16.50-19.50; ⏰ 7-11pm Sun-Thu, to midnight Fri & Sat) This small bakery boasts 91 varieties of pizza cooked in a wood-fired oven.

(Continued on page 401)

Expect an enthusiastic welcome from the caiman of the Pantanal (p415)

LEE FOSTER

Discover intriguing rock formations in the Parque
Nacional da Chapada dos Guimarães (p411)

JANE SWEENEY

JANE SWEENEY

Crested caracara (p85), a bird of prey common in the Pantanal and Amazonia

RICK GERHARTER

Plano Inclinado Gonçalves (p446) traversing Lower City and Upper City, Salvador

Perfecting the martial art of capoeira at Salvador's Terreiro de Jesus (p445)

Palácio Rio Branco (p446) cuts an impressive figure in downtown Salvador

Colonial architecture on display at the Igreja de NS da Corrente (p517), Penedo, Alagoas

JOHN PENNOCK

PAUL BERNHARDT

The restored art-deco masterpiece of Elevador Lacerda (p446), Salvador

Jangadas (sailboats) awaiting departure on Jatiúca beach (p510), Maceió, Alagoas

JOHN PENNOCK

Locals cool off at Praia da Boa Viagem (p448)

Snapshot of Olinda (p533)
streetlife, Pernambuco

Adrift off the coast of Porto de Galinhas (p537), Pernambuco

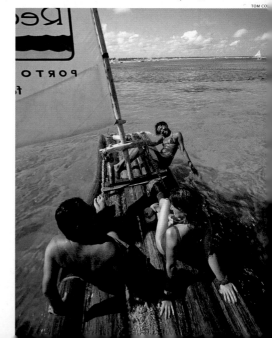

PAUL BERNHARDT

Fishermen try their luck in front of Forte dos Reis Magos (p556), Natal, Rio Grande do Norte

Take a buggy ride (p557) on the sand dunes of Genipabu

PAUL BERNHARDT

TOM COCKREM

The picture of happiness at popular Genipabu (p563) beach, near Natal, Rio Grande do Norte

Undulating aerial view of the Parque Nacional dos Lençóis Maranhenses (p597)
JOHN PENNOCK

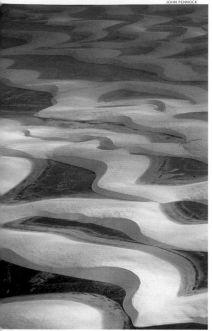

JOHN PENNOCK

Amble along the cobblestone streets of historic
São Luís, (p589), Maranhão

Deserted on the beach at Caburé (p598), access point for the Parque Nacional dos Lençóis Maranhenses
JOHN PEN

KRZYSZTOF DYDYNSKI

Catch of the day: colossal catfish at the Reserva Natural Palmari (665), Rio Javari

Next page:
Water-lily horizon, Rio Amazonas, Amazonas state (p641)
JOHN BORTHWICK

Generations of villagers from the Rio Negro basin (p655)

TOM COCKREM

The tranquillity of the Rio Negro (p655) at dusk

JOHN PENNOCK

(Continued from page 392)

Getting There & Away

The bus station is at the end of Rua Antônio Coelho de Godoy. Regular buses run to Brasília (R$41.50, six hours, two daily) and Goiânia (R$23.50, three hours, 10 daily), as well as to Rio de Janeiro (R$138) and São Paulo (R$97).

PARQUE NACIONAL DA CHAPADA DOS VEADEIROS

☎ 0xx61

This spectacular national park in the highest area of the Central West showcases the unique landscape and flora of high-altitude cerrado across 650 sq km of pristine beauty.

With high waterfalls, raging canyons, natural swimming pools and oasislike stands of wine palms, the park is a popular destination for ecotourists. In fact, the whole area is beautiful, with its big skies, exotic flora – check out the fascinating, sea urchin–like symbol of the cerrado, the *chuveirinho* – and dramatic hills rising up like waves breaking across the plains.

The sublime landscape, much of it based on quartz crystal and multihued sandstone, has also attracted New Agers who have established alternative communities and a burgeoning 'esoturismo' industry in the area. It is also noticeably well maintained – you won't find a Skol beer can within miles.

Crystals, dreadlocks and dirty feet are ubiquitous in **Alto Paraíso de Goiás** (commonly known as Alto Paraíso), 38km from the park, one of Brazil's kookiest towns. Unfortunately, there is not much more of

---

DETOUR: RIO QUENTE

The aquatic playground of **Rio Quente**, about 18km from Caldas Novas, is home to the world's only thermal-water river and enough water-themed entertainment to ensure you'd rather drown by the time it's all over. **Hot Park** (☎ 3453 7757; adult/child R$42/26; ☺ 9:30am-5pm, closed Thu) is the epicenter of the fun, a sort of waterlogged Disney for bronzed Brazilian beauties. Its 22,000 sq meters of slippery amusement, including a $2.5 million mega half-pipe imported from Canada, is the only one of its kind in Latin America.

---

interest to travelers here, so most use the former crystal-mining hamlet of **São Jorge** (2km from the national park entrance) as a base. You'll need two days to see the main attractions within the park.

Mammals in the area include maned wolves, banded anteaters, giant armadillos, deer, capybaras, pumas and tapirs. Birds include rheas, toucans, macaws, hawks and vultures. The best time to visit the park is between April and October, before the rivers flood during the rainy season and access becomes very slippery.

Information

Banco do Brasil (Av Ari Valadão Filho 690, Alto Paraíso; ☺ 10am-3pm Mon-Fri) Visa/MasterCard ATM.

CAT tourist office (☎ 3446 1159; Av Ari Valadão Filho s/n, Alto Paraíso; ☺ 8am-5pm) On the town's main street, 200m from the bus station. It offers information on pousadas and activities in and out of the park and can help arrange guides. There is also a smaller one in São Jorge.

Sights & Activities

All visitors to the **park** (☎ 3455 1114; admission R$3; ☺ 8am-6pm Tue-Sun) must be accompanied by an accredited guide. Guides can be organized at the visitors' center, through the local guide association, ACV-CV, or at most hotels in São Jorge. Guides usually cost R$60 (Portuguese) or R$80 (English) per day, plus R$100 (up to four passengers) if you need transport to/from Alto Paraíso.

The guides run half-day tours to the park's three main attractions – *canions* (canyons) and *cariocas* (rocks), which are usually combined as they transverse the same trail in the park; and *cachoeiras* (waterfalls). The tours are included in the price of the guide and can be divided by up to 10 people.

The **canions-cariocas tour** weaves along the Rio Preto, which runs through the middle of the park. The river has cut two large canyons (imaginatively named Canyon I and Canyon II) through sandstone, with sheer, 20m-high walls on either side. It's a spectacular sight. There are natural platforms for diving into the cold water at the bottom of the rushing river. Canyon I is usually flooded from September to May and inaccessible. The *cariocas* (named for two girls from Rio who went missing here in the '80s) picks up at the end of the river valley on the trail from Canyon II and leads to interesting rock formations and a huge cascading waterfall.

GOIÁS

The more difficult (and rewarding) **cachoeiras tour** takes in Salto do Rio Preto I and II, two spectacular waterfalls (80m and 120m respectively) that cascade to the ground just 30m apart. The falls are set in a picturesque valley at the end of a trail that weaves through a classic cerrado landscape of meadows and gallery forests. There is a small lake for swimming under II, where the sun creates a dazzling celestial effect under the water. Take loads of water and sunscreen; it's about a 6km ascent all the way back and the sun can be brutal.

VALE DA LUA

A unique sight in the Chapada dos Veadeiros area is the **Valley of the Moon** (admission R$5; ☻ 7am-5:30pm). Over millions of years, the rushing waters of the Rio São Miguel have sculpted rock formations and craters with a striking resemblance to a lunar landscape. Small *kalango* lizards dart across the ethereal metaconglomerate of quartz, sand and clay as shades of silver, gray, white and occasional patches of red (from rose quartz) reflect off the rocks. The chilly emerald waters add to the otherworldly atmosphere.

Vale da Lua is outside the national park, so you don't need a guide, but the area is subject to flash flooding during the rainy season (it takes all of three minutes for a flood of biblical proportions to rise), so check with locals before you head off. Walk out on the road to Alto Paraíso and take the first unmarked trail on the right – from there it's a 4km hike (there is no sign, as some guides remove them to enslave you to their services). If you miss this, it will be an 11km jaunt on the main road. Take sunscreen and water with you.

Tours

Trans Chapada Turismo (☎ 3446 1345; www.transchapada.com.br; Rua dos Cristais 219, Alto Paraíso; ☻ 1-6pm Mon-Fri) A short walk down a residential street from the bus station. It organizes transportation and guides for a variety of tours and activities, including trekking, mountain biking and canyoning.

Travessia Ecoturismo (☎ 3446 1595; www.travessia.tur.br in Portuguese; Av Ari Valadão Filho 979, Alto Paraíso; ☻ 8am-7pm Mon-Fri, 9am-2pm Sat & Sun) An excellent eco-agency on the main road in Alto Paraíso that can arrange everything in Chapada, including more-adventurous canyoning and rappelling trips, transportation, and English-speaking guides.

Sleeping & Eating

Alto Paraíso has a wide range of accommodations, but most travelers stay in the village of São Jorge because it is prettier, closer to the park and has more of a village atmosphere. But if you arrive there too late in the evening to arrange transport to São Jorge, Alto Paraíso is a good spot to base yourself for one night and make arrangements for tours in the area. Prices quoted below are for weekdays; they sometimes rise by up to 30% on weekends.

ALTO PARAÍSO

There are several good options to rest and refuel in Alto Paraíso.

Pousada Rubi (☎ 3446 1200; www.pousadarubi.com.br in Portuguese; Rua Coleto Paulino 732; s/d R$50/80; ☐) Superfriendly and cheap option not far from the bus station. Take your first left after CAT and walk one block. It's on your right. Ring the bell if you arrive in the middle of the night.

Casa Rosa (☎ 3446 1319; www.pousadacasarosa.com.br in Portuguese; Rua Gumercindo Barbosa 233; apt R$90-120, chalets R$104-138; ☐ ☒) A more upmarket, B&B-style option in a large pink house at the end of the main road.

Oca Lila (☎ 3446 1006; Av João Bernardes Rabelo 449; meals R$9-15; ☻ noon-midnight daily, closed Tue) The all-natural vegetarian lunch kilo is highly recommended and shockingly cheap. Oca Lila turns à la carte for dinner (excellent pizza) and there's a bit of *vida nocturna* in the evenings.

SÃO JORGE

Quality pousadas are plentiful here and they are usually very fairly priced. The hamlet also has some delicious restaurants.

Pousada Trilha Violeta (☎ 3455 1088; www.trilhavioleta.com.br; s/d R$52/74) Somebody here likes purple. It's a violet-hued oasis with rooms facing onto a lovely garden, each with a small verandah and hammock. The upstairs ones are reached via an ornate spiral staircase.

Pousada Casa das Flores (☎ 3455 1055; www.pousadacasasflores.com.br; R$128/137; ☒ ☐ ☒) Lighting is all from candles or gas lamps at this borderline New Age-y choice, making it ideal for romance and very ecofriendly. Go for the cheaper, two-level chalets with mosaic stone showers – they're more charming than the higher priced *apartamentos*.

our pick Baguá Pousada (☎ 3455 1046; www.baguapousada.com.br; bungalows R$220; ☒ ☐) The überstylish, massive bungalows (82 sq meters!) at this designer ecopousada have raised the bar on sophistication in Goiás: solar showers and reforested eucalyptus highlight the sustainable edge, while safari-chic lounge furnishings in the common area should suit Brazil's fashion *cognoscenti*. It's closest to the park's entrance as well.

Lua do São Jorge (☎ 3455 1054; pizzas R$18-31; ☻ from 6pm Thu-Sun) Intensely researched conclusion: the best of the numerous wood-fired pizzerias in town.

Fetiço da Vila (☎ 3455 1104; meals R$8-20; ☻ 5-10:30pm Mon-Thu, to midnight Fri, noon-12:30am Sat, noon-6pm Sun) The open kitchen and menu are very simple, but the food is a gourmet knockout. Try the filet with edible *capuchinha* flowers.

Getting There & Away

From Goiânia there's a daily bus to Alto Paraíso (R$53.50, six hours, 8:30pm). There are four buses a day from Brasília to Alto Paraíso (R$22.50, 3½ hours).

There is one daily bus from Alto Paraíso to São Jorge (R$6.50, one hour, 3pm) for access to the park. The bus returns from São Jorge to Alto Paraíso daily at 9am. The only other alternative is to hire private transport from a guide for around R$70 to R$100. In the past, tourists could hop on the school bus for a ride back to Alto Paraíso, but authorities in São Jorge quashed that idea a few years back, which is probably for the best. I mean, seriously.

Mato Grosso & Mato Grosso do Sul

Mato Grosso was once Brazil's wild, wild West, where explorers, Indian hunters, animal poachers, gold seekers and naturalists collided under miraculous sunsets and marvelous moons. Today, the massive area, split into the two separate states of Mato Grosso and Mato Grosso do Sul in the late 1970s, is still a wonderfully feral region that is home to some of Brazil's most spectacular wildlife and incredible scenery. It is a prime destination for ecotourists and anglers, the majority of whom come to visit the star attraction of the region, the Pantanal, an enormous floodplain that extends its watery tentacles across parts of both states as well as into Bolivia and Paraguay.

Though the Amazon has a larger marketing budget, it is the Pantanal that shines as Brazil's top destination for wildlife-viewing and bird-watching. Encompassing an area more than half the size of France, it is one of the most important and fragile ecosystems on the planet and home to an impressive concentration of cohabiting mammals. Jaguars, caiman, anacondas, giant river otters and capybaras are here in great numbers, as are seemingly endless collections of extraordinary birds, including macaws, toucans and jabiru storks.

Cuiabá, Corumbá and Campo Grande are all gateways to this celebrated wetland, but the region's offerings certainly don't stop there. There's the far-north town of Alta Floresta, where the cerrado morphs into the Amazon in a vast, fervently preserved forest full of copious bird species and picturesque waterways; and the Serra do Bodoquena surrounding Bonito, where high waterfalls, deep canyons, caves and crystal-clear rivers present world-class ecotourism opportunities. Between the two is the stunning Parque Nacional da Chapada dos Guimarães, an imposing tablelands with some of the most commanding views in Brazil.

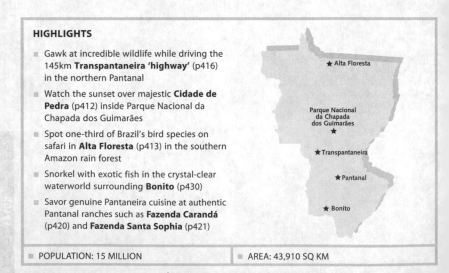

HIGHLIGHTS

- Gawk at incredible wildlife while driving the 145km **Transpantaneira 'highway'** (p416) in the northern Pantanal

- Watch the sunset over majestic **Cidade de Pedra** (p412) inside Parque Nacional da Chapada dos Guimarães

- Spot one-third of Brazil's bird species on safari in **Alta Floresta** (p413) in the southern Amazon rain forest

- Snorkel with exotic fish in the crystal-clear waterworld surrounding **Bonito** (p430)

- Savor genuine Pantaneira cuisine at authentic Pantanal ranches such as **Fazenda Carandá** (p420) and **Fazenda Santa Sophia** (p421)

★ Alta Floresta

Parque Nacional da Chapada dos Guimarães
★

★ Transpantaneira

★ Pantanal

★ Bonito

■ POPULATION: 15 MILLION   ■ AREA: 43,910 SQ KM

History

According to the Treaty of Tordesillas, the state of Mato Grosso belonged to Spain. For years its exploration was limited to occasional expeditions by adventurers and Jesuit missionaries.

With the discovery of gold in the early 18th century, the region was invaded by thousands of fortune hunters. To reach Cuiabá, they had to cross the lands of several groups of Indians, many of whom were formidable warriors. They included the Caiapó (who even attacked the settlement at Goiás), the Bororo of the Pantanal, the Parecis (who were enslaved to mine gold), the Paiaguá (who defeated several large Portuguese flotillas and caused periodic panic in Cuiabá) and the Guaicuru (skilled riders and warriors who gained many years of experience fighting the Europeans).

As the gold cycle declined, Mato Grosso again became just another isolated province, with its inhabitants eking out a living from subsistence farming and fishing. In the 19th century, the only way to get from Mato Grosso to Rio de Janeiro was by ship via the Rio Paraguai, a journey of several weeks.

This isolation from the capital fueled several separatist movements but, with the coming of the republic in 1889, the arrival of the telegraph in the early 20th century and the opening of a few rough roads, Mato Grosso slowly emerged from its slumber.

The government policy of developing the interior in the 1940s and '50s and the construction of Brasília in 1960 brought huge waves of migrants from both the Northeast and the South of the country. Today, using modern agricultural methods, the area has developed into Brazil's breadbasket, cultivating soy, corn, rice and cotton in vast plantations. Huge cattle ranches also abound.

Mato Grosso is still home to a large population of indigenous Brazilians. Several tribes remain in northern Mato Grosso, living as they have for centuries. The Erikbatsa, noted for their fine featherwork, live near Fontanilles and Juima; the Nhambikuraa are near Padroal; and the Cayabi live near Juara. The only tribe left in the Pantanal still subsisting by hunting and fishing is the Bororo. There are also the Cinta Larga Indians of Parque Indígena Aripuanã and the tribes under the care of Fundação Nacional do Indio (Funai) in the Parque Indígena do Xingu, which was set up in the 1950s as a safe haven for several groups of Indians.

In the late '70s, the massive area of Mato Grosso was cut in half, creating the new state of Mato Grosso do Sul, officially inaugurated in 1979. Agriculture pays the bills in both states, with massive cattle, sugarcane, and soy plantations peppering whatever landscape isn't protected by national parks and the *reserva particular patrimônio natural* (national private heritage reserve).

Climate

Given its geographic diversity, the climate varies considerably throughout Mato Grosso. In the north, Cuiabá remains hot and humid year-round, with marked rainfall from October through to March. Just 1½ hours north, in the higher Chapada dos Guimarães, you can expect much cooler temperatures year-round. In Mato Grosso do Sul, cold fronts coming up from the south during winter can cause dramatic temperature drops. In the Pantanal, expect the most rainfall from October to March. The climate here is generally hot and humid, but it can get cold at night during winter as fronts push up from the south.

National Parks

Deep in the Pantanal is the isolated Parque Nacional do Pantanal, a 1380-sq-km national park encompassing the confluence of the mighty Paraguai and Cuiabá Rivers. It's usually only visited by researchers, as access is by boat only. Most foreign travelers experience the Pantanal outside the park.

The 330-sq-km Parque Nacional Chapada dos Guimarães (p411) is located in the tablelands that mark the western edge of the Brazilian central plateau. The park is only 1½ hours from Cuiabá.

Getting There & Away

The gateway cities to Mato Grosso are Cuiabá and Campo Grande, with daily flights to Rio, São Paulo and Brasília. The majority of travelers coming from Bolivia take the scenic (though white-knuckled) train journey from Santa Cruz to Quijarro and cross into the Brazilian town of Corumbá, which is connected by road to all points east. Mato Grosso also borders Paraguay to the south. There are regular bus services to the Paraguayan border from Campo Grande.

Getting Around

Although distances are great, Mato Grosso has a well-developed road network, and regular bus services connect its towns and cities. Most travelers visiting the Pantanal will travel on either the Estrada Parque (p419) in Mato Grosso do Sul or the Transpantaneira (p416) in Mato Grosso. Both are dirt roads and conditions can be precarious.

MATO GROSSO

Mato Grosso means 'thick forest.' Part of the highland plain that runs through Brazil's interior, it's a dusty land of rolling hills, endless plantations, abundant savannas and some of the best fishing rivers in the world. South America's three major ecosystems – Pantanal, Amazon and cerrado – thrive within its borders.

CUIABÁ

☎ 0xx65 / pop 524,000

Cuiabá is a frontier boomtown basking in the relentless Mato Grosso sun. The town's name is a Bororo Indian word meaning 'arrow-fishing,' though it was first gold and later agriculture that led to the city becoming one of the fastest-growing capitals in Brazil over the last 30 years. The population explosion has tailed off in recent times, but Cuiabá is still a lively place and a good starting point for excursions to the Pantanal and Chapada dos Guimarães.

History

In 1719 a Paulista, Pascoal Moreira Cabral, was hunting Indians along the Rio Cuiabá when he found gold. A gold rush followed, but many of those seeking gold never reached the new settlement at Cuiabá. Traveling more than 3000km from São Paulo by river took five months; along the way, gold seekers found little food, many mosquitoes, dangerous rapids, lengthy portages, disease and incredible heat.

With the end of the gold boom and the decay of the mines, Cuiabá would have disappeared, except that the soil along the Rio Cuiabá allowed subsistence agriculture, while the river itself provided fish.

By 1835 the town was the capital of Mato Grosso but, apart from a brief resurgence as a staging point for the war against Para-

guay in the 1860s, it remained a backwater. Today, thanks mostly to the construction of Brasília and a massive agri-economy, Cuiabá has finally been propelled into the modern world.

Orientation

The city is actually two sister cities separated by the Rio Cuiabá: Old Cuiabá and Várzea Grande (where the airport is located). The center of the city is approximately 2.5km north of the river.

Information

EMERGENCY

Ambulance (☎ 192)
Fire department (☎ 193)
Police (☎ 190)

INTERNET ACCESS

Onix LAN House (Map p409; ☎ 3624 1127; Rua Pedro Celestino 8; per hr R$2.50; ☯ 7am-8pm Mon-Sat) Entrance through Mistura Cuiabana.

MEDICAL SERVICES

Hospital Geral (☎ 3616 7091; Rua 13 de Junho 2101)

MONEY

There are ATMs outside the airport for Visa/ MasterCard withdrawals.

Banco do Brasil (Map p409; Rua Getúlio Vargas 915; ☯ 11am-4pm Mon-Fri) Visa/MasterCard ATMs and money exchange.

HSBC (Map p409; Rua Getúlio Vargas 346; ☯ 9am-5pm Mon-Fri) Visa/MasterCard ATM.

POST

Post office (Map p409; Praça da República 101; ☯ 9am-5pm Mon-Fri, 8am-noon Sat)

TOURIST INFORMATION

CAT tourist office (☯ 8am-6pm Mon-Fri) There is a small tourist-info booth in the arrivals hall of the airport. A new location was under construction on Praça Rahidy Jaudy at the time of research.

Sedtur (Map p409; ☎ 3613 9340; Rua Voluntários da Pátria 118; ☯ 8am-6pm Mon-Fri) An alternative source of information in the city center is the office of the secretary of tourism, which has loads of helpful maps and brochures.

TRAVEL AGENCIES

Mundial Viagens (Map p409; ☎ 3623 3499; Av Isaac Póvoas 586) Helpful agency, west of downtown, for domestic and international flights.

Sights

Inside a beautifully restored colonial building on Praça da República, the **Museu Histórico de Mato Grosso** (Map p409; ☎ 3613 9234; admission free; ⏲ 8am-noon & 2-6pm Tue-Fri) is an interesting stroll through the state's history. Each room represents a different period and houses extensive collections of silver, military paraphernalia, and other historical odds and ends.

The small **Museu Rondon** (Map p408; ☎ 3615 8489; Av Fernando Correia da Costa; admission free; ⏲ 1:30-5:30pm Mon, 7:30-11:30am & 1:30-5:30pm Tue-Sat, 9am-5:30pm Sun) has exhibits on the Xavante, Bororo and Karajá tribes and is well worth a visit to check out the ornate Indian

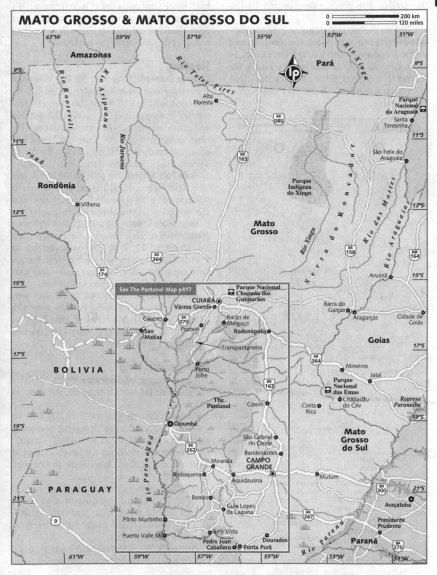

MATO GROSSO & MATO GROSSO DO SUL

headdresses and some vicious weaponry. It is on the grounds of the Federal University of Mato Grosso (UFMT), which also has a small **zoo** (admission free; ☺ 7:30-11:30am & 1:30-5:30pm Tue-Sun). To get there, catch a 103 Jd Universitário bus (R$1.85) on Av Tenente Coronel Duarte. Once you hit campus, the museum is behind the Aquatic Park and the zoo is directly across campus in the opposite direction.

Close to the municipal aquarium, the **Mercado do Porto** (Map p408; ☺ 6am-6pm Mon-Sat, to noon Sun) houses the new fish market, with a variety of species, as well as a vegetable and spice market. It's a good place to check out what the region's fish look like before they arrive at your table.

CUIABÁ

INFORMATION
Pantanal Explorer .....(see 8)

SIGHTS & ACTIVITIES
Mercado do Porto.......1 A2
Museu do Rondon......2 B2
Zoo..........................(see 2)

SLEEPING 🏠
Skala Palace Hotel......3 A1

EATING 🍴
Al Manzul..................4 B2

ENTERTAINMENT 🎭
Haus Bier.....................5 A2
Tom Choppin.................6 A2

SHOPPING 🛍
Casa do Artesão 7 A2

TRANSPORT
Marechal Rondon
Airport....................8 A3

Tours

For details about excursions from Cuiabá into the Pantanal, see p419.

Festivals

The **Festa de São Benedito** takes place during the first week of July at the Igreja NS do Rosário and the Capela de São Benedito. The holiday has a more Umbanda than Catholic flavor; it's celebrated with traditional foods such as *bolos de queijo* (cheese balls) and *bolos de arroz* (rice balls), and colorful regional dances.

Sleeping

Pousada Ecoverde (Map p409; ☎ 3624 1386; www.ecoverdetours.com; Rua Pedro Celestino 391; s/d R$25/40) This pousada is well worn, but owner/local wildlife ecologist Joel Souza is so hospitable and knowledgeable, you won't much care. He runs things out of a 100-year-old house full of antique radios and books on the Pantanal. There's also a small courtyard and garden.

Skala Palace Hotel (Map p408; ☎ 621 3067; Av Jules Rimet 26; s/d R$45/65; 🍴 🖥) There's not much to it, but it's directly opposite the bus station and a good option if you're just overnighting.

Hotel Mato Grosso (Map p409; ☎ 3614 7777; www.hotelmatogrosso.com.br in Portuguese; Rua Comandante Costa 2522; s/d R$70/90; 🍴 🖥 🏊) For basic comfort in a central location, the simple but clean rooms here are good value for your real – and that pool looks a lot like heaven in this heat.

Amazon Plaza Hotel (Map p409; ☎ 2121 2000; www.hotelamazon.com.br in Portuguese; Av Getúlio Vargas 600; s/d R$220/280; 🍴 🖥 🏊) Jungle-themed option with kitschy pool area and extra-large rooms. Highly recommended.

Eating & Drinking

The center is almost deserted at night, but there are good restaurants nearby on Av Getúlio Vargas.

Mistura Cuiabana (Map p409; ☎ 3624 1127; cnr Rua Pedro Celestino & Rua Cândido Mariano; meals per kg R$12.90; ☺ 11am-2:30pm Mon-Fri) A excellent buffet of regional selections for lunch (the fried bananas are divine). It's inside the orange colonial building on the corner.

Choppão (☎ 3623 9101; Praça 8 de Abril s/n; meals for 2 R$26-50; ☺ 24hr) A Cuiabá institution offering huge portions of meat and fish for two, all chased with frigid *chope* (draft beer) in specially iced tankards.

Pizza na Pedra (p409 ☎ 3622 0060; Praça Eurico Gaspar Dutra 45; pizza R$16-51; ☺ 6pm-midnight Sun-Thu, to 1am

CENTRAL CUIABÁ

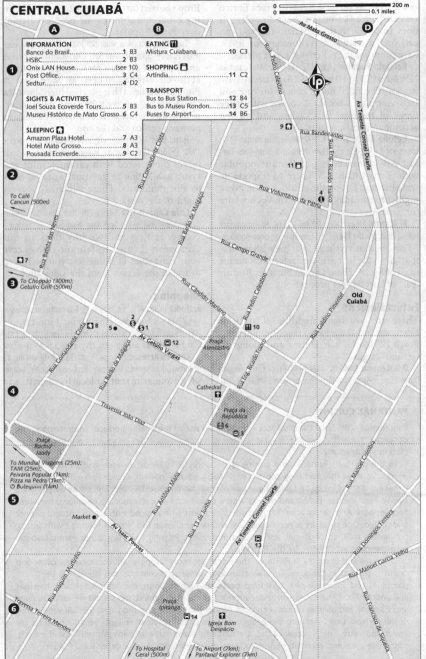

INFORMATION
Banco do Brasil..............................**1**	B3
HSBC..**2**	B3
Onix LAN House..................(see 10)	
Post Office....................................**3**	C4
Sedtur...**4**	D2

SIGHTS & ACTIVITIES
Joel Souza Ecoverde Tours...........**5**	B3
Museu Histórico de Mato Grosso..**6**	C4

SLEEPING
Amazon Plaza Hotel.......................**7**	A3
Hotel Mato Grosso........................**8**	A3
Pousada Ecoverde.........................**9**	C2

EATING
Mistura Cuiabana.........................**10**	C3

SHOPPING
Artíndia......................................**11**	C2

TRANSPORT
Bus to Bus Station.......................**12**	B4
Bus to Museu Rondon..................**13**	C5
Buses to Airport..........................**14**	B6

0   200 m
0   0.1 miles

To Café
Cancun (500m)

To Choppão (300m);
Getulio Grill (500m)

Rua Batista das Neves

Rua Comandante Costa

Rua Barão de Malgaço

Rua Pedro Celestino

Rua Elíe. Ricardo Franco

Rua Galdino Pimentel

Av Mato Grosso

Av Tenente Coronel Duarte

Rua Bandeirantes

Rua Voluntários da Pátria

Rua Campo Grande

Rua Cândido Mariano

**Old
Cuiabá**

Av Getúlio Vargas

Praça
Alencastro

Travessia João Dias

Cathedral

Praça da
República

Praça
Rachid
Jaudy

To Mundial Viagens (25m);
TAM (25m);
Peixaria Popular (1km);
Pizza na Pedra (1km);
O Buteguim (1km)

Rua Comandante Costa

Rua Barão de Malgaço

Market ●

Av Isaac Póvoas

Rua Antônio Maria

Rua 13 de Junho

Av Tenente Coronel Duarte

Rua Manoel Colômbia

Rua Domingos Ferreira

Rua Manoel Garcia Velho

Rua Joaquim Murtinho

Travessa Tereira Mendes

Praça
Ipiranga

**Igreja Bom
Despácio**

Rua Francisco de Siqueira

To Hospital
Geral (500m)

To Airport (7km);
Pantanal Explorer (7km)

Fri & Sat) A lively pizzeria right on Praça Eurico Gaspar Dutra (known as Praça Popular). It does an excellent pizza *rodízio* (all you can eat) on Tuesday and Wednesday for R$17. Save room for the ridiculous sweet pizzas.

Peixaria Popular (☎ 3322 5471; Av São Sebastião 2324; dishes R$20; ☺ 11am-3pm & 7-11pm Tue-Sat, 11am-5pm Sun) The R$20 lunch course for one will feed you plus a horse. It comes with three types of regional fish dishes and all the accompaniments. A must.

Getúlio Grill (☎ 3624 9992; Av Getúlio Vargas 1147; meals for 2 R$22-55; ☺ 11am-2:30pm & from 5pm Tue-Sun) An upmarket bar-restaurant popular with young Cuiabános. There's a respectable wine list, and DJs on the outdoor patio every night. On Saturday, the party moves upstairs for dancing.

Al Manzul (Map p408; ☎ 3663 2237; Av Arquimedes Pereira Lima; prix fixe R$89; ☺ 11am-3pm Sat, noon-4pm Sun, 7-11pm Thu-Sat) It's difficult to argue with reports that this is the best Middle Eastern restaurant in all of Brazil. There's no menu: it's a 30-dish feast of Last Supper proportions.

Entertainment

There are two main nightlife clusters in town, around the lovely Praça Popular (aka Praça Eurico Gaspar Dutra) and along Av Getúlio Vargas.

O Botequim (p409 ☎ 3324 0740; Praça Eurico Gaspar Dutra 35; ☺ 6pm-1am Mon-Thu, to 6pm-3am Fri & Sat)

Prop yourself up on the deck here for refreshing *chope* and some prime people-watching over Praça Popular.

Tom Choppin (Map p408; ☎ 3627 7227; Rua das Laranjeiras 701; ☺ 5pm-late Mon-Sat) Outstanding brews and views are the draw for Cuiabá's well-to-do at this cleverly named open-air MPB (Música Popular Brasileira) bar perched high above the city. Mondays get lively for *chorinho*, an informal, instrumental style of music. It's halfway between centro and the zoo.

Haus Bier (Map p408; ☎ 3027 2000; Av Mato Grosso 1000; ☺ 5pm-late) A massive microbrewery that offers *chope* laced with caramel, mint and syrup in addition to the usual suspects. Stick to the standards. There's live MPB every night of the week.

Café Cancun (☎ 3316 8120; Rua Cândido Mariano 1160; cover R$15; ☺ 9pm-late Wed-Sun) Cuiabá's young, restless and wealthy flock to this Caribbean-themed restaurant-club. Leave your Havaianas at home lest you be forced to watch the action from the sidewalk.

Shopping

Artíndia (Map p409; ☎ 3623 1675; Rua Pedro Celestino s/n; ☺ 8-11am & 1-5pm Mon-Fri) Excellent indigenous handicrafts from all over Brazil, including rattan handbags and a healthy arsenal of spears.

Casa do Artesão (Map p408; ☎ 3322 2047; cnr Rua 13 de Junho & Rua Senador Mello; ☺ 9am-6pm Mon-Fri, to 2pm Sat) A wonderful spot for local handicrafts and

---

PANTANAL CUISINE

Pantaneiros – the local Pantanal folk – make good use of regional ingredients in preparing their delicacies. You'll find lots of restaurants offering regional specialties on your travels in the area – stop in and try some.

In the northern Pantanal, the cuisine is decidedly fishy. *Pacu, dourado* and *pintado* are the most consumed fish, and they come *frito* (fried), *grelhado* (grilled), *assado* (baked) or *defumado* (smoked). Both *dourado* and *pacu* have lots of small bones, but they separate easily when baked slowly. *Pacu* is often baked and served with an *escabeche* sauce consisting of onions, tomatoes and peppers. Another favorite fish is *pintado,* excellent when spiced with rough salt and pepper and grilled. One specialty is *peixe à urucum,* where the chosen fish is served topped with spices, condensed milk, coconut milk and melted mozzarella. Piranha soup is another exotic favorite, considered an aphrodisiac by the Pantaneiros.

On farms and in southern Pantanal, the dishes are more strongly influenced by the cattle and grains produced in the area. Specialties include *carne seca com abobora* (sun-dried beef with pumpkin) and *paçoca-de-pilã* (sun-dried beef with manioc flour), the latter eaten with bananas and unsalted rice. There's also *arroz de carreteiro* (rice with sun-dried beef served with fried manioc and banana) and *galinha caipira* – chicken served with white rice and *pequi,* a small yellow fruit of the cerrado. Don't bite into the *pequi* – its seed contains lots of spines! Pantanal desserts are sweet and tasty. Some popular ones are *furrundu* – a mixture of papaya trunk (not the fruit), sugarcane juice and coconut – and ice cream made from *bocaiúva,* another local fruit.

sweets, including ceramics, woodcarvings, straw baskets and *pequi* crème liquor.

Getting There & Away

There are flights between Cuiabá and many airports in Brazil (with the notable omission of Corumbá in Mato Grosso do Sul) by **TAM** (☎ 3614 2557), **Gol** (☎ 3682 1645) and **OceanAir** (☎ 3614 2550). The latter and **Trip** (☎ 3682 2555) fly to Alta Floresta.

Frequent buses make the trip to Poconé (R$15.85, 2½ hours, six daily); the first leaves at 6am. To Barão de Melgaço (R$24.85, 2½ hours, two daily). For Chapada dos Guimarães (R$8.50, one hour, hourly) there are buses every hour from 7am, but take an early bus if you're doing a day trip.

Buses go to Cáceres (R$34.50, four hours, seven daily), with connections to Santa Cruz in Bolivia. Porto Velho (R$99, 24 hours, two daily) is a long ride. There are buses daily to Goiânia (R$95, 15 hours, six daily) and Brasília (R$107, 15 hours, five daily). Most of the buses to Campo Grande (R$80.50, 11 hours, four daily) stop at Coxim (R$52.10, seven hours). To Alta Floresta (R$125.50, 13½ hours, four daily), the first bus leaves at 6am.

Getting Around

Marechal Rondon airport (☎ 3614 2500) is in Várzea Grande, 7km from Cuiabá. To catch the local bus to town, turn left as you leave the airport and walk to the Las Velas Hotel. On the left side of the hotel, catch a bus labeled Shopping Pantanal and get off at Av Getúlio Vargas and Av Tenente Coronel Duarte. Praça da República is 200m northwest on Getúlio Vargas. A taxi costs R$28.

Cuiabá's **bus station** (Map p408; ☎ 3621 3629) is 3km north of the center on the highway toward Chapada dos Guimarães. From inside the bus station, you can get a Centro bus to Praça Alencastro. More frequent buses marked 'Centro' leave from outside the bus station and can drop you along Av Isaac Póvoas. A taxi from inside the bus station costs R$10 – or mototaxis run the trip for R$7.

All the car-rental places have branches in the center and in or near the airport. There are often promotional rates, so shop around. **Referência** (☎ 3682 6689) and **Localiza** (☎ 3624 7979) are a couple of reliable companies. The best car for the Pantanal is the Volkswagen Gol. A rental car with unlimited kilometers will cost around R$125 a day.

CHAPADA DOS GUIMARÃES

☎ 0xx65 / pop 17,300

After the Pantanal, the Parque Nacional da Chapada dos Guimarães is Mato Grosso's leading attraction. As little known as it is spectacular, the park is on a rocky plateau 64km northeast of Cuiabá and 800m higher, offering a cool change from the state capital. The region is reminiscent of the American Southwest and surprisingly different from the typical Mato Grosso terrain. The town of the same name is a convenient base for exploring the park and surrounding areas and is home to one of the lushest central squares in Brazil.

The area surrounding the park has numerous attractions. About 41km northeast of Chapada town is the 1100m-long **Aroe Jari** cavern and, in another cave close by, the **Lagoa Azul** (Blue Lake). On the way from Cuiabá to Chapada town, you pass **Rio dos Peixes**, **Rio Mutaca** and **Rio Claro**, which are popular weekend bathing spots for Cuiabános; and three commanding valleys, **Vale do Salgadeira**, **Vale do Paciência** and **Vale do Rio Claro**. The sheer 80m drop called **Portão do Inferno** (Hell's Gate) is also unforgettable – it was formerly the town 'prison' in the early 1900s (use your imagination). In **Salgadeira**, on the road to Cuiabá, you can take a waterfall shower or grab a beer at one of the four restaurants that sit under the imposing cliffs. The whole thing is one drawnout Kodak moment.

Parque Nacional da Chapada dos Guimarães

Only receiving national park status in 1989, the outstanding Parque Nacional da Chapada dos Guimarães remains a tad under the radar in the context of Brazil's most impressive national parks. Let us pray for status quo. As its offerings are as spectacular as anything in Brazil, you usually won't have to share them with anyone. Amen.

The two exceptional sights inside the park are the Véu de Noiva falls and the Cidade de Pedra. There is a **visitors center** (☎ 3301 1133; admission free; ☯ 8am-5pm) at the park entrance.

The impressive **Véu de Noiva** (Bridal Veil), an 86m free-falling waterfall, provides the park's ubiquitous postcard moment. It is around 15km west of the town of Chapada dos Guimarães. You can get off the bus from Cuiabá and walk from the road, spend a couple of hours there, then flag down the next bus coming through to the town of Chapada dos Guimarães. Start walking downhill over the bluff, slightly to your right. A small trail leads to a magical **lookout**, perched on top of rocks with the canyon below. This is one of Chapada's most dazzling spots.

From there, most visitors join the **Caminho das Águas**, a 6km hike that takes in seven swimmable waterfalls throughout the park. But it's **Cidade de Pedra** (Stone City) that provides Guimarães' most transcendent moment. Jagged sandstone rock formations reminiscent of stone temples jut up into the sky from the tops of enormous cliffs that drop down into the vast green valley below. The best time to visit is sunset, when fiery red light illuminates the whole area in a monumental display of color and light. It's 20km north of Chapada town along the road to Água Fria. The turnoff to Água Fria is 6km west of Chapada town on Hwy MT-251.

The best time to visit is fall, with clearer days, less rain and cooler nights.

Mirante

The Mirante (Lookout) is the unofficial geographic center of South America. It's a tad underwhelming, with nothing marking the occasion beyond a blank concrete slab that looks more like a manhole cover than a major geographical designator. That said, the views are miraculous; off to your right you can see the Cuiabá skyline, and beyond that, the flatlands that eventually become the Pantanal. It's outside the national park, 8km from town. Take the last road in Chapada on your right and go 8km; you'll see a dirt road. The rim of the canyon is a couple of hundred meters away.

Tours

Chapada Explorer (☎ 3301 1290; www.chapadaexplorer .com.br in Portuguese; Praça Dom Wunibaldo 57, Chapada dos Guimarães; ☒ 8-11:30am & 1:30-6:30pm Mon-Fri, 8-11:30am Sat & Sun) is an excellent agency run by a couple of young locals who have grown up around ecotourism. They are actively involved in teaching the benefits of low-impact tourism to locals. It runs excursions to all of the area's attractions in groups up to a maximum of 10. If you need transport, guided tours for four people run around R$100 (R$25 per person) to the park, R$130 (R$32.50 per person) to attractions further afield like Aroe Jari Cavern. Bring your own food; the price does not include admission prices, which range from R$2 to R$17.60.

If you're driving, drop by the official tourist office, **CAT** (☎ 3301 2085; Rua Penn Gomes s/n; ☒ 8am-6pm Mon-Fri, to noon & 1-5pm Sat & Sun), where a cartoonish map is available. You'll need it!

Sleeping & Eating

There is camping with good facilities at Salgadeira, just before the climb into the Chapada park. Chapada town has plenty of accommodations.

Pousada Bom Jardim (☎ 3301 2668; Praça Dom Wunibaldo 461; s/d R$35/50) There's no reason to spring for air-con at this cheapie right in the main square – the fans are high-octane. A favorite with backpackers.

Turismo Hotel (☎ 3301 1176; www.hotelturismo .com.br in Portuguese; Rua Fernando Corrêa Costa 1065; s/d R$135/180; ☒ ☒) A spotless place run by a German family. The traditional breakfast spread is encased in glass – no flies!

Solar do Inglês (☎ 3301 1389; www.solardoingles .com.br in Portuguese; Rua Cipriano Curvo 142; s/d R$198/242; ☒ ☒ ☒) This charming pousada owned by an English hunting enthusiast is full of Victorian charm and European antiques. The afternoon tea is one of Brazil's most authentic. No children.

Pousada do Parque Eco Lodge (☎ 3391 1346; www .pousadadoparque.com.br; Estrada do Parque Ecológico s/n; s/d R$210/235; ☒ ☒ ☒) This high-end eco-choice borders 150 hectares of newly preserved park land and is the closet accommodations to the park's entrance (4.5km). All the wood used in the construction of this pousada came from recycled sources and the roofs are made of recycled milk cartons.

Cantinho da Gula (☎ 9237 4454; Rua José de Souza Neves s/n; meals R$2-5; ☒ 6:30pm-late) Great outdoor spot serving small bites of delicious skewered barbeque and cheese (try the *queijo coalho*) for ridiculously low prices.

Da Mata Bistro (☎ 3301 3483; Estrada do Mirante, km1; dishes R$18-32; ☒ 8pm-2am Fri, 5pm-2am Sat, 11am-5pm Sun) A romantic bistro with stupendous views from the same owners as nearby Morro dos Ventos (also good). It's high-class contemporary Brazilian cuisine 4km east of town along Hwy MT-251 in the direction of Campo Verde. The homemade pasta buffet on Sunday is worth telling your grandchildren about.

Restaurante Cachoeirinha (MT-251, km51; meals for 2 R$39-68; ☒ 8am-6pm) An outstanding restaurant on private parkland under the nose of a beautiful waterfall. The pricy *pintado na telha* is unforgettable. R$2 of the R$4 admission price goes toward your check. Highly recommended.

Getting There & Away

Buses leave Cuiabá's bus station for Chapada town (R$8.50, 1½ hours) hourly from 5:45am to 7:30pm. In the other direction, the first bus leaves Chapada town at 6:30am and the last at 7:30pm. The miraculous views are out the right-side window from Cuiabá, vice versa coming back.

ALTA FLORESTA

☎ 0xx66 / pop 47,000

Technically, Alta Floresta, 873km from Cuiabá in the extreme north of Mato Grosso, sits at the transition point between two of Brazil's dominant ecosystems, cerrado and the pristine southern Amazon rain forest. Its landscapes, however, are all Amazon. The area around Cristalino Private Natural Heritage Preserve is considered Amazonia's best for spotting rare birds and mammals, including the endangered white-nosed bearded saki monkey, brown titi monkey, tapir, giant river otter, three-toed sloth and five species of macaws.

Alta Floresta is the end of the road: beyond it to the north is the vast expanse of the jungle, with the exception of a brief reappearance of cerrado in the northern neighbor state of Pará. The town itself has no attractions and has grown rapidly as an agricultural and logging center since its foundation in the early 1970s.

Tours

If you are short on time or money and can't spend the night at the Cristalino Jungle Lodge (the only way to see the abundant wildlife here unless you are on a fishing trip), **Floresta Tours** (☎ 3521 2221; www.florestatour .com.br in Portuguese; ⏱ 8am-5pm Mon-Fri, to noon Sat) offers day trips into the Cristalino Private Natural Heritage Preserve for R$210 per person. The trip takes nine hours and includes transfers, guides, excursions and lunch at the lodge. The agency is located at the Floresta Amazônica Hotel. Advance reservations are required.

Sleeping & Eating

Many visitors to the area are naturalists on expensive package tours to isolated jungle lodges, but independent travelers will find a few good accommodations in town.

Floresta Amazônica Hotel (☎ 3512 7180; www.fah .com.br; Av Perimetral Oeste 2001; s/d R$60/70; ⚴ 🖳 🖭) Not your average business hotel, set in jungly surroundings 5km from centro. It's in need of a touch-up, but the rooms with balconies around a lovely garden are pleasant, as is that wonderful pool. It's affiliated with the Cristalino Jungle Lodge.

Lisboa Palace (☎ 3521 2876; www.hotellisboa.com.br; Av Jaime Verissimo de Campos 251; s/d R$65/90; ⚴ 🖳) The sizable rooms here are clean and modern, though the beds are a tad hard. A suitable alternative if Floresta Amazônica is booked out.

Cristalino Jungle Lodge (☎ 3521 1349; www .cristalinolodge.com.br; s/d packages from R$490/405) On the banks of the Rio Cristalino (39km north of Alta Floresta) in an area rich in Amazon flora and fauna, the lodge offers a 50m-high observation tower and 20km of good bird-watching trails (it is considered one of the top 50 spots in the world for birding). The new VIP bungalows ooze creature comfort luxe. Rates include all meals, transfers, guides, excursions and insurance.

Café Mostarda (☎ 3521 3103; Av Ariosto da Riva 3493; meals per kg R$18; ⏱ 6am-6pm Mon-Fri, to 2pm Sat) An exceptionally well-to-do per-kilo place with excellent regional food.

Getting There & Away

From Cuiabá there are frequent buses to Alta Floresta (R$125, 13 hours, four daily). **Trip** (⏱ 0xx65-3682 2555) flies from Cuiabá to Alta Floresta (R$395) Monday to Friday at noon, returning at 2:15pm. **OceanAir** (⏱ 3614 2550) heads up (for considerably less money, no less) Monday to Friday at 9:20pm and Saturday at 11pm, returning Monday to Saturday at 5:50am (R$190).

CÁCERES

☎ 0xx65 / pop 85,000

Boats and bikes get top billing in sweltering Cáceres, a quiet little town that hugs the banks of the impressive Rio Paraguai. Anglers flock here for the rich fishing waters in the area, especially during September, when it attracts 150,000 visitors for the world's biggest fishing competition (p414). The main attractions here are the barco-hotels, floating accommodations for anglers that set off along the Rio Paraguai for days at a time. When not on the water, locals love to be on two wheels, and the town has a progressive amount of bike lanes for Brazil. It's also an access point for a few Pantanal lodges and Bolivia.

Information

Anvisa (⏱ 7-11am & 1-6:30pm) If you need a yellow fever vaccination for Bolivia, they are free at this small clinic in the bus station. The nurse tends to wander around the station, so stick around if it seems closed during business hours.

Bradesco (Rua José Dulce 183) Visa/MasterCard ATM.

Federal Police (☎ 3211 6300; Av Getúlio Vargas 2125; ⏱ 8am-6pm) If you're traveling on to Corixio and the Bolivian border, get a Brazilian exit stamp from here. It is 4km from town, close to the *prefeitura* (city hall).

Hospital São Luis (☎ 3223 1000; Praça Major João Carlos 99)

HSBC (Rua José Dulce 145; ⏱ 9am-3pm Mon-Fri) Visa/MasterCard ATM.

Post office (Av 7 de Setembro; ⏱ 9am-5pm Mon-Fri)

Scorpion LAN House (Praça Barão do Rio Branco 27; per hr R$2.50; ⏱ 1pm-midnight) Internet access.

Sematur (☎ 3223 5918; Rua Riachuelo 1; ⏱ noon-6pm Mon-Fri) For help hiring boats and arranging accommodations in the Pantanal, this local tourist office is pretty much the be all and end all.

Sleeping & Eating

All the action in Cáceres happens around the riverfront and nearby Praça Barão do Rio Branco, where there are many restaurants and bars.

Capri Hotel (☎ 3223 1771; Rua Getúlio Vargas 99; s/d R$30/50; ﹡) The best of the run-down options across the street from the bus station.

Hotel Porto Bello (☎ 3224 1937; Av São Luís 1888; s/d R$55/85; ﹡ ▢ ▩) Too bad the nicest digs in town sit 5km from the city center and doesn't

offer a pool. But it's otherwise the most colorful and comfortable option.

La Barca Hotel (☎ 3223 5047; Rua General Osório s/n; s/d R$60/108; ﹡ ▢ ▩) A good option 2km from the center, with rooms around a large courtyard and a wonderful pool. The singles are good value.

Riviera Pantanal Hotel (☎ 3223 1177; Rua General Osório 540; s/d R$120/$160; ﹡ ▢) This former family-run spot known as the Ipanema Hotel was sold and renovated post research. Previously, it was five-star luxury in comparison to other hotels in the center, but the verdict is still out on the new owners, who are less *simpatico* on the phone.

Restaurant Hispano (☎ 3223 1486; Praça Barão do Rio Branco 64; meals per kg R$16; ⏱ 11am-4pm) A solid per-kilo option on the main square with river views. The homemade potato chips are a nice surprise.

Corimba (☎ 3223 3002; Rua 6 de Outobro 27; meals for 2 R$20-45; ⏱ 10:30am-midnight) A lively outdoor spot overlooking the river with an extensive menu of regional fish dishes.

Kaskata Restaurante Flutuante (☎ 3223 2916; Beira-Rio; meals for 2 R$36-45; ⏱ 9:30am-11pm) The best floating restaurant in town. Regional fish is the specialty here, but if you're looking to try *jacaré* (caiman), it is served five ways.

Getting There & Away

The bus station is 10 blocks north of the riverfront, though the bus from Cuiabá first stops at the station just outside the city center in Vale do Araguaia. Frequent buses make the journey between Cuiabá and Cáceres (R$33.75, four hours, six daily). There are also bus services to Porto Velho (R$129.75, two daily). For information on buses to Bolivia, see p717.

POCONÉ

☎ 0xx65 / pop 22,000

The main entry point to the Pantanal for travelers heading south from Cuiabá, Poconé marks the beginning of the Transpantaneira 'highway.' Poconé still has a sleepy, frontier feel (as one local put it, 'In Poconé, even the restaurants close for lunch!'). The locals, many of whom are descended from the original tribe in the area, the Beripoconeses, have a strong sense of tradition.

In May, Poconé celebrates the week-long Semana do Fazendeiro e do Cavalo Pantaneiro with a cattle fair and rodeos.

CATCH OF THE DAY

Every September, 150,000 people, most of them toting fishing poles, descend on Cáceres for the **Festival Internacional de Pesca**, recognized by the *Guinness Book of World Records* as the world's largest fishing fête. Since 1979 the waters of the Rio Paraguai have been inundated by feverish fisherman from some 15 countries, all out to nab (and release) the largest *pintado*, *dourado* and *pacu* fish they can get their hooks on. Winners take home R$30,000 cars or boat motors. There are dance troupes by the river and local children – some 1500 strong – are taught the ecobenefits of catch-and-release fishing.

Orientation & Information

Buses to/from Cuiabá first stop at the Poconé bus station about 10 blocks from the center of town, then continue on to Praça da Matriz; behind the Matriz church is the road that leads to the beginning of the Transpantaneira. To get there, walk down Rua Dom Aquino, turn right at the Texaco station, then turn left at the end of SESC Estânica Ecológica. It's a straight shot from there.

At the time of research, there were no foreign-friendly ATMs in Poconé.

Future LAN House (Praça da Matriz; per hr R$2; ◯ 8am-11pm) Internet access.

Hospital (☎ 3345 1963; Rua Dom Aquino 406)

Police (☎ 3345 1456)

Post office (Rua Coronel Salvador Marques 335)

Tours

The only agency in town caters to serious fishers, **Transpantanal** (☎ 3345 2343; www.transpantanal.com.br in Portuguese; Av Aníbal de Toledo 1895; ◯ 7:30am-6pm Mon-Fri, to noon Sat) offers seven-day fishing packages along the rivers Cuiabá, São Lourenço, Piquiri and Paraguai for R$2400 per person (minimum 12).

Sleeping & Eating

The best places to stay, especially if you're trying to organize a lift down the Transpantaneira, are a couple of kilometers out of town near the beginning of the road.

Hotel Santa Cruz (☎ 3345 2634; Rodovia Transpantaneira 450; per person R$15) The least attractive option but will do if the others are full.

Pousada Pantaneira (☎ 3345 3357; Transpantaneira km0; s/d R$30/50; ◪ ▣) Newly remodeled, this simple pousada and *churrascaria* (barbecue restaurant) sits at the beginning of the Transpantaneira – a good base for hitchin' a ride down the highway.

Hotel Skala (☎ 3345 1407; Praça Bem Rondon 64; s/d R$30/60; ◪ ▣) The best option in the center, with spacious rooms and the most sophisticated restaurant in town, though don't expect Laguiole and Riedel.

Tulipa's Grill (☎ 8403 5401; Praça da Matriz; meals R$12-15) Great open-faced *picanha* (steak) sandwiches are the specialty here, but anything with meat is good. It's a simple little spot on the main square.

Getting There & Away

There are buses from Cuiabá to Poconé (R$15.85, two hours, six daily) from 6am to 7pm, and six in the opposite direction from 6am to 7:20pm. Alternatively, taxis leaving from the Ponto de Táxi at Praça da Matriz will drop you at your final destination in Cuiabá for a mere R$20 per person. Get a window seat if you want to appreciate the vegetation typical of the Pantanal's outskirts: *pequís* (a 5m- to 15m-tall plant with a thick, twisted trunk, the fruit of which is used in lots of local dishes); *piúvas* (one of the Pantanal's commonest trees, covered in pink flowers between July and September); *babaçus* (palm trees covered in spines, the fruit, wood and fiber of which are highly valued by locals); *ipês* (another common tree of the Pantanal that's covered in yellow flowers between August and September); and *buritis* (a variety of palm that's frequently used as an ornamental tree in Brazil's parks).

THE PANTANAL

The Amazon may attract more fame and glory, but the Pantanal is a better place to see wildlife. In the Amazon, the animals hide in the dense foliage, but in the open spaces of the Pantanal, wildlife is visible to the most casual observer. If you like to see animals in their natural environment, the Pantanal – with the greatest concentration of fauna in the New World – should not be missed.

Located in the center of South America, the world's largest contiguous wetland is 20 times the size of the famed Everglades in Florida – some 210,000 sq km. Something less than 100,000 sq km of this is in Bolivia and Paraguay; the rest is in Brazil, split between the states of Mato Grosso and Mato Grosso do Sul.

The Pantanal has few people and no towns. Distances are so great and ground transport so poor that people get around in small airplanes and motorboats; 4WD travel is restricted by the seasons. The only road that runs deep into the Pantanal is the Transpantaneira. This raised dirt road sectioned by around 125 small wooden bridges ends 145km south of Poconé, at Porto Jofre. Two-thirds of the intended route from Poconé to Corumbá (at the border with Bolivia) has been left incomplete for lack of funds and particularly for ecological concerns.

The Parque Nacional do Pantanal Matogrossense occupies 1350 sq km in the southwest of Mato Grosso, but most of the Pantanal is privately owned. The national park and three smaller private nature reserves nearby were given Unesco World Heritage listing in 2000.

GEOGRAPHY & CLIMATE

Although *pantano* means 'swamp' in both Spanish and Portuguese, the Pantanal is not a swamp but, rather, a vast alluvial plain. In geological terms, it is a sedimentary basin of quaternary origin, the drying remains of an ancient inland sea called the Xaraés, which began to dry out, along with the Amazon Sea, 65 million years ago.

First sea, then immense lake and now a periodically flooded plain, the Pantanal – 2000km upstream from the Atlantic Ocean yet just 100m to 200m above sea level – is bounded by higher lands: the mountains of the Serra de Maracaju to the east, the Serra da Bodoquena to the south, the Paraguayan and Bolivian Chaco to the west and the Serra dos Parecis and Serra do São Geronimo to the north. From these highlands the rains flow into the Pantanal, forming the Rio Paraguai and its tributaries (which flow south and then east, draining into the Atlantic Ocean).

DRIVING THE TRANSPANTANEIRA

In 1973 the government decided to push a road through the Pantanal from Cuiabá to Corumbá. After they had arrived at Porto Jofre, 145km from Poconé, they then made the wise choice of stopping and questioning the wisdom of putting a road through an area that was under water for six months a year. The result, or remnant, is the Transpantaneira, a raised dirt road that extends deep into the Pantanal. Wildlife is plentiful along the roadside and you'll typically see *jacarés*, capybaras and lots of birds. Once you get off the Transpantaneira and onto some of the farms, the impressive display of wildlife becomes even more varied. There are several places to stay along the Transpantaneira, with all offering horseback riding, walking and boating expeditions (p421).

If you are driving from Cuiabá, head out around 4am to reach the Transpantaneira by sunrise, when the animals come to life. Though the road officially starts in Poconé, most folks mark the wooden sign and guard station 17km south of the city as the beginning of the Transpantaneira. Don't forget to fill up your fuel tank in Poconé as the only other public gas station, at Pousada do Pixaim, is currently dry, though technically you should be able to make it to Porto Jofre and back on one tank. There is a gas station at Hotel Porto Jofre for client use only (at a whopping R$4.50 per liter!).

Heading south, it won't take long for a caiman or a macaw to cross your path as you navigate around 125 little wooden bridges and meter-wide potholes. Notice the interesting carved statue of São Francisco, Protector of Ecology, around km18. He was installed by a priest in Poconé a few years back. Barara is a small bar at km32, where you can stop for a beer and *galinhada* (boneless chicken and rice) or fried fish. You can also purchase a ticket here to go to the top of the lookout tower next door at **Araras Eco Lodge** (per person R$15), a real treat if you can't afford to empty your savings account for a night at the lodge.

At km65 you leave the electricity grid – everything for the next 40km is run on solar energy or generators. After km105, the landscape changes, with denser vegetation and an altogether wilder feel. You are now in jaguar country, where deep the Pantanal begins. Even if you don't spot a jaguar, you are rewarded for your intrepid efforts once you hit the beautiful wide-open spaces of Campo do Jofre, just north of Porto Jofre. Here the wildlife is so plentiful, you'll zap your camera batteries in a few kilometers.

Weekdays are better for driving, as there's less traffic kicking up dust. At the end of the road, check out the gigantic water lilies you always see in photos from the Amazon: there are hundreds in the pond at the back of Hotel Porto Jofre, out on the small wooden pier beyond the swimming pool.

In Cuiabá there are car-rental agencies just outside the airport grounds, and they're often cheaper than the agencies inside the airport. No matter what anyone tells you, you don't need a 4WD vehicle to drive the Transpantaneira. The best car is a Fiat Uno or VW Gol.

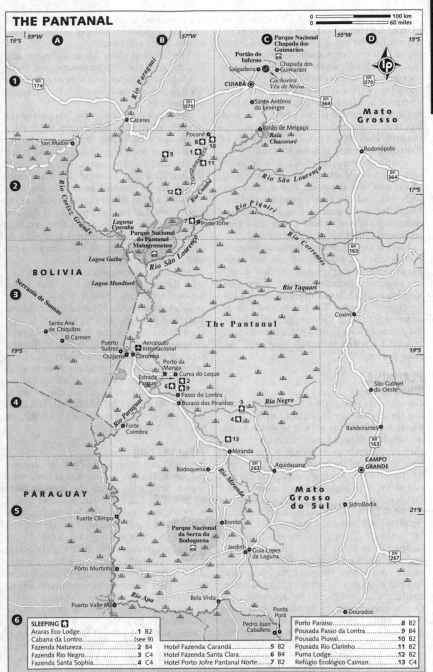

THE PANTANAL

During the wet season (November to March), the rivers flood their banks, inundating much of the low-lying Pantanal and creating *cordilheiras* (vegetation islands above the high-water level), where the animals cluster together. The waters reach their high mark – up to 3m – in January or February, then start to recede in March. This seasonal flooding has made systematic farming impossible and has severely limited human incursions into the area. However, it does provide an enormously rich feeding ground for wildlife.

The floodwaters replenish the soil's nutrients, which would otherwise be very poor, due to the excessive drainage. The waters teem with fish, and the ponds provide excellent niches for many animals and plants. Enormous flocks of wading birds gather in rookeries several square kilometers in area.

Later in the dry season, the water recedes, the lagoons and marshes dry out and fresh grasses emerge on the savanna (the Pantanal's vegetation includes savanna, forest and meadows, which blend together, often with no clear divisions). The hawks and *jacarés* compete for fish in the remaining ponds. As the ponds shrink and dry up, the *jacarés* crawl around for water, sweating it out until the rains return.

PLANNING
When to Go

Go whenever you can, but if possible go during the dry season (April/May to September/October). The best time to watch birds is from July to September, when they are at their rookeries in great numbers, the waters have receded and the bright-green grasses pop up from the muck. Temperatures are hot by day and cool by night, with occasional short bursts of rain.

Flooding, incessant rains and heat make travel difficult during the wet season (November to March), though this time is not without its special rewards – this is when the cattle and wildlife of the Pantanal clump together on the *cordilheiras*. However, the islands are covered with dense vegetation that can make spotting wildlife difficult. In September and October, the driest two months, the chances for spotting jaguar rise dramatically – the Pantanal is the last great stronghold for the biggest and most elusive of the American cats. The heat peaks in November and December, when temperatures higher than 40°C (104°F)

are common, roads turn to breakfast cereal, and the mosquitoes are out in force. Many hotels close at this time.

The heaviest rains fall in February and March. Roads become impassable and travel is a logistical nightmare. Every decade or so, the flooding is disastrous, killing both humans and animals.

Fishing is best during the first part of the dry season (April to May), when the flooded rivers settle back into their channels, but locals have been known to lasso 80kg fish throughout the dry season. This is some of the best fishing in the world. There are about 20 species of piranha, as well as the tasty *dourado*, a feisty fellow (known locally as the river tiger) that reaches upwards of 9kg and preys on hapless fellow fish. Other excellent catches include *pacu, suribim, bagre, giripoca, piraputanga, piapara, cachara, pirancajuva* and *pintado*, to name but a few.

Although hunting is not allowed, fishing – with the required permits – is encouraged between February and October. It is, however, prohibited during the *piracema* (breeding season) from November to the end of February, though the time frame varies year to year. Banco do Brasil branches in Cuiabá, Campo Grande and Coxim issue permits (from shore/boat R$24/60) valid for three months for fishing in the Pantanal. National fishing permits valid for one year are also available from **IBAMA offices** (☎ Cuiabá 0xx65-644 1200, Campo Grande 0xx67-3317 2952, Corumbá 0xx67-3231 6096, Coxim 0xx67-3291 2310).

What to Bring

You can't buy much in the Pantanal, so come prepared. The dry season is also the cooler season. Bring attire suitable for hot days, coolish nights, rain and mosquitoes. Leave behind red (it scares animals), yellow (mosquitoes love it) and black clothing (it's too hot and mosquitoes love it, too). You'll need sunscreen, sunglasses, a hat, lightweight clothes, sneakers or boots, light rain gear and something warmer for the evening. Mosquito relief means long pants and long-sleeved shirts, vitamin B12 and insect repellent.

Bring binoculars, a towel and a strong flashlight (to go searching for owls and anacondas after dark). Don't forget your camera and, if you're serious about photography, a tripod and a long lens (300mm is about right for wildlife).

Health

There is no malaria in the Pantanal, but dengue fever has been epidemic in Mato Grosso do Sul of late, with more than 55,000 documented cases in the first four months of 2007 alone. If you're concerned, consult a travel-health expert for the latest information before you leave home. For more on these and other traveler's health concerns, see p725, or check out Lonely Planet's *Healthy Travel – Central & South America* by Isabelle Young.

There are medical services available in Cuiabá, Corumbá and Campo Grande.

TOURS

There are three main approach routes to the Pantanal: via Cuiabá in Mato Grosso and via Corumbá or Campo Grande in Mato Grosso do Sul. You can arrange guided tours (or head off on your own) from any of these three towns (p423). As a reference, guides in Cuiabá tend to be more professional and better trained than those from Campo Grande. (They will point out every bird and tell you both its Portuguese and English name, for instance. In Campo Grande, they sometimes just point.)

Cuiabá

From Cuiabá, the capital of Mato Grosso, small tour operators arrange safaris into the Pantanal that include transportation, accommodations on farms and guides.

Fortunately, while there is healthy competition between tour operators in Cuiabá, it's not as intense as in Mato Grosso do Sul. Tours here are well-organized and quite comfortable.

Joel Souza Ecoverde Tours (Map p409; ☎ 0xx65-3624 4979; www.ecoverdetours.com; Getúlio Vargas 155; ☎ 8am-6pm Mon-Sat) Offers bird-watching and nature tours by land or boat, including accommodations on farms or camping, meals, hikes and horseback riding for around R$200 per day. You can also contact him at Pousada Ecoverde (p408). He speaks English, German and Spanish.

Natureco Natural Ecotours (☎ 0xx65-3321 1001; www.natureco.com.br; Rua Benedito Leite 570) Natureco is dead serious about sustainable tourism: owner Munir Nasr refuses to work with pousadas that mistreat the animals or harm the environment in any way. He has trained the local farmers on conservation and tourism since 1993. His highly recommended tours start at around R$210 per day and specialize in more traditional farms deeper into the Pantanal.

Pantanal Explorer (Map p408; 0xx65-3682 2800; www.pantanalexplorer.com.br; Av Governador Ponce de Arruda 670; Várzea Grande) Owner Andre Von Thuronyi has

been working with sustainable tourism in the area for 30 years and fights harmful government interference in the Pantanal with ferocity. He is actively involved in saving the blue macaw and giant river otter. Tours start at R$1221 for three nights (including everything). It is affiliated with Araras Eco Lodge.

If you want to go straight to the source, **Ailton Lara** (☎ 00xx67-9955 2632; www.wildbrazilpantanaltourguide.com) is an excellent freelance guide in the area and can arrange customized tours (p14).

Campo Grande

It won't take long for you to get hit up for a tour by Campo Grande operators – they are a pushy bunch and aggressively approach travelers as they get off the bus. Resist committing to anything in this situation and explore your options when you aren't being stampeded. You will be offered a free night in nearby hotels, but almost all of the operators offer this, so the one in your face at that moment isn't offering you anything above and beyond. Also, in an amazing feat of professional bullying, operators here forced the local tourist office to stop showing travelers their official complaint book, one even going so far as to try and rip the pages of a particularly scathing rant right out of the book in front of tourism officials. So, the book exists, but it is tucked away where you can't see it. Try begging.

Many budget travelers choose to go on cheap three- to four-day tours into the southern Pantanal from Campo Grande or Corumbá. Most trips are better organized than in the past, but they are still rough-and-tumble affairs. Accommodations are at basic lodges or bush camps in netted communal huts with hammocks or in tents. Food is generally OK, though you should take some extra snack food and water.

All the budget tour operators operating in Mato Grosso do Sul offer similar packages at camps along Estrada Parque, a 117km stretch of dirt road through the region known as Nhecolândia. Estrada Parque runs off the main Campo Grande–Corumbá road (Hwy BR-262) at Buraco das Piranhas, 72km from Corumbá and 324km from Campo Grande. The first stretch of Estrada Parque penetrates 47km into the Pantanal, before it doglegs back toward Corumbá. At Porto da Manga, a barge ferries vehicles over the Rio Paraguai (R$20) before Estrada Parque rejoins Hwy BR-262 at Lampião Aceso, about 12km from Corumbá.

IN THE FOOTSTEPS OF ARNE SUCKSDORFF

Swedish film-maker and photographer Arne Sucksdorff is considered the pioneer of ecotourism in the Pantanal. In the '60s, he packed a suitcase in Stockholm and left behind a film career and an Oscar (for the 1948 documentary *Symphony of a City*) and headed for Brazil. For 25 years he lived in a tent on the grounds of **Hotel Fazenda Carandá** (Map p417; ☎ 9971 1273; Boqueirão; s/d R$330/380), shooting wildlife and raising a family with his Brazilian wife, Maria. He taught the local Pantaneiros not to be ashamed of their simple way of life, because it was for this very reason that the Pantanal had been preserved with such ferocious tenacity.

His photographic book of the region, *Pantanal: Um Paraiso Perdido* (1984), is considered the visual bible of Pantanal wildlife. Through his images he showed the world both the beauty of and the threat to the Pantanal. When he died in 2001 his ashes were spread from a hot-air balloon over the Rio Paraguayzinho, very close to where he spent the bulk of his life at one with nature.

Estrada Parque is much closer to Corumbá than to Campo Grande. But unless you're traveling to or from Bolivia, there's no real need to travel all the way to Corumbá to join a tour. Campo Grande is a travel hub and more convenient for onward travel to other parts of Brazil. If you are also visiting Bonito, it's best to go to the Pantanal first as the tours end in Buraco das Piranhas, much closer to Bonito than Campo Grande.

Ecological Expeditions (Map p425; ☎ 0xx67-3321 0505; www.ecologicalexpeditions.com.br; Rua Joaquim Nabuco 185) A generally well-organized operation that attracts the bulk of the backpacking crowd due to its affiliation with Nosso Novo YHI hostel (p424). Tours leave daily and are usually kept to a maximum of eight people per guide. They claim no animals are touched or fed by their guides. Tours run to R$320 for three-night packages in lodges in Nhecolândia, R$280 for camping. Food and hospitality hover around orphanage level, though the tours and guides are a good time. It's across the street from the bus station and also has an office at the bus station in Corumbá.

Pantanal Discovery (Map p425; ☎ 0xx67-3384 7357; www.gilspantanaldiscovery.com.br) Inside the bus station, this operator recently merged with another recommended company, Natureza. It does not touch wildlife or employ macho machete-wielding guides who tear through the flora. Tours start at R$350 for three days and two nights and go a little deeper into the Pantanal than some of the competition. Accommodations are usually at the rustic Fazenda Natureza, which takes honors at this level for food and hospitality.

Pantanal Viagens & Turismo (Map p425; ☎ 0xx67-3321 3143; www.pantanalviagens.com.br) A slightly nicer agency working mainly with the excellent Hotel Fazenda Santa Clara (the two are a family-owned partnership) with excursions going as far as the Rio Paraguai. For a little extra cash (three nights camping from R$250, lodging from R$375), groups of up to eight are incalculably more comfortable. Also in the bus station.

Corumbá

Nearly all of the tour companies once in Corumbá have decamped to Campo Grande.

Canaã Viagens e Turismo (☎ 0xx67-3231 2208; www.corumba.com.br/canaa; Rua Colombo 245) is a recommended agency specializing in high-end fishing tours up the Rio Paraguai. It offers trips in two different barco-hotels and travels as far up the river as 300km. Mini tours of three days and two nights leave twice a week and start at R$1000 per person including all meals, fishing, guides and transfers.

SLEEPING

Pantanal accommodations are divided into three types: pousadas include all meals and range from simple to top-end; *fazendas* are ranch-style hotels that usually have horses and often boats for use; and *pesqueiros* cater for anglers and usually have boats and fishing gear for rent. Typical rental costs would be R$20 per person per hour for boat excursions and R$30 to R$40 for a couple of hours on horseback.

If you have doubts about roughing it on the budget tours, it is probably better to spend a bit more money for basic comforts – a bed, running water and some hope of avoiding a million mosquito bites.

Rates will usually include modest lodging, three meals and at least one excursion per day. Drinks – even soda and water – are extra. Transportation is almost never included in the room rates and can take a sizable chuck out of your budget. From Cuiabá, transfers in and out, via whatever combination of 4WD, boat, horseback and plane is necessary depending on the season, can run between R$250 to R$500 one way. For this reason, it is almost always cheaper – not to mention logistically less stressful – to go in under the services of a tour operator. Transportation in and out is then included and they often have access to more remote lodges.

Reservations are needed for all accommodations in July, when lots of Brazilians vacation here. If you want to avoid the crowds, go during the wet season, when occupancy rates drop by 45%. All listings that follow are shown on the Pantanal map (p417).

Mato Grosso
ALONG THE TRANSPANTANEIRA

Accommodations along the Transpantaneira are plentiful.

Porto Paraiso (☎ 0xx65-3345 2271; Transpantaneira km17; camping R$25, per person with full board R$100; ✖ ▢ ☎) An excellent budget option on a small working buffalo and cattle farm. There's good armadillo-spotting, though the real deal here is the excellent camping facilities around the luxe pool area. Reports are mixed, though, about the owner's tact.

Puma Lodge (☎ 0xx65-3345 1545; www.puma lodge.com.br; Transpantaneira km105; per person with full board R$100; ▢) The newest option along the Transpantaneira is completely solar powered – the owners, the same Pantaneiro family that opened Pousada Rio Claro years ago, want people to hear jaguars, not generators! The 12 rooms are comfy and they offer night safaris, horseback riding, bicycles and authentic cowboy cuisine. It's right next door to the Jaguar Ecological Preserve.

Pousada Rio Clarinho (☎ 0xx65-9998 8888; Transpantaneira km40; s/d R$120/200) An avian symphony is your wake-up call at this rustic *fazenda* right on the Rio Clarinho (there's a small river platform for swimming). There are more than 260 species of birds on the property, as well as capybaras and giant river otters. The food is authentic Pantanal. Rates include all excursions.

Pousada Piuval (☎ 0xx65-3345 1338; Transpantaneira km10; www.pousadapiuval.com.br; s/d with full board R$220/280; ✖ ▢ ☎) It's a trade-off at the first pousada along the Transpantaneira: it's more commercial (feeding caimans) but also more comfortable. It sits on 7000 hectares and is popular with bird-watchers and Germans. The pool is wonderful, as are sunset boat rides. It offers horseback riding, trekking and night safaris as well.

Pousada Araras Eco Lodge (☎ 0xx65-3682 2800; www.araraslodge.com.br; Transpantaneira km32; s/d

R$552/810; ✖ ▢ ☎) This pioneering lodge offers the most comfort and luxury along the Transpantaneira. Rooms have lovely artisanal bedspreads and all feature nice patios with hammocks separated by bamboo curtains, many looking out to a macaw nest. There is a tree-top tower for bird-watching and howler monkey–watching and an extensive bird list is available at check-in. Much of the food comes from its own farm. There is a cheaper, more rustic lodge, Passo da Ema, 4km into the property, which specializes in horseback riding.

PORTO JOFRE

Porto Jofre is where the Transpantaneira meets its end, at the Rio Cuiabá. It's a one-hotel town – in fact, it's not even a town; it's just a hotel.

Hotel Porto Jofre Pantanal Norte (☎ 0xx65-3623 0236; Transpantaneira km145; www.portojofre.com.br; s/d R$310/525; ✖ Mar-Oct; ✖ ▢ ☎) It's the only hotel at the end of the road, catering mostly to serious fishermen on expensive packages. There's an airstrip, a marina (3.6m, 115HP boats rent for R$990 per day for up to four people) and a nice restaurant.

Mato Grosso do Sul

Southern gateways to the Pantanal are the cities of Corumbá, Campo Grande, Aquidauana and Miranda. Most travelers head to Campo Grande or Corumbá – both cater mostly to backpackers – while Aquidauana and Miranda are popular with Brazilian anglers and more high-end travelers.

AROUND AQUIDAUANA

There are several excellent, high-end hotel-*fazendas* in this area.

Fazenda Rio Negro (☎ 0xx67-3326 0002; www.fazendarionegro.com.br; per person incl meals & excursions R$360; ✖ ▢) A traditional, adobe-style farm dating back to the 1920s on the banks of a tributary of the Rio Negro, surrounded by beautiful brackish lakes (an oddity in the Pantanal). Excellent bilingual guides lead guests on horseback rides, boat trips, canoes, Jeep and night safaris, and wilderness picnics. It's owned by Conservation International. In the wet season, it's a 40-minute plane ride from Aquidauana.

our pick Fazenda Santa Sophia (☎ 0xx67-9648 9352; www.fazendasantasophia.com.br; s/d incl meals & excursions R$520/900; ✖ May-Oct) Beautifully appointed

3400-sq-km cattle and horse ranch owned by fourth-generation Pantaneira Beatriz Rondon. It caters to high-end horse enthusiasts from around the world. Guests are welcomed as family, and the food, especially the *pudim de quejo* (cheese pudding), is miraculous. Access is by plane only.

Refúgio Ecológico Caiman (☎ 0xx11-3706 1800; www.caiman.com.br; s/d incl meals & 3 excursions R$877/884; ✖ ▣ ▨) This 520-sq-km, ecopioneering *fazenda* 36km north of Miranda is like a private Pantanal for a privileged few. There are three lodges: Sede, the main lodge, is the most luxurious; Cordilheiro, the most remote and rustic with a great lookout tower; and Baiazinha, a little more playful with the best pool deck and position for spotting jaguars. There are an estimated 40 jaguars and 300 macaws on the property. Multilingual guides who live on the *fazenda* lead tours. Prices include meals and numerous activities from canoeing to horseback riding; there is a three-night minimum in high season.

ESTRADA PARQUE

To get to the Estrada Parque you can take the Campo Grande–Corumbá bus and arrange for your lodge to pick you up (for a small fee) by the Posto Florestal guard station at the Buraco das Piranhas intersection. At Passo do Lontra, 7km from the Buraco das Piranhas, you cross Rio Miranda. There are lots of accommodations from here to Curva do Leque.

Fazenda Natureza (☎ 0xx67-9927 2404; dm per person incl meals & activities R$60) Off-the-beaten-path farm used often by Pantanal Discovery. It's a friendly family operation with dormitory facilities and the food is excellent for this budget. Ask Durvanil, the farm's patron, to cook up a Pantanal-style *churrasco*.

Cabana do Lontra (☑ 0xx67-9943 5783; per person incl meals R$60) This extremely rustic lodge is most often used by Campo Grande and Corumbá budget operators. It's nicely located right on Rio Miranda, but the staff is indifferent to visitors. One important note: the showers here drain your Axe shower gel and Herbal Essence shampoo straight into the water habitat. Definitely not eco.

Hotel Fazenda Santa Clara (☎ 0xx67-3364 3011; www.pousadasantaclara.com.br; camping per person incl meals R$58, apt per person incl meals R$90) A new elevated camping area along the Rio Abobral is an excellent choice for the more intrepid, while the comfortable lodge is the best value in the

south. For a few more reais, book a three-day package here and get all the same benefits with triple the comfort.

Pousada Passo do Lontra (☎ 0xx67-3231 9494; www .pousadapassodolontra.com.br in Portuguese; s/d apt incl meals R$165/187, s/d chalets incl meals R$300/340; ✖) A comfortable place with large *apartamentos* and riverside chalets. Safaris along Rio Miranda are the focus.

GETTING THERE & AWAY

From Cuiabá, the capital of Mato Grosso, there are three gateways to the Pantanal – Cáceres, Barão de Melgaço and Poconé.

Campo Grande, the capital of Mato Grosso do Sul, is a transportation hub, while Corumbá is best accessed by bus from Campo Grande. The route to Corumbá from Campo Grande runs via Aquidauana and Miranda. For transportation details, see the relevant city and town sections.

There are direct flights to Cuiabá and Campo Grande from Brasília and connecting flights from Rio and São Paulo. TAM is the only major Brazilian airline connecting other capitals, including Campo Grande and São Paulo, to Corumbá.

GETTING AROUND

Since the lodges are the only places to sleep, drink and eat, and public transportation is very limited, independent travel is difficult here. Driving is not easy. Only a few roads reach into the periphery of the Pantanal; they are frequently closed by rain, and reconstructed yearly. Only the Transpantaneira in Mato Grosso and Estrada Parque in Mato Grosso do Sul go deep into the region. Your options are hitching (never entirely safe), sticking to an operator or arranging transport in advance through a lodge.

MATO GROSSO DO SUL

Mato Grosso do Sul was created in 1979 when the military government decided it would be the best way to administer and develop such a large region (cynics claimed it was to provide more high-paying bureaucratic jobs for cronies). But even before the split, the area had a different economic and social make-up from the northern Mato Grosso.

In the late 19th century, many migrants from the south and southeast of Brazil arrived in the area, so the south has a greater number of smaller farms and a much more intensive agriculture when compared to the large farms and ranches in the north. All this is thanks to the rich, red earth, known as *terra rocha*.

The wealth created by the *terra rocha* has helped develop the state's modern agricultural sector. The main crop is soy, but there's also lots of corn, rice, cotton production and cattle farms. Mato Grosso do Sul also contains two-thirds of the Pantanal and the Serra da Bocaina, two wonderful natural areas that are popular with both Brazilian and foreign travelers.

CAMPO GRANDE

☎ 0xx67 / pop 734,134

Known as the Cidade Morena not for its beautiful women but rather its red earth, Campo Grande is the capital of Mato Grosso do Sul, a modern city that has become a major gateway to the Pantanal. Manganese, rice, soy and cattle are the traditional sources of its wealth, while education (there are four universities in the city), commerce and tourism are growing industries. Campo Grande lies 716km south of Cuiabá and 403km southeast of Corumbá. There's not much to see in the city itself, but it's a lively place, especially at night.

Founded around 1875 as the village of Santo Antônio de Campo Grande, Campo Grande really began to grow when the railway came through in 1914. By decree of military president Ernesto Giesel, the city became the capital of Mato Grosso do Sul in 1977 when the new state splintered off from Mato Grosso.

Orientation

The downtown area of Campo Grande is compact and easily navigated on foot. Av Afonso Pena, the main boulevard, runs east–west.

CHOOSING A GUIDE IN THE PANTANAL

Though it has nowhere near the tourism infrastructure of the Amazon, bringing tourists into the Pantanal is now big business, and whether you arrive in Cuiabá, Corumbá or Campo Grande you can expect to be approached by a guide fairly rapidly. Some of these individuals are simply opportunists looking to make a buck out of Brazil's ecotourism, but there are still a few old-timers out there who work to protect the environment while sharing its tremendous diversity with visitors.

A good guide can enhance your Pantanal experience by spotting and identifying animal and bird species, explaining the diverse ecology, and taking care of any hassles you may encounter along the way. Plus, if you're hoping to catch a glimpse of rarer animals, such as anteaters, anacondas, otters, iguanas and jaguars, a guide is indispensable. A guide who is familiar with the area will also know the location of nests of rare birds.

It can be hard to tell the good from the bad, but here are some suggestions to ensure you have a safe and enjoyable trip.

- Resist making a snap decision, especially if you've just climbed off an overnight bus.

- Go to the local tourism office. Most can't give independent advice, because they're government funded, but they do keep complaint books that you're free to peruse (unless you're in Campo Grande).

- Remember that the owner or salesperson is not always your guide, and it's the guide you're going to be with in the wilderness for three to five days. Ask to meet your guide if possible.

- Try to get things in writing and don't hand over your cash to any go-betweens.

- Compare your options. Most operators work out of the local bus station or airport, so it's easy to shop around.

- If you are even remotely concerned about sustainable tourism, do not use operators and lodges that harm this fragile environment. That means no picking up the animals for photographs or any touching them whatsoever.

- If time is a problem and money isn't, or if you'd just like a quality guide, contact **Focus Tours** (www.focustours.com) in the US. Focus Tours specializes in nature tours and is active in trying to preserve the Pantanal.

Going west, it becomes Av Duque de Caxias and then Hwy BR-262 before passing the airport (7km) and heading on to Corumbá. To the east, it runs past the Shopping Campo Grande and the Parque das Nações Indígenas. The center of the city is a grid, with the main commercial area concentrated around Afonso Pena and cross streets Av Calógeras and Rua 14 de Julho.

Information

EMERGENCY
Ambulance (☎ 192)
Fire department (☎ 193)
Police (☎ 190)

INTERNET ACCESS
Matrix Cyber Café (☎ 3029 6706; Av Calógeras 2069; per hr R$2.50; ☼ 7:30am-10pm Mon-Sat)

MEDICAL SERVICES
Clínica Campo Grande (☎ 3323 9000; Rua Marechal Rondon 1703)
Santa Casa (☎ 3322 4000; Rua 13 de Mayo s/n)

MONEY
Banco 24 Horas (Rua Joaquim Nabuco) Has an ATM beside the bus station that accepts Amex/Cirrus/MasterCard/Maestro cards when it's not suffering from a 'Communication Failure.'
Banco do Brasil (Av Afonso Pena 2202; ☼ 11am-4pm Mon-Fri) Visa/MasterCard ATM and money exchange.
Bradesco (cnr Av Afonso Pena & Av Calógeras; ☼ 11am-4pm Mon-Fri) Visa/MasterCard ATM.

POST
Post office (cnr Rua Dom Aquino & Av Calógeras; ☼ 8:30am-5:30pm Mon-Fri, 8am-noon Sat)
Post office (cnr Rua Barão do Rio Branco & Rua Rui Barbosa)

TOURIST INFORMATION
CAT tourist office (☎ 3314 9968; Av Noroeste 5140; ☼ 8am-7pm Tue-Sat, 9am-noon Sun) The best tourist office in the region, near the corner of Av Afonso Pena. Friendly staff (most are tourism students) offer an excellent city map and an extensive database with information about hotels and attractions throughout the state. There is a comment book here, but local operators pressured the office to stop showing tourists. There are smaller branches at the bus station and the Feira Central.

Sights
The **Museu das Culturas Dom Bosco** (Parque das Nações Indígenas; adult/child R$5/2.50; ☼ 8am-6pm Tue-Sun) has

undergone a R$2 million relocation to a new building designed by Italian architect Massimo Chiappetta a few kilometers from its old city-center location. The new space, a 3400-sq-meter expansion (set for completion in 2008), houses an excellent collection of over 10,000 insects. There is a beautiful new exhibit of Bororo Indian headdresses and other artifacts from the Moro, Karajá and Xavante Indians.

A great market worth a stroll is the **Feira Central** (☎ 3324 8129; cnr Av Calógeras & Rua 14 de Julho; ☼ 5pm-late Wed & Fri, 10am-late Sat), a massive open-air food and shopping court lined with Japanese soba-noodle joints (p426) and other food and merchandise stalls. It's packed with revelers on weekends.

Tours
For more information on tours into the Pantanal, see p419.

Sleeping
Most budget accommodations are clustered around the bus station, but this is a seedy area with no shortage of small-time crooks and prostitutes.

Nosso Novo Hotel (☎ 321 0505; Rua Joaquim Nabuco 185; s/d R$25/40; ☐ ☒) A nice YHI hostel associated with Ecological Expeditions. You get a free night if you sign up for a tour. The pool ain't bad, either.

Turis Hotel (☎ 3382 7688; Rua Allan Kardec 200; s/d R$45/62; ☒ ☐) Modern and minimalist, this newer option is entirely too trendy for its bus-station location.

Alkimia Hotel (☎ 3324 2621; Rua Afonso Pena 1413; s/d apt R$50/70; ☒ ☐) A new option just two blocks from the bus station in a slightly safer area. Rooms are spotless and the bathrooms are large.

Hotel Colonial (☎ 3382 6061; Rua Allan Kardec 211; s/d apt with air-con R$50/76; ☐) If you're not attached to air-conditioning, you can score the best deal in town here, a double for R$65 with breakfast and pool access at its more upmarket sister Hotel Internacional next door.

Pousada Dom Aquino (☎ 3382 9373; pousada_dom _aquino@hotmail.com; Rua Dom Aquino 1806; s/d apt R$60/90; ☒ ☐) A wonderful, relaxed pousada that is an oasis in the city and walking distance from nearly everything. The staff is very friendly and there's even international cable TV. Book ahead.

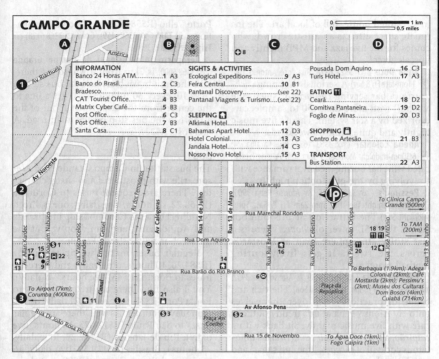

CAMPO GRANDE

INFORMATION		
Banco 24 Horas ATM	1	A3
Banco do Brasil	2	C3
Bradesco	3	B3
CAT Tourist Office	4	B3
Matrix Cyber Café	5	B3
Post Office	6	C3
Post Office	7	B3
Santa Casa	8	C1

SIGHTS & ACTIVITIES		
Ecological Expeditions	9	A3
Feira Central	10	B1
Pantanal Discovery	(see 22)	
Pantanal Viagens & Turismo	(see 22)	

SLEEPING		
Alkimia Hotel	11	A3
Bahamas Apart Hotel	12	D3
Hotel Colonial	13	A3
Jandaía Hotel	14	C3
Nosso Novo Hotel	15	A3

Pousada Dom Aquino	16	C3
Turis Hotel	17	A3

EATING		
Ceará	18	D2
Comitiva Pantaneira	19	D2
Fogão de Minas	20	D3

SHOPPING		
Centro de Artesão	21	B3

TRANSPORT		
Bus Station	22	A3

Bahamas Apart Hotel (☎ 3312 9393; www.bahamas aparthotel.com.br in Portuguese; Rua José Antônio 1117; s/d apt R$200/270; ❄ ▯ ▣) Sleek high-rise hotel with massive two-story *apartamentos* with kitchenette, living and dining areas and a small patio. By far the most luxury in town for the money.

Jandaía Hotel (☎ 3316 7700; www.jandaia.com.br; Rua Barão do Rio Branco 1271; s/d R$220/284; ❄ ▯ ▣) This upscale business hotel received new flooring and a décor makeover in a 2006 renovation. English is spoken and there are two decent restaurants.

Eating & Drinking

There is a distinctly Paraguayan influence on some of the culinary curiosities here. *Sopa Paraguaia*, a savory cake made with eggs, corn, milk, cheese and onions, is popular, as is *tereré*, a cold and refreshing maté tea.

Fogão de Minas (☎ 3325 5287; Rua Dom Aquino 2200; meals per kg R$19.80; ❄ 11am-2:30pm) An excellent lunch per-kilo specializing in the hearty food of Minas Gerais. Don't miss the old-style coffee with *rapadura* (dried sugarcane juice) on the way out.

Comitiva Pantaneira (☎ 3383 8799; Rua Dom Aquino 2221; meals per kg R$22.90; ❄ 11am-2pm Mon-Fri, to 3pm Sat, 11:30am-3pm Sun) A massive per-kilo swarming with locals digging into seriously good Pantaneira cowboy cuisine.

Ceará (☎ 3321 3927; Rua Dom Aquino 2249; meals for 2 R$31-42; ❄ 11:30am-2:30pm & 6:30-11pm Tue-Fri, 11am-3pm & 6:30-11pm Sat, 11am-3pm Sun) One of the city's best *peixarias* (fish restaurants). The *pintado* in a tomato stew with banana *mandioca* (cassava) incites tears of culinary joy.

Fogo Caipira (☎ 3324 1641; Rua José Antônio 145; dishes R$22-70; ❄ 11am-2pm & 7-11pm Thu-Fri, 11am-midnight Sat, 11am-4pm Sun) The best dishes at this regional institution require an advance order, such as the *galinhada* (chicken stew, six hours) or *pacu recheado* (a tasty fish stuffed with manioc and spices, three hours). It's pricey but worth it.

Entertainment

Campo Grande's nightlife knows no evening off, especially around the 3900 block of Av Afonso Pena, east of downtown.

Barbaquá (☎ 3321 8576; Rua Rio Grande do Sul 382; ❄ 6pm-late Mon-Sat) A beautiful candlelit bar in a restored house, full of local art. The intimate space attracts an artistic crowd, who comes for the live jazz and MPB nightly and upscale *tereré*.

Água Doce (☎ 3321 6978; Rua José Antonio 194; ☽ 11pm-late Fri & Sat) A seriously hopping *cachaçaria* (a bar serving *cachaça*, or sugarcane alcohol) with more than 150 to sample, categorized by a star system. There's live music nightly and quite a line on weekends.

Adega Colonial (☎ 3383 1633; Rua Paraíba 24; ☽ 6:30pm-midnight Mon-Sat, 1-3pm Sun) A sophisticated wine bar oozing medieval romance with a revolving by-the-glass option nightly.

Pessimu's (☎ 3383 6445; Av Afonso Pena 3901; ☽ 6pm-midnight Tue-Thu, 5pm-2am Fri & Sat, 5pm-midnight Sun) The attraction at this outdoor café is the 2.5L tower of *chope*. There is a less stuffy atmosphere than at Mostarda across the street. It gets lively during football matches.

Café Mostarda (☎ 3026 8439; Av Afonso Pena 3952; meals R$11-27; ☽ 5pm-late, closed Sun) The rich and beautiful practically trip over themselves onto Av Afonso Pena at this trendy outdoor café with live music nightly. Sit back with a *caipirão*, a five-fruit *caipirinha*,(Brazil's ubiquitous cocktail of *cachaça*, lime and sugar) and watch the show.

Shopping

Centro de Artesão (☎ 3383 2633; Av Calógeras 2050; ☽ 8am-6pm Mon-Fri, to noon Sat) sells colorful Indian ceramics, wooden crafts, sacred art and locally brewed liquor.

Getting There & Around
AIR

Daily connections link Campo Grande to São Paulo (R$344), Cuiabá (R$324), Corumbá (R$219.50), Rio (R$484), Brasília (R$344) and

Porto Velho (R$584). For additional information call **TAM** (☎ 3368 6159), **Gol** (☎ 3368 6128) or **Trip** (☎ 3368 6136).

Aeroporto Internacional de Campo Grande (☎ 3368 6000) is 7km from town; to get there, take the Indubrasil bus from the bus station (R$2.10, every 30 minutes). To get a bus to the center from the airport, walk out of the airport to the bus stop on the main road. A taxi costs R$22.

BUS

The bus station in Campo Grande is an eyesore, rife with prostitutes and shady characters. There are frequent buses to Corumbá (R$68.72, six hours, nine daily); one is direct. Nondirect buses to Corumbá stop in Miranda and Aquidauana, and can drop you at the intersection with Estrada Parque.

Regular buses make the trip to Cuiabá (R$84.20, 10 hours, nine daily) and there are buses to Bonito (R$46, five hours, six daily). You'll also find there are frequent buses to Ponta Porã (R$37, four hours, 21 daily) on the Paraguayan border. As well, there are regular buses to São Paulo (R$128.73, 15 hours, five daily), Rio de Janeiro (R$192.22, four daily, 23 hours), Brasília (R$129.50, two daily, 16 hours) and Foz do Iguaçu (R$80, one daily, 14 hours).

CORUMBÁ
☎ 0xx67 / pop 101,000

This port city close to the Bolivian border is the southernmost gateway to the Pantanal. The city sits atop a steep hill overlooking the Rio Paraguai; on the far side of the river, a huge expanse of the Pantanal stretches out on the horizon.

Corumbá is 403km northwest of Campo Grande by road. Its location near the Para-

---

CAMPO SOBÁ

What's with the fascination with Japanese soba noodles in Campo Grande? Well, there's an explanation. This Japanese delicacy was integrated into the culinary hierarchy here along with an influx of Japanese immigrants from Okinawa in the early 1900s – Campo Grande now boasts the third-highest Japanese population in Brazil (behind São Paulo and Paraná) – and eating sobá here is just about as popular as a Globo soap opera. The Okinawan version of the dish uses flour noodles instead of buckwheat and is served in a hot broth with pork and various other accompaniments. In Campo Grande, the Brazilianization of the dish includes options with filet mignon in place of pork and alongside *carne de sol* (salted beef) inside tapioca pancakes. The best place to try sobá is the Feira Central (p424), which is lined with *sobárias*. Slurp away…it's a nice antidote to rice and beans.

guayan and Bolivian borders ensures it sees its fair share of poaching and drug smuggling, but travelers are generally left alone. Surprisingly, the city has a very lively Carnaval, heavily influenced by Rio.

Corumbá, also known as Cidade Branca (White City), was founded in 1776 by Captain Luis de Albuquerque. By 1840 it had become the biggest river port in the world, boasting a dozen foreign consulates. Ships would enter the Rio de la Plata in the South Atlantic, sail up the Rio Paraná to its confluence with the Rio Paraguai, then continue on to the port of Corumbá. The impressive buildings along the waterfront reflect the wealth that passed through the town in the 19th century. However, with the coming of the railway, Corumbá lost its importance as a port and went into decline.

Orientation & Information

The city is divided into two parts: the upper city contains most of the commerce, and the lower city takes in the port. The streets are laid out in a grid pattern and are easy to navigate.

EMERGENCY

Federal Police (☎ 3231 5848; Praça da República 51; ☑ 8-11:30am & 1:30-5:30pm Mon-Fri) There's also an office at the bus station.

IMMIGRATION

At present all Brazilian border formalities (including entry and exit stamps) must be completed at the **Federal Police office** (☎ 3231 1224; ☑ 8am-noon & 2-4pm Mon-Fri, 2-5pm Sat & Sun) at the long-distance bus station. Bolivian entry/exit formalities can all be completed at the border post. If you're just crossing over to Bolivia for less than 24 hours, you don't need a Brazilian exit stamp.

Moneychangers at the border accept cash only and will change both reais and dollars.

You won't be allowed to enter Bolivia without a current yellow fever vaccination certificate, so organize one well in advance.

INTERNET ACCESS

Mega Net Cyber (☎ 3231 1009; Rua Frei Mariano 892; per hr R$2.50; ☑ 8am-midnight Mon-Fri, to noon Sat)

MEDICAL SERVICES

Hospital Sociedade Beneficência Corumbaense (☎ 3231 2441; Rua 15 de Novembro 854)

CORUMBÁ

INFORMATION			SLEEPING		
Banco do Brasil	1	A2	Corumbá Hostel		
Bradesco	2	A2	Internacional	15	A3
Federal Police	3	B2	Hotel Eldorado	16	B3
Hospital Sociedade			Hotel Nacional	17	A3
Beneficência			Santa Monica Palace	18	B2
Corumbaense	4	A3			
HSBC	5	A1	EATING		
Mega Net Cyber	6	A3	Antonellos	19	A3
Mutum Turismo	7	A1	Churrascaria Rodeio	20	B2
Pantur	8	A3	Peixaria do Lulu	21	B2
Post Office	9	B1	Vivabella	22	A1
Setur	10	A2			
Tentação	11	B2	DRINKING		
			Laço do Ouro	23	A2
SIGHTS & ACTIVITIES					
Art Izu	12	B2	TRANSPORT		
Casa de Artesão	13	B2	Bus to Bolivian border	24	A2
Instituto Luiz de			Local Bus Terminal	25	B2
Albuquerque	14	B2	Local Bus Terminal	26	B2

MONEY

It seems shady business, but some shopkeepers on Rua 13 de Junho change reais, dollars, euros and Bolivianos.

Banco do Brasil (Rua 13 de Junho 914) Usual high commissions for cash and traveler's checks.

Bradesco (Rua Delamare 1067) Visa/MasterCard ATM.

HSBC (Rua Delamare 1068) Visa/MasterCard ATM.

MATO GROSSO & MATO GROSSO DO SUL

Tentação (☎ 3232 4267; Rua 13 de Junho 883; ☽ 8am-6pm Mon-Sat) Money exchange.

POST

Post office (Rua Delamare 708; ☽ 8:30am-5pm Mon-Fri, 8-11:30am Sat)

TOURIST INFORMATION

Setur tourist office (☎ 3231 2886; Rua 15 de Novembro 659; ☽ 7:30am-1:30pm Mon-Fri) The office of the secretary of tourism can provide information on accommodations (including barco-hotels), restaurants, river trips and a helpful city map. There's also a small branch at the airport.

TRAVEL AGENCIES

Pantanal tours and boat and fishing tours of the Corumbá environs are available from all travel agencies. They also organize some day trips to Bolivia.

Mutum Turismo (☎ 3231 1818; www.mutumturismo .com.br; Rua Frei Mariano 17; ☽ 8am-6pm Mon-Fri, to noon Sat)

Pantur (☎ 3231 2000; Rua Frei Mariano 1013; ☽ 8am-6pm Mon-Fri, to noon Sat)

Sights & Activities

Corumbá's star attraction is the Pantanal; you can get a preview of it from the highest point in the area, **Morro Urucum** (1100m), 20km south of Corumbá. Otherwise, you could enjoy a boat trip on the Rio Paraguai. Between three and five hours long, these cruises usually take in the **Base Fluvial de Ladário**, Brazil's first river arsenal, dating from 1872. The longer trips also stop for a little fishing. These tours can be booked through any travel agent and usually cost between R$40 and R$60.

Around town, a pleasant spot to visit is the **Casa de Artesão** (Rua Dom Aquino 405; ☽ 8:30-11am & 1:30-5pm Mon-Sat). Here the old prison has swapped inmates for artists, who hawk their indigenous arts and crafts from former cells. **Art Izu** (Rua Cuiabá 558; ☽ 7-11am & 1-5pm Mon-Fri) is home to one of Corumbá's premier artists. You can't miss it – the giant bird sculptures and bronze statue of São Francisco in the front yard are stunning. The **Instituto Luiz de Albuquerque** (☎ 231 5757; Praça da República; ☽ 8am-noon & 2-5:30pm Mon-Fri) houses the Museu do Pantanal, which contains a reasonably interesting collection of stuffed local wildlife and Indian artifacts. It also displays modern local art.

Forte de Junqueira (☎ 3231 5828; Rua Cáceres 425; ☽ 9:30-11am & 2-4:30pm) is the only intact fort left near the city. It's a tiny hexagonal fort with 50cm-thick walls, though the real attraction is the excellent view of the Rio Paraguai and the Pantanal in the distance. To get there, go east along Rua Dom Aquino and turn left at the athletics ground. Once you hit the waterfront, continue east for another 10 minutes. The entrance is an unmarked door to the left of the main gate.

Sleeping

There are some cheap hotels close to the long-distance bus station if you're just spending a night in Corumbá. Otherwise, there are better places closer to the waterfront and the restaurants and bars in the center of town.

Corumbá Hostel Internacional (☎ 3231 1005; Rua Colombo 1419; s with/without air-con R$45/38, d R$75/60; ☐ ☒) YHI-affiliated hostel on a quiet residential street seven blocks from the river. Rooms are clean and spacious and the bathrooms are above and beyond. Breakfast isn't up to snuff, but it's served on better-than-average porcelain.

Hotel El Dorado (☎ 3231 6677; www.hotel-eldorado .net; Rua Porto Carreiro 554; s/d R$70/100; ☒) A fabulous option just off the corner of the bus station. The best value in town all said and done.

Santa Monica Palace (☎ 3234 3000; www.hsanta monica.com.br in Portuguese; Rua Antônio Maria Coelho 345; s/d R$85/105; ☒ ☐ ☒) A favorite with group tours, this is a good-value hotel in an aging building in the center of town.

Hotel Nacional (☎ 3234 6000; www.hnacional.com.br in Portuguese; Rua América 936; s/d R$100/140; ☒ ☐ ☒) The rooms here are a bit nicer than the institutionalized hallways suggest. It's the top option in town.

Eating & Drinking

Laço do Ouro (☎ 3231 7371; Rua Frei Mariano 556; meals for 2 R$18-34; ☽ 11am-1am) Corumbaense flock to this lively bar-restaurant to beat the heat: extra-large *garrafas* of beer line the outdoor tables, which fill up fast on the weekends.

Vivabella (☎ 3231 9464; Rua Arthur Mangabeira 1; meals for 2 $19-36; ☽ 5pm-late Mon-Sat) Beautiful sunsets over the Pantanal and Bolivia beyond are the main attraction on the outdoor deck at this small Italian restaurant and bar. Vivabella is perched precariously on a hillside over the Rio Paraguai.

Antonellos (☎ 3231 0010; Rua Frei Mariano 837; dishes R$18-24, pizzas R$12; ☽ 6pm-midnight Tue-Sun) Italian-leaning spot for great pizza, pasta and meat and fish dishes. Save room for dessert: the *petit gâteau* is decadent.

Churrascaria Rodeio (☎ 3231 6477; Rua 13 de Junho 760; meals per kg Mon-Fri R$23, Sat & Sun R$26; ⏰ 11am-3:30pm & 6-11pm Tue-Sat, 11am-3:30pm Sun) The owner is very proud of her 60 salads.

Peixaria do Lulu (☎ 3232 2142; Rua Dom Aquino 700; meals for 2 R$20; ⏰ 10:30am-3pm & 6:30-10pm Mon-Sat, 10:30am-3pm Sun) Lulu is the fried-fish king in Corumbá. Don't let the humble appearance fool you – Peixaria do Lulu offers superb regional fish dishes. It's a friendly, family-run place.

Getting There & Away

Corumbá is a transit point for travel to/from Bolivia and Paraguay.

AIR

Corumbá **international airport** (☎ 3231 3322) is 3km west of the town center. **TAM** (☎ 3232 2280) is currently the only airline serving Corumbá. There are regular flights to Campo Grande (R$259), São Paulo (R$479), Brasília (R$519), Rio (R$789) and other major cities. A taxi to the center from here will run between R$10 and R$15.

BUS

From the **long-distance bus station** (☎ 3231 2033; Rua Porto Carreiro), buses run to Campo Grande (R$67.30, 6½ hours, nine daily) and to Bonito (R$54, five hours, one daily at 2pm).

TO/FROM BOLIVIA

If you're heading from the city to the border, catch the Fronteira bus on Praça Independência or Rua Dom Aquino (R$1.70, every 30 minutes). If you're in a hurry, grab a moto-taxi for R$6. Taxis cost around R$20.

The Bolivian border town of Quijarro is not much more than a muddy little collection of shacks around the train station. Taxis navigate the 4km between the border and Quijarro station (trains travel to Santa Cruz in Bolivia from there) for around R$10.

Getting Around

A taxi from Corumbá's long-distance bus station to the center will cost R$10. A moto-taxi runs at R$4.

From the bus stop, located outside the long-distance bus station, the Cristo Redentor bus (R$2) runs to the **local bus terminal** (Rua 13 de Junho). To get to the long-distance

bus station, you can take a mototaxi (R$3) from the local bus station on Rua Antônio Maria Coelho if you're light on luggage.

From the local bus terminal on Rua 13 de Junho, you can catch the Popular Nova bus to the airport (R$1.70, every 50 minutes). Taxis usually cost R$15 for the same trip – make sure the taxi has a meter or establish a price before you get in, as some drivers like to play gringo rip-off.

COXIM

☎ 0xx67 / pop 33,200

Coxim is a small town about halfway between Cuiabá and Campo Grande, on the eastern border of the Pantanal. The town's main draw is the Piracema, when fish migrate up the Rios Taquari and Coxim, leaping through rapids to spawn. The Piracema takes place from November to late February; fishing is not allowed during this period, but if you're traveling through it's worth stopping off to have a look. The fishing is best from August to October.

The town itself is divided into the riverfront, a little older but still where most of the action is, and the more upscale Av Virginia Ferreira, which climbs up and away from the riverfront and is home to high-priced real estate and trendier boutiques and restaurants. Coxim is also an entry point to the Pantanal, but it has limited infrastructure for wildlife-spotting tours, with most operators catering exclusively to fishing tours. Due to migratory changes, fishing isn't what it used to be.

Information

Before you throw a line, you'll need to legalize your rod. Permits valid for three months cost R$60 if you want to fish from a boat, or R$24 from the banks. Pick one up at Banco do Brasil.

Banco do Brasil (Rua Antônio de Alberqueque 248; ⏰ 10am-3pm Mon-Fri)

Bradesco (Rua Filinto Müller 85; ⏰ 11am-4pm Mon-Fri) Visa/MasterCard ATM.

Directoria de Turismo e Meio Ambiente (☎ 3291 1143; cnr Rua Filinto Müller & Rua Antônio de Albuquerque) Inside Casa de Artesão.

Extreme LAN House (Av Virginia Ferreira 115; ⏰ 8am-1am; per hr R$2) Internet access.

Hospital (☎ 291 1398; Av Virginia Ferreira 2415) This hospital will soon be replaced by the new regional hospital on Rua Gasper Coelho.

Peixe Viva (☎ 3291 1798; Rua Getúlio Vargas 350; ⊙ 6am-6pm) In the center, this is the place to rent boats and fishing rods and buy bait. It can also provide information on fishing in the area.

Post office (Rua Antônio João 111; ⊙ 8:30am-5pm Mon-Fri, 8-11:30am Sat)

Sleeping & Eating

Hotel Rio (☎ 3291 1295; Rua Filinto Müller 651; s/d R$35/70; ⊙) A completely renovated riverfront option with a very pleasant patio practically spilling into the river.

Santa Ana Turismo Hotel (☎ 3291 1602; Rua Miranda Reis s/n; s/d R$55/95; ⊙ ⊙) It's hard to tell if it's the Stone Age or the future, but this concrete jungle of a hotel on the riverfront has a great pool and comfortable rooms.

Hotel Coxim (☎ 3291 1480; BR-163 km726; s/d R$48/94; ⊙ ⊙ ⊙) About 4km from town on the road to Campo Grande, the Coxim Hotel is the flashiest in town, though that's not saying much. There's a poolside pizzeria, and it is well equipped for fishing tours.

Cabana do Osmar (☎ 3291 3902; Av Coronel Pedro Severo 37; meals R$16; ⊙ 7am-10pm) The best of the riverside fish restaurants, run by Osmar, a fishing guide known all over Brazil. The shady riverside patio is also nice for a few cold Skol.

Getting There & Around

There are plenty of buses from both Cuiabá (R$52, seven hours) and Campo Grande (R$38, four hours) to Coxim. To get to the bus station, you can walk or catch a mototaxi (R$3).

The hotels along the river have small outboard boats for hire; daily rates start at about R$120.

BONITO & AROUND

☎ 0xx67 / pop 17,681

Bonito is *the* ecotourism model for Brazil. This small aquatic playground in the southwestern corner of Mato Grosso do Sul has few attractions of its own, but the natural resources of the area are spectacular, and local authorities have taken the high road in their regulation and maintenance. There are caves with lakes and amazing stalactite formations, beautiful waterfalls and incredibly clear rivers surrounded by lush forest where it's possible for divers to swim eyeball to eyeball with hundreds of fish. Since Bonito exploded on the ecotourism map in the early

1990s, the number of visitors has risen dramatically every year. A 770-sq-km national park is now in the works for 2009, further locking in the preservation of the area.

Orientation & Information

Bonito is a one-street show, Rua Coronel Pilad Rebuá, a 3km stretch that's home to bars, restaurants, tourism agencies and souvenir shops.

EMERGENCY

Police (☎ 3255 1104; Rua 24 de Fevereiro)

INTERNET ACCESS

Discovery LAN House (☎ 3255 4485; Rua Filinto Müller 609; per hr R$2.50; ⊙ 9am-midnight)

MEDICAL SERVICES

Hospital (☎ 3255 3455; Rua Pedro Apóstolo 201)

MONEY

Banco do Brasil (Rua Luiz da Costa Leite 2279; ⊙ 9am-2pm) Visa/MasterCard ATM.

Bradesco (Rua Coronel Pilad Rebuá 1942) Visa/MasterCard ATM.

POST

Post office (Rua Coronel Pilad Rebuá 1759)

TOURIST INFORMATION

Comtur (☎ 3255 2160; Rua Coronel Pilad Rebuá 1250; ⊙ 8am-5pm Mon-Fri) The office of the secretary of tourism.

TRAVEL AGENCIES

All agencies in Bonito are strictly regulated and all prices are fixed – no use shopping around. Some, however, are more helpful than others.

Agência Ar (☎ 3255 1008; www.agenciaar.com.br; Rua Coronel Pilad Rebuá 1184; ⊙ 24hr) A more commercial all-purpose agency handy if for no other reason than it's open 24 hours.

Bonito Adventure (☎ 3255 3050; www.bonito adventure.com.br in Portuguese; Rua Coronel Pilad Rebuá 2066; ⊙ 7am-10pm) The videos of excursions on offer are helpful.

Impacto Ecoturismo (☎ 3255 1414; www.impacto tour.com.br in Portuguese; Rua Coronel Pilad Rebuá 1555; ⊙ 6am-6:30pm) Nicely located in the middle of the strip. It has English capacity via email, not in person.

Muito Bonito Turismo (☎ 3255 1645; www.hotel muitobonito.com.br; Rua Coronel Pilad Rebuá 1444; ⊙ 7am-9pm) Travel agency located in the pousada of the same name. Multilingual and very helpful.

Sights & Activities

The only natural attraction in and around Bonito that doesn't need a guide is the **Balneário Municipal** (admission R$15; ☼ 8am-6pm), a natural swimming pool with clear water and lots of fish on the Rio Formoso, 7km southeast of town. You can spend the whole day here mingling with locals and have lunch at the kiosks. Macaws also make regular appearances. Grab a mototaxi to get there (R$6 one way).

Luckily, there is at least one activity in Bonito that has nothing to do with water at all. **Project Jibóia** (☎ 8419 0313; Rua Nestor Fernandes 610; admission R$15; ☼ 7pm) is a one-man crusade to change the world's opinion of snakes. It's an entertaining hour or so, complete with red tail boa constrictors that you nearly swap spit with by the end of the night.

Tours

The local government has strict regulations in place for visiting the area's natural attractions, partly because many are on private land and partly to minimize the impact on some pristine areas. Most attractions have a daily limit on the number of visitors they will accept, and a guide must accompany visitors at all sites. Sunscreen is not allowed in the river tours as it taints the water.

There are more than 30 travel agencies in Bonito offering almost as many different tours. Only guides from local travel agencies are authorized, so you're obliged to book

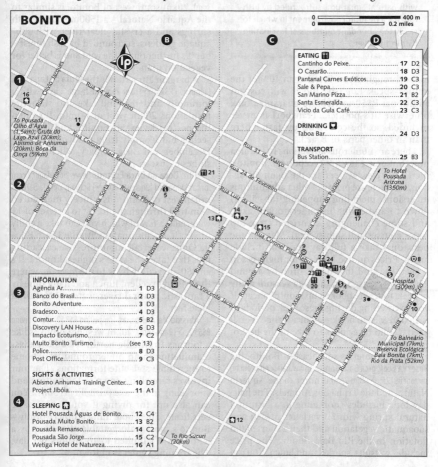

BONITO

0   400 m
0   0.2 miles

EATING 🍴
Cantinho do Peixe..........................**17** D2
O Casarão......................................**18** D3
Pantanal Carnes Exóticos................**19** C3
Sale & Pepa....................................**20** C3
San Marino Pizza............................**21** B2
Santa Esmeralda............................**22** C3
Vicio da Gula Café..........................**23** C3

DRINKING 🍷
Taboa Bar......................................**24** D3

TRANSPORT
Bus Station....................................**25** B3

To Hotel
Pousada
Arizona
(1350m)

To Pousada
Olho d'Água
(1.5km); Gruta do
Lago Azul (20km);
Abismo de Anhumas
(20km); Boca da
Onça (59km)

To Hospital
(300m)

To Balneário
Municipal (7km);
Reserva Ecológica
Baía Bonita (7km);
Rio da Prata (52km)

To Rio Sucuri
(20km)

INFORMATION
Agência Ar.......................................**1** D3
Banco do Brasil................................**2** D3
Bonito Adventure.............................**3** D3
Bradesco...**4** D3
Comtur..**5** B2
Discovery LAN House.......................**6** D3
Impacto Ecoturismo.........................**7** C2
Muito Bonito Turismo.................(see 13)
Police..**8** D3
Post Office......................................**9** C3

SIGHTS & ACTIVITIES
Abismo Anhumas Training Center....**10** D3
Project Jibóia..................................**11** A1

SLEEPING 🛏
Hotel Pousada Águas de Bonito......**12** C4
Pousada Muito Bonito......................**13** B2
Pousada Remanso............................**14** C2
Pousada São Jorge..........................**15** C2
Wetiga Hotel de Natureza................**16** A1

IT'S CLEAR TO SEE: BONITO IS BEAUTIFUL

If you bought a bunch of exotic fish and dumped them into your uncle's swimming pool, then jumped in with some goggles, you'd have an idea of what Bonito has to offer. But how did this happy accident of nature happen? The river waters spring from subterranean sources in a limestone base, almost entirely free of clay, which releases calcium carbonate into the water. The calcium carbonate calcifies all impurities in the water, which then sink to the riverbed (this is the reason you're asked to stay afloat and not touch the bottom during river tours). The result is an area filled with natural aquariums surrounded by lush forest – a beautiful environment in which to study the abundant numbers of fascinating fish in the rivers.

tours through them. Fewer than 10% of the guides speak English, and it will cost an additional R$50 to R$80 to guarantee one; otherwise, it's potluck. Transport is never included, so the costs add up faster here than in other parts of Brazil.

There are numerous attractions in the area now, but only a few are exceptional. Bonito's incredibly clear waters are the main attraction, but there are plenty of other adventurous diversions, including rappelling (abseiling) down to and diving in underground lakes, and some challenging *arvorismo* (tree-top ropes courses and sightseeing). Many of the best tours take a full day and will include lunch. Prices quoted here are for high season – keep in mind that prices drop by around 25% in low season. In the high season, many of these tours are booked up months ahead. If you're traveling during these peak periods, it is a good idea to book well in advance. You'll need a solid three days to take in the best of Bonito.

Seven kilometers southeast of Bonito, the **Reserva Ecológica Baía Bonita** (www.baiabonita.com.br; 3hr tour R$125; ☾ 6am-7pm) is home to the Aquário Natural and the Trilha dos Animais. The half-day tour includes snorkeling in a beautiful natural spring with 30 varieties of fish and subaquatic vegetation and then a short 900m flotation in the Rio Baía Bonita. The price includes wetsuits, snorkels and lunch. You can

also tack on an optional visit to the Trilha dos Animais, a zoo of regional animals including an impressive anaconda, a well-trained tapir and a cute little ocelot.

Within a *fazenda*, 52km south of Bonito, the marvelous **Rio da Prata** (5hr tour incl lunch R$134; ☾ 6:30am-2pm) program includes a short trek through rain forest and a 3km swim downstream along the Rio Olha d'Agua, amazingly crystal clear and full of 55 species of fish, and Rio da Prata, a little foggier but still great and fantastic for viewing massive *pacu* and curious *pirapitanga* varieties. This place should be near the top of your list. The afternoon visit to Buraco das Araras, often tagged on, is forgettable.

The **Rio Sucuri** (3hr tour incl lunch R$115; ☾ 8am-3pm), 20km southwest of Bonito, is similar to the Aquário Natural – a 1500m snorkel with springs and a crystal-clear river with sub-aquatic gardens, surrounded by lush forest – but it's further out in the wild and is better for vegetation than for fish.

A bargain attraction is the **Gruta do Lago Azul** (admission R$25; ☾ 6am-2pm), a large cave with a luminous underground lake and stalactite formations 20km west of Bonito. It's often the postcard view of Bonito, and is worth seeing, but it's only truly miraculous in late December and early January, when the sun shines in just so.

The **Boca da Onça Ecotour** (www.bocadaonca.com.br; trekking incl lunch R$100; ☾ 9:30am-6pm), 59km northwest of Bonito, is a nicely manicured 4km trail through the forest to a series of 11 waterfalls, a few of which you can take a chilly dip in. It all culminates with the 156m Boca da Onça waterfall, an impressive cascading falls that takes the state's highest honors. It's an 880-step climb back to the *fazenda*, where there is an excellent lunch and hang time by a fantastic natural river-water pool, full of local fish.

Abismo de Anhumas (rappelling R$360, scuba diving R$510; ☾ 7am-5pm), 20km west of Bonito, is like a journey to Middle Earth. It's a 72m abyss culminating in an underground lake, home to incredible stalactite formations. The tour involves rappelling down to the bottom and snorkeling in the lake (visibility is 30m). You can also opt for diving if you have a basic certificate. The whole thing is otherworldly – Bonito's most unforgettable attraction by a landslide. It's limited to 18 visitors per day. The training center is in town.

Sleeping

Accommodations in Bonito are tight and more expensive during the high season and on weekends throughout the year.

Pousada São Jorge (☎ 3255 4046; www.pousadasao jorge.com.br in Portuguese; Rua Coronel Pilad Rebuá 1605; s/d with air-con R$35/70; ✖ 🖵) There's decent English spoken and a nice breakfast at this good-value budget option, run by an extremely friendly couple – a good alternative if Muito Bonito is full. They can also book tours.

Pousada Muito Bonito (☎ 3255 1645; www.muito bonito.com.br; Rua Coronel Pilad Rebuá 1444; s/d R$40/70; ✖) Owner Mario Doblack speaks five languages and offers very well-appointed budget rooms around a small courtyard. Along the main road (200m from the bus station); excursions and transport can be organized.

Pousada Remanso (☎ 3255 1137; www.pousada remanso.com.br in Portuguese; Rua Coronel Pilad Rebuá 1515; s/d R$89/141; ✖) A good-value midrange option right in the heart of town, with leather hammocks, nicely maintained landscaping and a small pool.

Hotel Pousada Águas de Bonito (☎ 3255 2330; www.aguasdebonito.com.br; Rua 29 de Maio 1679; s/d R$125/170; ✖ 🖵 🔊) This pousada offers a little more character than others in town. Rooms are modern and spacious and the ones on the 2nd level have pleasant patios.

Pousada Olho d'Água (☎ 3255 1430; www.pousada olhodagua.com.br; Rua MS 382 s/n; s/d R$132/177; ✖ 🖵 🔊) Toucans often do flybys at this charming pousada about 1.5km west of the center. The spacious rooms with exposed brick, patios with hammocks, and excellent linens are good value.

Hotel Pousada Arizona (☎ 255 1040; http://hotel pousadaarizona.com.br in Portuguese; Rua das Águas Marinhas 680; s/d R$137/199; ✖ 🖵 🔊) Colorful brick and wood bungalows surround the best pool (and poolside bar) in town at this 16-room retreat 2km from the main drag.

Wetiga Hotel de Natureza (☎ 3255 1699; www .wetegahotel.com.br; Rua Coronel Pilad Rebuá 679; s/d R$370/400; ✖ 🖵 🔊) The remarkable wood and stone architecture is more interesting than the rather simple rooms, which all overlook a nice courtyard and pool. Rates include dinner.

Eating & Drinking

Vicio da Gula Café (☎ 3255 2041; Rua Coronel Pilad Rebuá 1852; sandwiches R$7; ✖ noon-2am) Popular corner spot for great burgers, fries and *açaí na tigela* (*açaí*, a berry-like fruit, in a bowl).

Sale & Pepe (☎ 3255 1822; Rua 29 de Maio 971; meals for 2 R$15-31; ✖ 6pm-2am) A decent selection of Chinese and Japanese dishes with a Pantaneiro slant, like Yakisoba *jacaré*.

O Casarão (☎ 3255 1970; Rua Coronel Pilad Rebuá 1843; meals for 2 R$24-34; ✖ 11am-3pm & 6-11:30pm) Go off menu for the *prato especial* – you get salad, meat, fish and chicken, rice, beans, and fries for R$12!

Cantinho do Peixe (☎ 3422 4992; Rua 31 de Março 1918; meals R$25-38; ✖ 11am-3pm & 6pm-1am Mon-Sat) *Pintado* (a type of catfish), fresh from Rio Miranda, ends up on plates 20 different ways at this simple but tasty spot just off the main drag. Try the *pintado à urucum*, a lasagnalike dish of *pintado* smothered in a tomato, condensed milk and mozzarella sauce.

Santa Esmeralda (☎ 3255 1943; Rua Coronel Pilad Rebuá 1831; meals for 2 R$25-42; ✖ 11am-2:30pm & 6pm-midnight) Pastas (R$14 to R$18) with your choice of sauce, and excellent barbecue meat served on lengthy *espetinhos* (skewers).

San Marino Pizza (☎ 3282 2656; Rua Luiz da Costa Leite 1543; pizzas R$16-24; ✖ 6pm-midnight, closed Tue) The four-cheese pizza from this outlet of the Campo Grande pizzeria of the same name is the best pie in town.

Pantanal Carnes Exóticas (☎ 3255 2763; Rua Coronel Pilad Rebuá 1808; meals for 2 R$37-60; ✖ 11am-2pm & 6pm-11pm) Got a craving for capybara with bacon? What about peccary with pineapple? Make a beeline for Pantanal Carnes Exóticas.

Taboa Bar (☎ 3255 1862; Rua Coronel Pilad Rebuá 1841; ✖ 6pm-late Sun-Thu, 5pm-late Fri & Sat) A graffitifueled institution on the main drag where locals and travelers converge over the house special: *pinga (cachaça)* mixed with honey, cinnamon and guaraná.

Getting There & Away

Only one bus company serves Bonito, Cruzeiro do Sul. There are buses to Bonito from Campo Grande (R$47, five hours, six daily) and six in the opposite direction beginning at 5:30am. There is one bus to Ponta Porã (R$38.50, four hours, noon), but you must switch buses in Jardim, and one to Corumbá (R$53, seven hours, 6am).

Getting Around

Unfortunately, many of Bonito's attractions are a fair hike from town, and there's no public transportation. To make matters worse, tours booked with travel agencies in Bonito don't include transport. The best solution is to make quick friends with Brazilians with their own vehicles (this is best done with *cachaça*). Otherwise, there are a few options. Local agencies can arrange a shuttle service, driven by a friendly local named Hallem, for R$34 per person for full-day excursions and R$17 for half-day. The catch is, Hallem only goes to one specific excursion each day, so you have to plan accordingly. Another local shuttle service, **Vanzella** (☎ 3255 3005), will take you to any excursion on any day so long as there is a minimum of four people. If you speak Portuguese, you can call direct; otherwise, Pousada Muito Bonito corrals foreigners together and can make the arrangements. The costs are R$25 for half-day tours and R$35 for a full day.

If you are part of a group, it might end up being more economical to hire a taxi for the full day (R$120, the same as renting a car, but without the gas bill) from any Ponto de Táxi. Lastly, there are your friendly neighborhood mototaxis, whose prices are negotiable. to the Rio Sucuri (38km round-trip) and Gruta do Lago Azul (38km round-trip) and back to town costs around R$30 per person; to Rio da Prata (100km round-trip) costs R$60; and to Boca da Onça (120km round-trip) R$80. The drivers will wait around for the duration of the tour. No matter which form of transportation you choose to take, remember to keep an eye on the landscape. It's not uncommon to see some impressive wildlife along the way, including deer, emas and even an occasional anteater.

PONTA PORÃ

☎ 0xx67 / pop 66,000

It's a strange feeling to cross a street and change countries, but you can do just that in Ponta Porã, a bustling little border town divided from the Paraguayan town of Pedro Juan Caballero by Av Internacional. The beer changes from Skol to Pilsen and prices on electronics are slashed – other than that, it's hard to even notice there is a border here (Portunhol vernacular is rampant). It once prospered as a center for the *yerba maté* trade in the late 19th century; now it caters to Brazilians by the truckload, who flock to the Paraguayan shopping centers. It's a get-in, get-out town – if you spend more than one night here, it had better be due to hospitalization.

Information

Banco do Brasil (Av Brasil 2623) Visa/MasterCard ATM.

Bradesco (Av Brasil 2665) Visa/Mastercard ATM.

Centro Digital (☎ 3431 2446; Rua 7 de Setembro 223; per hr R$1.50; ⏰ 8am-9pm Mon-Fri, to 5pm Sat, 2-9pm Sun) Internet access.

Federal Police (☎ 3431 1428; Av Presidente Vargas, Ponta Porã; ⏰ 9am-noon & 1-4pm Mon-Fri) Near the Paraguayan consulate. This is where you get Brazilian exit/entry stamps; this involves a bit of legwork, so if you're in a hurry, grab a cab.

Norte Cambios (cnr Calle Mariscal López & Calle Curupayty, Pedro Juan Caballero) Changes cash at a reasonable rate.

Paraguayan immigration office (☎ 3431 6312; Av Dr Francis; ⏰ 7am-noon & 1:30-9pm Mon-Fri, 8am-noon

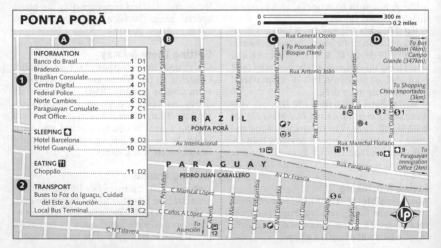

PONTA PORÃ

0 _____ 300 m
0 _____ 0.2 miles

INFORMATION	
Banco do Brasil	1 D1
Bradesco	2 D1
Brazilian Consulate	3 C2
Centro Digital	4 D1
Federal Police	5 D2
Norte Cambios	6 D2
Paraguayan Consulate	7 C1
Post Office	8 D1

SLEEPING	
Hotel Barcelona	9 D2
Hotel Guarujá	10 D2

EATING	
Choppão	11 D2

TRANSPORT	
Buses to Foz do Iguaçu, Cuidad del Este & Asunción	12 B2
Local Bus Terminal	13 C2

Rua General Osorio
To Pousada do Bosque (1km)
To Bus Station (4km); Campo Grande (347km)
Rua Antonio João
To Shopping China Importados (3km)
Av Brasil
B R A Z I L
PONTA PORÃ
Av Internacional
P A R A G U A Y
PEDRO JUAN CABALLERO
Av Dr Francia
Rua Marechal Floriano
Rua Paraguay
To Paraguayan Immigration Office (2km)
C Mariscal López
C Aquidaban
C Carlos A López
To Asunción
C N.Talavera
Av Presidente Vargas
Rua Baltazar Saldanha
Rua Joaquim Teixeira
Rua Aral Moreira
Rua Tradentes
Rua 7 de Setembro
Rua Guia Lopes
C Martinez
C D Martinez
C Júlia C Estigarribia
C Mal Estigarribia
C Gral Díaz
C Curupayty
C Perpétuo Socorro
C Alberdi

& 1:30-9pm Sat, 7-9pm Sun) For Paraguayan entry/exit stamps. The office is about 2km east of the local bus terminal. It's a large, yellow building next to Goodyear.

Post office (Av Brasil 2861)

Shopping

If you want to see what all the fuss is about, **Shopping China Importados** (☎ 0xx36-74343; Ruta V c/Callejón Internacional; Pedro Juan Caballero; ⊙ 8:30am-7pm Mon-Sat, 9am-2pm Sun) is a good place to start. This megastore near the bus station has…well, *everything* and is teeming with wide-eyed Brazilians throwing down real after real for massive discounts on everything from Johnny Walker to Canon.

Sleeping & Eating

This area is not suburban Rio by any means, but drug trafficking is widespread and assignations along the border are not uncommon (there were four during the week of research). Travelers are generally left alone, but it's a good idea to use extra caution, especially at night.

Hotel Guarujá (☎ 3431 9515; Rua Guia Lopes 63; s/d apt R$26/45; ❄) A bit ratty but still a good budget option with large *apartamentos*.

Pousada do Bosque (☎ 3431 1741; www.hotelpousada dobosque.com.br in Portuguese; Av Presidente Vargas 1151; s/d apt R$65/110; ❄ ⅏) A little forested oasis just outside the center in the ritzy side of town. It's too nice for Ponta Porá, truth be told.

Hotel Barcelona (☎ 3431 3061; Av Guia Lopes 45; s/d R$72/110; ❄) The nicest digs in the center, with big rooms (aged furniture free of charge) and a nice pool.

Choppão (☎ 3432 1992; Rua Marechal Floriano 1877; burgers R$5-7, meals for 2 R$23-43; ⊙ 6:30am-late) Pizza, fish, omelets, milk shakes – this classic spot has everything, including an old-timey fountain counter with 24 seats.

Getting There & Around

From the **bus station** (☎ 3431 4145), about 4km from the center of Ponta Porã, frequent buses go to Campo Grande (R$49, six hours, 11 daily). There are also buses to Corumbá (R$118, 13½ hours) and Paulo (R$213, 25 hours, two daily). For Bonito, you must first travel to Jardim (R$35, 6am) and then on to Bonito (R$7, seven daily).

For Foz do Iguaçu, take a bus from the bus station on Calle Alberdi in Pedro Juan Caballero (on the Paraguayan side) to Ciudad del Este. Cuidad del Este (Paraguay) is just across the border from the Brazilian town of Foz do Iguaçu. There are daily buses to Ciudad del Este (Gs 70,000), eight hours, three daily). You don't need a Paraguayan visa to transit through Paraguay on your way to Foz do Iguaçu. From the same bus station in Pedro Juan Caballero, there are also buses to Asunción, the capital of Paraguay (Gs 70,000, six hours, two daily).

Bahia

Boasting more than 900km of coastline and a rich culture spanning five centuries and two continents, Bahia is a state of massive proportions. With World Heritage–listed sites, deserted beaches, idyllic islands and festivals throughout the year, there is much to discover.

Bahia's centerpiece is Salvador, where the jewelbox colonial old town has gilded churches, cobblestone streets and an incredibly vibrant culture deeply connected to its Afro-Brazilian heritage. Music and dance seem to be everywhere, with the powerful sounds of drum corps reverberating off old stone walls as capoeiristas battle against the backdrop of a 16th-century cathedral. Catching open-air concerts, Candomblé ceremonies and impromptu fests are just a few of the ways to celebrate an evening in Salvador, Bahian-style.

Nearby scenic colonial towns like Cachoeira have picturesque river settings and a long tradition of wood carving. Just a short journey north and south lead to idyllic coastal spots like the car-free island of Morro de São Paulo or lovely Praia do Forte.

In the south, the small idyllic villages of Arraial d'Ajuda and Trancoso perch on hillsides near vast stretches of white-sand beaches. A fun, diverse crowd gathers at outdoor restaurants and bars, and there's a charming assortment of guesthouses. More off-the-beaten-track locales lie further south, including the sleepy fishing village of Caraíva, sandwiched between a mangrove-lined river and pounding waves on the beach. Other untouristy gems include the rustic island of Barra Grande, the beach village of Mangue Seco and the Parque Nacional Marinho de Abrolhos, its crystal-clear waters great for diving and whale watching.

Inland, the peaceful town of Lençóis, once a center for diamond-mining, lies amid breathtaking scenery, with waterfalls and rushing rivers setting the stage for hiking and exploring.

HIGHLIGHTS

- Follow the sounds of the pounding rhythms in **Salvador** (p439), Latin America's inspiring Afro-Brazilian capital

- Hike across dramatic plateaus and swim in mountain streams in the magnificent **Parque Nacional da Chapada Diamantina** (p498)

- Island-hop across lovely **Morro de São Paulo** (p470) and traditional **Boipeba** (p472), with a visit to the unspoiled peninsula **Barra Grande** (p474)

- Eat at outdoor restaurants, take long coastal walks and join the beach fests at **Arraial d'Ajuda** (p486)

- Watch tiny sea turtles hatch outside of **Praia do Forte** (p466) or **Mangue Seco** (p469)

Mangue Seco ★

Parque Nacional da Chapada ★ Diamantina

Praia do Forte ★

Morro de ★ Salvador São Paulo ★
★ Boipeba
★ Barra Grande

★ Arraial d'Ajuda

- POPULATION: 13.4 MILLION
- AREA: 567,295 SQ KM

History

Prior to the Portuguese arrival, the region known today as Bahia had a wide variety of ethnic groups scattered inland and along the coast, speaking dozens of languages. Many of the tribes were wiped out by the Portuguese, though some – like the Pataxó (boxed text, p491) – are still around today. The indigenous tribes practiced some form of agriculture, raising manioc, sweet potatoes and maize, and practiced hunting and fishing, while gathering fruits from the forests. Little else is known of the area's native population, who, for the most part, would disappear following the European arrival.

Portuguese sailors first made landfall near Porto Seguro in 1500, but it wasn't until one year later – All Saints' Day (November 1), according to legend – that Italian navigator Amerigo Vespucci sailed into Salvador's bay and named it Baía de Todos os Santos. Two generations later, in 1549, Tomé de Souza returned under orders by the Portuguese crown to found Brazil's first capital, Salvador da Bahia.

To fuel this new country, the colonists grew sugarcane and later tobacco in the fertile *recôncavo* (region named after the concave shape of the bay) that surrounds the Baía de Todos os Santos. The Portuguese enslaved the indigenous people to work these fields, and when they proved insufficient, they brought over Africans in staggering numbers. From 1550 to 1850, at least 3.6 million slaves were brought from Africa to Brazil, and the great majority of them ended up in the northeast.

In such numbers, the slaves managed to maintain much of their African culture. When their own religious practices were prohibited, for instance, slaves moved their Candomblé *terreiros* (venues) underground and syncretized their gods with Catholic saints. African food and music enriched the homes of both Blacks and Whites, and the African culture deeply influenced the newly developing Brazilian culture.

Throughout the life of the colony, the Portuguese utilized a harsh plantation system that would keep African slaves tied to the land until their emancipation in 1888. In addition to sugar and tobacco, the Portuguese created cattle ranches, which spread inland, radiating west into the *sertão* (backlands) and Minas Gerais, then northwest into Piauí.

Primary products were shipped out, while slaves and European luxury goods were shipped in. Bahia was colonial Brazil's economic heartland, with Salvador da Bahia the capital of colonial Brazil between 1549 and 1763. The city was the center of the sugar industry, which sustained the prosperity of the country until the collapse in international sugar prices in the 1820s. During the gold and coffee booms in the south, Salvador continued its decline.

Industrialization in Bahia began in the mid-19th century and continued slowly, with developments in banking and industry, as new rail lines brought goods from the interior to Salvador's large port. Factories appeared and the economy, once a monoculture of the sugarcane industry, diversified. The most important event of the late 19th century was the emancipation of slaves, which brought freedom for many of Bahia's inhabitants.

In the 20th century, oil discoveries in the 1940s helped bring Bahia out of economic stagnation and contributed to the state's continued modernization. Today, Salvador remains an important port, exporting soy, fruits, cocoa, petrochemicals and sugarcane – which is once again achieving prominence for its role as a highly efficient biofuel. In recent decades, tourism has emerged as an important industry and, with the influx of cash, the state has invested in much-needed infrastructure and public-health projects.

Climate

Bahia's tropical Atlantic coast remains hot and humid all year long, with high temperatures averaging between 26°C (79°F) and 30°C (86°F) and lows between 22°C (72°F) and 24°C (75°F). The southern coast (from about Porto Seguro south) is cooler during winter months, with low temperatures dropping as low as 17°C (63°F). Monthly rainfall averages on the coast run between 100mm and 350mm, with the period between March and June being the wettest. The southern coast has smaller monthly rainfall averages, between 100mm and 170mm, and though there is more rain from April to July, rain is seen pretty consistently throughout the year.

The Chapada Diamantina remains hot during the day and pleasantly cool at night throughout the year. High temperatures average between 27°C (81°F) and 32°C (90°F), with lows between 16°C (61°F) and 20°C (68°F). Monthly rainfall averages range between 50mm and 170mm, with November to March being the wettest months, making for greener scenery and fuller rivers and waterfalls.

National Parks
Set well west of Salvador, the 1520-sq-km Parque Nacional da Chapada Diamantina (p498) is by far Bahia's most spectacular national park. A well-developed network of tour providers and guides offer treks and a range of adventure sports in and around the park, with its waterfalls, green valleys and towering peaks. Divers and snorkelers will enjoy the clear waters and colorful variety of

coral and marine life in the Parque Nacional Marinho de Abrolhos (p492). The 913-sq-km marine park includes an archipelago and expanses of coral reef off the very south of the Bahian coast. Also in southern Bahia, coastal Parque Nacional de Monte Pascoal (p490) offers limited hiking and excellent views from its peak, and is overseen by the indigenous Pataxó tribe.

Getting There & Away
Bahia's primary airport (see p458) is located in its capital, Salvador, though Porto Seguro also has frequent and inexpensive flights.

Hwy BR-101 skirts the Bahian coastline but remains between 50km and 75km inland. It is the main thoroughfare through

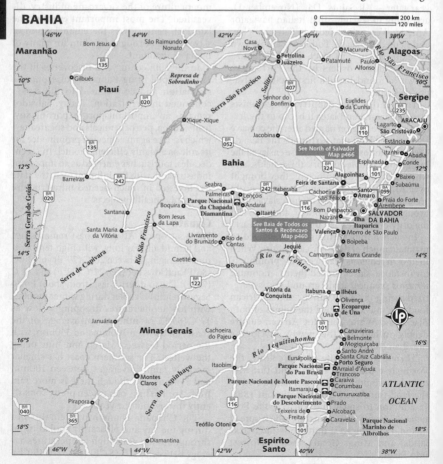

the state and the chosen route of most long-distance buses. There are good coastal highways only between Canavieiras and Itacaré and from Salvador north to the border with Sergipe.

Getting Around

Throughout Bahia there is always some form of transportation between where you are and where you want to go. Aside from buses, Kombis and *bestas* (vans that run a specific route and will stop anywhere to drop off or pick up passengers) are common in rural areas, as are collective taxis. Mototaxi (motorcycle taxis) and taxis are usually available in small to mid-sized towns.

SALVADOR

☎ 0xx71 / pop 2.7 million

Salvador da Bahia has an energy and unadorned beauty that few cities can match. Often called simply Bahia by locals, Salvador is the country's Afro-Brazilian jewel and the once magnificent capital of Portugal's great New World colony. Its brilliantly hued center is a living museum of 17th- and 18th-century architecture and gold-laden churches. More importantly, Salvador is the nexus of an incredible arts movement. Wild festivals happen frequently, with drum corps pounding out powerful rhythms against the backdrop of colonial buildings almost daily. At night, capoeira circles form on plazas and open spaces, while the scent of *acarajé* (bean and shrimp fritters) and other African delights fills the evening air. Elsewhere in town, a different spirit flows through the crowd as religious followers celebrate and reconnect with African gods at mystical Candomblé ceremonies. In fact, there's no other place in the world where descendants of African slaves have preserved their heritage as well as in Salvador – from music and religion to food, dance and martial arts traditions.

Aside from the many attractions within Salvador, gorgeous coastline lies right outside the city – a suitable introduction to the tropical splendor of Bahia.

HISTORY

In 1549, Tomé de Souza landed on Praia Porto da Barra under Portuguese royal orders to found Brazil's first capital, bringing city plans, a statue, 400 soldiers and 400 settlers, including priests and prostitutes. He founded the city in a defensive location: on a cliff top facing the sea. After the first year a city of mud and straw had been erected, and by 1550 the surrounding walls were in place to protect against attacks from hostile Indians. Salvador da Bahia remained Brazil's most important city for the next three centuries.

During its early years, the city depended upon the export of sugarcane and later tobacco from the fertile *recôncavo* region at the northern end of Baía de Todos os Santos. Later cattle ranching was introduced, which, coupled with gold and diamonds from the Bahian interior, provided Salvador with immense wealth, as is visible in the city's opulent baroque architecture.

African slaves were first brought to Salvador in the mid-1500s, and in 1587 historian Gabriel Soares tallied an estimated 12,000 Whites, 8000 converted Indians and 4000 Black slaves. The number of Blacks eventually increased to constitute half of the city's population, and uprisings of Blacks threatened Salvador's stability several times.

After Lisbon, Salvador was the second most important city in the Portuguese empire. It was the glory of colonial Brazil, famed for its many gold-filled churches, beautiful mansions and numerous festivals. It was also renowned as early as the 17th century for its bawdy public life, sensuality and decadence – so much so that its bay won the nickname Baía de Todos os Santos e de Quase Todos os Pecados (Bay of All Saints and of Nearly All Sins)!

Salvador remained Brazil's seat of colonial government until 1763 when, with the decline of the sugarcane industry, the capital was moved to Rio.

In 1798, the city was the stage for the Conjuração dos Alfaiates (Conspiracy of the Tailors) – the beginning of a wave of battles between Portuguese loyalists and those wanting independence. It was only on July 2, 1823, with the defeat of Portuguese troops in Cabrito and Pirajá, that the city found peace. At that time, Salvador numbered 45,000 inhabitants and was the commercial center of a vast territory.

For most of the 19th and 20th centuries the city stagnated as the agricultural economy foundered on its disorganized labor and production. Today, Salvador is Brazil's third-largest city, and it has only begun moving forward in the last few decades. New

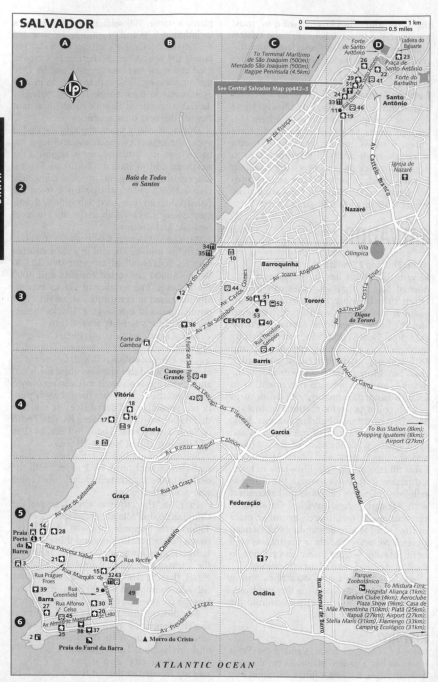

SALVADOR

0 ————— 1 km
0 ————— 0.5 miles

Ⓐ   Ⓑ   Ⓒ   Ⓓ

Forte de Santo Antônio

Ladeira do Baluarte
23
Praça de Santo Antônio
26
29
31
22 41
6 24
33 46
110 19

Santo Antônio

See Central Salvador Map pp442–3

To Terminal Marítimo de São Joaquim (500m); Mercado São Joaquim (500m); Itapipe Peninsula (4.5km)

Av da França

Baía de Todos os Santos

Igreja de Nazaré

Nazaré

Av Castelo Branco

Vila Olímpica

34
35
10

Barroquinha

Av Joana Angélica

12
44
50 51
52
53
40

CENTRO

Tororó

Av Marechal Costa Silva

Dique do Tororó

36

Forte de Gamboa

Rua Theodoro Sampaio
47

Barris

Av Vasco da Gama

Campo Grande
48

42

Vitória
18
16
17
9
8

Canela

Av Reitor Miguel Calmon

Garcia

To Bus Station (8km); Shopping Iguatemi (8km); Airport (27km)

Av Sete de Setembro

Graça

Rua da Graça

Federação

Av Centenário

Av Garibaldi

Praia Porto da Barra
4 14
28
1
3
21
13 Rua Recife
15
3243
5
39
27
45
24
2
25
38 37

Rua Princesa Isabel

Rua Marquês de

Rua Práguer Froes

Rua Greenfield

Rua Alfonso Celso

Av Almirante Marques de Leão

Barra

7

49

Ondina

Rua Ademar de Barro

Parque Zoobotânico

To Mistura Fina; Hospital Aliança (1km); Fashion Clube (4km); Aeroclube Plaza Show (9km); Casa de Mãe Pimentinha (10km); Piatã (25km); Itapuã (27km); Airport (27km); Stella Maris (31km); Flamengo (33km); Camping Ecológico (31km);

▲ Morro do Cristo

Praia do Farol da Barra

Av Presidente Vargas

ATLANTIC OCEAN

BAHIA

BAHIA

industries such as petroleum, chemicals and tourism have brought wealth to the city's coffers, but the rapidly increasing population is still faced with major economic and social problems.

ORIENTATION

Salvador sits at the southern tip of a V-shaped peninsula at the mouth of the Baía de Todos os Santos. The city can be difficult to navigate as there are many one-way, no-left-turn streets that wind through Salvador's hills and valleys. The center of the city is on the bay side of the peninsula and is divided by a steep bluff into two parts: Cidade Alta (Upper City) and Cidade Baixa (Lower City).

The heart of historic Cidade Alta is the Pelourinho (or Pelô), which is also the heart of Salvador's tourism and nightlife. This roughly refers to the area from Praça da Sé to Largo do Pelourinho.

From Praça Castro Alves, Av 7 de Setembro runs through the Centro to the wide Praça Campo Grande, then continues southwest through the well-to-do Vitória neighborhood, and down to the mouth of the bay. Here, at the tip of the peninsula, is the affluent Barra district, with its lighthouse, forts and popular beach.

A main thoroughfare, which constantly changes names, snakes east from Barra along the Atlantic coast. It passes through middle-class coastal suburbs such as Rio Vermelho, and a chain of beaches all the way to Itapuã.

Cidade Baixa contains the Comércio (the city's commercial and financial center), the ferry terminals and port. North, the land curves around the bay to create the Itapagipe Peninsula, including the Bonfim and Boa Viagem neighborhoods. The suburbs along the bay are poor, and the level of poverty generally increases with the distance from the center.

Maps

Tourist information offices give out free basic maps, but for a more in-depth map, look for the Geocad *Mapa de Salvador* (R$10), sold in newsstands about town.

INFORMATION
Bookstores

Berinjela (Map pp442–3; ☎ 3322 0247; Travessa da Ajuda 1, Cidade Alta; ⏰ 9am-5pm Mon-Fri, 9am-2pm Sat; 🖥) Sells used foreign-language books, CDs and LPs; the café serves vegetarian food.

Livraria Brandão (Map pp442–3; ☎ 3243 5383; Rua Rui Barbosa 15B, Cidade Alta; ⏰ 8am-6pm Mon-Fri, 8am-2pm Sat) Sells and trades used foreign-language books.

Emergency

Deltur (Map pp442–3; ☎ 3322 7155; Cruzeiro de São Francisco 14, Pelourinho; ⏰ 24hr) Any crime involving a tourist must be handled by the city's tourist police. A few speak English or French.

Pronto Socorro (first aid; ☎ 192)

BAHIA

CENTRAL SALVADOR

A **B** **C** **D**

INFORMATION
BahiaCafe.com..................................1 E4
Bahiatursa...2 F3
Bahiatursa....................................(see 69)
Banco do Brasil................................3 F4
Berinjela.....................................(see 48)
Bradesco...4 D4
Café Conosco...................................5 F4
Central Post Office...........................6 C3
Deltur...7 F4
Emtursa...8 D4
Grupo Gay da Bahia.........................9 F3
Internet Café.com...........................10 E3
Livraria Brandão..............................11 D5
Post Office......................................12 F4
Post Office......................................13 E4
Toursbahia......................................14 E4

SIGHTS & ACTIVITIES
Associação Brasileira de Capoeira
   Angola..15 F3
Câmara Municipal...........................16 D4
Catedral Basílica..............................17 E3
Diáspora Art Center.........................18 F4
Elevador Lacerda.......................(see 71)
Escadas do Carmo...........................19 F2
Escola de Dança..............................20 E4
Faculdade de Medicina Building...21 E3
Federação Baiana do Culto
   Afro-Brasileiro............................22 F2
Fundação Casa de Jorge Amado..23 F2
Fundação Mestre Bimba................24 F3
Igreja da Ordem Terceira de São
   Domingus....................................25 E3
Igreja da Ordem Terceira do
   Carmo...26 F1
Igreja da Terceira Ordem de São
   Francisco.....................................27 F4
Igreja do Santíssimo Sacramento
   do Passo......................................28 F2
Igreja e Convento São Francisco...29 F4
Igreja NS do Rosário dos Pretos...30 F2
Igreja São Pedro dos Clérigos......31 E3
Mercado Modelo.......................(see 69)
Mestre Lua......................................32 F3
Mestre Souza.............................(see 64)
Museu Afro-Brasileiro...............(see 21)
Museu da Cidade............................33 F3
Museu da Misericórdia...................34 D4
Museu de Arqueologia e
   Etnologia...............................(see 21)
Palácio Rio Branco..........................35 D4
Plano Inclinado Gonçalves........(see 73)
Senac...(see 65)

SLEEPING
Albergue da Juventude do Pelô...36 F2
Albergue das Laranjeiras................37 F4
Albergue do Passo...........................38 F2
Convento do Carmo........................39 F1
Hotel Arthemis................................40 E4
Hotel Maridina................................41 C6
Hotel Villa Bahia.............................42 F4
Pousada da Praça Hotel...................43 D6
Solar dos Romanos.........................44 F2
Studio do Carmo.............................45 F2

EATING
A Cubana..46 D4
A Cubana..47 F3
Berinjela..48 D5
Cafélier..49 F1
Coliseu..50 E4
Don Rafaello....................................51 F3
Dona Chika-ka................................52 F3
La Lupa..53 F4
Mamabahia.....................................54 E3
Maria Mata Mouro..........................55 F4

O Nilo..56 F4
Panorâmico.....................................57 F4
Pisseria Romolo e Remo.................58 F4
Restaurante Matusalem...................59 F4
Senac...(see 65)
Sorriso da Dadá...............................60 F3

DRINKING
Cantina da Lua................................61 E3
Estação de Pelô..............................62 F3
Habeus Copus.................................63 F3

ENTERTAINMENT
Teatro Miguel Santana....................64 F3
Teatro SESC-Senac..........................65 F2

SHOPPING
Artesanato São Domingos...............66 E4
Bahia Online....................................67 F3
Bau Bau...68 F4
Mercado Modelo.............................69 C4

TRANSPORT
Bus Stop..70 C4
Elevador Lacerda.............................71 D4
Marlin Ecotours..............................72 F3
Plano Inclinado Gonçalves..............73 E3
Praça da Sé Bus Stop.......................74 D5
Terminal da França..........................75 C3
Terminal Marítimo Turístico...........76 B3
VASP...77 D3

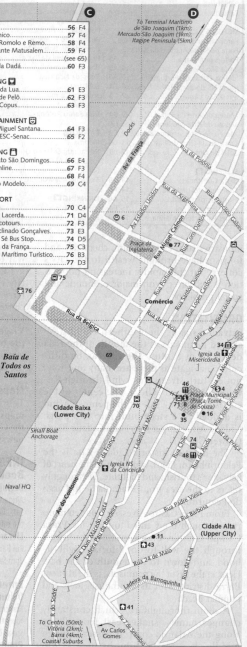

To Terminal Marítimo
de São Joaquim (1km);
Mercado São Joaquim (1km);
Itagipe Peninsula (5km)

Docks

Av da França

Rua da Polônia

Rua da Argentina

Av Estados Unidos

Rua Francisco Gálves

Rua Cons Dantas

Praça da
Inglaterra

Rua Miguel Calmon

Rua Santos Dumont

Comércio

Rua Portugal

Rua Lopes Cardoso

Rua da Grécia

Ladeira da Misericórdia

Rua da Bélgica

Igreja da
Misericórdia

Baía de
Todos os
Santos

Praça Municipal
(Praça Tomé
de Souza)

Rua José Gonçalves

Cald da Praça

Cidade Baixa
(Lower City)

Ladeira da Montanha

Rua Chile

Rua da Ajuda

Small Boat
Anchorage

Av da França

Igreja NS
da Conceição

Naval HQ

Av do Contorno

Cidade Alta
(Upper City)

Rua Pádre Vieira

Rua Rui Barbosa

Rua da Lama

Rua Dom Macedo Costa

Ladeira Paulo da Bandeira

Rua 24 de Maio

Ladeira da Barroquinha

R do Sodré

Av 7 de Setembro

Av Carlos
Gomes

To Centro (50m);
Vitória (2km);
Barra (4km);
Coastal Suburbs

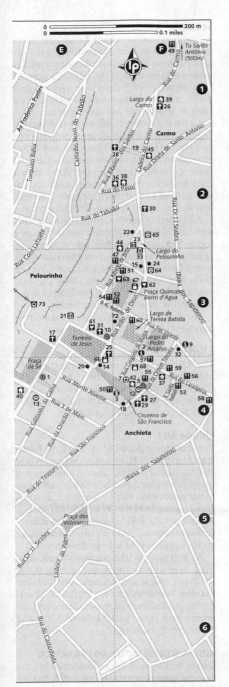

Internet Access

BahiaCafe.com (Map pp442-3; Praça da Sé 20, Pelourinho; per hr R$4; ☹ 10am-midnight)

Café Conosco (Map pp442-3; Rua da Ordem Terceira 4, Pelourinho; per hr R$3; ☹ 9am-9pm)

Internet Café.com (Map pp442-3; 2nd fl, Rua João de Deus 2; per hr R$4; ☹ 9am-9pm Mon-Fri, 9am-6pm Sat, 10am-6pm Sun)

Left Luggage

Airport (☎ 3204 1150; per 24 hr R$5-8; ☹ 24hr)

Bus station (☎ 3460 8300; per 24 hr R$3; ☹ 24hr)

Medical Services

Hospital Aliança (☎ 3350 5700; Av Lucaia Juracy Magalhaes Jr, Itaigara) English spoken.

Money

Banco do Brasil (Map pp442-3; Cruzeiro de São Francisco 11, Pelourinho) Also in the airport.

Bradesco (Map pp442-3; Rua da Misericórdia, Cidade Alta) Also with international ATMs in the Pelourinho, the bus station and the airport.

Toursbahia (Map pp442-3; ☎ 3320 3280; www.toursbahia.com.br; Cruzeiro de São Francisco 4, Pelourinho; ☹ 9am-6pm Mon-Fri, 10am-2pm Sat) One of Salvador's two official money changers changes cash or traveler's checks. Nearby imposters do the same thing.

Post

Central post office (Map pp442-3; Praça da Inglaterra, Comércio)

Post office Cruzeiro de São Francisco (Map pp442-3; Cruzeiro de São Francisco, Pelourinho); Rua 3 de Maio (Map pp442-3; Rua 3 de Maio, Pelourinho)

Tourist Information

Bahiatursa (www.bahiatursa.ba.gov.br, in Portuguese) airport (☎ 3204 1244; ☹ 7:30am-11pm); bus station (☎ 3450 3871; ☹ 7:30am-9pm); Mercado Modelo (Map pp442-3; ☎ 3241 0242; ☹ 9am-6pm Mon-Sat, 9am-2pm Sun); Pelourinho (Map pp442-3; ☎ 3321 2463; Rua Francisco Muniz Barreto 12; ☹ 8:30am-9pm Mon-Thu, 8:30am-10pm Fri-Sun); Porto da Barra (Map pp440-1; ☎ 3264 5440; Instituto Mauá, Av 7 de Setembro; ☹ 9am-7pm Mon-Fri, 10am-3pm Sat); Shopping Barra (Map pp440-1; ☎ 3264 4566; SAC; ☹ 9am-10pm Mon-Fri, 9am-2pm Sat) The multilingual state tourism authority is friendly and helpful, particularly the Pelourinho office, which has a noticeboard listing what's happening around town.

Disque Turismo (Dial Tourism; ☎ 0800 716 622) For general tourist information or help (in English).

Emtursa (Map pp442-3; ☎ 3321 3127; www.emtursa .salvador.ba.gov.br, in Portuguese; Elevador Lacerda,

Cidade Alta; 9am-8pm Mon-Fri, 9am-6pm Sat, 9am-1pm Sun) The city's tourism office can be helpful.

Grupo Gay da Bahia (Map pp442-3; ☎ 3321 1848; www.ggb.org.br, in Portuguese; Rua Frei Vicente 24, Pelourinho) A cultural center for gays, lesbians and transgenders.

Travel Agencies

STB (☎ 3334 7566; Rua Fonte do Boi, Rio Vermelho) Finds student discounts on international flights.

Toursbahia (Map pp442-3; ☎ 3320 3280; www.toursbahia .com.br; Cruzeiro de São Francisco 4, Pelourinho; 9am-6pm Mon-Fri, 10am-2pm Sat) An extremely professional multilingual travel agency offering local and national tours.

DANGERS & ANNOYANCES

The city has a reputation for theft and muggings, and pickpocketing is common on buses and in crowded places. Tourists are easily singled out. Paranoia is counterproductive, but be aware of the dangers and minimize the risks. The following small sacrifices could assure a trouble-free visit (for more tips, see p698).

When visiting Salvador: dress down; wear cheap jewelry and watches, if any at all; take only enough money with you for your outing; carry only a photocopy of your passport; and be roughly orientated before you set out. Don't hesitate to use taxis after dusk or in areas where you feel apprehensive, though taking buses in the evening is not necessarily unsafe.

In the center, tourist police maintain a visible presence, particularly in the Pelourinho. However, it is best not to rely solely on their protection, and you may find them apathetic should something occur.

Crime in the Pelô increases during the high season (especially around Carnaval) and on crowded Tuesday nights. Avoid empty areas. Not carrying a bag (and therefore little money and no valuables) at night will make you less of a target.

The Pelourinho shifts quickly into sketchy areas, so avoid wandering off the beaten path. Cidade Baixa is deserted and unsafe at night and on weekends, and the *ladeiras* (steep roads) that connect it to Cidade Alta should never be taken on foot.

On the beaches, keep a close eye on juvenile thieves – or *capitães d'areia* (captains of the sand) – who are quick to make off with unguarded possessions.

Women will attract annoying attention from men, especially in the Pelourinho. The best tactic is to simply ignore the comments, *psssu*-ing and beckoning.

Scams

A common way for bars and their customers to keep track of how many drinks were ordered without dispute is to place empty bottles underneath or next to the table. To prevent your server from pulling one over on you, make sure the area under and around your table is clear before you open your tab.

Be wary of motley bands of hotshots playing capoeira on the Terreiro de Jesus. Not only can you see better capoeira elsewhere, but if you even bat an eyelash in their direction, they will come scurrying across the plaza demanding a contribution. When you don't cough up, you will likely be accused of not supporting the arts. Just walk away, it's happened to them before.

Meandering vendors, especially the kids with the ribbons, will offer you things as a *regalo* (present; they often say 'presente,' as Spanish and English speakers understand this term). But as the street-weary say, nothing in life is free. Once you accept a free 'present,' you'll likely have to buy something in order to be free of your new vendor buddy.

See the boxed text on opposite for another prevalent scam.

SIGHTS

The Cidade Alta is packed with the city's most impressive sights, though you'll also find worthwhile museums in Vitória, scenic lighthouses in Barra and other fascinating attractions scattered about the city.

Cidade Alta

The centerpiece of the Cidade Alta is the **Pelourinho** (Map pp442–3), a Unesco-declared World Heritage site of colorful colonial buildings and magnificent churches. The area has undergone major restoration work – which remains ongoing – since 1993 thanks to Unesco funding. Admittedly, the Pelô has lost a lot of its character in the process, but to say that it is now safer and better preserved is an understatement.

As you wander the narrow streets, tripping over cobblestones and gazing up at the city's oldest architecture, you'll realize that the Pelô is not just for tourists. Cultural centers and schools of music, dance and capoeira pack these pastel-colored 17th- and 18th-century buildings.

IGREJA E CONVENTO SÃO FRANCISCO

One of Brazil's most magnificent churches, the baroque **Igreja e Convento São Francisco** (Map pp442-3;

Cruzeiro de São Francisco; admission R$3; 8:30am-5:30pm Mon-Sat, 1-5pm Sun) is crammed with displays of wealth and splendor. An 80kg silver chandelier dangles over ornate wood carvings smothered in gold leaf, and the convent courtyard is paneled with hand-painted *azulejos* (Portuguese tiles). The complex was finished in 1723.

Forced to build their masters' church and yet prohibited from practicing their own religion, African slave artisans responded through their work: the faces of the cherubs are distorted, some angels are endowed with huge sex organs, while others appear pregnant. Most of these creative touches were chastely covered by 20th-century sacristans.

The polychrome figure of São Pedro da Alcântara by Manoel Inácio da Costa shows a figure suffering from tuberculosis – just like the artist himself. One side of the saint's face is more ashen than the other, so he appears to become more ill as you walk past him. José Joaquim da Rocha painted the entry hall's ceiling using perspective technique, a novelty during the baroque period.

TERREIRO DE JESUS

A colorful intersection of vendors, tourists, capoeiristas and colorful locals, the **Terreiro de Jesus** (Map pp442-3; Praça 15 de Novembro) is a historic site of religious celebrations, and is ringed by four churches, as well as the 19th-century **Faculdade de Medicina Building**. The plaza feeds into the **Cruzeiro de São Francisco**, named for the cross in the square's center.

MUSEU AFRO-BRASILEIRO

Holding one of Bahia's most important collections, the **Museu Afro-Brasileiro** (Map pp442-3; 3321 2013; Terreiro de Jesus; admission R$5; 9am-6pm Mon-Fri, 10am-5pm Sat & Sun) exhibits wood carvings, baskets, pottery and other artwork and crafts linking Brazilian and African artistic traditions. The highlight of the museum is a room lined with 27 huge, breathtaking carved wooden panels by Argentine-born Carybé, who is perhaps Salvador's most renowned 20th-century fine artist. The panels are stylized depictions of *orixás* (deities of the Afro-Brazilian religions), inlaid with shells and metals. There's also a worthwhile exhibit of photography, sacred objects and ceremonial apparel demonstrating the African roots of Brazilian Candomblé (p450).

IGREJA DA ORDEM TERCEIRA DO CARMO

The original **Igreja da Ordem Terceira do Carmo** (Map pp442-3; Largo do Carmo; admission R$2; 8am-noon & 2-5pm Mon-Fri), founded in 1636, burnt to the ground; the present crumbling neoclassical structure dates from 1828. The nave has a French organ and a baroque altar with a scandalous statue of Nossa Senhora do Carmo. Church historians claim the statue was modeled in the likeness of Isabel II, the daughter of Garcia d'Ávila (of Praia do Forte fame), the largest landholder in the Northeast. The artist, known as O Cabra (Half-caste), was a slave with no artistic training, who was supposedly besotted with Isabel II. The Christ-child cradled in the statue's arms has Black features – could this be what O Cabra imagined their love child would look like? O Cabra took eight years to finish the life-size image of Christ (1630), with blood made from 2000 rubies. It's on display in the church's small museum.

CATEDRAL BASÍLICA

The **Catedral Basílica** (Map pp442-3; Terreiro de Jesus; admission R$2; 9-11am & 2-5pm Mon-Sat, 10am-noon Sun) dates from 1672 and is a marvelous example of Jesuit architecture. The interior is elegant and simple, with marble-covered walls and pillars that emphasize verticality. The sacristy has a beautiful carved jacaranda archway and a painted dome and floor.

HELPING HAND OR AIDING THE PROBLEM?

In the Pelourinho, everyone and their mother will ask you for something, even if it's just a sip of your water. You will be shown unfilled prescriptions, broken limbs, infants and empty bellies. Street kids may lead you to the store to buy them powdered milk. It is of course up to you whether you believe their stories, but it should be remembered that the use of drugs such as crack and solvents is high in this impoverished community. Everything from the can of milk, a sandwich, your wrapped-up dinner leftovers and, obviously, cash is capable of being traded for drugs. The best way to help someone out – and make sure you aren't being had – is to buy them food and have a chat with them as they eat it in front of you.

BAHIA

CHURCH SECRETS

A little-known fact is that the churches in the historic center are connected by a network of underground tunnels that feed to the port and the Forte de Santo Antônio. Supposedly they were constructed for defensive purposes, but one can't help but wonder what else they were used for. (Romantic encounters? Illegal slave trade? Contraband smuggling?)

LARGO DO PELOURINHO

The steep **Largo do Pelourinho** (Map pp442-3; Praça José de Alencar) is a wide square that was once the site of the *pelourinho* (whipping post), where slaves were auctioned (historians disagree about whether slaves were publicly tortured here).

MUSEU DA CIDADE

Rather like the city itself, **Museu da Cidade** (Map pp442-3; Largo do Pelourinho; admission R$3; ☺ 9am-6pm Mon & Wed-Fri, 1-5pm Sat, 9am-1pm Sun) contains an eclectic assortment of the old and the modern, the sacred and the profane. Exhibits include Candomblé *orixá* costumes, the personal effects of the poet Castro Alves (author of *Návio Negreiro*, Slave Ship, and one of the first public figures to protest slavery), and traditional rag dolls enacting quotidian colonial life, as well as paintings and sculptures.

IGREJA NS DO ROSÁRIO DOS PRETOS

The king of Portugal gave the Irmanidade dos Homens Pretos (Brotherhood of Black Men) the land for the periwinkle-blue **Igreja NS do Rosário dos Pretos** (Map pp442-3; Largo do Pelourinho; admission by donation; ☺ 9am-6pm Mon-Fri, 9am-2pm Sat & Sun) in 1704. Building in their free time, it took these slaves and freed slaves almost 100 years to complete it. The rococo facade includes design elements pertaining to Candomblé (ask a guide to point them out) and tiled towers with an Indian flavor.

FUNDAÇÃO CASA DE JORGE AMADO

If you read Portuguese, pay a visit to the **Fundação Casa de Jorge Amado** (Map pp442-3; ☎ 3321 0070; Largo do Pelourinho; admission free; ☺ 9am-6pm Mon-Sat) and learn about the life of Brazil's best-known international novelist (see the boxed text, p479). A wall of Amado's book covers in every major language demonstrates his widespread popularity. Free

screenings of the films based on his books are sometimes shown.

PRAÇA DA SÉ

The slick, L-shaped **Praça da Sé** has cool fountains and the fenced-off ruins of the foundations of its namesake church. A motley assortment of street performers congregate here, attracting crowds of locals and tourists alike. At the far end of the plaza, the 1874 funicular railway **Plano Inclinado Gonçalves** (Map pp442-3; fare R$0.05; ☺ 7am-7pm Mon-Fri, 7am-1pm Sat) rolls 30-passenger cars between Cidade Alta and Cidade Baixa on terrifyingly steep tracks.

ELEVADOR LACERDA

The beautifully restored, art-deco **Elevador Lacerda** (Map pp442-3; ☎ 3322 7049; R$0.05; ☺ 24hr) connects the Cidade Alta with Comércio, via four elevators traveling 72m in about 20 seconds. Jesuits installed the first manual rope-and-pulley elevator around 1610 to transport goods and passengers from the port to the settlement. In 1868 an iron structure with clanking steam elevators was inaugurated, replaced by an electric system in 1928. Facing the elevator are the impressive arches of the **Câmara Municipal**, the 17th-century city hall, which occasionally puts on cultural exhibitions.

PRAÇA MUNICIPAL & PALÁCIO RIO BRANCO

Once the political seat of colonial Brazil, the **Praça Municipal** (Map pp442-3; Praça Tomé de Souza) is now a lively place to people watch while enjoying a cool breeze. There are fine panoramic views over the bay – and free viewing telescopes for getting in close.

Overlooking the plaza, the impressive **Palácio Rio Branco** (Map pp442-3; ☎ 3322 7255; admission free; ☺ 2-7pm Mon, 9am-5pm Tue-Sat) was reconstructed in 1919 after being partially ruined in a bombing and subsequent fire. The original 1549 structure housed the offices of Tomé de Souza, Brazil's first governor general.

IGREJA DA ORDEM TERCEIRA DE SÃO FRANCISCO

Displeased with the inclusion of a Mason symbol – an eagle – in the facade of the **Igreja da Ordem Terceira de São Francisco** (Map pp442-3; Rua São Francisco; admission R$3; ☺ 8am-5pm), church fathers ordered the whole thing covered over in the late 18th century. It wasn't seen until a workman installing wiring in the 1930s serendipitously discovered the beautiful, baroque sandstone facade (the only one of its kind in Brazil). The church contains a museum with a random collection of priestly appurtenances and a room of Franciscan tombs.

MUSEU DE ARQUEOLOGIA E ETNOLOGIA

Below the Museu Afro-Brasileiro, the **Museu de Arqueologia e Etnologia** (Archaeology & Ethnology Museum; Map pp442-3; ☎ 3321 3971; Faculdade de Medicina Bldg, Terreiro de Jesus; admission R$5; ☉ 10am-5pm) exhibits indigenous Brazilian pottery, bows and arrows, masks and feather headpieces. Also tucked between the building's arching stone foundations is 19th-century glass and porcelain found during the excavations for the metro (a project halted due to a redirection of funds).

MUSEU DE ARTE SACRA DA BAHIA

Housed in a tranquil 17th-century cloister, the **Museu de Arte Sacra da Bahia** (Map pp440-1; ☎ 3243 6511; Rua do Sodré 276; admission R$5; ☉ 11:30am-5:30pm Mon-Fri) has high stone walls, a shady courtyard and bay views. Displayed in the former monks' quarters (of the Carmelitas Descalços, or Barefoot Carmelites order) is a collection of 17th- and 18th-century sacred art, including carvings from the demolished Igreja da Sé.

MUSEU DA MISERICÓRDIA

The newly opened **Museu da Misericórdia** (Map pp442-3; ☎ 3322 7355; Rua da Misericórdia 6; admission R$5; ☉ 10am-5pm Mon-Sat, 1-5pm Sun) is housed in yet another marvelous 17th-century edifice, this one serving as Brazil's first hospital. Visits here include a guided tour (in Portuguese) that allows a glimpse of fine period furnishings, portraits and assorted finery dating back four centuries. You'll also see the attached Igreja da Misericórdia, with its *azulejos* and a sacristy featuring impressive 18th-century woodwork.

LADEIRA DO CARMO

Leading away from the Pelourinho, the steep Ladeira do Carmo provides access to the **Escadas do Carmo** (Map pp442-3), a wide set of steps that were the setting of *O Pagador de Promessas* (1962). This was the first Brazilian film to win a Cannes film festival award. They lead to the eternally 'closed for renovation' **Igreja do Santíssimo Sacramento do Passo** (1737).

Also on this street is the **Oratório da Cruz do Pascoal** (Map pp440-1), plunked in the middle of the road, where believers gathered to pray for protection against demons and wayward souls.

Cidade Baixa

Interspersed between the Comércio's modern skyscrapers is some fantastic 19th-century architecture in various stages of decay.

MERCADO MODELO

The original 1861 Customs House was partially destroyed in a fire in 1986. After reconstruction, it was transformed into a tourist market, the Mercado Modelo (Map pp442-3). When shipments of new slaves arrived into port, they were stored in the watery depths of this building while awaiting auction. Night guards report all sorts of phantasmic activity after closing hours. Live music and free capoeira demonstrations often occur out back – be sure to ask the price before snapping photos of the capoeiristas. On a side note, you can see why the huge modernist sculpture beside the market is affectionately called *bunda* (butt) by locals.

SOLAR DO UNHÃO

The **Solar do Unhão** (Map pp440-1; Av do Contorno) is an 18th-century complex that served as a transfer point for sugar shipments. Legends say it is haunted by the ghosts of murdered slaves. Today, this dark place houses the **Museu de Arte Moderna** (☎ 3329 0660; admission free), with a changing display of avant-garde exhibits (and erratic opening times). A fine restaurant and an art workshop occupy the former store house. The hillside sculpture garden is a pleasant place to take a breath and enjoy the fine bay views. Take a taxi there, as it is off bus routes and the desolate walk is known for tourist muggings.

Vitória

This leafy suburb has several worthwhile museums on its main boulevard, and makes for a pleasant stop on a day out exploring the city beyond the Pelourinho.

MUSEU CARLOS COSTA PINTO

In a lovely two-story mansion, the **Museu Carlos Costa Pinto** (Map pp440-1; ☎ 3336 6081; www.museu costapinto.com.br; Av 7 de Setembro 2490; admission R$5, free on Thu; ☉ 2:30-7pm Wed-Mon) houses one of Salvador's best collections of decorative art.

Nicely lit displays highlight the unique works of talented artisans working in gold, crystal, porcelain and silver. Beautifully carved coral jewelry, tortoiseshell fans and elaborate *balangandans* (ethnic waist chains with attached charms) are among the highlights. Don't miss the charming outdoor café.

MUSE DE ARTE DA BAHIA

Set in an attractive neo-colonial edifice, the **Museu de Arte da Bahia** (Map pp440-1; ☎ 3117 6902; Av 7 de Setembro 2340; admission free; ☷ 2-7pm Tue-Sun) showcases works from Bahian artists, with paintings by José Teófilo de Jesus (1758–1817) among others. There's also an assortment of furniture and other antiques from the 18th and 19th centuries, as well as sacred art pieces.

North of the Center

To reach these sights north of the center, take a Ribeira or Bonfim bus from the base of the Elevador Lacerda.

The die-hard market fan will enjoy **Mercado São Joaquim** (☷ 6am-6pm Mon-Sat, 6am-2pm Sun), a small city of sketchy waterfront stalls about 2km north of the Elevador Lacerda. Puddles of green slime, a meat neighborhood capable of converting the unprepared into a devout vegetarian and bar stalls where rough hands grip glasses of rougher *cachaça* (sugarcane alcohol) let you know this is the real thing.

ITAPAGIPE PENINSULA

Jutting into the bay, a few kilometers north of Comércio, the Itapagipe Peninsula is a much-visited destination for the 18th-century **Igreja NS do Bonfim** (☎ 316 2196; admission free; ☷ 8am-noon & 2-5:30pm Tue-Sun). If you wonder where Pelourinho vendors get all their *fitas* (colored ribbons), look no further. As is printed on them, *fitas* are a souvenir of the Igreja NS do Bonfim and have come to symbolize Bahia itself. (If you sign on, and tie a *fita* around your wrist, you are making a commitment that lasts for months. With each of the three knots a wish is made, which come true by the time the *fita* falls off. Cutting it off is inviting doom.)

Bonfim's fame derives from its power to effect miraculous cures, which has transformed it from a rather ordinary church into a popular shrine. In the Sala dos Milagres (Room of Miracles) on the right side of the church, devotees leave photos, letters and *ex votos*: wooden and wax replicas of body parts left by those in need of curing (see the boxed text, p508).

Due to Candomblistas' syncretization of Jesus Christ (Nosso Senhor do Bonfim) with Oxalá, their highest deity, Bonfim is their most important church. Huge services are held hourly from 6am to 9am and at 5pm and 6pm on Fridays, Oxalá's day of the week. The 6am mass (first Friday of the month) attracts the most followers – wearing white is essential.

For a great view back to the center, walk 100m up the hill facing the church and stick to the left. By following the road around, down the hill and straight on for about 1km, you enter the Boa Viagem neighborhood and encounter the 16th-century **Forte de São Felipe** (☎ 3313 7339; Monte Serrat; ☷ 9am-5pm Tue-Sun). Below it is the **Praia da Boa Viagem**, which is lined with *barracas* (stalls) and is packed with locals from the surrounding neighborhoods on weekends. To the right is the **Ponta de Humaitá**, which has the Igreja NS de Monte Serrat (1650; closed to the public), a **lighthouse** and a 270-degree view over the bay. To return to the center, catch a bus to Terminal da França.

Barra

Barra's busy waterfront has three jutting points of land, occupied by the colonial forts of **Forte São Diogo**, **Forte Santa Maria** and the most impressive of the bunch, **Forte de Santo Antônio da Barra** (Map pp440-1; ☎ 3264 3296; admission R$6; ☷ 9am-7pm Tue-Sun). Built in 1698, Bahia's oldest fort is more commonly called the Farol da Barra for the lighthouse (South America's oldest) within its walls. In addition to having great views, the fort houses a small nautical museum, with relics and displays from the days of Portuguese seafaring. As you catch the sunset here, realize that Salvador's peninsula is the only location in Brazil where the sun appears to set over the ocean.

Beaches

Praia Porto da Barra (Map pp440-1) is rather like the Pelourinho: small, picturesque, usually crowded, loaded with vendors selling everything imaginable, and roughly half those present are foreigners. The bay's waters are clear and calm, and the people-watching is fantastic. To the left of the lighthouse, **Praia do Farol da Barra** has a beach break popular with surfers. Barra's waterfront is lined with bars and restaurants and is well lit at night, but it gets a bit sleazy in the later hours.

Smaller crowds and an unpolluted Atlantic are about 40 minutes' bus travel east from the center (or more with traffic), but it's worth it. Calm seas lap on flat white sands with *barracas* and swaying palms at popular city beaches **Piatã** (25km) and **Itapuã** (27km). As you reach **Stella Maris** (31km) and **Flamengo** (33km) beaches, the waves get progressively stronger, *barracas* begin to space out, and sand dunes and more greenery create a more natural setting. Catch an Itapuã, Aeroporto or Praia do Flamengo bus, making sure it goes up the coast *(via orla)* and as far as you are going.

COURSES
Capoeira, Dance & Percussion
Individual class prices range from R$10 to R$20, with discounts for longer commitments. The following are in the Pelourinho (Map pp442–3):

Associação Brasileira de Capoeira Angola (☎ 3387 4972; Rua Gregório de Mattos 38)

Diáspora Art Center (☎ 3323 0016; 3rd fl, Largo de São Francisco 21) Classes in traditional and contemporary Afro-Brazilian dance, capoeira and percussion.

Escola de Dança (☎ 3322 5350; Rua da Oração 1) Traditional and contemporary Afro-Brazilian dance, capoeira and percussion.

Fundação Mestre Bimba (☎ 3322 5082; Rua Gregório de Mattos 51) A school run by the son of the founder of Capoeira Regional, Mestre Bimba.

Mestre Lua (☎ 3488 3600; Rua Frei Vicente 19) To set up a percussion class, pass by this shop of instruments hand-made by the *mestre* himself.

Mestre Souza (☎ 3321 9783; Rua Frei Vicente 14) Afro-Brazilian drumming classes.

Cooking
Senac (☎ 3321 5502; Largo do Pelourinho 13-19) Cooking classes for tourists can be arranged at this cooking school and restaurant – contact the *coordenadora*, Profesora Celuta.

Language
The following schools offer group and private classes, and can set you up with a host family. A minimum one-week commitment is common. Contact the schools for the latest prices.

Associação Cultural Brasil-Estados Unidos (☎ 3336 4411; www.acbeubahia.org.br; Av 7 de Setembro, Vitória)

Diálogo (☎ 3264 0007; www.dialogo-brazilstudy.com; Rua Dr João Pondé 240, Barra) Music classes (singing), dance, cooking and capoeira are also offered.

Idioma Escola de Portuguêes (Map pp440-1; ☎ 3267 7012; www.portugueseinbrazil.com; 1st fl, Rua Greenfeld 46, Barra) Offers courses in capoeira and Bahian cooking.

CAPOEIRA

Capoeira was developed by slaves in Brazil as a means of maintaining a ready self-defense against their masters. It is said to have originated from a ritualistic African dance. Capoeira was prohibited by slave owners and banished from the *senzalas* (slave barracks), forcing slaves to practice clandestinely in the forest. Later, in an attempt to disguise this act of defiance from the authorities, capoeira was developed into a kind of acrobatic dance. The clapping of hands and striking of the *berimbau*, a one-string musical instrument that looks like a fishing rod, originally served to alert fighters to the approach of the boss and subsequently became incorporated into the dance to maintain the rhythm.

As recently as the 1920s, capoeira was still prohibited and Salvador's police chief sent out cavalry squads to ban it from the streets. In the 1930s, Mestre Bimba established his academy and changed the emphasis of capoeira from its original function as a tool of insurrection to a form of artistic expression that has become an institution in Bahia.

Today, there are two schools of capoeira: the slow and low Capoeira de Angola, led by Mestre Pastinha, and the more aggressive Capoeira Regional, initiated by Mestre Bimba. The former school believes capoeira came from Angola; the latter maintains it was born in the plantations of Cachoeira and other cities of the *recôncavo* region.

Capoeira combines the forms of the fight, the game and the dance. The movements are always fluid and circular, the fighters always playful and respectful as they exchange mock blows. Capoeira is typically practiced by two fighters at a time inside a *roda* (circle) of spectators/fighters who clap and sing. In addition to the *berimbau*, other instruments such as the *pandeiro* (tambourine), *agogô* (bell) and *atabaque* (drum) provide musical accompaniment. Capoeira gains more followers by the year, both nationally and abroad. Throughout Brazil – particularly Bahia – you will see people practicing their moves on the beach and street *rodas* popping up in touristy areas.

BAHIA

FESTIVALS & EVENTS

Salvador delights in its wild festivals, which have links to both Catholicism and Candomblé. Though Carnaval steals the show, there are numerous festivals, particularly in January and February. Check with Bahiatursa (p440) for dates.

Other Festivals

Processão do Senhor Bom Jesus dos Navegantes (January 1) A maritime procession transports the image of Bom Jesus from Igreja NS da Conceição in Cidade Baixa north along the bay to Igreja de NS da Boa Viagem. A festival ensues on Praia da Boa Viagem.

Festa da Lapinha (January 6) On the Dia de Reis, a procession of the *reis magos* (wise men) statues travels to a crèche in the Igreja da Lapinha.

Lavagem do Bonfim (second Thursday in January) In the morning, a procession of *baianas* (women dressed as Bahian 'aunts') in ritual dress carrying buckets of flowers walks 6km from Igreja NS da Conceição in Cidade Baixa to the Igreja NS do Bonfim. Here they perform a ritual *lavagem* (washing) of the church steps overseen by Catholic priests together with *mães de santo* (Candomblé

A NIGHT AMONG THE GODS *Regis St. Louis*

The wild and little understood Candomblé religion is deeply rooted in Bahian culture and connects countless Afro-Brazilians to a long line of West African ancestry. Ceremonies, held frequently throughout the year, take place in spacious, richly decorated halls called *terreiros*, and they can last for hours.

The celebrants are mostly women who arrive dressed in lace and hooped skirts. Drummers – all male – pound out powerful rhythms behind a gauzy curtain, and the dance begins. Around and around they go, with light steps at first, graceful hand motions accompanied by twirling skirts. The dancers, chanting in Yoruba, glide in a counter-clockwise circle, which represents the rolling back of the centuries, as they reach out to their ancestors. A festive, celebratory atmosphere prevails, with the *mãe de santo* or *pai de santo* (literally saint's mother or father – the Candomblé priests) and attendants watching over everyone from the center.

As the evening progresses, the music picks up, the dance becomes more heated, and over the drumming one can hear the chiming of bells – a haunting sound to conjure the spirits. The second phase of the ceremony is all about the dancers and the *orixás* – and the possession of one by the other.

Each candomblista has an *orixá*, and if a person has the gift (which not all have), he or she can become a medium for the spirit – going into a trance or becoming filled with frenetic energy. One's *orixá* can be male or female, regardless of one's own sex. Usually, when the spirit arrives, those dancing take on the attributes of that spirit.

On one recent steamy evening, I visited the Casa Brava, one of Salvador's oldest *terreiros*, and watched as a man shook and writhed – and even shrieked – as the spirit of Iansã, goddess of wind, entered him. As he shuttled about the room, another woman felt the presence of Changó. She stood in the center of the room for much of the evening as silent as a stone until the song dedicated to Changó was played and her energy was suddenly released. Other dancers showed the powerful strides of Ogun, god of war, or the predatory movements of Oxossi, god of hunters, while others simply danced madly about, occasionally letting out a loud cry.

Although it's discouraged, sometimes spectators go into trances, swooning and possibly collapsing as the ceremony continues. Others are just grateful to feel the energy from the celebrants. When those in the trance come by, they sometimes interact with spectators, exchanging hugs and caresses, in hopes of passing on the god's powerful energy from one to another.

The last part of the ceremony features elaborate costumes. The dancers leave the floor and return dressed as Orixás, and the dancing resumes long into the night.

Those interested in attending a ceremony should contact the **Federação Baiana do Culto Afro-Brasileiro** (Map pp442-3; ☎ 3321 1548; Rua Alfredo de Brito 39, Pelourinho; ◷ 9am-noon & 2-5pm Mon-Fri), which can provide schedules and addresses for some *terreiros*. Pelourinho travel agencies can arrange group visits. If you go without a guide, make sure there will be taxis for the return trip. Wear clean, light-colored clothes (no shorts).

For more on Candomblé, read the vivid tale *Tent of Miracles* by Jorge Amado, a Baiano and Candomblé initiate himself (Changó was his *orixá*).

priestesses). Then the Filhos de Gandhi and *trios elétricos* (trucks loaded with speakers) take the scene for a rowdy street party lasting into the night. This is Salvador's largest festival outside of Carnaval.

Festa de São Lázaro (last Sunday in January) A procession, ritual cleansing of the Igreja São Lázaro (Map pp440-1; end of Rua Professor Aristides Novis, São Lázaro) and festival honors the saint's Candomblé *orixá* counterpart Omolú (the god of plague and disease).

Festa de Iemanjá (February 2) Groups from local *terreiros* and other devotees of the *orixá* Iemanjá, goddess of the sea and fertility, descend on Praia Rio Vermelho in the morning, where ceremonies are held to bless offerings of flowers, cakes, effigies, cans of beer and bottles of perfume. Larger offerings are taken out to sea by boat to ensure they reach Iemanjá's hands. The ensuing street festival packs with people, some of Salvador's best bands and lasts into the night. This is probably Candomblé's most important festival.

Lavagem da Igreja de Itapuã (15 days before Carnaval) The actual church washing is a mini-version of Bonfim's, but the street party in Itapuã is loaded with *trios elétricos* and is equally raucous.

Festa de São João (June 23 to 24) Pyrotechnics and street parties spring up all over town and *genipapo* (local fruit) liqueur flows like water.

Festa Santa Bárbara (December 4 to 6) Rio Vermelho's Mercado do Peixe is probably the best place to catch this Candomblé festival celebrating markets.

Festa de NS da Conceição (December 8) Candomblistas honor the saint's *orixá* alter ego, Iemanjá, with a procession and ceremonies in Cidade Baixa.

Passagem do Ano Novo (December 31) New Year's Eve is celebrated with all the zest of Carnaval, especially on the beaches.

SLEEPING

Staying in Cidade Alta means being close to the action, but the beach suburbs are mellower. Santo Antônio is a peaceful neighborhood with classy pousadas in renovated old buildings, just a short walk from the Pelourinho. Reservations during Carnaval are essential.

Pelourinho
BUDGET

Albergue do Passo (Map pp442-3; ☎ 3326 1951; www .passoyouthhostel.com.br; Rua do Passo 3; dm/d R$20/70) This friendly, basic hostel has six-bed dorms, which are popular with a wide range of travelers.

Pousada da Praça Hotel (Map pp442-3; ☎ 3321 0642; www.pousadadapracahotel.com.br; Rua Rui Barbosa 5; dm R$27, s/d without bathroom R$38/65, with bathroom R$45/77) A few blocks south of the cobblestones, this

popular budget hotel has attractive two-tone wood floors and tidy fan-cooled rooms that open onto the street. The quiet back porch is a fine place to unwind.

Albergue da Juventude do Pelô (Map pp442-3; ☎ 3242 8061; www.alberguedopelo.com.br; Rua do Passo 5; dm R$28) A popular option among Salvador's many hostels, the Albergue da Juventude do Pelô has basic rooms (with six to 12 beds in each) and a small but comfy lounge.

Albergue das Laranjeiras (Map pp442-3; ☎ 3321 1366; www.laranjeirashostel.com.br; Rua Inácio Accioli 13; dm R$32, d without/with bathroom R$92/120) This attractive, well-organized HI hostel is set in a restored colonial building in the heart of the action. Dorm rooms have staggered beds like hanging trays, while private rooms are artfully designed (though small). Hammocks are strung about, and there's an inviting café on the first floor.

Hotel Arthemis (Map pp442-3; ☎ 3322 0724; www .arthemishotel.com.br, in Portuguese; Edifício Themis, Praça da Sé 398; s/d R$35/55, with view R$55/65) The view over the bay and Pelourinho makes a stunning addition to your breakfast at this hotel occupying the entire 7th floor of an apartment building. Rooms are large but extremely basic – cinderblock windows on one side, glass windows with bay view on the other. The location and price, however, are unbeatable.

MIDRANGE & TOP END

Hotel Maridina (Map pp442-3; ☎ 3242 7176; www.hotel maridina.com.br; Av 7 de Setembro 6; s/d from R$60/90; ⊠) A 10-minute walk south of Pelô, Maridina is a friendly, simple hotel where small, clean rooms have polished wood floors and decent natural light.

Solar dos Romanos (Map pp442-3; ☎ 3322 6158; www .hotelsolardosromanos.com.br; Rua Alfredo de Brito 14; s/d with fan R$100/115, with air-con R$120/135; ⊠) Run by a friendly older couple, this guesthouse has an assortment of rooms scattered over four floors. All are clean, a little dark and sparsely furnished; some have partial bay views, while others have decorative balconies overlooking the (noisy) pedestrian street.

Hotel Villa Bahia (Map pp442-3; ☎ 3322 4271; www .lavillabahia.com; Largo do Cruzeiro de São Francisco 16; s/d R$600/800; ⊠ ⊠) In a lovely colonial building near the Igreja São Francisco, this boutique hotel has just 17 rooms, each with wood floors, shuttered windows and antique furnishings (solid armoires, chandeliers). There's an excellent restaurant on the 1st floor.

Carmo & Santo Antônio

BUDGET

Nega Maluca (Map pp440-1; ☎ 3242 9249; www.nega maluca.com.br; Rua dos Marchantes 15; dm with fan R$24, d without/with bathroom R$52/60; ☐) This small, friendly guesthouse is a favorite for its warm welcome and the good mix of travelers it seems to attract. Guests have access to the kitchen, the peaceful back deck and lots of local insight from the well-traveled expat owners.

Pousada Hilmar (Map pp440-1; ☎ 3243 4959; www .pousadahilmar.com.br; Rua Direita de Santo Antônio 136; s/d with fan R$45/65, with air-con R$55/75; ☒) One of the more affordable options in the neighborhood, Hilmar has basic rooms with tile floors and tiny bathrooms. Rooms vary in size and ventilation, so have a look before committing.

CARNAVAL

Salvador's Carnaval is the second largest in Brazil and, according to Brazil's youth, the best. Usually held in February or March, it always begins on a Thursday night and ends the next Wednesday at dawn. In the days between, two million revelers take to the streets to dance, drink and kiss until they drop, get up the next day and start again.

The focus is on nationally famous city bands playing *axé* and *pagode* (Bahia's pop music) atop creeping *trios elétricos* (long trucks loaded with huge speakers). Between them march a few *blocos afros* (groups with powerful drum corps promoting Afro-Brazilian culture) and *afoxés* (groups tied to Candomblé traditions).

Each year the city designates a theme for Carnaval, and decorates the city accordingly. Since the *trios elétricos* are not decorated, and the bands dress like rock stars, the only elements of pageantry come from the *blocos afros* and the *afoxés*. The brotherhood Filhos de Gandhi (Sons of Gandhi) fills the avenue with its *afoxé* group, dressed alike in white terrycloth turbans, white sari-esque robes and their characteristic blue-and-white beads. Their favorite trick is splashing onlookers with cologne.

A *trio eléctrico* or a drum corps, together with its followers grouped in a roped-off area around it, form a *bloco*. People pay up to R$500 for the *abadá* (shirt or costume required for entry to a *bloco*) for their favorite band, mostly for prestige and the safety of those ropes.

Choosing to *fazer pipoca* (be popcorn) in the street is still a fine way to spend Carnaval, as you'll see a variety of music and be spared the hassle involved with picking up the *abadá*. You can also escape some of the madness by buying a day in a *camarote*, the walled-off, roadside bleachers with their own facilities. Head to the tourist office for information on *camarote* tickets.

There are three main Carnaval circuits: the beachside Barra to Rio Vermelho circuit (where most tourists hang out), the narrow Campo Grande to Praça Castro Alves circuit, and the Pelourinho (no *trios* here, mostly concerts and parading drum corps). Some neighborhoods also hold their own parties. Bahiatursa and Emtursa publish a schedule of events with a route map.

Crowds clearing (in order to escape a fight) pose the greatest threat during Carnaval, so be aware of your surroundings. A large police presence helps to keep violence to a minimum. On the Barra–Rio Vermelho circuit, avoid the section where the coastal road narrows near the Morro do Cristo – the tension heats up there. Hands will be all over you, searching your pockets and groping the ladies. To have a trouble-free Carnaval, take note of the following:

■ Carry only a small amount of money and stash it in your shoe.

■ Stash a photocopy of your passport somewhere private.

■ Leave any jewelry, watches or nice-looking sunglasses in your hotel.

■ Don't challenge pickpockets – the ensuing fight isn't worth it.

■ Form small groups.

■ Women should not walk alone or wear skirts (hands will be up them in no time).

■ Avoid deserted places, especially narrow alleyways.

For more info on Salvador's Carnaval, visit www.portaldocarnaval.ba.gov.br (in Portuguese).

MIDRANGE

our pick **Studio do Carmo** (Map pp442-3; ☎ 3243 0646; www.studiodocarmo.com.br; Ladeira do Carmo 17; d R$135-150) Above an art gallery, this guesthouse offers just four rooms – each beautifully set with polished wood floors, big windows, artwork and fresh flowers. All have small kitchen units, and a delightful breakfast is brought to your door.

Pousada do Baluarte (Map pp440-1; ☎ 3327 0367; www.pousadabaluarte.com; Ladeira do Baluarte 13; s/d from R$130/150; 🔲) Run by a friendly French-Brazilian couple, Baluarte feels more like a B&B, with just six rooms amid a welcoming, home-like ambience. All the rooms feature two-toned wood floors, and are hung with the marvelous block prints of local artist Nilo. Several rooms are ensuite, while others share a bathroom. Baluarte is just around the corner from the Forte de Santo Antônio.

Pousada do Boqueirão (Map pp440-1; ☎ 3241 2262; www.pousadaboqueirao.com.br; Rua Direita de Santo Antônio 48, Santo Antônio; s/d without bathroom R$65/85, with bathroom R$150/180) Two early-20th-century houses have been joined together to form this elegant pousada, tastefully decorated with antiques and artwork. Spacious common rooms back onto a porch with a fantastic bay view. Upper-story rooms have verandas with views.

TOP END

Solar do Carmo (Map pp440-1; ☎ 3323 0644; www.solardocarmo.com.br; Rua Direita de Santo Antônio 108; d R$168-210; 🔲) In a recently restored colonial building, Solar do Carmo has clean, modern rooms with exposed brick walls. The best rooms have decorative balconies overlooking the street.

Pousada das Flores (Map pp440-1; ☎ 3243 1836; www.pflores.com.br; Rua Direita de Santo Antônio 442; d from R$200) In a charming 18th-century home, Pousada das Flores has a mix of attractive spacious rooms with vaulted ceilings and wide-plank wooden floors. The cheapest rooms lack windows, while upper-floor rooms have verandas with potted plants and idyllic views over the neighborhood.

Villa Santo Antônio (Map pp440-1; ☎ 3326 1270; www.hotel-santoantonio.com; Rua Direita de Santo Antônio 130; d with fan/air-con/terrace R$200/250/300; 🔲) Among a growing crop of well-dressed guesthouses in Santo Antônio, this one offers value for the money. Its stylish rooms have polished wood floors and are decorated with original artwork and other thoughtful touches. Rooms with a terrace overlook the bay.

Convento do Carmo (Map pp442-3; ☎ 3327 8400; www.pousadas.pt; Rua do Carmo 1; d from R$600; 🔲 🔲 🔲) Set in a restored 17th-century convent, this magnificent hotel has elegantly furnished rooms with old-world details and modern comforts, and even more impressive common areas. There's a stone chapel, arched walkways around the cloister (set with a pool and greenery) and an excellent restaurant.

Vitória

Hotel Vila Velha (Map pp440-1; ☎ 3336 8722; www.hotelvilavelha.com.br, in Portuguese; Av 7 de Setembro 1971; d R$105; 🔲 🔲) Vila Velha is a friendly spot with small, somewhat worn rooms, the best with partial bay views.

Hotel Bahia do Sol (Map pp440-1; ☎ 3338 8800; www.bahiadosol.com.br, in Portuguese; Av 7 de Setembro 2009, Vitória; s/d R$148/165; 🔲) This pleasant, recently renovated hotel has cheerful yellow rooms with tile floors, sizeable windows and sleek modern bathrooms.

Hotel Sol Victória Marina (Map pp440-1; ☎ 3336 7736; www.solbahia.com.br; Av 7 de Setembro 2068, Vitória; s/d R$280/300; 🔲 🔲) Surrounded by other highrises, this modern hotel offers comfortably furnished rooms with somewhat dated décor, and the best rooms have bay views. The best feature is the private cable car that descends the steep cliff to the bay where a sun deck, swimming dock and bar/restaurant await.

Barra & Coastal Suburbs

Of all the beachside suburbs, happening Barra attracts the majority of visitors due to its proximity to the Pelourinho (roughly 5km). During Carnaval, the further from the waterfront between the Farol da Barra and Praia de Ondina, the quieter it should be.

BUDGET

Camping Ecológico (☎ 3374 0102; Alameda da Praia, Stella Maris; per person R$12) Flat, shady campsites near Praia de Catussaba with hot showers and a restaurant serving breakfast.

Hostel Jardim Brasil (Map pp440-1; ☎ 3264 9637; www.hostelbrasil.com.br; Rua Recife 4, Jardim Brasil, Barra; dm with fan/air-con R$26/32, d with fan/air-con R$62/70; 🔲 🔲) Close to lively bars and restaurants, Hostel Jardim Brasil has simple dorms separated by sex and a few basic private rooms. While lacking in charm, the location is excellent, and there's a good mix of travelers here. Guests have access to a kitchen and laundry.Behind Shopping Barra.

BAHIA

Pousada Âmbar (Map pp440-1; ☎ 3264 6956; www .ambarpousada.com.br; Rua Afonso Celso 485, Barra; dm R$35, d with fan R$100) A favorite among travelers, this lovely pousada has a relaxed atmosphere and a welcoming vibe. Private rooms are small, but there's ample outdoor lounge space with hammocks. Dorms have eight beds.

MIDRANGE

Barra Guesthouse (Map pp440-1; ☎ 3235 3245; www .barraguesthouse.com.br; Rua Recife 234, Barra; dm/s/d R$35/70/120; ✉ ▭) Located on a residential street, Barra Guesthouse is run by a friendly British-Brazilian couple who open their house and make travelers feel right at home. Rooms have wood parquet floors and vary in size. The beach, restaurants and bars are within walking distance.

Pousada Farol da Barra (Map pp440-1; ☎ 3264 7032; www.pousadasjovelina.com; Av Oceânica 171, Barra; s/d R$90/110; ✉) One of Barra's best deals, this charming guesthouse has spacious rooms with wood floors and marvelous bay views. Although there are just three rooms here, the owner runs a network of other cozy, similarly priced guesthouses in Barra.

Pousada Noa Noa (Map pp440-1; ☎ 3264 1148; www .pousadanoanoa.com; Av Sete de Setembro 4295, Barra; d R$110-130; ✉) This small, welcoming guest-house offers 15 nicely decorated rooms (four have views) and attractive common areas making good use of its oceanside location.

Pousada Azul (Map pp440-1; ☎ 3264 9798; www .pousadaazul.com.br; Rua Praguer Froes 102, Barra; s/d R$90/120; ✉) Azul is a sweet, safe, well-cared-for pousada close to the beach and bus stops. Spacious, comfortable rooms are sparsely furnished with polished wood floors and gleaming white bathrooms.

TOP END

Villa Romana (Map pp440-1; ☎ 3264 6748; www.villa romana.com.br; Rua Prof Lemos de Brito 14, Barra; s/d R$150/210; ✉ ▭) Set on a hill in a quiet part of Barra, Villa Romana has polished wood floors and an inviting lobby/sitting room laden with antiques. The rooms are pleasant, but much simpler, and some are rather small. Several rooms have sea views.

Hotel Catharina Paraguaçu (☎ 3334 0089; www.hotel catharinaparaguacu.com.br; Rua João Gomes 128, Rio Vermelho; s/d R$170/190; ✉) A mix colonial-modern mix, this charming hotel is decorated with beautiful tiles and antiques. The gardens and rooms are quite nice, but loud traffic noise from the busy avenues on either side does detract. Just off Largo de Santana.

Pousada Encanto de Itapoan (☎ 3285 3505; www .encantodeitapoan.com.br; Rua Nova Canaã 48, Farol de Itapuã; s/d R$180/200; ✉ ▭ ▣) A beach-lovers retreat outside the busy city center, this guesthouse has small, pleasantly set rooms, each with sliding glass doors opening onto a balcony facing a vine- and orchid-covered wall. The beach and good restaurants are just a short stroll from your door.

Grande Hotel da Barra (Map pp440-1; ☎ 2106 8600; www.grandehoteldabarra.com.br; Av Sete de Setembro 3564; d R$194-210; ✉ ▭ ▣) Across the road from the Forte São Diogo, the six-story Grande Hotel has plain but modern rooms, with tile floors and sizeable windows. It's worth the extra reais for the small balcony with ocean view. There's a restaurant serving local and international fare onsite.

Sol Barra (Map pp440-1; ☎ 3264 7011; www.solexpress .com.br; Av Sete de Setembro 3564; d from R$210; ✉ ▭ ▣) This enormous high-rise offers clean, simple rooms with white tile floors and big windows, the best of which offer partial ocean views.

EATING

Salvador has an excellent assortment of restaurants, some with great ambience and live music (cover charges are around R$5). Typical Bahian cuisine has a heavy African influence and features ingredients like coconut cream, tomato, bell pepper and spices of ginger, hot peppers and coriander. Seafood and *dendê* oil (a heavy palm oil) are also thrown into the mix. *Dendê* has a reputation for stirring up trouble in travelers' bellies, so sample sparingly until you've become accustomed.

Pelourinho

The Pelourinho is packed with restaurants of every description and price level. It's also worth wandering up Rua do Carmo and out the Rua Direita de Santo Antônio for a mix of bohemian and bourgeois.

A Cubana Pelourinho (Map pp442-3; ☎ 321 6162; Rua Alfredo de Brito 12; ◷ 9am-10pm Sun-Thu, 9am-midnight Fri & Sat); Praça Municipal (Map pp442-3; ☎ 322 7000; Praça Municipal; ◷ 9am-10pm Mon-Wed, 9am-midnight Thu-Sun) One of Salvador's oldest and best ice-cream shops.

Berinjela (Map pp442-3; ☎ 3322 0247; Travessa da Ajuda 1, Cidade Alta; mains R$4-6; ◷ lunch Mon-Sat) This atmospheric used bookstore serves a tasty, inexpensive vegetarian plate of the day as well as sandwiches and juices.

Panorámico (Map pp442-3; ☎ 3321 2243; Rua das Laranjeiras 18; per kg R$19; ❂ lunch & dinner) Popular for its filling lunch buffet, Panorámica is hidden on the 2nd floor of an old, characterful building.

Coliseu (Map pp442-3; ☎ 3321 5585; Cruzeiro de São Francisco 9; per kg R$22; ❂ lunch) Look for a costumed *baiana* (Bahian aunt) handing out tickets in the doorway to find this excellent restaurant on an upper floor. Vegetarians will love the huge salad bar, and many of the dishes are regional.

Don Rafaello (Map pp442-3; ☎ 323 0078; Rua Alfredo de Brito 31; mains R$15-24; ❂ lunch & dinner) Although there's better pizza elsewhere, Don Rafaello serves up fast, decent bites that won't break the bank. Grab a seat in back for nightly jam sessions on Praça Quincas Berro d'Agua.

La Lupa (Map pp442-3; ☎ 3322 0066; Rua das Laranjeiras 17; mains R$15-25; ❂ lunch & dinner) This small, elegant Italian restaurant serves tasty plates of gnocchi, risotto and other Mediterranean plates, though the seafood pastas are tops.

O Nilo (Map pp442-3; ☎ 3495 3578; Rua Laranjeiras 44; mains R$15-30; ❂ lunch Thu-Sun, dinner daily) On a restaurant-lined stretch of cobblestones, Nilo offers delicious falafel plates, Moroccan couscous with beef and other satisfying Middle Eastern dishes.

Mamabahia (Map pp442-3; ☎ 3322 4397; Rua das Portas do Carmo 21; mains R$15-40; ❂ lunch & dinner) Although the décor is uninspiring, this *churrascaria* (barbecued meat house) is an excellent place to enjoy fresh-grilled plates of steak.

Pizzeria Romolo e Remo (Map pp442-3; ☎ 3321 8060; Rua das Laranjeiras 27; mains R$18-22; ❂ dinner) Serving up some of Salvador's best thin-crust pizzas, this airy pizzeria has a pleasant outdoor terrace, where crowds feast on pizza, crostini and *dolci* like tiramisu or panna cotta.

Restaurante Matusalem (Map pp442-3; ☎ 3321 5598; Rua das Laranjeiras 28; mains for 2 R$40-70; ❂ lunch & dinner) A top choice for Bahian food, welcoming Matusalem has excellent *moquecas* (fish stew in clay pots) and other Northeastern favorites, plus fresh grilled meats served up Mineiran style.

Maria Mata Mouro (Map pp442-3; ☎ 3321 3929; Rua Inácio Accioli 8; mains for 2 R$40-80; ❂ lunch & dinner) The cozy garden patio or classically set dining room are fine settings to enjoy one of Pelô's top menus. Among an excellent range of pastas, seafood, grilled meats and all the Bahian favorites, you'll find unique dishes like lamb in tamarind sauce and rich paella.

Dona Chika-ka (Map pp442-3; ☎ 3321 1712; Rua João Castro Rabelo 10; mains for 2 R$45-60; ❂ dinner Mon-Sat) Flickering candles lead the way up to a charmingly decorated 2nd-floor dining room, where you can feast on Dona Chika-ka's famous *bobó de camarão* and other Bahian delights.

Sorriso da Dadá (Map pp442-3; ☎ 321 9642; Rua Frei Vicente 5; mains for 2 R$45-65; ❂ lunch & dinner) This casual, lively restaurant is known for its seafood – try the *moqueca*. Photos along the wall attest to Sorriso's celebrity status.

Senac (Map pp442-3; ☎ 321 5502; Largo do Pelourinho 13-19; buffet R$30; ❂ lunch & dinner Mon-Sat) With the best buffet in town, the cooking school Senac spreads a tempting array of Bahian dishes. Sample some 40 regional dishes plus desserts. There's also a small self-service restaurant (*por-kilo* R$18) open for lunch Monday to Friday.

Carmo & Santo Antônio

Cafélier (Map pp442-3; ☎ 3241 5095; Rua do Carmo 50; snacks R$2-8; ❂ 2-9pm Mon & Wed-Sat) Hidden behind a small storefront of antiques, this pleasant hideaway café has strong coffee, rich desserts and other snacks, and bay views.

Ristorante Al Carmo (Map pp440-1; ☎ 3242 0283; Rua do Carmo 66; mains R$16-25; ❂ lunch Tue-Sat, dinner Mon-Sat) In a charming 19th-century building, this inviting Italian restaurant has an upstairs terrace where you can enjoy rich pasta dishes (pumpkin tortellini in gorgonzola sauce) or fresh plates of grilled fish and steak.

Cidade Baixa

In the Comércio, cheap *lancheonetes* (snack bars) and self-service restaurants abound. For something more memorable, grab a bite at one of the casual restaurants on the 2nd floor of the Mercado Modelo. South along the bay are several excellent restaurants.

OUR PICK Restaurant Solar do Unhão (Map pp440-1; ☎ 329 5551; Av do Contorno 8; mains for 2 R$48-64; ❂ lunch & dinner Mon-Sat, show 8:30pm) The Solar do Unhão is set in an 18th-century *senzala* (slave quarters) that was part of the larger surrounding sugar mill. Thankfully, that oppressive era is long over, and you can experience something for which the place seems better suited – serving up fantastic plates of fresh seafood. Grab a table on the breezy back dock. The restaurant hosts an impressive nightly folkloric show (R$25). Take a taxi as it's unsafe to walk here.

Soho (Map pp440-1; ☎ 3322 4554; Av do Contorno 1010; dinner for 2 R$50-80; ❂ lunch Tue-Sun, dinner daily; ❂)

BAHIA

This stylish Japanese restaurant has an impressive bay view and spreads succulent plates of sashimi, sushi, along with other traditional Japanese fare.

Trapiche Adelaide (Map pp440-1; ☎ 3326 2211; Av do Contorno; mains R$40-60; ☺ lunch & dinner Mon-Sat) One of Salvador's finest restaurants serves creative and delectable cuisine in a lovely setting overlooking the bay. Top-notch service, fine views and unique flavors (octopus carpaccio, lamb chops, sesame-crusted tuna with wasabi) mean you'll be dining among Salvador's A-list crowd.

Barra & Coastal Suburbs

Some of the restaurants in the coastal suburbs have superb tropical ambience – dining with sea views.

Ramma (Map pp440-1; ☎ 3264 0044; Rua Lord Cochrane 76, Barra; per kg R$22; ☺ lunch Sun-Fri; ☒) Specializing in freshly prepared organic food (including vegetarian options), Ramma is a good place for a healthy lunch.

Casa da Dinha (☎ 3334 1703; Largo de Santana 25, Rio Vermelho; mains R$20-25; ☺ noon-last client) Dinha is the most famous *baiana* in the city, and her *acarajé* (shrimp croquettes) are renowned. Her nearby counterpart, Cira on Largo da Mariquita, is equally good (and is also on the water in Itapuã).

Paraíso Tropical (☎ 3335 0557; Rua Feira de Santana 354, Rio Vermelho; mains R$30-50; ☺ lunch & dinner) One of Salvador's top restaurants, Paraíso Tropical serves beautifully prepared Bahian cuisine with a twist. Expect long waits on weekends.

Mistura Fina (☎ 3375 2623; Rua Prof Souza Brito 41, Itapúa; mains R$30-50; ☺ lunch & dinner; ☒) The ambience is airy and bright at this fantastic seafood restaurant with outdoor seating.

DRINKING

The Pelourinho is Salvador's nightlife capital and is filled with bars offering outside tables on the cobbled streets. In Barra, outdoor ambience and live music are found along Av Almirante Marques de Leão and the waterfront between the Farol da Barra; Rua Recife and the Morro do Cristo also have some popular bars. Bohemian Rio Vermelho has by far the hottest nightlife scene along the Atlantic shore and a reputation for drawing all types. Its Largo de Santana and Largo de Mariquita are lined with outdoor restaurants and bars that fill up nightly.

Pelourinho & Santo Antônio

Habeas Copus Barra (Map pp440-1; ☎ 3267 4996; Av Almirante Marquês de Leão 172; ☺ 5:30pm-last client Tue-Sat, 10am-last client Sun); Pelourinho (Map pp442-3; ☎ 3321 1798; Rua Alfredo de Brito 31; ☺ 8pm-last client) Habeas Copus is a popular old favorite in the Pelô's Praça Quincas Berro d'Agua, which has a few bars that back onto it and face a common stage area. Things get a little seedy as the evening wears on. The Barra location tends to draw an older crowd.

Estação de Pelô (Map pp442-3; cnr Rua João de Deus & Gregório de Matos, Pelourinho; ☺ 5pm-1am) One of many bar/restaurants with live music in the Pelô, this one is particularly charming, with tables spilling onto the small plaza, and vendors and local characters adding to the colorful scene.

Cantina da Lua (Map pp442-3; ☎ 3241 7383; Terreiro de Jesus, Pelourinho; ☺ 11am-last client) This outdoor patio bar and restaurant is prime people-watching territory, given its setting in the heart of the Pelourinho. Live music nightly ranges from vocals to salsa.

Cidade Baixa

Bahia Café (Map pp440-1; ☎ 3328 1332; Mirante dos Aflitos; ☺ 5:30pm-last client Tue-Sun) Located just south of the Pelô, this slightly upscale bar has an eclectic environment, great food and a choice of three dozen cocktails to enjoy with those great bay views.

Bar da Ponta (Map pp440-1; ☎ 3326 2211; Av do Contorno; ☺ 5pm-1am Tue-Sat) This small, stylish bar is set on the end of a pier perched over the bay, making it a draw around sunset. Expect a well-dressed crowd and pricey cocktails as well as excellent *petiscos* (bar bites).

Quixabeira (Map pp440-1; ☎ 328 3286; Travessa dos Barris 30, Barris) A mixed crowd frequents this gay-friendly bar to enjoy drinks and small bites in a charming old house; there's often live music in the pleasant back patio.

Barra & Coastal Suburbs

Pereira (Map pp440-1; ☎ 3264 6464; Av Sete de Setembro 3959, Barra; mains $22; ☺ lunch Thu-Sun & 6pm-late) On Barra's seaside road, Pereira is a stylish indoor and outdoor bar with a Japanese restaurant and a wine bar attached. Excellent *chope* (draft beer) is on tap.

Bar do Chico (Map pp440-1; ☎ 3267 4386; Rua Recife 86, Barra; ☺ noon-2am) In an area of lively bars, this spot attracts a fun, festive crowd; there are other indoor-outdoor spots next door.

Barra Vento (Map pp440-1; ☎ 247 2577; Av Oceanica, Barra; ☯ 10-3am) Barra's only waterfront bar and restaurant is a choice spot for a sundowner.

Póstudo (☎ 3334 0484; Rua João Gomes 87, Rio Vermelho; ☯ noon-3pm & 6pm-last client Mon-Sat) This perpetually cool bar and restaurant has an ocean view and is known for its flavorful fare.

Extudo (☎ 3334 0671; Rua Lídio Mesquita 4, Rio Vermelho; ☯ noon-last client Tue-Sun; ☒) Frequented by those dialed in on Salvador's arts scene, it has dishes appropriately named after famous cinematic and literary works. Choose between a tranquil enclosed space or a rowdier open-air patio.

Mercado do Peixe (Largo da Mariquita, Rio Vermelho; ☯ 11am-last client) In the wee hours the Mercado is the 'end up' spot, where partiers can fill their bellies with any type of Bahian street food from its dozen or so stalls.

ENTERTAINMENT

Bars and clubs tend to come and go quickly in Salvador, so ask around to see what's hot at the moment. Good sources of information are the Friday editions of *A Tarde* and *Correio da Bahia*.

The Pelourinho explodes with people and action on Tuesday nights, which are called Terça da Bencão (Blessing Tuesday).

Live Music

Salvador is the pulsing center of an incredible music scene, where a blend of African and Brazilian traditions has produced mind-blowing forms of percussion that Salvadorenhos mix into their reggae, pop and rock, *pagode* and *axé*. The city has also produced unique styles such as *afoxé* and samba reggae. Since hardly a bar or restaurant in the city lacks live music at least one night of the week, catching some of Salvador's talented artists shouldn't be hard.

During the high season, there are almost nightly concerts in the inner courtyards of the Pelourinho, with cover charges ranging from free to R$30. Take a stroll by the following places and find out what's on for the evening: Largo de Tereza Batista, Largo de Pedro Arcanjo and Praça Quincas Berro d'Água (usually free). There are also occasional concerts on the Terreiro de Jesus. You can also frequently hear drum corps, which rehearse by walking through the Pelourinho, blocking traffic and gathering a following as they go.

Traditional groups (characterized by strong Afro drum corps) to be on the lookout for

include Ilê Aiyê (the first exclusively Black Carnaval group), the all-female Dida, Muzenza and Male Debalê. More pop and with strong percussion sections are world-famous Olodum – a Tuesday-night Pelourinho institution – Araketu and Timbalada, brainchild of master composer and musician Carlinhos Brown. The queens of Salvador pop music – Margareth Menezes, Ivete Sangalo and Daniela Mercury – also often 'rehearse' publicly.

If you aren't going to experience Carnaval in Salvador, don't worry: the two months leading up to it are the next best thing. *Ensaios* showcase secret big-name guests and clubs around the city put on special balls.

For the biggest acts, keep your eye on Salvador's finest venue, the **Teatro Castro Alves** (Map pp440-1; ☎ 3339 8033; Campo Grande). Its Concha Acústica (amphitheater) has weekly concerts throughout summer.

Alphorria (Map pp440-1; ☎ 3242 0053; Rua Direito de Santo Antônio 43, Santo Antônio; ☯ 11pm-last client) This bar in Santo Antônio packs a diverse crowd and even more eclectic sounds. Live bands play *forró*, rock, Afro pop and even salsa.

Casa de Mãe Iemanja (☎ 3334 3041; Rua Guedes Cabral 81, Rio Vermelho; ☯ 2pm-2am Fri-Sun) Named after the Yoruba goddess of the sea (the Festa de Iemanja happens nearby), this Rio Vermelho bistro/cultural center is a great space to hear live music. It's on the coastal road, just up from Largo de Santana.

Olivier (Map pp440-1; ☎ 3241 3829; Rua Direita de Santo Antônio 61, Santo Antônio; mains R$20-25; ☯ lunch & dinner) This attractive restaurant has a cozy backyard setting where you can catch live jazz and bossa nova several nights of the week.

Bohemia Music Bar (Map pp440-1; ☎ 3332 5774; Rua Belo Horizonte 177, Barra; admission R$5-15; ☯ 7pm-late Tue-Sun) This Barra favourite sees live pop and rock bands playing throughout the week

Pimentinha (☎ 3230 1725; Rua Dom Eugênio Sales 11, Boca do Rio; admission R$20; ☯ 9pm-3am Mon) On Monday nights, Pimentinha is the place to head. Decorated with LPs, mannequins, old umbrellas and other found materials, Pimentinha hosts spirited bands (often playing MPB or Música Popular Brasileira) and a diverse crowd.

Folkloric Shows

Seeing a folkloric show in the Pelourinho shouldn't be missed. The shows include Afro-Brazilian dance, the dances of the *orixás*, *maculêlê* (stick dance) and capoeira, to live percussion and vocals. The most astounding professional show is put on by the world-renowned Balé Folclórico da Bahia at **Teatro Miguel Santana** (Map pp442-3; ☎ 3322 1962; Rua Gregório de Matos 49; admission R$20; ☙ 8pm Mon & Wed-Sat). The Grupo de Danças Folclóricas SESC also puts on a lively show at **Teatro SESC-Senac** (Map pp442-3; ☎ 3324 4529; Largo do Pelourinho 19; admission R$15; ☙ 8pm Thu-Sat), as does Restaurant Solar do Unhão.

Capoeira

Most capoeira schools in the Pelourinho charge a few reais for watching a class (often called a 'show') and for taking pictures. Just remember that you are helping to support the studio. See p449 for a list of studios.

Nightclubs

Fashion Clube (☎ 3346 0012; Av Otávio Mangabeira 2471, Jardim dos Namorados, Pituba; cover R$20; ☙ 11pm-last client Thu-Sat) A large, terminally hip dance club with nights ranging from salsa to electronic music. Minimum age for women is 21; for men, 18.

The young and wealthy head for **Aeroclube Plaza Show** (Av Otávio Mangabeira, Boca do Rio), an outdoor entertainment complex with a few bars, dance clubs and free live *forró* nights. **Rock in Rio** (☎ 3461 0300; ☙ 10pm-last client Tue-Sun) is a 1700-sq-m dance club with eight bars that gets packed on weekends. Also in Aeroclube, **Café Cancun** (☎ 3461 0603; ☙ 9pm-last client Tue-Sat) has a Mexican theme to its food and décor, and makes for a fun night of dancing and tequila drinking.

Gay & Lesbian Venues

Beco dos Artistas (Map pp440-1; Av Cerqueira Lima, Garcia) Art mavens and a young, gay-friendly crowd flock to this small alley with its several bars (and a dance club). Enter next to Pizzaria Giovanni on Rua Leovigildo Filgueira.

Queens Club (Map pp440-1; ☎ 3328 6220; www.queens clube.com.br; Rua Theodoro Sampaio 160, Barris; ☙ 10pm-6am Fri & Sat) This mega-club is one of the biggest, best places to dance. Expect throbbing electronic beats, go-go boys and a dark room. There's also a sex shop, DVD rental and movie screening area open daily from 10am to 10pm.

Off Club (Map pp440-1; ☎ 3267 6215; www.offclub.com. br; Rua Dias D'Ávila 33, Barra; ☙ 10pm-6am Thu-Sun) Another great spot for dancing, this one brings in a mixed and assorted crowd of drag queens,

gays, lesbians, straights, go-go boys and more. Saturday house music nights are packed.

Club Mix Ozone (Map pp440-1; ☎ 3234 0362; Rua Augusto França 55, Largo 2 de Julio; ☙ 11pm-last client) In the center, people of all description come here to get down to electronic beats.

SHOPPING

Mercado Modelo (Map pp442-3; ☎ 241 2893; Praça Cayru; ☙ 9am-7pm Mon-Sat, 9am-2pm Sun) This two-story, enclosed tourist market has dozens of stalls selling local handicrafts. More of the same can be purchased in Pelourinho shops.

Artesanato São Domingos (Map pp442-3; ☎ 3322 6979; Terreiro de Jesus, Pelourinho; ☙ 10am-6pm Mon-Sat) Adjoining the Igreja São Domingos, this small shop sells lovely Bahian lacework – dresses, tablecloths, blouses and the like.

Bahia Online (Map pp442-3; ☎ 3321 0536; Rua João de Deus 22, Pelourinho; ☙ 10am-10pm Mon-Sat) This Pelourinho music store has a great selection of Bahian artists as well as samba, electronica and MPB CDs.

Bau Bau (Map pp442-3; ☎ 3323 0008; Rua Gregória de Matos 37, Pelourinho; ☙ 10am-7pm Mon-Sat) One of a growing crop of colorful boutiques.

GETTING THERE & AWAY
Air

Aeroporto Deputado Luis Eduardo do Magalhães (code SSA; ☎ 3204 1010; São Cristóvão) is serviced by **Gol** (☎ 3204 1603; airport), **TAM** (☎ 3365 2324; airport), **Varig** (☎ 3204 1050) and **BRA** (☎ 3204 1027; airport). There are daily flights to any Brazilian destination, but multiple stops are common. One-way fares from Salvador to São Paulo start around R$220, to Rio R$220, to Recife R$150 and to Fortaleza R$190.

TAP (Air Portugal; ☎ 3204 1531; airport) connects Salvador with Europe. Flights to other international destinations go via São Paulo or Rio.

Boat

Boats to points on Baía de Todos os Santos leave from the **Terminal Marítimo Turístico** (Map pp442-3; ☎ 326 6603; Av da França), behind the Mercado Modelo, and the **Terminal Marítimo de São Joaquim** (☎ 633 1248; Av Oscar Pontes, Água de Menino). See p461 for more information.

Boats heading for Morro de São Paulo also leave from the Terminal Marítimo Turístico. Four companies have *lanchas rapidas* (speed boats; R$60, two hours) and two run catamarans (R$50, two hours). The number of daily departures varies according to demand.

Bus

Most Salvador buses coming from the south go around the Baía de Todos os Santos, but alternately you can disembark at Bom Despacho on the Ilha de Itaparica and catch a boat across the bay. Some bus companies sell their tickets at convenient locations throughout the city, usually at malls. Ask Emtursa or Bahiatursa for more information. **Ticket Center** (Map pp440-1; ☎ 3329 5433; Rua Portão da Piedade, Piedade), facing Shopping Piedade, sells tickets for a variety of bus companies. More convenient is **Marlin Ecotours** (Map pp442-3; ☎ 3321 2125; cnr Rua João de Deus & Rua JC Rabelo), though they tack on R$10 per ticket.

GETTING AROUND
To/From the Airport

The airport is located about 30km east of the center. A taxi to the center will cost you around R$50 in a metered taxi, or R$76 for a radio taxi, paid in advance at the airport. There are also air-conditioned minibuses (R$5) that head to the center, marked 'Praça da Sé/Aeroporto.' City buses leave from a depot behind the parking garage.

Buses to the airport depart regularly from the so-called Praça da Sé bus stop (Map pp442-3), actually a block southeast of Praça Municipal. Supposedly they leave every 30 minutes, but the schedule is rather flexible, so leave plenty of time. The bus goes down Av 7 de Setembro to Barra, and continues along the coast before heading inland to the airport. In light traffic, the ride takes about an hour; with traffic allow 1¾ hours.

> **FOLK ART**
>
> Bahia has some of Brazil's best artisans, who usually have small shops or sell in the local market. You can buy their folk art in Salvador, but the best place to see or purchase the real stuff is in the town of origin. Feira de Santana is known for its leatherwork. Maragojipinho, Rio Real and Cachoeira produce earthenware. Caldas do Jorro, Caldas de Cipo and Itaparica specialize in straw crafts. Rio de Contas and Muritiba do metalwork. Ilha de Maré is famous for lacework. Jequié, Valença and Feira de Santana are woodworking centers. Santo Antônio de Jesus, Rio de Contas and Monte Santo manufacture goods made of leather and silver.

A municipal Aeroporto bus follows the same route to the airport, but gets very crowded and isn't recommended if you're carrying a bag.

To/From the Bus Station

Salvador's **bus station** (☎ 460 8300) is 8km east of the city center. A taxi to Cidade Alta or Barra runs R$18. Air-con minibuses (R$5) marked 'Praça da Sé' go to the center from in front of Shopping Iguatemi, just across the footbridge out front. For Barra, catch the Barra 1 bus in front of the bus station. Any bus that goes to Shopping Iguatemi will get you to the bus station.

BUSES FROM SALVADOR

Destination	Duration	Cost	Frequency	Company
Aracaju	6hr	R$40	3 daily	Bonfim (☎ 3460 0000)
Belo Horizonte	24hr	R$190	daily	São Geraldo (☎ 3450 4488)
Fortaleza	21hr	R$156	daily	Itapemirim (☎ 3450 5644)
Ilhéus	8hr	R$73-113	3 daily	Águia Branca (☎ 4004 1010)
João Pessoa	14hr	R$105	4 weekly	Bonfim (☎ 3460 0000)
Lençóis	6hr	R$42	2 daily	Real Expresso (☎ 3450 2991)
Maceió	10hr	R$58	2 daily	Bonfim (☎ 3460 0000)
Natal	21hr	R$134-167	2 daily	São Geraldo (☎ 3450 4488)
Penedo	7hr	R$43	daily	Bonfim (☎ 3460 0000)
Porto Seguro	12hr	R$110-172	daily	Águia Branca (☎ 4004 1010)
Recife	12hr	R$110	2 daily	Itapemirim (☎ 3450 5644)
Rio	25-28hr	R$200-218	4 daily	Águia Branca (☎ 4004 1010) & Itapemirim (☎ 3450 5644)
São Paulo	33hr	R$178-205	3 daily	São Geraldo (☎ 3450 4488)
Vitória	19hr	R$147	daily	Águia Branca (☎ 4004 1010)

Public Transportation

Linking Cidade Alta and Cidade Baixa are the **Elevador Lacerda** (Map pp442-3; ☎ 322 7049; R$0.05; ⏰ 24hr) and the **Plano Inclinado Gonçalves** (funicular railway; Map pp442-3; R$0.05; ⏰ 7am-7pm Mon-Fri, 7am-1pm Sat).

There are two main city bus terminals in the center that can serve as destinations or transfer points: Terminal da França (Map pp442–3) in the Comércio and Lapa (Map pp440-1), behind Shoppings Lapa and Pie-dade. The air-con minibuses are sometimes four times the cost of a regular fare. Taxis can be taken at meter price (legal) or negotiated.

BAÍA DE TODOS OS SANTOS

The Baía de Todos os Santos is Brazil's largest bay, and was at one time among the hemisphere's most important. The 56 islands contained in the 1000-sq-km bay have lush vegetation and architectural remnants of their historic past.

ILHA DE ITAPARICA

☎ 0xx71 / pop 51,000

Itaparica has long been an escape for the residents of Salvador, and its shores are lined with vacation homes. Though the beaches can't compare with those on Salvador's northern coast, and Club Med has privatized the best one, they are still fine places if you'd rather not head up the coast. Mar Grande (9km south of Bom Despacho) is perhaps the most likeable town on the island, with bars, restaurants and a relaxed atmosphere.

Sights & Activities

Guarding the northern tip of the island, the **Forte de São Lourenço** (1711) was built by Dutch invaders and figured prominently in Bahia's battle for independence in 1823. Nearby, the city of Itaparica has a few historic constructions, including the **Solar Tenente Botas** (Lieutenant Botas Manor; Praça Tenente Botas), the **Igreja Matriz do Santíssimo Sacramento** (Rua Luís Gama), built in 1715, and the **Fonte da Bica** (mineral-water fountain), from 1842. In the center of the island, a huge tree wraps its roots around the ruins of the **Igreja Baiacu** and grows right out of them.

BAÍA DE TODOS OS SANTOS & RECÔNCAVO

BEACHES

Praia Ponta da Areia (2km north of Bom Despacho) is a thin strip of sand with clear, shallow water and *barracas* serving good seafood. **Praia da Penha** (10km south of Bom Despacho) is a nice beach with excellent views of Salvador. **Praia Barra Grande** (7km further south) is Itaparica's finest public beach. It has clear water and weekend homes, and lies in front of its namesake village. Bahians, who love a beach with lots of people on it, consider **Praia Cacha Pregos** (20km further south) the island's best.

Sleeping & Eating

Camping Praia de Berlinque (☎ 3638 2435; per person R$10) Shaded campsites are spread around an enticing area just a few steps from the beach. Services are minimal, so bring food and essentials with you. It's located 30km south of Bom Despacho.

Pousada e Restaurante Koisa Nossa (☎ 3633 1028; Av Juvenal João Vinagre 173; d with fan/air-con R$65/90; 🖳) In Mar Grande, 200m straight up from the dock, this pousada has two floors of simple, slightly run-down rooms surrounding a small grassy yard. It's above a simple self-service restaurant (*por-kilo* R$13).

Pousada Arco-Íris (☎ 3633 1130; www.parcoiris .na-web.net, in Portuguese; Estrada da Gamboa 102; d with fan R$90-110; 🖳) Around the corner from Koisa Nossa, Arco-Íris is set on the unmanicured grounds of an old mango ranch. A variety of rooms are available in the antique-laden main house, and cabins overlook the yard. The whole place has an air of neglect.

Zimbo Tropical (☎ 3638 1148; zimbo_tropical@zipmail .com.br; Aratuba; s/d/tr with fan R$60/100/130) Sweet bungalows are spread through a gorgeously lush garden just 400m from the beach. The laid-back owners offer group meals and excursions to local sights, and can make tiny monkeys magically emerge from the trees. Ask the Kombi driver to let you off at the Brazil Gás store at the northern entrance to Aratuba (28km south of Bom Despacho), and walk 200m down Rua Iemanjá toward the beach. A taxi from Bom Despacho or Mar Grande is R$30.

Manga Rosa (☎ 3633 1130; Estrada de Gamboa 102; mains R$25-32; 🕑 lunch & dinner) Attached to the Arco-Íris, this restaurant serves large portions of acclaimed Bahian and international cuisine and its tropical ambience is a great setting for a meal.

Restaurante Philippe (☎ 3633 1060; Praça São Bento 113; mains R$28-44; 🕑 lunch & dinner) Near the dock in Mar Grande, the well-respected Restaurante Philippe serves a rich variety of Brazilian and European fare in an oceanfront setting. Simpler restaurants are next door.

Getting There & Away

BOAT

Schedules change with the seasons, so verify departure times.

Passenger ferries (R$4, 50 minutes, every 30 minutes from 7am to 6:50pm) leave from Salvador's Terminal Marítimo Turístico for Mar Grande's **terminal** (☎ 3633 1248), and return from 6:30am to 7:30pm. Buy your return ticket ahead of time on summer days.

A car ferry (R$7, car R$27, one hour, hourly from 5am to 11:30pm) and a catamaran (R$7, 30 minutes, seven daily) run between Salvador's Terminal Marítimo de São Joaquim and Bom Despacho. Expect a long wait to drive onto the ferry on weekends, especially in summer.

BUS

Frequent buses leave from Bom Despacho's **bus/ferry terminal** (☎ 3319 2890) for Valença (R$14, two hours, five daily).

Getting Around

Kombis leave from the boat terminals in both Bom Despacho and Mar Grande and run a circuit around the island until about 8pm. Some unscrupulous drivers overcharge tourists, so remember that no fare should be over R$8. Rental bicycles are widely available (R$20 per day).

OTHER ISLANDS

The lesser Baía de Todos os Santos islands include **Ilha Bom Jesus dos Passos**, which has traditional fishing boats and artisans; **Ilha dos Frades** (named after two monks who were killed and cannibalized there by local Indians), which has attractive waterfalls and palm trees; and **Ilha da Maré**, with the quiet beaches of **Itamoabo** and **Bacia das Neves** and the 17th-century **Igreja de NS das Neves**.

Tour companies in Salvador offer boat tours of the bay to either Ilha da Maré, or Ilha dos Frades and Ilha de Itaparica, from Salvador's Terminal Marítimo Turístico. Alternatively, boats to Ilha da Maré (R$4, 20 minutes, every

40 minutes from 8am to 5:30pm) leave from São Tomé de Paripe's **terminal** (☎ 3307 1447), 25km north of the city. To get there, take the Base Naval/São Tomé bus to the end of the line (ask at tourist information about the best place to catch the bus). For Ilha dos Frades, take an Oxalá bus from Salvador's main bus station to Madre de Deus (70km northwest of the city) and catch a boat for Paramana (R$2). You could also try hiring a boat from the small port next to the Mercado Modelo in Salvador.

RECÔNCAVO

A region of green, fertile lands surrounding the Baía de Todos os Santos, the *recôncavo* brought riches to Salvador (and the Portuguese crown) with its sugar and tobacco crops. The profits reaped off these lands also spurred the growth of once-rich towns like Cachoeira, which is resplendent with colonial architecture and history. For more of an adventure, hire a boat across Baía de Todos os Santos to Maragojipe, a sweet colonial village, and then catch a bus on to Cachoeira and São Félix.

CACHOEIRA & SÃO FÉLIX

☎ 0xx75 / pop 32,400

Cachoeira, affectionately known as the jewel of the *recôncavo*, is a sleepy place, full of colorful, mostly preserved colonial architecture uncompromised by the presence of modern buildings. The town sits below a series of hills, strung along the banks of the Rio Paraguaçu in a face-off with its twin, São Félix. A steady trickle of tourism flows through the area, attracted by Brazil's best tobacco, its reputation as a renowned center of Candomblé and a strong wood-sculpting tradition. If you get an early start, Cachoeira and São Félix make a great day trip from Salvador, or stay the night and explore at a more relaxed pace.

History

Diego Álvares, the father of Cachoeira's founders, was the sole survivor of a ship bound for the West Indies that was wrecked in 1510 on a reef near Salvador. This Portuguese Robinson Crusoe was saved by the Tupinambá Indians of Rio Vermelho, who dubbed the strange white sea creature Caramuru, or 'Fish-Man.' Álvares lived 20 years with the Indians and married Catarina do Paraguaçu, the daughter of the most power-

ful Tupinambá chief. Their sons João Gaspar Aderno Álvares and Rodrigues Martins Álvares killed off the local indigenous people, set up the first sugarcane *fazendas* (ranches) and founded Cachoeira.

By the 18th century, tobacco from Cachoeira was considered the world's finest, sought by rulers in China and Africa. The 'holy herb' also became popular in Brazil, taken as snuff, smoked in a pipe or chewed.

Early in the 19th century, Cachoeira achieved fame as a center for military operations in Bahia to oust the Portuguese rulers, and was the first place to recognize Dom Pedro I as the independent ruler of Brazil. Since then, not much has happened in this sleepy town.

Information

There is a helpful **tourist office** (☎ 3425 1123; Rua Ana Nery 4; ☾ 8am-noon & 1-5pm Mon-Fri, 1-4pm Sat & Sun) in Cachoeira, as well as a Bradesco bank and a post office, both overlooking Praça Dr Milton. São Félix also has a bank.

Sights & Activities

At some sights here, especially at churches, theft has been a problem, so you may have to pre-arrange a visit through the tourist office. When visiting São Félix, watch your footing while crossing the narrow and dilapidated bridge (built by the British in 1885). Loose planks have claimed at least one life in recent years.

CHURCHES & HISTORIC BUILDINGS

The **Igreja da Ordem Terceira do Carmo** (Praça da Aclamação, Cachoeira; admission R$2; ☾ 2-5pm Tue-Sat, 9am-noon Sun) has a gilded baroque altar, paneled ceilings and *azulejos*, and dates from 1702. A side gallery contains several polychrome Christs, imported from the Portuguese colony in Macao, and dripping with bovine blood mixed with Chinese herbs and sparkling rubies.

The **Igreja Matriz NS do Rosário** (Rua Ana Nery, Cachoeira) dates between 1693 and 1754. It has beautiful *azulejos* and a ceiling painted by Teófilo de Jesus. On the 2nd floor, the Museu das Alfaias contains remnants from the abandoned 17th-century Convento de São Francisco do Paraguaçu. The church is usually open mornings, but try knocking if it's closed.

Cachoeira's oldest church is the tiny **Igreja de NS da Ajuda** (Largo da Ajuda), built in

CACHOEIRA

INFORMATION	
Bradesco	1 D2
Post Office	2 D2
Tourist Office	3 D3

SIGHTS & ACTIVITIES	
Atelier do Doidão	4 D3
Atelier do Louco	5 C3
Casa da Câmara e Cadeia	6 D4
Igreja da Ordem Terceira do Carmo	7 D4
Igreja de NS da Ajuda	8 C3
Igreja Matriz NS do Rosário	9 C3
Museu da Boa Morte	10 C3
Museu Hansen Bahia	11 C3
Museu IPHAN	12 C4
Santa Casa de Misericórdia	13 D2

SLEEPING	
Pensão Tia Rosa	14 D3
Pousada do Convento do Carmo	15 D4
Pousada do Guerreiro	16 C3

EATING	
Baiana's Point	17 C4
Cabana do Pai Tomaz	18 C4
Gruta Azul	19 A2
Pizzaria Shambhalah	20 D4
Restaurante Beira Rio	21 C3

TRANSPORT	
Bus Station	22 A2

1595 when the town was known as Arraial d'Ajuda.

The climb to the 18th-century Igreja de NS do Conceição do Monte is rewarded only by views as it is closed to visitors.

At the **Casa da Câmara e Cadeia** (Prefecture & Jail; Praça da Aclamação, Cachoeira) organized criminals ran the show upstairs and disorganized criminals were kept behind bars downstairs. The building dates to 1698 and served as the seat of the Bahian government in 1822. The old marble pillory was removed from out front after abolition.

The municipality's oldest hospital, the **Santa Casa de Misericórdia** (Praça Dr Mílton, Cachoeira; 2-5pm Mon-Fri) has a pretty chapel (1734) with a painted ceiling, gardens and an ossuary.

MUSEUMS & CULTURAL CENTERS

The **Museu Hansen Bahia** (3425 1453; Rua 13 de Maio, Cachoeira; admission free; 9am-5pm Tue-Fri, 9am-2pm Sat & Sun) occupies the birthplace and former home of Brazilian heroine Ana Nery, who organized the nursing corps during the Paraguay War. Today, it houses the work of German-Brazilian artist Hansen Bahia. Among his powerful block prints and paintings on the theme of human suffering, depicting primarily prostitutes and Christ, is a series of illustrations of Castro Alves' poem *Návio Negreiro* (Slave Ship).

For a small donation, members of the exclusively female Boa Morte (Good Death) religious society will lead you around their barren one-room **Museu da Boa Morte** (Rua 13 de Maio, Cachoeira; admission free; 10am-6pm). There are some good photos and usually members sit around in their whites, smoking pipes and gossiping. The society began as a sisterhood of slaves that assured dead slaves a proper burial and bought old slaves freedom, while on the side they passed information regarding slave uprisings and carefully disguised Candomblé events.

Housed in an 18th-century colonial mansion, the humble **Museu IPHAN** (☎ 3425 1123; Praça da Aclamação, Cachoeira; admission R$2; ✆ 8am-noon & 2-5pm Mon-Fri, 8am-noon Sat) displays colonial furnishings and priestly vestments.

In São Felix, the riverfront **Centro Cultural Dannemann** (☎ 3425 2208; Av Salvador Pinto 29; admission free; ✆ 8am-noon & 1-4:30pm Tue-Sat, gallery only 1-4pm Sun) has modern art displayed throughout its converted warehouse. In a large room in the rear of the building, heavy with the rich smell of tobacco, women dressed in white with flowered head wraps sit at antique wooden tables rolling *charutos* (cigars), as has been done here since 1873. Dannemann cigars are considered Brazil's finest.

WOODCARVING

Cachoeira has maintained a tradition of woodcarving with a heavy African flavor. Stop in on the *ateliers* (studios) of two of the best sculptors in town, **Doidão** (Rua Ana Nery) and **Louco** (Rua 13 de Maio), to get a sense of the local style.

CANDOMBLÉ

Cachoeira is one of Candomblé's strongest and perhaps purest spiritual and religious centers. The *terreiros* are in small homes and shacks in the hills, where long ceremonies are usually held on Friday and Saturday nights. You can try contacting the tourist office for Candomblé information; or get in touch with **Luiz Magno** (☎ 3425 1133), who takes visitors to ceremonies, charging around R$50 per person.

Tours

For boat trips along the river, contact the owner of **Restaurante Beira Rio** (☎ 3425 5050; beira riotour@uol.com.br; Rua Manoel Paulo Filho 19, Cachoeira; per person R$10-60), who offers trips to Maragogipe, riverside convents and other nearby destinations.

Festivals & Events

Festa de São João (June 22 to 24) The largest popular festival of Bahia's interior, celebrated with folklore, music, dancing and a generous amount of food and drink.

Festa da NS da Boa Morte (Friday, Saturday and Sunday closest to August 15) Organized by the Boa Morte sisterhood: slave descendants pay tribute to their liberation with dance and prayer in a mix of Candomblé and Catholicism.
NS do Rosário (second half of October) Includes games, music and food.
NS da Ajuda (first half of November) Features a ritual *lavagem* (washing) of the church and a street festival.
Santa Bárbara or **Iansã** (December 4) Candomblé ceremony held in São Félix.

Sleeping & Eating

Accommodation prices double during festivals.

Pensão Tia Rosa (☎ 3425 1792; Rua Ana Nery 12, Cachoeira; s/d R$25/40) Tia Rosa is a friendly born and bred Cachoeiran who rents rustic rooms in her home. The best room is upstairs, with a view of the neighboring rooftops. She can also help arrange outings to Candomblé ceremonies.

Pousada do Guerreiro (☎ 3425 4509; Rua 13 de Maio 14, Cachoeira; s/d from R$30/60) This simple guesthouse has fan-cooled rooms with wood floors; the best are rather spacious, and one room has a small balcony.

Pousada e Restaurante Paraguassú (☎ 3438 3386; p-paraguassu@uol.com.br; Av Salvador Pinto 1, São Félix; s/d from R$45/65; ✖) Located on the riverfront in São Félix, Paraguassú has clean, cozy rooms surrounding a small garden. The restaurant is open for lunch and dinner and serves good typical food and pizza with riverside seating.

Pousada do Convento do Carmo (☎ 3425 1716; www.pousadadoconvento.com.br; Praça da Aclamação, Cachoeira; s/d R$105/110; ✖ ✚) The 18th-century convent attached to the Igreja da Ordem Terceira do Carmo has been converted into a comfortable pousada, with no loss of atmosphere. Rooms are spacious, with tall ceilings and heavy wood floors. A restaurant serves traditional Bahian fare.

Gruta Azul (☎ 3425 1295; Praça Manoel Vitorino 2, Cachoeira; ✆ Sat & Sun) A pleasant spot for a cocktail or a snack.

Pizzaria Shambhalah (☎ 3425 5318; Rua Inocência Bonaventura, Cachoeira; mains R$8-20; ✆ dinner) This small cozy pizzeria has brick walls and nicely lit tables with views onto the plaza.

Cabana do Pai Thomaz (☎ 3425 1288; Rua 25 de Junho 12, Cachoeira; mains R$12-22; ✆ lunch & dinner) Pai Thomaz serves good Bahian food and is filled with carved wooden panels and furniture.

Restaurante Beira Rio (☎ 3425 5050; Rua Manoel Paulo Filho 19, Cachoeira; mains R$14-27; ✆ lunch & dinner) This laid-back spot serves tasty seafood and Bahian fare with bench tables and old-fashioned décor. There are decent wines, outdoor river-facing tables and inexpensive lunch plates.

Baiana's Point (☎ 3425 5302; Rua Virgílio Reis, Cachoeira; mains R$25-35; ☺ dinner) Perched over the river, this place makes a great setting for an early evening drink; fine Bahian fare is available.

Getting There & Away

The Cachoeira bus station is located at the base of the bridge in Praça Manoel Vitorino. Numerous daily buses depart Salvador for Cachoeira (R$12, two hours, from 5:30am to 7pm). Hourly buses can be caught in either town from 4:30am to 6:30pm. You can also continue on to Feira de Santana (R$5, 1½ hours, 12 daily) to make further connections. For Valença, take one of the two daily buses going from São Félix to Santo Antônio (R$7) and connect from there.

SANTO AMARO

☎ 0xx75 / pop 61,200

Santo Amaro is a friendly colonial sugar town that sees very few tourists and has an unpretentious charm. It is most well known for being the hometown of the brother-sister pair Caetano Veloso and Maria Betânia, two of Brazil's most popular singers (who often put in an appearance during Carnaval). The center bustles with people, especially around the small outdoor market. Paper production has replaced sugar as the major industry, visible in the invasion of bamboo on the hillsides where sugarcane once flourished, and a large paper mill outside of town.

The decrepit sugar-baron mansions along the old commercial street, Rua General Câmara, and the numerous churches are reminders of Santo Amaro's prosperous days. The ornate **Matriz de NS da Purificação** (1668) is the largest church, with *azulejos* and a painted ceiling. Unfortunately, a gang of thieves stole most of the church's holy images and exported them to France.

The **Lavagem da Purificação** (January 23 to February 2) is celebrated by a procession and ritual washing of the church steps by *baianas* in traditional dress, before bands and *trios elétricos* take over the streets.

Some of the good nighttime local music is played at the sterile **Hotel Lôbo** (☎ 3241 1721; Rua Conselheiro Paranhos 52; s/d from R$35/50; ﹖), which has modern, tiled rooms.

Buses leave Salvador for Santo Amaro (R$8, one hour 10 minutes, almost every 30 minutes from 5:30am to 9:30pm). Most continue on to Cachoeira/São Félix (R$5, 50 minutes).

NORTH OF SALVADOR

Bahia's northern coast is not as startling as its southern, but the beaches here are still lovely, boasting tall bluffs with rustling palms and white sands (that grow finer the further north you go), which front a mix of calm inlets and wild surfable breaks. Keep in mind that when Salvadorenhos want a day at the beach, they naturally head for Bahia's northern coast. As a result, the sands close to the city get packed on weekends. To escape the crowds, head further north where there are many kilometers of deserted pristine shoreline.

The Estrada do Coco (Coconut Hwy) runs as far north as Praia do Forte, where the Linha Verde (Green Line) picks up, continuing all the way to the Sergipe border. You may feel that you are going against the grain if you are trying to access this coast heading north to south. Grassy medians in the highways require buses to pass town entrances and then double back, so few do. Instead, they drop passengers on the highway, leaving you to walk or pick up other transportation into the small towns and fishing communities along this stretch of coast. Traveling from south to north is a much smoother process.

AREMBEPE

☎ 0xx71 / pop 6200

Arembepe's proximity to Salvador and its past fame keep visitors packing the beaches on weekends or swinging through to check out the *aldeia hippy*, a hippie village that Mick Jagger and Janis Joplin got rolling in the 1960s. Unfortunately, pollution from the giant chemical plant to the south and an abundance of weekend homes detract from the beauty of the rocky coast. If you're looking for a quick escape from Salvador, there are prettier beaches and more charming coastal villages. For a taste of a simpler life, however, the *aldeia* is a curious place to explore. Today, it's home to a community of artisans, who sell from their small beachside community. To get there, take a left at the roundabout when arriving in town, and follow the signs. You can

BAHIA

also reach the *aldeia* by walking north from Arembepe along the beach (3km).

In town, the **Pousada Cores do Mar** (☎ 3624 1155; Rua das Flores; d with fan/air-con R$80/90; ⊠) is a friendly place with airy, modern rooms, some with verandas and partial sea views. On the road to the *aldeia hippy*, the **Arembepe Refugio Ecológico Hotel** (☎ 3624 1031; www.aldeiadearembepe. com.br; s/d from R$80/90; ⊠) has an excellent location perched on a small grassy dune overlooking the beach. Quarters consist of freestanding concrete cabins, some with sea views. There's a good restaurant and a pool.

From Salvador, catch an Arembepe bus from Terminal da França, or a Monte Gordo bus from Lapa (both R$6, 1¼ hours). Arembepe is 2km off the highway. Frequent buses continue on to Praia do Forte.

PRAIA DO FORTE
☎ 0xx71

Praia do Forte is a pleasant and attractive tourist village that was intentionally developed into an upmarket, somewhat ecologically sensitive beach resort. The main drag (Alameda do Sol) is a pedestrian walkway lined with nice restaurants and boutiques and dotted with trees. It leads to an adorably tiny church, a sea turtle reserve and fantastic, palm-lined beaches with sparkling white sands that fill up on weekends. Surrounding the village are castle ruins, a lagoon for canoeing, and the Sapiranga forest reserve, which has hiking and biking trails and a zip line. If you can, time your visit for the full moon and walk along the beach past the resort at sunset, when the sun turns the waters of the Rio Timeantube red as the moon rises over the sea.

Orientation & Information
Buses stop at the northern end of the pedestrian thoroughfare, Alameda do Sol (also called Av ACM). Opposite the bus stop, **Bahiatursa** (⏰ 3676 0283; Av de Farol; ⏰ 8:30am-4pm Tue-Sun) distributes maps and brochures and gives the low-down on Praia do Forte. A few doors down, along Alameda do Sol, there's an **HSBC ATM**, though you'll also find an ATM inside the **Albergue Praia do Forte** (Rua da Aurora 3).

Sights
The extremely worthwhile **Tamar Project station** (☎ 3676 1403; adult/child R$8/4; ⏰ 9am-6pm) is located on the beach next to the church and lighthouse. See the boxed text on opposite for a description of the station and details on this national project designed to protect endangered sea turtles.

The **Castelo do Garcia d'Ávila** (☎ 3676 1073; admission R$6; ⏰ 8:30am-6pm), dating from 1552, was the first great Portuguese edifice in Brazil. Today, it's an impressive ruin with great views. Desperate to colonize as a way to control his new territory, the king of Portugal had set about granting lands to merchants, soldiers and aristocrats. For no apparent reason, a poor, 12-cow farmer named Garcia d'Ávila was endowed with a tract of land that extended inland all the way to the state of Maranhão, with Praia do Forte as its seat. He became overnight the largest landholder in the Northeast. For the site of his home, Garcia chose an aquamarine ocean-view plot studded with palm trees. There's an excellent restaurant on-site. It's a 3km walk along the only road out of town and there is a sign indicating where to turn, or you can take a taxi or mototaxi.

A turn-off from the road to the castle leads down a dirt track to the **Reserva da Sapiranga** (☎ 3676 1144; sapiranga@fgd.org.br; admission R$6, guided hikes R$5-15; ⏰ 8am-5pm), where local student guides take visitors along trails skirting through 600 hectares of secondary Atlantic rain forest. Hikes range from 30 minutes to five hours, with one of the more popular hikes leading down to the Rio Pojuca (bring your swimsuit).

Tours
Worthwhile tours in the area include hiking and bird-watching treks, canopy tours, kayak-

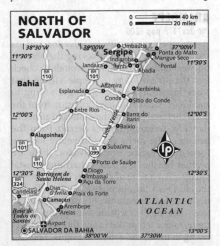

NORTH OF SALVADOR

THE SEA TURTLES OF TAMAR

Tamar, an abbreviation for sea turtles (TArtaruga MARinha), is a highly successful nonprofit organization (Fundação Pró Tamar; www.tamar.org.br) dedicated to saving five species of sea turtles in Brazil.

At the Praia do Forte station you can see several small exhibiting pools with marine turtles of various sizes and species, as well as urchins, eels and other sea life. If you visit during the turtles' nesting season (September to March) you will see the hatcheries functioning.

Tamar researchers protect around 550 nests a year along 50km of coast close to Praia do Forte. The moist, leathery, ping-pong-size eggs are buried in the sand when laid and either left on the beach or brought to the hatcheries for incubation. When they hatch, the baby turtles are immediately released into the sea.

Tamar has another 18 stations along the coast and two stations on oceanic islands, in all protecting some 1000km of coastline. Tamar estimates that under their protection some 600,000 baby turtles hatch per year. Of these only about 600 will reach adulthood. The Comboios station (Espírito Santo state, north of Vitória and near Linhares) protects the loggerhead and leatherback turtles. The Fernando de Noronha station protects green and hawksbill turtles. Praia do Forte station protects loggerhead, hawksbill, olive ridley and green turtles. Of the 60km of beach under Tamar's jurisdiction in Bahia, 13km are patrolled by the scientists alone; the remainder is protected by a cooperative effort in which fishermen – the very ones who used to collect the eggs for food – are contracted to collect eggs for the scientists.

ing, and whale watching (in season). **Centrotur** (☎ 3676 1091; www.centrotur.com.br; Alameda do Sol; ☼ 9am-7pm) is one of a handful of professional outfits in Forte offering excursions.

Sleeping & Eating

Praia do Forte has an abundance of attractive midrange guesthouses, with fewer budget options (Rua da Aurora, parallel to Alameda do Sol, has a handful of budget hotels).

Camping da Sapiranga (☎ 9976 9450; www.camping reservadasapiranga.cjb.net; per person R$12) One of several campsites 3km outside of town, Sapiranga has shady, grass and sand sites, with a kitchen available (R$3 extra). It's on a signed turn-off from the road to Castelo da Garcia d'Ávila.

Albergue Praia do Forte (☎ 3676 1094; www .albergue.com.br; Rua da Aurora 3; dm/d with fan R$35/100, d with air-con R$120; ☒ ⌨) The popular HI hostel has six-bed tile-floor dorm rooms, which face onto a grassy courtyard. There's a kitchen, and bikes and surfboards are available for hire.

Tia Helena (☎ 3676 1198; Alameda das Estrelas; s/d with fan R$50/70) Tia Helena offers clean, simple rooms, a warm welcome and rock-bottom prices that make her guesthouse a favorite among budget travelers.

Montreux Pousada (☎ 3676 1494; rolandruch@terra .com.br; Rua da Aurora 22; s/d with fan R$50/100, d with air-con R$140; ☒) One of Forte's better deals, Montreux is a friendly Swiss Brazilian–run guesthouse with clean, pleasant rooms with balconies.

Pousada Balanço do Mar (☎ 3676 1059; www .pousadabalancodomar.com.br; Rua da Aurora 25; s/d with fan R$80/100, with air-con R$100/150; ☒) This tidy guesthouse has seven cozy, simply furnished rooms, the best with small verandas and hammocks.

Pousada dos Artistas (☎ 376 1147; www.pousada dosartistas.tur.br; Praça dos Artistas; s/d R$150/180; ☒) This is a friendly pousada where lovely rooms look out on a lush, tropical garden.

Pousada Ogum Marinho (☎ 3676 1165; www .ogummarinho.com.br; Alameda do Sol; d R$175-260; ☒) One block from the beach, Ogum Marinho has attractive rooms with stone-slab floors, comfortable furnishings and private decks strung with hammocks.

Praia do Forte Eco-Resort (☎ 3676 4000; www .ecoresort.com.br; Av do Farol; s/d with dinner from R$540/690; ☒ ⌨ ☒) It's all luxury at this excellent resort, where walkways wind through groomed gardens to the beach out front and the food is fabulous. Rooms all have verandas with hammocks and the spa offers a wide range of treatments. Although there's nothing particularly 'eco' about the design, the hotel does contribute to social and educational programs.

Casa da Nati (☎ 3676 1239; Alameda do Sol; per kg R$23; ☼ lunch & dinner) A longtime Forte favorite, Casa da Nati spreads an excellent self-serve lunch buffet, with tasty a la carte dishes by night.

Sabor da Vila (☎ 3676 1156; Alameda do Sol; mains for 2 R$35-50; ☼ lunch & dinner) One of the top Bahian restaurants in town, Sabor da Vila serves excellent *moquecas*, *picanha*, grilled fish and other mouth-watering dishes.

Restaurante do Castelo (☎ 3329 3939; mains R$24-42; ☺ 9am-5pm) Located at the Castelo do Garcia d'Ávila, this elegant, breezy restaurant serves a small selection of seafood, grilled steak and Brazilian favorites to marvelous views.

Getting There & Around

Praia do Forte is 3km off the highway. **Linha Verde** (☎ 3460 3636) has regular departures to Praia do Forte from Salvador's Terminal da Calçada (R$8, 1¾ hours, 14 daily between 5am and 6pm). Buses return every 30 minutes between 7am and 6:30pm. **Catuense** (☎ 3450 4004) has one to three daily buses to Praia do Forte from Salvador's bus station.

Bicycles are available for hire at **Ciclo Forte** (☎ 3676 0309; Alameda do Sol; per hr/day R$5/50; ☺ 7am-5pm Mon-Sat, 7am-noon Sun).

PRAIA DO FORTE TO SÍTIO DO CONDE

Imbassaí is a rustic beach town 16km north of Praia do Forte. A tall sand dune and the peaceful Rio Barroso, which runs parallel to the beach, separate the village from a fine beach with choppy, rough surf. Most guesthouses in town are midrange and top-end options, though **Albergue Lujimba** (☎ 3677 1056; www.hostel lujimba.com.br; dm/d from R$20/90) offers good value for its pleasant wood-floor rooms in a rustic, thatch-roof guesthouse amid greenery. Hammocks, fruit trees and excursions add to the allure. It's a 20-minute walk to the beach.

A few kilometers north of Imbassaí lies the more rustic town of **Diogo**, which sees fewer visitors and retains the charm of village life. It's located along a river, about a 1km walk to the beach. **Too Cool Na Bahia** (☎ 9952 2190; www. toocoolnabahia.com; d from R$120) has eight colorfully designed chalets with verandas overlooking the lush surroundings. The friendly owner can arrange kite-surfing, kayaking, horseback riding and other activities. For a delicious meal stop in **Sombra da Mangueira** (☎ 9943 2745; Rua do Diogo; mains R$20-30; ☺ 10am-5pm), which serves excellent *moquecas* and other Bahian fare in a charming setting beneath a large *mangueira* (mango tree).

Another 6km north is the immense **Costa do Sauípe** tourist resort complex, with luxury hotels, a golf course, an equestrian center and a windsurfing lake, but no good natural beach. A further 6km north lies **Porto Sauípe**, a working-class fishing village with a few midrange pousadas and a pretty stretch of beach that gets wild a few kilometers from town.

To reach any of the places listed above, take the **Linha Verde** (☎ 3460 3636) bus from Salvador's Terminal da Calçada (almost hourly between 5am and 6pm) and alert the driver to your destination.

SÍTIO DO CONDE & BARRA

☎ 0xx75

Wet lowlands full of cattle surround this quiet, working-class beach retreat. While there's little to the town itself – just a few main streets and a sleepy central plaza – Sítio has a lovely beach with pounding surf (located 1km from the plaza). North or south along the coast quickly leads to deserted shore with churning seas and flat sands backed by bluffs topped with coconut trees.

Overlooking the beach, **Pousada Praiamar** (☎ 3449 1150; www.praiamarpousada.com.br; s/d from R$60/85; ☒) has comfortable rooms surrounding a sandy, palm-studded yard, a sea-facing porch with hammocks, and a constant breeze. Next door, **Pousada Talismã** (☎ 3449 1252; s/d with fan R$40/60) offers more rustic accommodation but the same great view.

Between the main plaza and the ocean, the flowery **Pousada Laia** (☎ 3449 1254; s/d/tr with fan R$30/40/60) has well-kept, good-value rooms and great home cooking. **Zecas & Zecas** (☎ 3449 1298; Praça Arsênio Mendes; mains for 2 R$24-36; ☺ lunch & dinner), on the main square, is a colorful seafood restaurant serving the town's best *moqueca*.

Direct transportation to Sítio do Conde is infrequent. You will most likely travel through Conde on the Linha Verde. From Salvador, São Luís has buses to Conde (R$22, 3½ hours, nine daily) from 6am to 5pm. Buses and more-frequent *topiques* (vans) make the 8km trip on to Sítio until about 5:30pm (R$1), or you can get a taxi (R$12).

Heading north, buses go through a picturesque coconut-palm forest to **Seribinha** (16km north), a small fishing community with a pretty riverside setting and good beach. From here, boats cross the Rio Itapicuru, from where it's a 30-minute walk to **Cavalo Russo**, a tea-colored lake with a sand dune sliding into it.

Down a rough dirt road, some 13km from Sítio do Conde, lies the pretty beach of **Barra** (Barra do Itarirí). Comprising a tiny community of weekend homes and beachfront restaurants, Barra has a wide, white sand bar

BAHIA

that curves into the bank of the idyllic Rio Itarirí. A tall sand bluff on the facing side and palm trees all around create a picturesque setting. Outside of Sundays and Carnaval, Barra is pretty much deserted. To get there take one of three daily São Luis buses from Sítio do Conde (R$1.50, 30 minutes). The last bus back leaves at 2pm.

MANGUE SECO

☎ 0xx75 / pop 920

Mangue Seco is a tiny, beautifully rustic riverfront village at the tip of a peninsula formed by the Rio Real, which delineates the Bahia/Sergipe border. The town itself is just a scattering of simple dwellings along sandy paths, a tiny church and plaza, a modern lighthouse (yielding lovely views for intrepid climbers) and a few friendly guesthouses and restaurants. The town ends at the edge of an enormous expanse of tall white sand dunes, beyond which the wide flat sands of the Bahian coast stretch to the south. Mangue Seco's remote location causes most visitors to come on guided day tours, preventing rapid growth and leaving nights decidedly quiet. Guesthouses can arrange dune-buggy trips through the sand dunes (R$50 for up to four people). It's about a 1½km walk to the ocean (or a R$10 dune-buggy ride), which has a handful of simple barracas strung with hammocks.

Sleeping & Eating

Pousada Grão de Areia (☎ 345 9064; www.praiademan gueseco.com.br; s/d with fan R$40/60, with air-con R$80/100; 🗱) In the village (stay to the right when exiting the dock), this is a simple, economical option with clean, light-colored rooms.

Pousada Suruby (☎ 9121 0803; www.praiademan gueseco.com.br; s/d with fan R$50/60) Suruby has a row of simple, fan-cooled rooms lined with hammocks that overlook a small front yard and the river beyond. The breezy restaurant serves seafood (mains R$27 to R$40). To get to this riverfront pousada, exit the dock and follow the riverfront to the left (toward the beach).

Pousada O Forte (☎ 3445 9039; www.pousada oforte.com; s/d with fan R$70/80, with air-con R$110/120; 🗱 🗱) Located 300m from the village center on the riverfront (past Suruby) and on the way to the beach, this friendly French Brazilian–owned pousada is in a prime, isolated spot overlooking river and mangroves.

Many activities are available: kayaking, sailing trips and even dune-buggy parasailing. There's also a good restaurant. Note that high tides swallow the riverbank 'road' to the village center, leaving you to either wait, wade or take a lengthy detour through the sand dunes.

Fantasias do Agreste (☎ 3445 9070; www.pousada fantasiasdoagreste.com; d with fan/air-con R$150/180; 🗱) In the center of the village, Fantasias do Agreste is the most comfortable guesthouse in town, with modern, colorfully painted rooms, with big windows (no view) and terra-cotta tile floors. Rooms face onto a garden courtyard. A good restaurant is here.

Mangue Seco's culinary specialty is aratu, a tiny red shellfish sometimes prepared in moquecas. In addition to restaurants at the pousadas Suruby, Fantasias do Agreste and O Forte, visitors can sample seafood at **Restaurant Frutas do Mar** (☎ 3445 9049; mains R$15-30; ☯ lunch & dinner), a pleasant outdoor spot located on the riverbank.

To satisfy sweet cravings, stop in **Recanto de Dona Sula** (☎ 3445 9008; ☯ 9am-5pm), where homemade candies, ice creams and liqueurs are made from local fruits. The café next door opens in the evenings and serves sandwiches, pizzas and light meals. It's located next to the church, facing a sandy plaza.

Getting There & Around

The easiest access to Mangue Seco is through Pontal, though boats also leave from Ponto do Mato; both are in Sergipe. Since there are few direct buses to Pontal, you'll have to route through either Indiaroba or Estância. From Salvador, Linha Verde has one daily bus to Indiaroba (R$24, five hours). Senhor do Bonfim buses go once daily to Estância (R$25, four hours). From Aracaju, Rota Sul has one daily bus to Pontal (R$10, 2½ hours) as well as three daily departures to Indiaroba (R$8, 2¼ hours) at 4pm. Upon arriving in Indiaroba you can hire a taxi for R$30 to Pontal.

Alternately, frequent topiques for Pontal leave from in front of Estância's hospital. If coming from the north, ask to be let off at the posto de gasolina (gas station) before Estância's bus station and walk one block up into town to the hospital. A taxi from Estância to Pontal costs R$40.

From Pontal, speed boats charge R$25 for up to six people. Slow boats (R$3) leave when they have 15 people together, which could take hours on quiet days.

Topiques depart Pontal (R$4, 90 minutes, hourly from 5:30am to 8:30am Monday to Saturday) and Ponto do Mato (R$4, two hours, hourly until 6pm) for Estância.

SOUTH OF SALVADOR

MORRO DE SÃO PAULO

☎ 0xx75

For some, the picturesque holiday village of Morro de São Paulo has exceeded acceptable limits of touristiness. For others, it is Bahia's best beach town. All agree it is charming. Remotely perched at the northern tip of the Ilha de Tinharé, Morro's appeal stems from its relaxed pace (no cars on the island) and unique geography: three jungle-topped hills on a point at the meeting of the mangrove-lined Canal de Taperoá and a clear, shallow Atlantic. Wheelbarrows help lug cargo (and luggage) along sandy lanes, past pousadas, restaurants and boutiques. During the high season the village booms, and there are parties on the beaches every night.

Orientation

Unless arriving by chartered flight, all visitors to the island disembark on the northern tip of the island. Uphill lies the main square (Praça Aureliano Lima) in the Vila, with an information office and a few restaurants. To reach the beaches, take a left at the square; this passes along the main street, Rua Caminho da Praia, and is lined with restaurants and shops. Continue downhill to access the shores, reaching Primeira Praia (first beach), then Segunda Praia, and so on. Heading right from the main plaza, you'll go through an archway down Rua da Fonte and pass the spring-fed fountain that was once the village's freshwater source. Pousadas are scattered about the island, with the cheapest options in the Vila area.

Information

There is a Bradesco ATM on Segunda Praia, but as it's often nonfunctional, get necessary funds before you arrive. Many establishments also accept credit cards. Internet cafés are plentiful (R$4 to R$6 per hour).

At the top of the hill up from the dock, **Centro de Informações ao Turista** (☎ 3652 1083; www .morrodesaopaulo.com.br; Praça Aureliano Lima s/n; ☻ 8am-

8pm) sells boat and domestic airline tickets, organizes excursions and distributes maps.

Sights & Activities

The town's icon is a 17th-century carved-stone **fortress gate**, which welcomes each arrival from its position above the dock. Around the corner at the point are the **fort ruins** (1630). Catching the rare sight of the sun setting over the river and mangroves from the fort is a visitor ritual. The **lighthouse** (1835) above the fort affords a fantastic view over Morro's beaches and has a **zip line** descending to Primeira Praia.

The waters of Morro's four conveniently named main beaches are mostly calm, shallow and warm, and their sands are narrow and swallowed by the high tides. Tiny **Primeira Praia** is lined with pousadas and has a decent surf break. Deep **Segunda Praia** (500m) is the 'action' beach with pousadas, restaurants, nightclubs and a sea of tables and chairs. Pousadas and anchored boats dominate one end of **Terceira Praia** (1km). Once you pass a pair of restaurants, **Quarta Praia** (2km) is a long, lovely stretch of sand graced by tall, swaying palms. For even more isolated peace, continue on at low tide to **Praia do Encanto** (5km) or further down the island to **Garapuá**, which has one pousada.

At low tide, take a walk to **Gamboa**, the next village on the river side of the island. The coast between the villages is filled with nooks to hide in and rocks to climb on. To start, head down Rua Fonte Grande and head right at the crossroads. You can catch the ferry back.

Tours

A boat trip around the island, with stops at the Garapuá and Moreré offshore reefs and the villages of Boipeba (p472) and historical Cairu, is obligatory (R$65). You'll fly over waves in a 10-person speedboat past gorgeous beach and mangrove scenery, swim, snorkel and stop at a floating oyster restaurant outside

---

TAX TO THE PEOPLE

In 2007, the authorities at Morro de São Paulo introduced a one-time 'tourist tax' of R$6.50 to all nonlocals entering the island. The money is earmarked for island upkeep and infrastructure, and you'll be asked to pay up when you disembark on the town dock.

Caravelas. Jeep trips to Boipeba are also possible (R$50). Also worthwhile is a hike to the small Fonte do Ceu waterfall, passing through the neighboring village of Gamboa, with an opportunity to do a bit of body painting from a cliff of colored clays (R$20). Horseback rides can also be arranged (R$20 per hour). All these tours can be booked through the many local agencies.

Sleeping

Reservations for Morro's 100 or so pousadas are required for all major holidays, especially Carnaval and *resaca* (five days of post-Carnaval hangover). Be forewarned that staying on Segunda Praia means sleeping to the nightclubs' pounding beats.

VILA

Pousada Cairu (☎ 3652 1074; pousadacairu@hotmail .com; Rua da Fonte Grande; s/d with fan R$25/50, with air-con R$35/70; ✷) To the right after arriving in the main plaza, this is a bare-bones choice for budget travelers, with basic, poorly ventilated rooms on the first floor, and breezier, more pleasant rooms upstairs.

Pousada Gaucho (☎ 3652 1243; www.pousadagaucho .com.br, in Portuguese; Rua Caminho da Praia 79; s/d from R$30/60; ✷) This tidy, family-run place has fine cheap rooms that can be a little noisy. Pricier, better rooms are on the upper floors and are run by a separate pousada of the same name.

Pousada Ninho da Águia (☎ 3652 1537; Rua Caminho do Farol 8; s/d from $40/50; ✷) On the hill above the dock, the tranquilly set Ninho da Águia is indeed at eagle's-nest heights. It's a friendly, family-run affair with tidy, simple rooms (upstairs rooms have great views). To get there, turn left after ascending from the dock; turn right after passing Pousada Natureza.

Hostel Morro de São Paulo (☎ 3652 1521; www .hosteldomorro.com.br; Rua da Fonte Grande; dm/d $40/80; ✷) This pleasant hostel has fine rooms with big shuttered windows, a little garden, hammocks and a guest kitchen. To get there, take the first left after passing through the archway leading to the spring.

Pousada Aconchego (☎ 3652 1005; www.pousada conchego.com.br; Rua da Fonte s/n; s/d R$50/70; ✷) To the right after arriving in the main plaza, this friendly modern pousada has small but comfortable rooms that are well maintained.

Pousada Colibri (☎ 3652 1056; www.pousada-colibri .com; d $125-145; ✷) In a marvelous hilltop posi-tion, the lushly landscaped Colibri has round cabins and well-finished two-room suites with verandas and hammocks. Two hectares of surrounding jungle assure beauty and quiet. To reach Colibri, take the path to the spring, then turn right up a quiet forested lane.

O Casarão (☎ 3652 1049; www.ocasarao.net; Praça Aureliano Lima 190; d/bungalow from $180/220; ✷ ✷) Reigning over the wide, main plaza, this renovated colonial mansion has lovely rooms with classical furnishings and large windows. Eclectically furnished chalets in back overlook a small garden. Excellent on-site restaurant.

BEACHES

Pousada e Camping Oxum (☎ 3652 1048; Segunda Praia; campsite/d R$20/70) One of several campsites near the beaches, Oxum has a small back-yard of equal parts grass and sand, with some shade. The rooms are boxy wooden cabins without charm.

Pousada Aradhia (☎ 3652 1116; www.pousadaaradhia .net; Terceira Praia; s/d R$70/80; ✷ ✷) Popular with young travelers, Aradhia offers fair value for its worn, basic rooms. Hammocks and a pool sweeten the deal. Aradhia lies on a narrow lane, just off Terceira Praia.

Pousada Ilha do Sol (☎ 3652 1576; Rua da Prainha; s/d from R$80/100; ✷) At the base of the steep road leading to the ocean, this well-established guesthouse is good value for its open, two-room suites catching the ocean breeze, and porches for people-watching.

Morro Praia Hotel (☎ 3652 1244; www.morropraia hotel.com.br; Terceira Praia; d R$100-200; ✷) Decent value among beachfront hotels, Morro Praia has small, simple rooms with colorful murals and decent windows, some opening onto the sea.

Pousada Paraíso do Morro (☎ 3652 1121; www .pousadaparaisodomorro.com.br; Terceira Praia; d without/with sea view R$160/230; ✷) This charming guesthouse is all about peace and tranquility: colorful, stylish rooms overlooking the sea or a small garden in back; guests receive a free yoga class.

Eating

Tia Lita (☎ 3652 1532; www.pousadatialita.com.br; Terceira Praia; mains R$8-10; ☉ lunch & dinner) This inexpensive, popular restaurant serves home-cooked grilled fish, chicken or beef. It's down a narrow lane, just off the beach. Tia Lita also rents out a few basic rooms.

Ponto de Encontro (☎ 3652 1165; Rua Caminho da Praia; mains R$15-25; ☉ lunch & dinner) This colorfully decorated spot serves eclectic dishes, including vegetarian options (such as baked stuffed eggplant).

Sabor da Terra (☎ 3652 1156; Rua Caminho da Praia; mains R$15-30; ✆ lunch & dinner) Excellent seafood is prepared simply or with Bahian spice. Fish *moqueca* and *casquinha de siri* (shredded crab meat) are excellent.

Forno a Lenha (☎ 3652 1347; Rua Caminho da Praia 24; rodízio R$18; ✆ dinner) This all-you-can-eat pizzeria is a favorite after a day at the beach.

Ristorante Mediterraneo (☎ 3652 1019; Rua Caminho da Praia; mains R$18-25; ✆ lunch & dinner) This quaint open-sided Italian restaurant serves fettuccine with shrimp and pesto, grilled fish, pasta al arrabiata and other old-world offerings. It's on the main strip.

Chez Max (☎ 3652 1103; Terceira Praia; mains R$18-26; ✆ lunch & dinner) Overlooking Terceira Praia, Chez Max is an idyllic retreat where you can dine on a grassy lawn facing the sea. Sizzling grilled dishes, seafood and plenty of Bahian cuisine fill out the menu.

Drinking

Don't miss dexterous vendors along Caminho da Praia and on Segundo Praia mixing delicious *caipirinhas* – made with fresh fruit. Outdoor bars are scattered along Segunda Praia. Current favorites are **Music Bar 87**, with its live music nightly (usually a bossa nova guitarist), and the reggae-infused **Jamaica Bar**. Pick up fliers for current dance parties (admission R$10 to R$30) at shops along Caminho da Praia.

Getting There & Away

Both catamarans (R$50, two hours, three daily) and *lanchas rapidas* (speedboats; R$60, two hours, daily) travel between Morro and the Terminal Marítimo Turístico in Salvador. The ride can be rough. Extra departures are added when there's sufficient demand.

If coming from the south, passenger ferries travel upriver to Morro from Valença (R$5, 1½ hours, hourly from 7am to 5pm), stopping first in Gamboa. At low tide, passengers are bussed to Atracadoro, then transferred to a waiting ferry. *Lanchas rapidas* (R$11, 40 minutes) leave whenever they have a full load.

Three daily flights go between Salvador and Morro (20 minutes, R$170 to R$180). Contact **Aerostar** (☎ 3652 1312, in Salvador ☎ 0xx71-3377 4406), **Adey Taxi** (☎ 3652 1242, in Salvador ☎ 0xx71-3377 1993) or a travel agency.

BOIPEBA

☎ 0xx75 / pop 4900

South of the Ilha da Tinharé, across the narrow Rio do Inferno, sits the Ilha de Boipeba. The village of Boipeba, on the northeastern tip of the island, is quiet, rustic and said to be what Morro de São Paulo was 20 years ago. The island's coastline is pristine, with more than 20km of beautiful, deserted beaches, including **Ponta de Castelhanos**, known for its diving.

Sleeping & Eating

Restaurants serving great seafood line the beach where the river meets the sea. Rounding the point, a string of top-end pousadas face Praia Boca da Barra.

Small Vila de Moreré, 40 minutes south by boat, has rustic accommodation.

Pousada 7 (☎ 3653 6135; www.ilhaboipeba.org .br/sete.html; Praça Santo Antônio; s/d from R$40/80; ✆) In the village center, overlooking the main plaza/football pitch, this friendly place has small attractive rooms with stone-slab floors and hammocks outside the door. A restaurant serves up tasty seafood for dinner daily.

Pousada Pérola do Atlântico (☎ 3653 6096; www .ilhaboipeba.org.br; s/d with fan R$100/150) On the beach, this welcoming guesthouse has lush gardens with winding pathways leading to pretty wooden cabins spread about the tranquil setting.

Pousada Pouso da Maré (☎ 3653 6069; www .ilhaboipeba.org.br; d R$140-180) Set amid abundant greenery, this guesthouse offers large, comfortable fan-cooled rooms facing gardens or the ocean.

Pousada Vila Sereia (☎ 3653 6054; www.ilhaboipeba .org.br; d with fan R$187) Brightly painted, thatched-roof cabins sit raised on stilts throughout a beachfront garden at this inviting pousada. Breakfast is served right on your porch.

Getting There & Away

From Valença, passenger ferries for Boipeba (R$10, four hours) leave daily Monday to Saturday (currently at noon). Two daily buses (11am and 2pm) leave Valença for Torrinhas, where passengers are transferred to a ferry for Boipeba (R$9, bus and ferry 2½ hours). Ferries stop first at the historic town of Cairu, a recommended stopover if you can catch a later boat on to Boipeba.

From Morro de São Paulo, options are to negotiate a boat ride with tour providers, or take a jeep (R$50) and then the ferry across the river.

VALENÇA
☎ 0xx75 / pop 84,200

Valença is a colonial fishing town on the banks of the Rio Una, historically the site of Portuguese struggles with both indigenous tribes and the Dutch. For most it is simply the gateway to Morro de São Paulo, but it has its own little-known secrets. Local shipbuilders maintain 15th-century techniques to such a degree that the town was chosen to produce a replica of the Spanish galleon *La Niña* for the American epic film *1492* (1992) about Christopher Columbus's journey.

To see the building of *saveiro* fishing boats in action, wander to the far end of the port where the smell of sap and sawdust, old fish and sea salt mingles with the wonderful odor of nutmeg drying in the sun. For a good walk and a beautiful view, follow the river's left bank upstream toward the **Igreja NS de Amparo** (1757) on the hill.

Orientation
From the port, walk straight uphill to reach the pedestrian center of town. If you keep going straight up along this main street, named Rua Governador Gonçalves, you will eventually reach the bus station (which is located 1km from the port). The Praça da Independencia is one block west of Rua Governador Gonçalves.

Information
All of the following are within a short walk of the port.

Banco do Brasil (Rua Governador Gonçalves 10)
Bradesco (Rua Governador Gonçalves 178)
Lys.com (Praça Admar Briga Guimarães; per hr R$2.50; ☽ 8am-10pm) Internet access near the port.
Tourist office (☎ 3641 0553; www.valenca.tur.br, in Portuguese; Rua Comandante Madureira 10; ☽ 8am-noon & 2-5pm Mon-Fri, 8am-noon Sat) Facing the port (go to the left), this office is mildly helpful.

Festivals & Events
During Carnaval and at Christmas, people dressed as cowhands accompany Catarina the *baiana* throughout the city while chanting and playing tambourines in the celebration of **Boi Estrela**. **Carnaval** and **Micareta** (held 15 days after the end of Lent) are lively, with *trios elétricos* blasting *axé* music. A weeklong

festival in honor of **NS do Amparo**, the patron saint of workers, climaxes on November 8. On New Year's Eve, **Zambiapumba** is celebrated by musical groups running through the streets playing improvised instruments.

Sleeping
Hotel Valença (☎ 3641 3807; Rua Dr Heitor Guedes De Melo 15; s/d with fan R$25/50, with air-con R$35/65; ☒) A few blocks off Praça da República, Hotel Valença is a good value for its clean, basic rooms.

Hotel Guaibim (☎ 3641 0018; Praça da Independência 74; s/d with fan R$40/60, with air-con R$50/80; ☒) Up from the port, this nice, simple hotel has friendly staff and clean rooms with tile floors. There's a cheap *por-kilo* restaurant here.

Onda Azul Hotel (☎ 3641 4964; Rua Conselheiro Ferraz 5; s/d with fan R$55/80, with air-con R$70/100; ☒) One block from the Praça da Independencia, Onda Azul is a sprightlier option, with stone-slab floors and pleasant furnishings.

Hotel Portal Rio Una (☎ 3641 5050; www.portal hoteis.tur.br in Portuguese; Rua Maestro Barrinha; d from R$215; ☒ ☒) This large, attractive hotel has Valença's best restaurant and its best rooms, each with verandas overlooking the river. It's 1km from the river (on the opposite side of the port).

Eating & Drinking
Casual outdoor bars/snack stands are scattered along the riverfront near the bridge.

Mega Chic (☎ 3641 4704; Av Maçônica 11; per kg R$15; ☽ lunch) Across the bridge from the town center, Mega Chic spreads a decent self-service buffet.

Sabor do Sol (Rua Governador Gonçalves 113; ☽ lunch) This low-key *churrascaria* and *por-kilo* restaurant is a popular lunch spot. It's on the pedestrian walkway.

Getting There & Away
Valença's tiny airport, served only by small air-taxi companies, is 15km from the center.

There is daily boat service to Boipeba, Gamboa and Morro de São Paulo from the port in the center.

The **bus station** (☎ 3641 4805) is a 1km hike from the port (or a R$8 taxi ride). Buses go to Porto Seguro (R$51, nine hours, one daily), Ilhéus via Itabuna (R$25, five hours, three daily) and Camamu (R$9, 1½ hours, hourly from 5am to 8pm). For Salvador, take a bus to

BAHIA

BAHIA

Bom Despacho (R$13, two hours, hourly from 5am to 11:45pm) on the Ilha de Itaparica and then a ferry (p461) across the bay.

CAMAMU

☎ 0xx73 / pop 34,300

On the mainland, shielded from the open ocean by the Peninsula de Maraú, Camamu is primarily the jumping-off point for Barra Grande. This picturesque town is the port of call for the many tiny fishing villages in the region and overlooks a maze of mangrove-filled islets and narrow channels. *Saveiro* fishing boats are built and repaired right outside the port. The beautiful **Açaraí Waterfalls** are 5km away by local bus or taxi (R$40 round trip).

The **Pousada Green House** (☎ 3255 2178; Rua Djalma Dutra 61; s/d with fan R$30/50), where the buses stop, is friendly, family-run and great value. Up a steep road from the port, the **Hotel Rio Açaraí** (☎ 3255 2315; www.hotelrioacarai.com.br; Praça Dr Francisco Xavier; s/d R$70/85; 🞰 🞰) is a rather bland modern hotel, but it boasts a fine setting overlooking the river. Rooms are small but tidy with decent natural light and wood-paneled ceilings. Several pleasant riverside cafés lie just past the boat dock.

There is no real bus station here; buses stop near the port. **Águia Branca** (☎ 3255 1823) and **São Geraldo** (☎ 3255 2508) have adjoining offices, and run buses to Ilhéus (R$17, three hours, four daily), Bom Despacho (R$17, 3½ hours, four daily) and Ubaitaba (R$7, 1¼ hours, four daily), where connections south can be found.

BARRA GRANDE

☎ 0xx73

Deliciously off the beaten path, Barra Grande is a remote, tranquil fishing village at the northern tip of the Peninsula de Maraú. It has the same charm and tree-shaded magic that originally attracted bohemian types to similar sand-street villages further south, but it hasn't yet experienced a tourism boom. With a fair number of pousadas and restaurants, Barra Grande makes a great base for checking out the rest of the peninsula. Much of the village closes in winter.

Separating the peninsula from the mainland is the island-riddled Baía de Camamu, Brazil's third-largest bay. One long, dirt road (often impassable after rain) heads down the peninsula, providing access to stunning beaches with crystal-clear water, such as **Praia**

Taipús de Fora (7km, rated among Brazil's top beaches), and a handful of very small fishing villages. Pricey excursions to **Lagoa Azul**, viewpoints, bay islands and down the Rio Maraú are offered by local providers.

Other lovely destinations are accessible on foot. At the base of the village lies the 2km-long **Barra Grande beach**, where the calm waters are fine for swimming. A short walk along the beach leads to the **Ponta da Mutá**, the northeast point of the peninsula, with a lighthouse marking the bay's entrance. Round the rocky point, and you access a long stretch of coast, with **Praia da Bombaça** the next notable beach (3.5km from Barra Grande) before reaching **Praia Taipús de Fora** (located another 3.5km further).

Information

Get funds before going to Barra Grande, as there are no banks. Check www.barragrande .net for the complete lowdown on the area.

Sleeping & Eating

Cantinho da Ivete (☎ 8105 7579; campsite per person R$7, d without bathroom R$30) On the beach path, Ivete offers campsites on a shaded lawn; shabby wooden cabins are also available.

Pousada Canto do Sol (☎ 3258 6018; Rua José Melo Pirajá; s R$50, d R$60-80; 🞰) Near the main plaza, this is a good budget choice for its small, spotless rooms. Hammocks and greenery are part of the setting.

Maria de Firmino (☎ 3258 6482; marilialuana@hotmail .com.br; s/d R$50/80; 🞰) The first pousada as you leave the pier, Maria de Firmino has spacious, somewhat worn rooms.

Portal do Mutá (☎ 3258 6036; www.pousadaportal domuta.com.br; Av José Melo Pirajá; s/d R$60/100; 🞰 🞰) Straight up from the dock, this guesthouse has clean, simple rooms on two levels that open onto a small garden and pool.

Pousada Porto da Barra (☎ 3258 6349; www.pousada portodabarra.com.br; s/d R$90/130; 🞰 🞰) On the beach, this mustard-yellow two-story pousada offers clean, simple rooms with tile floors and hammocks strung outside the doors; the beach is steps away.

Ponta do Mutá (☎ 3258 6028; www.pousadaponta domuta.com.br; Rua do Anjo; s/d/tr R$150/220/280; 🞰) This welcoming guesthouse has 10 simple, pleasantly decorated rooms, each with a veranda, hammock and seaviews. Bicycles and kayaks are available for rental. It's on the beach, left from the dock.

Churrascaria Barra Grande (Praça das Mangueiras; mains for 2 R$25-38; ☺ lunch & dinner) In the main plaza, this steak restaurant serves decent grilled meats.

Café Latino (☎ 3258 6188; Rua Dr Chiriquinho 19; mains R$15-25; ☺ dinner Wed-Mon) On a street leading off the main plaza (go left), this charming bistro and photo gallery serves tasty grilled dishes, pastas and desserts alongside wine and refreshing cocktails.

A Tapera (☎ 3258 6119; Rua Dr Lili; mains for 2 R$30-50; ☺ 3-8pm) Just off the plaza, this traditional Bahian restaurant serves seafood, including amazing squid *moqueca*.

Getting There & Around

Passenger ferries (R$5.50, 1¼ hours, five to six daily from 7:30am to 5:30pm) and *lanchas* (R$25, 25 minutes, four daily) depart for Barra Grande from Camamu. Heading to or from Itacaré, you will need to negotiate a ride with a tour provider (around R$70 per person).

Four-wheel-drive *jardineiras* (R$6) park off the main path in town, and leave for the beaches as soon as they have a full load.

ITACARÉ

☎ 0xx73 / pop 18,300

At its heart, Itacaré is a quiet, colonial fishing town, long sought out by hippies and surfers mesmerized by wide stretches of virgin Atlantic rain forest, postcard-perfect beaches and reliable surf breaks. In recent years, the paving of the road into town has led to a tourism boom, with dozens of pousadas and restaurants now packing the streets. In spite of this, the mellow, youthful vibe prevails. Deviating from the Bahian norm, Carnaval here is all about reggae.

Orientation

Itacaré lies at the mouth of Rio de Contas, where the river meets the sea. A short walk east of the working-class neighborhoods around the fishing port leads to the area known as Pituba, which is essentially one long street, Rua Pedro Longo, lined with pousadas, restaurants and shops. Follow this road east out of town to access Itacaré's prettiest beaches. North of the Pituba strip is known as Condomínio Conchas do Mar, and has higher-end restaurants and pousadas in a more verdant setting. The neighborhood ends at the small beach of Praia da Concha.

Information

There are several exchange offices near Praça dos Cachorros as well as a **Banco do Brasil ATM** (Rua João de Deus 150) just off the main strip. Internet cafés are plentiful, costing around R$6 per hour.

Dangers & Annoyances

There has been a rash of muggings at and around Itacaré's beaches, so take little money and nothing of value. Avoid the trails through the forests past late afternoon.

Activities

The coast south of Itacaré is characterized by rough surf (which is better for surfing than for swimming) and cove beaches separated by hills covered with rain forest. Some beaches, such as idyllic **Prainha** (reachable by trail from Praia do Ribeira), are private and charge entrance fees. **Praia da Concha** is an ordinary city beach. **Resende**, **Tiririca** and **Ribeira** beaches lie within 1.5km south of town and are frequented by surfers. Highly recommended are the paradisiacal **Engenhoca**, **Havaizinho** and **Itacarezinho** beaches, located 12km south of town.

Many travel agencies and seemingly every hotel offer canoe trips upriver, rafting, mountain biking, rappelling and excursions on foot or horseback to local sights. The principal excursion is up the Peninsula of Maraú, with stops at **Lagoa Azul** and **Praia Taipús de Fora** (R$60). A word of advice: maximize your comfort by assuring that the vehicle's seats face forward.

Several reliable agencies offering these kinds of adventures include **V9** (☎ 3251 2000; www.v9centraldepasseiositacare.com.br; Rua do Campo 100) and **Zebra & Pepê** (☎ 3251 2267; mestrezebra@hotmail .com; Rua Pedro Longo 385).

Surfboard rental and surf lessons are easily arranged. Zebra & Pepê offer board rentals for R$20 per day and three-day classes for R$180.

For a do-it-yourself excursion and a swim, catch a bus leaving town and hop off at the **Cachoeira Tijuipe** (admission R$5), a wide waterfall of tea-colored water on private, forested land.

Sleeping

The majority of guesthouses are scattered along Rua Pedro Longo. For a quieter, more idyllic stay that's still close to the action, look for guesthouses in Condomínios do Mar.

BAHIA

Tropical Camping (☎ 3251 3531; Rua Pedro Longo 187; per person R$10) In the middle of town, this grassy campsite has decent shade.

Albergue O Farol (☎ 3251 2527; www.albergueopharol .com.br; Praça Santos Dumont 7; dm/d with fan R$25/70) A favorite among young backpackers, this low-key hostel has tidy rooms, some with private verandas.

Pousada Estrela (☎ 3251 2006; Rua Pedro Longo 34; s R$40-60, d R$50-80; ▨) One of Itacaré's better deals, Estrela has a range of fine rooms, some quite spacious with big windows. There are hammocks and a garden in back.

Pousada Cores do Mar (☎ 3251 3418; Condomínio Conchas do Mar; s/d with fan R$50/75) This simple, inexpensive pousada has a row of tidy, fan-cooled rooms facing a small grassy courtyard.

Pousada Maresia (☎ 3251 2338; www.maresia pousada.com.br; Rua Pedro Longo 388; d R$80; ▨) Simple but nicely painted rooms and a lush garden courtyard are part of the charm of this fairly priced guesthouse. Rooms have verandas with hammocks.

Casa Zaza (☎ 3251 3022; www.itacare.com; Condomínio Conchas do Mar; d R$100; ▨ ▧) Run by a welcoming Dutch owner, Casa Zaza has a warm, home-like feel with nicely furnished rooms, some with small balconies. There's a tree-shaded backyard, a pool and plenty of relaxing lounge space.

Sítio Paraíso (☎ 3251 2113; www.sitioparaiso.tur.br; Rua Leonardo Magalhães 148; d/ste/chalet R$110/130/200; ▨ ▧) Spread across 2 hectares, Sítio Paraíso is a tranquil setting complete with pool, sauna and games room. Accommodations range from simple boxy rooms to spacious chalets with small kitchens.

Itacaré Hostel (☎ /fax 251 2030; www.itacarehostel .com.br; Rua Lodônio Almeida 120; dm/d R$40/120; ▣ ▧) In the heart of the action, this HI hostel has small, tidy rooms fronted by hammocks and a narrow courtyard with a pool. Discounts for HI members.

Pousada Nainas (☎ 3251 2683; www.nainas.com.br; Praia da Concha; d R$140; ▨) Set around a pretty garden, Pousada Nainas has uniquely designed rooms, painted in vibrant colors. All have private verandas strung with hammocks for soaking up the tropical vibe.

our pick Pousada Ilha Verde (☎ 3251 2056; www .ilhaverde.com.br; Rua Ataíde Setúbal 234; d R$170-190; ▨ ▧) In a lush setting, Ilha Verde has seven handsome, uniquely decorated rooms and one family bungalow. There's a Jacuzzi, a pool, and abundant outdoor lounge space for soak-ing up the greenery. It's run by a welcoming Franco-Brazilian family.

Burundanga (☎ 3251 2543; www.burundanga.com.br; Condomínio Conchas do Mar; d R$200; ▨ ▧) This bou-tique hotel has beautifully furnished rooms, hung with artwork and uniquely decorated with tropical woods and textures. Common to all rooms are private wooden decks overlook-ing the greenery.

Sage Point (☎ 3251 2030; www.pousadasagepoint .com.br; d with fan from R$329) Perched on a hill overlooking Praia Tiririca are beautiful wooden chalets with ocean views. It's run by a friendly Cuban-American.

Eating & Drinking

A browse up and down Itacaré's main strip, Rua Lodônia Almeida (which turns into Rua Pedro Longo), is the best way to discover what's on offer.

Gelato Grão (☎ 3251 3500; Rua Lodônio Almeida; 1/2 scoops R$2.50/4; ◷ noon-10pm) Although service doesn't come with a smile, this ice-cream shop serves creamy rich *sorvete* (ice cream).

Sahara (☎ 3251 3313; Rua Pedro Longo 500; sandwiches R$4-7; ◷ noon-10pm Wed-Mon) The new favourite in town is this small, inviting café serving up heavenly falafel sandwiches, plates of hummus and tabbouleh and refreshing lassis (yogurt drinks).

Habitat Café (☎ 3251 2480; Praia da Concha; sand-wiches R$8.50-10.50; ◷ 4-10pm) A casual grassy spot one block from the beach, this outdoor café serves addictive sandwiches (including burg-ers and soy burgers), juices and salads.

Almazen (☎ 3251 2483; Rua Pedro Longo 69; main R$12; ◷ lunch & dinner) Healthy natural food is served here, including sandwiches on homemade bread, and a delicious vegetarian *prato feito* (plate of the day).

Restaurante Mediterrâneo (☎ 3251 3444; Rua João Coutinho 70; mains R$18-26; ◷ dinner) In a colonial building near the Praça dos Cachorros, this lovely Italian restaurant serves tasty home-made pastas, grilled dishes, salads and more.

Boca do Forno (☎ 3251 2174; Rua Lodônia Almeida 108; pizzas R$18-35; ◷ dinner) This place serves pizzas everyone raves about in a beautiful floral out-door setting. Live music some nights.

our pick Jardim dos Sabores (☎ 3251 2966; Con-domínio Conchas do Mar; mains R$18-36; ◷ dinner) Sur-rounded by palms and a tropical garden, this is a lovely spot to linger over a meal. Top picks include paella, fresh grilled fish or filet mignon. Live jazz or bossa most nights.

Estrela do Mar (☎ 3251 2230; Praia da Concha; mains R$23-30; ✆ noon-10pm) Overlooking Concha beach, the elegant Estrela do Mar serves expertly prepared seafood, as well as pastas, salads and crepes. It has huge windows for taking in the sea, and outdoor seating.

Mistura Fina (☎ 3251 2289; Rua Pedro Longo 265; mains for 2 R$50-60; ✆ dinner) Serves fish *moqueca*, seafood risottos and other rich but satisfying fare.

Restaurante Mar e Mel (☎ 3251 2358; Praia da Concha; ✆ 7pm-midnight) This is the place to hear (and dance to) live *forró*. There's a spacious wooden deck in front and abundant seafood and drink choices.

Getting There & Around

Itacaré's **bus station** (☎ 3288 2019) is located just out of the center, but it's a bit of a hike from many of the pousadas. To get to Itacaré, you will most likely need to connect through Itabuna or Ilhéus. **Rota** (☎ 3251 2181) has frequent buses to Ilheus (R$7.50, 1½ hours, from 5:15am to 7:30pm) and Itabuna (R$10.50, 2½ hours, from 6am to 7:30pm). Several daily buses go to Porto Seguro (R$38, eight hours).

A ferry carries cars and passengers across the river to the Peninsula de Maraú (R$10). Several agencies in town hire cars, including **Pituba** (☎ 3251 3648; Rua Pedro Longo 235; per day R$90).

ILHÉUS

☎ 0xx73 / pop 224,000

Bright, early-20th-century architecture and oddly angled streets lend a vibrant and rather playful air to Ilhéus.

The town's fame comes from its history as a prosperous cocoa port, as well as being the hometown of Jorge Amado (Brazil's best-known novelist). He used it as the setting for one of his best novels, *Gabriela, Cravo e Canela* ('Gabriela, Clove and Cinnamon'). When you combine all this with Ilhéus' attractive city geography, its affable people and the nearby Atlantic rain-forest reserves, you can argue it's worth a quick stopover.

Lively during the day, the center clears out after dark, making it unsafe to wander.

History

Ilhéus was a sleepy place until cacao was introduced into the region from Belém in 1881. With the sugar plantations in the doldrums,

impoverished agricultural workers and freed or escaped slaves flocked from all over the Northeast to the hills surrounding Ilhéus to participate in the new boom: cacao, known as the *ouro branco* (white gold) of Brazil.

Sudden, lawless and violent, the scramble to plant cacao displayed all the characteristics of a gold rush. When the dust settled, the land and power belonged to a few ruthless *coroneis* (so-called 'colonels') and their hired guns. The landless were left to work, and usually live, on the *fazendas*, where they were subjected to a harsh and paternalistic labor system. This history is graphically told by Amado, who grew up on a cacao plantation, in his book *Terras do Sem Fim* (published in English as *The Violent Land*).

In the early 1990s, the *vassoura de bruxa* (witch's broom) disease left cacao trees shriveled and unable to bear fruit, hurting the area's economy dramatically. Though the disease persists to this day, you can still see cacao *fazendas* and rural workers like those Amado described throughout the lush, tropical hills.

Orientation

The city center is located on a beach-lined point that reaches into the mouth of the Rio Cachoeira, and is sandwiched between two hills. On the southern side of the s-curving river mouth is the modern neighborhood of Pontal.

Information

There are ATMs next to the cathedral.

Banco do Brasil (Rua Marquês de Paranagua 112, Centro)

Órbita Expedições (☎ 3634 7700; www.orbita expedicoes.com.br; Rua Marquês de Paranaguá 270) This adventure outfit offers a wide range of tours, including rafting, canoeing, hiking and cycling trips.

Post office (Rua Marquês de Paranagua)

Reality Internet (Rua Dom Eduardo, Centro; per hr R$4) Speedy internet access.

Tourist office (☎ 2101 5588; Praça Dom Eduardo, Centro; ✆ 9am-7pm)

Sights & Activities

The best thing to do in Ilhéus is explore the old streets. The center has several old, gargoyled buildings such as the **Prefeitura** (Praça Seabra).

The **Casa de Jorge Amado** (Rua Jorge Amado 21; admission R$1; ✆ 9am-noon & 2-6pm Mon-Fri, 9am-1pm Sat, 3-5pm Sun), where the great writer lived with his parents while working on his first novel, has been restored and turned into a Casa de

BAHIA

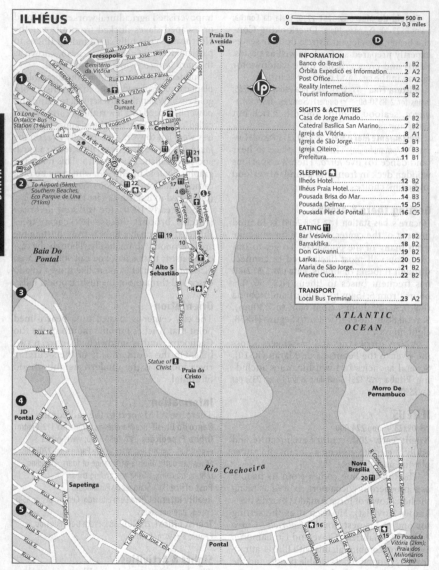

ILHÉUS

Cultura, complete with an interesting display about the man himself. Not many writers can boast this sort of recognition while still alive, but Amado became a national treasure well before his death in 2001. For more on Amado, see the boxed text on opposite.

The **Catedral Basílica San Marino** (Praça Dom Eduardo) is the city's icon and a unique, eclectic mix of architectural styles. The **Igreja de São Jorge** (Praça Rui Barbosa; Tue-Sun) is the city's oldest church, dating from 1534, and houses a small sacred-art museum.

BEACHES
City beaches are dirty. Your best bet is to head south, but even then you'll find that

the area's beaches are best for a *futebol* game (broad and flat), and it takes kilometers for the water to lose the muddy color of the river outflow. **Praia dos Milionários** (7km) has some *barracas* and is popular with locals, as is the prettier **Praia Cururupe** (12km), where a small river curves into the sea.

Tours

Trips to a tree-sloth recuperation center, a chocolate factory and Primavera Fazenda, where you'll be taken through the process of cacao production, can all be arranged through local travel agencies. Tours are also given of Lagoa Encantada, a state-protected area of Atlantic rain forest with waterfalls and wildlife; Rio do Engenho, an estate with Bahia's first sugarcane mill; and the Capela de Santana (1537), Brazil's third-oldest church. For information on the Ecoparque de Una tour, see the boxed text, p480.

Festivals & Events

As any knowledgeable Amado fan would guess, Ilhéus has highly spirited festivals. The best are the **Gincana da Pesca** in early January, **Festa de São Sebastião** (much samba and capoeira) from January 11 to 20, **Festa de São Jorge** (featuring Candomblé) on April 23 and **Festa das Águas** (Candomblé) in December. **Carnaval** has a full complement of *trios elétricos*.

Sleeping

Ilhéus' best hotels are located south of the city along the road to Olivença, making them convenient only for those traveling by car. Accommodations in the center are generally a bit run down, while Pontal has more modern options.

BUDGET

Pousada Brisa do Mar (☎ 231 2644; Av 2 de Julho 136; s/d R$40/50;) This pleasant modern pousada really does have a sea breeze (*brisa do mar*) and a privileged view over the river. The walk to the center at night, though short, is dark and desolate. Take a taxi.

Pousada Delmar (☎ 3632 8435; mamorim@cepec.gov .br; Rua Castro Alves 322, Pontal; s/d from R$45/60;) This is a popular modern hotel, with an open-air breakfast patio. It's nicely set on the Pontal.

MIDRANGE & TOP END

Ilhéos Hotel (☎ 3634 4242; Rua Eustáquio Bastos 144, Centro; s/d R$80/100;) This multistoried 1930s hotel has a fading grandeur and a vintage elevator that was hand-cranked until electrified in 1950. The rooms are fairly comfortable and have views over the bay. Rooms without window are cheaper.

Ilhéus Praia Hotel (☎ 3634 2533; www.ilheuspraia .com.br; Praça Dom Eduardo, Centro; s/d R$120/150;   ) This standard, high-rise hotel has fine views and lies in the heart of the center.

BAHIA'S FAVORITE SON

Nobody is more responsible for bringing Bahian culture to the rest of the world than Jorge Amado, Brazil's most famous romanticist author. Amado's tales have been translated into 49 languages and read the world over.

Born in 1912, Jorge spent his youth in Ilheús, the scene of many of his later novels. After secondary studies in Salvador, Amado studied law in Rio, but instead of going into practice he decided to become a writer. He surprised critics and the public by publishing his first novel, *O País do Carnaval*, when he was only 19 years old.

An avowed communist, Amado participated in the rebel literary movement of the time, launching two romances set in the cacao zone around Ilheús: *Cacau* and *Suor*. The first novel was banned by the fascist-leaning Vargas government, which only increased Amado's popularity. Sent to prison several times for his beliefs, Amado was elected a federal deputy for the Brazilian communist party (PCB) in 1945, but he lost his seat after a disagreement with the party several years later. He left Brazil and lived for more than five years in Europe and Asia, finally breaking ties with the communist party after the crimes of Stalin were revealed to the world.

With *Gabriela, Cravo e Canela* ('Gabriela, Clove and Cinnamon'), published in 1958, he entered a new writing phase, marked by a picturesque style that intimately described the colorful escapades of his Bahian heroes and heroines.

Amado died in Salvador in August 2001, just short of his 89th birthday.

Pousada Pier do Pontal (☎ 3632 4000; www .pierdopontal.com.br; Av Lamanto Jr 1650, Pontal; d from R$150; 🖭 🖭) In a peaceful location across the river, this guesthouse has simple, colorfully decorated rooms, some with sea-fronting verandas. There's also a pool, sauna and Japanese restaurant here.

Pousada Vitória (☎ 3632 4997; Sítio São Paulo, Praia do Sul; d from R$170; 🖭) Overlooking the pretty Praia do Sul, this attractive guesthouse resembles a Swiss chalet. Rooms are comfortably furnished, the best with verandas overlooking the sea. Decent restaurant on-site.

Eating

Barrakítika (☎ 3231 8300; Praça Antônio Muniz 39; per kg R$11; ⏱ lunch & dinner) This casual hangout has outdoor tables and an inexpensive lunch buffet. There's live music on weekend evenings.

Mestre Cuca (☎ 3634 1092; 2nd fl, Rua Eustáquio Bastos 126; per kg R$19; ⏱ lunch) This popular spot spreads an excellent self-service lunch, and the airy dining room has partial sea views.

Maria de São Jorge (☎ 3634 1798; Rua A Lavigne de Lemos 33; per kg R$22; ⏱ lunch Mon-Sat) In a colonial building in the old quarter, this charming spot has a small but top-quality lunch buffet. Bahian artwork and colorful décor adds to the allure.

Don Giovanni (☎ 3634 4459; Av 2 de Julho 1067; mains R$15-30; ⏱ dinner Tue-Sun) One of Ilheus' classiest dining rooms, this Italian restaurant overlooking the water serves tasty pastas and pizzas.

Bar Vesúvio (☎ 3634 2164; Praça Dom Eduardo, Centro; mains R$18-25; ⏱ lunch & dinner) Attracts both Amado fans and those interested in Arabic food and a cold beer at the outdoor tables facing the cathedral. Across the road, Ponto Chic has ice-cream flavors of tasty local fruits.

In Pontal, major traffic turns south off the road along the bay, creating a quiet area near the end of the point with great views back to the center. Nearby are a few restaurants, including **Larika** (Av Getúlio Vargas; sandwiches R$6; ⏱ 6pm-1am), a stand serving sandwiches and fresh fruit juices at bayside tables.

Getting There & Away
AIR
TAM (☎ 3234 5259; airport) and **Gol** (☎ 0800 280 0465) can fly or connect you to anywhere in Brazil from Ilhéus' **Aeroporto Jorge Amado** (code IOS; ☎ 3231 7629).

BUS
The **long-distance bus station** (☎ 3634 4121) is 15km from the center. Buses go to Valença (R$26, five hours, two daily), Porto Seguro (R$37, six hours, four daily), Vitória (R$91 to R$130, 13 hours, two daily) and Rio (R$162 to R$186, 22 hours, two daily).

Buses to Salvador (R$73, seven hours, three daily) make a long sweep around the Baía de Todos os Santos, recommended if you are stopping in the *recôncavo* on the way. Otherwise, catch a bus to Bom Despacho on the Ilha de Itaparica, and then a ferry into Salvador. For ferry information, see p461.

More frequent connections can be made in Itabuna, located 30km inland. Local buses to Itabuna leave from the local bus terminal in the town center and also from outside the long-distance bus station (R$3.50, 40 minutes) every 15 minutes from 5:30am to midnight.

ECOPARQUE DE UNA

The **Ecoparque de Una** (☎ 3633 1121; www.ecoparque.org.br in Portuguese; admission R$15; ⏱ 8am-5pm Tue-Sun) is a lush Atlantic rain forest reserve 63km south of Ilhéus. Here, guides lead visitors on a 2km trail, including four suspended tree-canopy walkways. The tour lasts two hours and ends with a cool pond dip.

Taking refuge in the park are rare species such as the golden-headed lion tamarin *(Leontopithecus chrysomelas)*. These unusual monkeys have the look and proud gaze of miniature lions: a blazing yellow, orange and brown striped coat, a golden mane and a long, scruffy tail. If you're lucky you'll also see *tatus* (armadillos), *pacas* (agoutis), capybaras and *veados* (deer), all native to the area.

Visits can be arranged through a travel agency or you can make a direct appointment – but you'll need to call at least one day in advance. If you go on your own, the bus to Canavieiras drops you at the park gate, where a park jeep picks you up.

Getting Around

The local bus terminal (*terminal urbano*) is on the edge of the center in a super-sinister area of abandoned-looking warehouses – not where you want to be at night or with your bags.

TO/FROM THE AIRPORT

The airport is in Pontal, 3.5km from the center. Taxis cost R$12.

TO/FROM THE BUS STATION

From the center, Teotónio Vilela, Circular and Santo Brinto buses pass the bus station. Taxis cost R$18.

OLIVENÇA

☎ 0xx73

Olivença is a small, charming beach town 16km south of Ilhéus. Sights include a spa, where the baths are believed to have healing powers, and a nearby indigenous village. The grassy town shore has beautiful cove beaches with rock formations and flat sand, powerful waves and a restaurant or two. Deserted beaches with calmer water stretch south of Olivença.

There are great waves just north of town at **Batuba** and **Backdoor**, Brazil's third-best surf break. The multilingual Marcio of **Pokoloco Surf Shop** (☎ 3269 1493) rents long and short boards (per day R$20) and gives surf lessons (for six hours private R$100).

The artfully decorated **Pousada Fazenda Tororomba Hostel** (☎ 9141 4372; www.fazendatororomba.com .br; Rua Eduardo Magalhães; dm/s/d with fan R$40/50/70, d chalet with kitchen R$130; ☒) is spread over a large grassy property with big trees and a pond. A house with a living room and full kitchen has several collective rooms. There are also comfortably set doubles and rustic chalets, some with outdoor spa baths. **Camping Estância das Fontes** (☎ 3269 1480; per person R$8), 15km south of Ilhéus, is close to the beach and has hot showers.

City buses leave every 30 minutes from the Ilhéus bus station (passing the city bus terminal) for Olivença (30 minutes) from 6am to 11pm. The bus travels close to the beaches, so you can hop off when you see one you like.

PORTO SEGURO

☎ 0xx73 / pop 128,000

The state's second most visited destination, Porto Seguro swarms with Brazilian package tourists who come from all across the country for partying and beach action. Not surprisingly, there's well-developed infrastructure here, with hundreds of hotels and colorful buildings (none over two stories) that lean toward a colonial aesthetic. This is, after all, the region where Portuguese sailors first landed in the New World, and you can see relics from those early settlement days. Aside from history, Porto Seguro is really only for inveterate nightlife seekers who don't mind the crowds. Otherwise, most travelers linger in town only long enough to change money and catch the ferry toward Arraial d'Ajuda.

History

Pedro Cabral's landing 16km north of Porto Seguro (Safe Port) at Coroa Vermelha is officially considered the first Portuguese landfall in Brazil. The sailors didn't stay long, just long enough to stock up on supplies. Three years later Gonçalvo Coelho's expedition arrived and planted a marker in what is now Porto Seguro's Cidade Histórica (Historic City). Jesuits on the same expedition built a church, now in ruins, in Outeiro da Glória. In 1526, a naval outpost, convent and chapel (Igreja NS da Misericórdia) were built in the present-day Cidade Histórica.

The Tupininquin, not the Pataxó, were the indigenous tribe around the site of Porto Seguro when the Portuguese landed. They were rapidly conquered and enslaved by the colonists, but the Aimoré, Pataxó, Cataxó and other inland tribes resisted Portuguese colonization and constantly threatened Porto Seguro. Military outposts were built along the coast in Belmonte, Vila Viçosa, Prado and Alcobaça to defend against both European attacks by sea and Indian attacks by land.

The Indians managed to take Porto Seguro twice and, according to colonial documents, reduced Porto Seguro to rubble in 1612 (thus undermining the city's claims to have 16th-century buildings).

Information

Adeltour (☎ 3288 1888; www.adeltour.com.br, in Portuguese; Shopping Avenida, Av 22 de Abril 100; ☺ 9am-7:30pm Mon-Fri, 9am-3pm Sat) For national and international air travel. Changes cash and traveler's checks. Also in the airport.

Banco do Brasil (Av 22 de Abril)

Bradesco ATM (Praça do Relógio) Also on Av dos Navegantes.

Brazil Travel (☎ 3288 1824; www.braziltravel.tur.br; Av 22 de Abril 200; ☺ 8am-10pm Mon-Sat) Offers local tours by multilingual guides.

Clínica NS d'Ajuda (☎ 3288 1307; Av dos Navegantes 640) Medical service.

Glória Viagens e Turismo (☎ 3288 0758; Av 22 de Abril 286; ☀ 7am-10pm) Offers a range of tours.

Internet Point (☎ 3268 4191; Av dos Navegantes 90; per hr R$4; ☀ 9am-11pm) Internet access; also changes US dollars and euros.

Pataxó (☎ 3288 1256; Praça dos Pataxós; ☀ 9am-6pm Mon-Sat) This tourism outfit and handicrafts shop provides information.

Police station (Rua Itagibá)

Post office (Rua Itagibá)

Dangers & Annoyances

It's best to take a taxi or the bus on Av Beira Mar at night as muggings are all too common.

Sights & Activities
BEACHES

North of town is one long bay dotted with *barracas* and clubs with invisible divisions creating **Praia Curuípe** (3km), **Praia Itacimirim** (4km), **Praia Mundaí** (6km) and **Praia Taperapuã** (7km). The sands are white and fluffy, backed by green vegetation and lapped by a tranquil sea. **Tôa Tôa** (Praia de Taperapuã), **Axé Moi** (Praia Mundaí) and **Barramares** (Praia de Taperapuã) are the biggest beach clubs and all have MCs and dancers leading crowds through popular dances. The best advice is to get off the bus at Tôa Tôa and walk north until you find your spot.

CIDADE HISTÓRICA

Motivation is required to climb the stairs to the Cidade Histórica. Rewards include a sweeping view, colorful old buildings, and free and humorous capoeira demonstrations given under the round roof behind the churches (hourly in high season). Housed in the former Câmara Municipal (Town Council), the **Museu Porto Seguro** (☎ 3288 5182; admission R$3; ☀ 9am-5pm) contains exhibits on Brazil's early settlement, with rooms dedicated to exploration and colonial life; even more interesting are the museum's exhibits on indigenous life, including films covering important rites and celebrations. Opposite the museum is Gonçalo Coelho's **marker stone**, now encased in glass and ringed with a fence. Other reminders of the past are the **Igreja NS da Misericórdia** (1526), which houses the **Museu de Arte Sacra**, with a collection of chalices, crucifixes and other religious pieces. Other old stone churches to peer inside include the **Igreja NS da Pena** (1772)

and the **Capela de São Benedito**, dating from the 16th century.

Warning: the area is beautifully illuminated at night, and definitely worth a look, but the steps are not safe after dark. Take a bus or taxi.

Courses

The friendly **Capoeira Sul da Bahia** (☎ 3268 2247; Rua Benedito Claudio 98; per class R$12) welcomes visitors to watch or take a class at its academy.

Tours

Local agencies offer schooner tours to Praia do Espelho (R$40) as well as trips to Trancoso (R$100), Caraíva (R$150) and the Parque Nacional Monte Pascoal (R$50). Trips are also offered to Recife de Fora (R$20) and Coroa Alta (R$50) offshore reefs, but we don't recommend it, as visitors are encouraged to walk over coral reefs in order to enter internal pools. Travel agencies are scattered along Av 22 de Abril.

Festivals & Events

Porto Seguro's **Carnaval** is Bahia's most famous after Salvador's. It is relatively small and safe, consisting of a few *trios elétricos* cruising the main drag blasting *axé* music, and lasts until the Saturday after Ash Wednesday, an additional four days longer than in other places. Well-known groups play here after finishing up in Salvador.

On April 19 to 22 the discovery of Brazil is commemorated with an outdoor mass and Indian celebrations on Av do Descobrimento. This seems a rather baffling celebration since the Indians lived here before the 'discoverers' and fared poorly after their arrival. The **Festa de São Benedito** is celebrated in the Cidade Histórica on December 25 to 27. Children blacken their faces and perform African dances, such as *congo da alma, ole* or *lalá,* to the percussion of drums, *cuica* and *xeque-xeque.*

Sleeping

Porto Seguro overflows with hotels, meaning decent low-cost rooms are easy to find. Reservations are still essential for major holidays.

BUDGET

Camping Mundaí Praia (☎ 3679 2287; www.camping mundai.com.br, in Portuguese; per person R$14; ☀) Opposite the beach, 4km north of town, this place

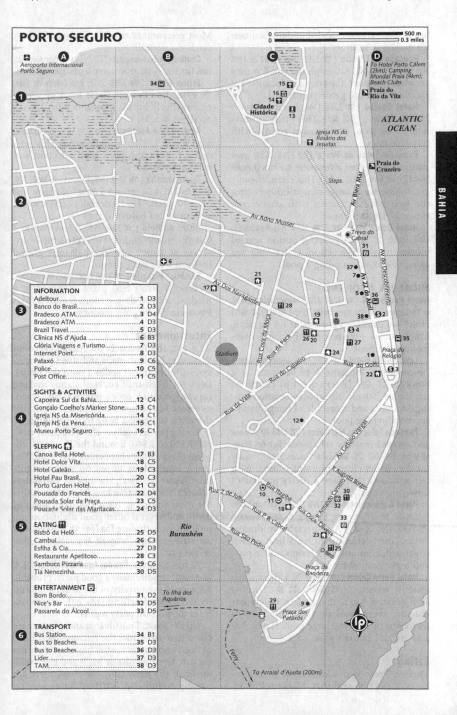

PORTO SEGURO

| 0 | 500 m |
| 0 | 0.3 miles |

BAHIA

Aeroporto Internacional
Porto Seguro

To Hotel Porto Cálem
(2km); Camping
Mundaí Praia (4km);
Beach Clubs

Praia do
Rio da Vila

Cidade
Histórica

ATLANTIC
OCEAN

Igreja NS do
Rosário dos
Jesuítas

Praia do
Cruzeiro

Steps

Av Beira Mar

Av Adno Musser

Trevo do
Cabral

Av do Descobrimento

Av 22 de Abril

Av Dos Navegantes

Stadium

Praça do
Relógio

Rua Cova da Moça

Rua da Faca

Rua do Cajueiro

Rua do Golfo

Rua da Vala

Av Getúlio Vargas

R Augusta Borges

Rua Itagibá

R. Oscar Amando Cerneiro

Rua Oscar Oliveira

Rua 2 de Julho

Rua P. P. Cabral

Rua São Pedro

Rio
Buranhém

Praça da
Bandeira

O Beco

To Ilha dos
Aquários

Praça dos
Pataxós

To Arraial d'Ajuda (200m)

Ferry

has shaded campsites and abundant facilities; it's packed in summer.

Pousada do Francês (☎ 3288 2469; Av 22 de Abril 180; s/d R$30/50; ❄) Although the small rooms are worn and dark, the price and location are excellent. Pleasant garden courtyard.

Hotel Galeão (☎ 3288 1141; Av dos Navegantes 250; s/d R$40/60; ❄ ⌨) This tidy guesthouse has trim, inexpensive rooms with tiny balconies.

Pousada Solar da Praça (☎ 3288 2585; www .pousadasolardapraca.com, in Portuguese; Rua Assis Chateaubriand 75; s/d from R$40/70; ❄) This clean, friendly guesthouse has a range of small tidy rooms; the best have balconies with partial sea views. Noisy at night.

Hotel Dolce Vita (☎ 3288 1058; Rua Itagibá 67; s/d R$60/70; ❄ ⌨) A peaceful option several blocks from all the action, Dolce Vita has aging rooms surrounding a pool.

MIDRANGE & TOP END

Hotel Pau Brasil (☎ 3288 2226; www.paubrasil.net, in Portuguese; Av dos Navegantes 255; d R$80; ❄ ⌨) Hotel Pau Brasil is a good value for its clean, simple rooms – the best have balconies overlooking the pool.

Canoa Bella Hotel (☎ 3288 1510; www.portoseguro .net/canoabella, in Portuguese; Av dos Navegantes 555; d from R$80; ❄ ⌨) There's a bit of charm to the Canoa Bella, with exposed beamed ceilings, mosaics and a cascade of bougainvillea surrounding the pool.

Pousada Solar das Maritacas (☎ 3288 2082; www .portonet.com.br/maritacas, in Portuguese; Rua dos Periquitos 50; d R$100; ❄ ⌨) Maritacas has homey touches in its clean, pleasant rooms, with tall windows that face a pretty garden of flowering vines.

Porto Garden Hotel (☎ 3288 2621; www.hotelporto garden.com.br, in Portuguese; Rua Oscar da Rosa Teixeira 1; s/d R$100/120; ❄ ⌨) A respectable midrange option, the Porto Garden has a lush garden courtyard, trim and tidy rooms and a pool and a playground for kids.

Hotel Porto Cálem (☎ 3268 8400; www.portocalem .com.br, in Portuguese; s/d R$150/170; ❄ ⌨) Located 2km north of town, the modern Cálem has spacious rooms looking across the road to the ocean or over the large pool. It also has a sauna and games room.

Eating

Though Porto is not known for its restaurants, it can't be said that it lacks selection.

Most restaurants are found along the Passarela do Álcool.

Cambuí (Av dos Navegantes 222; ❄ 8am-10pm Mon-Sat, 8am-1pm Sun) A large, convenient supermarket.

Esfíha & Cia (☎ 3288 5917; Rua Cidade de Fafe; ❄ 9:30am-10pm Mon-Sat) These meat or veggie *esfíhas* (fluffy breads topped or filled) make excellent snacks.

Restaurante Apetitoso (☎ 3288 1537; Av dos Navegantes 404; per kg R$16; ❄ lunch & dinner) This self-service restaurant has a good selection and is always packed.

Tia Nenezinha (☎ 3288 1846; Passarela do Álcool 170; mains for 2 R$34-60; ❄ lunch & dinner) A classic for over 30 years, Tia Nenezinha serves a fine assortment of Bahian dishes.

Bistrô da Helô (☎ 3288 3940; O Beco; mains for 2 R$35-45; ❄ dinner Tue-Sun) This cute little bistro serves gourmet fare like balsamic glazed shellfish with basil risotto.

Sambuca Pizzaria (☎ 3288 2366; Praça dos Pataxós; ❄ dinner) Porto's best pizza is served in a nicely decorated dining room removed from Passarela do Álcool's madness.

Entertainment

At night, the Passarela do Álcool (Alcohol Walkway) has craft stalls and street performers, with live music spilling onto the plazas. Look for fresh-fruit cocktail stands making *capeta* (*guaraná*, cocoa powder, cinnamon, sweetened condensed milk and vodka), just the thing to bring a bang to the evening.

Young partiers selling club and party tickets (R$20 to R$40) around the Passarela will let you know what's happening that night. The major beach clubs all put on weekly nighttime *luaus* (parties); the one at **Barramares** (☎ 3679 2980; Av Beira Mar km 6, Praia de Taperapuã) is the most stunning. It's about 6km north of town, and several other good nightspots are on the way, including **Tôa Tôa** (☎ 3679 1555; www .portaltoatoa.com.br, in Portuguese; Av Beira Mar km 5, Praia de Taperapuã).

Across the river, **Ilha dos Aquários** (☎ 3268 2828; Ilha Pacuío) is traditionally a good party, probably because of the novelty of the aquariums and its river-island setting (reachable by boats from the port on party nights).

Up the coast, Transilvânia and Alcatraz are clubs decorated like their namesakes. Each of these enormous venues has separate areas for *axé*, *forró*, samba or MPB and electronic music. If the party is up the coast, there are usually round-trip courtesy buses leaving from the *trevo do Cabral* (traffic circle at the entrance of town). For further information about these *luaus* and clubs, call **Porto Night** (☎ 3268 2828; www.portonight.com.br, in Portuguese).

In town, **Bom Bordo** (☎ 3288 4113; Av 22 de Abril 151) can be fun when it fills up with people swinging to *axé* and *forró*. Near the Passarela, **Nice's Bar** (Rua Armando Carneiro 19) is a laid-back reggae bar just off the mayhem.

Getting There & Away
AIR
BRA (☎ 3288 8917; airport), **Gol** (☎ 3268 4460; airport) and **TAM** (☎ 3288 3399; Av 22 de Abril 245) can connect you anywhere in Brazil from **Aeroporto Internacional Porto Seguro** (code BPS; ☎ 3288 1880), about 2km northeast of town. There are no buses to the airport. Taxis run to R$20.

BUS
The turnoff for Porto Seguro from Hwy BR-101 is at Eunápolis. The **bus station** (☎ 3288 1914) is 1.5km outside town on the road to Eunápolis. Additional buses run during high season.

São Geraldo (☎ 3288 1198) goes to São Paulo (R$175 to R$228, 26 hours, two daily), Rio (R$178, 19 hours, one daily) and Belo Horizonte (R$116 to R$156, 18 hours, two daily), and its tickets can be purchased through travel agencies in the center. **Águia Branca** (☎ 3288 1039) goes to Vitória (R$69 to R$99, 10 hours, two daily), Valença (R$51, nine hours, one daily), Bom Despacho (R$62, 12 hours, one daily) and Salvador (R$110 to R$140, 11 hours, two daily). **Rota Sul** (☎ 3288 3065) goes to Ilhéus (R$37, six hours, four daily) and shares the Itabuna (R$30, five hours, eight daily) route with Águia Branca. **Brasileiro** (☎ 3288 3065) goes to Itamaraju (R$17, three hours, six daily) for access to Corumbau, and Teixeira de Freitas (R$25, five hours, six daily) for access to Caravelas.

For more frequent connections, three companies run buses to Eunápolis (R$8, one hour, every 30 minutes from 5:30am to 10pm).

Getting Around
From Porto Seguro, take the Riacho Doce, Alto do Mundaí, Campinho-Barramares or Cabralia buses to the beach. On the return trip, hop off at the traffic circle if your bus is heading up to the bus station. Taxis and mototaxi are widely available throughout the city. For car and buggy rental, try **Lider** (☎ 3288 1505; www.alugueldecarrosportoseguro.com; Av 22 de Abril

397; per day R$90), which also has a branch at the airport.

NORTH OF PORTO SEGURO
The beaches maintain the same look from Porto Seguro north: long, gently curving bays of powdery sands and gentle seas backed by flowering vines. A good paved road runs along the coast, so it is much more developed than the southern coast.

Coroa Vermelha, a village 13km north of Porto Seguro, has a beach lined with *barracas* and reefs, and several pousadas. A walkway bordered by Pataxó craft stands selling bow-and-arrow packs and smooth wooden bowls leads to a monument to the discovery of Brazil. Just off the walkway is the **Museu do Índio** (admission R$1; ◷ 8:30am-5pm), displaying color photos and traditional objects.

Much more attractive, but still not worth staying overnight in, is **Santa Cruz Cabrália**, 23km north of Porto Seguro. Climb up the bluff to visit the **Igreja NS da Imaculada Conceição**, a small church built by Jesuits in 1630, and for a rewarding view over terracotta roofs, colorful lobster boats and the Rio João de Tiba. Departing with the morning low tide (usually around 9am to 10am), schooners cruise upriver and then out to **Coroa Alta coral platform** (R$15). Santa Cruz Cabrália buses (R$8, 40 minutes, hourly from 6am to 7pm) leave from Porto Seguro's bus station and pass through the center.

To continue north, a ferry (pedestrian/car R$1/8, every 30 minutes from 6am to 8pm, hourly from 8pm to midnight, every two hours from midnight to 8am) crosses the river. It's 2.5km further along to **Santo André**, a tiny fishing village with a lovely, tree-shaded magic similar to Arraial d'Ajuda's. There are four pousadas ranging from super simple to a deluxe luxury resort, and a pair of bohemian restaurants and bars. **Victor Hugo** (☎ 3671 4064; www.portonet.com.br/victorhugo; s/d R$100/120; ◷) has elegantly simple chalets with décor from the owner's travels, a beachfront garden area and a gay-pride flag in the lobby. Surfers will be interested to know that **Mogiquiçaba** (22km north) has waves.

SOUTH OF PORTO SEGURO
South of Porto Seguro is a series of touristy villages, each with their own unique charms. The comforts of civilization decrease with each kilometer traveled south. The coast from

Arraial d'Ajuda to Trancoso is a long stretch of pristine beaches backed by colored cliffs. From Trancoso to south of Corumbau, the beaches remain just as attractive, though the cliffs begin to flatten out.

Arraial d'Ajuda

☎ 0xx73 / pop 12,000

Atop a bluff overlooking an enchanting stretch of coastline, Arraial d'Ajuda is a peaceful tourist village with indisputable appeal. Its narrow paved roads and dusty lanes wind beneath large, shady trees, with lovely pousadas and open-air restaurants hidden among the greenery. Solid, brightly painted façades surround its plazas, and the air remains tinged with the scent of tropical vegetation. In the past, Arraial was the playground of the wealthy, which isn't far removed from the upmarket tourists the town tends to attract. More recently, however, a new wave of international backpackers and nouveau hippies have brought a little diversity to the idyllic surroundings. Consequently, there's a good range of eating and sleeping options, covering all budgets. There's also decent nightlife (at least during the high season), both in town and down on the beach.

INFORMATION

A few places on Broadway (spelled Bróduei by locals) and the Praça São Brás exchange US dollars and euros and offer internet access for around R$6 per hour. The **Banco do Brasil ATM** (Rua do Mucugé 333) is the best bet for cash withdrawal.

SIGHTS & ACTIVITIES

Billed as the largest water park in Latin America, **Eco Parque** (☎ 3575 8600; Praia d'Ajuda; www.arraialecoparque.com.br; adult/child R$45/23; ❧ changes seasonally) has long, twisting water slides, a wave pool and a slow 'river' you can float down on rafts. There's also a *tiroleza* (zipline), kayaks for rent and heaps of other activities. Big-name bands from Salvador play here for summer concerts.

Praia Mucugê is Arraial's main tourist beach and is crowded with *barracas* and blasted by music. As you continue south, **Praia do Parracho** is also built up, but with beach clubs and a few condominium complexes. Both of these beaches are sheltered by offshore reefs. Around the point, beautiful **Praia Pitinga** has red striped sandstone cliffs, pretty, calm waters and a few *barracas*. South of Pitinga, **Praia da Lagoa Azul** and **Praia Taípe** are backed by tall cliffs, and face stronger waves.

COURSES

Newcomers are warmly received at **Capoeira Sul da Bahia** (☎ 3575 2981; www.capoeirasuldabahia.com.br; Rua da Capoeira 57; per class R$12), which also offers lambada, samba and Afro-Brazilian dance classes.

TOURS

Arco-Íris Turismo (☎ 3575 1672; Rua do Mucugê 199) organizes schooner and van trips to Caraíva, Praias Espelho and Curuípe (both south of Trancoso), Trancoso and the offshore reefs Recife de Fora and Coroa Alta. It also occasionally runs three-day catamaran trips to the Parque Nacional Marinho de Abrolhos (p492).

SLEEPING

The road from the ferry dock to the center is lined with places to stay (some of them quite chic) but you'll find the center to be much more convenient. Reservations are a must for major holidays.

Pousada Alto Mar (☎ 3575 1935; Rua Bela Vista 114; dm/d with fan from R$25/50; ⌨) Pousada Alto Mar remains a travelers' favorite for the good mix of youthful international guests that arrive. Rooms are basic with fans and mosquito nets. To get there, turn down the road on the right side of the church.

Saudosa Maloca (☎ 3575 1266; www.saudosamaloca.tur.br; Alameda das Eugênias 31; s R$45, d R$70-90; ❍ ⌨ ⌚) A favorite among Israelis, Saudosa Maloca has clean, well-kept rooms – some with verandas – overlooking a pool and grassy lawn. It's a few blocks from the main drag.

Vila do Beco (☎ 3575 1230; fax 3575 1270; Beco do Jegue 173; s/d with fan R$60/80, with air-con R$80/100; ❍ ⌚) On a side street off Rua do Mucugê, this tranquil property spreads toward the edge of the bluff. White buildings are spread through lush grounds, ending at a pool with ocean views. Rooms are small, trim and simple, and an excellent value overall.

Le Grand Bleu (☎ 3575 1272; Beco do Jegue 160; www.pousadalegrandbleu.com.br; d with fan/air-con R$80/100; ❍ ⌚) Tucked down a side street off Rua do Mucugê, this pretty pousada with gardens has unique, well-kept rooms.

Pousada Erva Doce (☎ 3575 1113; www.ervadoce.com.br; Rua do Mucugê 200; d R$140; ❍ ⌚) Off the main strip, this peaceful guesthouse has spacious, nicely designed rooms surrounding a pool and tropical garden. There's ample outdoor lounge space with hammocks and a thatch-roof bar.

EATING

Arraial's excellent restaurants serve a wide variety of cuisine.

Beco dos Cores (Rua do Mucugê; ☺ Mon-Sat) This galleria is a big draw for its variety: you'll find great sushi, crepes, pizza and fancier fare; there's usually live music on summer weekend nights.

Soveteria Sumatra (☎ 3575 1951; Rua do Mucugê 118; 1/2 scoops R$2.50/3.50; ☺ noon-11pm) Delicious, creamy ice cream made right here in Arraial. Rich flavors like guava or pistachio are great, but the coffee with chocolate chips is famous.

Paulo Pescador (☎ 3575 1242; Praça São Braz 116; mains R$3; ☺ noon-10pm) The ordering couldn't be easier at this incredibly friendly, good-quality *prato feito* restaurant: the menu has large photos of its Bahian dishes, and there is only one price.

A Portinha (☎ 3575 1289; Rua do Campo; per kg R$22; ☺ lunch & dinner) This excellent self-service restaurant serves a rotating menu of veggie quiches, salads, seafood stews and meats of all kinds – all kept hot over a wood fire. Save room for dessert.

Rosa dos Ventos (☎ 3575 1271; Alameda dos Flamboyants 24; mains R$20-30; ☺ dinner Thu-Tue) One of Arraial's most delightful restaurants, Rosa dos Ventos offers an eclectic array of seafood, meats and crepes. The candlelit front patio is a great spot to unwind.

Boi nos Aires (☎ 3575 2554; Rua do Mucugê; mains R$20-35; ☺ dinner) Steak lovers shouldn't miss this stylish place, which serves fine Argentine beef.

Thai Garden (☎ 3575 1100; Rua do Mucugê 402; mains R$20-36; ☺ dinner) For a break from rich Bahian fare, try this nicely decorated Thai restaurant. Seafood dishes are particularly tempting.

Aipim (☎ 3575 3222; Beco do Jeque 131; mains R$20-40; ☺ dinner) This stylish restaurant exudes tropical chic with its old-world décor, new-world music and superb grilled seafood.

La Plage Blanche (☎ 8814 9787; Praia do Mucugê; mains R$30-50; ☺ 9am-6pm) Down on the beach, this open-air French-run café is an inviting place to linger between dips in the ocean. In addition to cocktails, you'll find a small menu of grilled fish and shrimp and roasted eggplant.

ENTERTAINMENT

Arraial has great nightlife throughout the summer, when beach clubs like **Magnolia** (☎ 3575 1576; Estrada da Pitinga 1770, Praia do Mucugê) host dance parties (cover R$25 to R$35).

Girasol (☎ 3575 1717; Rua do Mucugê; ☺ 5pm-last client) Here, dancers surround the pool tables on crowded nights, and pillowed window seats offer a comfortable vantage point. The tables out front are great spots to begin the night.

Beco dos Cores (Estrada do Mucugê; ☺ Mon-Sat) This shop and restaurant galleria has a few bars with magical atmosphere and always attracts a crowd with live music from Thursday through Saturday.

The enclosed **Doc** (Shopping d'Ajuda, Rua do Mucugê; cover around R$20) and smaller but more open **Limelight** (☎ 3575 2171; Estrada Trocoso; cover R$20) provide more typical dance-club environments with pounding techno.

Sweaty nights spent dancing rootsy lambada and *forró* are an Arraial staple. Ask around for the current hot spot.

GETTING THERE & AROUND

Two ferries travel between Porto Seguro and Arraial d'Ajuda. The passenger ferry (R$2.50 to Arraial, free return) runs every 30 minutes from 7:15am to 7:45pm. The car ferry (car R$9.50 to R$11.50) runs every 30 minutes from 7am to midnight, then hourly between 1am and 7am. From the dock, jump on a bus or Kombi van to Arraial (R$1.60). It's also possible to walk the 4km along the beach, but be cautious about carrying valuables or walking alone during hours when the beaches are deserted. Tourist muggings have occurred.

Bicycles and motorcycles are available for hire in the village.

Trancoso

☎ 0xx73 / pop 5900

Smaller in scale than Arraial, youthful Trancoso is also quite captivating. Sitting atop a grassy bluff overlooking fantastic beaches, this tiny rustic village has a relaxed air with a pretty assortment of guesthouses. It's known for its wide, grassy and, most importantly, car-free *quadrado* (square). This central plaza has a grazing horse or two and football-playing lads and a small church at one end. Surrounding it are tropical foliage and colorful buildings, which house expensive boutiques and open-air bars and restaurants. The sight of the *quadrado* at night is magical. Rave culture still thrives in 'Transe-coso,' and it's famous for full-moon beach parties. The village fills nicely in summer, but in the low season you'll find it in hibernation.

INFORMATION

Near the Praça da Independencia, there is one **Banco do Brasil ATM** (Rua Dudero 3) inside Supermercado Nogueira that sometimes functions. Several places offer internet access for around R$6 per hour.

SLEEPING

Reservations are a must during January and major holidays.

Café Esmeralda Albergue (☎ 3668 1527; cafe esmeralda@terra.com.br; quadrado; d without/with bathroom R$30/40) The cheapest overnight on the quadrado is a friendly multilingual guesthouse with extremely basic, fan-cooled rooms. It's behind the café of the same name. No breakfast.

Bom Astral (☎ 3668 1270; www.bomastral.com.br; quadrado; d from R$70; ❄) Another quadrado cheapie, Bom Astral has pleasant, simple rooms, small but well maintained. Several rooms have air-conditioning and kitchens, but most quarters are fan-cooled only. There's a handicrafts store in front.

Pousada Jequitibá (☎ 3668 1028; www.trancoso bahia.com.br/jequitiba; s/d R$60/80; ❄) On the grassy plaza to the right of the quadrado, Jequitibá has tidy well-ventilated rooms, which open onto a shared veranda.

Pousada Quarto Crescente (☎ 3668 1014; www .quartocrescente.net; s/d from R$90/110; ❄ ☐) Gardens surround handsomely decorated rooms with thoughtful touches. There's also a well-stocked library, a pool and a fine breakfast spread. It's on the road into town next to the school, a short walk from the quadrado.

Pousada Mundo Verde (☎ 3668 1279; www.pousada mundoverde.com.br; d R$160-220; ❄ ☐) Set on a quiet bluff overlooking the ocean, Mundo Verde has spacious, airy rooms painted in cheerful colors. The rooms are scattered around a natural garden, and there's a pool with a spectacular view. A short walk from the quadrado.

Pousada Porto Bananas (☎ 3668 1017; www.porto bananas.com.br; quadrado; d/ste from R$200/250; ❄) Spread through a towering jungle-like garden, Porto Bananas has lovely rooms with smooth cement floors stained dark blue,

bright bathrooms (the shower faces greenery), and comfortable beds.

Hotel da Praça (☎ 3668 2121; www.hoteldapraca .com.br; quadrado; d/ste from R$240/320; ❄) The loveliest hotel on the quadrado is a great place for a splurge, with beautifully designed rooms, each with a veranda to take in the lush landscaping.

EATING

Restaurants ring the quadrado, so take a stroll before settling into a seat.

Pandora (☎ 3668 1158; Rua 9 de Agosto 117; snacks R$2-4; ☺ 7am-10pm) A few steps from the entrance to the quadrado, this popular bakery and snack spot has coffee, pastries, and homemade sandwiches. There's often a buzz around the place in the evening, with live music and a good mixed crowd.

Café e Creperia du Blè Noir (☎ 3668 1258; Rua do Telégrafo 300; crepes R$9-12; ☺ dinner) In a small galleria en route to the quadrado, this crepe stand serves tasty savory and sweet crepes. Try the vaunted chocolate and banana crepe.

A Portinha (☎ 3668 1054; quadrado; per kg R$22; ☺ lunch & dinner) A Trancoso favorite (with a bigger branch in Arraial), A Portinha serves mouth-watering por-kilo food; quiches, salads and more.

Cantinho Doce (☎ 3668 1410; quadrado; mains for 2 R$45-70; ☺ dinner) One of several candlelit quadrado gems, Cantinho Doce features delectable seafood dishes, plus the famed doces (desserts) for which the restaurant is named.

Maritaca (☎ 3668 1258; Rua do Telégrafo 388; mains R$28-32; ☺ dinner daily Jul & Dec-Feb, Thu-Tue Mar-Jun & Aug-Nov) On the road leading to the quadrado, elegant and airy Maritaca cooks up pastas, grilled meats and rich desserts, though delicious thin-crust pizzas are the real draw.

Japaiano (☎ 3668 2121; quadrado; mains R$45; ☺ dinner) Amid lush surroundings, this elegant restaurant and lounge serves Japanese-Bahian fusion with surprising success. There are enticing cocktails, giving prominence to Brazil's tropical fruits.

ENTERTAINMENT

The two main night spots are on the road leading to the quadrado. **Loucos** (Av Principal) has hip-hop, reggae, axé and lambada nights, but its Friday-night forró is renowned with locals. **Pára-Raio** (Av Principal) is an ambient restaurant with outdoor tables under massive trees and an enclosed dance space.

There is always live music somewhere on the *quadrado*, but if local legend Elba Ramalho is giving a show, don't miss it. Beach *barracas* such as Pé na Praia sometimes have nighttime parties with pumping trance music and psychedelic décor.

GETTING THERE & AWAY

Hourly buses depart connect Trancoso with Arraial d'Ajuda and the ferry dock and run from 7:15am to 8pm (R$5, 50 minutes). Many informal Kombi vans run the same route for the same price. Two buses a day travel between Trancoso and Porto Seguro (R$6, two hours). It is also possible to walk the entirely beautiful 13km along the beach from Arraial d'Ajuda, but be cautious about carrying valuables or walking alone during hours when the beaches are deserted. For further connections north or south, head for Eunápolis (R$8, 2½ hours, five daily) on Hwy BR-101.

TRANCOSO TO CARAÍVA

Rated among Brazil's top-10 beaches, **Praia do Espelho** is 27km south of Trancoso and 14km north of Caraíva. Protective offshore reefs create calm, warm, transparent waters, while reefs closer to shore create natural pools at low tide. The shore is thick with coconut palms. White and orange cliffs divide Espelho from **Praia do Curuípe**, its neighboring beach, which has a collection of top-end pousadas.

Caraíva

☎ 0xx73 / pop 4800

Without electricity, cars, banks or even decent phone lines, the village of Caraíva is remote and beautiful, a combination that has attracted hippies and others looking for a quiet pace of life. The village is strung along the eastern bank of the mangrove lined Rio Caraíva and a long deserted beach kissed by strong waves. Noisy generators light up the dozen-or-so shops and restaurants lining the sand streets, and most importantly keep the *forró* hopping on Friday night. In the low season, the town all but shuts down.

Boat trips upriver, south to Parque Nacional de Monte Pascoal or Corumbau, and north to Praia do Espelho and Praia do Curuípe are easily organized through pousadas or with **Passeios Rio e Mar** (☎ 9191 3317; 3hr boat trip per person R$50). Horseback riding along the beach to **Barra Velha**, the Pataxó Indian village, is also an option if walking or boating the 6km

isn't appealing. When going to the village, bring lots of water and small bills. On April 19 the village celebrates the **Festa do Indio** with traditional games and dancing.

SLEEPING & EATING

Due to the lack of electricity, air-con isn't available (though essential mosquito nets are usually provided). Most budget places don't commonly serve breakfast.

Camping Caraíva (☎ 0xx24-2231 4892; www.camping caraiva.com.br; per person R$10) On the main riverside road, this place has sandy shaded campsites.

Brilho do Mar (☎ 3668 5053; d with fan R$80) This guesthouse has a sparkling bleached facade, matched by spotless rooms, with windows opening on two sides, allowing a nice cross-breeze. A restaurant serves excellent Bahian food.

Pousada Casinhas da Bahia (☎ 9985 6826; www.casinhasdabahia.com.br, in Portuguese; d with fan R$80-100) Tucked around behind the *forró* club, and sharing the same owner, are a grouping of quality rooms in a pretty garden setting. If the music doesn't bother you, the generator noise might, the benefit being 24-hour electricity.

Pousada da Lagoa (☎ 9985 6862; www.caraiva.com.br; d R$90-100) Surrounding a small pond are seven brightly painted, nicely decorated cottages with small verandas slung with hammocks. There is no electricity, except in the bar/restaurant, which is a popular nighttime hangout.

Pousada San Antonio (☎ 9962 2123; www.caraiva.com.br/sanantonio; d with fan R$100) Overlooking the sea, San Antonio is set with free-standing cabins scattered about a grassy lawn and garden. Rooms are bright, comfortable and inviting, and there's pleasant lounge space outside.

Casa da Praia (☎ 9113 3747; www.pousadapraia caraiva.com.br, in Portuguese; s/d with fan from R$70/110) Small, clean rooms are fair value at this simple beachside pousada. Upstairs rooms have the best views.

Pousada da Terra (☎ 9985 4417; www.terracaraiva.com.br; d R$110) Terra has small attractive bungalows, and a relaxing café and communal space with hammocks and pillows.

Canto da Duca (☎ 9985 0044; mains R$11; ⏰ 9am-2pm) Duca is a local artist who's skilled at creating art-naïf works from her small studio-home; she also whips up enormous vegetarian *prato feito* lunch plates.

Mangue Sereno (☎ 9991 1711; www.caraiva.tur.br; mains R$28-32; d R$150; ⏰ dinner) This marvelous restaurant serves eclectic dishes including pumpkin ravioli, bruschetta, curry shrimp and other seafood in a romantic but rustic setting. The hosts also rent a cozy chalet in back.

GETTING THERE & AWAY

Buses travel twice daily along a reasonable dirt road (keep an eye out for grazing buffalo) between Trancoso and Caraíva (R$10, two hours). The bus stops on the far side of the river in Caraíva, where small dugout canoes ferry passengers across to the village (R$2.50).

There is no road south along the coast from Caraíva.

If heading for other destinations north or south, catch the daily bus to Eunápolis via Itabela, both on Hwy BR-101.

Corumbau

☎ 0xx73

Corumbau sits at the mouth of a river on a sand spit reaching into the ocean. It is barely the semblance of a hamlet, just a charming collection of buildings without electricity. The spit creates calm, blue waters for a long white-sand beach dotted with a few simple restaurants.

The very comfortable, German-run **Jocotoka Eco Resort** (☎ 3288 2291; www.jocotoka.com.br; s/d R$180/220; ✗ ⊠) is a collection of round, thatched-roof bungalows 100m from the ocean. Included in the room price is an excellent buffet dinner served in the dining room. The resort offers activities such as snorkeling, river trips by canoe, kayak or boat, trekking in the national park, a visit to the nearby Pataxó village and whale watching (August to October).

For something simpler, try **Pousada Lourinho** (☎ 3294 5656; s/d with fan R$40/60), one of several inexpensive guesthouses offering basic concrete bungalows 200m from the beach.

One daily bus leaves Itamaraju on Hwy BR-101 for Corumbau (R$14, three hours). Otherwise, access is via beach buggy (R$25), boat (R$25) or on foot along the beach from Caraíva, 12km north.

PARQUE NACIONAL DE MONTE PASCOAL

On April 22, 1500, the Portuguese, sailing under the command of Pedro Álvares Cabral, sighted the broad, 536m-high hump of Monte Pascoal (Mt Easter), their first glimpse of the New World. The sailors called the land Terra da Vera Cruz (Land of the True Cross).

The 225-sq-km national park contains a variety of ecosystems: Atlantic rain forest, secondary forests, swamplands and shallows, mangroves, beaches and reefs. Wildlife includes several monkey species, including the endangered spider monkey, two types of sloth, anteaters, rare porcupines, capybara, deer, jaguars and numerous species of bird.

The northeastern corner of the park, below Caraíva, is home to a small number of Pataxó Indians, who took over control of the park in 2000. They allow visitors access to two trails while accompanied by a guide (settle fees before setting out), one of which climbs the mountain. The **visitors' center** (☎ 3294 1110) is 14km from the western (Hwy BR-101) end of the park. The coastal side is accessible by boat or on foot from Caraíva to the north and Corumbau to the south.

There are no direct buses to the park. A taxi from the closest town, Itamaraju, runs about R$40.

CARAVELAS

☎ 0xx73 / pop 21,300

Caravelas is a calm fishing town on the banks of the mangrove-lined Rio Caravelas. Though it has a friendly, down-home Carnaval and a pleasant enough atmosphere, the primary reason visitors come here is to visit the Parque Nacional Marinho de Abrolhos and other offshore reefs.

Information

Abrolhos Turismo (☎ 3297 1149; www.abrolhosturismo .com.br; Praça Dr Imbassaí) Travel agency; also acts as a kind of unofficial tourist office. Runs recommended tours (diving, whale-watching, trips to Parque Nacional Monte Pascoal).

Banco do Brasil (Praça Dr Imbassaí) ATMs with Visa connections.

Sights & Activities

To get a feel for the town's thriving fishing industry, check out the **Cooperativa Mista dos Pescadores** (Rua da Cooperativa), opposite the hospital, or wander along the riverfront where the fishers return with the day's catch. The **Instituto Baleia Jubarte** (Humpback Whale Institute; ☎ 3297 1320; www.baleiajubarte.com.br; Rua 7 de Setembro 214; ⊠ Mon-Fri) shows videos and offers information about its projects and Abrolhos at its visitors' center.

When the locals go to the beach, most head north for **Praia Grauçá** (10km) or the more isolated **Praia Iemanjá** (20km). Both have calm

BAHIA

THE PATAXÓ

Bahia's largest indigenous group, the Pataxó (pa-ta-SHO), who number 3500, are among Brazil's many indigenous groups facing an uncertain future. Historically, the Pataxó are survivors. They were a strong tribe who held out against the Portuguese, and up until the 1800s were one of the most feared Indian groups of the interior. Their resistance hindered frontier expansion, though by the early 19th century their power had waned.

Today, the Pataxó practice subsistence agriculture in the south of Bahia, supplemented by hunting, fishing and gathering. Similar to Amazonian indigenous groups, the Pataxó utilize local plants as their pharmacy, with the rain forests of southern Bahia providing a vital source for traditional medicine. The region boasts incredible biodiversity, with many of its plants and animals found nowhere else on earth.

In all, the Pataxó use more than 90 different plant species to treat colds, asthma, fever, toothaches, rheumatism, anemia and dozens of other illnesses. They have remedies to relieve menstrual pain, coagulants to stop bleeding and heal wounds, and antidotes for snake bites.

Despite the wide acceptance of the healer's powers within the community, the Pataxó are struggling to maintain their traditions. As elsewhere in many indigenous communities, the youth are not actively embracing the customs of the older generation. Traditional healers (*curandeiros*), who can be male or female, haven't passed their knowledge down to the next generation. In Barra Velha, the largest Pataxó community (numbering some 1800), all of the healers are over 60, meaning that if nothing changes, their knowledge will be lost within two decades. Today's *curandeiros* may be the final generation of traditional healers in Pataxó culture.

In addition to internal struggles, the Pataxó face severe threats from outside. As Bahia's population grows, farmers have pushed them off their lands, leading to violent skirmishes. In 2007, 15 Pataxó Indians went to Brasília to settle the matter of their land rights. Yet whether the tribe can flourish – and successfully preserve its customs – may be a matter less for government officials to decide than for Pataxó youth, who will be instrumental in ensuring the tribe's longevity.

water colored brown with river silt. Reachable by boat are **Praia Pontal do Sul** (across Rio Caravelas) and the island beach **Coroa da Barra** (30 minutes offshore).

Tours

Travel agencies offer snorkeling day trips (R$120) to nearby reefs and islands such as Parcel das Paredes, Sebastião Gomes and Coroa Vermelha. Since most tourists head for Abrolhos, these trips rarely meet the minimum number of people required (five) for departure. River trips up the Rio Caravelas or down the Rio Caribê to the next beach town to the south, Nova Viçosa, are also possible.

Sleeping

Pousada Canto do Atobá (☎ 3297 1009; www.geo cities.com/pousadacantodoatoba, in Portuguese; Rua de Palmeira; s/d with fan R$60/90; ⊠) A few friendly dogs and cats wander through the garden of this pretty pousada just outside the entrance of town. Airy, bright rooms open onto a hammock-strung veranda.

Pousada & Spa da Ilha (☎ 3297 2218; http://netpage .em.com.br/jelihovs; s/d R$90/130) Across the river, on Ilha da Caçumba, this multilingual bohemian pousada has two sweet and simple rooms with furniture built by the owners, and solar power. To get there, contact the pousada. Lots of mosquitoes.

Hotel Marina Porto Abrolhos (☎ 3674 1059; www .marinaportoabrolhos.com.br; Rua da Baleia 333, Praia Grauçá; s/d R$150/165; ⊠ ⊠) The fanciest hotel in town is located 7km from Caravelas, and has round, thatched-roof, beachfront chalets surrounding a gigantic pool. Rooms have TV and minibar.

Eating

Restaurants at Praia Grauçá serve great seafood.

Carenagem (☎ 3297 1280; Rua das Palmeiras; mains R$18-30; ⊠ lunch & dinner) This corner meeting spot has an extensive menu of seafood and meat dishes.

Encontro dos Amigos (☎ 3297 1600; Rua das Palmeiras 370; mains R$25-50; ⊠ lunch & dinner) A top place in town for seafood.

Getting There & Around

One daily bus goes between Porto Seguro and Caravelas (R$30, five hours). Otherwise, access to Caravelas is via Teixeira de Freitas, 74km east. The **bus station** (☎ 3297 1151) is in the center of town. Brasileiro goes to Teixeira de Freitas via Alcobaça (R$11, two hours, five daily).

Local buses do a round trip between Caravelas and the neighboring village of Barra (providing access to Praia Grauçá), leaving every 30 minutes from 6:30am until 10:30pm.

PARQUE NACIONAL MARINHO DE ABROLHOS

It is thought that the name of Brazil's first marine park comes from a sailor's warning: when approaching land, open your eyes *(abre os olhos)*. Abrolhos covers an area of 913 sq km, including reefs noted for the variety of colors and a five-island archipelago that Charles Darwin, aboard the HMS *Beagle*, visited in 1832. These days the primary residents of the archipelago are migrating birds and humpback whales (June to October), which come here to rest and give birth. Only the Ilha de Santa Bárbara has a handful of buildings, including a lighthouse built in 1861. The preservation of the islands is important to IBAMA (Instituto Brasileiro do Meio Ambiente e dos Recursos Naturais Renováveis; Brazilian Institute of the Environment and Renewable Natural Resources), so visitor land access is limited to daytime hours on only the Ilha da Siriba. But you didn't come to a marine park for land; you came to snorkel and dive in crystal-clear waters, the visibility of which can reach 20m in the dry season (May to September).

Getting There & Around

Abrolhos is located 80km offshore from Caravelas, the primary gateway, where travel agencies (p490) offer one- to three-day trips to the park. Day trips run to R$180 per person, including park fees and lunch. Abrolhos Turismo runs a two-day schooner trip, with an overnight stay on board, starting at R$360 per person including park fees, all meals, soft drinks and water. Snorkel kit rental is R$10 per day. Trips require around a 10-person minimum to go out, but by working together, tour operators usually manage to get trips out even in the low season.

From Arraial d'Ajuda, **Arco-Íris Turismo** (☎ 3575 1672; Rua do Mucugê 199) occasionally organizes three-day catamaran trips that cruise south along the Bahian coast, then on to Abrolhos.

WEST OF SALVADOR

The great attraction in Bahia's interior is the Parque Nacional da Chapada Diamantina, a verdant area of scenic plateaus, grassy valleys, waterfalls and rushing rivers. Opportunities for trekking and outdoor adventures abound.

In contrast to this verdant area, the rest of this region comprises the bizarre moonscapes of the *sertão*, a vast and parched land on which a struggling people eke out a living raising cattle and tilling the earth. When the periodic tremendous droughts sweep the land, thousands of Sertanejos (inhabitants of the *sertão*) pile their belongings on their backs and head out in search of jobs. But with the first hint of rain they return to renew their strong bond with this land.

FEIRA DE SANTANA

☎ 0xx75 / pop 524,000

Feira de Santana is the main city of Bahia's interior, and a great cattle center. There's not much to do or see here except the **Feira do Couro**, the big Monday cattle market, which is great fun, with lots of leather bargains, and the **Mercado de Arte Popular** (☯ Mon-Sat), which has folk art for sale.

Festivals & Events

Feira invented the now widespread concept of **Micareta**, an out-of-season Carnaval. In 1937 a flood caused the city's Carnaval to be celebrated late, a tradition the citizens decided to adopt and rename. In April or early May thousands of spectators fill the city to see Salvador's best *trios elétricos* parade for four days along with local samba schools and folklore groups. For those who missed out on Carnaval in Salvador, this could be the next best thing.

Sleeping & Eating

There are several cheap hotels near the bus station, such **Hotel Samburá** (☎ 3623 8511; Praça Dr Jackson do Amauri 132; s/d R$35/50; ✷). **Acalanto** (☎ 3625 3612; www.hotelacalanto.com.br; Av Torres 77; s/d R$80/120; ✷), nearby, offers sprightlier rooms.

O Picuí (☎ 3221 1018; Av Maria Quitéria 2463; mains R$15-25; ☷ lunch & dinner) has good regional food.

Getting There & Away

At the crossroads of three major highways, Feira is a major transportation hub. The **bus station** (☎ 3623 3667) features an eye-catching mural painted by Lénio Braga in 1967. Frequent buses go to Salvador (R$11, two hours). Buses for Lençóis originating in Salvador pass through Feira de Santana.

LENÇÓIS

☎ 0xx75 / pop 9700

Lençóis is the prettiest of the old diamond-mining towns in the Chapada Diamantina, a mountainous wooded oasis in the dusty *sertão*. While the town itself has charming cobbled streets and brightly painted 19th-century buildings, which are framed against lush green hills, the surrounding areas are the real attraction. Caves, waterfalls, idyllic rivers and panoramic plateaus set the stage for some fantastic adventures, with the town of Lençóis serving as a base for treks into the surrounding Parque Nacional da Chapada Diamantina (p498) and for sights outside the park. Lençóis is also noted for Jarê, the regional variation of Candomblé. If you want to see a flip side to surf-and-sand Brazil, or have time for only one excursion into the Northeastern interior, this is it.

BAHIA

GREAT CREATURES OF THE SEA

One of the world's great migratory animals, the humpback whale travels up to 25,000km each year. Massive in scale, adults can reach 17m long and weigh up to 36,000kg. Although they were hunted to near extinction by the turn of the 20th century, the population is slowly recovering following a moratorium on whale hunting in 1966. Biologists estimate that 30,000 to 60,000 now remain.

Identified by their long pectoral fins, distinct humps and knob-covered heads, the humpbacks feed only during the summer in polar waters on a diet of krill and small fish. In the winter, they migrate from the poles to tropical waters, where mating occurs. Thus, the austral winter (June to September) is the best time to observe them off the coast of Brazil, when they come in large numbers to mate and give birth.

During this time, the humpbacks fast and live off their fat reserves. Competition for females is intense, with groups of two to 20 males (called escorts) sometimes trailing a lone female. To win her over, each male competes to establish dominance, tail slapping, charging and parrying over the course of several hours.

The whale song is perhaps one of the most fascinating and least understood attributes of these mammals. Whales within an area sing the same song – or variations of the same song – while those from different regions sing entirely different songs. Performed only by males, each song lasts 10 to 20 minutes and can be repeated over several hours (some scientists have recorded whales singing continuously for over 24 hours). The songs are staggeringly complex. One research team from the Universidade Estadual de Campinas studied whales off Abrolhos in Bahia one winter and identified 24 note types, organized in five themes.

No one knows the purpose of the song, which changes from year to year, though scientists originally thought it had a role in mating (observations of males singing far from the presence of a female has thrown doubt onto this).

In Bahia, whale watching is a growing tourist industry, with numerous places from which to embark on a seagoing observation trip. During the winter, they can often be observed outside of Salvador, while Parque Nacional Marinho de Abrolhos (opposite) is among the world's best places to observe them.

Elsewhere in Brazil, other good sighting spots are Praia do Rosa (p350) in Santa Catarina state, where mother and calf pairs can come within 30m of the shore, and Arraial do Cabo (p213) in Rio state.

Those who want a deeper understanding of the great mammals can volunteer at the **Brazilian Humpback Whale Project** (www.gvi.co.uk), based in Praia do Forte (p466). Volunteers spend much time out on the sea, collecting data and contributing to the whale's long-term conservation. The program is offered through UK organization **Global Vision International** (www.gvi.co.uk).

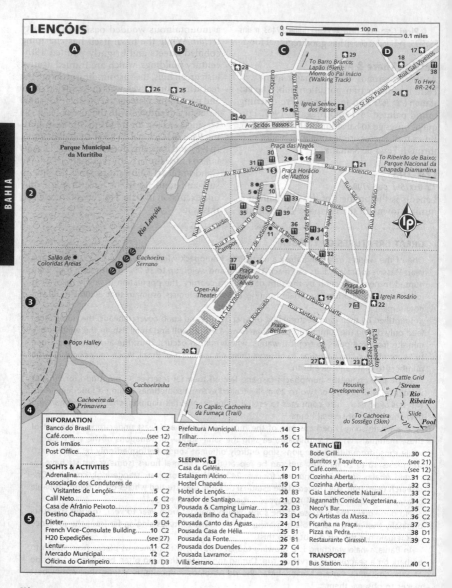

LENÇÓIS

History

The history of Lençóis epitomizes the story of the diamond boom and subsequent bust. After earlier expeditions by *bandeirantes* (Paulista explorers and hired guns) proved fruitless, the first diamonds were found in Chapada Velha in 1822. After large strikes in the Rio Mucujê in 1844, a motley collection of prospectors from across Brazil arrived seeking their fortunes.

Miners began searching for diamonds in alluvial deposits. They settled in makeshift tents, which, from the hills above, looked like bed sheets drying in the wind – hence the town's name: Lençóis (sheets). The tents of these diamond prospectors grew into villages: Vila Velha de Palmeiras, Andaraí, Piatã, Igatu and Lençóis. Exaggerated stories of endless riches in the Diamantina mines precipitated mass migrations, but the area proved rich in clouded industrial stones, not display-quality gems.

At the height of the diamond boom, the French – who purchased diamonds and used them to drill the Panama Canal (1881–89), St Gothard Tunnel and London Underground – built a vice-consulate in Lençóis. French fashions and bons mots made their way into town, but with the depletion of diamonds, the fall-off in French demand and the newly discovered South African mines, the boom went bust at the beginning of the 20th century.

Despite these developments, mining held on. Powerful and destructive water pumps were introduced in the 1980s, which increased production until they were finally banned in 1995. The few remaining miners have returned to traditional methods to extract diamonds from the riverbeds. With the establishment of the national park in 1985, the town's economy turned instead to tourism, which continues to be the major industry of Lençóis.

Information

Associação dos Condutores de Visitantes de Lençóis (☎ 3334 1425; Rua 10 de Novembro 22; ☽ 8am-noon & 2-8pm) Information about tour guides.

Banco do Brasil (Praça Horácio de Mattos 56) Has ATMs.

Café.com (Mercado Municipal; Rua José Florencio; per hr R$6; ☽ 4-11pm Mon-Sat) Internet access.

Dois Irmãos (Praça Horácio de Mattos 14) Sells town maps (R$8).

Post office (Av 7 de Setembro)

Sights & Activities

Take a stroll by the 19th-century **French vice-consulate building** (Praça Horácio de Mattos), where diamond commerce was negotiated, and the beautiful **Prefeitura Municipal** (Praça Otaviano Alves), which displays interesting old photos of Lençóis. The **Casa de Afrânio Peixoto** (Praça do Rosário; admission free) displays the works and personal effects of Lençóis' most illustrious native in addition to yet more old town photos. Peixoto was a writer, doctor, politician and academic.

The photo gallery of **Calil Neto** (Rua da Baderna; ☽ 8am-1pm & 6-11pm Wed-Mon, 6-11pm Tue) will leave no doubts about this area's beauty. Small prints of the artist's shots are for sale.

One of the more curious attractions is the **Oficina do Garimpeiro** (Rua São Benedito 140), which is a reconstructed *garimpeiro* (prospector) dwelling built by Coriolando Rocha, a local character and former prospector. A guided tour in Portuguese reveals the lifestyle and skills of freelance diamond hunters.

For handicrafts, stop by the lively **Mercado Municipal** (Rua José Florencio; ☽ 8am-11pm Mon-Sat) overlooking the river.

Local agencies offer a wide range of outdoor activities, including hiking, rappelling, climbing, kayaking, mountain biking and horseback riding. There are also great hikes leaving from town that the adventurous can undertake without a guide.

One is a 3km walk out of town, following the Rio Lençóis upstream through the Parque Municipal da Muritiba. You first pass a series of rapids known as **Cachoeira Serrano**. Off to the right is the **Salão de Coloridas Areias** (Room of Colored Sands), where artisans gather material for bottled sand paintings, so its original 40 colors have been greatly diminished. You then pass **Poço Halley** (Swimming Hole), before seeing **Cachoeirinha** (Little Waterfall) on a tributary to your left. Continuing upriver, **Cachoeira da Primavera** (Spring Waterfall) is on another tributary on your left.

Another relaxing 4km hike is to follow Rua São Benedito (known as the Rua dos Negros) out of town, ignoring the left turn 100m after Pousada Lumiar. Continue until the road ends at an upmarket housing development. Continue a short distance, then take a left fork onto a trail that descends and crosses a stream. Keep following the track until you reach a ridge overlooking Rio Ribeirão. At the foot of the ridge, is **Ribeirão do Meio**, a series of swimming holes with a natural waterslide (bring shorts or something to slide on). Avoid assured injury by climbing the dry rocks (not the slide's wet ones) before launching off.

For more swimming, catch the morning bus to Seabra and hop off at Mucugêzinho Bar (25km). About 2km downstream is **Poço do Diabo** (Devil's Well), a beautiful swimming hole on the Rio Mucugêzinho with a 25m waterfall.

The German masseur **Dieter** (☎ 9984 2720; Rua São Benedito 45) is highly recommended for walking pains.

Tours

Many of the area's best-known sights are outside of the national park on private land. Given the lack of public transportation, the easiest way to visit them is by taking a tour through a local agency. For information on longer treks, and tours within the national park, see (p499). The following are recommended Lençóis agencies:

Andrenalina (☎ 334 1689; Rua das Pedras 121) Specializes in adventure sports and treks.

H2O Expedições (☎ 3334 1229; www.pousada dosduendes.com; Pousada dos Duendes, Rua do Pires) Run by Olivia Taylor, a very helpful British guide. Both day trips and treks offered.

Destino Chapada (☎ 3334 1484; Rua 10 de Novembro 14) A well-staffed multilingual agency.

Lentur (☎ 3334 1271; www.lentur.com.br; Av 7 de Setembro 10) Day trips and treks organized. Multilingual guides available, but not every day.

Trilhar (☎ 3334 1045; Rua Perílio Benjamin 37)

Zentur (☎ 3334 1397; www.zentur.tur.br; Praça das Nagôs 1) Popular agency, though mostly Portuguese-speaking guides.

A popular tour visits Rio Mucugêzinho and its swimming hole Poço do Diabo, Gruta da Lapa Doce (an 850m-long cave, formed by a subterranean river, with an impressive assortment of stalagmites and stalactites), Gruta da Pratinha (a cave and river with clear, light blue waters), Gruta Azul (Blue Cave) and Morro do Pai Inácio (an 1120m peak affording an awesome view over a plateau-filled valley). Though this makes for a long day in the car, the tour includes memorable walks and swimming opportunities (R$50 plus R$17 admission fees).

Tours to Poço Encantado (the Lençóis poster child: a cave filled with stunningly beautiful blue water) and Poço Azul (another rainwater-filled cave you can swim in) are also offered (R$60 plus R$16 admission fees). Verify with agencies the quality of the light; after rains, the water remains murky.

Festivals & Events

The **Festa de Senhor dos Passos** begins on January 24 and culminates on February 2 with the Noite dos Garimpeiros (Prospectors' Night). **Lamentação das Almas** is a mystical festival held during Lent. Celebrated from June 23 to 25, the **Festa de São João** is a huge street party with traditional dancing and bonfires outside every house. The **Semana de Afrânio Peixoto** is held from December 11 to 18 and coincides with the municipality's emancipation from slavery.

Sleeping

Lençóis' best pousadas are famous for their fantastic breakfast spreads.

BUDGET

Pousada & Camping Lumiar (☎ 3334 1241; lumiar .camping@gmail.com; Praça do Rosário; camping per person R$10, s/d with fan R$35/70, bungalows R$150; ❷) Lumiar has grassy campsites in an attractive, tree-filled setting, along with simple rooms in a converted colonial home (bathrooms are shared). There are also roomier bungalows with private terraces and an excellent restaurant.

Pousada Brilho da Chapada (☎ 3334 1343; brilho dachapada@bol.com.br; Rua São Benedito 27; s/d with fan R$25/50) A modern pousada that offers a range of rooms from small and cramped to bright and breezy. Request a 2nd-floor room with an exterior window for the latter.

Hostel Chapada (☎ 3334 1497; www.hostelchapada .com.br; Rua Boa Vista 121; dm/d with fan R$25/55; ☐) This HI hostel attracts young travelers to its simple, fan-cooled dorm rooms (sleeping between four and six). There's a small interior garden, kitchen use (R$5 extra), excursions, and discounts for HI card-holders.

Pousada dos Duendes (☎ 3334 1229; www.pousada dosduendes.com.br; Rua do Pires; dm/s/d R$30/60/80, s/d without bathroom R$40/60) A relaxed atmosphere, good budget rooms and open-air lounge space makes Duendes a backpacker favorite. It serves group dinners with vegetarian options, and runs tours around the area.

Pousada Lavramor (☎ 3334 1280; lavramor@yahoo .com.br; Rua do Cajueiro; s/d with fan R$40/60) On the hill across the river from the center of town, Lavramor has six bright, modern rooms, one of which has fantastic views.

Pousada da Fonte (☎ 3334 1953; www.pousada dafonte.com.br, in Portuguese; Rua da Muritiba; s/d with fan R$45/70) With stone walls, outdoor hammocks and an open breakfast porch surrounded by lush forest, this quaint six-room pousada has the feel of a weekend mountain home.

Pousada Casa de Hélia (☎ 3334 1143; www.casa dehelia.com.br; Rua da Muritiba; s/d from R$50/80) Casa de Hélia has beautifully done rooms featuring stone-slab floors and furniture fashioned out of twisted branches. Walkways through the guesthouse are bordered by flowering plants, and its hillside locale affords fine views over the river valley below.

MIDRANGE

Parador de Santiago (☎ 3334 1083; Rua Cel José Florêncio; d with fan R$95) In a privileged position beside the river, this smartly decorated pousada has just four rooms. Though only two have river views, the sound of rushing water fills every room. There's an excellent Mexican restaurant on the first floor.

Estalagem Alcino (☎ 3334 1171; Rua Tomba Surrão 139; s/d R$90/120) This lovely yellow mansion has tastefully decorated rooms all designed and built by local artist Alcino. His artwork from his ceramic workshop out back is visible throughout the comfortable rooms and common areas.

Casa da Geléia (☎ 3334 1151; www.casadageleia.com .br; Rua Gal Viveiros 178; d R$100) A row of large rooms looks out onto a grassy yard, and the surrounding countryside beyond. In addition to pretty rooms, the Casa da Geléia (House of Jams) is open to the public and stocks an unbelievable range of homemade jams, chutneys, canned veggies, liqueurs and dried fruits and vegetables. It often appears closed; just ring the bell.

Villa Serrano (☎ 3334 1486; www.vilaserrano.com.br; Rua Alto do Bonfim; s/d R$115/150) In a lush setting, the classy and environmentally friendly Vila Serrano offers nine spacious apartments, each handsomely designed, with a veranda attached. There's a library/lounge area for meeting other travelers, and the friendly owners have a wealth of local insight.

TOP END

Pousada Canto das Águas (☎ 3334 1154; www.lencois .com.br, in Portuguese; Av Senhor dos Passos; d R$205-325; 🅿 🅿) At the river's edge, this attractively designed hotel has classically furnished rooms, ranging from comfortable to luxurious. The sound of the river fills the rooms, with large toads adding a countermelody to the flowing water at night.

Hotel de Lençóis (☎ 3334 1102; www.hoteldelencois .com.br; Rua Altina Alves 747; s/d $234/260; 🅿 🅿) This environmentally friendly hotel has attractive rooms set with hammocks overlooking greenery and a pretty pool area. There's also a pleasant restaurant.

Eating

Lençóis has some excellent cuisine, including vegetarian choices. Many cafés can pack lunches for hikes if you pre-arrange it.

Café.com (Rua José Florencio; 🕑 4-11pm Mon-Sat) Inside the Mercado Municipal, this cozy café overlooking the river makes a fine afternoon retreat.

Jagannath Comida Vegeteriana (☎ 3334 1980; Rua das Pedras 133; 🕑 lunch & dinner) A colorful veg-

etarian café serving tasty sandwiches (like ricotta cheese and sundried tomatoes), soy burgers and satisfying juices.

Bode Grill (☎ 3334 1600; Rua 10 de Novembro 26; per kg R$14; 🕑 lunch & dinner) On an open-sided terrace over the river, this pleasant, well-liked *por-kilo* restaurant spreads a small but enticing buffet that includes meats, chicken, pasta and salads.

Burritos y Taquitos (☎ 3334 1083; Rua Cel José Florêncio; mains R$9-14; 🕑 dinner Tue-Sun) Below the pousada Parador de Santiago, this Mexican restaurant serves incredibly tasty burritos, tacos, chips and guacamole and other delectable fare. A back patio overlooks the river.

Neco's Bar (☎ 3334 1179; Praça Clarim Pacheco 15; meals R$14; 🕑 dinner) Neco's is renowned for having the best regional food in town. Orders must be placed the day before.

Picanha na Praça (☎ 3334 1080; Praça Otaviano Alves 62; mains for 2 R$28-35; 🕑 lunch & dinner Tue-Sun) Choice cuts of beef, chicken and fish are brought sizzling to your table at this well-frequented institution. The half-portions, with their heaping side dishes, feed two.

Os Artistas da Massa (☎ 3334 1886; Rua da Baderna 49; mains R$14-24; 🕑 lunch & dinner) Fantastically fresh pastas and other Italian dishes are served to the jazz and pop tunes you pick off the menu at this gourmet restaurant.

Pizza na Pedra (☎ 3334 1475; Av Senhor dos Passos; mains for 2 R$30-35; 🕑 dinner) Stone slab tables and tree-trunk stools create a rustic atmosphere at this pizzeria tucked away on the road leaving town. The pizzas are agreed to be the best around. Tasty calzones and pastas as well.

Cozinha Aberta (☎ 3334 1066; Rua da Baderna 111 & Rua Barbosa 42; mains R$18-24; 🕑 lunch & dinner) With two branches in town, this gourmet bistro serves satisfying, eclectic fare like Thai-style chicken in coconut milk and Indian curry in a charming homelike setting.

Restaurante Girassol (☎ 3334 1663; Av 7 de Setembro 19; mains R$20-30; 🕑 lunch & dinner) Serving a mix of Asian and Brazilian fare, Girassol is an enticing spot for a meal, with tables spilling onto the street.

Getting There & Away

BUS

If coming from the south, the journey, though indirect, will be a lot quicker if you route through Salvador.

Real Express (☎ 3334 1112) buses for Salvador (R$38, six hours) leave two to three times

BAHIA

daily. Buses stop in Feira de Santana (R$28, 4½ hours), where connections can be made to just about anywhere, but are not always well timed.

CAR

Lençóis is 13km off Hwy BR-242, the main Salvador–Brasília route. There's a gas station 22km east of Lençóis on Hwy BR-242, in Tanquinho. The nearest station to the west is around 30km away. There's an improvised fuel station in Lençóis, which is usually open.

PARQUE NACIONAL DA CHAPADA DIAMANTINA

☎ 0xx75

Within this national park's 1520 sq km, waterfalls cascade over the Sincora Range's mountains and plateaus, dropping into rivers and streams that wind their way through grassy valleys and clean swimming holes. An endless network of trails is dotted with cactus and strawflowers in some places, and the philodendrons, velosiaceas, orchids and other bromeliads that have escaped poaching in others. Several species of monkey swing through trees where *araras* (macaws) perch. *Veados* (deer) pick their way past gaping caves, while *mocós* (native rodents) and *cutia* (agouti) scurry underfoot. Even an *onça pintada* (jaguar) or two sharpens its claws on a towering tree, but you're much more likely to cross paths with a cute *quati* (small, furry carnivore with a brown-and-yellow-ringed tail).

The region's unique natural beauty and the tranquility of its small, colonial towns have attracted a steady trickle of Brazilian and foreign travelers for several decades; some have never left. These introduced residents, moved by the degradation of the environment and depletion of the wild-animal population, spearheaded an active ecological movement, in direct opposition to the extractive mentality of diamond miners and many locals. After six years of bureaucratic battles, biologist Roy Funch helped convince the government to create the Parque Nacional da Chapada Diamantina in 1985.

The park has little, if any, infrastructure for visitors. Bus service is infrequent and scarce, particularly to the remote parts of the park. However, camping or sleeping in the park's small caves is free and can be done without a permit. You'll want gear such as backpacks, sleeping bags or tents, which can easily be rented in Lençóis, and reasonably warm clothes.

Geology

According to geologists, the diamonds in Chapada Diamantina were formed millions of years ago near present-day Namibia (Bahia was contiguous with Africa before continental drift). The diamonds were mixed with pebbles, swept into the depths of the sea that covered what is now inland Brazil, and imprisoned when the seabed turned to stone. Ultimately this layer of conglomerate stone was elevated, and the forces of erosion released the trapped diamonds, which then came to rest in the riverbeds.

Day Hikes & Trips

The most popular day trip into the park is to the top of Brazil's tallest waterfall, **Cachoeira da Fumaça** (Smoke Waterfall), so named because before it has plummeted the entire 420m, the water evaporates into mist. This 6km hike requires a guide, so contact an agency in Lençóis. Alternately, you can originate from the closest village, **Capão** (80km west of Lençóis by road), which has a number of pousadas and a few travel agencies. The nearby mystical Vale do Capão, or **Caeté-Açu**, has attracted an international community of folks interested in an alternative, back-to-the-land lifestyle.

Up the road and outside the park, **Palmeiras** (54km west of Lençóis by car) is a drowsy little town with a scenic riverside position. The streets are lined with colorful houses and a couple of cheap pousadas.

Hikers may want to take the trail along Barro Branco between Lençóis and **Morro do Pai Inácio**, an 1120m peak affording an awesome view over a plateau-filled valley. Allow four or five hours one way for the hike.

Just southwest of Lençóis, upstream from Ribeirão do Meio (p495), is the lovely **Cachoeira do Sossêgo** waterfall, with a deep pool at its base and rock ledges for diving. The 7km hike involves a great deal of stone-hopping along the riverbed and should not be attempted without a guide, or when rain or high water has made the lichen-covered rocks slippery.

Gruta do Lapão is probably the largest sandstone cave in South America and is just a 5km hike north of Lençóis. A guide is required as access is tricky.

'Chapada's Pantanal', or **Marimbus**, is a marshy microregion 94km south of Lençóis where you can canoe or kayak while fishing for *tucunaré* (peacock bass) and keeping a lookout for capybaras and *jacarés* (caimans). **H20 Expedições** (☎ 3334 1229; www.pousadadosduendes .com; Pousada dos Duendes, Rua do Pires, Lençóis) and several other Lençóis agencies offer kayak tours here (R$70).

Treks

Navigating the correct routes for these treks can be very difficult, so using a guide is strongly recommended. Treks organized with a guide can last anywhere from two to eight days, and can be custom fitted to the group. They usually involve a combination of camping and staying in local homes and pousadas.

THE BASE OF FUMAÇA

This extremely beautiful yet tiring 36km trek traverses the park from Lençóis to Capão in three days. Detours to other waterfalls are taken along the way, in addition to reaching the base of **Cachoeira da Fumaça**. An extra day can be added walking back to Lençóis or you can continue with the Grand Circuit. Be forewarned that the area around Fumaça's base gets extremely crowded at times, so you may find yourself sharing your sleeping cave with unexpected companions.

VALE DO PATÍ

Much easier than the Fumaça trek, this recommended hike starts and ends in Vale do Capão, and can last from four to six days depending on detours. You are more likely to have the trails to yourself here, and the views over the plains and Chapada's table mountains are spectacular. Stopping in at a local home for a meal or a night is a wonderful possibility. For those who don't want to carry anything, pack mules can be used.

GRAND CIRCUIT

The grand circuit of the park covers about 100km, best done in a counterclockwise direction. It takes about five days, but eight days are required to include side trips. Many of these sights have been described on opposite.

On the first day, you hike from Lençóis via Vale do Capão (Caeté Açu) to Capão. While there, you can take a side trip to the top of **Cachoeira da Fumaça**. In Capão, you can camp

or stay at a pousada such as the pleasantly alternative **Pousada Candombá** (☎ 3344 1102; www.infochapada.com, in Portuguese; Rua das Mangas; d R$100-120).

From Capão, you can take one very long day or two comfortable ones to cross the beautiful plains region of Gerais do Vieira to the **Vale do Patí**. You can camp overnight on the plains or sleep in the Toca do Gaucho cave.

You can power on in one day to Andaraí, or take a recommended day to putter around the Vale do Patí, checking out **Cachoeirão** (a delightful waterfall) or the tiny ghost settlement of **Ruinha**, before heading out.

Once in Andaraí, side trips to **Poço Encantado** (56km from Andaraí) and the intriguing diamond-era stone ruins in **Igatu** (12km from Andaraí) are highly recommended. In Andaraí, either camp or try the comfortable, riverside **Pousada Ecológica** (☎ 3335 2176; pousada .ecologica@terra.com.br; s/d R$90/110; 🏊 🖳).

In Igatu, the charming **Hospedagem Flor de Açucena** (☎ 3335 7003; www.igatu.com.br, in Portuguese; Rua Nova; campsite per person R$12, s/d with fan R$50/80; 🖳) has wildly natural rooms built into the rocky hillside, abundant greenery and striking views, with a trail leading down to the river.

Another Igatu option is the **Pousada Pedras do Igatu** (☎ 3335 2281; www.igatu.com.br, in Portuguese; Rua São Sebastião; d with fan R$136; 🖳 🖳), which has lovely views over the hillsides.

Most choose to drive from Andaraí to Lençóis as the walk is on an uninteresting dirt road passing scenery destroyed by machine mining. If you decide to walk, allow two days, camping the first night near Rio Roncador. The next day you'll pass the **Marimbus** microregion, which you could arrange to explore if you set it up ahead of time.

Tours

See p495 for a list of reputable travel agencies offering tours into the park.

Otherwise, knowledgeable guides can greatly enhance enjoyment of any trip into the park, and we recommend you take one, especially as park trails are not marked. Whether you take a guide or not, you should definitely not go alone. Be wary of guides off the street who offer rock-bottom prices; they are often insufficiently trained. In the past, groups led by undertrained guides have gotten lost, gone hungry and even been abandoned!

American-born **Roy Funch** (☎ 3334 1305; Fundação Chapada Diamantina, Rua Pé de Ladeira 212, Lençóis)

BAHIA

has very detailed knowledge of the region, as you can guess from all of his work in, and research on, this area. His book *A Visitor's Guide to the Chapada Diamantina Mountains* expertly demystifies the local flora, fauna, history and geology. It's available at **Dois Irmãos** (Praça Horácio de Mattos 14) in Lençóis.

Another excellent guide is British Olivia Taylor at **Pousada dos Duendes** (☎ 3334 1229; www .pousadadosduendes.com.br; Rua do Pires, Lençóis), who is familiar with the history, geography and biology of the area, as well as the trails.

Reputable pousadas in Lençóis like Villa Serrano and Hotel de Lençóis can also recommend excellent guides. For further information about guides, contact the **Associação dos Condutores de Visitantes de Lençóis** (☎ 3334 1425; Rua 10 de Novembro 22; 🕑 8am-noon & 2-8pm) in Lençóis.

Sergipe & Alagoas

Overshadowed by big Bahia to the south, Sergipe and Alagoas are often overlooked by travelers. Those seeking off-the-beaten-path gems would do well to explore these tiny twin states.

Although Sergipe's provincial capital has few attractions of its own, Aracaju is a great place to arrange a scenic tour up the Rio São Francisco, which at times is unrivalled in beauty. Aracaju is also a gateway to several sleepy colonial towns, where the sound of horse and cart still clatters through the streets, and the scattering of 17th-century churches attests to the area's prominence in Brazil's early settlement days.

Even more enticing than Sergipe is the state of Alagoas, which is known by the cognoscenti for its beautiful coastline. Highlights here include bumping around quaint coastal towns planted among swaying palms and vast stretches of isolated white-sand beaches. The ocean here is often a magnificent emerald green. Alagoas' laid-back capital, Maceió, overlooks such impressive coast, and has good restaurants and an eclectic nightlife – with evenings spent at beachside bars dining on local seafood specialties as the moon rises over the sea.

North and south of Maceió lie surfing beaches, tiny fishing villages and the dazzling, ever-present coastline, with a mix of rustic lodging and lovely, high-end pousadas (guesthouses). Inland travel offers its own rewards: Penedo, along the Rio São Francisco, is a charming riverfront town with picturesque churches, hilly cobblestone streets and a welcoming atmosphere that's hard to leave behind. If you visit just one inland town in the Northeast, Penedo is an excellent choice.

HIGHLIGHTS

- Playing in the surf and sipping refreshing *agua de côco* (coconut juice) on enchanting **Praia do Gunga** (p515)

- Dancing to the addictive rhythms of *forró* music in an old-school bar in **Maceió** (p513)

- Dining on fresh seafood at a riverside restaurant in colonial **Penedo** (p517)

- Snorkeling the coral reefs and exploring the breathtaking coastline outside of **Barra de Santo Antônio** (p518)

- Walking beautiful, untouched shores outside of idyllic **Pontal de Coruripe** (p516)

Barra de Santo Antônio ★

★ Maceió

Pontal de Coruripe ★   ★ Praia do Gunga

★ Penedo

| POPULATION: 4.6 MILLION | AREA: 49,983 SQ KM |

History

During the invasion by the Dutch in 1630, many slaves took advantage of the confusion and escaped to the mountains behind the coasts of northern Alagoas and southern Pernambuco. Where the Alagoan towns of Atalaia, Capela, Viçosa, União dos Palmares and Porto Calvo stand today, virgin forests with fruit and wildlife once provided for colonies of runaway slaves. Palmares, the mightiest republic of escaped slaves, led by the former African king Zumbi, covered present-day Alagoas and Pernambuco. In the 18th and 19th centuries, sugarcane and cotton brought the region prominence, and important commercial centers like Laranjeiras and Penedo still show the wealth from that era. Today,

sugarcane is still an important crop in the area, alongside oranges and cassava, though tourism is making in-roads in Maceió. The states are also known for extreme poverty in the interior and rampant corruption (former president Fernando Collor de Mello, who was accused of siphoning US$2 billion from Brazilian savings accounts, hails from Alagoas).

Climate

The tropical Atlantic coast of Sergipe and Alagoas remains hot and humid throughout the year. High temperatures range from 30°C (86°F) to 36°C (97°F) and low temperatures run between 20°C (68°F) and 25°C (77°F). Monthly rainfall averages run from 60mm in dry months (August to March) to 325mm in

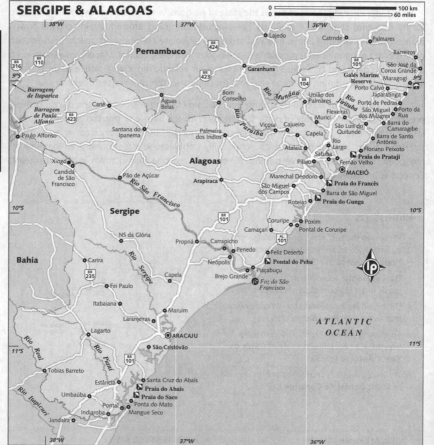

SERGIPE & ALAGOAS

the rainy months (April to July). The interior of Sergipe is part of the semiarid drought-prone *sertão* (backlands), that receives 500mm to 800mm of rainfall a year – though it falls only during a few months of the year (March to June), if at all.

Getting There & Away

Hwy BR-101 skirts the coastline of both Sergipe and Alagoas between 25km and 50km inland. It is the main thoroughfare through the region and the chosen route of most long-distance buses. The main airports in the region are in the capital cities, Aracaju and Maceió.

Getting Around

As is the norm in the Northeast, there is always some form of transportation between where you are and where you need to go, whether by buses, Kombi vans (aka *bestas*), *taxis coletivos* (collective taxis) or mototaxis (motorcycle taxis).

SERGIPE

Brazil's smallest state, Sergipe is a land of sugarcane fields with a coastline of swamp, mangrove and sandy shores. In addition to attractive beaches just south of Aracaju, the state capital, Sergipe is home to the sleepy, picturesque colonial towns of Sao Cristóvão and Laranjeiras.

ARACAJU

☎ 0xx79 / pop 495,000

Aracaju has a friendly, relaxed environment, and if you're coming from the South, it's the first city with a real Northeastern feel about it. Pedestrian malls slow the center to walking pace, and many attractive buildings surrounding the leafy main square have been restored. Though not a major tourist draw, Aracaju is a pleasant enough place to take care of business before continuing on to your next destination.

History

The seat of state government was moved from São Cristóvão to Aracaju in 1855, in part because of its good, deep harbor – badly needed to handle large ships transporting sugar to Europe – and because residents of the old capital were on the verge of armed revolt. Within a year, an epidemic broke out and decimated Aracaju's population, which the residents of São Cristóvão naturally saw as an omen that the new capital had a doomed future. The city received a makeover in the early 1900s with the advent of streetcars and other urbanizing elements. In recent days, the newest addition to Aracaju is the bridge over the Rio Sergipe (completed in 2006), connecting the capital to the suburb of Barra dos Coqueiros, and bringing steady development to this quiet coastal area.

Orientation

Aracaju's Centro sits on the Rio Sergipe, guarded from the ocean by a sandy barrier island, the Ilha de Santa Luzia. To the south, past the river mouth, are the city beach neighborhoods of Coroa do Meio, Jardim Atlantico (Praia dos Artistas) and Atalaia, collectively referred to as the *orla* (waterfront). Most of the action and nightlife concentrates in these suburban neighborhoods.

Information

EMERGENCY

Police (☎ 190)

INTERNET ACCESS

Centernet (Rua João Pessoa 64, Centro; per hr R$3; 🕑 8am-6.30pm Mon-Fri, 9am-2.30pm Sat)

Timer Web Café (Praça Olímpio Campos, Centro; per hr R$3; 🕑 9am-9pm Mon-Fri, to 3pm Sat)

MEDICAL SERVICES

Hospital Governador João Alves Filho (☎ 3216 2600; Av Tancredo Neves, América)

MONEY

Banco do Brasil (Rua Geru 341, Centro)

Bradesco (cnr Rua Geru & Praça Fausto Cardoso, Centro)

HSBC Rua São Cristóvão (Rua São Cristóvão 56, Centro); Rua Estancia (Rua Estancia 168, Centro)

POST

Central post office (Rua Laranjeiras 229, Centro)

TOURIST INFORMATION

Emsetur (www.emsetur.gov.br); Centro (☎ 3179 1947; Rua Propriá, Centro; 🕑 8am-5.30pm Mon-Fri, 9am-5pm Sat, 9am-2pm Sun); Rodoviária Nova (🕑 8am-10pm Mon-Fri, 9am-9pm Sat & Sun) The friendly, helpful main office of the state tourism authority is in the town center and distributes free maps of Aracaju.

TRAVEL AGENCIES

Nozes Tur (☎ 3243 7177; www.nozestur.com.br; Av Santos Dumont 348, Atalaia; ☽ 7am-9pm) Offers a range of day tours, including catamaran departures to Foz do São Francisco (R$65 including lunch) and all-day trips to Xingó (R$75) along the Rio São Francisco.

Sergitur (☎ 3214 2525; www.sergitur.com.br in Portuguese; Rua João Pessoa 71/75, Centro) Offers a similar assortment of day tours. Enter from Rua Laranjeiras.

Sights & Activities

The Tamar Project's small, interesting **Oceanário** (Aquarium; ☎ 3243 3214; Av Santos Dumont, Atalaia; adult/ student/child R$7/3/free; ☽ 2-8pm Tue-Fri, 9am-9pm Sat & Sun) has tanks with sea turtles, rays and eels as well as examples of specific local freshwater environments and their species. For more on Tamar, see p467.

For a more concentrated look at this conservation and education project, go and visit its **biological reserve** (☎ 3276 1202; Pirambú; admission free; ☽ 8am-5pm), where you can see tanks of sea turtles and have a talk with the biologists. To get there, take a Pirambu-bound bus, which passes in front of the Mercado Municipal in the center.

Speaking of the market, the **Mercado Municipal** (Rua José do Prado Franco, Centro; ☽ 6am-6pm Mon-Sat, to noon Sun) is one of the livelier attractions in town, with a wide range of goods sold and bartered inside the two-story building.

BEACHES

With rustling palms and a relative lack of buildings, **Praia Atalaia Nova** (6km), on the Ilha de Santa Luzia, is preferred over the city beaches of **Praia dos Artistas** (7km), **Praia Atalaia** (9km) and **Praia Aruana** (11km) to the south. These beaches are heavily developed but are popular with locals; they are also good sources of inexpensive seafood. Further south, **Praia do Refúgio** (18km) is the prettiest and most secluded nearby beach.

Tours

Local travel agencies offer a variety of day tours, including catamaran trips on the Rio São Francisco to the green waters of the canyon of Xingó, or to the **Foz de São Francisco**, where the river meets the sea. A tour is also a pretty good way to check out difficult-to-reach **Mangue Seco** (R$50, p469), on the border with Bahia.

Festivals & Events

On January 1 a huge fleet of fishing boats sails along the Rio Sergipe following the image of their patron saint to celebrate **Bom Jesus dos Navegantes**. The largest festival of all is the **Festa de São João**, which runs for the entire month of June and includes live *forró* (music and dance style of the Northeast; see p531) bands and *quadrilha* (a type of square dancing) presentations. The **Festa de Iemanjá** is celebrated on December 8, when followers perform ceremonies and make offerings to the sea goddess. Aracaju celebrates **Carnaval** a full two weeks before Shrove Tuesday, with street parties and other Salvador-style revelry.

Sleeping

The majority of Aracaju's hotels are on the waterfront at Praia dos Artistas and Atalaia (around 7km and 9km from the center respectively). For a short stay, you'll find those in the center cheaper and more convenient, though lacking charm.

BUDGET & MIDRANGE

Grande Hotel (☎ 3211 1388; Rua Itabaiana 371, Centro; s/d R$35/55; ☒) The best budget option in town, Grande Hotel has sizable, aging rooms with wood floors and decent natural light.

Hotel Amado (☎ 3211 9937; www.infonet.com.br /hotelamado; Rua Laranjeiras 532, Centro; s/d R$40/80; ☒) Potted plants line the porch of this old house, adapted and expanded into a hotel, making it almost pretty. The rooms are spacious, but most lack windows.

Pousada do Farol (☎ 3255 1513; www.pousadadofarol .com.br; Rua Delmiro Golveia 663, Coroa do Meio; s/d R$50/80; ☒ ☒) About 6km south of the center, this simple guesthouse offers small, trim rooms done in blue and gray that are fair value. Several other similarly priced options are near.

Pousada Mirante das Águas (☎ 3255 2610; www .mirantedasaguas.com.br; Rua Delmiro Golveia 711, Atalaia; s/d with fan R$60/80, with air-con R$70/90; ☒) Two blocks from the waterfront, the Pousada Mirante das Águas has quarters ranging from roomy and well-ventilated to dark and cramped. There's an elaborate games-lounge area (mini-golf, anyone?).

Hotel Jangadeiro (☎ 3211 1350; www.janga deirose.com.br; Rua Santa Luzia 269, Centro; s/d from R$71/82; ☒ ☒) The plain gray-walled Jangadeiro features an uninspiring lobby, but rooms are nicely kept with big beds and modern bathrooms.

Tropical Praia Hotel (☎ 3255 2799; Rua Renato Fonseca Oliveira 55, Praia dos Artistas; s/d R$100/140; ☒ ☒) This basic waterfront place has clean rooms

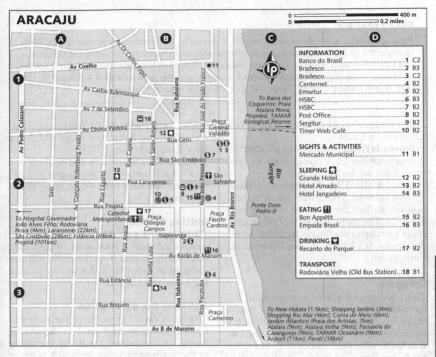

ARACAJU

SERGIPE & ALAGOAS

of varying size. Overall, it's a little worn but is better value than other waterfront hotels.

TOP END

San Manuel Praia Hotel (☎ 3218 5200; www.sanmanuel-praiahotel.com.br; Rua Niceu Dantas 75, Atalaia; s/d R$138/162; 🌫 🖥 🐟) This fairly new waterfront hotel has spacious modern rooms with a touch of Zenlike style. The best rooms have sea-facing balconies; a few restaurants are nearby.

Aquarios Praia Hotel (☎ 2107 5200; www.aquari-oshotel.com.br; Av Santos Dumont 1378, Praia dos Artistas; s/d R$200/210; 🌫 🖥 🐟) This respected place has trim, modern rooms with balconies and colorful decor. The best rooms overlook the waterfront. A restaurant complex lies across the street.

Eating & Drinking

The best selection of restaurants and drinking spots stretches out along the waterfront in Atalaia; it's a good spot to stroll at night, when the center is empty (and unsafe for wandering).

Praça de Eventos (Av Santos Dumont, Atalaia; snacks R$4-8; ⏲ lunch & dinner) This waterfront restaurant complex has many options, including seafood.

Out back, snack stands sell crepes and sandwiches. Look for the hangarlike building.

Bon Appétit (☎ 3221 1113; Rua João Pessoa 75, Centro; per kg R$14; ⏲ lunch Mon-Sat) One of several simple per-kilo lunch spots in the center.

Empada Brasil (☎ 3211 0676; Rua Pacatuba 113, Centro; per kg R$19; ⏲ 8am-7pm Mon-Fri, 8.30am-3pm Sat) This pleasant, modern spot serves the best per-kilo lunch in the center, though it's also a popular gathering spot for the small, signature *empadas* (savory or sweet pies).

O Miguel (☎ 243 1444; Av Antônio Alves 340, Atalaia Velha; mains R$18-36; ⏲ lunch daily, dinner Tue-Sun) A top place in town for Northeastern food, specializing in *carne de sol* (tasty, salted meat, grilled and served with beans, rice and vegetables).

our pick Parati (☎ 3227 2100; Rodovia José Sarnei 47, Praia do Refúgio; mains R$20-40; ⏲ lunch & dinner) Aracaju's best restaurant serves excellent seafood plates, with crab and shrimp dishes earning top billing. The idyllic outdoor tables overlook one of Aracaju's prettiest beaches.

New Hakata (☎ 3213 1202; Av Beira Mar s/n; dinner for 2 R$80; ⏲ dinner) Aracaju's top sushi restaurant draws crowds for its all-you-can-eat sushi

---

CRAB FEASTING

Although Aracaju is hardly a culinary capital, it does offer one particularly succulent dish: fresh, savory crabs. Just south of Atalaia, you'll find the popular Passarela do Caranguejo (Crab Lane), a row of open-sided restaurants facing the waterfront that serve the respected local dish. Look for signs advertising 'caranguejo dobrado' (two-for-one crabs). **Bar e Restaurante Amanda** (☎ 3243 2029; Praia de Atalaia s/n; per crab R$3.50; ✆ lunch & dinner) is a current favorite.

---

night (Wednesday, R$35). It's next to the Iate Clube (Yacht Club).

Recanto do Parque (Praça Olímpio Campos; drinks R$2-6; ✆ noon-8pm Mon-Sat) A casual, open-air spot for a drink on the leafy plaza.

Cariri (☎ 3243 1379; Av Santos Dumont s/n, Atalaia; ✆ 10pm-last client) This Northeastern restaurant lets its hair down in the evening with live forró. The traditional style of pé de serra (Luis Gonzaga's signature 'foothills' forró) dominates. It's located on the Passarela do Caranguejo.

Shopping

There are several places in town good for handicraft-browsing, including the dozen shops specializing in handmade embroidery surrounding the courtyard behind the **Emsetur tourist office** (Rua Propriá, Centro; ✆ 8am-5.30pm Mon-Fri, 9am-5pm Sat, 9am-2pm Sun). A wider selection of handicrafts can be found at the **Praça de Eventos** (Av Santos Dumont, Atalaia), the hangar-like structure on the waterfront.

Getting There & Away

AIR

BRA (☎ 3243 7333; airport), **Gol** (☎ 0800-280 0465; www .voegol.com.br) and **TAM** (☎ 3212 8567; airport) can fly or connect you to other Brazilian cities from Aracaju's **airport** (code AJU; ☎ 3212 8500).

BUS

Most long-distance buses leave from the **Rodoviária Nova** (New Bus Station; ☎ 3259 2848), 4km east of the center.

Bonfim (☎ 3259 2788) runs three daily buses to Salvador (R$40 to R$62) along the coastal Linha Verde highway (four hours), and two along Hwy BR-101 via Entre Rios (six hours). Bonfim buses also go to Maceió (R$24 to R$36, four hours, four daily) and Penedo (R$18, three hours, one daily). Both **Progresso** (☎ 3259 3020) and **Real Alagoas** (☎ 3259 2832) go to Recife (R$68, nine hours, four daily). For further access to Penedo,

catch a **Santa Maria** (☎ 3259 3000) bus to Neópolis (R$11, two hours, five daily) and then a ferry from there (see p517).

Coopertalse (☎ 3259 3028) and Santa Maria depart for Propriá (R$7, two hours, 10 daily) from the **Rodoviária Velha** (Old Bus Station; ☎ 3214 2578; Centro).

Getting Around

TO/FROM THE AIRPORT

Aracaju's airport is 11km south of the center. A taxi to the airport from the center will cost about R$20. From the Rodoviária Velha, take the Aeroporto city bus.

TO/FROM THE BUS STATION

City buses depart from a large shelter with a series of triangular roofs beside the Rodoviária Nova. For the center, catch any bus going to the Rodoviária Velha, such as Centro or Terminal Rodoviário/Desembarcador.

TO/FROM THE SOUTHERN BEACHES

The Circular Cidade 02 bus (R$1.65) leaves from the Rodoviária Velha and runs down Av Rio Branco south to Atalaia, terminating at the Terminal Integração Atalaia. From there, change to a Circular Praias 01 bus to reach the southern beaches. A taxi from the center to Atalaia costs about R$15.

CAR HIRE

Most car-rental agencies are in Atalaia, along the waterfront, including **ST** (☎ 3255 4005; Aquarios Praia Hotel, Av Santos Dumont 1378, Praia dos Artistas), with prices starting at R$80 per day, including unlimited kilometers.

LARANJEIRAS

☎ 0xx79 / pop 26,000

Nestled between three grassy, church-topped hills, Laranjeiras is the colonial gem of Sergipe. Although it lacks the quiet grandeur of Penedo (p516), Laranjeiras has picturesque cobblestone roads, colonial buildings topped by terracotta roofs and views over the meandering Rio Cotinguiba, and the whole town seems unblemished by modern development. Churches here are simple, while the museums offer a glimpse of the region's rich cultural heritage. The surrounding countryside hides crumbling ruins of old sugar mills and estates. Laranjeiras can be a pretty quick day trip from Aracaju, or a full day if you set out to explore the surrounding area.

History

First settled in 1605, Laranjeiras became the commercial center for its surrounding verdant sugar and cotton fields during the 18th and 19th centuries. At one point there were more than 60 sugar mills in and around Laranjeiras sending sugar down the Rio Cotinguiba to Aracaju for export to Europe.

Information

There is usually someone lingering inside the Trapiche building who can answer questions about local sights. Free guides paid by the city, or private guides charging around R$15, can be picked up around the bus station and Trapiche. To arrange guides, call ☎ 3281 2401.

Sights

Facing the bus station, the **Trapiche** is an imposing 19th-century structure that historically held cargo waiting to be shipped downriver.

A few kilometers from town is a partly restored sugar mill, known simply as **Engenho** (Mill), in a lovely setting. It is privately owned and not generally open to the public, but it may be possible to arrange a visit through a guide.

CHURCHES

At the top of Alto do Bonfim (Bonfim Heights), is the picturesque 19th-century **Igreja NS do Bonfim**. Although the church is often closed, the fine views make it worth the climb. Reach it by following the street to the left of Nice's Restaurant.

Out at the Engenho Boa Sorte, 4km upriver from town, is the baroque **Igreja de Comandaroba**, constructed by Jesuits in 1734. Only a few guides have keys to it, and unfortunately the church is not well maintained, despite past restoration efforts. A 1km tunnel leads from the church to the **Gruta da Pedra Furada** (a large cave built by the Jesuits to escape their persecutors and used for Mass in the early days).

MUSEUMS

The **Museu de Arte Sacra** (Museum of Sacred Art; Praça Dr Heráclito Diniz Gonçalves; admission R$2; ☺ 10am-5pm Tue-Fri, 1-5pm Sat & Sun) is located in a beautifully restored colonial house next door to the Igreja da Matriz on the main plaza. The house, built in 1897, still has its original wood floors and walls bordered with handpainted flowers. Guided tours (in Portuguese) reveal pieces gathered from area churches. The last room includes life-size wooden statues of saintly figures, including several used in the town's religious processions. Christ beneath the cross and NS das Dores have real human hair – donated by the faithful for prayers answered.

Laranjeiras is considered to be the stronghold of Afro-Brazilian culture in Sergipe. At the **Museu Afro-Brasileiro** (☎ 3281 2418; Rua José do Prado Franco 19; admission R$2; ☺ 10am-5pm Tue-Fri, 1-5pm Sat & Sun), a knowledgeable docent will explain (in Portuguese) displays on sugar production, slave torture methods, Afro-Brazilian religions and Laranjeiras' cultural traditions.

Festivals & Events

During the last week of January, Laranjeiras hosts the **Festa de Reis** (also called **Encontro Cultural**), a religious and folklore festival of traditional music and dance. More folklore revelry occurs during **Semana Folclórico** (Folklore Week), usually the second week of August. You can also catch colorful religious processions during **Semana Santa** (Holy Week).

Sleeping & Eating

Pousada Vale dos Outeiros (☎ 3281 1096; Rua João Prado Franco 124; s/d with fan R$15/30, with air-con R$20/45; ☒) The only pousada in town has rooms that are small, simple and fairly clean. Those in back have views of the surrounding hills.

Nice's Restaurant (☎ 3281 2883; Praça da Matriz; mains R$9-12; ☺ lunch & dinner) This inviting, breezy restaurant has large windows opening onto the main square with excellent grilled meats, as well as seafood and lasagne.

Getting There & Away

Both Coopertalse and São Pedro buses make the 21km trip between Laranjeiras and Aracaju's Rodoviária Velha (R$2, 35 minutes, half-hourly from 6am to 9:30pm). Unofficial collective taxis run the same route at the same

---

MIRACLE MAKERS

In many shrines and churches in the Northeast, visitors come face-to-face with carved wooden heads, arms, feet and other body parts, hung from ceilings or piled in baskets in a special room. A unique mixture of faith and folk art, these ex-votos are called *milagres* (miracles) and are left by supplicants seeking a cure for a specific ailment such as an injured limb or a congenital deformity. In exchange, the petitioner makes a vow (usually to a particular saint) promising to give up their wicked ways or perhaps make a long pilgrimage – which may even be performed on the knees.

The makers of these ex-votos are often self-taught artisans and their work has a primitive, almost cubist, quality. If the artisans are particularly skilled they may model their work – made of either of wood or clay – on the sufferer. No one knows exactly how this custom originated, but the *milagre* probably has links to old Iberian traditions, mingled with African and indigenous customs. In some communities, there is an element of mysticism to these carved objects, as if they could absorb the ills of the sufferer.

Many churches and shrines in the *sertão* have a *casa dos milagres* (miracle house), where such objects are displayed. During religious festivals, *milagre* artisans make the rounds, offering their services for a small fee.

---

price. If you're coming from the north on Hwy BR-101, get off at the turnoff for Laranjeiras and catch a ride or walk the 4km into town.

SÃO CRISTÓVÃO
☎ 0xx79 / pop 74,000

Atop a steep hill with expansive views over the countryside, the historic center of São Cristóvão houses a sleepy concentration of 17th- and 18th-century colonial buildings along narrow stone roads and a few wide plazas. Founded in 1590, São Cristóvão is reputedly Brazil's fourth-oldest town and was the capital of Sergipe until 1855. There are no pousadas in São Cristóvão, but it's an easy and worthwhile day trip from Aracaju.

São Cristóvão does not lack for churches. Of particular distinction are **Igreja de Senhor dos Passos** (Praça NS dos Passos; free admission), with a ceiling painted by José Teófilo de Jesus. The artist's work also appears in the sacristy with panels depicting the life of St Teresa of Avila.

Igreja e Convento de São Francisco houses the excellent **Museu de Arte Sacra** (Praça São Francisco; admission R$2; ⏰ 9am-5pm Tue-Fri, 1-5pm Sat & Sun), which contains some 500 pieces dating back to the 17th century. On the opposite side of the plaza, the **Museu Histórico Sergipe** (☎ 3261 1435; Praça São Francisco; admission R$2; ⏰ 1-5pm Tue-Sun) is housed in the former **Palácio do Governo**. It has paintings from Carybé and other Northeastern artists, a room for aficionados of the outlaw Lampião and antique furniture and other relics recalling bygone days.

During one weekend in mid-December, the town comes alive for the **Festival de Arte de São Cristóvão**, featuring popular bands and dance troupes from all over Brazil as well as theater and art exhibitions. If you're around then, don't miss it.

Restaurante O Sobrado (☎ 3261 1310; Praça da Matriz 40; mains R$10-14; ⏰ 7.30am-9.30pm) serves grilled meats and other standards in an old building overlooking a grassy plaza. Next door, the **Casa de Queijada** (Praça da Matriz 36; sweets R$1; ⏰ 8am-noon & 2-6pm) is a friendly place to sample *queijadas* (cheese pastries) and other local delicacies.

Frequent buses make the 25km trip between São Cristóvão and Aracaju's Rodoviária Velha (R$2, 45 minutes). The town is 8km off Hwy BR-101.

ALAGOAS

MACEIÓ
☎ 0xx82 / pop 890,000

One of the hot, up-and-coming destinations in the Northeast, Maceió is a navigable modern city set on some truly beautiful beachfront. It has a small but buzzing bar and restaurant scene and fairly laid-back streets; it's also the gateway to wonderfully idyllic shoreline to the north and south. On the city's beaches, vivid, emerald-hued water laps the powdery sands that are lined with palms and brightly painted *jangadas* (traditional sailboats). By night, local residents follow the meandering beachside path as it weaves past thatched-roof restaurants and palm-shaded football pitches. Maceió's sights are relatively few, leaving you plenty of time to enjoy a great meal, catch some rays and soak up the relaxed atmosphere.

Orientation

Maceió sits on a jagged peninsula between the Lagoa Mundaú and the ocean. The peninsula features two main points: one is the site of the city's port, and the other divides Praia de Pajuçara and Praia dos Sete Coqueiros from the more northern Praia de Ponta Verde and Praia de Jatiúca. The Centro is located near the oceanfront, 2km from Pajuçara and 4km from Ponta Verde. Local phone books have detailed maps of the city.

Information

EMERGENCY
Police (☎ 190)
Pronto Socorro (First Aid; ☎ 3221 5939)

INTERNET ACCESS
Internet Cybercafé (Av Dr Antônio Gouveia 1113, Pajuçara; per hr R$3; ✆ 9am-10pm Mon-Sat, 2-10pm Sun) Inside a shopping arcade.

MEDICAL SERVICES
Unimed (☎ 3215 2000; Av Dom Antônio Brandão, Farol)

MONEY
Major bank ATMs can also be found at the 24-hour Bom Preço grocery store in Pajuçara.
Aeroturismo Centro (☎ 3218 2030; Rua Barão do Penedo 61, Centro; ✆ 9am-noon & 2-6pm Mon-Fri);

VELHO CHICO: THE RIVER OF NATIONAL UNITY

For the Nordestino, it's impossible to speak about the Rio São Francisco without a swelling of pride. There is no river like the São Francisco, which is Brazil's third most important river, after the Amazon and the Paraguay. Those who live along its banks speak of it as a friend – hence the affectionate nickname Velho Chico or Chicão (Chico is a diminutive for Francisco).

The location of the São Francisco gave it great prominence during the colonial history of Brazil. With its headwaters in the Serra da Canastra, 1500m high in Minas Gerais, the Rio São Francisco flows north across the greater part of the Northeast *sertão* and completes its 3160km journey at the Atlantic Ocean after slicing through the states of Minas Gerais and Bahia, and delineating the Bahia–Pernambuco and Sergipe–Alagoas state borders.

For three centuries the São Francisco, also referred to as the 'river of national unity,' represented the only connection between the small towns at the extremes of the *sertão* and the coast. 'Discovered' in the 17th century, the river was the best of the few routes available to penetrate the semiarid Northeastern interior. Thus, the frontier grew along the margins of the river. The economy of these settlements was based on cattle, which provided desperately needed food for the gold miners in Minas Gerais in the 18th century and later fed workers in the *cacao* (cocoa) plantations throughout southern Bahia.

Although the inhabitants of the region were often separated by enormous distances, cattle ranching proved a common bond and produced a culture that can be seen today in the region's folklore, music and art.

The history of this area is legendary in Brazil: the tough *vaqueiros* (cowboys of the Northeast) who drove the cattle; the commerce in salt (to fatten the cows); the cultivation of rice; the rise in banditry; the battles between the big landowners; and the odd developments, like Canudos with its strange religious fanaticism (and later its horrific destruction).

The slow waters of the São Francisco have been so vital to Brazil because, in a region with devastating periodic droughts, the river provides one of the only guaranteed water sources. Today the river valley is irrigated to produce a huge amount of produce for local consumption and export.

Owing to its life-sustaining importance, the São Francisco has been the source of much myth-making and storytelling. The *bicho da água* (water beast), for example, is part animal and part human. It walks on the bottom of the river and snores. The crews on the riverboats placate the *bicho da água* by throwing handfuls of tobacco into the water. Nordestinos also believe that São Francisco is a gift from God to the people of the *sertão* to recompense all their suffering in the drought-plagued land.

Pajuçara (☎ 3327 5448; Av Antônio Gouveia 971, Pajuçara; ⏱ 8am-6pm) Both branches change traveler's checks with no fee.

Banco do Brasil (Rua João Pessoa, Centro)

Bradesco ATM (Av Senador Robert Kennedy, Ponta Verde)

POST

Central post office (Rua João Pessoa, Centro)

Sights & Activities

The **Museu Théo Brandão** (☎ 3221 2651; Av da Paz 1490, Centro; admission R$2; ⏱ 9am-5pm Tue-Fri, 2-5pm Sat-Mon) is housed in a handsomely renovated colonial building on the seafront. Excellent exhibits cover the state's history and popular culture, including high-quality samples of local crafts. The most impressive displays are festival headpieces modeled after churches, which are loaded with mirrors, beads and multicolored ribbons and weigh up to 35kg. To see traditional dancing in action, stop in for a free weekly show (Wednesday at 8pm).

BEACHES

Protected by an offshore coral reef, Maceió's ocean waters are calm and a deep emerald color. The most popular and beautiful of the city beaches are **Praia de Ponta Verde** (5km from the city center) and **Jatiúca** (6km). Be forewarned that Praia do Sobral and Praia da Avenida, close to the center, are polluted. **Praia de Pajuçara** and **Praia dos Sete Coqueiros** sometimes suffer from pollution as well.

The nicest beaches north of the city are thought to be **Garça Torta** (14km) and **Pratagi** (17km), but **Jacarecica** (9km), **Guaxuma** (12km) and **Riacho Doce** (16km) are also tropical paradises. The Riacho Doce bus runs up the coast to these northern beaches.

Tours

From Praia de Pajuçara, *jangadas* sail out 2km at low tide to natural pools formed by the reef (R$13). On a busy day, the pools fill up with people (clouding the water for those interested in snorkeling) and waiters run around serving drinks from floating bars. You can arrange trips with any boat captain – stop in early to find out when the boats are sailing.

From the nearby village of Pontal da Barra (see Shopping, p513), schooners leave at around 9am and 1pm on the Nove Ilhas

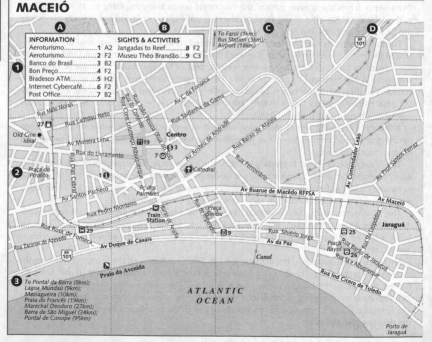

MACEIÓ

INFORMATION	
Aeroturismo................1 A2	
Aeroturismo................2 F2	
Banco do Brasil............3 B2	
Bon Preço....................4 F2	
Bradesco ATM.............5 H2	
Internet Cybercafé.....6 F2	
Post Office..................7 B2	

SIGHTS & ACTIVITIES	
Jangadas to Reef...........8 F2	
Museu Théo Brandão....9 C3	

(Nine Islands) tour (R$20). The trip lasts four hours and, in addition to cruising the Lagoa Mundaú, you'll stop at the outlet of the lake into the ocean. Departures are from Pontal da Barra's lakefront restaurants, such as **O Peixarão** (☎ 3325 7011) or **Alípio** (☎ 3351 9151). A five-person minimum is required, so call ahead.

Festivals & Events

Maceió Fest, a Salvador-style, out-of-season Carnaval in the third week of November, is the city's largest festival. As for Carnaval, the city empties and locals head for the beaches, especially Barra de São Miguel (p515).

Sleeping

The best selection of hotels is out at the beaches, with accommodations in Pajuçara being cheaper than in other beach neighborhoods. In general, Maceió's lodging options are on the pricey side.

BUDGET

Mar Amar (☎ 3231 1551; Rua Dr Antônio Pedro de Mendonça 343, Pajuçara; s/d R$25/50; ✸) The whole place

is pretty banged up, but the small rooms with mismatched furniture are clean.

Albergue Algamar (☎ 3231 2246; alag@superig .com.br; Rua Pref Abdon Arroxelas 327, Ponta Verde; dm/d R$32/60; ✸) Maceió's only hostel is rather disappointing. This large converted house has a wide front veranda and a TV room as well as the usual hostel amenities (laundry, kitchen). It is located on a quiet street two blocks from the beach. The dorm rooms are separate sex and sleep six; the private rooms are small and cramped.

Pousada Glória (☎ 3337 2348; Rua Jangadeiros Alagoanos 1119, Pajuçara; s/d R$40/60; ✸) A local family rents fair-sized rooms above its bakery. The amiability and decent room quality make this the best budget option.

MIDRANGE

Hotel Ibis (☎ 2121 6699; www.accorhotels.com.br; Av Dr Antônio Gouveia 277, Pajuçara; s/d R$80/100; ✸) The Ibis is a clean but generic modern high-rise hotel that offers good prices for the area.

Pousada Girassol (☎ 3231 4000; Rua Jangadeiros Alagoanos 535, Pajuçara; s/d R$80/100; ✸) Girassol has clean, simply furnished rooms. Those in

SERGIPE & ALAGOAS

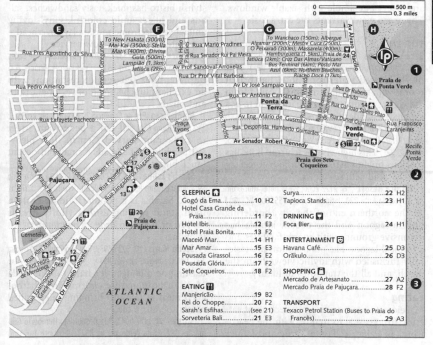

SLEEPING	
Gogó da Ema	10 H2
Hotel Casa Grande da Praia	11 F2
Hotel Ibis	12 E3
Hotel Praia Bonita	13 F2
Maceió Mar	14 H1
Mar Amar	15 E3
Pousada Girassol	16 E2
Pousada Glória	17 F2
Sete Coqueiros	18 F2

EATING	
Manjericão	19 B2
Rei do Choppe	20 F2
Sarah's Esfihas	(see 21)
Sorveteria Bali	21 E3

Surya	22 H2
Tapioca Stands	23 H1

DRINKING	
Foca Bier	24 H1

ENTERTAINMENT	
Havana Café	25 D3
Orákulo	26 D3

SHOPPING	
Mercado de Artesanato	27 A2
Mercado Praia de Pajuçara	28 F2

TRANSPORT	
Texaco Petrol Station (Buses to Praia do Francês)	29 A3

front are bright and breezy, but noisy. Those out back are short on natural light.

Gogó da Ema (☎ 3327 0329; www.hotelgogodaema .com.br; Rua Francisco Laranjeiras 97, Ponta Verde; s/d/tr R$80/100/120) On a quiet street near two lovely beaches, Gogó da Ema is a five-story guest-house with bright murals along the hallways but rather bland, aging rooms.

Hotel Casa Grande da Praia (☎ 3231 3332; www .hotelcasagrandedapraia.com.br; Rua Jangadeiros Alagoanos 1528, Pajuçara; s/d R$100; 🗷) Offers clean, comfort-able sensibly designed rooms overlooking a quiet garden courtyard.

Pousada Cavalo Marinho (☎ 3355 1247; www .pousadacavalomarinho.com; Rua da Praia 55, Riacho Doce; s R$55-100, d R$66-110) Located 17km northeast of the city in the fishing village of Riacho Doce (it's well-signed), the Cavalo Marinho is Swiss-owned quality: white walls and terracotta tile floors, lounge areas, and the ocean lapping right outside. There are canoes, bicycles and bodyboards available. Splash out for the rooms that open onto the sea.

Hotel Praia Bonita (☎ 2121 3700; www.praiabonita .com.br; Av Dr Antônio Gouveia 943, Pajuçara; s/d from R$140/160; 🗷 🗷) This two-story waterfront hotel has an attractive, modern design. Rooms are cheery but simple with sizable windows. The ocean view warrants the extra cash.

TOP END

Sete Coqueiros (☎ 3213 8583; Av Dr Antonio Gouveia 1335, Pajuçara; s/d from R$180/210; 🗷 🖳 🗷) This nicely located waterfront hotel has bright rooms with modern furnishings. Apart from the view, seafront rooms are identical to less expensive standard rooms.

Maceió Mar (☎ 2122 8000; www.maceiomarhotel.com .br; Av Álvaro Otacílio 2991, Ponta Verde; s/d from R$215/285; 🗷 🖳 🗷) This high-rise, beachfront hotel has spacious, brightly lit rooms with floor-to-ceiling windows, all with sea views.

Jatiúca Resort (☎ 2122 2000; www.hoteljatiuca.com .br; Lagoa da Anta 220, Jatiúca; d from US$300; 🗷 🗷) At the northern end of the city, bordering both a lagoon and the ocean, Jatiúca has expansive grounds with sports facilities and a tropical-lagoon-like pool. Rooms are taste-fully furnished with idyllic views from the porch, and all the trappings of luxury.

Eating

Maceió offers an impressive selection of eat-eries, from casual to trendy, with the beach-fronts of Pajuçara, Ponta Verde and Jatiúca

sprinkled with snack stands and restaurants. A good culinary street for browsing is Rua Eng Paulo B Nogueira in Jatiúca.

Local seafood specialties worth trying are *sururu* (small mussels) and *maçunim* (shellfish) cooked in coconut sauce, served as main courses or in a *caldo* (soup). Other seafood treats include *peixe agulha* (needle-fish) and *siri na casca com coral* (crab in its shell with roe). Stands clustered on the Ponta Verde shoreline make the Northeast-ern specialty *beiju de tapioca* by heating manioc flour until it solidifies, folding it like a taco, then filling it with savory or sweet fillings. The most traditional is *queijo coalho* (curd cheese) and coconut (R$4).

Simple restaurants serve up massive por-tions of extremely tasty and cheap seafood in Massagueira (10km south), on the southern shore of Lagoa Mundaú.

Sorveteria Bali (☎ 3231 8833; Av Dr Antônio Gou-veia 45, Pajuçara; one scoop R$2.50; 🕙 noon-10pm) Grab an outdoor table and enjoy Maceió's best ice cream. Among favorites are walnut, guava and tapioca.

Hamburgueria (☎ 3235 3772; Av Álvaro Otacílio 6595, Ponta Verde; mains R$7-14; 🕙 lunch & dinner) This new, stylish bistro has thick, tasty sandwiches, sal-ads and juices amid colorful, vinyl-loving ambience. Electronic music plays overhead – a counterpoint to the slow service.

Mestre Cuca (☎ 3327 1970; Av Deputado José Lages 593, Ponta Verde; per kg R$17; 🕙 lunch & dinner) An unpretentious self-service restaurant with an excellent lunch spread of regional dishes and salads.

Manjericão (Rua do Comércio 290, Centro; per kg R$20; 🕙 6am-10pm Mon-Sat) On a pedestrian street in restaurant-starved Centro, this pleas-ant per-kilo spot spreads a small but decent lunch buffet.

Sarah's Esfihas (☎ 3327 8877; Rua Dr Lessa de Azevedo 59, Pajuçara; mains R$13; 🕙 3-10pm) Great for a light snack, Sarah's is a popular Middle Eastern food stand making *esfihas* (fluffy breads topped or filled) to order. The *quatro qeijos* is divine.

Stella Maris (☎ 3235 3939; Rua Eng Paulo B Nogueira 290, Jatiúca; all-you-can-eat R$14; 🕙 lunch & dinner) For feasting on a budget, it's hard to beat Stella Maris, a no-nonsense *churrascaria* (barbe-cued meat restaurant) bringing juicy grilled meats to your table.

Surya (☎ 3377 0042; Rua Desportista Humberto Gui-marães 882, Ponta Verde; per kg R$23; 🕙 lunch Tue-Sun)

One of the city's best vegetarian restaurants recently reopened in Ponta Verde and provides a peaceful setting for healthy salads, sandwiches and juices.

Rei do Choppe (☎ 3327 5279; Av Antônio Gouveia s/n, Pajuçara; mains for 2 R$24-33; ☯ lunch & dinner) The 'king of beer' is a beachside spot serving a good selection of grilled fish, meat and seafood. There's live music some nights.

Massarela (☎ 3325 6000; Rua José Pontes Magalhães 271, Jatiúca; mains R$12-25; ☒) This is the place to come for homemade pastas and brick-oven pizzas. Decor consisting of hanging cheese and decorative plates adds authenticity.

Divina Gula (☎ 3235 1016; Rua Eng Paulo B Nogueira 85, Jatiúca; mains R$16-24; ☯ lunch & dinner Tue-Sun) A Maceió institution, Divina Gula specializes in the hearty cuisine of Minas Gerais and the Northeast. The *picanha* (steak) is excellent as is the *carne de sol* with plantains, corn, zucchini and *inhame* (a starchy root) purée. The outdoor tables in front are a good spot to sample one of 50 different kinds of *cachaça* (sugarcane spirit).

Peixarão (☎ 3325 7011; Av Dr Júlio Marques Luz 50, Jatiúca; mains for 2 R$28-36; ☯ lunch & dinner) This casual restaurant is a longtime local favorite for its filling seafood dishes. Grilled fish with shrimp sauce and *caldeirada* (Portuguese seafood stew) are top picks.

our pick **Wanchaco** (☎ 3377 6114; Rua São Francisco de Assis 93, Jatiúca; mains R$20-40; ☯ lunch Mon-Fri, dinner Mon-Sat; ☒) This highly acclaimed Peruvian restaurant serves excellent seafood in a cozy, creatively decorated setting.

New Hakata (☎ 3325 6160; Rua Eng Paulo B Nogueira 95, Jatiúca; buffet R$35; ☯ lunch & dinner) Maceió's top Japanese restaurant is a popular spot for sashimi and sushi, particularly on Tuesday's all-you-can-eat buffet night.

Drinking & Entertainment

Maceió's nightlife is scattered among the beach areas, with a few places in Jaraguá, a semi-restored colonial area located near the port.

Mai Kai (☎ 3305 4400; www.maikaimaceio.com.br; Rua Alfredo G de Mendonça s/n, Jatiúca; cover R$10; ☯ 9pm-last client Thu-Sun) This Polynesian-themed bar features live pop, rock or *axé* (Bahian pop music). The crowd can be young, especially on *axé* nights. Another Mai Kai (Rua Eng Paulo B Nogueira 215, Jatiúca, open 5pm to 2am) is a more casual spot for a drink with the same grass-roofed decor.

Lampião (☎ 3325 4376; Av Álvaro Otacílio, Jatiúca; cover R$6-10; ☯ 9pm-last client Tue-Sun) A mix of locals and tourists gathers at this well-known beachfront bar for dancing to Northeastern beats on the breezy shoreline.

Foca Bier (☎ 3304 3100; Av Álvaro Otacílio 3115, Ponta Verde; cover R$3-8; ☯ 4pm-2am Tue-Sun) This castle-like bar and music venue hosts live Música Popular Brasileira (MPB) and *forró* bands throughout the week. Foca serves decent plates (mains R$15 to R$25), and there's outdoor seating.

Orákulo (☎ 3326 7616; Rua Barão de Jaraguá 717, Jaraguá; cover R$10; ☯ 9pm-last client Tue-Sun) In an old building in Jaraguá, this dancehall is a favorite destination for Maceió's many *forró* lovers. The plaza in front is a lively meeting spot on weekends, with casual drink and snack stands in an otherwise barren neighborhood.

Havana Café (Av Comendador Leão 85, Jaraguá) This gay venue attracts gays and straights, who pack the dance floors on weekend nights to house music.

Shopping

The Mercado Praia de Pajuçara is an enclosed craft market on Pajuçara's waterfront selling lacework, hammocks, baskets and ceramics. However, you'll get a better deal at the **Mercado do Artesanato** (Centro; ☯ 8am-6pm Mon-Sat, to noon Sun). To get there, catch a bus that stops in front of the *antigo* (old) Cine Ideal.

If you are interested in doing some shopping for Alagoas' characteristic *filé* crochetwork, head for Pontal da Barra (8km south), a fishing/crafts village beside the Lagoa Mundaú. Women weave outside the shops that line the streets, and prices are generally the lowest around. To get there, catch any bus heading south with Barra in its name.

Getting There & Away
AIR

BRA (☎ 3214 4124; airport), **Gol** (☎ 3214 4078; airport) and **TAM** (☎ 3214 4048; airport) can fly you or connect you to anywhere in Brazil from **Aeroporto Zumbi dos Palmares** (code MCZ; ☎ 3214 4000).

BUS

The **bus station** (☎ 3221 4615) is 4km north of the city center.

Bonfim (☎ 3335 4629, 3336 1112) buses go to Salvador on Hwy BR-101 via Entre Rios (R$50, 10½ hours, daily) or along the coastal Linha Verde highway (R$65, nine hours, three daily).

There is a direct Linha Verde bus (R$40, eight hours, one weekly). Bonfim also has a daily *comercial* (R$25, six hours) and *executivo* (R$34, 4½ hours) bus to Aracaju.

São Geraldo (☎ 3223 4560) goes to João Pessoa (R$40, six hours, three weekly), Recife (R$30 to R$44, four hours, 14 daily) and Natal (R$78, nine hours, daily).

For Penedo, **Real** (☎ 3356 1324) has an *expresso litoral* (coastal express; R$17, 2½ hours, two daily), *pinga litoral* (coastal drip; R$17, four hours, two daily) and numerous *bestas* (R$17, 2½ hours). These buses provide access to Barra de São Miguel and Pontal do Coruripe. For more on the *pinga* see p518.

Transportation for the northern coast (except Maragogi) can be caught at the bus station or at the *posto* (gas station) Mar Azul at the northern edge of town, two blocks from the Cruz das Almas/Vaticano city bus terminal.

To reach Praia do Francês and nearby points south, there are frequent minibuses departing from a stop behind a Texaco petrol station (Rua Dias Cabral & Zacarias de Azevedo) southwest of Maceió's center.

Getting Around
TO/FROM THE AIRPORT
Maceió's airport is 20km north of the center. To get there, catch a taxi (R$26). Buses also run between Ponta Verde and the airport (signed Aeroporto-Ponta Verde) every 45 minutes or so (R$2).

TO/FROM THE BUS STATION
To reach the center, take the Ouro Prêto bus; for the beaches, catch the Circular 1. A taxi to the center costs R$7, and around R$14 to the beaches.

SOUTH OF MACEIÓ
This stretch of coast is characterized by small, quaint coastal villages – some with amazing beaches – surrounded by wide stretches of coconut plantations. The tourism hot spots on Alagoas' south coast are Praia do Francês and Barra de São Miguel, though entire neighborhoods of summer homes for Maceió's wealthy pop up in other areas as well.

Praia do Francês
☎ 0xx82
Given its proximity to Maceió (22km), Praia do Francês functions much like a remote city beach: cars and buses roll in on weekend days

and completely clear out by 5pm. Everyone concentrates on one end of Francês' fine, white sands, where just-offshore reefs create calm green waters and a string of restaurants provide beer and fried shrimp. A grouping of weekend homes, pousadas and a few restaurants, Francês lacks the infrastructure of a real town (or even a pharmacy). Surfers cluster at the southern end, where you'll find Alagoas' best surf, while swimmers opt for the protected reef at the beach's northern end. Walk 15 minutes in either direction to escape the crowds.

SLEEPING & EATING
Pousada Tortuga (☎ 3260 1539; Av dos Arrecifes 14; s/d with fan R$30/60) Among the battered cheapies in town, Tortuga is the best value, with sealed, painted cement floors. Right on the beach.

Pousada Lua Cheia (☎ 3260 1622; www.pousadaluacheia.com.br; Rua das Conchas 85; d R$100; ☒ ☒) The rooms are dark here, but most guests don't mind as the garden, hammock space and pool provide plenty of relaxing lounge space.

Pousada Miroku (☎ 3260 1187; www.pousadamiroku.com.br; Rua Cavalo Marinho 16; d R$110; ☒ ☒) A few blocks from the beach, Miroku is a tastefully decorated hotel; rooms have verandas strung with hammocks overlooking a garden.

Pousada do Aconchego (☎ 3260 1193; www.pousadaaconchego.com.br; Rua Carapeba 159; d R$150; ☒ ☒) Aconchego has pleasant, well-ventilated rooms set around a lush garden. Hammocks, a pool and friendly service add to the charm.

Cesar's Lanches (hamburgers R$2-5; ☒ 10am-5pm) Worth seeking out, Cesar's cooks up fantastic burgers on the beach. Look for young locals gathering around the tiny stand.

Restaurant Chez Patrick (☎ 3260 1377; Rua Marisia 15; mains R$25-35; ☒ lunch Tue-Sat, dinner Tue-Sun) Run by a French chef, this charming bistro serves seafood casserole, risottos and other tasty fare in a lovely setting.

GETTING THERE & AWAY
From Maceió, catch a minibus (R$2, 35 minutes, every 15 minutes from 5am to 10:30pm) from a stop behind the Texaco petrol station (Rua Dias Cabral and Zacarias de Azevedo) southwest of Maceió's center.

Marechal Deodoro
☎ 0xx82 / pop 38,000
On the banks of the tranquil Lagoa Manguaba, Marechal Deodoro is a small, peaceful

town with pretty churches and a few streets of colonial architecture dating back to early settlement days. Marechal served as capital of Alagoas between 1823 and 1839, and although there's not a lot to see, it's an easy and relaxing day trip from Maceió. The Saturday market, held until noon along the waterfront, is particularly lively. Arrive early in the morning to see fishermen working their nets out along the water.

SIGHTS

Marechal Deodoro has picturesque churches, though several of these are crumbling and not open to the public. At the top of the hill above the lagoon, the **Igreja de NS da Conceição** (8am-1pm Mon-Sat) has a white and yellow façade with a modern interior. Nearer to the water, the 17th-century **Igreja e Convento São Francisco** (8am-1pm Mon-Sat) houses the **Museu de Arte Sacra** (Sacred Art Museum; 8am-1pm Mon-Sat), which was closed for renovations at the time of research.

A block from the lagoon, the **Museu Deodoro** (Rua Marechal Deodoro 92; donations accepted; 8am-5.30pm), is set inside the house where Brazil's first president was born. The exhibits give a deodorized view of Manuel Deodoro da Fonseca, emphasizing his role as a military hero and president, but omitting to mention that he achieved this position with a military putsch in 1889 and that he later proved to be a poor politician. Next door **Artesanato NS Aparecido** (Rua Marechal Deodoro 82; 9am-6pm) sells the lace for which the town is renowned.

A few simple restaurants on the water sell plates of fried fish.

GETTING THERE & AWAY

Buses and minibuses for Marechal Deodoro (R$2, 35 minutes) via Praia do Francês depart frequently from a stop behind a Texaco petrol station (Rua Dias Cabral and Zacarias de Azevedo) southwest of Maceió's center. Buses, Kombi vans and collective taxis leave from Marechal's plaza for Praia do Francês (R$2, 15 minutes) and back to Maceió.

Barra de São Miguel

 0xx82 / pop 7300

Barra de São Miguel is best known as the gateway to **Praia do Gunga**, an idyllic, white-sand beach that curves to a point at the meeting of the Rio São Miguel and the sea. The center of this small village sits on the riverbank, facing

Praia do Gunga. The river mouth and local beaches are protected by a huge offshore reef, leaving the waters calm for bathing or kayaking. A daytime destination throughout the year, Barra only explodes with people during the high season and during Carnaval, when *trios elétricos* (electrically amplified bands playing atop trucks) take over the scene.

Boats for Praia do Gunga (R$20 to R$30) leave in the morning from the town's port, as well as from Praia de Barra de São Miguel.

SLEEPING

Most hotels are located 3km from the center at Praia Niquin, which is a better option for overnighting if you want to be near the beach.

Pousada Aconchego (3272 2090; Rua João Florêncio 97, Centro; d R$50;) Just a short walk to the boat dock, this modern, simple hotel offers a range of clean, sparsely furnished rooms, some rather spacious.

Hotel Portal Duleste (3272 1089; www.hotelportalduleste.com.br; Rua Edison Frazão 108, Niquin; s/d/tr R$90/130/165;) Overlooking the beach, this modern hotel has tidy rooms, many with beach views.

Pousada Sete Mares (3272 1054; fax 3272 1989; Av Leonita Cavalcante 371, Niquin; d R$150;) Opening onto a palm-shaded pool area, the spacious rooms of Sete Mares are fairly charming, with decorative touches.

EATING

Dining options are extremely limited. Restaurants at Praia do Gunga are infamously overpriced.

Sarah's Esfiha's (3272 1637; Rua Leonita Cavalcante 403, Niquin; snacks R$2-4; 2-10pm Wed-Sun) A favorite after a day in the sun, Sarah's serves Middle Eastern snacks and a few substantial plates.

Bar e Restaurante do Tio (Cais do São Pedro s/n, Centro; mains for 2 R$25-35; lunch Tue-Sun) On the waterfront near the boat dock, this simple restaurant serves seafood and Brazilian standards (try the shrimp with coconut sauce).

GETTING THERE & AWAY

Buses leave Maceió hourly for the 35km trip to Barra de São Miguel from a petrol station in the west of town.

From here, buses to Maceió (R$4, one hour) via Praia do Francês (R$4, 20 minutes)

leave hourly until 7pm. Collective taxis run the same route for the same price, leaving from behind the church in the center. Both buses and taxis pass through Praias Niquin and Barra de São Miguel.

Pontal de Coruripe

☎ 0xx82

A traditional fishing village that sees few visitors, Pontal de Coruripe lies in an area of verdant coconut plantations, on the edge of a long, deserted beach with beautiful emerald waters. On the peaceful streets of town, women sit in front of their homes gossiping and weaving palm baskets, placemats and handbags, while out at the cove just opposite the lighthouse, fishermen guide their boats across the sunlit sea.

SLEEPING & EATING

Pousada da Ada (☎ 273 7209; www.adapousada.com; s/d with fan from R$50/70; ❄) Travelers breathe a sigh of relief upon entering this pousada, with its shelves of books, lush, unmanicured garden, pets loafing about and the generally bohemian atmosphere. Ada speaks Italian, French, German and English and offers Portuguese lessons in her garden. Her rooms are tastefully simple and bright, and her breakfast and meals (with vegetarian options) are unforgettable.

Pousada Surf Paradise (☎ 3273 7303; www.surf paradise.com.br; d/chalet with 3 meals from R$280/330; ❄ ❖) Boasting marvelous views over the ocean, Surf Paradise comprises 15 chalets and four guest rooms spread about a grassy area above the beach. You'll find attractive decor and thoughtful touches (free bicycles, free DVDs to watch). You can also rent surfboards.

Of the restaurants clustered at the lighthouse, **Peixada da Madalena** (☎ 3273 7120; mains R$15-30; ❄ lunch) cooks up the town's best seafood, alongside tasty Italian dishes.

GETTING THERE & AWAY

The *pinga litoral* bus heading for Maceió (R$7, two hours) passes through Pontal de Coruripe twice daily. You can also catch a daily bus to Penedo (R$7, 2½ hours), which leaves around 3:30pm. There's also more frequent collective transport (R$7 to R$10, one hour) to Maceió, with many more options out of Coruripe (9km); or you can get a ride up to the highway (1km) and catch a passing *besta*.

PENEDO

☎ 0xx82 / pop 60,600

Penedo, known as the capital of the lower São Francisco, is the colonial masterpiece of the state and is almost unaltered by tourism. Attractions include the city's many baroque churches and colonial buildings and the opportunity to travel the sometimes-jade-colored waters of the Rio São Francisco. Penedo's downtown bustles with a daily market, Saturday being the biggest day, when people from surrounding villages pour in to do their shopping.

History

Since its founding, Penedo has been a commercial center, owing to its prime position on the Rio São Francisco. The town was founded sometime between 1535 and 1560 by Duarte Coelho Pereira, who descended the Rio São Francisco in pursuit of Caete Indians responsible for killing a bishop. Penedo is claimed to be the river's first colonial settlement. It was also the scene of a fierce 17th-century battle between the Dutch and the Portuguese for control of the Northeast. In the 19th century, Penedo was one of the focal points of the abolitionist movement in Alagoas. In the 20th century, the city lost its prominence as a commercial center, which probably saved its colonial buildings from destruction.

Information

You'll find a **Bradesco bank** (Av Duque de Caixas 71) with ATM on the riverfront.

Tourist office (☎ 3551 2727; Praça Barão de Penedo; ❄ 9am-3pm) Located in the Casa da Aposentadoria; staff hand out maps and offer city walking tours (for a fee and in Portuguese).

Sights & Activities

Penedo has a rich collection of 17th- and 18th-century colonial buildings, including many churches.

CHURCHES

The **Convento de São Francisco e Igreja NS dos Anjos** (Praça Rui Barbosa; admission R$2; ❄ 8-11am & 2-5pm Tue-Fri, 8-11am Sat & Sun) was under construction for nearly 100 years before its completion in 1759, and is considered the finest church in the state. Even Dom Pedro II (Brazil's second and last emperor) paid a visit. Of particular note are the richly colored ceiling, the gold rococo altar and the statue of St Francis to the left of it that was carved by Aleijadinho.

The **Igreja de NS da Corrente** (Praça 12 de Abril; � 8am-6pm Tue-Sun), completed in 1765, has some fine Portuguese *azulejos* (tiles), painted in green, purple and gold – colors rarely seen in Brazil – or Portugal for that matter. The Lemos family were big benefactors of the church (their family seal is marked on the floor) and abolitionists; slaves fled to the church for protection – some were even hidden behind panels of the church walls. A guide explains historical details (in Portuguese).

The **Igreja NS do Rosário dos Pretos** (Catedral do Penedo; Praça Marechal Deodoro; ☘ 8am-6pm) was built by slaves. The **Igreja de São Gonçalo Garcia** (Av Floriano Peixoto; ☘ 8am-6pm Tue-Sun) was built at the end of the 18th century. The small **oratório** (Praça Barão de Penedo) is where the condemned spent their last night praying before being hanged.

MUSEUMS

Occupying the top floor of the house Dom Pedro II once slept in, the **Museu do Paço Imperial** (Praça 12 de Abril 9; admission R$3; ☘ 11am-5pm Tue-Sat, 8am-noon Sun) displays lamps, portraits, furniture and elegant finery from the imperial period (17th and 18th centuries); it's tiny but nicely presented. The **Casa do Penedo** (Rua João Pessoa 126; admission R$2; ☘ 9am-noon & 2-6pm Tue-Sun) is a modest museum of relics and photographs from Penedo's history.

RIVER TRIPS

Regular ferries depart from the center for **Neópolis**, a colonial town on a hill with some interesting buildings and good crafts for sale, and **Carrapicho** (officially Santana de São Francisco; R$1, every 30 minutes), a small town noted for its ceramics.

An organized tour takes visitors to the **Foz do São Francisco** (R$20), where the river meets the sea at a beach with dunes and natural pools. The most frequent departures for this trip leave 28km downriver from Piaçabuçu.

Festivals & Events

The **Festa do Senhor Bom Jesus dos Navegantes** is held over four days from the second Sunday of January, and features an elaborate procession of boats and a sailboat race.

Sleeping

Hotel Turista (☎ 3551 2237; Rua Siqueira Campos 143; s/d with fan R$15/30) Traffic noise fills this simple hotel, and the rooms are small and bare, but it is clean and cheap.

Pousada Ribeirinha (☎ 3551 2691; Av Comendador Peixoto 49; s/d with fan R$15/30) This bare-bones option lies on the waterfront and has simple rooms (some without windows), though one room overlooks the river. No breakfast.

Pousada Estilo (☎ 3551 2429; Praça Jácome Calheiros 79; s/d with fan from R$20/30, s/d with air-con R$55/60; ❄) A local family rents clean, simple *apartamentos* (rooms with a private bathroom) in its home on a colonial plaza. Its breezy rooms here are nicer than those in its pousada (Rua Dâmaso do Monte 86), closer to the river.

our pick **Pousada Colonial** (☎ 3551 2355; Praça 12 de Abril 21; r with/without view R$80/60; ❄) The rooms in this beautifully converted colonial home on the waterfront have stained wood floors and antique furniture – you'll get extra space and marvelous river views for the added reais.

Hotel São Francisco (☎ 3551 2273; www.hotelsaofrancisco.tur.br; Av Floriano Peixoto 237; s R$77-133, d R$103-172; ❄ ▣) The rooms in this 1960s-style hotel have varnished wood floors and trim furniture. The place is quiet (could they ever hope to fill so many rooms?), has great hot showers and usually offers discounts for cash payment. The best rooms face the river.

Eating

Several supermarkets are on the main waterfront plaza near the bus stop.

Padaria São Francisco (Rua Nilo Pessanha 149; pastries R$1; ☘ lunch & dinner; ❄) Up the street from the São Francisco convent, this atmospheric bakery has a small selection of fresh baked goods.

Esquina Imperial (☎ 3551 5858; Av Floriano Peixoto 61; lunch R$6; ☘ lunch & dinner) A favorite budget spot, Esquina Imperial has a simple self-service lunch, and soups and sandwiches at night.

Oratório (☎ 9909 4777; Av Beira Rio 301; mains for 2 R$23-45; ☘ lunch & dinner) Penedo's best restaurant, Oratório serves excellent plates of seafood stews and grilled fish in a pleasant outdoor river setting. When in season, the *pitu* (giant river shrimp) should not be missed.

Forte da Rocheira (☎ 3551 3273; Rua da Rocheira 2; mains for 2 R$25-45; ☘ lunch & dinner) This former Dutch fortification has a splendid view out over the water. The food, which includes seafood, steak and *jacaré*, is less impressive, but it's still worth a visit.

Getting There & Away

The **bus station** (☎ 3551 2602) is on a riverfront traffic island. For Maceió, bus options are the expresso litoral (R$17, 2½ hours, two daily) and the pinga litoral (R$17, four hours, two daily). Bestas leaving from the same spot run a more frequent service to Maceió (R$15 to R$20, every 30 minutes). Any of these options provide access to Pontal do Coruripe, Barra de São Miguel and Praia do Francês. For more on the pinga see below.

There is one daily bus to Salvador (R$50, nine hours) via Propriá (R$6, 1½ hours) and Aracaju (R$13, three hours). It could be more convenient to take a ferry to Neópolis (R$1.50, 15 minutes, every 30 minutes from 5:30am to 10pm), where there are more frequent buses.

Topiques (vans) also go to Aracaju, Propriá and most frequently to Piaçabuçu (R$2, 40 minutes, every 30 minutes from 6am to 6pm). Ask the topique drivers hanging out on the riverfront for departure times.

If you're traveling by car, a car ferry runs between Penedo and Passagem (R$10, 10 minutes, hourly from 5:30am to 10pm), a short drive from Neópolis.

NORTH OF MACEIÓ

The coast up to Barra de Santo Antônio has fluffy sands, green waters and no shortage of coconut palms. From that point to Maragogi, the ocean takes on a calm, shallow and warm aspect due to the many reefs close to shore.

Low tides can allow you to walk 1km out to sea. The stretch from Barra do Camaragibe to Porto de Pedras is a sweet little pocket off the highway and a great place to treat yourself. Strung along one road are tiny villages with barely the basics to support tourism, save for a few luxury pousadas. Maragogi is the seat of tourism in the area. Wherever you go, it's advisable to get cash before heading out. The only reliable bank between Maceió and Recife is in Maragogi.

Getting There & Around

There are a variety of transport options to reach northern destinations. The Real Alagoas bus to Porto de Pedras (R$12, 3½ hours, five daily) runs via Barra do Camaragibe, São Miguel dos Milagres and Porto da Rua from the bus station in Maceió. This bus, as well as minibuses, bestas and collective taxis traveling the same route, can be caught at the posto Mar Azul at the northern edge of Maceió. Travel between these little towns is extremely easy up until about 7pm.

Barra de Santo Antônio

☎ 0xx82 / pop 13,500

Barra de Santo Antônio is a mellow fishing village built along the mouth of the Rio Jirituba. Across the river, on the narrow Ilha da

---

DRIPPING ALONG THE COAST

When traveling from Penedo to Maceió, throw in the extra two hours and opt for the pinga litoral (coastal drip) bus. If constant stops and deviations off the main road don't drive you crazy, you'll get a refreshing glimpse into rural life, passing tiny churches, dusty roads leading off into jungle and rustic fishing huts, with children waving as the bus rolls by.

From Penedo, the bus travels along the river toward the coast, passing the scattered fishing community in Piaçabuçu, then swings in from the river and north to Pontal do Peba, where it does a U-turn on the beach. From there it passes through Feliz Deserto, which has lots of cowboys and coconuts, one pousada and plenty of seafood.

The bus turns off Hwy AL-101 a bit further north at Miaí de Cima, where there are no pousadas, but many locals on the beach on weekends. The next time the bus turns off the main road is into Barreiras, also with good beaches but no pousadas. It then comes to pretty Coruripe before continuing to Pontal de Coruripe.

Next stop is Lagoa do Pau, with shrimp cultivation, weekend homes and a couple of pousadas. Then it's on to Poxim, past sugarcane fields and coconut palms. Approaching Maceió, it stops at the turnoffs for Barra de São Miguel and Praia do Francês. Passing the huge estuaries of the Mundaú and Manguaba lagoons, it's not long before the bus reaches the capital.

If you plan to stay at Pajuçara or beaches further north, get off the bus as soon as it turns off the coast road and before it continues into the center of Maceió. This will save you a long ride up to the bus station. As city buses travel through Pajuçara, they don't follow the beach but run along the first road parallel.

Croa, is a small settlement known as 'Barra II' and a collection of weekend houses. The main attraction of the area is the deserted **Praia de Carro Quebrado**, an exotic white-sand beach backed by thick palms. It is a 7km walk or beach-buggy ride (R$20 per car) from Barra II.

Praia Tabuba is a pretty, tranquil bay with a few bars and a couple of pousadas 4km south of Barra de Santo Antônio. There are reef tidal pools off the beach – ask at the bars about a ride there by *jangada*.

SLEEPING & EATING

our pick **Pousada Arco-Íris** (☎ 3291 1250; www.tabuba .tk; Rua 10, Praia Tabuba; d with fan/air-con R$100/120; ⊠) Arco-Íris is an attractive, high-quality pousada surrounded by greenery, 30m from the beach. The comfortable rooms are tastefully decorated and open onto a leafy back veranda, equipped with a hammock. Windsurf rigs, kayaks and bicycles are available for rent, and the pousada offers *jangada* trips. Heinz, the friendly, multilingual Swiss owner, has a wealth of information about the area. The delightful restaurant (mains R$13 to R$25, open for lunch and dinner Tuesday to Sunday) is a good place to enjoy fondues, pizzas, pastas, chicken curry and other unique dishes. Just follow the signs.

Chalés Costa Dourada (☎ 3327 9327; luizmen donca@nornet.com.br; s/d with fan R$80/100) Barra II has three pousadas, and the Costa Dourada's two-bedroom brick chalets are surprisingly the most economical. Though they feel a little like government housing, each one has a full kitchen and a hammock hung on the porch. No breakfast.

GETTING THERE & AROUND

You can catch minibuses to Barra de Santo Antônio (R$4.50, one hour, every 30 minutes from 5am to 6:30pm) at Maceió's bus station or *posto* Mar Azul at the northern edge of town. Collective taxis also leave from the Mar Azul but charge extra to enter the town.

For Maceió, catch one of the frequent buses leaving Barra de Santo Antônio's bus station. To head north, walk or catch a ride to the main highway, where you can flag down a bus, *besta* or collective taxi.

Canoes cross the river from behind the bus station (R$1), while the car ferry (return R$10 per car) leaves from beside the Banco do Brasil, up the road from the bus station.

Barra do Camaragibe
☎ 0xx82

This idyllic fishing village is strung along the road, on the edge of a small, reef-laden bay. *Jangadas* make trips south to **Praia do Morro**, a deserted beach with cliffs and clear waters. On the main road, **Restaurante & Pousada Foz do Camaragibe** (☎ 3258 5140; Rua São José s/n; s/d R$25/50; ⊠) has clean, simple rooms, several with tiny (frosted-glass) windows that open onto the sea. The seafood at the outdoor restaurant is quite good (mains R$20 to R$30). A few doors down, the **Pousada & Restaurante Barra Mar** (☎ 3258 5141; s/d R$25/50; ⊠) has a similar mix of simple rooms and a good seafood restaurant. It's 7km to São Miguel dos Milagres.

São Miguel dos Milagres
☎ 0xx82 / pop 6500

São Miguel dos Milagres has fine beaches with warm, shallow seas protected by offshore reefs. **Pousada e Restaurante do Gordo** (☎ 3295 1181; s/d with fan R$20/40), on the main road, rents out extremely basic rooms. The restaurant in front serves hearty, home-cooked fare (mains R$10 to R$25). It's a five-minute walk through coconut-palm plantations to the beach and 4km to Porto da Rua.

Porto da Rua
☎ 0xx82

Much like its neighbors, Porto da Rua is a small and sweet village of colorful houses spread along the road. A stretch of coconut plantation about 2km deep separates the center from the beach, where there are a few bars. The area's accommodations options are fairly spread out and set up for those traveling by car. The nicer pousadas have no problem picking up guests from as far away as Maceió; just call them.

SLEEPING

Pousada das Acácias (☎ 3295 1142; s/d R$70; ⊠) On the main road in Porto da Rua, this friendly, family-run guesthouse has simple, modern rooms, and the owners offer hiking and biking excursions around the area.

Pousada Um Milhão de Estrelas (☎ 3298 6223; www .pousadaummilhaodeestrelas.com.br; Praia de Tatuamunha; d with 2 meals R$400; ⊠ ⛲) Three kilometers north of Porto da Rua, this pousada sits 1800m off the main road, secluded in a sea of palms near the beach. Nicely designed cottages are spread through the grounds, each with its own wooden deck and some with Jacuzzi tubs.

The following two pousadas are 1½km down a dirt road (look for the signs), south of Porto da Rua.

Pousada do Caju (☎ 3295 1103; www.caju-al.com.br; d from R$160; 🔀) This estate house with a wraparound porch achieves the cool, urban-antique look in its lovely rooms. It has gorgeous gardens, an inviting restaurant (mains R$28 to R$35) and is just a short stroll to the beach. The owners speak French and a little English.

Pousada do Toque (☎ 3295 1127; www.pousada dotoque.com.br; d with 2 meals from R$400; 🔀 🏊) Truly one of the top pousadas in the state, Toque is an oceanfront property with a lushly landscaped garden and beautiful thatched-roof bungalows (with decks and unique features like private saunas and pools). You'll have the beach to yourself.

Porto de Pedras

☎ 0xx82 / pop 11,100

Porto de Pedras is a sweet little fishing town and, as it is the most established on this stretch of road, it boasts a few shops, bars and restaurants. It is located where the Rio Manguaba meets the sea, with a hilltop lighthouse offering great views.

Pousada Quinta do Coqueirais (☎ 3298 1375; Rua Seu Avelinho Cunha 39; s/d without bathroom & with fan R$35/55) On a quiet street on the way to the water (turn right after passing the church), this friendly spot has pleasant rooms with stained, sealed cement floors, mosquito nets and charming decor. A row of decent seafood restaurants is on the same street.

Pousada Costa das Pedras (☎ 3298 1176; www .costadaspedras.com.br; Rua Dr Fernandes Lima s/n; s/d R$100/110; 🔀) On the main road into town, this new guesthouse has five rooms that are handsome but a little dark. There's also a restaurant – its outdoor tables on the grassy lawn make a charming setting for the eclectic cuisine.

Peixada da Marinete (☎ 3298 1267; Rua Seu Avelinho Cunha s/n; mains R$35/55; 🕑 lunch & dinner) One of the best restaurants in town, this modest family-run spot serves tasty plates of shrimp, octopus and other fresh catch.

GETTING THERE & AWAY

A pedestrian ferry (R$2, 6am to 7pm) and a car ferry (car/pedestrian R$7/free, 6am to midnight) provide access to Japaratinga. Once across the river, you'll need to catch a collective taxi (R$4) the rest of the 9km into Japaratinga.

Japaratinga

☎ 0xx82 / pop 7000

Japaratinga's shallow waters are protected by coral reefs, and the beaches are backed by coconut trees and fishing huts. Under the moonlight, you can walk a couple of kilometers into the sea. The town is small but more touristy than the beach towns to its south, and it has a bustle to it. Accommodations on the whole are overpriced, but **Pousada dos Mares** (☎ 3297 1398; www.pousadadosmares.com.br; d with fan/air-con R$50/60; 🔀) is a cute place with simple, economical rooms. Kombi vans regularly make the 10km trip north to Maragogi (R$2).

Maragogi

☎ 0xx82 / pop 25,200

Maragogi is a small town with a waterfront strip along a white-sand beach and amazingly turquoise sea. It is probably the most visited beach in the state, due to its major draw: the sandbars and reefs that make up the **Galés marine reserve**, 6km offshore. Trips to the reserve (R$20 to R$25) are easily organized through the beachfront restaurants or hotels. It is a very touristy affair, with touts trying to sell you everything from fish food (unnecessary) to underwater photos, but if you grab a mask and snorkel and swim away from the crowd, the reefs are rich with sea life. Maragogi has a Banco do Brasil.

Maragogi's tourism is mostly day-use but, despite this, it has quite a few pousadas and Pernambucano weekend homes. On the waterfront, **Pousada Solar da Praia** (☎ 296 2025; www.solardapraia.com.br; s/d R$80/100; 🔀) has small, clean, simple rooms, but no views. On the same street, **Pousada Mariluz** (☎ 3296 1511; www .pousadamariluz.com.br; Av Beira Mar 885; s/d R$90/130, d with view R$170; 🔀) is also fair value (for the area), offering small but cheerfully painted rooms, some with verandas facing the ocean.

One of numerous seafood restaurants on the water, **Restaurante Frutas do Mar** (Av Beira Mar s/n; mains for 2 R$35-50; 🕑 lunch & dinner) is particularly noted for its *caldeirada*. It has relaxing outdoor seating near the water.

A casual open-air dining spot, **Pizzeria Regina** (☎ 3296 1279; Av Beira Mar s/n; pizzas R$10-20; 🕑 dinner) serves many varieties of pizza, as well as pasta, lasagne and desserts.

Real Alagoas runs buses to Maragogi (R$15, 4½ hours, two daily) from Maceió's bus station and from Recife (R$15, two hours, two daily).

Pernambuco

The small state of Pernambuco is one of the most exciting and varied destinations in the Northeast. Among the earliest centers of Portuguese settlement in Brazil, it has had five centuries to develop rich cultural traditions melding European, African and indigenous influences, especially in music and dance. Pernambuco gave Brazil the now universally popular *forró* but, especially in Recife and Olinda, you'll discover a whole gamut of musical styles from frenetic *frevo* to the big drum beats of *maracatu* – particularly at those cities' wild and euphoric Carnavals.

Recife, Pernambuco's capital, is one of Brazil's biggest cities, a very urban place with a rich cultural and entertainment scene and a fascinating history. By contrast its much smaller and calmer neighbor, Olinda, is a charming, historic town, full of pretty colonial churches, art and artisans.

North and south of these centers stretches a short but glorious coast with dozens of palm-fringed sandy beaches, great surfing waves and crystal-clear reef pools. Porto de Galinhas, south of Recife, is fast developing into one of Brazil's more popular coastal resorts; Tamandaré and Itamaracá are mellower spots for a more relaxed beach stay.

But Pernambuco's most glittering gem sits 500km out into the Atlantic. The archipelago of Fernando de Noronha is a tropical-island getaway to dream about, its spectacular scenery lined with near-empty, postcard-perfect beaches and surrounded by warm, brilliantly clear waters with world-class diving.

From its narrow coast, Pernambuco stretches 600km inland. Some irrigated agriculture now provides an alternative to sugarcane and ranching in the unforgiving interior, but sprawling Recife is still a magnet for many.

HIGHLIGHTS

- Dance in the streets of **Olinda** (p535) and **Recife** (p527) during euphoric Carnaval
- Dive, surf, snorkel, swim or just gaze at the crystalline waters of **Fernando de Noronha** (p541)
- Bliss out on the sand at **Praia dos Carneiros** (p538)
- Soak up the sun and fun at the beautiful beaches around **Porto de Galinhas** (p537)
- Discover the quirky history and creative art scenes of **Recife** (p525) and **Olinda** (p533)

Fernando de Noronha (525km)

Olinda
Recife ★
Porto de Galinhas ★
Praia dos Carneiros ★

| ■ POPULATION: 8.4 MILLION | ■ AREA: 98,938 SQ KM |

History

The history of Pernambuco centers on Recife and Olinda. Both were founded in the 1530s at the same time as sugarcane was introduced to Brazil. With the indigenous population brutally subdued, coastal Pernambuco quickly became one of Brazil's most important sugar-cane producers, using the labor of African slaves. This was one of the few areas where early Portuguese settlements prospered. Plantation owners built their homes and churches on the hills of Olinda, the original capital of the captaincy of Pernambuco. Recife was Olinda's port.

Dutch invaders sacked Olinda in 1630 but, doubtless feeling more at home among the waterways of Recife, developed it as the capital of ambitiously named New Holland. In 1637 they shipped in Prince Maurice of Nassau to govern the colony. Maurice's enlightened freedom-of-worship policy helped keep things calm while the Dutch extended their control as far north as Maranhão. But after the prince was ordered home in 1644, uprisings against Protestant Dutch rule eventually led to their expulsion in 1654.

Olinda was rebuilt, but Recife outgrew it to become South America's biggest city in the late 17th century. Recife's merchants eclipsed the power of Olinda's sugar barons in a bloody feud called the Guerra dos Mascates in the 18th century. The city finally became Pernambuco's capital in 1837. As the sugar economy floundered in the 19th century, Brazil's balance of population and power tipped from the Northeast to the Southeast, and Pernambuco declined to backwater status. Recife remained a significant port and commercial center, however, and industries developed in the 20th century. But the city still has double the Brazilian average number of households living below the official poverty line.

In recent years tourism has become a new commodity for Pernambuco, helping to waken Olinda from its slumber and turning the fishing village of Porto de Galinhas into one of Brazil's booming beach towns.

Climate

Pernambuco is hot and dry, and has a light rainy season from December to March. Temperatures along the coast rarely dip below the

PERNAMBUCO

high 20C°s (low 80F°s) and the interior is a lot hotter. Any time of the year is a good time to visit, but the temperatures are a bit more moderate and the foliage greener during the rainy season.

National Parks

Approximately 70% of the 21-island Fernando de Noronha archipelago (p539), 525km from Recife, is a marine national park, featuring crystal-clear waters and abundant marine life, from iridescent fish and hundreds of dolphins to giant sea turtles. The park is tightly controlled by the Instituto Brasileiro do Meio Ambiente e dos Recursos Naturais Renováveis (Ibama; Brazilian Institute of the Environment and Renewable Natural Resources) and the government of Pernambuco.

Getting There & Away

Recife's Guararapes airport receives regular scheduled flights from Lisbon, Madrid and all over Brazil, and charter flights from a few European and North American cities. Direct buses to nearly all major Brazilian cities serve Recife's large bus station.

Getting Around

Bus transport around Pernambuco is straightforward and easy. Buses are more frequent in the coastal areas than in the more provincial interior. To reach Fernando de Noronha, you must fly from Recife or Natal.

THE COAST

RECIFE

☎ 0xx81 / pop 2.5 million

Recife ('heh-*see*-fee'), capital of Pernambuco, is the Northeast's most exciting city after Salvador, with a vibrant cultural and entertainment scene, an intriguing coastal setting and a fabulous Carnaval. It's a very urban place of glassy high-rises, crowded commercial areas, thundering traffic and sprawling suburbs, both wealthy and poverty-stricken. It will take a little time to negotiate your way round the city and unlock its secrets. There are no must-visit beaches, but if you like your cities gutsy, gritty and proud, and can bear a whiff of putrefaction from the waterways, Recife is for you.

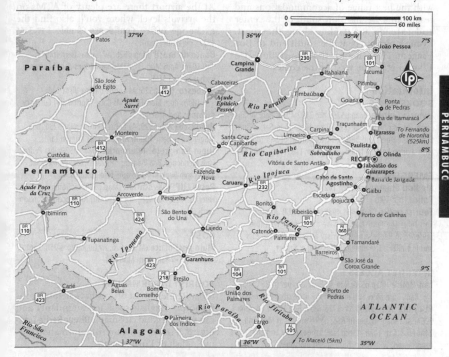

It takes its name from the offshore *recifes* (reefs) that calm the waters of the city's ports and shoreline.

The charming and far more tranquil historic town of Olinda lies on Recife's northern edge, just 6km from the city center, and many visitors opt to stay in Olinda and visit Recife during the day, or venture in for the animated nightlife.

Orientation

Recife is sprawling and more difficult to negotiate than most cities in the Northeast. The city center, a jumble of high-rise offices, colonial churches and thronged market areas, is spread over a number of islands and peninsulas at the mouths of the Rio Capibaribe and other, lesser rivers, with a dozen bridges crisscrossing the waterways. The main districts of interest are the historic Recife Antigo on the ocean side; Santo Antônio (the governmental area) in the middle, with a bustling commercial district to its south; and Boa Vista to the west. After dark and on Sunday afternoon many streets in the center are empty.

The middle-class suburb of Boa Viagem, with the best range of accommodations and restaurants, begins 3km south of the center and extends about 5km along the coast. Recife's airport is at the south end of Boa Viagem, 2km inland; the bus station is a 17km metro ride west of the center.

Information

BOOKSTORES

Livraria Cultura (Map p526; ☎ 2102 4033; Paço Alfândega, Rua da Alfândega; ☯ 10am-10pm Mon-Sat, 2-8pm Sun) The biggest and best bookstore north of Salvador, with a huge English-language section, CDs, DVDs and café.

EMERGENCY

Medical emergency (☎ 192)
Police (☎ 190)
Tourist police (☎ 3464 4935/4177; 3rd fl, Airport; ☯ 24hr) The tourist police have a reassuringly visible presence in Recife's more touristy areas, on foot, in cars and in trailers. The main office is at the airport.

INTERNET ACCESS

Lan-House (Map p526; Rua do Hospício; per hr R$1.50; ☯ 8am-8pm Mon-Sat) Inexpensive little city-center spot.
Pl@ylink (Map p529; ☎ 3326 1857; Rua Maria Carolina 2964, Boa Viagem; per hr R$6; ☯ 8am-11pm Mon-Thu, 24hr Fri & Sat, 10am-11pm Sun) Large, quiet and air-conditioned, with good, high-speed machines.

INTERNET RESOURCES

Destino Pernambuco (www.destinopernambuco.com.br) Site of the Recife Convention & Visitors Bureau, partly in English.
Guia Pernambuco (www.guiapernambuco.com.br) Useful info in English and Portuguese.

LAUNDRY

Most hotels will arrange affordable laundry services for guests.
Vivaz Lavanderia (Map p529; ☎ 3466 3755; Av Conselheiro Aguiar 2775; per 5/10 items R$12/20; ☯ 7am-7pm Mon-Fri, 7am-5pm Sat) Efficient laundry with wash-and-dry service.

MEDICAL SERVICES

Hospital Albert Sabin (☎ 3421 5411; www.hospital albertsabin.com.br in Portuguese; Rua Senador José Henrique 141) Highly regarded private hospital, west of the city center.
Real Hospital Português (☎ 3416 1122; www.rhp.com.br in Portuguese; Av Agamenon Magalhães) Well-reputed private hospital with 24-hour emergency service, west of downtown.

MONEY

At the airport there are plenty of ATMs on the arrivals level, where you'll also find the exchange office **Confidence Câmbio** (☎ 3464 4222; ☯ 8am-11pm).
Banco do Brasil (Map p526; Av Dantas Barreto 541; ☯ 10am-4pm Mon-Fri, ATMs 6am-10pm daily) Currency exchange and ATM.
Bradesco (Map p526; Av Conde da Boa Vista 126; ☯ 10am-4pm Mon-Fri, ATMs 6am-10pm daily) Currency exchange and ATM.
Bradesco (Map p529; Av Conselheiro Aguiar 3236, Boa Viagem; ☯ 6am-10pm) ATM; accepts foreign cards.
Hiper Bompreço supermarket (Map p529; Rua Pedro Paes Mendonça, Boa Viagem; ☯ 7am-midnight Mon-Sat, 8am-10pm Sun) ATM; accepts foreign cards.
Posto LUPP gas station (Map p529; Av Domingos Ferreira 1222, Boa Viagem; ☯ 24hr) ATM; accepts foreign cards.

POST

Main post office (Map p526; Av Guararapes 250, Santo Antônio; ☯ 8am-6pm Mon-Fri)

TOURIST INFORMATION

Most Recife tourist offices have helpful, professional, English-speaking attendants and can provide good city maps. **Disque Recife Turístico** (☎ 3232 8409) is the tourist information line, in English or Portuguese.

Airport (☎ 3462 4960; ☺ 24hr)
Boa Viagem (Map p529; ☎ 3463 3621; Praça de Boa
Viagem; ☺ 8am-8pm)
Casa da Cultura (Map p526; ☎ 3224 7626; ☺ 9am-
6pm Mon-Sat, 9am-2pm Sun) In the shopping complex.
Recife Antigo (Map p526; ☎ 3232 2942; Praça do
Arsenal; ☺ 9am-10pm)
TIP (bus station; ☎ 3452 1892; ☺ 8am-7pm)

TRAVEL AGENCIES
Asa Branca (Map p529; ☎ 3466 2244; www.asabranca
turismo.com.br in Portuguese; Shop 11, Av Conselheiro
Aguiar 3150, Boa Viagem) This professional agency sells
bus and air tickets, books hotels and offers car rentals and
tours. There are other agencies in the same block.

Dangers & Annoyances
Surfing is prohibited at Boa Viagem beach due
to the danger of shark attacks. Swimmers there
are advised to stay out of the water at high tide
and not go beyond the reef at any time. We
wouldn't recommend anything more than
paddling there in any case, as the water ain't
too clean. Since 1992, 19 fatal shark attacks,
and more than 30 other incidents, have been
recorded along a 20km stretch of coast that
includes Boa Viagem.

Recife has a reputation as a dangerous city,
and indeed it has the highest murder rate of
any Brazilian state capital. Tourists are more
at risk from pickpockets and bag snatchers, so
stay alert to your surroundings and be sure to
take the usual precautions (p698).

Sights
RECIFE ANTIGO
The narrow streets of Recife Antigo are a re-
minder that this was where the city began. The
waterside **Marco Zero** (Map p526; Praça Rio Branco), a
small monument on a broad square, marks
the spot where Recife was founded by the
Portuguese in 1537. Just north is **Rua Bom Jesus**,
formerly known as Rua dos Judeos (Jews' St)
because a number of Jewish businesses opened
here during Dutch rule (1630–54). The first
synagogue in the Americas, **Sinagoga Kahal
Zur Israel** (Map p526; ☎ 3224 2128; Rua Bom Jesus 197;
admission R$3; ☺ 9am-5pm Tue-Fri, 3-7pm Sat & Sun),
now a Jewish Cultural Center open to visitors, still has a bit of its original 17th-century
structure and interesting murals depicting
the role of Jews in Recife's development. This
area is at its best during the colorful Sunday
crafts market (see p531). On Recife Antigo's
southern waterfront stands the **Paço Alfândega**

(Map p526; ☺ 10am-10pm Mon-Sat, noon-9pm Sun), the
19th-century customs house converted into a
glitzy shopping mall.

SANTO ANTÔNIO
Praça da República (Map p526) at the northern
end of Santo Antônio has a formal park with tall
trees and a pretty fountain, and is surrounded
by imposing 19th-century buildings.

Just south is the **Capela Dourada** (Golden Chapel;
Map p526; Rua do Imperador; ☺ 8-11:30am & 2-5pm
Mon-Fri, 8-11:30am Sat), a church begun in 1696
that is a gem of Brazilian baroque. Further
south stretches a bustling commercial area
with shops and stalls lining every street, dotted with dilapidated colonial churches and
fine facades. This district throbs with city life
during the week but is deserted on Sundays.
In its midst is the **Pátio de São Pedro**, a traffic-
free square lined with bars, restaurants and
colorfully painted 19th-century houses. The
Concatedral de São Pedro dos Clérigos (Map p526;
☺ 8am-noon & 2-4pm Mon-Fri), an 18th-century
baroque church with incredibly fine wood
carvings, overlooks the Pátio.

The **Museu da Cidade do Recife** (Map p526; ☎ 3232
2812; Praça das Cinco Pontas; admission R$1; ☺ 9am-5pm
Tue-Fri, 1-5pm Sat & Sun) is housed in the Forte das
Cinco Pontas, a fort built by the Dutch in
1630. It has interesting exhibits on Recife's
history and popular culture.

PARQUE 13 DE MAIO
A great place to hang out, especially on a
Sunday, is Parque 13 de Maio (Map p526)
in the Boa Vista district. There's a lot of action in the park, including capoeira, heated
domino games and even more heated
political debates.

OFICINA CERÂMICA FRANCISCO BREN-
NAND & INSTITUTO RICARDO BRENNAND
A surreal sculpture garden of bizarre sexual-
ized earthworms, frogs and turtles covers
the landscape at the unique **Oficina Cerâmica
Francisco Brennand** (☎ 3271 2466; Várzea; admission
R$4; ☺ 8am-5pm Mon-Fri). The artist Francisco
Brennand, descended from 19th-century Irish
immigrants and considered Brazil's greatest
ceramicist, revitalized his family's abandoned
tile factory to create his own line of decorative
ceramic tiles. The rest of the huge space is dedicated to a seemingly exhaustive exhibition
of his peculiar sculptures, including gardens
with Moorish arches and rows of contorted

PERNAMBUCO

busts. A trip out to the Oficina Cerâmica, set amid thick Atlantic rain forest some 10km west of downtown, is a regional highlight, so set aside some time. From Tuesday to Friday afternoons, you can combine it with a visit to the scenic **Instituto Ricardo Brennand** (☎ 2121 0352; www.institutoricardobrennand.org.br in Portuguese; Alameda Antônio Brennand, Várzea; admission R$4; ☼ 1-5pm

Tue-Sun), Francisco's cousin's museum, 10 minutes south by taxi. This contains a massive collection of European and Brazilian art, swords, armor and historical artifacts in a fake medieval castle on lovely grounds.

The best way to reach these exhibitions is to arrange a round-trip by taxi. From Boa Viagem, with about 1½ hours at each place,

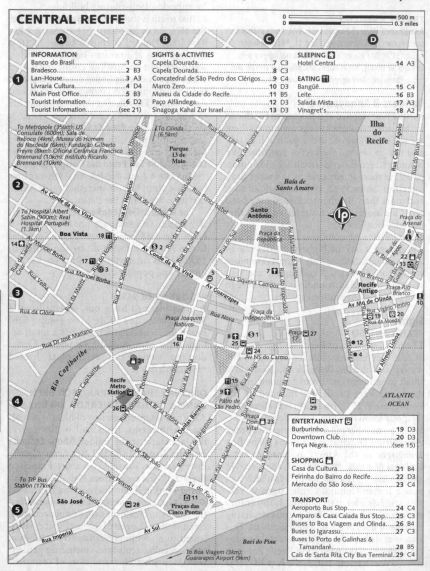

CENTRAL RECIFE

INFORMATION		SIGHTS & ACTIVITIES		SLEEPING 🏠	
Banco do Brasil..............1 C3		Capela Dourada.....................7 C3		Hotel Central...................14 A3	
Bradesco..............2 B3		Capela Dourada.....................8 C3			
Lan-House..............3 A3		Concatedral de São Pedro dos Clérigos..9 C4		EATING 🍴	
Livraria Cultura..............4 D4		Marco Zero.....................10 D3		Bangüê..................15 C4	
Main Post Office..............5 B3		Museu da Cidade do Recife........11 B5		Leite..................16 B3	
Tourist Information..............6 D2		Paço Alfândega.....................12 D3		Salada Mista..................17 A3	
Tourist Information..............(see 21)		Sinagoga Kahal Zur Israel........13 D3		Vinagret's..................18 A2	

To Metrópole (350m); US
Consulate (600m); Sala de
Reboco (4km); Museu do Homem
do Nordeste (6km); Fundação Gilberto
Freyre (8km); Oficina Cerâmica Francisco
Brennand (10km); Instituto Ricardo
Brennand (10km)

To Olinda
(6.5km)

Ilha
do
Recife

Parque
13 de
Maio

Baía de
Santo Amaro

To Hospital Albert
Sabin (900m); Real
Hospital Português
(1.3km)

Boa Vista

Santo
Antônio

Praça do
Arsenal

Praça da
República

Recife
Antigo

Praça Rio
Branco

Av Mq de Olinda

Rua da Glória

Praça Joaquim
Nabuco

Praça da
Independência

Rua Nova

Praça
17

Av NS do Carmo

Recife
Metro
Station

Pátio de
São Pedro

ATLANTIC
OCEAN

Praça
Dom
Vital

ENTERTAINMENT 🎭	
Burburinho.....................19 D3	
Downtown Club.....................20 D3	
Terça Negra.....................(see 15)	

SHOPPING 🛍	
Casa da Cultura.....................21 B4	
Feirinha do Bairro do Recife........22 D3	
Mercado do São José.....................23 C4	

To TIP Bus
Station (17km)

São José

Praças das
Cinco Pontas

TRANSPORT	
Aeroporto Bus Stop.....................24 C4	
Amparo & Casa Caiada Bus Stop.....25 C3	
Buses to Boa Viagem and Olinda.....26 C3	
Buses to Igarassu.....................27 C3	
Buses to Porto de Galinhas & Tamandaré.....................28 B5	
Cais de Santa Rita City Bus Terminal..29 C4	

Rua Imperial

To Boa Viagem (3km);
Guararapes Airport (9km)

Baci do Pina

PERNAMBUCO

this costs around R$60. The alternative is to take a CDU/Várzea bus west along Av Conde da Boa Vista in central Recife, get off at the end of the line and then take taxis to the Oficina Cerâmica, from there to the Instituto, and back to the bus stop. A taxi round-trip from the bus stop to both sites and back should be R$40 to R$50.

OTHER MUSEUMS

The **Museu do Homem do Nordeste** (Museum of Northeastern Man; ☎ 3441 5500; Av 17 de Agosto 2187, Casa Forte; ☯ 11am-5pm Mon-Fri, 1-5pm Sat & Sun), 6km northwest of downtown, has anthropological exhibits on Northeastern life ranging from slave chains to Carnaval costumes, with good photos throughout. It's extensive and well done, but was closed for renovations at research time, so check to see if it has reopened. Fans of Brazilian literature and history should visit the **Fundação Gilberto Freyre** (☎ 3441 1733; www.fgf .org.br in Portuguese; Rua Dois Irmãos 320, Apipucos; admission R$3; ☯ 9am-5pm Mon-Fri), 8km northwest of downtown, home of the author of the revolutionary 1933 book *Casa Grande e Senzala* (published as *The Masters and the Slaves* in English) about life on Pernambuco sugar plantations.

To get to either museum, catch the Sitio dos Pintos/Dois Irmãos bus west from Av Conde da Boa Vista, downtown.

BEACHES

The only beach worth visiting in Recife is at **Boa Viagem** (Map p529). It's a busy urban beach, packed on weekends and a good place to watch or play beach sports, but very few people enter the water, which is unclean and subject to shark attacks (see p525).

Festivals & Events

The Recife **Carnaval** is one of Brazil's most colorful and folkloric festivals, and has its claims to being the best in the country. It is a participatory event with an infectious euphoria and fabulous dancing: people don't sit and watch here, they join in. It also attracts far fewer tourists than Carnaval in the cities of Salvador or Rio. The months leading up to Carnaval, which are filled with parties and public rehearsals, are almost as much fun as the actual event, especially the week before (which is known as *semana pre*). Carnaval groups and spectators don elaborate costumes (see the boxed text on p528) and dance for days to most conceivable Brazilian

rhythms, but especially to Recife's very own, frenetic *frevo*.

Galo da Madrugada, which is claimed, probably correctly, to be the largest Carnaval *bloco* (themed singing/dancing group) in the world, brings a million and a half people cramming onto the streets of central Recife for the official Saturday-morning Carnaval opening. Activity generally focuses around a number of *pólos* (poles) dotted about the city center. Av Guararapes is the *pólo de frevo*; the Alfândega area is for mangue and electronica; Marco Zero and the Pátio de São Pedro feature varied rhythms. Programs are widely available including on the **Prefeitura website** (www.recife.pe.gov.br in Portuguese).

Carnaval in Olinda is so close that you could participate in both on the same day, and there is a lot of crossover in the events.

Recife also hosts one of Brazil's best out-of-season Carnavals, **Recifolia**, for four days in late October or November. In recent years it has taken place on the beach at Jaboatão dos Guararapes, south of Boa Viagem.

Sleeping

The city center has limited accommodations. The beach suburb Boa Viagem, with options from hostels to five-star hotels, is a much nicer place to stay.

CITY CENTER

Hotel Central (Map p526; ☎ 3222 4001; www.hotelcentral recife.com.br in Portuguese; Av Manoel Borba 209; s/d with shared bathroom R$25/40, s R$35-100, d R$50-100; ☒) The eight-story Central, on a tree-shaded street, was once Recife's most fashionable hotel and tallest building, but the rise of Boa Viagem left it stranded long ago. With antiquated furnishings and a 1930s caged elevator, it's now the best budget option in the center. High-ceiling rooms are bright enough and reasonably well maintained.

BOA VIAGEM

Albergue Maracatus do Recife (Map p529; ☎ 3326 1221; www.geocities.com/alberguemaracatus in Portuguese; Rua Maria Carolina 185; dm R$30, sheets & towel extra R$36) This is a well-located place with basic but airy bunk dorms for four to 10 people. There's a steady stream of travelers here.

Albergue Boa Viagem (Map p529; ☎ 3326 9572; www .hostelboaviagem.com.br in Portuguese; Rua Aviador Severiano Lins 455; dm R$37/75, d with air-con R$85; ☒ ☐ ☒) A newer hostel with separate-sex dorms, small rooms for couples and ample common areas, including a nice green garden with pool. It's well kept, sociable and has friendly staff.

Navegantes Praia Hotel (Map p529; ☎ 3326 9609; Rua dos Navegantes 1997; s/d R$70/90; ☒) Although a little past its best, the Navegantes is good value considering its location a block from the beach, with a quality breakfast and tidy rooms.

Bianca Praia Hotel (Map p529; ☎ 3327 9725; www .biancapraiahotel.com.br; Rua Mamanguape 142; s/d R$78/98; ☒) A modern, spick-and-span, small hotel just two blocks from the beach, Bianca is welcoming and professionally run, with nice artistic touches.

Pousada Casuarinas (Map p529; ☎ 3325 4708; www .pousadacasuarinas.com.br; Rua Antônio Pedro Figueiredo 151; s/d R$80/105; ☒ 🖳 🔊) This tranquil pousada in a former family home run by two friendly, English-speaking sisters is a marvelous retreat from the heat and bustle outside. Spotless rooms are set around a shady courtyard and folk art spices up the decor. Call ahead; it's a popular place.

Hotel Aconchego (Map p529; ☎ 3464 2989; www .hotelaconchego.com.br; Rua Félix de Brito Melo 382; s/d from R$108/125; ☒ 🔊) The well-run Aconchego

has immaculate rooms, substantial common areas, an affordable 24-hour restaurant and good service. It is popular with Brazilian tourists, and is a good deal in its price range.

Hotel Jangadeiro (Map p529; ☎ 3086 5050; www .jangadeirohotel.com.br in Portuguese; Av Boa Viagem 3114; r R$153-171; ☒ 🖳 🔊) One of the few midrange places on the beachfront, the high-rise Jangadeiro has amiable staff and colorful rooms with good-size bathrooms. All rooms have a sea view of some kind.

Recife Palace Hotel (Map p529; ☎ 4009 2500; www .lucsimhoteis.com.br; Av Boa Viagem 4070; s/d from R$243/274; ☒ 🖳 🔊) The mid-80s beachfront Recife Palace is still one of Boa Viagem's most luxurious hotels. Public areas are all black marble, polished woods and gleaming brass, and the rooms are ample and very comfortable, all with sea views and wireless internet. Contact reception directly for the best rates.

Eating

Recife has great places to eat, from the cheerful-and-bustling kind to refined establishments comparable with Rio's and São Paulo's finest.

MUSIC OF RECIFE & OLINDA

In Recife and Olinda you'll hear plenty of the very popular, typically Northeastern country music called *forró* (p531). There is also music from further south in Brazil like samba and its offshoots, *pagode* and *choro*. But these two towns are also an exciting music-and-dance world of their own – home to a variety of original genres, mostly bound up with Carnaval.

Top of the list has to be *frevo*. Its name is said to come from the Portuguese *ferver* (to boil). *Frevo* (in its most common form, known as *frevo-de-rua*) is feverishly fast brass music that inspires feverishly energetic dancing. People in performing troupes dress in supercolorful shiny costumes and twirl, for some reason, mini-umbrellas. The spectacular dance features a lot of high leaps and jumps. Its origins are thought to lie in a fusion of 19th-century marching-band music (polkas, quadrilles, tangos) with the movements of capoeira. *Frevo* really began to take over Recife Carnaval in the 1960s and celebrated its official 100th birthday in 2007.

Maracatu nação involves large African-style drum ensembles with dancers dressed as members of the Portuguese royal court from the baroque era – another curious juxtaposition that is said to derive from investiture ceremonies for the Reis do Congo (Kings of the Congo), leaders of the African community in times past.

Then there's *caboclinho* in which a set of characters from kings and queens to Indians and witch doctors and the *caboclinhos* themselves (Indian/African mixed-race characters wearing loincloths, bead and seed necklaces, and feathered headdresses) dance with much agility to pipe and percussion music.

All these combined music-and-dance styles, with clear origins in African, indigenous and European influences, play prominent parts in Carnaval in Recife and Olinda. A more recent arrival is mangue beat, which emerged in the 1990s among young bands who combined traditional local forms like *maracatu* with electrified rock instruments and rhythms of rap, hip-hop and electronica. Leader of the genre was singer Chico Science with his group Nação Zumbi. Science died in a car crash in 1997 and is still much mourned: Nação Zumbi plays on.

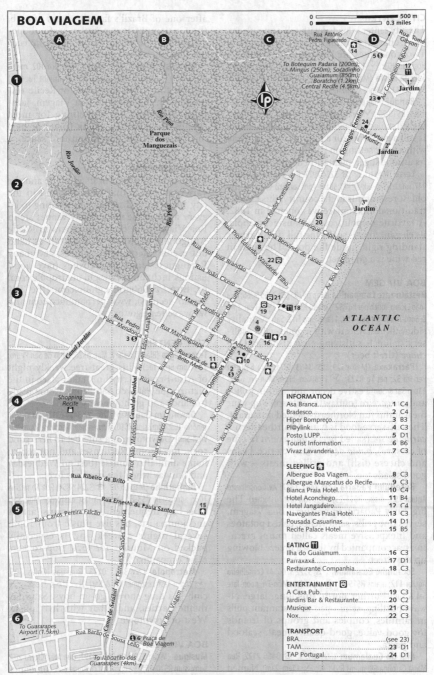

BOA VIAGEM

0	500 m
0	0.3 miles

To Botequim Padaria (200m);
Mingus (250m); Socadinho
Guaiamum (850m);
Boratcho (1.2km);
Central Recife (4.5km)

Parque
dos
Manguezais

ATLANTIC
OCEAN

Shopping
Recife

To Guararapes
Airport (1.5km)

To Jaboatão dos
Guararapes (4km)

PERNAMBUCO

INFORMATION
Asa Branca	**1** C4
Bradesco	**2** C4
Hiper Bompreço	**3** B3
Pl@ylink	**4** C3
Posto LUPP	**5** D1
Tourist Information	**6** B6
Vivaz Lavanderia	**7** C3

SLEEPING
Albergue Boa Viagem	**8** C3
Albergue Maracatus do Recife	**9** C3
Bianca Praia Hotel	**10** C4
Hotel Aconchego	**11** B4
Hotel Jangadeiro	**12** C4
Navegantes Praia Hotel	**13** C3
Pousada Casuarinas	**14** D1
Recife Palace Hotel	**15** B5

EATING
Ilha do Guaiamum	**16** C3
Parraxaxá	**17** D1
Restaurante Companhia	**18** C3

ENTERTAINMENT
A Casa Pub	**19** C3
Jardins Bar & Restaurante	**20** C2
Musique	**21** C3
Nox	**22** C3

TRANSPORT
BRA	(see 23)
TAM	**23** D1
TAP Portugal	**24** D1

CITY CENTER

The city center is loaded with self-serve places, most charging around R$17 per kilogram. Two good ones are **Vinagret's** (Map p526; Rua do Hospício 203; ☼ 11am-4pm Mon-Fri) and the nearby **Salada Mista** (Map p526; ☎ 3231 0583; Rua do Hospício 59; ☼ 11am-8pm Mon-Fri, 11am-4pm Sat).

Bangüê (Map p526; ☎ 3224 3649; Pátio de São Pedro 20; mains R$10-25; ☼ lunch & dinner) The restaurant lovingly detailed in Peter Robb's *A Death in Brazil* is still a good spot for a meat or seafood meal, with a great setting on Pátio de São Pedro and its unique sugar-plantation décor intact.

Leite (Map p526; ☎ 3224 7977; Praça Joaquim Nabuco 147; lunch R$30-60; ☼ 11:30am-4pm Sun-Fri) One of the oldest restaurants in the country, this famous traditional lunch place was opened in 1882. A favorite of politicos and businesspeople, its elegant tone is set by the full suit of armor standing right inside the door. The lamb in red wine is a good bet.

BOA VIAGEM

Restaurante Companhia (Map p529; ☎ 3465 9066; Rua João Cicero; lunch per kg R$21, mains R$13-20; ☼ 11am-3pm & 5pm-midnight Sun-Thu, 11am-2am Fri & Sat) A quality sidewalk restaurant with a good-value, self-service lunch, satisfying meat dishes and top *chope* (draft beer).

Parraxaxá (Map p529; ☎ 3463 7874; Rua Baltazar Pereira 32; per kg R$23; ☼ 11:30am-11pm Mon-Fri, 6am-11pm Sat & Sun) Festive decor and staff in police and *cangaceiro* (outlaw) outfits spice up your meal at this fun Northeast-themed restaurant. The self-serve food is typical Northeastern – *carne de sol* (salted beef), *macaxeira* (a type of cassava), *baião de dois* (a spicy rice, beans and cheese dish) and grilled meats – with good salads too.

Botequim Padaria (☎ 3467 7777; Av Conselheiro Aguiar 793; mains R$11-23; ☼ noon-last customer) The big, busy Padaria, in northern Boa Viagem, serves fine grills, sandwiches, baked potatoes and inexpensive meals called *pratos executivos*, accompanied by the sea breeze blowing up the street.

Socadinho Guaiamum (☎ 3322 3766; Av Conselheiro Aguiar 112; mains R$15-35; ☼ 4pm-late Mon-Fri, noon-late Sat & Sun) Further north, this long, large, always bustling, semi-open-air restaurant pulls in families, couples and groups of friends for good-value, good-quality meat, seafood and pasta.

Ilha do Guaiamum (Map p529; ☎ 3466 2122; Rua Maria Carolina 68; mains R$18-40; ☼ 11am-2am) Named after one of Brazil's favorite types of crab, the Guaiamum is a popular seafood specialist. Try the *camarão ao molho de coco* (shrimp in coconut sauce).

Mingus (☎ 3465 4000; Rua do Atlântico 102; meals R$60-90; ☼ noon-3:30pm daily, 7pm-midnight Tue-Sat) Sample the stylish new wave of Recife restaurants in the north of Boa Viagem. Jazz-themed Mingus has something for most palates, from herbed snook (pike) or beef medallions to foie gras in mustard sauce.

Entertainment

Recife is justly proud of its nightlife and the variety of music that can be found in the city. You can find somewhere exciting to go every night of the week. Many venues are in Boa Viagem but there are others in Recife Antigo and elsewhere. Tourist offices hand out useful entertainment guides, and many Portuguese-language websites have good listings including www.guiametropole.com. br, http://pe360graus.globo.com (the 'Diversão' section), www.pernambuco.com and www.recife.pe.gov.br.

CITY CENTER

Terça Negra (Black Tuesday; Map p526; Pátio de São Pedro; ☼ from 8pm Tue) This great free weekly night of Afro-Brazilian rhythms takes place in the picturesque Pátio de São Pedro. Come ready to dance and go home very late.

Downtown Club (Map p526; ☎ 3424 6317; Rua Vigário Tenório 105; admission R$10, women free Wed; ☼ 10pm-late Wed-Sun) Downtown is a sure bet to hear good rock, meet some Recifenses and not return home until after sunrise (best on Wednesday and Sunday when the music is live).

Burburinho (Map p526; ☎ 3224 5854; Rua Tomazina 106; admission R$3-8; ☼ 6pm-last customer Mon-Sat) This bar, frequented by musicians, artists and journalists, has live music from 10pm several nights a week and is especially packed on Monday for local pop-rockers Má Companhia.

Metrópole (☎ 3423 0123; Rua das Nínfas 125; ☼ 10pm-last customer Fri & Sat) Recife's best gay club has drag shows, go-go boys, Saturday theme parties, and a bar with live music. West of downtown.

BOA VIAGEM

Musique (Map p529; ☎ 2102 9191; Rua João Cicero 202; admission R$10-15; ☼ 6pm-last customer) A fun dance

FORRÓ

During WWII, the officers' clubs at the American military bases in Pernambuco would have balls open to the general public under the title 'For All'. The music was provided by local bands that played the accordion, triangle and a hand-held African drum, the *zabumba*. The rhythm was a fast-paced, two-by-four dance beat originally called *baião*. Couples danced to songs with simple lyrics speaking of the hard life of the countryside, the trials and tribulations of love and the beauty of dance. 'For All' became *forró* (fo-*hoh*) in Portuguese and the name became synonymous not only with the events, but with the spirit, the dance and the music.

The first icon of *forró* was the late Luiz Gonzaga (1912–89). 'Gonzagão' was responsible for taking the sound of Pernambuco to the rest of the country, later becoming the musical influence for some internationally renowned Brazilian musicians. Despite his personal popularity, *forró* continued to be looked down upon by São Paulo, Rio de Janeiro and other southern cities as backwoods Northeastern music.

During the 1990s, after the international success of lambada, and inspired by the country bands of São Paulo, *forró* musicians modernized their sound. They added electric guitars, keyboards and drum sets. The music and the dance became a national craze, with *forró* events throughout Brazil. It filled a void for an upbeat music that is easily danced with a partner – it's a simple two steps to the left and two steps to the right. The music is now known around the world.

Today the most commercially successful *forró* artists, such as Recife's Geraldinho Lins and Fortaleza's Aviões do Forró, have about 10 musicians with a solitary accordionist often looking a little uneasy in their midst. The Aviões do Forró even feature scantily clad dancing girls. But some of the most enjoyable *forró* is still played by traditional three-piece ensembles and this '*pé-da-serra*' (foot-of-the-hills, ie down-home) *forró* now carries the cachet of the genuine article. In any case, the best dancing goes occurs the dance floor where locals will thrill you with their fabulous innate rhythm and super-slick twists and turns.

bar with good house DJs and also live bands at 9pm most nights (pop-rock Friday and Saturday, *forró* Monday). Attracts locals and tourists.

A Casa Pub (Map p529; ☎ 2102 9191; Rua João Cicero; admission after 11pm R$15; ☺ from 5pm Tue-Sun) This lively British-cum-Brazilian pub sits opposite Musique, with an airy veranda and live music most nights from 11pm. Music ranges from samba and *axé* (a contemporary Afro-Brazilian pop style, incorporating samba, rock, soul and other influences) to *forró* and rock.

Nox (Map p529; ☎ 3326 8836; Av Domingos Ferreira 2422; women/men R$25/30; ☺ from 10pm Thu-Sat) Nox is the trendiest dance club in town, with a rave-like atmosphere, huge dance floor and spectacular lighting.

Jardins Bar & Restaurante (Map p529; ☎ 3326 8080; Av Domingos Ferreira 2045; admission for music R$15; ☺ from 6pm) A two-level restaurant in slick black, white and chrome with an roomy dance floor, Jardins hosts top local *forró*, rock and *axé* bands from 10pm or later several nights a week.

Boratcho (☎ 3327 1168; Galeria Joana d'Arc, Av Herculano Bandeira 513; ☺ 7pm-3am Wed-Sat) This groovy dance club with an artsy crowd often plays Recife's own mangue beat (modernized *ma-*

racatu). Thursday is a big DJ party night. It's located at the northern end of Boa Viagem.

OTHER AREAS

Sala de Reboco (☎ 3228 7052; Rua Gregório Junior 264, Cordeiro; admission R$10-15; ☺ 10pm-4am Thu-Sat) The best down-home *forró* in town is played – and danced – at this rustic-style place 4km west of the center.

Shopping

Pernambuco's traditional handicrafts, such as clay figurines, wood sculptures, lace and leather goods, plus plenty of T-shirts, are found at the **Mercado do São José** (Map p526; Praça Dom Vital; ☺ 6am-5:30pm Mon-Sat, to 11:30pm Sun), or the **Casa da Cultura** (Map p526; Rua Floriano Peixoto; ☺ 9am-7pm Mon-Fri, to 6pm Sat, to 2pm Sun). The latter is a creepy colonial-era prison with shops in cells where prisoners languished until 1973 (cell 106 is preserved as it was). Surrounding streets are also thronged with stores and stalls.

The **Feirinha do Bairro do Recife** (Map p526; Rua Bom Jesus; ☺ 2-10pm Sun), an interesting street market specializing in high-class artisanry – dresses, jewelry, ceramics – brings Recife Antigo to life on Sundays.

PERNAMBUCO

Getting There & Away

AIR

From Recife's **Guararapes Airport** (code REC; ☎ 3464 4188), there are direct flights to most major Brazilian cities, often on a choice of several airlines, plus Lisbon and Madrid with TAP Portugal and BRA. The following airlines have offices in Recife.

BRA Airport (☎ 3464 4655); Boa Viagem (☎ 3327 9911; Av Conselheiro Aguiar 1360)

Gol (☎ 0800 280 0465; Airport)

Ocean Air (☎ 4004 4040, 0300-789 8160; Airport)

TAM (☎ 3227 8813; Av Conselheiro Aguiar 1360, Boa Viagem)

TAP Portugal Airport (☎ 3341 0654); Boa Viagem (☎ 0300-210 6060; Av Conselheiro Aguiar 1472)

Trip (☎ 3464 4610; Airport)

Varig (☎ 3464 4846; Airport)

BUS

Recife's bus station is the large **Terminal Integrado de Passageiros** (TIP; ☎ 3452 2824), 17km west of the center. TIP handles all interstate buses and many destinations within Pernambuco. You can purchase many bus tickets at outlets in town, or by calling **Disk Rodoviária** (☎ 3452 3990), a bus-ticket delivery service.

Destinations include Caruaru (R$14 to R$18, two hours, hourly, 6am to 8pm), Fortaleza (R$73 to R$93, 12 hours, four daily), João Pessoa (R$15 to R$21, two hours, 31 daily), Maceió (R$30 to R$46, four hours, 11 daily), Natal (R$48, 4½ hours, eight daily), Rio (R$242 to R$257, 38 to 42 hours, three daily) and Salvador (R$93, 14 hours, one or two daily).

CAR & MOTORCYCLE

These recommended car-rental agencies have airport offices.

Avis (☎ 0800-725 2847)

Budget (☎ 3464 4030)

Localiza (☎ 3341 2082)

Getting Around

Recife is spread out and the buses (R$1.60) take some circuitous, confusing routes. A few taxis will save you time and stress.

TO/FROM THE AIRPORT

Taxis from the airport cost approximately R$10 to Boa Viagem, R$20 to the city center, R$25 to the bus station and R$30 to Olinda. Catch a regular cab, not a special airport taxi, which is more expensive.

City buses marked 'Aeroporto' run to Boa Viagem and the center from a stop five minutes' walk from the airport. Once outside the terminal, walk to the right and across busy Av Mascarenhas de Moraes, then turn left onto Rua 10 de Julho between the car showrooms and the gas station. Different Aeroporto buses go to different destinations, so check with the driver. For Olinda, you can get off on Av Conselheiro Aguiar in Boa Viagem and take a Rio Doce/Piedade bus from there to Olinda.

Going to the airport from Boa Viagem, get any Aeroporto bus on Av Domingos Ferreira; from the center, take an Aeroporto bus from the Cais de Santa Rita terminal (Map p526) on Av Martins de Barros, or from Av Dantas Barreto or Av NS do Carmo.

The Aeroporto metro station on Rua 10 de Julho, when it opens, will be a 15-minute ride from the central Recife station.

TO/FROM THE BUS STATION

From the TIP to all Recife and Olinda destinations, catch a metro train to the central Recife station (R$1.20, 25 minutes) and take a bus or taxi from there. Going out to the TIP, take a Camaragibe-bound metro train to the Rodoviária stop.

TO/FROM BOA VIAGEM

From the center, take a Setúbal/Príncipe bus from outside Recife metro station; an 033 Aeroporto bus from Av NS do Carmo; or a Setúbal/Conde da Boa Vista bus from Av Marques de Olinda (Recife Antigo)/Praça da Independencia/Av Conde da Boa Vista.

In Boa Viagem, southbound buses run along Av Domingos Ferreira; northbound buses run along Av Conselheiro Aguiar. The Setúbal/Conde da Boa Vista bus runs to Recife Antigo, Av Guararapes and Av Conde da Boa Vista; bus 160 Aeroporto heads to the Cais de Santa Rita city bus terminal (Map p526) along Av Martins de Barros and Av Dantas Barreto.

A taxi between central Recife and Boa Viagem costs R$10 to R$15.

From Boa Viagem to Olinda take a Rio Doce/Piedade bus (R$2.45).

TO/FROM OLINDA

From central Recife to Olinda's main bus stop on Praça do Carmo, take a Pau Amarelo or Rio Doce bus from outside the

Recife metro station; or a Casa Caiada bus from Av Dantas Barreto; or a Rio Doce bus westbound on Av Conde da Boa Vista. From Praça do Carmo, Rio Doce/Princesa Isabel buses go to the Recife metro station; Casa Caiada buses also go to central Recife. The Amparo bus shuttles between Av Dantas Barreto in central Recife and the street below the Igreja NS do Amparo in Olinda.

A taxi between central Recife and Olinda is R$15.

OLINDA

☎ 0xx81 / pop 369,000

Picturesque Olinda, set around a tree-covered hill, is the historic and artsy counterpart to the big-city hubbub of Recife. It's full of galleries, artisans' workshops, museums, lovely colonial churches, music in the streets, and there's always some kind of celebration in the works. With twisting streets of colorful old houses and gorgeous vistas over trees, church towers and red-tile roofs, this is one of the best-preserved colonial cities in Brazil. It has some lovely pousadas and makes a much more tranquil base for exploring the area than the bigger neighbor that it overlooks.

Olinda was the original capital of Pernambuco, founded in 1535. Sacked and burnt with all its Catholic churches by the Calvinist Dutch in 1631, it was rebuilt but lost its ascendancy to Recife in the 18th century. Although many buildings were originally constructed in the 16th century, most of what you see today dates from a later period.

Orientation

Olinda is 6km north of central Recife. The historic district, about 10% of the city, is concentrated on and around the hill and is easily visited on foot. The main bus stop is on Praça do Carmo, in the lower part of town near the coast.

Information

EMERGENCY

Tourist police (☎ 3439 9022; Rua Bernardo Vieira de Melo 80; ☼ 24hr)

INTERNET ACCESS

Click Brazil (Av Sigismundo Gonçalves 487; per hr R$1.50; ☼ 8am-10pm Mon-Sat)

Pontocerto (Ladeira da Sé 15; per hr R$3; ☼ 9am-10pm)

INTERNET RESOURCES

Most Recife information sites (p524 and p530) cover Olinda too.

Pousada Peter (www.pousadapeter.com.br) This pousada's site is full of fascinating information on Olinda and Recife, with lots of photos and videos.

MONEY

There are no ATMs in the old town. The nearest dependable ATMs for international cards are at **HSBC** (Av Getúlio Vargas 1050, Bairro Novo; ☼ 9am-5pm Mon-Fri, ATMs 6am-10pm daily); to reach it catch any Kombi van heading north from Praça do Carmo for 2km.

TOURIST INFORMATION

Casa do Turista (☎ 3305 1060; cnr Rua Prudente de Morais & Rua Bernardo Veira de Melo; ☼ 8am-8pm) The city's tourist information office has helpful staff, some speak English.

TRAVEL AGENCIES

Olinda is thin on travel agencies and you may need to go to Recife to arrange your travel needs, but **Amiga Viagens e Turismo** (☎ 3429 7811; www.amigaturismo.com.br; Casa Maloca, Rua do Amparo 183) can book flights, tours and some packages.

Dangers & Annoyances

Crime (mostly petty) exists, especially during Carnaval. To avoid false information or payment discrepancies it's best to use only accredited guides (see p535).

Sights

Olinda's sights are easy and enjoyable to visit on a walking tour, although highly random opening hours make it impossible to look in on everything in one day.

A good place to start is Praça do Carmo, overlooked by the **Igreja NS do Carmo** (1580; currently under restoration). Up Rua de São Francisco, the **Convento de São Francisco** (admission R$1; ☼ 7am-noon & 2-5pm Mon-Fri, 7am-noon Sat) is a large structure containing the 16th-century **Igreja NS das Neves** and two later chapels, with rich baroque detailing and lovely *azulejos* (Portuguese ceramic tiles).

Climb up to **Alto da Sé** (Cathedral Heights), which affords superb views of Olinda and Recife. There are food and drink stalls here and a small craft market with woodcarvings, figurines and jewelry. The imposing **Igreja da Sé** (☼ 8am-noon & 2-5pm Mon-Sat) was originally built in 1537. Burnt in 1631, it has been

PERNAMBUCO

reconstructed four times since, most recently from 1974 to 1984 in a Mannerist style that attempts to re-create the original 16th-century look. Check the touching inscription in simple Portuguese on the wooden door to the left inside the entrance.

The **Museu de Arte Sacra de Pernambuco** (Rua Bispo Coutinho 726; admission R$1; ⊙ 9am-12:45pm Mon-Fri)

is housed in Olinda's former Episcopal Palace, built in 1676. It contains a good collection of sacred art and a photographic homage to the city. Along the street, the **Igreja da Misericórdia** (⊙ 11:30am-12:30pm & 5:30-6:30pm), built in 1540, has fine *azulejos* and gilded carvings.

Head down Rua Saldanha Marinho to look at the restored 1613 **Igreja NS do Amparo**

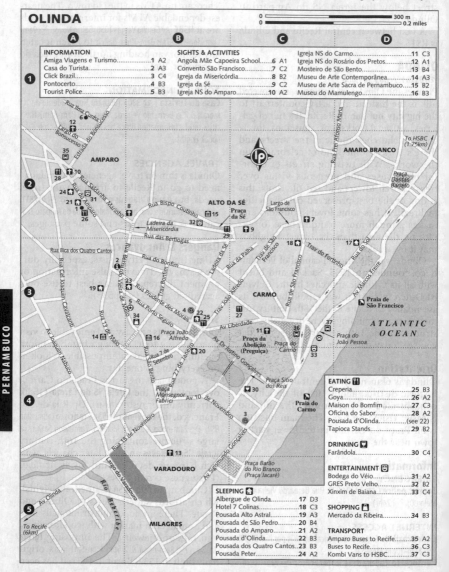

OLINDA

0   300 m
0   0.2 miles

AMARO BRANCO

To HSBC (1.75km)

Praça Dantas Barreto

AMPARO

ALTO DA SÉ

Praça da Sé

Largo de São Francisco

Rua Bispo Coutinho

Ladeira da Misericórdia

Rua das Bertiogas

Rua Bica dos Quatro Cantos

CARMO

ATLANTIC OCEAN

Praia de São Francisco

Praça do João Pessoa

Praça do Carmo

Praia do Carmo

Praça da Abolição (Preguiça)

Praça João Alfredo

Av Liberdade

Praça Sítio dos Reis

Praça Monsenhor Fabrici

Av 10 de Novembro

VARADOURO

Praça Barão do Rio Branco (Praça Jacaré)

MILAGRES

To Recife (6km)

Av Olinda

PERNAMBUCO

(🕑 9-11:30am Sun), and then round the corner to the **Igreja NS do Rosário dos Pretos** (Largo do Bonsucesso 45; admission R$2; 🕑 8-11am), built by an African brotherhood in the 17th century. Frescoes painted by slaves were revealed here during a recent restoration.

The **Museu de Arte Contemporânea** (Rua 13 de Maio 149; admission R$1; 🕑 9am-12:30pm) is recommended for both its permanent and temporary exhibits. It's housed in an 18th-century Inquisition jail.

The **Museu do Mamulengo** (Rua São Bento 344; admission R$1; 🕑 10am-5pm Tue-Sun) has a unique collection of over 1000 pieces devoted to the traveling puppet shows called Mamulengos, an authentic popular tradition of the Northeast.

The huge **Mosteiro de São Bento** (🕑 8-11am & 2-5pm), built in 1582, has some exceptional woodcarving in its church. Brazil's first law school was housed here for 24 years. The monastery celebrates mass complete with Gregorian chants at 10am on Sunday. Delicious homemade liqueurs are sold here too.

The city beaches are polluted and not recommended for swimming.

Activities

If you'd like to check out a capoeira school, **Angola Mãe** (☎ 3429 2671; Rua Ilma Cunha 243; per 2hr class R$15; 🕑 classes 9am & 7pm Mon, Wed & Fri) teaches the slower and more traditional Angola style. To find it, turn up the dirt street and look for the wall with the zebra mural. The school welcomes visitors to take classes or watch an open *roda* (circle) at 6pm on Sunday. Come with a respectful attitude and unaccompanied by a guide.

Tours

Throughout Olinda you'll no doubt hear the offer *'Guia!'* ('Guide!'). The best guides are those accredited by the local guides association, the Assocação de Conductores Nativos de Olinda (ACNO). They wear white shirts and an ACNO badge, and charge R$25 per hour. Some speak foreign languages.

Festivals & Events

Olinda's **Carnaval** lasts a full 11 days and has a spontaneity and inclusiveness that you don't get in big-city Carnavals.

There are organized Carnaval events, including balls, a night of *maracatu* and a night of *afoxé* (Afro-Brazilian music and dance based on the rhythms and spirit of Candomblé), but everything else happens in impromptu fashion on the streets. The official opening events – with all the pomp and ceremony of the Olympic Games – commence with the parade of As Virgens do Bairro Novo, a *bloco* of more than 400 'virgins' (men in drag), and awards for the most beautiful, the most risqué and the biggest prude.

Fabulously costumed groups of musicians and dancers, some thousands strong, parade right through the day from early morning to evening, with spectators joining them to dance *frevo* and *maracatu* through the narrow streets. It's playful and very lewd. Five separate areas have orchestras (as the bands call themselves) playing nonstop from 8pm to 6am every night. For schedules see www .olinda.pe.gov.br in Portuguese.

The **Folclore Nordestino** festival, in late August, features dance, music and folklore from many parts of the Northeast. It's highly recommended.

Sleeping

Book several months ahead for accommodations during Carnaval and be prepared for massive price hikes. Some of the quasi-official pousadas that crop up for Carnaval are among the best deals.

Albergue de Olinda (☎ 3429 1592; www.albergue deolinda.com.br in Portuguese; Rua do Sol 233; dm R$28, s/d/ tr R$45/65/75; 🖳 🗶) Olinda's excellent HI hostel has modern installations, spotless rooms and a sizable garden with pool. Rooms toward the back are quieter.

Pousada d'Olinda (☎ 3493 6011; www.pousada dolinda.com.br in Portuguese; Praça João Alfredo 178; dm R$25, s R$45-55, d R$75-105; 🗶 🖳 🗶) A central dining area, pool and lawn make this pretty pousada a good place to socialize with other travelers, and management is helpful. The plain rooms range from small economy-size to larger rooms.

Pousada Alto Astral (☎ 3439 3453; www.pousada altoastral.com; Rua 13 de Maio 305; s R$50-60, d R$80-90; 🗶 🗶) This colorful pousada has airy, bright rooms opening onto the leafy rear garden, but other rooms are dark. Discounts often available.

Pousada Peter (☎ 3439 2171; www.pousadapeter.com .br; Rua do Amparo 215; s R$55-132, d R$83-160; 🗶 🗶) A tasteful place on attractive Rua do Amparo, Pousada Peter is clean, quaint and well run,

PERNAMBUCO

and decked with art of its German owner. Varied rooms come at varied prices. Great views to Recife from the pool area.

Pousada de São Pedro (☎ /fax 3439 9546; www .pousadapedro.com; Rua 27 de Janeiro 95; s/d/tr R$70/110/150; ☒ ☏) Charming and friendly, the São Pedro occupies a 19th-century house full of art and antiques and has a lovely pool in the leafy garden.

Pousada dos Quatro Cantos (☎ 3429 0220; www .pousada4cantos.com.br; Rua Prudente de Morais 441; s R$89-280, d R$102-321; ☒ ☏) High ceilings, tall windows, hardwood floors and attractive art make this colonial home a delightful place to stay. There's a range of rooms at different prices: the splurge option is the suite, with four-poster bed and terrace. English spoken.

ourpick Pousada do Amparo (☎ 3439 1749; www .pousadadoamparo.com.br in Portuguese; Rua do Amparo 199; s R$215-415, d R$240-460; ☒ ☏) Charming Amparo occupies two 17th-century houses with lovely gardens and views back toward Recife. It's full of character and very comfortable, and will give you the full Olinda experience. English, Italian and Spanish are spoken.

Hotel 7 Colinas (☎ 3439 7766; www.hotel7colinas.com .br; Ladeira de São Francisco 307; r R$222-563; ☒ ☐ ☏) In spacious, leafy grounds in the heart of old Olinda, this more modern hotel is a nice change from the tight colonial streets. The rooms are comfortable and bright, and it has a quality restaurant and lovely pool.

Eating

A variety of restaurants is tucked away among the old city's cobblestone streets. A great way to start an evening is with a beer and a tapioca snack (R$2 to R$3) from the **tapioca stands** on Praça da Sé. The tapioca is lightly fried into a shell, and filled with prawns, cheese, ham, *carne de sol*, coconut or even chocolate.

Creperia (☎ 3429 2935; Praça João Alfredo 168; crepes R$5-18; ⏱ 11am-11pm) The spinach-and-ricotta crepe makes for a nice break from rice and beans, and the veggie salad comes with a true vinaigrette dressing.

Pousada d'Olinda (☎ 3494 2559; Praça João Alfredo 178; per kg R$17; ⏱ noon-3:30pm) Reasonably priced self-service lunch open to the public, with plenty of salad and veggies.

Goya (☎ 3439 4875; Rua do Amparo 157; mains R$15-30; ⏱ noon-5pm & 6pm-midnight Sun & Mon, 6pm-midnight Wed-Sat) The owners here are artists who dis-

play their work in the restaurant. The food is creative too, with fish and delicious shrimp dishes served in coconuts or banana leaves.

Maison do Bomfim (☎ 3429 1674; Rua do Bonfim 115; mains R$18-28; ⏱ 6pm-midnight Mon, noon-4pm & 6pm-1am Wed-Sat, noon-9pm Sun) A smart French place that has been around more than a decade, with nice decor and even better filet mignon, fish and prawns.

ourpick Oficina do Sabor (☎ 3429 3331; Rua do Amparo 335; mains R$18-35; ⏱ noon-4pm & 6pm-midnight Tue-Fri, noon-1am Sat, noon-5pm Sun) This well-known restaurant with a nice view is worth the prices. It's famed for its baked pumpkins stuffed with delicacies such as shrimp or fish in coconut or mango sauce.

Drinking & Entertainment

Alto da Sé gets busy in the evening as locals and visitors buy drinks and snacks from the street vendors, watch capoeira and savor the view and the breeze. Later in the evening the bars around Praça do Carmo are the center of the action, especially Xinxim de Baiana and the adjacent sidewalk places.

Bodega do Véio (☎ 3429 0185; Rua do Amparo 212; ⏱ 8am-11pm Mon-Sat, 8am-2pm Sun) Part small store, part bar, the Véio serves ice-cold beer, and locals and tourists alike congregate on the street or the small side terraces. A *choro* group plays here most Thursday evenings.

GRES Preto Velho (☎ 9927 1474; Rua Bispo Coutinho 681; admission R$2-5; ⏱ 9pm-late) This Alto da Sé bar is worth checking out late in the evening – it holds varied Brazilian music sessions, fills up with local partygoers and has a spectacular view.

Xinxim de Baiana (☎ 9627 3651; admission R$3; Praça do Carmo; ⏱ 9pm-late) Dark, sweaty Xinxim really fills with a hip crowd for the live *forró* from 10pm on Wednesday and Saturday.

Farândola (☎ 3491 0198; Praça Sitio dos Reis; admission free; ⏱ 5:30pm-late Tue-Sat) This lounge lizard–like bar with a red interior is a great place to sit at a table with friends, have a drink and check out live Música Popular Brasileira (MPB) and bossa nova.

Shopping

Olinda is full of small shops and galleries selling a plethora of art and artisanry such as ceramics, textiles, wood and stone carvings. Much of the work is incredibly colorful and browsing these places is one of the town's great pleasures. The hub of the creative scene is Rua do Amparo, where many of the best artists and artisans have their homes, workshops and galleries.

The **Mercado da Ribeira** (Rua Bernardo Vieira de Melo; ☺ 9am-6pm) houses art and souvenir shops and a room of *bonecos gigantes*, giant papier-mâché puppets used in Olinda's Carnaval.

Getting There & Away

Recife is the stepping stone to Olinda. See p532 for information on transport between Recife and Olinda.

BEACHES SOUTH OF RECIFE

South of the capital, the sea is calm, the waters are clear and the beaches are lined with coconut palms. The coastal Hwy PE-060 doesn't hug the ocean like the road in northern Alagoas, so you have to travel a dozen or so kilometers on an access road to see what each beach is like. Porto de Galinhas, 70km south of Recife, has mushroomed into one of the most popular beach resorts in the Northeast. Further south, the Tamandaré area is much less frenetic.

Around Gaibu

Ilha do Paiva, nicknamed the island of lovers, is popular for its nude beaches. Take a boat (R$10, 15 minutes) from Barra de Jangada, 15km south of Boa Viagem – it's worth a visit. You'll see boats along the beach.

Praia Calhetas, just outside the popular beach town of Gaibu, 45km from Recife, is the nicest beach in the initial stretch south of the city. It is a small bay surrounded by rocks and is a decent spot for snorkeling.

Porto de Galinhas
☎ 0xx81 / pop 10,000

Less than 20 years ago, Porto de Galinhas was just another fishing village at the end of a dirt road, with a palm-fringed beach and a few Recifenses' holiday homes. Today it is one of Brazil's booming beach destinations, with seven large resort-hotels strung along Praia Muro Alto and Praia do Cupe, north of the center. The development has been vertiginous and dense crowds flock to Porto at holiday times, but some village ambience has been preserved by pedestrianizing the few streets that make up the town center, where the odd restaurant opens right onto the beach. These streets are mainly lined with eateries, travel agencies and shiny little shopping galleries. Porto is a place for fun

and festivity, and beautiful white-sand beaches stretch several kilometers in both directions from the town. Some of the outer beaches are good for board sports, including Praia de Maracaípe, a lower-key spot 3km south of town.

Porto de Galinhas (Port of Chickens) gets its name from the fact that between 1853, when Brazil outlawed the slave trade, and 1888, when it abolished slavery itself, illicit slaving ships would land here loaded with crates of chickens *(galinhas)* as cover for their human cargo. Today, sculptures of brainless-looking chickens are dotted round town as a kind of on-street tourism logo.

INFORMATION
Banco 24 Horas (Rua Beijupirá; ☺ 24hr) ATMs; next to Beijupirá restaurant.
Diretoria de Turismo (☎ 3552 1728; ☺ 9am-3pm Mon-Sat) Tourist information is available at this office beside the main bus stop. There's another information office on Rua da Esperança, the street leading from the bus stop into the center.
Pé No Mangüe (Rua da Esperança; internet per hr R$4; ☺ 10am-11pm)

ACTIVITIES
Porto's fisherfolk have mostly given up fishing and now ferry tourists out to the **piscinas naturais** (tide pools) in the coral reefs, 100m in front of the main beach. Clusters of their triangular-sailed *jangadas* (boats) on the aquamarine waters are Porto's main postcard image. Take a snorkel to scrutinize the abundant marine life in these pools. The one-hour outing costs R$8 per person and you can rent snorkel and mask from most accommodations for around R$5. Just walk onto the beach and you'll find a *jangadeiro*. A longer outing to Maracaípe costs R$15 per person. There are further tide pools in front of Praias Muro Alto and do Cupe, and the latter, like Praia de Maracaípe, has competition-standard **surfing** waves. Some small bars and shops at Maracaípe rent boards.

The breezes are often good for **windsurfing** and **kitesurfing** off Pontal de Maracaípe, just south of Praia de Maracaípe, especially from June to September. **Beach-buggy rides** are popular; a three-hour trip from Muro Alto to Pontal de Maracaípe costs R$100 for up to four people. Drivers are easy to find in town.

SLEEPING
Pousada A Casa Branca (☎ 3552 1808; Loteamento Recanto Porto de Galinhas, Praça 18; dm R$37, s/d R$70/80; ⚹)

This HI hostel is a few hundred meters back from the beach, but sits on a quiet plaza and is one of the few decent budget options.

Pousada dos Coqueiros (☎ 3552 1294; www.pousada doscoqueiros.com.br; Praia de Maracaípe; s/d R$112/140; ☒ ☒) A relaxing pousada in Maracaípe, the Coqueiros is good value for its simple but attractive rooms, with hammock-strung verandas, and bar and pool in neat grassy gardens.

Pousada Beira Mar (☎ /fax 3552 1052; http://pousada beiramar.com.br; Av Beira Mar 12; r R$130; ☒) In a great location right on the beach in the middle of town, comfortable Beira Mar offers worthwhile discounts in the low season.

Pousada Marahú (☎ 3552 1700; www.pousadamarahu .com.br in Portuguese; Loteamento Recanto Porto de Galinhas, Praça 2; s/d R$140/150; ☒ ☒) One block from the beach just south of the central area, Marahú has very attractive rooms with terraces and pleasing fishy decor, plus a neat pool area.

EATING

Famed for its seafood, Porto de Galinhas has several good eateries. The beach bars serve inexpensive, fresh crabs.

La Crêperie (☎ 3552 1831; Rua Beijupirá; crepes R$10-13; ☒ 1:30-11pm) A quiet and affordable little place with a small garden area, La Crêperie serves soups, salads and pasta as well as tasty crepes.

Picanha Tio Dadá (☎ 3552 1319; Rua da Esperança 167; picanha for 1/2 R$20/35; ☒ 11am-2pm) The place to go for a good-value meat feast, though it can be overwhelmed by large, noisy groups of celebrating Recifenses. Come prepared to eat, as you will be stuffed with steak.

Peixe na Telha (☎ 3552 1323; Av Beira Mar; mains R$25-55; ☒ 11am-10pm) Peixe na Telha also serves quality seafood dishes and is right on the beach.

Beijupirá (☎ 3552 2354; Rua Beijupirá; mains R$30-40; ☒ noon-midnight) The most renowned of the seafood restaurants, it serves succulent dishes under romantic lighting. Don't miss the *camarulu* – shrimp in sugarcane syrup with passion-fruit sauce.

ENTERTAINMENT

The bars at Maracaípe get pretty lively after dark and sometimes big open-air concerts are held there. In town, **Chicken Club** (☎ 3552 1751; Av Beira Mar; women/men R$10/15; ☒ from 7pm) happily combines a beach bar (with live *forró* some nights) with a small, loud, dark disco.

GETTING THERE & AROUND

Buses to Porto de Galinhas (R$5.45, two hours) depart about twice an hour between 5am and 7.55pm from Av Dantas Barreto, just south of Rua do Peixoto, in central Recife. Coming from the south, get off your bus at Ipojuca, where buses run to Porto de Galinhas (R$2, 45 minutes) about every half-hour. Buses and Kombi vans to Maracaípe (R$1.50, 10 minutes) stop every 15 to 30 minutes across the road from the Recife bus stop in Porto.

Tamandaré

☎ 0xx81 / pop 17,000

Tamandaré, 30km south of Porto de Galinhas (75km by road), is a small beach town set on another series of lovely palm-fringed beaches – a far less hyper place than Galinhas, but with plenty of local tourism on weekends and holidays. Fishing boats will take you out to the tidal pools here for R$10 per person. Eight kilometers north up the beach, ultra-relaxed **Praia dos Carneiros** is the area's newly fashionable strand. It has wonderful, calm, shallow waters and more tidal pools formed by a rocky bar stretching across the wide mouth of the Rio Formosa.

Tamandaré has plenty of places to stay. **Pousada Recanto dos Corais** (☎ 3676 2155; www .pousadarecantodoscorais.com.br in Portuguese; Rua Hermes Samico 317; r R$80; ☒) is run by a welcoming, German-speaking, southern Brazilian couple and has comfy, spotless little rooms and a good breakfast. **Pousada Beira Mar** (☎ 3676 2829; kellytinaide@hotmail.com; Rua Almirante Tamandaré 140; r R$100; ☒) provides bright rooms right on the beach. **Restaurante Frente de Quintal** (☎ 3676 1863; Rua José Paulo Lins; mains R$15-50; ☒ 10am-10pm) serves generous portions of seafood and meat.

Praia dos Carneiros is lined by private coconut groves and, unless you're staying in one of the handful of lodgings there, beach access is only via two beach restaurant-bars, **Bora Bora** (☎ 3676 1482; minimum consumption per vehicle R$20-30; ☒ 9am-5pm) and **Sitio da Prainha** (☎ 3676 1498; admission incl buffet lunch R$30; ☒ 9:30am-5pm). Both are fine bases for a day of swimming, snorkeling, snoozing and strolling. **Bangalôs do Gameleiro** (☎ 3427 1808; www.praiadoscarneiros .com.br in Portuguese; d R$150-200; ☒) offers five brick-and-tile cottages, most with kitchen, spaced among the palms, and has its own good little restaurant.

Buses to Tamandaré (R$8, three hours) leave at 10am and 5:30pm Monday to Saturday, and 4pm Sunday, from Av Dantas Barreto in central Recife, just south of Rua do Peixoto. If you're coming north up Hwy PE-060 from Alagoas, get off your bus at Barreiros, where buses and Kombi vans to Tamandaré (R\$2, 40 minutes) leave about every half-hour till 8pm.

Mototaxis (R\$5 each way) will take you from Tamandaré to Praia dos Carneiros.

ILHA DE ITAMARACÁ
☎ 0xx81/pop 18,000

Less than 40km north of Olinda, Ilha de Itamaracá (separated from the mainland by a wide channel) is a pleasant weekend beach scene. During the week it's pretty calm.

Sights & Activities

The best area to head for is the southeast tip of the island. Here, **Forte Orange** (☎ 3544 1193; admission R\$2; ⏰ 9am-5pm Mon-Sat, 8am-5pm Sun) was built by the Dutch in 1631 and reconstructed by the Portuguese in 1654. It's an impressive citadel, with a nice view, right on the water. A short distance back along the road, the **Ecoparque Peixe-Boi** (☎ 3544 1056; admission R\$3; ⏰ 10am-4pm Tue-Sun) exists to study and rehabilitate the endangered West Indian manatee. You can watch up to 10 manatees, some rescued from injury or captivity, in a series of tanks, and see displays and films about them.

In front of the fort is the small sand island of **Coroa do Avião**, with several *barracas* (stalls). Small boats from the beach will run you across to the island for R\$7 per person, or take a boatload to the nearby reef pools and mangroves for R\$40.

Three kilometers west of Forte Orange is **Vila Velha**, a small port founded in 1540, one of the earliest Portuguese settlements in Brazil. A walking trail, the **Trilha dos Holandeses**, leads here from a chapel about 500m back up the road from the Ecoparque Peixe-Boi.

Itamaracá island has plenty more beaches, strung out along its 15km ocean shore. The quietest and prettiest are north of the central, most built-up part of the coast around **Jaguaribe** and **Pilar**. If you don't have a vehicle you need to hike 3km or 4km north along the coast from Jaguaribe to **Praia do Sossego** and palm-lined **Praia do Fortinho**.

Sleeping & Eating

Pousada Refúgio do Forte (☎ 3544 1675; Estrada do Forte Orange km4, Praia Forno da Cal; s/d R\$60/80; 🍴 🛏)

About 1km back from Forte Orange, this friendly place has clean, freshly painted rooms with hammock-strung verandahs.

Orange Praia Hotel (☎ 3544 1170; www.hotelorange.com.br in Portuguese; Praia do Forte Orange; s/d R\$125/153; 🍴 🛏) At Forte Orange beach, the Orange Praia is past its youth but still comfortable with a nice big central pool area and a good restaurant.

Recanto da Cigana Euzanira (☎ 3544 2971; Praia do Forte Orange 3400; mains R\$20-35; ⏰ 10am-6pm) The best of several beach restaurants near the fort, serving seafood, meat and salads.

GETTING THERE & AWAY

To reach Itamaracá, take a bus to Igarassu (R\$2.45, one hour, departures every few minutes) from Av Martins de Barros in central Recife. At Igarassu's Terminal Integração bus station, change to one of the frequent Itamaracá buses (free). A few of these go to Forte Orange; most of the others head to Jaguaribe but you can get off at the Forte Orange turn-off (the *entrada do Forte*) and catch a frequent Kombi van or shared taxi (R\$1) for the remaining 5km.

FERNANDO DE NORONHA

☎ 0xx81 / pop 3500

With its crystal-clear water, rich marine life and spectacular tropical landscapes, the Fernando de Noronha archipelago, in the Atlantic 525km from Recife and 350km from Natal, is one of the most stunning places in Brazil, if not the entire world. Brazil's 'Beach Bible,' *Guia Quatro Rodas Praias,* awards five stars to just four beaches in the whole country – and three of them are right here.

Although Noronha used to be the domain of regulated package tours, it's now easy for independent travelers to visit. Give yourself plenty of time because Noronha is addictive. The average stay is five nights. It's a wonderful place for doing things both water-based (diving, surfing, snorkeling) and on land (hiking, horseback riding, touring), and has a reputation as one of Brazil's top 'eco' destinations. Thanks in large part to the Fernando de Noronha Marine National Park and conservation projects based here, the marine and coastal environment is well preserved.

With little more than 200 plane seats per day available to Noronha, the islands can

PERNAMBUCO

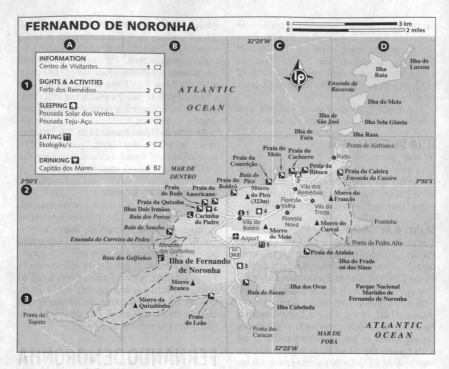

FERNANDO DE NORONHA

INFORMATION	
Centro de Visitantes........................1	C2
SIGHTS & ACTIVITIES	
Forte dos Remédios........................2	C2
SLEEPING	
Pousada Solar dos Ventos................3	C3
Pousada Teju-Açu..........................4	C2
EATING	
Ekologiku's..................................5	C2
DRINKING	
Capitão dos Mares..........................6	B2

PERNAMBUCO

never get overwhelmed by tourism. However, it's advisable to reserve accommodations and flights well ahead for December to February, and July and August. The week or so either side of New Year's can get booked up six months in advance. The showery season is from February to July and the islands are blessed by fresh breezes year-round. The time zone here is one hour ahead of Brasília time.

Prices are high due to the cost of transporting goods from the mainland. But as a guaranteed highlight of any trip to Brazil, Fernando de Noronha is well worth the expense.

HISTORY

The archipelago appeared on a Portuguese map in 1502 with the name Quaresma (Lent). A Portuguese aristocrat, Fernão de Loronha, was awarded the islands by his friend King Dom Manoel in 1504. He never set foot on the islands and forgot about them. They were occupied intermittently by the English, the French (twice) and the Dutch (twice), before Portugal definitively retook them in 1737, building 10 forts to defend the islands. Since

then, Noronha has been used as a penal colony, a military base (including for US troops in WWII), a US missile-tracking station, and now a tourist destination.

There has been some misguided tampering with the island's ecology. The teju, a black-and-white lizard, was introduced to eat the rats that had come ashore in colonial days. Unfortunately, the teju prefers small birds and crabs to rats.

A struggle between developers and environmentalists over the islands' future was resolved in 1988 when 70% of the archipelago, including much of the main island, was declared a marine national park, to protect its natural treasures. It was included on the Unesco World Heritage List in 2002.

ORIENTATION

Fernando de Noronha has 21 islands. The largest and only inhabited island, Ilha de Fernando de Noronha, is 10km long. The population is concentrated toward its northeastern end in the village of Vila dos Remédios and the adjoining, spread-out neighborhoods of Vila do Trinta, Floresta

Velha and Floresta Nova. The airport is in the middle of the island. A single paved road, the BR-363 (or Transnoronha Hwy!), runs 7km from the port near the island's northeast tip, through the populated area then to the airport and down to Baía do Sueste on the southeast coast. Unpaved side roads lead from the BR-363 to several of the island's other beaches. Morro do Pico, an extinct volcanic cone and the most spectacular of the islands' many striking rock formations, is the highest point, 323m above sea level – and more than 4300m above the ocean floor.

INFORMATION
Internet Access
Internet services here are the most expensive in Brazil.

Cia da Lua (☎ 3619 1631; Bosque Flamboyant, Vila dos Remédios; per hr R$18; ☽ 9am-11pm)

Creperia (☎ 3619 1120; Floresta Velha; per hr R$18; ☽ noon-11pm Tue-Sat, 6-11pm Sun & Mon)

Internet Resources
Fernando de Noronha (www.noronha.pe.gov.br) Has every detail imaginable, in English and Portuguese.

Medical Services
Hospital São Lucas (☎ 3619 1377; Bosque Flamboyant, Vila dos Remédios)

Money
ATMs at the airport and the Centro de Visitantes (right) accept international cards, but they sometimes run out of cash, so it's a good idea to withdraw a fair amount at Natal or Recife airport before you come (there is no need to worry about anyone stealing it on Noronha).

Post
Post office (Vila dos Remédios; ☽ 8am-1pm Mon-Fri, 9am-noon Sat)

Travel Agencies
Pirata Passeios (☎ 3619 0467/1318; www.pirata noronha.com; Pousada Aleffawi, Vila do Boldró) Fábio 'Pirata' knows the place backwards, speaks several languages and is an experienced dive instructor. He and his team can organize any tour or activity you want, as well as accommodations and flights.

Your Way (☎ 3619 1796; www.yourway.com.br; Native Lounge Hostel, Rua Antônio Álves Cordeiro, Floresta Velha) An indispensable contact on the island, this small agency

is perfect for independent travelers of all budgets. Fluent English-speaker Adriana will help you find the best-value flights to the island and the accommodations and activities that suit you best (at no additional cost), and will provide free airport transfers. It also runs the island's only inexpensive hostel.

Visitors' Tax
The state government imposes an environment-preservation tax on visitors to the island. The first day costs R$33, four days R$132, a week R$205, two weeks R$546 and a month R$2733. You pay by cash or credit card on arrival at the airport. If you decide to stay longer than planned, you must go to the airport at least one day before your original departure date and pay the tax for your extra days – otherwise you'll have to pay double for them when you finally leave.

SIGHTS
Centro de Visitantes
The visitors center, at Vila do Boldró, on the road between Vila dos Remédios and the airport, includes an open-air **turtle museum** (☽ 24hr) with displays on sea turtles by **Projeto Tamar** (☎ 3619 1171; www.tamar.org.br), as well as on Noronha's spinner dolphins by **Projeto Golfinho Rotador** (www.golfinhorotador.org.br in Portuguese). There are also Tamar information desks and a good café.

Forte dos Remédios
Easily the best preserved of the island's Portuguese forts, **Forte dos Remédios** (admission free; ☽ 24hr) is well worth a visit and has great views from its hilltop above Vila dos Remédios.

ACTIVITIES
Beaches
All the 26 beaches are clean, beautiful and almost deserted. The 'five-star' **Baia do Sancho**, **Baía dos Porcos** (named after the infamous Cuban Bay of Pigs) and **Praia do Leão** are all impossibly gorgeous. However, there is a lot of competition. The sandy beaches facing the Mar de Dentro (Inner Sea) on the northwest side of the island – **Cachorro** (at Vila dos Remédios), **Conceição**, **Boldró**, **Americano**, **Quixaba** and **Cacimba do Padre** – are also good for surfing.

Inside the national park, Ibama restricts access to some beaches in the interest of protecting marine life. Praia do Leão is closed off from 6pm to 8am from December to July, the turtle-nesting season. **Praia**

PERNAMBUCO

do Atalaia, which has shallow tide pools great for snorkeling, can only be accessed by a guided hike (see below) or by vehicle from Baía do Sueste four times daily (maximum 25 people per session – times are posted at Sueste). No flippers and minimal sunscreen are permitted.

Baía dos Golfinhos (below) is strictly off-limits to swimmers.

Boat Tours

A number of boats make enjoyable daily three-hour tours from the port, out to the Ilhas Secundárias (Secondary Islands) to the northeast, then back along the main island's northwest coast. Spinner dolphins like to swim and perform acrobatics near the boats, and a 40-minute snorkeling stop at Baía do Sancho is normally part of the trip. Naonda (☎ 3619 1307; www.barconaonda.com .br) is a recommended boat, charging R$80 including pick-up.

Dolphin Watching

From the clifftop lookout Mirante dos Golfinhos you can watch an average of more than 300 spinner dolphins cavorting in the Baía dos Golfinhos at approximately 5:30am (the dolphins come into the bay to take a rest from feeding out in the ocean). Trainee biologists provide Portuguese commentary Monday to Saturday. Two-hour early-morning tours here cost R$45 per person.

Hiking

Most trails within the national park can only be walked with a local guide. A great one runs from Praia da Caieira near the port to Praia do Atalaia, with cliff scenery and good snorkeling along the way – three to four hours in all. Portuguese-language guides charge R$45 per person for this hike; Fábio from Pirata Passeios travel agency (p541) does it in English, Italian or Spanish for R$80.

Scuba Diving

With 30m to 40m of visibility (at its very best in October), beautifully warm seas, abundant marine life and a well-preserved underwater environment, the diving around Noronha is world class. There are 230 fish species, 15 coral varieties and five types of (harmless) shark. Some of the best places to dive, including Ilha Rata, Ilha de Fora (Ilha da Viuvinha),

Enseada da Rasureta and Ponta da Sapata, are only accessible by boat. There are three dive operators, all well reputed:

Águas Claras (☎ 3619 1225; www.aguasclaras-fn.com .br; Alameda do Boldró) Friendly operation based near the Centro de Visitantes (where it also has a kiosk).

Atlantis Divers (☎ 3619 1371; www.atlantisdivers.com .br in Portuguese; Vila dos Remédios) French-run and very professional.

Noronha Divers (☎ 3619 1112; www.noronhadivers.com .br; Vila dos Remédios) The only locally owned operator.

For certified divers, two dives in one day at different sites normally cost R$250 including transfers and all equipment. All the operators also offer a range of courses, and batismo (baptism) dives for first-timers for around R$200.

Snorkeling

There are simply hundreds of good places to snorkel on the islands, from the rocks in Baía do Sancho to the tranquil tide pool of Atalaia (left), or Baía do Sueste where you can swim with marine turtles at high tide (local guides on the spot will swim you to the turtles for R$25). Masks and flippers can be rented for R$10 to R$15 per day at numerous stores and pousadas. A popular activity is a tow-dive, where you are slowly pulled along behind a boat, enabling you to cover greater distances; try Santuário (☎ 3619 1247; Porto; 2 half-hour tows incl transfers R$70). A novelty is Scooter Dive (☎ 9214 0017; Porto; per hr R$70), where you tour the harbor underwater steering a small torpedo-shaped motor – there are two wrecks and one sunken tractor to check out.

Surfing

Cacimba do Padre is the most famous surfing beach here and it hosts surf championships during the December to March season. Waves can reach 5m in height. Other surfing beaches on the Mar de Dentro, including Boldró and Bode, are also good, and in a big swell there are some thrilling waves among the Ilhas Secundárias. Most people bring their own boards but you can rent at Bar do Jacaré (☎ 3619 1947; Vila dos Remédios; per day R$30-45), which also offers classes for R$50 per hour.

SLEEPING

Noronha has around 120 pousadas, mostly in the Remédios/Trinta/Floresta area. Prices are very inflated, so most 'budget' pousadas here cost as much as midrange places on the mainland.

Budget

Native Lounge (☎ 3619 1796; www.yourway.com.br; Rua Antônio Álves Cordeiro, Floresta Velha; per person without breakfast R$40-60; 🖳) This sociable and relaxed little hostel is also the base of Your Way travel agency. Dorms and rooms are available, and there's a kitchen, outdoor BBQ and a mix-your-own *caipirinha* (*cachaça* cocktail) stand! They'll pick you up at the airport.

Some family homes in Vila dos Remédios function as simple pousadas. **Pousada Golfinho** (☎ 3619 1837; www.pousadagolfinhofn.com.br; Rua São Miguel 144; s/d R$70/150; 🔀), **Solymar** (☎ 3619 1965; Rua São Miguel 169; s/d R$100/150; 🔀) and **Pousada Tubarão** (☎ 3619 1391; Rua Sã Miguel 361; s/d R$70/120, with shared bathroom R$50/90; 🔀) are all no-frills but welcoming and adequate.

Midrange

Pousada Alamoa (☎ 3619 1839; pousadaalamoa@hotmail.com; Alameda das Acácias 2, Floresta Nova; s/d R$130/220; 🔀 🖳) On a street lined with pousadas close to Vila dos Remédios, small, attractive Alamoa is good value, with attentive service.

Pousada Barcelar (☎ 3619 1249; Rua Major Costa 128, Vila do Trinta; s/d R$165/260; 🔀) A friendly and spotlessly clean option, with mint and other green tones prevailing. Rooms at the front are airier.

Pousada Tia Zete (☎ 3619 1242; zetefn@ig.com.br; Rua Nice Cordeiro 8, Floresta Velha; s/d R$170/220; 🔀) Just outside Vila dos Remédios, this mustard-colored favorite has 12 comfortable rooms, hammocks and partial solar power. Airport transfers included.

Pousada Mabuya (☎ 3619 1205; www.pousada mabuya.com.br in Portuguese; Rua Major Costa 124, Vila do Trinta; s/d/tr R$195/260/351, chalet d/tr R$300/405; 🔀) Mabuya offers both cozy rooms and neat brick-and-wood chalets in the pretty garden. It's a friendly place providing a tasty breakfast, and the water is solar-heated.

Pousada Colina dos Ventos (☎ 3619 1257; pousada colinadosventos.com.br in Portuguese; Estrada da Colina 6, Vila do Trinta; d R$300; 🔀) This lilac-painted and pine-furnished hilltop pousada, just outside Vila dos Remédios, stands out for its fabulous views.

Beco de Noronha (☎ 3619 1568/9; www.becode noronha.com.br; Alameda das Acácias, Floresta Nova; s/d R$394/515; 🔀) A small place with nice wood paneling, good light and quirky, attractive decor using recycled wood and bottles.

Though not cheap, it's popular, especially with couples.

Top End

Pousada Solar dos Ventos (☎ 3619 1347; www.pousada solardosventos.com.br in Portuguese; Estrada do Sueste; r R$605; 🔀 🖳) With comfy wood-and-brick bungalows around extensive lawns and a gorgeous view down to Baía do Sueste, this pousada is very popular, so call ahead.

Pousada Zé Maria (☎ 3619 1258; www.pousada zemaria.com.br; Rua Nice Cordeiro 1, Floresta Velha; s/d R$607/638, bungalows from R$943/1100; 🔀 🖳 🌅) Luxurious Zé Maria boasts a stunning view of the Morro do Pico from its pool, and a fine restaurant.

Pousada Teju-Açu (☎ 3619 1277; www.pousadateju .com.br; Estrada da Alamoa, Boldró; s R$688-743, d R$770-825; 🔀 🌅) Almost underneath Morro do Pico, Pousada Teju-Açu is a relaxed, friendly eco-pousada with a good restaurant, spacious rooms and pleasant wood-decked pool area.

EATING

Creperia (☎ 3619 1120; Floresta Velha; crepes R$10-20; 🕑 noon-3:30pm Tue-Sat, 6-11pm daily) Dependable spot for tasty sweet and savory crepes; also has the island's best T-shirt selection.

Flamboyant (☎ 3619 1510; Bosque dos Flamboyant, Vila dos Remédios; per kg R$24; 🕑 noon-4pm & 7-10:30pm) Well-prepared food including good fresh salads makes this buffet very popular with visitors and locals.

Restaurante do Biu (☎ 3619 1458; Floresta Nova; buffet R$15; 🕑 11:45am-2:30pm & 6:30-10pm) Biu is an inexpensive log-cabin place with a huge variety of self-service food – a good place to stuff yourself after a long day of snorkeling or surfing. Get here soon after it opens to enjoy the full variety.

Cacimba Bistrô (☎ 3619 1200; Praça Eurico Dutra, Vila dos Remedios; mains R$23-40; 🕑 noon-3pm & 6:30-11.30pm) Run by three young Paulistas, Cacimba serves up tasty, carefully prepared pastas, risottos, steaks and salads.

Trattoria di Morena (☎ 3619 1142; Rua Nice Cordeiro 2600, Floresta Velha; mains R$25-40; 🕑 7-11:30pm Mon-Sat) Fine Italian dishes are served at this restaurant in the attractive Pousada da Morena. Have a glass of wine and try one of the seafood pastas or a steak.

Ekologiku's (☎ 3619 1807; Antiga Vila DPV; mains for 2 R$70-80; 🕑 7-10:30pm) A consistently good seafood restaurant behind the airport. Go for the superb *moqueca* (fish stew normally served in

PERNAMBUCO

a clay pot) or the *sinfonia ecológica*, a great mixed seafood platter.

DRINKING & ENTERTAINMENT

Most of the beaches outside the national park area have one bar/café. The clifftop bar **Capitão dos Mares**, beside the ruined Forte de São Pedro do Boldró, is a spectacular favorite for a sunset drink.

Visual do Porto (☎ 3619 1129; BR-363, Vila do Porto; ◷ 11am-10pm) With a great view of the harbor, Visual is nice for a sunset drink after water activities and usually has live music from 5pm. You can eat here too (mains R$15 to R$30).

Bar do Cachorro (Vila dos Remédios; ◷ 5pm-late) The famous 'Dog Bar' is the hub of Noronha social life, busy almost every night but really packed Thursday through Sunday. There's *forró* nightly from about 11pm (occasionally live), and if you don't know how to dance *forró* this is as good a place as any to learn. It's also a relaxingly breezy place to watch the sunset.

Feitiço Da Vila (Vila dos Remédios; ◷ 5pm-late) After-dark lighting gives this bar-pizzeria, next to the church, a special atmosphere and it packs in a crowd for the live music (reggae, rock, bossa nova etc) from 11pm to 1am, Thursday and Saturday.

GETTING THERE & AWAY

Fernando de Noronha's **airport** (code FEN; ☎ 3619 1311) sits in the middle of the island. Most incoming flights do a loop round the island as they arrive: views are best from the left side of the plane.

Trip (☎ Noronha 3619 1148) and **Varig** (☎ Noronha 3619 1144) both fly from Recife to Noronha and back daily. Trip also flies Natal–Noronha–Natal daily. Other airlines such as BRA and Ocean Air operate these routes from time to time, depending on the licensing situation. When they do, they are usually the most economical option.

Round-trip fares with Trip and Varig are normally R$750 to R$900 from Recife, slightly less from Natal, but they can rise to R$1100 or RS1200 at short notice in the high season. BRA fares can be as low as R$550. All the airlines issue e-tickets. Buy your flight as early as you can. Your Way travel agency can usually find you the best deal.

All seats on the Varig flights are available to Brazil airpass holders; Trip codeshares with TAM but only five seats are available to airpass holders.

GETTING AROUND

A good bus service (R$2.85) runs the length of the BR-363 between the port, Vila dos Remédios, the airport and Baía do Sueste, about every 20 to 30 minutes during daylight and early evening. You'll see bus-stop signs along the road. Hitchhiking is possible too.

Buggy taxis charge R$10 to R$20 for any ride. There's a stand by the central park in Vila dos Remédios.

A popular way to get around is to rent your own buggy. Rates are R$100 to R$150 per 24 hours, plus fuel (no insurance). Ask your pousada to find you one, or contact **Mulungu** (☎ 3619 1755, 3619 1970) or **Flor do Atlântico** (☎ 3619 1160), who will deliver the buggy to you. You can also rent motorcycles; Solymar (p543) charges R$50 to R$80 per day.

INLAND

CARUARU

☎ 0xx81 / pop 243,000

Though modern and without architectural appeal, this city 137km west of Recife does have cultural riches. Caruaru is known as the capital of *forró*, and its big Festa de São João (late May to late June) is, among other things, the largest *forró* festival in the country – 30 straight days of couples swaying to the accordion and triangle. It is also a huge market town and South America's biggest center for ceramic-figurine art, famous for its brightly painted little people captured in activities such as dancing and chasing chickens.

Sights

FEIRA DE CARUARU

This enormous **market** (Parque 18 de Maio; ◷ 6am-6pm) is the largest in the Northeast and has become a popular tourist attraction. It's busiest on Saturday. Among the thousands of stalls selling flowers, shoes, food, medicinal herbs, clothes and household goods is a large area devoted to handicrafts, the **Feira de Artesanato**, with leather goods, woven baskets, representations of strange beasts and mythical monsters, colorful figurines and much more. Also here is the **Feira do Troca-Troca** (Barter Market), where junk and treasure are traded without money. On Mondays, the **Feira da Sulanca**, the Northeast's biggest textiles market, happens here too.

In addition, you can hear singers and poets perform *literatura de cordel* (pamphlet literature), poetry by and for the people, which is sold in little booklets hanging from the market stands.

If you're interested in buying some figurines and seeing the ceramic artists at work, visit Alto de Moura (below) before buying at the Feira.

MUSEUMS

The **Museu do Forró** (☎ 3701 1533; Praça José de Vasconcellos; admission R$1; 8am-5pm Tue-Sat, 9am-1pm Sun) holds every bit of memorabilia on Luis Gonzaga, the father of *forró*, that it could get its hands on. There is a bonus side room on the Northeastern singer Elba Ramalho, a kind of Brazilian Tina Turner.

Museu do Barro (☎ 3701 1533; Praça José de Vasconcellos; 8am-5pm Tue-Sat, 9am-1pm Sun), upstairs from the Museu do Forró, displays nearly 70 original pieces by Mestre Vitalino (1909–63), Caruaru's original ceramic-figurine genius, and numerous works by other accomplished local potters. This is the best place to see Vitalino's work.

ALTO DE MOURA

The home village of Mestre Vitalino, 7km west of the city center, is a small **community of potters** that still specializes in producing *figurinhas* (figurines). Their pieces sell for anything from R$1 to R$3000. Many of the potters are descendants of Mestre Vitalino himself. Other noted artists include Manuel Eudócio, Luiz Galdino and the family of Zé Caboclo. The **Museu Casa do Mestre Vitalino** (☎ 3725 0805; Rua Mestre Vitalino; 8am-noon & 2-5pm Mon-Sat, 9am-5pm Sun), in the simple home of the master, contains his tools and personal effects.

Catch a taxi (R$8 to R$10) or bus (from Praça Porto, in the center of Caruaru) to Alto de Moura, then browse the dozens of workshops and galleries. The quality of the figurines here is generally higher than in Caruaru.

Sleeping & Eating

Caruaru is a long day trip from Recife, but there's no real need to stay overnight. Lots of places in the center serve regional food at good prices.

Hotel Vila Rica (☎ 3722 9666; Rua Dalvino Pedrosa 160; s/d R$60/95;) If you do decide to stay, this hotel in the southwestern Pinheirópolis district is decent value, with clean, basic rooms and a restaurant, and within easy reach of the bus station.

Bode Assado do Luciano (☎ 3722 0413; Rua Mestre Vitalino 511; mains R$8-15; 10am-5pm Tue-Sun) For lunch in Alto de Moura, head for this place. The specialty is the village's traditional roast goat and there are other options.

Getting There & Around

Buses run at least hourly to Caruaru from Recife (R$14 to R$18, two hours). Caruaru's **bus station** (☎ 3721 2480; Hwy BR-104, km68) is 3km southwest of the center. It's easy to get a taxi, Kombi van or local bus into town.

FAZENDA NOVA & NOVA JERUSALÉM
☎ 0xx81 / pop 4000

The small town of Fazenda Nova, 50km northwest of Caruaru, is famous for its theater-city reconstruction of Jerusalem, known as Nova Jerusalém. Surrounded by a 3m-high wall with seven gateways, 70 towers and 12 granite stages, the reconstruction occupies an area equivalent to one-third of the walled city of Jerusalem in the time of Jesus.

The time to visit is during Semana Santa (Holy Week, the week before Easter), when several hundred inhabitants of Fazenda Nova plus imported *novela* (soap opera) stars from Rio perform the *Paixão de Cristo* (Passion of Christ) play. Tickets cost R$30 to R$40.

For the full experience stay at the Passion Play–themed **Pousada da Paixão** (☎ 3732 1602; www.pousadadapaixao.com.br; Teatro de Nova Jerusalém; s/d incl dinner R$86/148;), inside the theater-city. During Semana Santa the cast stays here and other guests are invited to participate as extras. The restaurant is open to the public. The **Grande Hotel** (☎ 3732 1137; Av Poeta Carlos Pena Filho; d from R$80;) is a plain but adequate alternative. During Semana Santa doubles go up to R$120.

During Semana Santa, there are bus services direct from Recife, and travel agencies sell packages to see the spectacle. The rest of the year, there are daily buses from Caruaru (R$3, one hour).

GARANHUNS
☎ 0xx87 / pop 125,000

Garanhuns, 109km southwest of Caruaru, is popular as a holiday resort because of its relatively high altitude (842m). Its pleasant parks

PERNAMBUCO

and gardens and cool air give respite from the oppressive heat of the interior. President 'Lula' da Silva was born not far away in a tiny house (no longer standing) in the valley of Várzea Comprida, in 1945.

Hotel Village (☎ 3761 3624; Av Santo Antônio 149; s/d R$40/55; 🞮) is a plain but good-value central hotel, or you can enjoy the Pernambuco countryside at a few ranch-hotels in the area. **Fazenda Colônia da Serra** (☎ 3789 1104; off Hwy PE-218, Brejão; s/d R$70/140), 24km southwest of town, has its own lake and you can go horseback riding or fishing here.

The local food specialty, not for the faint-hearted, is *buchada de bode* (goat stomach stuffed with goat offal, herbs and vegetables). If you want to delve into this aspect of local culture, the unassuming but celebrated **Buchada do Gago** (☎ 3761 3894; Rua Mariano Filho 1, Vila do Quartel; mains R$10-25; 🕐 11am-3pm Mon, 11am-7pm Tue-Sun), on the outskirts of town, is the place to do it. Fondue lovers prepared to pay a bit extra should visit **Chez Pascal** (☎ 3761 2643; Av Rui Barbosa 891; mains R$20-40; 🕐 lunch & dinner), which has a variety of dishes.

The **bus station** (☎ 3761 0237; Av Caruaru) is 3km from the center. There are taxis and local buses from there. Eleven or more buses a day run to and from Recife (R$25 to R$31, three to four hours).

Paraíba & Rio Grande do Norte

This northeastern corner of Brazil has one huge advantage in life – kilometer upon kilometer of glorious beaches, some of them small palm-lined bays, others 20km long and backed by huge dune fields piled up by the coastal winds. Settlements along the shore vary from the large-ish, somewhat bland cities of Natal and João Pessoa to tiny undeveloped fishing villages, with an assortment of intermediate-size beach towns with varying degrees of tourism in between. João Pessoa and, especially, Natal serve as touristic entry points and bases for exploring the coasts to their north and south, either in day trips or – better, if you have the independence to travel freely – in lengthier explorations. For many travelers the hip international beach town of Praia da Pipa, a kind of 'global village' south of Natal, is the highlight of the region. For others it's the adventure of traveling itself that excites most, and it's even possible to make your way right along the coast all the way from Natal to Fortaleza in Ceará by beach buggy.

A different type of adventure awaits those willing to venture inland. The parched, drought-prone interior is home to dramatic landscapes and some of Brazil's most spectacular ancient remains, from fossilized dinosaur footprints to rock art many millennia old. The ideal months to head inland are June and July, when temperatures are less extreme.

The relatively sedate cities of João Pessoa and Natal do cut loose when it comes to festival time – especially in Natal's famous out-of-season carnival, Carnatal, in December.

HIGHLIGHTS

- Enjoy the stylish but unpretentious international scene of beautiful **Praia da Pipa** (p561)
- Cruise the spectacular, dune-lined coasts at **Genipabu** (p563) by buggy
- Explore the dramatic landscapes and intriguing archaeological remains of the arid interior at **Lajedo de Pai Mateus** (p554) and **Vale dos Dinossauros** (p554)
- Take to the streets for **Carnatal** (p558), Natal's lively out-of-season Carnaval
- Unwind at the remote beach village of **Galinhos** (p563)

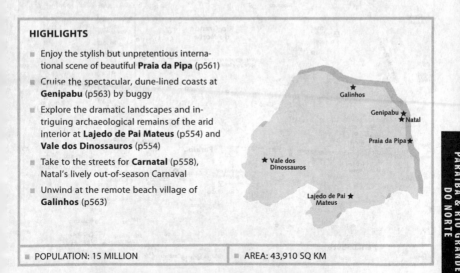

- POPULATION: 15 MILLION
- AREA: 43,910 SQ KM

History

This area of Brazil was a hotly contested colonial property, with both the French and Dutch vying for control against the Portuguese. French brazilwood traders had a decent foothold in Rio Grande do Norte until the Portuguese sent a fleet from Paraíba to kick them out in 1597. Natal was lost again to the Dutch from 1633 to 1654 before being retaken by the Portuguese.

Thereafter, the states of Paraíba and Rio Grande do Norte largely languished in obscurity until the early 20th century. Paraíba made a name for itself as the home state of João Pessoa, who allied himself with Getúlio Vargas in 1929 in a bid for the vice-presidency. Judging by the sheer number of João Pessoa tributes in the state, it seems that not much has happened since.

In 1935 rioting in Natal led to the declaration of a short-lived communist government in Rio Grande do Norte. The communist movement was suppressed and before long Rio Grande do Norte's strategic location as Brazil's closest point to Africa saw it become a supply base for the US in WWII. The injection of military money spurred significant development in the region. Today, the region's fabulous beaches bring in major income from tourism, especially in Rio Grande do Norte.

Climate

Although this area is no hotter than neighboring states, Rio Grande do Norte in particular is really dry and the sun can be very strong in the almost-always-clear skies. Temperatures in both states can top 40°C (104°F) in January and February. Although the weather is nice year-round, some find it the most pleasant in the slightly cooler months of June to August.

Getting There & Away
AIR

Natal has direct and indirect flights from every major Brazilian city and Lisbon (Portugal). It has seen an increasing number of European charter flights and, once in a while, an American charter flight. João Pessoa's airport also has a few European charters, plus domestic flights.

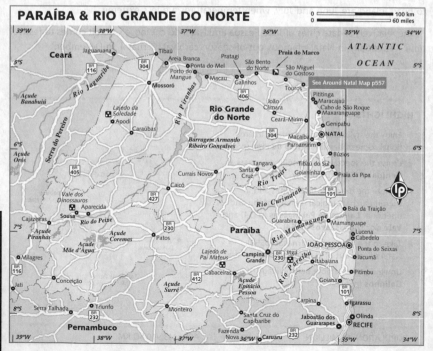

PARAÍBA & RIO GRANDE DO NORTE

BUS

Both state capitals, Natal and João Pessoa, are served by buses from the main Northeastern cities. Natal also has direct connections from Rio.

Getting Around

The bus network is good for travel between larger towns and more popular beach spots. Rental cars are available too. For anything more remote you should get a group together to hire a 4WD or buggy with a driver.

PARAÍBA

Sandwiched between Pernambuco and Rio Grande do Norte, the small, sunny state of Paraíba contains the easternmost point of the continent, Ponta do Seixas, where you are considerably closer to Senegal than you are to southern Brazil. The tranquil and reasonably well-developed coast is this small state's most important economic region, fueled by the farming of sugarcane and pineapples, and aided by a bit of tourism. Cattle ranching dominates the drought-affected interior, which also harbors some intriguing archaeological sites.

JOÃO PESSOA

☎ 0xx83 / pop 674,000

The coastal city of João Pessoa is the capital of Paraíba and the third-oldest city in Brazil. It claims to have more trees than any other capital city, including an Atlantic rain forest preserve, and has a reputation for being friendly and safe (some would say boring). Tourism is developing gradually here, and the city is an increasingly popular destination for Brazilian families. The city center has a few interesting churches, and Praia de Tambaú is particularly clean and relaxed for an urban beach.

History

Founded in 1585, the city was originally known as Vila de Felipéia de NS das Neves. It was later renamed for João Pessoa, the governor of Paraíba who formed an alliance with Getúlio Vargas to run for the presidency of Brazil in 1929. When courted by opposing political parties, João Pessoa uttered a pithy '*nego*'

CENTRAL JOÃO PESSOA

INFORMATION	
Banco do Brasil...............1	B3

SIGHTS & ACTIVITIES	
Igreja São Francisco...........2	C1

SLEEPING 🛏	
Hotel Aurora....................3	B3

TRANSPORT	
Bus Station.......................4	A1
Buses to Jacumã................5	A2
Buses to Tambaú................6	C3
Terminal de Integração....7	A1

To Airport (11km)

To BRA (500m); Casa do Artista Popular (500m); Praia de Tambaú (8km); Praia do Jacaré (13km)

PARAÍBA & RIO GRANDE DO NORTE

(I refuse), which is now given prominence in all Brazilian history books and is emblazoned in bold letters on the state flag of Paraíba.

Yet João Pessoa's aspirations to the vice-presidency were short-lived. In July 1930 he was assassinated, an event that sparked a revolutionary backlash that swept Getúlio Vargas to power (with plenty of help from the military) later that year.

Orientation

The bus station is on the western edge of the center, a little over 1km from the central Parque Solon de Lucena with its lake, called the Lagoa. Praia de Tambaú, 8km east of the center, is the heart of João Pessoa's tourist area. The airport is 11km west of the center.

Information

EMERGENCY

Deatur (Tourist Police; Map p550; ☎ 3214 8022; Av Almirante Tamandaré 100, Tambaú; ☺ 24hr)

INTERNET ACCESS

Varanda do Mar (Map p550; Av João Maurício 157, Tambaú; per hr R$3; ☺ 9:30am-1am) Enjoy an espresso, beer or

caipirinha (national cocktail made from limes, sugar, ice and high-proof sugarcane alcohol) while you check your mail.

INTERNET RESOURCES

Prefeitura (www.joaopessoa.pb.gov.br in Portuguese) City-hall site with some useful stuff.

MONEY

Banco do Brasil Centro (Map p549; Praça 1817 No 129; ☺ 10am-4pm Mon-Fri, ATMs 6am-10pm daily); Tambaú (Map p550; Av Senador Rui Carneiro; ☺ 10am-4pm Mon-Fri, ATMs 7am-10pm daily)

TOURIST INFORMATION

PBTUR (☎ 0800-281 9229) Tambaú (Map p550; Av Almirante Tamandaré 100, Tambaú; ☺ 8:30am-7pm) Bus Station (Map p549; ☺ 8am-6pm) These state tourism offices are reasonably well informed. The Tambaú office usually has an English speaker.

TRAVEL AGENCIES

Cliotur (Map p550; ☎ /fax 3247 4460; www.cliotur.com.br; Victory Business Hotel, Av Almirante Tamandaré 310, Tambaú; ☺ 8am-6pm) This very organized agency, with a comprehensive website, offers a range of tours in João Pessoa and Paraíba, from sedate city tours to hiking and adventure trips.

Orlando Berton (☎ 9984 8010; orlandopessoa@hotmail.com) Orlando speaks English and is the most professional and knowledgeable guide you will encounter in João Pessoa. He can be contacted through the Pousada do Caju (opposite), where he is the 'public relations'.

Sights & Activities

IGREJA SÃO FRANCISCO

This **church** (Map p549; ☎ 3218 4505; Praça São Francisco; admission free by guided tour; ☺ 9am-noon & 2-5pm Tue-Sun), the principal tourist attraction in the center, is one of Brazil's finest. Construction was interrupted by battles with the Dutch and French, resulting in a beautiful but architecturally confused complex built over two centuries (1589–1779). The facade, the church towers and the adjoining Santo Antônio monastery display a hodgepodge of styles. Portuguese-tile walls lead up to the church's carved jacaranda doors. The complex also contains a cultural center and an exhibition hall with art exhibits.

CASA DO ARTISTA POPULAR

This permanent **crafts exhibition** (☎ 3221 8852; Praça da Independencia 56, Centro; ☺ 9am-5pm Tue-Fri, 10am-6pm Sat & Sun) displays and sells some of the

TAMBAÚ

0 ——— 400 m
0 ——— 0.2 miles

To Manu's Lariches (350m);
Praia Camboinha (13km);
Fortaleza de Santa
Catarina (20km)

Praia de Manaíra

Coração
de Jesus

ATLANTIC
OCEAN

Praia de Tambaú

To Manga (1km)

Av João Maurício

Rua Carlos Alverga

Av Aurico Franca

Rua Cel Pedro Ramalho

Av Senador Rui Carneiro

Rua Isidro Gomes

To TAM (200m)

Av Talpino Marques

Av Olinda

Av Nego

Rua Prof Maria Sales

Av N S Dos Navegantes

Av Infante D Henrique

Av Helena Meira Lima

Av Antônio Lira

Av Almirante Tamandaré

Av José Augusto Trindade

To Praia Cabo
Branco (300m);
Ponta do
Seixas (8km)

INFORMATION	
Bahamas Chopp	1 A1
Cliotur	2 A2
Deatur	(see 3)
PBTUR	3 A1
Varanda do Mar	4 A1

SLEEPING	
Hotel Littoral Express	5 A2
Hotel Mar Azul	6 A1
Hotel Pousada Rhema	7 A2
Pousada do Caju	8 A2
Tropical Hotel Tambaú	9 B1

EATING	
Boi Bumbar	10 A1
Chiringuito La Espanhola	11 B2

ENTERTAINMENT	
Ponto das Francesinhas	12 A1
Ponto do Turista	13 A1

best Paraíba artisanship – ceramics, woodcut prints, textiles, *cachaça* (high-proof sugarcane alcohol) and more.

BEACHES

Praia de Tambaú (Map p550), 8km directly east of the center, is an urban beach but an enjoyable area to spend time. Bars, restaurants, coconut palms and fig trees are strung along Av João Maurício (north) and Av Almirante Tamandaré (south). A whole series of good urban beaches stretches north along the bay.

Ilha de Areia Vermelha is an island of red sand that emerges off the northern coast at low tide about half the days in each month. Boats park around the island and the party lasts until the tide comes in. You can catch a boat out there from Praia Camboinha (13km north of Tambaú) for R$10. At Cabedelo, 20km north of Tambaú, visit the 16th-century fort **Fortaleza de Santa Catarina** (☎ 3228 3959; admission R$2; ☼ 8am-5:30pm).

Praia Cabo Branco, a beautiful stretch of sand, cliffs and palms, runs south to **Ponta do Seixas**, the easternmost tip of the Americas, 8km from Tambaú, with calm, blue waters, a restaurant, camping ground and lighthouse at the point.

Festivals & Events

João Pessoa cuts loose in the **Folia da Rua** (Party in the Streets), the week before Carnaval proper (Saturday to Saturday), with *blocos* (drumming and dancing processions) parading through parts of the city. The city's **Paixão do Cristo** (Passion of Christ play) is second in size and fame only to the spectacle at Nova Jerusalém (p545). It's staged outdoors on Praça Dom Adauto and recruits well-known actors.

Sleeping

BUDGET

Hotel Aurora (Map p549; ☎ 3241 3238; Praça João Pessoa 41, Centro; s/d R$22/42, without bathroom R$14/28, with air-con R$34/54; ✖) The Aurora has shabby rooms but is adequate if you just need a bed for one night not too far from the bus station. The best thing about it is the handsome square it overlooks, surrounded by state government buildings, complete with a João Pessoa monument bearing his 'Nego' dictum.

Hotel Mar Azul (Map p550; ☎ 3226 2660; fax 3226 4614; Av João Maurício 315, Manaíra; r R$40-50) No frills here, but the beach is across the road and the rooms are very large.

MIDRANGE

Hotel Pousada Rhema (Map p550; ☎ 3247 1900; rhema_pb@hotmail.com; Av Antônio Lira 127, Tambaú; s R$60, d R$100-120; ✖) This plain, modern option near the beach is clean, quiet and well kept.

Pousada do Caju (Map p550; ☎ 2107 8700; www .pousadadocaju.com.br; Av Helena Meira Lima 269, Tambaú; s/d R$95/100; ✖ ✖ ✖) This rambling guesthouse is two blocks from the beach and contains two swimming pools, a games area and numerous giant *caju* (cashew) and dolphin sculptures (among other random accoutrements). Some rooms are airier and brighter than others, so ask to see another if you don't like the first they show you. The Caju has three other, similar branches within a few blocks.

ourpick Hotel Littoral Express (Map p550; ☎ 2106 9900; www.littoral.com.br; Av Almirante Tamandaré 370, Tambaú; s/d R$158/189; ✖ ⬚ ✖) A cut above other midrange choices in comfort and facilities, with touches like modern art on the walls and good glass-door showers. English is spoken and there are 30% discounts in the low season.

TOP END

Tropical Hotel Tambaú (Map p550; ☎ 2107 1900; www .tropicalhotel.com.br; Av Almirante Tamandaré 229, Tambaú; s/d from R$214/246; ✖ ⬚ ✖) The Tropical must have looked very space-age when it was built in 1971. It's a large, circular construction surrounded by grassy banks, with rooms looking either onto large central gardens (with a lovely big pool) or out to sea. Rooms are not super-luxurious, but it's fair value for an upmarket hotel.

Eating

Manu's Lanches (☎ 3247 6275; Cuadra de Manaíra; açaí na tigela R$3-7; ☼ 9am-1am) This little open-air café is packed in the evenings with people tucking into *tigelas* (bowls) of the Amazonian super-fruit *açaí* with honey and your choice of granola, nuts or fruit.

ourpick Mangai (☎ 3226 1615; Av General Edson Ramalho 696, Manaíra; per kg R$24; ☼ 7am-10pm Tue-Sun) The very good buffet at this festive restaurant gives you the chance to sample a variety of regional food. It's all labeled in English as well as Portuguese and there's plenty for vegetarians. Staff sport outfits in *cangaceiro* (Northeastern bandit) style. No alcohol served.

Chiringuito La Espanhola (Map p550; ☎ 3246 4592; Av Almirante Tamandaré s/n, Tambaú; mains R$18-30; ☼ 24 hr) The busiest and probably the best of the open-air restaurants along the Tambaú beach sidewalk, La Espanhola serves up good fish, meat and prawn dishes, with live music from 8pm nightly.

Boi Bumbar (Map p550; ☎ 3247 2847; Rua Isidro Gomes 246, Tambaú; per kg R$31; 🕙 11:30am-3pm Mon-Fri, noon-4pm Sat & Sun) The best self-serve lunch place in Tambaú; good for meats and fish, and great for salads and cheeses. At weekends drinks are served to customers waiting in line outside.

Entertainment

Praia do Jacaré (🕙 sunset) Almost every Brazilian tourist who comes to João Pessoa comes to this river beach in the north of the city to hear sax-ophonist Jurandy play Ravel's *Bolero* at sunset. Sounds corny but definitely worth witnessing. A taxi from Tambaú is R$15 to R$20.

Ponto do Turista (Map p550; Av Almirante Tamandaré s/n, Tambaú) Several restaurants and bars along the Tambaú beachfront sidewalk stage live music. Ponto do Turista has genuine *pé-da-serra forró*, a down-home version of the popu-lar Northeastern music style, from 9:30pm Thursday to Saturday.

Porto das Francesinhas (Map p550; ☎ 3247 6866; Rua Coração de Jesus 103, Tambaú; admission up to R$8) The most stylish of several bars along Rua Coração de Jesus, a block behind Tambaú beach, that fill up with teens and 20s from about 11pm on weekend nights. Some have live music in the second half of the week.

Getting There & Away

AIR

Presidente Castro Pinto Airport (☎ 3232 1200) has flights to Rio, São Paulo and the major cities of the Northeast and the Amazon, plus some charter flights from Europe.

BRA Centro (☎ 3222-6222; Rua Corálio Soares de Oliveira 541); airport (☎ 3232 2520)

Gol (☎ airport 0300-789 2121)

TAM Tambaú (☎ 3247 2400; Av Senador Rui Carneiro 512); airport (☎ 3232 2002)

Varig (☎ airport 3232 1515)

BUS

From the **bus station** (Map p549; ☎ 3221 9611; Rua Francisco Londres) there are services to many des-tinations, including Fortaleza (R$80 to R$120, 10 hours, two daily), Natal (R$21 to R$31, 2½ hours, eight daily), Recife (R$16 to R$21, two hours, 26 daily, 6am to 7:30pm), Salvador (R$122, 16 hours, 7:30pm except Saturday) and Sousa (R$54, six hours, up to six daily).

Getting Around

Local buses run from the Terminal de Inte-gração (Map p549), across the street outside the bus station. Buses 510, 511 and 513 run frequently to Tambaú (R$1.60, 25 minutes) via Parque Solon de Lucena. A taxi from the bus station to Tambaú is R$22.

From the airport, the 'Aeroporto Direto' bus goes to the bus station. A taxi from the airport to Tambaú costs around R$30.

JACUMÃ & AROUND

☎ 0xx83 / pop 4500

The string of good beaches and small, spread-out villages from Jacumã to Tambaba, halfway between João Pessoa and the Pernambuco state border, make a relaxed and inexpensive stop on a journey north from Recife or south from João Pessoa. They are popular on week-ends with people from the city, some of whom have holiday homes here.

Jacumã, the biggest of the villages, has a long, thin beach featuring colored sand-bars and natural pools, and *forró* (popular music of the Northeast) bars by night. **Praia de Carapibus**, 2km south, is also narrow, and is backed by low cliffs, with more natural pools. The broader **Praia da Tabatinga** curves south from the end of Carapibus, with a lagoon behind it after high tides. The most beautiful beach is **Praia dos Coqueirinhos**, a 2km walk from the end of Tabatinga, with lots of coconut palms, high red cliffs, freshwater springs and a dozen *barracas* (stalls). **Praia de Tambaba**, 6km further south, is 'famed as the only official nudist beach in the region (it also has a clothing-optional section at the north end). Attendants will explain the rules of the nude section: photography is not al-lowed, and men can only enter if accompa-nied by a woman. Tambaba is popular with families and others.

SLEEPING & EATING

Pousada Beija-Flor (☎ 3290 1822; Rua Maria Amélia, Jacumã; s/d without breakfast R$20/30, with air-con R$30/40; ⛶ 🛋) Inland from the main road in Jacumã and a short walk from the main bus stop, the Beija-Flor is a neat new place with spot-less rooms and a grassy garden with a small pool – excellent value.

Pousada dos Mundos (☎ 3290 1460; www.pousada dosmundos.com.ar; Rua dos Juazeiros, Tabatinga; s/d R$55/60, air-con R$65/70; ⛶ 🛋) Run by a young Argentine couple, Mundos has just half-a-dozen airy rooms, with simple but pleasing decorations and good bathrooms, around a nice garden with pool. It's 400m back from Tabatinga beach. The owners will collect you from the Jacumã bus stop, and they speak English, Spanish and Italian. The excellent Restaurante Bela Vista (below) will deliver meals here.

Pousada das Conchas (☎ 3290 1303; www.conchas hotel.com.br; Praia de Tabatinga; s/d R$70/85, chalets R$80/95; ✖ ☒) Just above Tabatinga beach, this is a comfortable, Swedish-owned place built in rustic style, with rooms and the brighter chalets around spacious gardens. All have verandas and hammocks. There's a restaurant here too.

Restaurante Bela Vista (☎ 9311 9769; Hwy PB-008, Tabatinga; mains R$10-16; ☒ 9am-5:30pm Tue-Thu, to 10pm Fri-Sun Mar-Nov, to 10pm daily Dec-Feb) Portuguese run and English speaking, the clean, well-run Bela Vista does great seafood and meat. Try the prawns in coconut sauce or the *picanha argentina* (rump steak).

GETTING THERE & AROUND

A car makes things easier around here. Buses run every 20 to 30 minutes to Jacumã (R$4, 45 minutes to 1¼ hours) from Rua Cícero Meireles near João Pessoa bus station (see Map p549). Those marked 'Jacumã PB-008' take a quicker route to Jacumã and also continue to Carapibus. Buses to Tambaba (R$4, 1¼ hours) leave the same stop in João Pessoa at 5:50am, 11am and 4:30pm. The last bus back to the city from Jacumã is at 10:30pm. Traveling north from Pernambuco on Hwy BR-101, ask to be dropped off at the turnoff for Conde and Jacumã, and catch a local bus from there.

A taxi from João Pessoa to any of these beaches costs R$30 to R$40.

Mototaxis from opposite the gasoline station on the main road in Jacumã will take you to the other beaches (R$5 to Carapibus).

BAÍA DA TRAIÇÃO

☎ 0xx83 / pop 7000

This fishing village with peaceful, reef-sheltered waters, coconut palms, gentle breezes, a few pousadas (guesthouses) and a smattering of weekend homes, is 90km north of João Pessoa. It's set on a sparsely settled stretch of coast with access to even better beaches within a few kilometers. At **Praia do Forte**, 2km north of Baía da Traição, are a Potiguar Indian village and some cannons of the old Portuguese fort. **Praia de Tambá**, 3km

further north, is empty and wild, with good surfing waves: here you'll also find Aldeia Galego, another Potiguar settlement, with crafts and native-fruit preserves for sale.

Baía da Traição was the scene of some conflict in colonial times. In the late 16th century the Portuguese defeated a French force here. In 1625 a Dutch fleet fleeing from Salvador stopped and took six Potiguars back to Holland, some of whom returned to Brazil as interpreters when the Dutch invaded Pernambuco in 1630. And in 1645 the Portuguese put to death 23 Potiguar prisoners who had sided with the Dutch.

Pousada Âncora (☎ 3296 1494; Av Dom Pedro II 871, Baía do Traição; s/d R$30/60; ✖ ☒) is a good-value centrally located pousada, with its own bar and restaurant.

Catumbaé Pousada (☎ 3296 1515; www.baia-da-traicao .com.br; Rua do Coronel 100, Trincheiras; s/d R$44/65, with air-con R$58/78; ✖), near Trincheiras beach at the south end of town, is slightly more upmarket, with comfortable, brick-walled rooms and a menagerie of domestic animals.

Buses to Baía da Traição (R$11, two hours) leave João Pessoa's bus station at 6am, 11am and 4pm Monday to Saturday, and at 6am only on Sunday.

SOUSA

☎ 0xx83 / pop 49,000

Sousa, 436km west of João Pessoa in far western Paraíba, is known for an offbeat tourist attraction: dinosaur footprints. The tracks were first found in 1897 by a cattle herder, and identified in 1924 by a geologist who was researching drought – a major preoccupation in the *sertão* (the interior of the Northeast). Later discoveries of tracks at many different sites along the Rio do Peixe showed that the whole region had once been a *vale dos dinossauros* (valley of dinosaurs). The best site is the **Parque dos Dinossauros** (☎ 3522 3055; Estrada para Uiraúna; admission free; ☒ 7am-5pm), 6km northwest of Sousa, where 52 prints were left 110 million years ago by dinosaurs that, judging by the depth and size of the imprints, weighed between three and four tons each. A stretch of the river has been diverted here to leave the fossilized footprints – one of the largest and best-preserved sets in the world – open to viewing year round, and there's a museum with models of dinosaurs and information panels. A taxi there and back from Sousa will cost R$30.

THE TIMELESS SERTÃO

The interior of the Northeast is not all drought-stricken countryside and dirt-poor towns, as its stereo-type might have us believe. There's no denying it gets broiling hot and dry in the second half of the year, nor that the cattle-dominated economy makes only a few rich. But the Sertanejos (residents of the interior) are a proud people with a rich popular culture evident in their music, their festivals and their artisanship. There is also amazing natural beauty out there in the rocky backlands – and fascinating evidence of a history and prehistory stretching right back to the dinosaurs. For those tempted to adventure into the *sertão*, the ideal months are June and July, when it is at its greenest and coolest. The towns of the *sertão* are equipped with adequate hotels and pousadas and well enough served by buses. Natal-based Cariri Ecotours (p556) specializes in tours to these areas. There are a few highlight destinations to find your way to:

- Ingá, Paraíba – features beautiful prehistoric carvings covering a rock 23m long and nearly 4m high. Located 46km east of Campina Grande, a city famed for its huge Festa Junina, a party lasting all June.
- Lajedo da Soledade, Rio Grande do Norte – rock paintings (including the world's oldest macaw pictures), ancient ceremonial sites and ice-age animal fossils are all found here. Guided visits are run from the **Museu da Soledade** (☎ 0xx84-3333 1017; ⊙ closed Mon), 85km southwest of Mossoró, near Apodi.
- Lajedo de Pai Mateus, Cariri, Paraíba – with its bizarre, otherworldly, rocky landscape of round boulders, granite blocks, caves and ancient petroglyphs. It's some 70km southwest of Campina Grande; several recent Brazilian films were shot here. Good lodgings are available at **Fazenda Pai Mateus** (www.paimateus.com.br).
- Serra da Capivara, Piauí (p588) – this has the earliest evidence of humanity in the Americas and 30,000 rock paintings in a dramatic rocky landscape near São Raimundo Nonato.
- Vale dos Dinossauros, Paraíba (p553) – home of the dinosaur footprints, near Sousa.

Travelers interested in handicrafts should take in **Aparecida**, 14km east of Sousa, which is famed as a center for the production of superb hammocks, textiles, and leather and straw goods.

The best place to sleep and eat is the **Jardins Plaza Hotel** (☎ 3522 4212; www.newline.com.br/jardins; Rua João Bosco Marques de Sousa, Gato Preto; s/d R$90/105; ⊗ ⊠), with modern rooms, a large pool and the **Restaurante Flamboyant** (mains R$13-25; ⊙ lunch & dinner), serving good meat and seafood. It's about 500m from the bus station.

From the **bus station** (☎ 3521 1458; Rua José Facundo de Lira) there are up to six daily buses via Patos and Campina Grande to and from João Pessoa (R$54, six hours). There are also daily buses to and from Juazeiro do Norte.

RIO GRANDE DO NORTE

Pure air, sun, fine beaches and sand dunes symbolize this small state in the extreme Northeast of Brazil. Rio Grande do Norte has one of the most spectacular coastlines in Brazil, some 400km of beautiful beach after beautiful beach interspersed with rivers, many of them fronted by reefs with natural pools and backed by tall dunes or cliffs. The most famous dunes are the 50m-tall piles at Genipabu. The locals, known as Potiguenses, are generally friendly and welcoming. As in Paraíba, the interior of the state is drought-prone, and many former inhabitants have already migrated to other parts of Brazil.

NATAL

☎ 0xx84 / pop 786,000

Natal, the capital of Rio Grande do Norte, is a clean, bright and rather bland city that has swelled as the entry point for coastal package tourism. Surrounded by impressively large sand dunes, Natal's main attractions are beaches, buggy rides and nightlife – don't come here if you seek museums and theater.

The city's northern beaches of Praia do Meio and Praia dos Artistas are no longer the attraction they once were. These days, most visitors stay in the southern beach neighborhood of Ponta Negra, 12km from the center. It is a striking location, overlooked by fantastic dunes, and with steady surf and some great nightlife in the Alto de Ponta Negra area.

Natal's Carnatal (out-of-season Carnaval), at the beginning of December, draws huge crowds from all over Brazil, and is a much bigger deal here than Carnaval itself.

History

An early attempt to settle the Natal area by a Portuguese contingent sailing from Recife in 1535 failed thanks to the hostility of the local Potiguar Indians and French brazilwood traders. The Portuguese didn't return until December 1597, when a fleet arrived at the mouth of the Rio Potengi with orders to build a fort to keep the French and Potiguars at bay. On January 6, 1598, the day of Os Reis Magos (Three Wise Men), the Portuguese began building the fortress, the Forte dos Reis Magos. The following year, on December 25, 1599, a town was founded nearby and christened Natal (Portuguese for Christmas). Apart from a period of Dutch occupation (1633 to 1654), Natal remained under Portuguese control thereafter. It stayed relatively unimportant until WWII, when its strategic location close to

Brazil's northeastern tip prompted Presidents Getúlio Vargas and Franklin D Roosevelt to turn the sleepy city into a supply base for Allied operations in North Africa. Thousands of US military were stationed here and the city became known as the 'Trampoline to Victory.' These days, it's known as the Cidade do Sol (Sun City), for good reason.

Orientation

The older part of Natal is on a peninsula flanked to the west by the Rio Potengi and to the east by Atlantic beaches and reefs. The Forte dos Reis Magos sits just off the peninsula's northern point. The unexciting city center, Cidade Alta, was developed around the river port, which was built in 1892. The beach neighborhood of Ponta Negra is 12km southeast of the center. Via Costeira, the coast road running north from Ponta Negra towards the Forte dos Reis Magos, is lined by resort hotels.

The bus station is 6km south of the center and 10km northwest of Ponta Negra; the airport is 15km south of the center and 8km west of Ponta Negra.

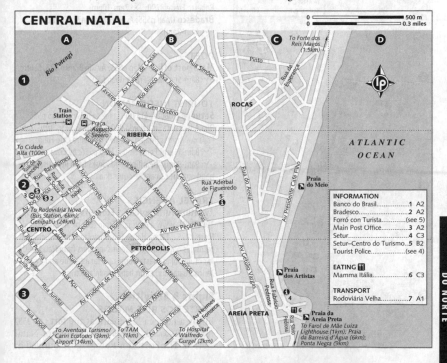

Information

BOOKSTORES

Livraria Laselva (☎ 3643 3807; airport; ☼ 9am-9pm) Has books in a variety of languages. Bookstores are hard to find in town.

EMERGENCY

Ambulance (☎ 192)

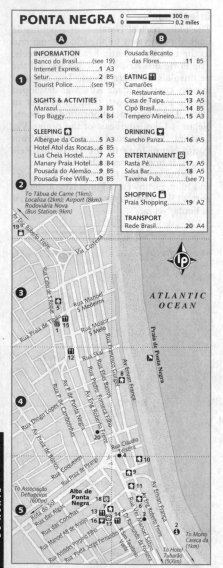

PONTA NEGRA

0 — 300 m
0 — 0.2 miles

INFORMATION	
Banco do Brasil	(see 19)
Internet Express	**1** A3
Setur	**2** B5
Tourist Police	(see 19)

SIGHTS & ACTIVITIES	
Marazul	**3** B5
Top Buggy	**4** B4

SLEEPING ⬛	
Albergue da Costa	**5** A3
Hotel Atol das Rocas	**6** B5
Lua Cheia Hostel	**7** A5
Manary Praia Hotel	**8** B4
Pousada do Alemão	**9** B5
Pousada Free Willy	**10** B5
Pousada Recanto das Flores	**11** B5

EATING ⬛	
Camarões Restaurante	**12** A4
Casa de Taipa	**13** A5
Cipó Brasil	**14** B5
Tempero Mineiro	**15** A3

DRINKING ⬛	
Sancho Panza	**16** A5

ENTERTAINMENT ⬛	
Rasta Pé	**17** A5
Salsa Bar	**18** A5
Taverna Pub	(see 7)

SHOPPING ⬛	
Praia Shopping	**19** A2

TRANSPORT	
Rede Brasil	**20** A4

To Tábua de Carne (1km);
Localiza (2km); Airport (8km);
Rodoviária Nova
(Bus Station; 9km)

ATLANTIC OCEAN

To Associação
Debujeiros
(600m)

Alto de
Ponta
Negra

To Morro
Careca da
(1km)

To Hotel
Tubarão
(500m)

Tourist Police Praia dos Artistas (Map p555; ☎ 3202 2920; Av Presidente Café Filho; ☼ 8am-11pm); Praia Shopping (Map p556; ☎ 3232 7234; Central do Cidadão, Av Engenheiro Roberto Freire 8790)

INTERNET ACCESS

Internet Express (Map p556; ☎ 3219 5552; Av Praia de Ponta Negra 8956; per hr R$3; ☼ 8am-10pm Mon-Sat, 1-9pm Sun) Good, air-conditioned, high-speed facility.

INTERNET RESOURCES

Natal Brazil (www.natal-brazil.com) Fairly useful tourism site.
Setur (www.setur.rn.gov.br) The Rio Grande do Norte state tourism site, with a variety of helpful introductory information.

MEDICAL SERVICES

Hospital Walfredo Gurgel (☎ 3232 7500; Av Senador Salgado Filho, Tirol) The main public hospital, with emergency service.

MONEY

These banks have ATMs that normally accept foreign cards:
Banco do Brasil Centro (Map p555; Av Rio Branco 510; ☼ 6am-8pm); Praia Shopping (Map p556; Av Engenheiro Roberto Freire 8790; ☼ 7am-10pm)
Bradesco (Map p555; Av Rio Branco 477, Centro; ☼ 6am-8pm)

POST

Main post office (Map p555; Av Rio Branco 538, Centro; ☼ 8am-5pm Mon-Fri, to noon Sat)

TOURIST INFORMATION

Setur (☎ 0800-841516) Centro de Turismo (Map p555; Rua Aderbal de Figueiredo 980, Petrópolis; ☼ 9am-7pm) Praia dos Artistas (Map p555; Av Presidente Café Filho; ☼ 8am-11pm) Ponta Negra (Map p556; Av Erivan França; ☼ 9am-9pm) The offices and kiosks have little useful to hand out but can answer questions.

TRAVEL AGENCIES

Aventura Turismo/Cariri Ecotours (☎ 3206 4949, 3086 3601; www.aventuraturismo.com.br; Av Prudente de Morais 4262, Lagoa Nova) This organized and experienced pairing is one of the best teams for tours from Natal, with Aventura doing coastal routes (as far as Recife and even Jericoacoara) and Cariri handling inland trips.

Sights & Activities

FORTE DOS REIS MAGOS

Enjoy a tapioca ice cream at the **fort** (☎ 3502 1099; admission R$3; ☼ 8am-4:30pm) that got Natal started. The Forte dos Reis Magos, founded in

1598, is still in its original five-point star shape and contains a chapel, a well, cannons and soldiers' quarters. The views of the city and the dunes across the Rio Potengi are fantastic from this prime location on the reef at the tip of the peninsula north of town.

BEACHES

Natal's northern beaches stretch 5km south from the fort to Farol de Mãe Luiza lighthouse. **Praia do Meio** (Map p555), 2km south of the Forte dos Reis Magos, is an urban beach with reefs and a lot of people getting drunk. **Praia dos Artistas** (Map p555) is another urban spot, with good surfing waves. It used to be the hub of Natal nightlife but is now pretty sketchy after dark.

South of the lighthouse, the coast road Via Costeira continues 7km south to Ponta Negra, passing the calm **Praia da Barreira d'Água** with its resort hotels. **Ponta Negra** (Map p556), at the far south end of the city, is the nicest beach in Natal – nearly 3km long and full of hotels, pousadas, restaurants, beach bars, surfers and sailing boats. On weekends it gets pretty packed: the northern part of the beach, with its pedestrian-only walkway, is less crowded. The surf here is consistent if small: you can rent boards from a few places along the beach for around R$25 a day. At the south end of the beach is **Morro da Careca**, a spectacularly high sand dune with a steep face that drops straight into the sea. Access to the dune has been closed off to prevent further erosion and damage to the primary Atlantic rain forest that covers it.

BUGGY RIDES

Dune-buggy excursions are offered by a host of would-be Ayrton Senna *bugeiros* (buggy drivers), mostly in Brazilian-built vehicles with brand names such as Bird, Baby, Praya or Malibuggy. To the north are the dunes of **Genipabu** (p563), which are the biggest around. You'll be asked if you want the trip *com emoção* (with emotion), and if you agree you'll be treated to thrills such as Wall of Death and Vertical Descent. It is possible to go as far as you like in either direction along the coast – even all the way to Fortaleza – covering 750km of gorgeous coastline (see p558).

There are pirate *bugeiros* and accredited *bugeiros;* the latter are represented by the **Associação de Bugeiros** (☎ 3219 3758; Posto VIP, Rota do Sol, Ponta Negra). A typical price for a half-day trip is R$240 for up to four passengers.

You can arrange buggy trips through most pousadas, agencies or, if you speak some Portuguese, directly with drivers. Two recommended operators are **Top Buggy** (Map p556; ☎ 3219 2820; www.topbuggy.com.br; Rua Claudio G Teixeira, Ponta Negra) and **Marazul** (Map p556; ☎ 3219 2221; www.passeiodebuggy.com.br; Rua Vereador Manoel Sátiro 1, Ponta Negra).

NATAL TO FORTALEZA BY BUGGY

Adventurous travelers who have time on their hands and don't mind sand in their faces or wind in their hair can make a fabulous trip of approximately 750km along the shore from Natal to Fortaleza by beach buggy. You can travel in either direction. The trip takes three to five days and you'll pass approximately 92 beaches.

This stretch of coastline is one of the most beautiful and undeveloped in Brazil. There are cliffs of colored sands, rolling dunes, salt flats, reefs, palm-lined beaches, beaches with freshwater lagoons, tiny traditional fishing villages and some larger settlements popular with local weekenders. The stretch between Zumbi, some 60km north of Natal, and Galinhos, about 130km further, is particularly rugged and in parts quite isolated. Between Galinhos and Porto do Mangue you have to head inland along roads to get round the mangrove and salt swamps near the coast.

You'll spend nights in pousadas along the way, in places like São Miguel do Gostoso, Praia do Marco, Galinhos, Ponta do Mel and Canoa Quebrada.

Anyone can hire a buggy in Fortaleza or Natal and drive on the beaches, but a trip of this kind requires an experienced driver. Beach buggies average 40km/h, and it takes a skilled driver to negotiate the uneven tracks, soft sand and small rivers that empty into the sea. You also have to drive certain parts only at low tide. Locals will ferry the buggies on rafts over the wide river mouths.

The average cost for the trip is R$1500 to R$2000 for up to three passengers, including lodgings, breakfast and the driver. Make sure you go with an accredited (credenciado) driver. Your accommodations can normally put you in touch with a suitable agency or driver. A recommended agency in Natal is Top Buggy (p557). It's also possible to do the trip in Jeeps, with firms such as Aventura Turismo (p556) in Natal, or Nordeste Off Road (p571) in Fortaleza.

Few people in Brazil seem overly concerned about the environmental impact of beach buggies, and many stretches of beach are routinely used as highways by off-road vehicles. But before signing up for a trip you may want to weigh the potential consequences against the fun you'll undoubtedly have and the employment that buggies provide for thousands of locals along Brazil's coasts.

While the impact of vehicles on dune configurations seems less than that of natural factors such as wind and rain, research in some countries, notably the US, has indicated that living beach and dune organisms, while largely invisible to the casual passer-by, can be seriously affected by the repeated passage of noisy, heavy vehicles. It's also true that dune buggies consume a liter of gasoline about every 6km (making them about twice as thirsty as normal cars) – and that they make an unholy racket!

Festivals & Events

Natal's out-of-season Carnaval, **Carnatal** (www .carnatal.com.br), takes to the streets at the beginning of December with Salvador-style *trios elétricos* (electrically amplified bands playing atop huge trucks) and *blocos* sporting names like *Jerimum* (Pumpkin) and *Burro Elétrico* (Electric Donkey). It's the wildest out-of-season Carnaval in the country and is a great substitute for anyone who can't make it to the real deal.

Sleeping

Ponta Negra has options for all budgets.

BUDGET

Albergue da Costa (Map p556; ☎ 3219 0095; www .alberguedacosta.com.br; Av Praia de Ponta Negra 8832, Ponta Negra; dm R$30, d R$75; 🖳 🖳) This hostel is small, relaxed and a touch bohemian. Run by two brothers who speak English, Italian, Spanish and Portuguese, it has a good kitchen and hammock area, three double rooms, and dorms for up to five people. Surfing lessons are offered for R$50 per hour.

Lua Cheia Hostel (Map p556; ☎ 3236 3696; www .luacheia.com.br; Rua Manoel AB de Araújo 500, Ponta Negra; dm with/without HI membership R$31/40; 🖳) In a famous castlelike building (drawbridge, turrets and all), Lua Cheia has a bizarre Halloween theme that you may as well go along with. Facilities are good, staff are helpful, and it is located in the heart of the Alto de Ponta Negra nightlife and restaurant area. It has its own pub and you can organize buggy rides and other trips from here. Don't expect to go to sleep early, but if you are looking for party fun in Natal, this is the place.

MIDRANGE

Pousada Recanto das Flores (Map p556; ☎ 3219 4065; www.pousadarecantodasflores.com.br; Av Engenheiro Roberto Freire 3161, Ponta Negra; s R$55, d R$85-120; ✿ ▣ ▦) This small pousada has nicely kept rooms with bamboo furnishings and offers good discounts in the low season. Some rooms suffer traffic noise from the busy street outside.

Pousada do Alemão (Map p556; ☎ 3219 2655; www .pousadadoalemao.com; Rua Pedro Fonseca Filho 2030, Ponta Negra; s R$70-100, d R$80-120; ✿) Spacious, plain rooms are set around a garden of palms in this extended family home. German spoken.

Hotel Tubarão (Map p556; ☎ 3641 1029; www.hotel tubarao.com.br; Rua Manoel Coringa Lemos 259, Ponta Negra; s/d R$95/115; ✿ ▦) An attractive smallish hotel set on the hill above Ponta Negra beach, Tubarão has a beautiful sea view, good pool and common areas and unadorned but pleasant rooms. Desk staff speak good English and are very helpful.

Pousada Free Willy (Map p556; ☎ 3236 2825; www .freewilly.com.br; Rua Francisco Gurgel 9292, Ponta Negra; r R$160; ✿ ▦) Free Willy, named for a 1990s whale movie, doesn't look that great from outside but it has clean if rather old-fashioned rooms, helpful and friendly staff and an excellent beachfront location.

TOP END

Hotel Atol das Rocas (Map p556; ☎ 3219 2072; www .atoldasrocas.com.br; Av Engenheiro Roberto Freire 3220, Ponta Negra; r/tr R$178/269; ✿ ▦) The plain, clean, one- and two-bedroom apartments here all have sea views, and share a pool in attractive gardens. English is spoken, and prices come down by about one-third in the low season.

our pick **Manary Praia Hotel** (Map p556; ☎ 3204 2900; www.manary.com.br; Rua Francisco Gurgel 9067, Ponta Negra; s R$483-675, d R$537-772; ✿ ▣ ▦) All 24 rooms have a sea view at this charming hotel, which combines traditional Northeastern style with modern facilities and comforts and solar-heated hot water. The pool and patio are idyllic and the hotel incorporates one of the best seafood restaurants in town (mains R$27 to R$43) – you can't beat its superb *misto di mare* (seafood mixed grill).

Eating

our pick **Casa de Taipa** (Map p556; ☎ 3219 5798; Rua Manoel AB de Araújo 130A, Alto de Ponta Negra; dishes R$5-15; ⏱ 5pm-midnight) This folksy, palm-thatched eatery specializes in great local tapioca and couscous creations. The tapiocas come with a lightly-fried tapioca shell around fillings ranging from vegetables and cheeses to *carne de sol* (see boxed text, below) or prawns.

Tempero Mineiro (Map p556; ☎ 3219 0356; Feira de Artesanato de Ponta Negra, Av Praia de Ponta Negra; dishes R$9-15; ⏱ 9am-10pm) A simple, open-air place handy to the Albergue da Costa, Tempero Mineiro does good-value *pratos feitos* (plates of the day) of steak, chicken, pasta or fish.

Tábua de Carne (☎ 3642 1236; Av Eng Roberto Freire 3241, Capim Macio; rodízio R$20; ⏱ 11:30am-11pm) This restaurant, 1.5km north of the north end of Ponta Negra, serves a great all-you-can-eat meat *rodízio* (smorgasbord), including that regional favorite, *carne de sol*.

Mamma Itália (Map p555; ☎ 3202 1622; Rua Silvio Pedrosa 43, Praia dos Artistas; dishes R$15-25; ⏱ lunch Fri-Sun, dinner daily) If you're in the center or the northern part of town, it's worth stopping in

---

CARNE DE SOL

Carne de sol (meat of the sun) is a lightly salted and partly dehydrated meat that is the dish most commonly associated with Rio Grande do Norte. Typically made from beef (although sometimes from goat), *carne de sol* has a somewhat salty taste and looks like a thin steak with a brownish tinge. It was developed generations ago due to a lack of proper food storage and has a shelf life comparable to refrigerated fresh meat.

Despite its name, *carne de sol* is rarely exposed to the sun. Its original name, *carne de vento* (meat of the wind), is closer to the truth, as it is dried in covered, ventilated areas, allowing for greater control of the process (and a better way to keep the insects out).

Before drying, the flattened meat is dusted with ground sea salt and stacked on a salted floor. The pile is remade and inverted after four to six hours. It is then covered with a heavy layer of salt for another four to six hours. The meat is washed and moved to a covered area where it's hung over rails with the fatty side up for eight to 14 hours.

Refrigerators or no refrigerators, *carne de sol* is the favorite dish of Rio Grande do Norte and it can be found everywhere from kitchens in the smallest towns to the fanciest city restaurants.

here for quality Italian fare. The spinach-and-ricotta ravioli is divine.

Cipó Brasil (Map p556; ☎ 3219 5227; Rua Aristides Porpino Filho 3111, Alto de Ponta Negra; mains R$15-30; ☺ 6pm-midnight) With a jungle theme, this is a fun place for pizza and pancakes, both savory and sweet.

Camarões Restaurante (Map p556; ☎ 3209 2424; Av Engenheiro Roberto Freire 3161, Ponta Negra; mains R$20-40; ☺ lunch & dinner) Prawn lovers are in heaven at this top seafood place in Ponta Negra.

Entertainment

The Alto de Ponta Negra neighborhood in the upper part of Ponta Negra (Map p556), around Rua Manoel AB de Araújo and Rua Aristides Porpino Filho, away from the tackier after-dark scene nearer the beach, is dense with a variety of fun bars and restaurants. It's packed with locals and visitors having a good time till dawn, Wednesday to Saturday nights. Just wander along after 11pm and see which places draw you in. **Sancho Panza** (Rua Aristides Porpino Filho), with tapas and *chope* (draft beer), and **Salsa Bar** (Rua Manoel AB de Araújo) are two of the more stylish bars.

Taverna Pub (Map p556; ☎ 3236 3696; Rua Manoel AB de Araújo 500; admission free-R$10; ☺ 11pm-late Mon-Sat) Attached to the Lua Cheia hostel and resembling a pub inside a medieval castle, this ever-popular tavern has nightly music from live Brazilian rhythms to '70s disco.

Rasta Pé (Map p556; Rua Aristides Porpino Filho 2198; admission R$10; ☺ 10pm-4am Wed, Fri & Sat) The place to dance to live *forró* – no shorts, microskirts, bare feet or bare torsos permitted here!

Getting There & Away
AIR

Natal's **Augusto Severo Airport** (☎ 3644 1000) has scheduled flights from Lisbon with TAP Portugal, charter flights from other European cities, and flights to many Brazilian cities with several airlines.
BRA (☎ airport 3643 2132)
Gol (☎ airport 3644 1264)
TAM Tirol (☎ 3201 2020; Av Afonso Pena 844); airport (☎ 3643 1261)
TAP Portugal airport (☎ airport 3644 1184)
Trip (☎ airport 3643 1450)

BUS

Long-distance buses go from the **Rodoviária Nova** (New Bus Station; ☎ 3232 7312; Av Capitão Mor Gouveia 1237). Destinations include Aracati (near

Canoa Quebrada, R$43 to R$69, six hours, seven or more daily), Fortaleza (R$62 to R$110, eight hours, eight daily), João Pessoa (R$21 to R$31, 2½ hours, eight daily), Recife (R$34 to R$48, four hours, 10 daily), Rio de Janeiro (R$300 to R$315, 44 hours, one or two daily) and Salvador (R$131 to R$163, 20 hours, 9am and 5pm).

Disk Passagens (☎ 3205 2428) will deliver bus tickets to you for a R$5 fee.

CAR & MOTORCYCLE

Recommended car-rental companies include the following:
Avis (☎ airport 3644 2503)
Localiza Capim Macio (☎ 4005 0400; Av Engenheiro Roberto Freire 1452A); airport (☎ 3643 1557)
Rede Brasil (Map p556; ☎ 3236 3344; Av Engenheiro Roberto Freire 9100, Ponta Negra)

Getting Around
TO/FROM THE AIRPORT

The 'Aeroporto' bus runs between the airport and the city center. For Ponta Negra, get off opposite Natal Shopping, cross the footbridge and take bus 46 or 54, which go along Av Engenheiro Roberto Freire and Rua Manoel Coringa Lemos in Ponta Negra. A taxi from the airport costs about R$50 to the city center or R$20 to Ponta Negra.

TO/FROM THE BUS STATION

Bus 66 runs from the Rodoviária Nova to Ponta Negra (Av Engenheiro Roberto Freire); a taxi is R$25 to R$30. Buses 19, 20 and 38 run between the Rodoviária Nova and the **Rodoviária Velha** (Map p555; Praça Augusto Severo), a local bus terminal in the city center.

BUS

From Av Engenheiro Roberto Freire in Ponta Negra, buses 46 and 54 run to the Praia Shopping mall and on to the center; 56 goes along the Via Costeira then heads inland to the Rodoviária Velha. To get to the Forte dos Reis Magos, you can take 56 as far as the north end of Praia de Areia Preta, where the bus leaves the coast, and walk the remaining 3km up the coast. Buses 54 and 56 go from the Rodoviária Velha to Ponta Negra.

If you're arriving in Natal by bus from the south and want to get to Ponta Negra, ask to be let off opposite Natal Shopping, cross the footbridge and catch bus 46 or 54.

City bus fares are R$1.60.

SOUTH OF NATAL

Like the rest of the Rio Grande do Norte coast, the stretch south of Natal has some fantastic beaches – it's difficult to find one that's not worth raving about. Praia da Pipa is famous and a great place to hang around for a few days, but there are other quieter places to be discovered too.

Pirangi do Sul & Pirangi do Norte

☎ 0xx84

The pretty twin beach towns of Pirangi do Sul and Pirangi do Norte, 15km south of Ponta Negra, are split by a river that weaves through palm-crested dunes on its way to the ocean. It's a quiet area where wealthy folk from Natal have weekend homes and people come to snorkel in the clear tide pools offshore. There are a few pousadas in the palm grove where the road crosses the river. The town is home to the **world's largest cashew tree**: its sprawl of branches is over 500m in circumference, and it's still growing! South of Pirangi do Sul is the beach town of Búzios, then the road runs along a coast with nothing but small waves crashing against the beach, white dunes, coconut palms, uncut jungle and little farms.

    Pousada Esquina do Sol (☎ 3238 2078; www.esquina dosol.com.br; Av Márcio Marinho 2210, Pirangi do Norte; r R$70, with air-con R$80-90; ✖ ☒) is a friendly place right on the main street, with tidy rooms and a good breakfast.

    Buses to Pirangi (R$2.70, one hour) and Búzios (R$4, 1¼ hours) go 14 times daily from Natal's Rodoviária Nova and 17 times (seven on Sunday) from the Rodoviária Velha.

Praia da Pipa

☎ 0xx84 / pop 4500

Pipa rivals Jericoacoara as the Northeast's hippest beach town, with a strongly international feel. It boasts pristine beaches backed by tall cliffs, decent surfing, dolphin-filled waters, a decent selection of restaurants, some upscale boutiques and good nightlife. Just another small, roadless, fishing village when discovered by surfers in the 1970s, it has changed beyond recognition since then and now attracts partiers from Natal, João Pessoa, Recife and beyond at holiday times and weekends. But don't let the weekend noise and the bright lights along the main drag fool you; a laid-back vibe still dominates Pipa, which is considered by locals to be a 'global village.'

ORIENTATION & INFORMATION

Pipa is small but it can be a little hard to get your bearings on arrival. The narrow main street, Av Baía dos Golfinhos, runs about 2km through town from west to east, parallel to the main beach and curving south at its eastern end. The main bus stop is at the west end. Small streets and lanes run down to the beach or uphill inland from Av Baía dos Golfinhos.

    Pipa is extraordinarily well endowed with helpful, informative websites. **Pipa** (www.pipa .com.br) is probably the best organized and most comprehensive, but **Pipa On Line** (www.pipaonline .com.br) and **Guia da Pipa** (www.guiadapipa.com.br) are good too.

Banco do Brasil ATM (Falésia Galeria, Av Baía dos Golfinhos 369; ⏰ 8am-10pm) 150m east of the main bus stop.

Bookshop (☎ 9937 1242; Rua Beija-Flor; ⏰ 4-10pm Mon-Sat) A good selection of books in a variety of languages, for rent or trade only.

Internet Telefone (per hr R$3; Rua da Gameleira; ⏰ 10am-midnight) Internet access

Pipatour (☎ 3246 2234; Galeria das Cores, Av Baía dos Golfinhos 767; ⏰ 9am-noon & 2:30-9pm) This central travel agency can arrange most travel needs.

SIGHTS & ACTIVITIES

The main beach, **Praia da Pipa** or **Praia do Centro**, about 1.5km long, has fishing boats, several bars, and rock pools at low tide. **Baía dos Golfinhos**, to its north, is where dolphins are most often seen: it's backed by cliffs and is only accessible by walking from the main beach at low tide. **Praia do Madeiro** curves northwards from the headland at the far end of Baía dos Golfinhos and has a few upmarket hotels dotted along its length. You can get down to it from the Santuário Ecológico (below). **Praia do Amor**, the favorite surf beach, is round the headland at the east end of the main beach, accessed off the eastern part of Av Baía dos Golfinhos. You can rent surfboards here and in town for around R$40 a day. Classes are also available.

    The privately owned **Santuário Ecológico de Pipa** (☎ 9982 8044; www.ecopipa.org.br; admission R$5; ⏰ 8am-5pm), 1.5km west along the road from the main bus stop, does a valuable job of protecting at least some of the Pipa coast from development. Well-marked trails lead through secondary forest to impressive lookouts over Baía dos Golfinhos and Praia do Madeiro, from which you can often see large green turtles at high tide.

SLEEPING

Pipa has dozens of pousadas and a few hotels, ranging from the dumpy to the charming. Some are along the main street, some up the hill behind it, and some near Praia do Amor. The following is just a selection of the best-value places. Most offer good discounts in low season.

Pousada Xamã (☎ 3246 2267; www.pousadaxama .com; Rua dos Cajueiros 12; s/d R$40/80; ✕ ▯ ▨) This pousada, off the far end of Av Baía dos Golf-inhos, ticks every box with hammocks all around, a good pool at the center of things, a great breakfast including your hostess's homemade pies, and colorful, comfortable rooms.

Pousada da Pipa (☎ 3246 2271; pousadapipa@yahoo .com.br; Rua do Cruzeiro 29; s R$55-75, d R$75-95; ✕) A green front patio and an entire veranda of hammocks with a partial sea view make this a very social pousada. It's just down from the middle of the main street. A recently opened annex known as PP2, just up on the main street, actually has nicer rooms in cheerful oranges and ochres, with silent air-con.

Pousada Aconchego (☎ 3246 2439; www.pipa online.com/aconchego, www.pipa.org.br; Rua do Céu 100; s/d R$60/80) Up a quiet lane from the heart of Av Baía dos Golfinhos, Aconchego has spacious chalets with hammocks in a garden setting, and is owned by a friendly Swiss and Brazilian couple.

Marlin's Pousada (☎ 3246 2219; Rua Beija-Flor; www .pousdamarlins.com.br; s R$90-170, d R$120-190; ✕ ▨) Marlin's big plus is that it's one of the very few central pousadas that actually look onto the sea (though not all the rooms do). It's friendly and well looked after, and the more expensive 'super luxo' rooms are spacious, bright and colorful.

Toca da Coruja (☎ 3246 2226; www.tocadacoruja .com.br; Av Baía dos Golfinhos; r R$406, chalets R$487-890; ✕ ▯ ▨) Quite possibly the most charming luxury pousada in the Northeast, Toca da Coruja is wrapped in an oasis of sprawling tropical gardens with monkeys, birds and two gorgeous pools. It's an eco-conscious place built with some recycled materials and using low-energy lighting and copper ionization treatment for the pools. The exquisite large deluxe chalets, in the style of old Northeast ranch houses, have broad, breezy verandas and outdoor Jacuzzis. Children under 12 not permitted.

Other options:

Pousada Alto da Pipa (☎ 3246 2281; www.pousada altodapipa.com.br; Rua da Gameleira 555; s/d R$90/120; ✕ ▨) Well-managed pousada with nice garden, up on the hill above the main street.

Hotel Ponta do Madeiro (☎ 3246 4220; www.ponta domadeiro.com.br; Praia do Madeiro; s/d R$325/420; ✕ ▯ ▨) Lovely medium-size hotel with chalets above Praia do Madeiro.

EATING

Restaurants abound, but it's harder to find an inexpensive one than a quality one.

Tapas Restaurante (☎ 9414 4675; Rua dos Bem-Te-Vis; dishes R$10-17; ☯ 6:30-11pm) Just up from the main street, Tapas provides some original and delicious combinations like organic shrimp with honey and ginger, or fish with red curry and coconut cream. Servings are about halfway in size between a full plate and real Spanish tapas, so you'll probably need a salad to go with it.

Água na Boca (☎ 3246 2641; Av Baía dos Golfinhos 687; mains for 2 R$20-50; ☯ 6pm-midnight, closed Jun & Sun Mar-May & Oct-Dec) One of the more refined places along the main street, Água na Boca serves well-prepared meat, pasta and seafood – including a pretty good *moqueca*.

Pacífico (☎ 9982 8981; Rua dos Bem-Te-Vis 8; mains R$13-23; ☯ 6:30-11:30pm, closed Tue Mar-Nov) The Californian owner-chef here offers a short but exceptional menu with Mexican and Asian tinges – fish tacos, beef croquettes in peanut sauce and so on. The cognac-flambé pepper steak is a treat. Order a salad or sautéed veggies to fill up.

Panela de Barro (☎ 3246 2611; Rua Beija-Flor; mains R$15-25; ☯ noon-11pm) Nice sea view and good seafood, especially the *moqueca capixaba* (a fish stew from the state of Espírito Santo), at reasonable prices, though the atmosphere is a little staid.

Calígula (☎ 3246 2383; Av Baía dos Golfinhos; dishes R$18-35; ☯ 4pm-midnight) With pseudo-Ionic columns and a giant mango tree rising between the tables, this Italian place has probably the best pizza in town – in a generous size too.

ENTERTAINMENT

Nightlife tends to start off at and outside Tribus and Oz bars, opposite each other on Av Baía dos Golfinhos, or the more relaxed China's just past Tribus. Around midnight or later, people move on to one of the venues with live music, of which there is an ever-changing array. A few that have lasted the course are the ever-popular disco **Calangos** (☎ 3246 2396; ☽ from 11pm Fri-Sun) at the end of Av Baía dos Golfinhos, which has live *forró* on Sunday and Euro-style DJs the other nights; **Zion Casa de Reggae** (☎ 9115 9015; Rua da Gameleira 69; ☽ 9pm-3am or later Tue-Sat), with a breezy terrace and usually live reggae from 11pm Thursday to Saturday; and the more sedate **Garagem** (☎ 3246 2154; Ladeira do Cruzeiro; ☽ from 10pm Tue-Sun) down by the beach, sometimes with live Brazilian/Latin music from about midnight.

Sometimes one of the pousadas will host a party with a DJ. Ask around to find out where it is, and don't expect to come home before sunrise.

GETTING THERE & AWAY
Ten daily buses (only four on Sunday) run to Pipa from the Rodoviária Nova in Natal (R$8.50, two hours). If you are arriving from the south, get out at Goianinha (1½ hours from João Pessoa), where Kombi vans run frequently to Pipa (R$2.50, 40 minutes, 5am to 10pm) from behind the blue church, 250m off the main road.

For travelers heading south from Pipa, Pipatour (p561) can reserve bus seats from Goianinha for a R$6 fee.

NORTH OF NATAL
The coast is relatively built-up as far as Zumbi, some 60km north of Natal, but it still has some spectacular stretches with sand dunes plunging into the surf. Settlement thins out as the coast bends westward and you can find some truly gorgeous, largely empty beaches and traditional fishing villages on the way to the Ceará border.

Genipabu
☎ 0xx84 / pop 5000
Only about 12km north of Natal as the crow flies, but 24km by road (unless you take the ferry across the Rio Potengi), is Genipabu, where palm trees, dune buggies and enormous golden sand dunes converge on a beach lined with bars, pousadas and restaurants. It's a popular, crowded place, where you can enjoy adrenalized buggy rides in the high dunes of the nearby **Parque das Dunas** (per hr R$140, up to 4 passengers), swim, surf and even take camel rides. The **buggy-drivers' association** (APCBA; ☎ 3225 2077) in the center of town also offers trips up the coast. You can even get a buggy all the way to Fortaleza from Genipabu.

The nicest places to stay are along the beach running northwest from the town center towards Barra do Rio – the buses from Natal come along here.

Pousada Três Coqueiros (☎ 3225 2061; Av da Praia; r R$75-95; ⚡ ⚡) is friendly, clean and only 300m from the center.

Pousada Villa do Sol (☎ 3225 2132; www.villadosol.com.br; Enseada de Genipabu; s/d R$160/200; ⚡ ⚡), 3km from the center and next to the Rio Ceará-Mirim, is a more upmarket place with beautiful grounds and even better views. Lon, the American owner, is a good source of local knowledge.

Restaurante 21 (☎ 3224 2484; Praia de Genipabu; mains R$10-30; ☽ 10am-6pm) has great seafood. Try Italian chef Lúcio's *peixada* (fish cooked in broth with vegetables and tomatoes). It will feed two easily.

Buses to Genipabu (R$2.30, 45 minutes) leave every half-hour until evening from Natal's Rodoviária Velha.

Genipabu to Galinhos
This stretch of nearly 200km, in which the coast veers from east-facing to north-facing, is a growing playground for weekenders and day-trippers from Natal, but there are still dozens of lovely beaches. The further from Natal you go, the more isolated and empty they become. Several beaches on the east-facing coast have reef pools that are good for snorkeling at low tide, notably the popular **Maracajaú**, 40km north of Genipabu, where speedboats (R$52 including snorkel gear) will whisk you out to reefs 7km offshore with floating platforms.

São Miguel do Gostoso, 110km from Natal, is one increasingly popular weekend destination, with pousadas, restaurants and bars, but also with several nearby beaches that are for the most part near-empty. Buses run there at least three times daily from Natal's Rodoviária Nova (R$12, 2½ hours).

Galinhos
☎ 0xx84 / pop 1000
Perched on a sandbar between a river and the ocean 160km northwest of Natal, the isolated fishing village of Galinhos is only just beginning to develop as a beach destination. With sandy streets and warm, gentle waters, it's a great place to unwind. Pristine beaches and dunes stretch 2km west to a small lighthouse at the river mouth, and endlessly along the

coast to the east. You can take an enjoyable four- or five-hour boat excursion (R$40 to R$50 per boat) up the estuary to Galos, an even smaller fishing village, via mangroves, dunes and the local saltworks.

SLEEPING & EATING

Pousada Galinhos (☎ 3552 0047; www.pousadagalinhos .com.br; Rua Walfran Ribeiro 207; s/d R$50/60) This budget option has small but clean rooms with verandas on a quiet side street.

Pousada das Velas (Rua Walfran Ribeiro; r R$100) A more comfortable new, Portuguese-owned pousada. The owners are also building a new place with pool along the street and plan to open a kitesurfing school (the winds are best here in June and July).

Pousada Retiro das Velas (☎ 3552 0077; Rua Senador Dinarte Mariz 224; r R$100; 🐾) This French-owned place has lovely, large, cool rooms adorned with art prints, in a pretty garden dotted with Mexican ceramics.

Pousada Brésil Aventure (☎ 3552 0085; www.bresil -aventure.com; mains R$12-25; 🕙 10am-3pm & 7-10pm) The best place to eat is this sometimes busy pousada belonging to a French tour company, right on the beach. The open-air restaurant serves satisfying meat, pasta, seafood and desserts.

GETTING THERE & AWAY

Access to Galinhos is not particularly easy, which is part of its charm. You can only get there by 4WD or buggy along the beach via São Bento do Norte, some 30km east, or by small boats along the river from Pratagi, 2km southeast (R$2 per person). If you have a vehicle you can leave it safely parked at Pratagi for free.

Just three buses a week leave Natal's Rodoviária Nova for Galinhos (R$16, 3½ hours), at 6:30am Sunday, and noon Monday and Friday.

Ponta do Mel

If you're traveling along this coast, the most charming and relaxing place you can find to stay is **Costa Branca Eco Resort** (☎ 0xx84-3332 7071; www.costabranca.com.br; Praia da Ponta do Mel; s R$150-468, d R$215-585; 🐾 🖥 🐾). Set above a gorgeous sweep of beach and beautifully designed with 360-degree views, it's 30km east of the town of Areia Branca. Despite the name it's much more like a particularly tasteful pousada or small hotel than a resort, with chalets of varied degrees of luxury dotted around attractive gardens. There's a quality restaurant, two pools, a pub-style bar and trails through the grounds. The coast in this area is spectacular, with the pink dunes of Praia do Rosado 10km east.

Ceará, Piauí & Maranhão

The Northwest's three northernmost states stretch along Brazil's only north-facing coast and deep into the arid interior. While Ceará in the east is mostly caatinga (semiarid land) country, the west of Maranhão is on the fringe of the Amazonian rain forest. For many visitors, this part of Brazil primarily means the beaches of Ceará, stretching either side of Fortaleza, easily the region's biggest city. Fortaleza itself, while not big on culture or charm, is a fun-loving beach town where you can dance to *forró* (popular music of the Northeast), electronic and other beats any night of the week. To its east and west stretch hundreds of kilometers of some of the best beaches in Brazil, some supporting growing resort towns, others with at most a small, traditional fishing village. Canoa Quebrada, with its weekend party atmosphere, and super-relaxed Jericoacoara are the places most travelers head for.

Further west, in Piauí, tranquil Parnaíba is the gateway to the large and intriguing Delta do Parnaíba. An adventurous coastal route leads west from here to the enormous expanses of high dunes and clear lagoons known as the Lençóis Maranhenses. Further west still is the half-decayed, half-restored colonial gem of São Luís, one of Brazil's most picturesque cities that also happens to be the country's reggae capital and home to one of its most extraordinary annual festivals, the Bumba Meu Boi.

The interior of all these states, known as the *sertão*, is a land where life has never been easy for its predominantly agricultural and ranching inhabitants, who suffer periodic horrific droughts. But there is spectacular country to explore here, with the bonus of fascinating rock art and archaeological remains in the Serra da Capivara and Sete Cidades national parks.

HIGHLIGHTS

- Forget the world in the remote backpacker village of **Jericoacoara** (p578)
- Soak up the tropical colonial ambience and dance to reggae in historical **São Luís** (p589)
- Take the adventurous coastal route from Jericoacoara to the endless dunes and pristine lakes of the **Lençóis Maranhenses** (p597)
- Surf, windsurf or kitesurf at **Fortaleza** (p570) and many other spots along the breezy Ceará Coast
- Explore the spectacular inland national park of **Serra da Capivara** (p588)

★ São Luís   Parque Nacional dos Lençóis Maranhenses
★ Jericoacoara
★ Fortaleza

Parque Nacional Serra da Capivara

■ POPULATION: 17 MILLION   ■ AREA: 732,092 SQ KM

History

The Portuguese were slow off the mark in occupying these distant northern parts of Brazil, and it was the French who founded São Luís, the capital of Maranhão (in 1612), and the Dutch who founded Fortaleza, the capital of Ceará (in 1637). These incursions spurred the Portuguese into action and they expelled both rival colonial powers within a few years. The main settlers in Ceará were from Portugal's Azores islands. Colonial sugar and cotton plantations, worked by slave labor, were developed in both states but cattle ranching dominated their economies, as it still does to a large extent today.

Initially Maranhão was governed together with Pará to its west as a separate entity from the rest of Brazil, with their capital at São Luís. They were placed under the same administration as the rest of Brazil in 1774. Piauí, between Ceará and Maranhão, was first settled inland, by poor cattle herders moving westwards from Ceará and north from São Paulo in the 17th and 18th centuries.

Despite resistance, the indigenous population of all three states was subdued by the 18th century. Once the wars ended, the colonists in the interior were faced with serious droughts. As many as two million people died in droughts in Ceará in the 1870s, with survivors flooding into Fortaleza. Neighboring Piauí was initially landlocked but eventually arranged a land swap with Ceará in the 19th century so that it could enjoy the benefits of a coastline. Piauí still has the lowest population density of any Brazilian state.

The city of Fortaleza, with its commerce and tourism, is the region's economic powerhouse. Some large industrial projects have been sited near São Luís in the last couple of decades in an effort to boost its economy. But all three states are still among Brazil's poorest.

Climate

These states are warm year-round and experience a rainier season, with some tropical downpours, from about December to March in the west (Maranhão) and February to May in the east (Ceará). Temperatures are higher in the interior as the coast receives ocean breezes off the ocean. Nowhere in this region does it ever get particularly cold or rainy, and the interior of Piauí claims to be the hottest part of the country. The interior is slightly less broiling in June and July.

National Parks

Lençóis Maranhenses (p597), east of São Luís, is one of the highlights of the region, a vast expanse of high sand dunes only interrupted by clear pools of water.

In deep southern Piauí, Serra da Capivara (p588) contains 128 visitable archaeological sites and 30,000 prehistoric rock paintings, in a dramatic rocky landscape. It is a Unesco World Heritage site and well worth the trip if you have time.

Nearer the coast, Sete Cidades (p587) contains bizarre rock formations that resemble seven cities, and hundreds more prehistoric rock paintings.

The small Ubajara (p582) is famous for its vast caves, accessed on foot or by cable car. It also contains lush forests and impressive waterfalls.

Chapada das Mesas (p600) is a zone of impressive rocky bluffs and gorgeous waterfalls near Carolina in southern Maranhão.

Nascentes do Rio Parnaíba (p588), straddling the far south of Piauí and Maranhão as well as bits of Tocantins and Bahia states, is a superb wildlife-viewing location for those who can get there. It's famed for its beautiful hyacinth macaws and ultra-intelligent capuchin monkeys.

Getting There & Away

AIR

Fortaleza has an international airport with flights from Europe, the US and most Brazilian cities. São Luís and Teresina are served by domestic flights.

BUS

You can get to Fortaleza by bus from Brasília, Rio or São Paulo to the south, Natal or Recife to the east, or Belém to the west. For the longest trips, airfares can be little more expensive than buses. Teresina and São Luís receive buses from Fortaleza, Belém, Brasilia, Rio and São Paulo.

Getting Around

Buses link pretty much every town and village in this region. Road quality is steadily improving, though much of the São Luís–Belém road within Maranhão is in poor shape, and access to some coastal villages including Jericoacoara is partly unpaved. Beach buggies and 4WDs with drivers provide trips along the coasts and dunes. A hire car is useful if you plan to visit some smaller places with limited bus service, but you should research road conditions first as some less-traveled routes require 4WD. Fortaleza is the easiest place to get a rental vehicle.

CEARÁ

In a country of glorious coastlines, Ceará has one of the most glorious of all – nearly 600km of beautiful and varied beaches, from idyllic little palm-fringed bays to 20km strips washed by ocean breakers. From the busy urban beaches of Fortaleza to hip Jericoacoara and Canoa Quebrada to the smallest of fishing villages where people continue to sail *jangadas* (distinctive single-sailed boats of the Northeast) and live in thatch-roofed homes, Ceará has anything you could wish for in terms of beach ambience. Much of the coast is backed by large expanses of high, white dunes, lending a starkly elemental touch to the landscape, while the waves and winds provide some of the best conditions in the world for surfing, windsurfing and kitesurfing.

FORTALEZA

☎ 0xx85 / pop 2.4 million

Considering its isolation on the Brazilian map, Fortaleza is a surprisingly large and sprawling place. With 3.3 million people in its metropolitan area, it's one of Brazil's biggest cities

CEARÁ, PIAUÍ & MARANHÃO

CEARÁ, PIAUÍ & MARANHÃO

and an economic magnet for people from all of Ceará and beyond. It's also a magnet for tourists from Brazil and overseas, who come for the beaches and the party atmosphere. Some of the city beaches are reasonably attractive and the nightlife is definitely a lot of fun. With its international and domestic airport, Fortaleza also serves as the jumping-off point for many visitors to truly spectacular beaches, rolling dunes and idyllic fishing villages up and down the Ceará coast.

History

According to many historians, the Spanish navigator Vicente Yañez Pinzón landed on Praia Mucuripe on February 2, 1500, more than two months before Pedro Álvares Cabral first sighted Monte Pascoal in Bahia (the officially recognized European discovery of Brazil). The first Portuguese attempts to settle here, in the early 17th century, were short-lived, and it was the Dutch who founded what ended up as Fortaleza by building Fort Schoonenborch in 1637. When the Dutch abandoned their Brazilian possessions in 1654, the Portuguese renamed this fort the

Fortaleza de NS da Assunção (Fortress of Our Lady of the Assumption). Around it grew a village, then a town, then a city that came to be called Fortaleza.

Indian resistance slowed Portuguese colonization of interior Ceará until the 18th century, but cattle ranchers, and later cotton growers, occupied land. It was cotton exports in the 19th century that made Fortaleza into an important town (it had previously played second fiddle to Aracati). Droughts in the interior and growing commerce and industry in Fortaleza have since attracted ever more migrants to the city. Since the early 1990s tourism has joined textiles and food among the leading industries here. Under Workers' Party mayor Luizianne Lins, elected in 2004, Fortaleza has had some success in shrugging off an unwanted reputation as a capital of sex tourism.

Orientation

Fortaleza stretches 20km along the coast and up to 10km inland. Centro is the oldest part of town, on a slight elevation beginning 200m from the seafront, and has many busy streets full of small stores. The main areas of interest

FORTALEZA

INFORMATION		In Out Turismo..................7 G3	SIGHTS & ACTIVITIES
Banco do Brasil..................1 G3		Lav & Lev..................8 G3	Academia de Surf Chandler.......13 F3
Banco do Brasil..................2 B3		Libratur..................9 G3	Centro de Turismo..................14 A2
Brazilian Internet		Setfor..................10 A3	Centro Dragão do Mar
Café..................3 G3		Setfor..................11 G3	de Arte e Cultura..................15 C2
Central Post Office..................4 B3		Setfor..................(see 34)	Memorial da Cultura Cearense..(see 15)
Coffee Image..................5 B3		Setur..................(see 14)	Museu de Arte e Cultura
HSBC..................6 E3		Tourist Police..................12 D2	Popular..................(see 14)

are east of Centro. First is Praia de Iracema, a tightly packed nightlife and restaurant area – with some hotels and pousadas (guesthouses), but no real beach. Then there's Meireles, the middle-class beach suburb with many of the best places to stay, 2km to 4km east of Centro. There's the port area, Mucuripe, and finally, starting some 8km east of Centro, Praia do Futuro, with the best beach, stretching 5km south along an east-facing coast.

The bus station is 4km south of Centro and the airport is 2km further south.

Information

BOOKSTORES

Fortaleza is principally a beach town and bookstores are hard to come by. The following are good for maps and guides.

Livraria Laselva (☎ 3477 1547; Aeroporto Pinto Martins) Upstairs in the airport.

Livraria Siciliana (☎ 3241 3642; Shopping Iguatemi, Av Washington Soares 85; ☯ 10am-10pm Mon-Sat)

EMERGENCY

Ambulance (☎ 192)

Police (Polícia; ☎ 190)

Tourist Police (Delegacia de Proteção ao Turista; ☎ 3101 2488; Av Almirante Barroso 805, Praia de Iracema)

INTERNET ACCESS

Brazilian Internet Café (☎ 3458 1675; Av Abolição 2300, Meireles; per hr R$6; ☯ 8am-10pm) Bright and busy.

Coffee Image (☎ 3217 7500; Rua Floriano Peixoto 489, Centro; per hr R$3; ☯ 9am-6pm) Also a good coffee lounge.

INTERNET RESOURCES

Setfor (www.setfor.fortaleza.ce.gov.br) The city tourism site, in Portuguese only but a useful reference.

Setur (www.setur.ce.gov.br) Ceará's official tourism site, with good information in English and Portuguese.

LAUNDRY

There are laundries all over town and most will pick up and deliver. Many hotels and pousadas also offer services.

Lav & Lev (☎ 3242 3345; Av Abolição 2685, Meireles; per load R$15.60; ☯ 8am-7pm Mon-Fri, to 6pm Sat)

MEDICAL SERVICES

The following recommended private hospitals have some English-speaking doctors.

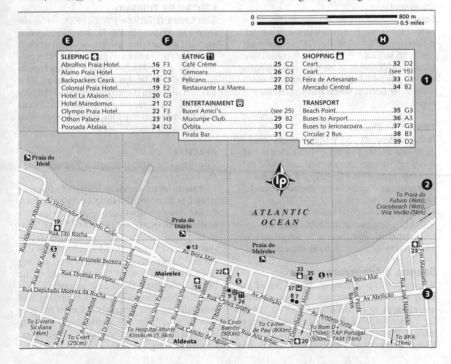

SLEEPING		
Abrolhos Praia Hotel	16	F3
Alamo Praia Hotel	17	D2
Backpackers Ceará	18	C3
Colonial Praia Hotel	19	E2
Hotel La Maison	20	G3
Hotel Maredomus	21	D2
Olympo Praia Hotel	22	F3
Othon Palace	23	H3
Pousada Atalaia	24	D2

EATING		
Café Créme	25	C2
Cemoara	26	G3
Pelicano	27	D2
Restaurante La Marea	28	D2

ENTERTAINMENT		
Buoni Amici's	(see 25)	
Mucuripe Club	29	B2
Órbita	30	C2
Pirata Bar	31	C2

SHOPPING		
Ceart	32	D2
Ceart	(see 15)	
Feira de Artesanato	33	G3
Mercado Central	34	B2

TRANSPORT		
Beach Point	35	G3
Buses to Airport	36	A3
Buses to Jericoacoara	37	G3
Circular 2 Bus	38	B3
TSC	39	D2

Hospital Monte Klinikum (☎ 4012 0012; Rua República do Líbano 747, Meireles)
Hospital São Mateus (☎ 3234 1444; Av Santos Dumont 5633, Papicu)

MONEY
ATMs on the upper level of the airport accept international cards. Elsewhere, avoid stand-alone ATM booths as these are most at risk of card-cloning fraud.
Banco do Brasil Centro (Praça Waldemar Falcao; ☾ 10am-4pm Mon-Fri, ATMs 6am-10pm daily); Meireles (Av Abolição 2311; ☾ 10am-4pm Mon-Fri, ATMs 6am-10pm daily) These branches do currency exchange and have ATMs.
HSBC (Av Monsenhor Tabosa 1200, Praia de Iracema) The ATMs here accept international cards.

POST
Central post office (Rua Senador Alencar 38; ☾ 8am-5pm Mon-Fri, to noon Sat)

TOURIST INFORMATION
Setfor Centro (☎ 3105 1444; Praça da Ferreira; ☾ 9am-5pm Mon-Sat); Meireles (☎ 3105 2670; Av Beira Mar; ☾ 9am-8pm); Mercado Central (☎ 3105 1321; ☾ 9am-5pm Mon-Fri) The city tourism department operates a few information booths.
Setur Centro de Turismo (☎ 3101 5508; Rua Senador Pompeu 350, Centro; ☾ 8am-5pm Mon-Fri, to 4pm Sat, to noon Sun); bus station (☎ 3101 3397; ☾ 6am-8pm); airport (☎ 3477 1667; ☾ 6am-11pm) The Ceará tourism organization has more useful information offices providing good city maps, with English-speaking attendants usually available. The Centro de Turismo branch is particularly helpful.

TRAVEL AGENCIES
In Out Turismo (☎ 3242 4347; www.inoutturismo.com .br; Av Abolição 2687, Meireles; ☾ 9am-6:30pm Mon-Fri, to 1pm Sat) This small agency is friendly and helpful, and the owner, Jonas, speaks excellent English and several other languages. It can help design your travels around Ceará or further afield.
Libratur (☎ 3248 3355; Av Abolição 2194; ☾ 8.30am-6pm Mon-Fri, 8am-noon Sat) This helpful agency has bilingual staff and competitive prices for national and international ticketing. It also runs a money-exchange service.

Dangers & Annoyances
Beware of pickpocketing in the city center and petty theft on the beaches. Tourists waiting at bus stops to return from Praia do Futuro have been targeted. Empty streets in Centro after dark are best avoided. There is prostitution in Meireles and especially Iracema, but the city has had some success in combating sex tourism.

Sights & Activities
CENTRO DRAGÃO DO MAR DE ARTE E CULTURA
This excellent modern **cultural center** (☎ 3488 8600; www.dragaodomar.org.br; Rua Dragão do Mar 81) in-cludes museums, cinemas, theatres, galleries, a good café and a planetarium in an exten-sive complex with elevated walkways join-ing blocks on different streets. It blends well with the surrounding older buildings, many of which have been restored to house bars, restaurants and artisans' workshops. It's a suc-cessful social focus for the city, very popular with locals especially on weekends. The **Memo-rial da Cultura Cearense** (admission R$2; ☾ 9am-7pm Tue-Thu, 2-9pm Fri-Sun) is a museum dedicated to the popular culture of Ceará, with permanent displays on the cowboys of the interior and the Padre Cícero cult of Juazeiro do Norte, and temporary exhibits focusing on crafts. Free capoeira lessons are given at 6pm Tuesday and Friday under the planetarium.

CENTRO DE TURISMO
The **Centro de Turismo** (☎ 3101 5508; Rua Senador Pompeu 350; ☾ 8am-6pm Mon-Sat, to noon Sun), a con-verted 19th-century jail, houses a lot of craft stalls and, upstairs from the tourist informa-tion office, the **Museu de Arte e Cultura Popular** (admission R$1; ☾ 8am-4pm Mon-Sat, to 11am Sun). This folk-art museum has an impressive collection of Ceará crafts, ranging from musical instru-ments and weaving looms to puppets and wooden sculptures.

BEACHES
The greatest attractions in Fortaleza are the beaches.
Praia do Futuro is a clean length of sand that stretches 5km south along Fortaleza's east-facing coast to the Clube Caça e Pesca. It's easily the best city beach, although far from most accommodations. *Barracas* (kiosks) line the beach, serving seafood and beer, and it is packed on weekends. It doesn't start getting really nice until you are 1km to 2km down the beach, away from the industrial port. This is also the best city beach for kitesurfing and windsurfing – participants frequent the *bar-raca* Vira Verão (p572). Swimming is OK here too, but unless you are a strong swimmer, beware of rough waves.

Praia do Meireles fronts Avenida Beira Mar, and this area contains most of the midrange and upmarket hotels and restaurants. The frantic pace of high-rise hotel construction has created what looks like a northeastern Copacabana. Meireles' numerous beach bars, shaded among the leafy trees, are popular places to hang out by day or evening. The water here is less clean than at Praia do Futuro, although that doesn't deter surfers. **Academia de Surf Chandler** (☎ 8803 4487; surfboard rental per day/hr R$15/30, ☀ 1-6pm Wed-Fri, 9am-6pm Sat & Sun), under a yellow awning on the beach, rents boards and gives classes for R$10 per hour.

Near the Ponte Metálica or Ponte dos Ingleses, the city's old dock built in the 1920s, **Praia de Iracema** was a source of inspiration to Luís Assunção and Milton Dias, Ceará's bohemian poets of the 1950s. Today Iracema has mainly been taken over by larger restaurants and bars catering to visiting partygoers. It also has an obvious prostitution scene. The beach itself is not worth your time.

Northwest of Fortaleza, **Icaraí** (20km from the center) and **Cumbuco** (35km from the center), are much cleaner than the city beaches and are easy day trips. Cumbuco, with its dunes, is popular for buggy rides, especially on weekends. Kitesurfing (best from July to February) is also good at Cumbuco beach and at Lagoa do Cauípe, 10km west of Cumbuco – rental and classes are available. Cumbuco has several hotels and pousadas if you want to stay over. **Vitória** (☎ 3342 1148) runs minibuses to Icaraí and Cumbuco (R$4 to either) from Praia do Meireles at 6:30am and 10am and 2:35pm and 5pm. They run east along Av Beira Mar, then westward along Av Abolição.

Tours

Day-trips to beaches along the coast to the east and west are very popular from Fortaleza. Dozens of travel agencies, hotels and pousadas will arrange these for you, and minivan and dune-buggy operators line up on Av Beira Mar near the Meireles tourist office in the early evening, looking for business for the next day. They will normally come and pick you up from your accommodations. The main destinations are Beach Park (R$20 per person, transport only), Cumbuco (R$20), Morro Branco (R$30), Canoa Quebrada (R$35), Lagoinha (R$30) and Mundaú (R$35). The tours are easier than taking public buses and you can use them just one way if you want to stay over.

Some agencies also offer longer-distance 4WD or beach-buggy tours, along Ceará's glorious beaches wherever possible, as far afield as Jericoacoara or even Natal or the Lençóis Maranhenses. A three-day return trip to Jericoacoara costs around R$1000 to R$1500 for up to four people, with accommodations and outings from Jeri included; a five-day one-way jaunt to Natal is around R$2000 for two. These trips can be done in less time for less money. Try Hotel La Maison (p572), **Nordeste Off Road** (☎ 3088 1708; www.nordesteoffroad.com; Rua Julio César 237, Benfica) or **Dunnas Expedições** (☎ 3264 2514; www.dunnas.com.br).

Festivals & Events

Fortal, Fortaleza's lively out-of-season Carnaval, is held during the last week of July. The **Iemanjá festival**, which celebrates the sea goddess, is held on August 15 at Praia do Futuro. The **Regata de Jangadas**, a sailing regatta with traditional northeastern *jangadas* (triangular-sailed fishing boats), takes place between Praia do Meireles and Praia Mucuripe during the second half of July.

Sleeping

There are endless accommodations for all budgets in Fortaleza. If you are here strictly for nightlife, stay in Iracema; for beaches and relaxation, stay in Meireles (or nearby).

BUDGET

Backpackers Ceará (☎ 3091 8997; www.backpackers ce.cjb.net; Av Don Manuel 89; per person R$20-25) The vibe is super informal at this sociable hostel with English-speaking Brazilian owners. Prettily decorated rooms line up on two floors alongside a pleasant lawn, and there are ample kitchen and hangout areas. The hostel is a stone's throw from the Centro Dragão do Mar, and bus 078 Siqueira/Mucuripe from the bus station comes right along here.

Alamo Praia Hotel (☎ 3219 7979; www.alamo.cjb .net; Av Almirante Barroso 885, Iracema; s/d R$50/70; ☀) Well put together by Iracema standards, this hotel is a block back from the action. There's lots of competition in the area, but this place is friendlier and cleaner than most.

MIDRANGE

Discounts of 25% to 35% are offered at many of these places outside the short mid-December-to-late-January high season.

Pousada Atalaia (☎ 3219 0755; www.atalaiahostel .com.br; Av Beira Mar 814, Iracema; dm/s/d R$32/70/95; ❄ 🖳) The rooms are bright and modern at this HI hostel, which is the nicest in Iracema and better than many of the pousadas. It has a good kitchen, common areas and location. The dorms, for up to four people, have lockers.

our pick **Hotel La Maison** (☎ 3242 6836; www.hotel lamaison.com.br; Av Desembargador Moreira 201, Meireles; r R$100; ❄ 🖳) The best-value midrange place in Meireles, La Maison is just a couple of blocks from the beach, with bright, spotless rooms. The attentive French owner knows the city very well, speaks English too, and can point you in the right direction, no matter what your interest. His son offers buggy and 4WD trips as far as Jericoacoara and Natal.

Abrolhos Praia Hotel (☎ 3248 1217; www.abrolhos praiahotel.com.br; Av Abolição 2030, Meireles; s/d R$90/110; ❄ 🖳) Busy Abrolhos, a couple of blocks back from the beach, is friendly, clean and well run, with one of the best breakfasts you'll find anywhere in the Northeast. Some English spoken.

Hotel Maredomus (☎ 4005 4500; www.maredomus hotel.com.br; Av Almirante Barroso 1030, Iracema; r R$128-148; ❄ 🖳 🖳) This gleaming, stylish 10-story hotel is a cut above most of its Iracema rivals, with a friendly atmosphere, a rooftop pool and spotless, colorful rooms that are equipped with bedside spot-lighting, 40-channel TV and sparkling bathrooms.

Colonial Praia Hotel (☎ 4005 4644; www.colonial praiahotel.com.br; Rua Barão de Aracati 145; s/d R$129/161; ❄ 🖳 🖳) With gardens of tropical fruit trees designed by Robert Burle Marx and a good pool area, this is one of the more charming spots in the Iracema area.

TOP END

Because of the competition between Meireles' many fancy hotels, some good prices can be found.

Othon Palace (☎ 3466 5500; www.othon.com.br; Av Beira Mar 3470, Meireles; s/d from R$200/242; ❄ 🖳 🖳) This landmark hotel, looking right along Meireles from its eastern end, boasts a panoramic external elevator, good service and quality, pine-furnished rooms, all with a sea view – good value.

Olympo Praia Hotel (☎ 3266 7200; www.olympo .com.br; Av Beira Mar 2380, Meireles; r R$207-278; ❄ 🖳) Olympo is located in the main beach area but set back from the busy beachfront. With all the modern amenities including a big pool area, it's worth the price – but avoid the rear rooms overlooking noisy Av Abolição.

Eating

Many restaurant dishes here are meant for two people to share, and this may not always be stated on menus: don't hesitate to ask if in doubt!

Bom D+ (☎ 3086 9194; Av Desembargador Moreira 469, Meireles; per kg R$20-24; ☽ 11am-3pm Mon-Sat) Top-value self-service place with great grilled meats, good fresh salads, vegetable fritters, and rice and bean dishes.

Café Crème (☎ 3219 7821; Rua Dragão do Mar 92; rodízio de pizza R$12; ☽ 4pm-1am Mon-Thu, to 3am Fri-Sun) Crème is one of the main restaurants at Dragão do Mar, with tables out front for watching the action. The pizza rodízio (smorgasbord) is unbeatable value.

Pelicano (☎ 3219 1726; Av Beira Mar 914, Iracema; mains R$15-30; ☽ lunch & dinner) Serves a variety of well-prepared food, including pizzas and grilled meats, with the beach right across the street.

our pick **Coco Bambu** (☎ 3242-7557; Rua Canuto de Aguiar 1317, Varjota; mains R$15-35; ☽ noon-1am) This huge and festive eatery has both a sand-floored, outdoor area and an air-conditioned interior. Options range from pancakes and tapiocas to meat and fish grills and a big choice of pizzas. Don't miss the chance to round off your meal with a banana, chocolate, cinnamon and cashew pizza.

Colher de Pau (☎ 3267 3773; Rua Frederico Borges 204, Varjota; mains R$17-30; ☽ 11am-midnight) This is one of the best places on a street lined with good-value, medium-range restaurants, many of them started by waiters from fancier places elsewhere in Fortaleza (a pizzeria and a sushi bar are among the others). It's especially good for fish and meat grills, in enormous proportions.

Restaurante La Marea (☎ 3219 2284; cnr Rua dos Tabajaras & Rua Tremembés, Iracema; mains R$20-30; ☽ 6pm-1am) Good two-level grill house on Iracema's 'restaurant corner', with meat cooked over red-hot coals. Staff grill the picanha (Brazil's favorite cut of beef comes from the cow's rump and is eaten pinkish, salty and fresh from the grill) at your table.

Vira Verão (☎ 3262 6227; Av Zezé Diogo 3345, Praia do Futuro; fish & seafood dishes R$20-40; ☽ 8am-8pm Fri-Wed, 8am-2am Thu) Praia do Futuro is lined with enormous barracas, some with hundreds of tables under sunshades on the sand. They're good for seafood meals and snacks – *pargo assado* (grilled sea bream) with salad is a favorite dish here. Vira Verão (watch out for its sign as you approach the beach, heading along Av Dioguinho) has a bright atmosphere and is frequented by surfers, windsurfers and kitesurfers.

Cemoara (☎ 3242 8500; Rua Joaquim Nabuco 166, Meireles; mains R$30-60; ⏰ noon-3pm & 7pm-midnight Mon-Sat, noon-5pm Sun) This is a renowned seafood restaurant, with no shorts or sandals allowed. It boasts some of the best seafood dishes in the city but still has reasonable prices for what you get. Try the fish in mussel sauce; you won't be disappointed.

Entertainment

Fortaleza is famed for its nightlife. Many tourists head for Iracema, which is packed with bars and clubs playing everything from *forró* (the quintessential music and dance of the Northeast) to techno, but has a big prostitution scene. The nearby Centro Dragão do Mar area is more popular with locals and is one of the best places to go out in the city. The *barracas* on Meireles beach serve icy beer from morning to night.

Buoni Amici's (☎ 3219 5454; Rua Dragão do Mar 80; admission R$5-15 after 10pm Thu-Sun; ⏰ 4pm-midnight) The Dragão do Mar area has several open-air restaurant/bars where people flock for evening drinks and to see what live music, street theater or other action starts up. Amici's is an attraction in itself, with Brazilian music (live or DJ) from about 9pm Thursday to Sunday.

Órbita (☎ 3453 1421; Rua Almirante Jaceguai 81; admission R$12-15; ⏰ 9pm-3am Thu-Sun) This large, black-and-purple Dragão do Mar bar hosts reggae, rock, techno and snooker.

Mucuripe Club (☎ 3254 3020; Travessa Maranguape 108, Centro; admission R$25; ⏰ 9:30pm-late Fri & Sat) The best, most stylish disco in town, a huge, modern, nontouristic venue with five different dance areas where you can move from techno or pop to jazz or *forró*.

Pirata Bar (☎ 4011 6161; www.pirata.com.br; Rua dos Tabajaras 325, Iracema; admission R$20; ⏰ 8pm-late Mon) Long-standing Pirata is famous for its '*segunda-feira mais louca do planeta*' (craziest Monday on the planet). The pirate ship-themed spot stages hours of live *forró* and other Brazilian rhythms for the packed crowd to dance through the night. The surrounding bars also get very lively.

Clube do Vaqueiro (☎ 3278 2000; Anel Viário IV s/n, Estrada do Eusebio; admission R$7; ⏰ 8pm-5am Sat) For more of a *sertão* (backlands of the Northeast) experience, try this enormous, cowboy-themed *forró* club where five different bands play on Saturday nights. It's popular with students. The Vaqueiro is out on the city's southeast outskirts, and best reached by taxi.

Crocobeach (☎ 3265 6667; Av Zezé Diogo 3125, Praia do Futuro; ⏰ 8:15pm-late Thu) The huge *barracas* on Praia do Futuro open on Thursday evening for nights of live music, dancing and a crab feast. Crocobeach is the most fun, with comedy acts as well as music.

Shopping

You can find handicrafts from all around Ceará here. Some of the finest work is in delicate lace, a tradition that came with the Portuguese. Artisans also work with *carnaúba* palm fronds, bamboo, vines and leather.

Ceart Dragão do Mar (☎ 3226 6917; Centro Dragão do Mar; ⏰ 9am-9pm Tue-Sat, 3-9pm Sun); Iracema (☎ 3101 2747; cnr Av Monsenhor Tabosa & Rua João Cordeiro; ⏰ 9am-6pm Mon-Fri, to 5pm Sat); Aldeota (☎ 3224 7291; Av Santos Dumont 1589; ⏰ 9am-8pm Mon-Sat) These state-run craft stores sell lace, ceramics, woven baskets and bags, leather goods, and textiles.

Mercado Central (☎ 3454 8586; Av Alberto Nepomuceno 199, Centro; ⏰ 8am-6pm Mon-Fri, to 4pm Sat, to noon Sun) Mainly geared to a tourist clientele, the three-story Central Market has good prices at over 500 stalls selling everything from hammocks and leather bags to excellent local cashews and a huge variety of *cachaça* (white spirit made from sugarcane) – some bottles have fruit salad or crabs pickled inside.

Feira de Artesanato (Náutico, Praia do Meireles; ⏰ 4-10pm) This large open-air craft market has an awful lot of T-shirts, but you can also find some real artisanry.

Centro de Turismo (☎ 3101 5508; Rua Senador Pompeu 350, Centro; ⏰ 8am-6pm Mon-Sat, to noon Sun) The many stalls here focus on lace and embroidery and you can usually see lace-makers at work.

Getting There & Away

AIR

Pinto Martins airport (☎ 3477 1200; airport code FOR) has daily flights to/from Miami with TAM, Lisbon with TAP or BRA, plus every major Brazilian destination with a variety of Brazilian airlines. There are also regular charter flights from several European cities. Airline offices include the following (at the airport unless otherwise stated):

BRA Aldeota (☎ 3261 1919; Av Padre Antônio Tomáz 585); airport (☎ 3477 1420)

Gol (☎ 3477 1318)

Ocean Air (☎ 3477 1527)

TACV (Cabo Verde Airlines; ☎ 3268 1020)

TAF (☎ 3272 7333)

TAM Aldeota (☎ 4002 5700; Av Desembargador Moreira 1940); airport (☎ 3477 1192)

TAP Portugal Aldeota (☎ 3458 1540; Sala 910, Shopping Aldeota, Av Dom Luís 500); airport (☎ 3477 1799)

Varig (☎ 3477 1078)

BUS

From the **bus station** (☎ 3256 2100; Av Oswaldo Studart) buses run to destinations including Belém (R$160, 28 hours, noon), Canoa Quebrada (R$18, three hours, five daily), Juazeiro do Norte (R$52 to R$79, 11 hours, 11 daily), Natal (R$65 to R$113, eight hours, seven daily), Parnaíba (R$58, nine hours, three daily), Recife (R$73 to R$93, 12 hours, four daily), Rio de Janeiro (R$294, 50 hours, 10am), Salvador (R$156, 22 hours, 7pm), Teresina (R$52 to R$82, 10 hours, seven daily), São Luís (R$118, 20 hours, three daily) and Ubajara (R$27 to R$31, six hours, eight daily). You can buy tickets in town at agencies including **TSC** (☎ 3086 2633; Rua Gonçalves Ledo 27, Iracema).

For Jericoacoara, **Redenção** (☎ 3256 1973) runs two or three buses daily from the **Praiano Palace Hotel** (Av Beira Mar 2800) on Meireles beach. The 9:30am and 5:30pm departures (R$35.50, seven hours) go every day and also pick up passengers at the airport (10am and 6pm) and bus station (10:30am and 6:30pm). The 3pm departure from the Praiano Palace (R$50, six hours, also daily but often canceled during Jericoacoara's low season, mid-March to June), picks up at the Hotel Amuarama opposite the bus station, at 3:30pm. It's a good idea to buy your ticket a day ahead: one outlet is **Beach Point** (☎ 3242 2946; Náutico, Meireles). The fare includes a 23km ride in an open-sided 4WD bus known as a *jardineira* for the final stretch from Jijoca to Jericoacoara along sandy tracks and the beach.

CAR & MOTORCYCLE

Recommended rental agencies, all with airport offices:

Avis (☎ 3477 1369)

Hertz (☎ 3477 5055)

Localiza (☎ 3477 5050)

Getting Around

TO/FROM THE AIRPORT

A taxi from the airport to Meireles, Iracema or Centro costs R$33. Bus 404 'Aeroporto' (R$1.60) runs both ways between the airport and Rua Pedro Pereira (corner of Rua General Sampaio) in Centro, every 20 minutes from 6am to 10pm, taking about 20 minutes. In Centro you can get another bus to Iracema or Meireles, but, for safety reasons, it's not advisable to change buses in Centro after late afternoon.

TO/FROM THE BUS STATION

To get bus 078 'Siqueira/Mucuripe' (R$1.60) to Iracema and Meireles, walk left outside the bus station, turn right at the traffic signal along Av Borges de Melo, and the stop is about 200m along on the far (south) side of the street, in front of the Telemar building. The bus stops opposite the Centro Dragão do Mar, then heads east along Av Almirante Barroso (Iracema) and Av Abolição (Meireles). Going out to the bus station, you can pick it up westbound on Av Abolição or southbound on Av Dom Manuel south of Rua Tenente Benévolo.

BUS

From Centro to Iracema and Meireles take the Circular 2 bus (R$1.60) from Rua Castro e Silva or the Iguatemi–Centro bus (R$2.50) from Praça da Ferreira or the Igreja da Sé. The Circular 2 follows Av Almirante Barroso and Av Abolição. The Iguatemi–Centro goes along Av Monsenhor Tabosa and Av Abolição.

The Circular 1 bus (R$1.60) runs from Meireles (Av Abolição) to Iracema (Av Almirante Barroso), Centro Dragão do Mar and Centro (Av Alberto Nepomuceno and Rua João Moreira).

For Praia do Futuro you can take Top Bus 049 from the Mercado Central, Av Almirante Barroso or Av Abolição, or a Caça e Pesca bus from Av Beira Mar, Meireles.

BEACHES SOUTHEAST OF FORTALEZA

The coast southeast of Fortaleza, dubbed the Costa Sol Nascente (Sunrise Coast) by the publicity folk, has many fine beaches, a lot of them backed by dunes, but is increasingly developed and built-up in the first 100km from Fortaleza. Hwy CE-040 runs about 10km inland, through a mostly flat, dry landscape of shrubs, stunted trees and some lakes.

Another attraction of this stretch is the full-blown water park, **Beach Park** (Map pp576-7; ☎ 0xx85-4012 3000; www.beachpark.com.br; Praia Porto das Dunas; over/under 13 yr R$80/70; ☯ 11am-5pm, closed most Thu & Fri except Jan, Jul & 2nd half Dec), 22km from Fortaleza. It's one of the biggest, best and most modern in Brazil, featuring wave pools, a huge water-playground of jets and showers, and various water slides including the highest in the country – the adrenaline-inducing Insano (Insane), 41m high with speeds up to 110km per hour. Children under 1m tall get in free. Day-trip transport from Fortaleza costs R$20.

CANOA QUEBRADA
☎ 0xx88 / pop 3000

Once a tiny village cut off from the world by its huge, pink sand dunes and beloved of early hippy travelers, Canoa Quebrada is now one of the most popular beach destinations in Ceará. The road from Aracati was paved and electricity was hooked up in the 1990s, and now many of the sandy streets are even rustically cobbled. Canoa claims dozens of pousadas, plenty of restaurants and the best nightlife in Ceará outside Fortaleza. The craggy, eroding sand cliffs behind the narrow beach still lend a touch of the otherworldly feel for which Canoa was famous. Other than the beach, the main attractions are exploring the endless beaches and dunes by buggy, kitesurfing (the season is from July to December), horseback riding, sailing in *jangadas,* dancing until the sun comes up or simply relaxing. It is a social town, particularly on weekends, and a good place to meet locals and other travelers.

Orientation & Information
The main street, known as Rua Principal or Rua Dragão do Mar, runs along the ridge of the hill from which Canoa slopes down to the beach. A pedestrianized strip of Rua Principal with most of the restaurants and bars is known as Broadway.

There's a stand-alone **Banco de Brasil ATM** (Rua Dragão do Mar) opposite the bus stop. The nearest banks, both with ATMs accepting international cards, are Bradesco and Banco do Brasil in Aracati, 13km southwest. **Planet Canoa** (Rua Principal; per hr R$3; ☯ 9am-11pm Mon-Fri, 4-11pm Sat & Sun) offers internet access and used books.

Activities & Tours
There are lots of high dunes and secluded beaches in both directions from Canoa and it's a shame not to get out and see them. Ask your pousada to recommend a buggy driver. A one- to two-hour buggy tour of the dunes on the northern side of town costs around R$100 for up to four people. Some of the dunes here have zip lines that you can race down and drop off into the pools below. A longer trip along the beautiful, cliff-lined coast to Ponta Grossa, 30km southeast (p577) is about R$150 round-trip (1½ hours each way). It's possible to get a buggy all the way to Natal for R$1500.

Kitesurfing is best around the mouth of the Rio Jaguaribe, 12km northwest. **Kite Holiday** (☎ 8806 3583; www.kiteholiday.com; Rua Principal; classes 9/15hr R$790/900) and **Kite Surf Adventure** (☎ 8806 6526, 8813 5891; www.kitesurfcanoa.com .br; classes 6/12 hr R$470/900) are recommended schools. Kite Holiday also rents gear (R$230 per day).

Paragliding is good here too (November to June): a half-hour tandem flight costs R$75.

Sleeping
There are lots of foreign-owned pousadas in Canoa Quebrada, and standards are generally high. In July, August, December and January it's best to make a reservation.

Pousada Europa (☎ 3421 7004; Rua Nataniel Pereira; s/d R$25/35; ☲) Canoa's only real budget pousada is a sociable spot with sea views, a garden, rooms in a two-story wooden building and unheated showers.

Quebramar Pousada (☎ 3421 7421; quebramar pousada@hotmail.com; Rua Caminho do Mar, s/d R$60/80) Set just above the beach, Quebramar doesn't have some of the frills of other pousadas, but the large thatch-roofed rooms with balcony views over the water are excellent value.

our pick **Pousada Califórnia** (☎ 3421 7039; www .californiacanoa.com; Rua Nascer do Sol 136; s R$70-130, d R$80-150; ☲ ☐ ☲) This popular 28-room pousada has a variety of neat, comfortable rooms on two sides of the street, and an attractive courtyard with a bar and pool. Free fruit and coffee are available all day.

Pousada Dolce Vita (☎ 3421 7213; www.canoa-quebrada.it; Rua Descida da Praia; s/d with fan R$90/100, with air-con R$100/130; ☲ ☐ ☲) The Dolce Vita is

CEARÁ COAST

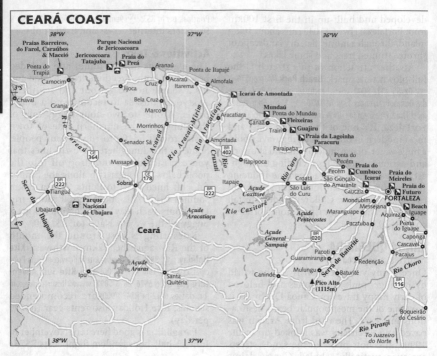

friendly and relaxed, with a pool set in gardens of palms, flowers and lawns. The cabins have more character than your average pousada, each named after a Fellini film and decorated with movie memorabilia. There's a restaurant serving Italian food.

Pousada do Toby (☎ 3421 7094; pousadadotoby .com; Rua Nascer do Sol 148; r R$90-360; ❄ ☐ ☒) Here since 1990, the Toby is a Canoa landmark, with rooms ranging from modest to upscale. All are clean, cool and attractive. The rooftop pools and deck have panoramic views and the restaurant serves breakfast until 4pm (for those who have truly enjoyed the nightlife). It's a good place to unwind and meet other guests from all over the world. If you don't meet Toby himself, you haven't experienced Canoa Quebrada.

Tranquilandia Village (☎ 3421 7012; www.tran quilandia.it; Rua Caminho do Mar; d R$130-200; ❄ ☒) The comfortable cabins at Tranquilandia Village are set around a rare grassy courtyard with a good ocean view from the nice big pool area. The son of the Italian owner is an avid kite-surfer and can facilitate outings for everyone from beginners to pros.

Eating

Artesanal (☎ 3421 7083; Rua Principal; mains R$12-18; ☽ 5pm-midnight mon, Tue & Thu, 11am-midnight Fri-Sun) This small place is good for inexpensive grilled fish or chicken curry.

ourpick Sarué (Rua Principal; mains R$12-24; ☽ dinner) Enjoy well-prepared dishes like prawn and mango curry or *filet mignon ao gorgonzola* in Sarué's pretty courtyard full of greenery and flowers. There's live music some nights.

El Argentino (☎ 3421 7123; Rua Nascer do Sol; mains R$13-25 ☽ 6pm-midnight Mon & Wed-Fri, noon-midnight Sat & Sun) Off-Broadway (just), Argentino is the best spot for grilled meats and does an all-you-can-eat R$20 *rodizio*.

Natural Bistrô (☎ 3421 7162; Rua Principal; mains R$18-30; ☽ 6:30pm-midnight) Natural serves tasty and original seafood, meat, pasta and salad concoctions.

The beach is lined with *barracas* where you can while away the days and put away a good lunch. Two of the most welcoming are **Barraca Antonio Côco** (☎ 3421 7000; mains R$20-40) at the western end, and **Lazy Days** (☎ 0xx85-8801 5996; mains R$10-20) at the eastern end, which does excellent seafood and chicken curries.

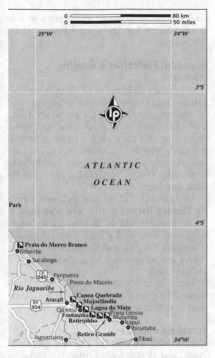

Drinking & Entertainment

There's no need to structure your evening, just walk along Broadway and you'll find what's going on. Caverna (towards the beach end of the street, with darts and pool) and Regart (at the inland end) open early and are smaller bars good for drinks from late afternoon onward. The larger, internationally-themed Canoa Central, around the middle of the strip, fills up later and is one of the main weekend party places. Opposite the Central are several more places, generally opening around 10pm or 11pm (often Friday to Sunday only outside the peak seasons) – Meu Xodó, which packs in *forró* fans; Bar do Reggae; Bar No Meio; and Canoa's only disco, No Name, where partiers flock to dance to everything from samba to house spun by resident and guest DJs.

Reggae parties start every Sunday night about 1am at **Freedom** *barraca* on the beach.

Getting There & Away

BUS

There are five daily buses to/from Fortaleza (R$18, three hours), or you can go by tour van

(R$35, two hours; see p571). Coming from Rio Grande do Norte, get off your bus at Aracati, 13km southwest of Canoa. Minibuses (R$1.50, about every half-hour, 6am to 6pm) and taxis (R$15) run from Aracati to Canoa.

SOUTHEAST TO RIO GRANDE DO NORTE

Road access to this stretch of coast is limited, so there are some great deserted beaches and small fishing villages. It's classic beach-buggy territory, and a great outing from Canoa Quebrada is the buggy ride along the beach to Ponta Grossa (30km).

The first town after Canoa Quebrada is **Majorlândia**, 7km southeast, a popular local resort that gets crowded on weekends. Another 4km southeast are the distinctive, chalky-white sandstone bluffs of **Quixaba**, a fishing village famed for its prawns. From the bluffs, cut by gullies between cacti and palms, you can see back to the pink hills of Canoa Quebrada.

The beach at the next fishing village, **Lagoa do Mato**, combines dunes, cliffs and coconut palms. It's a good snorkeling spot too. Picturesque **Fontainha**, **Retirinho** and **Retiro Grande** follow at intervals of a few kilometers before you reach **Ponta Grossa**, with its curve of beach backed by colorful cliffs. Just beyond Ponta Grossa, **Redondas** is a great place to eat lobster at lower-than-usual prices – try the restaurants in Pousada Oh Linda or Pousada Beija-Flor. These places also have good rooms at around R$100 a double.

From Barreiras, 8km beyond Redondas, a paved road continues to Icapuí and on to Tibau in Rio Grande do Norte.

BEACHES NORTHWEST OF FORTALEZA

The 'Costa Sol Poente' (Sunset Coast), northwest of Fortaleza, is strung with beautiful beaches and villages that are great for unwinding and exploring dunes, bays, lakes and rivers. The winds and waves along here provide some perfect conditions for surfing, windsurfing and kitesurfing.

Paracuru

☎ 0xx85 / pop 30,000

Paracuru, on a curving bay 95km northwest of Fortaleza with palms and rustic fishing boats, is a popular weekend retreat from the city and a fairly affluent coastal town in its own right. Although it can get crowded on weekends, it's quiet the rest of the week. Paracuru also has a good Carnaval for a town of its size.

Surfing can be good here year-round, and the kitesurf conditions from August to January are among the best in Brazil, with November and December optimal. The best kite spot is 4km east of the town center. Try the **Swiss Kite School** (☎ 9903 2761; www.kiteboardbrazil.com; classes per hr R$80) for classes and rentals.

SLEEPING & EATING

Pousada Villa Verde (☎ 3344 1181; Rua Professora Maria Luísa Sabóia 205; s R$40-50, d R$50-70; 🍴) This friendly place has nice, clean rooms with verandas in a lovely big green garden with huge, shady trees. It's just 150m west of the church on the central square, close to the beach.

Fórmula 1 (☎ 3344 2048; Praia da Munguba; mains R$9-19; 🕙 10am-midnight) A well-known restaurant on Paracuru's central beach, Fórmula 1 serves a variety of dishes including its specialty snails, and is also a good place just for a drink. The French owner, Michel, has seven good, large, colorful rooms (R$50 singles, R$60 to R$80 doubles) with air-con and access to a pool at his house, 2km back from the beach. This is also the site of his organic snail farm!

Paiol (☎ 3344 2890; Rua Ormezinda Sampaio 811; mains R$12-25; 🕙 11am-3am) Serves a range of pasta, pizza, seafood and meat in a pleasant courtyard setting.

GETTING THERE & AROUND

Eleven plus buses a day run to Paracuru from Fortaleza (R$9.50, two hours, 6am to 6pm).

Praia da Lagoinha

☎ 0xx85

Round the headland northwest of Paracuru (45km by road), Praia da Lagoinha has coconut palms, *jangadas* and a small, deep lagoon near the dunes. The beach is one of the best and prettiest in the state (and it has some competition). Stretching 15km to the northwest, it is still not heavily developed and is a good choice for a short visit from Fortaleza.

Milton Pousada (☎ 3363 5078; Praia da Lagoinha; s/d R$70/80; 🍴 🏊) is in a scenic location right on the beachfront, and has a popular restaurant – try the delicious fish stew. You should ask for one of the remodeled rooms.

The cliff-top **Pousada Mar à Vista** (☎ 3363 5038; www.pousadamaravista.cjb.net; Av Azevedo 170; s/d R$50/80; 🍴 🏊) has small, well-equipped rooms and a great view.

Four buses a day run to Lagoinha from Fortaleza (R$10, 2½ hours), the first at 6:30am

and the last at 5:30pm. There are also two a day (except Sunday) from Paracuru (R$4, 1½ hours).

Mundaú, Fleixeiras & Guajiru

☎ 0xx85

The beaches of Mundaú (150km from Fortaleza along Hwys CE-085 and CE-163) and Fleixeiras and Guajiru (respectively 13km and 18km east of Mundaú), are traditional fishing areas with wide stretches of beautiful sand, offshore reefs and dunes. They are increasingly popular weekend and holiday destinations from Fortaleza but still relatively little developed.

In Mundaú village the well-run **Estrela de Mundaú Hotel** (☎ 3351 9063; www.estrela.cc; Rua Vila Nova 50; r R$80; 🍴 🏊) has some rooms with sea views and a huge tropical garden with pool. English and German are spoken. There are some more basic pousadas right on the beach.

Buses leave Fortaleza bus station for Fleixeiras (R$16, three hours) and Mundaú (R$18, four hours) at 9:45am and 4pm daily.

Icaraí de Amontada

On a beautiful bay at the end of a 30km dirt road (and 195km from Fortaleza), Icaraí de Amontada is beyond the reach of Fortaleza tour buses and is a top windsurfing spot (best from July to December). It's a place to completely unwind: apart from windsurfing, the arrival of the morning fish catch is the day's main event. There's a small handful of good-standard pousadas including **Pousada Les Alizés** (☎ 0xx88-3636 3006; lesalizes@itanetce.com.br; r R$80; 🍴 🏊), with nice gardens right on the beach at the eastern end of the bay. Buses run here from Fortaleza bus station (R$14, 4½ hours, seven daily).

JERICOACOARA

☎ 0xx88 / pop 3000

Jericoacoara, more simply known as 'Jeri,' magnetizes travelers with its perfect combination of isolated location, stunning coastal scenery, enjoyable activities, good-value pousadas and restaurants, and nightlife. The village's six sandy streets are wedged between a broad beach, a series of grassy hills and the majestic Pôr do Sol (Sunset) dune. It is an easy place to make new friends and many people end up staying longer than they planned. The high season runs from July to January and it is advised to make a room reservation during those months, as the accommodations can get full.

Orientation & Information

The main streets run parallel to each other, towards the beach. In the middle is Rua Principal: buses from Fortaleza arrive at the central square here. To the east are Rua do Forró and Rua da Igreja; to the west (the dune side) are Rua São Francisco, Rua das Dunas and Rua Novo Jeri.

INTERNET ACCESS

Click Mania (Rua Principal; per hr R$7.80; ☽ 9am-midnight) Air-con.

Cyber Cachaça (Rua Principal; per hr R$6; ☽ 9am-midnight Mon-Sat, 2pm-midnight Sun) No air-con.

MONEY

Many pousadas and restaurants will accept Visa or MasterCard.

Banco do Brasil (Jijoca; ☽ ATM 6am-5pm) This is the nearest ATM and is 23km away in Jijoca. It accepts international cards. A buggy there and back should cost R$50 to R$60.

Sabor da Terra (Rua do Forró) This restaurant usually changes dollars or euros for reais, at poor rates. Knock if it isn't open.

Activities

The steady winds between July and January make Jericoacoara a top destination for windsurfing and kitesurfing, and the gigantic dunes mean good sandboarding. There are also nightly capoeira classes on the beach and decent waves for surfing. If you are of a calmer demeanor, you can visit the dunes and lakes outside town by buggy, sail on a *jangada*, take yoga classes or stroll to **Pedra Furada**, an arched rock 3km east of town.

BUGGY RIDES

Organize buggy rides through your pousada or agencies in town or the **Associação dos Bugueiros** (Buggy Drivers' Association; ☎ 3669 2284; central square, Rua Principal). The buggies take up to four passengers and prices are for the vehicle (with driver), so if you join with others it's cheaper. **Beach Sun** (☎ 8848 5955; Beco do Guaxeló) is a helpful agency that will try to organize group trips.

It's a memorable trip to the crystal-clear **Lagoa do Paraíso** and **Lagoa Azul**, inland near Jijoca. A five-hour trip costs R$120. Another good outing is to **Tatajuba**, 18km west, a fish-

ing village with a beach at the mouth of a tidal river, and a large lagoon among the dunes behind the village. There are *barracas* beside the lagoon. One of the dunes actually overtook the old Tatajuba, which had to be moved out of the way – brick by brick. You can still see evidence of where the church used to be. A five-hour Tatajuba trip costs R$180.

CAPOEIRA

Classes (R$10, 1½ hours) are held in the late afternoon on the beach followed by a sunset *roda* (open capoeira performance), which always attracts a crowd. There are also classes at 8pm nightly except Sunday at **Pousada Solar da Malhada** (☎ 3669 2094; Rua da Igreja) – all welcome.

KITESURFING

The best spot in the area is Praia do Preá, 10km east of Jeri along the beach. Here **Kite Club Preá** (☎ 3669 2359; www.kiteclubprea.com), an official IKO (International Kiteboarding Organization) center, offers classes (R$380 for four hours), equipment rental (around R$150 for four hours) and guided kiting. Clube dos Ventos (see below) also gives kite classes.

SURFING & SANDBOARDING

There are good waves for surfing (best from about March to May) right out in front of Jeri beach. **Varanasi** (☎ 3669 2252; Rua do Forró; boogie/funboard/longboard rental per hr R$10/18/20), just east from the beach, rents boards and gives classes. It also rents sandboards (R$8 per hour).

WINDSURFING

The east–west-aligned coast here brings excellent breezes almost any time of year, but July to January is best. Jeri hosts international competitions. **Clube dos Ventos** (☎ 3669 2288; www.clubventos.com; classes beginner/advanced per 1½ hr R$115/207, rentals per 3 hr/1 day/2 day R$126/154/276), on Jeri beach just east of Rua do Forró, is professional and well-equipped, though there are cheaper operators.

Tours

Apart from buggy day-trips (left) you can also take buggy or 4WD trips as far west as Parnaíba and the Lençóis Maranhenses (p597) –easier though more expensive than public transport. Good agencies to talk to are **Jeri Moon** (☎ 3669 2231; Rua da Farmacia; jeri moontour@hotmail.com), on a lane between Rua Principal and Rua do Forró and operated by the highly knowledgeable Dadinho (aka Ronaldo), and **Koala Passeios** (☎ 3621 0243; Rua do Forró). You can also organize trips from Jeri through a number of Fortaleza agencies.

Sleeping

There are dozens of pousadas and small hotels in Jericoacoara. The pousadas listed below are standouts: if they are full, ask them to suggest one of the many other fine places in town.

Pousada Calanda (☎ 3669 2285; www.pousada calanda.com; Rua das Dunas; s/d R$40/70, air-con R$50/80; 🔀 🖳) Close to the dune, this romantic pousada with a pretty garden has a relaxing charm, similar to the town itself. It serves a good breakfast and uses some solar power. English, Italian and Spanish spoken.

Pousada Atlantis (☎ 3669 2041; www.jericoacoara.tur .br/atlantis; Rua das Dunas; s/d R$50/70, with air-con R$60/80; 🔀) Immediately behind the Calanda, the Atlantis has a row of simple, well-kept rooms, each with outdoor hammock and table, looking onto a strip of leafy plants.

our pick Vila dos Ipês (☎ 3669 2241; www.vilados ipespousada.com.br; Rua São Francisco 50; s R$55-110, d R$80-160; 🔀) A charming little pousada with a palm-shaded garden a stone's throw from the beach. The bright rooms, some on two levels, have attractive wooden floors, doors and staircases, and you'll enjoy the sea view as you breakfast on the deck.

Pousada Casa do Turismo (☎ 3669 2000; www .casadoturismo.com; Rua das Dunas; s/d R$90/120; 🔀 🖳) This reasonably priced, professional pousada with a nice garden is a reliable choice for a comfortable stay.

Pousada Morada do Sol (☎ 3669 2318; www.jeri coacoara.tur.br/moradadosol; Rua das Dunas; r R$110-120; 🔀) Folksy cushions, mirrors, lamps and tiles prettify the good-sized rooms at this small new pousada. There's a neat little courtyard with a palm-thatched hangout zone.

Mosquito Blue (☎ 3669 2203; www.mosquitoblue.com .br; Rua da Farmacia; s R$215-270, d R$240-300, 🔀 🖳) On a lane off the central square, Mosquito Blue is one of Jeri's few luxury places. Rooms look out on the beach or attractive gardens with two very inviting pools. It lacks the character of most pousadas but is a good choice if you want international hotel standards.

Eating

Jeri offers a great variety of food for such a small place and a number of restaurants serve vegetarian dishes.

Café Brasil (☎ 3669 2272; sandwiches R$4-9; Beco do Guaxeló 65A; 🕙 8am-11pm Tue-Sun) In an alley between Rua Principal and Rua São Francisco, Café Brasil makes terrific pancakes, salads (R$8 to R$12), sandwiches (wholegrain if you like), cakes, coffee, juices and smoothies. Consistently some of the best food in town.

Tudo na Brasa (Rua Principal; mains R$12-25; 🕙 dinner) Always busy in the evening, Tudo na Brasa specializes in good-value barbecued beef, pork and fish.

Pimenta Tropical (☎ 9625 9303; Rua Principal; mains R$13-25; 🕙 dinner) A cheerful spot on the main street, Pimenta packs in diners for well-prepared, well-priced steaks, chicken and seafood.

our pick Restaurante Carcará (☎ 3669 2013; Rua do Forró 530; mains R$15-25; 🕙 noon-11pm Mon-Sat) The best meals in town are here at this inviting and romantic spot back up Rua do Forró. The menu ranges over seafood, pasta, steaks and salads, and the fish and prawn *moquecas* (Bahian fish stews cooked in a clay pot with *dendê* oil, coconut milk and spicy peppers) are superb.

Pizza Nômade (☎ 3669 2103; Rua da Farmacia; pizza & pasta R$16-28; 🕙 6pm-midnight) Jeri has a glut of pizzerias, most of similar quality, but this venerated spot, opposite the Mosquito Blue, wins for its wood-oven pies, chilled ambience and good music.

Entertainment

Everything starts – and frequently ends – at **Planeta Jerii** (Rua Principal), near the beach. Things don't get going until at least 10pm, the *caipirinhas* (the unofficial Brazilian national drink: *cachaça* with crushed lime, sugar and ice; R$3) are divine, and the music runs the gamut from hip-hop to samba. It's also a fine place to learn the local rules for snooker. Sky Restaurante in front of Planeta Jerii is open from 11am and may have live music in the evening. Nocturnal cocktail carts parked on the street here provide an alternative source of inebriation with concoctions like *maracujaroska* (passionfruit and vodka).

Past midnight the late-night crowd moves on to dance at **Bar do Forró** (Rua do Forró; 🕙 Wed & Sat) or the reggae/electronic **Mama África** (Rua Nova Jeri; admission R$3-7; 🕙 Tue, Thu & Sun).

Getting There & Away

Buses to Fortaleza leave from Pousada Casa do Turismo at 2pm and 10:30pm daily (R$35.50, seven hours), and at 7am (R$50, six hours) daily except during the low season from mid-March to June. You can buy tickets in advance at the Casa do Turismo and it's advisable to do so.

If you are coming to Jeri by non-4WD car, leave it parked in Jijoca, where some of the pousada owners can keep an eye on it. The ride to Jericoacoara – over and around sweeping dunes, lagoons and flat scrub terrain – is beautiful, but very hard on people and machines.

Moving on westward from Jeri, the easiest and costliest option is a tour (p579). Second easiest is to get a buggy ride about 40km along the coast to Camocim, where you can pick up a bus to Parnaíba or Sobral. The buggy will be about R$200 for up to four people. Thirdly, you can take the 10:30pm Fortaleza-bound bus as far as Jijoca (R$5), then find the minibus that's going to Sobral (R$25, three hours) and snooze inside it till it leaves at 2am (not Sunday). Sobral has bus connections to Ubajara, Teresina, Camocim and Parnaíba. Finally, a 4WD passenger truck and/or Jeep leave for Camocim (R$25) early in the morning (4:30am to 6:30am), Monday to Friday, from Rua Principal. The Jeep takes 1½ hours along the beach; the truck takes about three hours inland.

Coming to Jeri from the west, you have the same options in reverse. The 4WD trucks leave Camocim between 9am and 11am; the Sobral–Jijoca minibus departs from near Sobral bus station about 10:30am (not Sunday).

CAMOCIM

☎ 0xx88 / pop 46,000

Camocim is a low-key fishing port and market town near the mouth of the Rio Coreaú in northwestern Ceará, 40km west of Jericoacoara near the Piauí border. After Jericoacoara's blissed-out traveler vibe, Camocim is a reintroduction to the rest of Brazil.

Just a short distance from town, you can sip coconuts while tanning at **Praia Barreiras**, **Praia do Farol**, **Praia Caraúbas** or **Praia de Maceió**. However, for the great majority of travelers, Camocim is just a stop on the road.

Information

Banco do Brasil (Rua José de Alencar; ⏰ 10am-3pm Mon-Fri, ATM 7am-8pm daily) Exchange and ATM.

Ilha Digital (Av Beira Mar; internet free; ⏰ 8am-8pm) Opposite Hotel Ilha.

Inc-Camocim (☎ 3621 6800; www.incomingcamocim .com.br; Rua Alcindo Rocha 56; ⏰ 8am-6pm Mon-Fri, 8am-noon Sat) This helpful agency can help you to maneuver through a region with little public transportation.

Sleeping & Eating

Hotel Ilha (☎ 3621 1570; www.hotelilhadoamor.com .br; Av Beira Mar 2081; r R$50-75; 🖵 🖭) The dated interior may need a bit of renovation, but, hey, you're in Camocim. The Ilha is spacious, with comfortable rooms set around a pool.

O Fortim (Av Beira Mar; mains R$12-28; ⏰ 11am-9pm Mon-Sat) This simple restaurant on the waterfront, 650m from Hotel Ilha, has excellent and affordable fresh seafood dishes.

Getting There & Away

From Camocim's **bus station** (☎ 3621 0028; Praça Sinhá Trévia) buses run to Parnaíba (R$15, 2½ hours, 1am and 3:45pm), Sobral (R$12.50, 2½ hours, five daily) and Fortaleza (R$35, seven hours, four daily).

A 4WD truck and/or Jeep leave the Mercado Central for Jericoacoara (R$25, 1½ to three hours) between 9am and 11am Monday to Friday. Or you can hire a beach buggy in Camocim for the ride to Jericoacoara. Prices go up to R$200 but are negotiable.

SOBRAL

☎ 0xx88 / pop 170,000

Although Sobral is an industrial center of some importance and has a spiffy new bus station and riverside walkway along the Rio Acaraú, it's a hot, characterless place where you don't need to do more than change buses.

There are buses to Camocim (R$12.50, 2½ hours, five daily, 5:30am to 7:30pm), Fortaleza (R$22, four hours, eight or more daily), Parnaíba (R$35, five hours, three daily), Ubajara ($12, two hours, four daily) and points beyond.

SERRA DE BATURITÉ

☎ 0xx85

The interior of Ceará is not limited to the harsh landscapes of the *sertão*. There are also ranges of hills breaking up the monotony of the sun-scorched land. The Serra de Baturité is the range closest to Fortaleza – an island of green, with coffee, bananas and flowers cultivated around the cliffs and jagged spines of the hills. The climate is tempered by rain and the evenings are cool.

The two prettiest villages on the heights of the *serra* are Guaramiranga and Pacoti, 99km and 92km respectively from Fortaleza and reached by roads that wind uphill between lushly vegetated slopes with flowering trees. Everywhere you turn here seems to have a fantastic view. The villages are dotted with prettily painted houses and the tropical flowers cultivated here add further splashes of color. A visit here is good for a change of temperature, beautiful scenery, and walks and horseback rides along the many trails. A paved road leads to Pico Alto (1115m), the highest point in the range, 13km from Guaramiranga. When the morning mist clears the views over the *sertão* from here are fantastic.

Sleeping & Eating

There are plenty of places to stay and eat in Guaramiranga at a range of budgets, and other lodgings dotted around the countryside. As the hills are a popular weekend retreat from Fortaleza, prices can go up from Friday to Sunday. Many hotels offer lunch and dinner as well as breakfast.

Hotel Senac Guaramiranga (☎ /fax 3321 1106; Sítio Guaramiranga; s R$90-120, d R$115-150; ✗ ☒) The Senac doubles as a training center for hotel staff in Guaramiranga. It has ample rooms with wooden shutters, and in most cases verandas, in luxuriant grounds with a good pool. It's 750m from the main street, up Rua Matos Brito.

Estância Vale das Flores (☎ 3325 1233; www.valedas flores.com.br; Sítio São Francisco; r R$100; ✗ ☒) An attractive country hotel close to Pacoti, Vale das Flores offers plenty to do, with a swimming pool, a fishing lake, games and horse rental.

Hofbräuhaus (☎ 328 0004; www.hofbrauhaus-brasil .com; Estrada de Aratuba; d R$100-180; ✗) The mountain chalets of Hofbräuhaus are your little bit of Deutschland in Ceará. Each of the 20-odd chalets was designed by a different Ceará architect/artist. With hearty food and plentiful beers, a stay at Hofbräuhaus makes for a fun change of pace. It's about 20km from Guaramiranga, past the village of Mulungu.

Getting There & Away

Buses to Pacoti (R$9.50, three hours) and Guaramiranga (R$11.50, 3½ hours) leave Fortaleza's bus station at 5am, 8am, 1pm and 4:30pm.

PARQUE NACIONAL DE UBAJARA

☎ 0xx88

The entrance to this **national park** (admission R$2; ✇ 8am-5pm Tue-Sun) is 3km from the small town of Ubajara, 325km west of Fortaleza. The main attractions are giant caves, the cable car down to them, and walks in the surrounding forest. At 850m above sea level, the surrounding area has relatively cool temperatures that provide a welcome respite from the searing heat of the *sertão*.

Caves

Nine chambers with strange limestone formations extend more than 500m into the side of a mountain. The main formations seen inside the caves are **Pedra do Sino** (Bell Stone), **Salas da Rosa** (Rose Rooms), **Sala do Cavalo** (Horse Room) and **Sala dos Retratos** (Portrait Room). A **cable car** (per person each way R$2; ✇ 9am-2:30pm) makes the descent from the park entrance to the cave quick and easy. Last entry to the cave is at 2pm and the last cable car up is at 2:30pm. But if you fancy a beautiful hike take the 7km trail down to the caves via two waterfalls and a lookout point. Hikers must be accompanied by a park guide (included in the park admission fee), leaving from the entrance at 8am, 9am and 10am. Wear sturdy footwear and take enough to drink. You can take the cable car back up. You can also just walk the first, mainly flat, half of the trail, including the waterfalls and lookout. Guides are available for this till early afternoon.

Sleeping & Eating

Sítio do Alemão (☎ 9961 4645; www.sitio-do-alemao.20fr .com; Sítio Santana; s R$20-40, d R$30-60; ✗) There are wonderful vistas over the *sertão* from this property, 4km from Ubajara and 1.5km from the park entrance. It's run by a German-Brazilian couple who can provide loads of information about spectacular local walks and other attractions. Trips to the beautiful Cachoeira do Frade, a series of waterfalls in a canyon 25km away, and to the Parque Nacional de Sete Cidades (p587), are also offered. The chalets, in lushly vegetated grounds, are simple but well kept.

Neblina Park Hotel (☎ /fax 3634 1270; Estrada do Teleférico; s R$60-120, d R$80-150; ✗ ☒) Just 400m from the park entrance, this larger hotel has rooms ranging from small and dingy to bigger and better with their own patios. The pool is nice after a strenuous hike.

Pousada Gruta de Ubajara (☎ 3634 1375; mains for 2 R$15; ☺ lunch & dinner) Opposite the Neblina Park, the restaurant here serves excellent-value chicken and *churrasco* (grilled meat).

Getting There & Around
Buses leave Ubajara for Fortaleza (R$27 to R$31, six hours, eight daily) via Sobral, and for Piripiri (R$11, two hours) and Teresina (R$32, six hours) at 7:30am and 11:30am. There are more connections from Tianguá, on Hwy BR-222 17km north of Ubajara. Frequent minibuses link Tianguá to Ubajara; a taxi is R$25 to R$30.

To reach the park entrance from Ubajara, either walk or take a taxi (R$10).

JUAZEIRO DO NORTE
☎ 0xx88 / pop 232,000

Juazeiro do Norte (Map p567) 528km from Fortaleza in the deep south of Ceará, is a magnet for followers of Padre Cícero (1844–1934), who lived here in the early 20th century and became a controversial figure of the *sertão*. Not only was he a priest with several miracles to his credit and a great record of care for the poor, he also exercised a strong political influence. His astonishing rise to fame started when an elderly woman received the host from him at Mass and claimed that it had miraculously turned to blood. Soon he was being credited with all kinds of miracles, and thousands of his followers settled in Juazeiro. Padre Cícero and his followers were later drawn into the rivalry between different factions of the Ceará elite, with Juazeiro becoming a scene of armed conflict in the so-called Sedition of Juazeiro (1913–14). Despite the Catholic Church's unwillingness to beatify Padre Cícero, the adoration of his followers is as strong as ever. Some two million pilgrims come to Juazeiro every year.

Though the town itself is not particularly attractive, Juazeiro lies close to the main roads across the *sertão*, and the Cícero phenomenon makes it an interesting detour.

Sights
On the hill above town, the Colina do Horto, accessible either by road or along a path laid out like a cross, is the colossal **statue of Padre Cícero** (25m), built in 1969 and claimed to be the third-highest concrete statue in the world – only beaten by

Cristo Redentor on Corcovado (Rio) and the Statue of Liberty (New York). Nearby are a small chapel and a building filled with wooden and wax replicas of every conceivable body part – offerings that represent areas of the body supposedly cured by Padre Cícero's miraculous powers. **Padre Cícero's tomb** (Praça do Socorro) is beside the Capela NS do Perpétua Socorro.

If you are interested in *literatura de cordel*, popular pamphlet literature for the masses with woodcut illustrations and verses on topics such as biographies of famous figures, love stories, opinions and views, visit the **Gráfica de Literatura de Cordel** (cnr Av Castelo Branco & Rua José de Alencar; ☺ 7-11am & 1-5pm Mon-Fri, 8am-noon Sat), a workshop where you can see the pamphlets being produced for sale.

Festivals & Events
The best time to witness the devotion Padre Cícero inspires is during the festivals and pilgrimages. On March 24, the **Aniversário do Padre Cícero** celebrates Padre Cícero in legend and song. The commemoration of his death takes place on July 20. The **Dia do Romeiro e Festa do Padre Cícero**, November 1, sees 200,000 worshippers processing from the city's Igreja Matriz to his tomb. The four days leading up to it are filled with *romarias* (pilgrimage processions).

Sleeping & Eating
There is no lack of accommodations, except during the main festivals.

Hotel San Felipe (☎ 3511 7904; www.sanfelipehotel .com.br; Rua Dr Floro Bartolomeu 285; s R$36-67, d R$53-84; ☒) This centrally located hotel has comfortable rooms at a range of prices.

Panorama (☎ 3512 -3100; www.panoramahotel .com .br; Rua Santo Agostinho 58; s/d R$87/129; ☒ ☒) The Panorama is older but nicer, with a good restaurant and bar.

Mão de Vaca (☎ 3512 2543; Rua Rui Barbosa 25; mains R$12-26; ☺ 11am-3pm & 6pm-midnight Mon-Fri, 11am-midnight Sat) Mão de Vaca is recommended for regional food at a decent price.

Getting There & Away
From the **bus station** (☎ 571 2868; Rua Delmiro Gouvéia) there are 11 daily departures for Fortaleza (R$52 to R$59, 11 hours), and daily buses to all other major cities in the Northeast.

PIAUÍ

Piauí, one of the largest states in the Northeast, boasts several fantastic natural attractions, including the Delta do Parnaíba, the Parque Nacional de Sete Cidades and the Parque Nacional da Serra da Capivara (one of the top prehistoric sites in South America). Colonial settlement in Piauí began in the arid southern *sertão* and gradually moved north toward the coast, creating an oddly shaped territory with underdeveloped infrastructure. Today, Piauí is Brazil's poorest state.

If you're heading into the interior, the best time for festivals and bearable temperatures is July and August. The worst time, unless you want to cook yourself, is between September and December. The climate on the coast is kept cool(er) by sea breezes.

TERESINA

☎ 0xx86 / pop 773,000

Teresina, the flat and sun-baked capital of Piauí, is famed as the hottest city in Brazil. Founded in 1852, it was Brazil's first planned city. It has a lot of hospitals and, as a regional medical center, receives patients from neighboring states. However, most people who have a choice in the matter don't make it to Teresina or, if they do, are simply in transit.

Locals seem to be interested in meeting foreigners and they instantly warm to discussion of the weather, especially of their favorite topic: *o calor* (the heat). If you are keen to see a provincial Brazilian city unadulterated by tourism, this is your chance; otherwise, keep moving.

Information

Banco do Brasil (Rua Álvaro Mendes; ☒ 10am-4pm Mon-Fri, ATMs 6am-10pm daily) Just one of the ATMs here accepts international cards.

Café Paris (Av Frei Serafim; internet per hr R$2; ☒ 9am-10:30pm)

Piemtur (www.piemtur.pi.giv.br) The state tourism department's website has some useful information in English.

Setdetur (☎ 3221 9502; Central de Artesanato, Praça Dom Pedro II; ☒ 8am-6pm Mon-Fri, 9am-3pm Sat) Small information desk with erratically present staff.

Sights & Activities

The **Central de Artesanato** (☎ 221 3368; Praça Dom Pedro II; ☒ 8am-6pm Mon-Fri, 9am-3pm Sat) has crafts from all over Piauí and is Teresina's main focus of interest for visitors. It is pleasant to browse among the shops around a broad courtyard, selling small sculptures, leather articles, extremely intricate lacework, colorful hammocks, opals and soapstone from the town of Pedro Segundo. There are also liqueurs and sweet preserves made from such native plants as *genipapo* (genipap), *caju* (cashew), *buriti* (a palm-tree fruit) and *maracujá* (passionfruit). There's a café here and the courtyard is enlivened by sculptures including an interesting iron creation of a prehistoric giant sloth.

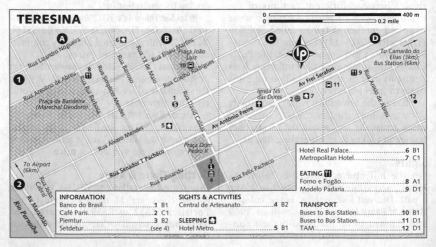

TERESINA

INFORMATION			SIGHTS & ACTIVITIES			TRANSPORT		
Banco do Brasil	1	B1	Central de Artesanato	4	B2	Buses to Bus Station	10	B1
Café Paris	2	C1				Buses to Bus Station	11	D1
Piemtur	3	B2	SLEEPING			TAM	12	D1
Setdetur	(see 4)		Hotel Metro	5	B1			

SLEEPING		
Hotel Real Palace	6	B1
Metropolitan Hotel	7	C1

EATING		
Forno e Fogão	8	A1
Modelo Padaria	9	D1

To Camarão do Elias (3km); Bus Station (6km)

To Airport (6km)

Praça da Bandeira (Marechal Deodoro)

Praça Dom Pedro II

Praça João Luiz

Igreja NS das Dores

Rio Parnaíba

Sleeping

Hotel Metro (☎ 3226 1010; metrohotel@webone.com.br; Rua 13 de Maio 85; s/d R$55/65; 🌊) Rooms are bland but staff friendly and the breakfast sizable at this nicely central hotel.

Hotel Real Palace (☎ 2107 2700; www.realpalace hotel.com.br; Rua Areolino de Abreu 1217; s/d R$89/109; 🌊 🌊) This is a smooth midrange option that guarantees a comfortable stay in central Teresina and has a good restaurant.

Metropolitan Hotel (☎ 3216 8000; metropolitan hotel.com.br; Av Frei Serafim 1696; s/d from R$275/330; 🌊 📶 🌊) This glassy modern high-rise is the poshest place in town, offering a variety of suites and luxury rooms, two restaurants and three bars. Promotional rates can cut prices by 40% during slow seasons.

Eating

Modelo Padaria (☎ 3221 8595; Av Frei Serafim 1910; per kg R$18; 🕑 6:30am-10pm) The per-kilo selection is OK (if less appetizing by evening); the desserts are very tempting.

Forno e Fogão (☎ 3222 9700; Luxor Piauí Hotel, Praça Marechal Deodoro 310; buffet R$18; 🕑 1-3pm) The gigantic buffet lunch here is excellent value.

Camarão do Elias (☎ 3232 5025; Av Pedro Almeida 457; mains R$18-36; 🕑 5:30pm-1am Mon-Sat, 11am-4pm Sun) A 10-minute taxi ride east of the center (about R$10), Camarão do Elias is famed for its original seafood recipes. Try the house specialty *moqueca á moda do Elias*, a delicious fish stew with lemon sauce, garlic and vegetables.

Getting There & Away

AIR

The **airport** (☎ 3225 2947) is on Avenida Centenário, 6km north of the center. Direct flights go to Fortaleza and Brasília.

Gol (☎ 0300-789 2121; airport)

TAM (☎ 3221 1912; Rua Félix Pacheco 2008)

BUS

Teresina's **bus station** (☎ 3222 8276) is 6km southeast of the center on Hwy BR-343. Destinations include Belém (R$98, 18 hours, 11 daily), Fortaleza (R$52 to R$82, 10 hours, nine daily, via Sobral), Parnaíba (R$42 to R$57, six hours, eight daily), Piripiri (R$22, three hours, 23 daily), São Luís (R$46, seven hours, eight daily) and Ubajara (R$32, six hours, noon).

Getting Around

Any bus marked 'Praça João Luiz' (R$1.50), across the road outside the bus station, will take you to the center – this is OK if you arrive at night, when it's cooler, but during the day it can be unbearably hot. Taxis cost around R$16. Buses 601 or 602 from Praça João Luiz or Av Frei Serafim go out to the bus station.

PARNAÍBA

☎ 0xx86 / pop 143,000

Parnaíba (Map p567) was a major port until its river silted up (the port was moved to nearby Luís Correia) and its carnaúba-palm wax industry died when artificial waxes were invented for cosmetics and car polish. These days it is a charmingly peaceful town, with its warm, sedate evenings only interrupted by the occasional sound of a truck or children's fireworks. It's a key stepping stone on the coastal route from Jericoacoara to the Lençóis Maranhenses, and the starting point for trips into the beautiful Delta do Parnaíba.

Orientation

Visitors gravitate to Porto das Barcas on the Rio Igaraçu waterfront, a complex of craft shops, galleries, restaurants and travel agencies in converted 18th- and 19th-century warehouses. The main street, Av Presidente Vargas, runs 1km south from here, with commercial streets to its west and residential streets to its east. The bus station is 5km south of the center.

Information

INTERNET ACCESS

Terr@ (Av Presidente Vargas 205; per hr R$3; 🕑 8am-9pm) Good facilities; 250m from Porto das Barcas.

MONEY

Bradesco (Av Presidente Vargas 403; 🕑 10am-3pm Mon-Fri, ATMs 6am-10pm daily) Does currency exchange and has ATMs accepting international cards.

TOURIST INFORMATION

Piemtur (☎ 3321 1532; Porto das Barcas; 🕑 7am-7pm Mon-Sat Jan & Jul, to 1pm Mon-Sat other months) Staff here are friendly and willing. Private agencies have more practical information about excursions.

TRAVEL AGENCIES

Casa do Turismo (☎ 3321 1243; www.deltaparnaiba .com; Porto das Barcas; 🕑 8am-10pm Mon-Sat, 7:30-10am & 5-10pm Sun) This very helpful agency offers boat tours of the delta and 4WD trips to the Lençóis Maranhenses, Sete Cidades and Jericoacoara, at reasonable prices (around R$450

CEARÁ, PIAUÍ & MARANHÃO

for a one-day trip to Jericoacoara or Caburé for up to seven people, for example). It will try to combine lone travelers with groups if you like. English and German spoken.

Ecoadventure Tour (☎ 3323 9595; www.ecoadventure .tur.br; Porto das Barcas)

Morais Brito (☎ 3321 1969; www.deltadoparnaiba.com .br; Porto das Barcas)

Sights

DELTA DO PARNAÍBA

The **Delta of the Rio Parnaíba** (sometimes called the Delta das Américas) is a 2700-sq-km expanse of islands, beaches, lagoons, channels, sand dunes and mangrove forest, teeming with wildlife. Around 65% of its area is in the state of Maranhão, but the easiest access is from Parnaíba. Tour boats leave from Porto dos Tatus, 14km north of Parnaíba. Two types of day-trips lasting eight or nine hours are offered by the agencies at Porto das Barcas. The better option for getting to know the delta is the small-boat trips costing R$50 per person (minimum R$200) including transfer to and from Porto dos Tatus but not including food or drink. You should see caimans, monkeys, iguanas and if you're lucky, highly colorful red ibis (*guará* in Portuguese). There's usually a beach stop and the option of a seafood meal at a small waterside restaurant. Casa do Turismo (p585) is a good agency to organize this trip. The other option, offered by all Porto das Barcas agencies, is larger boats holding 40 to 80 people. These go daily in high season (Christmas to Carnaval, July and August), but otherwise Saturday only, and have more of a party atmosphere. The price of R$40, plus R$10 for transfers to/from Porto dos Tatus, includes meals.

Sleeping

Residencial Pousada (☎ 3322 2931; www.residencial pousada.com.br; Rua Almirante Sampaio 375; s/d R$26/37, with air-con R$32/47; 🅿 🖵) A friendly budget spot in a neat, cottagelike building, one block east of Av Presidente Vargas. The rooms are large and have high ceilings.

Hotel Cívico (☎ 3322 2470; www.hotelcivico.com .br; Av Chagas Rodrigues 474; s/d R$55/80, with air-con R$75/105; 🅿 🖵) Just off the south end of Av Presidente Vargas, the well-run Cívico has pleasantly campy 1970s décor, a big buffet breakfast and an attractive pool area, and it slashes prices in the low season.

Refúgio Ecológica Ilha do Caju (☎ 3321 1308; www.ilhadocaju.com.br; office Av Presidente Vargas 235,

Parnaíba; r R$160-195, chalets R$220) This famous pousada, on the Ilha do Caju, is three hours by boat from Parnaíba. The 100-sq-km island has been owned for several generations by a family of English origin and is now an Environmental Protection Area. With its dunes, beaches, forests, mangroves, lakes and abundant varied wildlife, it's a great place to experience the Parnaíba delta to the full. If you are going all this way, you may as well opt for the more comfortable chalets. Boat transfers, activities (horseback riding, guided walks, wildlife spotting, boat trips), meals other than breakfast and an environmental charge are not included in room rates – budget around R$80 to R$120 per person per day for these.

Eating

Sabor e Arte (☎ 3321 1234; Porto das Barcas; dishes R$8-30; 🕑 11am-last customer, closed some Sun low season) This Porto das Barcas favorite is a relaxed place with interesting original art on the walls. The dishes themselves are works of art – beautifully presented, delicious seafood and meat dishes. The owners also run the Casa do Turismo agency two doors away.

Caranguejo Expresso (Rua Quentinha Peres 64; mains R$9-25; 🕑 11am-11pm) Locally famous for its enormous and delicious *torta de caranguejo* (crab omelette; R$22). Don't expect *expresso* service but do expect it to be worth the wait. Take mosquito repellent in the evening.

Shopping

Porto das Barcas is a good place to shop for Piauí handicrafts such as hammocks, carnaúba-palm bags, soapstone carvings, handmade leather sandals, and opals. **Cerámica Serra da Capivara** (☎ 3321 2718; Rua Oscar Clark 555), just off Av Vargas, specializes in the attractive Serra da Capivara ceramics.

Getting There & Around

From the **bus station** (☎ 3323 7300; Av Pinheiro Machado) there are services to Fortaleza (R$55 to R$92, nine hours, three daily, via Camocim and/or Sobral), São Luís (R$51 to R$56, 11 hours, 6:30am and 8:15pm), Teresina (R$42 to R$57, six hours, eight daily via Piripiri), and Tutóia (R$12, three hours, five a day Monday to Saturday, two on Sunday). You can buy tickets for these destinations (except Tutóia) at **Clip** (☎ 3322 3129; Av Presidente Vargas 274).

Any city bus (R$1) outside the bus station will take you to Av Presidente Vargas. A taxi should be R$10. Going back, you can catch them on Praça Santo Antônio, three blocks west of southern Av Presidente Vargas.

TO/FROM THE LENÇÓIS MARANHENSES

The adventurous and fun direct route to the Lençóis Maranhenses (p597) involves getting to Tutóia, 65km west of Parnaíba, then via rough tracks to the town of Barreirinhas or along the beach to the tiny village of Caburé. To Tutóia, the options are bus or a chartered boat through the delta costing around R$450 for the five- to six-hour trip (ask at the Casa do Turismo, p585). From Tutóia, passenger trucks run to Paulino Neves and from there to Barreirinhas. You would be lucky to get through in one day but there are accommodations in Tutóia and Paulino Neves. Alternatively, Parnaíba agencies offer 4WD trips to Barreirinhas or Caburé for around R$450 per vehicle.

AROUND PARNAÍBA

Piauí's 66km coastline is the result of a land swap with Ceará in the 19th century. There are some fine beaches, many of which are fast being developed. **Praia Pedra do Sal**, 15km northeast of Parnaíba on Ilha Grande Santa Isabel, is quite built-up but is still a good beach, divided by rocks into a calm section suitable for swimming and a rough section preferred by surfers. **Lagoa do Portinho** is a lagoon surrounded by dunes about 14km east of Parnaíba on the road to Luís Correia. It's a popular spot for swimming, boating, sailing and fishing.

The busiest beaches east of Luís Correia are **Praia do Coqueiro** and **Praia Atalaia**. Coqueiro has been discovered by kitesurfers. Atalaia is very popular on weekends and is lined with bars selling drinks and seafood. **Carnaubinhas**, 15km east of Luís Correia, is another fine beach but much more tranquil. **Lagoa do Sobradinho**, 6km inland here, is renowned for its shifting sands that bury surrounding trees. **Macapá**, 43km east of Luís Correia, has a few pousadas and is a possible base for exploring the deserted beaches further east – including **Barra Grande** (considered by many to be the pick of the bunch) and, just before the border with Ceará, **Cajueiro da Praia**. Adventurous travelers should bring their hammocks if they want to stay at these beaches.

Aimberê Eco Resort (☎ 3366 1144; www.aimbere ecoresorthotel.com.br; Rua Projetada s/n, Praia do Coqueiro; s/d R$130/150; ✷ ☒) is a former beach mansion that's been transformed into a resort. It has good views and is a stylish way to experience the coastline of Piauí.

Local buses to Luís Correia leave Parnaíba's Praça Santo Antônio about hourly, but the best way to get around this coast is in your own vehicle or a taxi, or to take a tour. A taxi from Parnaíba to Praia Atalaia costs R$30.

PARQUE NACIONAL DE SETE CIDADES
☎ 0xx86

Sete Cidades is a small national park (62 sq km) with bizarre rock formations that some have claimed are *sete cidades* (seven cities) left behind by some mysterious long-departed culture (aliens, Vikings etc). The place doesn't need such fantasies to make it worth visiting, however. The rock formations are indeed fantastic – some look like giant turtle shells, others resemble a castle, an elephant, a map of Brazil or the head of emperor Dom Pedro II – but there are also superb vistas over a landscape that combines caatinga and cerrado (savanna) vegetation. There are some 1500 intriguing rock paintings between 3000 and 5000 years old, wildlife that includes marmosets, small rodents called *mocós* that like to pose for photos, tarantulas and (we're told) rattlesnakes, and two delectable natural bathing pools.

The park **entrance** (☎ 3343 1342; admission R$3; ☽ 8am-5pm) is 190km northeast of Teresina, 26km northeast of Piripiri and 8km north by paved road off Hwy BR-222. From the entrance it's another 5km (unpaved) to the visitors' center, where you must get a guide. Guides cost R$15 for a three-hour tour by vehicle; or it's R$30 for a six-hour walking tour or R$20 for a three-hour circuit on not very good bicycles (both up to six people). Shortened tours are also available by foot (R$20, four hours) or bike (R$15, two hours). Be sure to bring insect repellent, water, a hat and sunscreen.

Sleeping & Eating

Califórnia Hotel (☎ 3276 1645; Rua Antenor Freitas 546, Piripiri; s/d R$35/45; ✷) A modern hotel with well-kept rooms, the California is the place to stay in Piripiri. It's 700m from the bus station and two blocks off the central square.

Parque Hotel Sete Cidades (☎ 3223 3366; www
.hotelsetecidades.com.br; camp sites per person R$10, s/d
R$45/57; ✷ ⚊) This good-value hotel inside
the park, 2km from the visitors' center, has
an inviting natural pool and its own restaurant. It's a great place to crash after a hot
day in the park.

Getting There & Around

A taxi from Piripiri costs R$40 to or from
the park, or R$80 round-trip including a
three-hour driving tour of the park. A mototaxi is R$15 and R$30 respectively. There is
no public transport to the park.

From **Piripiri bus station** (☎ 3276 2333) there
are buses to Fortaleza (R$38, seven hours,
six daily, via Tianguá and Sobral), Parnaíba
(R$24, three hours, seven daily), São Luís
(R$74, 11 hours, 8pm and 12:30am), Tere-
sina (R$22, three hours, up to 22 daily) and
Ubajara (R$14, two hours, 3pm).

PARQUE NACIONAL DA SERRA DA CAPIVARA

In the south of Piauí, near the small town of
São Raimundo Nonato, the dramatic rocky
landscape of the 1300-sq-km **Parque Nacional
da Serra da Capivara** (admission R$3; ⏰ 6am-6pm) con-
tains over 30,000 rock paintings – claimed to
be the greatest concentration on the planet. It
has 800 archaeological sites and has yielded
what's considered the oldest evidence of
human presence in the Americas, at least
50,000 years ago. The dates put forward by

researchers here were revolutionary in the archaeological world because they predated other
'earliest' finds by about 30,000 years, but they
are now gaining increasing acceptance. The
rock art is mostly 6000 to 12,000 years old and
includes depictions of deer and caimans, and
people dancing, hunting and having sex.

Over R$50 million has spent on developing
the park's facilities and the museum in São
Raimundo, and a surprising number of visitors do find their way to these distant parts.
The park has wooden walkways, disabled access to many sites, good vehicle tracks, walking trails, a visitors' center, lookout points and
helpful bilingual signs. The landscape is one
of canyons and rocky outcrops amid classic
caatinga vegetation. Some rock-art clusters
are on cliffs 100m high.

Up to 128 sites are open to the public,
organized into 14 circuits helping visitors
appreciate the landscape, geology, vegetation and wildlife as well as the evidence of
ancient humanity. The outstanding sites
include the **Boqueirão da Pedro Furada**, where
remains of cooking fires provided evidence of
human presence 50,000 years ago (this site is
equipped with illumination for night visits);
and the **Baixão do Sítio do Meio** and **Desfiladero da
Capivara**, both with a wealth of rock art.

A local guide is obligatory for visiting the
park, costing R$45 per day for up to 10 people.
It's best to organize a guide through your
accommodations in São Raimundo Nonato.
Don't miss the recently modernized **Museu do**

THE EINSTEIN MONKEYS OF PIAUÍ

In the deep, deep south of Piauí, the Parque Nacional das Nascentes do Rio Parnaíba (Parnaíba
River Headwaters National Park), Brazil's biggest national park outside the Amazon region, was
only declared in 2002. The park's beautiful landscape of red rock mesas rising from cerrado
grasslands straddles neighboring Maranhão, Tocantins and Bahia states as well. It is already
celebrated as the home not only to a sizable population of the endangered hyacinth macaw (a
gorgeous, large, deep blue–colored bird), but also to the most technologically advanced monkeys on the planet.

Brown capuchin monkeys here, dubbed 'Einstein monkeys' by scientists, have the intelligence
to select exceptionally hard igneous stones from a river bed – sometimes half their own weight –
and drag them hundreds of meters to a clearing where they use them to crack open their favored
diet of palm nuts by slamming them down on the nuts from above their heads. No such advanced
tool use by monkeys anywhere else on the planet is known to scientists.

The monkeys, macaws and plenty more wildlife can all be seen at Hyacinth Camps, a comfortable three-site lodge in the park. Visits are available through **Tropical Nature Travel** (www
.tropicalnaturetravel.com): a five-day stay costs US$1296 per person, based on double occupancy. The
price includes transfers from Barreiras, some 300km south in Bahia state, which can be reached
by bus or flight from Brasília.

Homem Americano (☎ 3582 1612; www.fumdham.org.br; Bairro Campestre; admission R$6; ☯ 9am-5pm Tue-Sun) in São Raimundo, with exhibits from the park including the oldest human skull found in the Americas, 12,000 years old.

São Raimundo has half a dozen hotels and pousadas, the best value being **Hotel Serra da Capivara** (☎ /fax 3582 1389; Santa Luzia; s/d R$61/76; ☒ ☒), 2km north of the center on Hwy PI-140, with rustic but comfortable facilities including a restaurant.

Another attraction of the area is the appealing ceramics decorated with designs from Capivara rock art, produced by the villagers of Barreirinho just outside the park.

Fourteen daily buses make the 509km odyssey from Teresina to São Raimundo Nonato (R$58, nine hours). There are also buses from Petrolina in Pernambuco, 350km east, to which you can fly from Recife, Salvador or São Paulo.

MARANHÃO

The atmosphere-laden colonial city of São Luís and the wild natural beauty of the Parque Nacional dos Lençóis Maranhenses have put the Northeast's farthest-flung state firmly on the travel map. The coastal route from Jericoacoara (Ceará) to the Lençóis Maranhenses is an adventure in itself.

Although the southern and eastern areas of Maranhão are characterized by vast expanses of *babaçu* palms and typical *sertão* landscapes, the western and northwestern regions of the state merge into humid Amazon rain forests.

SÃO LUÍS

☎ 0xx98 / pop 954,000

The historic center of São Luís is an enchanting neighborhood of steamy cobbled streets and pastel-colored colonial mansions, some handsomely restored, some still deep in tropical decay, and 1100 of them on the Unesco World Heritage list. It's a charming area with a unique atmosphere, and also has one of the best concentrations of museums, galleries and craft stores in the Northeast. But Maranhão's capital is more than just this colonial heart. São Luís is also the reggae capital of Brazil, it is home to the highly colorful and unusual Bumba Meu Boi festivities, and it has a lively beach scene.

The trip across Baía de São Marcos to Alcântara, an impressive historic town slipping regally into decay, is an added reason to put São Luís on your itinerary.

History

São Luís is the only city in Brazil that was founded by the French. In 1612 three French ships sailed for Maranhão to try to commandeer a piece of South America. Once established at São Luís, the French used the local Indian population, the Tupinambá, to attack tribes around the mouth of the Amazon to try to expand their foothold in the region. But the French colony could not hold off the imminent Portuguese attack, which came in 1614. Within a year, the French fled and before long the Portuguese had 'pacified' the Tupinambá.

After a brief Dutch occupation between 1641 and 1644, São Luís developed slowly as a port for the export of sugar, and later cotton. Despite relatively poor land, the plantation owners prospered and by the early 19th century São Luís was one of the wealthiest cities in Brazil. All this was achieved through the labor of African slaves and today the city has the third highest Afro-Brazilian population in the country (after Rio and Salvador).

When demand for São Luís' crops slackened later in the 19th century, the city went into a long decline, but the economy has been stimulated by several megaprojects in the past two decades. In the 1980s a big port complex was constructed at Itaqui, just west of São Luís, to export the mineral riches of the Carajás in neighboring Pará state, and Alcoa built an enormous aluminum-processing plant on the highway south of the city. A missile station was established in Alcântara, and oil was discovered in the bay. And thanks to the restoration of many of São Luís' beautiful old buildings, domestic and international tourism are now important to the city's economy.

Orientation

São Luís sits at the northwest corner of a 50km-long island, Ilha de São Luís, which is separated from the mainland only by narrow channels. The city itself is divided by the Rio Anil. South of the Anil, the Centro Histórico's street grid rambles up and down over hilly terrain, with its heart in the lower, tourism-dominated area known as Praia Grande. East of Praia Grande is the city's commercial heart; north of the Anil are the more modern suburbs, such as São Francisco, as well as the city's beaches stretched along the island's north coast.

The bus station is 8km southeast of the center and the airport 3km further southeast.

Roteiro e Mapa Turístico São Luís (R$3), sold at many shops, pousadas and museums, is an excellent map and information guide to the historic center.

Information

EMERGENCY
Ambulance (Pronto Socorro; ☎ 192; ☾ 24 hr)
Tourist Police (Map p591; ☎ 190; Rua Portugal 165; ☾ 24 hr)

INTERNET ACCESS
Livraria Poeme-se (Map p591; Rua João Gualberto 52; per hr R$3; ☾ 8am-6pm Mon-Fri, to 1pm Sat) Also sells Portuguese secondhand books, CDs and postcards.

INTERNET RESOURCES
Guiasaoluis (www.guiasaoluis.com.br) This site has some useful information, but only in Portuguese.
Maranhão (www.turismo.ma.gov.br) Maranhão's official tourism site, in English and Portuguese, has helpful descriptions, though less in English than in Portuguese.

MEDICAL SERVICES
These are some of the better private hospitals.
Cemed Hospital Português (Map p595; ☎ 3231 3216; Rua Passeio 365, Centro Histórico)
Hospital São Domingos (Map p595; ☎ 3216 8100; Av Jerônimo de Albuquerque 540, Bequimão)

MONEY
These bank branches do currency exchange and have ATMs accepting foreign cards.
Bradesco (Map p591; Av Dom Pedro II 120; ☾ 10am-4pm Mon-Fri, ATMs 6am-10pm daily)
Banco do Brasil Dom Pedro (Map p591; Av Dom Pedro II 78; ☾ 10am-4pm Mon-Fri, ATMs 6am-8pm daily); Boa Ventura (Map p591; Travessa Boa Ventura 26; ☾ 10am-4pm Mon-Fri, ATMs 6am-10pm daily)

TOURIST INFORMATION
These information offices usually have helpful, English-speaking attendants.
Airport (☎ 3244 4500; ☾ 24 hr)
Bus station (☎ 3249 4500; ☾ 8am-8pm)
Central de Informações Turísticas (Map p591; ☎ 3212 6211; Praça Benedito Leite; ☾ 8am-7pm Mon-Fri, to 2pm Sat) The main information office of Setur, the city tourism department.

Praia Grande (☎ 3231 4996; Rua Portugal 165; ☾ 8am-7pm Mon-Fri, 9am-2pm Sat & Sun)

TRAVEL AGENCIES
São Luís is full of agencies offering city tours and trips to the Lençóis Maranhenses and other destinations around Maranhão and beyond.
Giltur (Map p591; ☎ 3231 7065; www.giltur.com.br; ☾ 8am-6pm Mon-Fri, to 1pm Sat) Palma (Rua da Palma 196B); Montanha Russa (Rua Montanha Russa 22) A helpful and trustworthy agency with an ecotouristic focus and reasonable prices; English-speakers are usually on hand.
Interturismo (☎ 3227 0791; www.interturismo.com.br; ☾ 8:30am-9pm Mon-Fri, to 2pm Sat) Centro Histórico (Map p591; Rua do Giz 127) Ponta d'Areia (Map p595; Av dos Holandeses 14) This efficient English-speaking agency is a good place to buy air tickets and also offers good-value city tours.

Sights
The historic center of São Luís is the best-preserved colonial neighborhood in the Northeast, full of 18th- and 19th-century mansions covered in colorful 19th-century *azulejos* (decorative ceramic tiles, often blue or blue-and-white) from Portugal, France, Belgium and Germany. The tiles provided a durable means of protecting walls from São Luís' ever-present humidity and heat. The historic center has been under piecemeal restoration under Projeto Reviver (Project Revival) since the late 1980s, after many decades of neglect and decay. Many of the restored buildings house interesting museums, galleries, craft shops and restaurants.

CASA DO MARANHÃO
Inside a gigantic converted warehouse, the **Casa do Maranhão** (Map p591; ☎ 3218 9955; Rua do Trapiche; admission free; ☾ 9am-7pm Tue-Fri, to 6pm Sat & Sun) houses a comprehensive exhibit on the different regional flavors of Bumba Meu Boi (p593), with guided tours in Portuguese. The ground floor has videos on Maranhão's main tourist attractions.

CASA DO NHÔZINHO
At the eclectic **Casa do Nhôzinho** (Map p591; ☎ 3218 9951; Rua Portugal 185; admission free; ☾ 9am-7pm Tue-Fri, to 6pm Sat & Sun), you can see a collection of ingenious fish traps, a room of Maranhão Indian artisanry, a great range of textiles and baskets made from cotton and the *buriti* palm, and hosts of colorful, delicate Bumba Meu Boi

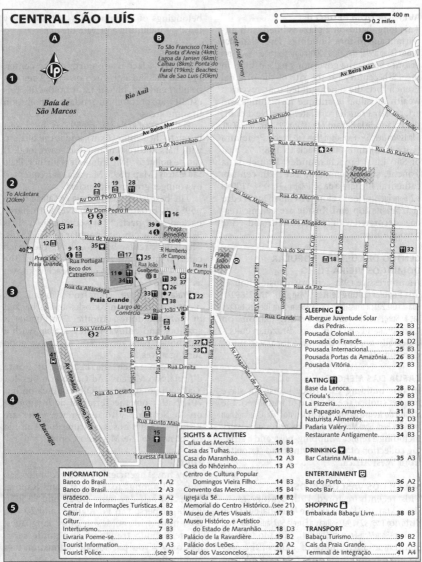

CENTRAL SÃO LUÍS

0 _____ 400 m
0 _____ 0.2 miles

figurines made by the 20th-century master artisan Mestre Nhôzinho.

MUSEU DE ARTES VISUAIS

There's a fine collection of old *azulejos*, engravings and paintings at the **Visual Arts Museum** (Map p591; ☎ 3218 9938; Rua Portugal 273; admission R$1; ☒ 9am-6pm Tue-Sun).

CASA DAS TULHAS

Opposite the Museu de Artes Visuais, this 19th-century **market building** (Map p591; Largo do Comércio; ☒ 6am-8pm Mon-Fri, to 6pm Sat, to 1pm Sun) now trades in a fascinating variety of typical Maranhão crafts and foods, from dried prawns and live ducks to big bags of cashews and a bright purple cassava liquor called *tiquira*.

AVENIDA DOM PEDRO II

This long, handsome plaza is lined with important and historic buildings. The **Palácio dos Leões** (Map p591; ☎ 2108 9000; admission free; ☼ 2-5pm Mon, Wed & Fri) is the governor's palace, built in the 18th century on the site of the original French fort; the quick guided tour reveals a wealth of valuable antique furnishings and art, mostly French from later eras. Next door, the **Palácio de la Ravardière** (Map p591; ☎ 3212 8000; admission free; ☼ 8am-6pm Mon-Fri) is the Prefeitura (City Hall) and dates back to 1689. A bust of São Luís' French founder, Daniel de la Touche, stands before it. The 17th-century cathedral, the **Igreja da Sé** (Map p591; ☼ 8-11:30am & 2-6pm Tue-Sun) looks along Avenida Dom Pedro II from its top end. Inside are ceiling frescoes decorated with *babaçu* motifs and a fine baroque altar.

CENTRO DE CULTURA POPULAR DOMINGOS VIEIRA FILHO

An impressive 19th-century mansion houses this **Popular Culture Center** ((Map p591; ☎ 3218 9925; Rua do Giz 221; admission free; ☼ 9am-7pm Tue-Fri, to 6pm Sat & Sun), with very interesting exhibits on Carnaval and São Luís' Afro-Brazilian cults – especially *tambor de mina,* a local variant of Candomblé.

CAFUA DAS MERCÊS

In this building that once housed a slave market (notice the absence of windows), the **Museu do Negro** (Map p591; Rua Jacinto Maia 43; admission free; ☼ 9am-6pm Mon-Fri) exhibits relics of slavery including a replica whipping-post, and a striking collection of wood carvings and statuettes from West Africa.

SOLAR DOS VASCONCELOS

This recently-restored 19th-century mansion (Map p591) houses the **Memorial do Centro Histórico** (☎ 3231 9075; Rua da Estrela 562; admission free; ☼ 7am-6pm Mon-Fri, 9am-5pm Sat), with models and before-and-after photos of some of the outstanding restoration works, plus a display on traditional boats of Maranhão.

MUSEU HISTÓRICO E ARTÍSTICO DO ESTADO DE MARANHÃO

In a restored 1836 mansion, the **Museu Histórico e Artístico** (Map p591; ☎ 3221 4537; Rua do Sol 302; admission R$1; ☼ 9am-7pm Tue-Fri, to 6pm Sat & Sun) is set out as it might have been in days of yore, displaying all the furnishings, valuables and everyday belongings of an upper-class 19th-century family – including a private theater.

BEACHES

The city's beaches are north of the center, beyond the São Francisco district. They can be busy and fun, but are far from Brazil's finest. Beware of rough surf, tides and pollution in some areas.

Praia Ponta d'Areia (Map p595) is the closest beach to the center (4km), and is the busiest, with bars and restaurants for beach food. It can be polluted. Two kilometers further, **Praia São Marcos** (Map p595; Marcela) is frequented by younger groups and surfers.

The best local beach, **Praia de Calhau** (Map p595), is broad and attractive, with hard-packed sand perfect for soccer games. It is 9km from the city and popular on weekends. The large circular *barracas* along the beach cater to late-night partiers throughout the week. The calm far end of the beach is known as Praia do Caolho.

Praia Olho d'Água, 12km from São Luís, has plenty of houses and kiosks and is backed by cliffs and dunes. Another 7km further is spacious and enjoyable **Praia Araçagi**, with a lighthouse, bars, restaurants and more good surfing waves.

You can reach the beaches of Ponta d'Areia, São Marcos and Calhau on bus 403 'Calhau/Litorânea,' and Olho d'Água on bus 701, both from the Terminal de Integração on Av Senador Vitorino Freire. Fares are R$1.70. Araçagi buses go from Rua António Rayol next to the Mercado Central.

Tours

Many travel agencies offer city tours of São Luís and outings to Alcântara and Raposa. Prices for half-day tours are around R$50 to R$70 per person in Portuguese, and 20% to 30% more with guides in other languages. These include transport and guide services only – you pay for any admission fees and food.

Interturismo (p590) does an interesting Tambores da Fé tour, visiting three Afro-Brazilian cult houses, in English, French, Italian or Spanish for R$66 per person (minimum two), or in Portuguese for R$55.

Festivals & Events

São Luís has one of Brazil's richest folkloric traditions, evident in its many festivals. The

BUMBA MEU BOI

São Luís is famous for its Bumba Meu Boi – a fascinating, wild, folkloric festival. Derived from African, Indian and Portuguese influences that mingled in colonial times, it's a rich mixture of music, dance and theater, with fantastic and colorful costumes and masks. In a Carnavalesque atmosphere, participants dance, sing, act and tell the story of the death and resurrection of the bull – with plenty of room for improvization. It happens all over Maranhão, and in São Luís alone some 400 groups take to the streets every June. New songs, dances, costumes and poetry are created every year.

The story and its portrayal differ throughout the Northeast, but the general plot is as follows: Catrina, goddaughter of the local farmowner, is pregnant and feels a craving to eat the tongue of the best *boi* (bull) on the farm. She cajoles her husband, Chico, into killing the beast. When the dead bull is discovered, several characters (caricatures drawn from all levels of society) track down the perpetrator of the crime. Chico is brought to trial, but the bull is resuscitated by magic incantations and tunes. A pardon is granted, and the story reaches its happy ending when Chico is reunited with Catrina.

Most groups start rehearsing at the end of Semana Santa (Easter week) in preparation for the 'baptism' of their *boi* on June 13, the feast of Santo Antônio, or June 23 (São João). Several groups perform in different places in the city every night from June 13 to 30. The more commercial performances may last only one hour, while local community celebrations can go on all night. Things get especially lively on the nights of June 23–24 and 29–30.

A smaller, but still genuine, Bumba Meu Boi festival happens at the **Convento das Mercês** (Map p591; Rua da Palma 502) on Thursday to Sunday evening in July. In addition, many rehearsals are open to the public and some groups begin months before the traditional Easter Saturday start (check with tourist offices or your accommodations for schedules).

city's famous **Bumba Meu Boi** festival (above) commences in mid-June. The **Tambor de Mina** festivals, in July, are important events for followers of the Afro-Brazilian religions. **Marafolia**, the out-of-season Carnaval, is held in mid-October, and can be livelier than the main one.

Sleeping

BUDGET

Pousada Internacional (Map p591; ☎ 3231 5154; www .pousadahotelinternacional.com; Rua da Estrela 175; s/d with shared bath without window R$15/25, with window R$20/30) Friendly, basic budget spot with fan-cooled rooms, kept clean enough.

Albergue de Juventude Solar das Pedras (Map p591; ☎ 3232 6694; www.ajsolardaspedras.com.br; Rua da Palma 127; dm/s/d R$18/40/50; 🖳) This hostel in a restored colonial home has decent facilities including a sizable sitting area, though the rooms are rather dark and poorly ventilated. It has separate-sex dorms and gives discounts for HI members.

Pousada Vitória (Map p591; ☎ 3231 2816; pousada vitoria@hotmail.com; Rua Afonso Pena 98; s/d R$40/65, with air-con R$50/75; 🖳 🖳) Near the more expensive Pousada Colonial, the Vitória has ample rooms with improvised bathrooms, along an inner patio. It's also a family home, with a friendly welcome.

MIDRANGE

Pousada Tia Maria (Map p595; ☎ 3227 1534; br.geocities .com/pousadatiamaria; Rua Das Angélicas Quadra 2, Lote 11, Ponta d'Areia; s/d R$60/110; 🖳 🖳) The Tia Maria is a smart option for those who want to enjoy the beach bars but be relatively close to the historic center.

our pick Pousada Colonial (Map p591; ☎ 3232 2834; www.clickcolonial.com.br; Rua Afonso Pena 112; s/d R$90/110; 🖳 🖳) Pousada Colonial offers comfortable rooms and luxurious suites in a lovely restored colonial mansion. Some rooms have fantastic views over the old city. The building is covered inside and out with unique raised *azulejos*, which the tourism authority has adopted as its mascot for brochure covers. A 20% discount is offered for cash payment.

Pousada do Francês (Map p591; ☎ 3231 4844; pousada @elo.com.br; Rua 7 de Setembro 121; s/d R$105/135; 🖳 🖳) In a beautifully restored colonial building, all polished wood and cool floor tiles, this is one of the nicest pousadas though slightly away from the heart of the Centro Histórico. Ancient phonograph, radio and telephone equipment at reception set a bygone-era tone, but the rooms are up-to-date and comfortable, and some have good river views. There's also a nice restaurant and bar. Discounts of 15% often available.

Pousada Portas da Amazônia (Map p591; ☎ 3222 9937; www.portasdaamazonia.com.br; Rua do Giz 129; s R$89-139, d R$139-189; ❷ ▣) Rambling corridors in another restored mansion lead around two patio-gardens to attractive rooms with polished wood floors and furniture. There's a good street-view lounge.

Calhau Praia Hotel (Map p595; ☎ 3214 4800; www.calhaupraiahotel.com.br; Av Litorânea 1, Praia do Calhau; s/d R$138/162; ❷ ▣) This is a bright and modern but small-scale and friendly hotel opposite the center of Calhau beach. Only a few rooms face the sea, though.

TOP END

Hotel Brisamar (Map p595; ☎ 2106 0606; www.brisamar.com.br; Av São Marcos 12, Ponta d'Areia; s/d R$157/181; ❷ ▣ ▣) The Brisamar is a good-value high-end beach option, with particularly clean rooms, a spacious pool area and sea views from some rooms. The beach just here is rather rocky, though.

Pestana São Luís (Map p595; ☎ 2106 0505; www.pestana.com; Av Avicênia 1, Calhau; s/d R$260/320; ❷ ▣ ▣) Recently renovated, this stylish resort hotel surrounded by attractive gardens is considered the nicest place to stay in town. Beyond having all the amenities of a fancy hotel, it is close to Calhau beach.

Eating

The best Maranhense food comes from the sea. Regional specialties include *casquinha de caranguejo* (stuffed crab), *caldeirada de camarão* (shrimp stew) and the city's specialty, *arroz de cuxá* (rice with shrimp, toasted sesame and the slightly bitter herb *vinagreira*). Unfortunately, compared with São Luís' other attractions, the restaurant and café choice is rather sparse.

Padaria Valéry (Map p591; ☎ 221 3677; Rua do Giz 164; quiche & pastries R$1.25-2.50; ❧ 7am-10pm Mon-Fri, to 8pm Sat) A relaxingly informal café with decent coffee, French breads and pastries.

Base da Lenoca (Map p591; ☎ 3227 5545; Rua Montanha Russa 181; mains for 2 R$16-40; ❧ noon-11pm) Base da Lenoca is a popular seafood restaurant in a great location overlooking the Rio Anil – order a beer and a crab dish and enjoy the breeze.

Naturista Alimentos (Map p591; ☎ 3221 0318; Rua do Sol 517; buffet per kg R$16; ❧ 8am-6pm Mon-Fri) This legitimate vegetarian buffet is a real treat for vegetarians who have been surviving on cheese sandwiches.

La Pizzeria (Map p591; ☎ 3221 4193; Rua do Giz 129; pizza R$12-22; ❧ 6-11:30pm Wed-Mon) Serves nothing but large pizzas in a long 19th-century warehouse.

Crioula's (Map p591; ☎ 3221 0985; cnr Rua do Giz & Rua João Vital; per kg US$19; ❧ lunch & dinner Mon-Sat) Offers a decent-quality buffet in a tall barnlike space with colorful art and murals.

A Varanda (Map p595; ☎ 3232 8428; Rua Genésio Rego 185, Monte Castelo; mains for 2 R$30-45; ❧ noon-midnight Mon-Sat) The lush patio and excellent fish, shrimp and beef dishes make up for the slow service at this restaurant set in its owner's home. It's 4km east of the historic center: take a 'Vicente Fiaro' or 'Santa Clara' bus from the Terminal de Integração, get off at CEFET and take your first right.

ourpick Restaurante Antigamente (Map p591; ☎ 3232 3964; Rua da Estrela 220; mains R$15-30; ❧ lunch & dinner Mon-Sat) It's a bit of a tourist trap, but it's worth dining here just to soak up the feeling of the historic center. Amid rows of *cachaça* bottles and sepia photos, or outside on the sidewalk, you can choose from a long list of seafood, rice, meat, pasta and salads. It's not haute cuisine but it's fun. There's live music outside in the evening. Neighboring **Le Papagaio Amarelo** (Map p591; ☎ 3221 3855; Rua da Estrela 210; mains R$13-26; ❧ 5pm-2am Tue-Sun) provides similar fare, and you can enjoy the same music.

Drinking

The sidewalk tables of Restaurante Antigamente and Le Papagaio Amarelo (left) are good for evening drinks in the heart of the old town, to the sound of live Música Popular Brasileira (MPB) Monday to Saturday. Around the corner and up a quaint, staired street, the tables from **Bar Catarina Mina** (Map p591; ☎ 3221 5997; Beco Catarina Mina 121; ❧ closed Sun) spill outside – a good place to drink beer and possibly start dancing on the steps.

The *barracas* along Ponta d'Areia, São Marcos and Calhau beaches are also popular drinking spots, with the added attraction of a sea breeze. On weekends, middle-class locals go to Lagoa da Jansen to listen to relaxing music and sip drinks at lakeside bars like **Academia do Chopp** (Map p595; Lagoa da Jansen).

Entertainment

São Luís is the reggae center of Brazil, and many bars and clubs have regular reggae

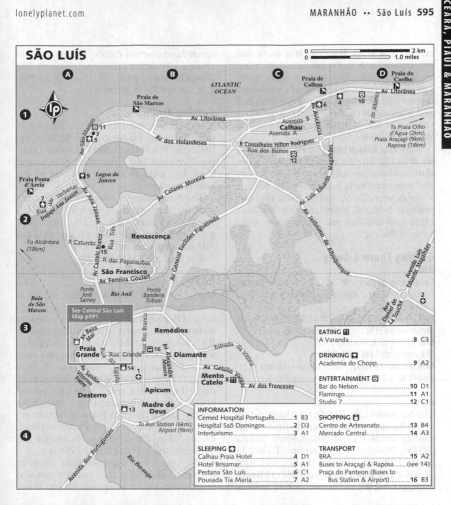

SÃO LUÍS

nights, sometimes live, other times just with DJs and vast banks of speakers. It's worth asking locals or tourist offices for recommendations – or check the entertainment listings in *Estado do Maranhão* newspaper or **São Luís On Line** (www.farolweb.com.b r/saoluis_online).

Bar do Porto (Map p591; ☎ 3232 1115; Rua do Trapiche 49; admission R$4; ☼ 6pm-late Mon-Sat) This vast club hosts live reggae on Wednesday and Friday night, when the street out front becomes a party and reggae fans pack the inside.

Roots Bar (Map p591; ☎ 3221 7580; Rua da Palma 86; admission R$2; ☼ 6pm-2am Wed-Fri) Another old-town live reggae venue.

Bar do Nelson (Map p595; Avenida Litorânea, Calhau; men/women R$2/free; ☼ 7pm-7am Sat & Sun) With its shanty clubhouse feel, Bar do Nelson is the most famous reggae spot in town and is good for live music (sometimes) and dancing.

Flamingo (Map p595; ☎ 3235 1186; Rio Poty Hotel, Ponta d'Areia; admission R$10-25) and **Studio 7** (Map p595; ☎ 3235 9090; Rua dos Buzios, Quadra 33 No 20, Calhau; admission R$10-25) are popular clubs that play music other than reggae, eg electronica and Rio-style funk. Large crowds on weekends.

Shopping

São Luís is the place for Maranhão handicrafts such as painted tiles, woodcarving, basketry, lace, ceramics and leather work. There are plenty of shops around Rua Portugal and Rua da Estrela in the historic center. The large **Centro de Artesanato** (Map p595; Ceprama; Rua de São Pantaleão 1332, Madre de Deus; ☯ 9am-7pm Mon-Sat, 10am-2pm Sun), 2km southeast of the center, is housed in a renovated factory and functions as an exhibition hall and sales outlet for handicrafts. Also worth visiting is the **Mercado Central** (Map p595; Av Magalhães de Almeida).

Embaixada Babaçu Livre (Map p591; ☎ 3221 0462; Rua do Giz 175) Run by a rural workers' association, this shop sells soap, boxes, jewelry and other products made from the *babaçu*, a highly versatile Maranhão palm that also provides food, oil, timber, roofing, fertilizer, cattle feed and charcoal for people in rural parts of the state.

Getting There & Away

AIR

From the **airport** (☎ 3217 6101; Av Santos Dumont, Tirirical) there are direct flights to many Brazilian cities.

BRA São Francisco (Map p595; ☎ 3235 0112; Av Marechal Castelo Branco 333); airport (☎ 3217 6175)

GOL airport (☎ 3217 6216)

TAF airport (☎ 3244 1262)

TAM Renascença (☎ 3227 0816; Av Colares Moreira 23); airport (☎ 3217 6174)

BUS

The **bus station** (☎ 3249 2488; Av dos Franceses, Santo Antônio) has departures to many destinations including Belém (R$76, 12 hours, 8pm), Brasília (R$191, 26 hours, 5pm), Carolina (R$103, 17 hours, 7:30pm), Fortaleza (R$116, 20 hours, 11:30am and 4pm), Parnaíba (R$57, 11 hours, 8:30am and 8pm) and Teresina (R$46 to R$76,

seven hours, seven daily). Tickets are sold at some city-center travel agencies including **Babaçu Turismo** (Map p591; ☎ 3231 4747; Av Dom Pedro II; ☯ 8am-6pm Mon-Fri, to noon Sat).

Getting Around

A taxi costs around R$30 from the airport to the Centro Histórico and R$22 going back. The bus marked 'São Cristovão' (note: not 'Terminal São Cristovão') runs to and from Praça do Panteon, 1km east of the historic center.

The bus station is connected by bus 903 with the Terminal de Integração, a city bus terminal in Praia Grande, and by 'Rodoviária' buses with Praça do Panteon. It's an R$18 cab ride from the Centro Histórico.

Bus fares are R$1.70.

RAPOSA

Out at the tip of the Ilha de São Luís, 30km from the city, is the small and poor fishing town of Raposa, built on stilts above mangrove swamps, which gives it an unusual appearance. It's best known for the intricate lacework of its women, sold from their homes along the main street. But Raposa also attracts visitors from São Luís for good seafood meals; visits to long, dune-lined Praia Carimã, a R$1 per person boat ride from Raposa; and trips through the nearby coastal channels between islands and beaches. The bulk of Raposa's population is descended from two families of Cearense immigrants who founded it in the 1940s.

São Luís travel agencies offer tours to both the following places, but you can also reach them under your own steam. Buses

---

THE BRAZILIAN SPACE PROGRAM

The Brazilian space program is pulling itself back together after an accident on August 22, 2003, in which a US$6 million, 20m-tall, Brazilian-designed VLS rocket exploded on the launch pad in Alcântara. Sadly, 21 engineers and technicians were killed. It was later determined that a booster with solid rocket fuel had ignited.

The accident was unfortunately not the Brazilian space program's first failure. The two previous VLS rockets had also failed: in 1997, a rocket crashed into the ocean shortly after liftoff, and in 1999 officials destroyed a rocket after it veered off course three minutes into flight. The next VLS launch is not now expected before 2009.

VLS stands for Veículo Lançador de Satélites (Satellite-Launching Vehicle) and the rocket is designed to put satellites into orbit. Alcântara's location near the equator enables rockets to reach orbit with less fuel and bigger payloads than from other launch sites, and Brazil has hopes of commercial success for Alcântara by marketing its facilities to other nations. Ukraine and Brazil were due to start work in late 2007 on a launch facility here for Ukrainian satellite-carrying Tsyklon-4 rockets.

to both destinations (both R$2, 45 minutes) leave about every 30 minutes from the Mercado Central.

ALCÂNTARA

☎ 0xx98 / pop 6000

Across the Baía de São Marcos from São Luís is the colonial town of Alcântara. Built between the 17th and 19th centuries with slave labor, Alcântara was the preferred residence of Maranhão's rich plantation owners. In decline since the latter half of the 19th century, Alcântara today is an atmospheric amalgam of ruined, maintained and restored mansions, houses and churches. Some experts claim that it is the most homogeneous group of 17th- and 18th-century colonial buildings in Brazil. Some restoration and improvement works since 2001 have given it a brighter face than it had a decade ago.

Since 1990 the Centro de Lançamento de Alcântara (CLA), the rocket-launching facility for the Brazilian space program (opposite), has operated near the town. It is an odd juxtaposition: rockets alongside a slumbering colonial town.

Bring a copy of the excellent *Alcântara Roteiro e Mapa Turístico*, sold in São Luís for R$3. Keep an eye out for *guará*, beautiful red ibises that are unusually plentiful around here.

Sights

Don't miss **Praça da Matriz**, where the best-preserved **pelourinho** (whipping post) in Brazil stands beside the ruined 17th-century **Igreja de São Matias**. Around the *praça* (plaza or town square) are the interesting **Museu Histórico de Alcântara** (admission R$1; ☾ 9am-2pm) where each room has its own guardian, a source of employment for the locals; the 18th-century **Casa Histórica** (☾ 10am-4pm Mon-Fri) with exhibits of colonial artifacts; and the **Prefeitura**, originally the town's 18th-century jail. Moving along Rua Grande, with its beautiful row of two-story houses, you come to the pretty, two-towered **Igreja de NS do Carmo** (1665), recently restored, on Largo do Carmo, with the ruins of the 18th-century **1° Palácio do Imperador** (First Palace of the Emperor) beside it.

Festivals & Events

The **Festa do Divino**, on the first Sunday after Ascension Day (usually in May), is one of the most colorful annual festivals in Maranhão. It represents a fusion of African and Catholic elements and features two children dressed as emperor and empress, who are paraded through the town accompanied by musicians.

Sleeping & Eating

Alcântara is a straightforward day trip from São Luís, but if you want to stay, there are a few inexpensive pousadas.

Pousada dos Guarás (☎ 3337 1339; pousadados guaras@terra.com.br; Praia da Baronesa; r R$26-70) Right on the beach at the east end of town, this is a very relaxing place to stay, with chalets in a pretty tropical garden, and a good, open-sided restaurant-bar. You can organize a boat here to see the *guarás* themselves.

Restaurante da Josefa (☎ 3337 1109; Rua Direita; mains R$11-24; ☾ 7am-10pm) This is a basic and decent seafood restaurant near the Igreja do Carmo where you can eat locally caught fish.

Getting There & Away

Boats to Alcântara leave from the Cais da Praia Grande (Map p591) on Av Senador Vitorino Freire in São Luís. Motorboats normally leave at 7am and 9:30am, starting back from Alcântara at 4pm and 7:30am next day (R$10 each way, 1¼ hours). There are also often yachts at 1pm (R$5 each way), returning at 7am the next day. It's a good idea to buy your ticket the day before, and check the departure times, which vary with tides.

PARQUE NACIONAL DOS LENÇÓIS MARANHENSES

☎ 0xx98

The name of this 1550-sq-km national park refers to its immense expanses of dunes, which look like *lençóis* (bed sheets) strewn across the landscape and stretch 70km along the coast and up to 50km inland. Halfway between São Luís and the Piauí border, the park also includes beaches, mangroves, lagoons and some interesting fauna, especially turtles and migratory birds. The area's designation as a national park in 1981 staved off potentially ruinous land and oil speculation. It is a spectacular place, especially from March to September, when rain that has filtered through the sand forms crystal-clear pools and lakes between the dunes.

The main base for visiting the park, on 4WD tours, is the small town of Barreirinhas on the Rio Preguiças near its southeast corner, 260km from São Luís. Other access points are Atins and Caburé, on the Preguiças near the park's northeast corner, and remote Santo Amaro on the park's western border, where the dunes come right to the edge of the village. Atins is a small, untidy village from which you can walk to the dunes in about an hour (a four-hour guided hike costs R$30 to R$40 for two people). Tiny, sandy Caburé, on a sandbar between the river and an ocean beach, is a fine place to bliss out with the sun, surf and stars.

The park has no admission fee. A highlight of the surrounding area is the boat trip along the tall-mangrove-lined Preguiças between Barreirinhas, Caburé and Atins. Between the last two you can call at the fishing village of Mandacaru and climb its **lighthouse** (admission R$1; [clock] 9am-3pm) for a great panorama.

Barreirinhas has a couple of cybercafés, and a branch of **Banco do Brasil** (Av Joaquim Soeiro de Carvalho; [clock] 9am-2pm Mon-Fri, ATMs 6am-10pm daily) on the main street.

Tours

Several agencies in Barreirinhas offer daily 4WD trips to Lagoa Azul and Lagoa Bonita, two of the park's biggest lakes, northwest of town. The five-hour trip to either lake costs R$40 per person in open-sided 4WD buses, or R$250 for up to four people in a Jeep. Alternatively, you can take a R$50, eight-hour boat tour down the Rio Preguiças to Caburé, Mandacaru, and Atins, at the river mouth. On a private basis for up to four people, this trip costs R$250.

A tour to Santo Amaro from Barreirinhas, with a visit to the nearby Lagoa da Gaivota, costs R$350 to R$450 for up to 10 people. Santo Amaro is 40km north by a sandy track off Hwy MA-402.

Recommended agencies in Barreirinhas include **Seaandair/Rota das Trilhas** ([phone] 3349 0372; Av Joaquim Soeiro de Carvalho 682A) and **Ecodunas** ([phone] 3349 0545; Rua Inácio Lins 164).

You can also take tours to the Lençóis Maranhenses from São Luís. Giltur (p590) offers some interesting options including a four-day trip with a night at Caburé for R$840 per person (minimum two people) or R$1369 (minimum four) traveling by small plane between São Luís and Barreirinhas – the aerial view of the park is fantastic. A three-day land tour staying at Santo Amaro is R$840 (minimum two people).

São Luís–based **Terra Nordeste** ([phone] /fax 3221 1188; www.terra-nordeste.com; São Luís) arranges well-organized hikes right across the Lençóis from east to west (or vice versa) – the walk takes three or four days, plus a day getting there and a day getting back. English, French and Spanish spoken.

Cururupu Táxi Aéreo (see opposite) does half-hour flights over the park from Barreirinhas for R$160 per person (minimum three).

Sleeping & Eating
BARREIRINHAS
Barreirinhas has plenty of accommodations options.

Pousada do Porto ([phone] 3349 1910; Rua Anacleto de Carvalho; s/d R$20/40, with air-con R$30/60; [icon]) On a street with several pousadas, this is a good budget bet, with just six simple rooms, four of them looking out over the river.

Pousada d'Areia ([phone] 3349 0550; www.pousadadareia .com.br; Av Joaquim Soeiro de Cavalho 888; s/d R$55/70; [icon]) Friendly owners and neat, pleasant rooms.

Pousada Lins ([phone] 3349 1494; pousadalins@hotmail.com; Av Joaquim Soeiro de Cavalho 550; s/d R$50/85; [icon] [icon]) A nice place to stay on the main street. Helpful staff and bare but comfortable rooms.

Several restaurants are dotted along pedestrianized Av Beira Rio on the riverfront.

Restaurante Barlavento ([phone] 3349 0627; mains R$7-16) This place does well-prepared seafood. Try the *filet de peixe al molho de maracujá* (fish fillet in passionfruit sauce).

Restaurante Bela Vista ([phone] 3349 1746; Rua Anacleto de Carvalho 617; mains R$15) Enjoy the shady deck built over the river.

CABURÉ
There are half a dozen pousadas here, and no electricity between 10pm and 6am.

Pousada do Mirante ([phone] 0xx99-9608 2852; s/d R$40/70) Closest to the beach, this place has rustic, clean cabins with tile floors and mosquito nets, and a large restaurant/hammock area where you can eat good fish, prawn and chicken dishes for R$13 to R$18.

Pousada do Paturi ([phone] 3349 9902; www.pousada dopaturi.com.br; s/d R$60/95) By the river, this is a bit fancier than Mirante. The cabins have brick walls, tile roofs and hammocks and are set round a spotless, brick-laid courtyard.

ATINS
Pousada Rancho dos Lençóis ([phone] 9616 9646; www .ranchopousada.com; s/d R$60/90; [icon]) Set around a large central *rancho*, this is easily the best pousada, with comfortable cabins, a good common area and well-prepared food. It's a

little way from Atins' main strip, but you're not missing much. The owner, Buna, can arrange guides, horseback rides and a boat to Barreirinhas.

Getting There & Around

A good paved road, Hwy MA-402, runs east to Barreirinhas from Hwy BR-135 south of São Luís. Minibuses and shared taxis run between São Luís and Barreirinhas (R$30 to R$35, three hours) with door-to-door service. You can arrange these through your accommodations at either end, or in Barreirinhas through **Coopcart** (☎ 3349 1511; Av Joaquim Soeiro de Cavalho). Buses make the same journey (R$26, four hours, five daily) but start and finish at São Luís' bus station, way out of the city center. The most spectacular way to go is by small plane with **Cururupu Táxi Aéreo** (☎ 3244 1511, airport, São Luís; ☎ 3349 0730, Av Joaquim Soeiro de Carvalho, Barreirinhas) for R$250 per person one way (three to six people).

Approaching the Lençóis from the east, a paved road from Parnaíba in Piauí state runs as far as the small port of Tutóia. Up to five daily buses link the two towns. From Tutóia an unpaved road runs 40km west to Paulino Neves, and from there sandy tracks head 30km or so west to Barreirinhas and Caburé. 4WD passenger trucks normally leave Tutóia for Paulino Neves (R$5, 1½ hours) at 9:30am and 5:30pm Monday to Saturday, and vice versa at 5am and 1pm. Similar vehicles normally leave Paulino Neves for Barreirinhas (R$10, two hours) at about 6am and 12:30pm, Monday to Saturday, starting back from Barreirinhas (opposite Banco do Brasil) at 9am and 5pm. Schedules on these routes are not precise. On Sunday there may be one service in each direction. The Paulino Neves–Barreirinhas track is a very poor one passing by (and over) some superb dune-scapes and isolated fishing communities.

To reach Caburé from the east without going via Barreirinhas, you need 4WD transport that can make it along the beach for the final stretch from Paulino Neves – see p587 for more information.

A public passenger boat leaves Atins for Caburé and Barreirinhas (R$5, 3½ hours) at about 3am or 4am Monday to Saturday (depending on tides), and starts back downriver from Barreirinhas about 10:30am. You can usually find other boats to take you up or down the Rio Preguiças if you don't leave

it too late in the afternoon. Ask at your pousada. The trip between Barreirinhas and Caburé could cost from R$30 for one seat to R$150 or R$200 for a whole fast launch taking 1¼ hours.

PAULINO NEVES/RIO NOVO

☎ 0xx98

Due to political redistricting, this town has ended up with two names that are used interchangeably. A small fishing and farming community between Barreirinhas and Tutóia, it's a tranquil place with one main attraction: its coastal dunes, the Pequenos Lençóis. These are almost an extension of those in the park to the west, and they're much more accessible – just a 20-minute walk from the village.

The venerated **Pousada Oásis dos Lençóis** (☎ 3487 1012; s/d R$20/40, r with air-con R$60; ⊠) is very comfortable and has a garden running down to the Rio Novo. Dona Mazé oozes tranquility and cooks a fabulous *moqueca* or *mariscada* (seafood stew).

TUTÓIA

☎ 0xx98 / pop 44,000

Tutóia is a relatively large yet somewhat underdeveloped town at the western end of the Delta do Parnaíba (p586). People from all over the countryside descend on Tutóia to do their shopping. The main plaza is lined with 4WD trucks that wait until they are filled with people, sacks of rice, rolls of toilet paper and plastic broom handles before departing. Trips of a few hours into the delta from here cost around R$150 per boat.

Pousada Tremembés (☎ 3347 9354; s R$20-30, d R$30-50; ⊠ 🖳) has some bright, fairly spacious new rooms with verandas. The owner, Cacau, may look intimidating but is a friendly and helpful character of some local renown. He can arrange for the 4WD to Paulino Neves to pick you up in the morning. The last stop of the bus from Parnaíba is directly in front of the pousada.

If you'd like to stay on the beach (1km from Praça Tremembes), **Pousada Em-Bar-Cação** (☎ 3479 1309; Rua Magalhães de Almeida 1105; r R$28-56; ⊠) has reasonable rooms in pastel and primary hues and gets breezes.

THE NORTH COAST

Beyond Alcântara, the Maranhão coast is a maze of estuaries, islands and mangrove-lined channels. The region is starting to be promoted as the **Floresta dos Guarás** (Forest of the Red Ibis) for its colonies of these colorful birds. The main town is Cururupu, with a couple of hotels and half a dozen pousadas. The **Ilha dos Lençóis** is a large sand island with beaches, a fishing village, dunes like the Lençóis Maranhenses and a mangrove forest that is a sanctuary for red ibis. It's reached by a 3½-hour boat ride from the small fishing port of Apicum-Açu, 80km beyond Cururupu. The area has not yet been developed at all for tourism.

Two buses a day go to Cururupu from São Luís' bus station (11 hours), or you can charter a small plane for around R$1000 roundtrip (maximum six people) from **Cururupu Táxi Aéreo** (☎ 3244 1511; airport, São Luís). Some agencies in São Luís can organize trips to the Ilha dos Lençóis – try **Lotus Turismo** (☎ 0xx98-3221 0942; www.lotusturismo.com.br; Travessa Marcelino Almeida 85).

IMPERATRIZ
☎ 0xx99 / pop 218,000

An expanding city 636km southwest of São Luís, Imperatriz is on the border with Tocantins state. The growth is due to the rabid logging and mining of the surrounding region. The Belém–Brasília highway comes through Imperatriz, so you might need to change buses here en route between São Luís and Tocantins or Brasília. There are seven daily buses from São Luís (R$65 to R$75, 12 hours).

CAROLINA
☎ 0xx99 / pop 17,000

The town of Carolina, 242km south of Imperatriz, lies beside the Rio Tocantins and is the best base for visiting the recently designated (2006) **Parque Nacional da Chapada das Mesas**, east of town. The park's attractions are its dramatic flat-topped rocky bluffs (the *mesas,* or tables, of its name) and its many beautiful waterfalls, canyons and crystalline swimming holes. Contact **Companhia do Cerrado** (☎ 3531 3222; www.ciadocerrado.com.br; Praça José Alcides de Carvalho 236) or **Moropóia Aventurismo** (☎ 3531 8508; www.carolina.com.br/moropoia) for 4WD day-trips into the park.

One of the best routes takes in the 76m-high **Cachoeira Santa Bárbara** waterfall and the lovely **Poço Azul** and **Encanto Azul** bathing pools, for R$70 per person, with the option of doing some abseiling for an extra R$30. Slightly cheaper is the trip to the thundering, 33m-wide **Cachoeira de São Romão** and the **Cachoeira de Prata**. Outside the national park are **Pedra Caída** (admission by guided tour R$5; ⏰ 10am-2pm Mon-Fri, to 4pm Sat & Sun), a dramatic combination of canyons and waterfalls 37km north of Carolina on the Estreito road; and the twin falls of **Cachoeira do Itapecuru** (admission R$2; ⏰ 7am-7pm), 33km east of town on the BR-230.

Sleeping & Eating
Pousada do Lajes (☎ 3531 2499; www.pousadadolajes .com.br; Hwy BR-230 km2, Sucupira; s/d R$70/80; ❉ ☎) This family-run pousada, 3km east of the center towards Riachão, has straightforward but well-kept rooms, a nice garden, and a good pool and restaurant.

Restaurante K-Funé (☎ 3531 2468; Rua José Augusto dos Santos 90; mains R$12-20; ⏰ lunch & dinner) Head here for good home-style cooking.

Getting There & Around
There's one overnight bus to Carolina from São Luís (R$103, 17 hours) and a few daily services from Imperatriz (R$10, four hours).

The Amazon

Every traveler has fantasized about a trip to the Amazon. Just the name evokes images of dense rain forest, indigenous tribes, and abundant wildlife.

The numbers are certainly mind-boggling: the Amazon basin is twice the size of India, and spans eight countries. At its height, the river can measure 40km across and dump 300 million liters of fresh water into the ocean per second. That's more than the next eight largest rivers combined.

Yet many travelers leave the Amazon underwhelmed, having come expecting a Discovery channel–like encounter with jaguars, anaconda and spear-toting Indians. That simply doesn't happen – surprise, surprise – much less on the schedule or budget of most travelers.

The Amazon's quintessential experiences are more sublime than they are superlative: canoeing through a flooded forest, dozing in a hammock on a boat chugging upriver, waking up in the jungle to the call of a thousand birds or the otherworldly cry of howler monkeys.

It's only in the halogen glare of unreasonable expectations (or too short a visit) that a trip to the Amazon will feel disappointing. The river itself is massive and unrelenting, as much a living thing as the plants and animals that depend on it. Wildlife is hard to see, but that much more special when you do; the rain forest is everywhere and awesome. Indigenous tribes are extremely reclusive, but the Caboclo (mixed Indian and European) communities that populate the riverbanks are vital and compelling.

On a river whose size is legendary, it's actually the little things that make it special. Give it some time, forget your expectations, and the Amazon cannot fail to impress.

HIGHLIGHTS

- Glide through the flooded forest at **Mamirauá Reserve** (p659), in search of the shaggy-coated uakari monkey
- Soak up night sounds and river life on **jungle tours** (p651) outside Manaus
- Rough it with rubber tappers in **Tapajós National Forest** (p625) outside Santarém
- Become a beach bum at **Alter do Chão** (p627), the Caribbean of the Amazon
- Ply the windy Atlantic beaches at **Ilha de Marajó** (p618) – steer clear of the buffalos!

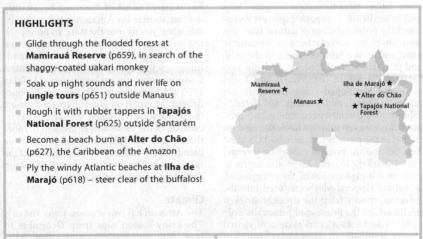

Mamirauá Reserve ★   Ilha de Marajó ★
          ★ Alter do Chão
Manaus ★   ★ Tapajós National Forest

■ POPULATION: 14.7 MILLION   ■ AREA: 3,850,000 SQ KM

History

The Amazon basin has been continuously inhabited for at least 10,000 years, possibly more. Its earliest inhabitants were stone-age peoples, living in hundreds of far-flung tribes, some tiny, others numbering in the tens of thousands. It was from the west that Europeans explorers first arrived. In 1541 a Spanish expedition from Quito, led by Gonzalo Pizarro, ran short of supplies while exploring east of the Andes in what is today Peru. Pizarro's cousin Francisco de Orellana offered to take 60 men along with the boats from the expedition and forage for supplies. De Orellana floated down the Rio Napo to its confluence with the Amazon, near Iquitos (Peru), and then to the mouth of the Amazon. Along the way his expedition suffered numerous attacks by Indians; some of the Indian warriors, they reported, were female, like the Amazons of Greek mythology, and thus the world's greatest river got its name. No one made a serious effort to claim this sweaty territory, however, until the Portuguese built a fort near the mouth of the river at Belém in 1616, and sent Pedro Teixeira up the river to Quito and back between 1637 and 1639. During the 17th and 18th centuries, Portuguese *bandeirantes* (groups of roaming adventurers) penetrated ever further into the rain forest in pursuit of gold and Indian slaves, exploring as far as present-day Rondônia, and the Guaporé and Madeira river valleys.

Amazonian Indians had long used the sap from rubber trees to make waterproof bags and other items. European explorers recognized the potential value of natural latex, but were unable to market it because it tended to grow soft in the heat, or brittle in the cold, and thus had limited appeal outside the rain forest. However, in 1842 American Charles Goodyear developed vulcanization (made natural rubber durable) and in 1890 Ireland's John Dunlop patented pneumatic rubber tires. Soon there was an unquenchable demand for rubber in the recently industrialized USA and Europe, and the price of rubber on international markets soared. As profits skyrocketed, so did exploitation of the *seringueiros,* or rubber tappers, who were lured into the Amazon, mostly from the drought-stricken northeast, by the promise of prosperity only to be locked into a cruel system of virtual slavery dominated by *seringalistas* (owners of rubber-bearing forests). Rigged scales, hired guns, widespread illiteracy among the rubber tappers, and monopoly of sales and purchases all combined to perpetuate the workers' debt and misery. In addition, *seringueiros* had to contend with jungle fevers, Indian attacks and all manner of deprivation.

Despite Brazilian efforts to protect the country's world rubber monopoly, a Briton named Henry Wickham managed to smuggle rubber seeds from the Amazon back to London. Before long, rubber trees were growing in neat and efficient groves in the British colonies of Ceylon and Malay, and Brazil's rubber monopoly was punctured. The price of latex plummeted and by the 1920s the rubber boom was over. It was briefly revived during WWII, when Malay was occupied by Japan, and the Allies turned to Brazil for its Amazon rubber. Another 150,000 *seringueiros* – this time hailed as 'rubber soldiers' – flooded the Amazon from the northeast again, only to have rubber prices fall shortly after the war was over.

Brazil has always feared foreign domination of the Amazon region. One of the official slogans of the military government of the 1970s was *'Integrar para não entregar'* (essentially, 'Use it or lose it'). Governments have made a determined attempt to consolidate Brazilian control of Amazonia by cutting roads through the jungle and colonizing the interior. Unfortunately, those roads became the arteries from which rampant destruction of the Amazon rain forest was – and is – fed. The state of Pará has suffered some of the most devastating deforestation in the Amazon, a fact easily visible when you fly over the state. In Rondônia, the infamous Polonoroeste program opened the state to agricultural colonization by land-hungry settlers from all over the country. Rondônia's population leapt from 111,000 in 1970 to 1.13 million in 1991, while about one-fifth of the virgin jungle that covered almost the whole state was felled. The rate of deforestation in the 1980s was equivalent to more than a football field a minute, for a whole decade. International pressure has brought the rate of deforestation down, but the Amazon continues to shrink at an alarming rate.

Climate

The Amazon has two seasons, rainy and dry. The rainy season runs from December to June, with temperatures ranging from 23°C (73°F) to 30°C (86°F) and frequent, even daily,

lonelyplanet.com

THE AMAZON

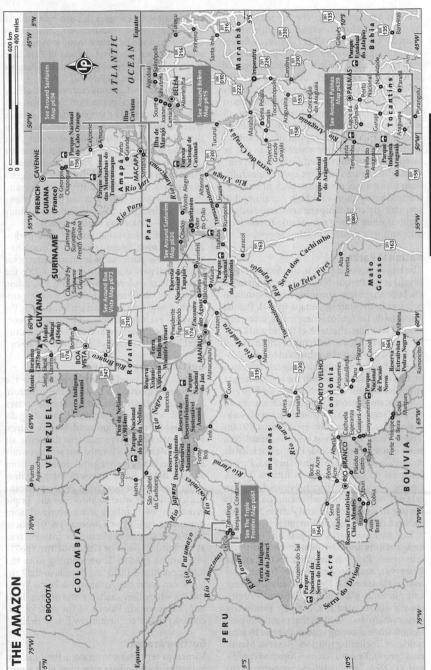

THE AMAZON

rains in April and May. The dry season lasts from July to November, with temperatures from 26°C (78°F) to 40°C (104°F), with less rain, though showers are still possible. As with any area as large as the Amazon, regional differences can be stark. Belém is one of the rainiest cities in the world, with no true dry season. Downpours can be expected almost daily from December to June, tapering off somewhat in October, the driest month. By contrast, Palmas, the capital of Tocantins, lies in a low river valley where the sun can be intense and uninterrupted for weeks on end, even while nearby hills are cool, even chilly. Rain forest areas manage to pack in both extremes: heavy rains and high humidity, but surprisingly cool temperatures, especially at night or when there's rain, thanks to relatively little sunlight penetrating the canopy.

National Parks

The largest national park in the Amazon (and Brazil) is the Parque Nacional das Montanhas do Tumucumaque, spanning nearly 4 million hectares in the state of Amapá (p634). Parque Nacional do Jaú (p656) is next in line, protecting around 2.3 million hectares of the Jaú and Carabinani river systems, both major tributaries of the Rio Negro located northwest of Manaus. Tocantins' Parque Nacional do Araguaia is located on Ilha do Bananal, arguably the world's largest river island, while Parque Nacional do Pico Neblina, located almost a thousand kilometers up the Rio Negro in the northwest corner of Amazonas state, contains the eponymous 3014m 'Foggy Peak,' the highest point in Brazil. Still other national parks include Parque Nacional da Amazonia (p626), near Itaituba in Pará, Parque Nacional do Cabo Orange in Amapá (p634), Parque Nacional de Pacaás Novos (p682) in central Rondônia, Parque Nacional da Serra do Divisor in western Acre, and Parque Nacional da Serra da Mocidade in Roraima.

But national parks are just one of many designations used to protect the Amazon rain forest. *Reservas Extrativistas* (Extractive Reserves), *Reservas de Desenvolvimento Sustenável* (Sustainable Development Reserves), and *Florestas Nacionales* (National Forests, usually abbreviated FLONA) are innovative preservation designations that maximize protection while allowing sustainable use by local residents, including tourism. Reserva Mamirauá (p659), Reserva Xixuaú-Xipariná (p655), and FLONA Tapajós (p625) are three of the better known examples of such reserves, all with excellent eco-tourism programs. Other reserves include Reserva Amaná in Amazonas state, Reserva Tapajós Arapiuns in Pará, and Reserva Pedras Negras (p682) in the Guaporé Valley in southern Rondônia.

Of course, indigenous reserves also afford effective ecological protection by limiting access to outsiders. The largest and best known is Terra Indígena Yanomami (Yanomani Indian Reserve) in northern Amazonas state (see the boxed text on p667), but there are dozens more, including Parque Indigena do Tumucumaque in Pará, Reserva Indígena Waimiri Atroari straddling Roraima and Amazonas states (see the boxed text on p669), and Área Indígena Vale do Rio Javari along the Brazil—Colombia border (p665).

There is at least one notable state park – Parque Estadual Jalapão (p639), in Tocantins – though state park status is often a precursor to national park designation. And in 2006 the state of Pará ordered a whopping 15 million hectares of the Guayana Shield – a mostly untouched swatch of tropical rain forest along the Guyana, French Guiana, and Suriname borders – to be preserved and used for the future establishment of various parks and reserves

Getting There & Away

Manaus (p641) and Belém (opposite) are the major transportation hubs of the Amazon. Most travelers arrive by air – Manaus receives the bulk of international flights, including direct flights from Miami and Buenos Aires, while both cities have frequent domestic air service. Manaus has limited bus service, while Belém has buses arriving and departing from all over Brazil. Some travelers enter the Brazilian Amazon by boat from Peru or Colombia, crossing at what is known as the Triple Frontier (p660); others arrive overland from Venezuela (p671) or Guyana (p670) where there's bus service to Manaus, or from Bolivia, at the border towns of Gujará-Mirim (p677) or Brasiléia (p688). Those coming from the interior of Brazil, including Brasília or the Pantanal, can enter the Amazon via Porto Velho (p674), where they catch a plane or river boat to Manaus, or via Palmas in the state of Tocantins (p635), connecting by bus to Belém.

Getting Around

Virtually every major town along the Amazon, Solimões, and Madeira rivers has both a port and an airstrip – but no roads in or out – so travel is limited to plane or boat. Choosing between flying and boating is really a matter of time, money and preference. Boat travel is certainly an experience, and most travelers cover at least one or two legs by water. But the distances are enormous and the boats very slow, especially going upstream. Flying gives you more time to do the fun stuff (hiking, canoeing etc) and frequent promotions can make the cost of flying surprisingly close to that of taking a boat. Bus service is available in states along the edges of the rain forest, like Pará, Tocantins, and Rondônia. Highways conditions are improving, and there are more deluxe and direct options available, which help make the invariably long bus routes a bit less taxing.

PARÁ

Pará doesn't have the name 'Amazonas' like the state next door, so it might be easy to think it's not part of 'the Amazon' either. In fact, Pará has some terrific Amazonian destinations, and not ones you may have expected to find. You can wander deserted beaches on the islands of Algodoal and Marajó, or chill out on the white sands of Alter do Chão, a thousand kilometers from the ocean. The Tapajós river and national forest offer plenty of rain forest and riverboat options, plus a fascinating living history of rubber boom and bust. Pará has a lively modern city in Belém, and South America's oldest cave paintings just upriver in Monte Alegre.

Pará is also ground zero for Amazonian deforestation, the front lines of a pitched battle between preservationists and agro-industrialists, especially soy farmers and cattle ranchers. It's here in 2005 that an American nun and environmentalist was gunned down on the orders of a landowner she accused of illegally cutting trees. But it is also the state that, in 2007, set aside 15 million hectares – more than twice the size of Ireland – as protected territory.

Travelers understandably see Pará as 'not deep enough' in the Amazon to warrant an extended visit. But it doesn't take long to see that Pará has plenty to offer, and those who give it a chance are rarely disappointed.

BELÉM
☎ 0xx91 / pop 1.4 million

Belém is a surprisingly rewarding city, with streets and parks shaded by mango trees, and a number of fascinating monuments and museums. The sloping central park is quiet during the week and bustling on weekends, when locals come out en masse for free performances and tasty street food. Nightlife tends toward the bohemian intellectual sort: art house theaters, small music venues, heady café-bars. From Belém you can take overnight trips to Algodoal and Ilha de Marajó, both appealing coastal destinations, and it's an important launch pad for journeys up the Rio Amazonas. The Amazon is not known for its cities, and Belém can't compete with places like São Luis or Salvador for charm or urban flair. But given time to explore, most find Belém is not nearly as rough around the edges as they expected.

History

Belém was one of the first Portuguese settlements on the Amazon, founded in 1616. It prospered for over two centuries, relying on enslaved Indians (and later enslaved Africans) for finding and harvesting Amazonian treasures like cacao, indigo and animal skins, all for export to Europe. It was a fragile success, though, and an economic downturn in the early 19th century helped spark a popular uprising and bloody civil war.

The rubber boom at the turn of the century sent Belém's population rocketing, from 40,000 in 1875 to more than 100,000 in 1900. The city suddenly had electricity, telephones, streetcars and a distinctly European feel. Officials erected a few grand monuments such as the Teatro da Paz, earning the city the nickname 'the tropical Paris.'

By 1910 rubber constituted 39% of Brazil's total exports and new ports and wharfs were commissioned and built in Belém to handle the flow. Rubber eventually crashed, but the ports have remained active ever since. Today some 800,000 tons of cargo pass through Belém, mostly timber, but also soy, fish, shrimp, Brazil nuts and palm hearts.

Orientation

Belém's central park is called Praça da República, a quiet leafy spot despite the fact that several major avenues converge there. West of there, and closer to the water, is Comercio, a gritty commercial district that's not terribly pleasant or safe, especially at night. Further south is Cidade Velha, or the Old City, where Belém's best museums are located. East of the center is an upscale neighborhood called

Nazaré, with cafés, a few hotels, and Basílica Santuario de Nazaré, Belém's most important church.

Information

BOOKSTORES

Clio (☎ 210 6369, 210 6368; airport; ☼ 24hr) Belém's best English-language selection, including guidebooks.

Livraría Newstime Estaçáo das Docas (☎ 3212 3298; ☼ noon-midnight Mon-Fri, 10am-midnight Sat & Sun); Iguatemi Shopping (☎ 3250 5398, 3250 5321; 1st & 3rd fl; ☼ 10am-10pm Mon-Sat, noon-10pm Sun)

EMERGENCY

Police (☎ 190)
Tourist Police (CIPTUR) Central station (☎ 3222 2602;

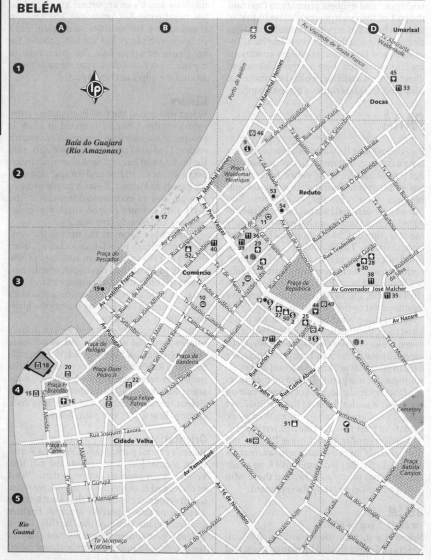

THE AMAZON

BELÉM

Rua 28 de Setembro); Paratur office (☎ 3212 0948; Praça Waldemar Henrique s/n)

INTERNET ACCESS
Equilibrium (Rua Ó de Almeida; per hr R$3; ✆ 8am-8pm Mon-Sat)
Hilton Belém (Av Presidente Vargas 882; per hr R$6; ✆ 8am-10:30 Mon-Fri, 8am-6:30pm Sat & Sun) Public

business center that charges by the minute, handy if you don't need a whole hour online.
Órbitas (Av Serzedelo Correia; per hr R$2; ✆ 9am-10:30pm)

LAUNDRY
Many hotels do laundry for guests; it's rarely cheap, but neither is going to a launderette.

Lav & Lev (☎ 3223 7247; Travessa Dr Moraes 576; ⏲ 8am-8pm Mon-Sat) Charges by the load, up to 7kg. Self-serve R$17, drop-off R$24; no discount for smaller loads.

MEDICAL SERVICES
Airport health post (⏲ 8am-noon & 2-6pm Mon-Fri) Provides free yellow-fever vaccinations.
Hospital Adventista de Belém (☎ 3246 8686, 0800 91 0022; Av Almirante Barroso 1758) One of the better private hospitals.

MONEY
Banco da Amazônia (Av Presidente Vargas; ⏲ 10am-1pm, 2-4pm Mon-Sat) Changes traveler's checks.
Bradesco (Av Presidente Vargas 988; ⏲ 10am-1pm, 2-4pm Mon-Fri) Changes Amex traveler's checks on the 4th floor in the morning only; passport required.
Estação das Docas Has numerous cash machines in secure settings.
HSBC (Av Presidente Vargas 670; ⏲ 10am-5pm Mon-Sat)

POST
Main post office (☎ 211 3147; Av Presidente Vargas 498; ⏲ 9am-4pm Mon-Fri)
Post office (☎ 212 7093; Travessa Frutuoso Guimarães; ⏲ 9am-3pm Mon-Fri)

TOURIST INFORMATION
Paratur (☎ 3212 0575; www.paraturismo.pa.gov.br; Praça Waldemar Henrique s/n; ⏲ 8am-6pm Mon-Fri) Reasonably helpful state tourism agency.

TRAVEL AGENCIES
Amazon Star Turismo (☎ 3212 6244; www.amazonstar.com.br; Rua Henrique Gurjão 210) Organizes day trips around Belém, including bird-watching and city tours (per person R$70 to R$180; see right), plus pricey multiday packages to Ilha de Marajó (per person R$525 to R$875).
Turvicam (☎ 3241 5465; Av Presidente Vargas 636) Sells plane tickets.

Dangers & Annoyances
The Mercado Ver-o-Peso is a prime place to get pickpocketed – this shouldn't prevent you from going, but do take care. As always, consider taking cabs at night.

Sights & Activities
CENTRAL AREA
Estação das Docas
An ambitious renovation project converted three down-at-heel riverfront warehouses into a terrific commercial and gathering center. **Estação das Docas** (Av Marechal Hermes) has restaurants, artsy shops, a small theater, plus a post office and ATMs. There are also interesting displays, in Portuguese and English, about the founding of Belém and the growth and importance of the shipping trade here. The waterfront promenade is lined with attractive yellow cranes, further reminders of Belém's port-town roots, and outdoor tables with great lunchtime views. There's live music most nights, performed from a moving platform up in the rafters, slowly rolling the length of the dining area.

Teatro da Paz
One of Belém's finest buildings, the **Teatro da Paz** (☎ 3224 7355, 212 7915; Praça da República) was built between 1869 and 1874 overlooking Praça da República. Built in neoclassical style, the architecture has all the sumptuous trappings of the rubber-boom era: columns, busts, crystal mirrors and an interior decorated in Italian theatrical style. Half-hour guided tours (R$5) are offered hourly from 9am to 5pm weekdays, and 9am to 1pm weekends.

Mercado Ver-o-Peso
A symbol of the city, the name of this **waterfront market** (Av Castilho França) comes from colonial times, when the Portuguese would *ver o peso* (check the weight) of merchandise in order to impose taxes. The market's four-turreted iron structure is known, aptly enough, as the Mercado do Ferro. It was brought over in parts from Britain, and assembled and inaugurated in 1901. A profile of the turrets is commonly used as a symbol of Belém.

The display of fruits and animals, not to mention the people, is fascinating. It's best to get there early, when the fishing boats are unloading at the southwest end of the market. Other shops sell medicinal plants, shoes, clothes, food and more, all at cut-rate prices. Pickpocketing is a persistent problem, so be alert when you visit (and avoid going after 5pm). Also, don't be fooled by tricksters who pose as foreigners who've been robbed and then ask you for money.

River Tours
Valeverde (☎ 3213 3388; Estação das Docas; ⏲ 9am-10pm Tue-Sun) and **Amazon Star Turismo** (☎ 3212 6244; www.amazonstar.com.br; Rua Henrique Gurjão 210) offer a variety of short tours on the river (per person R$25 to R$80). The former has an office and daily schedule at the pier at Estação das Docas; in most cases you can simply show

up. Amazon Star requires reservations and will usually fetch you from your hotel. Both have a similar selection, including sunrise bird-watching tours, pleasant evening cruises, and a standard (none too exciting) daytime tour to a nearby river island.

CIDADE VELHA
The 'Old City' has most of the city's museums and galleries, fronting the river and four nearly adjoining plazas. The area is safe during the day, with plenty of people about, but is tucked below the Comercio neighborhood, which gets seedy at night. Take a taxi if you stay late.

Forte do Presépio
The city of Belém was founded in 1616 with the construction of the **Forte do Presépio** (Praça Frei Brandão; admission R$2, free Tue; 10am-6pm Tue-Sun), which was intended to protect Portuguese interests upriver against incursions by the French and Dutch. Today it houses a small but excellent museum, primarily about Parás indigenous communities (displays in Portuguese only). There are great views of the city and Amazon river from atop the fort's thick stone walls.

Palácio Antonio Lemos & MABE
This rubber-boom palace served as city hall between 1860 and 1883, and now houses, among other things, the **Museo de Arte de Belém** (MABE; 3283 4665; Praça Dom Pedro II; admission free; 10am-6pm Tue-Fri, 10am-1pm Sat). The museum has gorgeous wood floors – cloth slippers are provided at the entrance – and a fine collection of Brazilian 20th-century paintings, including Cândido Portinari's 1957 oil *Seringal*.

Palácio Lauro Sodré & Museo do Estado do Pará
This grand rambling building was once the residence of Portugal's royal representatives in Belém, and later of various governors of Pará state. One governor, Ernesto Lobo, was killed on the staircase during the Cabanagem Rebellion in 1835. Today it's the home of the **Museo do Estado do Pará** (Pará State Museum; 3225 2414; Praça Dom Pedro II; admission R$4; 8am-6pm Mon-Fri) a mildly interesting collection on the founding and growth of Belém and Pará.

Casa das Onze Janelas
Once the home of a sugar baron, then a military hospital, the **Casa das Onze Janelas** (3219 1165; Praça Frei Brandão; adult/student R$2/1, free Tue;

10am-6pm Tue-Sun) now houses an excellent art gallery and one of Belém's finest restaurants, Boteco das Onze (see p612). The medium-sized gallery contains a mix of classical and modern artwork, plus a good photography exhibit upstairs. The café in back has a view of the mouth of the Amazon.

Museu de Arte Sacra
The **Museu de Arte Sacra** (Museum of Sacred Art; Praça Frei Brandão; adult/student R$4/2, Tue free; 10am-6pm Tue-Sun) consists of the impressive Igreja do Santo Alexandre and the adjoining Palácio Episcopal (Bishop's Palace). Santo Alexandre was Belém's first church, founded by Jesuits in the early 17th century. Impressive in size alone, the church nave also contains brilliant sculpture and detailing, virtually all done by indentured Indians using plaster and local red cedar. The rambling Bishop's Palace has a decent collection of modern art and installation pieces, plus a café and gift shop.

Catedral da Sé
Belém's **cathedral** (Praça Frei Brandão; 7am-noon & 2-7:30pm) is a 1750s colonial baroque-cum-neoclassical construction by Antônio Landi. The cathedral's twin-towered main facade has long outshined the rather bland interior, but a major renovation (which was still underway at the time of research) is sure to help even the score.

EAST OF THE CENTER
Basílica Santuario de Nazaré
A bit humdrum from the outside, the **Basílica Santuario de Nazaré** (Praça Justo Chermont; admission free; 5:30am-8pm) has a truly spectacular interior, with soaring marble columns, brilliant stained glass windows and ornate wood and tile work in every direction, even the ceiling, with faces peering straight down. The basilica is the focal point of Brazil's largest religious festival, Círio de Nazaré (see p610) drawing more than a million worshippers to Belém every October.

Museu Emílio Goeldi & Parque Zoobotánico
The best **museum and zoo** (3249 1233; Av Governador Magalhães Barata 376; park, aquarium & permanent exhibit each R$4; 9am-11:30am & 2-5pm Tue-Thu, 9am-11:30am Fri, 9am-5pm Sat & Sun) in Belém contains many Amazonian animal species, from manatees and anacondas to jaguars and giant otters, plus

an aviary, aquarium and excellent permanent exhibit of artifacts from ancient Amazonian peoples. Sundays are popular with families.

Festivals & Events

Every year on the morning of the second Sunday of October, Belém explodes with the sounds of hymns, bells and fireworks. Started in 1793, the **Círio de Nazaré** is Brazil's biggest religious festival. People from all over the country flock to Belém, and even camp in the streets, to participate in the grand event.

The diminutive image of *Nossa Senhora de Nazaré* (Our Lady of Nazareth) is believed to have been sculpted in Nazareth (Galilee) and to have performed miracles in medieval Portugal before getting lost in Brazil. It was rediscovered in 1700 by a humble cattleman on the site of the basilica, to which it later returned of its own accord after being moved away several times.

The day before the main annual event, the little statue, having previously been taken 23km north to Icoaraci, is carried in a river procession back to the cathedral in Belém. On the Sunday itself, well over a million people fill the streets to accompany the image from the Catedral da Sé (p609) to the Basílica Santuario de Nazaré (p609). The image is placed on a flower-bedecked carriage, and thousands squirm and grope in an emotional frenzy to get a hand on the 300m rope pulling the carriage. Five hours and just 3.5km from the cathedral, the Virgin reaches the basilica, where she remains for the duration of the festivities.

Sleeping

BUDGET

Hotel Amazônia (☎ 3222 8456; Rua Ó de Almeida 548; dm R$10, s/d with fan R$18/26) Not to be confused with the hostel of the same name, rooms here are itty-bitty makeshift cubbies with thin plywood walls, but the sheets are clean and the price can't be beat. Shared bathrooms are tolerable, and there's a small living room with TV; breakfast is not included, however. The dorm has 10 or so beds, but no lockers – better to spring for a room you can lock.

Amazônia Hostel (☎ 4008 4800; www.amazoniahostel .com.br; Av Governador José Malcher 592; dm with hostelling card R$28, without card R$38) A century-old rubber baron mansion in a safe area is the perfect home for Belém's one and only youth hostel. Smallish women's and men's dorms have

new bunks and large lockers, plus 4m ceilings and gorgeous wood floors. Internet, common kitchen, and laundry service are welcome features. Prices are high for a hostel, but it's still an attractive place.

MIDRANGE

Many midrange options are only slightly more expensive than budget listings, so even if you're on a tight budget you might want to consider one of these options.

Hotel Unidos (☎ 3224 0660; hotel.unidos@bol.com .br; Rua Ó de Almeida 545; s/d R$65/85; ☒) One of Belém's best values, the Unidos has large spotless rooms and competent, welcoming staff. The corridors are spacious and well-lit – so often overlooked in the Amazon – and there's no skimping on the complimentary *café de manhã* (breakfast). The decor is admittedly plain, but the rates here are significantly lower than comparably equipped hotels around town. And just a half-block off Av Presidente Vargas, the hotel is within walking distance of most places, and close to the bus stops for everything else.

Hotel Grão Pará (☎ 3224 4100; www.hotelgraopara .com.br; Av Presidente Vargas 718; s/d R$71/91; ☒) Another great value, rooms here are a bit newer than at the Unidos – especially the bathrooms, with glass showers and marble counters – though with 150 rooms, service is necessarily less personalized. The street can be quite noisy, but then again you're right across from Praça da República – ask for an upper floor to minimize the former and maximize the view of the latter.

Manacá Hotel Residência (☎ /fax 3242 5665; manaca@veloxmail.com.br; Travessa Quintino Bocaiúva 1645; s/d/tr R$98/119/139; ☒ ☐) The common areas of this converted colonial mansion are superb: beautiful wood and stone floors, and creative artwork – the original wooden front door hangs like a painting in the hallway. The neighborhood is equally appealing, with stylish shops and restaurants, and the Basílica Nazaré and zoo a short walk away. All of which makes the rooms just a bit disappointing: aging bathrooms, weak lighting, and springy mattresses (and no double beds, only singles!).

Hotel Le Massilia (☎ 3224 7147; le_massilia@yahoo .com; Rua Henrique Gurjão 236; s/d standard R$120/140, deluxe R$130/150; ☒ ☐ ☒) Close to Praça da República, this French-run hotel has a guesthouse atmosphere, small swimming pool and recommended French restaurant. Most rooms have homey details like beanbag chairs, hair driers and writing tables. Deluxe units have lofts and can sleep up to four, though the space can feel a bit enclosed. All rooms open onto a long leafy garden, and the pool is tempting after (or instead of!) a day of sightseeing.

TOP END

Machado's Plaza Hotel (☎ 4008 9800; www.machados plazahotel.com.br; Rua Henrique Gurjão 200; s/d R$160-220; ✗ ▢ ⅊) Next door to Hotel Le Massilia. Come here if you want more modern digs, and don't mind sacrificing elbow room to get it. Rooms are notably small, but have great beds, new TVs, spiffy decor, miniature balconies and in-room internet. Same goes for the rooftop bar and pool area: cool, but tiny. Don't bother with the lone 'executive' room; the huge TV and whirlpool tub don't make up for the fact it opens into the parking garage.

Hilton Belém (☎ 4006 7000, toll free 0800 728 0888; www.hilton.com; Av Presidente Vargas 882; s R$470-490, d R$495-515; ✗ ▢ ⅊) This is Belém's top hotel, opposite Praça da República and offering all the expected services, including a business center, exercise room, lobby bar and small swimming pool. And the rooms are spacious. That said, the hotel could really use updating, especially its gaudy fabrics and aging furniture. (Or else stick with it for a few more years – the '70s are making a comeback.) Reserve in advance for discounts of up to 40%.

Eating

CENTER

Restaurante Belo Centro (☎ 241 8677; 2nd fl, Rua Santo Antônio 264; per kg $16; ✓ lunch Mon-Fri) This friendly, airy restaurant cooks up tasty self-serve, with plenty of options for vegetarians and carnivores. It can be hard to find – look for a sandwich-board sign and narrow stairway at the back of an eyeglasses store, at least when we passed through.

Mãe Natureza (☎ 3212 8032; Rua Sen Manoel Barata 889; per kg R$20; ✓ lunch Mon-Sat) The sterile dining room doesn't do justice to the unique vegan lunch buffet, though the air-conditioning will have you ahh-ing even before you get to the food. Mãe Natureza – the name is Portuguese for 'Mother Nature' – uses only fresh veggies and ingredients (even raw sugar) and makes its own soy milk.

Do Campo (☎ 3241 7512; Travessa Dr Moraes 21; mains R$10-45; ✓ lunch & dinner) This new restaurant's

R$10 all-you-can-eat lunch buffet – not per kilo – is one of the best deals in town, especially considering the quality of the spread, including grilled meats, stewed veggies and pasta. Knock on wood it's a permanent feature, but even if the prices go up, the classy setting and lively nighttime bar would still make this a worthy stop.

K'Delícias IV (Rua Carlos Gomes 237; per kg R$23-24; ✓ lunch) One of the few eateries open on Sunday, its extensive and smartly displayed spread makes this one of the center's best per-kilo spots, and with air-con blasting, one of the most comfortable too. The original K'Delícias I (lunch Monday to Saturday) is smaller but better located, on Rua 28 de Setembro 276 just off Av Presidente Vargas.

Restaurant Açaí (☎ 4006 7000; Hilton Belém, Av Presidente Vargas 882; buffet $29-35; menu R$20-50; ✓ 24hr) Though lacking in character – and with prices that are high even for a hotel restaurant – this is a decent option late or on weekends, when many other places are closed.

Estação das Docas (Av Marechal Hermes; ✓ lunch & dinner) is one of the best places in Belém to get a meal, no matter what you're in the mood for. The complex has almost a dozen restaurants, most with indoor and outdoor seating and serving per-kilo lunches and à la carte dinners. Many stay open well past midnight on Friday and Saturday. **Restaurante Hatobá** (mains R$18-45) serves quality Asian food including sushi, while **Capone** (mains R$18-40) has a large selection of pasta and pizza.

OUTSIDE THE CENTER

Tia Maria (Travessa Benjamin Constant; mains R$4.50-10; ✓ 10am-8pm Mon-Sat) It's hard not to stop at the sight of the chairs here, whose shaggy, multicolored upholstering makes them look like pom-poms, or the Fry Guys from the '70s McDonald's commercials. And once you stop, you may as well pop in for a piece of pie, which comes in a dozen or so varieties. Better yet, come here for dessert after Italian dinner across the street.

Santo Antonio (Travessa Quintino Bocaiúva; dishes R$5-15; ✓ breakfast, lunch & dinner) The high burgundy walls and old-fashioned wood shutters give this place an appealing chic-bohemian look. Inside are a bakery and deli that live up to the promise, with creative sandwiches composed on fresh-made bread. There's a chain bookstore too, though it's very out of place.

Cosanostra Caffé (Travessa Benjamin Constant 1499; mains R$7-20; ☾ noon-1am) The dim lighting and unmarked entrance lend a certain *Goodfellas* ambience, and Frank Sinatra happened to be playing when we visited, but the beefy guys at the bar are mostly business people on break, and probably not packing heat. Lunch specials include a main dish, side dish and soda for R$7, or order larger plates off the menu. The bar is open late, and there's live music after 11pm (see right).

Cantina Italiana (Travessa Benjamin Constant 1401; mains US$9-13; ☒) The pink walls of this cozy pasta and pizza restaurant are covered with framed photos and artwork.

Restaurante Le Massilia (Hotel Le Massilia, Rua Henrique Gurjão 236; mains R$12-35; ☾ lunch & dinner Mon-Sat) Quality French cuisine served in an attractive dining area.

Xicara da Silva (☎ 3241 0167; Av Visconde de Souza Franco 978-A; mains R$12-35; ☾ dinner) Plenty of people say this popular restaurant prepares the city's best pizza and pasta, and you won't find any arguments to the contrary here. With artful and comfortable dining areas indoors and on a raised patio, the atmosphere is just as appealing. For something smaller, try the quiche. Squeezed into a small leafy lot near the huge Lider Z mall.

Lá em Casa (☎ 3242 4222; Av Governador José Malcher 247) A little-known fact is that this Belém institution is in fact two restaurants side by side, neither of them called Lá em Casa. That's the old name, but the owners haven't bothered to take down the sign, and besides, you'll only get funny looks asking for the real names: 'Vero-o-Pesinho' (per kilo R$29; open for lunch, closed Saturday) has a tasty self-serve spread in a casual bistro-like setting, while 'O Outro' (mains R$16 to R$50; open for lunch Sunday only) is a formal glass-walled restaurant with international fare and expert service.

Cia Paulista de Pizza (☎ 3212 2200; Av Visconde de Souza Franca 559; dishes R$20-30; ☾ noon-5pm & 6pm-1:30am) You wouldn't know from the dining room that this is actually a chain restaurant, as the wineglasses, tablecloths, attentive waiters and recorded jazz create a unique and classy ambience. Prices are quite affordable, and the pizza and pasta excellent.

Boteco das Onze (Casa das Onze Janelas, Praça Frei Brandão; mains R$20-55; ☾ lunch & dinner) Part of Casa das Onze Janelas gallery (see p609), this classy joint is one of the city's best restaurant-bars for lunch, dinner and beyond. You can sit in either the dining room with modern art on the walls, or on the breezy back patio overlooking the river. Meals include *muqueca de filhote*, a tasty stew prepared with catfish, shrimp and lobster. There's live music virtually every night (cover R$4), and plenty of good beer and drinks to choose from.

Drinking

Cervejaria Amazonas (Estação das Docas, Av Marechal Hermes; ☾ 5pm-1am or 2am) This boutique brewery has five different beers brewed on the premises and good German-inspired food.

Bohemio Cervejaria (Av Visconde de Souza Franco; ☾ 6pm-3am Mon-Fri, noon-3am Sat & Sun) Cool, laid-back bar with dark wood tables and a huge bank of beer bottles as modern art against the back wall (pray for no earthquakes). There's live music most nights – and a R$3 to R$4 cover when there is – varying from rock to pop to Música Popular Brasileira (MPB).

Cosanostra Caffé (Travessa Benjamin Constant 1499; ☾ noon-1am) Already a pleasant wood-beamed lunch and dinner spot, the bar stays open late and is popular among intellectuals and professionals, with varied live instrumental music starting at 11pm nightly (8pm on Sunday).

Bar do Parque (Praça da República s/n; ☾ 24hr) This outdoor bar is a popular spot for beers and people-watching. Prostitutes may approach male travelers here, but the area isn't intolerably seedy thanks to plenty of foot traffic.

Entertainment

Av Visconde de Souza Franco has several bars and clubs, where you can simply follow the music to find the latest hot spot. Elsewhere in the city, try the following:

Mormaço (☎ 9983 4320; Praço do Arsenal; ☾ Sat & Sun) At the end of a pier overlooking the river, this open-air club is hard to find but worth the effort. Known by some as the *Templo do Rock* (Temple of Rock), it offers some of the best dancing in the city.

African Bar (☎ 3241 1085; cnr Av Marechal Hermes & Travessa da Piedade) Across from the state tourist office, this longtime club often stages samba groups on Saturday nights. Check the posters by the door for upcoming events.

Casa do Gilson (☎ 3272 7306; Travessa Padre Eutíquio 3172 btwn Ruas Nova & Tambés; ☾ 8pm-3am Fri, noon-3am Sat & Sun) Frequently voted as having Belém's best live music, to no one's surprise. Opened in 1987, Gilson's draws intellectuals and hipsters alike with first-rate samba, *choro* (improvised samba-like music) and other music, and terrific food and atmosphere to boot – don't miss the *patinha de carenguejo* (crab cake).

Belém had three art film houses at last count: **Cine Olimpia** (☎ 3223 1882; Av Presidente Vargas & Rua Silva Santos) and **Cine Estação** (☎ 3212 552; Estação das Docas) are the most convenient to the center. The former hosts international film festivals while the latter shows Brazilian and international art films on weekends. In the Centur complex, **Cine Líbero Luxardo** (☎ 3202 4321; Av Gentil Bittencourt at Travessa Quintino Bocaiúva) shows similar fare, usually for three- to seven-day runs.

For Hollywood flicks, try **Cinema 1-2-3** (Travessa São Pedro) located behind Iguatemi Shopping. Tickets are R$12 from Friday to Sunday, $10 Monday, Tuesday and Thursday, and R$7 on Wednesday.

Shopping

Feira de Artesanato (Praça da República; ☻ Fri-Sun) A large crafts fair that has the city's biggest range of attractive artwork, and a lot of it is homemade. Sundays are especially busy.

Natural Ervas (☎ 3230 4667; Rua Gaspar Viana 228; ☻ 8am-6:30pm Mon-Fri, to 4pm Sat) One of a handful of shops on Rua Gaspar Viana that specialize in natural Amazonian medicines, good for everything from dandruff to cancer.

Mercado Ver-o-Peso (Av Castilho França) This and the surrounding area is probably the most interesting place to shop, whether for pants or piranha or anything in between. There are no set hours, but there is something interesting to see from 5:30am to 8:30pm every day. However, you should be especially wary of pickpockets and assailants in the early and late hours.

Artíndia (☎ 223 6248; end of arcade, Av Presidente Vargas 762; ☻ 9am-5pm Mon-Fri) Sells authentic and inexpensive Indian crafts at its main shop in the center and from a kiosk (open from noon to midnight) in Estação das Docas.

Iguatemi Shopping (Travessa Padre Eutíquio) A modern shopping center with designer clothes, bookshops and music stores. Most shops are open from 10am to 10pm Monday to Saturday, and from 2pm to 10pm on Sunday.

Getting There & Away

AIR

Belém's **Aeroporto Val de Cães** is a hub for international, domestic and regional flights.

Air Caraibes (☎ 3224 0000; www.aircaraibes.com)
Gol (☎ 3210 6312 or 0300 115 2121; www.voegol.com.br)

Rico (www.voerico.com.br) airport (☎ 3210 6456); Belém (☎ 3241 4433; Av Assis de Vasconcelos 207)
Surinam Airways (☎ 3210 6436; surinam@amazon.com.br)
TAF (☎ 3210 6501; www.voetaf.com.br)
TAM (☎ 3212 2166; www.tamairlines.com; Av Assis de Vasconcelos 265)

BOAT

All long-distance boats leave Belém from the **Terminal Hidroviária** (Av Marechal Hermes). Purchase tickets from the booths just inside the entrance, preferably a day or two in advance. See boxed text, p614, for tips on riverboat travel.

Marques Pinto Navigação (☎ 3272 3847) and **ENART** (☎ 3224 1225) offer service to and from Manaus, and most points along the way. At last check, boats to Manaus left Tuesday, Wednesday and Friday evenings, with stops at Monte Alegre (hammock/cabin R$150/200, two days), Santarém (R$160/250, 2½ days), Óbidos (R$180/260, three days), Parantins (R$210/300, four days), and Manaus (R$250/350, five days). Remember that cabins fit two people for the listed price; some boats have an air-conditioned hammock area and/or suites.

Arapari Navigação (☎ 3241 4977) and **Rodofluvial BANAV** (☎ 3269 4494) alternate service to Ilha de Marajó, with daily ferries from Belém to Foz do Rio Camará, better known as Camará, (R$13.50, three hours) twice daily from Monday to Saturday, once on Sunday.

São Francisco de Paula (☎ 3242 2070) has service to Macapá (hammock/cabin R$110/150, 24 hours, departure 10am Wednesday and Saturday) with return trips Tuesday and Friday.

BUS

Belém's long-distance bus station is 3km east of town. Major destinations may be served by several lines, while *leito* and *semi-leito* (luxury and semi-luxury) seats are available on some longer routes.

Beira-Dão (☎ 3226 1162) Runs buses to Vila Mosqueiro (R$3.50, with air-con $4, 1½ hours, departures every 30 minutes 6am to 11pm, until 10pm Sat, until 9pm Sun).
Itaperim (☎ 3235 2880) Serves Fortaleza (R$160, 24 hours, once daily), Salvador (R$269, 36 hours, three departures weekly) and Rio de Janeiro (R$329, 53 hours, three departures weekly).
Rápido Excelsior (☎ 3249 6365) Has service to Marudá (R$15, three to four hours, four departures daily, five on Friday and Saturday).
SIPROVAN (☎ 3226 5872) Also has van service to Marudá (R$15, 3½ hours, six departures daily).

BUSES OF THE WATERWAYS

Rivers are roads in Amazonia, and riverboat trips are a uniquely Amazonian experience: the slow pace, sleeping in hammocks, watching the river and forest and local life glide by. But they can also be tedious, with day after day of the same food, same scenery, same ear-splitting music and drunken banter on the top deck.

For most people two or three days is enough to get the experience, but not tire of it. Instead of taking those five- or six-day trips (like Belém to Manaus, or Manaus to Tabatinga) consider stopping off halfway, doing some fun stuff, and then either continuing or even flying the rest. In many cases, boat and plane tickets cost the same.

- You'll need a hammock (R$15 to R$40) and some rope to hang it. A sheet or sleep sack is nice if the temperature dips.

- Your gear probably won't get wet, but play it safe by keeping it in a large plastic bag, tied at the top. This also helps keep prying fingers out of any side-pockets.

- Get to the boat six to eight hours early to secure a good hammock spot. By departure time, the hammock areas will be jammed – you may end up with fellow passengers swinging above or beneath you!

- Most boats have three decks. The top deck is for hanging out, while the middle and lower ones are for hammocks. The middle deck is definitely better, since the engine is on the first. Try to get a spot away from the toilets (in case they smell) and the buffet area (crowded and noisy during meal times). A porter may offer to help you pick a spot and tie up your hammock, a service that's well worth the R$2 to R$3 tip that's expected. A few boats have air-conditioned or women-only hammock areas – ask when you buy your ticket.

- Theft isn't rampant, but you should take common-sense precautions, like locking your zippers and knotting all drawstrings. Don't leave valuables unattended and be especially alert when the boat stops in port. Be friendly with the passengers around you, as they can keep an eye on your gear. The captain may stow your bag in a secure area on request, though it may be hard to access mid-trip.

- Most boats have a few *camarotes* (cabins with two to four bunks and a fan) and suites, with air-conditioning and private bathrooms. The advantage is you sleep in a bed instead of a hammock, can lock up your gear, and usually get better food. The disadvantage is you miss out on the comradeship (and bragging rights) that come from sleeping in a hammock along-side everyone else. If you do book a cabin or suite, avoid those on the top deck, where there's no escape from blasting music.

- Three simple meals a day are included in the fare and served buffet-style. Consider skipping them – though probably okay, you really don't want the shits in the middle of a boat trip. You can always order cheap hot sandwiches at the kitchen on the upper deck. And pack some food that travels well, like apples, nuts or energy bars.

- Bring a couple liters of water and extra toilet paper.

Transbrasília (☎ 3226 1942) Serves dozens of cities, near and far, including São Luís (R$77, 20 hours, one departure daily), Rio de Janeiro (R$313, 50 hours, four departures weekly), and Palmas (R$143, 20 hours, once daily).

Getting Around

Aeroporto Val de Cães is 8km north of the center on Av Júlio César. The 'Pratinha – Pres Vargas' bus (number 638) runs between the airport and Av Presidente Vargas (R$1.50, 40 minutes); the 'E Marex' bus also goes there, but you may have to change buses at the depot (no extra charge). At the airport, turn left as you leave the terminal; buses stop at the traffic circle about 50m past the end of the airport terminal building. A taxi between the airport and center is a fixed R$30 when booked inside the terminal, but can be negotiated to R$15 to R$25 at the bus stop.

The long-distance bus station is on the corner of Av Almirante Barroso and Av Ceará, 3km east of the city center. Going into town, catch almost any westbound bus on Av Governador José Malcher or cross to the far side of

Av Almirante Barroso and catch any bus saying 'Aero Club' or 'P Vargas' – both can drop you at Praça de República. Going out to the bus station, take any 'Guama – P Vargas' bus (number 316) from Av Presidente Vargas.

AROUND BELÉM
Ilha do Mosqueiro
☎ 0xx91 / pop 25,000

Thousands of Belenenses (Belém residents) beat the heat by flocking to Mosqueiro's 18 freshwater beaches. The area gets particularly crowded on weekends between July and October. The beaches on Ilha de Marajó and the Atlantic coast are nicer overall, but if you just want to get out of Belém for a day or so, Mosqueiro on a weekday is a decent option.

ORIENTATION
The island's main town, Vila Mosqueiro, is on the southwest tip of the island. Av Beira Mar, the main drag, starts in town at Praia Farol and runs northward along the shore past Praia Chapéu, Praia do Murubira, Praia Marahú and Praia Paraíso. The other main road is Av 16 de Novembro, which intersects with Av Beira Mar between Praia Farol and Praia Chapéu, at a small plaza and church.

SIGHTS & ACTIVITIES
The best beaches are **Praia do Farol** (in town) and **Praia do Paraíso** and the more remote **Baía do Sol** in the north. Stingrays may be present – shuffle your feet when entering the water to scare them off.

THE AMAZON

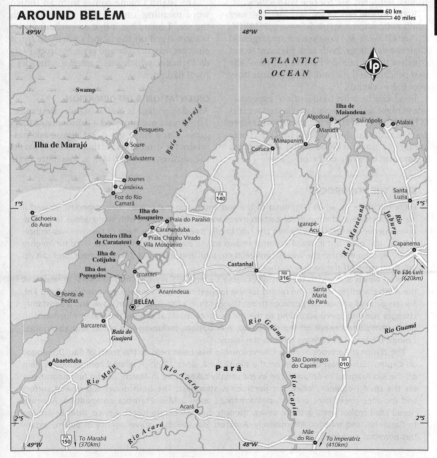

AROUND BELÉM

Mosqueiro's traditional **folklore festival**, in June, features plenty of Amazonian *carimbó* music and *boi-bumba* performances, from the popular regional celebration. The **Círio de NS do 0** is celebrated on the second Sunday of December. Like Belém's Círio, this is a beautiful and joyous event, well worth seeing if you're in the area.

SLEEPING & EATING

Hotel Farol (☎ 3771 1219; Praia do Farol; r with air-con R$90-100, with fan R$80, without bathroom R$60; 🖳) In a converted lighthouse overlooking the south end of Farol (Lighthouse) beach, this unique hotel is reasonable value and easy to get to even if you don't have a car. The building's circular shape makes for interestingly shaped rooms; definitely ask for one with a view.

Hotel Fazenda Paraíso (☎ 3618 2022 hotel; www .hotelfazendaparaiso.com.br; Praia do Paraíso; s/d R$100/150, t/q chalet R$180/220; 🖳) Rooms here are large and chalets even larger, both with pleasant wood construction. Praia do Paraíso is one of the best beaches on the island, but gets quite busy over the weekends.

Food can be a bit hard to find, especially late at night and on weekdays. The restaurants at Hotel Farol and Hotel Fazenda Paraíso serve good, standard dishes for R$12 to R$25. There are lots of *barracas* (food stalls) in the main square and on Praia do Farol.

GETTING THERE & AROUND

Buses from Belém (R$3.50, with air-con R$4, 1½ hours) pass Praia Murubira and Praia Chapéu Virado, then turn up Av 16 de Novembro just before Praia Farol. The actual terminal is another 4.5km away from the beach, but you can ask the driver to let you off anywhere along the line.

Algodoal

☎ 0xx91 / pop 1000

The small fishing village of Algodoal on Ilha de Maiandeua, 180km northeast of Belém, attracts younger Belenenses and a few foreign travelers. It's an attractive natural retreat with hard, windswept beaches and a sometimes turbulent sea.

The island's name comes from an Indian word meaning 'uncountable riches beneath the sea.' Legend has it that an enchanted city is submerged off the island's northern tip; it emerges occasionally and is visible from Praia da Princesa, which was named for the city's royal daughter.

ORIENTATION & INFORMATION

Algodoal village is on the island's west coast. The streets are unpaved – some dirt, others grass – and have no street signs; ask passersby for directions. A tidal channel marks the northern end of town; across it are Praia

---

SURF THE POROROCA!

Every month or so, when alignment of the sun and moon make tides their strongest, powerful waves can form at the mouth of certain rivers and barrel upstream with tremendous force. The phenomenon – which occurs when the tide briefly overpowers the force of the river – is technically a 'tidal bore' but in Brazil is better known as the *pororoca,* an indigenous word for 'mighty noise.' And no wonder: the waves can reach 4m high and speeds of 30km per hour, and can rip full-sized trees off the bank with their force.

All of which is music to the ears of extreme surfers (and wave-surfing kayakers) in search of the mythic 'endless wave.' The record for the longest ride is 37 minutes, covering nearly 13 km. Surfers generally report the *pororoca* to be stronger than a like-sized ocean wave, and it constantly changes size and speed according to the river's contours. What's more, the water is loaded with debris that's been swept off the shore and river bottom, including tree trunks and abandoned canoes. (At least the caimans tend to stay away.)

The National Pororoca Surfing Championship has been held at the town of São Domingos do Capim, 120km east of Belém on the Rio Guamá, since 1999. (A related competition is held on the Rio Araguari in Amapá.) The event usually takes place in March, on the full moon nearest the spring equinox, when the *pororoca* is strongest. The bash draws top-ranked surfers and includes street fairs, cultural performances, even a Miss Pororoca competition. A newly paved road makes getting there easier, though there still is no direct service; from Belém, go to Castanhal and transfer. Alternatively, Amazon Star (p608), a travel agency in Belém, organizes *pororoca* packages.

do Farol and, beyond that, Praia da Princesa. Around the island are three more small communities: Fortalezinha, Mocoóca, and Camboinha.

There is no bank or ATM in Algodoal or elsewhere on the island, and no businesses accepted credit cards at the time of research. Pousada Kakuri and Jardim do Eden have internet access, but the connection is spotty at best.

A São Paulo–based tour operator called Viagens Ecológico maintains a surprisingly handy website about Algodoal (www.algo doal.com) with info on the island's history and hotels.

DANGERS & ANNOYANCES

The island has several tidal channels (known as *furos*, or 'punctures', in Portuguese) that connect inland lagoons to the ocean, and vary in size and strength according to the tide. The channel separating Algodoal from Praia do Farol can be waded at low tide, while canoes ferry people across in high water (R$0.50). A second channel, Furo Velho, is just over halfway between Algodoal and Fortalezinha (walking clockwise). It's larger and deeper than the others and should *never* be crossed on foot, even at low tide.

SIGHTS & ACTIVITIES

Across the channel from town is **Praia do Farol**, a broad attractive beach that's good (and convenient) for swimming and sunbathing. Continuing clockwise along the shore, a rocky outcrop called Ponta do Boiador marks the beginning of **Praia da Princesa**. This is the island's best beach, stretching 8km, with rough surf and backed by dunes, palms and the occasional structure or rocky outcrop.

Jardim do Éden (☎ 9623-9690; www.algodoal-amazon tourism.com; Praia do Farol) and **Kanoa Tur** (☎ 9978 2572; algodoal91@hotmail.com; at Le Café) offer personalized tours around the island, including canoeing upriver and hiking upriver to Lago da Princesa, then returning by foot via the beach; or walking across the island to Fortalezinha and returning by boat. Tour prices range from R$50 to $150 per person.

SLEEPING

It can be hard to find a room during high season, especially at Carnaval, Semana Santa, the month of July and all holiday weekends. Otherwise, there are many more beds than bods to fill them.

Pousada Kakurí (☎ 3854 1156, 8157 9619; hammock without breakfast R$15; s/d without bathroom R$25/30, with bathroom R$35/40) The second little pig evidently oversaw the construction of this hotel, the largest stick house you may ever see. Accommodations are very basic – you can literally peek through the walls – but the laid-back atmosphere keeps it popular with backpackers and young Brazilians. The hammock area is in another building, two blocks away.

Le Café (☎ 9978 2572; algodoal91@hotmail.com; dm R$20) Still being completed when we passed through, this promises to be a good alternative for backpackers. Five dorm rooms have single and double beds and clean collective bathrooms, while the café-bar in front is a mellow hangout spot. The French owner also runs Kanoa Tur, next door, which arranges tours around the island, including sport fishing.

Pousada Bela Mar (☎ 3854 1128, www.belamar .hpgvip.com.br; s/d without bathroom R$25/50, with bathroom & fan R$30/60, with air-con & minibar R$50/80; 🖭) Another clean, reliable choice, this is the first hotel you reach from the boat drop-off. Fifteen tidy rooms are arranged around a pretty central garden, all with high ceilings and attractive decor. An ample breakfast spread is served in the hotel's spacious restaurant.

Estrela Sol Hotel (☎ 3854 1107; www.estrelasolhotel .hpgvip.com.br; s/d with fan R$35/50, with air-con R$45/60; 🖭 🕮) A good value, rooms here are plain but clean, and surround a large leafy garden. The swimming pool is a rare and lovely bonus, though keeping it full and clean is a challenge the staff isn't always up to. Visa cards accepted.

Pousada Marhesias (☎ 3854 1129, 9123 9483; Rua Bertoldo Costa 47; s R$40-50, d R$80-100, t R$130) Just three spacious chalets here face a quiet rear courtyard. All have air-conditioning, firm comfortable beds, private bathrooms with hot water, and a small patio for hanging a hammock. One of the young owners is a painter and not only supplies the rooms with artwork, but offers painting classes as well, all materials included. The restaurant here is well-recommended; located at the end of town, across the channel from Praia do Farol.

Pousada do Boiador (☎ 3279 0060; r with fan R$55, with air-con R$80; 🖳) All-wood construction gives rooms here a clean, dry air, a pleasant change from the stuffy concrete cubicles you usually see. Rooms are small and tidy, with adequate beds and bathrooms, but the best features are the patios with hammocks and great sea views.

The shore is no good for swimming or sunbathing, but there's a deck, and Praia do Farol is just across the channel. Good value.

Jardim do Éden (☎ 9623-9690; www.algodoal-amazon -tourism.com; Praia do Farol; hammock or tent per person R$25, r without bathroom R$75, d cabin R$130-150, extra person R$25) Located across the channel from town on Praia do Farol, the appealingly eclectic main house has large comfortable rooms with fan; three private cabins (one tiny and cute, the others large enough for four) are nearby. Meals are served on a 2nd-floor deck on the main house, which also has hammocks for chilling out. Room prices are steep, but it's the only true beach hotel on the island. The multi-lingual owner can lead or arrange tours around the island. The Marudá ferry may drop you here if you ask; if not, walk or donkey-cart across town to the channel, which is wade-able in low tide, and served by canoe taxis otherwise (R$0.50).

EATING

Virtually all the recommendable places to eat in Algodoal are at hotels, which are always open to their own guests, but in the low season may close to non guests (or cut back to, say, just dinner). Fortunately, the town is small enough that it's not hard to find a place that's open.

Pousada Kakurí (☎ 3854 1156, 8157 9619; mains R$7-20) The dining area consists of a few tables set up on the porch, but that's all you need to enjoy the kitchen's tasty creations – mostly fresh fish, grilled or fried, with veggies and rice – and a couple cold beers. Usually has great music playing, to boot.

Jardim do Éden (☎ 9623-9690; www.algodoal-amazon -tourism.com; Praia do Farol; mains R$8-35; ☺ lunch & dinner) Tasty creative meals, including plenty of vegetarian options, are served on the hotel's 2nd-floor deck, with great sea views and breezes. Canoes are available to cross the channel day and night, so don't worry about staying late.

Pousada Marhesias (☎ 3854 1129, 9123 9483; Rua Bertoldo Costa 47; mains R$8-40; ☺ lunch & dinner, bar till late) Serving a little of everything, from fish and seafood to pasta and pizza, all freshly made and served in a large 2nd-floor dining area with views across the channel to Praia do Farol. You can count on hearing some great jazz over your meal – it's all they play. Live music is presented here every once in a while.

Pousada Bela Mar (☎ 3854 1128; www.belamar .hpgvip.com.br; mains R$10-25; ☺ breakfast, lunch & dinner)

Yet another hotel restaurant, this one serving good no-frills Brazilian fare in a spacious indoor dining area.

Le Café (☺ lunch & dinner, bar open late) Mellow café and bar.

GETTING THERE & AROUND

Access to Algodoal is via the mainland village of Marudá. Boats leave there for Algodoal (R$5, 40 minutes) four to five times daily, with the last departure at 5pm. If you're arriving by bus from Belém, be sure to leave by 12:30pm in order to catch a boat to Algodoal.

Arriving at Algodoal, the boat drops you at the beach, where a slew of donkey carts will vie for the chance to take you to your hotel (per person R$3 to R$5). Be aware that some hotels pay commissions to drivers to bring tourists there; it's possible that 'such-and-such hotel burned down' is true, but you can still insist on seeing for yourself, usually at no extra cost.

Boats return to the mainland five to seven times per day; the first is always at 6am, the last at 1:30pm Monday to Thursday, 3pm on Friday and 5pm on Sunday.

Ilha de Marajó
☎ 0xx91 / pop 250,000

The 50,000-sq-km Ilha de Marajó, slightly larger than Switzerland, lies at the mouths of the Amazonas and Tocantins rivers. It was the ancient home of the Marajoaras indigenous culture, notable for their large ceramic burial urns. Today, Marajó's friendly residents live in a few towns and villages and on the many *fazendas* (ranches) spread across the island. This is a world apart, where bicycles outnumber cars and water buffalo graze around town. Legend has it the buffalo are descended from animals that swam ashore from a French ship that sank while en route from India to French Guiana. The island is well-known for its buffalo cheese, buffalo steaks and buffalo-mounted police force.

Only the island's eastern shore is easily accessible to tourists, and has three small sleepy towns: Joanes and Salvaterra have the best beaches and most interesting accommodations, while Soure has better restaurants and all the services. A number of *fazendas* are open to visitors, and make for interesting though somewhat pricey day-trips. Much of the island's interior is wetland, and is home to tens of thousands of birds, including the graceful scarlet ibis (*guará* in Portuguese), with its long, curved beak.

It's a good idea to bring extra cash from Belém, as credit cards are rarely accepted and the one ATM in Soure does not recognize all foreign cards. Also be aware that Marajó is very wet from January to June, with almost daily rain.

GETTING THERE & AWAY

Ferries to and from Belém (R$13.50, three hours) come and go from a port south of Joanes called Foz do Rio Camará, or Camará for short. There are two daily departures in either direction, and one on Sunday.

GETTING AROUND

Buses and minivans meet ferries arriving from Belém and at Camará, Marajó's main port. Each has a sign to its destination; simply look for the place you're going and get on. It's R$3.50 to Joanes, R$3.50 to Salvaterra, and R$8 to Soure, including the barge across the river. Vans cost slightly more than buses, but will drop you right at your hotel door. When you're leaving, ask your hotel to call for the shuttle to swing by the next day.

Moto taxis are common in all three towns, and cost R$1 to R$2 around town, and R$15 between Joanes and Salvaterra.

In Salvaterra, boats to Soure leave from the town pier (R$2, 15 minutes, 7am to 6:30pm) but you may have to wait a half-hour or more for enough passengers to gather. Alternatively, take a cab or moto taxi to the car ferry port (R$3 to R$8) about 8km from town, where small passenger boats cross day and night, even with just one passenger (R$1, five minutes). If the barge happens to be leaving (hourly 6am to 6pm), you can hop on it for free.

Coming from Soure, the boats that go directly to Salvaterra – the ones you may have to wait a half-hour for – leave from a dock at the end of Travessa 14. The car ferry and motorized canoes leave from a dock at the end of Travessa 15.

JOANES

Head to sleepy Joanes for total isolation. It's got one of the island's most appealing hotels, a good sandy beach, the remains of a 17th-century Jesuit church – and not much else. It is thought that Spanish navigator Vicente Yáñez Pinzón landed on Joanes beach on February 26, 1500 – a couple of months before Pedro Cabral's 'discovery' of Brazil for Portugal.

There are no services in Joanes, save a **post office** (🕙 8am-noon Mon-Fri) on the main road. Shuttles from the ferry port cost R$3.50; moto taxi are an easy way to get elsewhere around the island (R$15 to Salvaterra) or you can rent bikes from Pousada Ventania do Rio-Mar (see below).

Sleeping & Eating

Pousada Ventania do Rio-Mar (🕿 3646 2067, 9992 5716; www.pousadaventania.com; s/d/t/q R$50/60/70/100) sits atop a breezy headland overlooking the shore. Large rooms have whimsical decor and oversized paintings, private bathrooms (but no TV or air-conditioning), and open onto a large patio. The owners, a Belgian-Brazilian couple, organize all sorts of outings, including hiking and fishing with local guides (around R$60 for two people). They also rent bikes so you can explore on your own, and of course the beach – a few steps away – is a great place to while away the day (and no stingrays!). Pay in reais, dollars or euros.

Three **beach restaurants** (mains R$12-25) serve Joanes's best lunch and dinner, especially the Marajoana favorites of grilled fish and buffalo steaks. One is even open 24 hours, for those late-night munchies.

A **no-name pizzeria** (behind post office; mains R$12-25; 🕙 dinner) has no menus and only one table (set up in the driveway of a private home) but serves tasty pizzas made of whatever ingredients are on hand. A large feeds two.

SALVATERRA

Eighteen kilometers north from Joanes, Salvaterra (population 5800) has the island's best and longest beach, the aptly named Praia Grande, a short walk outside town. Salvaterra isn't as big as Soure, but is more compact, so it can feel busier.

Orientation & Information

The main street through town is Av Victor Engelhard, which ends at the town pier. The cross streets are numbered starting at the pier – 1a Rua, 2a Rua etc – though few people refer to them as such. Along the main drag is the **post office** (🕙 8am-noon, 2-5pm Mon-Fri) and the internet café **Cyber Marajó Online** (per hr R$3; 🕙 8am-midnight Mon-Sat, 8am-noon, 6pm-midnight Sun). **Pousada Bosque dos Aruãs** (🕿 3765 1115; per hr R$5) also has internet access as well as **bike rental** (per hr/day R$2/12). Praia Grande is about 500m south of town.

See p619 for info on getting from Salvaterra to Soure and Salvaterra, and vice versa.

Sleeping & Eating

Hotel Beira Mar (☎ 3765 1400; Rua 5 at Travessa 2; s/d with fan R$25/35, with air-con R$35/45; ✳) A short walk from the center and Praia Grande, rooms here are of the large and plain variety, with graying tile floors, TV, and thin mattresses and linens. Those with air-con also have minibars, while fan-cooled rooms are appealing mainly for their low price. Breakfast is included, and the restaurant served decent meals.

Pousada Bosque dos Aruãs (☎ 3765 1115; s/d/t R$50/60/70; ✳) Set on an oceanfront lot shaded by mango trees, large wood cabins have two smallish rooms apiece, each with private bathroom, hot water, air-con, and polished wood floors. The fixtures are definitely aging, but the sound of the ocean waves and mangos thudding in the courtyard makes for a peaceful stay. Too rocky to swim in front, but Praia Grande is a 10-minute walk away. The patio restaurant is quite good.

Pousada dos Guarás (☎ 3765 1149; in Belém 4005 5658; www.pousadadosguaras.com.br; s/d R$125/139; ✳ ✳) This upscale resort caters to package tourists from Belém, but is still a decent value for independent travelers, especially considering it's right on Praia Grande. Suites here are spacious and attractively decorated, with solar-heated water, and are surrounded by large grassy grounds. There's a midsized swimming pool if you tire of the ocean.

Pousada Bosque dos Aruãs and **Pousada dos Guarás** both have recommended restaurants, serving lunch and dinner (mains R$15 to R$35). The first is small, with tables set up on wooden patio and mellow music playing, while the latter is huge and befitting the resort groups it serves. Both serve fairly standard chicken and fish dishes, along with rice, beans and veggies.

There are several beach restaurants on Praia Grande, where you can fill up for around R$7 to R$15.

SOURE

The 'Capital of Marajó,' Soure (population 19,000) is on the far side of the Rio Paracauari and the biggest town on the island. Most travelers assume it's less appealing than Salvaterra and Joanes, yet it's got fewer cars than Salva-

terra and is less isolated than Joanes, which can be just the right balance. Something about the water buffalo grazing on the soccer field and the double-wide streets – many of them grass with just a bike track weaving down the middle – lends Soure a certain charm. And the opening of several new hotels suggests things are looking up here.

Orientation & Information

The streets running parallel to the river are Ruas (with Rua 1 closest to the river). The perpendicular streets are Travessas, with Travessa 1 closest to the seashore. Getting off the car ferry, you will be nearest the corner of Rua 1 and Travessa 15. See Getting Around (p619) for more info on getting to and from Soure and the rest of the island.

Banco do Brasil (Rua 3, btwn Travessas 17 & 18; ☽ 10am-3pm Mon-Fri) has an ATM that accepts most Plus and Cirrus cards. It's still a good idea to bring plenty of cash from Belém, however.

Cyber Gigabyte (Travessa 15 at Rua 2; per hr R$2-3; ☽ 8am-midnight) has a fast internet connection and long hours. You can also rent bikes here for R$1.50 per hour

You'll get a better price on bike rentals from a guy named **Bimba** (☎ 8135 1065; Rua 4 btwn Travessas 18 & 19), who charges R$1 per hour or R$7 per day.

Beaches

The bay beaches near Soure, fronting on water that is a mixture of salt and fresh, are often covered with fantastic seeds washed down from the Amazonian forests. You can easily bicycle or walk the 3km to **Praia Barra Velho**. Follow Travessa 14 out of town till you see a path diverging to the right. If you continue past the Barra Velho turnoff, you'll reach a river where you will see the ruins of a footbridge. If a boat is on hand to take you over, you can reach **Praia de Araruna**, the most beautiful beach, just beyond the river. At low tide you can walk about 5km in either direction along the beach, which is practically deserted most of the time. **Praia do Pesqueiro**, 9km from town (reached by heading inland along Rua 4), is another very nice beach, popular on weekends.

Beware: stingrays are common at all three of Soure's beaches and it is not recommended you swim or wade there. If you must, enter the water where other people have recently done so, as the rays are likely to have been scared off. If the beach is deserted, use a stick to poke the sand as you enter and leave the shallows, and shuffle your feet to kick up a cloud of sand in front of you.

Festivals & Events
On the second Sunday in November, Soure has its own **Círio de Nazaré** (see p610) with a beautiful procession. Hotels can be booked up.

Sleeping & Eating
Hotel Araruna (☎ 8163 7731; Travessa 14 btwn Ruas 7 & 8; s/d R$40/50) Soure's best option, located next to the tall Cosampa water towers. Clean, simple rooms opening on a breezy outdoor corridor. Friendly owners.

Pousada O Canto do Francês (☎ 3741 1298; Rua 5 at Travessa 8; R$65-80; 🏊) An attractive foyer gives way to nine elegantly decorated suites, with whitewashed walls, fine woodwork and comfortable beds. Breakfast is served on a patio overlooking a huge private grassy yard. Well removed from the center, but the hotel rents bikes; the French owner can also arrange guided excursions.

Hotel Ilha do Marajó (☎ 3741 1315; ocean end of Rua 8; s/d R$130/160; 🛈 🏊) For many years Soure's best hotel, though the competition is getting stiffer (and the hotel isn't getting any newer). Long buildings linked by raised walkways have clean rooms. The swimming pool is a welcome diversion after a long hot day. Quite far from the center – you'll definitely want a bike.

Hotel Casarão da Amazônia (☎ 8188 3495; www .amazzonia.info; cnr Rua 4 & Travessa 9) Nearly completed at time of research, this Italian-owned hotel occupies a huge blue colonial-era *casarão* (mansion). Plans for a pizzeria and wine bar were also in the works.

Restaurante Patú Anú (☎ 3741 1359; Rua 2 at Travessa 14; mains R$7-20; 🕓 breakfast, lunch & dinner) A simple place, but one of the island's best. Large servings of chicken, beef, fish or shrimp, plus rice and beans.

Shopping
Cerâmica Mbara-yo (Travessa 20 btwn Ruas 3 & 4) This is the modest shop of ceramicist Carlos Amaral, who combines traditional Aruã and Marajoara ceramic traditions with award-winning results. You can have a short tour of the workshop to see how the pieces are made. Numerous small, affordable pieces are for sale, and each has a particular tale or significance behind it.

FAZENDAS
Ilha Majaró has a number of semi-working *fazendas* (ranches) that are open to visitors. They vary in style and substance, but the good ones are a place for bird-watching, animal spotting and canoeing on narrow rivers in the forest. They're a staple of tour packages booked in Belém – in which case riding a water buffalo is invariably included – but can be rewarding for independent travelers as well.

Fazenda Bon Jesus (in Soure ☎ 3741 1243; admission R$15) Located a short distance outside Soure, this has terrific bird-watching and beautiful natural surroundings. It's rarely visited, so you're liable to have it to yourself. Reservations required; budget a couple hours for the visit.

Fazenda do Carmo (☎ in Belém 3241 2202; admission R$130) Has canoeing, horseback riding, and plenty of animal and bird life. It's on the Rio Camará, 30km from the main highway on the way to Cachoiera do Arari. Getting there solo can be difficult and pricey; ask about tagging along with a group.

SANTARÉM
☎ 0xx93 / pop 275,000
Santarém is a pleasant city, blessed with river breezes and a mild climate. Its location at the confluence of the creamy-brown Rio Amazonas and the much darker Rio Tapajós means Santarém has its very own 'Meeting of the Waters,' as the two rivers flow side-by-side without mixing, two bands of different-colored water clearly distinguishable from the waterfront. A stop here is a good way to break up the five-day boat trip between Belém and Manaus.

Most travelers who do stop in Santarém hop right on a bus to Alter do Chão, a cool little town 35km away with white-sand river beaches and a laid-back backpacker ambience. Both towns provide easy access to the Floresta Nacional do Tapajós (FLONA Tapajós), a beautiful national forest where you can hike, canoe, and stay the night with rubber-tapper families. And while Alter do Chão has good tours to FLONA (and elsewhere), Santarém is where you catch the bus to go there independently. Santarém also has a couple of good museums, a nearby private reserve, and an agreeable waterfront, all handy for a day or two's stay.

History
The Santarém region has been a center of human settlement for many thousands of years (see 'Prehistoric Amazonia,' p600). In

THE AMAZON

1661, more than 20 years after Pedro Teixeira's expedition first contacted the local Tupaiu Indians, a Jesuit mission was established at the meeting of the Tapajós and Amazonas, and officially named Santarém in 1758.

The later history of Santarém was marked by the rubber boom and bust, and a series of gold rushes that started in the 1950s. The economy today is based on rubber, soy and hardwoods, plus Brazil nuts, black pepper, mangoes, jute and fish. The discovery of gold and bauxite and the construction of the Curuá-Una hydroelectric dam, 60km southeast of Santarém, have brought some development in the last 25 years, but it is still largely isolated. A movement to form a new state of Tapajós has some popular support here, but little traction outside the region.

Information

EMERGENCY

24-hour police kiosk (☎ 190) Kitty-corner from the post office.
Ambulance (☎ 192)

INTERNET ACCESS

Amazon's Star Cyber (☎ 3522 3648; Av Tapajós; per hr R$3; ☼ 8am-10pm Mon-Sat, 10am-10pm Sun)
Cinerama DVD Cyber (Av Rui Barbosa; per hr R$2.50; ☼ 9am-9pm Mon-Sat)

LAUNDRY

Lavandería Storil (☎ 3523 1329; Travessa Turiano Meira 167; per kg R$11; ☼ 8am-6pm Mon-Sat) Same-day service if you drop off clothes in the morning.

MEDICAL SERVICES

Hospital Municipal (Av Presidente Vargas & Travessa Barão do Rio Branco) Has an emergency room.

MONEY

Bradesco (Av Rui Barbosa) Reliable ATMs.
HSBC (Av Rui Barbosa) Reliable ATMs.
Ourominas (☎ 3522 7655; Travessa dos Mártires 198; ☼ 7:30am-5:30pm Mon-Fri, 8am-noon Sat) Good rates for euros, British pounds and US dollars.

POST

Main post office (Rua Siqueira Campos; ☼ 8am-4pm Mon-Fri) Facing Praça da Matriz.

TELEPHONE

Posto TeleTrin (☎ 3522 1657; Rua Siqueira Campos 511) Air-conditioned call center sells a variety of prepaid phone cards and has a bank of pay phones at which to use them.

TRAVEL AGENCIES

Getting out of Santarém is evidently big business, as there's a travel agency on virtually every street. The below offer additional services.

Amazon Tours (☎ 3522 1928, 9122 0299; www.amazon river.com; Travessa Turiano Meira 1084; ☼ 8am-noon, 2-5:30pm Mon-Fri, 8am-noon Sat) Organizes trips to Bosque Santa Lucia and area sites. Can also offer tourist information.
Santarém Tur (☎ 3522 4847; www.santaremtur.com.br; Rua Adriano Pimentel 44) Plane tickets and tour packages, including city tours, day trips to Alter de Chão by boat or car, and overnight riverboat tours to FLONA. Friendly and helpful staff.

Sights

MUSEU DE SANTARÉM

Housed in a large yellow waterfront mansion, the **Museu de Santarém** (Rua do Imperador, Praça Barão de Santarém; admission by donation; ☼ 8am-5pm Mon-Fri, 8am-1pm Sat) is also known as the Centro Cultural João Fona, after the Pará artist who painted the frescoes on its interior walls. The building dates from 1867 and has been a jail, city hall and courthouse. In addition to several paintings and documents related to the city's founding, the museum features a small but excellent collection of stone pieces and pottery, including burial urns and ceremonial figurines, from the Tapajoara culture that flourished locally more than 6000 years ago.

MUSEU DICA FRAZÃO

Octogenarian Dona Dica Frazão (b 1920) is the creator, namesake, tour guide and No 1 advocate of the **Museu Dica Frazão** (☎ 522 1026; Rua Floriano Peixoto 281; admission free; ☼ daytime). Slight and cheerful, Dona Dica has spent more than 50 years making women's clothing and fabrics from natural fibers, including grasses and wood pulp. Pieces on display include reproductions of a dress made for a Belgian queen, a tablecloth for Pope John Paul II and costumes for the Boi-Bumbá festival at Parintins.

IGREJA MATRIZ

Facing Praça da Matriz, the city's pretty bluepainted church dates from 1761. Its predecessor church, made of palm fronds in 1661, was Santarém's first building.

WATERFRONT PROMENADE

The Nova Orla Fluvial promenade follows Av Tapajós over a mile from the Museu de Santarém almost as far as the Docas do Para.

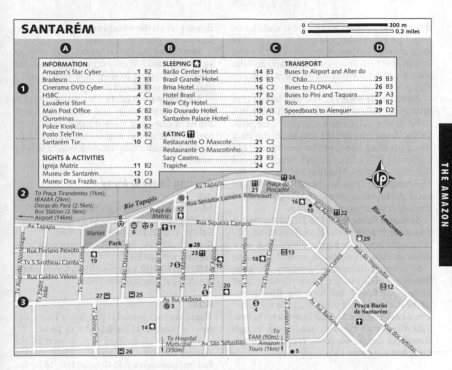

SANTARÉM

0 — 300 m
0 — 0.2 miles

INFORMATION
Amazon's Star Cyber.................1 B2
Bradesco..................................2 B3
Cinerama DVD Cyber...............3 B3
HSBC......................................4 C3
Lavadería Storil.......................5 C3
Main Post Office......................6 B2
Ourominas...............................7 B3
Police Kiosk.............................8 B2
Posto TeleTrin.........................9 B2
Santarém Tur.........................10 C2

SIGHTS & ACTIVITIES
Igreja Matriz..........................11 B2
Museu de Santarém................12 D3
Museu Dica Frazão.................13 C3

SLEEPING
Barão Center Hotel................14 B3
Brasil Grande Hotel................15 B3
Brisa Hotel.............................16 C2
Hotel Brasil............................17 B2
New City Hotel.......................18 C3
Rio Dourado Hotel.................19 A3
Santarém Palace Hotel............20 C3

EATING
Restaurante O Mascote..........21 C2
Restaurante O Mascotinho......22 D2
Sacy Caseiro..........................23 B3
Trapiche.................................24 C2

TRANSPORT
Buses to Airport and Alter do
  Chão..................................25 B3
Buses to FLONA....................26 B3
Buses to Pini and Taquara.......27 A3
Rico......................................28 B2
Speedboats to Alenquer..........29 D2

A nice stroll starts from Praça Matriz heading west, passing colorful boats before ending in the shadow of the massive Cargill facility, a symbol of Brazil's burgeoning soy trade. There is little shade, so bring a hat.

Festivals

The patron saint of fishermen, São Pedro, is honored on June 29, when boats decorated with flags and flowers sail in procession before the city.

Sleeping

BUDGET

Hotel Brasil (☎ 3523 5177; Travessa dos Mártires 30; s/d R$20/35, with air-con 50/60) In a big old building in the commercial area, this backpacker favorite doesn't look like much from outside, but has simple and surprisingly comfortable rooms at bargain prices. Large shutter windows allow for plenty of light and air, though you'll have to close them when the mosquitoes come out. Rooms share a reasonably clean bathroom (cold water only), and breakfast is served in the spacious 2nd-floor dining room. Often full, so call ahead.

Brisa Hotel (☎ 3522 1018; brisahotel@hotmail.com; Rua Senador Lameira Bittencourt 5; s/d/t R$45/60/70; 🌀) *Apartamentos* here are small, clean and straight-laced – the mint-green exterior even matches the room doors, like shoes and belt (or is it socks and tie?). Upstairs rooms have more charm but are often occupied. Still, for reliable digs, a waterfront location and a reasonable price, this is a perfectly adequate choice.

New City Hotel (☎ 3523 3149; Travessa Francisco Corrêa 200; s/d R$75/95) Rooms come in all shapes and sizes (as do the furnishings) in this big rambling hotel with a maze of stairs and hallways. If it weren't for the peppy peach paint job, it'd be straight out of a horror movie. A few rooms have balconies or large windows, which help considerably; all have crisp, clean linens. The official price is inflated, so definitely ask for a discount.

MIDRANGE

Rio Dourado Hotel (☎ 3522 4021; riodouradohotel@yahoo.com.br; Rua Floriano Peixoto 799; s R$65-95, d R$85-115; 🌀) Upstairs rooms are well worth their higher rate, with polished floors, gleaming bathrooms, mini-split air conditioners, even fake

THE AMAZON

flowers and a proper writing table and chairs. Don't be put off the proximity to the market area; it's busy but not overwhelmingly so, and you're near restaurants, internet cafés and the waterfront promenade An excellent choice in this price range.

Brasil Grande Hotel (☎ 3522 5660; Travessa 15 de Agosto 213; s/d R$75/90) You half expect Lucille Ball to be staying in the room next door here, with 1950s decor everywhere you look: the faux wood paneling, pea-green bathrooms and old fashioned TVs with a button for each channel (all nine of them). Not that we're complaining: rooms are large, bright and come with an excellent breakfast spread, making this one of the better values in town.

Santarém Palace Hotel (☎ 3523 2820; stmpalace @netsan.com.br; Av Rui Barbosa 726; s/d/t R$95/105/125; 🔀) All rooms here have high ceilings, large windows and spare, eclectic decor with the same '70s veneer common in so many Amazon hotels – check out the groovy wood-panel ceilings. Definitely ask for a top-floor room as they're newer and provide a little more distance between you and the busy street below. Side rooms have even less street noise, though somewhat smaller windows. You get hot water here, but not cable TV.

TOP END
Barão Center Hotel (☎ 3064 9950; www.baraocenter hotel.com; Av Barão do Rio Branco; r R$165-220; 🔀 💻) Santarém's best hotel, and the second home for business people connected to the massive soy and timber river ports just outside of town. The rooms are comfortable and well equipped – wireless internet, electronic key cards, mini-splits, in-room safes – though the minimalist decor goes too far: with stark white walls and curiously few windows, you might feel a little like a lab rat. Fortunately, you can always escape to the rooftop restaurant, which has a terrific view of the city and river.

Eating
Restaurante O Mascotinho (Rua Adriana Pimentel; mains R$6-25; 🕑 5pm-midnight) On a terrace overlooking the river, this large open-air restaurant is a great low-key place to enjoy a beer, burger, pizza or sandwich.

Trapiche (☎ 3522 0509; Av Tapajós opposite Praça do Pescador; R$7-25; 🕑 dinner) Right on the waterfront, a table along the rail gives you a view of both rivers – the regular one and the one made up of joggers, families and teenage couples

flowing down the wide promenade. The menu has mostly pizza and pasta.

Sacy Caseiro (Rua Floriano Peixoto 521; self-service per kg R$18; 🕑 lunch) Well-prepared self-service spread, including fresh-grilled meats, and a clean, air-conditioned dining area.

Restaurante O Mascote (☎ 3523 2844; Praça do Pescador; dishes R$14-40; 🕑 lunch & dinner) The lunch buffet is tasty and a good value. Fish plates are the specialty at night – try the *tucunaré ao molho de camarão* (peacock bass in shrimp sauce).

Getting There & Away
AIR
Most flights go through Manaus (R$170 to R$200) or Belém (R$190 to R$250).
Gol (☎ 0300 115 2121; www.voegol.com.br)
Rico (☎ 3523 3997, 3064 0192; www.voerico.com.br; Rua Floriano Peixoto 556)
TAM (☎ 3523 9450; www.tamairlines.com; Av Mendoça Furtado 913 at Travessa Turiano Meira)

BOAT
There are two ports for passenger boats. For tips on boat travel see boxed text, p614.

From Docas do Pará (2.5km west of the center) you can catch a *recreo* (slow boat) to Belém (hammock R$140 to R$160; 48 hours; 10am, noon and 5pm Friday to Sunday), which stops at Monte Alegre (R$25, six to seven hours) along the way; or to Manaus (hammock R$100 to R$120, 2½ to three days, 2pm Monday to Saturday), with a stop at Parantíns (R$50, 18 hours); or to Macapá (hammock R$100 to R$120, 36 hours, 6pm daily). Buy your ticket a day or two in advance, especially in high season, to be sure you'll get a spot. Competing ticket booths at the port can make buying a ticket somewhat confusing, unfortunately.

Praça Tiradentes (1km east of center on Av Tapajós) has a port with additional services to midrange destinations such as Parantíns (same price and duration, 3pm Wednesday) and Monte Alegre (same price and duration, 6pm Monday to Saturday). To Alenquer, you can take a slow boat (R$10, six hours, 6pm) from Praça Tiradentes, or a speedboat (R$30, three hours), which departs daily at 3pm from near Restaurante O Mascotinho (left).

BUS
Buses to Alter do Chão (R$2, 45 minutes) stop on Av Rui Barbosa, Av Barão do Rio Branco

and Travessa João Otaviano roughly every hour between 5am and 6:30pm.

Buses to Maguary and Jamaraquá (R$10, four hours, 11am Mon-Sat) in the Floresta Nacional do Tapajós (FLONA) depart from a stop on Av São Sebastião between Av Barão do Rio Branco and Travessa Silvino Pinto, near the Telemar building. Also going to FLONA, buses to Pini and Taquara (R$15, six hours, 1pm Monday to Saturday) leave from a different stop, on Rui Barbosa between Travessas João Otaviano and Senador Lemos.

The **bus station** (☎ 523 4940) is 2.5km west of town. However, departures from there – primarily to Rurópolis, Itaituba, Cuiabá, and Marabá – are unreliable in the rainy season, and can be dangerous year-round due to highway robberies.

Getting Around

The airport is 14km west of the city center; buses (R$1) run to the city every hour or so between 6:15am and 6:15pm. Going to the airport, catch a bus marked 'Aeroporto' on Av Rui Barbosa just west of Travessa Barão do Rio Branco, between 5:30am and 5:30pm. Avoid buses marked 'Aeroporto Velho'; these go elsewhere. Taxis cost an exorbitant R$48 from the airport; or R$35 the other direction.

Arriving by boat, 'Orla Fluvial' minibuses (R$1) shuttle between the city center and Docas do Pará, passing the Praça Tiradentes port every 20 to 30 minutes until 7pm. The 'Circular Esperança' bus (R$1) runs from the center to the Docas and then the bus station; avoid it returning from the Docas, however, as it does not go directly to the center. A taxi costs R$10 to R$15.

Moto taxis are the best way, beyond walking, to get around town. Most trips cost R$2.

AROUND SANTARÉM
Floresta Nacional (FLONA) do Tapajós

Behemoth *sumaúna* trees, with trunks too big for even 10 people to stretch their arms around, are a highlight of this 544,000 hectare (5440 sq km) reserve on the east side of the Rio Tapajós. The forest also is home to numerous communities dedicated mostly to rubber and Brazil nuts, but which also host and guide a small number of tourists. It makes for a memorable Amazon experience: exploring the forest, staying with local villagers, and learning more about extractive trades that are so important to preserving the Amazon.

Four rustic communities have eco-tourism initiatives. Maguary and Jamaraquá have longer, more developed trails and the most experienced guides, simply because they have been doing it longer. Maguary has the longest trail and biggest trees, while at Jamaraquá the tour often includes paddling through the *igapó* (flooded forest). Tauri and Pini are further down the Rio Tapajós, and offer canoeing, bird watching, fishing, even snorkeling. You can visit more than one community, though transport can be tricky.

You need authorization from **IBAMA** (☎ 3523 2815; Av Tapajós 2267, Santarém; ⊙ 7am-noon & 2-5pm Mon-Fri) before visiting FLONA Tapajós or villages. There's also a park admission fee of R$3 per person per day. You're supposed to visit the office in Santarém, but in truth you get permission and pay your fee at the IBAMA post (open daily) at the entrance to the reserve in São Domingo. If you book a tour, confirm whether admission is included in the price.

Indie travelers will have to stop at the IBAMA post in São Domingo anyway, to find out which family will be hosting you. It's a rotating schedule and not always perfectly oiled; if the IBAMA guard gives you a blank stare, the bus driver might know where to drop you. Needless to say a go-with-the-flow attitude helps immensely. And don't worry: someone will definitely take you in.

Lodging prices vary by family and community, but are roughly R$20 to R$30 per person, including simple meals. Hiking and/or canoeing excursions vary in length, from a few hours to all day, and cost from R$15 to R$50 for groups of one to five people. There is also a R$5 to R$7 per person *taxa comunitaria* (community tax) for all outings. Be sure to bring a hammock, bottled water, toilet paper, mosquito repellent, flashlight, cash (in small bills!) and any additional food you may want. There are no stores or restaurants.

Buses to Maguary and Jamaraquá (R$10, three to four hours) leave Santarém at 11am Monday to Saturday. Buses to Tauri and Pini (R$15, six hours) leave at 1pm from a different stop. Prainha I, Paraíso and Itapuama are only reachable by boat; ask on the waterfront in Santarém for the boat to 'Aveiro,' which unfortunately has no fixed schedule or departure point.

Tour agencies in Santarém and Alter do Chão offer tours to FLONA Tapajós. The best use a riverboat to get there, and stay a night or two; you sleep on board, and take day trips with local guides.

Bosque Santa Lúcia

An enjoyable excursion from Santarém is to Bosque Santa Lúcia (Santa Lucia Woods), a private protected forest that's home to over 400 different species of native plants. Guided walking tours (R$75 per person, minimum two people) are an easy and excellent introduction to Amazonian flora, from ironwood and Brazil-nut trees to famously medicinal plants like *andiroba* (decongestant, insect repellant, heals minor cuts) and *guaraná* (said to cure just about everything; see box on p650), and much more. The reception center has a 'Museum of Wood' of sorts, with samples, cuttings and descriptions of the many types of Amazonian trees and their wood.

The forest is owned by American Steve Alexander, who does most of the guiding himself, and manages visits through his agency **Amazon Tours** (☎ 3522 1928, 9122 0299; www.amazon river.com; Travessa Turiano Meira 1084; ☉ 8am-noon, 2-5:30pm Mon-Fri, 8am-noon Sat). The forest is 18km south of Santarém; hotel pick-up and drop-off are included (and the ride there affords a first-hand look at how farming and logging impact the rain forest, too). Tours are available most days; a day's advance notice is preferred.

Parque Nacional da Amazônia

This large (9940 sq km) Amazonian rain-forest national park lies west of the town of

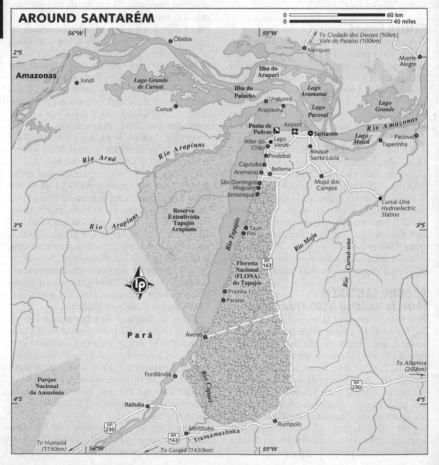

AROUND SANTARÉM

0 _____ 60 km
0 _____ 40 miles

Itaituba (population 65,000), which is 250km southwest of Santarém. To visit, you must obtain prior permission from the **IBAMA office** (☎ 0xx93-3518 1530; Av Marechal Rondon s/n, Itaituba) and an IBAMA staff member must accompany you on your visit. It is possible to stay at rudimentary facilities at an IBAMA post inside the park, but there's no real visitor infrastructure here. **Mãe Natureza** (☎ 3527 1264, 9125 8721; www.maenaturezaecoturismo.com.br; Praça 7 de Setembro, Alter do Chão; ☺ 8am-late) can arrange trips here as well.

Monte Alegre
☎ 0xx93 / pop 23,300
The sandstone hills behind Monte Alegre, about 120km downstream from Santarém, are dotted with caves and bizarre rock outcroppings. They, in turn, are adorned with dozens of rock paintings believed to be around 11,000 years old, the oldest known human creations in Amazonia and possibly Brazil. Most are in red and yellow, and depict human and animal figures, plus geometric designs and handprints of the painters themselves. Some are clustered tightly together, others appear to be isolated doodling.

Tour agencies in Santarém and Alter do Chão also arrange trips to Monte Alegre; see those sections for details. To do it yourself, contact **Nelsí Sadeck** (☎ 3533 1430; nelsi@netsan.com .br; Rua da Jaquara 320), a local teacher and engineer who bears much of the credit for the paintings' conservation, and is the go-to guide for visiting them.

Hotel Panorámica (☎ 3533 1282; s/d with fan R$20/40, with air-con R$40/60; ✖) is one of the better places in town, with a variety of rooms. The cheapies are small with no frills. For a bit more you get air-con, TV and a bit more room to stretch out.

Restaurante Panorama (Travessa Oriental 100; dishes R$7-18) is a reasonable fish restaurant.

Most boats to and from Belém and Santarém stop at Monte Alegre, but there are faster direct boats from Santarém as well; see p625 for more info.

Alenquer
☎ 0xx93 / pop 27,300
Across the Amazon from Santarém, the village of Alenquer was founded in the 18th century by missionaries attempting to convert the local Abaré Indians. Alenquer has several impressive waterfalls relatively nearby, including **Cachoeira Açu das Pedras**. The town is also the gateway to **Ciudade dos Deuses** (City of the Gods), a field of bizarre rock formations 50km north of the town. Another 50km further is the **Vale do Paraíso** (Valley of Paradise), which has a fine pousada and additional waterfalls.

Tour agencies in Santarém and Alter do Chão offer trips here, which are advisable considering the lack of transportation and tourism infrastructure in there. Adventurous travelers can try renting motorcycles in Alenquer and making it to the waterfalls on their own; however, the road is unpaved and can be quite rutted, so only experienced motorcyclists should attempt it. Hiring a taxi is another option: you'll have to negotiate a price, but it is unlikely to be less than US$100 each way.

Pousada Vale do Paraíso (per person R$30) in Vale do Paraíso has quaint, comfortable bungalows sleeping four to seven people.

Speedboats to Alenquer (R$30, three hours) depart Santarém once a day from a pier east of the center, near the Restaurante O Mascotinho. Slow boats (R$10, six hours) leave twice daily from Praça Tiradentes. Most riverboats to and from Belém stop there as well.

Alter do Chão
☎ 0xx93 / pop 7000
Alter do Chão, 33km west of Santarém, is justly the subject of a thousand postcards. A sandbar directly in front of the town forms a picturesque white-sand island, known as Ilha do Amor (Island of Love). The island is largest and most attractive when the water is low, usually June to December. In the wet season it's greatly reduced, though still pretty.

Besides its famous beach, Alter do Chão also stands at the entrance to a huge lagoon, Lago Verde, which you can explore in rented canoes. FLONA do Tapajós and other spots on the Rio Tapajós make for good boat tours. Also accessible is the lesser-known Rio Arapiunes, whose nickname, 'the Caribbean of the Amazon,' is a forgivable exaggeration: the dry season reveals white-sand beaches and, on sunny days, transparent, even turquoise water. And don't miss Arariba, one of the best indigenous art stores in the Amazon region.

ORIENTATION
Only a handful of Alter do Chão's streets are paved. Buses stop at the corner of Travessa Antônio A Lobato, in front of Hotel Tia Marilda and Arariba store. There's an official bus

PREHISTORIC AMAZONIA

Archaeologist Anna C Roosevelt (a great-granddaughter of Theodore Roosevelt) caused a stir in her field when she reported, in 1996, that remains of an ancient settlement in the Amazon were 11,100 years old. If true, it means humans got to South America at least a thousand years earlier than thought. The site is near the town of Monte Alegre (p627) in Pará state, and includes a plethora of intriguing rock paintings that travelers can visit with a guide or on a tour from Alter do Chão.

The Roosevelt controversy notwithstanding, most archaeologists agree that stone-age peoples had definitely populated the Amazon basin by 10,000 years ago, living in extended family groups and practicing primitive hunting and gathering. And it was around 6000 years ago that the Tapajoara people, living near present-day Santarém, carved stone representations of animals and humans, and created simple clay urns, the oldest known pottery in the Americas. At the same time indigenous Amazonians started fishing and collecting shellfish, and mastering rudimentary agriculture.

By the last few centuries of the pre-Christian era, the Amazon was home to numerous cohesive communities, numbering in the thousands and led by chiefs. They produced good-quality pottery and cultivated maize and manioc intensively. It was in this time that the techniques of itinerate agriculture still used today were first developed, including selective burning, crop rotation, and allowing the land periodic 'rest periods' to regenerate.

On Ilha de Marajó, in the mouth of the Rio Amazonas, early people built earth platforms called *aterros* to escape the annual floods, and buried their dead in elaborate urns. The Marajó cultures reached their most advanced stage in the Marajoara phase (AD 400–1350), when hundreds of *aterros* up to 6m high and 250m long were built around Lago Arari. Marajoara ceramics – elaborate funerary and ceremonial vases and simpler domestic ones – are the most sophisticated artifacts known from pre-colonial Brazil, exhibiting exuberant decoration in red, black and white. Marajoara influence reached as far as Lago de Silves, 200km east of Manaus, and the Rio Cunani in northern Amapá.

station a bit further, but by disembarking at that corner – as most people do – you'll be within a couple blocks of just about everything, including Praça 7 de Septembro, the main square.

Alter do Chão's riverfront area has been completely refurbished, with a new *orla fluvial* (waterfront promenade) that extends several hundred meters along what was once just a muddy bank. Stairs, rails, and a new dock area make catching a rowboat to Ilha do Amor easier and safer, while the wide walkway and numerous benches make the riverfront a nice place for a stroll.

INFORMATION

Alter do Chão is growing year by year, but there were still no banks, ATMs or exchange offices in town at the time of research. A few hotels accept credit cards, but better to bring a stash of cash from Santarém.

You can use the internet at **Mãe Natureza** (☎ 3527 1264, 9125 8721; www.maenaturezaecoturismo .com.br; Praça 7 de Setembro; ☺ 8am-late) and at hotels **Belas Praias Pousada** (☎ 3527 1365; belaspraias@gmail

.com; Praça 7 de Setembro) and **Mirante de Ilha** (☎ 3527 1268; www.hotelmirantedailha.com.br; Rua Lauro Sodré 369); all are open late and charge R$4 per hour. **Pousada Tupaiulândia** (☎ 3527 1157; Rua Pedro Teixeira 300) serves as the local post office and there are public phones in the main plaza.

DANGERS & ANNOYANCES

Stingrays are a concern in shallow areas of Ilha do Amor, Lago Verde and in the river. One of their nicknames is 'Wish-You-Were-Dead Fish' which indicates the painfulness of their sting. Fortunately, rays are very skittish and prefer muddy areas over sandy ones, which means they're fairly uncommon in busy areas of Ilha do Amor. That said, always shuffle your feet when entering and exiting the water – this will kick up a cloud of sand in front of you and scare rays away. You can also use a long reed or stick to poke the sand in front of you. They only sting when stepped on, so a little caution goes a long way. Be especially alert in the morning and afternoon, and any in shallow areas that don't commonly have swimmers.

SIGHTS & ACTIVITIES
Beaches
When the water is low, you can wade from the waterfront to **Ilha do Amor**. Otherwise, rowboats will take you across for R$2 per person. On the tip of the island closest town, a bevy of shacks serve food and drinks year-round, and have chairs set up along the water's edge. For a little more solitude, simply walk further down the island (but be especially careful of stingrays if you do.) Another good sandy beach, **Praia do Cajuiero**, faces the Rio Tapajós on the west side of the village. Beaches further afield are best reached in a car, including **Pindobal** (8km), **Cajutuba** (16km), **Aramanai** (26km) and **Ponta de Pedras** (28km). And tour operators in town offer day trips that include stopping at isolated **no-name beaches** along the main channel.

Lago Verde
This huge three-fingered lake is surrounded by forest, and has places to swim, snorkel, and spot birds and animals (including a resident family of monkeys). Tour operators offer enjoyable **boat tours** (per person R$60 to R$100, minimum two people); if you go in the afternoon, the tour usually ends at Ponta de Cururú, a good spot to see the sunset and river dolphins. Freelance boatmen on the waterfront do the same for cheaper, but typically don't have the same service or equipment that agencies do. Or you can rent a kayak at the waterfront and explore the lagoon on your own; just be alert to strong waves and currents.

Lago Verde is also home to the **Centro de Proteçã ao Peixe-Boi** (Manatee Protection Center, better known as the *projeto peixe-boi* – 'manatee project'), which rehabilitates orphaned and injured manatees. Most are juveniles, and are kept in floating enclosures in the lake. Do not approach the enclosures! Rather, go to the lakeshore shack for a some interesting background, then you can tag along in the boat to see the feedings (7:30am, 10:30am, 1:30pm and 4:30pm; per person R$5).

Jungle Tours
Tour operators in town (p630) offer multiday jungle trips from Alter do Chão. Most are on riverboats, where you eat and sleep onboard (in hammocks or small cabins) and stop at different locations for outings. Prices vary, but expect to pay R$120 to R$250 per person per day for most trips, with a minimum of two people.

As anywhere in the Amazon, there is no guarantee you will see wildlife; in fact, this region is better known for its flora, like massive *sumaúna* trees and *Vitória Régia* water lilies, than its animal life. That said, it is possible to spot dolphins, sloth, monkeys, caimans and numerous bird species.

THE TRANSAMAZÔNICA

The idea of the *Rodoviaria Transamazônica* (Trans-Amazon Highway) was born in 1970, during the military dictatorship, when President Garrastazu Médici decided that drought-stricken Northeasterners should colonize Amazonia. A 5600km 'Highway of National Integration' was proposed, cutting across the savanna and rain forests from João Pessoa on the Atlantic coast to Boquerão da Esperança on the Peruvian border.

The vast hardships of the project – disease, dense vegetation, intense rain, encounters with Indians – are legendary. Only about 2500km were actually constructed, and most of the Amazonian portion – from the Pará—Tocantins border westward – is unpaved and poorly maintained. Passenger buses struggle for 36 hours to cover the 1000km from Marabá to Itaituba, negotiating potholes big enough to tip them over; In the rainy season, it's utterly impassable. The section beyond that, from Itaiuba to Porto Velho, and a northward fork to Manaus, have been closed since 1999.

Which is a good thing. Environmentalists have long recognized the serious ecological impact of building roads in the Amazon. Even a poorly maintained road provides access to the forest for illegal logging, ranching and mining, and not just by big-time interests: in 1981, the rumor that Hwy BR-364 between Cuibá and Porto Velho would be paved attracted more than 350,000 settlers into Rodônia's rain forest over the next three years, destroying 5% of the forest every year in the process. Any flight over the Amazon – or even perusing Google Earth – makes the process abundantly clear: Wherever a road weaves through the forest, the deforestation extends in malignant tendrils on either side.

There are various options including visiting rubber tapper communities in FLONA Tapajós and Tapajós Arapiuns extractive reserve; bird and animal spotting in Canal do Jarí; or hiking and chilling on the beach in Rio Arapiuns. With six to eight days you can pretty much see it all, though most people go for three or four.

TOURS

Mãe Natureza (☎ 3527 1264, 9125 8721; www.mae naturezaecoturismo.com.br; Praça 7 de Setembro; ☯ 8am-late) Experienced agency offering recommended excursions and multiday tours throughout the area, including Lago Verde, FLONA, Rio Tapajós, Rio Arapiuns, Monte Alegre, Alenquer, and others. Operated by amiable Argentinean transplants Jorge Bassi and Claudio Chena (who lives on-site).

Vento em Popa (☎ 9654 4245; ventoempopa@netsan .com.br; Praça 7 de Setembro; 9am-noon & 4-10pm) Next door to Mãe Natureza, and offering most of the same tours at similar prices.

FESTIVALS

The **Festa do Çairé** in the second week of September is the major folkloric event in western Pará. The Çairé is a standard held aloft to lead a flower-bedecked procession; its origins may go back to symbols used by early missionaries to help convert Indians.

SLEEPING

Albergue Pousada da Floresta (☎ 9651 7193; www .alberguepousadadafloresta.com.br; Travessa Antônio Pedrosa s/n; hammock or camping per person R$10-15, cabin R$60-90) Super laid-back, this backpacker favorite has an open-air area for hammocks, and four simple cabins, all nestled in the trees a short walk from the center. The cabins are overpriced – you may as well stay in a proper hotel – although you won't find this atmosphere anywhere else. Guests can rent bikes and kayaks (per day R$10 to R$15), and use the small outdoor kitchen. Run by a young friendly multilingual Brazilian-Uruguayan couple, who live on-site and offer guided tours to lesser-known spots. Follow the sign past Pousada Alter-do-Cháo, and turn left on the fifth side-road.

Pousada Tia Marilda (☎ 3527-1144/1131; Travessa Antônio A Lobato 559; s/d R$30/40; ☒) Literally steps from where everyone piles off the bus from Santarém, this simple place has decent-sized rooms and friendly owners. The decor is an honest attempt at cute – well, it's the thought that counts. Second floor rooms are larger and breezier than the somewhat stuffy ones below.

Pousada Tupaiulândia (☎ 3527 1157; Rua Pedro Teixeira 300; s/d $50/70; ☒) The suites here occupy two circular buildings, making for curving walls and uncommon angles. No matter, the units are spacious and clean, all with TV, minibar and air-conditioning. Decor is rather bare, but the shellacked brick interior walls make up for it. Good value.

Pousada do Mingote (☎ 3527 1158; www.pousada domingote.com.br; Travessa Antônio A Lobato s/n; s/d R$60/75; ☒) Two floors of clean, modern rooms are comfortable, if a bit small, facing a compact shady courtyard. Well located, just 50m from both the bus stop and the plaza.

Belas Praias Pousada (☎ 3527 1365; belaspraias @gmail.com; Praça 7 de Setembro; r R$80; ☒ ▢) Right on the corner of the plaza, the location may be almost too good, as music from restaurants and bars can last late into the night. But it's mostly a weekend and holiday issue, and the view of Ilha do Amor from the upstairs rooms is superb. Spacious, clean rooms.

Mirante da Ilha (☎ 3527 1268; www.hotelmirante dailha.com.br; Rua Lauro Sodré 369; s/d R$100-130; ☒ ▢) Alter do Chão's newest hotel is a big babyblue box facing the waterfront and featuring crisp modern furnishings. Only a handful of rooms have, as the name suggests, a view of Ilha do Amor, which makes all the difference. If you don't get one, the rooftop is a close second.

Beloalter Hotel (☎ 3527 1230; www.beloalter.com .br; end of Rua Pedro Teixeira; s/d R$175/205, 2-room suite R$465; ☒) Alter do Chão's most upscale hotel is near Lago Verde, about 500m east of the highway down a shady dirt road. Standard rooms are spacious and modern, with ceramic floors, tasteful decor and small terraces. Split-level 'ecological' rooms have wood interiors, shutter windows and, in at least one case, a huge tree trunk angling through the room. A private beach and clean pool make this a comfortable getaway.

EATING & DRINKING

La Oca (Rua Jo Caisi de Arrimo s/n; dishes R$12-35; ☯ lunch & dinner) With good views of the river and Ilha do Amor, this recommended restaurant (formerly Farol da Vila) serves excellent fish and seafood, including *mosques*, a sort of seafood stew that serves two easily. Next to Belas Praias Pousada.

Tribal (☎ 3527 1226; Travessa Antônio A Lobato s/n; mains R$15-40; ☉ lunch & dinner) Huge, well- prepared fish dishes serve two easily, with potato salad to spare at this popular open-air restaurant. Good grilled beef and chicken also served. Single portions available.

Mãe Natureza (☎ 3527 1264, 9125 8721; www.mae naturezaecoturismo.com.br; Praça 7 de Setembro; R$7-24) Nightly bar and pizza service, with great international music and tables set up on the street right outside the shop. Good place to meet other travelers.

SHOPPING
Arariba (☎ 3527 1251; www.araribah.com.br; cnr Travessa Antônio A Lobato & Rua Dom Macêdo Costa; ☉ 8am-noon & 3-8pm Tue-Sun) Arguably the best indigenous art store in the Amazon, with items ranging from inexpensive necklaces to museum-quality masks and ceremonial figures. Credit cards accepted.

GETTING THERE & AWAY
Buses from Alter do Chão to Santarém (R$2, 45 minutes) depart hourly from 6am to 7:20pm, except on Sunday, when service ends around 6pm. Catch the bus opposite Hotel Tia Marilda. There is no bus to the airport from Alter do Chão; if you've got plenty of time, you can take the bus as far as the airport turnoff, and wait for the shuttle from Santarém to pass, usually once an hour. Otherwise, a taxi to the airport (or to Santarém or the riverboat ports) costs a painful R$60 to R$70.

AMAPÁ

Stretching from the Amazon delta to the borders of French Guiana and Suriname, Amapá has just over a half-million inhabitants, most of whom live in the capital, Macapá. The climate is equatorial and super humid, though drier from September to November. Owing to the proximity of French Guiana, many Amapaenses speak some French.

Amapá is home to the huge – and hugely promising – Tumucumaque National Park (p634). The park is Brazil's largest, and just now opening for tourism. It's an untouched swath of tropical rain forest blanketing a cluster of mountains, rich in flora and fauna.

Beyond that, however, Amapá has precious little to offer most travelers, except those looking for a land route into French Guiana.

MACAPÁ
☎ 0xx96 / pop 350,000
The state capital lies on the equator, in a strategic position on the north side of the Rio Amazonas estuary. Though not really worth a trip on its own, anyone headed to French Guiana must pass though Macapá and won't regret spending a day or two here, with its delectable sea breezes and a couple of nice sights. If you have extra time, visiting the San Antônio waterfall or forging a path to the national parks can be rewarding (though tough) before you head up to the border.

Information
EMERGENCY
Ambulance (☎ 192)
Police (☎ 190)

INTERNET ACCESS
TV Som (Av Mendonça Furtado 253; per hr R$3; ☉ 8am-10pm)

MONEY
Bradesco (Rua Cândido Mendes 1316) Reliable ATMs.
FITTA (☎ 3223 2788; airport; ☉ 9am-5pm Mon-Fri) Changes euros, US dollars and traveler's checks.

POST
Post office (☎ 3223 3803; btwn Ruas São José & Cândido Mendes; ☉ 9am-4pm Mon-Fri)

TOURIST INFORMATION
IBAMA (☎ 3214 1122, 3214 1116; Rua Hamilton Silva at Av Antônio Coelho de Carvalho; ☉ 8am-noon & 2-6pm Mon-Fri) For info on national parks.
Setur (☎ 3212 5335; www.setur.ap.gov.br; Rua Independência 29; ☉ 8am-noon & 2-6pm Mon-Fri) Friendly state tourism office.

Sights
FORTALEZA DE SÃO JOSÉ DE MACAPÁ
The Portuguese built the large stone **Fortaleza de São José de Macapá** (entrance Av Henrique Galúcio; admission free; ☉ 9am-6pm) between 1764 and 1782 to defend the north side of the Amazon against French incursions from the Guianas. More than 800 laborers were involved in the construction, mostly Indians, blacks and Caboclos (people of mixed Indian and Portuguese parentage).

The long pier just north of the Fortaleza, the **Trapiche Eliezer Levy**, dates from the 1930s. Reconstructed in 1998, it makes a pleasant stroll, and has a restaurant at the end (see p632).

THE AMAZON

MUSEU SACACA

About 2km west of the city center is the unique **Sacaca Sustainable Development Museum** (☎ 3212 5361; Av Feliciano Coelho 1509 at Rua Manoel Cudoxo Perreira; admission free; ☽ 9am-6pm Tue-Sun). The primary exhibits, arranged in a large outdoor plot, are reconstructions of various rural homes, from the thatched huts of *castanheiros* (Brazil-nut harvesters) to riverboats used by traveling merchants. Slightly corny, yes, but Portuguese-speaking guides give interesting explanations.

There are no convenient buses here, and it's a long, hot walk. Moto taxis are a good option (R$3).

MONUMENTO DO MARCO ZERO

The **Zero Line Monument** (Av Equatorial at Rodovía Juscelino Kubitscheck), a large obelisk-cum-sundial, stands on the equator, about 6km southwest of the city center. A hemisphere-straddling sports stadium and a sambadrome (a stadium built for the express purpose of holding huge samba concerts and dances) are part of the same complex.

To get there, take a southbound 'Fortaleza' or orange 'Universidad' bus on Rua Tiradentes at Av Mendonça Furtado, behind Igreja de São José. The same bus returns to the centro. The Zerão bus also works, but takes a more roundabout route.

PRAIA DA FAZENDINHA

A reasonably attractive beach 16km southwest of Macapá, which has a number of beachside restaurants with good seafood. From Macapá, take a 'Fortaleza' or 'Santana – Vila Fazendinha' bus southbound from the stop on Rua Tiradentes behind Igreja de São José (R$1.50, 20 minutes).

Festivals & Events

O Marabaixo is an Afro-Brazilian celebration, with music and dance, held 40 days after Semana Santa (Holy Week). In mid-August, the nearby town of Curiaú hosts an exuberant Afro-Brazilian celebration called **Festa de São Joaquim**.

Sleeping

Hotel América Novo Mundo (☎ 3223-2819; Av Coaracy Nunes 333; s/d R$40/55, without bathroom R$25/30; ☒) This place has friendly service and good rooms – get a breezy one in front.

Hotel Glória (☎ 3222-0984; Rua Leopoldo Machado 2085; s/d R$65/85; ☒) Neat rooms and hot showers.

Pousada Ékinox (☎ 3223 0086; www.ekinox.com.br; Rua Jovino Dinoá 1693; s/d R$130/150; ☒) Run by a hospitable French honorary consul and his Brazilian wife, these are Macapás choicest accommodations. Pleasant rooms have hot shower, TV, VCR and minibar, and guests can use the hotel's fitness area, video and book library, courtyard and excellent restaurant. Advance booking recommended.

Eating & Drinking

Food kiosks lining the waterfront, north of the fort, are popular for cheap evening snacks, served at plastic tables and customarily accompanied by a tall beer.

Peixaria Amazonas (☎ 225 2008; Rua Beira Rio; dishes for 2 US$8-10; ☽ lunch & dinner Mon-Sat, lunch only Sun) The 2nd-floor open-air dining area has fine river views and breezes. The chef's special is an ample fillet of *tucanaré* (peacock bass) stuffed with shrimp, tomato and cheese, served with rice, beans and *farofa* (manioc flour sautéed with butter).

Bom Paladar Kilos (Av Presidente Getúlio Vargas 456; per kg R$22; ☽ lunch) Excellent self-service including daily vegetarian dishes, creative seafood and fresh-grilled meats. Clean air-con dining area and good service.

Trapiche Restaurante (Trapiche Eliezer Levy; mains R$15-35; ☽ 10am-midnight Tue-Sun, dinner only Mon) This would be just another typical restaurant if it weren't on the end of a long pier sticking into the Amazon river. Dishes are large enough for two (mostly fish with a few meat and chicken options) and come with a terrific view – during the rainy season you can watch storm clouds march up and down the river.

Shopping

APITU (☎ 222 4329; Av Mendonça Jr at Rua Azarias Neto; ☽ 8am-noon & 2-6pm Mon-Sat) A small but authentic selection of art and jewelry of the Tumucumaque indigenous people who come from the mountainous borders of Amapá, Pará and Surinam.

Mercado dos Produtos da Floresta (Rua São José 1500; ☽ 8am-6pm Mon-Fri) All-natural medicines, oils, shampoos and more.

Getting There & Away

TO/FROM THE AIRPORT

Taxis from the airport cost R$15 to most hotels. There are buses into town, but the nearest stop is about a kilometer away on Avenida Fab.

MACAPÁ

INFORMATION	
Bradesco	1 B2
Post Office	2 B1
Setur	3 B2
TV Som	4 A2

SIGHTS & ACTIVITIES	
Fortaleza de São José de Macapá	5 C3
Igreja de São José	6 B2
Trapiche Eliezer Levy	7 C2

SLEEPING	
Hotel América Novo Mundo	8 B3

EATING	
Bom Paladar Kilos	9 B2
Food Kiosks	10 C2
Peixaria Amazonas	11 B4
Trapiche Restaurante	12 C2

SHOPPING	
APITU	13 C2
Mercado dos Produtos da Floresta	14 B1

TRANSPORT	
Agencia Solnave	15 C2
Buses to airport	16 B2
Buses to Santana	17 B2
TAM	18 B2

TO/FROM THE BUS STATION

To get to the bus station, take bus 'Jardim' or bus 'Pedrinhas Novo Horizonte' on Rua São José, in front of Igreja de São José (R$1.50, 20 minutes). The same buses return.

AIR

Gol (☎ 3222 4857, 0300 115 2121; www.voegol.com.br; airport only)

TAF (0300 313 2000; www.voetaf.com.br; airport only)

TAM (☎ 3223 8100, 3223 2688; www.tamairlines.com; Av Júlio Maria Lombaerd 520)

BOAT

Agencia Solnave (☎ 3223 9090; Rua Padre Júlio M Lombaerd 48; ⏰ 8am-6pm Mon-Fri, to 9am-3pm Sat) sells tickets in Macapa, but the boats leave from a port in the town of Santana, 25km southwest of Macapá. A taxi there costs around R$30. Otherwise take a southbound 'Santana' bus from the stop on Rua Tiradentes behind Igreja de São José (R$1.50, 30 minutes).

Slow boats for Belém depart twice a week (hammock R$100, double cabin R$300, 24 hours). There are daily departures for Santarém (hammock R$125, double cabin R$350, 48 hours) and continuing to Manaus (hammock only R$260, 72 hours). See the boxed text on p614 for tips on riverboat travel.

BUS

Macapá's bus station is on the BR-156 in Barrio São Lázaro, about 3km north of the center. Rain and mud make long-distance bus travel in Amapá very rough, especially January to June, and temporary cancellations are common year-round.

Bus service to Oiapoque and the French Guiana border (R$65, 16 to 24 hours, four departures daily) take Hwy BR-156, which is paved for the first 140km only. If service is suspended, freelancers offer *camioneta* (truck) service for R$120 to R$150.

For Cachoeira Santo Antonio, take a bus to Laranjal do Jarí (US$35, seven to 12 hours, two departures daily); dirt road the entire way.

TRAIN

An enjoyable train ride links Santana, 25km south of Macapá where the docks are located, and Serra do Navio (R$7, five hours), near the Parque Nacional Montanhas do Tumucumaque. Departures are on Monday, Wednesday and Friday.

AROUND MACAPÁ
Tumucumaque National Park

Parque Nacional Montanhas de Tumucumaque is Brazil's largest national park, spanning nearly 3.9 million hectares (39,000 sq km). It borders the similarly immense Parque Indígena do Tumucumaque, in Pará. Together they form the largest swath of protected rain forest. That distinction will only be strengthened by the expected establishment of new parks in the Guyana shield area, established in 2006, and spanning a whopping 15 million hectares (150,000 sq km).

IBAMA is in the very early stages of opening Tumucumaque park to visitation, following a lengthy period of environmental review. Call or visit the IBAMA office in Macapá (p631) for the latest. There are already guided trips around the small town of Serra do Navio, which although outside the park enjoys much of the same ecology. Local guide **Gilson** (☎ 9964 2774) can arrange a tour. **Pousada Cupuaçu** (☎ 3321 1374; s/d R$55/75) has simple rooms with air-conditioning, TV, and shared bathrooms. Or contact **Michiel Swanborn** (http://members.lycos.nl/swanborntours), a friendly Dutch freelance guide based in Rio de Janeiro who's enthusiastic about Amapá for its off-the-beaten-path potential.

Other protected areas in Amapá include **Ilha de Maracá**, the **Floresta Nacional do Amapá** and **Parque Nacional do Cabo Orange**. Like Tumucumaque, they are not yet open to tourism, but plans are in the works. Check with IBAMA.

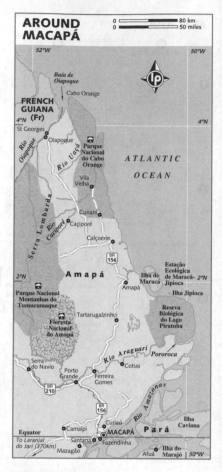

AROUND MACAPÁ

OIAPOQUE
☎ 0xx96 / pop 15,000

Oiaoque is a rough and tumble border town at the end of Highway BR-156, with muddy streets and aggressive money changers. It's separated by the Rio Oiapoque from St Georges, French Guiana, which itself is about four hours (200km) southeast of Cayenne, the French Guiana capital. The town is notable for its substantial indigenous population – nearly half the city belongs to one of four local ethnic groups – but is primarily a way to cross between Brazil and French Guiana.

Oiapoque was long thought to mark the northernmost point of Brazil. The saying *Do Oiapoque ao Chuí* (from Oiapoque to Chuí) is still a common phrase meaning all of Brazil.

The town itself has a monument – **Marco Inicial do Brazil** and a motto, *Aqui começa o Brazil* (Brazil starts here) – to mark the distinction. The only problem is that it is *not* the northernmost point: Monte Caburaí, on the Venezuelan border in Roraima, beats it by a good hundred kilometers! Oiapoque took the news in its stride, tweaking its claim to say the town has the northernmost coastline, which is true.

Orientation & Information

The Rio Oiapoque forms the curving northern edge of town. Av Barão do Rio Branco is the principal avenue in town, running from the Marco Inicial do Brasil on the riverfront south past Igreja NS das Graças and through the residential part of town.

The pier is a block west of Av Barão do Rio Branco. The **Hospital Geral** (☎ 3521 1280; Rua Presidente Vargas & Av Veiga Cabral) is four blocks south of the pier.

The **Polícia Federal** (☎ 3521 1380; ⏰ 6am-10pm) handles passport control, coming or going from Brazil.

Oiapoque has branches of Banco do Brasil and Bradesco.

Sleeping & Eating

Arizona Hotel (☎ 3521 2185; Av Coaracy Nunes 551; s/tw R$50/65) A few blocks inland from the waterfront. Rooms here are basic but clean with TV, minibar and air-conditioning.

Restaurante Beija Flor (Rua Joaquim C da Silva near the pier; mains R$12-30) Recommended for Brazilian and French food.

Getting There & Away

The bus station is on BR-156, a few hundred meters southeast of the center. The airport is further east, also off BR-156. A motorboat ride across the Rio Oiapoque to St Georges costs R$15 and takes about 20 minutes.

See Getting There & Away in the Macapá section (p632) for information on bus and air transportation.

TOCANTINS

The state of Tocantins was created in 1989 by hiving off what was previously the northern half of Goiás. It's in a transition zone between the Amazon rain forest to the north and the *cerrado* (scrubland) in the southeast. This makes for plenty of outdoor opportunities, and the state is making a concerted effort to portray itself as Brazil's next eco-tourism hot spot. It certainly has the potential, from easy-reach hiking and waterfalls around Taquaruçu to vast protected areas like Jalapão state park and Ilha do Bananal, a Pantanal-like wetland. But progress has been slow: the fact that Palmas is 14 hours by bus from Brasília and 20 hours from Belém, and that flights remain expensive, surely has something to do with it.

PALMAS

☎ 0xx63 / pop 175,000

Less than 20 years ago, the broad valley bisected by the Rio Tocantins held just a scattering of rural *fazendas*. Starting in 1989, a new state capital was built from scratch, and construction, state government and economic incentives brought thousands of Brazilians to this unlikely landscape, 1000km north of Brasília and 1600km south of Belém.

There is a surprising number of good outdoor options around Palmas, which are the main reason to make a trip here. The city itself is sure to strike most first-timers as sterile and shadeless, but has a way of growing on you. It's basically a smaller, newer version of Brasília, with a handful of interesting sites and that same planned-city weirdness.

Orientation

Palmas' layout is confusing to most first-time visitors. The current system is actually a simplified version of the original one, which was scrapped because even the mailmen couldn't find the correct addresses.

Praça Girossóis is the center of town, the lake is to the west, and the hills are to the east. Palmas' two primary thoroughfares – Av Juscelino Kubitschek (known as Av JK, or 'Jota-Kah') and Av Teotônio Segurado – are the only streets with regular names. All other roads are named according to their direction and location. Main avenues start with either 'NS' (*norte–sul*, or north–south) or 'LO' (*leste–oeste*, or east–west), depending on which direction they run. Between the avenues are smaller ruas (roads), which are named according to their quadrant, like 'NO' for the northwest or 'SE' for southeast, plus a number: east–west ruas have odd numbers, north–south ruas have evens. Finally, every block is numbered, eg Quadra 101 Norte or Quadra 104 Sul, with numbers increasing as they get further from the center.

Most hotels and restaurants listed here are on the west side of Praça Girossóis, near a small commercial center called Galería Bela Palma on Avenida NS-01. Buses to and from the airport, the bus station and Taquaruçú (p638) stop right in front. Palmas Shopping, a large red-painted mall with movies and restaurants, is on the south side of the plaza at Avenidas LO-01 and NS-01.

To really enjoy Palmas' outdoors areas, you will need to rent a car. Fortunately, driving in Palmas is a blast, with huge roundabouts at most intersections instead of street lights.

Information

MSD Inform@tica (☎ 3215 8562; Quadra 103 Nte, Rua NO-03; per hr R$2; ⏰ 8am-10pm Mon-Sat, 1-10pm Sun) is already the cheapest internet option in town, yet usually offers three hours for the price of two. On the other side of the plaza, try the **Posto Telefônica** (Quadra 104 Nte, Av Juscelino Kubitschek; per hr R$3; ⏰ 7:30am-6pm).

Hospital Oswaldo Cruz (☎ 3219 9000; Quadra 501 Sul; Av NS-01 btwn Avs LO-09 & LO-11) is a recommended private hospital in Palmas' medical district. **Hospital Geral de Palmas** (☎ 3218 7802; Quadra 201 Sul, Av LO-5 btwn Av Teotônio Segurado & NS-01) is the city's main public hospital. Both have 24-hour emergency rooms. **Droganita** (☎ 3228 5804; ⏰ 24hr) is one of several pharmacies in Galería Bela Palma. In emergencies, dial ☎ 192 for an ambulance or ☎ 190 for the police.

Banco do Brasil (Quadra 103-Sul, cnr Av Juscelino Kubitschek at Av NS-01) is handy to the listed hotels, while directly across the plaza **Bradesco** (Quadra 104 Nte, cnr Av Juscelino Kubitschek at Av NS-02) and **HSBC** (Av Juscelino Kubitschek, near NS-02) also have reliable ATMs. There's a **post office** (⏰ 10am-9pm Mon-Fri, 10am-1pm Sat) on the 2nd floor of the Palmas Shopping mall on the south side of Praça Girossóis.

The **Centro de Atendimento ao Turista** (CATUR; ☎ 3218 5339, 3218 5570; Av LO-11, btwn Av NS-02 & Av NS-04; ⏰ 8am-noon & 2-6pm Mon-Fri) is the city's tourist office, inconveniently located in Parque Cesamar, in Quadra 506 Sul. It's a long hot walk southeast of the center; better to drive or take a moto taxi there. You can also try the **Agência de Desenvolvimento Turístico** (ADETUR; ☎ 3218 2396; east side of Praça Girossóis; ⏰ 8am-noon, 2-6pm Mon-Fri), the state tourism agency, though it's more an administrative office than a public one.

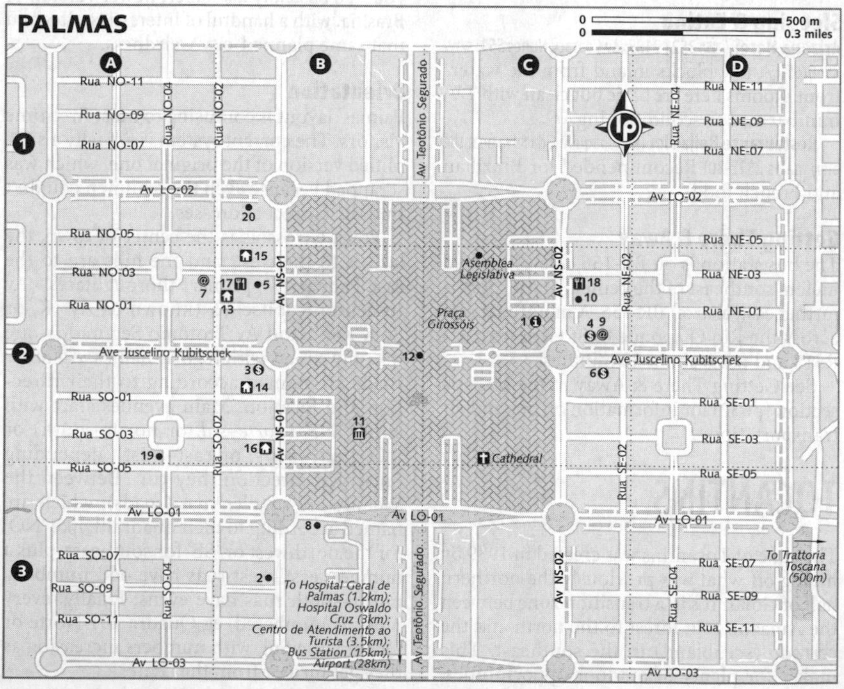

Bananal Ecotour (☎ 3219 4200; www.bananalecotour .com.br; Quadra 103 Sul, Av NS-01) offers tours to the Ilha Bananal and Jalapão areas, and operates a well-recommended ecolodge near Taquaruçu (p639). You can also buy plane tickets there, at **Viagem & Cia** (☎ 3215 2040; www.viagemecia.com.br; Quadra 104 Nte; Av NS-02).

Sights & Activities

Most of the sights of interest are in **Praça Girossóis**, purportedly Brazil's largest municipal plaza and the second-largest in the world (after Moscow's Red Square).

PALACIO ARAGUAIA

Built on the only hill in town, the **Palacio Araguaia** (☎ 3218 1000; admission free; ☉ 8am-6pm), the state capitol, looks over the plaza and Palmas itself. The lobby is adorned with huge colorful mosaics and in one corner there's an impressive scale model of Praça Girossóis, which you can then compare to the real thing from windows on the 2nd floor.

Be aware that you may not enter the palace with shorts or tank tops, and the 2nd floor is closed on weekends.

MEMORIAL COLUNA PRESTES

Housed in a curious white, tubular structure near Palacio Araguaia, the **Memorial Coluna Prestes** (admission free; ☉ 8am-noon & 2-6pm Tue-Sun) tells the life story of Captain Luis Carlos Prestes, who led 1500 rebel soldiers against the military dictatorship in 1924. The march lasted three years and covered 25,000km, and is credited with helping bring democracy to Brazil, especially its long-isolated interior.

SERRA DO LAJEADO

East of town, **Serra do Lajeado** has scores of beautiful ecological attractions, especially waterfalls, swimming holes, trails and even ancient cave paintings. Its sheer cliffs make it a popular destination for rappelling and paragliding as well. Unfortunately, most of the land is privately owned, and at the time of research the best and most accessible attractions were closed to visitors by the landowners. Call **CATUR** (☎ 3218 5339, 3218 5570; ☉ 8am-noon & 2-6pm Mon-Fri) for the latest info.

Sleeping

Hotel Serra Azul (☎ 3215 1505; Rua NO-03; s/d R$50/60; ☒) Clean rooms, affordable price and convenient location make this Palmas' best budget option. Rooms are small with no frills, but face onto a sunny courtyard and a quaint dining room where breakfast is served. Close to the bus stop for those who don't have a car, and secure parking for those who do.

Hotel Estrela (☎ 3215 1895; hotelestrela@bol.com .br; Rua SO-03; s/d R$75/100; ☐ ☒) Rooms here are less expensive than at Eduardu's or Girassóis, but larger than at Serra Azul (and come with internet access and a swimming pool). On the other hand, it's got neither the super low price of a budget hotel nor the bells and whistles of a true midranger.

Eduardu's Palace Hotel (☎ 3215 9300; www.eduardos photel.com.br; cnr Rua NO-01 & NO-02; s/d standard R$92/123, deluxe R$123/154; ☒ ☐ ☒) Whatever you do, don't miss the rooftop pool and patio, which has a terrific view of the city and lake. Large rooms have fresh paint and modern appointments; deluxe rooms are larger, but standards have balconies. Street parking only.

Pousada dos Girassóis (☎ 3219 4500; www.pousada dosgirassois.com.br; Av NS-01, btwn Ruas SO-03 and SO-05; s/d deluxe R$135/145, r superior R$165; ☒ ☐ ☒) Superior rooms are definitely that, with large windows and private verandas. Rooms in both categories are rather small, but have details like a writing desk with leather chair, modern paintings and glass showers. The pool area is oddly small and uninviting.

Eating

Restaurante Cerrados (☎ 3215 5026; Quadra 103 Nte, Rua NO-03; per kg R$14; ☽ lunch & dinner) Opposite the Hotel Serra Azul, serving reliable and reasonably priced per-kilo fare, including freshly grilled meats sliced right onto your plate.

Restaurante Finezza (☎ 3212 1717; Av NS-02 at Rua NE-03; per kg R$17; ☽ lunch Mon-Sat) Directly across from the Miniterio Público building, this popular low-key lunch spot has good self-service with covered outdoor seating. At night, come here for beer and bar food.

Trattoria Toscana (☎ 3218 2795; Quadra 104 Sul, Av NS-04 btwn Avs SE-07 & SE-09; mains R$16-$27; ☽ lunch Sat & Sun, dinner Mon-Sat) The gnocchi, ravioli and lasagna are all made in-house, and served in hefty portions. The spaghetti and linguini use store-bought noodles, but the sauces – salmon, putanesca, and others – are excellent. For dessert, splurge on the divine *petit gateau di cioccolato* (chocolate cake; R$10).

Entertainment

Cine Blue (☎ 3228 0110; www.cineblue.com.br; tickets R$12) Shows mostly Hollywood films; tickets are half-price on Thursday.

Getting There & Around

AIR

GOL (☎ 3218 3738; airport only) and **TAM** (☎ 3219 3777; airport only) are the primary airlines serving Palmas. All flights go via Brasília.

The airport is located 28km south of the city center. A taxi from the airport to the hotel area costs R$40 to R$45, and the same to return. Alternatively, catch the red number 75 bus at the airport curb (hourly 7am to 7pm) to the 'Terminal,' where you can switch to Bus 20 (hourly 7:35am to 7:35pm), which passes Galeria Bela Palma in the center. Do the reverse to get back. Either direction, the first leg is R$1.70; the second leg is free.

BUS

The **bus station** (Av NS-06 at Av LO-27) is at the far southeast corner of town. Taxi fare to/from the station is R$25. To get into town, use the bus stop across the main road from the terminal – almost every bus that passes is headed to the center and stops in front of Galería Bela Palma.

Transbrasiliana (☎ 3217 5600) has daily buses to Natividade (R$22, three hours), Belém (R$143, 20 hours), Brasília (R$74, 13 hours) and Fortaleza (R$192, 36 hours). **Imperatriz** (☎ 3228 5613) runs buses to São Luis (R$140 to 150, 23 hours) daily except Saturday.

For Taquaruçú, take Bus 90 from Praça Girossóis in front of Galería Bela Palma.

CAR

Car rental agencies include **Avis** (☎ 3215 3336, airport 3219 3802; Rua SO-03), **Hertz** (☎ 3215 1900; Av LO-02 at Av NS-01) and **Localiza** (☎ 9978 9995, toll-free 0800 979 2020).

AROUND PALMAS

Taquaruçú

This cozy town is nestled in the green Serra do Carmo hills, 30km southeast of Palmas, in an area studded with beautiful waterfalls and healthy forest. The state and local tourism boards have dedicated themselves to making Taquaruçu an eco-tourism mecca, with modest success. There's no local transportation, however, so you'll need a rental car from Palmas to really enjoy the area's attractions (some sites even require a 4WD during the rainy season). Weekends and holidays can be quite busy.

ORIENTATION & INFORMATION

Street signs are few and far between in Taquaruçú, but it's a small town, and locals and the folks at CATUR are happy to give directions. There's a Banco do Brasil cash machine next to CATUR, and a small **clinic** (☽ 24hr) on the road toward Fazenda Encantada. Look for a couple of small artesanato shops as you enter town.

Near the plaza, **Centro de Atendimento ao Turista** (CATUR; ☎ 3554 1515; Rua 20-A; ☽ 8am-noon & 2-6pm Mon-Fri, to 4pm Sat & Sun) is the best place for information about the area, and to hire a guide to visit the falls and other sites (per half/full day R$20/45).

ACTIVITIES

There are 80 identified waterfalls, caves and pools in the area, of which 10 to 15 are open and accessible to the public during most of the year. The tourist office encourages visitors to use guides for all the sites, though several of the most popular ones are perfectly easy to visit on your own. **Cachoeria de Roncadeira** is the tallest in the area (70m), and **Cachoiera Escorrega Macaco**, just a hundred meters away, is nearly

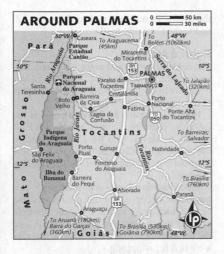

AROUND PALMAS

as tall (60m). Both tumble picturesquely down sheer rust-brown cliffs, fringed by green vegetation and moss-covered stones. Both have small pools for wading and swimming, while Roncadeira is sometimes used for rappelling (per person R$30). The falls are located 1.5km down a leafy well-marked trail; follow signs toward Hotel Fazenda Encantada and look for a large turnoff and parking area as the road ascends just out of town. **Cachoiera Taquaruçú** is a beefy cascade with a choppy swimming hole that can get crowded on hot summer weekends. (There's even a restaurant here.) Look for the large roadside parking area along the highway from Palmas, about 4.5km before reaching Taquaruçú; the falls are a 150m walk from there. A R$3 per person trail fee applies if you come without a guide.

Other popular spots that are best visited with a guide include the **Cachoeira do Rappel**, on the Fazenda Encantada grounds and used for rappelling (naturally), and **Vale do Vai-Quem-Quer**, a broad valley with a series of falls and good swimming spots. Before setting out, discuss with your guide what type of falls you'd like to see, how much hiking and driving you want, and whether the car you have is adequate for all sites (some require 4WD, especially in the rainy season).

SLEEPING & EATING
You can stay in town or a nearby eco-lodge. All accommodations come with free breakfast.

Pousada Lokau (☎ 3554 1238; 3a Av; r per person R$25) Part art gallery, part pousada, the Lokau

has five clean, comfortable rooms that open onto a pleasant garden. The heat and vegetation can make some rooms a bit musty, though high ceilings and stand-up fans help. To get here, turn left after the plaza, right just before Restaurante Mandala, and left at the roundabout. The pousada is at the next corner on your left.

Pousada Catarse (☎ 3554 1237; Rua 20, 2 blocks from CATUR; s R$30-40, d R$60-70) Very homey, with a common kitchen and small TV room, complete with aquarium. One room has a private bathroom, while the other two share one in the hallway; all have ceiling fans and simple cozy decor. Usually open on weekends only; call ahead if you'll be visiting during the week.

Hotel Fazenda Encantada (☎ 3533 1054, 9973 2294; www.hotelfazendaencantada.com.br; 10.5km from Taquaruçú; s/d with full board R$170/250; 🏊) Taquaruçú's best accommodations, the Fazenda Ecantada is a complete eco-resort, with comfortable upscale rooms and bungalows, and 9km of private trails (and several waterfalls, including one for rappelling) on the hotel's extensive property. Open to walk-ins Saturday and Sunday only.

Restaurante Mandala (Av Belo Horizonte; 🕐 lunch daily, dinner Wed-Sun) Right around the corner from the plaza, on the road toward Fazenda Encantada. The fixed-plate lunch comes with pasta, rice, beans, salad, *farofa* (manioc flour sautéed with butter) and a choice of meat, all for R$5.

GETTING THERE & AWAY
By car, take Hwy TO-010 past the bus station and follow the signs, passing first through the town of Taquaralto.

Bus 90 passes Galería Bela Palma on its way to and from Taquaruçú (US$1.50; 45 minutes). Remember that you need a car to visit the falls there.

Parque Estadual do Jalapão
Jalapão State Park is a unique 34,000-sq-km area in far eastern Tocantins, combining cerrado vegetation, hills, caves, crystalline rivers and springs, 40m-high sand dunes, waterfalls, freshwater bathing spots, odd rock formations, quite a range of wildlife – including anteaters, armadillos, macaws and rheas – and very few people indeed. The best season to explore Jalapão is the dry season from June to September.

THE AMAZON

THE AMAZON

Bananal Ecotour (☎ 3219 4200; www.bananal ecotour.com.br; Quadra 103 Sul, Av NS-01, Palmas) and **Jalapão Adventure** (☎ 3224 4378, 9977 2233; jalapao adventure@hotmail.com) arrange wide-ranging tours of the park, lasting from three to seven days. You typically travel in vans or converted trucks, stopping for hiking, swimming and other excursions, and staying in tents or simple camps. Prices start at around R$600 per person, varying widely according to the number of days, number of people, and the type of transport and accommodations used on the trip.

Ilha do Bananal

Ilha do Bananal is arguably the world's biggest river island – only Ilha do Marajó in Pará state is bigger, and some say Marajó doesn't qualify since part of it faces the ocean. Bananal covers 19,000 sq km, slightly less than the size of Israel, and is formed where the Rio Javaés splits from the Rio Araguaia and rejoins it 350km downstream. The island is so big it has its own rivers, stretching over 250km. Three distinct ecosystems converge here – rain forest, cerrado and wetland – and the island teems with plant and animal life; the bird-watching is especially noteworthy. Tours are available during the dry season only, from roughly June through October.

Bananal Ecotour (☎ 3219 4200; www.bananalecotour .com.br; Quadra 103 Sul, Av NS-01, Palmas) arranges three-day, two-night all-inclusive tours to Ilha do Bananal and Lagoa da Confuão, a large lake east of the island (per person R$710 to R$980 for groups of two to four people). The trips include mild forest walks, nighttime caiman spotting, fishing, boat trips, and visits to a freshwater turtle rescue program and an indigenous community. The birding is great and you can count on seeing dolphins, caimans and giant river turtles. It's possible – but quite difficult – to see the island's other inhabitants, including tapirs, fox and marhays, and jaguar.

NATIVIDADE

☎ 0xx63 / pop 6200

The pleasant little town of Natividade is 230km from Palmas in southeast Tocantins, in a valley beneath the green and wooded Serra Geral. Natividade is Tocantins' oldest town, founded in 1734. The Portuguese and their African slaves came to the Serra Geral in a minor gold rush in the 1720s, but when

the gold gave out they moved down the hill and turned to cattle herding.

Sights & Activities

The cobbled streets and prettily painted, tile-roofed, 18th- and 19th-century houses of Natividade's historic center are protected as part of the national historic heritage.

Igreja NS do Rosário dos Pretos, known as the Igreja dos Escravos (Slaves' Church), was built in 1828 by slaves, who were not allowed to use the Whites' Church. Construction was reportedly never completed, and it remains roofless.

Museu Municipal (Praça Leopoldo de Bulhões; ☉ 8am-1pm Mon-Fri) occupies the old prison, evident by the thick walls and heavy doors. Simple exhibits tell the story of Natividade; among the artifacts is a tree trunk to which slaves were tied for whipping.

Half a kilometer from Praça Leopoldo de Bulhões – and reputedly connected to it by a tunnel – are the **Poções**, a series of small waterfalls and refreshing natural bathing pools, and beyond that the remains of **São Luiz**, the original settlement of the 1720s gold prospectors. About 4km from town are **Cachoeiras do Paraíso**, another series of natural bathing pools, though they often dry to a trickle from June to September. Local kids can lead you to either for a small tip.

Dona Romana is a local spiritual medium who awaits the end of the world at her home 1.5km north along Hwy TO-280, toward Dianópolis. She will cleanse your spirit in exchange for a bit of *pinga* (high-proof sugarcane alcohol), then walk you through her fantastic garden.

Sleeping

Hotel Serra Geral (☎ 3372 1160; 1.7km north of the center, 300m before the Trevo Norte; s/d with fan R$40/55, with air-con R$66/100). Natividade's best hotel is a short distance from town, with friendly management and clean, modern rooms that open onto breezy corridors.

Getting There & Away

Natividade is on the best road between Palmas and Brasília (Hwy TO-050); longer but in much better condition than Hwy BR-153).

Buses or vans for Palmas (R$25, three hours) leave every one to two hours from 7am to 3pm; arrive 30 minutes early as the bus is known to leave ahead of schedule. There are also night buses to Brasília (US$95, eight hours) with connections to Lençóis, Salvador and Goiânia.

AMAZONAS

Amazonas is Brazil's largest state, spanning almost 1.6 million sq km. You could fit four Germanys within its borders with room left over for, say, Greece. It is here that the massive Solimões, Negro and Madeira-Mamoré rivers converge to form the Rio Amazonas, the granddaddy of them all. Life in Amazonas state is lashed inextricably to those waterways, and the thousands of smaller ones: transportation, food, water, waste removal and, of course, tourism. For travelers, Amazonas state is not the only place to visit 'the Amazon' but certainly the most popular, with Manaus as the main hub. Tour operators in Manaus specialize in three- to six-day excursions into the forest, or you can book a stay at one of the nearby jungle lodges. Manaus also is a jumping-off point for trips deeper into the state's vast rain forest, whether up the Rio Negro to reserves like Jaú or Xixuaú or the Rio Solimões, to Mamirauá and the 'Triple Frontier.'

History

The modern history of the Amazon begins in 1842, in the US, when Charles Goodyear developed the vulcanization process that made natural rubber durable. Fifty years later Irishman John Dunlop invented pneumatic rubber tires, and soon there was an unquenchable demand for the milky white sap of *Hevea brasiliensis*, the Brazilian rubber tree.

Poor farmers in Brazil's drought-ridden northeast were lured into the Amazon by the promise of land and prosperity as *seringueiros* (rubber tappers). A feudal system quickly took root, with rubber tappers trapped in virtual serfdom by debt, illiteracy, and the trickery and brutality of rubber barons and their armed thugs. As if that weren't enough, *seringueiros* also had to contend with jungle fevers, Indian attacks and all manner of deprivation. It was primarily on their backs that Manaus was built, a grand prosperous city rising improbably from the Amazon rain forest.

Despite Brazilian efforts to protect the country's world rubber monopoly, rubber tree seeds were smuggled to London, and before long cultivated in massive planta-

tions in British colonies in the South Pacific. By the 1920s, prices fell and the Amazon's great rubber boom was over. WWII brought a temporary revival, as thousands of 'rubber soldiers' were recruited to gather rubber for the Allied cause.

In the 1970s, the slogan '*Integrar para não entregar*' (essentially, 'Use it or lose it') was part of the rationale for building roads deep into the Amazon, including the infamous Trans-Amazonian highway. Speculators and squatters poured into the rain forest, and the trees fell at prodigious rates. Satellite images of thousands of fires burning across the Amazon – slash and burn being the easiest way to clear the dense forest – eventually awakened the international environmental community. Eco-tourism was promoted here, as elsewhere, as a new and better way to 'Use it or Lose it.'

MANAUS

☎ 0xx92 / pop 2 million

Manaus is the Amazon's largest city, an incongruous pocket of urbanity in the middle of the jungle, a major port for ocean vessels that's 1500km from the ocean. The rain forest has a population density half that of Mongolia's, but the journey there invariably begins in (or passes through) this bustling city of two million souls. Don't be surprised if you feel a little out of whack.

The city itself has some genuinely rewarding sights, including a leafy zoo with as many animals out of the cages as in them, and a beach-and-museum combo that gets you out of the city center. It's a place to stock up on anything you forgot to pack, or to refill your tank with beer and internet after a week in the forest.

Manaus is also where most Amazon tour operators are based; plenty are honest professionals, but the city is also full of scammers. See p655 for tips on avoiding them, including right when you step off the plane. And remember that Manaus is not the only place to book a jungle tour! There are numerous options in cities further up- and downstream that may give more options off-the-beaten path than possible in well-worn Manaus.

Information
EMERGENCY
Police stations are located across from the bus station on Praça da Matriz and at the Centro de Atendimento ao Turista.

THE AMAZON

Ambulance (☎ 192)

State Police (☎ 190)

Tourist Police (Map p643; ☎ 3215 7125; Av Lourenço da Silva Braga & Rua Lima Bacuri; ☺ 24hr)

INTERNET ACCESS

Amazon Cyber Café (Map p643; Av Getúlio Vargas; per hr R$3.50; ☺ 9:30am-11pm Mon-Thu, 9:30am-10pm Fri, 10am-9pm Sat, noon-8pm Sun)

Juliana Cyber Café (Map p643; Av Joaquím Nabuco; per hr R$2; ☺ 8am-11pm)

LogiNet Cyber Café (Map p643; ☎ 3248 4498; Rua 10 de Julho 625; per hr R$3-4; ☺ 8am-10pm Mon-Sat, 2-9pm Sun)

Selva Cyber Café (Map p643; Rua Joaquim Sarmento; per hr R$2.50; ☺ 7am-7:30pm Mon-Fri, 7am-6pm Sat)

LAUNDRY

In addition to the below, most hotels offer laundry service to guests.

Lavandería Paradise (Map p643; ☎ 3633 6092; Rua Quintino Bocaiuva; per piece R$1.50-3, per kg R$10; ☺ 8am-6pm Mon-Sat)

LEFT LUGGAGE

Most hotels will store extra luggage (for free or a small fee) for guests who are taking short excursions, even if you do not plan to stay there when you return. The airport and long distance bus station also have left-luggage service.

MEDICAL SERVICES

Hospital de Doenças Tropicais (Hospital of Tropical Illnesses; Map p643; ☎ 3238 1146; Av Pedro Teixeira 25) Specializes in tropical diseases.

Unimed (Map p643; ☎ 3633 4431; Av Japurá 241; emergency ☺ 24hr) One of the best private hospitals in the city.

Yellow fever vaccines airport (☺ 24hr); long distance bus station (☺ 8am-noon & 2-5pm Mon-Fri); Hospital de Doenças (☺ 9am-6pm) Yellow fever vaccines are free, but are not effective until 10 days after administration. A yellow fever vaccine certificate is usually required when entering Brazil by land or water.

MONEY

Amazônia Turismo (Map p643; ☎ 3622 7206; Av Sete de Setembro 1251) Decent exchange rates for US dollars and euros, plus Amex and Visa traveler's checks. A branch at Millennium Shopping Mall is open 10am-10pm.

Banco do Brasil (Map p643; Rua Guilherme Moreira 315; exchange office ☺ 9am-3pm Mon-Fri) Exchange foreign cash and traveler's checks at the exchange office on the 3rd floor.

Bradesco Av Sete de Setembro (Map p643; Av Sete de Setembro at Rua Barroso); Av Eduardo Ribeiro (Map p643; Av

Eduardo Ribeiro at Rua Saldanha Marinho) Both branches have reliable ATMs.

HSBC Rua Dr Moreira 226 (Map p643; Rua Dr Moreira 226; ☺ 9am-3pm Mon-Fri); Rua 24 de Maio (Map p643; Rua 24 de Maio at Rua Azevedo; ☺ 9am-3pm Mon-Fri)

Selvatur (Map p643; ☎ 3622 2577; Praça Tenreiro Aranha 17; ☺ 8am-6pm Mon-Fri, 8am-noon Sat, 8-9am Sun) The local Amex representative.

POST

Airport branch office (lower level; ☺ 9:30am-12:30pm & 1:30-5pm)

Main post office (Map p643; Rua Marcílio Dias 160; ☺ 8am-4pm Mon-Fri, 8am-noon Sat)

Selvatur (Map p643; ☎ 3622 2577; Praça Tenreiro Aranha 17; ☺ 8am-6pm Mon-Fri, 8am-noon Sat, 8-9am Sun) Local American Express representative; will hold packages sent to Amex cardholders for up to 30 days.

TELEPHONE

Embratel cards, available at the post office, are best for making international calls from payphones (per minute R$0.50-1). Most internet cafés have Skype-ready computers.

Discover Internet (Map p643; ☎ 3233 0121; Rua Marcílio Dias; per min R$1-3; ☺ 8:30am-6pm Mon-Fri, 8:30am-5pm Sat) Offers web-based international phone service. This and other internet cafés have Skype-ready computers and headsets as well.

TOURIST INFORMATION

Centro de Atendimento ao Turista (Map p643; www.amazonastur.am.gov.br) Tourist Assistance Centers operated by Amazonastur, the state tourism agency, are located at the corner of Rua Ramos Ferreira and Rua Tapajos (☎ 3622 0767) and at the corner of Av Eduardo Ribeiro and Rua José Clemente. The administrative office (☎ 2123 3800) is on Rua Saldanha Marinho near Rua Lobo D'Almada. There is also a kiosk at the airport, though it is manned only sporadically.

TRAVEL AGENCIES

Paradise Turismo (Map p643; ☎ 3633 8301; Av Eduardo Ribeiro 656; ☺ 8am-6pm Mon-Fri, 8:30am-noon Sat)

Selvatur (Map p643; ☎ 3622 2577; Praça Tenreiro Aranha 17; ☺ 8am-6pm Mon-Fri, 8am-noon Sat, 8-9am Sun)

Sights

TEATRO AMAZONAS

Manaus' famous opera house, the **Teatro Amazonas** (Map p643; ☎ 3232 1768; Rua Jose Clemente; ☺ 9am-5pm), was designed in eclectic neoclassical style by engineers from Lisbon and a team of interior designers at the height of the rubber boom. Opened in 1896, this beautiful

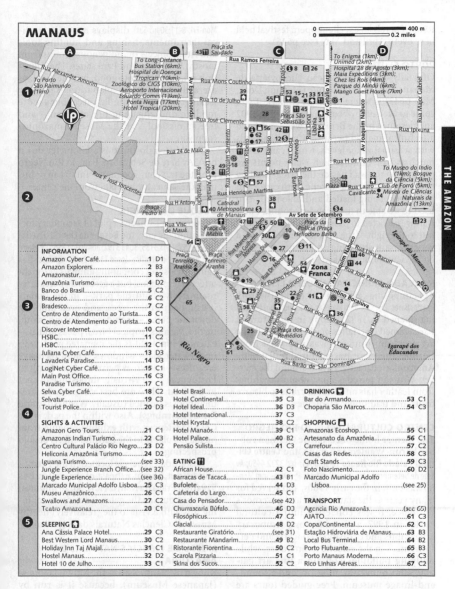

INFORMATION
Amazon Cyber Café	1 D1
Amazon Explorers	2 B3
Amazonastur	3 B2
Amazônia Turismo	4 D2
Banco do Brasil	5 C2
Bradesco	6 C2
Bradesco	7 C3
Centro de Atendimento ao Turista	8 C1
Centro de Atendimento ao Turista	9 C1
Discover Internet	10 C2
HSBC	11 C1
HSBC	12 C1
Juliana Cyber Café	13 D3
Lavadería Paradise	14 C2
LogiNet Cyber Café	15 C1
Main Post Office	16 C3
Paradise Turismo	17 C1
Selva Cyber Café	18 C3
Selvatur	19 C3
Tourist Police	20 D3

SIGHTS & ACTIVITIES
Amazon Gero Tours	21 C1
Amazonas Indian Turismo	22 C3
Centro Cultural Palácio Rio Negro	23 D2
Heliconia Amazônia Turismo	24 D2
Iguana Turismo	(see 33)
Jungle Experience Branch Office	(see 32)
Jungle Experience	(see 36)
Marcado Municipal Adolfo Lisboa	25 C3
Museu Amazônico	26 C1
Swallows and Amazons	27 C3
Teatro Amazonas	28 C1

SLEEPING 🏠
Ana Cássia Palace Hotel	29 C3
Best Western Lord Manaus	30 C3
Holiday Inn Taj Majal	31 C1
Hostel Manaus	32 D2
Hotel 10 de Julho	33 C1

Hotel Brasil	34 C1
Hotel Continental	35 C3
Hotel Ideal	36 D3
Hotel Internacional	37 C3
Hotel Krystal	38 C2
Hotel Manaós	39 C1
Hotel Palace	40 B2
Pensão Sulista	41 C3

EATING 🍴
African House	42 C1
Barracas de Tacacá	43 B1
Bufolete	44 D3
Cafeteria do Largo	45 C1
Casa do Pensador	(see 42)
Churrascaria Búfalo	46 D3
Filosóphicus	47 C2
Glacial	48 D2
Restaurante Giratório	(see 31)
Restaurante Mandarim	49 B2
Ristorante Fiorentina	50 C2
Scarola Pizzaria	51 C1
Skina dos Sucos	52 C2

DRINKING 🍷
Bar do Armando	53 C1
Choparia São Marcos	54 C3

SHOPPING 🛍
Amazonas Ecoshop	55 C1
Artesanato da Amazônia	56 C1
Carrefour	57 C2
Casas das Redes	58 C3
Craft Stands	59 C3
Foto Nascimento	60 D2
Marcado Municipal Adolfo Lisboa	(see 25)

TRANSPORT
Agência Rio Amazonas	(see 65)
AJATO	61 C3
Copa/Continental	62 C1
Estação Hidroviária de Manaus	63 B3
Local Bus Terminal	64 B2
Porto Flutuante	65 B3
Porto Manaus Moderna	66 C3
Rico Linhas Aéreas	67 C2

theater symbolizes the opulence that once was Manaus. The artists and most of the materials (Italian marble and glass, Scottish cast iron) were imported from Europe. The wood is Brazilian but even some of that was sent to Europe to be carved. One truly homespun feature was the roadway outside the entrance; it is made of rubber, so that late-arriving car-

riages wouldn't create too much noise. The theater has been restored four times (most recently in 1990).

Interesting guided tours (R$10, 30 minutes, 9am to 4pm) are offered every day except Sunday, often in English. Concerts (classical and popular), opera, theater and dance events are held all year, with tickets ranging from R$5 to

R$60. There's an excellent opera festival held here every April and May (see p646).

PORTO FLUTUANTE

Officially called the Estaçáo Hidroviária de Manaus, the Porto Flutuante (Floating Dock; Map p643) is where you'll disembark if you come to Manaus by boat. Inaugurated in 1902 and designed by the British, it was considered a technical marvel because it rises and falls with seasonal water levels, which can vary as much as 14m (annual high-water points are marked on the wall beside the bridge leading to the dock). It's quite a scene, with cargo and passengers being loaded and unloaded. You used to be able to just wander around, but it is now restricted to passengers only. A bridge just to the right of the port entrance leads to a very pleasant shopping and eating area with good views of the docks.

MERCADO MUNICIPAL ADOLFO LISBOA

This imposing cast-iron city **market** (Map p643; Rua dos Barés; 8am-5pm Mon-Sat, 6am-noon Sun) building opened in 1882, a copy in miniature of Paris' famed Les Halles market. Although the art nouveau ironwork was imported from Europe, the place has acquired a distinctly Amazonian character. In and around the market, you can purchase just about anything, from leather hats and Indian crafts to bizarre fruits and traditional medicines.

CENTRO CULTURAL PALÁCIO RIO NEGRO

The former home of eccentric German rubber baron Waldemar Scholz, the **Centro Cultural Palácio Rio Negro** (Map p643; 3232 4450; Av Sete de Setembro 1546; admission free; 9am-5pm Mon-Fri) was built in the early 1900s, and served for many years as the state capital and governor's residence. It was converted into a cultural center in 1997, and today hosts temporary art exhibits and occasional concerts and performances in the eclectic main house, while outlying buildings contain a fine art gallery, a ho-hum coin museum, and a sound-and-image museum. Free guided tours are available, usually in Portuguese, though you may get lucky and find an English-speaking docent.

MUSEU DO ÍNDIO

Sandwiched between two churches and run by Salesian nuns, the **Museu do Índio** (Rua Duque de Caxias 296; admission R$5; 8:30-11:30am & 2-4:30pm Mon-Fri, 8-11:30am Sat) displays artwork, musical instruments, fishing and hunting tools and ritual objects of indigenous groups from mostly Amazonas and Pará states. The collection is large and quite good, but the displays are artless and the explanations seriously lacking. You'll find similar pieces but a more modern and engaging presentation – and free admission! – at the Museu Amazônico (opposite).

The Museu do Índio is a kilometer down busy Av Sete de Setembro. Palácio Rio Negro is on the way, but you may want to cab or bus it all the same; try bus 606 from the center.

BOSQUE DA CIÊNCIA

Occupying a 13-hectare plot of secondary forest within the city, the **Bosque da Ciência** (Forest of Science; 3643 3135, 3643 3192; admission R$6; 9am-4pm Tue-Sun, ticket office closed 11am-2pm weekdays) has aging enclosures containing animals like giant otters and caimans, but a great many creatures roam freely about the park – in the underbrush, high in the trees, and even ambling down the paths – including monkeys, sloth, turtles, various tropical birds, pacas and anteaters. A highlight is the manatee pool, with underwater glass windows. These reclusive creatures – known as *peixe boi* (cow fish), in Portuguese – are virtually impossible to spot in the wild. They are best viewed here after their pool is cleaned (usually Wednesday and Friday mornings). Also within the park is the Casa da Ciência, with exhibits ranging from medicinal plants to the harmful effects of gold prospecting.

Bosque da Ciência is located in the Petrópolis district, 5km northeast of the center. Bus 519 from Praça da Matriz (R$1.50, 20 minutes) stops just outside the gates. Consider combining this with a visit to the (relatively) nearby Museu de Ciências Naturais da Amazônia.

MUSEU DE CIÊNCIAS NATURAIS DA AMAZÔNIA

Known by many locals as the Museu Japonesa (Japanese Museum), because it is run by Japanese-Brazilians and located in a predominately Japanese-Brazilian area, the **Museu de Ciências Naturais da Amazônia** (Amazon Natural Sciences Museum; 3644 2799; Estrada Belém s/n; adult/child R$12/6; 9am-noon, 2-5pm Mon-Sat) has an extensive exhibit of stuffed fish, preserved butterflies and some unnervingly large beetles and spiders from the region, with descriptions in

English, Portuguese and Japanese. A modest aquarium contains live Amazon fish, including the impressive 2m-long *pirarucú*.

Take bus 519 from Praça da Matriz; it's the same bus that passes Bosque da Ciência, so you can visit both places in a day. Follow the 'Museu' signs from the stop; it's about a 10 to 20 minute walk. An easier option is to take the bus to the Bosque da Ciência and then cab it from there (R$15); to get back, ask the taxi driver to return (an hour ought to be enough) or ask in the museum gift shop for directions back to the main road.

PARQUE DO MINDÚ

Believe it or not, Manaus has its own endemic primate: the tiny *Sanguinus bicolor*, better known as the pied bare-face tamarin. The species is critically endangered, with no known groups in the open forest – they seem to have evolved to thrive only in areas of secondary growth – yet notoriously difficult to breed in captivity. The best place to observe this curious and vanishing creature is **Parque do Mindú** (Av Perimetral s/n; admission free; 8am-5pm Tue-Sun), a 33-hectare park in a residential area of Manaus about 6km from the center. The park has a system of eight intersecting trails, including sections of elevated walkways and an orchid house. Volunteer guides can help visitors locate the tamarins (early morning and late afternoon are best) and point out other flora and fauna along the way, from *açaí* palms to *jacaré* (caimans). This is by no means a journey into the wild – the trails are wide and the river running through the park is heavily polluted from upstream dumping – but it's a worthwhile outing nonetheless, especially if you manage to spot the resident monkeys. Sunday can be very crowded, however, when locals turn out for a buffet breakfast spread. Parque do Mindu is in the Parque Dez district; from the center, take bus 423, 433, 407 or 427 (R$1.50, 30 minutes).

ZOOLÓGICO DO CIGS

Operated by the Brazilian army, the **zoo** (CIGS; 3625 2044; admission R$2.50; 9am-4:30pm Tue-Sat, 9am-6:30pm Sun) contains jaguars, anaconda, tapir and other animals supposedly 'rescued' by soldiers training in the jungle, but the sorry little enclosures make you wonder just how dedicated to animal welfare the place really is. Take bus 120 from Praça da Matriz (R$1, 20 minutes).

MUSEU AMAZÔNICO

Housed in a converted mansion a short walk from the center, the **Museu Amazônico** (Map p643; 3234 3242; www.museuamazonico.ufam.edu.br; Rua Ramos Ferreira; admission free; 8am-noon & 2-5pm Mon-Fri) has a small but excellent collection of indigenous items and artifacts from around the Amazon. Highlights include Xingu feather headdresses, Yanomami weapons, and terrific masks and costumes used in Kobewa and Ticuna rituals.

MUSEU DO SERINGAL VILA PARAÍSO

This **museum** (Rubber Museum; Map p654; admission R$5; 8am-4pm Wed-Sun) is a 25-minute boat ride from Ponta Negra, which is itself a 20-minute bus ride from the center. Fortunately, the trip there is part of the fun, and can be combined with a stop at Praia da Lua, Manaus's best beach. Guided tours include an opulent rubber baron's townhouse and a replica rubber tapper shack, and walking a short trail to see how rubber trees are tapped, and the latex processed in a thatch smoke house. It's a bit gimmicky but still interesting, and the only place in Manaus to learn about this all-important history.

Boats to the museum (R$6, 25 minutes) leave frequently from Marina Davi, just past Ponta Negra. Take Bus 011, 012, or 120 (R$1.50, 20 minutes) from the center, get off at the turnaround (right in front of the Hotel Tropical) and hop onto the free 'Especial' to the marina.

PRAIA DA LUA

Manaus's best beach is a short boat ride up the Rio Negro and can be coupled with a visit to the Museu do Seringal for a nice city escape. The sand is surprisingly fine and the water good for swimming, despite the tea color. Like all river beaches, Lua is biggest when the water is low (November and December) and smallest when it's high (June and July). Trees provide some shade, but the midday sun can be intense. Semi-permanent eateries serve fish and beer at tables set up along the water. The big drawback: no toilets.

Catch a boat to Praia da Lua (R$2 to R$3, 10 minutes) from Marina Davi, just past Ponta Negra. Take Bus 011, 012, or 120 (R$1; 20 minutes) to the turnaround and wait for the free 'Especial' bus to the marina.

ENCONTRO DAS ÁGUAS

Downriver from Manaus, the 'black' (actually reddish-brown) water of the Rio Negro meets the 'white' (light brown) water of the Rio Solimões, but owing to differences in speed, density and temperature, the waters don't immediately mix. Instead, they flow side by side for several kilometers, an occurrence known as the Encontro das Águas (Meeting of the Waters; Map p654). The phenomenon, which occurs in several places along the river, was the inspiration for the wavy black-and-white tile work in front of the Opera House, and was borrowed again for Rio de Janeiro's famous beach promenade.

Boat trips to see the meeting of the waters are typically combined with a highly packaged tour of **Parque Ecológico Janauary** (Janauary Ecological Park; Map p654), where you'll cut the same rubber tree, admire the same water lilies, and looks at the same captured animals as thousands before you. Then lunch, then shopping, then home.

Amazon Explorers (Map p643; ☎ 3232 3052; www .amazonexplorers.com.br, Estação Hidroviária/Porto Flutuante; ☷ 8am-6pm Mon-Sat, 8-9:30am Sun) is the go-to agency for such outings (adult/child R$78/39, including lunch; depart 9am daily except Monday).

Festivals & Events

The June **Festival Foldórico do Amazonas** features a wide variety of regional folklore performances, including rehearsals of the Parintins Boi-Bumbá teams. The festival culminates on June 29 with the Procissão Fluvial de São Pedro (St Peter River Procession), when hundreds of riverboats parade on the Rio Negro before Manaus to honor the patron saint of fishers.

Inaugurated in 1997, the annual **Manaus Opera Festival** brings high-quality opera deep into the rain forest at the Teatro Amazonas. The three-week gala usually takes place in late-April and early-May, and audience apparel ranges from tuxedos and ballroom gowns, to jeans and T-shirts that have obviously done duty in the jungle (they do draw the line at shorts, tank tops and flip flops, however). Tickets (R$5 to R$60) are available at the Teatro Amazonas (p642) several weeks before the festival opens.

Sleeping

The below are hotels in Manaus itself; for jungle lodges outside the city, see p652.

BUDGET

Hostel Manaus (Map p643; ☎ 32334545; www.hostel manaus.com; Rua Lauro Cavalcante 231; dm with fan R$19, with air-con R$23, r with air-con R$55) It took a while, but hostels have finally arrived in the Amazon, here as well as Belém. This HI-registered, Australian-operated hostel has small comfortable dorms (including a women's only room), self-serve laundry machine, and two open-air patios ideal for nursing a beer – the one on the roof has great city views. You also get lockers, luggage storage, kitchen access, and internet service, and the neighborhood, while not problem-free, is safer than the Zona Franca area.

Hotel Ideal (Map p643; ☎ 3622 0038; www.geocities .com/hotelidealmanaus; Rua dos Andradas 491; s/d with fan R$22/33, with air-con R$33/41, with air-con, TV & minibar $40/50; ☷) A multistory block of plain but adequate rooms coated in gray and white highgloss paint. Ask for a room with a window, or one on the top floor where at least the corridor is sunny. There's a recommended tour operator based here, and another across the street, but be wary of freelance guides touting cutrate tours on the sidewalk. The hotel doesn't allow them in the lobby or up to the rooms, but be ready to be pounced on once you step outside the door.

Hotel Continental (Map p643; ☎ 3233 3342; Rua Coronel Sérgio Pessoa 189; s/d with fan R$25/30, with air-con R$45/65; ☷) A small step up from other budget hotels, with cleaner and brighter rooms, all with TV and windows facing the street, and convenient to the port for speedboats to Tefé and Tabatinga. It's also a favorite haunt of freelance guides – be very clear with the receptionist that you do not want guides knocking on your door.

Pensão Sulista (Map p643; ☎ 3234 5814; Av Joaquim Nabuco 347; s/d/tr without bathroom, R$30/30/45, d/t with bathroom & air-con R$40/60; ☷) Occupying a former hospital of all things, this tenement-style budget hotel has attractive blond and chocolate wood floors, and large rooms that open onto a sunny corridor. The charm flags considerably with the saggy beds, ancient bathrooms and walls that don't quite reach the high ceilings, but it's still a decent value and (as a result) often full. Call ahead.

Hotel 10 de Julho (Map p643; ☎ 3232 6280; www .hoteldezdejulho.com; Rua 10 de Julho 679; s/d R$55/60, with hot water & minibar R$70/75; ☷) Rooms are pretty sterile, especially for the price – R$15 extra for hot water? – but Manaus isn't exactly awash in clean affordable digs. The location is ideal, in a safe area, with two recommended tour agencies nearby and the Teatro Amazonas a block away. Check out the interior patios with potted plants and molded Amazonian murals.

Hotel Brasil (Map p643; ☎ 3233 6575 or 2101 5000; Av Getúlio Vargas 657; s/d R$59/69; 🔀 🔳) An eight-story hotel on safe, busy Av Getúlio Vargas. Rooms here are spacious enough for two beds, a table and chair, even a sofa. The bathrooms are weirdly tiny, but it's a minor inconvenience for an otherwise good value. The breakfast spread is ample, and buses to and from the airport and bus station stop a half-block away. Listed prices are technically a promotion, but it's being going for years with no sign of alteration.

Hotel Palace (Map p643; ☎ 3622 4622; Av Sete de Setembro 593; s/d/tr R$75/95/115; 🔀 🔳) Historical preservation laws have helped preserve this hotel's ornate, 18th-century façade, a one-of-a-kind in downtown Manaus. The rooms are pleasant and bright, with high ceilings, crisp sheets and wood furniture. The tiny bathrooms have brown, 50s-style tile work. Busy avenues run along either side of the hotel – ask for a room facing front or back for a bit more peace and quiet. Easy access to the plaza and bus stop.

MIDRANGE
Ana Cássia Palace Hotel (Map p643; ☎ 3622 3637; www.hotelanacassia.com.br; Rua dos Andradas 14; s/d/tr R$90/110/130; 🔀 🔳) Definitely request a room with a view – the river, port, market and theater are all within sight from the Ana Cássia's upper floors, as well as vast stretches of green forest beyond. If none are available, you can still get that Wow-I'm-in-the-Amazon feeling from the rooftop pool and restaurant areas. Rooms here are modern and clean, despite their painfully dated decor. Some single rooms are quite tight, while doubles are more reasonably sized. The area has an appealing hustle and bustle during the day, but is not a place to stroll about at night.

Chez les Rois (Map p643; ☎ 3234 5860; www.amazonnut.com; Conjunto Manauense Q/G 01, Barrio Vieiralves; s/d/t R$95/128/155; 🔳 🔳) Occupying an attractive colonial home in a swanky neighborhood, Chez les Rois is technically Manaus' one and only boutique hotel. The lobby, garden and pool areas live up to the promise, with beautiful wood floors, comfy sofas and chairs, and plenty of nooks and crannies to read a book or soak up the sun. Yet most of the nine rooms are disappointingly plain, or small, or both.

True, the rates are quite low by comparison, but what's the point of a half-boutique hotel? The center is a R$12 cab ride away.

Hotel Krystal (Map p643; ☎ 3233 7535; www.krystalhotel.com.br; Rua Barroso 54; s/d/tr R$105/130/175; 🔀) The lobby could be more, 80s only if the Charlie's Angels themselves were chilling on the pleather sofas; then again, the painfully slow automatic front doors would probably cramp their style. Rooms here are clean though rather dark, with bold mint-green walls, attractive wood headboards, granite-topped writing desks, pedestal sinks and tinted glass shower doors. And you gotta dig the brown sheets with the hotel logo printed on them. If you don't mind the decor, it's a well-located and reliable option in this price range.

Mango Guest House (Map p643; ☎ 3656 6033; www.naturesafaris.com; Rua Flávio Espírito Santo 01, Barrio Kissia II; s/d R$125/145; 🔳 🔳) The hotel grounds are the highlight here, shaded by giant mango trees and located well outside the center's hustle and bustle. The rooms are admittedly a bit cement-block sterile, but attractive hand-painted murals, printed cotton sheets and good towels do a lot to soften them up. The pool is appealing. Operated by Nature Safaris, which also runs the Amazon Rainforest Adventure Station outside Manaus (p652).

Hotel Internacional (Map p643; ☎ 3633 7034; www.hotelinternaional.brasilcomercial.com; Rua Dr Moreira 168; s/d R$128/154; 🔀 🔳) The Internacional wins no awards for decor – the rooms and lobby could teach most hospitals a thing or two about austerity – but the spotless, sizable rooms are perfectly comfortable, with high ceilings, aircon, TV and fridge. A cable internet connection is available in most rooms, and there's a computer for guest-use near reception. It's the best of several hotels in this busy, safe commercial area.

TOP END
Hotel Tropical (Map p654; ☎ 658 5000; fax 658 5026; www.tropicalhotel.com.br; Av Coronel Teixeira 1320, Ponta Negra; d/tr/ste from US$121/182/242; 🔳) Manaus' premier luxury hotel is a self-contained resort built in a sprawling hacienda style that never rises more than three stories. The newest rooms (3104 to 3142) have granite bathroom counters, dark wood floors, and furniture brightened by bird-of-paradise bedspreads over the firm mattresses; definitely better than the older, 70s style units. The hotel has a wave pool, a mini-zoo, an orchid house, various sports

fields (including archery) and no fewer than five bars.

Hotel Manaós (Map p643; ☎ 3633 5744; www.hotel manaos.com.br; Av Eduardo Ribeiro 881; s/d R$149/179) Most of the center's top end hotels offer disappointingly unattractive rooms, and the boxy, mint-green exterior here seems to promise more of the same. Not so: rooms, albeit generic, have sharp modern touches like honey-colored wood trim and polished stone bathroom counters. Most have large windows, including some with a view of the Teatro Amazonas.

Best Western Lord Manaus (Map p643; ☎ 3622 2844; www.bestwestern.com.br/manaus; Rua Marcílio Dias 217; s/d R$175/203; ☒ ☐) Rooms come with either carpet or white tile floors, here called *piso frio*, literally 'cold floor.' If the carpet sounds nicer, that's because it is. Carpet rooms tend to be larger, and some are split level, with a small raised area with table and chairs. The air-cooled lobby is welcome respite from the busy commercial district area. A bit high, but at least you know what to expect.

Holiday Inn Taj Mahal (Map p643; ☎ /fax 3627 3737; www.grupotajmahal.com.br; Av Getúlio Vargas 741; s/d R$225/270, with view R$385/420; ☒) Find every excuse to spend time in the hotel's rooftop revolving restaurant – the view and food are excellent, and after enough revolutions you'll know all the wait-staff's children's names. Rooms have the expected fixings, though the hodge-podge of colors, textures and styles are definitely dated (brace yourself for the bathrooms). There is a small pool on the roof, and a travel agency, a jewelry shop and wireless internet in the lobby.

Eating

Skina dos Sucos (Map p643; cnr Av Eduardo Ribeiro & Rua 24 de Maio; sandwiches & snacks R$2-8; ☒ 7am-8pm Mon-Fri, 7am-7pm Sat) Stake out some counter space at this busy eatery, where you can order snacks and sandwiches to go along with *sucos* (fresh juices) made from Amazonian fruits, including *guaraná* (a tropical berry thought to have numerous medicinal properties), *cupuaçú* (sweet cousin of the cacao fruit) and *graviola* (custard apple).

African House (Map p643; Praça São Sebastião; mains R$2.50-6; ☒ breakfast, lunch & dinner Mon-Sat, 3-11pm Sun) Right next door to Casa do Pensador is African House, the same in every way but the menu. Here, you can order hamburgers and sandwiches instead of pizza and *prato feito* (plate of the day).

Glacial (Map p643; Av Getúlio Vargas 161 & 188; R$3-7) The most popular ice-cream chain in town. There are two branches on this one corner – No 161 sells per kilo, a good way to sample flavors.

Cafeteria do Largo (Map p643; Praça São Sebastião; mains R$4-20; ☒ 2-10:30pm) This unassuming boutique eatery specializes in all-natural *tapas*-style appetizers, and they may well be the most creative and well-prepared edibles anywhere in Manaus. Most are distinctly Amazonian, like smoked *pirarucú* pâté with *açaí* (berry-like fruit) rolls or a miniature log cabin made of tender palm hearts. The *caipirinhas* are stellar, and the setting – a scattering of outdoor stainless steel tables opposite Teatro Amazonas – is hard to beat.

Restaurante Mandarim (Map p643; Rua Joaquim Sarmento 224; self-service per kg R$22, dishes US$5-10; ☒ lunch Mon-Sat) The Mandarim has been serving quality affordable Chinese food for more than three decades, always with a low-key atmosphere and style. The per-kilo spread includes Chinese staples like egg rolls, chop suey, and sweet-and-sour pork, plus a smattering of other Asian and Brazilian items, like sushi, shrimp tempura and of course rice and beans.

Barracas de Tacacá (Map p643; Praça da Saudade; R$5-15; ☒ 4pm-midnight) These are street stalls serving *tacacá*, a classic Brazilian stew made from dried shrimp, manioc root, and *jambú*, an Amazonian herb that leaves tingly, jumpy feeling in your lips.

Restaurante Giratório (Map p643; Taj Mahal; ☎ /fax 3627 3737; tajmahal@internext.com.br; Av Getúlio Vargas 741; dishes US$7-10; ☒ lunch & dinner) She's starting to creak and groan a bit, but the revolving restaurant atop the Taj Majal hotel still offers unbeatable views and better-than-average meals. Snag a table just upstream from the view of Teatro Amazonas so you're sure to get at least two passes. The menu is a bit pricey, but not outrageously so; try the filete mignon or *tucanaré* in *cupuaçu* (a tart, tropical fruit) sauce.

Filosóphicus (Map p643; 3rd fl, Av Sete de Setembro 752; self-service per kg R$17; ☒ lunch Mon-Fri) Vegetarians should head to this small upstairs restaurant, serving a creative, genuinely meat-free lunch buffet. A bit hard to find, and not exactly bursting with atmosphere, but worth the effort all the same.

Scarola Pizzaria (Map p643; ☎ 3234 8542; Rua 10 de Julho 739; mains R$10-30, per kg R$15.50; ☒ lunch & dinner) Good food, good service and good *chope* (draft beer) makes for a varied clientele, from backpackers back from jungle trips to professionals pontificating on the latest opera performance. The affordable lunch spread has all the standards, including fresh grilled meats, while pizza and beer are the dinner of choice. One of the few places around that's open late, even on Sunday.

Bufolete (Map p643; Av Joaquim Nabuco; per kg R$23; ☺ lunch) If Churrascaria Búfalo is a little rich for your blood, try its smaller sister restaurant next door. The service and ambience are less refined – and the dining area rather cave-like, with low ceilings and arches – but the food is nearly as good and the prices much more palatable.

Casa do Pensador (Map p643; Praça São Sebastião; mains R$13-22; ☺ 3-11pm Mon-Fri, 4-11pm Sat & Sun) Simple wood tables set up on the plaza facing Teatro Amazonas make this an easy low-key place for dinner and a beer. The menu is equally low-key, mostly pizza (including a couple veggie options) and standard rice-beans-meat dishes.

Ristorante Fiorentina (Map p643; ☎ 3215 2231; Rua José Paranaguá 44; per kg R$34.50, dishes R$18-35; ☺ lunch & dinner) The pasta, fresh meats, sangria and homemade desserts are all first-rate, even at the per-kilo lunch buffet, but bring some extra moolah to cover your meal. The dining area features the obligatory Italian restaurant red-and-white checkered tablecloths; the upstairs area mixes things up a bit with blue and white checkers.

Churrascaria Búfalo (Map p643; Av Joaquim Nabuco 628; lunch R$40, dinner R$24; ☺ lunch & dinner) There's no better place in Manaus for *rodizio*, an all-you-can-eat meat extravaganza in which a cadre of tuxedoed waiters bring skewer after skewer of sizzling meat right to your table. Accompanied by a full salad and pasta bar, there's no chance of leaving here hungry. The price is rather steep, and some travelers complain about being approached by freelance guides here, but it's still a Manaus institution and a worthwhile splurge.

Entertainment

There are a few quiet bars in town, but for more of a party scene, head to Ponta Negra.

Bar do Armando (Map p643; Rua 10 de Julho 593; ☺ noon-midnight Mon-Sat) Near the opera house, this is a traditional rendezvous place for Manaus' intellectual and bohemian types, but all

sorts of people crowd around the outdoor tables for beers and conversation.

Choparia São Marcos (Map p643; Rua Quintino Bocaiúva 369; ☺ 8am-8pm Mon-Sat) On the noisy corner of Av Floriano Peixoto, this is another traditional bar recommended for *chope* and *bolinhos de bacalhau* (cod fish balls).

Laranjinha Bar (Ponta Negra; ☺ from 9pm Mon-Sat) On the waterfront in Ponta Negra, Laranjinha is a good place to start out your night. You can order beer and burgers, and check out a live music and dance shows, held most nights at the bar's large outdoor stage. A small cover charge may be added to your bill if you're there for the show.

Club de Forró (Estrada do Aleixo s/n, near Bosque de Ciência, Ponta Negra; ☺ from 11pm Thu only) A good *forró* spot, also known as the Club dos Sargentos da Aeronautica (Sergeants Aeronuatical Club).

Enigma (☎ 3234 7985; Rua Silva Ramos 1054; ☺ 11pm-late Thu-Sat) A mixed gay/lesbian/straight *boate* (nightclub) about 1km north of the center, with beach music and dancing.

Purão do Alemão (Ponta Negra; ☺ from 11pm Fri & Sat) and **Coração Blue** (Ponta Negra; ☎ 3658 4057; ☺ from 9pm Mon-Sat) are both located on Estrada de Ponta Negra, and are lively, safe bars frequented by tourists and locals alike. Coração Blue is good for dancing, with a different theme every night, including *forró* and 'Tourist Night.'

Shopping

Artesanato da Amazônia (Map p643; ☎ 3232 3979; Rua José Clemente 500; ☺ 9am-6:30pm Mon-Fri, 9am-3pm Sat) Once a terrific store for folk art, the good stuff here is getting buried by a growing amount of predictable kitsch. But you can still find some quality items, especially indigenous masks and handmade weapons.

Amazonas Ecoshop (Map p643; ☎ 3633 3569; www .ecoshop.com.br; Rua 10 de Julho) Smallish store with quality art, jewelry and other gift items, all made in the region. An in-store coffee shop has appealing coffees and pastries.

Foto Nascimento (Map p643; ☎ 3215 8900; Av Sete de Setembro 1194) You've got a jungle trip tomorrow and that new 2GB memory chip you bought online isn't £$&%!! formatting. You can buy a replacement here – and other photo supplies – but don't count on eBay prices.

Carrefour (Map p643; Av Eduardo Ribeiro; ☺ 7:30am-9pm Mon-Sat, 7:30am-2pm Sun) The biggest and best downtown supermarket. Also a good place to buy batteries, flashlights and rain ponchos.

THE AMAZON

GUARANÁ: FOUNTAIN OF ETERNAL YOUTH

Amazonian Indians have revered the guaraná plant for centuries. The Sateré-Maúé Indians, in particular, believe they are descended from a guaraná bush, and use the bright-red fruit to prepare a ritual drink known as *çapo*. The berry-like fruits are collected before they are opened, and cooked in earthen ovens. Water is added to form a paste, which is molded into black sticks and dried in a smokehouse. Flakes are shaved from the sticks using a rough stone or even the raspy tongue of the giant *pirarucu* fish, then mixed with water to make the *çapo*. The drink is believed to cure all illness, to bring strength, and enhance fertility.

Guaraná seeds contain a host of compounds with long names ending in 'ine,' 'ide' and 'oid,' including caffeine, in concentrations of 4–8%, roughly three times that of coffee beans. It's a common ingredient in herbal remedies, including weight loss pills and energy boosters (with mixed results). Travelers are most likely to encounter guaraná in soda – Antarctica, Brahma and Kuat are the main brands. No matter what the form, guaraná is said to improve blood circulation, reduce menstrual pains, and cure hemorrhoids and hangovers, among other things. In late November or early December the Festa do Guaraná is celebrated in the town of Maués (about 200km east of Manaus), in the main guaraná-cultivating area.

For hammocks, head to any of numerous casa das redes (house of hammocks; Map p643) on Rua Rocha dos Santos and the side streets, or the street vendors around Praça Tenreiro Aranha. For riverboat trips, suitable cloth hammocks start at US$5 to US$7 and go up to US$12 to US$20 for larger, prettier, or more durable ones.

Near Porto Manaus Moderno, the **Mercado Municipal Adolfo Lisboa** (Map p643; Rua dos Barés; 8am-5pm Mon-Sat, 6am-noon Sun) is good for inexpensive crafts and T-shirts, cheap stuffed piranhas and natural medicines.

Numerous **crafts stands** (9am-6pm Mon-Sat) sell mostly identical souvenir-type items in Praça Tenreiro Aranha.

Getting There & Away
AIR
The **Aeroporto Internacional Eduardo Gomes** (Map p654; Av Santos Dumont 1350) is 13km north of the city center. Smaller regional airlines may use a smaller airport (known as 'Eduardinho'), about 600m east of the main one. The large modern airport terminal has a tourism office (open from 7am to 11pm), cash machines, an exchange booth, an internet café, and a clinic for yellow fever vaccinations.

Fares fluctuate greatly – ask travel agents about promotions, especially when flying within the Amazon region. All flights from Gomes airport are subject to a R$20 departure tax; those from Eduardinho pay R$16. The tax is usually charged to your ticket at the time of purchase.

Gol (airport only ☎ 3652 1634; www.voegol.com.br)

Copa/Continental (centro ☎ 3622 1381; www.copaair .com; Av Eduardo Ribeiro 654)

Rico Linhas Aéreas (www.voerico.com.br) centro (☎ 3633 5166; Rua 24 de Maio 60; 7am-6pm Mon-Fri, 7am-noon Sat); airport (☎ 3652 1655; 5am-7pm Mon-Fri, 5am-5pm Sat)

TAF (airport only ☎ 3652 1355; www.voetaf.com.br; 8am-5:30pm Mon-Fri, 8am-4:30pm Sat)

TAM (airport ☎ 3652 1300; www.tam.com.br)

Varig (airport only ☎ 4003 7000; www.varig.com.br; 9am-3pm)

BOAT
Large passenger boats arrive and depart at the **Estação Hidroviária de Manaus** (Map p643; at Porto Flutuante). Speedboats to Tefé, Tabatinga and Parintins use the **Porto Manaus Moderna** (Map p643; behind Mercado Municipal Adolfo Lisboa). See the boxed text on p614 for tips on riverboat travel.

Agencia Rio Amazônas (Map p643; ☎ 3621 4319, 3621 4310; 6am-6pm) sells passenger-boat tickets inside the terminal at the Porto Flutuante. Boats going downstream to Belém usually make stops in Itacoatiara, Parintins, Santarém and Monte Alegre. Up the Rio Solimões, boats call at Tefé, Benjamin Constant and Tabatinga. Boats to Porto Velho, along the Rio Madeira, make stops at Manicoré and Humaitá. You can buy tickets at slightly discounted prices from the men hanging around the entrance, but you may be bumped if the boat is full.

AJATO (Map p643; ☎ 3622 6047, 9984 9091; Porto Manaus Moderna; 8am-5pm Mon-Fri, 8am-noon Sat) operates comfortable speedboats upstream to Tefé (R$180, 14 hours, twice weekly) and Tabatinga (R$360, 36 hours, once weekly), and downstream to Parantins (R$140, 10 hours, twice weekly). There is also service up the Rio Madeira as far as Manicoré (R$150, 14 hours, twice weekly). Service to Santarém was suspended at last check, but it's worth asking whether it's been reinstated. All trips include meals. Boats can fill up, so plan on buying your ticket a day or two in advance.

Slow boats going up the Rio Negro leave from Porto São Raimundo, in the Bairro São Raimundo, an unsavory district 1.5km northwest of the Porto Flutuante. A few boats a week go to Barcelos (two days) and onward to São Gabriel da Cachoeira (five to six days), typically leaving in the evening.

BUS
Manaus's **long-distance bus station** (Rua Recife 2784) is rather small and dumpy, probably a consequence of the fact that there aren't many places you can get to by bus. It's 6km north of town, in the same direction as the airport.

Eucatur (☎ 3648 1493) has service to Boa Vista (R$91 to R$107, 12 hours, five departures daily) and to Itacoatiara (R$24, four hours, four departures daily). One of the departures continues into Venezuela, including Santa Elena (R$110), Puerto Ordaz (R$170) and Puerto La Cruz (R$190).

Aruanã (☎ 3236 8305) has a bus service to Presidente Figueiredo (R$12.50, 1½ hours, 107km, five daily) and to Silves (R$32, seven hours, departing at 7am).

CAR
Few travelers rent cars in Manaus, but if you feel the need there are several agencies at the airport that can put you behind a wheel in no time. They include **Localiza** (☎ 3652 1176), **Unidas** (☎ 3652 1327), **Avis** (☎ 3652 1579) and **Hertz** (☎ 3652 1421).

Getting Around
City buses and downtown streets get super busy around 1pm to 2pm and 5pm to 7pm; avoid trying to move too far across the city at these times. Bus fare is R$1 to R$1.50 on most routes. Taxis are plentiful, but rather expensive.

TO/FROM THE AIRPORT
Buses 306 'Aeroporto' (R$1.50) and 813 'Aeroporto-Ejecutivo' (R$2.50) run about every half-hour between the airport and Praça da Matriz in the center of town; the latter is air-conditioned, less crowded, and definitely worth the extra *real*. At the airport, turn right out of the main doors and walk to the bus stop at the end of the terminal. In town, the most convenient stops are Praça da Matriz and on Av Getúlio Vargas near Rua José Clemente.

Taxis at the airport charge a fixed R$49 for the 20-minute ride into town. The return trip costs roughly the same, though you may be able to bargain the price down a bit.

TO/FROM THE BUS STATION
Buses 306 and 813 (the same ones you take to the airport) also pass the bus station; pick up either at Praça da Matriz or on Av Getulio Vargas. The bus station is small and easy to miss, so be sure to tell the driver where you're headed and keep your eyes peeled. It's the second stop after the stadium on the left.

You can catch the same buses back into town. Leaving the bus station, use the pedestrian bridge to cross Rua Recife and turn left along the busy street on the far side of the gas station there. The bus stop is 100m further along, on the far side of the street.

A taxi between the bus station and the center costs R$20 to R$25.

AROUND MANAUS
Jungle Trips
JUNGLE TOUR OPERATORS
Most agencies have a small lodge or jungle camp where they can set up almost anything you might want to do, but some have certain experience and expertise in particular kinds of trip. Prices start at around R$170 per person per day, and vary somewhat according to the season, and the number of days you go for. They can reach significantly higher of course for specialized trips, but there's a limit to how low an agency can go and still maintain quality and safety. Be wary of prices that seem too good to be true.

Amazon Gero Tours (Map p643; ☎ 3232 4755, cell 9983 6273; www.amazongerotours.com; next to Hotel 10 de Julho, Rua 10 de Julho 679) Gero Mesquita, an all-around good guy who goes out of his way to help travelers, runs tours from a new lodge on Lago Ararinha, in the Lago de Juma area. Accommodations range from dorms (hammocks or beds) to private cabins with bathroom and screened patio. Groups are typically small, and always accompanied by two guides, one from the area and one who's

RIVERBOAT SCHEDULE

Riverboats from Manaus (Estação Hidroviária)

Destination	Days	Time	Upper Deck	Lower Deck	Cabin
Belém	Wed & Fri; noon	4 days	R$200	R$180	R$700
Porto Velho	Tue & Fri; 2pm	4 days	R$200	R$180	R$500
Santarém	Tue-Sat; noon	36hr	R$100	R$90	R$350
Tabatinga	Tue, Wed, Fri & Sat; 4pm	6 days	R$268	n/a	R$700
Tefé	Tue-Sat; 7am	30hr	R$115	n/a	R$300

bilingual. In addition to the standard excursions (caimans- or dolphin-spotting, paddling through the flooded forest etc) you can arrange for overnights with a local family or at camps deep in the forest.

Iguana Turismo (Map p643; ☎ 3633 6507, cell 9627 4151; www.amazonbrasil.com.br; Hotel 10 de Julho, Rua 10 de Julho 679), branch office (next to Hotel Rio Branco, Rua dos Andradas 484) Run by Guyanese transplant Gerry Hardy – not to be confused with Gero, whose office is next door – Iguana has an appealing lodge at the mouth of Lago de Juma. A large dorm area has hammocks and beds, while six wood cabins have private bathrooms and partial views of the river. There are a couple large decks for spotting dolphins and hanging out between excursions, and a cow pasture in back (which explains the occasional moo). Daily excursions include all the usuals, including overnighting in the forest.

Amazonas Indian Turismo (Map p643; ☎ 3633 5578; www.amazonasindianturismo.tur.br; 2nd fl, Rua dos Andradas 311) This long-time budget agency has a rustic camp on the Rio Urubú, 200km northeast of Manaus, with hammocks, latrine toilets and no electricity. The agency specializes in long hikes in the forest, so you may spend a night or two roughing it even more, in a makeshift camp and your hammock slung between two trees. The Rio Urubú is black water, so there are blessedly few mosquitoes. This agency is notable for being indigenous-owned and operated; most guides are Wapixano, and all speak English.

Jungle Experience (Map p643; ☎ 3233 9423, cell 9961-8314; jungleexperience@bol.com.br) Hotel Ideal (Rua dos Andradas 491) branch office in Hostel Manaus (Rua Lauro Cavalcante 231) This long-established agency also takes guests to the Rio Urubú, using a thatch-roof camp with just hammocks and latrine toilets, and offering long hikes into the forest, including overnights. Night hikes and visits to local families can also be arranged. There's a

second camp nearer the main Amazon channel, where you spend more time canoeing, though you'll encounter more mosquitoes.

Swallows and Amazons (Map p643; ☎ 3622 1246; www.swallowsandamazonstours.com; 2nd fl, Rua Quintino Bocaiúva 189) Another long-established tour operator, Swallows and Amazons specializes in riverboat tours, where you sleep onboard – either in hammocks or in private cabins, depending on the boat – and visit several areas in one trip. Tours go up the Rio Negro, exploring smaller tributaries along the way; with enough time, you can reach as far as Anavilhanes Archipelago (a profusion of islands known for their bird-watching) and even Jaú national park. The agency recently began offering multiday jungle hikes as well.

Maia Expeditions (☎ 3613 4683, cell 9983 7141; www.maiaexpeditions.com; Rua Dr Odilon 16-A Raiz) This highly professional outfit specializes in boat excursions, from deluxe yachts to simple riverboats for groups of two to eight people. It also has a well-maintained lodge in the Lago Juma area (roughly between Amazon Gero's and Iguana's) with eight small cabins, all with high thatched roof and most with private bathroom. The dining room and screened hammock area are great for relaxing. Most independent travelers book trips just at the lodge – from which you take standard excursions – but combination boat-and-lodge tours are possible.

Heliconia Amazônia Turismo (Map p643; ☎ 3234 5915; www.heliconia-amazon.com; Rua Lauro Cavalcante 250; ⏰ 9am-noon, 2-7pm Mon-Fri) Loosely affiliated with the Alliance Française, this agency does not have facilities of its own, but can help travelers find and book the tour operator or jungle lodge that's best for them.

JUNGLE LODGES

Within 250km of Manaus are at least two dozen jungle lodges, ranging from super luxurious to very basic. Visits are normally by two- to four-day packages (but a week or more is certainly possible) including transportation, meals and a program of outings and activities.

The deluxe lakefront cabins at **Juma Lodge** (Map p643; ☎ 3232 2707; www.jumalodge.com; all-inclusive packages from 3 days/2 nights s/d jungle view US$604/1026, lake view US$906/1540) stand on 15m stilts, connected by wood walkways, and have huge screened windows and a private patio overlooking the lake. They can get hot in the late afternoon sun, but that's when you might be sipping a *caipirinha* in the lodge's shady deck, having just returned from a canoe trip in the forest. All cabins have private bathrooms, and meals are served in a spacious communal dining area.

Amazon Rainforest Adventure Station (Map p643; ☎ 3656 6033; www.naturesafaris.com; Manaus office at Mango Guest House, Rua Flávio Espirito Santo 01, Barrio Kissia II; all-inclusive packages from 4 days/3 nights per person US$599) is a homey floating lodge in Juma Lake, about 80km from Manaus. Standard rooms are comfortable but tiny, while two larger suites, each with private outdoor showers, are well-worth the extra cost. (None have private toilets, however). Packages are a bit overpriced, but the setting and service are top-notch. It used to be called Amazon Eco-Lodge, and was the area's first eco-lodge.

Tiwa Amazonas Ecoresort (☎ 3088 4676; www .tiwaamazone.nl; 2-/3-/4-night all-inclusive packages per person US$407/515/615; ⛺ ▣) About 10km from Manaus, Tiwa has 20-plus wooden cabins on stilts and a small natural lake in the middle. There's a large pool and a sandy sunbathing area – you might momentarily forget you're a thousand miles from the ocean. Rooms have

---

JUNGLE TRIPPING

The top priority for most foreign visitors to Manaus is a jungle trip. While anything's possible, the most common trip is two to four days, including hiking in the jungle, fishing for piranha, spotting caiman at night and visiting a local village. Best of all, you'll canoe through narrow river channels and eerie flooded forests (in the high water), which are beautiful and better for spotting wildlife than the main river.

Different tour operators specialize in different things; thinking carefully about what sort of trip you want can help determine which operator is best for you. How much do you want to rough it? Do you want a bed or a hammock? What about sleeping aboard a boat? Private bathroom, shared, or pit toilet? Do you want to spend a night or two in the forest or do day trips from the lodge? How much do mosquitoes bother you? Do you prefer hiking or canoeing? There is no shame in choosing more or less comfort – you are there to enjoy yourself after all.

There are also a few questions to ask the tour operator: does the guide speak English (or a language you understand)? How long will you spend getting there? What is the trip itinerary? How much hiking and/or canoeing will you do? Ask to see recent pictures of the accommodations and activities, and a guest comment book.

And talk to other travelers! Virtually every foreigner you see in Manaus is planning a trip or returning from one, and they are the best source of honest, up-to-date info.

A word about what you'll see: many travelers come to the Amazon expecting to see jaguars in every tree and a village of spear-toting Indians around every river bend. This just doesn't happen, not in Manaus and not anywhere in the Amazon. On a typical trip, you are likely to see dolphins and a slew of birds, including herons, parrots and macaws. Monkeys, sloth and caiman are relatively common, but seeing them is no sure thing. Manatees, anacondas and jaguars are extremely hard to spot. Some tour operators may dissuade you from taking a trip on 'black' rivers, claiming they have fewer animals. While this is technically true, white rivers also have more mosquitoes and thicker vegetation, inhibiting even the keenest observer. The single biggest factor in seeing animals is luck. The diligence of your guide is also important: during your trip, politely insist that morning excursions leave on time, and that they last the full allotted time.

Bring sturdy shoes or boots, long-sleeve shirt and pants, mosquito repellent, a hat and sunscreen, a raincoat, flashlight, extra batteries, roll of toilet paper, daypack and a water bottle. If you don't have binoculars, ask your tour operator if you can borrow or rent a pair. For photos, high-speed film and/or flash are often necessary. Pack as light as possible: most hotels in Manaus offer secure luggage storage for whatever you don't bring along.

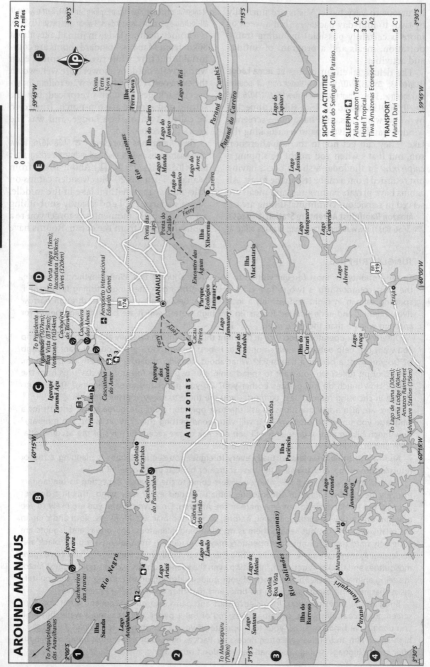

AROUND MANAUS

THE AMAZON

THE AMAZON

JUNGLE TRiP SCAMS

Manaus is teeming with scammers and touts. Most go after budget-conscience travelers, selling cut-rate tours that turn out to be woefully uninspired: overcrowded, surly guides, caged animals, hiking through cow pastures, skipping activities etc. Worse, in 2007, a tourist drowned after the boat he was in capsized in a storm. The boat had no life jackets, was driven by an inexperienced guide, and had been booked by an agency known for snagging tourists off the street (and which is still operating today). Some precautions worth taking include the following:

- **Never pay for a tour anywhere except the agency's main office in town.** Touts often pretend they are with a legitimate agency but steer you to a café or airport bench to make the deal. They even make phony phone calls to convince you the main office is closed, or that you must to commit right away to get the best price or the 'last seat on the boat.' These are all scams.

- **Firmly turn down anyone who approaches you at the airport about booking a tour.** No legitimate agency fishes for tourists there, so anyone who does so is a tout. If you've reserved ahead of time and are being picked up, look for a sign with your name on it.

- **Do not tell touts what hotel you are in, nor accept 'help' getting to a hotel from the airport.** They just want to be able to hound you to take their tour, or steer you to a hotel that pays commissions, or both.

- **Confirm the agency is registered with the state tourism authority.** Go to www.amazon astur.am.gov.br, select the Portuguese version (it's more up-to-date than the English one), then *Agências de Turismo*.

- **Don't risk your life to save a little money.** In the end, the reason there are so many scammers is because travelers keep booking with them. Be smart: the Amazon is not a place to cut corners.

private decks, hot shower and thick wooden furniture. Guided excursions and 4km of do-it-yourself hiking trails offer a chance to spot crocodiles, pink dolphins, monkeys and macaws.

Ariaú Amazon Towers (☎ 2121 5000, toll free 0800 702 5005, in US 877 442 7428; www.ariautowers.com; all-inclusive packages from 3 days/2 nights per person US$407, 1-time room upgrades US$200–$1000; ✷ ▣) Two hours by boat from Manaus, this city on stilts has eight huge round towers (with 300-odd rooms) and a handful of 'Tarzan Suites' – glorified tree-houses with private swimming pools. No mercy is spared in the decoration: Amazonian-themed paintings, fake vines and palm thatch, even a huge fiberglass Indian towering over the pool. Everything is connected by raised walkways, which extend well beyond the hotel – 7km in all – and offer fine walking and animal-spotting, perhaps the most authentic part of the whole experience.

Rio Negro Basin

Trips up the Rio Negro tend to be a week or more, simply because it takes 24 to 36 hours on a boat to get most places. You'll do many of the same activities as elsewhere – hiking, canoeing, fishing – but the area is far less developed so you'll encounter fewer villages, pastures and other human footprints. That is not to say you will necessarily see more animals; as always, that depends on luck and the skill of your guide. One advantage: most of the rivers here are 'black,' meaning they are blissfully mosquito-free.

RESERVA XIXUAÚ-XIPARINÁ

This 1780 sq km ecological reserve – which is in the process of being expanded to over 4000 sq km and converted into an extractive reserve – covers a virtually untouched area of primary rain forest along the Rio Jauaperí in southern Roraima, some 500km (35 to 40 hours by boat) from Manaus. It is one of the best places in the Amazon to see giant river otters, and monkeys, dolphins, wild boars and caimans, including a 15ft one named 'Lucy' who trolls for fish guts tossed from the kitchen.

A handful of guest rooms in a large *maloca* (Indian dwelling) have thinning beds and hooks for hammocks, plus clean shared bathrooms and a great deck overlooking the river. The tiny nearby community has a public telephone and satellite internet, amazingly enough. Visits here are typically 12 to 14 days and cost US$100 per person per day, including transportation; a week is the bare minimum, considering how long it takes to get there and back. Most guests spend a couple nights camping in the forest or on beaches upstream, while deep jungle expeditions, including a grueling 10-day journey into the heart of the reserve to a macaw nesting site, can be arranged with advance notice.

The reserve is owned and operated by the nearby community, whose residents are members of **Asociação Amazônia** (in Manaus ☎ 6344 0127; www.amazonia.org). The association was founded by Scottish transplant Chris Clark, who still lives on-site and arranges your visit. Unlike some lodges that plan your every last minute, Clark takes a more hands-off approach; to make the most of each day, be sure to discuss your options the night before, including what time to leave (the earlier the better, usually), how long you'll be gone, what to do in the afternoon etc. Clark accompanies some outings, but most are guided by local community members.

The reserve is open year round, though April and May aren't recommended because of heavy rain. The river is highest in June and July (best for canoeing the flooded forest, and spotting animals) and lowest in December to February (more hiking options).

PARQUE NACIONAL DO JAÚ

Spanning nearly 2.3 million hectares (22,720 sq km, to be exact), the Jaú national park is Brazil's second-biggest national park, and one of the largest tracts of protected tropical rain forest in the world. It stretches west from the Rio Negro along the Jaú and Carabinani rivers, and is rich in flora and fauna. The park was designated a Unesco World Heritage listing in 2000.

There are no lodges in the park, so it's best to visit with a tour operator that specializes in riverboat tours, like Swallows and Amazons or Maia Expeditions, both in Manaus. Advance booking is essential, as the operator must obtain special permission to enter the park.

PRESIDENTE FIGUEIREDO

☎ 0xx92 / pop 30,000

Self-named the 'Terra de Cachoeiras' (Land of Waterfalls), this dusty little town is surrounded by dozens of waterfalls and caves.

Just 100km north of Manaus by good highway, this is the only leisure spot easily accessible by road from the capital, and it gets obscenely packed on weekends. A midweek visit can be a nice diversion if you've got time to kill.

Sights & Activities

You need a vehicle to visit the waterfalls here. You can rent a car from Manaus, or take the bus and hire a taxi in Presidente Figueiredo. Or book a guided tour at Pousada das Pedras (see below), which is certainly the easiest and more informative route.

The best and easiest falls to visit are Iracema (12km from town), Santuario (16km), Portera (19km) and Suframa (11km); further away is Pedra Furada (60km). About 12km from town is the town of Balbina, where the **Water Mammals Preservation Center** (☎ 3312 1202; admission free; ☺ 8am-noon & 2-4pm Mon-Sat, 8am-noon Sun) shelters manatees and other animals. Nearby, Caverna Maruaga – an attractive cave with a waterfall at its entrance and a clear shallow river running over its floor – was closed for fears of contaminating the river, and special permission from the tourist office is required to visit.

The **tourist office** (☎ 3324 1158; ☺ 7:30am-noon & 2-6pm) has an office in the bus station and across the street, above the grocery store.

Sleeping & Eating

All hotels listed here include breakfast.

Pousada das Pedras (☎ 3324 1296, 9141 4523; s/d weekday R$35/50, weekend R$50/70) Operated by friendly Francisco 'Pimenta' de Mazi, this is easily the best and most convenient place to base your visit. Rooms are small but attractive with private bathroom; suites are quite spacious. Meals are served in a nice garden patio. De Mazi arranges guided trips in the area, including long hikes to beautiful Neblina and Natal falls (per person R$50, negotiable) A taxi from the bus station is R$5, but de Mazi will pick you up if you call ahead.

Hotel Marauga (☎ 3324 1110; across from bus station; r R$60-80; ☷) Large but plain rooms have air-con, TV and minibar. The hotel owner can arrange tours.

Delícias no Esteto (☺ 8am-10pm; R$8-20) Basic self-serve and menu restaurant, across from the bus station, with soups, fish and more.

Getting There & Away

Aruanã (in Manaus ☎ 3642 5757) has five daily buses from Manaus to Presidente Figueiredo (US$1.50, 1½ hours). Buses north to Boa Vista and the Venezuela pass several times per day.

PARINTINS

☎ 0xx92 / pop 70,000

The Boi-Bumbá festival held here June 28 to 30 is the biggest annual shindig in Amazonas. It's an Amazonian version of Bumba Meu Boi, a traditional festival of mixed African and European origins that uses music, theater and dancing to enact the kidnapping, death and resurrection of an ox – a metaphor for agricultural cycles. In Parintins the event incorporates a rivalry between two 'clans,' the Caprichoso, who dress all in blue, and Garantido who dress red.

Tens of thousands of people descend on Parintins for the event, for which the tiny town has a 35,000 capacity purpose-built stadium known as the *bumbódromo*. Parintins' few hotels are booked months in advance, but hundreds of riverboats go especially for the festival, and passengers sleep onboard. A five-night boat trip from Manaus (transportation, hammock space and meals) costs around US$350. Private houses also rent rooms during the festival. Most travel agencies in Manaus can arrange a trip.

If you arrive any other time, the **Hotel Avenida** (☎ 3533 1158; Av Amazonas 2416; s/d R$30/40; ✴) and **Pousada Ilha Bela** (☎ 3533 2737; Rua Agostinho Cunha 2052; R$30/40; ✴) offer passable rooms with air-conditioning, TV and minibar.

Most riverboats between Manaus and Belém stop at Parantins, and **AJATO** (Map p643; ☎ 3622 6047, 9984 9091; Porto Manaus Moderna; ⏲ 8am-5pm Mon-Fri, 8am-noon Sat) has speedboat service there from Manaus (R$140, 10 hours, twice weekly).

Rico (reservations ☎ 92/4009 8333; www.voerico.com.br) flies to Parintins from Manaus (R$245) and Belém (R$512) four days a week.

TEFÉ

☎ 0xx97 / pop 80,000

Tefé is the jumping-off point to the Mamirauá reserve (p659), one of the best ecotourism

---

BLACK & WHITE

The Amazon has not always flowed west to east. About 150 million years ago, when South America and Africa went their separate ways, it flowed east to west. Then, 15 to 20 million years ago, the Andes shot up and blocked the water's exit. At the same time, a smaller ridge of land, now called the Purus Arch, rose like a spine in the middle of the continent. East of the Purus Arch the river starting draining into the Atlantic Ocean, but west of there, the water was trapped and a huge inland sea formed. Eventually the water poured over the Purus Arch, gouging a deep channel near present-day Parantins, and the Amazon returned to being a river, but now flowing west to east. Scientists of various fields have helped confirm the theory: biologists showed that Amazonian stingrays are more closely related to Pacific species than Atlantic ones, and geologists discovered tell-tale sediment from eastern South America deep in the central Amazon basin.

The Amazon basin's early geology is one reason there are three different types of rivers there: *negro* (black), *branco* (white) and *claro* (clear). White rivers (actually more a creamy beige) come from the Andes, and get their color from sediment eroded from those 'young' mountains. These rivers – including the Solimões and Madeira – are loaded with nutrients and can support more plants and animals along their path.

Black rivers, like the Rio Negro and Rio Urubu, originate in northern Amazonia and flow over much older land, long swept clean of sediment. Black rivers tend to be slower and warmer than white ones (which start as snowpack in the Andes, after all) and the vegetation in them has time to rot, releasing organic acids. Those acids turn the water 'black,' actually a tea-like color. The same acids kill mosquito larvae, meaning black water areas have amazingly few mosquitoes and low incidence of malaria and other diseases.

Clear rivers have neither the sediment nor the organic acids that would make them white or black. The massive Tapajós and Arapiuns rivers are clear, and small tributaries in predominantly white or black water areas can be clear if their course happens to allow it.

One last note: both white and black water rivers flood seasonally, but the result is not the same, at least in name. Forest flooded with black water is referred to as *igapó*, while forest flooded with white water is called *várzea*.

experiences in the Amazon. Visits there are closely coordinated with airline schedules, so those coming and going by plane generally have little or no time to explore the town. Those traveling by boat may have a day or two to spare, which is plenty. It's not that there is anything wrong – it's a perfectly safe, agreeable place, just not particularly memorable.

Orientation

Most of the listed hotels, restaurants and services are within a block of two Tefé's two central plazas. The main plaza – not because it's larger, but because it has the church – is Praça Santa Tereza, a long tapered wedge running roughly east-to-west, with the church on the western end. A block north is Praça Tulio Azevêdo, a more traditional square with trees, benches, and newsstands. Beyond that is the municipal market and the waterfront. Both plazas are bordered by busy streets, down which flow a constant stream of scooters and moto taxi.

Information

EMERGENCY
Ambulance (☎ 192)
Hospital São Miguel (☎ 3343 2469; Rua Marachal Deodoro 66)
Police (☎ 190)

INTERNET ACCESS
Arenna (1½ blocks west of Praça Santa Teresa; per hr US$3; ◔ 9am-midnight) Fast connection and air-con blasting.
Eganet (Rua Getulio Vargas; per hr R$3; ◔ 8am-11pm Mon-Sat, 2-11pm Sun) Opposite Ega's Hotel.

LAUNDRY
Lavandaría do Paulo (Rua Daniel Servalho 345; per item R$0.50-2)

MONEY
Banco do Brasil (Rua Olavo Bilac at Praça Tulio Azevêdo; ◔ 9am-2pm Mon-Fri)
Bradesco (Ruas Getúlio Vargas & Daniel Servalho)

POST
Post office (Estrada Aeroporto; ◔ 8am-4pm Mon-Fri)

TOURIST OFFICES
Instituto Mamirauá (☎ 3343 4160; www.mamiraua .org.br; Rua Brasil 197; ◔ 8am-noon, 2-6pm Mon-Fri, 8am-noon Sat) Oversees the Mamirauá reserve and Pousada Uakari; stop in or call for info and reservations. English spoken.

TRAVEL AGENCIES
Instituto Mamirauá (☎ 3343 4160; www.mamiraua .org.br; Rua Brasil 197; ◔ 8am-noon, 2-6pm Mon-Fri, 8am-noon Sat) Can purchase advance plane and boat tickets for visitors to the reserve, with a 10-15% service fee.
Motivos Viagens e Turismo (☎ 3343 5633; Rua Benjamin Constant 382) Purchase plane tickets here.

Sights & Activities

There are a few sights and activities in Tefé if you happen to have time to spare.

In town, **O Seminario** (◔ 8-11:30am Mon-Fri) is a striking structure that occupies the entire northern side of Praça Tulio Avevêdo. Oddly New England-ish in its design, it was once a seminary and is now the local headquarters of a Portuguese mission with numerous congregations in the Amazon. It's not technically open for visitation, but you might finagle a tour if you ask nicely.

Operated by the same Portuguese mission, **As Misões** (☎ 3343 3011) is a mildly interesting complex overlooking the mouth of Lago de Tefé and the main channel of the Rio Solimões. Founded in 1897, it has a well-kept garden, huge decaying church, and a cemetery full of former missionaries. The main building was a church-run vocational school where many of Tefé's masons, metalworkers and other skilled tradesmen were trained. The elfish priest, Padre Altino from the north of Portugal, gives spirited tours to anyone who's interested. The best time to come is Tuesday to Friday; to get there, hire a boat from the waterfront.

Sleeping & Eating

Hotel Patricia (☎ 3343 2541; Praça Tulio Azevêdo; s/d R$25/40) The best of Tefé's cheap hotels is run like a guesthouse by a friendly grandma figure. Some rooms are bright and tolerable, others musty and unpleasant, all have air-con and satellite TV.

Hotel Vendadores (☎ 3343 6587; Praça Santa Tereza; s/d R$25/35) Right next door to the Hotel Anilce, but in another time zone in terms of quality and comfort. The rooms here are musty, the beds saggy, and the bathrooms grimy. Stay here only if your budget really demands it.

Hotel Anilçe (☎ 3343 2416; Praça Santa Tereza; s/d R$45/70) A reasonable alternative to Ega's if the latter is full or hosting a party, though the rooms aren't as large nor the bathrooms as clean. The top-floor breakfast area is pleasant enough, as is the location – opposite the church and plaza.

Ega's Hotel (☎ 3343 2929; egashoteltur@hotmail.com; Ruas Getúlio Vargas & Daniel Servalho; s/d/t R$50/70/90) Tefé's best hotel has large clean rooms and bathrooms, and a convenient location near both parks and opposite a bank and cyber café. There's no hot water, but that's a luxury you won't find in any of Tefé's hotels. Just be sure there isn't loud music coming from inside – the hotel occasionally rents out its interior courtyard for private parties, which last into the wee hours.

Petisco (Praça Santa Tereza 286; per kg R$16; mains R$5-12; ☽ lunch & dinner) A popular hang-out spot at night, when they set up tables on the sidewalk facing the plaza. The per-kilo lunch spread is simple and reliable, and includes an ice cream bar. You can also order grilled beef kebabs with rice, or big cheap *prato feito* (plate of the day).

Stylos (Rua Floriano Peixoto 190; mains R$8-35; ☽ lunch & dinner Mon-Sat) The most reliable eatery in the center, with hefty, well-prepared dishes served at outdoor tables right on the street corner. The menu includes all the standard fish, meat and chicken dishes, plus a few less common ones, like huge portions of *lingua na brasa* (grilled tongue).

Trapiche (mains R$12-30; ☽ dinner) A short moto taxi ride from the center will get you to this small pizza joint and bar, where the service is slow but the pizza is worth the wait. Cold beer and cool music help the wait go faster.

Barzinho (Rua Olavo Bilac) Perched on a small rise above one of Tefé's main drags – with a tree growing through the floor and out the roof – this is a cool little spot to have a beer or two and listen to live music, mostly of the singer-songwriter variety.

Getting There & Away
AIR
Rico (reservations ☎ 92/4009 8333; www.voerico.com.br) and **TRIP** (reservations ☎ 0300 789 8747; www.airtrip .com.br) serve Tefé to and from Manaus (R$260 to R$330) and Tabatinga (R$330 to R$345). TRIP typically uses small propeller planes and stops at smaller towns along the way, like Coari, Fonte Boa and Eriunepé.

BOAT
Slow boats to Manaus depart six days per week (hammock R$150, cabin R$350, 30 to 36 hours). Prices vary somewhat according to the boat, and you should always bargain, as a 'gringo tax' is commonly applied here.

AJATO (☎ 3343 5306) has twice weekly speedboat service to Manaus (R$180, 10 hours). Advance reservations are recommended, as the boats frequently fill up. Unfortunately you can't book a return ticket in Manaus; the Instituto Mamirauá office can do it for you in Tefé, but a 15% surcharge applies.

Boats going upriver to Tabatinga do not enter Tefé proper, so catching them is a little trickier. For a slow boat, catch a regional boat to the towns of Fonte Boa or Jutaí (R$50 to R$80, 18 hours) and wait for the daily Tabatinga boat to pass (hammock R$190, cabin R$1000, three to four days). AJATO speedboats to Tabatinga (R$350, 16 hours) stop once a week in Alvarães, a small town across the lake from Tefé. To get there, take a motorboat to the village of Nogueira (R$5, 15 minutes) and then a truck or taxi to the dock in Alvarães (R$5, 15 minutes).

MAMIRAUÁ RESERVE
One of the Amazon's best eco tourism options, Mamirauá offers pristine rain forest, comfortable lodging, excellent guide service, and affordable prices, plus it's just 1½ hours by boat from a large town with reliable air and boat service. With so many places claiming to be eco-this and eco-that, Mamirauá is one of few places in the Amazon that really does it right.

The Reserva de Desenvolvimento Sustentável Mamirauá (Mamirauá Sustainable Development Reserve) is Brazil's last large area of *várzea* (forests seasonally flooded with sediment-rich 'white water'). It covers 1.24 million hectares (12,400 sq km) northwest of Tefé between the Solimões and Japurá rivers. The park's eastern edge merges with the Amanã reserve, which in turn borders Jaú national park. Together the three reserves span 5.7 million hectares (57,000 sq km), the second-largest block of protected tropical rain forest in the world.

Mamirauá was Brazil's first sustainable development reserve (there are now five). Their purpose is to combine nature conservation and scientific research, while promoting sustainable practices and improved opportunities for the local population. There are numerous small communities within the Mamirauá reserve; many residents work part-time as tour guides, cooks and boat drivers while continuing traditional work like fishing, planting and hunting under a mutually agreed sustainable-use plan.

THE AMAZON

The reserve is ably managed by the **Instituto Mamirauá** (☎ 3343 4160; www.mamiraua.org.br; Rua Brasil 197, Tefé; ⏰ 8am-noon, 2-6pm Mon-Fri, 8am-noon Sat). Packages are coordinated with the Manaus–Tefé flight schedule, and priced according to the length of stay: US$500 per person for four days/three nights (Saturday to Tuesday); US$580 per person for five days/four nights (Tuesday to Saturday); and US$900 per person for eight days/seven nights or US$800 per person for groups of four or more (Saturday to Saturday). Accommodations are the **Pousada Uacari** (www.pousadauacari.com.br), an excellent floating lodge run by the ecotourism wing of the institute. It has spacious comfortable bungalows, each with private bathrooms and a small patio with hammock, and a large common area where generous meals are served. Tours include food, lodging, guides, and boat transfer to and from Tefé, plus pick-up and drop-off at airport or speedboat port.

Visitors to Mamirauá can be reasonably assured of seeing sloth, caiman, and dolphins, and dozens of birds, such as macaws and toucans. There are five species of monkeys, including howlers, capuchins, and the highly elusive white uakari, an endemic species that's notable for its crimson face and shaggy white coat. Manatees, anaconda and jaguars also live in the reserve but are extremely difficult to spot.

You'll also visit a local village and one of the reserve's ongoing research projects. Both can be fascinating, and you'll likely see dolphins, birds and even monkeys along the way. A new option is a night in the 'tree house,' a one-room cabin on 5m stilts a short way into the forest with great early morning bird-watching. An English-speaking naturalist is at the main lodge at all times (and accompanies some excursions) but most guides speak Portuguese only. Binoculars can be rented, and are highly recommended.

High water here is in June and July, when the forest is completely flooded and you glide through the water in canoes. (This is not to be confused with rainy season, which peaks in April and May.) This is when monkeys and sloth are most visible, and tends to be the busiest time. In low water, roughly October and November, hiking is possible and aquatic animals, especially fish and caiman, are more concentrated.

THE TRIPLE FRONTIER

The Brazilian town of Tabatinga and the Colombian town of Leticia lie side-by-side on the eastern bank of the Amazon, about 1100km west of Manaus, while the far bank belongs to Peru. A logical travel hub, the 'triple frontier' also happens to be a good area for taking jungle trips, particularly to remote areas up the Rio Javari (the Brazil–Peru border) and further up the Rio Amazonas in Colombia.

Most travelers base themselves in Leticia, which is more pleasant and better equipped than Tabatinga or the small villages on the Peruvian side.

Tabatinga

☎ 0xx97 / pop 32,000

Tabatinga is most notable as the place where the Amazon River enters Brazil; otherwise, it's a nondescript border town. Boats headed down to Manaus and up to Iquitos depart from Tabatinga's two ports, and its airport serves Brazilian and Peruvian destinations.

ORIENTATION

Tabatinga's main artery is Avenida da Amizade (aka Avenida Principal), which runs parallel to the river for 3km from Tabatinga's airport to Leticia and the international border. The most useful cross streets include Rua Marechal Rondon (250m south of the border), Rua Rui Barbosa (650m), Av Marechal Mallet (900m), Rua Santos Dumont (1.2km) and Rua Duarte Coelho (1.7km). Rua Santos Dumont leads to Porto da Feira, Tabatinga's small-boat port; you can also get there by going down Av Marechal Mallet, turning left at the end and passing the market. Porto Fluvial, where boats for Manaus dock, is at the end of Rua Duarte Coelho.

INFORMATION
Consulates
Colombian consulate (☎ 3412 2104; Rua General Sampaio 623; ⏰ 8am-1pm Mon-Fri)

Emergency
Hospital Militar (☎ 192, 3412 2403, 3412 2117; Rua Duarte Coelho at Av da Amizade)
Police (☎ 190)

Immigration
Federal Police (Polícia Federal; ☎ 3412 2180; Av da Amizade 650; ⏰ 8am-6pm) 100m south of Rua Duarte Coelho.

Internet Access
Digital Net (☎ 3412 3505; Rua Pedro Teixera 397; per hr R$2; ⏰ 8am-noon, 1:30-9pm Mon-Fri, 9am-noon Sat, 2-6pm Sun) On the street parallel to Av Marechal Mallet, one block south.

Money
Banco do Brasil (🕙 8am-1pm Mon-Thu) Across from Bradesco.

Bradesco (Av da Amizade at Av Marechal Mallet)

CNM Câmbio e Turismo (☎ 3412 3281; Av da Amizade 2017) Five hundred meters south of border. Changes cash and traveler's checks, but rates usually lower than in Leticia.

Post
Post office (Av da Amizade s/n; 🕙 8am-5pm Mon-Fri) Located 300m north of the federal police station.

Travel Agencies
CNM Câmbio e Turismo (☎ 3412 3281; Av da Amizade 2017)

Turamazon (☎ 3412 2026; Av da Amizade 2271)

SLEEPING
Hotel Bela Vista (☎ 3412 3093; Rua Marechal Rondon 1806; s/d R$25/30; 🟦) It may not be fancy, but this place packs a great combination – cheap, clean, air-conditioned and steps from the morning boat to Iquitos. And it's friendly to boot.

Hotel Restaurant Te Contei? (☎ 3412 4548; Av da Amizade 1813; s/d R$40/45) Large rooms with air-conditioning off a breezy upstairs patio and corridor. The back rooms have less street noise, and there's a popular per-kilo restaurant and bar on the ground floor.

Pousada Takanás (☎ 3412 3557; Rua Oswaldo Cruz 970; s/d R$60/90; 🟦 🟦) Tabatinga's best hotel, with a lush courtyard and a small swimming pool in the works. Rooms are reasonably modern, with air-conditioned and simple furnishings and decor. A bit removed from the main drag, but that's not necessarily a bad thing.

EATING
Cozinha da Fazenda (☎ 3412 3406; Av da Amizade 1961; per kg R$14; 🕙 breakfast, lunch & dinner) Reliable per-kilo joint.

Restaurante Tres Fronteiras do Amazonas (☎ 3412 2341; Rua Rui Barbosa, 200m west of Av da Amizade; mains R$8-15; 🕙 breakfast, lunch & dinner) Try the *peixe tres fronteiras*, a fish fillet with spices from Peru, Brazil and Colombia, served on a large banana leaf. Wash it down with a beer or *caipirinha*.

Churrascaria Tia Helena (☎ 3412 2165; Rua Marechal Mallet 12; all-you-can-eat per person R$15; 🕙 lunch & dinner) Waiters bring skewered meats directly from the grill and carve it at the table in classic *churrascaria* fashion. Decor is austere (think cement floors and fluorescent lights) but the food is good and the ambience cheerful.

THE TRIPLE FRONTIER

GETTING THERE & AWAY
Air
Between **Rico** (reservations ☎ 92/4009 8333; www.voe rico.com.br) and **TRIP** (reservations ☎ 0300 789 8747; www.airtrip.com.br) there are flights every day from Tabatinga to Manaus (R$500 to R$625), always via Tefé (R$345). Some TRIP flights make additional stops at the towns of Carauari and Coari.

Boat
Slow boats to Manaus (hammock R$150; three to four days) leave from the Porto Fluvial on Wednesday, Friday, and Saturday afternoons. Arrive in the morning to stake out good hammock space, as boats can be quite crowded. See the boxed text, p614, for more tips on riverboat travel.

Speedboats operated by **AJATO** (Map p643; ☎ Porto Manaus Moderna 3622 6047, 9984 9091, Tabatinga 3412 2227; 🕙 8am-5pm Mon-Fri, 8am-noon Sat) leave Tabatinga for Manaus (R$360, 31 hours) once a week, usually in the morning. The boats have airplane-style seating and TVs playing movies, and good meals are included. Call for more information.

To get to Tefé, take Manaus-bound slow boat to Fonte Boa or Jutaí, and transfer to a regional boat that enters Tefé proper. AJATO has a once weekly speedboat service to Tefé (R$300, 20 hours).

To/from Colombia

The international border is marked by nothing more than a few moneychangers on the Brazilian side and a Colombian police officer directing traffic on the other side. You are free to move between Tabatinga and Leticia as much as you like, but if you plan to travel onward, even to Amacayacu national park, you should clear immigration for both countries – DAS in Colombia, the Polícia federal in Brazil – before leaving town. If you need it, there's a Colombian consulate in Tabatinga (p660).

To/from Peru

Transtur (☎ 3412 2945; Rua Marechal Mallet 248) runs high-speed passenger boats – known in Portuguese as *rápidos* – from Tabatinga and Iquitos (US$60, nine to 10 hours, two meals served). Boats depart Tabatinga's Porto da Feira six days per week at 5am. Be sure to get a Brazilian exit stamp the day before; you'll stop at Santa Rosa for Peruvian immigration on the way out.

If you just want to get to Santa Rosa, small motor boats go back and forth frequently from Porto da Feria (R$2, five minutes) from around 6am to 6pm.

There is a Peruvian consulate in Leticia, Colombia (right).

GETTING AROUND

For a *colectivo* (minibus) from the airport to town (R$1.50), walk to the left outside the airport terminal and down the approach road to the corner of the main road. Some continue into Leticia. Taxis and mototaxi are ubiquitous and inexpensive.

A taxi from the airport costs R$15 to hotels in Tabatinga and R$20 to those Leticia. Mototaxi are ubiquitous and cheap (R$2 to R$5) but most cannot cross the international border.

Leticia (Colombia)

☎ 8 / pop 35,000

Leticia is a remarkably spruce little town, with brightly painted houses, pleasant outdoor eateries, and well-maintained parks and streets.

For travelers, it's got hotels in all price categories, regularly scheduled flights between Leticia and Bogota, and a long-standing military presence that keeps the city and surrounding region safe. It's also the starting point for trips to the Colombia's Parque Nacional Natural Amacayacu, and up the Rio Javari into Peru.

There are no border checkpoints between Tabatinga and Leticia, and you're free to pass back and forth provided you stay within either town. However, do clear immigration if you plan to go any further into Colombia or Peru, even on short-term jungle trips.

INFORMATION
Consulates
Brazilian consulate (☎ 592 7530; Carrera 9 No 13-84; ☽ 8am-noon & 1-4pm Mon-Fri)
Peruvian consulate (☎ 592 7204; Calle 13 No 10-70; ☽ 9am-2pm Mon-Fri)

Emergency
Hospital San Rafael (☎ 592 7075; Calle 13 btwn Carreras 9 & 10) 24-hour emergency room and pharmacy.
Police (☎ 112; Carr 11, btwn Calles 12 & 13)

Immigration
DAS (Departamento Administrativo de Seguridad; ☎ 592 7189); centro (Calle 9 btwn Carreras 9 & 10; ☽ 8am-noon & 2:30-6pm); airport (☽ 8am-noon & 2-6pm) You have to go to the airport for entry and exit stamps.

Internet Access
Indio.net (Centro Comercial Acuarios, Calle 8 at Carrera 7; per hr US$1; ☽ 9am-10pm Mon-Sat, 10am-10pm Sun)

Laundry
Lavandería Aseo Total (☎ 592 6051; Calle 9 No 9-85; wash & dry per pound C$2500-3200; ☽ 7am-8pm Mon-Sat, 8am-1pm Sun)

Money
Most businesses in Leticia accept Brazilian reais as well as Colombian pesos. At the time of research, the exchange rate was roughly C$1000 per R$1.
Banco de Bogotá (cnr Calle 7 & Carrera 10)
BBVA Banco Ganadero (cnr Calle 7 & Carrera 10; ☽ 8-11:30am & 2-4:30pm) Has reliable ATMs and will change Amex traveler's checks if you have a current Colombia entry stamp in your passport.
Casas de cambio (several at cnr Calle 8 & Carrera 11) Exchanges Colombian, Brazilian, Peruvian, US or European currency. Most are open until 5pm weekdays, until 2pm on Saturday, and closed Sunday.

Telephone
Telecabinas-Telecom (☎ 592 6725; Calle 8 & Carrera 10; ⏲ 7am-11pm; calls to USA/Europe/Australia per min C$600-750)

Tourist information
City tourist office (☎ 592 7569; Calle 8 No 9-75; ⏲ 7am-noon & 2pm-5:30pm Mon-Fri)

SIGHTS
Museo del Hombre Amazónico (☎ 592 7729; inside Banco de la República, Carrera 11 at Calle 10; admission free; ⏲ 9am-noon & 2:30-5pm Mon-Fri, 9am-1pm Sat) has a small collection of Indian artifacts and implements. Located inside the Banco de la República.

Museo Uirapuru (☎ 592 7056; Galería de Arte Indígena Uirapuru; Calle 8 No 10-35) is in the rear section of Leticia's largest craft shop, selling artifacts of indigenous Indian groups. Less a museum than the personal collection of the shop owner; displays include indigenous artifacts, dried plants and woods, and preserved reptiles and animals.

The **Jardín Zoológico Departamental** (Av Vásquez Cobo; admission C$2; ⏲ 8am-noon, 2-5pm) has animals typical of the region such as anacondas, tapirs, monkeys, caimans, ocelots, eagles, macaws and a friendly manatee named Polo. The small lake at the northern end of the zoo is plastered with *Victoria amazonica*, giant water lilies.

Visit **Parque Santander** before sunset for an impressive spectacle as thousands of small screeching parrots (*pericos*, in Spanish) arrive for their nightly rest in the park's trees.

SLEEPING
Unlike in Brazil, hotels do not commonly offer free breakfast.

Residencias El Divino Niño (☎ 592 5598; Av Internacional No 7-23; s/d C$30,000/40,000) Simple cheap hotel three blocks from the border with Brazil. All rooms have fan and private bath.

Hospedaje Los Delfines (☎ 592 7488 or 7488; Carrera 11 No 12-83; s/d C$30,000/40,000) A 10-minute walk from the center, this small, family-run guesthouse offers basic but spacious rooms around a lush courtyard. Rooms are clean, have fans and private baths; it's often full, so call ahead.

Hotel Yurupary (☎ 592 7983; www.hotelyurupary .col.nu; Calle 8 No 7-26; s C$62,000, d C$82,000-96,000, ste C$124,000-163,000; ☒) Recently refurbished, the large spotless rooms have cheerfully eclectic furnishings, including armchairs, fake flowers and oversize original paintings. All have air-conditioning and hot water, and face a bright courtyard.

Hotel Anaconda (☎ 592 7119; www.hotelanaconda .com.co; Carrera 11 No 7-36; s/d C$126,000/234,000; ☒) Located just across from Parque Orellana, rooms are comfortable and spacious, though they have a distinctly utilitarian feel. Those on the top floor are the best value, with less street noise and nice views over the Amazon. There's also a welcoming courtyard, lobby bar and swimming pool.

Decameron Decalodge Ticuna (☎ 592 6948; www .decameron.com; Carrera 11 No 6-11; s/d C$238,000/458,000; ☒ ☒ ☒) Leticia's only luxury option, this international resort chain has plush, stylish cabanas that open onto a leafy courtyard and pool area, complete with fountains and night lighting. Note that these are walk-in rates; multiday packages reserved in advance are a much better value.

EATING
Food in Leticia is generally good and reasonably priced. The local specialty is fish, including *gamitana* and *pirarucú*.

Restaurante El Sabor (☎ 592 4774; Calle 8 No 9-25; mains C$4000-8000; ⏲ 24hr) Leticia's best budget option serves set meals, vegetarian burgers, and fruit salads, plus unlimited free fruit juice with your meal. The banana pancakes are excellent. Best of all, it's open 24-7 (except Tuesday night).

La Casa del Pan (☎ 592 7660; Calle 11, 10-20; mains C$4000-$8000 ⏲ breakfast, lunch & dinner) Facing Parque Santander, this is an excellent spot for breakfast (eggs, French bread, coffee and juice for US$2) or an afternoon snack.

A Me K Tiar (☎ 592 6094; Carrera 9 No 8-15; mains C$6000-10,000; ⏲ lunch & dinner) Serving good *parillas* (grilled meats) at great prices, this place is popular with locals and tourists alike. Wash your meal down with cold beer or freshly blended juices.

Restaurante Acuarius (☎ 592 5025; Carrera 7 No 8-12; mains US$3-5/C$6000-10,000; ⏲ 7am-9pm) On a quiet corner slightly removed from the center, this pleasant, outdoor restaurant is a cut above the rest, with well-prepared meat and chicken and fish dishes.

DRINKING
Calle 8 has several bars and cafes, including **Tierras Amazónicas** (Calle 8 No 7-50, next to Hotel Yurupary), a mellow spot that specializes in *aguardiente* (powerful liquor made of sugarcane) and salsa music. **Taberna Americana** (Carrera 10 No 11-108) is a cheap, rustic bar playing salsa music till late.

THE AMAZON

For more contemporary Latin and hip-hop beats to groove to, try **Discoteca Tacones** (Carrera 11 No 6-14) near Parque Orellana.

GETTING THERE & AWAY
Air
AeroRepública (☎ 592 7666; Calle 7 No 10-36) is the only airline serving Leticia, with flights to Bogotá three to four days a week. For travel in August or December to January, try to book as early as possible, as flights fill up.

GETTING AROUND
Colectivos (minibuses) to Leticia airport leave from Parque Orellana (C$1000). A mototaxi will cost you C$1000 in town or C$2000 to Tabatinga.

Colectivos to Tabatinga wait at the corner of Carrera 10 and Calle 8 (C$2500) – in Tabatinga, they pass Porto da Feria, the turnoff for Porto Fluvial, the Policía Federal post and the airport, before turning back. A taxi from central Leticia to Tabatinga airport costs C$20,000; there's a stand on Carrera 10 between Calles 7 and 8.

Fast passenger boats to Parque Amacayacu (C$21,000; 1½ hours) and continuing to Puerto Nariño leave from a pier at the end of Calle 8 twice a day during the week, usually at 10am and 2pm.

Parque Nacional Natural Amacayacu
Spanning nearly 300,000 hectares (3000 sq km), Amacayacu national park is home to

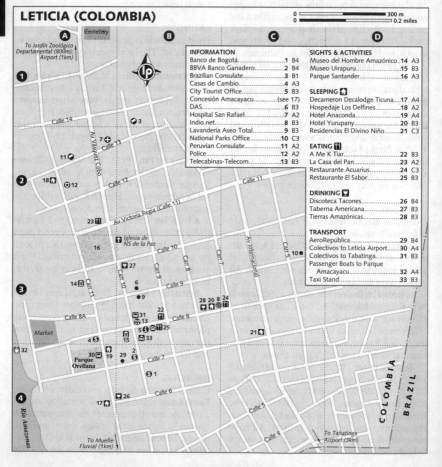

LETICIA (COLOMBIA)

0 — 300 m
0 — 0.2 miles

INFORMATION
Banco de Bogotá.......................1	B4
BBVA Banco Ganadero..............2	B4
Brazilian Consulate...................3	B1
Casas de Cambio.......................4	A3
City Tourist Office.....................5	B3
Concesión Amacayacu........(see 17)	
DAS...6	B3
Hospital San Rafael...................7	A2
Indio.net.................................8	B3
Lavandería Aseo Total...............9	B3
National Parks Office...............10	C3
Peruvian Consulate..................11	A2
Police.....................................12	A2
Telecabinas-Telecom...............13	B3

SIGHTS & ACTIVITIES
Museo del Hombre Amazónico..14	A3
Museo Uirapuru.......................15	B3
Parque Santander....................16	A3

SLEEPING
Decameron Decalodge Ticuna..17	A4
Hospedaje Los Delfines............18	A2
Hotel Anaconda......................19	A4
Hotel Yurupany......................20	B3
Residencias El Divino Niño........21	C3

EATING
A Me K Tiar.............................22	B3
La Casa del Pan.......................23	A2
Restaurante Acuarius...............24	C3
Restaurante El Sabor................25	B3

DRINKING
Discoteca Tacones...................26	B4
Taberna Americana..................27	B3
Tierras Amazónicas..................28	B3

TRANSPORT
AeroRepública........................29	B4
Colectivos to Leticia Airport......30	A4
Colectivos to Tabatinga...........31	B3
Passenger Boats to Parque	
Amacayacu..........................32	A4
Taxi Stand..............................33	B3

an impressive array of plant and animal life, including caimans, boas and various species of monkeys, not to mention a profusion of fish and some 450 bird species. (You'll also see a lot of mosquitoes – bring long clothes and plenty of repellent). The new **visitors center** (☎ 520-8654) serves as base camp for excursions into the park, whether hiking, canoeing, canopy tours, fishing, even visits to indigenous communities. The forest immediately around the center is mostly secondary growth – it was cleared for coca production, back in the day – but the forest is growing back nicely, and you can arrange overnight treks deeper into the reserve where the primary forest is.

The park fee is C$21,000. Accommodations are in large mosquito-proofed **dorms** (C$85,000) or **wooden cabins** (with bathroom incl breakfast & dinner per person C$140,000). Outings vary from C$35,000 to C$150,000 per group (one to five people) and are arranged right at the center. Be sure to bring enough Colombian pesos in small denominations, as credit cards aren't accepted.

You can go directly to the park, though it's recommended you call ahead to be sure there's room. Alternatively, **Concesión Amacayacu** (☎ 592 6600; ☺ 8am-noon, 2-6pm Mon-Fri) is a private agency located inside the Hotel Decameron Decalodge Ticuna (see p663) that handles advanced bookings, mainly for groups. The **national parks office** (☎ 592 7124; www.parquesnacionales.gov.co; Carrera 9 6-100 btwn Calles 5 & 6; ☺ 8am-5pm Mon-Fri) has general information about Amacayacu and other parks.

To get to Amacayucu from Leticia, take any Puerto Nariño–bound boat from the pier at the end of Calle 8 (C$21,000, 1½ hours).

RIO JAVARI

The meandering Rio Javari provides Brazil and Peru with a border, and travelers with excellent opportunities to see the Amazon rain forest up close and undisturbed. A handful of jungle lodges offer accommodations and activities similar to those found elsewhere in the Amazon basin, including forest walks, fishing, night-time caiman-spotting, bird-watching, and dolphin-watching. It's also possible to visit indigenous settlements (though be forewarned they are not the 'uncontacted' sort many travelers imagine). Petru Popescu's book *Amazon Beaming* relates photographer Loren McIntyre's extraordinary experiences among one of the indigenous groups here. Prices vary according to the number of days and types of activities you schedule, as well as

the season. In general, expect to pay US$75-125 per day per person.

Operated by Amazon Jungle Trips, **Zacambu Lodge** (☎ 592 7377; amazonjungletrips@yahoo.com; Av Internacional 6-25, Leticia) is on Lake Zacambú, in a beautiful lake region on the Peruvian side of the Javari river. It's the closest of the lodges to the triple frontier – about 70km from Tabatinga, or three hours by motorboat. Accommodations are simple but comfortable, in hammocks or small rooms, with shared toilets. Most excursions are by motorboat or canoe, for obvious reasons – the bird-watching is particularly good.

Reserva Natural Palmari (in Leticia ☎ 592 4156; www.palmari.org) is another 20km upstream on the south bank of the river, overlooking a bend where pink and gray dolphins are often seen. A slew of activities and outings are possible, from trekking and canoeing to sport fishing and zip-lines up in the canopy. The lodge receives a number of large groups; you may want to ask how many people will be at the lodge when you are (and adjust your schedule accordingly).

Even further still, **Reserva Natural Heliconia** (☎ 311-508 5666; www.amazonheliconia.com; Calle 13 No 11-74) provides room and board in thatch-covered cabins, plus tours via boat or foot of the river, creeks and jungle. There are also organized visits to indigenous villages and special tours devoted to bird-watching and dolphin-watching.

RORAIMA

The tropical rain forest that blankets Roraima's southern half (bisected by the equator) gives way to broad savanna in the middle of the state, and remote and beautiful mountains in the north. It includes most of the Brazilian territories of the Yanomami, one of the country's largest surviving indigenous peoples. The state capital, Boa Vista, still doesn't make the itinerary of most travelers, but has better and better tour options every year. Roraima is home to Monte Roraima, of course, but this intriguing flat-topped mountain sits right on the Brazil–Venezuela–Guyana border, and the best way up is from the Venezuelan side.

BOA VISTA

☎ 0xx95 / pop 197,000
The state capital, a planned city on the banks of the Rio Branco, is home to more than half

of Roraima's population. It's long been a transfer point for travelers headed to Guyana or to Venezuela's beautiful high plains, just three hours north. The town itself lacks pizzazz, but two quality tour outfits based here offer excursions to the pristine and little-visited regions of Serra Grande and Serra de Tepequém.

Information

BOOKSTORES

Nobel (☎ 3621 3422; Av Glaycon de Paiva 789-A; ☽ 9am-7pm Mon-Sat) Occasionally stocks English-language guidebooks.

CONSULATES

Guyana (☎ 3224 2674; Av Benjamin Constant 1020; ☽ 8am-noon Mon-Fri) One-room office at the back of an accounting firm.
Venezuela (☎ 3623 9285; Av Benjamin Constant 525E; ☽ 8am-noon Mon-Fri)

EMERGENCY

Both hospitals listed under 'Medical Services' have 24-hour emergency rooms.
Ambulance (☎ 192)
Police (☎ 190)

INTERNET ACCESS

Nobel (☎ 3621 3422; Av Glaycon de Paiva 789-A; per hr R$3; ☽ 9am-7pm Mon-Sat)
Red Zone (cnr Ruas Araújo Filho & Av Benjamin Constant; per hr R$2; ☽ 9am-midnight)

MEDICAL SERVICES

Hospital Geral (☎ 3236 0326; Rua Recife 1581) Boa Vista's main public hospital, located 2km from the center of town toward the airport.
Hospital Lotty Iris (☎ 3224 1433; Rua Floriana Peixoto) Private hospital convenient to the center.
Yellow fever vaccines are available for free at the airport clinic (☽ 8am-noon, 2-6pm Mon-Fri).

MONEY

Banco do Brasil (Av Glaycon de Paiva 56; ☽ 8am-2pm Mon-Fri) Changes euros and US dollars.
Bradesco (Av Sebastão Diniz & Rua Inácio Magalhães) Reliable ATMs.
Gold & pawn shops (Av Benjamin Constant) Numerous shops on this block change US, Venezuelan and Guyanese currencies.

POST

Main post office (☎ 3621 3535; Praça do Centro Cívico; ☽ 8am-4:30pm Mon-Fri, 8am-noon Sat)

TRAVEL AGENCIES

Timbo Turismo (☎ 3224 4077; timbotur@osite.com.br; Av Benjamin Constant at Rua Araujo Filho; ☽ 8am-noon, 2-6pm Mon-Fri, 8am-noon Sat) Sells plane and bus tickets, though you may need to go to the respective terminals to use credit cards.

Dangers & Annoyances

If you go to Praia Grande, be careful of stingrays, especially in low-water season. The sting hurts like a mother; fortunately, rays are quite skittish and you have to actually step on one for it to sting you. Shuffle your feet when entering or exiting the water – the cloud of sand will scare them away – or use a long stick to poke the shallow water in front of you.

Also, while Orla Taumanan is well lit and a popular watering hole at night, the surrounding streets can be a bit seedy – be alert walking home, or just take a cab.

Sights

PARQUE ANAUÁ & MUSEU INTEGRADO DE RORAIMA

About 2.5km northwest of the center, the vast grounds of **Parque Anauá** (Av Brigadeiro Eduardo Gomes) contain gardens, a lake, a museum, an amphitheater and various sporting facilities. Inside the park, the **Museu Integrado de Roraima** (admission free; ☽ 8am-6pm) has modest displays on the state's archaeology, indigenous peoples, wildlife and history.

PRAIA GRANDE

A tawny sandbar beach emerges on the far bank of the Rio Branco, opposite Boa Vista, during low water, roughly December to April. Known as **Praia Grande**, it is indeed big and beachy, and makes for a pleasant afternoon visit. Its transitory existence means there is no shade – bring an umbrella or consider waiting until the afternoon. **Porto do Babazinho** (☎ 3624 8382; Major William 1) offers ferry service for R$4 roundtrip, and can provide food and drinks.

Activities

HIKING & CAMPING

Porto do Babazinho (☎ 3224 9174, 9111 3511; babarinhorr@yahoo.com; Av Major William 1) is home-base for long-time local guide Sebastião de Souza e Silva (aka 'Babazinho'), who leads a variety of appealing excursions. **Boat trips** (per person R$30-50) can be two-hour excursions along the Rio Branco or all-day outings to Serra Grande, with good hiking. **Fazenda Bacabal** (per person per

THE YANOMAMI

The Yanomami are one of the largest indigenous peoples of Amazonia, and also among its most primitive, living a semi-nomadic life with stone implements, pottery, animal hides and plants in a remote area on the Brazil–Venezuela border. Despite their numbers – estimated at around 15,000 – they remained uncontacted until the 1950s, and then only occasionally until the 1970s. That's when the Brazilian government decided to build Hwy BR-210, abruptly dragging a Stone Age people into the 20th century. Predictably, the Yanomami began dying of measles, influenza and venereal diseases introduced through contact with the highway's construction workers. Several villages were wiped out.

A decade later, a gold rush sent some 40,000 miners swarming into Yanomami territory, polluting rivers and destroying the forest in the process. In 1988, the government attempted to strip the Yanomami of 70% of their traditional territory and open it to mining. It backed off the plan in the face of national and international uproar, but the plight of the Yanomami remained dire. Nearly a fifth of the tribe's population died between 1986 and 1993, mostly of disease.

In 1991 the Venezuelan government officially recognized its country's portion of the Yanomami territory as a special Indian reserve. Brazil followed suit a month later, creating the 96,650-sq-km Terra Indígena Yanomami, Brazil's largest single Indian territory. But conflicts continued: in 1993, a gang of goldminers used machetes and rifles to kill 16 Yanomami, including an infant. Four of the attackers were eventually convicted and jailed, but many more murders have gone uninvestigated.

The Yanomami are a slight people, with typical Amerindian features. The focal point of each community is the *yano*, a large round timber-and-thatch structure where each family has its own section facing onto an open central area used for communal dance and ceremony. Each family arranges its own area by slinging hammocks around a constantly burning fire that forms the center of family life.

Their diet includes monkey (a delicacy), tapir, wild pig and a variety of insects, plus fruits, yams, bananas and manioc. The Yanomami hold elaborate ceremonies and rituals and place great emphasis on intertribal alliances, primarily to minimize feuds. When nearby soil and hunting grounds are exhausted, the *yano* is dismantled and the village moves to a new site.

Disease is cured with shaman dances, healing hands and various herbs, including *yakoana* (a hallucinogenic herbal powder). When a tribe member dies, the body is hung from a tree until dry, then burned to ashes. The ashes are mixed with bananas, which are then eaten by friends and family of the deceased to incorporate and preserve the spirit.

Anthropologist Napoleon Chagnon lived with Yanomami off and on for three decades and described them in his best-selling book *The Fierce People* as aggressive and living in a state of 'chronic warfare.' He received acclaim when the book was published in 1968, but his methods and findings came under increasing scrutiny over the years. In 2001, activist Patrick Tierny wrote *Darkness in El Dorado* in which he accused Chagnon and a colleague of ethical breaches, from using gifts to pry information from subjects, to knowingly exacerbating a measles outbreak. The most serious accusations proved unfounded, but the controversy highlighted the ethical dilemmas inherent in studying isolated indigenous groups.

day R$145, transport per person R$15-60) is a lodge about 140km west of Boa Vista, with comfortable bungalows, excellent horseback riding and bird-watching. Even more remote, in the Serra do Tepequém, is **Baba's Place** (per person per day R$145, transport per person R$15-60), which has simple rooms with shared bathroom, and fine hiking, swimming and animal-spotting. Back in town, you can also **rent kayaks** (per hour R$5) or **learn to windsurf** (six lessons R$180; rentals available; best wind December to May).

Roraima Adventures (☎ 36249611; www.roraima-brasil .com.br; Rua Coronel Pinto; ⏰ 8am-noon, 2-6pm Mon-Fri, 8am-noon Sat) offers professional multiday camping tours all over Roraima, including Serra do Tepequém and Mt Roraima in Venezuela. Ask about excursions into the Yanomami reserve, as well.

Sleeping

Hotel Monte Líbano (☎ 3224 7232; Av Benjamin Constant 319 W; s/d with bathroom R$28/35, without bathroom

THE AMAZON

BOA VISTA

0	500 m
0	0.3 miles

INFORMATION
Banco do Brasil......................1 B1
Bradesco.............................2 C2
Gold & Pawn Shops.................3 B2
Guyanese Consulate................4 C1
Hospital Lotty Iris..................5 C3
Main Post Office....................6 C1
Nobel................................7 B2
Red Zone............................8 B2
Timbo Turismo......................9 B2
Venezuelan Consulate.............10 C1

SIGHTS & ACTIVITIES
Porto de Babazinho................11 D1
Roraima Adventures...............12 C2
Xerokão Center....................13 C1

SLEEPING
Aipana Plaza Hotel................14 B2
Hotel Barrudada...................15 B2
Hotel Euzébio's...................16 A1
Hotel Ideal........................17 B2
Hotel Monte Líbano...............18 B2
Uiramutam Palace.................19 A1

EATING
La Gondola.........................20 B2
Mister Quilo.......................21 C2
Open-Air Food Court..............22 A1
Peixada Tropical...................23 A1
Peixada Ver O Rio.................24 C3

ENTERTAINMENT
Orla Taumanan.....................25 C3
S69.................................26 B2

SHOPPING
Centro de Artesanato.............27 C3

TRANSPORT
Buses to Airport...................28 B1
Mini-Terminal Urbano.............29 B1
Municipal Bus Terminal..........30 C3

R$20/30, with air-con R$35/45; 🗙) The least worst of a string of cheap hotels in this area, the Monte Líbano still has drab rooms, grubby bathrooms, and no free breakfast. (Gotta dig the psychedelic designs on the cement floor, however.) Air-con rooms are slightly better, but then again the only good reason to stay here is to save every last *real*.

Hotel Euzébio's (☎ 3623 0300; Rua Cecília Brasil 1107; s/d standard R$35/49, superior R$56/70; 🗙) Standard rooms are clean but small; superiors are bigger, more cheerful and come with hot water, minibar and telephone. All rooms have air-con and TV. A bit removed from the center, but closer to the appealing walkways and nighttime restaurants in the center of Av Capital Ene Garcez.

Hotel Ideal (☎ 3224 6342; Rua Araújo Filho 533; s/d/t R$40/50/60; 🗙) Popular with travelers, rooms at this rambling hotel are sparsely decorated and on the small side, but definitely a step up from the Monte Líbano. All rooms have air-con and TV; for another R$6, you can have a frigobar as well.

Hotel Barrudada (☎ 2121 1700; www.hotelbarrudada .tur.br; Rua Araújo Filho 228; r R$59/69; 🗙 🖳) Spot-less rooms, a swimming pool, large breakfast and central location make this the best value in town – the bathrooms even have groovy motion-sensors instead of light switches. (Of course, they turn off during a long shower, but it's all good clean fun.) Rooms are on the small side, but those on the upper floors have large windows with views of the park and river.

Uiramutam Palace (☎ 3624 4700; www.uiramutam .com.br; Av Capitan Ene Garcêz 427; s/d/t R$60/80/100, with hot water R$100/130/150; 🗙 🖳 🖳) Standard rooms here are awfully plain for the price, and the cold shower only adds insult to injury. The de-luxe rooms are a better value if they're in your price range, not only for the hot water, but the newer furniture and amenities, including a small table and chair, and their larger and more cheerful interior. The pool is a welcome mid-afternoon diversion.

Aipana Plaza Hotel (☎ 3224 4800; www.aipana plaza.com.br; west side of Praça do Centro Cívico; s/d/tr R$145/165/190; 🗙 🖳 🖳) The reception area of Boa Vista's fanciest hotel has leather sofas, modern paintings and sculptures and a hip lobby bar. Rooms are no less classy, with muted decor, slate floors, glass showers and good beds. The well-maintained pool makes a nice escape from the heat.

Eating

La Gondola (Av Benjamin Constant 35 W; self-service per kg R$16.50; ⏰ lunch) Facing the plaza across a busy intersection, this smaller per-kilo place offers outdoor, fan-cooled or air-con dining areas, in addition to the typical per-kilo options: pasta, potatoes, roast chicken, grilled beef, rice, beans etc.

Mister Quilo (Rua Inácio Magalhães 346; per kg R$18, ⏰ lunch Mon-Sat) The tinted doors conceal a huge and perpetually busy dining area, with three levels, air-con machines blasting and a bevy of blue-shirted waitresses hustling to keep up with drink orders. Diners queue up for a large self-serve spread, including fresh grilled meats, pastas and desserts.

Peixada Tropical (cnr Rua Ajuricaba & Rua Pedro Rodrigues; dishes for 2 R$20-35; ☎ lunch) Another popular open-air lunch spot serving fish in every way imaginable, from Portuguese fish stew to fried-up spicy, Bahian style.

Peixada Ver O Rio (Olra; ☎ 3624 1683; Praça Barreto Leite; mains R$30-40; ⏰ lunch daily, dinner Tue-Sun) You can indeed 'see the river' from this open-air eatery, as the name promises. Fish is the specialty, served in a dozen different ways. Most dishes are designed for two people, but you can request a half-portion. Even so, prices are a bit steep – budget travelers might consider eating somewhere cheaper and migrating here for the beer and the breeze.

A busy **open-air food court** (mains R$2.50-20; ⏰ dinner) occupies part of the long narrow park between the split lanes of Av Capitan Garcez. A slew of mom-and-pop restaurants have tables set up under a high awning, serving cheap tasty Brazilian fare. There's occasionally live music, but the lively, family-friendly ambience is the real draw here.

At the top end of the same park are a restaurant quartet: a **pizza joint, upscale Italian restaurant, midrange churrascaria**, and **Bob's**, the ubiquitous fast-food burger chain. They occupy top and bottom floors of identical side-by-side buildings, and are open for lunch and dinner. Take your pick!

Entertainment

Boa Vista's recently refurbished waterfront, known as **Orla Taumanan**, has a handful of open-air beer gardens that fill up most weekend evenings and nights. The streets around the waterfront can get a little lonely, however – stay alert walking back to the hotel, or just grab a cab.

S69 (cnr Rua Araújo Filho & Av NS da Consolata; ⏰ midnight-6am Sat only) Boa Vista's most prominent gay club makes the most of its once-weekly schedule, with dancing and drinking until dawn. This is actually a GLS spot – *gay, lesbiana, e simpatizante* (gay, lesbian, and down straight people) – and foreigners are welcome.

Shopping

Centro de Artesanato (☎ 3623 1615; Rua Floriano Peixoto 158; ⏰ 8am-6pm Mon-Sat) A handful of storefronts sell a virtually identical selection of knickknacks and souvenirs, but you can sometimes find a few true quality items if you look hard.

Getting There & Away

AIR

Frequent promotions mean flying is often only slightly more expensive than the bus.

Gol (airport ☎ 3224 5824; www.voegol.com.br; ⏰ 11:30am-5:30pm & 10pm-4am)

THE ROAD THROUGH A RESERVE

The Manaus–Boa Vista highway (BR-174) has a violent history. A 125km stretch of this road cuts across the 25,000-sq-km Terra Indígena Waimiri Atroari.

The Waimiri fiercely defended their land against the construction of the road, combating the forces of the Brazilian army in the 1970s. During the confrontations more than 200 soldiers were killed by poison arrows. Casualties on the Indian side, however, were a lot higher. From a population of 1500 in 1974, their numbers were reduced to a mere 374 in 1986, when finally they agreed to negotiate with the government.

Today the population is increasing, with nearly a thousand people living in 14 *aldeias* (villages). On the part of the road that crosses Indian land, drivers are not allowed to get out of their vehicles, and (with a few exceptions such as the Manaus–Boa Vista bus service) the road through the reserve is closed between 6pm and 6am.

THE AMAZON

Meta (airport ☎ 3224 7490; www.voemeta.com.br; ☉ 8am-6pm Mon-Fri) Flights to Guyana and Suriname twice weekly.

TAM (airport ☎ 3623 0049; www.tamairlines.com.br; ☉ 8am-10pm Mon-Fri, 8am-6pm Sat & Sun)

BUS

Eucatur (☎ 3623 1318) has five daily buses to Manaus (R$91 to R$107, 12 hours) including one *semi-leito* at 8:30pm; and four daily to Pacaraima on the Venezuelan border (R$12, three to four hours). You can also take a collective taxi to Pacaraima, charging R$20 but making the trip in under three hours. A single Venezuela-bound bus passes Boa Vista once a day at 7:30am continuing to Santa Elena Uairén (R$20, four to five hours), Puerto Ordaz (R$80, 14 hours) and Puerto La Cruz (R$100, 20 hours).

Amatur (☎ 3224 0004) operates daily buses to Bonfim on the Guyana border (R$13, 1½ hours). From there, you cross the border to Lethem, and catch a bus to Georgetown (R$102, 10 hours, four days per week); you can buy the complete ticket (R$115) in Boa Vista.

Getting Around

Around town, taxis marked 'Lotação' operate like buses, following fixed routes and carrying up to four passengers. The fare is R$2, or R$4 if the driver veers off the route to drop you at a given spot. Private cabs use meters, and can be pricey.

The airport is 3.5km northwest of the city center. To get there, you can take a 206 'Aeroporto' bus (R$1.80) from the *terminal urbano* (municipal bus terminal) on Av Dr Silvio Botelho or across from the *mini-terminal*

urbano at the top of Praça do Centro Cívico. Buses depart roughly every 30 to 90 minutes from 6am until 11:15; the schedule is reduced on weekends. Taxis to/from the airport and center charge R$25.

The **bus station** (Av das Guianas, in Bairro São Vicente) is 2.5km southwest of the center. Several buses go there to/from the *terminal urbano* and the *mini-terminal urbano*, including 'Jockei Clube,' 'Raiar do Sol,' and 'Nova Ciudad' (all R$1.80). Catch any of the same buses back to the center. A private taxi from the center to the bus station costs about R$10, a *lotação* cab is R$2.

AROUND BOA VISTA
Bonfim & Lethem (Guyana)

Bonfim ☎ 0xx95 / pop 3000
Lethem (Guyana) ☎ 072 / pop 900

The small town of Bonfim, 125km northeast of Boa Vista, is the stepping stone to Guyana. The Guyanese town of Lethem is about 5km west across the Rio Tacutu. Neither Bonfim nor Lethem are exactly pleasant, but Lethem is the better of the two; both have hotels in case you get stuck.

Arriving from Boa Vista, bus drivers usually wait for passengers to get exit stamps at the Polícia Federal before continuing the short distance further to the pier on the river. From there, a canoe across the river costs R$3, and Guyanese immigration is another 1.5km from there.

Pousada Fronteira (☎ 3552 1294; Rua Aluísio de Menezes 26, Bonfim; s/d US$25/30) is one of various not-so-good options in Bonfim, with basic rooms and OK bathrooms.

See left for info on buses to Bonfim and continuing to Georgetown.

ENTERING VENEZUELA & GUYANA

Travelers of many nations, including USA, Canada, Australia and most EU countries, need to obtain a Venezuelan tourist card before entering Venezuela by land. The process can be completed in Boa Vista and takes about a half-hour; you'll need to present a passport photo, and copies of your passport data page, your Brazilian entry stamp, and the front and back of your Brazilian tourist slip and yellow fever vaccination certificate. Photos are available at booths in Boa Vista's main plaza, and there's a copy shop around the corner from the consulate **Xerokão Center** (Rua Barão do Rio Branco at Av Ville Roy). Be aware that the consulate is open weekdays until noon only, and Venezuelan border control is not as lax as it used to be. At the time of research, Israeli citizens were not allowed to enter Venezuela unless they had a confirmed international plane ticket out of the country, and even then were permitted to stay for 72 hours only.

Entering Guyana, citizens of the US, Canada, Australia and EU countries do not normally need an advance visa, and can proceed directly to the border. Israeli citizens, again, must obtain advance permission.

AROUND BOA VISTA

THE AMAZON

SANTA ELENA DE UAIRÉN (VENEZUELA)

☎ 0289 / pop 17,000

Santa Elena is dusty town a few kilometers north of the only land-border crossing between Brazil and Venezuela. It's higher and cooler than Boa Vista, and provides access to Venezuela's vast and beautiful Gran Sabana. The region is dotted with waterfalls and curious flat-topped mountains called *tepuis;* the largest and most famous *tepui* is Mt Roraima, a spectacular natural monument and the spot where Brazil, Venezuela and Guyana meet.

Brazilian and Venezuelan immigration procedures are all dealt with at the border, from posts situated about 1km apart from each other. Entering Venezuela, travelers of most nationalities are supposed to have a tourist visa (see the boxed text on opposite) and yellow fever vaccination card.

Orientation

Calle Bolivar is Santa Elena's main drag, with hotels, internet and shops. Where it intersects with Calle Udaneta is called Cuatro Esquinas (Four Corners) and is the spot moneychang-

ers typically hang out. Turn right on Calle Urdaneta and you hit Plaza Bolivar, the town's central square; turn left and in a couple blocks you'll pass backpacker central – a cluster of hotels, eateries and tour operators. At the end of the block is Av Perimetral, which runs along the edge of town.

Information

EMERGENCY

Police, Fire, Ambulance (☎ 171)

IMMIGRATION

Brazilian Consulate (☎ 995 1256, 995 1277; Av Antonio José de Sucre; ☽ 8am-noon Mon-Fri) Set back from the road, across from the gas station.

DIEX (☎ 995 1958, 885-1858; Av Mariscal Sucre, Sector Entrada de Acurima; ☽ 8am-noon & 2-5pm Mon-Fri) Issues permits to visit the El Paují area.

INTERNET

Cafe Iruk (☎ Calle Bolivar across from Hotel Panazarelli; per hr VZ$2500; ☽ 9am-11pm Mon-Sat, 1-11pm Sun)

Mundo Cyber (Calle Udaneta at Calle Ikabarú; per hr VZ$2500; ☽ 8am-10pm Mon-Sat, 1-10pm Sun)

LAUNDRY

Lavandaría Cristal (Calle Udaneta at Calle Ikabarú; per kg VZS$4000; ☽ 8am-noon Mon-Fri, 2-6pm Sat)

MEDICAL SERVICES

Hospital Rosario Vera Zurita (Calle Icabarú) No phone; linked to 171 emergency services via radio. Basic services.

MONEY

At the time of research, the exchange rate was roughly VZ$1150 per R$1. Freelance moneychangers at Calle Bolívar and Calle Urdaneta have good rates.

Banco Guyana (Plaza Bolivar; ☽ 8:30am-3:30pm Mon-Fri)

Banco Industrial de Venezuela (Calle Bolivar, 50m north of Hotel Augusta; ☽ 8:30am-3:30pm Mon-Fri)

POST

Ipostel (Calle Urdaneta btwn Calles Bolívar & Roscio)

Sights & Activities

GRAN SABANA

Santa Elena is at the southern tip of the massive Parque Nacional Canaima (three million hectares/30,000 sq km). At its heart is the **Gran Sabana**, a high savanna dotted with stark flat-topped mountains called *tepuis,* and crisscrossed by rivers. Trips here include great vista points, swimming in natural pools and visiting spectacular waterfalls, including the 100m Salto Aponwao. Other options include whitewater rafting and visiting the town/region of El Pauji, an interesting combination of natural attractions and counterculture community.

MT RORAIMA

The largest and highest of the *tepuis* is 2810m **Mt Roraima**, and climbing it is the reason most people come to Santa Elena. The standard trip is six days, including three spent exploring the wild 60-sq-km moonscape on top. Highlights up there include 'La Ventana' with terrific views; 'El Foso,' a round deep sinkhole with interior arches; and a series of freezing quartz-lined ponds called the 'Jacuzzis.' If a tour doesn't appeal, you can hire a guide and porters in the towns of San Francisco (66km north of Santa Elena) or Paraitepui (26km east). Reaching the top requires no technical climbing, but you definitely should be in good shape. Mt Roraima straddles Venezuela, Brazil and Guyana, but this is the only non-vertical route to the top.

Tours

Santa Elena is a logical base for exploring the Gran Sabana and Mt Roraima, and has a dozen or so tour agencies to prove it. Most offer five to six day Mt Roraima trips (five to six days, per person US$250 to US$450, including gear, transport, food and porters) as well as one- to three-day hiking, rafting and other trips for those with less time (US$60 to US$80 per person per day). Most require at least four people to form a group; some reduce their prices if you have your own gear, don't want porters etc.

Adventure Tours (☎ 0414 853 7903; www.adventuretours .com.ve; Calle Urdaneta) Photography tours are a specialty.

Backpacker Tours (☎ 995 1524, 0414 886 7227; www .backpacker-tours.com; Calle Urdaneta) An attentive and responsible German-run company with comfortable Roraima treks and some of the best camping equipment.

Jaime Rodriguez (☎ 808 8470, 0414 778 5234; germanjaimerodriguez@yahoo.com) An experienced local guide fluent in English, Spanish and Pemón, he leads excellent Roraima tours emphasizing local culture and customs.

Kamadac (☎ 995 1408, 0414 886 6526; www.abenteuer -venezuela.de; Calle Urdaneta btwn Calle Ikabarú & Av Perimetral) A German- and Venezuelan-owned agency, it offers staples (Gran Sabana, Roraima), as well as some more adventurous tours (Auyantepui, Akopán Tepui).

Roraima Trek (☎ 416 0558, 0414 886 1055; Calle Urdaneta) Some of the lowest prices for Roraima treks. They

also do tours to El Pauji and Gran Sabana trips incorporating a more spiritual flavor.

Ruta Salvaje Tours (☎ 995 1134, 0414 889 4164; www.rutasalvaje.com; Av Mariscal Sucre) Reliable company specializing in rafting trips. They also have the usual range of tours, including the Gran Sabana and Roraima.

Sleeping

Posada Hotel Michelle (☎ 416 0792; Calle Urdaneta btwn Calle Ikabarú & Av Perimetral; s/d/tr Bs. 15,000/20,000/27,000) The undisputed backpacker headquarters, and the best place to fill out a tour group. A clean and surprisingly quiet posada with 25 rooms with fans, hot water and a basic kitchen downstairs. Bulletin boards on the front patio announce upcoming trips.

Posada Backpacker Tours (☎ 995 1524 or 0414/886 7227; www.backpacker-tours.com; Calle Urdaneta btwn Calle Ikabarú & Av Perimetral; s/d/t incl breakfast Bs 20,000/40,000/60,000; 💻) Affiliated with the recommended tour operator of the same name (and right across the street). Rooms here are reasonably clean and comfortable. The agency is building a 20-room guesthouse with a pool across town; if this location appears shuttered, the new one is surely open and worth checking out.

Hotel Augusta (☎ 995 1654, 0414/886-0168; Calle Bolívar opposite Café Iruk; s/d/tr Bs 30,000/35,000/40,000) Spick-and-span rooms here have hot water and a cheerful tropical decor. Corridors and common areas are breezy and bright, and there's even a small courtyard with palm trees. The location gives you easy access to internet, restaurants and passing taxis. All in all, it's good value if air-conditioning isn't a requirement.

Hotel Lucrecia (☎ 995 1105; hotellucrecia@hotmail .com; Av Perimetral at Calle Las Apamates; s/d Bs 50,000/60,000; ❄ 💫) Fifteen aging but clean rooms face a nice garden area. The small pool is a treat, though it faces onto a somewhat busy road. The hotel is a bit further removed from the center than other hotels, but not inconveniently so. A good option if you really want air-conditioning.

Eating

Kamadac (☎ 995 1408; Calle Urdaneta; pizza Bs 5000-30,000; ☯ lunch & dinner) Across the street from the Michelle, this tour operator also runs a tasty pizza parlor. Fruit plates are highly sought-after, and the flan is a decadent indulgence.

Restaurant Michelle (☎ 995 1415; Calle Urdaneta; mains Bs 7000-14,000; ☯ lunch & dinner) Dig into huge portions at this popular Chinese restaurant, just two doors down from the hotel of the same name.

Alfredo's Restaurant (☎ 995 1628; Av Perimetral; pasta & pizza Bs 14,000-30,000; ☒) One of the best restaurants in town, Alfredo's has a lengthy menu, gourmet meals and tortellini with ricotta and spinach that melts in your mouth. The filling lunch special is a bargain.

Restaurant Nova Opção (☎ 995 1013; Plaza Bolívar; buffet per kg Bs 18,000; ☒ 11am-5pm Mon-Sat) You'll think you're back in Brazil at this popular lunch spot. The large spread includes dishes from both sides of the border, including grilled meats and a few vegetarian options. When the heat drives you to drink, revitalize with a freshly blended juice.

Inversiones Lakshmy (Calle Icabarú; Bs 5000-25,000; ☒ 8am-noon, 3-7pm Mon-Sat) A small health food store and bakery with fabulous vegan empanadas (really!), dried fruit and bags of TVP (texturized vegetable protein) that vegetarians covet on Roraima treks.

Scoop up a *cachapa* – a savory Venezuelan corn pancake, usually piled with a small mountain of shredded cheese, chicken or pork – from the doorway stall at the **Rivas Manrique carnecería** (cnr Calles Roscio & Icabarú; Bs 9000-22,000).

Getting There & Away

AIR

Rutaca (in Ciudad Bolívar ☎ 0285-632 6290) has flights most mornings to Ciudad Bolívar (Bs 425,100) usually via Canaima (same price) on five-seater Cessnas. Buy tickets at the airport, 7km south of town.

BUS

From the Santa Elena bus terminal, **Caribe Expresos** (☒ 0414/386 2997) has two daily buses to Puerto Ordaz (standard Bs 31,000, deluxe Bs 41,000, 10 hours) and Ciudad Bolívar (same price, 11 hours) and one to Puerto La Cruz (Bs 51,000; 15 hours). **Expresos Los Llanos** (☒ 089/995 1468) has one daily bus to Caracas (Bs 90,000; 20 hours). Alternatively, a bus operated by Brazil's **Eucatur** (☎ 3592 1147 in Pacaraima) passes the Pacaraima and Santa Elena bus terminals at around 10am and continues to Puerto Ordaz and Ciudad Bolívar (R$40), and Puerto La Cruz (R$60).

There is no direct service from Santa Elena into Brazil. Instead, take a taxi across the border to the Pacaraima bus terminal, where buses to Boa Vista (R$12, three to four hours) leave four times daily, and collective taxis leave whenever there are four passengers (R$20, two to three hours).

Entering Venezuela, you can easily walk the 300m from the Pacaraima bus terminal to the **Brazilian border post** (☒ 8am-7:30pm). From there it's a sweaty 750m to the **Venezuelan post** (☒ 8am-6pm) – fortunately, taxis pass frequently and typically don't charge for a quick stop at Venezuelan immigration before continuing to Santa Elena (collective/private VZ$5000/VZ$20,000).

Leaving Venezuela, taxis from Santa Elena to *la linea* (the border) charge the same as when arriving, though *por puesto* (collective) cabs may tag on a couple thousand if you take long passing immigration. Be sure to confirm they'll take you all the way to Brazilian immigration – some go only as far as the Venezuelan post.

RONDÔNIA

In 1943 President Getúlio Vargas created the Territory of Guaporé from chunks of Amazonas and Mato Grosso. In 1981 it became the state of Rondônia, named for Marechal Cândido Rondon, the enlightened and humane soldier who 'tamed' this region in the 1920s when he constructed a telegraph line linking it to the rest of Brazil. Rondon also founded the Serviço de Proteção ao Índio (SPI), predecessor of Funai (Fundação Nacional do Indio; government Indian agency). He exhorted SPI agents to '*Morrer, se preciso for, matar nunca !*' ('Die, if necessary, but never kill!').

Policies later in the century were not so forward-thinking. In 1981, the Brazilian government, with help from the World Bank, launched an initiative to distribute land to poor settlers. Called Polonoreste, the project spawned a land-rush, and Rondônia's population leapt from 111,000 in 1970 to 1.13 million in 1991. Environmental safeguards were flimsy, and about one-fifth of the state's primary virgin forest was cut down to make farmland. The rate of deforestation in the 1980s was equivalent to more than a football field a minute, for a whole decade.

Rondônia is a transition zone between dense Amazonian forests and cerrado (savanna), and despite its sad environmental past, it still has a rich diversity of fauna and flora.

THE AMAZON

PORTO VELHO

☎ 0xx69 / pop 311,500

Porto Velho is not high on anyone's list of favorite cities in the Amazon. It isn't one of the worst cities either, but few travelers find reason to linger long here. Charming or not, Porto Velho is a vital link in Brazil's agricultural economy, as soybeans and other products are shipped on huge barges from here up the Rio Madeira and transferred directly to ocean liners headed abroad. That same ride – albeit on a boat not a barge – draws some travelers up from Cuiabá and the Pantanal on the slow route to Manaus and the Amazon.

Information

EMERGENCY

Ambulance (☎ 192)
Emergency room (☎ 224 5225; Hospital Central, Rua Julio de Castiho 149)
Police (☎ 190)

INTERNET ACCESS

Titan Cyber Lan (2nd fl, Sanduba's restaurant; Av Campos Sales; per hr R$2, after 2pm R$3; ☺ 10am-10pm)

LAUNDRY

Many hotels offer laundry service.
Lavanderia Mamoré (☎ 3221 3266; Av Pinheiro Machado 1455; per piece US$4-10; ☺ 7:45am-6:15pm Mon-Fri, 7:45am-2pm Sat) Quick and professional, but prices are ridiculously high. Definitely request a discount, especially if you've got a lot.

MEDICAL SERVICES

Hospital Central (☎ 224 5225; Rua Julio de Castiho 149)

MONEY

Banco do Brasil (Rua Dom Pedro II 607; ☺ 10am-2pm Mon-Fri) Changes traveler's checks.
Bradesco (Av Carlos Gomes) Across from the cathedral. Reliable ATMs.
Casa de Câmbio Marco Aurélio (☎ 3221 4922; Rua José de Alencar 3353; ☺ 8:30am-3pm Mon-Fri) Changes foreign currencies.
HSBC (cnr Rua Prudente de Morais & Av Sete de Setembro) Reliable ATMs. There's another branch near the bus station.

POST

Post office (☎ 217 3667; cnr Av Presidente Dutra & Av Sete de Setembro; ☺ 8am-5pm Mon-Fri, 9am-noon Sat)

TOURIST INFORMATION

IBAMA (☎ 3223 2023; Av Jorge Teixeira 3559) Check here on progress toward opening nearby protected areas, including Lago do Cuniã (p677), for ecotourism. The office is a few kilometers north of the center – bus 201 signed 'Hospital de Base via Aeroporto' passes here.

TRAVEL AGENCIES

Nossa Viagens e Turismo (☎ 3224 4777; Rua Tenreiro Aranha 2125) Buy plane tickets in the air-con portion of the office, or bus tickets in the sweltering fan-only area – go figure. Cash only.
Vip's Tur (☎ 3224 2144; vipstur@mailcity.com; Av Carlos Gomes 1700) For air tickets. Credit cards accepted.

Sights & Activities

MUSEU DA ESTRADA DE FERRO MADEIRA-MAMORÉ

The city's only real sight of interest, the Museu da Estrada de Ferro Madeira-Mamoré (Madeira-Mamoré Railway Museum; admission free; ☺ 8am-5pm) is housed in one of several huge sheds that made up the original train station. It displays train relics, memorabilia, and photographs charting the railway's story, especially its early construction (both success and failures). The locomotive 'Colonel Church' has been restored and is on display here: built by the Baldwin Locomotive Works of Philadelphia, it became the first locomotive to run in Amazonia when it inaugurated the Madeira–Mamoré Railway in 1878. The Colonel Church has been restored and is on display here, alongside other old US- and German-made locomotives and rolling stock.

RIVER TRIPS

The broad Rio Madeira forms the western boundary of Porto Velho. Measurements of the length of the mud-brown river usually include its main tributary, the Rio Mamoré, and *its* tributaries, which originate in the Bolivian Andes, making the Madeira 3200km long. With an average flow of 1.4 billion liters a minute, the Madeira has the sixth-greatest volume of all the world's rivers. It enters the Rio Amazonas 150km downstream from Manaus.

From about 9am to 7pm daily, riverboats make 45-minute cruises along the Rio Madeira from the dock in front of the Madeira–Mamoré train station (R$5 per person). While not exactly thrilling, this is a reasonable way to idle away an hour or so – with luck you'll see a few pink dolphins. You can buy snacks and drinks on board.

Sleeping

Hotel Tia Carmem (☎ 3221 7910; Av Campos Sales 2895; s/d without bathroom & with fan R$22/34, with bathroom &

air-con R$35/50;) With just a handful of rooms, this family-run place feels more like a guesthouse than a hotel. Rooms are tiny but clean. You're removed from the bustle of downtown, but it's still an easy walk to and from nightlife on Av Pinheiro Machado. Breakfast is offered Monday to Saturday only.

Vitória Palace Hotel (3221 9232; Rua Duque de Caxias 745; s/d with fan R$35/45, with air-con & minibar R$45/55;) A small step up from the Tia Carmem, with somewhat bigger rooms and more central location, but the same guesthouse ambience. Simple, tidy rooms have private bathrooms (with hot water) and high ceilings for a bit more breathing space.

Hotel Yara (3221 2127; Rua General Osório 255; s/d R$45/65;) Ordinary, somewhat cramped

rooms are nevertheless clean and reasonably comfortable. The location isn't exactly charming, but it's safe and convenient to the bank, riverboat dock, airport buses. Definitely the best option on Av Sete de Setembro.

Hotel Central (2181 2500; www.enter-net.com .br/hcentral; Rua Tenreiro Aranha 2472; s/d R$96/124;) A classy modern hotel with comfortable rooms and prompt professional service. The location is a bit removed – and the street a bit lonely, especially at night – but that just makes getting here all the more comforting. Good value.

Hotel Vila Rica (3224 3433; www.hotelvilarica.com .br; Av Carlos Gomes 1616; s/d R$240/275;) Porto Velho's finest hotel has a spacious lobby, and excellent views from the upper

THE AMAZON

PORTO VELHO

0 — 500 m
0 — 0.3 miles

INFORMATION	
Banco do Brasil	**1** B3
Bradesco	**2** B3
Casa de Câmbio Marco Aurélio	**3** A3
Hospital Central	**4** B3
HSBC	**5** B4
Lavanderia Mamoré	**6** C2
Nossa Viagens e Turismo	**7** B4
Post Office	**8** A4
Titan Cyber Lan	**9** B3
Vip's Tur	**10** C3

SIGHTS & ACTIVITIES	
Museu da Estrada de Ferro Madeira-Mamoré	**11** A4

SLEEPING	
Hotel Central	**12** B3
Hotel Tia Carmem	**13** B3
Hotel Vila Rica	**14** C3
Hotel Yara	**15** B4
Vitória Palace Hotel	**16** B3

EATING	
Caffé Restaurante	**17** B3
Casa D'Italia	**18** B3
Mirante II	**19** A3
Praça Rondón	**20** A4
Remanso do Tucunaré	**21** C4

ENTERTAINMENT	
Buda's Bar	(see 24)
Cine Brasil	**22** B4
Cine Rio	**23** C3
Emporium	**24** A3
Estação do Porto	(see 24)
Food and Beer Stalls	**25** A4
Praça Rondón	(see 20)

SHOPPING	
Artes Brasil	**26** A3

TRANSPORT	
Agência Amazonas	**27** A4
Bus 201 to Bus Station & Airport	**28** B4
Porto Cai n'Água	**29** A4
Rico	**30** B3

floor rooms. A business center and swimming pool make this suitable for work or pleasure, and frequent promotions can draw the room rates into upper midrange territory. On Saturdays, the hotel hosts the popular *Feijoada do Vila*, a huge lunch buffet that attracts travelers and PV's upper crust alike (per plate R$25).

Eating

Praça Rondón (cnr Avs Sete de Setembro & Presidente Dutra; ☽ 4-11pm) Carts set up along the edges of the plaza serve *espetinho completo* – beef or chicken kabobs served with rice and farinha – and other street-food favorites for less than R$5 a plate. Afterward, migrate across the plaza to one of the outdoor bars for a tall beer at a plastic table.

Mirante II (end of Rua Dom Pedro II; ☽ lunch & dinner Tue-Sun) Fish figures prominently on the menu of this outdoor eatery, but the real reason to come is the great view of the Rio Madeira. You can also order simple sandwiches. There's a popular *feijoada* (bean-and-meat stew; per plate R$12 to R$18) on Saturdays. Very low key, with outdoor tables.

Caffé Restaurante (☎ 3224 3176; Av Carlos Gomes 1097; per kg R$20; ☽ lunch Mon-Sat) Come here for the excellent lunch buffet. A wide selection of mains – from shepherds pie to fried fish – and a slew of sides and a refrigerated case full of succulent desserts are served in a nice and cool dining area. Popular with professionals, but perfectly affordable.

Casa D'Italia (cnr Golçalves Dias & Av Pinheiro Machado; mains R$10-25; ☽ dinner, closed Tue) The *rodízio* concept works perfectly well for Italian food: instead of skewers of meat, waiters rotate by with dishes of lasagna, pastas with red or cream sauces, and of course pizza of all sorts, including chocolate and banana pizzas for dessert. It's all-you-can-eat, but don't get greedy: you pay extra if you leave anything on your plate.

Remanso do Tucunaré (☎ 3221 2353; Av Brasília 1506; dishes R$16-40; ☽ lunch & dinner) Good fish dishes serve two easily; try a delicious *caldeirada de tucunaré* (river-fish stew) or *tambaquí* – big fish chunks boiled with onion and tomatoes in a souplike sauce, accompanied by rice.

Shopping

Artes Brasil (☎ 3224 4774; Rua Euclides da Cunha 1952) The best items here are carved wooden animals, from pink dolphins to peacock bass, and ranging from keychain size to several feet long. The rest is fairly predictable *artesenato*, but still worth perusing. Facing the Mercado Central, a short distance from the railroad museum.

Entertainment

The corner of Avs Pinheiro Machado and Presidente Dutra is the epicenter of Porto Velho's nightlife. Three bars in row – Emporium, Estação do Porto and Buda's Bar – serve up beer, mixed drinks, and a cool, bohemian-ish atmosphere that draws a mixed-age crowd. Weekends are busiest, of course, and occasionally feature live music. Further down Av Pinheiro Machado – to about Rua Goncalves – are several more small bars, restaurants and cafés, if you're looking for something bit mellower (or just a bite to eat).

If you don't feel like walking up to Av Pinheiro Machado, **Praça Rondón** (cnr Avs Sete de Setembro & Presidente Dutra; ☽ 4-11pm) has a handful of restaurant-bars with tables set up in the plaza, where you can chill out over a cold beer or two.

For something a bit edgier, the riverbank area by the Madeira–Mamoré train station has a slew of outdoor stands serving beer, and a couple of floating docks that double as bars. Saturday and Sunday nights have live music and dancing; things can get a bit seedy as the night wears on, so definitely be alert.

Cine Rio (tickets R$10, R$5 on Mon) is a one-screen theater located on the 2nd floor of Rio Shopping, a small mall on Av Carlos Gomes, between Rua Joaquím Nabuco and Av Brasília; at least five people are required to run the movie, and some nights a quorum is not to be had. **Cine Brasil** (Av Sete de Setembro; tickets R$6) is even more modest, located in a run-down theater near Rua José de Alencar. Both show relatively recent Hollywood movies.

Getting There & Away

AIR

Porto Velho airport is 7km north of town. There are daily direct flights to Manaus and Brasília, from here you can connect to the rest of the country and world. Gol also has direct flights to Rio Branco and, most of the year, to Cruzeiro do Sul. The small airport has HSBC and Banco de Brasil cash machines, a post office, rental car agencies, an information desk and a strangely large food court.

Gol (☎ 3217 7494; www.voegol.com) At airport only, direct flights to Manaus, Brasilia, Rio Branco and Cruzeiro de Sul.

Rico (☎ 3224 2105, airport check-in desk ☎ 3222 0879; Av Pinheiro Machado 744; ◷ 8am-5:30pm Mon-Fri, 8am-noon Sat)

TAM (☎ 3217 7508; www.tam.com.br) At airport only; all flights connect through Brasilia.

BOAT
Slow boats to Manaus via the Rio Madeira and Rio Amazonas leave twice weekly from Porto Cai n'Água at the end of Rua 13 de Maio. Departures are on Tuesday (arriving in Manaus on Friday) and Friday (arriving on Sunday) between noon and 6pm. Tickets are R$100 for hammock, R$350 for *camarote* (one to two people, fan, no bathroom) and R$450 for a suite (one to two people, air-con, private bathroom); all include three meals per day, the latter two get somewhat better meals, and lunch and dinner are delivered to your room. **Agência Amazonas** (☎ 3223 9743; ◷ 7am-7pm Mon-Sat, 7am-11am Sun) is one of several ticket offices on Rua 13 de Maio near the port; ticket prices are negotiable, especially for groups. Most agencies can reserve good hammock spots for you, and even sell you a hammock (though you'll get better prices at the market); otherwise, arrive at the boat in the morning to secure a good place to hang your hammock. You can even arrive a day or two in advance, and stay for free on the boat before it departs (see p674).

BUS
The **bus station** (cnr Av Jorge Teixeira & Av Carlos Gomes) is 2km east of the center.

Real Norte (☎ 3225 2891) runs four daily buses to Rio Branco (R$50 to R$57 eight hours) departing at 7am, noon, 10pm and 11:55pm; the 10pm departure is direct. It also has service to Guajará-Mirim (R$30 to R$34, five hours) at 6am, 9:30am, 2pm, 6pm, 11:30pm and 1am; the 2pm and 1am departures are direct. Collective taxis also make the trip to Guajará-Mirim (per person R$40, four hours). The price is based on a minimum of four passengers; ask taxi drivers at the bus station.

Andorinha (☎ 3225 3025) has virtually identical services to Real Norte, including to Rio Branco (ordinary/direct R$50/57, eight hours, four departures daily), Guajará-Mirim (ordinary/direct R$30/34, five hours, six departures daily) and Cuiabá (R$130, 24 hours, two departures daily).

Eucatur (☎ 3222 2223) offers long-distance service to destinations like Cuiabá (R$130,

24 hours, five departures daily), São Paulo (R$260, 48 hours, one departure daily) and Brasília (R$240, 40 hours, one departure daily).

Tekla (☎ 3225 2867) serves the glutton-for-punishment route, with buses to Imperitriz (R$320, 2½ to three days, one departure weekly) connecting to Belém (R$380, three to 3½ days).

CAR
Rental agencies can be found at the airport, including **Localiza** (☎ 3224 6530, 0800/99 2000; www.localiza.com; Av Jorge Teixeira 151) and **Boa Sorte Rent a Car** (☎ 3229 4425).

Getting Around
Bus 201 (R$2), signed 'Hospital de Base via Aeroporto,' runs between the city center and the bus station and the airport, passing each roughly every hour. Pick it up opposite the north side of the bus terminal, right in front of airport terminal, or at designated stops along Av Sete de Setembro. A taxi between the bus station and town costs R$10; to or from the airport is R$25.

AROUND PORTO VELHO
Reserva Extrativista do Lago do Cuniã
This 558-sq-km reserve, created in 1999, lies 150km down the Rio Madeira from Porto Velho and is accessible only by river. It's Rondônia's largest fish-spawning ground (pirarucu and *aruanã* are among the species breeding here) and is renowned for its abundant bird life. Plans to open the reserve to tourism have been delayed by several years, as IBAMA completes required environmental studies. Contact **IBAMA** (☎ 223 2023; esecunia.ro@ibama.gov.br; Av Jorge Teixeira 3559) in Porto Velho to check the progress.

GUAJARÁ-MIRIM
☎ 0xx69 / pop 37,500
This low-key town on the Rio Mamoré came into existence as the southern terminus of the Madeira–Mamoré Railway. Both Guajará-Mirim and Bolivian Guayaramerín across the river are free-trade zones with a steady stream of shopping tourists.

Though exceedingly sleepy most of the year, Guajará-Mirim perks up in mid-August when it hosts its own Boi-Bumbá festival, a re-creation of the huge bash of the same name held in Parantins, near Manaus, and which is

THE AMAZON

THE AMAZON

UNCONTACTED

The notion that deep in the Amazon rain forest live indigenous tribes who have yet to be contacted by the outside world is not as illusory as you might think. In fact, Brazil has more uncontacted indigenous groups than any other country. A report in 2007 by Funai, Brazil's indigenous affairs agency, estimates there are 67 such groups, up from the previous estimate of 40.

Anthropologists have long known that uncontacted groups exist, though estimating how many, and how numerous they are, is obviously difficult. Contacted tribes often tell of uncontacted families living in remote areas of their territories. Occasionally members of an uncontacted group will emerge from the jungle, having left or been expelled from their land. Funai studied footprints, abandoned huts and other clues in its recent study. Experts believe most uncontacted groups have seen or even encountered non-Indians – and have probably seen and heard airplanes – but choose to remain hidden.

Several uncontacted groups are believed to live in Rondônia, including at least three in the Uru-eu-Wau-Wau Indian reserve, in the center of the state. The reserve suffers rampant illegal mining and logging, and hundreds of settlers have had to be expelled since the reserve's establishment in 1994. Rondônia is also home to an indigenous man believed to be the last member of an unknown tribe. He has refused all contact, despite being surrounded by pastures and plantations. When Funai arranged for a woman from a nearby tribe to meet him, and possibly reproduce, he chased away the would-be bride with bow and arrows. He is called the 'man in the hole' because he has a hole in his hut, protected by sharp spikes, where he hides when outsiders approach.

---

itself an adaptation of the Bomba Meu Boi festival celebrated in Sã Luis and other parts of the northeast. Guajará-Mirim's festival includes many of the same elements, including mock feuds between the 'Caprichosos' and 'Garantidos' (traditionally dressed in blue and red, respectively) and nighttime performances depicting the story of an ox that's killed and then resurrected. A R$5 admission is charged for some events.

Information

EMERGENCY
Emergency room (☎ 192; Hospital Regional, cnr Rua Marechal Deodoro & Av Costa Marques)
Police (☎ 190)

INTERNET ACCESS
Cyber Space (per hr R$1.50; ⏰ 8am-12:30pm Mon-Fri, 8am-12:30pm & 2:30-7pm Sat) Around the corner from Pizzaria Pit Stop.
Playnet (Av Dom Pedro; per hr R$2.50; ⏰ 9am-midnight) One of several shops at the local gas station.

MEDICAL SERVICES
Hospital Regional (☎ 3541 7129, or toll-free 192; cnr Rua Marechal Deodoro & Av Costa Marques)
Yellow fever vaccinations (cnr Av Beira Rio & Travessa do Navigante; ⏰ 7am-7pm Mon-Sat, 7am-noon Sun) Free of charge at the health post near the port. Note that the vaccine is not considered effective until 10 days after injection.

MONEY
There are numerous moneychangers at the port in Guayaramerín (p680), on the Bolivian side.
Banco do Brasil (Av Mendonça Lima 388; ⏰ 9am-2pm Mon-Fri) Exchanges US cash but not traveler's checks.
Bradesco (cnr Av Costa Marques) Reliable ATMs.

POST & TELEPHONE
Post office (☎ 3541 2777; cnr Av Presidente Dutras & Rua Marechal Deodoro; ⏰ 8am-noon & 2-6pm Mon-Fri, 8am-noon Sat)
Posto Telefónico (☎ 3541 3991; Av 15 de Novembro 620; ⏰ 8am-9pm) Sells telephone cards.

TRAVEL AGENCIES
Alfatur (☎ 3541 1073, 541 1811; alfatur@osite.com.br; Av 15 de Novembro 148-A) Friendly helpful office for air travel from Porto Velho.

Sights & Activities
MUSEU HISTÓRICO MUNICIPAL
'Have animal, will stuff' seems to be the motto at Guajará-Mirim's **Museu Histórico Municipal** (cnr Av Constituição & Av 15 de Novembro; admission free; ⏰ 8:30-11:30am & 2:30-5:30pm Mon-Fri, 8:30-11:30am Sat). Monkeys, falcons, and anteaters are among the slew of birds and mammals stuffed (none too recently, it seems) and posed in a tree in the museum's foyer. Inside the main room, a stuffed anaconda is stretched the length of the

main salon, while another is wrapped around a crocodile, also stuffed. A few other oddities, like conjoined-twin piglets preserved in formaldehyde, complete the bizarre natural history collection. The museum is housed in the old Madeira–Mamoré train station, and has some mildly interesting train memorabilia, and there are two genuine steam locomotives parked outside.

PAKAAS PALAFITAS LODGE
A visit to the upscale eco-hotel **Pakaas Palafitas Lodge** (☎ 3541 3058; www.pakaas.com.br; all-day entry incl lunch R$40) is an agreeable way to spend the day. You can walk along the 2.5km of raised scenic trails, and book a canoe tour through nearby channels and flooded forest. Or just relax beside the beautiful pool, which overlooks a 'meeting of the waters,' like the larger and more famous one near Manaus, and enjoy a fine buffet lunch. A taxi to the lodge from town costs R$50.

Sleeping & Eating
Hotel Mini-Estrela (☎ 3541 1206; Av 15 de Novembro 460; s/d with fan R$20/40, with air-con $30/50; 🆑) offers large basic rooms with cable TV, and a location that's convenient to restaurants, internet and passing taxis for getting to the port or bus station. By no means luxurious, but a reliable budget choice, especially if you're just passing through.

Hotel Jamaica (☎ 3541 3722; Av Leopoldo de Matos 755; s/d/tr R$50/65/80; 🆑 🖳) Near the cathedral, this is Guajará-Mirim's best hotel, with large comfortable rooms arranged along a long internal corridor and lobby. For not too much more than the Mini-Estrela, you are sure to have firm beds, fresh sheets, working air-con, and a well-supplied breakfast. Free wireless internet is available in the lobby, but doesn't reach most rooms.

Pakaas Palafitas Lodge (☎ 3541 3058; www .pakaas.com.br; s/d with jungle view R$159/282, with river view R$200/355; 🖳) A memorable, locally owned jungle lodge about 30 minutes by taxi from Guajará-Mirim whose price includes all meals. Built on stilts, the lodge overlooks the confluence of the Mamoré and Pacaas rivers, which – one being white, the other black – form a stark 'meeting of the waters' like the one near Manaus. The best view is from the

THE AMAZON

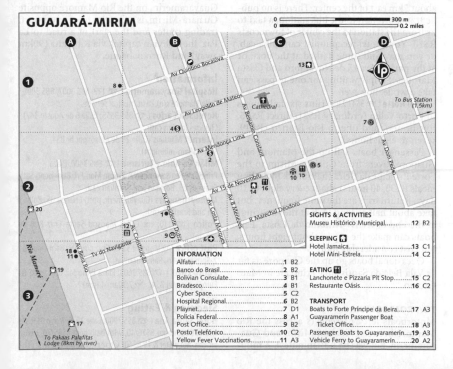

GUAJARÁ-MIRIM

0 — 300 m
0 — 0.2 miles

INFORMATION
Alfatur......................................	1 B2
Banco do Brasil.........................	2 B2
Bolivian Consulate.....................	3 B1
Bradesco..................................	4 B1
Cyber Space.............................	5 C2
Hospital Regional.......................	6 B2
Playnet.....................................	7 D1
Policia Federal..........................	8 A1
Post Office................................	9 B2
Posto Telefónico.......................	10 C2
Yellow Fever Vaccinations...........	11 A3

SIGHTS & ACTIVITIES
Museu Histórico Municipal............	12 B2

SLEEPING
Hotel Jamaica............................	13 C1
Hotel Mini-Estrela......................	14 C2

EATING
Lanchonete e Pizzaria Pit Stop......	15 C2
Restaurante Oásis.......................	16 C2

TRANSPORT
Boats to Forte Príncipe da Beira......	17 A3
Guayaramerín Passenger Boat Ticket Office..........................	18 A3
Passenger Boats to Guayaramerín....	19 A3
Vehicle Ferry to Guayaramerín........	20 A2

Rio Mamoré

To Bus Station (1.5km)

To Pakaas Palafitas Lodge (8km by river)

hotel's suspended pool – from the right angle, it looks like a meeting of *three* waters. The lodge has 28 comfortable chalets, and 2.5km of raised walkways through the surrounding forest – it's secondary growth, but home to many animals and birds. Guests can book various tours (R$90 to R$250 for one to five people), including nighttime caiman spotting and canoeing through the flooded forest. Closed December 23 to January 2nd.

Lanchonete e Pizzaria Pit Stop (☎ 3541 4213; Av 15 de Novembro 620; dishes US$4-6; ☯ dinner) A popular if somewhat sterile eatery serving decent pizzas. It has a huge wide-screen TV so you're sure not to miss a moment of the latest *novela* or soccer game.

Restaurante Oásis (☎ 541 1621; Av 15 de Novembro 460; self-service per kg US$5; ☯ lunch) This long-time favorite in Guajará-Mirim can be counted on for a tasty, well-prepared lunch buffet, including fresh grilled meats. The airy dining area gets some street noise, but is still a pleasant place for a midday break.

Getting There & Around

The **bus station** (☎ 541 2448; Av 15 de Novembro) is about 2km east of the center. There is no public transportation to the bus station; a taxi to or from the station to the center of town costs R$10. Your hotel receptionist can call a cab, or you may find some parked at the port, or at the park at Avs 15 de Novembro and Costa Marques. Simply waiting for one to pass can take a while, however.

Real Norte (☎ 3541 2302) runs six daily buses to Porto Velho (ordinary R$31, direct R$35, five hours), and one to Rio Branco (R$49, seven to eight hours).

Passenger boats sail up the Mamoré and Guaporé Rivers from Guajará-Mirim to the Forte Príncipe da Beira (hammock including meals R$90, 40 hours) about every eight to 10 days. Return trips are the same frequency, but take about half as long. Ask at the moorings at the end of Av Dr Antônio da Costa. Fast boats can make the trip in about eight hours, but cost considerably more.

Occasional boats go up the Guaporé as far as Vila Bela da Santíssima Trindade in Mato Grosso.

TO/FROM BOLIVIA

Motorboats ferry passengers across the Rio Mamoré between Guajará-Mirim and Guayaramerín, Bolivia (B$2, 10 minutes). A mini-

mum of 10 passengers is usually required, but boats often go with fewer. Mornings and afternoons are the busiest, and it's rare to wait more than 30 minutes at any time of the day. The port and **ticket office** (☎ 3541 7221; ☯ 24hr) in Guajará-Mirim are on Av Beira Rio, near the east end of 15 de Novembro. If you're driving, ask here about the vehicle ferry. Money changers on the Bolivian side change reais and bolivianos. Entering Bolivia, get your entry stamp and visa (up to 60 days) at the immigration office a block from the main port. Entering Brazil, you can request up to 90 days, and will be required to show a yellow fever vaccine certificate.

Bolivian consulate (Av Quintino Bocaiúva) Changes location frequently; ask at the Polícia Federal for the current location.

Polícia Federal (☎ 3541 2437; cnr Av Presidente Dutra & Av Quintino Bocaiúva; ☯ 8am-noon, 2-6pm) The immigration office is an unmarked door on Av Presidente Dutra, but you can use the main entrance on Av Quintino Bocaiúva after hours.

GUAYARAMERÍN (BOLIVIA)

☎ 0xx855 / pop 35,000

Guayaramerín, on the Rio Mamoré opposite Guajará-Mirim, is a frontier town, river port, trading center and the start of a road to La Paz, the Bolivian capital, via Riberalta (90km away) and Rurrenabaque.

Information

Hospital Guayaramerín (☎ 112, 885 3007, 885 3008; Calle Mamoré s/n) Basic medical services.

Hotel San Carlos (☎ 855 3555; Calle 6 de Agosto 347) Changes foreign cash.

Internet M@s@s (Calle 25 de Mayo; per hr B$4; ☯ 9:30am-midnight)

Milán Cambio y Turismo (☎ 885 3400; Plaza Principal; ☯ 8am-noon & 2-6pm Mon-Fri, 8am-noon Sat) Changes US, Bolivian and Brazilian cash.

Moneychangers (Guayaramerín port) Change US, Bolivian and Brazilian cash.

Police (☎ 110; cnr Calles Mariscal Santa Cruz & 6 de Agosto)

Post office (Av Mariscal Santa Cruz s/n; ☯ 8am-noon & 2-5pm Mon-Fri, 8am-noon Sat)

Punto Entel (☎ 885 3603; Plaza Principal; calls to US & Europe per min B$4; ☯ 7:30am-11pm)

Sleeping & Eating

Hotel Santa Ana (☎ 855 3900; Calle 25 de Mayo 611; s/d without bathroom B$20/40, with bathroom B$35/70, r with air-con, hot water & TV B$60) Operated by a cheerful

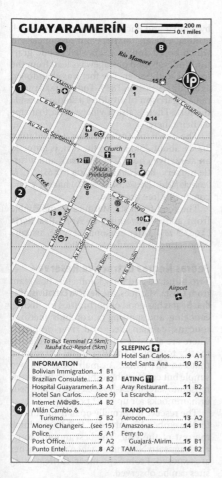

GUAYARAMERÍN

chalets in a large lakeshore complex. Stretching the concept of 'eco resort,' it is nevertheless a reasonably pleasant retreat, especially when there are no loud or boisterous school groups (as there sometimes are). Hiking, canoeing and horseback riding trips can be arranged. Prices include breakfast.

Aray Restaurant (cnr Av Federico Román & Av 24 de Septiembre; dishes B$7-35; ☺ lunch) has long been Guayaramerín's most popular restaurant, though it is certainly not the cleanest or most attractive option in town. The menu has the same standard meat, chicken and fish dishes found anywhere, but its large dining area can fill to overflowing at lunchtime.

La Escarcha (cnr Calle Mariscal Santa Cruz & Av 24 de Septiembre; mains B$5-25; ☺ 9am-11pm Tue-Sun) is a family-run eatery serving simple meals in a pleasant indoor dining area, and at wood tables set up on the sidewalk facing the plaza. Go light with a couple empanadas and a freshly blended fruit smoothie, or fill up on with grilled beef with rice, beans and salad.

Getting There & Away

AIR

Guayaramerín's small simple airport is on the eastern edge of town. At the time of research, there were three airlines with service here: **Amazonas** (☎ 855 3731; www.amazonas.com; Av Federico Roman 100 at Calle Mamoré; ☺ 8:30am-noon & 2:30-6pm Mon-Fri, open at airport Sat & Sun); **Aerocon** (☎ 885 3882, Calle Mariscal Santa Cruz; ☺ 8am-12:30pm & 2-6:30pm Mon-Fri, 8am-12:30pm Sat, 10am-12:30pm Sun); and **TAM** (☎ 885 3924, 885 3925; cnr Av 16 de Julio & Calle Sucre). The latter is operated by the Bolivian military, and while it typically offers cheaper fares, it reportedly is not held to the same strict safety standards that the commercial airlines are. TAM airplanes also tend to be less modern and comfortable, as they are mostly re-purposed military cargo planes.

All three airlines offer one flight daily to Trinidad, with connections from there to La Paz, Santa Cruz, Cochbamba and elsewhere. If you are connecting, be sure to confirm the flight is the same day, lest you are stuck in Trinidad unexpectedly. At the time of research, a one-way ticket to Trinidad cost B$580 on Amazonas and Aerocon, and B$495 on TAM, or B$1115 and B$812, respectively, to La Paz.

BOAT

Motorboats zip back and forth between Guayamerín and Guajará-Mirim. There was

---

INFORMATION

Bolivian Immigration...1	B1
Brazilian Consulate......2	B2
Hospital Guayaramerín.3	A1
Hotel San Carlos.......(see 9)	
Internet M@s@s.........4	B2
Milán Cambio &	
Turismo.................5	B2
Money Changers....(see 15)	
Police.....................6	A1
Post Office...............7	A2
Punto Entel..............8	A2

SLEEPING 🏠

Hotel San Carlos.........9	A1
Hotel Santa Ana........10	B2

EATING 🍴

Aray Restaurant........11	B2
La Escarcha..............12	A2

TRANSPORT

Aerocon...................13	A2
Amazonas................14	B1
Ferry to	
Guajará-Mirim...15	B1
TAM.......................16	B2

---

elderly couple, this hotel offers simple affordable lodging. Rooms are basic but clean, and most open onto a sunny courtyard brimming with potted plants. No food service, but water and coffee are always available.

Hotel San Carlos (☎ 855 3555; Calle 6 de Agosto 347; s/d B$150/220; ☒ ☒) By far the most upmarket place in town, with an attitude and parking area full of SUVs to prove it. Guests can make use of a pool, restaurant and billiards table; all rooms are modern and comfortable and include TV and air-con, while suites have an additional small sitting area. Breakfast is included in the price.

About 5km out of town, **Itauba Eco Resort** (☎ 855 3514, in Brazil 9951 1562; itaubaecoresort@bol.com .br; Av Federico Román s/n; s/d B$140/200) offers comfy no long distance passenger-boat travel at the time of research, but in the past it has been possible to catch boats up the Rio Mamoré to Trinidad (hammock only, five to seven days) and beyond. Ask at the office of the Capitanía del Puerto for current information.

BUS & TAXI
Think twice about getting onto any long-distance buses here, especially in the rainy season (roughly from November to April). Flooded roads and bridges can triple the estimated travel time, and two-, three- and even five-day epics are not uncommon. Most locals either fly or wait for the roads to clear. Depending on where you're headed, consider crossing into Brazil, where the roads are much better, and reentering Bolivia closer to your destination.

The bus terminal is 2.5km from the river along Av Federico Román. A taxi to the terminal will cost you B$5.

TO/FROM BRAZIL
See above for information about boats between Bolivia and Brazil. Thirty-day visas are standard on both sides, though you can request up to 60 days from the Bolivians and 90 days from the Brazilians. Officials on both sides usually look for the other's exit stamp, so definitely get one before crossing the river. **Bolivian immigration** (☎ 855 4413, after hours 7395 2902; cnr Av Costañera & Calle Mariscal Santa Cruz; ☯ 8am-12:30pm & 2:30-6:30pm Mon-Fri, 8:30am-noon Sat) **Brazilian consulate** (☎ 855 3766; cnr Av 24 de Septiembre & Av Beni; ☯ 9am-1pm & 3-5pm Mon-Fri)

Getting Around
The town is so small you can walk just about anywhere, except to the bus terminal. Moto-taxi charge B$1 to B$3.

GUAPORÉ VALLEY & CENTRAL RONDÔNIA
Forte Príncipe da Beira
Remote Forte Príncipe da Beira, beside the Rio Guaporé, 210km south of Guajará-Mirim, was constructed by the Portuguese between 1776 and 1783 to consolidate their hold on the lands east of the Guaporé and Mamoré against the Spanish. The star-shaped fort, one of only two ever constructed by Portugal in the Brazilian interior, has 10m-high walls and four corner bastions, each of which held 14 cannons. Today just one cannon remains. The walls, nearly 1km around, are surrounded by a moat and enclose the ruins of a chapel, armory, officers quarters and prison cells in which bored convicts scrawled poetic graffiti. Underground passageways lead from the fortress to the river. The fort was abandoned as a military post in 1889. Today Brazil maintains a garrison of around 70 soldiers beside the fort. There's also a village, Vila Príncipe da Beira, here.

The town of **Costa Marques** (population 7000), about 25km from the fort, is home to an attractive church, orchid park and a turtle nursery. **Hotel Girassol Palácio** (☎ 651 2215; Av Demétrio Melas 1796; s/d B$75/125; ⊠) have TV and come with free breakfast.

The road to Costa Marques is impassable from about November to April **Real Norte** (☎ 3225 2891) offer seasonal service, usually connecting in Presidente Medici.

Pedras Negras Extractive Reserve
Two hundred and forty kilometers upstream from Costa Marques, the **Reserva Extrativista Pedras Negras** has good opportunities for hiking, canoeing, and spotting rare orchids, macaws, toucans, caiman, deer and river dolphins. There are also a few rural villages, dedicated mostly to rubber and Brazil nut harvesting, that can be visited. A small lodge has two simple but comfortable cabins with hot water, mosquito screens, 24-hour electricity and beds or hammocks for up to 12 people.

The reserve is normally open from June 15 to November 15 only, due to heavy rainfall the rest of the year. The best months to go are August to November, when river beaches are exposed. From September, turtle nesting sites can be observed.

Visits to the reserve were suspended at the time of research, as a new agency was sought to manage them. Check with IBAMA in Porto Velho (p674) for the latest.

Parque Nacional de Pacaás Novos
This rugged, 7648-sq-km national park includes Rondônia's highest peak, Pico do Tracoá (1230m) and some spectacular waterfalls. Fauna includes jaguars, tapirs, giant anteaters, howler monkeys and rare blue macaws. The park lies inside an Indian reserve, Terra Indígena Uru-Eu-Wau-Wau. Ibama has plans to open the park to visitors, including constructing a research and visitor center, but as with other reserves in the state, the necessary studies have not been completed. Once

again, check with IBAMA in Porto Velho for the latest.

ACRE

Present-day Acre was originally part of Bolivia, but by the end of the 19th century it was mostly populated by Brazilian *seringueiros* (rubber tappers), spreading south from the Amazonas. In August 1902, Bolivia sent its army to assert control and was met by fierce resistance from the *seringueiros* in what is known here, a bit melodramatically, as the 'Acrean Revolution.' Bolivia eventually ceded the territory to Brazil in exchange for 2 million British pounds and a promise to build a railroad from the border to Porto Velho to facilitate Bolivian exports. (The railroad was never completed and some in Bolivia say the money was never paid.) The Brazilian government, however, had never really supported the upstart Acreans and refused to name Acre a state, designating it the nation's first 'federal territory' instead. Thus the 'autonomist' movement was born, a sometimes-armed conflict that took 60 years to be resolved.

Acre is the home state of martyred union and environmental leader Chico Mendes, and was a key battleground for battles over deforestation. Hundreds of union leaders, activists and ordinary workers died in the conflicts, including Mendes, who was assassinated in 1988. But thanks to those struggles, today a full third of the state is under environmental protection or designated as indigenous lands.

RIO BRANCO

☎ 0xx68 / pop 265,000

Rio Branco, the capital of Acre, was founded in 1882 by rubber tappers on the banks of the Rio Acre. Once a brash, uneasy town, Rio Branco has transformed itself into a genuinely pleasant place, with easy access to some interesting sites, including Xapuri, the hometown of union leader and environmentalist Chico Mendes. Unfortunately for Rio Branco, few travelers make it here for the simple reason that it's not on the way to or from anywhere travelers commonly go.

Note that Rio Branco (and the entire state of Acre) is an hour behind Porto Velho and Manaus, and two hours behind Brazilian Standard Time.

Information

EMERGENCY

Emergency room (☎ 192, 3223 3080; Hospital Geral, cnr Av Nações Unidos & Rua Hugo Carneiro)
Police (☎ 190)

INTERNET ACCESS

Viper.net (Av Ceará; per hr R$2; ☯ 7am-11pm Mon-Sat, 11am-11pm Sun)
Viarena Cyber Café (Rua Rui Barbosa; per hr R$3; ☯ 8:30am-10pm Mon-Sat, 2:30-10pm Sun)

MEDICAL SERVICES

Hospital Geral (☎ 192, 3223 3080; cnr Av Nações Unidos & Rua Hugo Carneiro)

MONEY

Banco do Brasil (Rua Porto Leal 85)
Bradesco (Rua Porto Leal 83)
HSBC (cnr Rua Rui Barbosa & Rua Marechal Deodoro)

POST

Post office (Rua Epaminondas Jácome 447; ☯ 7am-4pm Mon-Fri, 8am-noon Sat)

TOURIST INFORMATION

Centro de Atendimento ao Turista (☎ 0800/647 3998; Praça Povos da Floresta; ☯ 8am-6pm Mon-Sat, 4-9pm Sun) Not terribly helpful, but a good place to start. Otherwise, try asking at the Museu da Borracha, where staff are more used to encountering foreign tourists.

TRAVEL AGENCIES

Inácio's Tur (☎ 3224 9626; Pinheiro Palace Hotel, Rua Rui Barbosa 450; ☯ 8am-noon & 2-6pm Mon-Fri, 8am-noon Sat)

Sights

PALACIO RIO BRANCO

Acre's first capital building, the imposing **Palacio Rio Branco** (☯ 3223 9241, Av Getúlio Vargas facing Praça Povos da Floresta; admission free; 8am-6pm Tue-Fri, 4-9pm Sat & Sun) is now mostly a tourist attraction. A maze of interconnected rooms contain interesting and well-done displays on prehistoric artifacts, indigenous communities, Chico Mendes and the Acrean Revolution. Docents are available for free guided tours, though you'll have to understand Portuguese. (Same goes for the all displays.)

MEMORIAL DOS AUTONOMISTAS

In its spiffy home just uphill from the Palacio Rio Branco, the **Memorial dos Autonomistas** (Autonomists Memorial; ☎ 3224 2133; Praça Eurico Dutra; admission free; ⊙ 8am-6pm Tue-Fri, 2-9pm Sat & Sun) has a permanent display on the history of Acre's battle for statehood – hence the center's name – plus space for rotating art exhibits, typically paintings and sculptures by local artists. This is also the resting place of José Guiomard dos Santos and his wife; highly revered, Guiomard dos Santos served as federal administrator of Acre in the early 1940s and was later (by then a senator) the chief sponsor of the bill that eventually gave Acre its statehood. But blood runs thicker than water, especially in Acre – Guiomard, born in Minas Gerais, lost to Acre native José Augusto in the state's first gubernatorial election.

MUSEU DA BORRACHA

Housed in a beautifully restored mansion, the **Museu da Borracha** (Rubber Museum; ☎ 3224 6605; Av Ceará 1441; admission free; ⊙ 8am-6pm Tue-Fri, 4-9pm Sat & Sun) has three small rooms for permanent exhibits: one explains the extraction and processing of rubber, while the others have displays on archaeology, the Acrean Revolution and the cult of Santo Daime. The plaques are all in Portuguese, but there are several English-speakers among the cadre of staff and docents; they occasionally give free tours.

Sleeping

Hotel AFA (☎ 3224 1938; Rua Franco Ribeiro 99; s R$35-55, d R$50-80; ✖) Standard rooms are a little rough around the edges, though some are quite large with windows facing the street. Otherwise, the newer deluxe rooms are a decent value, with better beds, matching fixtures, even paintings on the walls. Next door to its sister-restaurant, AFA Bistro, one of the city's best per-kilo restaurants.

Rio Branco Hotel (☎ 3224 2681; Rua Rui Barbosa 354) Closed for renovation when we came through, this has long been the best deal in Rio Branco, with clean rooms with balconies in a great location. It's a good bet to stay that way once it reopens. Our main complaint before was the old-fashioned decor, which ought to be improved with the renovations.

Hotel do Papai (☎ 3223 2044; cnr Ruas Floriano Peixoto & Rui Barbosa; s/d/t R$40/70/90; ✖) A huge, sparsely decorated reception area gives way to smaller but equally sparse guest rooms, where high ceilings (and the lack of decor) lend an airy uncluttered feel, and the beds and bathrooms are aging, but clean. A reliable budget choice.

Hotel Guapindaia Centro (☎ 3223 5747; www.hoteis guapindaia.com.br; Rua Floriano Peixoto 550; s/d/t R$55/75/95) A great value, the Guapindaia Centro has clean comfortable rooms with sage-colored walls and amenities rare to find in hotels at this price, like glass shower doors and quiet air-conditioners. The huge breakfast spread may save you having to stop for lunch.

Pinheiro Palace Hotel (☎ 3223 7191; www.irmaos pinheiro.com.br; Rua Rui Barbosa 450; s R$65-130, d R$98-175; ✖ ▢ ▣) Most hotels offer discounts if you pay in cash, but here it's a whopping 50% off. Rooms are divided into luxo and granluxo: the former are hardly 'luxury' units, with brick walls, old fixtures, and a dark corridor between the elevator and your door. 'Grand luxury' rooms are a better deal, with more natural light and a fresh coat of paint. Breakfast is served in a modern dining area beside a clean medium-sized pool.

João Paulo Hotel (☎ 3223 8933; www.joaopaulohotel .com.br; Av Ceará 2090; s/d R$68/99; ✖ ▣) It doesn't look like much from the outside, or even from the lobby, but the incredibly wide hallways make the interior feel like a castle. Rooms are a bit small, ironically, but clean and nicely appointed. Four suites (R$145) are the nicest rooms in Rio Branco. All guests receive two tickets per day to the movie theater next door, and there's a R$25 airport drop-off service. Popular with business travelers.

Eating

Café do Theatro (☎ 3223 5862; cnr Av Brasil & Av Getúlio Vargas; dishes US$3-9; ⊙ 8am-9pm Tue-Sat, 4pm-midnight Sun) Part of the Memorial dos Autonomistas (see p683), this low-key café serves great coffee and light meals, including sandwiches and quiche. Daily specials (R$10 to R$18) are more substantial, and there's an extensive wine and cocktail menu.

Mercado Velho (Praça Bandeira; dishes R$5-15; ⊙ 7am-10pm) Dubbed the 'Old Market' this is in fact part of Rio Branco's newest and most successful urban renewal efforts. An old port building was transformed into a small, pleasant food court. Grilled beef, fried fish and other comfort foods are cooked up at clean booths. Eat inside or on benches overlooking the river.

Churrascaria Triângulo (☎ 3224 9265; Hotel Triângulo, Rua Floriano Peixoto 727; per kg R$18 or rodízio R$19; ⊙ lunch & dinner Mon-Sat, lunch only Sun) True, the ambience here is quite lacking – it's a hotel restaurant – but if you're famished and in the mood for meat, you are sure to get your fill here. The *rodízio* is sort of an all-you-can-eat meat buffet: waiters pass by your table with long skewers of fresh-grilled meats that you can sample as long as your stomach and chair hold up. It also includes all the self-serve side dishes you like, as if you'll have room.

AFA Bistrô D'Amazônia (☎ 3224 3936; Rua Franco Ribeiro 99; self-service per kg R$20; 🕑 lunch) The name has changed but this unassuming bistro remains one of the best *por kilo* lunch spots you'll find in the Amazonia. The city's professional classes pack in for fresh and original salad combinations, tender meat and fish dishes, and irresistible desserts. Sundays feature *frutas do mar* (seafood) and the price jumps to a hefty R$35 per kilo.

Entertainment

Praça Bandeira has a handful of outdoor **restaurant-bars** (Waterfront btwn Av Getulio Vargas & Rua Marechal Deodoro) overlooking the river. It's a popular place to nurse a few tall beers and contemplate the new pedestrian bridge, which at night is bathed in a hypnotic blue light.

Cine João Paulo (☎ 3223 3828; Av Ceará 2090; tickets Mon-Wed R$8, Thu-Sun R$12, shows at 5pm R$6) has two screens showing relatively recent Hollywood movies. Next to, and operated by, the Hotel João Paulo (guests get free passes).

Getting There & Away

Highway BR-364 is paved and well-maintained between Rio Branco and Porto Velho, and as far as Sena Madureira, 170km beyond Rio Branco. Likewise, the road from Rio Branco to Brasiléia (235km) and Assis Brasil on the Peruvian border are also paved, and have year-round bus service. Beyond those corridors, however, most of Acre's roads are unpaved, and can be difficult or impassable during the rainy season, usually October to May (most of the year, that is). Boat and plane may be the only options during those times.

AIR

Three airlines serve Rio Branco, with daily flights to Porto Velho and Brasilia (and onward connections from there) plus seasonal service to Cruzeiro do Sul.

Gol (☎ 0300 115 2121; at airport only)

Rico (☎ 3223 5902; Av Ceará 2090)

TAM (☎ 4002 5700; at airport only)

THE AMAZON

RIO BRANCO

| 0 | 300 m |
| 0 | 0.2 miles |

BOAT

The Rio Acre is navigable all the way to the Peruvian border at Assis Brasil but there's little river traffic (and none that follows a schedule). Headed the other direction, it's possible to catch a boat down the Rio Purus from the town of Boca do Acre, north of Rio Branco, theoretically all the way to Manaus. That said, if Manaus is your destination, there's much more frequent and reliable boat service on the Rio Madeiro, leaving from Porto Velho.

BUS

Real Norte (☎ 3224 4293; toll-free 0800 647 6666; www .realnorte.com.br) has service to Xapuri (R$18.50, 3½ hours, twice daily), Brasília (R$19, four hours, five departures daily), Assis Brasil (R$32.50, six hours, twice daily), Guajará-Mirim (R$49.50, seven to eight hours, once daily); and Porto Velho (ordinary/*semi-leito* R$58/63.50, seven to eight hours, four daily). The road to Cruzeiro do Sol ($108, 19 hours) is passable only in July and August; otherwise, the only way to get there is to fly.

Eucatur (☎ 3244 2233) and **Andorinha** (☎ 3224 2233) each have morning departures to Brasilia (R$260 to R$270, 50 to 55 hours services) with onward connections from there.

Getting Around

Rio Branco has an efficient **terminal urbano** (city bus terminal; Rua Sergipe btwn Av Ceará & Rua Benjamin Constant), next to the market. You pay your fare at a bank of turnstiles, and buses come and go from clearly marked platforms. You can board at bus stops around town as well; there's a handy one on Av Getulio Vargas, near the Palacio Rio Branco.

The airport is located 22km west of town, on Hwy BR-364. A taxi to or from town costs an eye-popping R$70 to R$80. Coming off the plane, you may be able to find another passenger or two to share the fare; taxi drivers sometimes help pair you up. Alternatively, bus 304, signed as 'Custódio Freire' and/or 'Aeroporto,' runs between the airport and town about once an hour (R$1.75, one hour, 5am-11pm). The Pinheiro Palace Hotel and Hotel João Poulo (see p684) both operate airport shuttles, R$25 to R$30 per person, to (but not from) the airport. The Pinheiro's is open to guests and non-guests, but is not always available. The João Poulo's is more reliable but is technically for hotel guests only; those staying elsewhere may be able to plead their case, however.

The **long distance bus station** (Av Uirapuru) is 1.25km southwest of the center, across the Rio Acre. At least three different city buses run between there and the center of town, including those marked 'Norte-Sul,' 'Taquarí' and 'Domoacir' (R$1.75, 25 minutes, every half hour). Catch them at either bus terminal or at the bus stop on Av Getúlio Vargas by the Palacio Rio Branco. A taxi to or from the city center costs R$10, a mototaxi R$3.

AROUND RIO BRANCO
Parque Ambiental Chico Mendes

Only 52 hectares in size, of which roughly half is native forest, **Parque Ambiental Chico Mendes** (admission free) is nevertheless the most interesting park easily accessible to Rio Branco. A memorial to Chico Mendes stands near the entrance. The park also has a picnic area, a funny cast-iron treetop lookout, bike paths and a small zoo. Along the paths are theme huts representing different aspects of life in the region, including rubber tapping, a *maloca* (Indian dwelling) and myths and legends. Some wildlife can be seen.

The park is located at Km 3 on Hwy AC-040, about 10km south of Rio Branco. To get here take a 'Vila Acre' bus from the terminal urbano of the stop on Av Getúlio Vargas (R$1.75, 45 minutes, every half hour).

Santo Daime Centers

There are several centers of the Santo Daime religious cult in and around Rio Branco, where it was founded in 1930 by Raimundo Irineu Serra (1892–1971), also known as Mestre Irineu. The cult's practices revolve around a sacred hallucinogenic drink called *ayahuasca*. Thursday is the group's holy day, and important ceremonies typically take place on the 15th and 30th of every month.

The ceremonial center at the cult's birthplace, called **Alto Santo**, is 7km from Rio Branco in Colônia Custódio Freire. You can reach it on an 'Irineu Serra' bus from the terminal urbano. A visitors center (of sorts) has been built there, next to Irineu Serra's tomb, though a visit here still requires a fair amount of simply asking around. Another community of Santo Daime followers, **Colônia Cinco Mil**, is 12km north of Rio Branco.

Although you can certainly just show up, it's ideal to try to find somebody from the community to organize your visit, especially if you're interested in witnessing or even participating in the group's ceremonies. The folks at the Museu da Borracha (p684) may be able to help, or at least point you in the right direction. You can reach the community by taxi (about R$30) or by catching a 'Porto Acre' bus along Hwy AC-010, which will drop you at the turnoff for Colônia Cinco Mil, from which it's a 2.5km walk.

XAPURI

☎ 0xx68 / pop 6200

This tidy little town of neat wooden houses along broad streets was home to environmental hero Chico Mendes. It lies about 12km northwest of Hwy BR-317, the main road between Rio Branco (241km away) and Brasiléia (74km away).

Information

Banco da Amazona (Rua C Bradão) Next to the gas station.

Sights

CASA CHICO MENDES

Just across the street from the Fundação Chico Mendes, the teal and pink **Chico Mendes House** is just that: the simple wood house where Mendes, his wife and two children lived until his murder. This is also where he was killed; tours conducted by docents from the Foundation (required) include a graphic description of the place and moment he was shot, with bloodstains still on the walls. Photos are not permitted inside the house, but outside is OK.

FUNDAÇÃO CHICO MENDES

The visitors center of the **Fundação Chico Mendes** (Chico Mendes Foundation; ☎ 3542 2651; admission free; ☽ 8am-6pm) contains poster-size photos of Chico Mendes with his wife and children, tapping rubber trees, and leading empates – work stoppages designed to stop clear-cutting in the rain forest. There are some personal effects, including the blood-stained clothes and bath towel he had when he was murdered, and numerous awards given to Mendes, both before and after he died. Though interesting, you're sure to leave wishing there was more about the life and legacy of this seminal figure in workers' and environmental activism. Unfortunately, the foundation – which is headed by Mendes' widow and daughter, both of whom live in Rio Branco – does virtually no work beyond maintaining the modest visitor's center, and Casa de Chico Mendes across the street.

MUSEU DO XAPURI

Museu do Xapuri (Rua C Brandão; admission free; ☽ 8am-6pm Tue-Sun) A modest museum with displays on the history of Acre and Xapuri. There's special emphasis on the state's rubber extraction, and the union and environmental struggles of Chico Mendes and others.

FÁBRICA DE PRESERVATIVOS

Acre's rubber tappers have fewer and fewer places to sell their product, pushed out by cheaper (but inferior) Asian and synthetic latex. However, condoms – called *preservativos* or *camisinhas* in Portuguese – are one of few mass-market items still commonly made from 100% natural latex. The Brazilian government has long promised Xapuri a condom factory, which will buy locally produced rubber, and employ a couple dozen factory workers at the same time. Nearly complete – finally! – the factory reportedly will offer tours to visitors. Done properly, the visits could be fascinating; ask at your hotel for the latest.

Sleeping & Eating

Pousada Floresta Viva (☎ 3542 2406; s/d R$30/60) The live-in owners of this hotel work elsewhere full-time, and the cleaning person isn't around all the time; ask across the street if no one answers the door. Rooms are large and clean, and while newer than the Chapurys, they seem to have less character. There's a pool, but it was in no condition to be used when we passed through. Located about 150m from the bus terminal, and a block past Casa de Chico Mendes.

Pousada das Chapurys (☎ 3542 2253; Rua Sadala Koury 1385; s/d/t R$35/60/75; ✖) A short walk from the bus terminal, this is the old stand-by of Xapuri's hotels, and still a pleasant and convenient place to stay. The friendly owners were close friends of Chico Mendes', and have photos and memorabilia in the hotel's dining area (not to mention some fascinating stories). Rooms are large and comfortable, though definitely showing their age.

Pousada Villa Verde (☎ 3542 3012; pousada-villa verde@hotmail.com; Rua Rodovaldo Nogueira 500; s/d R$55/85; ✖ ☐ ▣) Well worth the extra couple hundred meters you'll have to walk from the bus terminal, the Villa Verde has a huge leafy garden and just eight cozy rooms, all with air-con, comfortable beds, and in-room internet. Some have private patios, and there's a small clean pool for cooling off. Speaking

THE AMAZON

of cool, ask the owners about having a peek through their professional-grade telescope, housed in a shed-turned-observatory on the hotel grounds.

Pizzaria Tribos (☎ 3542 2531; Rua C Branbão; mains R$12-20; ☾ dinner) One of a handful of kiosks in a small park a block off the main plaza, Tribos serves up tasty pizzas at small outdoor tables and gets kudos for playing something other than *forró* or Brazilian pop (or simply blasting the TV). Select from one of the dozen or so usual suspects – shredded chicken, presunto, tuna, palm hearts – while head-bobbing to Maria Rita, Natiruts or some good ol' U2.

Bebum (Rua C Branbão) After pizza, you can migrate a few dozen meters down the park to this kiosk, a popular watering hole for Xapuri's young and restless.

Getting There & Away

Real Norte (☎ 3542 2324, toll-free 0800 647 6666; www .realnorte.com.br) has bus service from Xapuri to Rio Branco (R$17, four hours) twice daily at 6am and 3:30pm. There's only one bus from Xapuri to Brasiléia (R$7, 1½ hours) departing at 9:30am. Alternatively, you can catch a cab to the turnoff at Highway BR-317, where additional buses to Rio Branco pass at 7am, noon and 7pm, and to Brasiléia at 3pm.

BRASILÉIA

☎ 0xx68 / pop 10,500

The border town of Brasiléia is separated from Cobija, Bolivia, by the meandering Rio Acre and Igarapé Bahia. There's precious little to do here, unless you're in the market for a computer or DVD player – for that, you can join the crowds crossing into Cobija to take advantage of the lower prices and a duty-free border.

Orientation

Hwy BR-317 from Rio Branco approaches Brasiléia from the southeast, through the adjacent but independent town of Epitáciolândia. The Brasiléia bus terminal is just across a small bridge; from there it's a 300m walk (or R$5 taxi ride) to the center of town. If you do walk, bear right out of the bus terminal, and follow Rua Odilon Pratagi to Av Prefeito R Moreira, where most of the listings here are located.

A bridge over the Igarapé Bahia connects Epitáciolândia to Cobija, and is the official border crossing, with immigration offices for both

countries nearby. A smaller, more convenient bridge spans the Rio Acre, making it possible to walk from one downtown to the other in just a few minutes. The smaller bridge – which is dedicated to Wilson Pinheiro, a rubber tapper union president and friend of Chico Mendes who was assassinated in July 1980 – is at the end of Av Prefeito R Moriera; there is a customs post there, but no immigration officers.

Information

Banco das Amazonas (cnr Av Prefeito R Moreira & Rua Odilon Pratagi; ☾ 8am-1pm Mon-Fri) Has ATM and changes foreign cash.

Banco do Brasil (Av Prefeito R Moreira No 470) Has ATM.

No-name internet café (Rua Odilon Pratagi; per hr R$2; ☾ 8:30am-10pm) Two blocks from Pousada Las Palmeras.

Police (☎ 190, 3546 3207; Av Prefeito R Moreira No 456; ☾ 24hr)

Post office (Av Prefeito R Moreira btwn Banco das Amazonas & tourist information kiosk; ☾ 8am-noon & 2-5pm Mon-Fri)

Tourist information kiosk (Av Prefeito R Moreira near Restaurante Lili; ☾ 7am-6pm) Exceedingly unhelpful, more concerned with selling handicrafts than aiding visitors. You may find some worthwhile brochures here, however.

Sleeping

Pousada Orquidia Negra (☎ 9981 8967; Travessa 7 de Setembro 69; s/d R$30/40) Simple rooms have tile floors and clean private bathrooms; a few have hot water and all are painted cheerful colors. The owner, who lives on site with his family, worked alongside Chico Mendes, Wilson Pinheiro, and others back in the day, and has plenty of stories (many conspiratorial) for anyone who's interested.

Hotel Vitória Régia (☎ 3546 4743; Av Geny Assis 345; s/d/t R$40/65/85) A perfectly adequate alternative, rooms here are virtually identical in size and amenities to those at Las Palmeras – the main difference is the boxy unattractive exterior and somewhat less elaborate breakfast spread. On the other hand, an attached internet café is available 24 hours.

Pousada Las Palmeras (☎ 3546 3284; Rua Odilon Pratagi at Av Geny Assis; s/d/tr R$45/65/85; ☒) Brasiléia's most appealing hotel has a variety of rooms, from narrow singles to spacious doubles, all with air-con, TV, minibar and hot water; the breakfast is excellent. Newer units are spotless, although there's just no way to dress up faux-marble tile. Older ones have less tile and more character, but the amenities also creak and complain more. A wraparound covered passageway in front has chairs and sofas on one side, and breakfast area on the other.

Eating

Brasiléia's eating options are remarkably limited.

Restaurant Lili (Av Prefeito R Moreira; ☺ lunch & dinner) Lunch is by weight (per kilo R$14) while dinner is R$5 per plate at the same self-serve buffet – a chance to hone your stacking skills. Pickings are reliable, if uninspired. Located near the tourist office.

Saborella (Rua Odilon Pratagi s/n; mains R$7-15; ☺ lunch daily, dinner Tue-Sun) Daily specials make

---

CHICO MENDES & HIS LEGACY

In the mid-1970s an ambitious military government plan to tame the Amazon attracted a flood of developers, ranchers, logging companies and settlers into Acre, clear cutting rubber and Brazil trees to make room for ranches. Francisco Alves Mendes Filho, better known as Chico Mendes, was a 30-something rubber tapper, but one of few who could read and write, and had long taken an interest in improving the lives of rubber tappers like himself. In 1977, he co-founded the Sindicato dos Trabalhadores Rurais de Xapuri (Xapuri Rural Workers' Union) to defy the violent intimidation and dispossession practiced by the newcomers.

Mendes organized *empates* (stoppages), nonviolent human blockades to stop the clear-cutting. But Mendes was not initially an environmentalist – his motivation was to help rubber-tappers, whose livelihood happened to depend on a healthy, intact forest. Likewise, the environmental movement (largely based in the US at the time) was focused on preserving 'virgin' forest, which it assumed to empty of humans save a few Indian tribes.

The joining of those groups – rubber tappers and American environmentalists – was one of Mendes' key accomplishments. He convinced rubber-tappers to see themselves as stewards of the forest and allies of indigenous peoples. And he helped conceive of 'extractive reserves,' to this day an important means of protecting land and people there. He won numerous international awards in the process, including election to the UN Environment Organization's Global 500 Honor Roll in 1987.

Mendes' fame abroad made life increasingly dangerous at home. Killings of rural workers and activists, including priests and lawyers, jumped from single digits in the 1960s, to over a hundred in 1980, to nearly 500 between 1985 and 1987, according to Amnesty International.

In December 1988 he moved to establish his birthplace, Seringal Cachoeira, as an extractive reserve, defying a local rancher and strongman, Darly Alves da Silva, who claimed the land. Mendes had already denounced Silva to the police for threatening his life and for the murder of a union representative earlier that year. Mendes received innumerable death threats, but resisted the urging of colleagues to flee Acre state. On December 22, 1988, Mendes stepped onto the back porch of his home in Xapuri and was shot at close range by men hiding in the bushes. He staggered into the house, where his wife and children were watching TV, and bled to death.

Mendes' was the first of hundreds of murders to be thoroughly investigated and prosecuted, owing to the massive international reaction to his killing. Darly Alves da Silva and his son Darci Pereira da Silva, were sentenced to 19 years in prison for ordering and committing the crime. Both Silvas escaped from jail in 1993, apparently just walking free with the complicity of corrupt police, but were recaptured in 1996, after another outcry, and returned to jail. In 2000 they were granted day release, being required to spend only the nights in their prison. They complete their sentences in 2009.

Mendes' life and death brought unprecedented international attention to the environmental crisis in the Amazon. But activism on behalf of the forest and people who live there remains a dangerous undertaking. On February 12, 2005, an American-born nun named Dorothy Stang was gunned down in the small town of Anapú, in the soy and cattle country of Pará state. She was killed by men acting on the orders of a rancher Stang had accused of illegally clearing land. The rancher who ordered her killing was convicted in 2007 and sentenced to 30 years in prison. However, he is only the fourth such 'mastermind' to have been held to account for scores of murders that have taken place there, even since the assassination of Chico Mendes.

ordering easy at this small restaurant, one of few genuinely agreeable places in town. Options are same-old, same-old – chicken, beef, sometimes fish, served with rice and beans – but are well prepared and usually served with a smile. Half-a-block from the bus station, and about 300m from the internet café.

Getting There & Away
BUS
The bus station is 500m from the listed hotels and the main commercial strip; a taxi either direction costs R$5. **Real Norte** (☎ 3546 3257; www.realnorte.com.br) has daily services to Rio Branco (R$19, four hours, departing at 6am, 11am, 2pm, 3pm and 6pm), Xapuri (R$7, two hours, at 2pm only) and Assis Brasil (R$9, two hours, at 10:30am and 4pm). You can usually catch a collective taxi to any of the above as well; the fares are roughly double and you may need a minimum of four passengers, but the trip tends to be quicker and the driver will drop you at your hotel door.

TO/FROM COBIJA
You are free to cross back and forth between Cobija and Brasiléia without passing immigration, provided you're going for a short period. If you plan to continue inland, or stay longer than a couple days, you ought to clear immigration officially.

Bolivian immigration (⊗ 8:30am-8:30pm) is on the main international bridge. In Brazil, the **Polícia Federal** (☎ 3546 3204; ⊗ 24hr) handle immigration procedures; the office is in Epitáciolândia,

just across the main international bridge. In Cobija, the **Brazilian consulate** (⊗ 8am-1pm Mon-Fri) is a half-block from the main plaza, on Av General Rene Barrientos, next to the Banco Mercantil de Bolivia.

A Brazilian taxi from Brasiléia into Bolivia, with brief stops at the immigration offices, costs R$10 to R$15. A Bolivian cab charges R$5 for the same trip back.

COBIJA (BOLIVIA)
☎ 03 / pop 15,000
The capital of Bolivia's Pando department is the wettest spot in Bolivia, with 1770mm of precipitation annually. It is a hilly town on the banks of the Rio Acre, with a pleasant enough plaza but a somewhat gritty atmosphere. Prices in this section are listed in *bolivianos* (B$), which at the time of research was trading at roughly R$1 to B$4, or US$1 to B$8. That doesn't mean you'll need Bolivian money right away, however. In Cobija you can use Brazilian *reais* to pay for just about everything.

Orientation
Crossing the smaller bridge from Brasiléia, turn left after the military base and make your way up to Cobija's main plaza, at the top of the hill. Coming from the main international bridge, Av Internacional extends 600m to Av 9 de Febrero. Turn right, and follow Av 9 de Febrero about 1.5km to the center of town.

Information
Banco Mercantil de Bolivia (Av General Rene Barrientos, next to the Brazilian consulate) Also has cash machines.
Banco Union (Plaza Principal) Twenty-four-hour cash machine.
Casa de Cambio Cachito (☎ 842 3277; Calle Teniente Coronel Cornejo at Av 9 de Febrero; ⊗ 8am-noon & 3-6pm Mon-Fri, 8am-noon Sat) A block west of the central plaza. Exchanges Bolivian, Brazilian and US currencies.
Internet Jandy (☎ 842 2921; Av 9 de Febrero 156; per hr B$5; ⊗ 8am-midnight Mon-Sat, noon to 10pm Sun) A block downhill from Hotel Nanijo's.
Police (☎ 110)
Post Office (ECOBOL; main plaza; ⊗ 8am-noon, 3-7pm Mon-Fri, 9am-noon Sat)

Sleeping & Eating
Except for the Hotel Avenida, the places below are all within two blocks south of the central plaza. It is not custom in Bolivia to include free breakfast.

AROUND BRASILÉIA

0 — 3 km
0 — 2 miles

68°46'W   68°44'W

To Assis Brasil; Iñapari (110km)

Rio Acre

11°00'S   11°00'S

Rio Acre

BOLIVIA

New International Bridge

Brasiléia
Brasiléia Bus Station
Brasiléia

Av 9 de Febrero (Bus Terminals)   Cobija

BRAZIL

Policía Federal
Epitáciolândia

To Xapuri (50km); Rio Branco (290km)

Av Internacional   Main International Bridge

BR 317

11°02'S   11°02'S

Igarapé Bahia

To Airport (3km); Riberalta (350km)

Igarapé Emenexe

68°46'W   68°44'W

Residencial Cocodrilo (☎ 842 2215; Av Fernández Molina 48; s/d without bathroom B$30/60, r with bathroom & TV B$80) Safe, cheap, and centrally located, the Cocodrilo appeals equally to backpackers and smalltime businessmen on limited budgets. Rooms are small but reasonably tidy, and some face a little interior garden. The collective toilets and showers are surprisingly clean; however, they're on the 1st floor (and across the garden) while all the rooms that use them are on the second.

Residencial Frontera (☎ 842 2740; Calle Beni s/n; r B$120, without bathroom B$80) The fan-cooled rooms here are small but clean, and come with free breakfast; those with private bathrooms also have TVs. This is a step up from the Cocodrilo – cleaner and newer, overall – though you'd never know from the forgettable exterior and reception area.

Hotel Avenida (Av 9 de Febrero s/n; s/d with fan B$80/120, with air-con B$100/180; 🖭) Ask for Cobija's top hotel and most people point to this place, located 500m from the center, toward the airport and main international bridge. Rooms are fine, not great, with tile floors and sponge-painted walls; be sure to get an interior unit to escape the heavy traffic din. Breakfast is included, but given how far it is from the center, the hotel is still a smidge overpriced.

Hotel Nanijo's (☎ 842 2230; Av 9 de Febrero 147; s/d 130/220; 🖭 🖭) This is Cobija's very first hotel, originally owned and operated by the city (which may explain the bland design and exterior). The inside has been renovated, however, making this one of Cobija's best hotels. Clean comfy rooms are freshly painted and sport modern TVs. Best of all, there's a large clean pool in the center courtyard that's perfect for cooling off on hot humid days. Breakfast is included in the price.

Across from the Residencial Cocodrilo, the friendly **Esquina de la Abuela** (☎ 842 2364; cnr Av Fernández Molina & Calle Sucre; dishes B$35-40; 🕑 8am-noon, 12:30-3pm & 7-11pm Mon-Fri, 9am-noon Sat) has pleasant indoor and outdoor seating and standard meat and chicken fare. The morning service consists of *salteñas* (salty breakfast pastries) only.

Getting There & Away
AIR
Cobija's **airport** (☎ 842 2260) is 3km southeast of town on the Porvenir road. A taxi to/from the town center is B$15; there is no regular bus service. Flights in June, July, August,

December and January get heavily booked, and advance reservations are almost always required in those months.

AeroSur (☎ 842 3050; www.aerosur.com; cnr Av Fernández Molina & Calle Teniente Coronel Cornejo; 🕑 8am-noon, 3-6pm Mon-Fri, 8am-noon Sat) has flights to La Paz (B$956, 55 minutes) on Tuesday, Thursday and Saturday afternoons, with same-day connections to Santa Cruz and Cochabamba (both B$1139) and next-day connections for national and international destinations. Cash only; students receive a 5% discount with credentials, seniors get 20% off.

Aerocon (☎ 842 4166; www.aerocon.bo; Av Fernández Molina next to AeroSur; 🕑 8am-12:30pm, 3pm-6:30pm Mon-Sat, at airport on Sun) has one daily flight to Trinidad (B$759, 1½ hours) with onward connections from there. Cash only.

Amaszonas (☎ 842 3844; www.amaszonas.com; Av Fernández Molina) is just a block down from the other two airline offices and has daily service to Trinidad (B$759, 1½ hours) with connections to destinations throughout Bolivia, including Rurrenabaque (B$1350 total) and Santa Cruz (B$967 total). Credit cards accepted; discounts for advance purchase.

TAM (☎ 842 2267; road to airport; 🕑 8am-noon, 3-6pm Mon-Fri, 8am-noon Sat) has flights to La Paz on Monday, Wednesday and Friday at lower fares than other airlines. However, TAM is operated by the Bolivian military and some say it does not follow the same safety and maintenance guidelines that commercial airlines do.

BUS
Bus companies cluster at Km 2 of the road to airport, just past the turnoff for Av International and the main bridge to Brazil. Be aware that bus travel in this part of Bolivia is never deluxe, and can be especially arduous during the rainy season (roughly November to April). The roads are unpaved and there are numerous river crossings (four on the Cobija–Riberalta stretch alone). Travel times can easily double or triple due to mud and flooding. Prices and travel times are identical for all bus lines: to Riberalta (B$130, seven to 12 hours), Guayaramerín (B$140, nine to 14 hours), Trinidad (B$280, 24 to 36 hours), and La Paz (B$250, 48 to 72 hours).

Sindicato Unificado Guayaramerín (☎ 842 2703) and **Flota Vaca Diez** (☎ cell 7610-0319) both have service to Riberalta and Guayaramerín departing Tuesday and Saturday. The former has an additional departure on Thursday.

Transpando (☎ 842 3831) and **Flota Cobija** (☎ 842 3588) go to Riberalta on Sunday, Monday, Wednesday and Friday. Transpando buses continue to Trinidad.

Flota Yugeña (☎ 842 2833) is the only line with service to La Paz, departing on Tuesday, Thursday and Saturday.

TO/FROM BRASILÉIA

You are free to make short trips back and forth between Cobija and Brasiléia, without passing immigration. For longer stays, it's a good idea to get your passport stamped; remember that you will be required to show a valid yellow fever vaccination in order to enter (or re-enter) Brazil. See p690 for details on crossing between the two countries.

A taxi from Cobija into Brasiléia costs around B$15 or R$5, including stops at both countries' immigration offices. Mototaxis charge the same around town, but are not allowed to carry passengers into Brazil. A taxi from Brazil into Bolivia costs R$10 to R$15.

GETTING TO PERU

Access to Peru is through the village of Assis Brasil, 110km west of Brasiléia. Once an adventure route, the road is now paved and has daily bus services. Complete Brazilian immigration procedures in Brasiléia, and Peruvian immigration at the border town of Iñapari.

Real Norte has bus services to Assis Brasil to/from Rio Branco and Brasiléia; see those sections for schedules and fares.

GETTING TO BOLIVIA

Brazilian immigration procedures are handled at the Polícia Federal station in Epitáciolândia, while Bolivian border officials are at the main international bridge. Expect Brazilian officials to request your yellow fever vaccine certificate when entering.

Directory

CONTENTS

ACCOMMODATIONS

Brazilian accommodations range from battered, windowless cells to sumptuous, seaside guesthouses, with many options in between. Nearly every pousada (guesthouse), hostel and hotel serves some form of café da manha (breakfast). We note only when breakfast is not served. Private rooms with communal bathrooms are called quartos. Rooms with a private bathroom are apartamentos.

For our listings, all hostels as well as guesthouses where double rooms cost less than R$80 are placed in the budget category. At the bottom end of the scale, cheap hotel rooms sometimes cost as little as R$35/50 (US$17/25) for single/double quartos. At that price expect a bare room with nothing but a bed and maybe a fan.

Midrange listings run from R$80 to R$160 (US$40 to US$80) and are usually comfortable but not stylish, with decent beds, air-conditioning, hot-water bathrooms and cable TV. The top end runs from R$160 and up. Here you'll find spacious digs, with maybe a veranda, a pool in back and other amenities. Many midrange and top-end hotels have safes in the rooms for storing valuables. Note that R$160 buys you a lot less in pricier haunts like Rio, Salvador and Brasília than it does at smaller, less-visited towns.

In tourist centers, especially Rio, reservations are wise during July, and from Christmas to Carnaval. The same holds for any vacation mecca (eg Búzios, Ilha Bela, Morro de São Paulo) on weekends, and anywhere during major festivals. For prime peak times (eg Carnaval in Rio or Salvador), try to make contact months ahead. Many places allow you to book online, which can save you 30% or more. For Rio, visit www.ipanema.com to get good rates on many hotels.

Camping

Camping has limited popularity in Brazil and is a viable alternative in some parts of the country for those wanting to explore national or state parks. Obviously, you'll need your own tent and other necessary gear. The biggest concern is safety. Many camping grounds are near urban areas and it's unwise to camp in these spots, unless trustworthy locals have assured you it's safe.

The **Camping Clube do Brasil** (Map pp144-5; ☎ 0xx21-3479 4200; www.campingclube.com.br in Portuguese; 29th fl, Rua Senador Dantas 75, Centro, Rio de Janeiro) has 48

BOOK ACCOMMODATION ONLINE

For more accommodation reviews and recommendations by Lonely Planet authors, check out the online booking service at www.lonelyplanet.com. You'll find the true, insider low-down on the best places to stay. Reviews are thorough and independent. Best of all, you can book online.

camping grounds as far apart as Fortaleza and Porto Alegre. Check its website for info.

MINIMUM-IMPACT CAMPING

The following guidelines are recommended for those camping in wilderness or other fragile areas of Brazil.

- Select a well-drained camp site and, especially if it's raining, use some type of waterproof groundsheet to prevent having to dig trenches.
- Along popular routes, camp in established sites.
- Carry as little packaging in as possible, and carry out all your rubbish.
- Use established toilet facilities if available. Otherwise, select a site at least 100m from water sources and bury wastes in a small hole about 15cm deep. If possible, burn used toilet paper or bury it well.
- Use only biodegradable soap products (you'll probably have to bring them from home). Disperse wastewater at least 50m from watercourses.
- Try to select an established site for fires and keep them as small as possible. Use only fallen dead wood and make sure the fire is fully extinguished before leaving.

Hostels

Youth hostels in Brazil are called *albergues da juventude*. The HI-affiliated Federação Brasileira de Albergues da Juventude (FBAJ; www.hostel.org.br) has more than 80 hostels in the country, most with links on the website. There are also dozens of private hostels – with more opening each month. Rio is by far the country's hostel capital, with more than three dozen at last count. Quality varies considerably, but they're generally good places to meet young Brazilians.

A dormitory bed in an FBAJ hostel costs between R$20 and R$45 per person. At HI-hostels, nonmembers usually pay around 20% extra, but you can buy an HI guest card for R$40 at many hostels and at youth hostel association offices in Brazil.

Hotels

Brazil has good, modern, luxury hotels, old, shabby, moldy hotels, and everything in between. At more expensive places, taxes of 15% are often added to the basic price. Always ask for prices, as they're often lower than posted prices. Also it never hurts to ask *'Tem desconto?'* ('Is there a discount?'), which might net a saving of up to 30%. Prices typically rise by 30% to 40% in the high season, and room rates triple during Carnaval and around New Year's Eve. Hotels in business-oriented cities such as São Paulo, Curitiba, Porto Alegre and Brasília usually give discounts on weekends.

Jungle Lodges

One popular type of remote-area accommodations is the jungle lodge – a hotel catering to tourists in or on the edge of the forest. These usually have all the amenities of a midrange or even top-end hotel, with a considerably more exotic setting and architecture (they're usually made of wood and often stand on stilts). The largest number of jungle lodges are found in Manaus.

Pousadas

A pousada typically means a small family-owned guesthouse, though some hotels call themselves 'pousadas' to improve their charm

---

PRACTICALITIES

- The biggest Portuguese-language daily newspapers are *Jornal do Brasil* (www.jbonline.com.br) and *O Globo* (www.globo.com.br), both out of Rio, and *O Estado de São Paulo* and *Folha de São Paulo,* out of Sampa. The weekly *Veja* is an excellent current-affairs magazine, and in Rio and São Paulo it comes with a good pullout guide to what's happening locally.

- TV programming revolves around sports, comedy shows and the nightly *telenovelas* (soap operas). *O Globo* is the largest nationwide TV network.

- Brazil uses the PAL system for video.

- Electrical current is not standardized in Brazil and can be almost anywhere between 110V and 220V. Carry a converter and use a surge protector with electrical equipment.

- Brazilians use the metric system for weights and measures.

HOW TO CHOOSE AN ENVIRONMENTALLY FRIENDLY HOTEL

'Eco' is a much bandied-around word in certain parts of Brazil, but sometimes it's difficult for even the discerning traveler to know whether a business truly lives up to the label. An environmentally friendly hotel should adhere to strict conservation guidelines and make a positive impact on the local community. Here are a few questions that will help settle the matter.

- Is the hotel built on a sensitive site – or is it built right on the beach/riverbank, where erosion is likely to occur?
- Does the hotel have effective management of its wastewater and pollutants?
- Is solar energy or some other alternative energy system used?
- Are there recycling programs?
- Does it use natural illumination and avoid wasting energy whenever possible?
- Does the hotel maintain pesticide-free grounds using only native plants?
- Is the business involved in environmental-conservation programs, or is it an active member of regional or local organizations that address environmental problems?
- Are the majority of the employees from the local population?
- Does it support the community by associating with locally owned businesses and providing places where native handicrafts can be displayed for sale?
- Does it serve foods that support local markets and use local materials and products in order to maintain the health of the local economy?

While very few places in Brazil are likely to meet all of the above criteria, there are hotels that make a conscientious effort to have a low impact on the environment, while investing in the local community. We highly recommend you support those businesses that do.

quotient. Rustic pousadas can cost as little as R$50/80 per single/double and as much as R$500 for a lavish double – breakfast is typically included in these rates.

Rental Accommodations

It's possible to rent vacation, short- or long-term apartments through a number of sources. Real-estate agencies in most large cities will be able to provide information on rentals for foreigners. The best bet is to speak to other foreigners in Brazil to get an idea of current prices, which vary from city to city. In the classified real-estate sections of newspapers, apartments are usually listed under *temporada* or *apartamentos para aluguel*. If you just want a room in someone else's house or apartment, look under *vaga* or *quarto*. Generally, an apartment that costs R$400 per week in Belo Horizonte will cost you two to three times that in Rio or São Paulo.

ACTIVITIES

Mountains, coast and sea all provide some great opportunities for fresh-air adventure. Websites **360 Graus** (www.360graus.com.br) and

Guia Verde (www.guiaverde.com.br) cover a host of activities: canyoning, paragliding, kitesurfing or wakeboarding to rafting, surfing, trekking, diving or mountain climbing. The websites are in Portuguese, but they need little translation.

Climbing

Climbing in Brazil is best from April to October. The best thing about rock climbing in Brazil is that in one hour you can be on the beach, and the next on a world-class climb, 300m above a city. Brazil has lots of fantastic climbs, ranging from beginner level to routes yet to be conquered. Within 40 minutes of central Rio de Janeiro, the hub of Brazilian climbing, are some 350 documented climbs. The national parks of Serra dos Órgãos (p209) and Itatiaia (p203) and Caparaó (p270) have some particularly good climbs. For climbing clubs in Rio, see p159.

Hang Gliding & Paragliding

It's easy – and fantastic – to hang glide *duplo* (double) in Rio (p159). Paragliding (*parapente*) can be set up, too. Another place you

CLIMBING VOCABULARY

Although most Brazilians in the clubs know some English, a little Portuguese helps smooth the way.

baudrie – harness
corda – rope
dar segurança – to belay
equipamento – equipment
estar preso – to be secured
fenda – crack
fita – webbing
grampo – bolt
mochila – backpack
mosquetão – carabiner
pó de magnésio – chalk powder
queda – a fall
rocha – rock
tomar uma vaca – to make a stupid mistake and fall
topo – summit; also *cume*
uma agarra – a hold
via – route; also *rota*

can double hang glide is Rio da Barra, near Trancoso (p487), Bahia.

Hiking

Hiking in Brazil is highly popular. It's best done during the cooler months of April to October. During the summer, the tropical sun heats the rock to oven temperatures and turns the jungles into steamy saunas.

There are lots of great places to hike in Brazil, both in the national and state parks and along the coastline, and especially in the Southeast and South. Plenty of good hikes are mentioned in the regional chapters. Outstanding areas include the national parks of Chapada Diamantina (p498), Serra dos Órgãos (p209) and Itatiaia (p203), Chapada dos Veadeiros (p401) and Caparaó (p270), as well as the Parque Estadual Marumbi (p318), the Serra de São José (p258), near Tiradentes, and the Canela area (p362).

Contact some of the local hiking and rock-climbing clubs (see p159), which have details of trekking options.

Horseback Riding

In Minas Gerais you can ride stretches of the old gold road, the Estrada Real, or take a five-day horse trek from the state capital, Belo Horizonte (p233), to its most famous historic town, Ouro Prêto (p241). The Pantanal (p415) is another attractive riding area.

Surfing

Surfing is very popular, and several Brazilian professionals are usually to be found in the top 20 of the world rankings.

There's surf virtually all along the coast, with particularly good waves in the South. The best surf beaches are in Santa Catarina state and the Brazilian championships are held at Praia da Joaquina (p340), on Ilha de Santa Catarina. São Francisco do Sul (p347), Ilha do Mel (p321), Ubatuba (p303), Ilhabela (p305), Maresias (p306) and the Boiçucanga area (p306) all serve up good waves.

The best surf is in Rio state, Saquarema (p212). Búzios (p217) and Itacoatiara (p157) beach in Niterói are also popular breaks. There's plenty of surf close to the city of Rio and there are places to rent boards and take classes (p159). Prainha (see the boxed text, p158) is the best surfing beach near the city. The waves are best in the Brazilian winter (from June to August).

On other beaches surfing is still a way of life – even in Espírito Santo state with its breaks of only 1m to 3m – boogie boarding is popular too. Renting boards can be difficult outside of popular tourist areas. If you plan to do a lot of surfing in less traveled places, you'll need to bring your own board.

Further north, Itacaré (p475) and Sítio (p468) and Porto de Galinhas (p537) and Fernando de Noronha (p542) are among the better spots.

A curious event is the national *pororoca* (tidal bore) surf championship held at São Domingos do Capim (p616) at the time of the full moon nearest the March equinox. The waves here are formed by the tidal bore on a tributary of the Rio Amazonas, a long way from the ocean. Waves can reach a few meters in height.

Windsurfing

Windsurfing has caught on in Brazil. In Rio you can rent equipment at Barra da Tijuca, but there are better conditions, and again equipment to rent, at Búzios (p217) in eastern Rio state. In São Paulo state there's good windsurfing at Ilhabela (p305) and around Boiçucanga (p306). But Brazil's hardcore windsurfing mecca can be found much further north, along the Ceará coast, northwest of Fortaleza, where constant, regular, strong trade winds blow from July to December. Jericoacoara (p579) is one of the best spots in the country for windsurfing. Near Fortaleza, the beaches of Praia do Futuro (p570) and Praia de Iracema (p571) are also popular spots.

Other Water Sports

Sailing is big at Búzios in Rio state and the larger resorts along the coast.

Mergulho (diving) doesn't match the Caribbean, but is worthwhile if you're keen. You can arrange diving excursions or rent equipment in Rio (p158). Good dive spots are Arraial do Cabo (p214); the Reserva Biológica do Avoredo (p349), near Porto Belo in Santa Catarina state; Boipeba (p472); Ponta do Seixas (p551), near João Pessoa in Paraíba; and Fernando de Noronha (p542), perhaps the country's finest diving spot.

Fishing in the interior of Brazil is fantastic. The Rio Araguaia in Goiás and Tocantins is known as a fishing paradise with a large variety of fish, including the *pintado*, *dourado* and *tucunaré* (peacock bass). The legendary fighting qualities of the *tucunaré* attract sport fishers from far and wide to the Araguaia and other Amazonian rivers. Fishing for piranha is not undertaken by serious anglers, though it's good fun. Fishing is brilliant in the Pantanal (p418) too, and is allowed from February to October.

You can also ride an inner tube down the Rio Nhundiaquara (p319).

SURFING VOCABULARY

Despite their reputation for aggressiveness in the water, once on land Brazilian surfers are fairly keen on meeting foreign surfers and hearing about their travels. Some are even willing to lend you a board if you ask politely.

body board – boogie board
onda – wave
Pode me emprestar sua prancha por favor? – Could I borrow your board please?
prancha – surfboard
quebrar – to break
surfista – surfer
Tem ondas? – Are there any waves?
Vamos pegar ondas. – Let's go surfing.
vento – wind

BUSINESS HOURS

Most shops and government services (including post offices) are open from 9am to 6pm Monday to Friday and 9am to 1pm Saturday. Shopping malls usually stay open till 10pm Monday to Saturday, and some even open on Sunday (usually late, from 3pm to 9pm). Because many Brazilians have little free time during the week, Saturday morning is often spent shopping.

Restaurants tend to be open from noon till 2:30pm and from 6pm till 10pm; aside from juice stands and cafés, there aren't many restaurants open for breakfast. Those that do generally serve it between 8am and 10:30am. Bars typically open 7pm to 2am, staying open until 4am on weekends.

Banks, always in their own little world, are generally open from 9am or 10am to 2pm or 3pm Monday to Friday.

CHILDREN

Brazilians generally love well-behaved children, who are welcome at nearly all hotels, cafés and restaurants. Many hotels let children stay free, although the age limit varies. Babysitters are readily available, and most restaurants will be able to provide high chairs. The common bond shared by all parents of all nationalities will often bring you that welcome extra personal contact and attention from Brazilians.

Apart from the obvious attractions for children of beaches, coasts and swimming pools in Brazil, you can also find excellent special attractions in many areas, such as amusement parks, zoos, aquariums, and train and boat rides.

Diapers are widely available in Brazil, but you may not easily find creams, baby foods or familiar medicines if you are outside larger cities.

See Visas & Documents (p711) for information on special bureaucratic requirements for unaccompanied travelers under the age of 18.

Children under two years old generally fly for 10% of the adult fare. Those between two and 12 usually pay 50% on international flights and 67% on Brazilian domestic flights. Lonely Planet's *Travel with Children* book contains lots of practical advice on this subject, as well as firsthand stories from many parents who have traveled with kids.

CLIMATE CHARTS

For information about weather and seasonal patterns, see When to Go (p21). See right for climate charts.

COURSES

Aside from language instruction, very few courses are geared for foreigners. If you have a bit of Portuguese, you can join in classes of dance, percussion, capoeira and cooking. Rio and Salvador are the best places to find such activities.

Language

There are lots of ways to learn Portuguese in Brazil. It's easy to arrange classes through branches of the Instituto Brazil-Estados Unidos (IBEU), where Brazilians learn English. Rio de Janeiro offers the most opportunities for classes (see p163), but there'll be a language institute in each large city. Website www.onestoplanguage.net has a small database of Portuguese-language schools in Brazil. In the US, the **National Registration Center for Study Abroad** (☎ 414-278-0631; www.nrcsa .com) has information on Portuguese language schools in some Brazilian cities.

CUSTOMS

Travelers entering Brazil are allowed to bring in one radio, tape player, typewriter, notebook computer and video and still camera each. Plants and seeds must be declared on arrival. Apart from clothes, books, periodicals and other personal articles for domestic or professional use, or for consumption, goods that have cost more than US$500 (US$150 if you are arriving by land, river or lake) are subject to 50% import duty.

DANGERS & ANNOYANCES

Brazil receives a lot of bad press about its violence and high crime rate. While undoubtedly sensationalized by the media, many tourists do get robbed while in Brazil, and you'll want to minimize the risks of becoming a victim. Don't start your trip by wandering around touristy areas in a jet-lagged state soon after arrival: you'll be an obvious target. Accept the fact that you might be mugged, pickpocketed or have your bag snatched while you're in the country. If you carry only the minimum needed for the day (neither too much nor too little), and don't try to resist thieves,

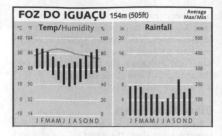

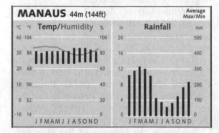

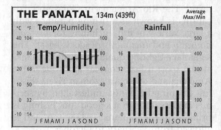

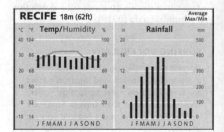

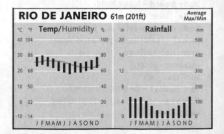

you're unlikely to come to any real harm. Other tips:

- Don't come to Brazil with jewelry, iPods, expensive watches and other items you'll worry about.
- Don't dress like a gringo. Avoid wearing baseball caps, shiny sunglasses and black socks (Brazilians, like North Americans, wear white socks with sneakers). Dress down in casual clothes that blend in. Bermuda shorts, T-shirts, a pair of Havaianas and other clothes bought in Brazil are a good choice.
- Keep small change handy so you don't have to flash a wallet to pay bus fare.
- Don't wear a backpack when out sightseeing.
- Don't wander around with a camera in view – keep it out of sight. Consider carrying it in a plastic bag from a local store. Disposable cameras are much less worry.
- Before arriving in a new place, get a map or at least have a rough idea of the area's

orientation. Use taxis to avoid walking through high-risk areas.

- Be alert and walk purposefully. Criminals will hone in on dopey, hesitant, disoriented-looking individuals.
- Use ATMs inside buildings. When using any ATM or exchanging money, be aware of those around you. Robbers sometimes watch these places looking for targets.
- Check the windows and doors of your room for security, and don't leave anything valuable lying around. If you consider your hotel to be reliable, place your valuables in its safe and get a receipt.
- If you're suspicious or uneasy about a situation, don't hesitate to make excuses and leave, change your route, or whatever else is needed to extricate yourself.
- Don't take anything to city beaches except your bathing suit, a towel and just enough money for food and drinks. No camera, no bag, no jewelry.

PREVENTING CHILD SEX TOURISM IN BRAZIL *Beyond Borders and ECPAT*

Tragically, the exploitation of local children by tourists is becoming more prevalent throughout Latin America, including Brazil. Various socio-economic factors make children susceptible to sexual exploitation, and some tourists choose to take advantage of their vulnerable position.

Sexual exploitation has serious, lifelong effects on children. It is a crime and a violation of human rights.

Brazil has laws against sexual exploitation of children. Many countries have enacted extraterritorial legislation that allows travelers to be charged as though the exploitation happened in their home country.

Responsible travelers can help stop child sex tourism by reporting it. It is important not to ignore suspicious behavior. **Cybertipline** (www.cybertipline.com) is a website where sexual exploitation of children can be reported. You can also report the incident to local authorities and if you know the nationality of the perpetrator, report it to their embassy.

Travelers interested in volunteering against sexual exploitation of children or learning more about the topic are encouraged to contact **ECPAT Brazil** (☎ 00 55 61-3347 8524; www.comitenacional .org.br in Portuguese; SFPN 506, Bl C, Sl 26, 70740-530, Brasília/DF). ECPAT Brazil is an advocacy, mobilization and monitoring agency that focuses on sexual exploitation of children. It is composed of representatives of the civil society, of the government and of international organizations.

A similar organization that may be contacted for further information is **Coletivo Mulher Vida** (☎ 00 55 85-3341 7926; www.mulhervida.com.br in Portuguese; Rua João Cardoso Ayres, 1005, Setúbal, Recife-PE, 51.130-300) which aims to prevent domestic violence, abuse and sexual exploration experienced by women, adolescents and children.

Beyond Borders (www.beyondborders.org) is the Canadian affiliate of ECPAT. It aims to advance the rights of children to be free from abuse and exploitation without regard to race, religion, gender or sexual orientation.

ECPAT – USA (End Child Prostitution and Trafficking; www.ecpatusa.org) is part of a global network working on these issues with over 70 affiliate organizations around the world.

- After dark, don't walk along empty or nearly empty streets or into deserted parks.
- Don't wander into the *favelas* (shantytowns) unless you're with a trustworthy guide who really knows the area.
- Never carry any more money than you need for the specific outing you're on, and keep it discreetly stashed away in a money belt, sock, secret pocket or shoe. But always have enough cash on hand to appease a mugger (R$20 to R$40).
- If something is stolen from you, you can report it to the police, but it can be an enormous hassle just to get a police report for your insurance company. The tourist police are the best equipped to deal with foreigners, but are rare outside of Rio.

Scams & Robbery Techniques

One of the biggest new scams to hit Brazil in recent years is the hacking into a person's bank account after he or she uses an ATM machine. There have been many reports of this by travelers throughout Brazil. When withdrawing money, try to use machines inside banks that get a lot of pedestrian traffic and always hide the number pad when you're inputting your PIN.

Distraction is a common tactic employed by street thieves in Brazil and elsewhere around the world. The aim is to throw potential victims off guard so that they're easier prey. It may be something as simple as asking you for a cigarette or a light so that you slow down and take your attention off other people around you.

Techniques are continually being developed, and imported or exported across national borders, to relieve the unwary of their belongings. Keep abreast of new scams by talking to other travelers. Theft and security are sources of endless fascination and stories.

A classic, revolting distraction method is the 'cream technique,' common the world over, including in Brazil. You're walking down the street or standing in some public place, when someone surreptitiously sprays a substance on your shoulder, your daypack or anything else connected with you. The substance can be anything from mustard to chocolate or even excrement. An assistant (young or old, male or female) then taps you on the shoulder and amicably offers to clean off the mess…if you'll just put down your bag for a second. The moment you do this, someone makes off with it in a flash. The golden rule is to ignore any such attempt or offer, and simply endure your mucky state until you can find a safe place, such as your hotel, where you can wash.

There have also been reports of druggings, including spiked drinks. While you're temporarily unconscious or semiconscious as a result of some noxious substance being slipped into your beverage, you're powerless to resist thieves. There have even been reported cases of rape in such circumstances. If you start to feel unaccountably dizzy, disoriented, fatigued, or just mentally vacant not long after imbibing, your drink may have been spiked. If you suspect this to be the case, quickly extricate yourself from the situation and get to a safe place – your hotel room.

Exercise *extreme* caution when someone you don't know and trust offers you a drink of *any* kind or even cigarettes, sweets etc. If the circumstances make you suspicious, the offer can be tactfully refused by claiming stomach or other medical problems.

EMBASSIES & CONSULATES
Brazilian Embassies & Consulates

Argentina (www.brasil.org.ar)
Australia (www.brasil.org.au)
Bolivia (www.brasil.org.bo)
Canada (www.consbrastoronto.org)
Colombia (www.brasil.org.co)
France (www.bresil.org)
French Guiana (www.nplus.gf/~cbrascay)
Germany (www.brasilianische-botschaft.de)
Guyana Georgetown (☎ 02-57970)
Ireland Dublin (☎ 01-475 6000)

GOVERNMENT TRAVEL ADVICE

The following government websites offer travel advisories and information on the security situation in Brazil and elsewhere.
Australian Department of Foreign Affairs (☎ 61-1300 139 281; www.smarttraveller.gov.au)
British Foreign Office (☎ 44-0845-850-2829; www.fco.gov.uk/travel)
Canadian Department of Foreign Affairs (☎ 1-800-267 6788; www.dfait-maeci.gc.ca)
US State Department (☎ 1-888-407 4747; http://travel.state.gov)

Netherlands The Hague (☎ 070-302 39 59)
New Zealand Wellington (☎ 04-473 3516)
Paraguay (www.embajadabrasil.org.py)
Peru Lima (☎ 01-421-2759)
Spain Madrid (☎ 91 700 4650)
UK (www.brazil.org.uk)
Uruguay (www.brasmont.org.uy)
USA (www.brasilemb.org)
Venezuela Caracas (☎ 02-261-7553); consulate in Santa Elena de Uairén (☎ 088-951262)

Embassies & Consulates in Brazil

Embassies are all in Brasília, but many countries have consulates in the cities of Rio and São Paulo, and often other cities too. For addresses in Brasília, SES stands for Setor de Embaixadas Sul.

Argentina Brasília embassy (Map pp374-5; ☎ 0xx61-3364 7600; www.brasil.embajada-argentina.gov.ar; SHIS Quadra 2, Conj 01, Casa 19, Lago Sul, Brasília); Foz do Iguaçu consulate (Map p326; ☎ 0xx45-3574 2969; Rua Dom Pedro II 28, Foz do Iguaçu; ☒ 10am-2:30pm Mon-Fri); Porto Alegre consulate (☎ 0xx51-3321 1360; Rua Coronel Bordini 1033, Porto Alegre); Rio consulate (Map pp142-3; ☎ 0xx21-2553 1646; Praia de Botafogo 228, Room 201, Botafogo, Rio de Janeiro); São Paulo consulate (☎ 0xx11-3284 1355; 9th fl, Av Paulista 1106, São Paulo)

Australia Brasília embassy (Map pp374-5; ☎ 0xx61-3226 3311; www.brazil.embassy.gov.au; SES, Av das Nações, Q 801, Conj K, Lota 7, Brasília); Rio consulate (Map pp144-5; ☎ 0xx21-3824 4624; 23rd fl, Av Presidente Wilson 231, Centro, Rio de Janeiro)

Bolivia Brasiléia consulate (☎ 0xx61-3366-3432; SHIS, QL 19, Conj 13, Casa 19 Brasiléia; ☒ 8am-noon Mon-Fri); Brasília embassy (☎ 0xx61-3364-3362; SHIS, Q L-10, Conj 01, Casa 06, Lago Sul, Brasília); Corumbá consulate (Map p427; ☎ 0xx67-3231-5605; Rua Antônio Maria Coelho 881, Corumbá; ☒ 8:30am-1:30pm Mon-Fri); Guajará-Mirim consulate (Map p679; ; ☎ 0xx69-3541 5876; 1st fl, Av Beira Rio 505, Guajará-Mirim; ☒ 8am-1:30pm Mon-Fri); Rio consulate (☎ 0xx21-2551 1796; Room 101, Av Rui Barbosa 664, Botafogo, Rio de Janeiro)

Canada Brasília embassy (Map pp374-5; ☎ 0xx61-3424 5400; www.dfait-maeci.gc.ca/brazil; SES, Av das Nações, Q 803, Lote 16, Brasília); Rio consulate (Map pp140-1; ☎ 0xx21-2543 3004; 5th fl, Av Atlântica 1130, Copacabana, Rio de Janeiro); São Paulo consulate (☎ 0xx11-5509 4321; 16th fl, Av Nações Unidas 12901, São Paulo)

Colombia Brasília embassy (Map pp374-5; ☎ 0xx61-3226 8897; www.embcol.org.br; SES, Av das Nações, Q 803, Lote 10, Brasília); Rio consulate (☎ 0xx21-2552 6248; Room 101, Praia do Flamengo 284, Rio de Janeiro); Tabatinga consulate (☎ 0xx92-3412 2597; Rua General Sampaio 623, Tabatinga)

France Belém honorary consulate (☎ 0xx91-3224 6818; Rua Aristides Lobo 651); Brasília embassy (Map pp374-5;

☎ 0xx61-3312 9100; www.ambafrance-br.org.br; SES, Av das Nações, Q 801, Lote 04, Brasília); Macapá honorary consulate (☎ 0xx96-3223 7554; Rua Jovino Dinoa 1693, Macapá; ☒ 9am-noon Mon & Tue, Thu & Fri); Rio consulate (Map pp144-5; ☎ 0xx21-2210 1272; 6th fl, Av Presidente Antônio Carlos 58, Rio de Janeiro) Note: French honorary consulates do not issue visas for French Guiana or France.

Germany Brasília embassy (Map pp374-5; ☎ 0xx61-3442 7000; www.brasilia.diplo.de; SES, Av das Nações, Q 807, Lote 25, Brasília); Rio consulate (☎ 0xx21-2553 6777; Rua Presidente Carlos de Campos 417, Laranjeiras, Rio de Janeiro)

Guyana Brasília embassy (Map pp374-5; ☎ 0xx61-3248 0874; SHIS Quadra 5, Conj 19, Casa 24, Brasília)

Ireland Rio honorary consulate (☎ 0xx21-2501 8455; Rua 24 de Maio 347, Riachuelo, Rio de Janeiro)

Israel Brasília embassy (Map pp374-5; ☎ 2105 0500; SES, Av das Nações, Q 809, Lote 38, Brasília)

Netherlands Brasília embassy (Map pp374-5; ☎ 0xx61-3961 3200; www.embaixada-holanda.org.br; SES, Av das Nações, Quadra 801, Lote 05, Brasília); Rio consulate (☎ 0xx21-2552 9028; 10th fl, Praia de Botafogo 242, Rio de Janeiro)

New Zealand São Paulo consulate (☎ 0xx11-3288 0307; 15th fl, Alameda Campinas 579, São Paulo)

Paraguay Brasília embassy (Map pp374-5; ☎ 0xx61-3242 3732; SES, Av das Nações, Quadra 811, Lote 42, Brasília); Foz do Iguaçu consulate (Map p326; ☎ 0xx45-3523-2898; Rua Marechal Deodoro da Fonseca 901, Foz do Iguaçu; ☒ 8:30am-4:30pm Mon-Fri); Rio consulate (☎ 0xx21-2553-2294; 2nd fl, Praia de Botafogo 242, Rio de Janeiro)

Peru Brasília embassy (Map pp374-5; ☎ 0xx61-3242 9933; www.embperu.org.br; SES, Av das Nações, Quadra 811, Lote 43, Brasília); Rio consulate (☎ 0xx21-2551-9596; 2nd fl, Av Rui Barbosa 314, Flamengo, Rio de Janeiro)

Spain Brasília embassy (Map pp374-5; ☎ 0xx61-3244 2121; SES, Av das Nações, Quadra 811, Lote 44, Brasília); Rio consulate (☎ 0xx21-2543 3200; Rooms 1601 & 1612, Rua Lauro Müller 116, Torre Rio Sul, Botafogo, Rio de Janeiro)

UK Brasília embassy (Map pp374-5; ☎ 0xx61-3329 2300; www.reinounido.org.br; SES, Av das Nações, Quadra 801, Conj K, Lote 08, Brasília); Rio consulate (Map pp142-3; ☎ 0xx21-2555 9600; 2nd fl, Praia do Flamengo 284, Flamengo, Rio de Janeiro); Salvador consulate (☎ 0xx71-3243 7399; 8th fl, Av Estados Unidos 18B, Comércio, Salvador); São Paulo consulate (☎ 0xx11-816 2303; Rua Fereira de Arauja 741, Pinheiros, São Paulo)

Uruguay Brasília embassy (Map pp374-5; ☎ 0xx61-3322 1200; www.emburuguai.org.br; SES Av das Nações, Quadra 803, Lote 14, Brasília); Porto Alegre consulate (☎ 0xx51-3224 3499; Rua Siqueira Campos 1171, Porto Alegre); Rio consulate (☎ 0xx21-2553 6030; 6th fl, Praia de Botafogo 242, Rio de Janeiro)

USA Brasília embassy (Map pp374-5; ☎ 0xx61-3312 7000; www.embaixada-americana.org.br; SES, Av das Nações,

Quadra 801, Lote 3, Brasília); Rio consulate (Map pp144-5; ☎ 0xx21-2292-7117; Av Presidente Wilson 147, Rio de Janeiro); Salvador consular agency (☎ 0xx71-3345 1545; Rua Pernambuco 51, Pituba, Salvador); São Paulo consulate (Map p277; ☎ 0xx11-3081 6511; Rua Padre João Manoel 933, Cerqueira César, São Paulo)

Venezuela Boa Vista consulate (Map p668; ☎ 0xx95-3623 9285; cnr Av Benjamín Constant & Rua Barão do Rio Branco; ☯ 8am-noon Mon-Fri); Brasília (Map pp374-5; ☎ 0xx61-3322 1011; SES, Av das Nações, Quadra 803, Lote 13, Brasília); Manaus consulate (☎ 0xx92-3233-6004; Rua Ferreira Pena 179, Centro, Manaus); Rio consulate (☎ 0xx21-3552 6699; 5th fl, Praia de Botafogo 242, Rio de Janeiro)

FESTIVALS & EVENTS

Highlights of Brazil's many festivals are listed below. See the regional chapters for details of these and many other events.

January

Bom Jesus dos Navegantes Four-day festival starting on the second Sunday in January; Penedo (p200), Alagoas.

Lavagem da Purifição (Festa de Santo Amaro; p465) January 23 to February 2; Santo Amaro, Bahia.

Lavagem do Bonfim (p450) Second Thursday in January; Salvador, Bahia.

Processão do Senhor Bom Jesus dos Navegantes (p450) January 1; Salvador, Bahia.

February

Festa de Iemanjá (p451) February 2; Salvador, Bahia.

Shrove Tuesday and Carnaval February or March depending on the Easter date; the famous Fat Tuesday celebration and the days preceding it. Nationwide.

March

Semana Santa The week before Easter, in March or April; celebrations in Congonhas (p252), Ouro Prêto (p246), Cidade de Goiás (p387).

April/May

Cavalhada (see the boxed text, p390) Held 50 days after Easter; Pirenópolis, Goiás.

Festa do Divino (p597) The first Sunday after Ascension Day; Alcântara, Maranhão.

Festa do Divino Espírito Santo (p196) In May or June, 40 days after Easter; Paraty, Rio de Janeiro state.

Micareta (p492) In April or early May; Feira de Santana, Bahia.

June

Boi-Bumbá (p657) Three days in late June, Parintins, Amazonas.

Bumba Meu Boi (see the boxed text, p593) From late June to the second week of August; São Luís, Maranhão.

Festa de São João (p464) Held June 22 to 24; Cachoeira, Bahia.

Festas Juninas Celebrated throughout June in Rio state and much of the rest of the country.

Festival Folclórico do Amazonas (p646) Throughout June, Manaus, Amazonas.

July

Festival de Dança Second half of July; Joinville (p342), Santa Catarina.

Fortal (p571) Last week of July; Fortaleza, Ceará.

Regata de Jangadas (p571) Second half of July; Fortaleza, Ceará.

August

Festa da NS de Boa Morte (p464) Held in mid-August; Cachoeira, Bahia.

Festa de Iemanjá (p571) Held August 15; Fortaleza, Ceará.

Folclore Nordestino (p535) In late August; Olinda, Pernambuco.

September

Festa de NS de Nazaré (p212) On September 7 and 8; Saquarema, Rio de Janeiro state.

Festa do Çairé (p630) Second week of September; Alter do Chão, Pará.

Jubileu do Senhor Bom Jesus do Matosinhos (p252) Takes place from September 7 to 14; Congonhas, Minas Gerais.

October

Círio de Nazaré (p610) Starts the second Sunday in October; Belém, Pará.

NS do Rosário Second half of October in Cachoeira (p464), Bahia, and October 23 to 25 in Ouro Prêto (p245), Minas Gerais.

Oktoberfest (p345) The middle two weeks in October; Blumenau, Santa Catarina.

Rio Jazz Festival (p164) Varying dates in October; Rio de Janeiro.

November

Dia do Romeiro e Festa do Padre Cícero (p583) Held November 1 and 2; Juazeiro do Norte, Ceará

Maceió Fest (p511) Held in the 3rd week of November; Maceió, Alagoas.

December

Carnatal (p558) First week of December; Natal, Rio Grande do Norte.

Festa Santa Barbara (p451) Celebrated December 4 to 6; Salvador, Bahia.

Reveillon & Festa de Iemanjá (p164) December 31; Rio de Janeiro.

FOOD

Check out the Food & Drink chapter (p103) for more details on Brazil's culinary breadth. Where we have divided our restaurant reviews into different price ranges, you can expect a main course to cost less than R$12 in a budget eatery, R$12 to R$25 in a midrange one and more than R$25 in a top-end restaurant.

GAY & LESBIAN TRAVELERS

Brazilians are pretty laid-back when it comes to most sexual issues, and homosexuality is more accepted here than in any other part of Latin America. That said, the degree to which you can be out in Brazil varies greatly by region, and in some smaller towns discrimination is prevalent.

Rio is the gay capital of Latin America, though Salvador and São Paulo also have a lively scene. Gay bars in Brazil are all-welcome affairs attended by GLS (Gays, Lesbians e Simpatizantes), crowds full of heterosexuals, homosexuals and who-gives-a-sexuals, who are far more concerned with dancing and having a good time than determining your sexual preference.

There is no law against homosexuality in Brazil, and the age of consent is 18, the same as for heterosexuals. Rio's **Arco Iris Association** (☎ 0xx21-2552 5995; www.arco-iris.org.br; Rua Mundo Novo 62, Botafogo, Rio de Janeiro) is a gay lobbying group that assists and informs the local gay and lesbian community. In Salvador you can contact the **Grupo Gay da Bahia** (Map pp442-3; ☎ 0xx71-322 2552; Rua Frei Vicente 24, Pelourinho).

Gay travelers interested in meeting others should consider booking an excursion with Rio's best (and only) gay travel agency, **G Brazil** (Map pp138-9; ☎ 0xx2247 4431; www.gbrazil.com in Portuguese; Suite 303, Rua Farme de Amoedo 76, Ipanema).

The Rio Gay Guide at www.riogayguide .com is an excellent resource for gay and lesbian travelers in Rio. Another informative site that has lots of good links is www.pridelinks.co m/Regional/Brazil.

HOLIDAYS

April 19, the **Dia do Índio** (Indian Day), is not a national holiday, but it's marked by festivities in indigenous villages around the country.

The official national holidays consist of the following:

New Year's Day January 1 – officially the Day of Universal Confraternization

Carnaval February/March – the two days before Ash Wednesday, which falls 46 days before Easter Sunday

Good Friday & Easter Sunday March/April

Tiradentes Day April 21 – in honor of Tiradentes, an 18th-century Brazilian nationalist martyr

May Day/Labor Day May 1

Corpus Christi Late May/June – 60 days after Easter Sunday

Independence Day September 7

Day of NS de Aparecida October 12 – holiday of Brazil's religious patron

All Souls' Day November 2

Proclamation of the Republic Day November 15

Christmas Day December 25

INSURANCE

A travel-insurance policy to cover theft, loss and medical problems is a good idea. The policies handled by STA Travel and other student travel organizations are usually good value. Some policies offer lower and higher medical-expense options; the higher ones are chiefly for countries, such as the US, that have extremely high medical costs. There is a wide variety of policies available, so check the fine print.

Some policies specifically exclude 'dangerous activities,' which can include scuba diving, motorcycling and even hiking. Note that a locally acquired motorcycle license is not valid under some policies.

You may prefer a policy that pays doctors or hospitals directly rather than you having to pay on the spot and claim later. If you have to claim later, make sure you keep all documentation.

Some policies ask you to call back (reverse charges) to a center in your home country for immediate assessment of your problem.

Check that the policy covers ambulances or an emergency flight home.

INTERNET ACCESS

Many top-end hotels and a few midrange ones in São Paulo and Rio have the technology to allow you to plug in your laptop – or go wireless – and access the internet from your room. Download the details of your ISP's access numbers before you leave home. The major internet providers in Brazil are **Universo Online** (www.uol.com.br in Portuguese) and **Brazil Online** (www.bol.com.br in Portuguese).

Internet cafés are prevalent throughout the country. Most places charge between R$4 and R$8 an hour.

DIRECTORY

LEGAL MATTERS

If something is stolen from you, you can report it to the police. No big investigation is going to occur, but you will get a police report to give to your insurance company. The police, however, aren't always to be trusted. Brazilian police have on occasion planted drugs and stung gringos for bribes.

Speaking of drugs, the former military regime had a pathological aversion to drugs and enacted stiff penalties. Although laws are slowly changing (giving more lenient sentences to users rather than sellers), drugs still provide a perfect excuse for the police to extract a fair amount of money from you, and you don't want to end up in a Brazilian prison.

Police checkpoints along the highways stop cars and buses at random. Some are even set up outside nightclubs to stop taxis and give the full pat down to club-goers on their way home (hint, don't carry anything!). Police along the coastal drive from Rio to Búzios and Rio to São Paulo are notorious for hassling young people and foreigners. Border areas are also dangerous, particularly around the Bolivian border.

A large amount of cocaine is smuggled out of Bolivia and Peru through Brazil. Be very careful with drugs. If you're going to buy, don't buy from strangers and don't carry anything around with you.

Marijuana is plentiful in Brazil and very illegal. Nevertheless, it's widely used, and, like many other things in Brazil, everyone except the military and the police has a rather tolerant attitude towards it. Bahia seems to have the most open climate.

If you're coming from one of the Andean countries and have been chewing coca leaves, be especially careful to clean out your pack before arriving in Brazil. Sentences are stiff even for possession of coca leaves.

Because of the harsh penalties involved with possession or apparent possession, we advise you to stay away from it in any form.

MAPS

The best maps in Brazil are the Quatro Rodas series. These good regional maps (Norte, Nordeste etc) are available throughout Brazil and sell for around R$10. It also publishes the *Atlas Rodoviário* road atlas, useful if you're driving, as well as excellent street atlases for the main cities.

In the US, **Omni Resources** (www.omnimap.com) is a good source of Brazil maps. It ships worldwide and you can order online.

Good topographical maps are published by the IBGE, the government geographical service, and the DSG, the army geographical service. Availability is erratic, but IBGE offices in most state capitals sell IBGE maps. Office locations can be found on the IBGE website (www.ibge.gov.br).

Telephone directories in many states include city maps.

One of the country's best sources of DSG and IBGE maps is **Editora Geográfica J Paulini** (Map pp144-5; ☎ 0xx21-2220 0181; Shop K, Rua Senador Dantas 75, Centro) in Rio de Janeiro.

MONEY

Brazil's currency is the real (hay-*ow;* often written R$); the plural is reais (hay-*ice*). One real is made up of 100 centavos. The real was introduced on a one-for-one parity with the US dollar in 1994 but after 13 years of modest fluctuations reached a value of around US$0.50 by 2007.

Banknotes are easy to distinguish from each other as they come in different colors with a different animal featured on each. There's a green one-real note (hummingbird), a blue two (hawksbill turtle), a violet five (egret), a scarlet 10 (macaw), a yellow twenty (lion-faced monkey), a golden-brown 50 (jaguar) and a blue 100 (grouper fish).

ATMs

ATMs are the easiest way of getting cash in big cities and are common. In many smaller towns, ATMs exist but rarely work for non-Brazilian cards. Make sure you have a four-digit PIN (longer PINs may not work). In general HSBC, Citibank, Banco do Brasil and Bradesco are the best ATMs to try. Look for the stickers on the machines that say Cirrus, Visa, or whatever system your card uses – though this may not mean the machine will necessarily work. Do take care when using ATMs; there have been a number of scams, where criminals have managed to hack into bank accounts of ATM users and subsequently drain them. See also Dangers & Annoyances (p700).

Bargaining

A little bargaining for hotel rooms should become second nature. Before you agree to take a room, ask for a better price. *'Tem desconto?'* (Is there a discount?) and *'Pode fazer um melhor preço?'* (Can you give a better price?) are the phrases to use. It's also possible to reduce the price if you state that you don't want a TV, private bathroom or air-conditioning. There's sometimes a discount for paying *à vista* (cash).

You should also bargain when shopping in markets, and when riding in unmetered taxis arrange the price before departing.

Cash & Traveler's Checks

Even if you are relying mainly on credit or debit cards as your source of funds, it's not a bad idea to take some cash and traveler's checks in reserve. You can change these in banks or in *casas de câmbio* (exchange offices). Banks have slower, more bureaucratic procedures but on the whole give better exchange rates (an exception being Banco do Brasil which charges R$40 commission for every traveler's check transaction). You'll usually get a 1% or 2% better exchange rate for cash than for traveler's checks. Checks, of course, have the advantage of being replaceable if lost or stolen.

Both cash and traveler's checks should be either in US dollars or euros, and Amex is easily the most recognized traveler's check. Thomas Cook, Barclays and Citibank traveler's checks are less widely accepted, but you should be able to cash them in large cities.

Credit Cards

You can use credit cards for many purchases and to make cash withdrawals from ATMs and banks. Visa is the most widely accepted card, followed by MasterCard. Amex and Diners Club cards are also useful. Visa cash advances are widely available, even in small towns with no other currency-exchange facilities; you'll need your passport, and the process can be time consuming, especially at the ubiquitous but bureaucratic Banco do Brasil. In Brazilian banks generally, it's preferable to deal with machines than to try to make contact with human beings. Credit-card fraud is extremely common in Brazil. Keep your card in sight at all times, especially in restaurants.

Tipping

Workers in most services get tipped 10%, and as they make the minimum wage – which is not enough to live on – you can be sure they need the money. In restaurants the service charge will usually be included in the bill and is mandatory. If a waitperson is friendly and helpful you can give more. When the service charge is not included, a 10% tip is customary.

There are many places where tipping is not customary but is a welcome gesture. The local juice stands, bars, coffee corners, street and beach vendors are all tipped on occasion. Parking assistants receive no wages and are dependent on tips, usually R$2. Gas-station attendants, shoe shiners and barbers are also frequently tipped. Most people round up taxi fares to the nearest real, but tipping is not expected.

PHOTOGRAPHY

Cameras will suffer on the road and they may get broken, lost or stolen. But there are so many good shots in Brazil that you'll kick yourself if you don't bring a camera along on your travels. If you're nervous about losing an expensive camera, disposable ones are readily available in most large cities.

Kodak and Fuji print film are sold and processed almost everywhere, but for high-quality results you should use a large lab in Rio city or São Paulo. For camera repairs and professional needs in Rio, **Unimagem** (Map pp144-5; ☎ 0xx21-2507 7745; Rua dos Andradas 29, Centro; ☯ 9am-6pm Mon-Fri, to noon Sat) is recommended.

Don't carry a flashy camera bag – it may attract the attention of thieves – and make sure your equipment is insured.

Technical Tips & Restrictions

When exposed to the forest's humid conditions for an extended period, your cameras and lenses may have their functioning impaired by fungus growth. The standard preventative measure is to keep your gear sealed in plastic bags together with silica-gel packs.

When shooting on beaches, remember to adjust for the glare from water or sand. Don't take a camera to a beach; theft is too big a risk.

Some Candomblé temples do not permit photography. Avoid taking photographs or video in banks or near military bases or other sensitive areas.

Be respectful of the locals and always ask before taking photos – this applies to indigenous peoples in the Amazon, who may not feel comfortable being photographed or filmed.

POST

A postcard or letter weighing up to 20g costs R$1.55 to the US, R$1.90 to Europe and R$2.10 to Australia.

Most post offices are open 9am to 6pm Monday to Friday, and Saturday morning. Airmail letters to the US and Europe arrive in a week or so. For Australia, allow about two weeks.

Brazilian postal codes are five numbers followed by three; the first five are the code for the city, the others specify the location.

For receiving mail, the *posta restante* (poste restante) system seems to function reasonably well. Post offices hold mail for 30 days. A reliable alternative for Amex customers is to have mail sent to one of its offices.

SHOPPING

Smart souvenir hunters can do well in Brazil, provided they know a little about Brazilian culture. Many people find the best souvenirs to be handicrafts, artwork, recorded music and fashion. Try to buy arts and crafts directly from the artist or artisan rather than giving most of your money to some guy simply because he has a storefront.

Glitzy, air-conditioned shopping malls – imaginatively called *shoppings* – are in every self-respecting medium-sized city, and São Paulo has hundreds of them. Browsing the many markets and small streetside stores yields, for better or worse, less predictable results.

Never buy products made from endangered plants or animals. In Brazil you will see numerous souvenirs made from coral, turtle shell, rare bird feathers, caiman skin and bits of jaguar skin. Don't be a sucker and fall for the story about how the jaguar was only slain in revenge for killing a baby in the Amazon. Remember that these products are only sold because there is a tourist demand for them.

Art & Crafts

Although nearly everything can be found in Rio and São Paulo, there is a premium for moving craft and art pieces from the hinterland into the fancy stores of the big cities. Rio has excellent shopping (p183) at markets like the Hippie Fair, the wild Feira Nordestina and the popular Babilônia Feira Hype. Among Rio's handicrafts shops (p183), O Sol in Jardim Botânico, Pé de Boi in Botafogo and La Vareda in Santa Teresa, offer good selections.

Outside the two big cities, your best bets for craftwork are artisan fairs – held on Saturday and Sunday in many cities – cooperative stores and government-run shops. The Northeast has a rich assortment of artistic items. Salvador and nearby Cachoeira are notable for their rough-hewn wood sculpture. Artisans in Fortaleza and the southeastern coast of Ceará specialize in fine lace. The interior of Pernambuco, in particular Caruaru, is famous for its wildly imaginative ceramic figurines.

Some Amazonian Indian peoples now make artifacts such as bows, arrows, baskets, feather headdresses, carvings, pottery and beads specifically as commodities to sell. Some are very attractive, even if not quite the genuine article.

Gemstones

Gemstones are the most famous souvenir/luxury items from Minas Gerais. But if you're in the market for fine jewelry and precious stones, wait until you return to the big cities to make your purchases. Buy from a large and reputable dealer such as Amsterdam Sauer (p127) or H Stern (p127) in Rio. Stern is an international dealership based in Ipanema, and its reputation for quality and honesty is beyond reproach. It isn't a discount store, but its jewelry is less expensive in Brazil than at its outlets in other parts of the world.

Leather

Brazilian leather goods are moderately priced, but the leather isn't particularly supple. The better Brazilian shoes, belts, wallets, purses and luggage are sold in the upmarket shops of Ipanema and Leblon. Shoes are extremely good value, but many of the best are reserved for export, and larger sizes are difficult to find. Good-quality, cheap, durable, leather soccer balls with hand-stitched panels are sold all over Brazil in sporting-goods stores. (Inflated soccer balls should not be put in the cargo hold of a plane.)

In interior Pernambuco, the Sertanejos' curious traditional leather hats appeal to some travelers.

Music

Don't leave the country without buying some music. Rio (p183) has great music stores, with plenty of used and new shops, places for DJs and open-air music markets. In other cities, your best bet for music may be the big malls.

New-release CDs cost anywhere from R$18 to R$45 in stores. Street stalls sell bootleg CDs for around R$5.

Brazil's many varieties of percussion, wind and string instruments make fun souvenirs and presents. You can often find inexpensive ones at craft markets as well as in music stores.

Other Purchases

Functional and decorative hammocks are available in cities throughout Amazonia. They're indispensable for travelers and make fine, portable gifts. A typical one-person hammock costs R$35 to R$60; a large *casal* (double) hammock might run around R$80.

Coffee-table picture books on Brazil, DVDs of Carnaval and of highlights of the national football team and Pelé in various World Cup matches are hawked in the streets of Copacabana – though better book selections are found in Ipanema bookshops. Guaraná powder, a stimulant (said to be an aphrodisiac) derived from an Amazonian fruit, is sold by health stores, like Rio's **Mundo Verde** (Map pp140-1; ☎ 2257 3183; Av NS de Copacabana 630, Copacabana) and some pharmacies. In the Amazon region itself, there are plenty of shops and market stalls devoted to herbal and natural medicines. Belém's **Mercado Ver-o-Peso** (p608) and Manaus' Mercado Municipal Adolfo Lisboa (p644) are fascinating places to browse.

A Brazilian *fio dental* (dental-floss bikini) is fun to have. Rio's Ipanema has dozens of shops selling stylish beachware for men and women.

Candomblé stores are a good source of curios. They range from magical incense guaranteed to bring good fortune and increase sexual allure, wisdom and health to amulets and ceramic figurines of Afro-Brazilian gods.

SOLO TRAVELERS

On your own, you need to be alert about what's going on around you, and be particularly prudent about where you go. These are cardinal rules for solo female travelers.

Brazil is an excellent place to meet other travelers. There's a large network of hostels, and many towns that are particularly suited for meeting travel companions (Rio, Salvador and Jericoacoara topping the list). Language schools, group tours and volunteer work provide fine opportunities for mingling with travelers and locals.

Since double rooms often cost only slightly more than single ones, solo travelers face higher accommodations costs than others. If you're on a tight budget – or simply want to meet other travelers – the hostels are your best bet.

TELEPHONE
Domestic Calls

You can make domestic calls – intercity or local – from normal card pay phones on the street and in telephone offices. The telephone cards you need are sold in denominations of 20, 50 and 90 units (costing between R$5 and R$20) by vendors, newsstands and anywhere you see advertising *cartãos telefônicos*.

For calls within the city you're in, just slide the card into the phone, then check the readout to see if it's given you proper credit, and dial the eight-digit number. Local fixed-line phone calls cost only a few units. For directory information, call ☎ 102.

For calls to other cities, you need to precede the number with 0, then the code of your selected carrier (see the boxed text, p708), then the two or three digits representing the city. City codes are therefore usually given in the format 0xx digit digit, with the 'xx' representing the carrier code. A long-distance call usually eats up between five and 10 phonecard units per minute.

You need to include the city code (0xx digit digit) when calling to another city even if that city has the same city code as the one you're calling from.

To make a *chamada a cobrar* (intercity collect) call, stick a 9 in front of the 0xx. To make a local collect call, dial 9090 and then the number. A recorded message in Portuguese will ask you to say your name and the name of the state where you're calling from, after the beep.

International Calls

To phone Brazil from abroad, dial your international access code, then 55 (Brazil's country code), then the city code (omitting the initial 0xx), then the number.

By far the least-expensive, most hassle-free way of calling abroad from Brazil is via Skype (www.skype.com), which you can access from many internet cafés.

The cost of international calls from a traditional line in Brazil is pricey. Expect to

BRAZILIAN CITY CODES & CARRIERS

Brazil has several rival long-distance telephone carriers. When making an international or inter-city call, you have to select a carrier and include its two-digit *código de prestadora* (code) in the number you dial. Brazilian city codes are commonly quoted with an xx representing the carrier code, eg ☎ 0xx21 for Rio de Janeiro or ☎ 0xx71 for Salvador. You'll find city codes listed in this way beneath each city and town heading in this book.

Different carriers cover different areas of the country, and you have to use one that covers both the place you are calling from and the place you're calling to. The carriers are as follows:

Carrier	Code	Area of Coverage
Brasil Telecom	☎ 14	Distrito Federal, states of Mato Grosso, Mato Grosso do Sul, Acre, Goiás, Tocantins, Rondônia, Santa Catarina, Paraná (except Sercontel area), Pelotas, Capão do Leão, Morro Redondo & Turuçu (Rio Grande do Sul)
Canbrá	☎ 85	states of Rio de Janeiro, Minas Gerais (except CTBC Telecom areas), Espírito Santo, Bahia, Sergipe, Alagoas, Pernambuco, Rio Grande do Norte, Ceará, Piauí, Maranhão, Pará, Amapá, Roraima & Amazonas
Ceterp	☎ 16	Guatapará & Ribeirão Preto (São Paulo state)
CRT	☎ 51	Rio Grande do Sul (except Brasil Telecom area)
CTBC Telecom	☎ 12	Some areas of São Paulo, Minas Gerais, Mato Grosso do Sul & Goiás states
Embratel	☎ 21	All of Brazil & international calls
Intelig	☎ 23	All of Brazil & international calls
Sercontel	☎ 43	Londrina & Tamarana (Paraná state)
Telefônica	☎ 15	São Paulo state (except CTBC Telecom & Ceterp areas)
Telemar	☎ 31	Same as Canbrá
Vésper	☎ 89	São Paulo state (except CTBC Telecom & Ceterp areas)

This may look complicated, but in practice it's straightforward. For one thing, you can use **Embratel** (☎ 21) or **Intelig** (☎ 23) for any call; for another, other major carriers usually have their names and codes widely displayed in their localities, so you absorb them unconsciously.

For example, to call from Rio de Janeiro to Fortaleza (city code ☎ 0xx85), in the state of Ceará, you dial 0 followed by 21 or 23 or 31 or 85 (the codes of the four carriers that cover both Rio and Ceará), followed by 85 for Fortaleza, followed by the number.

For an international call, dial 00 followed by 21 or 23 (the international carriers), followed by the country code, city code and number.

There appears to be little appreciable difference between the carriers, but at least the system gives you alternatives if the lines of your initial choice always seem to be busy.

pay a minimum of R$2 a minute to the US or Canada, and R$4 a minute to Europe or Australia. Prices are about 20% lower during off-peak hours, which is typically from 8pm to 6am daily and all day Sunday.

To make an international call at your own expense, ordinary card pay phones – nicknamed *orelhões* (big ears; you'll soon understand why when you see one) – are of little use unless you have an international calling card.

If you don't have an international calling card, you can buy Embratel phonecards from newsstands and pharmacies (sold in denominations of R$20 to R$50). These have a bar on the back that you scratch off to reveal a code to

enter along with the number you are calling. (Instructions are printed on the cards in English and Portuguese.) You can make calls from any phone. Rates are generally about R$1.50 a minute for calls to the US, R$2.50 to Europe and about twice that to Asia and Australia. Not all pay phones will work. You may have to try a few (a rare few are marked 'Este aparelho faz ligações internacionais;' 'This apparatus makes international calls').

Another option is to find an internet or phone café, where you pay in cash after you finish talking (don't forget to establish the cost per minute before you call). Normally you'll be directed to a booth and will dial the call yourself. Country codes include the following:

Argentina ☎ 54
Australia ☎ 61
Bolivia ☎ 591
Colombia ☎ 57
France ☎ 33
Germany ☎ 49
New Zealand ☎ 64
Paraguay ☎ 595
Peru ☎ 51
UK ☎ 44
USA & Canada ☎ 1
Venezuela ☎ 58

USEFUL TELEPHONE PHRASES

I would like to make an international
call to...
Quero fazer uma ligação internacional para...
I would like to reverse the charges.
Quero fazê-la a cobrar.
I am calling from a public (private)
telephone in Rio de Janeiro. *Estou falando
dum telefone público (particular) no Rio de Janeiro.*
My name is... *Meu nôme é...*
The area code is... *O código é...*
The number is... *O número é...*

You can also make calls from your hotel or
a private phone, but in hotels it's essential to
attempt to establish beforehand what it will
cost you. Hotels often charge astronomical
rates.

For *a cobrar* (international collect) calls,
dial ☎ 0800-703-2111 from any phone. Or try
dialing the local operator (☎ 103-31 or 103-
21) and asking to be transferred to a *telefonista
internacional* (international operator). Since
many operators do not speak English, you
could experiment with some of the phrases
in the boxed text on right.

Be careful with services advertised by stickers on some phones announcing free calls to
multilingual operators who can get you collect
calls to the US or international credit-card
calls. Make sure you establish the costs of any
call before making it.

Mobile Phones

Mobile phones are ubiquitous throughout
Brazil (103 million at last count). Known as
a *celular* (often shortened to *cel*), a mobile
phone has eight-digit numbers starting with
a 9 or 8, and calls to them run through your
phonecard units much faster than calls to
regular numbers. Mobiles have city codes
just like normal phone numbers (0xx digit
digit), and if you're calling from another city
you have to use them.

If you plan to carry your own, an unlocked
GSM tri- or quad-band cell phone is your
best bet. You can purchase a prepaid SIM
card, and refill with extra minutes as needed.
Cartões pre-pago (prepaid cards) to refill minutes are sold at newspaper kiosks throughout
Brazil. Charges vary but typically run R$1.30/
R$1.90 per minute for local/long-distance
calls (within Brazil). Brazil's major mobile
carriers, with the widest coverage, are Vivo,
TIM and Claro.

In several cities, you can rent a mobile phone for around R$10 a day plus call
charges. The following agencies rent mobile
phones, with pick-up and drop-off service
to your hotel:

ConnectCom (☎ 0xx21-2275 8461; www.connectcomrj
.com.br) Based in Rio de Janeiro.
Fast Cell (☎ 0xx61-3323 3662; www.fastcell.com.br)
Provides rental in São Paulo (R$10 per day) and Brasília
(R$15 per day).

TIME

Brazil has four time zones. Brasília time, which
is GMT/UTC minus three hours, covers the
whole of the Southeast, South and Northeast
regions, plus, in the Central West section, Distrito Federal (including Brasília) and the state
of Goiás, and, in the Amazon, the states of Tocantins, Amapá and the eastern half of Pará.

The remainder of the Central West (Mato
Grosso and Mato Grosso do Sul states) and
the rest of the Amazon (except Acre and far
southwest Amazonas state) are one hour
behind Brasília time (GMT/UTC minus
four hours). Acre and southwest Amazonas
(southwest of a line drawn between Tabatinga
and Porto Acre, which is on the Amazonas-
Acre border, just north of Rio Branco) are
two hours behind Brasília time (GMT/UTC
minus five hours). The Fernando de Noronha
archipelago, out in the Atlantic Ocean, 350km
off Natal, is one hour *ahead* of Brasília time
(GMT/UTC minus two hours).

Thus, when it's noon in London and 7am
in New York, it should be 9am in most of
Brazil, but 10am in Fernando de Noronha,
8am in Mato Grosso and most of the Amazon, and 7am in Acre. We say 'should be'
because daylight saving means that it usually isn't. Brazilian daylight-saving time runs

from mid-October to mid-February, during which period clocks are advanced one hour – but only in the Southeast, South and Central West and the states of Bahia and Tocantins! And of course northern hemisphere daylight saving happens in the other half of the year, so in reality the time difference between Rio and New York is three hours in December and one hour in July. And the time difference between Rio and Manaus is three hours from October to February but two hours otherwise. Got that clear then?

Not surprisingly, Brazilians, as well as foreign travelers, sometimes don't know what time of day it is, and a lot of travelers have a few tales to tell about connections missed due to temporal ignorance.

Even when they do know the time, Brazilians are not noted for respecting it. Don't be surprised, or angry, if they arrive a couple of hours later than expected. To them it is acceptable, and they always have the most inventive reasons for it.

TOILETS

Public toilets are not common but they exist at every bus station and airport and somewhere else in most cities and towns; there's usually an charge of around R$0.50 to R$1. Brazilians are quite nice about letting you use toilets in restaurants and bars. As in other Latin American countries, toilet paper isn't flushed. There's usually a nice smelly basket next to the toilet to put it in.

TOURIST INFORMATION

Most tourist offices in Brazil are sponsored by individual states and municipalities. In many places, they have shoestring budgets that are chopped or maintained according to the whims (or feuds!) of regional and local politicians. Some tourist offices clearly function only as a sinecure for politicians' relatives; others have dedicated, knowledgeable staff who care about tourism in their locality and are interested in providing information. Some offices are conveniently placed in the center of town; others are so far out of range that you'll spend an entire day getting there. Keep your sense of humor, prepare for potluck and don't expect too much!

Embratur (☎ 0xx61-429 7777; www.braziltour.com; Setor Comercial Norte, Quadra 2, Bloco G, 70712-907 Brasília, DF), the Brazilian tourism institute, has its headquarters in Brasília, but maintains an office (☎ 0xx21-2509 6017; 8th fl, Rua Uruguaiana 174, Centro) in Rio de Janeiro.

Outside of the country, Brazilian consulates and embassies (see p700) are able to provide limited tourist information, although the embassy in the UK actually has a dedicated tourist information section. Several Brazilian embassies and consulates provide useful tourist information on their websites.

TRAVELERS WITH DISABILITIES

Travelers in wheelchairs don't have the easiest of times in Brazil, but in the large cities there is a concerted effort to keep people mobile. Problems you'll encounter include immensely crowded public buses and restaurants with entrance steps. It pays to plan your trip through contact with some of the organizations listed here.

Rio is probably the most accessible city in Brazil for disabled travelers to get around, but that doesn't mean it's always easy. The metro system has electronic wheelchair lifts, but these aren't always operational. The streets and sidewalks along the main beaches have curb cuts and are wheelchair accessible but most other areas do not have cuts. Many restaurants also have entrance steps.

Most of the newer hotels have wheelchair-accessible rooms, and some cable TV is closed-captioned.

Useful Organizations

The **Centro de Vida Independente** (Map pp138-9; ☎ 0xx21-2512 1088; www.cvi-rio.org.br in Portuguese; Rua Marquês de São Vicente 225, Gávea) can provide advice for the disabled about travel in Brazil.

Those in the USA may like to contact the **Society for Accessible Travel & Hospitality** (SATH; ☎ 212-447 7284; www.sath.org). SATH's website is a good resource for disabled travelers. Another excellent website to check out is www.access-able.com.

Other useful organizations in the US include the following:

International Association for Medical Assistance to Travelers (IAMAT; ☎ 716-754 4883; www.iamat.org; 417 Center St, NY 14092)

Mobility International USA (☎ 541-343-1284; www.miusa.org) Advises disabled travelers on mobility issues, runs an exchange program and publishes the quarterly *Over the Rainbow* newsletter.

Moss Rehabilitation Hospital (☎ 215-456-5995; www.mossresourcenet.org) Offers an online travel information service with a disability fact sheet.

In Australia try **Acrod** (☎ 02-6282 4333; www.acrod .org.au; Acrod House, 33 Thesiger Ct, Deakin, ACT 2600). Its website has excellent links, among them the highly useful www.independentliving.org.

In the UK, **RADAR** (☎ 020-7250 3222; www .radar.org.uk) is run by and for disabled people. Its website is very organized, and, although travel is not a feature, there are travel-specific links to excellent sites such as www.holiday care.org.uk.

VISAS & DOCUMENTS

Brazil has a reciprocal visa system, so if your home country requires Brazilian nationals to secure a visa, then you will need one to enter Brazil. At the time of writing, American, Canadian, Australian and New Zealand citizens need visas, but citizens of the UK, Ireland and most other EU countries as well as South Africa do not. Check with the Brazilian embassy or consulate in your home country.

Tourist visas are issued by Brazilian diplomatic offices. They are valid from the date you arrive in Brazil for a 90-day stay. They are renewable in Brazil for an additional 90 days. In most embassies and consulates, visas can be processed within 24 hours.

In many Brazilian embassies and consulates it takes only a couple of hours to issue a visa if you go in person (it's instant in some places), but the processing can take a couple of weeks or more if you do it by mail. You will normally need to present a passport valid for at least six months beyond your intended arrival date, a passport photograph, and a round-trip or onward ticket or a photocopy of it or a statement from a travel agent that you have it. If you don't have the ticketing requirements, proof of means of support – such as credit cards or bank statements – may be acceptable.

If you decide to return to Brazil, your visa is valid for five years.

The fee for visas is also reciprocal. For most nationalities, a visa costs between US$20 and US$50, though for US citizens it's US$100 (which is what the US charges Brazilians for visas).

Applicants under 18 years of age who are traveling alone must also submit a notarized letter of authorization from a parent or legal guardian.

Business travelers may need a business visa. It's also valid for 90 days and has the same requirements as a tourist visa. You'll also need a letter on your company letterhead addressed to the Brazilian embassy or consulate, stating your business in Brazil, your arrival and departure dates and your contacts. The letter from your employer must also assume full financial and moral (!) responsibility for you during your stay.

Depending on where you are coming from when you arrive in Brazil, you may need a yellow-fever vaccination certificate. On your arrival in Brazil, immigration officials sometimes ask to see your onward or return ticket and/or proof of means of support such as credit cards or traveler's checks.

Visa regulations change from time to time, and you should always get the latest information from your local Brazilian embassy or consulate (see p700).

Entry/Exit Card

On entering Brazil, all tourists must fill out a *cartão de entrada/saida* (entry/exit card); immigration officials will keep half, you keep the other. They will also stamp your passport and, if for some reason they are not granting you the usual 90-day stay in Brazil, the number of days will be written beneath the word *Prazo* on the stamp in your passport.

When you leave Brazil, the second half of the entry/exit card will be taken by immigration officials. Tip: Don't lose your card while traveling around Brazil! If you do lose it, you could miss your flight dealing with immigration hassles. Typically, you'll be required to pay a fine (upwards of R$150) at the Banco do Brasil before you're allowed to leave.

EXTENSIONS TO ENTRY/EXIT CARDS & VISAS

These are handled by Brazil's Polícia Federal (Federal Police), which has offices in the state capitals and border towns. You must apply before your entry/exit card or visa lapses, and don't leave it until the last minute. Tourist offices can tell you where the nearest Polícia Federal office is. When you go, dress nicely! Some Fed stations don't take kindly to people in shorts.

In most cases an extension seems to be pretty automatic, but sometimes you may not be given the full 90 days. The police may well require that you have a ticket out of the country and proof of sufficient funds, though this seems to be at the discretion of the officer. You may be told to complete a Documento de Arrecadeção de Receitas

Federais (DARF; Federal Revenue Collection Document) form (R$3), which you have to buy from vendors outside the police station or from a *papelaria* (stationery shop). After filling it out, you must go to a bank and pay a fee of about R$100. You then return to the federal police with the DARF form stamped by the bank. The extension should then be routinely issued.

If you opt for the maximum 90-day extension and then leave the country before the end of that period, you cannot return until the full 90 days have elapsed.

Passport

By law you must carry a passport with you at all times, but many travelers opt to carry a photocopy (preferably certified) when traveling about town and leave their passport securely locked up at their hotel. It's convenient to have extra passport photos for any documents or visas you may need to acquire in Brazil. Travelers from other South American countries can travel from country to country without a passport.

WOMEN TRAVELERS
Attitudes Toward Women

Depending on where they travel in Brazil, women traveling alone will experience a range of responses. In São Paulo, for example, where there are many people of European ancestry, foreign women without traveling companions will scarcely be given a sideways glance. In the more traditional rural areas of the Northeast, where a large percentage of the population is of ethnically mixed origin, blonde-haired and light-skinned women, especially those without male escorts, will certainly arouse curiosity.

Although machismo is an undeniable element in the Brazilian social structure, it is less overt than in Spanish-speaking Latin America. Perhaps because attitudes towards sex and pornography are quite liberal in Brazil, males feel little need to assert their masculinity or prove their prowess in the eyes of peers.

Flirtation – often exaggerated – is a prominent element in Brazilian male/female relations. It goes both ways and is nearly always regarded as amusingly innocent banter; no sense of insult, exploitation or serious intent should be assumed.

Health & Safety Precautions

If you encounter unwelcome attention, you should be able to stop it by merely expressing displeasure.

Although most of Brazil is nearly as safe for women as for men, it's a good idea to keep a low profile in the cities at night and to avoid going alone to bars and nightclubs if you'd rather not chance your behavior being misinterpreted.

Similarly, women should not hitchhike alone or even in groups (even men or couples should exercise caution when hitching). Most importantly, the roughest areas of the north and west, where there are lots of men but few local women, should be considered off-limits by lone female travelers.

In the event of unwanted pregnancy or the risk thereof, most pharmacies in Brazil stock the 'morning-after' pill (*a pílula do dia seguinte*), which costs about R$20. Tampons and other sanitary items are widely available in most pharmacies, though you'll want to stock up before heading into rural areas.

What to Wear

Once you've spent an hour or two in Copacabana or Ipanema, where some women run their errands wearing *fio dental* (dental floss – the famous skimpy bikini) you'll be aware that in some parts of Brazil, the dress guidelines aren't quite as strict as in others. What works in Rio will probably not be appropriate in a Northeastern city or in a Piauí backwater. It's best to adapt your clothing to local standards.

WORK

Brazil has high unemployment, and visitors who enter the country as tourists are not legally allowed to take jobs. It's not unusual for foreigners to find English-teaching work in language schools. The pay isn't great (if you hustle you can make around R$1500 a month), but you can still live on it. For this kind of work it's always helpful to speak some Portuguese, although some schools insist that only English be spoken in class. Private language tutoring may pay a little more, but you'll have to do some legwork to get students.

To find this type of work, log on to a Brazilian web server such as **Terra** (www.terra.com.br in Portuguese), **UOL** (www.radaruol.com.br in Portuguese) or **Radix** (www.radix.com.br in Portuguese), and search for English academies. Also, look for 'Professor de Ingles' (English Teacher) in news-paper classified ads, and ask around at the language schools.

Volunteer Work

RíoVoluntário (☎ 0xx21-2262 1110; www.riovoluntario .org.br in Portuguese), headquartered in Rio de Janeiro, supports several hundred volun-teer organizations, from those involved in social work and the environment to health care. It's an excellent resource for finding volunteer work.

One excellent volunteer organization you can get involved with is Rio-based **Iko Poran** (☎ 0xx21-2205-1365; www.ikoporan.org), which links the diverse talents of volunteers with needy or-ganizations. Previous volunteers have worked as dance, music, art and language instructors, among other things. Iko Poran also provides housing for volunteers. It has plans to create volunteer opportunities in Salvador, Praia do Forte and Santarém.

The UK-based **Task Brasil** (www.taskbrasil.org.uk) is another laudable organization that places volunteers in Rio. Here, you'll have to make arrangements in advance and pay a fee that will go toward Task Brasil projects and your expenses as a volunteer.

The best website for browsing volunteer opportunities is **Action Without Borders** (www.ideal ist.org). Also check the website of the **Learning Abroad Center** (☎ 612-626-4782; www.istc. umn.edu).

A little doorknocking can help you find volunteer work in Brazil. There's plenty of need, and many local welfare organizations will gladly find you some rewarding work. Ask around at churches and community centers.

International NGOs (nongovernmental organizations) work in all sorts of fields in Brazil, including environmental, medi-cal and social-welfare projects. If you have some particular interest or skill, try con-tacting relevant organizations to volunteer your services.

Transportation

CONTENTS

GETTING THERE & AWAY

ENTERING THE COUNTRY

Most travelers start their Brazilian odyssey by flying down to Rio, but this is only one of many ways to arrive. The country has several other gateway airports and land borders with every other country in South America except Chile and Ecuador.

AIR
Airports & Airlines

The most popular international gateways are Aeroporto Galeão (GIG) in Rio de Janeiro and São Paulo's Aeroporto Guarulhos (GRU). From both, connecting flights to airports throughout the country leave regularly. Salvador (SSA) and Recife (REC) receive a few direct scheduled flights from Europe.

Since the downsizing of Varig, TAM is now Brazil's main international carrier, with flights to New York, Miami, Paris, London and seven South American cities. The US Federal Aviation Administration has assessed TAM as Category 1, which means they are in compliance with international aviation standards.

Airlines flying to/from Brazil are listed below. All numbers that begin with 0xx11 numbers are in São Paulo. For Brazil's regional carriers, see p720.

Aerolineas Argentinas (AR; ☎ 0800-707 3313; www.aerolineas.com.ar; Buenos Aires)

Aeroméxico (AM; ☎ 0xx11-3253 3888; www.aeromexico.com; Mexico City)

Aerosur (5L; ☎ 0xx11-3214 0484; www.aerosur.com; Santa Cruz, Bolivia)

Air Canada (AC; ☎ 0xx11-3254 6600; www.aircanada.ca; Toronto)

Air France (AF; ☎ 0800-888 9955; www.airfrance.com; Paris)

Alitalia (AZ; ☎ 0800-704 0206; www.alitalia.com; Rome)

American Airlines (AA; ☎ 0xx11-4502 4000; www.aa.com; Dallas & Miami)

Avianca (AV; ☎ 0800-891 8668; www.avianca.com; Bogotá)

British Airways (BA; ☎ 0xx1-4004 4440; www.britishairways.com; London)

Continental Airlines (CO; ☎ 0800-702 7500; www.continental.com; Houston & Newark)

COPA (CM; ☎ 0800-771 2672; www.copaair.com; Panama City)

Delta Airlines (DL; ☎ 0800-881 2121; www.delta.com; Atlanta)

Gol (G3; ☎ 0800-280 0465; www.voegol.com.br; São Paulo)

Iberia (IB; ☎ 0xx11-3218 7130; www.iberia.com; Madrid)

Japan Airlines (JL; ☎ 0xx11-3175 2270; www.jal.com; Tokyo)

KLM (KL; ☎ 0800-888 1888; www.klm.com; Amsterdam)

Lan Chile (LA; ☎ 0800-761 0056; www.lanchile.com; Santiago)

Lufthansa (LH; ☎ 0xx11-6445 2499; www.lufthansa.com; Frankfurt)

Penta (5P; ☎ 0300-789 2029; Belém, Brazil)

South African (SA; ☎ 0xx11-3065 5115; www.flysaa.com; Johannesburg)

Spanair (JK; ☎ 0800-550 002; www.spanair.com; Madrid)

Suriname Airways (PY; ☎ 0xx91-3210 6284; Paramaribo)

THINGS CHANGE...

The information in this chapter is particularly vulnerable to change. Check directly with the airline or a travel agent to make sure you understand how a fare (and ticket you may buy) works and be aware of the security requirements for international travel. Shop carefully. The details given in this chapter should be regarded as pointers and are not a substitute for your own careful, up-to-date research.

FLIGHTLESS

Following the bankruptcy and downsizing of Varig, Brazilian airlines have been in a serious state of turmoil. While still around, Varig continues to slash many of its flights both in Brazil and abroad. Although Gol is now the largest domestic carrier, neither it nor TAM has picked up many of Varig's international routes. LAB and some other South American airlines are also struggling. This means a big reduction in travel options to and from Brazil.

Swissair (LX; ☎ 0xx11-3049 2720; www.swiss.com; Zurich)
TAM (KK; ☎ 0800-570 5700; www.tam.com.br; São Paulo)
TAP Air Portugal (TP; ☎ 0300 210 6060; www.flytap.com; Lisbon)
United Airlines (UA; ☎ 0xx11-3145 4200; www.united.com; Los Angeles)
Varig (RG; ☎ 0xx11-4003 7000; www.varig.com.br; São Paulo)

Tickets

For high-season travel, which basically means flying to Brazil between mid-December and the end of February, tickets cost about US$300 more than they do during the rest of the year.

AIR PASSES

If you're combining travel in Brazil with other countries in southern South America, there are several air passes that can be decent value if you're covering a lot of ground and don't mind a fixed itinerary (among other restrictions). The Mercosur Airpass is valid for flights within Argentina, Brazil, Chile (except Easter Island), Uruguay and Paraguay. The cost is based on the number of standard air miles you want to cover (prices range from US$295 to US$1195 for 1900 to 9200 miles). The Visit South America air pass offered by airlines of the Oneworld Alliance (www.oneworld.com) allows stops in more than 30 cities in 10 South American countries. Prices are calculated on a per flight, per distance basis (US$80 to US$270 for 269 to 1850 miles). For more info on air passes, visit Last Frontiers (www.lastfrontiers.co.uk/flights_airpasses.php).

For information on air passes for flights solely within Brazil, see p720 in the Getting Around section.

COURIER FLIGHTS

Courier flights are a great bargain if you are lucky enough to find one. However, only the major cities are served, with London, New York and Los Angeles being the most common departure points. Visit www.courier.org for more information on being an air-courier. You'll have to pay an annual US$45 membership fee.

IN BRAZIL

Rio de Janeiro is Brazil's most popular international gateway, and has many travel agents. For student fares, try the **Student Travel Bureau** (STB; ☎ 0xx21-2512 8577; www.stb.com.br; Rua Visconde de Pirajá 550, Ipanema), which has some 30 branches around the country. Discount agencies in São Paulo include **US Tour** (☎ 0xx11-3815 8262; www.ustour.com.br). Websites with cheap flights include www.passage mbarata.net.

Australia & New Zealand

Lan Chile and several of its codeshare partners (including or Qantas) fly from Sydney to São Paulo, stopping in Santiago, Chile; some flights also pass through Auckland. Round-trip fares start at A$2800. If you're planning a longer trip through Latin America, an open-jaw (into one city, out of another) or even an around-the-world ticket will be your best bet.

Canada

Airlines flying between Canada and Brazil include Canadian Airlines and Air Canada, but many routings are with US airlines, involving a change of planes in the US.

DEPARTURE TAX

The airport tax for international departures from Brazil is a hefty US$36. This may be included in the price you pay for your ticket. If it is not, you will have to pay cash, in US dollars or in Brazilian reais, at the airport before or at check-in, so remember to keep that amount of cash in reserve. If your ticket price includes the tax, it may be shown in the taxes section at the bottom of your ticket by the letters BR following the amount – but to be absolutely certain, you should ask the agent about departure tax when you buy the ticket.

Continental Europe

A variety of European and Brazilian airlines fly direct to Rio and São Paulo. There are also less-frequent flights connecting Salvador with Madrid (Spanair) and Lisbon (TAP Air Portugal). From Lisbon you can also fly to Recife (TAP Air Portugal) and Fortaleza (TAP Air Portugal).

Fares are pretty similar from starting points across Western Europe, with fares to Rio or São Paulo starting around €800, and usually several hundred euros more for most other destinations.

South America

In addition to flights between South American capitals and the major Brazilian cities, shortish cross-border flights provide alternatives to some overland routes into or out of Brazil.

Meta, a Brazilian regional airline, flies from Georgetown (Guyana), Paramaribo (Suriname) and Cayenne (French Guiana) to Belém and Boa Vista. French Guiana carrier Air Caraïbes also flies between Belém and Cayenne. Puma, a Brazilian carrier, flies from Macapá to Oiapoque, just across the border from St Georges, French Guiana.

From Bolivia, Gol flies from Santa Cruz to Campo Grande. TAM and Aerosur fly from Santa Cruz and Cochabamba to São Paulo.

Inside Bolivia, Aerosur and Aerocon fly from other Bolivian cities to Cobija, Guayaramerin and Puerto Suárez, across the border from the Brazilian towns of Brasiléia, Guajará-Mirim and Corumbá respectively.

From Peru, Gol flies from Lima to São Paulo. From Iquitos, Peru, Peruvian airliner Aviaselva flies to Leticia, Colombia on the Brazil–Peru–Colombia triple frontier.

From Argentina, Gol flies from Buenos Aires to Rio or São Paulo. There are also Gol flights from Porto Alegre to Buenos Aires, Rosario and Córdoba, as well as Montevideo (Uruguay).

Gol and TAM fly between São Paulo and Santiago (Chile), with flights to Asunción (Paraguay) from Curitiba as well. For more information on flights to other South American destinations, see the relevant sections of the towns and cities listed above.

UK & Ireland

Varig and British Airways offer direct flights from London. Fares on average range from UK£750 to UK£900. You can often find cheaper fares on flights from Europe. At the time of writing, there were no direct flights from Ireland. The cheapest fares from Dublin are currently with Lufthansa, via Frankfurt.

CLIMATE CHANGE & TRAVEL

Climate change is a serious threat to the ecosystems that humans rely upon, and air travel is the fastest-growing contributor to the problem. Lonely Planet regards travel, overall, as a global benefit, but believes we all have a responsibility to limit our personal impact on global warming.

Flying & Climate Change

Pretty much every form of motorized travel generates CO2 (the main cause of human-induced climate change) but planes are far and away the worst offenders, not just because of the sheer distances they allow us to travel, but because they release greenhouse gases high into the atmosphere. The statistics are frightening: two people taking a return flight between Europe and the US will contribute as much to climate change as an average household's gas and electricity consumption over a whole year.

Carbon Offset Schemes

Climatecare.org and other websites use 'carbon calculators' that allow travelers to offset the level of greenhouse gases they are responsible for with financial contributions to sustainable travel schemes that reduce global warming – including projects in India, Honduras, Kazakhstan and Uganda.

Lonely Planet, together with Rough Guides and other concerned partners in the travel industry, support the carbon offset scheme run by climatecare.org. Lonely Planet offsets all of its staff and author travel.

For more information, check out our website: www.lonelyplanet.com.

USA

Nonstop flights to Brazil arrive from New York, Los Angeles, Miami and Atlanta. Prices can range from US$800 to US$1100. If you don't want to arrive in Rio or São Paulo, you can also fly to Fortaleza and Recife, though you'll have to connect through São Paulo or Rio.

LAND

There's direct land access to Brazil from nine countries. Several border towns can also be reached by air or river – see opposite and p718 for details.

Bus

International buses travel between Brazil and Argentina, Paraguay and Uruguay, along decent roads. Prices of bus tickets between countries are substantially more than you'd pay if you took a bus to the border, crossed on foot and caught another on the other side, but you'll lose a lot of time that way. If arriving by bus, make sure your papers are in order. See p711 for information on visas and documents.

Car & Motorcycle

If you plan to take a vehicle into Brazil, see p721 for information on essential documents, road rules, and info on fuel and spare parts. At the border you will be asked to sign a bond called a *termo de responsabilidade*, which lists the owner's identification details and home address, destination, and description of the vehicle (make, model, year, serial number, color and tag number). You will also be asked to pay a bank guarantee (the amount to be determined by customs) and sign a statement agreeing that if you stay for more than 90 days, you will contact customs in the area where the entry was registered to apply for an extension for the permit. This must be presented to customs at the time of departure. If your vehicle overstays its permitted time in Brazil, it is liable to be seized and the bank guarantee forfeited. It's illegal to sell the vehicle in Brazil.

Argentina

The main border point used by travelers is Puerto Iguazú–Foz do Iguaçu, a 20-hour bus ride from Buenos Aires (see p331 for more information). Further south, you can cross from Paso de los Libres (Argentina) to Uruguaiana (Brazil), which is also served by buses from Buenos Aires.

Direct buses run between Buenos Aires and Porto Alegre (R$150, 20 hours), Florianópolis, Curitiba, São Paulo and Rio de Janeiro (R$310, 46 hours).

Bolivia

Brazil's border with Bolivia is its longest. Most of it runs through remote wetlands and lowland forests, and it's much-used by smugglers. The main crossings are at Corumbá, Cáceres, Guajará-Mirim and Brasiléia.

Corumbá, opposite the Bolivian town of Quijarro, is the busiest crossing point. Corumbá is a good access point for the Pantanal and has bus connections with São Paulo, Rio de Janeiro, Campo Grande and southern Brazil. The Bolivian train service between Quijarro and Santa Cruz is known as the Death Train (because of what happens to some of those who attempt to ride free on the roof), but it's a beautiful ride. For more information, see p429.

The Bolivian border town of San Matías is 115km southwest of Cáceres in Mato Grosso, Brazil. Cáceres has several daily bus connections with Cuiabá, 215km east. A daily bus runs between Cáceres and Santa Cruz in Bolivia (R$120, 24 hours). The Cáceres–San Matías trip takes two hours (R$30).

Guajará-Mirim, in Rondônia (Brazil), is a short boat ride across the Rio Mamoré from Guayaramerín, Bolivia. Guajará-Mirim has daily bus service to Porto Velho (5½ hours), and buses run between Guayaramerín and the Bolivian towns of Riberalta, Cobija, Trinidad, Santa Rosa, Reyes, Rurrenabaque and La Paz. From late December to late February, rains can make the roads very difficult.

Brasiléia, a 4½-hour bus ride from Rio Branco, in Brazil's Acre state, stands opposite Cobija, Bolivia, which has bus connections to Riberalta, Guayaramerín and La Paz (see p681 for details). This route is less direct than the Guayaramerín–Guajará-Mirim route between Bolivia and Brazil, and buses face the same wet-season difficulties.

Chile

Chile does not share a border with Brazil, but direct buses run between Santiago and Brazilian cities such as Curitiba (R$340, 52 hours), Porto Alegre (R$280, 36 hours), São

Paulo (R$350, 56 hours) and Rio de Janeiro (R$362, 72 hours).

Colombia

Leticia, on the Rio Amazonas in far southeast Colombia, is contiguous with Tabatinga, Brazil. You can cross the border by foot, Kombi van or taxi. From within Colombia, Leticia is only really accessible by air. Tabatinga is a quick flight (or a several-day Amazon boat ride) from Manaus or Tefé. See p661 for details.

French Guiana

The Brazilian town of Oiapoque, a rugged 560km bus ride north of Macapá (R$130, 12 to 24 hours depending on weather conditions), stands across the Rio Oiapoque from St Georges in French Guiana. An unpaved road from St Georges to Régina, about halfway to the French Guiana capital of Cayenne, was recently cut through the jungle, though you'll find that travel along it is still arduous. Taxi-buses between Régina and Cayenne cost around US$10. Flights from St Georges to Cayenne cost around US$70.

Guyana

Lethem, in southwest Guyana and Bonfim, in Brazil's Roraima state, are a short boat ride apart. You can travel between Lethem and the Guyanese capital of Georgetown by plane or truck. The latter takes between two days and two weeks depending on weather conditions. Bonfim is a two-hour bus ride from Boa Vista, the Roraima state capital. See p670 for details.

Paraguay

The two major border crossings are Foz do Iguaçu–Ciudad del Este (see p331) and Ponta Porã–Pedro Juan Caballero (see p435). Use the latter if you're going to/from the Pantanal. Direct buses run between Asunción and Brazilian cities such as Curitiba (US$40, 14 hours), São Paulo (US$45, 20 hours) and Rio de Janeiro (US$60, 24 hours).

Peru

Peru and Brazil share a long border in the Amazon basin, but there are few land routes between them. The most accessible route is at the southeastern end of the border. Iñapari (Peru) is a four-hour minibus or truck ride north of Puerto Maldonado (Peru). From Iñapari,

cross the Rio Acre by ferry or bridge to the small Brazilian town of Assis Brasil, which is a three- to four-hour bus trip from Brasiléia.

Suriname

It isn't possible to travel overland between Suriname and Brazil without first passing through either French Guiana or Guyana.

Uruguay

The crossing most used by travelers is Chuy–Chuí. This is actually one town, with the international border running down the middle of its main street. See p370 for details.

Heading west along the border, other crossings are Río Branco–Jaguarão, Isidoro Noblia–Aceguá, Rivera–Santana do Livramento, Artigas–Quaraí and Bella Unión–Barra do Quaraí. Buses link Jaguarão with Pelotas and Santana do Livramento with Porto Alegre (p355).

Buses run between Montevideo and Brazilian cities such as Porto Alegre (US$70, 12 hours), Florianópolis (US$75, 19 hours) and Curitiba (US$80, 24 hours).

Venezuela

Roads from northern Venezuela go southeast to Ciudad Bolívar, Ciudad Guayana and Santa Elena de Uairén (p671), on the border near Pacaraíma, Brazil. From here, a paved road heads south to Boa Vista (215km) and Manaus (990km). Buses run to Manaus and Boa Vista from as far north as Venezuela's Puerto La Cruz. Santa Elena has buses to and from Caracas (p673).

RIVER
Bolivia

From Trinidad in Bolivia you can reach Brazil by a boat trip of about five days down the Río Mamoré to Guayaramerín, opposite the Brazilian town of Guajará-Mirim (p681).

Paraguay

The passenger-boat service on the Rio Paraguai between Corumbá (Mato Grosso do Sul) and Asunción (Paraguay) has been discontinued. You might be able to travel this route using a sequence of cargo and/or naval boats, but it would take time and luck.

Peru

Fast passenger boats make the 400km trip (US$50 to US$80, eight to 10 hours) along the Rio Amazonas between Iquitos (Peru) and Tabatinga (Brazil). From Tabatinga you can continue 3000km down the river to its mouth. See p661 for more information.

GETTING AROUND

AIR

Because of the great distances in Brazil, the occasional flight can be a necessity, and may not cost much more than a long-haul bus journey. If you intend to take more than just a couple of flights, a Brazil Airpass (p720) will probably save you money. Book ahead for busy travel times – from Christmas to Carnaval, Easter, July and August. Always reconfirm

your flights, as schedules frequently change. See below for air routes in Brazil.

Brazil's worst aviation disaster in the country's history occurred in 2007, when a TAM flight from Porto Alegre crashed on São Paulo's Congonhas runway. Pilots and industry experts have long claimed the runway

> **DOMESTIC DEPARTURE TAX**
>
> Embarkation tax on domestic flights ranges from R$8 to R$20, depending on the airport (the bigger the airport, the bigger the tax). If it isn't already included in the price of your ticket, you have to pay it in cash (reais) at check-in.

was too short, which was partially to blame in the tragic accident. This may mean changes on the horizon for Congonhas and other Brazilian airports.

Airlines

Brazil has three major national carriers and many smaller regional airlines. The biggest airlines are Gol, TAM and Varig. At least one of these flies to every major city. Gol tends to be the cheapest and have the most routes.

Tickets can only be purchased online with an Amex card, but you can buy them from any travel agent with cash.

Brazil's main carriers:

Gol (☎ 0800-280 0465; www.voegol.com.br)
Ocean Air (☎ 0300-789 8160; www.oceanair.com.br)
TAM (☎ 0800 570 5700; www.tam.com.br)
Trip (☎ 0800-789 8747; www.airtrip.com.br)
Varig (☎ 0xx11-4003 7000; www.varig.com.br)

Air Passes

A Brazil Airpass is a good investment if you're planning on covering a lot of ground in 21 days or less. TAM offers a Brazil Airpass, which gives you four flights on its domestic routes, for US$560 (US$480 if you fly TAM to Brazil). Additional flights cost US$120 each. You have to buy the pass before you go to Brazil, and you have to book your air pass itinerary at the time you buy it – or possibly pay penalties for changing reservations. Many travel agents sell the air pass, as does the Brazilian travel specialist **Brol** (www.brol.com).

If for any reason you do not fly on an air-pass flight you have reserved, you should reconfirm all your other flights. Travelers have sometimes found that all their air-pass reservations had been scrubbed from the computer after they missed, or were bumped from, one flight.

Air Taxis

Many areas, especially Amazonia, feature air-taxi companies that will fly you anywhere their small planes can reach. Unfortunately these planes and the runways they land on aren't always maintained. You might think twice before booking one of these flights.

BICYCLE

You don't see many long-distance cyclists in Brazil. Crazy drivers who only respect vehicles larger than themselves, lots of trucks on the main roads spewing out unfiltered ex-

haust fumes, roads without shoulder room and the threat of theft are just some of the reasons for this. Long-distance cycling in Brazil is not recommended; it's a dangerous thing to do.

If you're still determined to tackle Brazil by bike, go over your bike with a fine-tooth comb before you leave home and fill your repair kit with every imaginable spare part. There are a few decent bike shops in Rio for buying equipment and gear – as well as renting bikes (which averages R$50 per day). See p158 for details.

BOAT

The Amazon region is probably the last great bastion of passenger river travel in the world. Rivers still perform the function of highways throughout much of Amazonia, with passenger-carrying vessels of many shapes and sizes putt-putting up and down every river and creek that has anyone living near it. For information on river travel in the Amazon region, see the boxed text, p614.

Boat is also the only – or at least, the most interesting – way of getting around many parts of the Pantanal and to the many islands and beaches along the Atlantic coast.

BUS

Except in the Amazon Basin, buses are the primary form of long-distance transportation for the majority of Brazilians and many foreign travelers. Bus services are generally excellent. Departure times are usually strictly adhered to, and most of the buses are clean, comfortable and well-serviced Mercedes, Volvos and Scanias.

All major cities are linked by frequent buses – one leaves every 15 minutes from Rio to São Paulo during peak hours – and there are a surprising number of long-distance buses. It is rare that you will have to change buses between two major cities, no matter what the distance. Every big city, and most small ones, has at least one main long-distance bus station, known as a *rodoviária* (pronounced ho-do-vi-*ah*-ri-ya).

Bus service and road conditions vary by region. The South has the most and the best roads. Coastal highways are usually good; while the roads of Amazonia and the *sertão* (backlands of the Northeast) are quite bad. The Quatro Rodas *Atlas Rodoviário*, a very useful road atlas for any traveler, helpfully marks the worst stretches of road with lines of large Xs and classifies them as *estradas precárias*.

Brazil has numerous bus companies and the larger cities have several dozen rival agencies. Before buying a bus ticket from São Paulo or Rio de Janeiro to other destinations, be sure to shop around.

Classes

There are three main classes of long-distance bus. The ordinary *convencional* or *comum* is indeed the most common. It's fairly comfortable and usually has a toilet on board. An *executivo* is more comfortable (often with reclining seats), costs about 25% more and stops less often. A *leito* (overnight sleeper) can cost twice as much as a *comum* and is exceptionally comfortable. It has spacious, fully reclining seats with blankets and pillows, air-con, and more often than not, an attendant serving sandwiches, coffee, soda and *água mineral* (mineral water). If you don't mind missing the scenery, a *leito* can get you there in comfort and save you the additional cost of a hotel room.

With or without toilets, buses generally make pit stops every three or four hours. These stops are great places to meet other passengers, buy bizarre memorabilia, and load up on greasy plates of food.

Air-con on buses is quite strong; carry a light sweater or jacket to keep warm.

Costs

Bus travel throughout Brazil can be expensive; *convencional* fares average from R$6 to R$9 per hour. Sample fares from Rio are as follows: São Paulo (six hours), R$57 *convencional,* R$74 *leito*; Florianópolis (18 hours), R$146 *convencional,* R$179 *leito*; Salvador (25 hours), R$167 *convencional*; Foz do Iguaçu (22 hours), R$185 *convencional*; Belém (52 hours), R$313 *executivo*.

Reservations

Usually you can go down to the bus station and buy a ticket for the next departing bus. If this is not the case (eg in Ouro Prêto), it will be mentioned in the relevant destination chapter. In general, though, it's a good idea to buy a ticket at least a few hours in advance or, if it's convenient, the day before departure. On weekends, holidays and from December to February, advance purchase is always a good idea. It's sometimes possible to buy bus tickets from travel agencies. Although they tack on a small commission, it will save you an extra trip out to the bus station. Ask at local tourist offices for agencies that sell bus tickets.

CAR & MOTORCYCLE

Especially in Rio, the anarchic side of the Brazilian personality emerges from behind the driver's wheel as lane dividers, one-way streets and sidewalks are disregarded. The police take little interest in road safety.

Bringing Your Own Vehicle

All vehicles in Brazil must carry the registration document and proof of insurance. To take a vehicle in or out of Brazil, you might be asked for a *carnet de passage en douane*, which is kind of a vehicle passport, or a *libreta de pasos por aduana*, which is a booklet of customs passes; in practice these are not often required. Contact your local automobile association for details about all documentation.

Driver's License

Your home-country driver's license is valid in Brazil, but because local authorities probably won't be familiar with it, it's a good idea to carry an International Driver's Permit (IDP) as well. This gives police less scope for claiming that you are not driving with a legal license. IDPs are issued by your national motoring association and usually cost the equivalent of about US$10. It is illegal for foreigners to drive motorbikes in Brazil unless they have a Brazilian license.

Fuel & Spare Parts

Ordinary gasoline (called *combustível* or *gasolina*) costs around R$2.80 per liter. Travelers planning to take their own vehicles need to check in advance what spare parts and gasoline are likely to be available. Unleaded gas is not on sale across Brazil, and neither is every little part for your car (Brazil does have plenty of Volkswagen parts).

Hire

A small four-door car with insurance and unlimited kilometers costs around R$100 a day (R$130 with air-con). You can sometimes get discounts for longer rentals.

To rent a car you must be 25 years old (21 with some rental firms, including Avis), have a credit card in your name and a valid driver's license from your home country (not just an IDP).

There is little price variation among the major rental companies, except for the occasional promotional deals. Some agencies have been known to add extra charges onto your credit card long after you've returned the vehicle. This is less likely to happen with more-established agencies.

Insurance

Minimum coverage is always tacked onto the cost of renting, though you can get extra protection (a wise idea) for another R$20 to R$40.

Road Rules & Hazards

Brazil is a dangerous place to drive. Each year, approximately 35,000 people are killed in automobile accidents, with another 500,000 injured. Some roads are especially hazardous, such as the busy highways between Rio and São Paulo. This cult of speed is insatiable. Many drivers are racing fans, finding it impossible to slow down to anyone else's pace.

At night many motorists don't stop at red lights – they merely slow down. This is because of the danger of robbery at stoplights, and it's particularly common in São Paulo. In big cities, keep your windows closed and doors locked when stationary.

Drivers use their horns without restraint, and buses, which have no horns, rev their engines instead. Driving at night is particularly hazardous; other drivers are more likely to be drunk and, at least in the Northeast and the interior, the roads are often poor and unreliable. Poorly banked turns are the norm. To save a bit of fuel, some motorists drive at night with their headlights turned to low-beam or turned off completely.

Brazilian speed bumps are quite prevalent. Always slow down as you enter a town.

Further headaches for drivers in Brazil are posed by poor signposting; impossible one-way systems; tropical rainstorms; drivers overtaking on blind corners; flat tires (common, but there are *borracheiros*, or tire repairers, stationed at frequent intervals along the roads); and, of course, the police pulling you over for bogus moving violations.

For security, choose hotels with off-street parking; most in the midrange and above offer this option.

HITCHHIKING

Hitchhiking is never entirely safe in any country, and is not recommended. Travelers who decide to hitchhike should understand that they are taking a small but potentially serious risk. People who do choose to hitchhike will be safer if they travel in pairs and let someone know where they are planning to go.

Hitchhiking in Brazil, with the possible exception of the Pantanal and a few other areas where it's commonplace among local folk, is difficult. The Portuguese word for 'lift' is *carona*, so ask *'Pode dar carona?'* (Can you give us a lift?). The best way to hitchhike – practically the only way if you want rides – is to ask drivers when they're not in their vehicles, for example by waiting at a gas station or a truck stop. But even this can be difficult.

LOCAL TRANSPORTATION
Bus

Local bus services tend to be pretty good in Brazil. Since most Brazilians take the bus to work every day, municipal buses are usually frequent and their network of routes is comprehensive. Fares range from R$1.50 to R$2.10.

In most city buses, you get on at the front and exit from the back, though occasionally the reverse is true. Usually there's a money collector sitting at a turnstile just inside the entrance.

Crime can be a problem on buses. Don't take valuables onto the buses. See Dangers & Annoyances (p698) in the Directory for more information.

Jumping on a local bus is one of the best ways to get to know a city. With a map and a few dollars you can get an overview of the town.

Metro

Both Rio and São Paulo have excellent metro systems. These are a safe, cheap and efficient way of exploring the city. One-way fares cost around R$2.30.

Taxi

Taxi rides are reasonably priced, and are the best option for getting around cities at night, and across town in a hurry. Taxis in cities usually have meters that start at R$4.30 and rise by something like R$3 per km (more on nights and weekends). Occasionally, the driver will refer to a chart and revise slightly upwards. This reflects recent official hikes in taxi rates and the meter has not yet been adjusted.

In small towns, taxis often don't have meters, and you'll have to arrange a price beforehand.

Some airports and bus stations have a system for you to purchase a fixed-price taxi ticket from a *bilheteria* (ticket office). At a few such places it's much cheaper to go onto the street outside and find a cab that will take you for the meter fare or sometimes even less. In this book we've indicated places where this is the case. If you are carrying valuables, however, the special airport taxi, or a radio taxi, can be a worthwhile investment. These are probably the safest taxis on the road.

If possible, orient yourself before taking a taxi, and keep a map handy in case you find yourself being taken on a wild detour. The worst place to get a cab is where the tourists are. Don't get a cab near one of the expensive hotels. In Rio, for example, walk a block away from the beach at Copacabana to flag down a cab.

TRAIN

Brazil's passenger-train services have been scaled down to almost nothing, supplanted long ago by the personal automobile. There are still over 30,000km of track, but most trains carry only cargo. Rail enthusiasts should not quite despair, however, as there are still a couple of great rides. The outstanding trip goes from Curitiba to Paranaguá (see the boxed text, p318), descending the coastal mountain range with some unforgettable views. The Belo Horizonte–Vitória run (p240), via Santa Bárbara and Sabará, is far more pleasant than the bus ride.

Steam trains in Brazil are affectionately known as Marias Fumaça (Smoking Mary), and a couple of them still run as leisure attractions. One such is the 13km ride from São João del Rei to Tiradentes in Minas Gerais (see the boxed text, p257). Another pleasant short trip, this time by electric train, is the ride through the Serra da Mantiqueira of São Paulo state from Campos do Jordão to Santo Antônio do Pinhal, the highest stretch of track in the country (p311).

Health
Dr David Goldberg

CONTENTS

Prevention is the key to staying healthy while abroad. Travelers who receive the recommended vaccines and follow commonsense precautions usually come away with nothing more dangerous than a little diarrhea.

Medically speaking, Brazil is part of tropical South America, which includes most of the continent except for the southernmost portion. The diseases found in this area are comparable to those found in tropical areas in Africa and Asia. Particularly important are mosquito-borne infections, including malaria, yellow fever and dengue fever, which are not a significant concern in temperate regions.

BEFORE YOU GO

INSURANCE
If your health insurer doesn't cover you for medical expenses incurred abroad, you'll need to get some extra travel insurance. Find out in advance if your travel insurer will make payments directly to providers or reimburse you later for overseas health expenditures.

RECOMMENDED VACCINATIONS
Since most vaccines don't produce immunity until at least two weeks after they're given, visit a physician four to eight weeks before departure. Ask your doctor for an International Certificate of Vaccination (otherwise known as the yellow booklet), which will list all the vaccinations you've received. This is mandatory for countries that require proof of yellow-fever vaccination upon entry, but it's a good idea to carry it wherever you travel.

MEDICAL CHECKLIST
Bring medications in their original containers, clearly labeled. A signed, dated letter from your doctor describing your medical conditions and medications (including their generic names) is a good idea. If carrying syringes or needles, take a physician's letter documenting their medical necessity.

INTERNET RESOURCES
There is a wealth of travel-health advice on the internet. For further information, the Lonely Planet website at www.lonelyplanet .com is a good place to start. The World Health Organization (WHO) publishes a superb book called *International Travel and Health,* which is revised annually and is available online at no cost (www.who.int/ith/). Another website of general interest is the MD Travel Health website at www.mdtravelhealth. com, which provides free, complete travel-health recommendations for every country and is updated daily.

It's usually a good idea to consult your government's travel-health website before departure, if one is available:
Australia www.dfat.gov.au/travel/
Canada www.hc-sc.gc.ca/pphb-dgspsp/tmp-pmv/pub_e .html
UK www.doh.gov.uk/traveladvice/index.htm
US www.cdc.gov/travel/

FURTHER READING
For more detailed information on health matters, see *Healthy Travel Central & South America,* published by Lonely Planet. If you are traveling with children, Lonely Planet's *Travel with Children* provides useful advice. The *ABC of Healthy Travel* by E Walker et al is another valuable resource.

IN TRANSIT

DEEP VEIN THROMBOSIS (DVT)

Blood clots may form in the legs (deep vein thrombosis; DVT) during plane flights, chiefly because of prolonged immobility. The longer the flight, the greater the risk. Though most blood clots are reabsorbed uneventfully, some may break off and travel through the blood vessels to the lungs, where they could cause life-threatening complications.

The chief symptom of DVT is swelling or pain of the foot, ankle or calf, usually but not always on just one side. When a blood clot travels to the lungs, it may cause chest pain and difficulty breathing. Travelers with any of these symptoms should seek medical attention immediately.

To prevent DVT on long flights you should walk about the cabin, perform isometric compressions of the leg muscles (ie contract leg muscles while sitting), drink lots of fluids, and avoid alcohol and tobacco.

JET LAG & MOTION SICKNESS

Jet lag is common when crossing more than five time zones and can result in insomnia, fatigue, malaise or nausea. To avoid jet lag try drinking plenty of (nonalcoholic) fluids and eating light meals. Upon arrival, get exposure to natural sunlight and readjust your schedule (for meals, sleep etc) as soon as possible.

Antihistamines such as dimenhydrinate (Dramamine) and meclizine (Antivert, Bonine) are usually the first choice for treating motion sickness. Their main side effect is drowsiness. An herbal alternative is ginger, which works like a charm for some people.

IN BRAZIL

AVAILABILITY & COST OF HEALTH CARE

For an ambulance in Brazil, call ☎ 192, or an emergency number (listed following).

Good medical care is available in the larger cities, but may be difficult to find in rural areas. Medical care in Brazil may be extremely expensive. Most doctors and hospitals expect payment in cash, regardless of whether you have travel-health insurance.

The US embassy website at www.embai xada-americana.org.br has an extensive list of physicians, dentists, pharmacists, laboratories and emergency services. If you're pregnant, be sure to check this site before departure to find the name of one or two obstetricians in the area you'll be visiting, just in case.

The **Einstein Hospital** (☎ emergencies 55-11-3747 0200, ambulance & air ambulance 0xx11-3747 1000/1100; Av Albert Einstein 627, Morumbi) in São Paulo is used by expatriates throughout Brazil, including US government personnel. English is also spoken at **Hospital Sírio-Libânes** (Map pp292-3; ☎ information 0xx11-2344 8877, ambulance 0xx11-826 0111 or 926 0400; Rua da Adma Jafet 91, Bela Vista) in São Paulo.

If you develop a medical emergency while in Rio, you can call **Hospital Samaritano** (☎ 0xx21-2537 9722; Rua Bambina 98, Botafogo), **Clínica São Vicente** (☎ 0xx21-2529 4422; Rua João Borges 204, Gávea), **Hospital Ipanema** (Map pp138-9; ☎ 0xx21-3111 2300; Rua Antônio Parreiras 67, Ipanema), **Miguel Couto Hospital** (Map pp138-9; ☎ 0xx21-2274 2121; Av Bartolomeu Mitre 1108, Gávea) or **Pró-Cardíaco** (☎ information 0xx21-2537 4242, ambulance 0xx21-2527 6060; Rua General Polidoro 192, Botafogo) – the latter specializes in cardiac emergencies.

If you develop a life-threatening medical problem, you'll probably want to be evacuated to a country with state-of-the-art medical care. Since this may cost tens of thousands of dollars, be sure you have insurance to cover this before you depart. You can find a list of medical-evacuation and travel-insurance companies on the US State Department website at www.travel.state.gov/medical.html.

Each Brazilian pharmacy has a licensed pharmacist. Most are well supplied. Many medications that require prescriptions in the US are available over the counter in Brazil. If you're taking medication on a regular basis, be sure you know its generic (scientific) name, since many pharmaceuticals go under different names in Brazil. Droga Raia is a large pharmacy chain; many stores are open 24 hours.

INFECTIOUS DISEASES

Cholera

Cholera is an intestinal infection acquired through ingestion of contaminated food or water. The main symptom is profuse, watery diarrhea, which may be so severe that it causes life-threatening dehydration. The key treatment is drinking oral rehydration solution. Antibiotics are also given (tetracycline or doxycycline), though quinolone antibiotics such as ciprofloxacin and levofloxacin are also effective.

Cholera sometimes occurs in Brazil, but it's rare among travelers. Cholera vaccine is no longer required, and is in fact no longer available in some countries, including the US, because the old vaccine was relatively ineffective and caused side effects. There are new vaccines that are safer and more effective, but they're not available in many countries and are only recommended for those at particularly high risk.

Dengue

Dengue fever is a viral infection found throughout South America. A large outbreak of dengue was reported from the Rio area in early 2002, ultimately affecting almost 800,000 people. Dengue is transmitted by aedes mosquitoes, which bite preferentially during the daytime and are usually found close to human habitations, often indoors. They breed primarily in artificial water containers, such as jars, barrels, cans, cisterns, metal drums, plastic containers and discarded tires. As a result, dengue is especially common in densely populated, urban environments.

Dengue usually causes flulike symptoms, including fever, muscle aches, joint pains, headaches, nausea and vomiting, often followed by a rash. The body aches may be quite uncomfortable, but most cases resolve uneventfully in a few days. Severe cases usually occur in children under the age of 15 who are experiencing their second dengue infection.

There is no treatment for dengue fever except to take analgesics such as acetaminophen/paracetamol (Tylenol) and drink plenty of fluids. Severe cases may require hospitalization for intravenous fluids and supportive care. There is no vaccine. The cornerstone of prevention is protection against insect bites (see p730).

Hepatitis A

Hepatitis A is the second most common travel-related infection (after traveler's diarrhea). It's a viral infection of the liver that is usually acquired by ingestion of contaminated water, food or ice, though it may also be acquired by direct contact with infected persons. The illness occurs throughout the world, but the incidence is higher in developing nations. Symptoms may include fever, malaise, jaundice, nausea, vomiting and abdominal pain. Most cases resolve without complications, though hepatitis A occasionally causes severe liver damage. There is no treatment.

The vaccine for hepatitis A is extremely safe and highly effective. If you get a booster six to 12 months later, it lasts for at least 10 years.

You really should get it before you go to Brazil or any other developing nation. Because the safety of hepatitis A vaccine has not been established for pregnant women or children under the age of two, they should instead be given a gamma globulin injection.

Hepatitis B

Like hepatitis A, hepatitis B is a liver infection that occurs worldwide but is more common in developing nations. Unlike hepatitis A, the disease is usually acquired by sexual contact or by exposure to infected blood, generally through blood transfusions or contaminated needles. The vaccine is recommended only for long-term travelers (on the road more than six months) who expect to live in rural areas or have close physical contact with the local population. Additionally, the vaccine is recommended for anyone who anticipates sexual contact with the local inhabitants or a need for medical, dental or other treatments while abroad, especially transfusions or injections.

Hepatitis B vaccine is safe and highly effective. A total of three injections, however, is necessary to establish full immunity. Several countries added hepatitis B vaccine to the list of routine childhood immunizations in the 1980s, so many young adults are already protected.

Malaria

Malaria occurs in every South American country except Chile, Uruguay and the Falkland Islands. It's transmitted by mosquito bites, usually between dusk and dawn. The main symptoms are high spiking fevers, which may be accompanied by chills, sweats, headache, body aches, weakness, vomiting or diarrhea. Severe cases may involve the central nervous system and lead to seizures, confusion, coma and death.

Taking malaria pills is strongly recommended for forested areas within the nine states of the 'Legal Amazonia' region, including Acre, Amapá, Amazonas, Maranhão (western part), Mato Grosso (northern part), Pará (except Belém city), Rondônia, Roraima and Tocantins, and for urban areas within this region, including the cities of Porto Velho, Boa Vista, Macapá, Manaus, Santarém and Maraba. Transmission is greatest in remote jungle areas where mining, lumbering and agriculture occur and which have been settled for less than five years. Malaria risk is negligible outside the states of 'Legal Amazonia.'

Travelers visiting only the coastal states from the horn to the Uruguay border and Iguaçu Falls do not need prophylaxis.

There is a choice of three malaria pills, all of which work about equally well. Mefloquine (Lariam) is taken once weekly in a dosage of 250mg, starting one to two weeks before arrival and continuing through the trip and for four weeks after return. The problem is that a certain percentage of people (the number is debatable) develop neuropsychiatric side effects, which may range from mild to severe. Atovaquone/proguanil (Malarone) is a newly approved combination pill taken once daily with food starting two days before arrival and continuing through the trip and for seven days after departure. Side effects are typically mild. Doxycycline is a third alternative, but it may cause an exaggerated sunburn reaction.

In general, Malarone seems to cause fewer side effects than Lariam and is becoming more popular. The chief disadvantage is that it has to be taken daily. For longer trips, it's probably worth trying Lariam; for shorter trips, Malarone will be the drug of choice for most people.

Protecting yourself against mosquito bites is just as important as taking malaria pills (see p730), since none of the pills is 100% effective.

If you may not have access to medical care while traveling, you should bring along additional pills for emergency self-treatment, which you should take if you can't reach a doctor and you develop symptoms that suggest malaria, such as high spiking fevers. One option is to take four tablets of Malarone once daily for three days. Malarone should not be used for treatment, however, if you're already taking it for prevention. An alternative is to take 650mg of quinine three times daily and 100mg of doxycycline twice daily for one week. If you start self-medication, see a doctor at the earliest possible opportunity.

If you develop a fever after returning home, see a physician, as malaria symptoms may not occur for months.

Plague

The plague continues to occur among animals in the drier northern and eastern states, from Ceará south to Minas Gerais, but human cases are uncommon. Most occur in Bahia state. The infection is usually transmitted to humans by the bite of rodent fleas, typically when rodents die off. Symptoms include fever, chills, muscle aches and malaise, associated with the development of an acutely swollen, exquisitely painful lymph node, known as a bubo, most often in the groin. Most travelers are at extremely low risk of the plague. But if there's a chance you will have contact with rodents or their fleas, especially in the above areas, you should bring along a bottle of doxycycline, to be taken prophylactically during periods of exposure. Those less than eight years old or allergic to doxycycline should take trimethoprim-sulfamethoxazole instead. In addition, you should avoid areas containing rodent burrows or nests, never handle sick or dead animals, and follow the guidelines in this chapter for protecting yourself from insect bites (see p730).

Rabies

Rabies is a viral infection of the brain and spinal cord that is almost always fatal. The rabies virus is carried in the saliva of infected animals and is typically transmitted through an animal bite, though contamination of any break in the skin with infected saliva may result in rabies. Rabies occurs in all South American countries. In Brazil, most cases are reported from the extreme western Minas Gerais state and northeastern areas. Dog bites are the most common cause, but bites from other animals can also lead to rabies. In 2004 several dozen people in the Amazon died from rabies after being bitten by vampire bats.

Rabies vaccine is safe, but a full series requires three injections and is quite expensive. Those at high risk of rabies, such as animal handlers and spelunkers (cave explorers), should certainly get the vaccine. In addition, those at lower risk of animal bites should consider asking for the vaccine if they may be traveling to remote areas and may not have access to appropriate medical care if needed. The treatment for a possibly rabid bite consists of rabies vaccine with rabies immune globulin. It's effective, but must be given promptly. Most travelers don't need rabies vaccine.

All animal bites and scratches must be promptly and thoroughly cleansed with large amounts of soap and water and local health authorities contacted to determine whether or not further treatment is necessary (see p730).

Typhoid

Typhoid fever is caused by ingestion of food or water contaminated by a species of salmonella known as *Salmonella typhi*. Fever occurs in virtually all cases. Other symptoms may include headache, malaise, muscle aches, dizziness, loss of appetite, nausea and abdominal pain. Either diarrhea or constipation may occur. Possible complications include intestinal perforation, intestinal bleeding, confusion, delirium or (rarely) coma.

Unless you expect to take all your meals in major hotels and restaurants, typhoid vaccine is a good idea. It's usually given orally, but is also available as an injection. Neither vaccine is approved for use in children under the age of two.

The drug of choice for typhoid fever is usually a quinolone antibiotic such as ciprofloxacin (Cipro) or levofloxacin (Levaquin), which many travelers carry for treatment of traveler's diarrhea. However, if you self-treat for typhoid fever, you may also need to self-treat for malaria, since the symptoms of the two diseases may be indistinguishable.

Yellow Fever

Yellow fever is a life-threatening viral infection transmitted by mosquitoes in forested areas. The illness begins with flulike symptoms, which may include fever, chills, headache, muscle aches, backache, loss of appetite, nausea and vomiting. These symptoms usually subside in a few days, but one person in six enters a second, toxic phase characterized by recurrent fever, vomiting, listlessness, jaundice, kidney failure, and hemorrhage, leading to death in up to half of the cases. There is no treatment except for supportive care.

Yellow fever vaccine is strongly recommended for all travelers to Brazil, except those visiting only Rio de Janeiro, São Paulo, the central eastern area to the coast, and the coastal areas south of São Luís. Major outbreaks have recently been reported from Minas Gerais state, and additional cases occur elsewhere. Fatal cases of yellow fever among travelers who failed to get vaccinated are periodically reported. For an up-to-date map showing the distribution of yellow fever in Brazil, go to the Centers for Disease Control (CDC) website at www.cdc.gov/travel/diseases/maps/yellowfever_map2.htm.

Proof of vaccination is required from all travelers arriving from a yellow fever–infected country in Africa or the Americas.

Yellow fever vaccine is given only in approved yellow fever vaccination centers, which provide validated International Certificates of Vaccination. The vaccine should be given at least 10 days before any potential exposure to yellow fever and remains effective for approximately 10 years. Reactions to the vaccine are generally mild and may include headaches, muscle aches, low-grade fevers or discomfort at the injection site. Severe, life-threatening reactions have been described but are extremely rare. In general, the risk of becoming ill from the vaccine is far less than the risk of becoming ill from yellow fever, and you're strongly encouraged to get the vaccine.

Taking measures to protect yourself from mosquito bites (see p730) is an essential part of preventing yellow fever.

Other Infectious Diseases

SCHISTOSOMIASIS

This is a parasitic infection acquired by skin exposure to contaminated fresh water; it occurs in almost all states of the Northeast and two states (Minas Gerais and Espírito Santo) in the Southeast. When traveling in these areas, you should avoid swimming, wading, bathing or washing in bodies of fresh water, including lakes, ponds, streams and rivers. Salt water and chlorinated pools carry no risk of schistosomiasis.

TOXOPLASMOSIS

This has been reported from various areas, including northwestern Paraná state and northern Rio de Janeiro state. Most cases have been related to contaminated water supplies. Pregnant women should be particularly careful to avoid drinking unfiltered water, since toxoplasmosis may cause severe fetal illness. In nonpregnant people with normal immune systems, most cases of toxoplasmosis clear uneventfully.

CHAGAS' DISEASE

This parasitic infection is transmitted by triatomine insects (reduviid bugs), which inhabit crevices in the walls and roofs of substandard housing in South and Central America. In Brazil, the disease has been eliminated in every state except Bahia and Tocantins through an aggressive program of insecticide spraying.

The triatomine insect lays its feces on human skin as it bites, usually at night. A person becomes infected when they unknowingly rub the feces into the bite wound or any other open sore. Chagas' disease is extremely rare in travelers. If you sleep in a poorly constructed house, especially one made of mud, adobe or thatch, however, you should be sure to protect yourself with a bed net and a good insecticide.

LEISHMANIASIS

Leishmaniasis occurs in the mountains and jungles of all South American countries except for Chile, Uruguay and the Falkland Islands. The infection is transmitted by sand flies, which are about one-third the size of mosquitoes. In Brazil, leishmaniasis has been reported from suburban areas in Rio de Janeiro and São Paulo. Most cases are limited to the skin, causing slowly growing ulcers over exposed parts of the body. The more severe type of leishmaniasis, which disseminates to the bone marrow, liver and spleen, occurs mainly in the Northeast. Leishmaniasis may be particularly severe in those with HIV. There is no vaccine. To protect yourself from sand flies, follow the same precautions as for mosquitoes (see p730), except that netting must be made of a finer mesh (at least 18 holes per 2.54cm or to the linear inch).

HANTAVIRUS PULMONARY SYNDROME

A rapidly progressive, life-threatening infection, hantavirus is acquired through exposure to the excretions of wild rodents. Most cases occur in those people who live in rodent-infested dwellings in rural areas. In Brazil, hantavirus infections are reported from the states of Minas Gerais, Santa Catarina and São Paulo.

ECHINOCOCCUS

This is a parasite that infects the liver, usually in people who work with sheep. Echinococcus infections occur chiefly in the southernmost part of the country.

BRUCELLOSIS

Brucellosis is an infection of domestic and wild animals that may be transmitted to humans through animal contact or by consumption of unpasteurized dairy products from infected animals. In Brazil, most human cases are related to infected cattle. Symptoms include fever, malaise, depression, loss of appetite, headache, muscle aches and back pain. Complications may include arthritis, hepatitis, meningitis and endocarditis (heart-valve infection).

FASCIOLIASIS

This is a parasitic infection that is typically acquired by eating contaminated watercress grown in sheep-raising areas. Early symptoms may include fever, nausea, vomiting and painful enlargement of the liver.

ONCHOCERCIASIS

Also known as river blindness, onchocerciasis is caused by a roundworm that may invade the eye, leading to blindness. The infection is transmitted by black flies, which breed along the banks of rapidly flowing rivers and streams. In Brazil, onchocerciasis is reported among the indigenous Yanomami population living along the Venezuelan border, as well as in nearby tribes and non-Indians visiting the area. Most cases occur near swift-flowing streams in densely forested highlands.

VENEZUELAN EQUINE ENCEPHALITIS

Transmitted by mosquitoes and causing brain inflammation, this form of encephalitis occurs sporadically.

'CATERPILLAR PLAGUE'

Cases were reported from the Amazon delta region between 1983 and 1985 and from southern Brazil in 1995. The disease is caused by contact with the larvae (caterpillars) of the butterfly *Lamonia achelous*, which secrete venom through their skins. The illness is characterized by high fever, bleeding from the nose and ears, kidney failure, and death. The caterpillar is found from December through March. The adult and pupal forms are harmless.

HIV/AIDS

HIV/AIDS is a big problem in Brazil. An estimated 600,000 Brazilians carry the virus. Be sure to use condoms for all sexual encounters.

TRAVELER'S DIARRHEA

Traveler's diarrhea is defined as the passage of more than three watery bowel actions within 24 hours, plus at least one other symptom such as fever, cramps, nausea, vomiting or feeling generally unwell. In over 80% of cases, traveler's diarrhea is caused by a bacteria and therefore responds promptly to treatment

HEALTH

with antibiotics. Treatment with antibiotics will depend on your situation – how sick you are, how quickly you need to get better, where you are etc.

To prevent diarrhea, avoid tap water unless it has been boiled, filtered or chemically disinfected (iodine tablets); be wary of dairy products that may contain unpasteurized milk; and be highly selective when eating food from street vendors.

Treatment consists of staying well hydrated. Drink plenty of fluids, preferably an oral rehydration solution like Gastrolite. Coconut water, which is loaded with electrolytes, is also good for rehydration. Antibiotics such as Norfloxacin, Ciprofloxacin or Azithromycin will kill the bacteria quickly.

Loperamide is just a 'stopper' and doesn't get to the cause of the problem. It can be helpful, for example, on a long bus ride. Don't take Loperamide if you have a fever or blood in your stools. Seek medical attention quickly if you do not respond to an appropriate antibiotic.

If diarrhea is bloody, persists for more than 72 hours or is accompanied by fever, shaking chills or severe abdominal pain, you should seek medical attention.

ENVIRONMENTAL HAZARDS
Animal Bites

Do not attempt to pet, handle or feed any animal, with the exception of domestic animals known to be free of any infectious disease. Most animal injuries are directly related to a person's attempt to touch or feed the animal.

Any bite or scratch from a mammal, including bats, should be promptly and thoroughly cleansed with large amounts of soap and water, followed by application of an antiseptic such as iodine or alcohol. The local health authorities should be contacted immediately for possible post-exposure rabies treatment, whether or not you've been immunized against rabies. It may also be advisable to start an antibiotic, since wounds caused by animal bites and scratches frequently become infected. One of the newer quinolones, such as levofloxacin (Levaquin), which many travelers carry in case of diarrhea, would be an appropriate choice.

Insect Bites & Stings

To prevent mosquito bites, wear long sleeves, long pants, hats and shoes (rather than sandals). Bring along a good insect repellent,

preferably one containing DEET, which should be applied to exposed skin and clothing, but not to eyes, mouth, cuts, wounds or irritated skin. Products containing lower concentrations of DEET are as effective, but for shorter periods of time. In general, adults and children over the age of 12 should use preparations containing 25% to 35% DEET, which usually last about six hours. Children between two and 12 years of age should use preparations containing no more than 10% DEET, applied sparingly, which will usually last about three hours. Neurologic toxicity has been reported from DEET, especially in children, but appears to be extremely uncommon and generally related to overuse. DEET-containing compounds should not be used on children under the age of two.

Insect repellents containing certain botanical products, including oil of eucalyptus and soybean oil, are effective but last only 1½ to two hours. DEET-containing repellents are preferable for areas where there is a high risk of malaria or yellow fever. Products based on citronella are not effective.

For additional protection, you can apply permethrin to clothing, shoes, tents and bed nets. Permethrin treatments are safe and remain effective for at least two weeks, even when items are laundered. Permethrin should not be applied directly to skin.

Don't sleep with the window open unless there is a screen in the windowframe. If sleeping outdoors or in accommodations that allow entry of mosquitoes, use a bed net, preferably treated with permethrin, with edges tucked in under the mattress. The mesh size should be smaller than 1.5mm. If the sleeping area is not otherwise protected, use a mosquito coil, which will fill the room with insecticide throughout the night. Repellent-impregnated wristbands are not effective.

Snake Bites

Snakes and leeches are a hazard in some areas of South America. In the event of a venomous snake bite, place the victim at rest, keep the bitten area immobilized and move the victim immediately to the nearest medical facility. Avoid tourniquets, which are no longer recommended.

Sun

To protect yourself from excessive sun exposure, you should stay out of the midday sun, wear sunglasses and a wide-brimmed sun hat, and apply sunscreen with SPF15 or higher, with both UVA and UVB protection. Sunscreen should be generously applied to all exposed parts of the body approximately 30 minutes before sun exposure and should be reapplied after swimming or vigorous activity. Travelers should also drink plenty of fluids and avoid strenuous exercise when the temperature is high.

Water

Tap water in Brazil is not safe to drink. Vigorous boiling for one minute is the most effective means of water purification. At altitudes greater than 2000m (6500ft), boil for three minutes.

Another option is to disinfect water with iodine pills. Instructions are usually enclosed and should be carefully followed. Or you can add 2% tincture of iodine to one quart or liter of water (five drops to clear water, 10 drops to cloudy water) and let stand for 30 minutes. If the water is cold, longer times may be required. The taste of iodinated water may be improved by adding vitamin C (ascorbic acid). Iodinated water should not be consumed for more than a few weeks. Pregnant women, those with a history of thyroid disease, and those allergic to iodine should not drink iodinated water.

A number of water filters are on the market. Those with smaller pores (reverse-osmosis filters) provide the broadest protection, but they are relatively large and are readily plugged by debris. Those with somewhat larger pores (microstrainer filters) are ineffective against viruses, although they remove other organisms. Manufacturers' instructions must be carefully followed.

TRAVELING WITH CHILDREN

In general, children under the age of nine months should not be brought to areas where yellow fever occurs, since the vaccine is not safe in this age group.

When traveling with young children, be particularly careful about what you allow them to eat and drink, because diarrhea can be especially dangerous in this age group and because the vaccines for hepatitis A and typhoid fever are not approved for use in children who are under the age of two years.

The two main malaria medications, Lariam and Malarone, may be given to children, but insect repellents must be applied in lower concentrations.

TRAVELING WHILE PREGNANT

You can find an English-speaking obstetrician near your location in Brazil by going to the US embassy website at www.embixada -americana.org.br. However, medical facilities will probably not be comparable to those in your home country. It's safer to avoid travel to Brazil late in pregnancy, so that you don't have to risk delivering there.

If pregnant, it's preferable to avoid areas where yellow fever occurs, since the vaccine is not safe during pregnancy.

For malaria prevention, mefloquine (Lariam) is the safest during pregnancy.

HEALTH

Language

CONTENTS

Brazilians speak Portuguese, which looks similar to Spanish on paper but sounds completely different. You'll do quite well if you speak Spanish in Brazil. Brazilians will understand you, but you won't get much of what they say – so don't think studying Portuguese is a waste of time. Listen to language tapes and develop an ear for Portuguese – it's a beautiful-sounding language.

When the Portuguese arrived in 1500, an estimated 700 indigenous languages were spoken by Brazil's Indian peoples. About 180 survive, 130 of them being considered endangered because they have fewer than 600 speakers. These indigenous languages, together with the various idioms and dialects spoken by the Africans brought in as slaves, extensively changed the Portuguese spoken by the early settlers.

Along with Portuguese, the Tupi-Guarani language, simplified and given a written form by the Jesuits, became a common language that was understood by the majority of the population. It was spoken by the general public until the middle of the 18th century, but its usage diminished with the great number of Portuguese gold-rush immigrants and a royal proclamation in 1757 prohibiting its use. With the expulsion of the Jesuits in 1759, Portuguese was established as the national language.

Nevertheless, many words remain from Indian and African languages. From Tupi-Guarani come lots of place names (such as Guanabara, Carioca, Tijuca and Niterói), animal names (such as piranha, *capivara* and *urubu*) and plant names (such as *mandioca, abacaxí, caju* and *jacarandá*). Words from the African dialects, mainly those from Nigeria and Angola, are used in Afro-Brazilian religious ceremonies (eg Orixá, Exú and Iansã), cooking (eg *vatapá, acarajé* and *abará*) and in general conversation (eg samba, mocambo and moleque).

Brazilians are easy to befriend, but unfortunately the vast majority of them speak little or no English. This is changing, however, as practically all Brazilians in school are learning English. All the same, don't count on finding an English speaker, especially out of the cities. The more Portuguese you speak, the more rewarding your stay will be.

For information on Portuguese language courses in Brazil, see p698. For words and phrases for use when dining, see p109.

BODY LANGUAGE

Brazilians accompany their speech with a rich body language, a sort of parallel dialogue. The thumbs up *tudo bem* is used as a greeting, or to signify 'OK' or 'Thank you.' The authoritative *não-não* finger-wagging is most intimidating when done right under someone's nose, but it's not a threat.

The sign of the *figa,* a thumb inserted between the first and second fingers of a clenched fist, is a symbol of good luck that has been derived from an African sexual charm. It's more commonly used as jewelry than in body language. To indicate *rápido* (speed and haste), thumb and middle finger snap while rapidly shaking the wrist – a gesture it often seems only Brazilians can make. If you don't want something (*não quero),* slap the back of your hands as if ridding yourself of the entire affair. Touching a finger to the lateral corner of the eye means 'I'm wise to you.'

BOOKS

An excellent pocket phrasebook is Lonely Planet's *Brazilian Portuguese Phrasebook*. In addition to covering most travel situations, the book will also provide much help in social situations. It includes an easy-to-follow grammar guide, a comprehensive section on food and dining, plus a two-way dictionary.

Although Spanish and French take up far more shelf space at most bookstores, there's a growing selection of Portuguese language learning material. One of the best short-term introductions is *Portuguese Complete Course: Basic-Intermediate* by Living Language. In addition to an English-Portuguese dictionary, the kit includes a course book with 40 lessons and three audio CDs. The lessons are easy to follow and designed to get you speaking quickly.

For grammar, pick up a copy of *Essential Portuguese Grammar* by Alexander da Prista. Although it's old (published in 1966), this slim volume is still a gem, with clear and concise explanations of grammatical structures and the language in practice.

If you'd like to delve deeper into the language, and have the time to dedicate to a challenging self-study course, try the US Foreign Service Institute (FSI) series, which comes in two volumes. The first volume, *Mastering Portuguese,* includes 12 90-minute cassettes and a textbook that covers pronunciation, verb tenses and essential nouns and adjectives. Volume 2 is harder to find, but polishes your skills even more with 22 tapes and an additional textbook.

Combine these with a few old bossa nova albums, recent Brazilian cinema (seek out any Walter Salles or Fernando Meirelles film) and some Jorge Amado novels, and you're ready for the next level of instruction – on the streets and beaches of Brazil.

PRONUNCIATION

Brazilian Portuguese pronunciation can be tricky for the uninitiated. The big shocker is that, generally, an **r** is pronounced like an 'h': 'Rio' becomes 'hee-oh,' the currency is pronounced 'hay-ow' etc. In the same spirit of fun, a **t** (or **d**) followed by a vowel is pronounced 'ch' as in 'church' or 'j' as in 'judge', so the word *restaurante* is pronounced approximately 'hess-to-roch.'

The letter **ç** is pronounced like an English 's'; the letter **x** as the 'sh' as in 'ship.' So 'Iguaçu' is 'ig-wa-soo' and 'Caxambu' 'ka-sham-boo.'

You'll know you've mastered Brazilian Portuguese pronunciation when you've successfully ordered one of the country's more popular beers, *Antarctica* (that's right, you say 'ant-okt-chee-kah'!).

Within Brazil, accents, dialects and slang (*gíria*) vary regionally. The Carioca inserts the 'sh' sound in place of **s**. The *gaúcho* speaks a Spanish-sounding Portuguese, the Baiano (from Bahia) speaks slowly, and the accents of the Cearense (from Ceará) are often incomprehensible to outsiders.

Vowel Sounds

a	as the 'u' in 'run,' eg *camera*
a	as in 'father,' eg *padre*
ai	as in 'aisle,' eg *pai*
aw	as in 'saw,' eg *nó*
ay	as in 'day,' eg *lei*
e	as in 'bet,' eg *cedo*
ee	as in 'bee,' eg *fino*
o	as in 'go,' eg *gato*
oo	as in 'moon,' eg *azul*
ow	as in 'how,' eg *saudades*
oy	as in 'boy,' eg *noite*

Nasal Vowels

A characteristic feature of Brazilian Portuguese is the use of nasal vowels. Nasal vowels are pronounced as if you're trying to produce the sound through your nose rather than your mouth. English also has nasal vowels to some extent – when you say 'sing' in English, the 'i' is nasalized by the 'ng.' In Brazilian Portuguese, written vowels that have a nasal consonant after them (**m** or **n**), or a tilde over them (eg **ã**), will be nasal. In our pronunciation guide, we've used 'ng' after nasal vowels to indicate a nasal sound.

Consonants

The following lists a few of the letters used in our pronunciation guide that represent the trickier Portuguese consonant sounds.

ly	as the 'lli' in 'million'
ny	as in 'canyon'
r	as in 'run'
rr	as in 'run' but stronger and rolled
zh	as the 's' in 'pleasure'

Word Stress

Word stress generally occurs on the second last syllable of a word, though there are exceptions. When a word ends in -r or is pronounced with a nasalized vowel, the stress falls on the last syllable. Another exception is that if a written vowel has an accent marked over it, the stress falls on the syllable containing that vowel.

In our transliteration system, we have indicated the stressed syllable with italics.

GENDER

Portuguese has masculine and feminine forms of nouns and adjectives. Alternative endings appear separated by a slash, the masculine form first. Generally, 'o' indicates masculine and 'a' indicates feminine.

ACCOMMODATIONS

I'm looking for a ...
Estou procurando por ...   es·to pro·koo·rang·do porr ...
Where is a ...?
Onde tem ...?   on·de teng ...
  room
  um quarto   oom kwarr·to
  bed and breakfast
  uma pensão   oo·ma pen·sowng
  camping ground
  um local para   oom lo·kow pa·ra
    acampamento   a·kam·pa·meng·to
  guesthouse
  uma hospedaria   oo·ma os·pe·da·ree·a
  hotel
  um hotel   oom o·tel
  youth hostel
  um albergue   oom ow·berr·ge
    da juventude   da zhoo·veng·too·de

I'd like a ... room.
Eu gostaria um   e·oo gos·ta·ree·a oom
quarto de ...   kwarr·to de ...
  double
  casal   ka·zow
  single
  solteiro   sol·tay·ro
  twin
  duplo   doo·plo

What's the address?
Qual é o endereço?   kwow e o en·de·re·so
Do you have a ... room?
Tem um quarto de ...?   teng oom kwarr·to de ...
For (three) nights.
Para (três) noites.   pa·ra (tres) noy·tes

MAKING A RESERVATION
(for phone or written requests)

To ...   Para ...
From ...   De ...
Date   Data
I'd like to book ...   Eu gostaria de fazer uma
    reserva ... (see the list
    under 'Accommodations'
    for bed/room options)
in the name of ...   no nome de ...
for the nights of ...   para os dias ...
from ... to ...   de ... até ...
credit card ...   cartão de credito ...
  number   número
  expiry date   data de vencimento

Please confirm ...   Por favor confirme ...
  availability   a disponibilidade
  price   o preço

Does it include breakfast?
Inclui café da manhã?   eeng·kloo·ee ka·fe da ma·nyang
May I see it?
Posso ver?   po·so verr
I'll take it.
Eu fico com ele.   e·oo fee·ko kom e·lee
I don't like it.
Não gosto.   nowng gos·to
I'm leaving now.
Estou indo embora   es·to een·do em·bo·ra
agora.   a·go·ra

How much is it per ...?
Quanto custa por ...?   kwan·to koos·ta porr ...
  night
  noite   noy·te
  person
  pessoa   pe·so·a
  week
  semana   se·ma·na

Can I pay ...?
Posso pagar com ...?   po·so pa·garr kom ...
  by credit card
  cartão de crédito   karr·towng de kre·dee·to
  by traveler's check
  traveler cheque   tra·ve·ler she·kee

CONVERSATION & ESSENTIALS

Hello.
Olá.   o·la
Hi.
Oi.   oy

Good day.
Bom dia.   bong *dee*·a
Good evening.
Boa noite.   bo·a *noy*·te
See you later.
Até mais tarde.   a·*te* mais *tarr*·de
Goodbye.
Tchau.   chau
How are you?
Como vai?   *ko*·mo vai
Fine, and you?
Bem, e você?   beng e vo·*se*
I'm pleased to meet you.
Prazer em conhecê-lo.   pra·*zerr* eng ko·nye·*se*·lo (m)
Prazer em conhecê-la.   pra·*zerr* eng ko·nye·*se*·la (f)
Yes.
Sim.   seem
No.
Não.   nowng
Please.
Por favor.   por fa·*vorr*
Thank you (very much).
(Muito) obrigado/   (mween·to) o·bree·*ga*·do/
obrigada. (m/f)   o·bree·*ga*·da
You're welcome.
De nada.   de *na*·da
Excuse me.
Com licença   kom lee·*seng*·sa
Sorry.
Desculpa.   des·*kool*·pa
What's your name?
Qual é o seu nome?   kwow e o *se*·oo *no*·me
My name is ...
Meu nome é ...   *me*·oo *no*·me e ...
Where are you from?
De onde você é?   de *ong*·de vo·*se* e
I'm from ...
Eu sou (da/do/de) ...   e·oo so (da/do/de)
May I take a photo (of you)?
Posso tirar uma foto   po so tee *rarr* oo ma *fo* to
(de você)?   (de vo se)

DIRECTIONS
Where is ...?
Onde fica ...?   on·de *fee*·ka ...
Can you show me (on the map)?
Você poderia me   o·*se* po·de·*ree*·a me
mostrar (no mapa)?   mos·*trarr* (no *ma*·pa)
What's the address?
Qual é o endereço?   kwow e o en·de·*re*·so
How far is it?
Qual a distância   kwow a dees·*tan*·see·a
daqui?   da·*kee*
How do I get there?
Como é que eu chego lá?   *ko*·mo e ke *e*·oo *she*·go la

Turn ...	Vire ...	vee·re ...
at the corner	à esquina	a es·*kee*·na
at the traffic lights	no sinal de trânsito	no see·*now* de tran·zee·to
left	à esquerda	a es·*kerr*·da
right	à direita	a dee·*ray*·ta
here	aqui	a·*kee*
there	lá	la
near ...	perto ...	*perr*·to ...
straight ahead	em frente	eng *freng*·te

LANGUAGE

north	norte	norr·te
south	sul	sool
east	leste	les·te
west	oeste	o·es·te

HEALTH

I'm ill.
Estou doente.   es·to do·eng·te

I need a doctor (who speaks English).
Eu preciso de um médico   e·oo pre·see·zo de oom me·dee·ko
(que fale inglês).   (ke fa·le een·gles)

It hurts here.
Aqui dói.   a·kee doy

I've been vomiting.
Estive vomitando.   e·steev vo·mee·tan·do

(I think) I'm pregnant.
(Acho que) estou grávida.   (a·sho ke) es·to gra·vee·da

Where's the nearest ...?
Onde fica ...is perto?   on·de fee·ka ... mais perr·to
   (night) chemist
   a farmácia (noturna)   a farr·ma·see·a (no·toor·na)
   dentist
   o dentista   o deng·tees·ta
   doctor
   o médico   o me·dee·ko
   hospital
   o hospital   o os·pee·tow
   medical centre
   a clínica médica   a klee·nee·ka me·dee·ka

I feel ...
Estou me sentindo ...   es·to me seng·teeng·do ...
   dizzy
   tonto/tonta (m/f)   tong·to/tong·ta
   nauseous
   enjoado/enjoada (m/f)   eng·zho·a·do/en·zho·a·da

asthma	asma	as·ma
diarrhea	diarréia	dee·a·he·ee·a
fever	febre	fe·bre
nausea	náusea	now·ze·a
pain	dor	dorr

I'm allergic to ...
Tenho alergia à ...   te·nyo a·lerr·zhee·a a ...
   antibiotics
   antibióticos   an·tee·bee·o·tee·kos
   aspirin
   aspirina   as·pee·ree·na
   bees
   abelhas   a·be·lyas
   peanuts
   amendoims   a·meng·do·eengs
   penicillin
   penicilina   pe·nee·see·lee·na

EMERGENCIES

Help!
Socorro!   so·ko·ho

It's an emergency.
É uma emergência.   e oo·ma e·merr·zheng·see·a

I'm lost.
Estou perdido/a. (m/f)   es·to perr·dee·do/a

Where are the toilets?
Onde tem um banheiro?   on·de teng oom ba·nyay·ro

Go away!
Vai embora!   vai eng·bo·ra

Call ...!
   a doctor
   um médico!   oom me·dee·ko
   an ambulance
   uma ambulância   oo·ma am·boo·lan·see·a
   the police
   a polícia   a po·lee·see·a

antiseptic		
anti-séptico	an·tee·sep·tee·ko
contraceptives		
anticoncepcionais	an·tee·kon·sep·see·o·now
painkillers		
analgésicos	a·now·zhe·zee·ko

LANGUAGE DIFFICULTIES

Do you speak English?
Você fala inglês?   vo·se fa·la een·gles

Does anyone here speak English?
Alguém aqui fala inglês?   ow·geng a·kee fa·la een·gles

Do you understand?
Você entende?   vo·se en·teng·de

I (don't) understand.
Eu (não) entendo.   e·oo (nowng) en·teng·do

What does ... mean?
O que quer dizer ...?   o ke kerr dee·zerr ...

Could you please ...?
Você poderia por favor ...?   vo·se po·de·ree·a porr fa·vorr ...
   repeat that
   repetir isto   he·pe·teerr ees·to
   speak more slowly
   falar mais devagar   fa·larr mais de·va·garr
   write it down
   escrever num papel   es·kre·verr noom pa·pel

NUMBERS

0	zero	ze·ro
1	um	oom
2	dois	doys
3	três	tres

4	quatro	kwa·tro
5	cinco	seen·ko
6	seis	says
7	sete	se·te
8	oito	oy·to
9	nove	naw·ve
10	dez	dez
11	onze	ong·ze
12	doze	do·ze
13	treze	tre·ze
14	quatorze	ka·torr·ze
15	quinze	keen·ze
16	dezesseis	de·ze·says
17	dezesete	de·ze·se·te
18	dezoito	de·zoy·to
19	dezenove	de·ze·naw·ve
20	vinte	veen·te
21	vinte e um	veen·te e oom
22	vinte e dois	veen·te e doys
30	trinta	treen·ta
40	quarenta	kwa·ren·ta
50	cinquenta	seen·kwen·ta
60	sessenta	se·seng·ta
70	setenta	se·teng·ta
80	oitenta	oy·teng·ta
90	noventa	no·veng·ta
100	cem	seng
200	duzentos	doo·zeng·tos
1000	mil	mee·oo

QUESTION WORDS

Who?
 Quem? — keng
What?
 (O) Que? — (o) ke
When?
 Quando? — kwang·do
Where?
 Onde? — ong·de
Why?
 Por que? — porr ke
Which/What?
 Qual/Quais? (sg/pl) — kwow kais

SHOPPING & SERVICES

I'd like to buy ...
 Gostaria de comprar ... — gos·ta·ree·a de kom·prarr ...
I'm just looking.
 Estou só olhando. — es·to so o·lyan·do
May I look at it?
 Posso ver? — po·so verr
How much?
 Quanto? — kwan·to
That's too expensive.
 Está muito caro. — es·ta mweeng·to ka·ro

> **ON THE BEACH**
>
> | **I can't swim.** | *Eu não sei nadar.* |
> |---|---|
> | **Can I swim here?** | *Posso nadar aqui?* |
> | **Is it safe to swim here?** | *É seguro nadar aqui?* |
> | **What time is high/ low tide?** | *A que horas será a maré alta/baixa?* |
> | **How's the surf?** | *Como estão as ondas?* |
> | **Where's a good place to surf?** | *Onde tem um bom lugar para surfar?* |
> | **beach** | *praia* |
> | **beach towel** | *toalha de praia* |
> | **coast** | *costa* |
> | **lifeguard** | *salva-vidas* |
> | **rock** | *pedra* |
> | **sand** | *areia* |
> | **sea** | *mar* |
> | **sunblock** | *protetor solar* |
> | **wave** | *onda* |

Can you lower the price?
 Pode baixar o preço? — po·de ba·sharr o pre·so
Do you have something cheaper?
 Tem uma coisa mais barata? — teng oo·ma koy·za mais ba·ra·ta
I'll give you (five reals).
 Dou (cinco reais). — do (seen·ko he·ais)
I don't like it.
 Não gosto. — nowng gos·to
I'll take it.
 Vou levar isso. — vo le·var ee·so

Where is ...?
 Onde fica ...? — on·de fee·ka ...
 an ATM
  um caixa automático — oom kai·sha ow·to·ma·tee·ko
 a bank
  o banco — o ban·ko
 a bookstore
  uma livraria — oo ma lee vra ree a
 the ... embassy
  a embaixada do/da ... — a eng bai sha da do/da
 a foreign-exchange office
  uma loja de câmbio — oo·ma lo·zha de kam·bee·o
 a market
  o mercado — o merr·ka·do
 the police station
  a delegacia de polícia — a de·le·ga·see·a de po·lee·see·a
 a pharmacy/chemist
  uma farmácia — oo·ma far·ma·sya
 the post office
  o correio — o co·hay·o

a supermarket
o supermercado — o soo·perr·merr·*ka*·do
the tourist office
a secretaria de turismo — a se·kre·ta·*ree*·a de too·*rees*·mo
a laundrette
uma lavanderia — oo·ma la·vang·de·*ree*·a

less	*menos*	*me*·nos
more	*mais*	mais
large	*grande*	*grang*·de
small	*pequeno/a*	pe·*ke*·no/a

What time does ... open?
A que horas abre ...? — a ke *aw*·ras a·bre ...
Do you have any others?
Você tem outros? — vo·*se* teng *o*·tros
How many?
Quantos/Quantas? (m/f) — kwan·tos/kwan·tas

Do you accept ...?
Vocês aceitam ...? — vo·*ses* a·*say*·tam ...
  credit cards
  cartão de crédito — karr·*towng* de kre·dee·to
  traveler's checks
  traveler cheques — tra·ve·ler *she*·kes

letter
uma carta — oo·ma *karr*·ta
parcel
uma encomenda — oo·ma eng·ko·*meng*·da

I want to buy ...
Quero comprar ... — ke·ro kom·*prarr* ...
  an aerogram
  um aerograma — oom a·e·ro·*gra*·ma
  an envelope
  um envelope — oom eng·ve·*lo*·pe
  a phone card
  um cartão telefônico — oom kar·*towng* te·le·fo·nee·ko
  a postcard
  um cartão-postal — oom karr·*towng* pos·*tow*
  stamps
  selos — se·los

Where can I ...?
Onde posso ...? — on·de po·so ...
  change a traveler's check
  trocar traveler cheques — tro·*karr* tra·ve·ler *she*·kes
  change money
  trocar dinheiro — tro·kar dee·*nyay*·ro
  check my email
  checar meu e-mail — she·*karr* me·oo e·mail
  get internet access
  ter acesso à internet — terr a·*se*·so a een·terr·ne·tee

TIME & DATES
What time is it?
Que horas são? — ke *aw*·ras sowng
It's (ten) o'clock.
São (dez) horas. — sowng (des) *aw*·ras

now	*agora*	a·*go*·ra
this morning	*esta manhã*	es·ta ma·*nyang*
this afternoon	*esta tarde*	es·ta *tarr*·de
today	*hoje*	o·zhe
tonight	*hoje à noite*	o·zhe a *noy*·te
tomorrow	*amanhã*	a·ma·*nyang*
yesterday	*ontem*	on·teng

Monday	*segunda-feira*	se·*goon*·da·*fay*·ra
Tuesday	*terça-feira*	terr·sa·*fay*·ra
Wednesday	*quarta-feira*	kwarr·ta·*fay*·ra
Thursday	*quinta-feira*	keen·ta·*fay*·ra
Friday	*sexta-feira*	ses·ta·*fay*·ra
Saturday	*sábado*	sa·ba·doo
Sunday	*domingo*	do·*meen*·go

January	*janeiro*	zha·*nay*·ro
February	*fevereiro*	fe·ve·*ray*·ro
March	*março*	marr·so
April	*abril*	a·*bree*·oo
May	*maio*	ma·yo
June	*junho*	zhoo·nyo
July	*julho*	zhoo·lyo
August	*agosto*	a·*gos*·to
September	*setembro*	se·*teng*·bro
October	*outubro*	o·too·bro
November	*novembro*	no·*veng*·bro
December	*dezembro*	de·*zeng*·bro

TRANSPORT
Public Transport

Which ... goes to ...?	*Qual o ... que vai para ...?*	kwow o ... ke vai *pa*·ra ...
boat	*barco*	*barr*·ko
bus	*ônibus*	o·nee·boos
city/local bus	*ônibus local*	o·nee·boos lo·*kow*
ferry	*balsa*	*bal*·sa
inter-city bus	*ônibus inter-urbano*	o·nee·boos een·terr oorr·*ba*·no
plane	*avião*	a·vee·*owng*
train	*trem*	treng

When's the ... (bus)?	*Quando sai o ... (ônibus)?*	kwang·do sai o ... (o·nee·boos)
first	*primeiro*	pree·*may*·ro
last	*último*	ool·tee·mo
next	*próximo*	pro·see·mo

JUNGLE EXCURSIONS

Does the tour include ...?
A excursão inclui ...?

Will we sleep in hammocks?
Iremos dormir em redes?

What is the breakdown of costs?
Como é dividido o custo?

Is the water level high or low?
O nível das águas esta alto ou baixo?

Does the boat have life jackets?
O barco tem coletes salva-vidas?

How long does it take to get there?
Quanto tempo leva para chegar lá?

Can we shop for food together?
Podemos ir comprar comida juntos?

Do you have fishing gear?
Você tem equipamento de pesca?

Is it safe to go there?
É seguro ir lá?

Will we see animals?
Iremos ver animais?

Are there ...?	*Lá tem ...?*
dangerous animals	*animais perigosos*
snakes	*cobras*
spiders	*aranhas*
lots of mosquitos	*muitos pernilongos*
accommodations	*alojamento*
canoe	*canoa*
food/drinks	*comida/bebida*
fuel	*combustível*
guides	*guias*
jungle	*selva; mata; floresta*
tree	*arvore*

What time does it leave?
Que horas sai?   ke *aw*·ras sai

What time does it get to (Paraty)?
Que horas chega   ke *aw*·ras she·ga
em (Paraty)?   eng (pa·*ra*·tee)

A ... ticket	*Uma passagem*	oo·ma pa·*sa*·zhem
to (...)	*de ... para (...)*	de ... *pa*·ra (...)
1st-class	*primeira classe*	pree·*may*·ra *kla*·se
2nd-class	*segunda classe*	se·*goon*·da *kla*·se
one-way	*ida*	ee·da
round-trip	*ida e volta*	ee·da e *vol*·ta

How much is it?
Quanto é?   *kwan*·to e

Is this the bus to ...?
Este ônibus vai para ...?   es·te o·nee·boos vai *pa*·ra ...?

Do I need to change?
Preciso trocar de trem?   pre·*see*·so tro·*karr* de treng

the luggage check room
o balcão de guarda   o bal·*kowng* de *gwarr*·da
volumes   vo·*loo*·me

a luggage locker
um guarda volume   oom *gwarr*·da vo·*loo*·me

Is this taxi free?
Este táxi está livre?   es·te tak·see es·ta *lee*·vre

Please put the meter on.
Por favor ligue o   porr fa·*vorr lee*·ge o
taxímetro.   tak·*see*·me·tro

How much is it to ...?
Quanto custa até ...?   *kwan*·to *koos*·ta a·*te* ...

Please take me to (this address).
Me leve para este   me *le*·ve *pa*·ra es·te en·de·*re*·so
endereço por favor.   porr fa·*vorr*

Private Transport

I'd like to hire	*Gostaria de*	gos·ta·*ree*·a de
a/an ...	*alugar ...*	a·loo·*garr* ...
4WD	*um quatro*	oom *kwa*·tro
	por quatro	por *kwa*·tro
bicycle	*uma bicicleta*	oo·ma bee·see·*kle*·ta
car	*um carro*	oom *ka*·ho
motorbike	*uma motocicleta*	oo·ma mo·to·see·*kle*·ta

Is this the road to ...?
Esta é a estrada para ...?   es·ta e a es·*tra*·da *pa*·ra

(How long) Can I park here?
(Quanto tempo) Posso   (*kwan*·to teng·po) po·so
estacionar aqui?   es·ta·see·o·*narr* a·kee

Where's a gas/petrol station?
Onde tem um posto   on·de teng oom *pos*·to
de gasolina?   de ga·zo·*lee*·na

Please fill it up.
Enche o tanque, por   en·she o *tan*·ke porr
favor.   fa·*vorr*

I'd like ... liters.
Coloque ... litros.   ko·*lo*·ke ... *lee*·tros

diesel	*diesel*	*dee*·sel
LPG	*gás*	gas
ethanol	*álcool*	*ow*·kol
unleaded	*gasolina comum*	ga·zo·*lee*·na ko·*moon*

The (car/motorbike) has broken down at ...
(O carro/A motocicleta) quebrou em ...
(o ka·ho/a mo·to·se·kle·ta) ke·bro eng ...

The car won't start.
O carro não está pegando.
o ka·ho nowng es·ta pe·gang·do

I need a mechanic.
Preciso de um mecânico.
pre·see·so de oom me·ka·nee·ko

ROAD SIGNS

Entrada	Entrance
Estrada dê Preferência	Give Way
Mão Única	One-way
Pare	Stop
Pedágio	Toll
Proibido Entrar	No Entry
Rua Sem Saída	Dead End
Saída	Freeway Exit

I've run out of gas/petrol.
Estou sem gasolina.
es·*to* seng ga·zo·*lee*·na
I've had an accident.
Sofri um acidente.
so·*free* oom a·see·*den*·te

TRAVEL WITH CHILDREN
I need (a/an) ...
Preciso de ...
pre·*see*·zo de ...
Do you have (a/an) ...?
Aqui tem ...?
a·*kee* teng

baby change room
uma sala para trocar   oo·ma *sa*·la *pa*·ra tro·*karr*
  bebê   be·*be*

baby seat
um assento de criança   oom a·*seng*·to de kree·*an*·sa
booster seat
um assento de elevaçã   oom a·*seng*·to de e·le·va·*sowng*
child-minding service
um serviço de babá   oom serr·*vee*·so de ba·*ba*
children's menu
um cardápio para   oom kar·*da*·pee·o *pa*·ra
  criança   kree·*an*·sa
(English-speaking) babysitter
uma babá   oo·ma ba·*ba*
  (que fale ingles)   (ke *fa*·le een·*gles*)
formula (milk)
leite em pó (para bebê)   *lay*·te (*pa*·ra be·*be*)
high-chair
uma cadeira de criança   oo·ma ka·*day*·ra de kree·*an*·sa
potty
um troninho   oom tro·*nee*·nyo
pusher/stroller
um carrinho de bebê   oom ka·*hee*·nyo de be·*be*
(disposable) nappies/diapers
fraldas (descartáveis)   *frow*·das (des·karr·*ta*·vays)

Do you mind if I breast-feed here?
Você se importa se eu amamentar aqui?
vo·*se* se eeng·*porr*·ta se e·oo a·ma·meng·*tarr* a·*kee*
Are children allowed?
É permitida a entrada de crianças?
e perr·mee·*tee*·da a eng·*tra*·da de kree·*an*·sas

Also available from Lonely Planet:
Brazilian Portuguese Phrasebook

LANGUAGE

Glossary

For a glossary of food and drink items, see p110.

afoxé – music of Bahia, which has strong African rhythms and close ties to *Candomblé*

albergue – lodging house or hostel

albergue da juventude – youth hostel

aldeia – originally a village built by Jesuits to convert Indians to Christianity; now the term for any small, usually Indian, village

andar – walk; also a floor of a multistory building

apartamento – hotel room with a private bathroom

apelido – nickname

arara – macaw

artesanato – handcrafted workmanship

ayahuasca – hallucinogenic drink

azulejos – Portuguese ceramic tiles with a distinctive blue glaze, often seen in churches

babaçu – versatile palm tree that is the basis of the rural economy in Maranhão

bairro – district

bandeirantes – bands of 17th- and 18th-century roaming adventurers who explored the vast Brazilian interior while searching for gold and Indians to enslave; typically born of an Indian mother and a Portuguese father

barraca – any stall or hut, including food and drink stands common at beaches, parks etc

bateria – rhythm section of a band, including the enormous ones in samba parades

beija-flor – literally 'flower kisser'; hummingbird; also the name of Rio's most famous samba school

berimbau – musical instrument that accompanies *capoeira*

bilheteria – ticket office

bloco – large group, usually numbering in the hundreds, of singing or drumming Carnaval revelers in costume, organized around a neighborhood or theme

boate – nightclub with a dance floor, sometimes featuring strippers; also boîte

bonde – cable car, tram or trolley

bossa nova – music that mixes North American jazz with Brazilian influences

boteco – small, open-air bar

boto – freshwater dolphin of the Amazon

Bumba Meu Boi – the most important festival in Maranhão, a rich folkloric event that revolves around a Carnavalesque dance/procession

bunda – African word for buttocks

caatinga – scrub vegetation of the *sertão*

Caboclo – literally 'copper-colored'; person of mixed Caucasian and Indian ancestry

cachoeira – waterfall

camisinha – condom

Candomblé – Afro-Brazilian religion of Bahia

cangaceiros – legendary bandits of the *sertão*

capivara – capybara; the world's largest rodent, which looks like a large guinea pig and lives in the Pantanal

Capixaba – resident of Espírito Santo state

capoeira – martial art/dance developed by the slaves of Bahia

Carioca – resident of Rio de Janeiro

cartão telefônico – phonecard

casa de câmbio – money-exchange office

casa grande – big house or plantation owner's mansion

casal – married couple; also a double bed

chapada – tableland or plateau that divides a river basin

churrascaria – restaurant featuring barbecued meat

cidades históricas – historic colonial towns

Círio de Nazaré – Brazil's largest religious festival, which takes place in Belém

cobra – any snake

coronel – literally 'colonel'; rural landowner who typically controlled the local political, judicial and police systems; any powerful person

correio – post office

delegacia de polícia – police station

Embratur – Brazilian Tourist Board

engenho – sugar mill or sugar plantation

escolas de samba – large samba clubs that compete in the annual Carnaval parade

estalagem – inn

estrangeiro – foreigner

Exú – spirit that serves as messenger between the gods and humans in Afro-Brazilian religions

fantasia – Carnavalesque costume

favela – slum, shantytown

favelado – resident of a *favela*

fazenda – ranch or farm, usually a large landholding; also cloth, fabric

fazendeiro – estate owner

feira – produce market

ferroviária – railway station

festa – party

Filhos de Gandhi – Bahia's most famous Carnaval *bloco*

fio dental – literally 'dental floss'; Brazil's famous skimpy bikini

Flamengo – Rio's most popular football team; also one of Rio's most populated areas

Fluminense – native of Rio state; also the football team that is *Flamengo's* main rival

forró – popular music of the Northeast, recently enjoying a wave of nationwide popularity

frevo – fast-paced, popular music from Pernambuco

frigobar – minibar

Funai – Fundação Nacional do Indio; government Indian agency

Fusca – Volkswagen Beetle, Brazil's most popular car

futebol – football

futevôlei – volleyball played without hands

gafieira – dance hall

garimpeiro – prospector or miner; originally an illegal diamond prospector

garimpo – mining camp

gaúcho – cowboy of southern Brazil

gringo – foreigner or person with light hair and complexion; can even refer to light-skinned Brazilians

gruta – grotto or cavern

hidrovia – aquatic freeway

hidroviária – boat terminal

hospedagem – cheap boardinghouse used by locals

Iemanjá – Afro-Brazilian goddess of the sea

igapó – flooded Amazon forest

igarapé – creek or small river in Amazonia

igreja – church

ilha – island

jaburú – jabiru; a giant white stork of the Pantanal with a black head and a red band on its neck

jacaré – alligator or caiman

jangada – beautiful sailboat of the Northeast

jangadeiros – crews who use *jangadas*

jeito or jeitinho – possibly the most Brazilian expression, both a feeling and a form of action; from dar um jeito, meaning 'to find a way to get something done,' no matter how seemingly impossible, even if the solution may not be completely orthodox or legal

Jogo dos Búzios – Casting of Shells; type of fortune-telling performed by a *pai* or *mãe de santo*

leito – sleeping berth

literatura de cordel – literally 'string literature'; popular literature of the Northeast

litoral – coastal region

machista – male chauvinist

mãe de santo – female Afro-Brazilian spiritual leader

malandro do morro – vagabond; scoundrel from the hills; a popular figure in Rio's mythology

maloca – Indian dwelling

Maracanã – Rio's soccer stadium

mercado – market

mestiço – a person of mixed Indian and European parentage

Mineiro – resident of Minas Gerais

moço/a – waiter or other service industry worker

morro – hill; also a person or culture of the *favelas*

mulato/a – person of mixed Black and European parentage

novela – soap opera; Brazil's most popular TV shows

NS – Nosso Senhor (Our Lord) or Nossa Senhora (Our Lady)

O Globo – Brazil's biggest media empire, with the prime national TV station and several newspapers and magazines

orixá – deity of the Afro-Brazilian religions

pagode – popular samba music

pai de santo – male spiritual leader in Afro-Brazilian religions

palácio – palace or large government building

palafita – stilt or a house built on stilts

pampas – grassy plains of the interior of southern Brazil

parque nacional – national park

pau brasil – now-scarce brazilwood tree; a red dye made from the tree that was the colony's first commodity

Paulista – resident of São Paulo state

Paulistano – resident of São Paulo city

PCB – Communist Party of Brazil

pensão – guesthouse

posta restante – poste restante

posto – post; lifeguard posts along Rio de Janeiro's beaches, used as names for different sections of beach

posto de gasolina – a gas (petrol) station

posto telefônico – telephone office

pousada – guesthouse

praça – plaza or town square

praia – beach

prefeitura – city or town hall

PT – Partido dos Trabalhadores (Worker's Party); Brazil's newest and most radical political party

quarto – hotel room without a bathroom

quente – hot

quilombo – community of runaway slaves

Quimbanda – black magic

rápido – fast

real – Brazil's unit of currency since 1994; plural reais

rede – hammock

rio – river

rodoferroviária – bus and train station

rodoviária – bus station
s/n – abbreviation for sem número (without number) used in some street addresses
sambista – samba composer or dancer
sambódromo – street with tiers of seating built for samba parades
senzala – slave quarters
serra – mountain range
Sertanejo – resident of the *sertão*
sertão – the drought-prone backlands of the Northeast
shopping – shopping mall

telefonista internacional – international telephone operator
Terra da Vera Cruz – Land of the True Cross; the original Portuguese name for Brazil
terreiro – Afro-Brazilian house of worship
travessa – lane

travesti – transvestite; a popular figure throughout Brazil, considered by some to be the national symbol
trem – train
trio elétrico – three-pronged electrical outlet; electrically amplified bands that play atop trucks
tropicalismo – important cultural movement centered in Bahia in the late 1960s
Tupi – Indian people and language that predominated along the coast at the time of the European invasion

Umbanda – white magic, a mixture of Candomblé and spiritism

vaqueiro – cowboy of the Northeast
várzea – Amazonian floodplain

zona da mata – bushland just inside the *litoral* in the Northeastern states

The Authors

REGIS ST. LOUIS
Coordinating Author, Rio de Janeiro City, Sergipe & Alagoas, Bahia

Regis' longtime admiration for the music, scenery and wildlife of Brazil has led to his deep involvement with the country. Rio de Janeiro is among his great loves and is perhaps the biggest reason he returns so often. Favorite memories from this trip include catching a surprise Gilberto Gil concert in Rio's Lapa, watching freshly hatched sea turtles race to the sea in Mangue Seco, attending a mystical Candomblé ceremony in Salvador and discovering the unspoiled beauty of Alagoas. Regis has written many articles on Rio and the tropics, and he is also the author of Lonely Planet's *Rio de Janeiro* guide. He lives in New York City.

My Favorite Trip

Few cities in the world evoke the magic of Rio (p121), and I never miss the chance to hear sidewalk samba, take long walks on the beach and explore old neighborhoods of the *Cidade Maravilhosa* (Marvelous City). Afterwards, I catch a flight to Cuiabá (p406) and head into the Pantanal (p415), that bio-rich wonderland where I always see some astounding wildlife. Next is Bahia, one of my favorite states, where I spend a few days among the music and culture of Salvador (p439) before going south to enchanting Arraial d'Ajuda (p486) and Trancoso (p487). I finish my ramble out west at the peaceful and beautifully set town of Lençóis (p493), gateway to waterfalls, abandoned mining towns and exhilarating treks through the Parque Nacional da Chapada Diamantina (p498).

Parque Nacional da Chapada Diamantina ○ Lençóis
○ Salvador
○ Cuiabá
○ Arraial d'Ajuda
○ Pantanal
○ Trancoso
○ Rio de Janeiro

GARY CHANDLER
The Amazon

This was Gary's second time updating the Amazon chapter. Once again the mother of all rivers proved a mother to cover: in seven weeks Gary took eight flights, dozens of boat trips, crossed three time zones and four international borders, and caught a grand total of three piranha (one better than last time). Raised in California, Gary has degrees in ethnic studies from UC Berkeley and journalism from Columbia. He has worked on 15 guidebooks, including Lonely Planet's *Dominican Republic, Central America on a Shoestring*, and first editions of *Honduras* and *El Salvador & Nicaragua*. He lives in Oakland, CA, with his wife and frequent co-author, Liza Prado, and their new baby daughter, Eva Quetzal.

LONELY PLANET AUTHORS

Why is our travel information the best in the world? It's simple: our authors are independent, dedicated travelers. They don't research using just the internet or phone, and they don't take freebies in exchange for positive coverage. They travel widely, to all the popular spots and off the beaten track. They personally visit thousands of hotels, restaurants, cafés, bars, galleries, palaces, museums and more – and they take pride in getting all the details right, and telling it how it is. Think you can do it? Find out how at lonelyplanet.com.

GREGOR CLARK
Rio de Janeiro State, Espírito Santo, Minas Gerais

Gregor's passion for all things Brazilian dates back to his first Portuguese class at age 19, where he became enamored of Brazilians' exuberant vocal cadences. (Where else can you call a picnic 'peeky-neeky'?) His first three-month visit to Brazil in 1990 enhanced his appreciation for the country's vastness and diversity, and helped him understand why so many travelers rave as much about Brazil's people, music and welcoming atmosphere as about its must-see destinations. After seven subsequent trips to Latin America, he still agrees – it scarcely matters where you go in Brazil, it's really about the people. Gregor has written for Lonely Planet since 2000. He lives in Vermont with his wife and two daughters.

ROBERT LANDON
São Paulo State

In 2002, Robert went to Brazil for one week, stayed two, returned home only to quit his job and sell all his worldly goods, and a month later he was living in Copacabana. Now fluent in Portuguese, he has also spent extensive time in both São Paulo and the south of Brazil as well as in Rio. A graduate of Stanford University and the University of California at Irvine, Robert has been a travel writer for almost 15 years, including a two-year stint in Paris. His work has appeared in the *Los Angeles Times*, *Miami Herald*, *Houston Chronicle* and *San Jose Mercury News*.

JOHN NOBLE
Pernambuco, Paraíba & Rio Grande do Norte, Ceará, Piauí & Maranhão

Long-nurtured dreams of exploring the mother of all rivers and of all rain forests came true for John when he tramped the length and breadth of Amazonia for an earlier edition of *Brazil*. This time, he turned to Northeast Brazil and now knows that nowhere else on the planet has real beaches. A travel writer, John is from the UK and lives in Spain, but spends much of his life in Latin America. He especially loves Brazil for its musical and footballing genius, its varied regional cultures, the Portuguese language and, above all, the charm and grace of its people.

KEVIN RAUB
Brasília, Goiás, Mato Grosso & Mato Grosso do Sul

Kevin Raub grew up in Atlanta and received a degree in magazine journalism from the University of Georgia in Athens. He started his career as a music journalist in New York City, working for *Rolling Stone*. He now divides his time between music and travel, contributing regularly to *Travel+Leisure*, *American Way*, *Town and Country* and the *New York Post*. His fascination with Brazil began on New Year's Eve, 2001, when he was forced to leave Rio at the unheard of hour of 11:30pm – the only mileage flight he could get a seat on. He vowed to return. He has since visited over 15 times and now divides his time between Los Angeles and Fernando de Noronha. This is his first assignment for Lonely Planet.

MARA VORHEES — Paraná, Santa Catarina, Rio Grande do Sul

Mara's love for Brazil dates back to her college days, when she became a *futebol* fan thanks to the Carioca star of the Georgetown team. Years later, she found herself working at a Harvard University research center, studying issues of environment and development in the Brazilian cerrado. She finally got some first-hand, in-country experience in 2005, when she spent a month doing volunteer work and learning Portuguese in Salvador da Bahia. For this book she covered southern Brazil and learned to love yet another region. Mara lives with her husband and her cat in Somerville, Massachusetts, which could be called 'Mini Minas' for all its Brazilian boutiques, salons and *mercados*.

Behind the Scenes

THIS BOOK

This guidebook was commissioned in Lonely Planet's Oakland office, and produced by the following:

Commissioning Editor Kathleen Munnelly
Coordinating Editor Elisa Arduca
Coordinating Cartographer Kusnandar
Coordinating Layout Designer Jim Hsu
Managing Editor Melanie Dankel
Managing Cartographer Alison Lyall
Managing Layout Designer Celia Wood
Assisting Editors Holly Alexander, Sarah Bailey, Yvonne Byron, Gennifer Ciavarra, Melanie Dankel, Kate James, Susan Paterson, Phillip Tang, Gina Tsarouhas, Simon Williamson
Assisting Cartographers Jessica Dean, Diana Duggan, Joshua Geoghegan, Corey Hutchison, Jacqueline Nguyen, Andrew Smith
Cover Designer Marika Mercer

Project Manager Eoin Dunlevy, Fabrice Rocher
Language Content Coordinator Quentin Frayne
Thanks to David Connolly, Mark Germanchis, James Hardy, Lauren Hunt, Margot Kilgour, Adam McCrow, Sarah Sloane, David Zingarelli

THANKS
REGIS ST. LOUIS

Numerous Brazilians helped with this enormous project, and I'm grateful for the kind assistance I received in so many towns. Big thanks to commissioning editor Kathleen Munnelly for her enthusiasm and sharp ideas. Thanks go to Robert Landon for hosting me in Rio and sharing good times, Heinz for an excellent day around Barra de Santo Antônio, Marcelo Armstrong for a fascinating *favela* tour, Ada at Pontal de Coruripe and Dan, Bruna and Carina from Rio. I'd also like to thank Fabio and Carmen of Santa Teresa for the interview,

LONELY PLANET: TRAVEL WIDELY, TREAD LIGHTLY, GIVE SUSTAINABLY

The Lonely Planet Story

The story begins with a classic travel adventure: Tony and Maureen Wheeler's 1972 journey across Europe and Asia to Australia. There was no useful information about the overland trail then, so Tony and Maureen published the first Lonely Planet guidebook to meet a growing need.

From a kitchen table, Lonely Planet has grown to become the largest independent travel publisher in the world, with offices in Melbourne (Australia), Oakland (USA) and London (UK). Today Lonely Planet guidebooks cover the globe. There is an ever-growing list of books and information in a variety of media. Some things haven't changed. The main aim is still to make it possible for adventurous individuals to get out there – to explore and better understand the world.

The Lonely Planet Foundation

The Lonely Planet Foundation proudly supports nimble nonprofit institutions working for change in the world. Each year the foundation donates 5% of Lonely Planet company profits to projects selected by staff and authors. Our partners range from Kabissa, which provides small nonprofits across Africa with access to technology, to the Foundation for Developing Cambodian Orphans, which supports girls at risk of falling victim to sex traffickers.

Our nonprofit partners are linked by a grass-roots approach to the areas of health, education or sustainable tourism. Many projects we support – such as one with BaAka (Pygmy) children in the forested areas of Central African Republic – choose to focus on women and children as one of the most effective ways to support the whole community.

Sometimes foundation assistance is as simple as helping to preserve a local ruin like the Minaret of Jam in Afghanistan; this incredible monument now draws intrepid tourists to the area and its restoration has greatly improved options for local people.

Just as travel is often about learning to see with new eyes, so many of the groups we work with aim to change the way people see themselves and the future for their children and communities.

Jelon Vieira for insight into capoeira, and Cassandra for sharing the Bahian adventure.

GARY CHANDLER

Thank you to the innumerable people whose generous help and know-how were so essential to my research. I'm particularly grateful to Gero Mesquita of Amazon Gero's Tours in Manaus, Shirlei Piñeiro of the Mamirauá Institute, and Claudio Chena of Mãe Natureza in Alter do Chão. At Lonely Planet, thanks to Kathleen Munnelly, Regis St. Louis, and authors Robert Landon, Beth Kohn and Molly Green, whose work on overlapping books was a great help to my own. Thank you to my family, especially my brilliant and beautiful wife, Liza, and my new and impossibly precious daughter, Eva Quetzal.

GREGOR CLARK

Thanks to countless Brazilians whose thumbs-ups and warm smiles reminded me again why Brazil is my favorite country on earth. *Um abraço para* Ángela Inglez, Alex, Maíra, Bia, Maria Helena, Ricardo, Ángela, José, Jacqueline, Pete, Penny, Antonella, Rubem, Daniela, Mario, Bixão, Beatriz, Rafael, Christoph and Deolinda for showing me wonders I would never have discovered otherwise. Thanks to le Maître des Champs Rocheux, whose expert driving skills extricated me from Itatiaia. Thanks also to the wonderful editors and cartographers at Lonely Planet, especially Kathleen Munnelly, Elisa Arduca and Kusnandar. Above all, thanks to my beloved wife Gaen and sweet daughters Meigan and Chloe for helping me pursue my dreams and keeping the home fires burning in my heart always.

ROBERT LANDON

Thanks first to Carlos for keeping down the home front so lovingly; Kathleen Munnelly for her enthusiasm about São Paulo and choosing me to write about it; Regis St. Louis for his valuable third-party insights; Fernando Salis, a Carioca with a remarkable tolerance for *coisas paulistas*; Leland Haskins and Ricky Brown for their company; Ann Williams for her humor; and especially Paulo Bellot, who taught me first-hand about his beloved city. *Adeus*, Valeria da Silva. *Tanta saudade de você.*

JOHN NOBLE

Thanks to the very many Brazilians who helped me in my research, almost always with a smile and courtesy. Extra special thanks to Francis Jauneau, Gisele Leal, David Wagenaar, Steve Joynson, Herbert Klein, Adriana Schmidt, Kevin Raub, Fabiana Cava, Themis Nayle and Eduardo Bagnoli.

KEVIN RAUB

A *brigadão* to my fiancée, Adriana Schmidt, without whose love, support and late night phone calls, nothing in my chapters would have been written. At Lonely Planet, Kathleen Munnelly, Regis St. Louis and Thomas Kohnstamm. And to all those who helped over the years and along the way: Marcelo, Gracia and André Schmidt, Denise Wedren, Marcelo Armstrong, João Veloso, Dov Zylberman, Daniel Borges, Julia Segatto, Mara Alcamim, Maria Pinto, Ana Paula Barros, Marcus Serejo, Bruno Maia, Rodrigo Lopes, Alessandra Schneider, Tatoo, Paul and Maria Solis-Cohen, Oswaldo Murad, Alberto Krebs, Ailton Lara, Munir Nasr, Juliana Albuquerque, Al Macedo, Gilberto Motta, Beatriz Rondon, Paula Lago, and Ariane Janial.

MARA VORHEES

In my worldwide travels, I have never received such a warm welcome as I did in southern Brazil. I am indebted to my newfound friends, all of whom provided helpful hints and warm hospitality: Dina Moser, Lori and Decio Moser, Chica and

---

SEND US YOUR FEEDBACK

We love to hear from travelers – your comments keep us on our toes and help make our books better. Our well-traveled team reads every word on what you loved or loathed about this book. Although we cannot reply individually to postal submissions, we always guarantee that your feedback goes straight to the appropriate authors, in time for the next edition. Each person who sends us information is thanked in the next edition – and the most useful submissions are rewarded with a free book. See the Behind the Scenes section.

To send us your updates – and find out about Lonely Planet events, newsletters and travel news – visit our award-winning website: **www.lonelyplanet.com/contact**.

Note: we may edit, reproduce and incorporate your comments in Lonely Planet products such as guidebooks, websites and digital products, so let us know if you don't want your comments reproduced or your name acknowledged. For a copy of our privacy policy, go to www.lonelyplanet .com/privacy.

Octavio, Bruno Pritsch and Rita Michelon. A special *obrigada* to Sonia Nunes, for sharing Santa Catarina's 'beautiful places,' and Marco Ântonio, my *companheiro* in Rio Grande do Sul. I'm forever grateful to Kathleen Munnelly for sending me to the southern hemisphere in February. And Jerz, thanks for learning how to use Skype (and for everything else too).

OUR READERS

Many thanks to the travelers who used the last edition and wrote to us with helpful hints, useful advice and interesting anecdotes:

A Rachele Aiudi, Adam Alban, Keith Albee, Jonathan Algdal, Clarissa Altmann, Gabriella Amabile, Muriel Ammann, Jan Anderson, Frida Andrae, Axel Antoine-Feill, Patrik Aqvist, Angela Ariatti, Gill Armstrong, Tim Armstrong, Mercedes Arredondo, Federico Arrizabalaga, James Ash, Wilhelmina Asis-Mcnelis, Hilary Avertick, Mik Awake, Alberto Azevedo, Sarai Azkona **B** Joergen Baekgaard, William Baines, Jim Bakhaus, Marc Ballantine, Catherine Barrett, Lauren Barry, Jeff Beatty, Sara Beaudry, Karen Bedingfield, Mike Beedham, Stephen W Beidner, Vincent Belanger, Charli Rumsey Ben Waller, Luigi Benvenuti, Owe Berg, Russell Berg, Laura Beriola, Oya Berk Demirel, Tineke Berthelsen, René Beuchle, Anne Beuwer, Simone Blok, Enole Boedeker, Paul Boehlen, John Bonallack, Fabrizio Bori, Robert Bortner, Jorg Bosshart, Natalia Bougaevskaia, Denise Bouras, Terry Brady, Manuela Brambilla, Stephen Brand, Wendy Brazendale, Melissa Breedijk, Maria Bridger, Peter Bristot, Klaus Brokmeier, Martin Brookes, Cindy Brown, Hans Brown, Sharon A Browne, Jeroen Bruijns, Carol Buchman, Jan Peter Busscher **C** Assad Cahli Junior, Danira Caleta, Eduardo Camelo, Jim Camp, Fabiano Campos, João Cardadeiro, Eric Chambers, Vicki Chan, Bergman Wing Keung Chan, Brian Chang, Pedro Chaves, Kinga Choszcz, Peter Churchill, Jay Clark, Chantelle Clegg, Eduardo Coelho, Karel Coenen, Perrine Colignon, José Gabriel Coll, Matteo Collet, Johan Collier, Alice Conibear, Deborah Cook, Marcelo Corrê, Maurizio Corvino, Daniel Cote, Beverly Cothran, Licuri Couto, Eric Crawford, Carter Cromwell, Michael Crowley, Mike Crowley, Gina Cruickshank, Brooke Curtis **D** Paulo Da Costa, Carlos Augusto Da Cruz Neto, Carlos Damasceno, Andrea Dangelmayer, Paul Darbyshire, Annemarie Dautzenberg, Jerry Davila, Remco De Kok, Arjan De Meij, Mathieu De Patoul, Nuno Franco De Sousa, Marjella De Vries, Tom De Wilde, Hector Del Olmo, Dominique Desmoires, Robert Desproges, Marichat Devise, Nicole Disante, Paulo Dias, Joann Diaz, Mausi Digel, Sheila Domingues, Nuno Dos Santos, Karsten-Patrick Dr Urban, Nelson Duarte, Aniel Dutra **E** Achim Eckert, Frank Edelbroek, Belinda Edington, Elizabeth Edwards, Maria Edwards, Daniel Egenolf, Roland Ehrat, Martin Eidmann, Andreas Ekblad, Katrin Eliasson, Lisa Elstad, Peter Emmers, Helena Enflo **F** Cynthia Farrell, Valentina Fazio, Abigail Ferkin, Edoardo Ferreira Melo, Frederico Fick, Grahame Finnigan, Bob Finucane, Florian Fischer, Eric Fischer, Zoe Fisher, Gilian Fleet, Monika Fliegel, Ephraim Flores, Nadiá Fonseca, Pascal Fortin, Stuart Frank, Katya

Frank, Matt Frear, James French, Nir Fridler, Katrina Frith, Mark Fulcher, Eugene Fytche **G** Fraenze Gade, Rebeca Galaz, Angela Gall, Clemente Garcia Aguado, Julie Garnier, Petter Garnier, André Gauvreau, Vanessa Genier, Sarah George, Patrik Gerecke, Manoel Giffoni, Dani Gimeno, Eva Goedecke, Christian Gogolin, Gaurang Gohel, Tony Golding, Lisa Goldscheider, Michael Goldsmith, Micheangelo Gonzales, Coco González Pi, Lorea Gonzalez Rojas, Jan Goossens, Barry Grogan, Joachim Grohnwald, Barbara Grueble, Jonas Gunnarsson **H** Taeo Haas, Kevin Hakl, Knodishall Hall, Goetz Hanningsmann, Deb Harding, Glen Harmon, Bryan Harris, Nadia Harrison, Glenn Hayataka, Berry Hayter, Paul Hendrikx, Sam Henson, Stefan Herker, Jason Hobbie, Barnaby Hodgson, Kate Hoel, Richard Hoffer, Francis Holland, Malcolm Holmes, Chris Holt, Mikael Honda, Villa Bebek Hotel, Jordan Howard, Richard Huber, Cameron Hum **I** Keith Innes, Dave Iverson **J** Terri Jackson, Ulf Jacobson, Andreas Jaeger, Richard Jenkins, Richard Jenkins, Mark Jennings, Jim Jensen, Lars Harald Joakimsen, Mauri Johansson, Tim Jones, Jose Jueguen **K** Alicia Kamm, Frida Karlson, Amanda Katz, Wolfgang Kausch, Stewart Kennedy, Adam Kent, Toni Kesby, Taco Ketting, Matthias Kiepsch, Robert King, Sven Kistner, Rafael Kon, Stavroula Konidari, Nadège Konyn, Francesco Kostner, David Kratochvil, Ina Krause, Nikki Kreis, Monica Krupenski, Dirk Kruyder, Helmar Kurz **L** Janine Labletta, James Laban, Tanja Laier, Marie Lajaunie, Marcus Lamprecht, Jimmy Langman, Anne Lavandon, Louise Lavoie, Le Gousse, Barbara Lemberg, Rob Lensen, Treena Lewis, Henry Lindsay-Smith, Claudia Linker, Sergio Linzmeyer, Mauro Lombardi, Fausto Lopes De Almeida, Jonas Thomas Lopez, Frederic Lopez, Alejandro Lopez, Joel Lopez-Ferreiro, David Lord, Wanderson Louzada, Agata & Michal Lubienieccy, Adrian Lush **M** Simon Macenroe, Diogo Marcel, Dana Marino, Toni Marti, Stephanie Martins, Marian Masar, John Mcleod, Terry Mcninch, Gerry Mcdonald, Pablo Meglioli, Peter Meier, David Meissner, Vincent Merlin, Geraldo Neto Mesquita De Sousa, Matthew Metcalfe, Jefri Metheany, Julien Meyer, Torin Millar, Patrick Miscampbell, Sohil Mistry, Grégoire Monconduit, Juriaan Moolhuysen, Matt Morgan, Erich Morgenstern, Maxime Morneau, Anna Morris, Fernando Luiz Motta Dos Santos, Aloysius Mulder, Jeannine Mullan, Benjamin Murtagh, Emile Myburgh, John Myers **N** Sabina Nagpal, Youngho Nam, Maria Nauer, Chris Neale, Adriana Newell, Aricna Newell, Andreas Niklas, Vladislav Nodelman, Sabine Nönn, Kennet Nordstrom, Kit Nørgaard, Karin Nyffenegger **O** Michael O'Brien, Alan O'Dowd, John O'Heron, John O'Neill, Russell & Mitty O'Shea, Gustav Oberdörfer, Cecile Obertop, Blon Obrien, Jakob Oddershede, I Igo Odriozola Saez, Gabriela Oliva, Bruno Gomes Oliveira, Phil Oster, Elna Otter **P** Zilvinas Pakeltis, Ariane Paraskevopoulos, Jérôme Parnisari, Gisele Paula, Katharine Pearson, Marianne Pecht, Gary Peiser, Martin Pekarek, Ricardo Peng, Thaís Pereira, Fabrice Perrier, Chris Perry, Julia Persitzky, Caroline Pietermaat, John Potter, Laurent Pouvreau, Raphaelle Proulx, Markus Pscheidt, Josef Putschoegl **R** Vijay Ragoonanan, Nyoka Rajah, Sebastian Rank, Paulo Raymundo, Paulo Raymundo, Hans Reber, Christoph Reichold, Maureen Richey, Anton Rijsdijk, Sara Ringgaard, Kristen Ritter, Graeme Robinson, Felipe Rodrigues, Dana Rohde, Barbara Roos, Diana Ros, Ursula Rose, Harvey Rosenblum, Ben Ross, Jim Rowan-Parry, Caroline Ryder,

BEHIND THE SCENES

S Björn Salomonsson, Julio Sampaio, Sigrid Sanborn, Gary Sands, Paulo Santos, Ayami Sato Mock, Kimmie Sayas, Jane Scharf, Michael Scheiwein, Christoph Schinko, Simone Schmies, Rolf Schnyder, Erin Scholl, Dieter Schoop, Harvey Schwartz, Jason Scorse, Dario Scursatone, Leanna Seamans, David Senger, Hannah Senior, Mariana Sigail, Jean Sigel, Christoph Sigl, Coby Sikkens, Rogerio Aparecido Silva De Andrade, Neta Silveira, Anna and Chris Simon, Julie Sion, Tony Sirotkin, Ronaldo Soares E Silva, Kirsten Soerensen, Paul Soerensen, Maria Solé, Lucy Spilberg, Stefan Stallmann, Arthur Steele, Volker Steinhoff, Cecilia Stevens, Adrianne Stolaruk, Fess Stone, Ian C Story, Rebecca Stringer, Sangeetha Subramani, Sandra Sundberg, Sasha Sutherland, Carmen Söhngen **T** K Tan, Dora Taillefer, Nicoletta and Eugenio Tallachini, Amadeo Tapia, Abeline Tarp, Mehetia Taue, Mirko Tegeder, Frank Thomae, John Thomas, Franck Thomas, Aaron Thomas, David Thompson, Karina Tiekstra, Amelia Tienghi, Maria Tjønn **V** Marcos Valente Jr, Laetitia Van Der Elst, Jorine Van Der Vlag, Paul Van Egmond, Sophie Van Hadeln, Tamara Van Hal, Marcel Van Kampenhout, Bastiaan Van Leeuwen, Jack Van Messel, Arie Van Oosterwijk, Tomas Van Roosmalen, Cor Van Wijnen, Eric Vanoncini, Bruce Varley, Aimee Vegter, Joyce Veldsink, Emma Vernon-Harcourt, Kara Vertigan, Vincent Verweij, Albert Vila Mallarach, Rachael Vinyard, H Plenter Vledder, Hansjörg Volkart, Veronika Von Eltz **W** Monique Waalboer, Bonnie C Wade, Verena Wagner, Michelle Walsh, Tony Weald, Eveline Welschen, Stephanie West, Andrew West, Jodie Whitbread, Brian White, T J Wichmann, Arno Wicki, Erin Wignall, Greg Wilks, Tim Wilson, Matt Wilson, Ruediger Wittenberg, Martina Wunderli **Y** Ariel Yerushalmi, Maria Lucia Yolen, Monica Younghusband, Geir Ytredal **Z** Ivan Zabojnik, Deann Zampelli, Kênya Zanatta,

ACKNOWLEDGMENTS

Many thanks to the following for the use of their content:

Globe on title page ©Mountain High Maps 1993 Digital Wisdom, Inc.

Index

INDEX

000 Map pages
000 Photograph pages

000 Map pages
000 Photograph pages

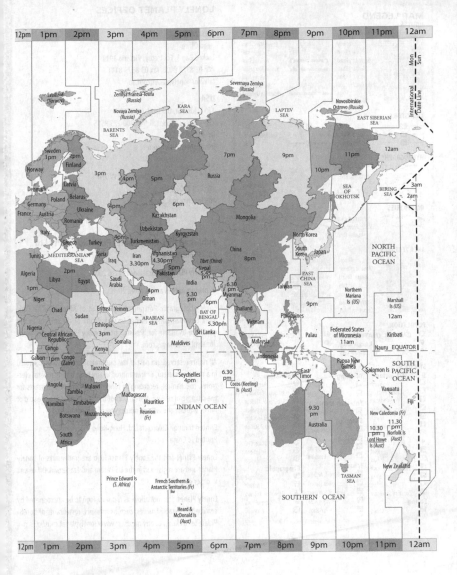

Mon
Sun

International
Date Line

Svalbard
(Norway)

Zemlya Frantsa-Iosifa
(Russia)

Severnaya Zemlya
(Russia)

Novosibirskie
Ostrovo (Russia)

KARA
SEA

LAPTEV
SEA

EAST SIBERIAN
SEA

Novaya Zemlya
(Russia)

BARENTS
SEA

Sweden
1pm
Finland
7pm

3pm

7pm

9pm

11pm

12am

Norway

Russia

10pm

3am

Denmark
Latvia
Germany Poland Belarus
France Austria
Ukraine
Romania
Italy

4pm

5pm

10pm

SEA
OF
OKHOTSK

BERING
SEA

2am

Greece Turkey
Tunisia MEDITERRANEAN
SEA

6pm

Kazakhstan

Mongolia

North Korea
South
Korea Japan

NORTH
PACIFIC
OCEAN

Algeria Syria
Libya Egypt
2pm

Iraq
Iran
3.30pm

4pm

Uzbekistan
Turkmenistan

Kyrgyzstan

China
8pm

EAST
CHINA
SEA

Taiwan

Afghanistan
4.30pm
Pakistan
5pm

Tibet (China)

Saudi
Arabia

Nepal
5.45

Northern
Mariana
Is (US)

Niger

1pm

Oman
4pm

India
5.30
pm

6.30

Myanmar
6pm

Philippines

9pm

Marshall
Is (US)

Chad
Sudan
Eritrea Yemen

BAY OF
BENGAL

Thailand
Vietnam

Palau

Federated States
of Micronesia
11am

12am

Nigeria
Ethiopia
3pm

ARABIAN
SEA

5.30pm

Sri Lanka

Central African
Republic
Congo
Somalia
Kenya

Maldives

Malaysia

Kiribati

Nauru EQUATOR

Gabon 1pm
Congo
(Zaire)

Indonesia

SOUTH
PACIFIC
OCEAN

Tanzania

Seychelles

6.30
pm

East
Timor

Papua New
Guinea
Solomon Is

Angola
Zambia Malawi

Madagascar

4pm

Cocos (Keeling)
Is (Aust)

Vanuatu

Fiji

Namibia Zimbabwe
Botswana Mozambique

Mauritius
Reunion
(Fr)

INDIAN OCEAN

9.30
pm

New Caledonia (Fr)

11.30
pm

South
Africa

Australia

10.30
pm
Lord Howe
Is (Aust)

Norfolk Is
(Aust)

New Zealand

Prince Edward Is
(S. Africa)

French Southern &
Antarctic Territories (Fr)

TASMAN
SEA

SOUTHERN OCEAN

Heard &
McDonald Is
(Aust)

MAP LEGEND

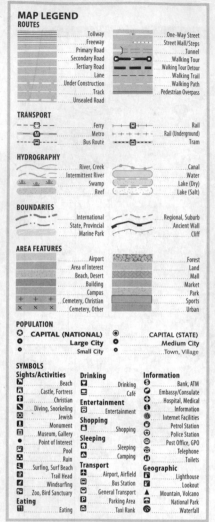

ROUTES

............Tollway
............Freeway
............Primary Road
............Secondary Road
............Tertiary Road
............Lane
............Under Construction
............Track
............Unsealed Road

............One-Way Street
............Street Mall/Steps
............Tunnel
............Walking Tour
............Walking Tour Detour
............Walking Trail
............Walking Path
............Pedestrian Overpass

TRANSPORT

............Ferry
............Metro
............Bus Route

............Rail
............Rail (Underground)
............Tram

HYDROGRAPHY

............River, Creek
............Intermittent River
............Swamp
............Reef

............Canal
............Water
............Lake (Dry)
............Lake (Salt)

BOUNDARIES

............International
............State, Provincial
............Marine Park

............Regional, Suburb
............Ancient Wall
............Cliff

AREA FEATURES

............Airport
............Area of Interest
............Beach, Desert
............Building
............Campus
............Cemetery, Christian
............Cemetery, Other

............Forest
............Land
............Mall
............Market
............Park
............Sports
............Urban

POPULATION

○ **CAPITAL (NATIONAL)**
● **Large City**
● Small City

◉ ....CAPITAL (STATE)
◉ ....Medium City
○ ....Town, Village

SYMBOLS

Sights/Activities
............Beach
............Castle, Fortress
............Christian
............Diving, Snorkeling
............Jewish
............Monument
............Museum, Gallery
● ....Point of Interest
............Pool
............Ruin
............Surfing, Surf Beach
............Trail Head
............Windsurfing
............Zoo, Bird Sanctuary

Eating
............Eating

Drinking
............Drinking
............Café

Entertainment
............Entertainment

Shopping
............Shopping

Sleeping
............Sleeping
............Camping

Transport
............Airport, Airfield
............Bus Station
............General Transport
............Parking Area
............Taxi Rank

Information
............Bank, ATM
............Embassy/Consulate
............Hospital, Medical
............Information
............Internet Facilities
............Petrol Station
............Police Station
............Post Office, GPO
............Telephone
............Toilets

Geographic
............Lighthouse
............Lookout
▲ ....Mountain, Volcano
............National Park
............Waterfall

LONELY PLANET OFFICES

Australia
Head Office
Locked Bag 1, Footscray, Victoria 3011
☎ 03 8379 8000, fax 03 8379 8111
talk2us@lonelyplanet.com.au

USA
150 Linden St, Oakland, CA 94607
☎ 510 893 8555, toll free 800 275 8555
fax 510 893 8572
info@lonelyplanet.com

UK
2nd floor 186 City Rd, London, EC1V 2NT
☎ 020 7106 2100
go@lonelyplanet.co.uk

Published by Lonely Planet Publications Pty Ltd
ABN 36 005 607 983

© Lonely Planet Publications Pty Ltd 2008

© photographers as indicated 2008

Cover photograph: Portrait of jaguar, Out of Africa Wildlife Park, Mark Newman/Lonely Planet Images. Many of the images in this guide are available for licensing from Lonely Planet Images: www .lonelyplanetimages.com.

Printed through Colorcraft Ltd, Hong Kong
Printed in China